MARKETING
AN INTRODUCTION

THIRD EDITION

GARY ARMSTRONG University of North Carolina

PHILIP KOTLER Northwestern University

MICHAEL HARKER University of Strathclyde, Glasgow

ROSS BRENNAN University of Hertfordshire Business School

Harlow, England • London • New York • Boston • San Francisco • Toronto • Sydney • Auckland • Singapore • Hong Kong
Tokyo • Seoul • Taipei • New Delhi • Cape Town • São Paulo • Mexico City • Madrid • Amsterdam • Munich • Paris • Milan

Pearson Education Limited
Edinburgh Gate
Harlow CM20 2JE
United Kingdom
Tel: +44 (0)1279 623623
Web: www.pearson.com/uk

Authorised adaptation from the United States edition, entitled Marketing: An Introduction, 12th Edition, ISBN 0133451275 by Armstrong, Gary; Kotler, Philip, published by Pearson Education, Inc, Copyright © 2011.

European adaptation edition published by Pearson Education Ltd, Copyright © 2015.

First published 2009 (print)
Second edition 2012 (print and electronic)
Third edition published 2015 (print and electronic)

The screenshots in this book are reprinted by permission of Microsoft Corporation.

Pearson Education is not responsible for the content of third-party internet sites.

ISBN: 978-1-292-01751-8 (print)
         978-1-292-01754-9 (PDF)
         978-1-292-01752-5 (eText)

British Library Cataloguing-in-Publication Data
A catalogue record for the print edition is available from the British Library

Library of Congress Cataloging-in-Publication Data
A catalog record for the print edition is available from the Library of Congress

10 9 8 7 6 5 4 3 2 1
19 18 17 16 15

Print edition typeset in 10/12 pt Sabon MT Pro by 71
Print edition printed and bound by L.E.G.O. S.p.A., Italy

NOTE THAT ANY PAGE CROSS-REFERENCES REFER TO THE PRINT EDITION

BRIEF CONTENTS

CONTENTS

PART THREE
DESIGNING A CUSTOMER-DRIVEN MARKETING STRATEGY AND MARKETING MIX   186

Putting marketing into action   187

PREFACE

WELCOME TO THE THIRD EDITION!

Our goal with the third European edition of *Marketing: An Introduction* has been to retain the great strengths of both the classic US original – among which are its clarity, coherence and authority – and those of the two prior European editions – among which are their contextual detail and incorporation of material on new and embryonic marketplaces – and to do so while fully incorporating the latest developments, evolutions and changes with respect to the practice and theory of marketing. Further, great effort has been expended in developing and diversifying the European-oriented material in order to create an even more effective text from which to learn about and teach marketing in a European context.

Most students learning marketing require a broad, complete picture of basic marketing principles and practices. They need a text that is complete yet easy to manage and master, one that guides them through the great variety of topics that come under the rubric of marketing without confusing or bewildering them – one that helps them prepare their assessments but also prepares them for careers in marketing or related fields. We hope that this text serves all of these important needs for marketing students, and that it strikes a careful balance between depth of coverage and ease of learning. Unlike more abbreviated texts, *Marketing: An Introduction* provides a complete overview of marketing in theory and in practice. Unlike longer, more complex texts, its moderate length makes it possible to use fully in one semester.

Marketing: An Introduction makes learning and teaching marketing more effective, easier and more enjoyable. The text's approachable style and design are well suited to cater to the enormous variety of students that may take introductory marketing classes. These students will be helped to learn, link and apply important concepts by generous use of up-to-date cases, exemplars and illustrations. Concepts are applied through many examples of situations in which companies from Spain to Russia and from Denmark to Turkey assess and solve their marketing problems. This third edition has no fewer than 48 cases – of which 10 are brand new and the remainder updated thoroughly. Integrated with accounts of contemporary practice, each chapter has had the roster of supporting academic literature updated to reflect the latest thinking and research.

Finally, this text presents the latest marketing thinking – as advocated and implemented by the reflective professional working in established or developing industries or job roles. It builds on an innovative and integrative marketing framework, one that positions marketing simply as the art and science of creating value *for* customers in order to capture value *from* customers in return. We hope that the great diversity to be found in Europe and marketing is found within.

Creating customer value and relationships

Today's marketing is all about building profitable customer relationships through interacting face to face or online. It starts with understanding consumer needs and wants, deciding which target markets the organisation can serve best, and developing a compelling value proposition by which the organisation can attract, keep and develop targeted consumers. If the organisation does these things well, it will reap the rewards in terms of market share, profits and customer equity. From beginning to end, *Marketing: An Introduction* presents and develops this integrative customer value/customer equity framework.

Marketing is much more than just an isolated business function – it is a philosophy that guides the entire organisation. The marketing department cannot build profitable customer relationships by itself. Marketing is a company-wide undertaking. It must drive the company's vision, mission and strategic planning. It involves broad decisions about who the company wants as its customers, which needs to satisfy, what products and services to offer, what prices to set, what communications to send and receive, and what partnerships to develop. Thus, marketing must work closely with other departments in the company and with other organisations throughout its entire value-delivery system to create superior customer value and satisfaction.

How do we get you learning?

This edition of *Marketing: An Introduction* builds on five major themes:

1 **Creating value for customers in order to capture value from customers in return** Today's marketers must be good at *creating customer value* and *managing customer relationships*. They must attract targeted customers with strong value propositions. Then, they must keep and grow customers by delivering superior customer value and effectively managing the company–customer interface. Today's outstanding marketing companies understand the marketplace and customer needs, design value-creating marketing strategies, deliver value and satisfaction, and build strong customer relationships. In return, they capture value from customers in the form of sales, profits and customer equity.

   Marketers must also be good at *relationship management*. They must work closely with partners inside and outside the company jointly to build profitable customer relationships. Successful marketers are now partnering effectively with other company departments to build strong company value chains. And they are joining with outside partners to build effective demand and supply chains and effective customer-focused alliances in virtual and real worlds.

2 **Building and managing strong brands to create brand equity** Well-positioned brands with strong brand equity provide the basis upon which to build profitable customer relationships. Today's marketers must be good at positioning their brands powerfully and managing them well across diverse and sometimes conflicting cultures.

3 **Measuring and managing return on marketing** Marketing managers must ensure that their marketing budget is being well spent. In the past, many marketers spent freely, often without sufficient care in respect of the financial returns on their spending. That attitude belongs to the past. Measuring and managing return on marketing investments has become an important part of strategic marketing decision making.

4 **Harnessing new marketing technologies in this digital age** New digital and other high-tech marketing developments are dramatically changing both buyers and the marketers who serve them. Today's marketers must know how to use new technologies to connect more effectively with customers and marketing partners in this new digital age – not to mention understanding how consumers are using these same technologies. Several of the new cases focus on the impact of social media and digital distribution on marketing and markets.

5 **Marketing in a socially responsible way around the globe** As technological developments make the world an increasingly smaller place, marketers must be good at marketing their brands globally and in socially responsible ways.

Important improvements and additions

Marketing is a set of extremely varied practices, and Europe is a diverse and exciting continent. In this book we will look at Spanish clothing being manufactured and shipped, Russian beer brands being launched in the UK, French cars being advertised in Germany, Scandinavian foods being sold in Arab supermarkets and European aircraft being marketed around the world – among many other examples of marketing in, to and from Europe by companies like Rolex, Google and Alibaba. The rise and rise of technology as an influence on businesses, customers and markets is reflected by examining the digital distribution of software, advertising in video and computer games, the use and abuse of social media, and the market impact of new digital markets – seen through the prisms of Angry Birds and 3D home printing.

This third European edition of *Marketing: An Introduction* has been thoroughly revised to reflect the major trends and forces that are affecting marketing in this age of customer value and relationships.

The first chapter on the importance of managing customer relationships effectively begins by looking at some of the marketing activities carried out by UEFA, the governing body of European football, and those past masters of attracting lucrative sponsorships deals – Manchester United. Later on the role and importance of marketing is discussed by three current managers – two from the well-known firms of Electrolux and Land Rover, and the third from Acme Whistles – who together show that marketing ideas are applicable to small firms as well as global mega-corporations. The new case in this chapter looks at the text and context of the use of metaphors in marketing in the dialogue between marketers and between marketing organisations and their stakeholders.

The second chapter considers the importance of marketing strategy and the difficulties inherent in managing complex businesses in the dynamic context of Europe. Examples of key issues are taken from companies including Monsanto, Danone and Under Armour. We hope that our book will act as a guide on marketing *to* Europe, as well as within and from it. The chapter contains a new case about the crucial logistics services provided by Maersk. The other case in this chapter about British Telecom (BT) is integrated with the stories of Taiwanese and Danish engineering companies hoping to deepen and broaden their European markets.

All firms operate within dynamic marketing environments. Recent economic turbulence has caused many managers to pause and reflect on their marketing environment – the context of business. Recent events, coupled with the perpetual complexity and variety of Europe geographically, demographically and politically, have meant that Chapter 3 is very different from the equivalent chapter in the second edition of the text. Cases for this edition consider a Scandinavian dairy products company having a torrid time in countries with radically different cultural and societal norms, a case looking at the story of how a shoe retailer has developed a business model to help disadvantaged children in South America, and a new case examining how companies are getting themselves into hot water quickly and on a global scale through the two-edged sword of social media. The unique nature of the European Union (EU) is examined in some detail – not just politically, but also the impact of the community on national and multinational economies and legal frameworks – and its relationships with other countries and trading blocs in and out of Europe.

In order to understand their customers, markets and environments, firms need to collect, process and manage marketing information. The opening case to Chapter 4 considers the importance of tourism to many European nations – large and small – and the efforts in Scotland to collect and interpret data from tourists at a national/sector level. The critical importance of information and relationship management hardware, software and marketing processes is brought home through the new case in this chapter on CRM at Air France and KLM. Privacy, and the increasing number and significance of companies that you've never heard of but who know a great deal about you, are discussed. As an aid to student learning and research, a comprehensive table is presented giving suggested sources of marketing intelligence across and within Europe. The final case in this chapter looks at how market researchers are collecting information using social media like Facebook and Twitter.

Airbus is a leading player in the global aerospace industry, and the particular problems in selling the new generation of large-capacity airliners are examined in the opening case to Chapter 5, which deals with consumer and business buying behaviour. Marketing to consumers is, of course, a major component of this chapter, and a second, brand-new case is presented on the lengths firms must go to in order to satisfy their older customers in the context of one company – Doro – offering simplified hi-tech products. The wide diversity of European customers is reflected in examples of financial services especially designed for Muslims, French anti-pollution technology, Italian tyre manufacturers and a final case looking at how General Electric is connecting with partners on a global scale.

Europe is more than the EU. Chapter 6, dealing with segmentation, targeting and positioning, opens with a case about a Russian brewery and its efforts to match the right beer to the right drinker in markets outside Russia. We look at the success Ryanair has garnered by targeting specific market segments for its cheap flights. The new case in this chapter looks at how men's suiting is an excellent demonstration of how markets can be segmented in subtle but powerful ways. Original examples include wealth management services for the increasing numbers of women with investment portfolios, the sophisticated ways and means by which companies such as Experian segment markets for their clients, and how one clothing retailer has tried to make itself stand out through a unique positioning strategy.

Every country in Europe has brands that are famous on the international stage and a near infinite number that are new or known only locally. Chapter 7, dealing with product, services and branding strategy, considers some of these famous brands, drawing on cases on Dunhill and Cloon Keen Atelier. While Dunhill epitomises cool Englishness, and has been world famous for many years, Cloon Keen Atelier is a quirky Irish brand of cosmetics which is at the other end of the spectrum from mega-brands such as Guinness, IBM and Intel. The chapter contains a detailed discussion of the impact of legal restrictions on the development and support of brands, and the case on naming brands has been updated to reflect recent examples of success and failure.

Chapter 8 explores new product development and product life-cycle strategies. In this chapter we look at the strategies employed by global brands such as Apple and Procter & Gamble. The first case looks at how Google is hot-housing innovation in order to stay ahead. We reflect on how Electrolux is bringing together diverse teams in order to improve product development. The final case in this chapter considers the development and marketing of products by VW and Alfa Romeo.

In Chapter 9 we look at pricing. Even though many countries in Europe have adopted the euro, there are still a lot of different currencies in use across the continent, which can complicate the pricing decision. Two of the companies that are discussed in this chapter have arrived at quite different answers to the problem of setting 'the right price'. The chapter opens with a case study about Primark, a clothing retailer that sets prices so low that some people think there just has to be something wrong! This provides us with the chance to explore the difficult issues associated with pricing ethics and in particular allegations that low prices in Europe may only be possible because of exploitation of workers in developing countries. On the other hand, German electrical appliance manufacturer Miele has arrived at an entirely different answer to the pricing question from Primark. The Miele answer? Offer products of such high quality and reliability that they win one consumer award after another, and have the confidence to charge a premium price for the value that you are offering to the consumer. That lesson is continued by Rolex, the subject of the second case in this chapter which has been reinforced by material to show how pricing impacts upon and is impacted by marketing strategy over the long term.

All organisations operate within complex networks of firms moving raw materials, components and finished manufactured goods up and down supply chains. Effective management of these channels is a key factor in becoming and staying a successful business.

Chapter 10, on marketing channels, gives many examples of companies large and small dealing with issues of logistics and distribution at the sector and company level – examples such as the European Plastics Distributors Association and the famous French hauliers Norbert Dentressangle appear alongside lesser-known family firms such as the Spanish company Pinturas Fierro – the focus of the opening case. Recent concepts, driven by the emergence of the Internet and e-marketing, such as disintermediation, are addressed in the case on Steam, the dominant player in the market for the digital distribution of computer games. On that theme, the increasing importance of partner relationship management and how it fits into the distribution mix are considered.

Chapter 11 on wholesaling and retailing opens with a case about the German discounter Aldi. The threat of these hard discounters to established supermarkets is timely in the context of multiple crises at Tesco. Alongside a second and highly evolved case on Dutch cooperative wholesaler The Greenery, there is a case discussing top retailing brands in key European markets. You may be surprised to learn that the biggest shopping mall in Europe is not in London or Paris but rather Istanbul. At the other end of the size scale, the chapter gives many examples of the small to medium-sized firms that make up the bulk of most European economies – firms like Henry Poole & Co. and the many members of the Euronics network.

Advertising, sales promotion and public relations management are the focus of Chapter 12. The opening case discusses French cars being advertised in Germany and another – significantly updated – case considers the rapid growth of advertising in computer and console games. New and up-to-date statistics and tables are presented on European advertising expenditures at the national and international level with special emphasis on social media spending, and there is a third case on how advertisers are using technology to narrowcast tailored promotional messages to individual customers.

The other elements in the promotional mix are covered in Chapter 13 on personal selling and direct marketing. Personal selling is illustrated with a case on Philips. The legal, ethical and technical issues of direct marketing in Europe are considered in depth. A new case in this chapter looks at the rise and near fall of Groupon. The European direct marketing industry is described in some detail with specific attention paid to governing and regulating bodies at national and EU level. A second case illustrates how even small firms can use modern IT equipment to target specific communications to individual customers.

Chapter 14 concerns marketing in the digital age, and is necessarily substantially altered and updated from the second edition of *Marketing: An Introduction*. Substantial changes were inevitable because of the rate of change in the technology and consequent developments in marketing techniques. The new chapter opening case shows how technologies associated with 3D printing – or additive manufacturing as it is more formally known – may well disrupt multiple areas of marketing activity. A second case illustrates how charities such as the International Red Cross are using these same technologies to advance their messages and causes at a reduced cost. The chapter presents a substantial set of statistics on the personal and commercial use of the Internet across different European countries – including expenditure on online advertising – and there is a renewed case giving the example of the Angry Birds app as a new type of product in a rapidly developing and growing market.

One of the characteristics of Europe, a continent with a large number of nation states squeezed into a rather compact land mass, is that often a firm will find that it has one or more 'international' markets closer at hand than the major markets of its own country. For example, Nice in south-east France is just over the border from Italy and is closer to the capital cities of Italy and Switzerland than it is to Paris. European customers are buying products and services across international boundaries with increasing regularity and confidence. Chapter 15 considers issues relevant to the global marketplace with a case on the trials and tribulations faced by Volkswagen in China. New figures show the leading brands globally, and the chapter now has numerous examples of firms marketing to and from Europe alongside a case looking at the past, present and future of McDonald's in Russia.

The brand-new case in this chapter looks at the complexities caused by culture and society when doing business in Asia.

Finally, Chapter 16 builds on the strength of the US original in respect of its detailed considerations of marketing ethics and social responsibility. There is enhanced coverage of social marketing: the use of marketing techniques to bring about desirable social changes and the coverage of sustainable marketing has been developed and improved – how can marketing contribute to a sustainable planet? The first case in this chapter looks at the success of a recent EU-wide campaign to reduce the number of young people who smoke, the second case at the international debate on who is to blame for obesity, and the final case at how a major European retailer is trying to reduce its environmental impact without inconveniencing its customers, while collaborating with a major charity to combat poverty in developing countries. The chapter asks readers to take a critical look at the issues involved in marketing ethics, social responsibility and sustainability.

This edition includes new and expanded material on a wide range of other topics, including social media, managing customer relationships, brand strategy and positioning, supplier satisfaction and partnering, supply chain management, data mining and data networks, marketing channel developments, environmental sustainability, cause-related marketing, marketing and diversity, socially responsible marketing, new marketing technologies, global marketing strategies, and much, much more.

Throughout all 16 chapters you'll find links to European bodies, political and sector specific, through new chapter-specific sets of weblinks. Each chapter refers to recent marketing journal articles with a European focus and many of the images contained within the book are new for this edition. Every chapter is supported by a matching set of lecture slides created by the authors themselves, which have been produced to a standard – not down to a price. Each chapter has an updated set of multiple-choice questions suitable for use with a variety of software platforms and many of the cases are supported by audio-visual material from the case authors and companies involved.

We don't think you'll find a better, fresher solution to teach and learn about marketing anywhere.

ABOUT THE AUTHORS

GARY ARMSTRONG is Crist W. Blackwell Distinguished Professor Emeritus of Undergraduate Education in the Kenan–Flagler Business School at the University of North Carolina at Chapel Hill. He holds undergraduate and masters degrees in business from Wayne State University in Detroit, and he received his PhD in marketing from Northwestern University. Professor Armstrong has contributed numerous articles to leading business journals. As a consultant and researcher, he has worked with many companies on marketing research, sales management and marketing strategy. But Professor Armstrong's first love is teaching. His Blackwell Distinguished Professorship is the only permanent endowed professorship for distinguished undergraduate teaching at the University of North Carolina at Chapel Hill. He has been very active in the teaching and administration of Kenan–Flagler's undergraduate programme. His recent administrative posts include Chair of the Marketing Faculty, Associate Director of the Undergraduate Business Program, Director of the Business Honors Program, and others. He works closely with business student groups and has received several campus-wide and business school teaching awards. He is the only repeat recipient of the school's highly regarded Award for Excellence in Undergraduate Teaching, which he has won three times. In 2004, Professor Armstrong received the UNC Board of Governors Award for Excellence in Teaching, the highest teaching honour bestowed at the University of North Carolina at Chapel Hill.

PHILIP KOTLER is one of the world's leading authorities on marketing. He is the S.C. Johnson & Son Distinguished Professor of International Marketing at the Kellogg Graduate School of Management, Northwestern University. He received his masters degree from the University of Chicago and his PhD from MIT, both in economics. Professor Kotler is the author of *Marketing Management,* now in its 12th edition and the most widely used marketing textbook in graduate schools of business. He has authored more than 20 other successful books and more than 100 articles in leading journals. He is the only three-time winner of the coveted Alpha Kappa Psi Award for the best annual article published in the *Journal of Marketing.* He was named the first recipient of two major awards: the Distinguished Marketing Educator of the Year Award given by the American Marketing Association; and the Philip Kotler Award for Excellence in Health Care Marketing presented by the Academy for Health Care Services Marketing. Other major honours include the 1978 Paul Converse Award of the American Marketing Association, honouring his original contribution to marketing, the European Association of Marketing Consultants and Sales Trainers Prize for Marketing Excellence, the 1995 Sales and Marketing Executives International (SMEI) Marketer of the Year Award, the 2002 Academy of Marketing Science Distinguished Educator Award, and honorary doctoral degrees from Stockholm University, the University of Zurich, Athens University of Economics and Business, DePaul University, the Cracow School of Business and Economics, Groupe HEC in Paris, the Budapest School of Economic Science and Public Administration, and the University of Economics and Business Administration in Vienna. Professor Kotler has been a consultant to many major US and foreign companies in the areas of marketing strategy and planning, marketing organisation and international marketing. He has been Chairman of the College of

Marketing of the Institute of Management Sciences, a Director of the American Marketing Association, a Trustee of the Marketing Science Institute, a Director of the MAC Group, a member of the Yankelovich Advisory Board, a member of the Copernicus Advisory Board, and a member of the Advisory Board of the Drucker Foundation. He has travelled extensively throughout Europe, Asia and South America, advising and lecturing to many companies about global marketing opportunities.

MICHAEL JOHN HARKER is a Lecturer in Marketing within the Business School at the University of Strathclyde in Glasgow, Scotland. Prior to this he was employed in a similar position in London at Middlesex University after completing his PhD at Nottingham Business School. He also holds BSc and MSc degrees in marketing – both from the University of Newcastle-upon-Tyne. At Strathclyde – among his other teaching duties – Dr Harker delivers the introductory marketing class to upwards of 500 students per year. A member of the Academy of Marketing, he is a familiar figure at the annual conference where he performs track chairing duties, often on the Marketing Cases track, which attracts interesting and innovative cases from across the world. He served for seven years as an editor of the journal *Marketing Intelligence and Planning*. His own research revolves around the twin tracks of consumer perspectives on relational marketing and pedagogic issues relevant to the teaching, learning and assessment of marketing at degree level. He has conducted work with a variety of companies including Porsche, The Body Shop, Toyota, NTL, Tesco and T-Mobile. His work has been published in journals such as *The Journal of Marketing Management, The Journal of Strategic Marketing, The International Small Business Journal, The European Business Review* and *Marketing Intelligence and Planning*. With John Egan he edited the three-volume series of papers published by Sage entitled *Relationship Marketing*.

ROSS BRENNAN is Professor of Industrial Marketing at the University of Hertfordshire Business School. He holds an undergraduate degree in economics from the University of Cambridge, a masters degree in management science from Imperial College, University of London, and a PhD in marketing from the University of Manchester. Prior to entering academia, Professor Brennan worked for BT Plc for 10 years in a number of marketing and strategic management roles. The principal focus of his research in recent years has been in the field of business-to-business marketing, where he has long been associated with the IMP Group. This group is a worldwide network of researchers who have interests in relationships and networks in business-to-business markets. Professor Brennan's research on business-to-business marketing, and on a range of other topics in marketing, strategy and business education, has been published in many journals. Within the academic community he has served as editor of *Marketing Intelligence and Planning*, where he is now a member of the editorial advisory board, and has been involved with the development of doctoral researchers in marketing as chairperson of the Academy of Marketing doctoral colloquium (2006) and as a doctoral colloquium panel member at both Academy of Marketing and IMP Group conferences. He has held Visiting Fellowships at both the University of Cambridge (Clare Hall) and the University of Oxford (University College), and is a Member of the Chartered Institute of Marketing (holding Chartered Marketer status), a Fellow of the Higher Education Academy, a Member of the Academy of Marketing, and a Member of the Economics and Business Education Association.

CASE MATRIX

Chapter	Page	Title of case study	Author(s)	Country	Chapter opening case study	Marketing at work case study
Chapter 1 Marketing: Managing profitable customer relationships	6	Marketing European football	Dr Michael Harker (Lecturer in Marketing), *Business School, University of Strathclyde, Glasgow, Scotland*		✓	
	17	Managers on marketing	[Dr Michael Harker]			MaW 1.1
	31	Metaphors in marketing	Professor Ross Brennan, University of Hertfordshire Business School.	UK		MaW 1.2
Chapter 2 Company and marketing strategy: Partnering to build customer relationships	42 47	BT: strategy in turbulent times Maersk Line	Dr Paurav Shukla Dr Steve Hogan and Ina Chang *Brighton Business School, University of Brighton*	Taiwan	✓	MaW 2.1
	61	Implementing customer relationship strategy at Danfoss	Professor Adam Lindgreen, *Cardiff University*, Dr Martin Hingley, *University of Lincoln*, Professor Michael Beverland, *RMIT University*, Jesper Krogh Jørgensen, *Stig Jørgensen & Partners* and John D. Nicholson, *Hull University Business School*	Denmark		MaW 2.2
Chapter 3 The marketing environment	76	The boycott of Arla Foods in the Middle East	Dr Ibrahim Abosag *Manchester Business School, University of Manchester*	The Middle East	✓	MaW 3.1
	84	TOMS shoes: '*be the change you want to see in the world*'	Sean Ennis *University of Strathclyde*	USA		MaW 3.2
	94	The two-edged sword of social media				

Chapter	Page	Title of case study	Author(s)	Country	Chapter opening case study	Marketing at work case study
Chapter 4 Managing marketing information	109	Visit Scotland!	[Dr Michael Harker]	Scotland	✓	MaW 4.1
	115	Air France–KLM: flying high with CRM	Michael Schellenberg, *University of Strathclyde*	UK		
	138	Doubleplusgood market research				MaW 4.2
Chapter 5 Consumer and business buyer behaviour	148	Airbus A380	George S. Low, *Associate Professor of Marketing, M.J. Neeley School of Business, Texas Christian University*	France	✓	MaW 5.1
	166	Understanding what older consumers want	Caroline Tynan, *Professor of Marketing*, and Sally McKechnie, *Associate Professor in Marketing, Nottingham University Business School*	England		MAW 5.2
	172	GE: building B2B customer partnerships				
Chapter 6 Segmentation, targeting and positioning: building the right relationships with the right customers	190	Baltika: segmenting the beer market in Russia and the West	Maria Smirnova, *Graduate School of Management, St Petersburg State University*	Russia	✓	MaW 6.1
	196	Sebiro – segmentation in men's clothing				
	219	Ryanair's value proposition: less for much less	[Dr Michael Harker]	Ireland		MaW 6.2
Chapter 7 Product, services and branding strategy	230 248 255	Alfred Dunhill Ltd: reconciling tradition and innovation in product and brand management	Dr Kim Lehman and Dr John Byrom, *School of Management, University of Tasmania*		✓	MaW 7.1
		Naming brands: just how much does a name matter?	[Dr Ross Brennan]			
		Cloon Keen Atelier: developing a premium brand	Ann M. Torres, *Cairns Graduate School of Business and Economics, National University of Ireland*	Ireland		MaW 7.2
Chapter 8 Developing new products and managing the product life cycle	270	Google: innovation at the speed of light			✓	MaW 8.1
	281	Electrolux: cleaning up with customer-centred, team-based new-product development				
	288	VW and Alfa Romeo: German engineering with Italian chic?				MaW 8.2

Chapter	Page	Title of case study	Author(s)	Country	Chapter opening case study	Marketing at work case study
Chapter 9 Pricing: understanding and capturing customer value	298	Primark – the cost of low prices?	[Dr Ross Brennan]	UK	✓	
	307	Rolex: much more than just a watch				MaW 9.1
	320	Quick, what's a good price for . . .? We'll give you a cue				MaW 9.2
Chapter 10 Marketing channels and supply chain management	334	Pinturas Fierro: slow but safe growth	Jesús Cambra-Fierro	Spain USA	✓	
	345	Steam-powered marketing: disintermediation in the computer game industry				MaW 10.1
	358	Zara: fast fashions – *really* fast				MaW 10.2
Chapter 11 Retailing and wholesaling	366	Aldi: don't discount them	Sean Ennis, *University of Strathclyde*		✓	
	377	Movers and shakers: leaders in European retailing	[Dr Michael Harker]			MaW 11.1
	382	The Greenery: a fresh approach		The Netherlands		MaW 11.2
Chapter 12 Communicating customer value: advertising, sales promotion and public relations	394	Renault: how a sausage, a sushi roll, a crispbread and a baguette have affected car sales in Europe	Barbara Caemmerer, *ESSCA, France*	France and Germany	✓	
	410	Narrowcasting – Savile Row and science fiction		USA		MaW 12.1
	416	Advertising in computer games	[Dr Michael Harker]			MaW 12.2
Chapter 13 Communicating customer value: personal selling and direct marketing	436	Innovating in business relationships: how Philips works with international retailers	Beth Rogers, *University of Portsmouth Business School*	The Netherlands	✓	
	453	Groupon: making life less boring through direct marketing on the Web				MaW 13.1
	463	Amorica Cookware: integrated direct marketing in a small firm	Adapted by Dr Michael Harker, *University of Strathclyde*, from 'Here's how direct marketing improved my business' (**www.businesslink.gov.uk**)	England		MaW 13.2

ACKNOWLEDGEMENTS

The authors and publisher would like to thank the following contributors who supplied material for the chapter opening and Marketing at Work case studies throughout the book:

Dr Paurav Shukla, **Dr Steve Hogan** and **Ina Chang**, Brighton Business School, University of Brighton

Professor Adam Lindgreen, Cardiff University, **Dr Martin Hingley**, University of Lincoln, **Professor Michael Beverland**, RMIT University, **Jesper Krogh Jørgensen**, Stig Jørgensen & Partners and **John D. Nicholson**, Hull University Business School

Dr Ibrahim Abosag, Manchester Business School, University of Manchester

George S. Low, Associate Professor of Marketing, M.J. Neeley School of Business, Texas Christian University

Caroline Tynan, Professor of Marketing and **Sally McKechnie**, Associate Professor in Marketing, Nottingham University Business School

Maria Smirnova, Graduate School of Management, St Petersburg State University

Dr Kim Lehman and **Dr John Byrom**, School of Management, University of Tasmania

Ann M. Torres, Cairns Graduate School of Business and Economics, National University of Ireland

Jesús Cambra-Fierro, University Pablo De Olavide

Barbara Caemmerer, ESSCA, Paris

Beth Rogers, University of Portsmouth Business School

Janet Ward, University of Leicester

Wing Lam, University of Durham

Dr Louise Hassan, Lancaster University

Professor Ken Peattie, BRASS Research Centre, Cardiff Business School

The authors and publisher would like to thank the following reviewers who commented and provided valuable feedback on the text throughout its development:

Jaya S. Akunuri, University of East London, UK

Jenny Balkow, Jönköping University, Sweden

Ton Borchert, Hogeschool Utrecht University of Applied Sciences, The Netherlands

Caroline Miller, Keele University, UK

Anna Nyberg, Stockholm School of Economics, Sweden

Beth Rogers, University of Portsmouth, UK

Paul van der Hoek, HAN University of Applied Sciences, The Netherlands

Peter Williams, Leeds Metropolitan University, UK

PUBLISHER'S ACKNOWLEDGEMENTS

We are grateful to the following for permission to reproduce copyright material:

Figures

Figure 1.5 adapted from *The Mismanagement of Customer Loyalty*, Harvard Business School Publishing Corporation by Reinartz, W. and Kumar, V., July 2002. Copyright © 2002 by the Harvard Business School Publishing Corporation; all rights reserved; Figure 2.2 from www.bcg.com, Adapted from the Product Portfolio Matrix,©1970,The Boston Consulting Group (BCG).; Figure 2.8 Republished with permission of American Marketing Association (AMA) from Return on marketing: Using consumer equity to focus marketing strategy, *Journal of Marketing,* January, p.112 (Rust, R.T., Lemon, K.N. and Zeithamel, V.A. 2004), © 2004 ; permission conveyed through Copyright Clearance Center, Inc.; Figure 5.3 from *Motivation and Personality,* 3 ed., Pearson Education, Inc., Upper Saddle River, New Jersey (Maslow, A. H., Frager, R. D.; Fadiman, J. 1987) Pearson Education Inc., © 1987. Printed and Electronically reproduced by permission of Pearson Education, Inc., Upper Saddle River, New Jersey.; Figures on page 204–5 courtesy of Experian; Figure 6.3 from Making sense of market segmentation, a fashion retailing case, *European Journal of Marketing,* 41 (5/6), pp. 439-465 (Quinn L, Hines, T. and Bennison, T. 2007), European journal of marketing by EMERALD GROUP PUBLISHING LIMITED. Reproduced with permission of EMERALD GROUP PUBLISHING LIMITED in the format Republish in a book via Copyright Clearance Center.; Figure 8.4a from http://eupocketbook.theicct.org/charts/pc-registrations-member-state, icct available under the Creative Commons Attribution-ShareAlike 3.0 Unported License at http://creativecommons.org/licenses/by-sa/3.0/; Figure 8.4b from http://eupocketbook.theicct.org/charts/pc-registrations-brand, iccticct available under the Creative Commons Attribution-ShareAlike 3.0 Unported License at http://creativecommons.org/licenses/by-sa/3.0; Figure on page 308 from http://www.minus4plus6.com/PriceEvolution.htm, Sheldon K. Smith, EdD., - Minus4Plus6.com; Figure 9.2 from *The Strategy and Tactics of Pricing: A Guide to Profitable Decision Making,* 3 ed., Pearson Education Inc. (Nagle, T. and Holden, R. 2002) © 2002. Printed and Electronically reproduced by permission of Pearson Education, Inc., Upper Saddle River, New Jersey.; Figure 9.6 Republished with permission of American Marketing Association (AMA) Pricing and Public Policy: A Research Agenda and Overview of Special Issue, *Journal of Public Policy and Marketing,* Spring, 3-10 (Compeau, L.D. and Grewel, D. 1999), © 1999 ; permission conveyed through Copyright Clearance Center, Inc.; Figure on page 477 from www.internetworldstats.com/stats.htm, Copyright © 2014 Miniwatts Marketing Group; Figures on page 481, page 483 from Dutton, William H. & Blank, Grant with Groselj, Darja. (2013) Cultures of the Internet: The Internet in Britain, Oxford Internet Survey 2013. Oxford Internet Institute. http://oxis.oii.ox.ac.uk/wp-content/uploads/2014/11/OxIS-2013.pdf, Source: Oxford Internet Survey (Dutton & Blank. 2013); Figure on page 483 from http://epp.eurostat.ec.europa.eu/statistics_explained/images/3/36/E-commerce_sales_and_purchases%2C_2012_%28%25_enterprises%29.png, Eurostat, Source: Eurostat, http://epp.eurostat.ec.europa.eu, © European Union, 1995-2015; Figure 16.1 adapted from Beyond Greening: Strategies for a Sustain-able World', *Harvard Business Review,* January-February, p. 74 (Hart, S.L. 1997), Copyright © 1997 by the Harvard Business School Publishing Corporation: all rights reserved.

Logos

Logo on page 132 courtesy of Experian; Logos on page 560 from http://help.marksandspencer.com/support/company-website/oxfam-clothing-exchange, Marks & Spencer Group plc

Screenshots

Screenshot on page 88 from www.diyaonline.com, DIYA by RFL Ltd, with permission from Mrs Rani Gill; Screenshot on page 153 from http://www.lloydsbank.com/current-accounts/islamic-account.asp, Lloyds Bank; Screenshot on page 221 from http://www.ryanair.com/, Ryanair Holdings plc; Screenshot on page 569 from https://www.aib.ie/servlet/Satellite?pagename=AIB_Investor_Relations/AIB_Article/aib_d_article&c=AIB_Article&cid=1004443230333&channel=IRHP, AIB

Tables

Table 4.4 adapted from *Marketing Research: Measurement and Method*, 7 ed., New York: Macmillan Publishing (Tull, D.S. and Hawkins, D.I. 1993) Tull, M.A., Adapted with permission. Reprinted with permission of Mrs Marjorie A. Tull.; Table 5.1 from http://www.iser.essex.ac.uk/research/esec/user-guide/the-european-socio-economic-classification. Institute for Social and Economic Research University of Essex; Table 6.4 from IATA World Air Transport Statistics, http://www.iata.org/wats., International Air Transport Association (IATA); Table 8.1 from *Marketing Management: Analysis, Planning, Implementation and Control,* 12 ed., Pearson Education Inc. (Philip, K. and Keller, K. L. 2006) © 2006. Printed and Electronically reproduced by permission of Pearson Education, Inc., Upper Saddle River, New Jersey.; Table 11.2 from www.interbrand.com, Interbrand; Table 12.1 from http://www.marketingmagazine.co.uk/article/1289560/top-100-uk-advertisers-bskyb-increases-lead-p-g-bt-unilever-reduce-adspend. Reproduced from *Marketing* magazine with the permission of the copyright holder, Haymarket Media Group Limited; Table 13.1 from Sales Compensation: In search of a better solution, *Compensation and Benefits Review* 25 (6), 53-60 (Johnson, S.T. 1993), Copyright © 1993 by Sage Publications.; Table 14.1 from http://www.pocketgamer.biz/metrics/app-store/app-prices/, pocketgamer.biz, Steel Media; Table 15.2 adapted from http://www.bestglobalbrands.com/2014/ranking/, Interbrand.

Text

Extract on page 7 from *Swiss cry foul as UEFA targets fans to fight 'Ambush Marketing'*, Bloomberg (Gallu J.) © 2008 Bloomberg L.P., All rights reserved. Used with permission.; Interview on page 17 from Richard Sells; Interview on page 17 from Colin Green; Interview on page 17 from Philip Popham; Interview on page 18 from Simon Topman; Box on pages 47–8 from Maersk Line's three-stage strategy for profit By Tom Malnight http://www.ft.com/cms/s/0/1f4c6068-1bbc-11e3-b678-00144feab7de.html#axzz3O3uF7CII, Financial Times, © The Financial Times Limited. All Rights Reserved; Box on pages 61–3 from Professor Adam Lindgreen, Cardiff University, UK, Dr Martin Hingley, University of Lincoln, UK, Professor Michael Beverland, RMIT University, Melbourne, Australia, Jesper Krogh Jørgensen, Stig Jørgensen & Partners, Denmark and John D. Nichol-son, Department of Marketing and Business Strategy, Hull University Business School, UK; Box on pages 76–7 from Dr Ibrahim Abosag; Box on pages 115–8 from Michael Schellenberg; Box on pages 148–50 from George S. Low, Associate Professor of Marketing, M.J. Neeley School of Business, Texas Christian University, USA; Quote on page 196 from *Civilization: The West and the Rest, 'Stitched up on Savile Row'*, Penguin, London (Ferguson, N. 2011) Reproduced by permission of Penguin Books Ltd.; Case Study on pages 190–1 from Maria Smirnova, Graduate School of Management, St Petersburg State University, Russia, This case was prepared with kind support of Marcho Kuyumdzhiev, Vice President for

Marketing at Baltika Breweries and Anna Balakina, Marketing Manager, International Marketing Group at Baltika Breweries.; Box on pages 230–2 from Dr Kim Lehman and Dr John Byrom, School of Management, University of Tasmania, Australia; Box on pages 255–6 from Ann M. Torres, Marketing Department, Cairns Graduate School of Business and Economics, National University of Ireland; Extract on page 279 from http://www.innocentdrinks.co.uk/, Innocent Ltd; Extract on page 303 from www.miele.co.uk, Miele Co. Ltd; Box on pages 320–1 adapted from Mind Your Pricing Cues', *Harvard Business Review,* September (Anderson, E. and Simester, D. 2003), Harvard Business School. Copyright © 2003 by the Harvard Business School Publishing Corporation; all rights reserved.; Case Study on pages 334–5 from Jesús Cambra Fierro; Case Study on pages 394–6 from Barbara Caemmerer, Professor of Marketing, ESSCA School of Management, France; Quote on page 416 from Jordan L. Howard www.officialplaystationmagazine.co.uk/2013/11/01/when-ads-invade-games-in-game-advertising-is-worth-over-1-billion-a-year/, Jordan L. Howard, RapidFire; Extract on page 416 adapted from http://www.digitaljournal.com/a-and-e/gaming/op-ed-the-potential-of-advertising-in-video-games/article/375665, DigitalJournal.com; Case Study on pages 436–8 from Beth Rogers, Principal Lecturer, University of Portsmouth Business School, UK, the author is very grateful for the help of Bart Logghe, Senior Director, IKAM Competence Centre, Philips, in producing this case study.; Case Study on page 463 adapted from www.businesslink.gov.uk, HMSO, Contains public sector information licensed under the Open Government Licence (OGL) v3.0.http://www.nationalarchives.gov.uk/doc/open-government-licence.; Extract on page 485 from http://www.huffingtonpost.co.uk/2013/01/31/hmv-twitter-goes-rogue-60-staff_n_2589922.html, The Huffington Post; Interview on page 497 from Kendell, P. (2011) Angry Birds: The Story Behind iPhone's Gaming Phenomenon, www.telegraph.co.uk/technology/video-games/8303173/Angry-Birds-the-story-behind-iPhones-gaming-phenomenon.html Daily Telegraph, copyright © Telegraph Media Group Limited; Case Study on pages 500–2 from Ann M. Torres, Marketing Department, Cairns Graduate School of Business and Economics, National University of Ireland; Case Study on pages 512–13 from Wing Lam, Durham University; Case Study on pages 558–60 from Professor Ken Peattie, BRASS Research Centre, Cardiff Business School, Wales; Extract on pages 569–70 from https://archive.ama.org/Archive/AboutAMA/Pages/Statement%20of%20Ethics.aspx, AMA

Photographs

The publisher would like to thank the following for their kind permission to reproduce their photographs:

(Key: b-bottom; c-centre; l-left; r-right; t-top)
6 Getty Images: AFP; 8 Corbis: Catherine Ivill / AMA / AMA (t); The Advertising Archives (b); 10 Getty Images: Mark Runnacles;18 Electrolux: (bl). Getty Images: Timothy Hiatt / Stringer (br); Frank Greenaway (tl); 20 Image courtesy of The Advertising Archives; 22 Dick Lovett.co.uk: Lloyd Precious; 23 ING Direct; 30 Alamy Images: RIA Novsoti (br); ITAR-TASS Photo Agency (bl); 32 Alamy Images: Stu Porter (b); Stocktrek Images, Inc. (t); 42 BT Image Library; 45 Alamy Images: Tompiodesign (br). WAGGS: (bl); 46 Monsanto Company: (c) 2005 Monsanto Company. All rights reserved; 47 Alamy Images: Søren Lund Hviid; 53 Corbis: Elipsa; 54 Alamy Images: Lou Linwei; 62 Danfoss; 76 Arla Foods; 82 Alamy Images: jake wyman; 93 Volkswagen Group; 97 Getty Images: Joseph Van Os; 102 Getty Images: David M. Benett / Getty Images for Converse; 110 Alamy Images: Nagelstock.com; 115 Getty Images: AFP; 120 Getty Images: Andy Reynolds; 125 Fisher-Price, Inc.: Photograph of Fisher-Price Playlab used with permission of Fisher-Price, Inc., East Aurora, New York 14052 (l); Photograph of Fisher-Price Playlab used with permission of Fisher-Price, Inc., East Aurora, New York 14052 (r); 136 Alamy Images: Webstream; 139 Alamy Images: Anatolii Babii; 148 Alamy Images: Antony Nettle; 156 Vauxhall General Motors; 160 Alamy Images: Tony Lockhart; 166 Getty Images: Bambu

Productions; 172 Getty Images: Daniel Acker / Bloomberg via Getty Images; 190 Getty Images: Scott Peterson; 195 Image courtesy of The Advertising Archives; 196 Getty Images: General Photographic Agency; 197 Rex Features: Times Newspapers (t); Alamy Images: Andrew Holt (b); 198 Shutterstock.com: Viorel Sima (l); Mark LaMoyne (r); 200 Courtesy of Fortnum and Mason; 208 Amanda Kamen; 211 DVLA; 217 Alamy Images: Alan King; 221 Ryanair; 230 The Advertising Archives (t); Alamy Images: Hugh Threlfall (b); 231 Alamy Images: Photos 12; 233 Alamy Images: AR Photo; 236 Photoshot Holdings Limited: Zuma; 240 Invotek Systems; 249 John Kuczala; 251 Alamy Images: David Pearson; 254 Victorinox; 256 Shutterstock.com: Andreka; 262 Getty Images: Ariel Jerozolimski / Bloomberg via Getty Images; 270 Getty Images: Bloomberg; 276 Volkswagen Group; 279 innocent ltd; 282 Getty Images: Martin Poole; 284 The Economist Newspaper Limited, London; 289 Getty Images: Valentin Flauraud / Bloomberg (b). Volkswagen Group; 298 Getty Images: Peter Macdiarmid; 304 Miele; 308 Alamy Images: carlodraisci; 316 Westland Horticultural; 318 Alamy Images: G I Dobner; 320 Getty Images: Tim Boyle; 326 Getty Images: WireImage; 334 Jesus Cambra Fierro; 340 Getty Images: Mike Ehrmann; 346 Alamy Images: Patriotic Alien; 347 Alamy Images: PhotoAlto; 355 Courtesy of Renault Trucks Ltd; 366 Alamy Images: Vario Images GmbH & Co KG; 370 Alamy Images: TNT Magazine; 374 Alamy Images: Lilyana Vynogradova; 375 Alamy Images: Kirsty Mclaren; 377 Alamy Images: Paul Mayall / Germany (br); M Itani (tr); Iain Masterton (l). Getty Images: Bloomberg (bc); AFP (tc); 383 Shutterstock.com: Kondor83; 400 Image courtesy of The Advertising Archives; 410 The Kobal Collection: 20th Century Fox / Dreamworks; 413 Image courtesy of The Advertising Archives; 426 Getty Images: Dave M. Bennett; 436 Courtesy of Philips Electronics; 439 Alamy Images: Jack Sullivan; 444 Schibsted: Gustav Martensson; 451 Boise Cascade Corporation; 454 Alamy Images: M4OS Photos; 463 Alamy Images: Foodfolio; 475 Alamy Images: Rik Hamilton (tl); Piero Cruciatti (tr); 479 Getty Images: Evrim Aydin / Anadolu Agency; 484 Shutterstock.com: Mark Shoon; 495 Alamy Images: Pumpkinpie; 496 Firemint.com; 499 Getty Images: Gareth Davies; 500 Getty Images: Roberto Schmidt / AFP; 501 Alamy Images: M4OS Photos; 512 Volkswagen Group; 514 Alamy Images: Rob Bartree; 517 Alamy Images: BL Images Ltd; 522 Getty Images: AFP; 531 Eyevine Ltd: Mark Leong / Redux; 532 Courtesy of Bernard Matussiere; 535 Alamy Images: mikecranephotography.com; 550 Corbis: Peter Dench; 552 Lawrence Journal-World; 560 Marks and Spencer plc (company): (l). Oxfam: (r); 563 Alamy Images: Helene Rogers; 565 innocent ltd.

In some instances we have been unable to trace the owners of copyright material, and we would appreciate any information that would enable us to do so.

PART ONE

DEFINING MARKETING AND THE MARKETING PROCESS

IS MARKETING FOR EVERYONE?

If someone told you that effective marketing was crucial in large companies with well-known brands like Electrolux or Land Rover you might readily agree. Do smaller firms need to think about their marketing? How about cities – can marketing ideas be useful to them? Is it possible that a charity like VSO could usefully spend time thinking about its marketing strategy? St Paul's Cathedral – surely marketing could never be something that might concern that august institution!

CHAPTER 1
MARKETING: MANAGING PROFITABLE CUSTOMER RELATIONSHIPS

AFTER STUDYING THIS CHAPTER, YOU SHOULD BE ABLE TO

- define marketing and outline the steps in the marketing process
- explain the importance of understanding customers and the marketplace and identify the five core marketplace concepts
- identify the key elements of a customer-driven marketing strategy and discuss the marketing management orientations that guide marketing strategy
- discuss customer relationship management and identify strategies for creating value *for* customers and capturing value *from* customers in return
- describe the major trends and forces that are changing the marketing landscape in this age of relationships

THE WAY AHEAD
Previewing the concepts

We'll start with a simple question: What *is* marketing? Simply put, marketing is managing profitable customer relationships. The aim of marketing is to create value for customers and to capture value in return. Chapter 1 is organised around five steps in the marketing process – from understanding customer needs, to designing customer-driven marketing strategies and programmes, to building customer relationships and capturing value for the firm. Understanding these basic concepts, and forming your own ideas about what they really mean to you, will give you a solid foundation for all that follows.

Our first stop is to look at an organisation that you might not think of as having much need for marketing ideas and concepts – UEFA, the governing body of European football.

MARKETING EUROPEAN FOOTBALL

What are the biggest sporting events in the world? Everyone has their own opinion, but if you weigh a number of factors like television audience size, number of countries or teams involved, revenues and expenditure – not to mention the ability to bring much of the world to a halt – then the top five probably include the World Cup, the summer Olympic Games, the European Football Championship, the Super Bowl and the European Champions League.

Source: Getty Images/AFP.

Of these five, three are football tournaments and two of those are overseen by UEFA – the Union of European Football Associations. There is a lot at stake here: regional and national pride, global TV audiences in the billions, and lots and lots of money. UEFA defines its core purpose as being to promote, protect and develop European football at every level of the game, to promote the principles of unity and solidarity, and to deal with all questions relating to European football. It does this by taking the excitement, the attention and the cash that big tournaments generate and using it to support its other activities.[1]

Because of this, a lot of what UEFA does is marketing related – whether sponsorship of an event or tournament by a commercial enterprise, a social programme to use the power of sport to alleviate problems like racism, the buying and selling of broadcasting and merchandising rights, public relations and managing relationships with governments, teams and an almost infinite number of journalists – not to mention the fans!

The marketing function of UEFA – people, resources and responsibilities for marketing affairs – is split across four divisions, each with its own focus.

The **Marketing and Media Rights Division** develops marketing and media strategies for all UEFA competitions – the Champions League, the UEFA Cup, the European Football Championships and less prominent competitions like women's football, junior-level tournaments and various 'futsal' events (the name is a contraction of the Portuguese term *futebol de salão* and the game is an indoor version of the standard sport). It has the responsibility to find the best price for broadcasting rights and agreeing terms and conditions with broadcasting partners and then maintaining relationships with these key partners.

UEFA Marketing and Media Management (UMMM) is the commercial division of UEFA responsible for generating revenue from sponsorship and licensing for competitions, and managing the relationships with all associated commercial partners. In essence, this division sells the rights to be associated with prestigious and exciting international events. It maintains high prices by strictly limiting the number of companies that are given these licences. Euro 2016 in France will have a core sponsorship panel of just six companies – big global names like Carlsberg, Continental, Coca-Cola, Hyundai and McDonald's will be joined by one company you've probably never heard of – SOCAR. That would be the State Oil Company of Azerbaijan Republic.

In the 2014–15 Champions League season, the competition had just seven sponsors – Heineken, Mastercard, Sony, Nissan, Heineken, UniCredit and HTC. Any number of merchandise items are produced for major tournaments – replica team strips, footballs, and even items for the desk-oriented like mouse mats and coffee mugs.[2]

UEFA Media Technologies SA (UMT) is the service company created by UEFA to support broadcast and sponsorship partners with multimedia content. It links with the TV companies to try to ensure the best possible coverage of games. Other than TV, this division is increasingly involved with supporting UEFA's online operations – whether providing and maintaining statistical databases or selling downloadable recordings of games in order to maintain and develop relationships with fans and journalists.

The **Communications and Public Affairs Division** (CPAD) is responsible for public relations activity – such as briefing and supporting the activities of journalists. The division also has the responsibility of managing the work UEFA does with various charity and social groups.

For example, CPAD works with the International Red Cross and FARE (Football Against Racism in Europe) on projects with other organisations that have charitable or social causes to advance through the money and publicity generated by the sport.

That UEFA expends so much effort on marketing activity may surprise you, but think about it – it has brands, it provides services, it has connections and relationships with various publics and it generates significant revenue. How much revenue? One senior UEFA marketing manager, Guy-Laurent Epstein, commented on the recent winning of the rights auction for the UK by BT, who took over from Sky:

> **UEFA is delighted to welcome newcomer BT Sport to the family of UEFA Champions League rights holders. Since its launch in the summer, BT Sport has been UEFA's partner for the UEFA Europa League and has demonstrated its ability to deliver premium sports coverage. We look forward to working with BT Sport on both competitions in the 2015–18 rights cycle.**[3]

How much did BT pay for these broadcasting rights? £900m.[4]

Is everyone happy with the marketing activities of UEFA? Not quite. Some people are not convinced that UEFA is sticking to its core mission of supporting football – they worry that it is moving too far towards becoming fully commercialised and that the sport is being used to make some people rich while traditional fans are being sidelined. UEFA's decision to award a future tournament to Russia has been rightly criticised, but let's consider one of the stories to come out of a recent tournament:

> **For Yves Stemmle, Switzerland's opening match against the Czech Republic in the 2008 European soccer championship won't be just about advancing to the next round. It will be about his civil rights.**
>
> **'They want me to drink only Carlsberg beer and wear things with this,' said Stemmle, 36, pointing to the Euro 2008 logo on his hat as he sat in a Lugano café before a warm-up game with Slovakia. 'They can't tell me what to wear.'**
>
> **Some fans say UEFA, European soccer's governing body, has put profits ahead of their interests and plans to turn them away from stadiums and 'fan zones' if they wear clothes bearing the logos of companies that aren't tournament sponsors. UEFA estimates the 23-day championship, which begins June 7 in Basel, will generate 2 billion Swiss francs ($1.9 billion) in revenue from media rights, tickets**

and sponsors. After expenses, it expects to retain 330 million francs to cover administrative costs and fund other tournaments.

> **A Swiss tabloid, SonntagsBlick, published a caricature showing UEFA President Michel Platini as Moses holding up 11 commandments to heed during the event. The first: Drink only Carlsberg beer. Lamp posts around Zurich are sprouting stickers saying, 'UEFA: We Care About Money,' a play on the group's slogan, 'We Care About Football.'**
>
> **Organisers of previous events have protected sponsors' rights inside stadiums by refusing entry to groups of fans paid to wear corporate logos. UEFA is extending its campaign against ambush marketers into fan zones, areas in each of the host cities where supporters gather to watch games on giant TV screens. That has aroused the ire of some fans.**
>
> **'Fan zones are paid for and run by the city and access is free,' says Patrick Cotting, who lectures on marketing and sponsorships at the University of Lugano. 'There's no legal precedent that would forbid individuals from entering a public space because they're wearing the wrong T-shirt.'**
>
> **Copenhagen-based Carlsberg is paying at least 100 million kroner ($21 million) for the sponsorship, its biggest ever, giving it the right to exclusive sales in the eight biggest fan zones in each host city.**
>
> **'There are plenty of other places in the local cities where fans can drink other beers and we totally respect that,' said Keld Strudahl, head of international marketing for the company.**
>
> **In Austria, beermaker Ottakringer Brauerei AG is taking advantage of the popular backlash by selling its beer with a red-white-red logo, the colours of Austria's flag, and calling it the 'unofficial fan beer' drunk by 'real fans who want to show their support in whatever way they want'.**
>
> **'Soccer used to belong to the people,' said Carlo Kuemin, 70, as he huddled under an umbrella in the standing-only curve of Lugano's Cornaredo Stadium during the Switzerland–Slovakia match. 'Not any more. The sponsors govern the events now. It's all about the money.'**
>
> **Stemmle, the fan in the café, isn't taking UEFA's actions lying down.**
>
> **'I have a ticket to the opening match between Switzerland and the Czech Republic,' he said. 'I'm only going to wear things they don't allow.'**[5]

UEFA then is an organisation that recognises the need to build and maintain relationships with its stakeholders – including customers. Our example shows, however, that marketing actions can have unintended consequences – care and attention is needed!

UEFA is not the only organisation involved with marketing in the sport of football. During the summer of 2011 it emerged that Manchester City had sold the naming rights to its stadium for an incredible £100m to Etihad – an Abu Dhabi airline.[6] In 2010, Barcelona ended a 111-year tradition of not having its shirts sponsored by signing a record £125m/five-year deal with the Qatar Foundation. Prior to this, the only non-club logo on the shirts was for UNICEF – and Barcelona made an annual donation to the charity for the privilege.[7]

Source: Corbis/Catherine Ivill / AMA / AMA.

One team above all, though, is master of attracting sponsorships, and that team is Manchester United.

The *Daily Mail*[8] takes us through the facts and figures:

Question: What do Mister Potato crisps and Smirnoff vodka have in common?

Answer: They are both official sponsors of Manchester United Football Club.

And they pay handsomely for the privilege.
These two distant products may appear to have little to do with football but they can wear the same badge as Robin van Persie, Wayne Rooney and Co because of United's exhaustive quest for maximum commercial revenue. That figure is now approaching an astonishing £130million a year and will only continue to rise. No wonder United recently became the first sports team in the world to be valued at $3BILLION.

There are no fewer than 32 companies listed as sponsors of the club on their official website and this does not even include three – somewhat peculiar – deals announced this month.

First there was the tie-up with Indonesian tyre manufacturer Multistrada on January 7, then came Wahaha, a Chinese soft drinks producer, a week later, and on January 18 we heard Japanese paint manufacturer Kansai had become the club's first 'paint partner'. Painting the town red, perhaps.

Each contract will run for three years and business experts speculate are worth between £1m to £2m annually. United announced such deals as part of last summer's listing agreement on the New York

Source: Image courtesy of The Advertising Archives.

Stock Exchange but the exact financial terms can be withheld unless they are large enough to affect market and shareholder interests.

Those numbers might not sound massive but when you consider that in return all United need provide is their logo and occasionally ambassadors for appearances the sums become startling. The link works for these companies because of the huge boost their brand receives from associating with arguably the most famous club in the world.

If you snigger at what you see as the prostitution of the club by the owners, consider this: Manchester United

TABLE 1.1 Manchester United's sponsors (according to club website)

AON	Principal sponsor of Manchester United – £20m a year
DHL	Official logistics partner of Manchester United – £10m
NIKE	Official kit supplier of Manchester United – £25.4m
CHEVROLET	Official automotive partner of Manchester United – £12m
SINGHA	Official beer of Manchester United – £2m
THOMAS COOK	Official travel partner of Manchester United – £1.3m
BWIN	Official online gaming and betting partner of Manchester United – £2.4m
CASILLERO DEL DIABLO	Official wine partner of Manchester United – £2m
HUBLOT	Official timekeeper of Manchester United – £4m
The below are all worth approximately £1m–£2m. . .	
SMIRNOFF	Official responsible drinking partner of Manchester United
TOSHIBA MEDICAL SYSTEMS	Official medical systems partner of Manchester United
STC	Official integrated telecommunications partner of Manchester United for Saudi Arabia
PCCW	Official integrated telecommunications partner of Manchester United in Hong Kong
TURKISH AIRLINES	Official airline partner
EPSON	Official office equipment partner of Manchester United
MISTER POTATO	Official savoury snack partner of Manchester United
YANMAR	Official global partner
TM	Official integrated telecommunications partner of Manchester United in Malaysia
GLOBACOM	Official integrated telecommunications partner of Manchester United for Nigeria, Ghana, Republic of Benin
VIVA KUWAIT	Official integrated telecommunications partner of Manchester United in Kuwait
MTN	Official integrated telecoms partner of Manchester United for South Africa/Zambia/Rwanda/Uganda/Swaziland/Botswana
AIRTEL	Official telecommunications partner of Manchester United in India/Sri Lanka/Seychelles/Bangladesh
ZONG	Official telecommunications partner of Manchester United in Pakistan
GLOBUL	Official telecommunications partner of Manchester United in Bulgaria
MAMEE	Official noodles partner of Manchester United for Asia, Oceania and Middle East
VIVA	Official integrated telecommunications partner of Manchester United in Bahrain
TURK TELEKOM	Official integrated telecommunications partner of Manchester United in Turkey
A.P. HONDA	Official motorcycle partner of Manchester United in Thailand
AIRTEL AFRICA	Official telecoms partner in Burkina Faso, Chad, DR Congo, Gabon, Kenya, Madagascar, Malawi, Niger, Sierra Leone, Tanzania, Congo Brazzaville
BEELINE	Official telecommunications partner of Manchester United in Vietnam, Cambodia and Laos
BAKCELL	Official telecommunications and broadcast partner of Manchester United for Azerbaijan
KAGOME	Official soft drink partner of Manchester United for Japan
WAHAHA	Official soft drink partner of Manchester United for China
PT MULTISTRADA	Official tyre partner of Manchester United
KANSAI	Official paint partner of Manchester United

Source: http://www.dailymail.co.uk/sport/football/article-2269599/Manchester-Uniteds-incredible-list-sponsors-helping-3billion-super-club.html

makes twice as much from these sponsorships as Celtic does from all sources of revenue *combined*. That extra money means more and better players attracted by higher salaries and reinforces the chances of success on the field, which in turn increases the opportunities for further sponsorships off it.

Manchester United is a globally recognised brand, which is why it has partners queuing up. Other sporting bodies and teams are not as fortunate as UEFA and MUFC, though. The SPFL is a rare example of a professional sports league without a main sponsor.

The SPFL is almost unique in being a football pyramid without a sponsor. Considerable effort is being expended to find one by senior management.

Source: Getty Images/Mark Runnacles.

Today's successful organisations have one thing in common: they are strongly customer focused and heavily committed to marketing. These organisations share a passion for satisfying customer needs in well-defined target markets. They motivate everyone in the organisation to help build lasting customer relationships through superior customer value and satisfaction. As Wal-Mart founder Sam Walton asserted: 'There is only one boss. The customer. And he can fire everybody in the company from the chairman on down, simply by spending his money somewhere else.'

WHAT IS MARKETING?

Marketing, more than any other business function, deals with customers. Although we will soon explore more detailed definitions of marketing, perhaps the simplest definition is this one: marketing is managing profitable customer relationships. The twofold goal of marketing is to attract new customers by promising superior value and to keep and grow current customers by delivering satisfaction.

Tesco states that 'customers are at the centre of what we do', and that 'no one tries harder for customers'. IKEA's vision is to 'create a better everyday life for the many people'. Dell is a leader in the personal computer industry by consistently making good on its promise to 'be direct'. Dell makes it easy for customers to custom-design their own computers and have them delivered quickly to their home or office. These and other highly successful companies know that if they take care of their customers, market share and profits will follow.

Sound marketing is critical to the success of every organisation. Large for-profit firms such as Procter & Gamble, Toyota and Zara use marketing. But so do not-for-profit organisations such as universities, museums, symphony orchestras and even churches.

You already know a lot about marketing – it is all around you. You see the results of marketing in the abundance of products in your nearby department store. You see marketing in the advertisements on your TV screen, your magazine pages that arrive in the post or border your web pages. At home, where you work, and where you study, you see marketing in almost everything you do. Yet there is much more to marketing than meets the consumer's casual eye. Behind it all is a massive network of people and activities competing for your attention and purchases. Marketing is a set of extremely varied practices, and Europe is a diverse and exciting continent. In this book we will look at Russian beer brands being launched in the UK, French cars being advertised in Germany, Danish foods being sold in Arab supermarkets and European aircraft being sold around the world – and many other examples of marketing in, to and from Europe.

This book will give you a complete and formal introduction to the basic concepts and practices of today's marketing. In this chapter, we begin by defining *marketing* and the marketing process.

Marketing defined

What *is* marketing? Many people think of marketing only as selling and advertising. Even if you have chosen to study marketing deliberately and with forethought, you might think the same. However, selling and advertising are only the tip of the marketing iceberg.

Today, marketing must be understood not in the old sense of making a sale – 'telling and selling' – but in the new sense of *satisfying customer needs*. If the marketer does a good job of understanding consumer needs, develops products and services that provide superior customer value, and prices, distributes and promotes them effectively, these products will sell very easily. Thus, selling and advertising are only part of a larger 'marketing mix' – a set of marketing tools that work together to satisfy customer needs and build customer relationships. Marketing is as much attitude as action, as much perspective as planning.

Broadly defined, marketing is a social and managerial process by which individuals and organisations obtain what they need and want through creating and exchanging value with others. In a narrower business context, marketing involves building profitable, value-creating exchange relationships with customers. Hence, we define **marketing** as the process by which companies create value for customers and build strong customer relationships in order to capture value from customers in return.[9]

The marketing process

Figure 1.1 presents a simple five-step model of the marketing process. In the first four steps, companies work to understand consumers, create customer value and build strong customer relationships. In the final step, companies reap the rewards of creating superior customer value. By creating value *for* consumers, they in turn capture value *from* consumers in the form of sales, profits and long-term customer equity.

In this and the next chapter we will examine the steps of this simple model of marketing. In this chapter, we will review each step but focus more on the customer relationship steps – understanding customers, building customer relationships and capturing value from customers. In the following chapter, we will look more deeply into the second and third steps – designing marketing strategies and constructing marketing programmes.

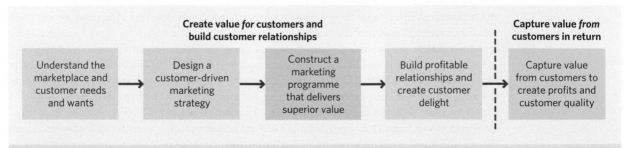

FIGURE 1.1
A simple model of the marketing process

UNDERSTANDING THE MARKETPLACE AND CUSTOMER NEEDS

As a first step, marketers need to understand customer needs and wants and the marketplace within which they operate. We now examine five core customer and marketplace concepts:

1   needs, wants and demands;

2   marketing offers (products, services and experiences);

3   value and satisfaction;

4   exchanges and relationships; and

5   markets.

Customer needs, wants and demands

The most basic concept underlying marketing is that of human needs. Human **needs** are states of felt deprivation. They include basic *physical* needs for food, clothing, warmth and safety; *social* needs for belonging and affection; and *individual* needs for knowledge and self-expression. These needs were not created by marketers; they are a basic part of the human make-up.

Wants are the form human needs take as they are shaped by culture and individual personality. A hungry person *needs* food but *wants* a burger, fries and a soft drink. A person in Mauritius *needs* food but *wants* a mango, rice, lentils and beans. Wants are shaped by one's society and are described in terms of objects that will satisfy needs. When backed by buying power, wants become **demands**. Given their wants and resources, people demand products with benefits that add up to the most value and satisfaction.

Outstanding marketing companies go to great lengths to learn about and understand their customers' needs, wants and demands. They conduct consumer research and analyse mountains of customer data – Tesco collects gigabytes per day through its Clubcards. Marketing people at all levels – including top management – stay close to customers. For example, at Richer Sounds audio-visual stores (**www.richersounds.com**) every after-sales questionnaire filled in and returned by a customer passes across the desk of the founder, Julian Richer.

Market offerings – products, services and experiences

Consumers' needs and wants are fulfilled through a **market offering** – some combination of products, services, information or experiences offered to a market to satisfy a need or want. Market offerings are not limited to physical *products*. They also include *services*, activities or benefits offered for sale that are essentially intangible and do not result in the ownership of anything. Examples include banking, airlines, hotels, accountancy and home repair services. More broadly, market offerings also include other entities, such as *persons, places, organisations, information* and *ideas*. For example, for the International Red Cross, the 'marketing offer' is health education and charitable workplace giving – not to mention efforts in recruiting blood donors.[10]

Many sellers make the mistake of paying more attention to the specific products they offer than to the benefits and experiences produced by these products. These sellers suffer from **marketing myopia**.[11] They are so obsessed with their products that they focus only on existing wants and lose sight of underlying customer needs. They forget that a product is only a means to solve a consumer problem. A manufacturer of drill bits may think that the customer needs a drill bit. But what the customer *really* needs is a neatly drilled hole. These sellers will have trouble if a new product comes along that serves the customer's need better or less expensively. The customer will have the same *need* but will *want* the new product.

Smart marketers look beyond the attributes of the products and services they sell. By coordinating several services and products, they create *brand experiences* for consumers. For example, Europe's biggest theme park is Parque Warner,[12] just outside Madrid. Visiting this is certainly an experience; so is a ride on a Harley-Davidson motorcycle. Your Nike's are more than just shoes: they are an empowering experience that makes you think you can 'just do it'. And you don't just watch AC Milan play: you immerse yourself in the San Siro experience.[13] 'What consumers really want [are offers] that dazzle their senses, touch their hearts, and stimulate their minds', declares one expert. 'They want [offers] that deliver an experience.'[14]

Customer value and satisfaction

Consumers usually face a broad array of products and services that might satisfy a given need. How do they choose among these many market offerings? Customers form expectations about the value and satisfaction that various market offerings will deliver and buy accordingly. Satisfied customers buy again and tell others about their good experiences. Dissatisfied customers often switch to competitors and disparage the product to others.

Marketers must be careful to set the right level of expectations. If they set expectations too low, they may satisfy those who buy but fail to attract enough buyers. If they raise expectations too high, buyers will be disappointed. Customer value and customer satisfaction are key building blocks for developing and managing customer relationships. We will revisit these core concepts later in the chapter.

Exchanges and relationships

Marketing occurs when people decide to satisfy needs and wants through exchange relationships. **Exchange** is the act of obtaining a desired object from someone by offering something in return. In the broadest sense, the marketer tries to bring about a response to some market offering. The response may be more than simply buying or trading products and services. For instance, a political candidate wants votes, a church wants a bigger congregation, an orchestra wants an audience, and a social action group wants to change government policy and public opinion.

Marketing consists of actions taken to build and maintain mutually beneficial exchange *relationships* with target audiences involving a product, service, idea or other object. Beyond simply attracting new customers and creating transactions, the goal is to retain customers and grow their business with the company. Marketers want to build strong relationships by consistently delivering superior customer value. We will expand on the important concept of managing customer relationships later in the chapter.

Markets

The concepts of exchange and relationships lead to the concept of a market. A **market** is the set of actual and potential buyers of a product. These buyers share a particular need or want that can be satisfied through exchange relationships.

Marketing means managing markets to bring about profitable customer relationships. However, creating these relationships takes work. Sellers must search for buyers, identify their needs, design good market offerings, set prices for them, promote them, and store and deliver them. Activities such as product development, research, communication, distribution, pricing and service are core marketing activities.

Although we normally think of marketing as being carried on by sellers, buyers also carry on marketing. Consumers do marketing when they search for the goods they need at prices they can afford. Company purchasing agents do marketing when they track down sellers and bargain for good terms.

Figure 1.2 shows the main elements in a modern marketing system. Most of the time we think of marketing as serving a market of final consumers in the face of competitors. The company and its competitors send their respective offers and messages to consumers, either directly or through marketing intermediaries. All the actors in the system are affected by major environmental forces (demographic, economic, physical, technological, political/ legal, social/cultural) that we discuss later (see Chapter 3).

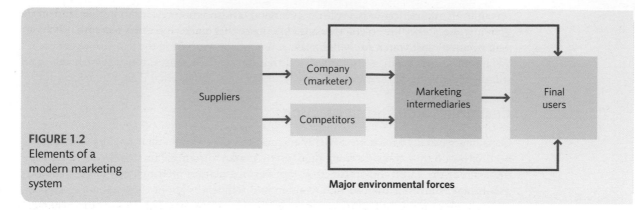

FIGURE 1.2
Elements of a
modern marketing
system

Each party in the system adds value for the next level. All of the arrows represent relation-ships that must be developed and managed. Thus, a company's success at building profitable relationships depends not only on its own actions, but also on how well the entire system serves the needs of final consumers. Aldi cannot fulfil its promise of low prices unless its suppliers provide merchandise at low costs. And BMW cannot deliver high quality to car buyers unless its dealers provide outstanding sales and service.

DESIGNING A CUSTOMER-DRIVEN MARKETING STRATEGY

Once it fully understands consumers and the marketplace, marketing management can design a customer-driven marketing strategy. We define **marketing management** as the art and science of choosing target markets and building profitable relationships with them. The marketing manager's aim is to find, attract, keep and grow target customers by creating, delivering and communicating superior customer value.

To design a winning marketing strategy, the marketing manager must answer two impor-tant questions: what customers will we serve (what's our target market) and how can we serve these customers best (what's our value proposition)? We will discuss these marketing strategy concepts briefly here, and then look at them in more detail in the next chapter.

Selecting customers to serve

The company must first decide *who* it will serve. It does this by dividing the market into segments of customers (*market segmentation*) and selecting which segments it will go after (*target marketing*). Some people think of marketing management as finding as many cus-tomers as possible and increasing demand. But marketing managers know that they cannot serve all customers in every way. By trying to serve all customers, they may not serve any customers well. Instead, the company wants to select only customers that it can serve well and profitably. For example, Marks & Spencer profitably targets the affluent; Lidl profitably targets families with modest means.

Some marketers may even seek *fewer* customers and lower demand. For example, some public transport systems have trouble meeting demand during peak usage periods. In these and other cases of excess demand, organisations may practise *demarketing* to reduce the number of customers or to shift their demand temporarily or permanently. In order to reduce demand for seats on trains, for example, London Underground has a price struc-ture to persuade tourists and other leisure travellers to take their trips after the morning rush hour, and many public healthcare organisations across Europe use demarketing to persuade people to use services only when they need them, and not simply when it is convenient.[15]

Thus, marketing managers must decide which customers they want to target, and on the level, timing and nature of their demand. Simply put, marketing management is *customer management* and *demand management*.

Choosing a value proposition

The company must also decide how it will serve targeted customers – how it will *differentiate and position* itself in the marketplace. A company's *value proposition* is the set of benefits or values it promises to deliver to consumers to satisfy their needs. Porsche promises driving performance and excitement and tells us that: 'There is no substitute.' Red Bull energy drink, on the other hand, captures a large part of the energy drink market by promising 'It gives you w-i-i-i-ngs!'

Such value propositions differentiate one brand from another. They answer the customer's question, 'Why should I buy your brand rather than a competitor's?' Companies must design strong value propositions that give them the greatest advantage in their target markets.

Marketing management orientations

Marketing management wants to design strategies that will build profitable relationships with target consumers. But what *overall approach* should guide these marketing strategies? What weight should be given to the interests of customers, the organisation and society? Very often, these interests conflict.

There are five alternative overall approaches, or 'concepts', to the design and implementation of marketing strategies: the *production, product, selling, marketing* and *societal marketing concepts*.

The production concept

The focus here is on production efficiency. The **production concept** holds that consumers will favour products that are available and highly affordable. Therefore, management should focus on improving production and distribution efficiency. This concept is one of the oldest orientations that guides sellers.

The production concept is still a useful philosophy in some situations. For example, Asian computer maker Legend dominates the highly competitive, price-sensitive Chinese PC market through low labour costs, high production efficiency and mass distribution. However, although useful in some situations, the production concept can lead to marketing myopia. Companies adopting this orientation run a major risk of focusing too narrowly on their own operations and losing sight of the real objective – satisfying customer needs and building customer relationships.

The product concept

Here, the focus is on the product itself. The **product concept** holds that consumers will favour products that offer the most in quality, performance and innovative features. Under this concept, marketing strategy focuses on making continuous product improvements.

Naturally, product quality and improvement are important parts of most marketing strategies. However, focusing *only* on the company's products can also lead to marketing myopia. For example, some manufacturers believe that if they can 'build a better mousetrap, the world will beat a path to their door'. But they are often rudely shocked. Buyers may well be looking for a better solution to a mouse problem but not necessarily for a better mousetrap. The better solution might be a chemical spray, an exterminating service, or something that works better than a mousetrap. Furthermore, a better mousetrap will not sell unless the manufacturer designs, packages and prices it attractively, places it in convenient distribution channels, brings it to the attention of people who need it, and convinces buyers that it is a better product.

The selling concept

Many companies follow the **selling concept**, which holds that consumers will not buy enough of the firm's products unless it undertakes a large-scale selling and promotion effort. The concept is typically practised with unsought goods – things that people often just do not think they need, such as insurance policies or donating blood. These industries must be good at tracking down prospects and selling them on product benefits.

Such aggressive selling, however, carries high risks. It focuses on creating sales transactions rather than on building long-term, profitable customer relationships. The aim often is to sell what the company makes rather than making what the market wants. It assumes that customers who are coaxed into buying the product will like it. Or, if they do not like it, they will possibly forget their disappointment and buy it again later. These are usually poor assumptions.

The marketing concept

The **marketing concept** holds that achieving organisational goals depends on knowing the needs and wants of target markets and delivering the desired satisfactions better than competitors do. Under the marketing concept, customer focus and value are the *paths* to sales and profits. Instead of a product-centred 'make and sell' philosophy, the marketing concept is a customer-centred 'sense and respond' philosophy. It views marketing not as 'hunting' but as 'gardening'. The job is not to find the right customers for your product, but to find the right products for your customers.

Figure 1.3 contrasts the selling concept and the marketing concept. The selling concept takes an *inside-out* perspective. It starts with the factory, focuses on the company's existing products, and calls for heavy selling and promotion to obtain profitable sales. It focuses primarily on customer conquest – getting short-term sales with little concern about who buys or why.

In contrast, the marketing concept takes an *outside-in* perspective. In the words of one Southwest Airlines blogger, 'we're NUTS about customers!'[16] The marketing concept starts with a well-defined market, focuses on customer needs, and integrates all the marketing activities that affect customers. In turn, it leads to profits by creating lasting relationships with the right customers based on customer value and satisfaction.

Implementing the marketing concept often means more than simply responding to customers' stated desires and obvious needs. *Customer-driven* companies research current customers in detail to learn about their desires, gather new product and service ideas, and test proposed product improvements. Such customer-driven marketing usually works well when a clear need exists and when customers know what they want.

In many cases, however, customers *do not* know what they want or even what is possible. For example, even 20 years ago, consumers would not have dreamt of asking for products we regard today as normal, like smartphones with face-time, tablet computers, 24-hour online buying, and satellite navigation systems for cars. Such situations call for *customer-driving* marketing – understanding customer needs even better than customers themselves do and creating products and services that meet existing and latent needs, now and in the future. As

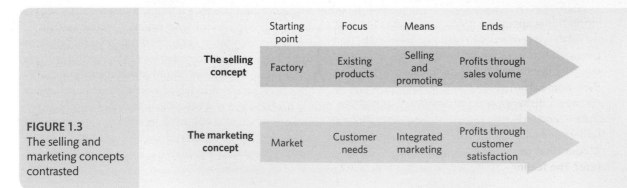

FIGURE 1.3
The selling and marketing concepts contrasted

an executive at 3M puts it: 'Our goal is to lead customers where they want to go before *they* know where they want to go.' In Marketing at Work 1.1 several managers from a variety of firms give their perspectives on what marketing is and how their companies implement it.

The societal marketing concept

The **societal marketing concept** questions whether the pure marketing concept overlooks possible conflicts between consumer *short-term wants* and consumer *long-term welfare*. Is a firm that satisfies the immediate needs and wants of target markets always doing what is best for consumers in the long run? The societal marketing concept holds that marketing strategy should deliver value to customers in a way that maintains or improves both the consumer's *and the society's* well-being.

Consider the fast-food industry. You may view today's giant fast-food chains as offering tasty and convenient food at reasonable prices. Yet many nutritionists and environmental groups have voiced concerns. They point to increasing levels of obesity in adults and in children at ever earlier ages. What's more, these products are wrapped in convenient packaging, leading to waste and pollution. Thus, in satisfying short-term consumer wants, the highly successful fast-food chains may be harming consumer health and causing environmental problems in the long run.[17]

Managers on marketing

MARKETING AT WORK 1.1

So how and why do businesses take marketing so seriously? Let's look at the personal perspectives from some current managers working in business today.

Electrolux – the Swedish manufacturer of household appliances – has been in business for nearly a hundred years and currently sells more than 40 million products globally for about €11 billion annually. The corporate motto is '*Thinking of you*' – but is the company's embracing of the marketing concept more than skin-deep? Richard Sells, the Chief Innovation Officer at Electrolux, gives his take as a designer on the importance of marketing:

> I think marketing ultimately is the bringing together of a consumer offer that is relevant and attractive to consumers, so whether you talk about that from the point of view of brand marketing, product marketing, marketing services, the offer in store – ultimately it's about bringing together an offer that is relevant and understanding the consumer well enough to know that that offer is relevant. Most of the home appliance markets are saturated, and therefore consumers are looking for more sophisticated appliances. They're looking for better designed appliances, things that add some value to their home. They're no longer simply saying, 'OK, I'll have a dishwasher because I've never had one before', and so in that respect it's important that we understand what their needs are. You know, does a product that we are offering give some unique feature? The feeling can be sort of, you know, 'Wow,

how did Electrolux know I needed that, because it really does solve my problem.'

Land Rover is a familiar name. For 60 years Land Rover has been producing high-quality utility vehicles. Colin Green is the Director of Global Marketing:

> I think marketing at its essence is understanding consumer needs, understanding whether you can satisfy those consumer needs and then presenting yourself in the marketplace through the principles of the four Ps – Price, Product, Promotion and Place – and getting those activities entirely focused on what the consumer is demanding and how you can meet those needs.

You'd expect a marketing manager to be onside with the idea of the importance of marketing, but what about at the very top level? Philip Popham, the Managing Director of Land Rover, comments:

> For me, marketing is all about positioning your brand and your product correctly. It's about developing and building desirability which really does take away the need for the selling process, it builds desirability of the product so people want it and it builds loyalty. It's about handling the customer in the right way, making him or her proud to be associated with the brand, proud to be associated with the product which he or she has purchased and wanting more of that in the future, that's what good marketing is.

Land Rover and Electrolux are huge companies employing thousands of people and marketing their products globally. What about smaller businesses – is marketing relevant there as well? Acme Whistles has been in business for more than 130 years, with its 100 employees making and selling 6 million whistles per year. Quite simply, they think they make the world's best whistles. Acme products are used by police forces and animal trainers around the globe, by referees in most professional football leagues, and in the early 1900s it supplied the whistles for use on the *Titanic!* Simon Topman, the MD at Acme, explains his take on how marketing is relevant to his business:

> **Our marketing is undoubtedly affected by the way that we make things. A very good example of that is a tradition that was laid down by Joseph Hudson, our founder, who like any founder of a business was perhaps a little eccentric and a very determined individual. One of the things he used to do was personally blow every whistle before it left the factory. The production now is about 6 million a year so, of course, that isn't possible anymore – but we still do test every single one. Everything that leaves this factory is as we say in our marketing literature: 'Individually tested and guaranteed.' There are rejects, but we find them, not the customers.**

Successful marketing for me is linking together all resources of the company with the demand of the customer. So that everybody within this place right down to the cleaners knows what the customer wants and understands that keeping the machinery clean and the floor space around it clean is yet another way of making sure that the plating isn't contaminated, or the solder isn't contaminated, so the whistle looks better and lasts longer. And when you have all that lined up properly, then I think you have a great story to tell, great marketing and a business that's truly tuned in to its customers.

Our ultimate aim is to make sure that that very famous brand name Acme, and our product link with it, is obligatory for the buyers of whistles. That such is the demand by the customer that retailers can't afford to not carry that product. To that extent we educate our entire workforce from the cleaners all the way through to those who are dealing with sales calls on what the customer wants, why the customer wants it, how they want it so that we're filling up that chain all the way from the very bottom right through to the customer. The whole company is focused on that customer – making our product the best they can possibly get, the one they've got to have.

Sources: Corporate websites for Acme Whistles (www.acmewhistles.co.uk), Electrolux (www.electrolux.com/), Land Rover (www.landrover.com/), and interviews with managers conducted by Pearson Education Ltd.

How firms market their products varies from industry to industry, as these images from Acme Whistles, Electrolux and Land Rover show – but there are commonalities as well

Source: Electrolux (bottom left); Getty Images/Frank Greenaway (top left); Getty Images/Tomothy Hiatt/Stringer (bottom left). All with permission.

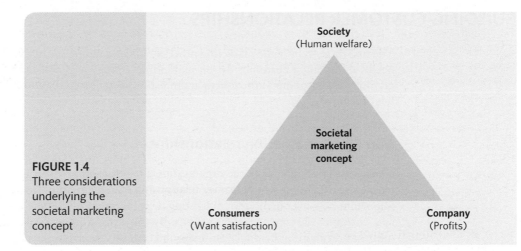

FIGURE 1.4
Three considerations underlying the societal marketing concept

As Figure 1.4 shows, companies should balance three considerations in setting their marketing strategies: company profits, consumer wants *and* society's interests. Cadbury had a problem in 2007 when warnings for nut-allergy sufferers were missed off the packaging of its Creme Eggs. Despite this happening at Easter, when sales are at their absolute peak, and such allergies affecting only a tiny proportion of the population, Cadbury felt it had no choice but to recall the products.[18]

PREPARING A MARKETING PLAN AND PROGRAMME

The company's marketing strategy outlines which customers the company will serve and how it will create value for these customers. Next, the marketer develops a marketing programme that will actually deliver the intended value to target customers. The marketing programme aims to build customer relationships by transforming the marketing strategy into action. It consists of the firm's *marketing mix*, the set of marketing tools the firm uses to implement its marketing strategy.

The best known, and simplest, way of classifying the major marketing mix tools is called the *four Ps* of marketing: product, price, place and promotion. Do not make the mistake of thinking that the well-known 4Ps classification is a profound marketing concept – rather, it is a simple framework that helps to classify the many tools available to the marketing manager into coherent groups. To deliver on its value proposition, the firm must first create a need-satisfying market offering (product). It must decide how much it will charge for the offer (price) and how it will make the offer available to target consumers (place). Finally, it must communicate with target customers about the offer and persuade them of its merits (promotion). We will explore marketing programmes and the marketing mix in much more detail in later chapters.

MAKING CONNECTIONS Linking the concepts

What have you learned so far about marketing? For the moment, set aside the more formal definitions we've examined and try to develop your own understanding of marketing.

- In *your own words*, what *is* marketing? Write down *your* definition. Does your definition include such key concepts as customer value and relationships?

- What does marketing *mean* to you? How does it affect your life on a daily basis?

- What brand of trainers did you purchase last? Describe your relationship with Nike, New Balance, Reebok, Adidas, or whichever company made the shoes you purchased.

BUILDING CUSTOMER RELATIONSHIPS

The first three steps in the marketing process – understanding the marketplace and customer needs, designing a customer-driven marketing strategy and constructing marketing programmes – all lead up to the fourth and most important step: building profitable customer relationships.

Managing marketing relationships

The necessity of managing the organisation's relationships, sometimes called relationship marketing[19] or, popularly, **customer relationship management** (CRM), is perhaps the most important new idea in modern marketing. Until recently, CRM has been defined narrowly as a customer data management activity. By this definition, it involves managing detailed information about individual customers and carefully managing customer 'touch points' in order to maximise customer loyalty – that is, the company uses its data about past transactions and interactions as a corporate memory, to help it more effectively engage with its customers in the present. We will discuss this narrower CRM activity later (see Chapter 4), when we deal with managing marketing information.

More recently, however, CRM has taken on a broader meaning. In this broader sense, it is the overall process of building and maintaining profitable customer relationships by delivering superior customer value and satisfaction. It deals with all aspects of acquiring, keeping and growing customers – the opening case of UEFA showed how complex this can be.

Perceived customer value: when deciding to purchase a Prius, customers will weigh its benefits against the benefits of owning another hybrid or non-hybrid brand

Source: Image courtesy of The Advertising Archives.

Relationship building blocks: customer value and satisfaction

The key to building lasting customer relationships is to create superior customer value and satisfaction. Satisfied customers are more likely to be loyal customers and to give the company a larger share of their business for longer.

Customer value

Attracting and retaining customers can be a difficult task. Customers often face a bewildering array of products and services from which to choose. A customer is likely to buy from the firm that offers the highest **customer perceived value** – the customer's evaluation of the difference between all the benefits and all the costs of a market offering relative to those of competing offers.

For example, Toyota Prius hybrid car owners gain a number of benefits. The most obvious benefit is fuel efficiency and hence reduced running costs. However, by purchasing a Prius the owners may also receive some status and image values. Driving a Prius makes owners feel and appear more environmentally responsible. When deciding whether to purchase a Prius, customers will weigh these and other perceived values of owning the car against the money, effort and psychic costs of acquiring it. Moreover, they will compare the value of owning a Prius against that of owning another hybrid or non-hybrid car. They will select the brand that gives them the greatest perceived value. Other drivers may prioritise factors other than efficiency and environmental impact – such as performance and social status reinforcement. These people would be more likely to buy a Ferrari or a Mercedes.

Customers often do not judge product values and costs accurately or objectively. They act on *perceived* value. For example, is the Prius really the most economical choice? Running costs may be significantly cheaper, but an alternative like a Skoda might be much cheaper to buy. In reality, it might take years to save enough in reduced fuel costs to offset the car's higher price. However, Prius buyers perceive that they are getting real value. A survey of the ownership experiences of 69,000 new car buyers showed that Prius owners *perceived* more overall value for their money than buyers of any other new car.[20] How many of them are likely to have considered it objectively – even to the extent of some calculations on the back of an envelope?

Customer satisfaction

Customer satisfaction depends on the product's perceived performance relative to a buyer's expectations. If the product's performance falls short of expectations, the customer is dissatisfied. If performance matches expectations, the customer is satisfied. If performance exceeds expectations, the customer is highly satisfied or delighted.

Outstanding marketing companies go out of their way to keep important customers satisfied. Highly satisfied customers make repeat purchases and tell others about their good experiences with the product. Most studies show that higher levels of customer satisfaction lead to greater customer loyalty, which in turn results in better company performance.[21] The key is to match customer expectations with company performance. Smart companies aim to *delight* customers by promising only what they can deliver, then delivering *more* than they promise.

However, although the customer-centred firm seeks to deliver high customer satisfaction relative to competitors, it does not attempt to *maximise* customer satisfaction. A company can always increase customer satisfaction by lowering its price or increasing its services. But this may result in lower profits. Thus, the purpose of marketing is to generate customer value profitably.

Customer relationship levels and tools

Companies can build customer relationships at many levels, depending on the nature of the target market. At one extreme, a company with many low-margin customers may seek to develop *basic relationships* with them. For example, Tesco has handed out millions of Clubcard loyalty cards which it uses to collect and analyse data on the shopping habits of a good proportion of the UK population. At the other extreme, in markets with few customers and high margins, sellers want to create *full partnerships* with key customers. This is often the case where one business is selling to another – P&G customer teams work closely with Sainsbury's, Asda, Carrefour and other major supermarkets – but also where the product is customised or tailored to the specific needs of a specific customer – such as a bespoke suit. In between these two extreme situations, other levels of customer relationships are appropriate.

Beyond offering consistently high value and satisfaction, marketers can use specific marketing tools to develop stronger bonds with consumers. For example, many companies now offer *frequency marketing programmes* that reward customers who buy frequently or in large amounts. Airlines offer frequent-flyer programmes and hotels give room upgrades to their frequent guests.

Other companies sponsor *club marketing programmes* that offer members special discounts and create member communities. For example, Porsche, the German sports car manufacturer, sponsors owners' clubs in many countries around the world. As well as organising purely social events like dinners, track days and charity fundraising events, the clubs also run trips to the Porsche manufacturing and development centres in Stuttgart, Leipzig and Weissach. Porsche as a commercial enterprise has a brand and human presence at all of these events and makes sure that the relationships with current owners are maintained and developed over time.[22]

To build customer relationships, companies can add structural ties as well as financial and social benefits. A business marketer might supply customers with special equipment or online linkages that help them manage their orders, payroll or inventory.

Building customer relationships. Porsche helps to maintain the community spirit of Porsche owners by sponsoring and endorsing owners' clubs across Europe

Source: Dick Lovett.co.uk/ LLoyd Precious.

The changing nature of customer relationships

Dramatic changes are occurring in the ways in which companies are relating to their customers. Yesterday's companies focused on mass marketing to all customers at arm's length. Today's companies are building more direct and lasting relationships with more carefully selected customers. Here are some important trends in the way companies are relating to their customers.

Relating with more carefully selected customers

Few firms today still practise true mass marketing – selling in a standardised way to any customer who comes along. Today, most marketers realise that they do not want relationships with every customer. Instead, companies now are targeting fewer, more profitable customers. Called *selective relationship management*, many companies now use customer profitability analysis to weed out customers that cost them money and to target ones that are profitable for pampering. Once they identify profitable customers, firms can create attractive offers and special handling to capture these customers and earn their loyalty.

But what should the company do with unprofitable customers? If it cannot turn them into profitable ones, it may even want to 'fire' customers that are too unreasonable or that cost more to serve than they are worth. For example, banks now routinely assess customer profitability based on such factors as an account's average balances, account activity, services usage, branch visits and other variables. For most banks, profitable customers with large balances are pampered with premium services, whereas unprofitable, low-balance ones get the cold shoulder. The Dutch bank ING Direct selects accounts differently. It seeks relationships with customers who do not need or want expensive pampering while firing those who do.

ING Direct is the fast-food chain of financial services. With a handful of offerings including savings accounts, mortgages and certificates of deposit (CDs) and home equity loans, the bank is about as no-frills as it gets. Yet its profits are downright gaudy. ING Direct's secret? Selective relationship management. The bank lures low-maintenance customers with high interest rates. Then, to offset that generosity, the bank does 91 per cent of its transactions online and offers bare-bones service. In fact, ING Direct USA routinely 'fires' overly demanding customers. By ditching clients who need the direction, hand-holding and personalised service of a branch bank, the company has driven its cost per account to a third of the industry average.

The CEO of ING Direct USA, Arkadi Kuhlmann, explains:

We need to keep expenses down, which doesn't work when customers want a lot of [hand-holding]. If the average customer phone call costs us $5.25 and the average account revenue is $12 per month, all it takes is 100,000 misbehaving customers for costs to go through the roof. So when a customer calls too many times or wants too many exceptions to the rule, our sales associate can basically say: 'Look, this doesn't fit you. You need to go back to your community bank and get the kind of contact you're comfortable with . . . .' It's all about finding customers who are comfortable with a self-serve business; we try to get you in and out fast . . . . Even though our touch is light and short, it's all about how you feel in the end. The smile at a take-out window can be just as satisfying as good service at a sit-down restaurant. While this makes for some unhappy customers, [those are the] ones you want out the door anyway.'[23]

Of course, marketing strategies and tactics like this can cause significant issues for society as a whole – as we saw with the dissatisfied football fans in the UEFA case – and we will discuss these later (see Chapter 16).

Relating for the long term

Just as companies are being more selective about which customers they choose to serve, they are serving chosen customers in a deeper, more lasting way. Today's companies are going beyond designing strategies to *attract* new customers and create *transactions* with them. They are using CRM to *retain* current customers and build profitable, long-term *relationships* with them. From this perspective marketing is the science and art of creating, developing and sustaining interactive relationships with profitable customers.[24]

Why the new emphasis on retaining and developing/growing customers? In the past, growing markets and an upbeat economy meant a plentiful supply of new customers. However, companies today face some new marketing realities. Changing demographics, more sophisticated competitors, and overcapacity in many industries mean that there are fewer customers to go around. Many companies are now fighting for shares of flat or fading markets.

As a result, the costs of attracting new consumers are rising. In fact, on average, it can cost a lot more to attract a new customer than it does to keep a current customer satisfied – meaning that some investment in keeping current customers can save a lot further down the line.

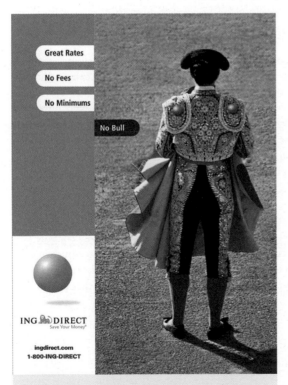

Selective relationship management: ING Direct seeks relationships with customers who do not need or want expensive pampering, routinely 'firing' overly demanding customers. The bank lures low-maintenance customers with high interest rates and no fees or minimums. 'No bull!'

Source: ING Direct. With permission.

Relating directly

Beyond connecting more deeply with their customers, many companies are also connecting more *directly*. In fact, direct marketing is booming. Consumers can now buy virtually any product without going to a shop – by telephone, mail-order catalogues, kiosks and online. Businesses routinely shop on the Web for items ranging from standard office supplies to high-priced, high-tech computer equipment.

Some companies sell *only* via direct channels – firms such as Dell, Expedia and **Amazon.com**, to name only a few. Other companies use direct connections to supplement their other communications and distribution channels. For example, Xbox consoles and games are available from many high-street retailers, but once set up and connected to the Web, customers can buy new games, add-ons for games they already own, music and films through the online marketplace – as well as being able to purchase trailers and demos of new games.

Some marketers have hailed direct marketing as the 'marketing model of the next century'. They foresee a day when all buying and selling will involve direct connections between companies and their customers. Others, while agreeing that direct marketing will play a growing and important role, see it as just one more way to approach the marketplace. We will take a closer look at the world of direct marketing later (see Chapters 13 and 14).

Partner relationship management

When it comes to creating customer value and building strong customer relationships, today's marketers know that they cannot go it alone. They must work closely with a variety of marketing partners. In addition to being good at CRM, marketers must also be good at **partner relationship management**. Major changes are occurring in how marketers partner with others inside and outside the company jointly to bring more value to customers.

Partners inside the company

Traditionally, marketers have been charged with understanding customers and representing customer needs to different company departments. The old thinking was that marketing is done only by marketing, sales and customer support people. However, in today's more connected world, marketing no longer has sole ownership of customer interactions. Every functional area can interact with customers, especially electronically. The new thinking is that every employee must be customer focused. David Packard, late co-founder of Hewlett-Packard, wisely said, 'Marketing is far too important to be left only to the marketing department.'[25] This has led to the idea of 'the part-time marketer' – someone who works for the organisation but not in the marketing department and who has, nevertheless, the opportunity to impact positively or negatively upon how customers think about the firm. Technicians can make a good or bad impression, as can shop-floor staff and anyone who answers the phone when a customer calls.[26]

Today, rather than letting each department go its own way, firms are linking all departments in the cause of creating customer value. Rather than assigning only sales and marketing people to customers, they are forming cross-functional customer teams. Marketing at Work 1.1 gave the perspectives of those not employed as marketers but who nevertheless understood the importance of marketing in their roles as senior managers or product designers. As an example of this culture, P&G assigns 'customer development teams' to each of its major retailer accounts. These teams – consisting of sales and marketing people, operations specialists, market and financial analysts, and others – coordinate the efforts of many P&G departments towards helping the retailer be more successful.

Marketing partners outside the firm

Changes are also occurring in how marketers connect with their suppliers, channel partners and even competitors. Most companies today are networked companies, relying heavily on partnerships with other firms.

Marketing channels consist of distributors, retailers and others who connect the company to its buyers. The *supply chain* describes a longer channel, stretching from raw materials through components to final products that are carried to final buyers. For example, the supply chain for PCs consists of suppliers of computer chips and other components, the computer manufacturer, and the distributors, retailers and others who sell the computers.

Through *supply chain management*, many companies today are strengthening their connections with partners all along the supply chain. They know that their fortunes rest not just on how well they perform. Success at building customer relationships also rests on how well their entire supply chain performs against competitors' supply chains. These companies do not just treat suppliers as vendors and distributors as customers. They treat both as partners in delivering customer value. On the one hand, for example, Mercedes works closely with carefully selected suppliers to improve quality and operations efficiency. On the other hand, it works with its franchise dealers to provide top-grade sales and service support that will bring customers through the door and keep them coming back.

Beyond managing the supply chain, today's companies are also discovering that they need *strategic* partners if they hope to be effective. In the new, more competitive global environment, going it alone is going out of style. *Strategic alliances* are booming across almost all industries and services. For example, Dell joins forces with software creators such as Oracle and Microsoft to help boost business sales of its servers and their software. And Volkswagen is working jointly with agricultural processing firm Archer Daniels Midland further to develop and utilise biodiesel fuel.

Sometimes even competitors work together for mutual benefit. For example, oral-care competitors P&G and Philips joined forces to create the innovative IntelliClean system, a combination power toothbrush and toothpaste dispensing system. For years Sony partnered with Ericsson to produce smartphones – the Japanese electronics giant brought decades of experience in manufacturing high-quality handheld gadgets and the Swedish telecoms giant brought detailed knowledge in respect of design and use of this product category by customers. This successful partnership came to an end in 2012 when Sony bought Ericsson's share of the Sony Ericsson venture.[27]

CAPTURING VALUE FROM CUSTOMERS

The first four steps in the marketing process involve building customer relationships by creating and delivering superior customer value. The final step involves capturing value in return, in the form of current and future sales, market share and profits. By creating superior customer value, the firm creates highly satisfied customers who stay loyal and buy more. This, in turn, means greater long-run returns for the firm. Here, we discuss the outcomes of creating customer value: customer loyalty and retention, share of market and share of customer, and customer equity.

Creating customer loyalty and retention

Good CRM creates customer delight. In turn, delighted customers remain loyal and talk favourably to others about the company and its products. Studies show big differences in the loyalty of customers who are less satisfied, somewhat satisfied and completely satisfied. Even a slight drop from complete satisfaction can create an enormous drop in loyalty. Thus, the aim of CRM is to create not just customer satisfaction, but customer delight.[28]

Companies are realising that losing a customer means losing more than a single sale. It means losing the entire stream of purchases that the customer would make over a lifetime of patronage. For example, Porsche believe that someone who buys a new Porsche will typically replace it with a new car after seven years. Five years after purchase, the company starts to target these owners with letters and other communications to make sure their next car is a Porsche as well – if this works, that is another £70,000 in revenue. Indeed, Lexus estimates that a single satisfied and loyal customer is worth $600,000 in lifetime sales. You almost certainly visit a supermarket once a week or more – you may not spend much per visit, but consider how this sum adds up over a year or two. Thus, working to retain and grow customers makes good economic sense. In fact, a company can lose money on a specific transaction but still benefit greatly from a long-term relationship. Banks recognise this when putting together account packages for students. While at university, it is likely they will cost rather than make their bank money – because of reduced rate loans and overdrafts, low-level balances and often free gifts for account opening. When the student becomes a full-time worker four or five years later, that is the point at which this customer will begin to become profitable – statistics tell us that you are more likely to get divorced than change your bank.

This means that companies must aim high in building customer relationships. Customer delight creates an emotional relationship with a product or service, not just a rational preference.

Growing share of customer

Beyond simply retaining good customers to capture customer lifetime value, good CRM can help marketers to increase their **share of customer** – the share they get of the customer's purchasing in their product categories. Thus, banks want to increase 'share of wallet'. Supermarkets and restaurants want to get more 'share of stomach'. Car companies want to increase 'share of garage' and airlines want greater 'share of travel'.

To increase share of customer, firms can offer greater variety to current customers. Or they can train employees to cross-sell and up-sell in order to market more products and services to existing customers. For example, Amazon is highly skilled at managing and developing relationships with its customers to increase its share of each customer's purchases.[29] Originally an online bookseller, Amazon now offers customers music, films, gifts, toys, consumer electronics, office products and home improvement items. In addition, based on each customer's purchase history, the company recommends related products that might be of interest – and the more you buy, the better it becomes at predicting what else will interest you – it even calls your personal, customised Amazon homepage 'the page you made'. In this way, Amazon captures a greater share of each customer's spending budget.

Building customer equity

We can now see the importance of not just acquiring customers, but of keeping and growing them as well. CRM takes a long-term view. Companies want not only to create profitable customers, but to 'own' them for life, capture their **customer lifetime value**, and earn a greater share of their purchases.

What is customer equity?

The ultimate aim of CRM is to produce high *customer equity*.[30] **Customer equity** is the combined discounted customer lifetime values of all of the company's current and potential customers. Clearly, the more loyal the firm's profitable customers, the higher the firm's customer equity. Customer equity may be a better measure of a firm's performance than current sales or market share. Whereas sales and market share reflect the past, customer equity suggests the future. Consider the US car manufacturer Cadillac:

> In the 1970s and 1980s Cadillac had some of the most loyal customers in the industry. To an entire generation of car buyers, the name 'Cadillac' defined American luxury. Cadillac's share of the luxury car market reached a whopping 51 per cent in 1976. Based on market share and sales, the brand's future looked rosy. However, measures of customer equity would have painted a bleaker picture. Cadillac customers were getting older (average age 60) and average customer lifetime value was falling. Many Cadillac buyers were on their last car. Thus, although Cadillac's market share was good, its customer equity was not. Compare this with BMW. Its more youthful and vigorous image didn't win BMW the early market share war. However, it did win BMW younger customers with higher customer lifetime values. The result? In the years that followed, BMW's market share and profits soared while Cadillac's fortunes eroded badly. Thus, market share is not the answer. We should care not just about current sales but also about future sales. Customer lifetime value and customer equity are the name of the game. Recognising this, Cadillac is now making the Caddy cool again by targeting a younger generation of consumers with new high-performance models and its highly successful Break Through advertising campaign.[31]

Building the right relationships with the right customers

Companies should manage customer equity carefully. They should view customers as assets that need to be managed and maximised. But not all customers, not even all loyal customers,

FIGURE 1.5
Customer
relationship groups

Source: Reprinted by
permission of *Harvard Business
Review.* Exhibit adapted from
'The Mismanagement of
Customer Loyalty', by Werner
Reinartz and V. Kumar, July
2002, p. 93. Copyright ©
2002 by the Harvard Business
School Publishing Corporation;
all rights reserved.

		Short-term customers	Long-term customers
Potential profitability	High profitability	**Butterflies** Good fit between company's offerings and customer's needs; high profit potential	**True Friends** Good fit between company's offerings and customer's needs; highest profit potential
	Low profitability	**Strangers** Little fit between company's offerings and customer's needs; lowest profit potential	**Barnacles** Limited fit between company's offerings and customer's needs; low profit potential

Projected loyalty

are good investments. Surprisingly, some loyal customers can be unprofitable, and some disloyal customers can be profitable. Which customers should the company acquire and retain? 'Up to a point, the choice is obvious: keep the consistent big spenders and lose the erratic small spenders', says one expert. 'But what about the erratic big spenders and the consistent small spenders? It's often unclear whether they should be acquired or retained, and at what cost.'[32]

The company can classify customers according to their potential profitability and manage its relationships with them accordingly. Figure 1.5 classifies customers into one of four relationship groups, according to their profitability and projected loyalty.[33] Each group requires a different relationship management strategy. 'Strangers' show low profitability and little projected loyalty. There is little fit between the company's offerings and their needs. The relationship management strategy for these customers is simple: do not invest anything in them.

'Butterflies' are profitable but not loyal. There is a good fit between the company's offerings and their needs. However, as with real butterflies, we can enjoy them for only a short while and then they are gone. Efforts to convert butterflies into loyal customers are rarely successful. Instead, the company should enjoy the butterflies for the moment. It should use promotional blitzes to attract them, create satisfying and profitable transactions with them, and then cease investing in them until the next time around.

'True Friends' are both profitable and loyal. There is a strong fit between their needs and the company's offerings. The firm wants to make continuous relationship investments to delight these customers and nurture, retain and grow them. It wants to turn true friends into 'true believers', who come back regularly and tell others about their good experiences with the company. Apple has succeeded in this – there is even a website called 'The Cult of Mac' (**www.cultofmac.com**).

'Barnacles' are highly loyal but not very profitable. There is a limited fit between their needs and the company's offerings. An example is smaller bank customers who bank regularly but do not generate enough returns to cover the costs of maintaining their accounts. Like barnacles on the hull of a ship, they create drag. Barnacles are perhaps the most problematic customers. The company might be able to improve their profitability by selling them more, raising their fees, or reducing service to them. However, if they cannot be made profitable, they should be 'fired'.

The point here is an important one: different types of customer require different relationship management strategies. The goal is to build the *right relationships* with the *right customers.*

MAKING CONNECTIONS Linking the concepts

We've covered a lot of territory. Again, slow down for a moment and develop *your own* thoughts about marketing.

● In *your own words*, what *is* marketing and what does it seek to accomplish?

● How well does Ford manage its relationships with customers? What CRM strategy does it use? Compare the relationship management strategies of Tesco and Asda.

● Think of a company for which you are a 'true friend'. What strategy does this company use to manage its relationship with you?

THE NEW MARKETING LANDSCAPE

As the world spins on, dramatic changes are occurring in the marketplace. Richard Love of Hewlett-Packard observes: 'The pace of change is so rapid that the ability to change has now become a competitive advantage.' As the marketplace changes, so must those who serve it.

In this section, we examine the major trends and forces that are changing the marketing landscape and challenging marketing strategy. We look at four major developments: the new digital age, rapid globalisation, the call for more ethics and social responsibility, and the growth in not-for-profit marketing.

The new digital age

The **Internet** has and is continuing to revolutionise how companies create value for customers and build and maintain customer relationships. The digital age has fundamentally changed customers' notions of convenience, speed, price, product information and service. Thus, today's marketing requires new thinking and action. Companies need to retain most of the skills and practices that have worked in the past. But they will also need to add major new competencies and practices if they hope to grow and prosper in the changing digital environment. Now, more than ever before, we are all connected to each other and to things near and far in the world around us. The Orient-Express took three days to travel between Paris and Istanbul. An air passenger could fly round the world twice or more in that time. Where it once took days or weeks to receive news about important world events, we now see them as they are occurring through live satellite broadcasts. Where it once took weeks to correspond with others in distant places, they are now only moments away by phone or email.

The technology boom has created exciting new ways to learn about and track customers, and to create products and services tailored to individual customer needs. Technology is also helping companies to distribute products more efficiently and effectively. And it's helping them to communicate with customers in large groups or one to one.

Through video conferencing, marketing researchers at a company's headquarters in Paris can look in on focus groups in Prague without ever stepping onto an aeroplane. With only a few clicks of a mouse button, a direct marketer can tap into online data services to learn anything from what car you drive, to what you read, to what flavour of ice cream you prefer. Or, using today's powerful computers, marketers can create their own detailed customer databases and use them to target individual customers with offers designed to meet their specific needs.

Technology has also brought a new wave of communication and advertising tools – on mobile phones, podcasts and even in virtual online worlds like Second Life. Marketers can use these tools to zero-in on selected customers with carefully targeted messages. Through e-commerce, customers can learn about, design, order and pay for products and services, without ever leaving home. For products like music, films and games, delivery can be almost instantaneous. From virtual reality displays that test new products to online virtual stores that sell them, the technology boom is affecting every aspect of marketing.

The Internet

Today, the Internet links individuals and businesses of all types to each other and to information all around the world. It allows anytime, anywhere connections to information, entertainment and communication. Companies are using the Internet to build closer relationships with customers and marketing partners. Beyond competing in traditional market*places,* they now have access to exciting new market*spaces.*

These days, it is hard to find a company that does not use the Web in a significant way – or one that does not have new opportunities and challenges for marketers. We will explore the impact of the new digital age in more detail later (see Chapter 14).

Rapid globalisation

As they are redefining their relationships with customers and partners, marketers are also taking a fresh look at the ways in which they connect with the broader world around them. In a rapidly shrinking world, many marketers are now connected *globally* with their customers and marketing partners.

Today, almost every company, large or small, is touched in some way by global competition. Your local florist might buy its flowers from the Netherlands, while BMW and Mercedes compete in their home market of Germany with giant Japanese rivals like Toyota and Nissan. A fledgling Internet retailer finds itself receiving orders from all over the world at the same time as an Italian consumer goods producer introduces new products into emerging markets abroad.

Coca-Cola offers a mind-boggling 400 different brands in more than 200 countries. MTV has joined the elite of global brands, delivering localised versions of its music channels in 30 languages to 161 countries.[34]

Today, companies are not only trying to sell more of their locally produced goods in international markets, but also buying more supplies and components abroad. For example, Isaac Mizrahi, one of the top US fashion designers, may choose cloth woven from Australian wool with designs printed in Italy. He will design a dress and email the drawing to a Hong Kong agent, who will place the order with a Chinese factory. Finished dresses will be flown to New York, where they will be redistributed to department and speciality stores around the country.

Thus, managers in countries around the world are increasingly taking a global, not just local, view of the company's industry, competitors and opportunities. They are asking: What is global marketing? How does it differ from domestic marketing? How do global competitors and forces affect our business? To what extent should we 'go global'? We will discuss the global marketplace in more detail later (see Chapter 15).

The call for more ethics and social responsibility

Marketers are re-examining their relationships with social values and responsibilities and with the very Earth that sustains us. As the worldwide consumerism and environmentalism movements mature, today's marketers are being called on to take greater responsibility for the social and environmental impact of their actions – whether it be the place of manufacture, the packaging surrounding the product or how far the finished item travels before being sold. Corporate ethics and social responsibility have become hot topics for almost every business and few companies can ignore the renewed and very demanding environmental movement.

The social responsibility and environmental movements will place even stricter demands on companies in the future. Some companies resist these movements, responding only when forced by legislation or organised consumer outcries. More forward-looking companies, however, readily accept their responsibilities to the world around them. They view socially responsible actions as an opportunity to do well by doing good. They seek ways to profit by serving the best long-term interests of their customers and communities.

Some companies – such as Ben & Jerry's, The Body Shop, the Co-op and others – are practising 'caring capitalism', setting themselves apart by being civic-minded and responsible. They are building social responsibility and action into their company value and mission statements. For example, the financial services division of the Co-op – the Co-operative Bank – is a leader in respect of investing the money of its clients. Armaments manufacturers, industries which pollute heavily and companies that provide poor conditions for their staff are all on the Co-op's investment blacklist. In turn, the supermarket portion of the business has been a pioneer on many consumer rights issues – genetically modified foods, sourcing from sustainable resources and clear labelling on all foods. We will revisit the relationship between marketing and social responsibility in greater detail later (see Chapter 16).

The growth of not-for-profit sector marketing

In the past, marketing has been most widely applied in the for-profit business sector. In recent years, however, marketing also has become a major part of the strategies of many not-for-profit organisations, such as universities, hospitals, museums, orchestras and even churches. Many performing arts groups – even Russia's famous Mariinsky Company, which performs opera and ballet to packed houses – face huge operating deficits that they must cover by more aggressive donor marketing from businesses like Gazprom, BP and Total, for example.[35] Finally, many long-standing not-for-profit organisations – the YMCA, the Salvation Army and the Scouts are now modernising their missions and 'products' to attract more members, visitors or donors.[36]

Government agencies have also shown an increased interest in marketing. For example, the national defence forces of most European countries – who rely on volunteers rather than conscripts – have a marketing plan to attract recruits, and various government agencies across the Continent are now designing *social marketing campaigns* to encourage energy conservation and concern for the environment or to discourage smoking, excessive drinking and drug use.

The Mariinsky Theatre in St Petersburg, Russia, uses marketing to raise money from sponsors

Sources: Alamy Images/ITAR-TASS Photo Agency (left); RIA Novsoti (right).

Metaphors in marketing

Metaphors are very important in everyday life, and they are very important in marketing too. In everyday life we might send a Facebook message to our friends telling them that we 'killed' a 10 km run, or that our football team 'destroyed' the opposition in an important match. Of course, everyone concerned understands that we are talking metaphorically. A 10 km run is not the sort of thing that can be killed; and it is to be hoped that when your football team destroyed the opposition this was only a figure of speech and the opponents were all perfectly healthy and able to walk home at the end of it. Much of the time metaphor becomes so much a part of our everyday language that we do not even notice that we are using it. Probably one of the most amusing developments in the use of the English language in recent years, particularly popular among young people, is to say that something is 'literally' the case when, in fact, what is meant is that it is metaphorically the case, as in 'I dropped a book on my foot and now my foot is *literally* killing me'. This is literally using the word literally to mean 'not literally', but we have to accept that the same word is now used with two exactly opposite meanings; yes, literally does mean both 'literally' and 'not literally' (so, metaphorically or figuratively). Language is that sort of thing. Meanings are fluid. Words with perfectly respectable meanings can be reinvented simply because people choose to use them in a different way. Literally means 'not literally'. Get over it!

Metaphors in particular, and the fluidity of the language more generally, greatly interest marketers. As an exercise, you could usefully spend a few minutes trying to think of some of the more prominent metaphors commonly used in marketing. Metaphors combine two different ideas or concepts to create a symbolic bridge between them that expresses something meaningful. Rather than hearing that Red Bull is a drink containing substances that may make you feel more alert, what we hear is that Red Bull gives you wings. Rather than hearing that Budweiser tastes great, we are told that 'Budweiser is the King of Beers'. The metaphor can even be the name of the product, as in the Ford Fiesta motorcar, or the name of the brand, like Jaguar cars.

One famous marketing theorist, Gerald Zaltman, has even argued that there are seven 'deep metaphors' that work across countries and cultures:

1 Balance: how justice, equilibrium and the interplay of elements affect consumer thinking.

2 Transformation: how changes in substance and circumstances affect consumer thinking.

3 Journey: how the meeting of past, present and future affect consumer thinking.

4 Container: how inclusion, exclusion and other boundaries affect consumer thinking.

5 Connection: how the need to relate to oneself and others affects consumer thinking.

6 Resource: how acquisitions and their consequences affect consumer thinking.

7 Control: how the sense of mastery, vulnerability and well-being affects consumer thinking.

Zaltman is famous for his Zaltman Metaphor Elicitation Technique (ZMET), a patented interview process based on a metaphor for carrying out deep research into the way that consumers go about making their decisions that has been used to help develop the marketing strategies of many well-known companies.

So, metaphors are widely used both in marketing research and in marketing practice. But can the use of metaphor help you to get a new or different perspective on marketing itself? We like to think it can. If you've never really thought about it much before then the first metaphor for marketing that may come to mind is the warfare or battleground metaphor: 'marketing is like warfare' (actually that's a simile, which is much the same as a metaphor but not quite so strongly phrased – if I say that my friend plays football *like a gorilla*, that's a simile, but if I say that when playing football my friend *is a gorilla*, that's a metaphor). The companies that own the products and the brands go into the marketplace to try to defeat or destroy the enemy, and they use all of the tools of the marketing mix as their weapons. You can even take the metaphor further if you feel like it. A big TV advertising campaign is like firing your artillery at the enemy, while a clever behind-the-scenes social media campaign is like guerrilla warfare (if you do a Google search for 'guerrilla marketing' you will find that this particular metaphor is very popular indeed). The owner of the biggest brand controls the most territory and rival brands have to consider whether they are going to engage in a frontal assault on the brand, or look for possible flanking manoeuvres to attack from an unexpected angle.

However, it has been argued that the warfare metaphor, although heavily used, is inappropriate for marketing. In warfare, much is permissible that would be considered unethical in any other aspect of life. For example, lying, deception and providing misinformation are all usually considered to be an acceptable part of warfare. Marketing professionals, on the other hand, know that lying, deception and misinformation are considered to be unethical practices in the marketplace. Those marketing professionals that are members of a professional body have signed up to a code of professional practice that prohibits them from using unethical methods. There are even circumstances where such unethical practices are illegal, so that marketers who engaged in them would risk prosecution.

Perhaps we need another metaphor for marketing. That is what Brent Smith thought when he wrote 'Gazelle, Lion, Hyena, Vulture and Worm' – the five-creature metaphor for marketing. While the warfare metaphor immediately suggests that marketing is a zero-sum game (if one person gains, then somebody else must lose), the beauty of the five-creature metaphor is that it is a positive-sum game (there is room for everyone to make gains). In addition, this is an ecological metaphor, which fits rather well with our present-day concerns about climate change, damage to the environment, and the need for business to be environmentally sustainable.

In simple terms the five-creature metaphor represents a food chain. Lions hunt gazelles; it takes considerable effort but a successful hunt feeds the lion pride; lions need substantial amounts of high-quality meat to survive. Hyenas take a close interest in this kind of activity, waiting patiently until the lions have eaten what they want, and then take over the kill. Sometimes a large pack of aggressive hyenas can even steal a kill from a weak pride of lions. Vultures and then worms feed on what is left behind by the hyenas. At the bottom of this particular food chain, worms need relatively small amounts of rather low-quality food; lots of worms can survive on small pieces of food overlooked by the larger animals.

The five-creature metaphor opens up new perspectives not illuminated by the warfare metaphor. While there is some competition between the creatures, it is only at the margins and generally they intend each other little harm. Hyenas will growl at vultures that get too close, but the conflict between them is mostly symbolic rather than physical. Between lions at the top of the food chain and worms at the bottom, it makes no sense to talk about competition at all, since they occupy entirely different ecological niches. The success of the lions in catching prey could be likened to Apple introducing a brilliant new product that is destined to be globally successful. As we descend the food chain, more and more creatures (companies) obtain their own sustenance (market

Metaphors are important in marketing, but which is a better metaphor for marketing itself, human warfare or the ecological niches of animals in their natural environment?

Source: Alamy Images/Stu Porter (b); Alamy/Stocktrek Images, Inc. (t).

opportunities) because of Apple's original success. Admittedly, this is probably not a great metaphor for gazelle-lovers, but then no metaphor is perfect.

Should the five-creature metaphor supersede the warfare metaphors with which we are more familiar? Probably not. Rather, it is a different way of looking at things that enriches our perspective on marketplace competition. Warfare metaphors have their place too.

Sources: Martha Gill, 'Have We Literally Broken the English Language?', theguardian.com, 13 August 2013, accessed at http://www.theguardian.com/commentis-free/2013/aug/13/literally-broken-english-language-definition, May 2014.

Edward F. McQuarrie and Barbara J. Phillips, 'Indirect Persuasion in Advertising: How Consumers Process Metaphors Presented in Pictures and Words', *Journal of Advertising*, 34(2), 2005, pp. 7–21

Brent Smith, 'Gazelle, Lion, Hyena, Vulture, and Worm: A Teaching Metaphor on Competition between Early and Late Market Entrants', *Marketing Education Review*, 20(1), 2010, pp. 9–16.

Details of Gerald Zaltman's work can be found at http://www.marketingmetaphoria.com/index.html

SO, WHAT IS MARKETING? PULLING IT ALL TOGETHER

At the start of this chapter, Figure 1.1 presented a simple model of the marketing process. Now that we have discussed all of the steps in the process, Figure 1.6 presents an expanded model that will help you pull it all together. What is marketing? Simply put, marketing is the process of building profitable customer relationships by creating value for customers and capturing value in return.

The first four steps of the marketing process focus on creating value for customers. The company first gains a full understanding of the marketplace by researching customer needs and managing marketing information. It then designs a customer-driven marketing strategy based on the answers to two simple questions. The first question is: What consumers will we serve? (Market segmentation and targeting.) Good marketing companies know that they cannot serve all customers in every way. Instead, they need to focus their resources on the customers they can serve best and most profitably. The second marketing strategy question is: How can we best serve targeted customers? (Differentiation and positioning.) Here, the marketer outlines a value proposition that spells out what values the company will deliver in order to win target customers.

With its marketing strategy decided, the company now constructs a marketing programme – consisting of the four marketing mix elements, or the four Ps – that transforms the marketing strategy into real value for customers. The company develops product offers and creates strong brand identities for them. It prices these offers to create real customer value and distributes the offers to make them available to target customers. Finally, the

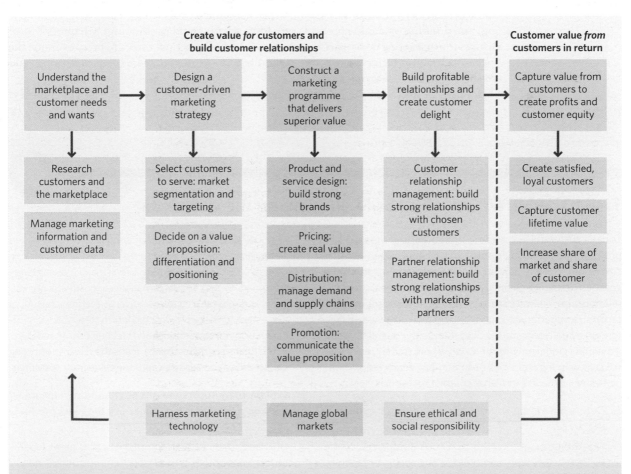

FIGURE 1.6
An expanded model of the marketing process

company designs promotional programmes that communicate the value proposition to target customers and persuade them to act on the market offering.

Perhaps the most important step in the marketing process involves building value-laden, profitable relationships with target customers. Throughout the process, marketers practise CRM to create customer satisfaction and delight. In creating customer value and relationships, however, the company cannot go it alone. It must work closely with marketing partners both inside the company and throughout the marketing system. Thus, beyond practising good CRM, firms must also practise good partner relationship management.

The first four steps in the marketing process create value *for* customers. In the final step, the company reaps the rewards of its strong customer relationships by capturing value *from* customers. Delivering superior customer value creates highly satisfied customers who will buy more and will buy again. This helps the company to capture customer lifetime value and greater share of customer. The result is increased long-term customer equity for the firm.

Finally, in the face of today's changing marketing landscape, companies must take into account three additional factors. In building customer and partner relationships, they must harness marketing technology, take advantage of global opportunities, and ensure that they act in an ethical and socially responsible way.

Figure 1.6 provides a good road map to future chapters of the text. Chapters 1 and 2 introduce the marketing process, with a focus on building customer relationships and capturing value from customers. Chapters 3, 4 and 5 address the first step of the marketing process – understanding the marketing environment, managing marketing information and understanding consumer behaviour. In Chapter 6, we look more deeply into the two major marketing strategy decisions: selecting which customers to serve (segmentation and targeting) and deciding on a value proposition (differentiation and positioning). Chapters 7 to 13 discuss the marketing mix variables, one by one. Then, the final three chapters examine the special marketing factors: marketing technology in the digital age, global marketing, and marketing ethics and social responsibility.

So, here we go, down the road to learning marketing. We hope you'll enjoy the journey!

THE JOURNEY YOU'VE TAKEN Reviewing the concepts

Today's successful companies – whether large or small, for-profit or not-for-profit, domestic or global – share a strong customer focus and a heavy commitment to marketing. The goal of marketing is to build and manage profitable customer relationships. Marketing seeks to attract new customers by promising superior value and to keep and grow current customers by delivering satisfaction. Marketing operates within a dynamic global environment, which can quickly make yesterday's winning strategies obsolete. To be successful, companies will have to be strongly market focused.

1 **Define marketing and outline the steps in the marketing process**

Marketing is the process by which companies create value for customers and build strong customer relationships in order to capture value from customers in return.

The marketing process involves five steps. The first four steps create value for customers. First, marketers need

to understand the marketplace and customer needs and wants. Next, marketers design a customer-driven marketing strategy with the goal of getting, keeping and growing target customers. In the third step, marketers construct a marketing programme that actually delivers superior value. All of these steps form the basis for the fourth step, building profitable customer relationships and creating customer delight. In the final step, the company reaps the rewards of strong customer relationships by capturing value from customers.

2 **Explain the importance of understanding customers and the marketplace, and identify the five core marketplace concepts**

Outstanding marketing companies go to great lengths to learn about and understand their customers' needs, wants and demands. This understanding helps them to design want-satisfying market offerings and build value-laden customer relationships by which they can capture customer lifetime value and greater share of customer. The result is increased long-term customer equity for the firm.

The core marketplace concepts are needs, wants and demands; market offerings (products, services and experiences); value and satisfaction; exchange and relationships; and markets. Wants are the form taken by human needs when shaped by culture and individual personality. When backed by buying power, wants become demands. Companies address needs by putting forth a value proposition, a set of benefits that they promise to consumers to satisfy their needs. The value proposition is fulfilled through a market offering, which delivers customer value and satisfaction, resulting in long-term exchange relationships with customers.

3 Identify the key elements of a customer-driven marketing strategy and discuss marketing management orientations that guide marketing strategy

To design a winning marketing strategy, the company must first decide who it will serve. It does this by dividing the market into segments of customers (market segmentation) and selecting which segments it will cultivate (target marketing). Next, the company must decide how it will serve targeted customers (how it will differentiate and position itself in the marketplace).

Marketing management can adopt one of five competing market orientations. The production concept holds that management's task is to improve production efficiency and bring down prices. The product concept holds that consumers favour products that offer the most in quality, performance and innovative features; thus, little promotional effort is required. The selling concept holds that consumers will not buy enough of the organisation's products unless it undertakes a large-scale selling and promotion effort. The marketing concept holds that achieving organisational goals depends on determining the needs and wants of target markets and delivering the desired satisfactions more effectively and efficiently than competitors do. The societal marketing concept holds that generating customer satisfaction and long-term societal well-being are the keys to both achieving the company's goals and fulfilling its responsibilities.

4 Discuss customer relationship management, and identify strategies for creating value for customers and capturing value from customers in return

Broadly defined, customer relationship management (CRM) is the process of building and maintaining profitable customer relationships by delivering superior customer value and satisfaction. The aim of CRM is to produce high customer equity, the total combined customer lifetime values of all of the company's customers. The key to building lasting relationships is the creation of superior customer value and satisfaction.

Companies want not only to acquire profitable customers, but to build relationships that will keep them and grow 'share of customer'. Different types of customer require different CRM strategies. The marketer's aim is to build the right relationships with the right customers. In return for creating value for targeted customers, the company captures value from customers in the form of profits and customer equity.

In building customer relationships, good marketers realise that they cannot go it alone. They must work closely with marketing partners inside and outside the company. In addition to being good at CRM, they must also be good at partner relationship management.

5 Describe the major trends and forces that are changing the marketing landscape in this new age of relationships

As the world spins on, dramatic changes are occurring in the marketing arena. The boom in computer, telecommunication, information, transportation and other technologies has created exciting new ways to learn about and track customers, and to create products and services tailored to individual customer needs.

In a rapidly shrinking world, many marketers are now connected globally with their customers and marketing partners. Today, almost every company, large or small, is touched in some way by global competition. Today's marketers are also re-examining their ethical and societal responsibilities. Marketers are being called upon to take greater responsibility for the social and environmental impact of their actions. In the past, marketing has been most widely applied in the for-profit business sector. In recent years, however, marketing has also become a major part of the strategies of many not-for-profit organisations, such as colleges, hospitals, museums, symphony orchestras and even churches.

Pulling it all together, as discussed throughout the chapter, the major new developments in marketing can be summed up in a single word: relationships. Today, marketers of all kinds are taking advantage of new opportunities for building relationships with their customers, their marketing partners and the world around them.

NAVIGATING THE KEY TERMS

Customer equity **26**
Customer lifetime value **26**
Customer perceived value **20**
Customer relationship
  management **20**
Customer satisfaction **21**
Demands **12**
Exchange **13**

Internet **28**
Market **13**
Marketing **11**
Marketing concept **16**
Marketing management **14**
Marketing myopia **12**
Market offering **12**
Needs **12**

Partner relationship
  management **24**
Product concept **15**
Production concept **15**
Selling concept **16**
Share of customer **26**
Societal marketing concept **17**
Wants **12**

NOTES AND REFERENCES

1 The main UEFA website is at **www.uefa.com** – navigate from there to find information on sponsors, competitions and marketing/press releases.

2 This merchandise is sold globally, not just in Europe. See for example the range of products sold at **america1.store.uefa.com/uefachampionsleague.html**

3 A press release about the victory in the auction can be found at: **sport.bt.com/ sportfootball/football/bt-sport-wins-all-live-uk-tv-rights-to-champions-league-and- europa-league-S11363847946944**

4 See the BBC News story 'Champions League: BT Sport Wins £897m Football Rights Deal' at **www.bbc.co.uk/sport/0/football/24879138**

5 Swiss cry foul as UEFA targets fans to fight 'Ambush Marketing', by J. Gallu, 4 June 2008 © 2008 Bloomberg L.P. All rights reserved. Used with permission.

6 See Daniel Taylor and Owen Gibson, 'Manchester City to Test Financial Fair Play with Naming Rights Deal', 7 July 2011, at **www.guardian.co.uk**

7 For more on the story about who sponsors Barcelona FC, see Paul Kelso, 'Barcelona Sell Shirt Sponsorship for the First Time as Qatar Foundation Pay £125m to Share Space with Unicef', *Telegraph,* **www.telegraph.co.uk**, 10 December 2010.

8 The whole column and tables of sponsors and values can be found at 'The Making of the $3BILLION Super Club: How Manchester United's bank balance is being boosted by beer, wine and crisps . . . and that's just for starters!', available from **www.dailymail. co.uk/sport/football/article-2269599/Manchester-Uniteds-incredible-list-sponsors- helping-3billion-super-club.html**, accessed September 2014.

9 The American Marketing Association offers this definition: 'Marketing is the activity, set of institutions, and processes for creating, communicating, delivering, and exchanging offerings that have value for customers, clients, partners, and society at large. (Approved July 2013)': **https://www.ama.org/AboutAMA/Pages/Definition-of-Marketing. aspx**. See also Lisa M. Keefe, 'What Is the Meaning of "Marketing"?', *Marketing News,* 15 September 2004, pp. 17–18; and Chekitan S. Dev and Don E. Schultz, 'A Customer-Focused Approach Can Bring the Current Marketing Mix into the 21st Century', *Marketing Management,* January–February 2005, pp. 18–24.

10 See for example an effort to recruit more blood donors from the Afro-Caribbean community in the UK: **http://www.blood.co.uk/news-media/events/daniel-de-gale/**

11 See Theodore Levitt's classic article, 'Marketing Myopia', *Harvard Business Review,* July–August 1960, pp. 45–56. For more recent discussions, see James R. Stock,

'Marketing Myopia Revisited: Lessons for Logistics', *International Journal of Physical Distribution & Logistics Management*, 2(1/2), 2002, pp. 12–21; and Yves Doz, Jose Santos and Peter J. Williamson, 'Marketing Myopia Re-Visited: Why Every Company Needs to Learn from the World', *Ivey Business Journal*, January–February 2004, p. 1.

12 More information on Parquewarner can be found at **www.parquewarner.com**

13 AC Milan have pages at **www.acmilan.com**

14 See Erika Rasmusson, 'Marketing More Than a Product', *Sales & Marketing Management*, February 2000, p. 99; and Lawrence A. Crosby and Sheree L. Johnson, 'Managing Experiences', *Marketing Management*, January–February 2005, pp. 12–14.

15 See Nigel Bradley and Jim Blythe, *Demarketing* (London: Routledge, 2013).

16 See the blog (December 2013) by Laura Wilkinson about Southwest Airlines here: **http://www.blogsouthwest.com/re-a-letter-of-luv/**. For more on market orientation and firm performance, see Ahmet H. Kirca, Satish Jayachandran and William O. Bearden, 'Marketing Orientation: A Meta-Analytic Review and Assessment of Its Antecedents and Impact on Performance', *Journal of Marketing*, April 2005, pp. 24–41.

17 See 'Deep Fried Mars Bar Myth is Dispelled', *BBC News*, **http://news.bbc.co.uk/1/hi/scotland/4103415.stm**, 17 December 2004; or 'America's Most Fattening Burger', *Time*, 3 January 2005, p. 186; and 'For the Health-Unconscious, Era of Mammoth Burger Is Here', *Wall Street Journal*, 27 January 2005, p. B.1.

18 'How Effective are Product Recalls?', *BBC News*, **http://news.bbc.co.uk/1/hi/magazine/6379389.stm**, 20 February 2007.

19 For more on relationship marketing, read M.J. Harker and J. Egan, 'The Past, Present and Future of Relationship Marketing', *Journal of Marketing Management* – special issue on relationship marketing, 22, 2006, pp. 215–42; or J. Egan and M.J. Harker (eds), *Relationship Marketing* (London: Sage, 2005).

20 'The 2004 Total Value Award7s: Incentives Don't Correlate to Value Says Strategic Vision', *Strategic Vision*, 4 October 2004, accessed at **www.strategicvision.com**, February 2005; Chad Lawhorn, 'Gas Costs Steer Study into Hybrids', *Knight Ridder Tribune Business News*, 29 April 2005, p. 1; and Ronald D. White, 'Car Buyers Think Hard and Long Distance about Mileage', *Los Angeles Times*, 30 April 2005, p. C.1.

21 Timothy L. Keiningham, Lerzan Aksoy, Bruce Cooil and Tor Wallin Andreassen, 'Linking customer loyalty to growth', *MIT Sloane Management Review*, 2008, available at **http://sloanreview.mit.edu/article/linking-customer-loyalty-to-growth/**, accessed May 2014; Catherine Arnold, 'Satisfaction's the Name of the Game', *Marketing News*, 15 October 2004, pp. 39, 45; Eugene W. Anderson, Claes Fornell and Sanal K. Mazvancheryl, 'Customer Satisfaction and Shareholder Value', *Journal of Marketing*, October 2004, pp. 172–85; and Christian Homburg, Nicole Koschate and Wayne D. Hoyer, 'Do Satisfied Customers Really Pay More? A Study Between Customer Satisfaction and Willingness to Pay', *Journal of Marketing*, April 2005, pp. 84–96.

22 The homepage of the UK Porsche owners club can be found at **www.porscheclubgb.com**

23 General information about the ING Group is available at **http://www.ing.com/About-us/Profile-Fast-facts/Profile.htm**, accessed May 2014. Other information adapted from Elizabeth Esfahani, 'How to Get Tough with Bad Customers', *Business 2.0*, October 2004, p. 52; see also Amey Stone, 'Bare Bones, Plump Profits', *BusinessWeek*, 14 March, 2005, p. 88. The UK savings and mortgage business of ING Direct was transferred to Barclay's Direct in March 2013.

24 See E. Gummesson, *Total Relationship Marketing* (Oxford: Butterworth–Heinemann, 1999); C. Grönroos, *Service Management and Marketing: Customer Management in Service Competition* (Chichester: Wiley, 1990); and M.J. Harker, 'Relationship Marketing Defined', *Marketing Intelligence and Planning*, 17(1), 1999, pp. 13–21.

25 Philip Kotler and Kevin Lane Keller, *Marketing Management*, 12th edn (Upper Saddle River, NJ: Prentice Hall, 2006), p. 27.

26 See E. Gummesson, 'Marketing Orientation Revisited: The Crucial Role of the Part-Time Marketer', *European Journal of Marketing*, 25(2), 1991, pp. 60–75.

27 http://www.digitaltrends.com/mobile/its-the-end-of-an-era-as-sony-completes-its-buyout-of-ericsson/, accessed May 2014.

28 For more discussion of customer loyalty, see Fred Reichheld and Christine Detrick, 'Loyalty: A Prescription for Cutting Costs', *Marketing Management*, September–October 2003, pp. 24–5; Jacquelyn S. Thomas, Robert C. Blattberg and Edward J. Fox, 'Recapturing Lost Customers', *Journal of Marketing Research*, February 2004, pp. 31–45; and Clara Agustin and Jagdip Singh, 'Curvilinear Effects of Consumer Loyalty Determinants in Relational Exchanges', *Journal of Marketing Research*, February 2005, pp. 96–108.

29 Next time you log into Amazon, look to see how the products given prominence might be selected based on your past consumption history.

30 See Roland T. Rust, Valerie A. Zeithaml and Katherine A. Lemon, *Driving Customer Equity* (New York: Free Press, 2000); Robert C. Blattberg, Gary Getz and Jacquelyn S. Thomas, *Customer Equity* (Boston, MA: Harvard Business School Press, 2001); Rust, Lemon and Zeithaml, 'Return on Marketing: Using Customer Equity to Focus Marketing Strategy', *Journal of Marketing*, January 2004, pp. 109–27; James D. Lenskold, 'Customer-Centered Marketing ROI', *Marketing Management*, January/February 2004, pp. 26–32; and Rust, Zeithaml and Lemon, 'Customer-Centered Brand Management', *Harvard Business Review*, September 2004, p. 110.

31 This example is adapted from information in Rust, Lemon and Zeithaml, 'Where Should the Next Marketing Dollar Go?', *Marketing Management*, September–October 2001, pp. 24–8. Also see David Welch and David Kiley, 'Can Caddy's Driver Make GM Cool?', *BusinessWeek*, 20 September 2004, pp. 105–6; John K. Teahen Jr, 'Cadillac Kid: "Gotta Compete"', *Knight Ridder Tribune Business News*, 7 May 2005, p. 1.

32 Ravi Dhar and Rashi Glazer, 'Hedging Customers', *Harvard Business Review*, May 2003, pp. 86–92.

33 Werner Reinartz and V. Kumar, 'The Mismanagement of Customer Loyalty', *Harvard Business Review*, July 2002, pp. 86–94. For more on customer equity management, see Sunil Gupta, Donald R. Lehman and Jennifer Ames Stuart, 'Valuing Customers', *Journal of Marketing Research*, February 2004, pp. 7–18; Michael D. Johnson and Fred Selnes, 'Customer Portfolio Management: Toward a Dynamic Theory of Exchange Relationships', *Journal of Marketing*, April 2004, pp. 1–17; Sunil Gupta and Donald R. Lehman, *Managing Customers as Investments* (Philadelphia, PA: Wharton School Publishing, 2005); and Roland T. Rust, Katherine N. Lemon and Das Narayandas, *Customer Equity Management* (Upper Saddle River, NJ: Prentice Hall, 2005).

34 Joshua Chaffin, 'MTV's Search for Global Harmony', *Financial Times*, 9 June 2008: http://www.ft.com/cms/s/0/f52e958c-3631-11dd-8bb8-0000779fd2ac.html

35 Information about the Mariinsky can be found in English at www.mariinsky.ru/en/

36 For other examples, and for a good review of non-profit marketing, see Philip Kotler and Alan R. Andreasen, *Strategic Marketing for Nonprofit Organizations*, 6th edn (Upper Saddle River, NJ: Prentice Hall, 2003); Philip Kotler and Karen Fox, *Strategic Marketing for Educational Institutions* (Upper Saddle River, NJ: Prentice Hall, 1995); Norman Shawchuck, Philip Kotler, Bruce Wren and Gustave Rath, *Marketing for Congregations: Choosing to Serve People More Effectively* (Nashville, TN: Abingdon Press, 1993); Philip Kotler, John Bowen and James Makens, *Marketing for Hospitality and Tourism*, 3rd edn (Upper Saddle River, NJ: Prentice Hall, 2003); and 'The Non-profit Marketing Landscape', special section, *Journal of Business Research*, June 2005, pp. 797–862.

CHAPTER 2

COMPANY AND MARKETING STRATEGY: PARTNERING TO BUILD CUSTOMER RELATIONSHIPS

AFTER STUDYING THIS CHAPTER, YOU SHOULD BE ABLE TO

- explain company-wide strategic planning and its four steps
- discuss how to design business portfolios and develop growth strategies
- explain marketing's role in strategic planning and how marketing works with its partners to create and deliver customer value
- describe the elements of a customer-driven marketing strategy and mix, and the forces that influence them
- list the marketing management functions, including the elements of a marketing plan, and discuss the importance of measuring and managing return on marketing

THE WAY AHEAD
Previewing the concepts

Ready to travel on? In the first chapter, we explored the marketing process by which companies create value for consumers in order to capture value in return. On this leg of our journey, we dig deeper into the second and third steps of the marketing process – designing customer-driven marketing strategies and constructing marketing programmes. To begin, we look at the organisation's overall strategic planning. Next, we discuss how marketers, guided by the strategic plan, work closely with others inside and outside the firm to serve customers. We then examine marketing strategy and planning – how marketers choose target markets, position their market offerings, develop a marketing mix and manage their marketing programmes. Finally, we look at the important step of measuring and managing return on marketing investment.

First stop: BT. During the past several decades, BT (British Telecommunications plc) has successfully adapted to a rapidly changing technological and political environment. In the process, it has evolved from a UK telephone company into a global player in the IT revolution. But the BT we know today is far, far different from the rather dull old telephone company it was 30 years ago. As BT has become slim and responsive, its marketing strategy has matured as well. To stay on top in the intensely competitive international communications business, BT will have to keep finding fresh ways to bring value to its customers.

BT: STRATEGY IN TURBULENT TIMES

When reflecting on the communications and IT revolution that has brought us laptops, netbooks, smartphones, tablet PCs, social media, broadband, online gaming and much more, most of us are inclined to think of businesses that were formed in the last few years, perhaps even the last few months. If you were asked to list businesses that were central to the information revolution, you would probably come up with Amazon (founded in 1994), Google (1998), LinkedIn (2003), Facebook (2004), Twitter (2006) and Foursquare (2009), among others. Of course, a lot of people would also mention those really old businesses that have been around since pre-WWW times, such as Intel

BT's strategy is to be a global player

Source: BT Image Library.

(1968), Apple (1976), Dell (1984) and Cisco (1984). Few people, however, unless heavily prompted, would mention France Télécom, Deutsche Telekom or BT. Of those who did, quite a few would probably trace the history of these telecommunications network providers to the 1980s and 1990s, and so regard them as fairly representative members of the information revolution's old guard. And it is true that France Télécom was incorporated in its present form in 1990, Deutsche Telekom in 1996 and BT in 1980. But each of these three companies can trace its corporate history back for more than 100 years, and each of them has a recently discarded corporate name that tells us something important about their history: France Télécom used to be the Direction Générale des Télécommunications, Deutsche Telekom was the telecommunications arm of the Deutsche Bundespost, and BT was the telecommunications division of the British Post Office. All three used to be state-owned monopoly providers of telecommunications services. Incidentally, the history of these companies can be traced much further back than that. For example, the origins of BT are to be found in the world's first ever electronic communication company, the Electric Telegraph Company, founded in 1846. Frankly, and no doubt this will come as a surprise to many people, the millions of SMS text messages and tweets flying through the ether today do not look much different from the telegrams that the Electric Telegraph Company was sending over 150 years ago. But the company doing the sending – today known as BT – has had to change radically. In particular, during the last 30 years BT has seen numerous major opportunities and threats arise as its

business has been buffeted by political factors, globalisation and massive technological change.

It may not be fashionable to say this, but the story of how a publicly owned monopoly provider – essentially a branch of government service – could transform itself into a successful, profitable, commercial business in a competitive and dynamic marketplace is at least as fascinating as the story of how an Internet start-up can go from zero to hero in practically no time. After all, there are millions of prospective Internet heroes, and by the laws of probability some of them are bound to be lucky; the unlucky ones are forgotten. On the other hand, taking a business that operated according to old-fashioned government procedures and enjoyed a legally protected monopoly on an essential service, and reinventing that as a highly competitive business fit to be a key player in the fast-moving technological world of the twenty-first century . . . well, that takes long-term strategy. The scale of the changes required to transform the old Post Office Telecommunications Division into the new BT, a fit competitor in 2015, is breathtaking. Consider this: in the 1970s, if you wanted a telephone line in the UK, there was only one place to go. If you didn't like the customer service, then too bad; if you didn't like the lengthy waiting list before you could have your phone installed, well, there was no alternative; if you didn't like the prices for the line rental, phone rental and call charges, tough. (Phone rental? Well, you didn't think you could just pop down to your local shop and *buy* a phone, did you? After all, there was only one phone network, and the only kind of phone you were allowed to connect to it was a Post Office phone. So, naturally, you had to rent one of those.) Of course, the organisation that provided those services – the company that became BT – was not held in high esteem for its commercial acumen, customer service or market orientation. Competition spurs companies to strive for innovation, efficiency and excellent customer service. A company that has no competition, like BT in the early 1980s, has little or no incentive to work hard to delight customers. In fact, BT was widely disliked. So, how does a company like that manage to survive and thrive in a completely new era? The answer is strategy.

Strategy operates at a number of different levels, across all of a business's main functions. The key drivers of strategy are the external opportunities and threats that a business faces, the resources it controls, and the overall corporate direction determined by the board of directors who, in the case of a limited company (a Public Limited Company in the UK, a Société Anonyme in France, an Aktiengesellschaft in Germany, Austria and Switzerland, an Aktiebolag in Sweden), operate on behalf of the owners, that is the shareholders. BT (British Telecommunications PLC as it then was) became a public company operating for the benefit of shareholders when it was privatised in 1984. Since then it has faced a formidable array of challenges, has seen numerous fabulous business opportunities arise, and has transformed its resources, both physical and human, to address these changing circumstances.

The principal challenge facing BT over the last 30 years has been competition. Competitors have been increasingly allowed to encroach on BT's core business of delivering telecommunications services to UK homes and businesses. Strategically, BT has responded to this consistently by extending its product portfolio through product development, and by expanding into international markets. Consequently, today, one of BT's biggest business units is BT Global Services, which, according to BT itself, is 'a global leader in the provision of networked IT services to multinational corporations, domestic businesses, government departments and other CPs [communication providers] in more than 170 countries'. This is a line of business that practically did not exist when BT became a PLC; it involves the development of purpose-built, complex private telecommunications networks for major public and private sector organisations. In providing global communications solutions to corporations such as the Singapore Exchange (which connects Asian companies seeking capital to global investors), the Australian power distribution company Western Power, automotive company Fiat Group, Air China, and many others, BT has transformed itself from a rather dull and plodding provider of telephone services in the UK into a major player in the highly competitive global telecommunications market. There have been many slip-ups along the way, and the complex details of the implementation of the strategy have changed frequently to adapt to new technologies, new political circumstances and new competitors. But the one straight line running from 1984, when BT was privatised, to the present day, has been the unswerving determination to pursue a strategy of succeeding as a global telecommunications provider. As we saw in the previous chapter, BT is now involved in the provision of content as well as infrastructure by means of the multi-billion-pound deal for the rights to broadcast football matches.[1]

Sources: See note 1 at the end of this chapter.

Marketing strategies and programmes are guided by broader, company-wide strategic plans. So, to understand the role of marketing, we must first understand the organisation's overall strategic planning process. Like BT, all companies must look ahead and develop long-term strategies to meet the changing conditions in their industries and ensure long-term survival.

COMPANY-WIDE STRATEGIC PLANNING: DEFINING MARKETING'S ROLE

Each company must find the overall plan for long-term survival and growth that makes the most sense given its specific situation, opportunities, objectives and resources. This is the focus of **strategic planning** – the process of developing and maintaining a strategic fit between the organisation's goals and capabilities and its changing marketing opportunities.

Strategic planning sets the stage for the rest of the planning in the firm. Companies usually prepare annual plans, long-range plans and strategic plans. The annual and long-range plans deal with the company's current businesses and how to keep them going. In contrast, the strategic plan involves adapting the firm to take advantage of opportunities in its constantly changing environment.

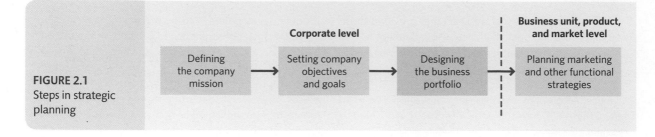

FIGURE 2.1
Steps in strategic planning

At the corporate level, the company starts the strategic planning process by defining its overall purpose and mission (see Figure 2.1). This mission is then turned into detailed supporting objectives that guide the whole company. Next, headquarters decides what portfolio of businesses and products is best for the company and how much support to give each one. In turn, each business and product develops detailed marketing and other departmental plans that support the company-wide plan. Thus, marketing planning occurs at the business unit, product and market levels. It supports company strategic planning with more detailed plans for specific marketing opportunities.[2]

Defining a market-oriented mission

An organisation exists to accomplish something. At first, it has a clear purpose or mission, but over time its mission may become unclear as the organisation grows, adds new products and markets, or faces new conditions in the environment. When management senses that the organisation is drifting, it must renew its search for purpose. It is time to ask: What is our business? Who is the customer? What do consumers value? What *should* our business be? These simple-sounding questions are among the most difficult the company will ever have to answer. Successful companies continuously raise these questions and answer them carefully and completely.

Many organisations develop formal mission statements that answer these questions. A **mission statement** is a statement of the organisation's purpose – what it wants to accomplish in the larger environment. Studies have shown that firms with well-crafted mission statements have better organisational and financial performance.[3]

Some companies define their missions only in product or technology terms ('We make and sell furniture' or 'We are a chemical processing firm'). But mission statements should be *market oriented* and defined in terms of customer needs. Products and technologies eventually become outdated, but basic market needs may last for ever.

A market-oriented mission statement defines the business in terms of satisfying basic customer needs. For example, publisher Wiley-Blackwell's mission is not just to publish books, but to be a 'global provider of content-enabled solutions to improve outcomes in research, education and professional practice with online tools, journals, books, databases, reference works and laboratory'. Likewise, eBay's mission is not simply to hold online auctions and trading. Instead, its aim is 'connecting people with the things they need and love'. Its mission is to be a unique web community in which people can shop around, have fun and get to know each other, for example by chatting at the eBay Café. Table 2.1 provides several other examples of product-oriented versus market-oriented business definitions.

Management should avoid making its mission too narrow or too broad. A pencil manufacturer that says it is in the communication equipment business is stating its mission too broadly. Missions should be *realistic*. Singapore Airlines would be deluding itself if it adopted the mission to become the world's largest airline. Missions should also be *specific*. Many mission statements are written for public relations purposes and lack specific, workable guidelines. Such generic statements sound good but provide little real guidance or inspiration. Missions should fit the *market environment*. For example, the World Association of Girl Guides and Girl Scouts no longer concentrates on preparing girls to fulfil traditional

TABLE 2.1 Market-oriented business definitions

Company	Product-oriented definition	Market-oriented definition
Allied Irish Bank	We run banks	We offer a distinctive value proposition to our customers by providing them with a distinctive combination of best products, best service, best relationships and best delivery
Amazon.com	We sell books, videos, CDs, toys, consumer electronics, hardware, housewares and other products	We make the Internet buying experience fast, easy and enjoyable – we're the place where you can find and discover anything you want to buy online
Asda	We run discount stores	We deliver low prices every day and give ordinary people the chance to buy the same things as rich people
Disney	We run theme parks	We create fantasies – a place where America still works the way it's supposed to
B&Q	We sell tools and home repair and improvement items	We enable consumers to achieve the homes of their dreams
eBay	We hold online auctions	We connect individual buyers and sellers in the world's online marketplace, a unique web community in which they can shop around, have fun and get to know each other
Nike	We sell shoes	We help people experience the emotion of competition, winning and crushing competitors
Revlon	We make cosmetics	We sell lifestyle and self-expression; success and status; memories, hopes and dreams
Ritz-Carlton Hotels	We rent rooms	We create the Ritz-Carlton experience – one that enlivens the senses, instils well-being, and fulfils even the unexpressed wishes and needs of our guests

female roles in society, but has as its mission 'to enable girls and young women to develop their fullest potential as responsible citizens of the world', and 'aims to engage and empower young women, so that they can make a difference in their communities'.[4]

The organisation should also base its mission on its *distinctive competencies*. Finally, mission statements should be *motivating*. A company's mission should not be stated as making more sales or profits – profits are only a reward for undertaking a useful activity. A company's employees need to feel that their work is significant and that it contributes to people's lives. For example, Microsoft's aim is to help people to 'realise their potential' – 'your potential,

The mission of the World Association of Girl Guides is 'to enable girls and young women to develop their fullest potential as responsible citizens of the world'

Sources: World Association of Girl Guides (left); Alamy Images/Tompiodesign (right).

our passion' says the company. Google's mission is to 'organise the world's information and make it universally accessible and useful'.

Setting company objectives and goals

The company needs to turn its mission into detailed supporting objectives for each level of management. Each manager should have objectives and be responsible for reaching them. For example, Monsanto operates globally in the agricultural biotechnology business. Its mission is 'focused on empowering farmers – large and small – to produce more from their land while conserving more of our world's natural resources such as water and energy'. It seeks to help feed the world's rapidly growing population while at the same time sustaining the environment. Monsanto ads ask us to 'Imagine innovative agriculture that creates incredible things today.'

This mission leads to a hierarchy of objectives, including business objectives and marketing objectives. Monsanto's overall objective is to build profitable customer relationships by developing better agricultural products and getting them to market faster at lower costs. It does this by researching products that safely help crops produce more nutrition and higher yields without chemical spraying. But research is expensive and requires improved profits to plough back into research programmes. So improving profits becomes another major Monsanto objective. Profits can be improved by increasing sales or reducing costs. Sales can be increased by improving the company's share of existing markets, by entering new markets, or both. These goals then become the company's current marketing objectives.[5]

Marketing strategies and programmes must be developed to support these marketing objectives. To increase its European market share, Monsanto might increase its products' availability and promotion. To enter new markets, the company may cut prices and target

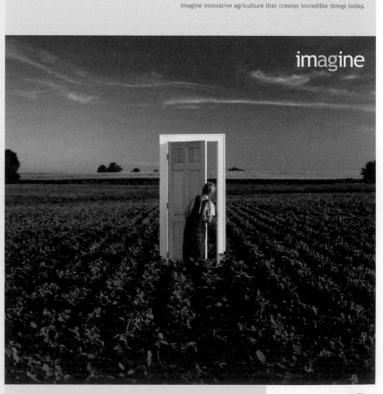

Monsanto defines its mission as 'improving the future of farming . . . improving the future of food . . . abundantly and safely'

Source: Monsanto Company © 2005. All rights reserved.

large farms in several different countries. These are its broad marketing strategies. Each broad marketing strategy must then be defined in greater detail. For example, increasing the product's promotion may require more salespeople and more advertising; if so, both requirements will have to be spelled out. In this way, the firm's mission is translated into a set of objectives for the current period.

Marketing at Work 2.1 looks at the development of company strategy in the world's largest container shipping company, Maersk Line.

Maersk Line

Although these days we think of them as mundane items, shipping containers were an important part of the revolution that enabled us to talk realistically about globalisation and global business. Without a means of transporting large quantities of goods thousands of miles between continents, global business simply could not happen. The so-called 'container revolution' in the shipping industry has made global business possible. Shipping containers are the standardised steel boxes that you see stacked up when you visit port cities like Rotterdam, Antwerp, Hamburg and Felixstowe. They are known as intermodal containers because they can be transferred between modes of transport, from ship to truck to train, without removing the contents. Perhaps the most characteristic sight, however, is the container ship piled unfeasibly high with these containers, crossing oceans to transport consumer and industrial goods from where they are manufactured to where they are marketed and consumed. And one of the most common sights on the high seas is a container ship prominently marked as belonging to the Maersk Line, a Danish company that carries more shipping containers than any other company in the world. You may remember the 2013 Tom Hanks movie *Captain Phillips* that featured a Maersk Line ship, the *Maersk Alabama*.

Maersk has a fleet of over 600 vessels and owns many of the largest container ships in the world; several vessels in the Maersk fleet are around 400 metres long. However, in business, size isn't everything. Maersk might be the biggest, but until recently it was struggling to deliver the level of profitability expected by its shareholders. The last few years have seen Maersk Line making a substantial move forwards in terms of profitability. It has taken a carefully crafted and well implemented company strategy to bring about this transformation. The following case study explains how Maersk Line achieved this.

Maersk Line is the world's largest container-shipping company

Source: Alamy Images/Søren Lund Hviid.

Maersk Line's Three-Stage Strategy for Profit

As the world's largest container-shipping company, Maersk Line operates in an industry with a poor overall record of delivering value to shareholders, high volatility and an uncertain outlook. When Soren Skou took over as CEO in January 2012, the Denmark-based company was losing $8m–$9m a day, reaching a total loss of about $600m in the first quarter.

The company plays an important strategic role in Denmark's AP Møller-Maersk Group; restoring profitability and maintaining its industry leadership position were central to its strategy.

The challenge

Mr Skou and his new leadership team faced the dual challenge of improving financial results in the short term while simultaneously breaking the cycle of volatility and delivering more sustainable shareholder value over the medium to long term. They quickly recognised that the best performers in the container-shipping industry created shareholder value throughout the cycles experienced by the sector. Maersk Line therefore had to identify and address the root causes of its own volatile performance.

The strategy

The team led by Mr Skou developed a three-stage strategy that would have overlapping phases:

- The first phase, 'Back to Black', was all about short-term financial results. Its specific aim was to restore profitability within one year, which meant engineering a swing in performance representing more than $1bn. Mr Skou's team quickly identified a number of measures to cut costs and increase revenues. This was the easiest stage, probably because Maersk Line executives worked in a volatile industry and were used to addressing immediate performance issues.

- The second stage, 'Finish the Foundation', involved the leadership team taking greater control of the mass of internal organisational initiatives that different parts of Maersk Line had launched to address the company's declining performance. Mr Skou's goal overall was to break down silos to make planning and operating systems more integrated and coherent as part of a general effort to create a strong organisational foundation for long-term success. This phase involved hard choices about how much the leadership team should intervene in shaping a new organisation, including how the business should be structured and which projects should be shelved. Ultimately, more than 40 per cent of projects were halted.

- The final phase, 'Sustainable Profitable Growth', was concerned with specific actions to make Maersk Line the best-performing container-shipping company, and not just the largest. Mr Skou and his team reflected on current and potential changes in their industry, and on what type of company they wanted to build. They identified clear 'must-win battles', the priority areas on which the leadership team would focus to address long-term underperformance.

Defining these priorities was the most difficult part of the strategy. It forced the team to consider not only how to reshape their individual areas of responsibility but also how the decisions would collectively help advance the business.

The results

In November 2013 Maersk Line reported net profit of $554m. Maersk had cut its target for its shipping unit's return on invested capital from 10 per cent to 8.5 per cent in September but Maersk Line delivered 10.9 per cent in the third quarter.

The lessons

The Maersk Line case shows that a CEO and leadership team can address both immediate short-term pressures and the need to reshape a company fundamentally to be successful in the future.

Source: 'Maersk Line's Three-Stage Strategy for Profit' was written by Tom Malnight and originally published by the Financial Times at ft.com/management.

Designing the business portfolio

Guided by the company's mission statement and objectives, management now must plan its **business portfolio** – the collection of businesses and products that make up the company. The best business portfolio is the one that best fits the company's strengths and weaknesses to opportunities in the environment. Business portfolio planning involves two steps. First, the company must analyse its *current* business portfolio and decide which businesses should receive more, less or no investment. Second, it must shape the *future* portfolio by developing strategies for growth and downsizing.

Analysing the current business portfolio

The major activity in strategic planning is business **portfolio analysis,** whereby management evaluates the products and businesses making up the company. The company will want to put strong resources into its more profitable businesses and phase down or drop its weaker ones.

Management's first step is to identify the key businesses making up the company. These can be called the strategic business units. A *strategic business unit* (SBU) is a unit of the company that has a separate mission and objectives and that can be planned independently from other company businesses. An SBU can be a company division, a product line within a division, or sometimes a single product or brand.

The next step in business portfolio analysis calls for management to assess the attractiveness of its various SBUs and decide how much support each deserves. Most companies are well advised to stick to what the company is good at when designing their business portfolios. It is usually a good idea to focus on adding products and businesses that fit closely with the firm's core philosophy and competencies.

The purpose of strategic planning is to find ways in which the company can best use its strengths to take advantage of attractive opportunities in the environment. So most standard portfolio analysis methods evaluate SBUs on two important dimensions – the attractiveness of the SBU's market or industry and the strength of the SBU's position in that market or industry. The best known portfolio planning method was developed by the Boston Consulting Group, a leading management consulting firm.[6]

The Boston Consulting Group approach

Using the Boston Consulting Group (BCG) approach, a company classifies all its SBUs according to the **growth–share matrix** shown in Figure 2.2. On the vertical axis, *market growth rate* provides a measure of market attractiveness. On the horizontal axis, *relative market share* serves as a measure of company strength in the market. The growth–share matrix defines four types of SBUs:

- *Stars*. Stars are high-growth, high-share businesses or products. They often need heavy investment to finance their rapid growth. Eventually their growth will slow down, and they will turn into cash cows.

- *Cash cows*. Cash cows are low-growth, high-share businesses or products. These established and successful SBUs need less investment to hold their market share. Thus, they produce a lot of cash that the company uses to pay its bills and to support other SBUs that need investment.

- *Question marks*. Question marks are low-share business units in high-growth markets. They require a lot of cash to hold their share, let alone increase it. Management has to think hard about which question marks it should try to build into stars and which should be phased out.

- *Dogs*. Dogs are low-growth, low-share businesses and products. They may generate enough cash to maintain themselves but do not promise to be large sources of cash.

The 10 circles in the growth–share matrix represent a company's 10 current SBUs. The company has two stars, two cash cows, three question marks and three dogs. The areas

FIGURE 2.2
The BCG growth–share matrix

Source: Adapted from the Product Portfolio Matrix,©1970,The Boston Consulting Group (BCG).

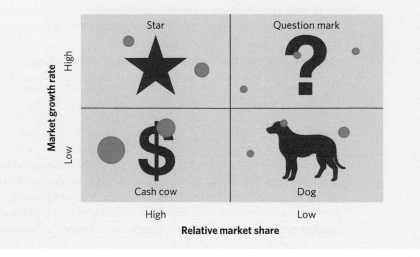

of the circles are proportional to each SBU's sales value. This company is in fair shape, although not in good shape. It wants to invest in the more promising question marks to make them stars and to maintain the stars so that they will become cash cows as their markets mature. Fortunately, it has two good-sized cash cows. The income from these cash cows will help finance the company's question marks, stars and dogs. The company should take some decisive action concerning its dogs and its question marks. The picture would be worse if the company had no stars, if it had too many dogs or if it had only one weak cash cow.

Once it has classified its SBUs, the company must determine what role each will play in the future. One of four strategies can be pursued for each SBU. The company can invest more in the business unit in order to *build* its share. Or it can invest just enough to *hold* the SBU's share at the current level. It can *harvest* the SBU, milking its short-term cash flow regardless of the long-term effect. Finally, the company can *divest* the SBU by selling it or phasing it out and using the resources elsewhere.

As time passes, SBUs change their positions in the growth–share matrix. Each SBU has a life cycle. Many SBUs start out as question marks and move into the star category if they succeed. They later become cash cows as market growth falls, then finally die off or turn into dogs towards the end of their life cycle. The company needs to add new products and units continuously so that some of them will become stars and, eventually, cash cows that will help finance other SBUs.

Problems with matrix approaches

The BCG and other formal methods revolutionised strategic planning. However, such centralised approaches have limitations. They can be difficult, time consuming and costly to implement. Management may find it difficult to define SBUs and measure market share and growth. In addition, these approaches focus on classifying current businesses but provide little advice for *future* planning.

Formal planning approaches can also place too much emphasis on market-share growth or growth through entry into attractive new markets. Using these approaches, many companies plunged into unrelated and new high-growth businesses that they did not know how to manage – with very bad results. At the same time, these companies were often too quick to abandon, sell or milk to death their healthy mature businesses. As a result, many companies that diversified too broadly in the past are now narrowing their focus and getting back to the basics of serving one or a few industries that they know best.

Because of such problems, many companies have dropped formal matrix methods in favour of more customised approaches that are better suited to their specific situations. Moreover, unlike former strategic planning efforts, which rested mostly in the hands of senior managers at company headquarters, today's strategic planning has been decentralised. Increasingly, companies are placing responsibility for strategic planning in the hands of cross-functional teams of divisional managers who are close to their markets.

Developing strategies for growth and downsizing

Beyond evaluating current businesses, designing the business portfolio involves finding businesses and products the company should consider in the future. Companies need growth if they are to compete more effectively, satisfy their stakeholders and attract top talent. 'Growth is pure oxygen,' states one executive. 'It creates a vital, enthusiastic corporation where people see genuine opportunity.' At the same time, a firm must be careful not to make growth itself an objective. The company's objective must be 'profitable growth'.

Marketing has the main responsibility for achieving profitable growth for the company. Marketing must identify, evaluate and select market opportunities, and lay down strategies for capturing them. One useful device for identifying growth opportunities is the **product–market expansion grid,** shown in Figure 2.3.[7] We apply it here to performance sports clothing

		Existing products	New products
	Existing markets	Market penetration	Product development
FIGURE 2.3 The product–market expansion grid	New markets	Market development	Diversification

maker Under Armour. In 1996, Under Armour introduced its innovative line of comfy, moisture-wicking shirts and shorts.[8] Since then, it has grown rapidly in its performance-wear niche. Until recently, sales have been growing at around 65 per cent a year. And even as retail sales slumped across the board in the recent recession, Under Armour's sales grew by nearly 20 per cent. Looking forward, the company must look for new ways to keep growing.

First, Under Armour might consider whether the company can achieve deeper **market penetration** – making more sales without changing its original product. It can spur growth through marketing mix improvements – adjustments to its product design, advertising, pricing and distribution efforts. For example, Under Armour offers an ever-increasing range of styles and colours in its original apparel lines, and it recently boosted its promotion spending in an effort to drive home its 'performance and authenticity' positioning. In 2013 Under Armour launched its largest-ever advertising campaign – themed 'I will'. The company also added direct-to-consumer distribution channels, including its own retail stores, website and toll-free call centre. Direct-to-consumer sales are growing at nearly 50 per cent a year and now account for more than 11 per cent of total revenues.

Second, Under Armour might consider possibilities for **market development** – identifying and developing new markets for its current products. Under Armour could review new *demographic markets*. For instance, the company recently stepped up its emphasis on women consumers, and could also pursue new *geographical markets*. For example, the brand has announced its intentions to expand internationally, bringing its products to more athletes throughout the world.

Third, Under Armour could consider **product development** – offering modified or new products to current markets. Recent years have seen Under Armour develop product lines in both cross-trainer and high-performance athletic shoes. Although this puts the company into direct competition with sports heavyweights such as Nike and Adidas, it also offers promise for big growth.

Finally, Under Armour might consider **diversification** – starting up or buying businesses outside of its current products and markets. For example, it could move into non-performance leisurewear or begin making and marketing Under Armour fitness equipment. When diversifying, companies must be careful not to overextend their brands' positioning.

Companies must develop not only strategies for *growing* their business portfolios, but also strategies for **downsizing** them. There are many reasons why a firm might want to abandon products or markets. The market environment might change, making some of the company's products or markets less profitable. The firm may have grown too fast or entered areas where it lacks experience. This can occur when a firm enters too many foreign markets without the proper research or when a company introduces new products that do not offer superior customer value. Finally, some products or business units simply age and die.

When a firm finds brands or businesses that are unprofitable or that no longer fit its overall strategy, it must carefully prune, harvest or divest them. Weak businesses usually require a disproportionate amount of management attention. Managers should focus on promising growth opportunities, not fritter away energy trying to salvage fading ones.

PLANNING MARKETING: PARTNERING TO BUILD CUSTOMER RELATIONSHIPS

The company's strategic plan establishes what kinds of businesses the company will operate in and its objectives for each. Then, within each business unit, more detailed planning takes place. The major functional departments in each unit – marketing, finance, accounting, purchasing, operations, information systems, human resources and others – must work together to accomplish strategic objectives.

Marketing plays a key role in the company's strategic planning in several ways. First, marketing provides a guiding *philosophy* – the marketing concept – that suggests that company strategy should revolve around building profitable relationships with important consumer groups. Second, marketing provides *inputs* to strategic planners by helping to identify attractive market opportunities and by assessing the firm's potential to take advantage of them. Finally, within individual business units, marketing designs *strategies* for reaching the unit's objectives. Once the unit's objectives are set, marketing's task is to help carry them out profitably.

Customer value and satisfaction are important ingredients in the marketer's formula for success. However, as we noted in the previous chapter, marketers alone cannot produce superior value for customers. Although it plays a leading role, marketing can be only a partner in attracting, keeping and growing customers. In addition to *customer relationship management*, marketers must also practise *partner relationship management*. They must work closely with partners in other company departments to form an effective *value chain* that serves the customer. Moreover, they must partner effectively with other companies in the marketing system to form a competitively superior *value-delivery network*. We now take a closer look at the concepts of a company value chain and value-delivery network.

Partnering with other company departments

Each company department can be thought of as a link in the company's **value chain.**[9] That is, each department carries out value-creating activities to design, produce, market, deliver and support the firm's products. The firm's success depends not only on how well each department performs its work, but also on how well the activities of various departments are coordinated.

For example, the French group Carrefour is the second-largest retailer in the world and the largest retailer in Europe. Carrefour's goal is to create customer value and satisfaction by providing shoppers with the products they want at the lowest possible prices. Marketers at Carrefour play an important role. They learn what customers need and stock the stores' shelves with the desired products at unbeatable low prices. They prepare advertising and merchandising programmes and assist shoppers with customer service. Through these and other activities, Carrefour's marketers help deliver value to customers.

However, the marketing department needs help from the company's other departments. Carrefour's ability to offer the right products at low prices depends on the purchasing department's skill in developing the needed suppliers and buying from them at low cost. Carrefour's IT department must provide fast and accurate information about which products are selling in each store. And its operations people must provide effective, low-cost merchandise handling.

A company's value chain is only as strong as its weakest link. Success depends on how well each department performs its work of adding customer value and on how well the activities of various departments are coordinated. At Carrefour, if purchasing cannot wring the lowest prices from suppliers, or if operations cannot distribute merchandise at the lowest costs, then marketing cannot deliver on its promise of lowest prices.

Ideally, then, a company's different functions should work in harmony to produce value for consumers. But, in practice, departmental relations are full of conflicts and

The value chain: Carrefour's ability to offer the right products at low prices depends on the contributions of people from all departments: marketing, purchasing, information systems and operations

Source: Corbis/Elipsa.

misunderstandings. The marketing department takes the consumer's point of view. But when marketing tries to develop customer satisfaction, it can cause other departments to do a poorer job *in their terms*. Marketing department actions can increase purchasing costs, disrupt production schedules, increase inventories and create budget headaches. Thus, the other departments may resist the marketing department's efforts.

Yet marketers must find ways to get all departments to 'think consumer' and to develop a smoothly functioning value chain. Marketing management can best gain support for its goal of customer satisfaction by working to understand the company's other departments. Marketing managers need to work closely with managers of other functions to develop a system of functional plans under which the different departments can work together to accomplish the company's overall strategic objectives.

Jack Welch, General Electric's highly regarded former CEO, told his employees: 'Companies can't give job security. Only customers can!' He emphasised that all General Electric people, regardless of their department, have an impact on customer satisfaction and retention. His message: 'If you are not thinking customer, you are not thinking.'[10]

Partnering with others in the marketing system

In its quest to create customer value, the firm needs to look beyond its own value chain and into the value chains of its suppliers, distributors and, ultimately, customers. Consider McDonald's. People do not swarm to McDonald's only because they love the chain's hamburgers. In fact, consumers typically rank McDonald's behind major competitors in taste. Consumers flock to the McDonald's *system*, not just to its food products. Throughout the world, its finely tuned system delivers a high standard of what the company calls QSCV (Quality, Service, Cleanliness and Value). McDonald's is effective only to the extent that it successfully partners with its franchisees, suppliers and others jointly to deliver exceptionally high customer value.

More companies today are partnering with the other members of the supply chain to improve the performance of the customer **value-delivery network**. For example, French cosmetics maker L'Oréal knows the importance of building close relationships with its extensive network of suppliers, who supply everything from polymers and fats to spray cans and packaging to production equipment and office supplies:

L'Oréal is the world's largest cosmetics manufacturer, with 25 brands ranging from Maybelline and Kiehl's to Lancôme and Redken. The company's supplier network is crucial to its success. As a result, L'Oréal treats suppliers as respected partners. On the one hand, it expects a lot from suppliers in terms of design innovation, quality, and socially responsible actions. The

Marketing plays a key role in delivering value to L'Oréal's customers

Source: Alamy Images/ Lou Linwei.

company carefully screens new suppliers and regularly assesses the performance of current suppliers. On the other hand, L'Oréal works closely with suppliers to help them meet its exacting standards. Whereas some companies make unreasonable demands of their suppliers and 'squeeze' them for short-term gains, L'Oréal builds long-term supplier relationships based on mutual benefit and growth. According to the company's supplier website, it treats suppliers with 'fundamental respect for their business, their culture, their growth, and the individuals who work there. Each relationship is based on . . . shared efforts aimed at promoting growth and mutual profits that make it possible for suppliers to invest, innovate, and compete'. As a result, more than 75 per cent of L'Oréal's supplier-partners have been working with the company for 10 years or more, and the majority of them for several decades. Says the company's head of purchasing, 'The CEO wants to make L'Oréal a top performer and one of the world's most respected companies. Being respected also means being respected by our suppliers.'[11]

Increasingly in today's marketplace, competition no longer takes place between individual competitors. Rather, it takes place between the entire value-delivery networks created by these competitors. Thus, Toyota's performance against Ford depends on the quality of Toyota's overall value-delivery network versus Ford's. Even if Toyota makes the best cars, it might lose in the marketplace if Ford's dealer network provides more customer-satisfying sales and service.

MAKING CONNECTIONS Linking the concepts

Here's a good place to pause for a moment to think about and apply what you've read in the first part of this chapter.

● Why are we talking about company-wide strategic planning in a marketing text? What *does* strategic planning have to do with marketing?

● What are L'Oréal's mission and strategy? What role does marketing play in helping L'Oréal to accomplish its mission and strategy?

● What roles do other L'Oréal departments play, and how can L'Oréal's marketers partner with these departments to maximise overall customer value?

MARKETING STRATEGY AND THE MARKETING MIX

The strategic plan defines the company's overall mission and objectives. Marketing's role and activities are shown in Figure 2.4, which summarises the major activities involved in managing marketing strategy and the marketing mix.

Consumers stand in the centre. The goal is to build strong and profitable customer relationships. Next comes **marketing strategy** – the marketing logic by which the company hopes to achieve these profitable relationships. Through market segmentation, targeting and positioning, the company decides which customers it will serve and how. It identifies the total market, then divides it into smaller segments, selects the most promising segments, and focuses on serving and satisfying customers in these segments.

Guided by marketing strategy, the company designs a *marketing mix* made up of factors under its control. To find the best marketing strategy and mix, the company engages in marketing analysis, planning, implementation and control. Through these activities, the company watches and adapts to the actors and forces in the marketing environment. We will now look briefly at each activity. Then, in later chapters, we will discuss each one in more depth.

Customer-centred marketing strategy

As we emphasised throughout the previous chapter, to succeed in today's competitive marketplace, companies need to be customer centred. They must win customers from competitors, then keep and grow them by delivering greater value. But before it can satisfy customers, a company must first understand their needs and wants. Thus, sound marketing requires a careful customer analysis.

Companies know that they cannot profitably serve all consumers in a given market – at least not all consumers in the same way. There are too many different kinds of consumers with too many different kinds of needs. And most companies are in a position to serve some

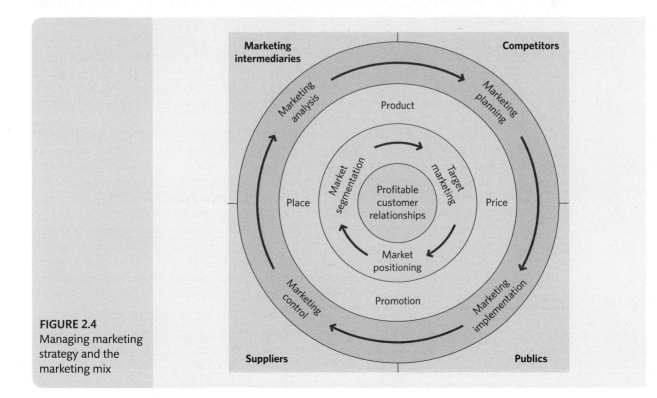

FIGURE 2.4
Managing marketing strategy and the marketing mix

segments better than others. Thus, each company must divide up the total market, choose the best segments, and design strategies for profitably serving chosen segments. This process involves three steps: *market segmentation, target marketing* and *market positioning.*

Market segmentation

The market consists of many types of customers, products and needs. The marketer has to determine which segments offer the best opportunities. Consumers can be grouped and served in various ways based on geographic, demographic, psychographic and behavioural factors. The process of dividing a market into distinct groups of buyers who have different needs, characteristics or behaviour and who might require separate products or marketing programmes is called **market segmentation.**

Every market has segments, but not all ways of segmenting a market are equally useful. For example, Nurofen (a leading painkiller provided by Reckitt Benckiser plc) would gain little by distinguishing between low-income and high-income painkiller users if both respond in the same way to marketing efforts. A **market segment** consists of consumers who respond in a similar way to a given set of marketing efforts. In the car market, for example, consumers who want the biggest, most comfortable car regardless of price make up one market segment. Customers who care mainly about price and running costs make up another segment. It would be difficult to make one car model that was the first choice of consumers in both segments. Companies are wise to focus their efforts on meeting the distinct needs of individual market segments.

Target marketing

After a company has defined market segments, it can enter one or many of these segments. **Target marketing** involves evaluating each market segment's attractiveness and selecting one or more segments to enter. A company should target segments in which it can profitably generate the greatest customer value and sustain it over time.

A company with limited resources might decide to serve only one or a few special segments or 'market niches'. Such 'nichers' specialise in serving customer segments that major competitors overlook or ignore. For example, Arm & Hammer is a leader in providing consumer goods that use baking soda as an ingredient, including toothpaste, deodorants and others. The Danish butter brand Lurpak has become established as a leader in many international markets because of the reputation of Denmark for producing high-quality dairy products (for more about the company that makes Lurpak, Arla Foods, you'll have to wait until the start of the next chapter).

A company might choose to serve several related segments – perhaps those with different kinds of customers but with the same basic wants. French food manufacturer Danone, for example, offers a wide range of yogurt-based products. Danone targets very young children with Danonino, older children with Danette, and adults with Activia and Actimel. In addition, Danone offers the Densia brand as a high-calcium brand aimed at middle-aged women who are worried about loss of bone density. Alternatively a large company might decide to offer a complete range of products to serve all market segments. Most companies enter a new market by serving a single segment, and if this proves successful, they add segments. Large companies eventually seek full market coverage. They want to be the General Motors of their industry. GM says that it makes a car for every 'person, purse, and personality'. The leading company normally has different products designed to meet the special needs of each segment.

Market positioning

After a company has decided which market segments to enter, it must decide what positions it wants to occupy in those segments. A product's *position* is the place the product occupies relative to competitors in consumers' minds. Marketers want to develop unique market positions for their products. If a product is perceived to be exactly like others on the market, consumers would have no reason to buy it.

Market positioning and differentiation is arranging for a product to occupy a clear, distinctive and desirable place relative to competing products in the minds of target consumers. As one positioning expert puts it, positioning is 'how you differentiate your product or company in the mind of your prospect. It's why a shopper will pay a little more for your brand. The trick is to figure out how to express the difference.'[12] Thus, marketers plan positions that distinguish their products from competing brands and give them the greatest advantage in their target markets.

BMW has offered customers 'the ultimate driving machine', then 'sheer driving pleasure' and most recently simply 'joy'. Sainsbury's used to be 'where good food costs less', and more recently says simply 'live well for less'. Kenco claims that 'when your coffee's this good, nothing else has to be'. MasterCard tell us that: 'There are some things money can't buy. For everything else there's MasterCard.' Visa is 'everywhere you want to be'. Tesco says 'every little helps'. Such deceptively simple statements form the backbone of a product's marketing strategy.

In positioning its product, the company first identifies possible competitive advantages upon which to build the position. The company can offer greater customer value either by charging lower prices than competitors do or by offering more benefits to justify higher prices. But if the company *promises* greater value, it must then *deliver* that greater value. Thus, effective positioning begins with actually *differentiating* the company's market offering so that it gives consumers more value. Once the company has chosen a desired position, it must take strong steps to deliver and communicate that position to target consumers. The company's entire marketing programme should support the chosen positioning strategy.

Developing the marketing mix

After deciding on its overall marketing strategy, the company is ready to begin planning the details of the marketing mix, one of the major concepts in modern marketing. The **marketing mix** is the set of controllable, tactical marketing tools that the firm blends to produce the response it wants in the target market. The marketing mix consists of everything the firm can do to influence the demand for its product. The many possibilities can be collected into four groups of variables known as the 'four Ps': *product, price, place* and *promotion*.[13] In service markets the 'four Ps' are often extended to 'seven Ps' by the addition of *people, process* and *physical* evidence. But for the moment we will concentrate on product, price, place and promotion. Figure 2.5 shows the marketing tools under each P.

Product means the goods and services combination the company offers to the target market. Thus, a Peugeot 208 product (produced by PSA Peugeot Citroën) consists of nuts and bolts, spark plugs, pistons, headlights and thousands of other parts. Peugeot offers several 208 models and dozens of optional features. The car comes fully serviced and with a comprehensive warranty that is as much a part of the product as the steering wheel.

Price is the amount of money customers have to pay to obtain the product. PSA Peugeot Citroën calculates suggested retail prices that its dealers might charge for each 208. But Peugeot dealers rarely charge the full list price. Instead, they negotiate the price with each customer, offering discounts, trade-in allowances and credit terms. These actions adjust prices for the current competitive situation and bring them into line with the buyer's perception of the car's value.

Place includes company activities that make the product available to target consumers. Peugeot partners with a large body of independently owned dealerships that sell the company's many different models. Peugeot selects its dealers carefully and supports them strongly. The dealers keep an inventory of Peugeot cars, demonstrate them to potential buyers, negotiate prices, close sales and service the cars after the sale.

Promotion means activities that communicate the merits of the product and persuade target customers to buy it. Peugeot spends more than €1.0bn each year on advertising, about €300 per vehicle, to tell consumers about the company and its many products. Dealership

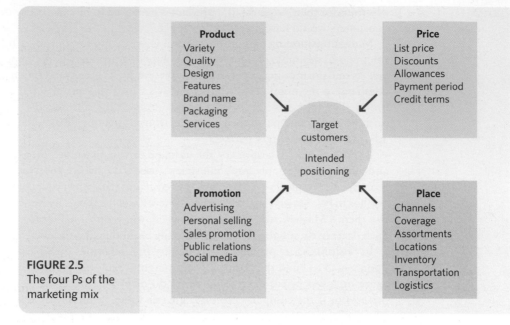

FIGURE 2.5
The four Ps of the marketing mix

salespeople assist potential buyers and persuade them that Peugeot is the best car for them. Peugeot and its dealers offer special promotions – sales, cash rebates, low financing rates – as added purchase incentives.

An effective marketing programme blends all of the marketing mix elements into a coordinated programme designed to achieve the company's marketing objectives by delivering value to consumers. The marketing mix constitutes the company's tactical toolkit for establishing strong positioning in target markets.

Some critics think that the four Ps may omit or under-emphasise certain important activities. For example, they ask, 'Where are services?' Just because they do not start with a *P* does not justify omitting them. The answer is that services, such as banking, airline and retailing services, are products too. We might call them *service products*. 'Where is packaging?' the critics might ask. Marketers would answer that they include packaging as just one of many product decisions. All said, as Figure 2.5 suggests, many marketing activities that might appear to be left out of the marketing mix are subsumed under one of the four Ps. The issue is not whether there should be four, six or ten Ps so much as what framework is most helpful in designing marketing programmes.

There is another concern, however, that is valid. It holds that the four Ps concept takes the seller's view of the market, not the buyer's view. From the buyer's viewpoint, in this age of customer relationships, the four Ps might be better described as the four Cs:[14]

4Ps	4Cs
Product	Customer solution
Price	Customer cost
Place	Convenience
Promotion	Communication

Thus, while marketers see themselves as selling products, customers see themselves as buying value or solutions to their problems. And customers are interested in more than just the price; they are interested in the total costs of obtaining, using and disposing of a product. Customers want the product and service to be as conveniently available as possible. Finally, they want two-way communication. Marketers would do well to think through the four Cs first and then build the four Ps on that platform.

MANAGING THE MARKETING EFFORT

In addition to being good at the *marketing* in marketing management, companies also need to pay attention to the *management*. Managing the marketing process requires the four marketing management functions shown in Figure 2.6: *analysis, planning, implementation* and *control*. The company first develops company-wide strategic plans and then translates them into marketing and other plans for each division, product and brand. Through implementation, the company turns the plans into actions. Control consists of measuring and evaluating the results of marketing activities and taking corrective action where needed. Finally, marketing analysis provides information and evaluations needed for all of the other marketing activities.

Marketing analysis

Managing the marketing function begins with a complete analysis of the company's situation. The marketer should conduct a **SWOT analysis,** by which it evaluates the company's overall strengths (S), weaknesses (W), opportunities (O) and threats (T) (see Figure 2.7). Strengths include internal capabilities, resources and positive situational factors that may help the company to serve its customers and achieve its objectives. Weaknesses include internal limitations and negative situational factors that may interfere with the company's performance. Opportunities are favourable factors or trends in the external environment that the company may be able to exploit to its advantage. And threats are unfavourable external factors or trends that may present challenges to performance.

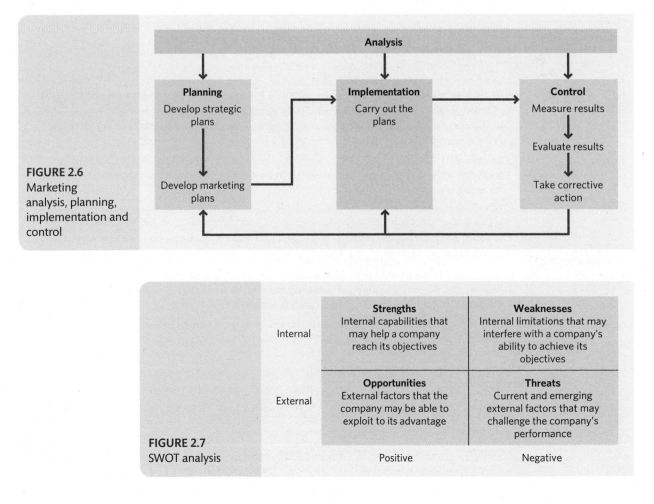

FIGURE 2.6
Marketing analysis, planning, implementation and control

FIGURE 2.7
SWOT analysis

The company must analyse its markets and marketing environment to find attractive opportunities and identify environmental threats. It must analyse company strengths and weaknesses as well as current and possible marketing actions to determine which opportunities it can best pursue. The goal is to match the company's strengths to attractive opportunities in the environment, while eliminating or overcoming the weaknesses and minimising the threats. Marketing analysis provides inputs to each of the other marketing management functions. We discuss marketing analysis more fully in the next chapter.

Marketing planning

Through strategic planning, the company decides what it wants to do with each business unit. Marketing planning involves deciding on marketing strategies that will help the company attain its overall strategic objectives. A detailed marketing plan is needed for each business, product or brand. What does a marketing plan look like? Our discussion focuses on product or brand marketing plans.

Table 2.2 outlines the major sections of a typical product or brand marketing plan. (See Appendix 1 for a sample marketing plan.) The plan begins with an executive summary,

TABLE 2.2 Contents of a marketing plan

Section	Purpose
Executive summary	Presents a brief summary of the main goals and recommendations of the plan for management review, helping top management to find the plan's major points quickly. A table of contents should follow the executive summary
Current marketing situation	Describes the target market and company's position in it, including information about the market, product performance, competition and distribution. This section includes: ● A market description that defines the market and major segments, then reviews customer needs and factors in the marketing environment that may affect customer purchasing ● A product review that shows sales, prices and gross margins of the major products in the product line ● A review of competition, which identifies major competitors and assesses their market positions and strategies for product quality, pricing, distribution and promotion ● A review of distribution, which evaluates recent sales trends and other developments in major distribution channels
Threats and opportunities analysis	Assesses major threats and opportunities that the product might face, helping management to anticipate important positive or negative developments that might have an impact on the firm and its strategies
Objectives and issues	States the marketing objectives that the company would like to attain during the plan's term and discusses key issues that will affect their attainment. For example, if the goal is to achieve a 15 per cent market share, this section looks at how this goal might be achieved
Marketing strategy	Outlines the broad marketing logic by which the business unit hopes to achieve its marketing objectives and the specifics of target markets, positioning and marketing expenditure levels. It outlines specific strategies for each marketing mix element and explains how each responds to the threats, opportunities and critical issues spelled out earlier in the plan
Action programmes	Spells out how marketing strategies will be turned into specific action programmes that answer the following questions: *What* will be done? *When* will it be done? *Who* is responsible for doing it? *How* much will it cost?
Budgets	Details a supporting marketing budget that is essentially a projected profit-and-loss statement. It shows expected revenues (forecasted number of units sold and the average net price) and expected costs (of production, distribution and marketing). The difference is the projected profit. Once approved by higher management, the budget becomes the basis for materials buying, production scheduling, personnel planning and marketing operations
Controls	Outlines the control that will be used to monitor progress and allow higher management to review implementation results and spot products that are not meeting their goals

which quickly overviews major assessments, goals and recommendations. The main section of the plan presents a detailed analysis of the current marketing situation as well as potential threats and opportunities. It next states major objectives for the brand and outlines the specifics of a marketing strategy for achieving them.

A marketing strategy consists of specific strategies for target markets, positioning, the marketing mix and marketing expenditure levels. In this section, the planner explains how each strategy responds to the threats, opportunities and critical issues spelled out earlier in the plan. Additional sections of the marketing plan lay out an action programme for implementing the marketing strategy along with the details of a supporting marketing budget. The last section outlines the controls that will be used to monitor progress and take corrective action.

Marketing implementation

Planning good strategies is only a start towards successful marketing. A brilliant marketing strategy counts for little if the company fails to implement it properly. **Marketing implementation** is the process that turns marketing *plans* into marketing *actions* in order to accomplish strategic marketing objectives. Whereas marketing planning addresses the *what* and *why* of marketing activities, implementation addresses the *who, where, when* and *how*.

Many managers think that 'doing things right' (implementation) is as important as, or even more important than, 'doing the right things' (strategy). The fact is that both are critical to success, and companies can gain competitive advantages through effective implementation. One firm can have essentially the same strategy as another, yet win in the marketplace through faster or better execution. Still, implementation is difficult – it is often easier to think up good marketing strategies than it is to carry them out. For example, the Danish industrial air-conditioning company Danfoss had a clear strategic vision to be a global leader in its core business, and a clear strategy to implement this by developing close relationships with its customers using a relationship marketing approach. The vision and the strategy were only the start, and had to be implemented through a detailed and lengthy process of gathering and analysing customer service information in order to understand and deliver what customers really wanted (see Marketing at Work 2.2).

Implementing customer relationship strategy at Danfoss

MARKETING AT WORK 2.2

Professor Adam Lindgreen, Cardiff University, UK, Dr Martin Hingley, University of Lincoln, UK, Professor Michael Beverland, RMIT University, Melbourne, Australia, Jesper Krogh Jørgensen, Stig Jørgensen & Partners, Denmark and John D. Nicholson, Department of Marketing and Business Strategy, Hull University Business School, UK

A lot of business-to-business companies talk about the need to develop closer relationships with their customers. In many cases this remains an unfulfilled wish, because they fail to invest in the basic tools to understand exactly what their customers want and exactly how their customers feel about what they are getting. Danish company Danfoss invested some serious time and money so that the desire of the management to get closer to its customers was matched by the information and the systems to enable this really to happen.

With 22,500 employees and net sales of DKr33.6bn in 2013, Danfoss ranks among the largest industrial companies in Denmark. The company's broad vision reflects its desire to become a global leader within its core businesses, as well as a highly respected company that improves quality of life through advanced customer application technologies that also create value for stakeholders. The company consists of 110 sales subsidiaries across the world, classified into 13 business units within three divisions: refrigeration and air-conditioning, heating, and motion controls. The global group manufactures products in 70 factories spread across 25 different countries and leads several industries in terms of research and development, production, and the sales and service of mechanical and electronic components.

Danfoss has for many years measured its customers' satisfaction using customer perception studies. At the beginning of 2003, however, the executive board of the Heating Division initiated a process with the goal of improving and coordinating its local customer surveys. In 2005, some of the elements from the solution developed by the Heating Division were absorbed, adopted and further developed to prepare for a company-wide and global rollout. The following sections describe this two-step process.

The first step: the process within the Heating Division

In 2003, the Danfoss Heating Division initiated a project to improve its customer surveys. The management team had a very clear idea of what they wanted to achieve: the objective was to develop a unified approach for the entire division to improve its ability to benchmark results, make the survey results more operational, and thereby improve their relevance and value for the frontline staff.

Danfoss, a Danish company with global reach, has recently implemented a comprehensive new strategy to gather better customer information and develop improved customer relationships

Source: Danfoss.

In this process, the Heating Division turned to Stig Jørgensen & Partners, a management consulting company that has specialised in the field of developing and implementing global solutions for measuring and managing customer loyalty. Together with the team at Danfoss, Stig Jørgensen & Partners developed and implemented a new solution that meets the requirements of the divisional management.

In short, the solution would create a knowledge base that could summarise the drivers of customer loyalty, the overall loyalty towards Danfoss Heating, and the division's 'share of wallet' among its existing customers. With such knowledge, Danfoss Heating could involve all its sales managers and employees in improving its customer relationships. Furthermore, the project aimed eventually to improve sales and marketing activities by measuring their effects on customer loyalty, and increase sales growth through greater share of customers' spending. Finally, Stig Jørgensen & Partners hoped to help Danfoss identify, select and implement some cost-effective loyalty and sales growth improvement projects, and provide customers with more relevant services, more effective customer-facing processes and better customer experiences.

From May 2003 to the end of 2005, the '4C programme' was created: Customer loyalty, Competence development, Cultural change and Customer relationship management. This programme was designed to increase the effectiveness of the sales, service and marketing processes within the Heating Division by analysing, developing and capitalising on customer loyalty. As a 'health check' for the division, the project attempted to help the company prioritise and improve its relationships with various direct and indirect customers so as to ensure future profitable growth.

The second step: the process within the Danfoss Sales Programme (DSP)

In 2005, Danfoss established the global, group-wide DSP that forms part of the Danfoss Business System (DBS). This was a change initiative designed to achieve global operational excellence throughout the group's value chain.

One of the working principles of DSP is to use the division's best existing methods and tools within the fields of sales and marketing. At the end of 2005, it was decided that DSP should use the customer loyalty measurement concept developed by the Heating Division. Because DSP already had the necessary support processes and tools in place, it only needed to integrate and further develop the core measurement methods and tools used by the Heating Division.

One of the key elements is the Customer Insight tool, with which Danfoss can follow developments in its market and obtain an objective evaluation of how well it is doing. The overview analysis from this tool includes details not only of the marketplace, but also of customer satisfaction, customer loyalty, average share of wallet per customer, and loyalty drivers for each specific customer segment, which then can be combined with existing internal data about customers and their purchasing patterns.

A key building block of the Customer Insight tool is the use of structured customer surveys (with telephone-based and online data captures); a proprietary Loyalty Simulator analysis tool uses customer feedback to identify the key drivers of customer loyalty among existing customers. Danfoss can upload the data and receive an automatic report in return. These easily understood summary reports go to frontline staff and form the basis of the information that sales managers and sales engineers use when they communicate with customers. With more customer information than ever before, including individual customer reports, Danfoss's sales engineers are in a far better position to understand what makes customers tick, and have a strong, objective basis for effective cross-selling (i.e. selling additional products and services to existing customers).

It also has become possible to give existing target customers better information about new products and services based on their specific business needs and their perceptions of Danfoss's performance and ability to fulfil those needs. Last but not least, the customer surveys function as a fact-based 'voice of customer' that the different sales companies can use as input for selecting and utilising the various other sales and marketing improvement modules provided by DSP.

Results

In general terms the new system enables Danfoss to understand the specific needs of individual business customers and to conduct market segment analysis using concrete, customer-based information. More specifically, the Customer Insight tool helps to increase sales to individual customers, makes it clearer which are the most important customers, reduces the risk of customers defecting to competitors, and increases the efficiency of the sales engineers. Certainly, the pioneers of the system, the Heating Division, have seen excellent financial performance recently. In Sweden, the Heating Division doubled its sales growth. It was estimated that the investment in the new customer survey system was repaid within seven months. The management team were very happy with the return on this investment. Danfoss has gained market share as a result of improved customer insight. If nothing else, it has more detailed information about its customers, including their preferred product ranges and sales, service and marketing activities. Sales engineers can now approach customers armed with much more information, and offer new business opportunities. Danfoss uses the information generated through the project as the basis of its marketing activities; it considers the project an ongoing process. Its marketing strategy is now based on concrete customer information combined with excellent analytical tools. The key question for Danfoss now? How can it be made even better?!

In an increasingly connected world, people at all levels of the marketing system must work together to implement marketing strategies and plans. At Bosch, for example, marketing implementation for the company's power tools, outdoor equipment and other products requires day-to-day decisions and actions by thousands of people both inside and outside the organisation. Marketing managers make decisions about target segments, branding, packaging, pricing, promotion and distribution. They talk with engineering about product design, with manufacturing about production and inventory levels, and with finance about funding and cash flows. They also connect with outside people, such as advertising agencies to plan ad campaigns and the news media to obtain publicity support. The sales force urges Homebase, Argos, B&Q and other retailers to advertise Bosch products, provide ample shelf space and use company displays.

Successful marketing implementation depends on how well the company blends its people, organisational structure, decision and reward systems, and company culture into a cohesive action programme that supports its strategies. At all levels, the company must be staffed by people who have the needed skills, motivation and personal characteristics. The company's formal organisation structure plays an important role in implementing marketing strategy; so do its decision and reward systems. For example, if a company's compensation system rewards managers for short-term profit results, they will have little incentive to work towards long-term market-building objectives.

Finally, to be successfully implemented, the firm's marketing strategies must fit with its company culture, the system of values and beliefs shared by people in the organisation. The most successful companies have almost cult-like cultures built around strong, market-oriented missions. At companies such as Ryanair, Innocent and BMW, employees share such a powerful vision that they have a very strong sense of what is right for their company.

Marketing department organisation

The company must design a marketing organisation that can carry out marketing strategies and plans. If the company is very small, one person might do all of the research, selling, advertising, customer service and other marketing work. As the company expands, a marketing department emerges to plan and carry out marketing activities. In large companies, this department contains many specialists. Thus, PSA Peugeot Citroën and Nestlé have product and market managers, sales managers and salespeople, market researchers, advertising experts and many other specialists. To head up such large marketing organisations, many companies have now created a *chief marketing officer* (or CMO) position.

Modern marketing departments can be arranged in several ways. The most common form of marketing organisation is the *functional organisation*. Under this organisation, different marketing activities are headed by a functional specialist – a sales manager, advertising manager, marketing research manager, customer service manager or new-product manager. A company that sells across the country or internationally often uses a *geographic organisation*. Its sales and marketing people are assigned to specific countries, regions and districts. Geographic organisation allows salespeople to settle into a territory, get to know their customers, and work with a minimum of travel time and cost.

Companies with many very different products or brands often create a *product management organisation*. Using this approach, a product manager develops and implements a complete strategy and marketing programme for a specific product or brand. Product management first appeared at Procter & Gamble in 1929. A new company soap, Camay, was not doing well, and a young P&G executive was assigned to give his exclusive attention to developing and promoting this product. He was successful, and the company soon added other product managers.[15] Since then, many firms, especially consumer products companies, have set up product management organisations.

For companies that sell one product line to many different types of markets and customers that have different needs and preferences, a *market* or *customer management organisation* might be best. A market management organisation is similar to the product management organisation. Market managers are responsible for developing marketing strategies and plans for their specific markets or customers. This system's main advantage is that the company is organised around the needs of specific customer segments.

Large companies that produce many different products flowing into many different geographic and customer markets usually employ some *combination* of the functional, geographic, product and market organisation forms. This ensures that each function, product and market receives its share of management attention. However, it can also add costly layers of management and reduce organisational flexibility. Still, the benefits of organisational specialisation usually outweigh the drawbacks.

Marketing organisation has become an increasingly important issue in recent years. As we discussed in the previous chapter, many companies are finding that today's marketing environment calls for less focus on products, brands and territories and more focus on customers and customer relationships. More and more companies are shifting their brand management focus towards *customer management* – moving away from managing just product or brand profitability and towards managing customer profitability and customer equity. And many companies now organise their marketing operations around major customers. For example, companies such as Nestlé and Bosch have large teams, or even whole divisions, set up to serve large customers like Asda, Homebase or Carrefour.

Marketing control

Because many surprises occur during the implementation of marketing plans, the marketing department must practise constant marketing control. **Marketing control** involves evaluating the results of marketing strategies and plans and taking corrective action to ensure that objectives are attained. Marketing control involves four steps. Management first sets specific marketing goals. It then measures the performance in the marketplace and evaluates the causes of any differences between expected and actual performance. Finally, management takes corrective action to close the gaps between its goals and performance. This may require changing the action programmes or even changing the goals.

Operating control involves checking ongoing performance against the annual plan and taking corrective action when necessary. Its purpose is to ensure that the company achieves the sales, profits and other goals set out in its annual plan. It also involves determining the profitability of different products, territories, markets and channels.

Strategic control involves looking at whether the company's basic strategies are well matched to its opportunities. Marketing strategies and programmes can quickly become outdated, and each company should periodically reassess its overall approach to the marketplace. A major tool for such strategic control is a **marketing audit**. The marketing audit is a comprehensive, systematic, independent and periodic examination of a company's environment, objectives, strategies and activities to determine problem areas and opportunities. The audit provides good input for a plan of action to improve the company's marketing performance.

The marketing audit covers *all* major marketing areas of a business, not just a few trouble spots. It assesses the marketing environment, marketing strategy, marketing organisation, marketing systems, marketing mix, and marketing productivity and profitability. The audit is normally conducted by an objective and experienced outside party. The findings may come as a surprise – and sometimes as a shock – to management. Management then decides which actions make sense and how and when to implement them.

MEASURING AND MANAGING RETURN ON MARKETING

Marketing managers must ensure that their marketing expenditure is being wisely invested. In the past, many marketers spent freely on big, expensive marketing programmes, often without thinking carefully about the financial returns on their spending. They believed that marketing produces intangible outcomes, which do not lend themselves readily to measures of productivity or return. But all that is changing:

> For years, corporate marketers have walked into budget meetings like neighbourhood junkies. They couldn't always justify how well they spent past handouts or what difference it all made. They just wanted more money – for flashy TV ads, for big-ticket events, for, you know, getting out the message and building up the brand. But those heady days of blind budget increases are fast being replaced with a new mantra: measurement and accountability. Armed with reams of data, increasingly sophisticated tools, and growing evidence that the old tricks simply don't work, there's hardly a marketing executive today who isn't demanding a more scientific approach to help defend marketing strategies in front of the chief financial officer. Marketers want to know the actual return on investment (ROI) of each dollar. They want to know it often, not just annually . . . Companies in every segment of business have become obsessed with honing the science of measuring marketing performance: 'Marketers have been pretty unaccountable for many years,' notes one expert. 'Now they are under big pressure to estimate their impact.'[16]

In response, marketers are developing better measures of *return on marketing*. **Return on marketing (or marketing ROI)** is the net return from a marketing investment divided by the costs of the marketing investment. It measures the profits generated by investments in marketing activities.

It is true that marketing returns can be difficult to measure. In measuring financial ROI, both the *R* and the *I* are uniformly measured in money terms. But there is as yet no consistent definition of marketing ROI. 'It's tough to measure, more so than for other business expenses,' says one analyst. 'You can imagine buying a piece of equipment . . . and then measuring the productivity gains that result from the purchase,' he says. 'But in marketing, benefits like advertising impact aren't easily put into dollar returns. It takes a leap of faith to come up with a number.'[17]

One recent survey found that although two-thirds of companies have implemented return on marketing investment programmes in recent years, only one-quarter of companies report making good progress in measuring marketing ROI. Another survey of chief financial officers (CFOs) reported that 93 per cent of those surveyed are dissatisfied with their ability to measure return on marketing. The major problem is figuring out what specific measures to use and obtaining good data on these measures.[18]

A company can assess return on marketing in terms of standard marketing performance measures, such as brand awareness, sales or market share. Many companies are assembling such measures into *marketing dashboards* – meaningful sets of marketing performance measures in a single display used to monitor strategic marketing performance. Just as automobile dashboards present drivers with details on how their cars are performing, the marketing dashboard gives marketers the detailed measures they need to assess and adjust their marketing strategies.

Increasingly, however, beyond standard performance measures, marketers are using customer-centred measures of marketing impact, such as customer acquisition, customer retention, customer lifetime value and customer equity. These measures capture not just current marketing performance but also future performance resulting from stronger customer relationships. Figure 2.8 views marketing expenditures as investments that produce returns in the form of more profitable customer relationships.[19] Marketing investments result in improved customer value and satisfaction, which in turn increases customer attraction and retention. This increases individual customer lifetime values and the firm's overall customer equity. Increased customer equity, in relation to the cost of the marketing investments, determines return on marketing investment.

Regardless of how it is defined or measured, the return on marketing concept is here to stay. 'All good marketers live and die by measurements of their results,' states the marketing productivity consultant. 'Projections are made, marketing is delivered, results are measured, and the knowledge is applied to guide future marketing . . . The return on marketing investments is integral to strategic decisions at [all levels] of the business.'[20]

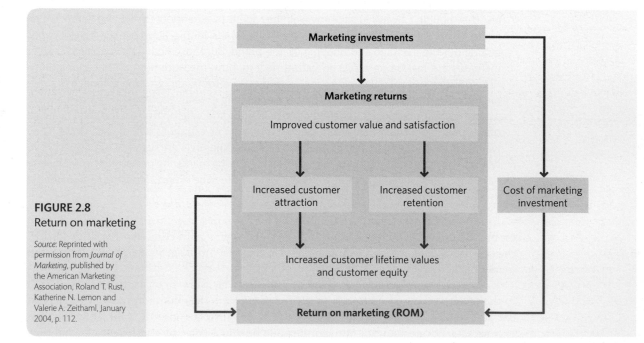

FIGURE 2.8
Return on marketing

Source: Reprinted with permission from *Journal of Marketing*, published by the American Marketing Association, Roland T. Rust, Katherine N. Lemon and Valerie A. Zeithaml, January 2004, p. 112.

THE JOURNEY YOU'VE TAKEN Reviewing the concepts

In the previous chapter, we defined *marketing* and outlined the steps in the marketing process. In this chapter, we examined company-wide strategic planning and marketing's role in the organisation. Then, we looked more deeply into marketing strategy and the marketing mix, and reviewed the major marketing management functions. So you've now had a pretty good overview of the fundamentals of modern marketing. In future chapters, we'll expand on these fundamentals.

1 Explain company-wide strategic planning and its four steps

Strategic planning sets the stage for the rest of the company's planning. Marketing contributes to strategic planning, and the overall plan defines marketing's role in the company. Although formal planning offers a variety of benefits to companies, not all companies use it or use it well.

Strategic planning involves developing a strategy for long-term survival and growth. It consists of four steps: defining the company's mission, setting goals and objectives, designing a business portfolio, and developing functional plans. Defining a clear company mission begins with drafting a formal mission statement, which should be market oriented, realistic, specific, motivating and consistent with the market environment. The mission is then transformed into detailed supporting goals and objectives to guide the entire company. Based on those goals and objectives, headquarters designs a business portfolio, deciding which businesses and products should receive more or fewer resources. In turn, each business and product unit must develop detailed marketing plans in line with the company-wide plan.

2 Discuss how to design business portfolios and develop strategies for growth and downsizing

Guided by the company's mission statement and objectives, management plans its business portfolio, or the collection of businesses and products that make up the company. The firm wants to produce a business portfolio that best fits its strengths and weaknesses to opportunities in the environment. To do this, it must analyse and adjust its current business portfolio and develop growth and downsizing strategies for adjusting the future portfolio. The company might use a formal portfolio-planning method. But many companies are now designing more customised portfolio-planning approaches that better suit their unique situations. The product/market

expansion grid suggests four possible growth paths: market penetration, market development, product development and diversification.

3 Assess marketing's role in strategic planning and explain how marketers partner with others inside and outside the firm to build profitable customer relationships

Under the strategic plan, the major functional departments – marketing, finance, accounting, purchasing, operations, information systems, human resources and others – must work together to accomplish strategic objectives. Marketing plays a key role in the company's strategic planning by providing a marketing-concept philosophy and inputs regarding attractive market opportunities. Within individual business units, marketing designs strategies for reaching the unit's objectives and helps to carry them out profitably.

Marketers alone cannot produce superior value for customers. A company's success depends on how well each department performs its customer value-adding activities and how well the departments work together to serve the customer. Thus, marketers must practise partner relationship management. They must work closely with partners in other company departments to form an effective value chain that serves the customer. And they must partner effectively with other companies in the marketing system to form a competitively superior value-delivery network.

4 Describe the elements of a customer-driven marketing strategy and mix, and the forces that influence them

Consumer relationships are at the centre of marketing strategy and programmes. Through market segmentation, target marketing and market positioning, the company divides the total market into smaller segments, selects segments it can best serve, and decides how it wants to bring value to target consumers. It then designs a marketing mix to produce the response it wants in the target market. The marketing mix consists of product, price, place and promotion decisions.

5 List the marketing management functions, including the elements of a marketing plan, and discuss the importance of measuring and managing return on marketing

To find the best strategy and mix and to put them into action, the company engages in marketing analysis, planning, implementation and control. The main components of a marketing plan are the executive summary, current marketing situation, threats and opportunities, objectives and issues, marketing strategies, action programmes, budgets and controls. To plan good strategies is often easier than to carry them out. To be successful, companies must also be effective at implementation – turning marketing strategies into marketing actions.

Much of the responsibility for implementation goes to the company's marketing department. Marketing departments can be organised in one or a combination of ways: functional marketing organisation, geographic organisation, product management organisation or market management organisation. In this age of customer relationships, more and more companies are now changing their organisational focus from product or territory management to customer relationship management. Marketing organisations carry out marketing control, both operating control and strategic control. They use marketing audits to determine marketing opportunities and problems and to recommend short-term and long-term actions to improve overall marketing performance.

Marketing managers must ensure that their marketing budget is being well spent. Today's marketers face growing pressures to show that they are adding value in line with their costs. In response, marketers are developing better measures of return on marketing. Increasingly, they are using customer-centred measures of marketing impact as a key input into their strategic decision making.

NAVIGATING THE KEY TERMS

Business portfolio **48**
Diversification **51**
Downsizing **51**
Growth–share matrix **49**
Market development **51**
Market penetration **51**
Market positioning **57**
Market segment **56**
Market segmentation **56**

Marketing audit **65**
Marketing control **64**
Marketing implementation **61**
Marketing mix **57**
Marketing strategy **55**
Mission statement **44**
Portfolio analysis **48**
Product development **51**
Product–market expansion grid **50**

Return on marketing (or marketing ROI) **65**
Strategic planning **43**
SWOT analysis **59**
Target marketing **56**
Value chain **52**
Value-delivery network **53**

NOTES AND REFERENCES

1 'BT Group Annual Report and Form 20-F: 2010', available from **www.bt.com**, accessed 18 April 2011; 'British Telecommunications plc A: The Strategic Dilemma' and 'British Telecommunications B: Tomorrow the World?', case studies 1 and 2 in *Contemporary Strategic Marketing*, by Ross Brennan, Paul Baines, Paul Garneau and Lynn Vos (Basingstoke: Palgrave Macmillan, 2008); additional material from **https://www.globalservices .bt.com**, accessed 1 May 2011.

2 For a more detailed discussion of corporate- and business-level strategic planning as they apply to marketing, see Ross Brennan, Paul Baines, Paul Garneau and Lynn Vos, *Contemporary Strategic Marketing*, 2nd edn (Basingstoke: Palgrave Macmillan, 2008).

3 See Forest David and Fred David, 'It's Time to Redraft Your Mission Statement', *Journal of Business Strategy*, January/February 2003, pp. 11–15; 'Crafting Mission Statements', *Association Management*, January 2004, p. 23; and Charles N. Toftoy and Joydeep Chartterjee, 'Mission Statements and the Small Business', *Business Strategy Review*, Autumn 2004, pp. 41–4.

4 http://www.wagggs.org/en/about/About

5 Monsanto Company: **http://www.monsanto.com/whoweare/pages/default.aspx**, accessed May 2014.

6 For a general description of the concepts one can go to **http://www.bcg.com/about_bcg/ vision/our_heritage/history/history_1968.aspx** (December 2014). For more on strategic planning, see Dennis Rheault, 'Freshening Up Strategic Planning: More than Fill-in-the-Blanks', *Journal of Business Strategy*, 24(6), 2004, pp. 33–7; Anthony Lavia, 'Strategic Planning in Times of Turmoil', *Business Communications Review*, March 2004, pp. 56–60; Rita Gunther McGrath and Ian C. MacMillan, 'Market Busting', *Harvard Business Review*, March 2005, pp. 80–9.

7 H. Igor Ansoff, 'Strategies for Diversification', *Harvard Business Review*, September–October 1957, pp. 113–24; also see Kevin Lane Keller, *Strategic Brand Management*, 2nd edn (Upper Saddle River, NJ: Prentice Hall, 2003), pp. 576–8; and Philip Kotler and Kevin Lane Keller, *Marketing Management* (Upper Saddle River, NJ: Pearson Education, 2011), pp. 47–8.

8 Information about Under Armour in this section is from Stephanie N. Metha, 'Under Armour Reboots,' *Fortune*, 2 February 2009, pp. 29–34; Elaine Wong, 'Under Armour Makes Long-Run Calculation', *Brandweek*, 19 January 2009, p. 28; Liz Farmer, 'Baltimore-Based Under Armour Says Revenue Will Be Lower', *Daily Record* (Baltimore), 15 January 2009; Farmer, 'This Super Bowl Weekend, Baltimore-Based Under Armour Taking Grass Roots Marketing Approach', *Daily Record* (Baltimore), 30 January 2009; 'Under Armour Reports 20% Top-Line Growth for the Full Year with 3% Growth for the Fourth Quarter', Under Armour press release, 29 January 2009, accessed at **http://investor .underarmour.com**; and Under Armour annual reports and other documents accessed at **www.underarmour.com**, April 2009.

9 Michael E. Porter, *Competitive Advantage: Creating and Sustaining Superior Performance* (New York: Free Press, 1985); and Michel E. Porter, 'What is Strategy?', *Harvard Business Review*, November–December 1996, pp. 61–78. See also Kim B. Clark, *et al.*, *Harvard Business School on Managing the Value Chain* (Boston, MA: Harvard Business School Press, 2000); 'Buyer Value and the Value Chain', *Business Owner*, September–October 2003, p. 1; and 'The Value Chain,' accessed at **www.quickmba.com/strategy/value-chain/**, July 2005.

10 Philip Kotler, *Kotler on Marketing* (New York: Free Press, 1999), pp. 20–2. See also Philip Kotler, *Marketing Insights from A to Z* (Hoboken, NJ: Wiley, 2003), pp. 102–7.

11 Rebecca Ellinor, 'Crowd Pleaser', *Supply Management*, 13 December 2007, pp. 26–29; and information from **www.loreal.com/_en/_ww/html/suppliers/index.aspx**, accessed August 2009.

12 Jack Trout, 'Branding Can't Exist without Positioning', *Advertising Age*, 14 March 2005, p. 28.

13 The four Ps classification was first suggested by E. Jerome McCarthy, *Basic Marketing: A Managerial Approach* (Homewood, IL: Irwin, 1960). For the 4Cs, other proposed classifications and more discussion, see Robert Lauterborn, 'New Marketing Litany: 4P's Passé; C-Words Take Over', *Advertising Age*, 1 October 1990, p. 26; Elliott Ettenberg, 'Goodbye 4Ps, Hello 4Rs', *Marketing Magazine*, 14 April 2003, p. 8; Michael R. Hyman, 'Revising the Structural Framework for Marketing Management', *Journal of Business Research*, September 2004, p. 923; and Don E. Schultz, 'New Definition of Marketing Reinforces Idea of Integration', *Marketing News*, 15 January 2005, p. 8.

14 For more on brand and product management, see Keller, *Strategic Brand Management*, 2nd edn, op. cit.

15 For details, see Kotler and Keller, *Marketing Management*, 12th edn, pp. 719–25. Also see Neil A. Morgan, Bruce H. Clark and Rich Gooner, 'Marketing Productivity, Marketing Audits, and Systems for Marketing Performance Assessment: Integrating Multiple Perspectives', *Journal of Marketing*, May 2002, pp. 363–75.

16 Diane Brady, 'Making Marketing Measure Up', *Business Week*, 13 December 2004, pp. 112–13; and 'Kotler Readies World for One-on-One', *Point*, June 2005, p. 3.

17 Mark McMaster, 'ROI: More Vital than Ever', *Sales & Marketing Management*, January 2002, pp. 51–2. Also see Paul Hyde, Ed Landry and Andrew Tipping, 'Are CMOs Irrelevant?' Association of National Advertisers/Booz, Allen, Hamilton white paper, p. 4, accessed at **http://www.strategyand.pwc.com/media/uploads/Are_CMOs_Irrelevant .pdf**, December 2014.

18 For a full discussion of this model and details on customer-centred measures of return on marketing, see Roland T. Rust, Katherine N. Lemon and Valerie A. Zeithaml, 'Return on Marketing: Using Customer Equity to Focus Marketing Strategy', *Journal of Marketing*, January 2004, pp. 109–27; and Roland T. Rust, Katherine N. Lemon and Das Narayandas, *Customer Equity Management* (Upper Saddle River, NJ: Prentice Hall, 2005).

19 Mark McMaster, 'ROI: More Vital than Ever', *Sales & Marketing Management*, January 2002, pp. 51–2. Also see Steven H. Seggie, Erin Cavusgil and Steven Phelan, 'Measurement of Return on Marketing Investment: A Conceptual Framework and the Future of Marketing Metrics', *Industrial Marketing Management*, August 2007, pp. 834–41; and David Armano, 'The New Focus Group: The Collective', *BusinessWeek Online*, 8 January 2009, accessed at **www.businessweek.com**

20 For more discussion, see Bruce H. Clark, Andrew V. Abela and Tim Ambler, 'Behind the Wheel', *Marketing Management*, May–June 2006, pp. 19–23; Christopher Hosford, 'Driving Business with Dashboards', *BtoB*, 11 December 2006, p. 18; Allison Enwright, 'Measure Up: Create a ROMI Dashboard That Shows Current and Future Value', *Marketing News*, 15 August 2007, pp. 12–13; and Lawrence A. Crosby, Bruce A. Corner and Cheryl G. Rieger, 'Breaking Up Should Be Hard to Do', *Marketing Management*, January/February 2009, pp. 14–16; James D. Lenskold, 'Marketing ROI: Playing to Win', *Marketing Management*, May–June 2002, pp. 30–6. Also see James D. Lenskold, *Marketing ROI: The Path to Campaign, Customer, and Corporate Profitability* (New York: McGraw-Hill, 2003); and Rishad Tobaccowala, 'The High Cost of Arrogance and the Need to Focus on Outputs', *Point*, May 2005, p. 6.

PART TWO

UNDERSTANDING THE MARKETPLACE AND CONSUMERS

MAKING AN EFFORT TO UNDERSTAND YOUR CUSTOMERS

Now that you have some idea about the basic concepts and objectives of marketing you should have realised that understanding both the context of the organisation you work for and the patterns in the behaviour of your customers are issues that must be confronted if the firm is to succeed. In this part of the book we will consider these problems – how companies understand their customers and how they acknowledge forces and trends within their environments.

CHAPTER 3
THE MARKETING ENVIRONMENT

AFTER STUDYING THIS CHAPTER, YOU SHOULD BE ABLE TO

- describe the environmental forces that affect the company's ability to serve its customers
- explain how changes in the demographic and economic environments affect marketing decisions
- identify the major trends in the firm's natural and technological environments
- explain the key changes in the political and cultural environments
- discuss how companies can react to the marketing environment

THE WAY AHEAD
Previewing the concepts

In Part One (see Chapters 1 and 2), you learned about the basic concepts of marketing and the steps in the marketing process for building profitable relationships with targeted consumers. In Part Two, as you continue your journey towards learning about marketing, we'll look deeper into the first step of the marketing process – understanding the marketplace and customer needs and wants. In this chapter, you'll discover that marketing does not operate in a vacuum but rather in a complex and changing environment. Other *actors* in this environment – suppliers, intermediaries, customers, competitors, publics and others – may work with or against the company. Major environmental *forces* – demographic, economic, natural, technological, political and cultural – shape marketing opportunities, pose threats and affect the company's ability to serve customers and develop lasting relationships with them. To understand marketing, and to develop effective marketing strategies, you must first understand the context in which marketing operates.

To illustrate just how swiftly and how unexpectedly serious damage can be inflicted on a company by something entirely outside its control, we start off by looking at the Danish company Arla Foods, and the damage that it suffered in Middle Eastern markets after a Danish newspaper published cartoons that many people of the Islamic faith found offensive. Through no fault of its own, Arla found its brand reputation damaged, its relationships with customers and retailers undermined, and its sales slashed. Read on to see how Arla set out to put this right.

THE BOYCOTT OF ARLA FOODS IN THE MIDDLE EAST

Dr Ibrahim Abosag, School of Oriental and African Studies, University of London

The Danish company Arla Foods is a global dairy group with production facilities in 11 countries and sales offices in 24 countries, and which sells its products in over 100 countries. Arla started its operation in the Middle East some 40 years ago. Soon after its entry into the market there it became the market leader, mainly because of the absence of any credible local competitors. Over the years, Arla has maintained its position as market leader in the Middle East in cheese, butter and cream production. In the mid-1980s, Arla started to operate the Danya Foods Dairy in Saudi Arabia's capital, Riyadh. The production facilities in Riyadh are seen to enhance and strengthen its position as market leader in the region. It employs more than 1,200 people across the Middle East, mostly in Saudi Arabia. From its early days in the Middle East until the end of 2005, Arla enjoyed excellent brand recognition and, according to the Executive Director of the Overseas Division (in 2005), Finn Hansen, 'consumer awareness of our brands is on a par with, say, Coca-Cola'.

However, in early 2006 Arla lost its market lead because of a boycott of Danish products in many parts of the Middle East. The publication in 2005 by a Danish tabloid newspaper of a series of cartoon caricatures of the Prophet Muhammad sparked uproar across the Middle East. Consumers started to boycott Danish products and a trade boycott followed shortly after; major local retailers such as Al-Othaim Holding and Azizia Panda announced the withdrawal of all Danish products from their shelves. Arla Foods' brands such as Lurpak butter, Puck cream cheese, Three Cows white cheese and Dano powdered milk felt the double impact of both the consumer and the trade boycott. The most intense boycotting campaigns were carried out in Saudi Arabia, the biggest market in the Middle East. Arla Foods' products were withdrawn from more than 50,000 stores across the region in less than five days, losing over 60 per cent of its market. The main Saudi competitor Almarai took advantage of the cartoon crisis and took the lead in the market. In 2008, Almarai was still the market leader.

The campaigners were successful in posting the images of Danish brands on the Internet and calling upon consumers to boycott these brands. Also, mobile phone messages carrying boycott lists of Danish products were widely circulated. Similarly, a number of retail stores put all Danish brands, including Arla's, in a special section on one side of the store accompanied by a large notice calling on consumers not to buy. At the same time, Western stores doing business in the region tried to limit the damage to their own reputations. For example, the French-owned supermarket chain Carrefour stopped selling Danish goods, while several firms, including the Swiss food multinational Nestlé, placed advertisements in Saudi newspapers to counter rumours that their products were made in Denmark.

Product boycotts are not new, but this one was organised, widespread and quite devastating in its impact. Demonstrations were organised and in some countries they reached riot level. Two drivers of Arla official cars and distribution lorries were attacked. The headquarters premises were stoned and threats were issued by demonstrators. The impact was such that Arla was forced to close its plant in Riyadh, lay off employees in Denmark for 10 weeks and postpone its plan to double sales in the region by 2010.

Over 40 years of marketing investment and brand building had been undermined in a blink of an eye. With a large-scale boycott happening and no previous experience of anything like this, the whole situation was new to the senior managers of Arla Foods. There were no tried and tested damage-limitation strategies because the campaign was unprecedented. Faced with an unenviable task, the General Manager, Erik Folden, and the Marketing

Arla Foods owns leading dairy brands in the Middle East

Source: Arla Foods. With permission.

Manager, Torben Terp Hansen, at Arla Foods' headquarters in Saudi Arabia, considered ways of restoring faith in Arla Foods' brands. They realised that successful boycotts can have a short-term impact on sales and a long-term impact on a company's most precious asset, its reputation. The main intention was to protect the brand by distancing Arla Foods' brands from the trigger of the boycott.

The initial reaction from Arla was to keep silent. 'Consumer sentiments were high and we knew it was not the right time yet to address our society. "Silence is golden" and we kept it for almost 45 days,' said Torben Terp Hansen. During this period, Arla Foods' executives worked on developing 'a comeback strategy' involving seven steps. The first step was to distance themselves from the cartoons, a message that was communicated by Arla managers widely through newspapers and TV stations. The second step revolved around the International Support of the Prophet Conference on 23 March 2006 in Bahrain. The conference discussed Arla Foods' statement and issued a religious recommendation to exempt the company from any boycott. The Bahrain statement cleared Arla of any responsibility and emphasised that Arla should not be punished for the action of others.

In the third step, the company made the Bahrain statement public. To serve this purpose, a statement was published in all newspapers and TV channels thanking the conference for removing Arla Foods from the boycott list. The Bahrain statement was attached alongside the company's statement. A printed version of the statement was placed on the doors of outlets. Soon after, Arla Foods organised a Press and Trade Conference in Riyadh, which was attended by the major retailers and spearheaded by Al-Othaim Holding. The aim was to persuade the retailers to make a collective decision to accept Arla Foods back onto their shelves. Although Arla Foods was successful in restarting its relationships with some of the retailers, it failed to secure the support from the big retailer, Azizia Panda, which continued to boycott Arla products. Nonetheless, Arla published another 'thank you statement' through the media for those retailers who accepted Arla Foods back. The statement contained the logos of the retailers who agreed to sell Arla Foods' brands.

The fourth step was getting back to the stores. Now the retailers were safe in taking back Arla products because Arla had distanced itself from the cartoons. Reuters television covered the return of Arla Foods' brands to stores across the region. Despite all of the statements and coverage, some customers maintained their boycott. This meant that the fifth step had to focus on promotion. Given the huge product stock returns from markets since the boycott started, and because customers are price sensitive, heavy consumer and trade offers were made to entice retailers and consumers to break their boycott.

In the sixth step Arla concentrated on corporate and brand communication. Two main messages were at the heart of its communication. First, it informed the public about its position on the cartoons. Second, it reminded consumers about the long heritage Arla Foods had in the region. The communication platform for all brands was aligned with the corporate one and phrases such as ' 40 years with you' and 'together for generations' were used. Brand communication was designed to show understanding of the region's values, culture and sentiments. However, this communication strategy was essentially a short-term measure. Two months later, the strategy was replaced in the seventh step by the long-term brand communication. This was seen as an important step to regain the hearts and minds of consumers. To achieve this, heavy investments were made in charities, social activities and social responsibility campaigns: namely, product donations, ties with official governmental bodies, children's cancer activities, and donations of ambulances to the Saudi Red Crescent. These activities, which endured for some considerable time, were designed to improve the perception of Arla Foods across the Middle East, and specifically in Saudi Arabia.

A year after the boycott started, at the end of 2006, Arla Foods had recovered most of its market share in most Middle Eastern countries with the exception of Saudi Arabia, where it had recovered only 50 per cent. By early 2008 Arla Foods had managed to recover 70 per cent of its market in Saudi Arabia.

The boycott against Arla lasted a lot longer than many others. A similar boycott of US products faded quite quickly, in only a few weeks. The intensity and the scale of the boycott against these products did not force US companies to react in the way Arla Foods had to. Even now, Arla still has more work to do to repair all of the damage inflicted by the boycott.

Source: With thanks to Torben Terp Hansen, General Manager of Arla Foods, Lebanon.

Marketers need to be good at building relationships with customers, others in the company and external partners. To do this effectively, they must understand the major environmental forces that surround all of these relationships. A company's **marketing environment** consists of the actors and forces outside marketing that affect marketing management's ability to build and maintain successful relationships with target customers. Successful companies know the vital importance of constantly watching and adapting to the changing environment.

The marketing environment is the *context of business*. All plans and strategies are made in that context, and will be successful or not in that context. As the context and facts change, so should minds and plans, and the environment may change rapidly, so both consumers and marketers will often wonder what the future will bring. More than any other group in the company, marketers must be the trend trackers and opportunity seekers. Although every manager in an organisation needs to observe the outside environment, marketers have two special aptitudes. They have disciplined methods – marketing research and marketing intelligence – for collecting information about the marketing environment. They also spend more time in the customer and competitor environments. By carefully studying the environment, marketers can adapt their strategies to meet new marketplace challenges and opportunities.

The marketing environment is made up of a *microenvironment* and a *macroenvironment*. The **microenvironment** consists of the actors close to the company that affect its ability to serve its customers – the company, suppliers, marketing intermediaries, customer markets, competitors and publics. The **macroenvironment** consists of the larger societal forces that affect the microenvironment – demographic, economic, natural, technological, political and cultural forces. We look first at the company's microenvironment.

THE COMPANY'S MICROENVIRONMENT

Marketing management's job is to build relationships with customers by creating customer value and satisfaction. However, marketing managers cannot do this alone. Figure 3.1 shows the major actors in the marketer's microenvironment. Marketing success will require building relationships with other company departments, suppliers, marketing intermediaries, customers, competitors and various publics, which combine to make up the company's value-delivery network.

The company

In designing marketing plans, marketing management takes other company groups into account – groups such as top management, finance, research and development (R&D), purchasing, operations and accounting. All these interrelated groups form the internal environment. Top management sets the company's mission, objectives, broad strategies and policies. Marketing managers make decisions within the strategies and plans made by top management.

Marketing managers must also work closely with other company departments. Finance is concerned with finding and using funds to carry out the marketing plan. The R&D department focuses on designing safe and attractive products. Purchasing worries about getting

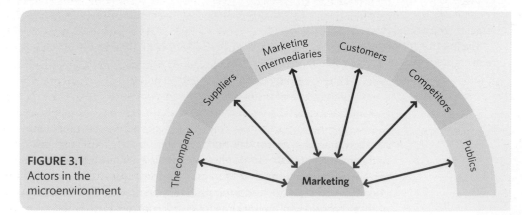

FIGURE 3.1
Actors in the microenvironment

supplies and materials, whereas operations is responsible for producing and distributing the desired quality and quantity of products. Accounting has to measure revenues and costs to help marketing know how well it is achieving its objectives. Together, all of these departments have an impact on the marketing department's plans and actions. Under the marketing concept, all of these functions must 'think consumer'. They should work in harmony to provide superior customer value and satisfaction.

Suppliers

Suppliers form an important link in the company's overall customer value-delivery system. They provide the resources needed by the company to produce its goods and services. Supplier problems can seriously affect marketing. Marketing managers must watch supply availability – supply shortages or delays, labour strikes and other events can cost sales in the short term and damage customer satisfaction in the long term. Marketing managers also monitor the price trends of their key inputs. Rising supply costs may force price increases that can harm the company's sales volume.

Most marketers today treat their suppliers as partners in creating and delivering customer value. Tesco goes to great lengths to work with its suppliers. For example, it helps them to test new products in its stores. Tesco has signed up to the Office of Fair Trading supermarket Code of Practice on the treatment of suppliers, which means that it undertakes to treat suppliers fairly at all times and to avoid such practices as delaying payments to suppliers or insisting that suppliers contribute financially to supermarket promotional activities. In the most recent audit by the Office of Fair Trading, Tesco was found to be implementing this code effectively.

Marketing intermediaries

Marketing intermediaries help the company to promote, sell and distribute its goods to final buyers. They include resellers, physical distribution firms, marketing services agencies and financial intermediaries. *Resellers* are distribution channel firms that help the company find customers or make sales to them. These include wholesalers and retailers, who buy and resell merchandise. Selecting and partnering with resellers is not easy. No longer do manufacturers have many small, independent resellers from which to choose. They now face large and growing reseller organisations such as Tesco, Carrefour, Aldi and Fnac. These organisations frequently have enough power to dictate terms or even shut the manufacturer out of large markets.

Physical distribution firms help the company to stock and move goods from their points of origin to their destinations. Maersk – a company that is a world leader in this field – made an appearance in an earlier case study (see Chapter 2). Working with warehouse and transportation firms, a company must determine the best ways to store and ship goods, balancing factors such as cost, delivery, speed and safety. *Marketing services agencies* are the marketing research firms, advertising agencies, media firms and marketing consulting firms that help the company target and promote its products to the right markets. *Media intermediaries* include the traditional print and television but also companies like Facebook, Pinterest and Twitter – organisations that shape, manage and target communications and allow interaction and engagement between firm and customers. *Financial intermediaries* include banks, credit companies, insurance companies and other businesses that help finance transactions or insure against the risks associated with the buying and selling of goods.

Like suppliers, marketing intermediaries form an important component of the company's overall value-delivery system. In its quest to create satisfying customer relationships, the company must do more than just optimise its own performance. It must partner effectively with marketing intermediaries to optimise the performance of the entire system.

Thus, today's marketers recognise the importance of working with their intermediaries as partners rather than simply as channels through which they sell their products. For example, when Coca-Cola signs on as the exclusive drinks provider for a fast-food chain, such as McDonald's or Subway, it provides much more than just soft drinks. It also pledges powerful marketing support. Coke assigns cross-functional teams dedicated to understanding the finer points of each retail partner's business. It conducts a staggering amount of research on beverage consumers and shares these insights with its partners. It analyses the demographics of geographical areas and helps partners to determine which Coke brands are preferred in their areas. Coca-Cola has even studied the design of drive-through menu boards to understand better which layouts, fonts, letter sizes, colours and visuals induce consumers to order more food and drink. Based on such insights, the Coca-Cola FoodService Group develops marketing programmes and merchandising tools that help its retail partners to improve their beverage sales and profits.[1]

Customers

The company needs to study five types of customer markets closely. *Consumer markets* consist of individuals and households that buy goods and services for personal consumption. *Business markets* buy goods and services for further processing or for use in their production process, whereas *reseller markets* buy goods and services to resell at a profit. *Government markets* are made up of government agencies that buy goods and services to produce public services or transfer the goods and services to others who need them. Finally, *international markets* consist of these buyers in other countries, including consumers, producers, resellers and governments. Each market type has special characteristics that call for careful study by the seller.

Competitors

The marketing concept states that to be successful a company must provide greater customer value and satisfaction than its competitors do. Thus, marketers must do more than simply adapt to the needs of target consumers. They also must gain strategic advantage by positioning their offerings strongly against competitors' offerings in the minds of consumers.

No single competitive marketing strategy is best for all companies. Each firm should consider its own size and industry position compared with those of its competitors. Large firms with dominant positions in an industry can use certain strategies that smaller firms cannot afford. But being large is not enough. There are winning strategies for large firms, but there are also losing ones. And small firms can develop strategies that give them better rates of return than large firms enjoy.

Publics

The company's marketing environment also includes various publics. A **public** is any group that has an actual or potential interest in or impact on an organisation's ability to achieve its objectives. We can identify seven types of publics:

- *Financial publics* influence the company's ability to obtain funds. Banks, investment houses and shareholders are the major financial publics.
- *Media publics* carry news, features and editorial opinion. They include newspapers, magazines, websites, social media and radio and TV stations.
- *Government publics*. Management must take government developments into account. Marketers must often consult the company's lawyers on issues of product safety, truth in advertising, and other matters.
- *Citizen-action publics*. A company's marketing decisions may be questioned by consumer organisations, environmental groups, minority groups and others. Its public relations department can help it stay in touch with consumer and citizen groups.

- *Local publics* include neighbourhood residents and community organisations. Large companies usually appoint a community relations officer to deal with the community, attend meetings, answer questions and contribute to worthwhile causes.
- *General public.* A company needs to be concerned about the general public's attitude towards its products and activities. The public's image of the company affects its buying.
- *Internal publics* include workers, managers, volunteers and the board of directors. Large companies use newsletters and other means to inform and motivate their internal publics. When employees feel good about their company, this positive attitude spills over to external publics.

A company can prepare marketing plans for these major publics as well as for its customer markets. Suppose the company wants a specific response from a particular public, such as goodwill, favourable word of mouth, or donations of time or money. The company would have to design an offer to this public that is attractive enough to produce the desired response.

THE COMPANY'S MACROENVIRONMENT

The company and all of the other actors operate in a larger macroenvironment of forces that shape opportunities and pose threats to the company. Figure 3.2 shows the six major forces in the company's macroenvironment. In the remaining sections of this chapter, we examine these forces and show how they affect marketing plans.

Demographic environment

Demography is the study of human populations in terms of size, density, location, age, gender, race, occupation and other statistics. The demographic environment is of major interest to marketers because it involves people, and people make up markets. The world population is growing at an explosive rate. It now totals more than 6.9 billion and will exceed 8.1 billion by the year 2030.[2] The world's large and highly diverse population poses both opportunities and challenges.

Changes in the world demographic environment have major implications for business. For example, consider China. More than a quarter of a century ago, to curb its rapidly growing population, the Chinese government passed regulations limiting families to one child each. As a result, Chinese children – known as 'little emperors and empresses' – are being showered with attention and luxuries under what's known as the 'six-pocket syndrome'. As many as six adults – two parents and four doting grandparents – may be indulging the

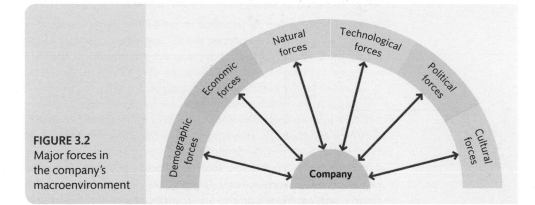

FIGURE 3.2
Major forces in the company's macroenvironment

China is now a key market for many luxury brands

Source: Alamy Images/Jake Wyman.

whims of each 'only child'. Parents in the average Beijing household now spend about 40 per cent of their income on their cherished only child:

> China's one-child rule created a generation who have been pampered by parents and grand-parents and have the means to make indulgent purchases. Instead of believing in traditional Chinese collective goals, these young people embrace individuality. 'Their view of this world is very different,' says the president of Starbucks Greater China. 'They have never gone through the hardships of our generation. Starbucks is in sync with that,' he says, 'given its customised drinks, personalised service, and original music compilations.'[3]

Interestingly, the one-child policy is creating another major Chinese demographic development – a rapidly ageing population. In what some deem a potential 'demographic earthquake', a large and growing proportion of the Chinese population is now aged over 40. And because of the one-child policy, close to 75 per cent of all Chinese households will be childless, either because they chose to have no children or because their only child has left the nest. The result is an ageing society that will need to be more self-reliant, which in turn will cause a large growth in service markets such as education for older people, leisure clubs and nursing homes.[4]

Thus, marketers keep close track of demographic trends and developments in their markets, both at home and abroad. They track changing age and family structures, geographic population shifts, educational characteristics and population diversity. Here, we discuss the most important demographic trends in Europe.

Changing age structure of the population

The population of the 28 member states of the EU stood at more than 503 million in 2013.[5] It is very difficult to forecast the EU population because of the very large inward and outward flows of migrants, and because the population of the EU depends on when, and whether, new countries such as Turkey are allowed to join. Net inward migration to the EU is expected to be the biggest factor leading to population growth, since the natural growth of the population (where births exceed deaths) is expected to decline as families across the EU choose to have fewer children. Birth rates in the richest countries of the EU, such as the UK, France and Italy, are already well below the 'replacement level' (where births and deaths are just in balance). The single most important demographic trend in the EU is the changing age structure of the population. Internationally, in Europe, North America and several other parts of the world (such as Australia and New Zealand) there are three generational groups that are considered particularly important by marketers: the baby boomers, Generation X and the Millennials (also known as Generation Y, or echo boomers).

The baby boomers

This is the generation born between 1946 and 1964, a period when birth rates in countries affected by the Second World War rose sharply (hence the 'baby boom'). Since then, the **baby boomers** have become one of the most powerful forces shaping the marketing environment. The baby boomers have now grown to maturity, many of them are property owners and they account for around a quarter of the population.

Marketers have typically paid the most attention to the smaller upper crust of the boomer generation – the more educated, mobile and wealthy segments. These segments have gone by many names. In the 1980s, they were called 'yuppies' (young urban professionals), and 'DINKs' (Dual-Income, No-Kids couples). In the 1990s, yuppies and DINKs gave way to a new breed, with names such as 'DEWKs' (Dual-Earners With Kids) and 'MOBYs' (Mother Older, Baby Younger). Now, to the chagrin of many in this generation, they are acquiring such titles as 'WOOFs' (Well-Off Older Folks) or even 'GRUMPIES' (just what the name suggests).

As a group, the baby boomers are the most affluent Europeans. However, although the more affluent boomers have grabbed most of the headlines, baby boomers cut across all walks of life, creating a diverse set of target segments for businesses. There are wealthy boomers but also boomers of more modest means. The Credit Crunch and associated volatility in share prices have created financial uncertainty for a lot of boomers, who thought that they had their retirement plans all figured out. Many of them have had to rethink their plans and are now thinking about working longer before retirement.

The youngest boomers are now in their fifties; the oldest are in their seventies. Thus, the boomers have evolved from the 'youthquake generation' to the 'backache generation'. The maturing boomers are rethinking the purpose and value of their work, responsibilities and relationships. They are approaching life with a new stability and reasonableness in the way they live, think, eat and spend. Even despite the setbacks they have suffered during the Credit Crunch, the boomers constitute a lucrative market for new housing and home remodelling, financial services, travel and entertainment, eating out, health and fitness products, and high-priced cars and other luxuries. Saga is one company which has specialised in catering to the older market.

It would be a mistake to think of boomers as ageing, staid retirees. In fact, boomers are spending large amounts each year on *anti*-ageing products and services. And unlike previous generations, boomers are likely to postpone retirement. Many boomers are rediscovering the excitement of life and have the money to enjoy themselves.

Generation X

The baby boom was followed by a 'birth dearth', creating another generation of people born between 1965 and 1976. The term **Generation X** was made famous in the book of that name by Douglas Coupland, published in 1991, although the term had been in use for several years before Coupland wrote his book.[6] People are named 'Generation X' because they lie in the shadow of the boomers and lack obvious distinguishing characteristics. Others call them the 'baby busters,' the 'yiffies' (young, individualistic, freedom-minded few), or the 'generation caught in the middle' (between the larger baby boomers and later Millennials).

Generation X people are defined as much by their shared experiences as by their age. Increasing divorce rates and higher employment for their mothers made them the first generation of latchkey kids (left to look after themselves after school). They grew up during the 1970s and 1980s, which were particularly troubled times in the world economy, with rampant inflation and high unemployment. Having grown up in times of recession when companies ceased to offer 'lifetime employment' and started to reduce their workforces ('downsizing'), they developed a more cautious economic outlook. They care about the environment and respond favourably to socially responsible companies. Although they seek success, they are less materialistic; they prize experience, not acquisition. They are cautious romantics who want a better quality of life and are more interested in job satisfaction than in sacrificing personal happiness and growth for promotion. Often, family comes first, career second.

As a result, the 'Gen Xers' are a more sceptical bunch. 'Marketing to Gen Xers is difficult,' says one marketer, 'and it's all about word of mouth. You can't tell them you're good, and they have zero interest in a slick brochure that says so. You have to rely on somebody they know and trust to give you instant credibility. They have a lot of "filters" in place.'[7]

Once labelled as 'the MTV generation' and viewed as body-piercing slackers who whined about 'McJobs', the Gen Xers have now grown up and are beginning to take over. They are displacing the lifestyles, culture and materialistic values of the baby boomers. Very soon they will overtake the baby boomers as a primary market for almost every product category.[8] With so much potential, many companies are focusing on Gen Xers as an important target segment.

Millennials

Both the baby boomers and Gen Xers will one day be passing the reins to the **Millennials** (also called **Generation Y** and echo boomers). This is the generation born between 1977 and 1995, when the number of births increased as the baby boomers entered their child-bearing years. The echo boom has created a large teen and young adult market.

Older members of the Millennials have now graduated from university and are moving up in their careers. One thing that all of the Millennials have in common is their utter fluency and comfort with digital technology. They do not just embrace technology, it is a way of life. The Millennials were the first generation to grow up in a world filled with computers, mobile phones, satellite TV and online social networks. 'All generations are comfortable with technology, but this is the generation that's been formed by technology,' says a Yahoo executive. For them, 'it's not something separate. It's just something they do'.[9]

The Millennials represent an attractive target for marketers. However, reaching this message-saturated segment effectively requires creative marketing approaches. For example, the popularity of action sports with Millennials has provided creative marketing opportunities for products ranging from clothes to video games, films and even beverages. Red Bull's edgy and irreverent positioning makes it a natural for the action-sport crowd. Red Bull has become a true action-sports supporter. It sponsors the Red Bull Air Race World Series and the Red Bull X-Alps adventure racing event, is endorsed by athletes from a wide range of sports including cricket, football and athletics, and sponsors top adventure sports stars such as the amazing Austrian base-jumping star Felix Baumgartner (if you were unaware of Felix's exploits, you should really check them out at **www.felixbaumgartner.com**).

What is the next generation going to be like? Ipsos MORI and the National Children's Bureau released 'Who is Generation Next?' in the summer of 2014, a study detailing the priorities and aspirations of young people between 11 and 16 years old. The report contained some surprising findings. Underage drinking was down – as was smoking. Interest in politics and environmental issues was up. It is a generation that has grown up under the surveillance of social media. Boyband idols were seen as shallow and ridiculous and have been replaced by socially campaigning cooks like Jack Monroe. This up-and-coming generation is perceived by some as being quite prim and dull, leading the *Telegraph* to label it Generation Yawn.[10]

TOMS shoes: '*be* the change you want to see in the world'

If the world were a village of 100 people, 14 of the 100 would be illiterate, 20 would be malnourished, 23 would drink polluted water, 25 would have no shelter, 33 would have no electricity and 40 would have *no shoes*. In 2006, these stark facts, especially the last one, struck Blake Mycoskie up close and personally as he visited Argentina to learn how to play polo, practise his tango and do some community service work. While there, the sight of barefooted children, too poor to have shoes, stunned him.

So in May 2006, Mycoskie launched TOMS Shoes with $300,000 of his own money. The founding concept was this: for every pair of TOMS shoes that customers bought, the company would donate another pair of shoes to a child in need around the world. Mycoskie had previously started five successful strictly for-profit businesses. 'But I was ready to do something more meaningful,' he says. 'I always knew I wanted to help others. Now, it was time to do something that wasn't just for profit.' Mycoskie remembered Mahatma Gandhi saying: '*Be* the change you want to see in the world.'

'Doing good' is an important part of TOMS' mission. But so is 'doing well' – the company is very much a for-profit venture. However, at TOMS Shoes, the two missions go hand in hand. Beyond being socially admirable, the buy-one–give-one-away concept is also a good business proposition. In addition to scratching Mycoskie's itch to help people, he says that the timing was right for the consumer: 'With the rise of social and eco-consciousness and the economy in a downturn, people were looking for innovative and affordable ways to make the world a better place.'

With all of these 'do good' and 'do well' goals swirling in his head, Mycoskie returned home from his Argentina trip, hired an intern and set about making 250 pairs of shoes in the loft of his home. Stuffing the shoes into three duffel bags, he made the fledgling company's first 'Shoe Drop' tour, returning to the Argentine village and giving one pair of shoes to each child. Mycoskie arrived back home to find an article about his project on the front page of the *Los Angeles Times* Calendar section. TOMS had been in business for only two weeks, but by that very afternoon, he had orders for 2,200 pairs of shoes on his website.

By October 2006, TOMS had sold 10,000 pairs of shoes. True to the company's one-for-one promise, Mycoskie undertook a second TOMS Shoe Drop tour. Consistent with his new title, Chief Shoe Giver of TOMS Shoes, he led 15 employees and volunteers back to Argentina, where they went from school to school, village to village, and gave away another 10,000 pairs of shoes.

'We don't just drop the shoes off, as the name might imply,' says Mycoskie. 'We place the shoes on each child's feet so that we can establish a connection, which is such an important part of our brand. We want to give the children the feeling of love, and warmth, and experience. But *we* also get those feelings as we give the shoes.'

The one-for-one idea caught fire. As word spread about TOMS, a non-profit organisation called 'Friends of TOMS' formed to 'create avenues for individuals to volunteer and experience [the TOMS] mission', participate in Shoe Drops and 'perform good works in their own communities and their own lives'. *Vogue* magazine and other major publications ran stories on the company's philosophy and good works. By 2010, in its *Giving Report*, TOMS could report that 1,000,000 pairs of shoes had been given away to children in need in 23 countries.

In Ethiopia, 11 million people are at risk of podoconiosis, a disease often caused by silica in volcanic soils. Children's bare feet absorb the silica, which can cause elephantiasis, severe swelling of the legs and feet.

The disease progresses until surgery is required. The simple preventative cure? Shoes. As part of the Christmas season in 2008, TOMS offered gift card packages, which included a certificate for a pair of shoes and a DVD telling the TOMS story. The goal was to give 30,000 pairs of shoes to Ethiopian children in 30 days.

TOMS started a grassroots marketing movement called 'TOMS Vagabonds'. These travelling groups of TOMS disciples hit the road in vans full of TOMS shoes and help to organise events on college and school campuses and in communities. The Vagabonds' goal is to raise awareness about TOMS, sell shoes and inspire more people to get involved with the company's movement. The Vagabonds chronicle their travels on TOMS Facebook page (**www.facebook.com/TOMSVagabonds**), blog (**http://www.toms.com/stories/**) and Twitter site (**http://twitter.com/tomsshoes**).

The company is profitable and growing exponentially. TOMS' rapid growth is the result of purchases by caring customers who then tell the TOMS story to their friends. Whereas the typical shoe company spends about 20 per cent of sales on traditional advertising and promotion, TOMS has not spent a single dollar on it. It has not had to. 'Ultimately, it is our customers who drive our success,' says Mycoskie. 'Giving not only makes you feel good, but it actually is a very good business strategy, especially in this day and age. Your customers become your marketers.'

Moreover, as TOMS success shows, consumers like to feel good. A recent global study found that 71 per cent of consumers said that despite the recession they had given just as much time and money to causes they deemed worthy; 55 per cent of respondents also indicated they would pay more for a brand if it supported a good cause.

TOMS Shoes is a great example of cause-related marketing – of 'doing well by doing good'. Mycoskie hopes that his company will inspire people to think differently about business. 'My thinking was that TOMS would show that entrepreneurs no longer had to choose between earning money or making a difference in the world,' he says. 'Business and charity or public service don't have to be mutually exclusive. In fact, when they come together, they can be very powerful.'

Sources: Quotes and other information from Stacy Perman, 'Making a Do-Gooder's Business Model Work', *BusinessWeek Online*, 26 January 2009, accessed at www.businessweek.com/smallbiz/content/jan2009/sb20090123_264702.htm; Blake Mycoskie, 'Shoes for a Better Tomorrow', Presentation made 13 March 2009, accessed at www.clintonschoolspeakers.com/lecture/view/toms-shoes-better-tomorrow. Also see Michael Bush, 'Consumers Continue to Stand by Their Causes During Downturn', *Advertising Age*, 17 November 2008, p. 4; 'TOMS Shoes', *Obesity, Fitness & Wellness Week*, 13 December 2008, p. 2937; Patricia Sellers, 'Be the Change You Want To See in the World', HuffingtonPost.com, 11 October 2008; and information found at www.tomsshoes.com, http://friendsoftoms.org/, and in the online TOMS *Giving Report 2010*, accessed April 2011.

Generational marketing

Do marketers have to create separate products and marketing programmes for each genera-tion? Some experts warn that marketers have to be careful about turning off one generation each time they craft a product or message that appeals effectively to another. Others caution that each generation spans decades of time and many socio-economic levels. For example, marketers often split the baby boomers into three smaller groups – leading boomers, core boomers and trailing boomers – each with its own beliefs and behaviours. Similarly, they split Millennials into tweens, teens and adults. Thus, marketers need to form more precise age-specific segments within each group. More importantly, defining people by their birth date may be less effective than segmenting them by their lifestyle or life stage.

The changing family

The 'traditional household' consists of a husband, wife and children (and sometimes grand-parents). But this stereotypical notion of a household is becoming less and less representa-tive of the way modern society really is.

In Europe today, couples with children now make up only about 31 per cent of house-holds, and this percentage is falling. Ireland and Poland have twice as many such households as Germany and Finland. Cyprus leads the way in people getting married, with 7.3 mar-riages per 1,000 people per year, while in Bulgaria it is only 2.9. Almost no one in Malta gets divorced – 0.1 per thousand per year – whereas in Latvia it is a rate 40 times higher.

The average size of a household is about 2.4 people, but this varies considerably across Europe, standing, for example, at 2.9 in Romania but only 1.9 in Sweden. More people are divorcing or separating, choosing not to marry, marrying later, or marrying without intending to have children. Marketers must increasingly consider the special needs of non-traditional households, because they are now growing more rapidly than traditional house-holds. Each group has distinctive needs and buying habits. The type of household that is most common across Europe? The single person living alone.[11]

Women are making up an increasing proportion of the working population. In 2013 in the EU, 70 per cent of men aged 15–64 were in paid employment, compared with 58 per cent of women of the same age group. Again, this figure varies considerably across Europe: for example, 70 per cent of women in Denmark were in paid employment and only 46 per cent of women in Greece.[12] The significant number of women in the workforce has spawned the child day-care business and increased consumption of career-oriented women's clothing, financial services, and convenience foods and services.

Geographic shifts in population

This is a period of great migratory movements between and within countries. Net migra-tion is the difference between immigration (the number of people entering a country) and emigration (the number of people leaving). In recent years the number of immigrants from the rest of the world into Europe has considerably exceeded the number of emigrants; it is estimated that net inward migration into the EU was between 1.5 million and 2 million people each year from 2009 to 2012. Within the EU countries there has been a net migration of people westwards; that is to say, Western European countries, particularly the UK and Germany, have seen large inflows of population from countries in Eastern Europe. Such population shifts interest marketers because people in different geographical regions buy differently. Tobacco consumption provides a good way of understanding this: in Finland, 23 per cent of adults smoke (27 per cent of men, 20 per cent of women); in France, 27 per cent of adults smoke (33 per cent of men, 21 per cent of women); in Denmark, 30 per cent of adults smoke (32 per cent of men, 29 per cent of women); while in Hungary, 42 per cent of adults smoke (53 per cent of men, 30 per cent of women).[13] As workers from Eastern European countries such as Hungary move west to find jobs, marketers have to ask them-selves whether their consumption behaviour will resemble more the country where they were born or the country where they choose to work.

The shift in where people live has also caused a shift in where they work. For example, the migration towards metropolitan and suburban areas has resulted in a rapid increase in the number of people who 'telecommute' – work at home or in a remote office and conduct their business by phone, fax, modem or the Internet. This trend, in turn, has created a booming SOHO (Small Office/Home Office) market.

A better-educated, more white-collar, more professional population

The European population is becoming better educated, and European workers are increasingly employed in professional or 'white-collar' (managerial or equivalent) jobs. This generalisation is valid more or less everywhere across the Continent and the proportion of those aged 25–54 with a degree or equivalent qualification is consistently higher than for previous generations. These proportions do vary from country to country and the gender differences can be quite stark. With an EU average of 29 per cent in 2013, it is 40 per cent or more in Finland, Ireland and the UK, but less than 20 per cent in Portugal, Italy and the Czech Republic. Across the EU for the 30–34 age bracket, 10 per cent more women than men have degrees. Greece and Luxembourg are nearly at parity, but in Norway and Slovenia there is a 20 per cent difference.

Four EU countries currently have 2 million or more university students: Germany, the UK, France and Poland. The EU contains about 4,000 universities and other providers of tertiary-level qualifications. Governments across Europe recognise that economic success is increasingly dependent on having a well-educated population, and are investing in education. Typically, public spending on education in European countries runs at about 5.4 per cent of gross domestic product (GDP, a measure of the total national income).[14] The rising number of educated people will increase the demand for good-quality products, books, magazines, travel, PCs and Internet services. Over the next decade, job growth is likely to be strongest for professional workers and weakest for jobs in manufacturing.

Increasing diversity

Countries vary in their ethnic and racial make-up. For example, in Japan almost everyone is Japanese. The situation is very different in the UK, with people from virtually all nations. Roughly 20 per cent of the births in the UK are to mothers born outside the country. Taking England alone, in 2011 it was estimated that 82.8 per cent of the population was White British, and another 4.5 per cent was White but not British (including Irish people and immigrants from Eastern Europe). The largest ethnic minority group in England was Asian (very largely of Indian, Pakistani or Bangladeshi origin), who made up 6.1 per cent of the population, followed by the Black population at 2.9 per cent (fairly equally divided between people of African and of Caribbean origin).[15] Focusing even more tightly on London alone, it is estimated that a third of Londoners were born outside the UK, but Londoners born outside the UK made up a higher proportion, around 38 per cent, of London's labour force; they are more likely to be parents than Londoners born in the UK.

Marketers in the public and private sectors often have to factor in the ethnic composition of their markets when devising marketing strategies. Lloyds TSB bank has launched an Islamic bank account (which conforms to Islamic, sharia law) aimed at a predominantly Asian target market that practises Islam. The Mayor of London's office makes publicity and information material available in Arabic, Bengali, Chinese, Greek, Gujurati, Hindi, Punjabi, Turkish, Urdu and Vietnamese as well as English. In a multiracial city, like London, opportunities for marketers to turn a profit by serving the specific needs of particular ethnic groups abound – just ask **www.afrotherapy.com** of London (suppliers of hair-care and beauty products for those with black skin), **www.diyaonline.com** of Luton near London (suppliers of traditional Indian clothing) or Polish Specialities, which has specialist food stores in Oxford and London (**www.polishspecialities.com**).

Diversity goes beyond ethnic heritage. For example, many major companies have recently begun explicitly to target gay and lesbian consumers. Evidence from countries in which a

Multicultural marketing: an increasing number of businesses in Europe target the large, and often affluent, ethnic minority markets

Source: http://www.diyaonline.com

gay lifestyle is widely accepted, such as the UK, the USA and Germany, suggests that gay men and lesbians represent a tremendous marketing opportunity – being, on average, better educated, more likely to be in a professional job and better paid. In addition, gay men and lesbians tend to be early adopters of trends that eventually are adopted by the mainstream. For example, according to one expert, 'in the weeks following an episode of the Bravo hit show *Queer Eye for the Straight Guy* – in which five gay men, known as the Fab 5, make over a low-maintenance straight man – many businesses whose products are featured have seen a significant sales boost'. Lucky Brand jeans saw a 17 per cent sales jump for the two months following a mention on *Queer Eye*.[16]

Companies in several industries are now waking up to the needs and potential of the gay and lesbian segment. For example, **Gay.com**, a website that attracts more than 2 million unique visitors each month from more than 100 countries, has also attracted a diverse set of well-known advertisers. In fact, holiday companies and holiday destinations have recently demonstrated a particularly strong interest in the large amounts of money that are being spent in what is called the 'gay tourism' or 'pink tourism' market.[17] A wide range of cities around the world are vying to attract gay and lesbian tourists. Many of them provide detailed information through their websites, and other media, to prospective gay and lesbian tourists. For example, the city of Manchester in northern England promotes its gay scene as one of the UK's friendliest, busiest and most welcoming. There is even a Manchester Gay Village channel on YouTube.[18] The city of Melbourne, Australia, says: 'Melbourne is a gay-tolerant and gay-friendly city with bars, clubs and accommodation places in the older inner-suburban areas',[19] and gay and lesbian tourists eager to visit Germany can find out everything they need to know at the 'Gay-friendly Germany' section of the official German tourism website.[20]

MAKING CONNECTIONS Linking the concepts

Pull over here for a moment and think about how deeply these demographic factors affect all of us and, as a result, marketers' strategies.

● Apply these demographic developments to your own life. Think of some specific examples of how the changing demographic factors affect you and your buying behaviour.

● Identify a specific company that has done a good job of reacting to the shifting demographic environment – generational segments (baby boomers, Generation X or Millennials), the changing family and increased diversity. Compare this company with one that's done a poor job.

Economic environment

Markets require buying power as well as people. The **economic environment** consists of factors that affect consumer purchasing power and spending patterns. Nations vary greatly in their levels and distribution of income. Some countries have *subsistence economies* – they consume most of their own agricultural and industrial output. These countries offer few market opportunities. At the other extreme are *industrial economies,* which constitute rich markets for many different kinds of goods. Marketers must pay close attention to major trends and consumer spending patterns both across and within their world markets. The following are some of the major economic trends in Europe.

Changes in income

The general trend in incomes throughout the EU over the last two decades has been upwards. Table 3.1 shows that among the European nations that make up the EU, there is a wide disparity. The columns in the left half are total GDP for the nation, showing that Belgium has an economy about a third the size of Spain, and Poland twice that of Portugal. The right-hand half is the more useful data. This portion of the table shows GDP per capita – that is, how much there is per person, where 100 indicates an average amount for the EU28 nations. From this we can see that Belgium – when measured on a per capita basis – is about 20 per cent wealthier than Spain, and the Netherlands twice as wealthy per head as Hungary. Italy meanwhile has gone from being 20 per cent better than average to just about average, indicating decline – or other countries catching up. A closer inspection will show that the growth rate of income per head has been a little higher in the poorer nations than in the richer nations, indicating a narrowing of the income gap between Europe's richest countries and its poorest countries. During the period from 1996 to 2008, when average EU GDP per capita rose by 54 per cent, GDP per capita in Lithuania rose by 68.4 per cent. When looking at figures like these it is important to remember that the largest economies in the EU are far larger than the smaller economies. Germany alone represents over a fifth of EU GDP, and the four largest economies combined – Germany, the UK, France and Italy – represent two-thirds of EU GDP. At the other end of the scale, there are nine EU member countries that each represent less than 1 per cent of total EU GDP – the Czech Republic, Cyprus, Latvia, Lithuania, Luxembourg, Hungary, Malta, Slovenia and Slovakia.

The growth of consumer spending in the EU was adversely affected in 2008–11 by the so-called Credit Crunch. Although this problem largely originated in the USA, where banks had lent large sums of money to people who, it turned out, did not have the means to repay it, it was also felt throughout the EU, particularly in countries such as the UK where consumers had borrowed heavily to buy houses, cars and durable consumer goods. As a consequence the supply of funds banks had to lend to consumers diminished sharply, and a lot of consumers found themselves worse off when their short-term discounted mortgage deals came to an end and they had to refinance at a higher interest rate. These financially squeezed consumers have adjusted to their changing financial situations and are spending more carefully. *Value marketing* has become the watchword for many marketers. Rather than offering high quality at a high price, or lesser quality at very low prices, marketers are looking for ways to offer today's more financially cautious buyers greater value – just the right combination of product quality and good service at a fair price.

Marketers should pay attention to *income distribution* as well as average income. Income distribution in Europe is very skewed. At the top are *upper-class* consumers, whose spending patterns are not affected by current economic events and who are a major market for luxury goods. There is a comfortable *middle class* that is fairly careful about its spending but can still afford the good life some of the time. The *working class* must stick close to the basics of food, clothing and shelter and must try hard to save. Finally, the *underclass* (persons on welfare and many pensioners) must count their pennies when making even the most basic purchases. This distribution of income creates a tiered market. Many companies – such as

TABLE 3.1 GDP at current market prices, 2001 and 2010–11

	GDP (1,000 million EUR)			GDP per capita (PPS, EU27 = 100)		
	2001	2010	2011	2001	2010	2011
EU27	9,584	12,264	12,638	100	100	100
EA17	7,085	9163	9413	112	108	108
BE	260	356	370	124	119	119
BG	16	36	38	30	44	45
CZ	72	149	155	73	80	80
DK	179	236	239	128	127	125
DE	2,102	2,496	2,593	116	119	121
EE	7	14	16	46	64	67
IE	118	156	156	134	127	–
EL	146	227	215	86	90	82
ES	680	1,051	1,073	98	100	99
FR	1,496	1,937	1,997	115	108	107
IT	1,256	1,553	1,580	118	100	101
CY	11	17	18	90	95	91
LV[1]	9	18	20	38	55	58
LT	14	28	31	42	57	62
LU	23	40	43	234	271	274
HU	59	97	101	58	65	66
MT	4	6	6	79	83	84
NL	448	589	602	134	133	131
AT	214	286	301	126	126	129
PL	212	355	370	48	63	65
PT	134	173	171	80	80	77
RO	45	124	136	28	47	49
SI[2]	23	35	36	80	85	84
SK	24	66	69	52	73	73
FI	139	179	189	115	114	115
SE	254	349	387	122	124	126
UK	1,640	1,710	1,747	119	112	109
IS	9	91	01	32	111	110
NO	191	315	349	161	181	189
CH	293	416	479	143	153	157
HR	26	45	45	51	59	61
MK	4	7	7	25	36	36
TR	218	550	554	37	49	53
JP	4,652	4,145	4,220	115	106	105
US	11,485	10,937	10,830	156	147	148

[1]2010 and 2011, break in series.
[2]GDP per capita, 2010, break in series.

Source: Key figures on Europe – 2013 digest of the online Eurostat yearbook. Available from **ec.europa.eu/eurostat**

Rolex and Dior – aggressively target the affluent. Others – such as Aldi and Lidl – target those of more modest means. Still other companies tailor their marketing offers across a range of markets, from the affluent to the less affluent.

Figure 3.3 shows what proportion of the population in each EU state is in trouble economically. The threshold is 60 per cent of the national median equivalised disposable income. More simply, if your personal income is 60 per cent or less than the national average you are considered at risk of poverty. Clearly this would mean that someone with a given income could be considered poor in Germany but rich in Romania. Almost half the population of Bulgaria is in a bad way, but just one in six in Iceland.

Changing consumer spending patterns

Consumers at different income levels have different spending patterns. Some of these differences were noted over a century ago by Ernst Engel, who studied how people shifted their spending as their income rose. He found that as family income rises, the percentage spent on food declines, the percentage spent on housing remains about constant (except for such

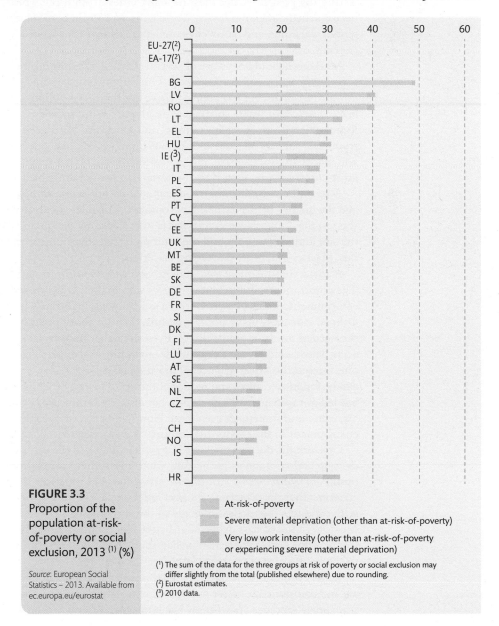

FIGURE 3.3
Proportion of the population at-risk-of-poverty or social exclusion, 2013 [1] (%)

Source: European Social Statistics – 2013. Available from ec.europa.eu/eurostat

At-risk-of-poverty

Severe material deprivation (other than at-risk-of-poverty)

Very low work intensity (other than at-risk-of-poverty or experiencing severe material deprivation)

[1] The sum of the data for the three groups at risk of poverty or social exclusion may differ slightly from the total (published elsewhere) due to rounding.
[2] Eurostat estimates.
[3] 2010 data.

utilities as gas, electricity and public services, which decrease), and both the percentage spent on most other categories and that devoted to savings increase. **Engel's laws** generally have been supported by later studies. However, since incomes are rising faster in poorer countries, such as Lithuania and Poland, the proportion of income spent on essentials is declining much faster there than elsewhere in Europe.

Changes in major economic variables such as income, cost of living, interest rates, and savings and borrowing patterns have a large impact on the marketplace. Companies watch these variables by using economic forecasting. Businesses do not have to be wiped out by an economic downturn or caught short in a boom. With adequate warning, they can take advantage of changes in the economic environment.

Natural environment

The **natural environment** involves the natural resources that are needed as inputs by marketers or that are affected by marketing activities. Environmental concerns have grown steadily during the past three decades. In many cities around the world, air and water pollution have reached dangerous levels. World concern continues to mount about the possibilities of global warming, and many environmentalists fear that soon we will be buried in our own rubbish.

Marketers should be aware of several trends in the natural environment. The first involves growing *shortages of raw materials*. Once upon a time air and water may have seemed to be infinite resources, but few people believe this today. Air pollution chokes many of the world's large cities, and water shortages are already a big problem in some parts of the world. Renewable resources, such as forests and food, also have to be used wisely. Non-renewable resources, such as oil, coal and various minerals, are likely to become more difficult to find and increasingly expensive. Firms making products that require these scarce resources face large cost increases, even if the materials do remain available.

A second environmental trend is *increased pollution*. Industry will almost always damage the quality of the natural environment. Consider the disposal of chemical and nuclear wastes, the dangerous mercury levels in the oceans, the quantity of chemical pollutants in the soil and food supply, and the littering of the environment with non-biodegradable bottles, plastics and other packaging materials.

A third trend is *increased government intervention* in natural resource management. The governments of different countries vary in their concern and efforts to promote a clean environment. Some, like the German government, vigorously pursue environmental quality. Others, especially many poorer nations, do little about pollution, largely because they lack the needed funds or political will. Even the richer nations lack the vast funds and political accord needed to mount a worldwide environmental effort. The general hope is that companies around the world will accept more social responsibility, and that less expensive devices can be found to control and reduce pollution. The rise of China as an industrial superpower has led to rapid increases in wealth, but also a vast increase in the pollution levels present in air, water and sometimes even food. How China responds to this damage to its local natural environment in the twenty-first century is a key issue for all of humanity.

Concern for the natural environment has spawned the so-called green movement. Today, enlightened companies go beyond what government regulations dictate. They are developing *environmentally sustainable* strategies and practices in an effort to create a world economy that the planet can support indefinitely. They are responding to consumer demands with products that do less damage to the environment. For example, the Volkswagen 'Blue Motion' range of cars delivers far better fuel economy and causes less damage to the environment for each kilometre travelled than previous generations of vehicles. We will return to the theme of sustainability later (see Chapter 16).

Other companies are developing recyclable or biodegradable packaging, recycled materials and components, better pollution controls and more energy-efficient operations. Public transport operator Stagecoach has announced plans to run the first carbon-neutral bus network in the UK, by offsetting the emissions from its fleet of buses with a huge tree-planting scheme. McDonald's has a long-standing rainforest policy and a commitment to purchasing recycled products and to energy-efficient restaurant construction techniques. Panasonic Europe is investing in technology to reduce the environmental impact of its factories, by using filtration systems for waste water that go far beyond regulatory requirements, by exercising strict control over exhaust emissions, and by keeping energy consumption to a minimum.

These companies are looking to do more than just good deeds. More and more, companies are recognising the link between a healthy ecology and a healthy economy. They are learning that environmentally responsible actions can also be good business.[21] Some, though, are cynical about what they label as *greenwashing* – adding a thin veneer of environmental action or protection to a product that remains inherently damaging to nature.

Technological environment

The **technological environment** is perhaps the most dramatic force now shaping our destiny. Technology has released such wonders as antibiotics, organ transplants, mobile phones, laptop computers and the Internet. It also has released such horrors as nuclear missiles, chemical weapons and assault rifles. It has created such mixed blessings as the car, TV and credit cards.

Our attitude towards technology depends on whether we are more impressed with its wonders or its blunders. For example, what would you think about having a tiny little transmitter implanted in all of the products you buy that would allow tracking products from their point of production through use and disposal? On the one hand, it would provide many advantages to both buyers and sellers. On the other hand, it could be a bit scary. Either way, it is already happening:

Envision a world in which every product contains a tiny transmitter, loaded with information. As you stroll through the supermarket aisles, shelf sensors detect your selections and beam ads to your shopping cart screen, offering special deals on related products. As your cart fills, scanners detect that you might be buying for a dinner party; the screen suggests a wine to go with the meal you've planned. When you leave the store, exit scanners total up your purchases and automatically charge them to your credit card. At home, readers track what goes into and out of your pantry, updating your shopping list when stocks run low. For Sunday dinner, you pop a Butterball turkey into your 'smart oven', which follows instructions from an embedded chip and cooks the bird to perfection.

Seem far-fetched? Not really. In fact, it might soon become a reality, thanks to tiny radio-frequency identification (RFID) transmitters – or 'smart chips' – that can be embedded in the products you buy. Beyond benefits to consumers, the RFID chips also give producers and retailers an amazing new way to track their products electronically – anywhere in the world, any time, automatically – from factories, to warehouses, to retail shelves, to recycling centres.[22]

The technological environment changes rapidly. Think of all of today's common products that were not available 100 years

Responding to consumer demands for more environmentally responsible products, Volkswagen has created the Blue motion range of cars

Source: Volkswagen Group.

ago, or even 30 years ago. Anyone who died 150 years ago did not know about cars, aeroplanes, radios or the electric light. Someone who died only 80 years ago did not know about TV, aerosol cans, automatic dishwashers, air-conditioners, antibiotics or computers. Anyone who died during the Second World War did not know about photocopying, synthetic detergents, tape recorders, birth control pills or communications satellites. Even people who died as recently as the 1960s did not know about PCs, mobile phones, MP3 players or the Internet.

New technologies create new markets and opportunities. However, every new technology replaces an older technology. Transistors damaged the vacuum tube (valve) industry, photocopying damaged the carbon-paper business, the car damaged the railway business, CDs damaged the record industry, and in turn music and video downloads have killed the CD and DVD businesses. When old industries fought or ignored new technologies, their businesses declined. Thus, marketers should watch the technological environment closely. Companies that do not keep up will soon find their products outdated. And they will miss new product and market opportunities. In addition, as Marketing at Work 3.2 shows, companies need to keep up to date with the new ways in which technology allows consumers to make their opinions about products and services quickly, and widely, known.

The two-edged sword of social media

MARKETING AT WORK 3.2

You almost certainly have a Facebook page. You are quite likely to have a Twitter account and an associated self-curated feed. How about a Pinterest board or two and some uploaded videos at YouTube?

As you've explored these online environments and become expert in their use and abuse you'll have noticed that many organisations have a presence there. The way these organisations use their social media profiles varies from simple to complex, but also from well to disastrous.

Let's look at a few examples of how companies have got things very wrong, and how the characteristics of social media have meant that their errors, disdain, incompetence and even occasional acts of aggression have been seen and read across the globe by highly tech-literate and engaged publics.

To err is human, but to really foul things up you need a computer.

Paul R. Ehrlich

Take for example the case of Hasan Syed. After his father's luggage went missing on a recently taken flight with British Airways (BA), Hasan became increasingly frustrated with the quality of service he was getting in respect of recovering it. How upset? Well, while it is not certain, he has a good claim on being the first private individual to buy a sponsored Tweet on Twitter. That is, he was willing to pay a fee so that his complaint about BA would not just be seen by people who followed him – less than 1,000 at the time – but would also crop up in the timelines of many thousands of others.

That being the situation, things were already looking pretty bad for BA. It got much worse very quickly, though. First, the novelty of the complaint and its manner of dissemination attracted attention and it went viral. Other professionals in the airline industry took note, and 'helpfully' added their retweets to the pile, further spreading the message.

BA still had not suffered the worst of it, though. Hours later, when the company finally got round to responding, the human behind the commercial account did not realise that it was a sponsored Tweet and replied as if it were an almost private conversation.

The moment of response was the point at which this building PR disaster could have been brought round to a success. Unfortunately for BA, their response was a generic request to send a direct message to begin to progress the matter during UK business hours. This failure was seen by tens if not hundreds of thousands worldwide. Hasan responded negatively, and he had a very fair point – if your company is operating globally across all time zones, and you are flying hundreds of thousands of people per day then you have to be ready to respond quickly, and not just when a work day begins in one country.

The final blow came as the story was passed on via retweets to online news aggregation sites like Mashable and Fark, until mainstream media got hold of it and it became headline news in dozens of newspapers around the world.

Hasan even came up with a name for his actions. He called it *complaintvertising*. Naturally, it now has its own hashtag. Hasan is not revealing how much this exercise cost him, but some have estimated it at about $1,000. It seems he got good value.

He also got his dad's luggage back.

British Airways is not the only airline to suffer a social media disaster. Qantas is a specialist in this area. Its bright ideas have included offering prizes for pictures of passengers in blackface, asking for feedback from passengers on what they thought about the company at a time when half the fleet was grounded for emergency mechanical checks and later asking passengers to describe what they would define as a luxury Qantas experience. Customers were very willing to share their ideas using the hashtag #QantasLuxury:

#QantasLuxury is a massive executive bonus while your workers starve and your former customers choke

A 'Full service' airline that gives apples or cookies for flights between 11am and 3pm#NoLunchForYou

A plane that doesn't have an exploding engine!#QantasLuxury

#QantasLuxury Planes that arrive intact and on time because they're staffed and maintained by properly paid, Australia-based personnel.

#QantasLuxury? 1. Plane takes off/arrives on time; 2. Baggage delivered promptly. This used to be called#QantasService

The clear lesson here is, if you have thousands of passengers tired, bored and frustrated at airports, be very, very careful what you ask them.

Both Qantas and BA operated on social media in an impersonal way. Michael O'Leary brought his inimitable personal touch to a Twitter Q&A on behalf of Ryanair when his first response to a journalistic query during a Twitter Q&A session was to make an inappropriate comment about the personal appearance of the journalist.

It is not just airlines that have had troubles, though. When horsemeat contamination in ready-meals was a big issue, it probably was not wise for Tesco to publish a series of horse-related jokes on its Facebook page. British Gas invited the world to pose questions via Twitter to the company just hours after announcing an 11 per cent price rise. One response: '24,000 pensioners died from cold last year, @BritishGas. Are you trying to round it up? #AskBG'.

Benadryl went for a sophisticated method. The company released a tool to allow users of its cough and allergy remedies to draw custom maps of pollen and pollution. Shockingly, many of the submitted returns contained jokes or foul language – or crude representations of genitalia. All of these were automatically published by Benadryl for its global audience to view. Nokia New Zealand went the other route, going for a simple, direct message easily comprehendible across cultures and nations and broadcasting it to the whole world, again via Twitter – 'Fuck you'.

Apple is normally a company that connects with customers well. You may recall the launch of the iPhone 6 and how Apple presumed to download a copy of a new U2 album to millions of iTunes users who did not want it? How many people did not want it, and in fact resented

TABLE 3.2 Facebook is naturally a very popular method for companies to engage with customers through social media. This table shows the most popular brands in five European countries.

	France	Germany	Italy	Poland	UK
1	Air France	Amazon.de	Nutella	Play	Wall's
2	Kiabi	Zalando	Amazon.it	Orange	Amazon.co.uk
3	Oasis Be Fruit	stylefruits	Samsung Italia	Plus	Topshop
4	Nutella	McDonald's	Calzedonia	Tymbark	New Look
5	Coca-Cola	Nutella	Kinder Cioccolato	McDonald's	Zoma
6	M&M's France	Samsung Mobile Deutschland	Coca-Cola	Allegro	Cadbury Creme Egg
7	Samsung France	kinder Riegel	KIKO Cosmetics Italia	Cropp	Coca-Cola
8	Dragibus	DefShop	Microsoft Lumia Italia	Samsung Polska	Bentley Motors
9	Samsung Mobile France	Lidl	Samsung Mobile Italia	Reserved	boohoo.com
10	Amazon.fr	Lufthansa	Valentino	House	River Island

Source: http://www.socialbakers.com/facebook-statistics/

music they had not chosen being added to their libraries? For the best part of a day, the article 'Apple releases U2 album removal tool' was the global top story on the BBC News website. It got worse. The comedienne Joan Rivers made her appreciation of the new handset known on Facebook and Instagram. The problem? She had died the week before but the sponsored messages were already set up to go.

Why are so many companies getting themselves into so much trouble? As is usually the case, it is for a mix of reasons. Senior management may not understand what and how social media works technically, or may treat it as an add-on to other operations. Possibly the management may just not support it with sufficient staffing and/or training. Often there is an element of bandwagonism, as companies feel a need to join other organisations in an arena where they are without experience and skill. As we have seen, the automation and speed of social media can catch companies out very easily. Problems and niggles can be blown out of proportion as global distribution and sharing occur instantly and adverts are placed in inappropriate contexts without human input or oversight.

So if crises are common, quick and uncontrollable, why are so many companies trying to incorporate social media into their marketing? Again, the reasons are many, and each of the over-numerous 'social media gurus' has their own list and ranking. Here are some commonly accepted advantages:

- **Branding** – social media place your brand imagery in places where current and potential customers give their attention, thus developing and supporting brand awareness and recognition.

- **Cost** – measured on a cost per conversion, or cost per eyeball basis, social media marketing does very well at getting and keeping attention when compared with other forms of promotion and does so relatively cheaply. If combined successfully with other forms of promotion these effects can be exponentially magnified.

- **E-commerce** – social media provide a gateway and connection between customers and your standard online retail presence, bringing them to where they can shop quickly and conveniently – often on the spur of the moment.

- **Customer relationships** – social media allow companies to listen as well as talk. The thoughts and opinions and concerns of customers are detectable and receivable. If used properly, social media can help humanise even the largest and most intimidating corporation.

- **The competition** – is most likely already engaging with customers in these spaces, and if your organisation does not follow suit, then it could be missing out on key dialogues, opportunities and sales.

Finally, have the travails of these companies amused you? A thought to ponder: if you were asked to look after the Twitter feed or Facebook page of a company as a tech-savvy young person recently appointed, would you feel confident that you could survive without being caught between (old-school idiom here) the Scylla of an enraged customer base and the Charybdis of an angry line manager whose professional life you have just ruined with a spelling mistake, a throwaway comment, an omission or simply by forgetting to log out of the corporate account and back into your personal one? Sleep well. You could wake up to a nightmare!

Sources: Social media disasters compiled from econsultancy.com/blog/63901-the-top-16-social-media-fails-of-2013 and www.marketingmagazine.co.uk/article/1217267/best-worst-ryanair-ceo-michael-olearys-grillmol-twitter-q-a Read about unwanted rock music and messages from beyond the grave at www.theguardian.com/technology/2014/sep/19/joan-rivers-apple-iphone-6-instagram and www.bbc.co.uk/news/technology-29208540, while one list of the advantages of social media for companies can be found at www.forbes.com/sites/jaysondemers/2014/08/11/the-top-10-benefits-of-social-media-marketing/

One of the keys to developing and exploiting new technologies is spending on R&D. Total R&D spending across the EU accounted for just over 2 per cent of collective GDP in 2012, but as you might expect there were wide differences between member nations. Cyprus and Malta, with relatively simple economies heavily reliant on agriculture and tourism, spent less than half that rate, while Germany, with a far larger and complex economy in which manufacturing plays a significant part, spent almost 50 per cent more, at 2.92 per cent of GDP. To put those figures into context, China spent 1.84 per cent, the USA 2.67 per cent and the EU has a target figure of 3 per cent.[23]

Scientists today are researching a wide range of promising new products and services, ranging from practical solar energy, improved electric cars, paint-on computer and entertainment video displays, and powerful computers that you can wear or fold into your pocket, to go-anywhere concentrators that produce drinkable water from the air. Almost every day you can read articles on the next ground-breaking technology that will be incorporated into mass-manufactured products in the years to come.

Today's research is carried out usually by research teams rather than by lone inventors such as Louis Pasteur, George Stephenson or Karl Benz. Many companies are adding marketing people to R&D teams to try to obtain a stronger marketing orientation. Scientists also speculate on fantasy products, such as flying cars, 3D TVs and space colonies. The challenge in each case is not only technical but also commercial – to make *practical, affordable* versions of these products.

As products and technology become more complex, the public needs to know that these are safe. Thus, government agencies investigate and ban potentially unsafe products. In the EU, the European Food Safety Authority (EFSA) works with the European Commission, the European Parliament and the authorities in individual countries to assess and eliminate food safety risks. The European Commissioner for Consumer Affairs is in charge of promoting consumer interests, health and safety throughout the EU. This involves working with national consumer protection organisations and recommending regulations to protect consumer interests. Such regulations can result in much higher research costs and in longer times between new-product ideas and their introduction. Marketers should be aware of these regulations when applying new technologies and developing new products.

Political environment

Marketing decisions are strongly affected by developments in the political environment. The **political environment** consists of laws, government agencies and pressure groups that influence or limit various organisations and individuals in a given society.

The European Union

How the EU was created

By 2013 the EU had expanded to include 28 countries after Croatia cleared the final hurdle. The combined population of the EU was 503 million people in 2014. The largest member states in terms of population are Germany (80 million), France (65 million), the UK (64 million), Italy (60 million), Spain (47 million) and Poland (39 million). All together, the EU represents the third-largest population block in the world after China and India. If the six countries currently candidates for EU membership – Albania, the Former Yugoslav Republic of Macedonia, Turkey, Iceland, Serbia and Montenegro – were to join, then the combined population would be close to 600 million. How did such a large and economically powerful international union come about?

The origins of the EU can be traced back at least as far as the 1950s. Initially there were six members of the European Coal and Steel Community (ECSC), which was established by

Technological environment: technology is perhaps the most dramatic force shaping the marketing environment. Here, a herder makes a call on his mobile phone

Source: Getty Images/Joseph Van Os.

Belgium, France, Germany, Italy, Luxembourg and the Netherlands in 1952. Politically, the principal motivation behind greater European cooperation could be found in the aftermath of the Second World War (1939–45), during which the major countries of Europe fought each other to a standstill and largely destroyed Europe's industrial capacity. In particular, the cooperation between those great European powers, and rivals, France and Germany was symbolic of the desire to avoid further major conflicts. (Remember that, at the time, the latter was 'West Germany', since Germany had been partitioned into East, the German Democratic Republic, and West, the Federal Republic of Germany, after the war. German reunification was not to occur until 1990.)

The most prominent forerunner of the EU was the European Economic Community (EEC), established by the six members of the ECSC in 1957 by the Treaty of Rome. During the next 30 years the EEC expanded periodically: Denmark, Ireland and the UK joined in 1973, Greece in 1981, Spain and Portugal in 1986. Then, in 1987, the Single European Act was passed which was designed to make real progress towards the goal of having a 'single European market'. By the beginning of 1993 the economic reforms to implement the Single European Act had been completed, establishing the free movement of goods, services, people and money within the EEC. In principle, nationals of the EEC states could work wherever they wished within the Community, and businesses could buy and sell as easily across national borders within the EEC as they could within their own countries. Around the same time, in 1992, the Treaty of Maastricht was signed, which was to lead to the creation of the single European currency (the euro) and to closer cooperation between member states on foreign and domestic policy. It was with the Maastricht Treaty that the name 'European Economic Community' was dropped in favour of the new term 'European Union' (EU).

Further major expansion of the EU followed, with three new member states joining in 1995, ten in 2004, a further two joining in 2007 and Croatia in 2013 to make up 28 in all. Here they are, with the year in which they joined the EU, or its predecessors (the ECSC or the EEC):

1952	Belgium, France, Germany, Italy, Luxembourg, the Netherlands
1973	Denmark, Ireland, the UK
1981	Greece
1986	Spain, Portugal
1995	Austria, Finland, Sweden
2004	Czech Republic, Estonia, Latvia, Lithuania, Hungary, Poland, Slovenia, Slovakia, Cyprus, Malta
2007	Bulgaria, Romania
2013	Croatia

The objectives of the EU

Initially, the main driving force behind European cooperation was the desire to avoid further major conflicts between the member states, and to promote peace more widely within Europe. However, the two principal factors promoting closer European cooperation for the last three or four decades have been politics and economics. Politically, there have always been some within Europe who wish to promote the concept of a 'United States of Europe': that is, ever-closer political union leading eventually to the creation of a European superstate. Economically, the main argument for closer European cooperation is that, through the creation of a huge single market for goods, services, labour and capital in Europe, all of the member states will reap substantial economic benefits. For example, by eliminating the barriers to the free movement of labour, skilled workers can travel across Europe to wherever they are most needed, and employers in search of skilled labour need not restrict themselves to the local economy but can search among all of the member states. Both the political and economic goals of the EU are reflected in the formal objectives, to be found in the key treaties that are the foundation of the Union.

The following are the formal, stated objectives of the EU:

To promote economic progress and social progress and a high level of employment and to achieve balanced and sustainable development, in particular through the creation of an area without internal frontiers, through the strengthening of economic and social cohesion and through the establishment of economic and monetary union, ultimately including a single currency . . .

To assert its identity on the international scene, in particular through the implementation of a common foreign and security policy including the progressive framing of a common defence policy, which might lead to a common defence . . .

To strengthen the protection of the rights and interests of the nationals of Member States through the introduction of a citizenship of the Union . . .

To maintain and develop the Union as an area of freedom, security and justice, in which the free movement of persons is assured in conjunction with appropriate measures with respect to external border controls, asylum, immigration and the prevention and combating of crime . . .

To maintain in full the *acquis communautaire* and build on it with a view to considering to what extent the policies and forms of cooperation introduced by this Treaty may need to be revised with the aim of ensuring the effectiveness of the mechanisms and the institutions of the Community.[24]

The *acquis communautaire* refers to the accumulated body of European laws developed by the EU so far; this covers a wide range of subjects, including the free movement of people, goods, services and money within the EU, laws on free competition, intellectual property, public procurement and many other topics.

Legislation regulating business

Even the most liberal advocates of free-market economies agree that the system works best with at least some regulation. Well-conceived regulation can encourage competition and ensure fair markets for goods and services. Thus, governments develop *public policy* to guide commerce – sets of laws and regulations that limit business for the good of society as a whole. Almost every marketing activity is subject to a wide range of laws and regulations.

Increasing legislation

Legislation affecting business around the world has increased steadily over the years. Europe has many laws covering issues such as competition, fair trade practices, environmental protection, product safety, truth in advertising, consumer privacy, packaging and labelling, pricing and other important areas. The Commission has been active in establishing a new framework of laws covering competitive behaviour, product standards, product liability, and commercial transactions for the nations of the EU.

Of course, marketers must become familiar with the relevant legislation in whichever markets they operate around the world. For example, Norway bans several forms of sales promotion – trading stamps, contests, premiums – as being inappropriate or unfair ways of promoting products. Thailand requires food processors selling national brands to market low-price brands also, so that low-income consumers can find economy brands on the shelves. In India, food companies must obtain special approval to launch brands that duplicate those already existing on the market, such as additional cola drinks or new brands of rice.

Understanding the public policy implications of a particular marketing activity is not a simple matter. For example, in Europe, there are laws created at the EU and at the national levels, and these regulations often overlap – one of the goals of the EU is progressively to harmonise national laws so that the same legal system applies throughout the Union, but it will be quite a while before that goal is achieved. For example, food products sold in Athens are governed both by relevant EU and Greek national laws. Moreover, regulations are constantly changing – what was allowed last year may now be prohibited, and what was prohibited may now be allowed. Marketers must work hard to keep up with changes in regulations and their interpretations.

Business legislation has been enacted for a number of reasons. The first is to *protect companies* from each other. Although business executives may praise competition, they sometimes try to neutralise it when it threatens them. So laws are passed to define and prevent unfair competition. In Europe, such laws are enforced by the Directorate General for Competition and by national competition authorities such as the Office of Fair Trading in the UK, the Competition Authority in Ireland, the Konkurrensverket in Sweden and the Conseil de la Concurrence in France.

The second purpose of government regulation is to *protect consumers* from unfair business practices. Some firms, if left alone, would make shoddy products, tell lies in their advertising and deceive consumers through their packaging and pricing. Unfair business practices have been defined and sanctions are enforced by various agencies.

The third purpose of government regulation is to *protect the interests of society* against unrestrained business behaviour. Profitable business activity does not always create a better quality of life. Regulation arises to ensure that firms take responsibility for the social costs of their production or products.

Changing government agency enforcement

International marketers will encounter dozens, or even hundreds, of agencies set up to enforce trade policies and regulations. We have mentioned several of those that will be found in Europe in the preceding paragraphs, while in the USA, for example, businesses have to consider the Federal Trade Commission, the Food and Drug Administration and the Federal Communications Commission, among others. Because such government agencies have some discretion in enforcing the laws, they can have a major impact on a company's marketing performance. Few of these agencies employ marketing professionals, however, so that it can be difficult to get them to understand the impact that their actions can have on company marketing strategies.

New laws and their enforcement will continue to increase. Business executives must watch these developments when planning their products and marketing programmes. Marketers need to know about the major laws protecting competition, consumers and society. They need to understand these laws at the local, state, national and international levels.

Increased emphasis on ethics and socially responsible actions

Written regulations cannot possibly cover all potential marketing abuses, and existing laws are often difficult to enforce. However, beyond written laws and regulations, business is also governed by social codes and rules of professional ethics.

Socially responsible behaviour

Enlightened companies encourage their managers to look beyond what the regulatory system allows and simply 'do the right thing'. These socially responsible firms actively seek out ways to protect the long-term interests of their consumers and the environment.

The recent rash of business scandals and increased concerns about the environment have created fresh interest in the issues of ethics and social responsibility. Almost every aspect of marketing involves such issues. Unfortunately, because these issues usually involve conflicting interests, well-meaning people can honestly disagree about the right course of action in a given situation. Thus, many industrial and professional trade associations have suggested codes of ethics. And more companies are now developing policies, guidelines and other responses to complex social responsibility issues.

The boom in e-commerce and Internet marketing has created a new set of social and ethical issues. Online privacy issues are the primary concern. For example, website visitors and users of social networking sites such as Facebook, Pinterest, Twitter and Instagram continually reveal extensive amounts of personal information that may leave them open to abuse by unscrupulous marketers. Much of the information is systematically developed by businesses seeking to learn more about their customers, often without consumers realising that they are under the microscope and handing over digital data through every mouse click, like, share and upvote. Critics are concerned that companies may now know *too* much, and that some companies might use digital data to take unfair advantage of consumers. Although many companies fully disclose their Internet privacy policies, and some work to use data to benefit their customers, abuses do occur. As a result, consumer advocates and policy makers are taking action to protect consumer privacy. If forced to pick the one issue that will dominate marketing-related legislation, policy and standards of practice in the next decade, many would choose online data collection and consumer privacy.

Throughout the text, we present examples that summarise the main public policy and social responsibility issues surrounding major marketing decisions. These exhibits discuss the legal issues that marketers should understand and the common ethical and societal concerns that marketers face. Later, we discuss a broad range of societal marketing issues in greater depth (see Chapter 16).

Cause-related marketing

To exercise their social responsibility and build more positive images, many companies are now linking themselves to worthwhile causes. These days, every product seems to be tied to some cause. Buy women's underwear or swimwear from a Debenhams store and support breast cancer research. Shop at Tesco and collect free vouchers that your local school can use to buy computer equipment. Pay for these purchases with the right credit or debit card and you can support a local cultural arts group or help fight heart disease.

Cause-related marketing has become a primary form of corporate giving. It lets companies 'do well by doing good', by linking purchases of the company's products or services with fundraising for worthwhile causes or charitable organisations. Companies now sponsor dozens of cause-related marketing campaigns each year. Many are backed by large budgets and a full complement of marketing activities. Consider this example:

> The Pantene Beautiful Lengths campaign has involved a broad-based marketing effort, including a campaign website, public service TV and prints ads, and promotional items and events. P&G kicked off the Pantene Beautiful Lengths with celebrity spokeswoman Diane Lane having her hair cut for donation on the Today Show. Since then the campaign has generated more than 700 million media impressions in major publications, TV shows, and websites. To date, the campaign has received more than 24,000 donated ponytails and more than 3,000 free wigs have been distributed through the American Cancer Society's nationwide network of wig banks. Compare that to the 2,000 wigs created over the past ten years by charity Locks of Love. Pantene Beautiful Lengths has also contributed more than $1 million to the EIF Women's Cancer Research Fund, which raises funds and awareness for millions of women and their families affected by cancer.[25]

Cause-related marketing has stirred some controversy. Critics worry that cause-related marketing is more a strategy for selling than a strategy for giving – that 'cause-related' marketing is really 'cause-exploitative' marketing. Thus, companies using cause-related marketing might find themselves walking a fine line between increased sales and an improved image, and facing charges of exploitation.

However, if handled well, cause-related marketing can greatly benefit both the company and the cause. The company gains an effective marketing tool while building a more positive public image. The charitable organisation or cause gains greater visibility and important new sources of funding.

Cultural environment

The **cultural environment** is made up of institutions and other forces that affect a society's basic values, perceptions, preferences and behaviours. People grow up in a particular society

The Telegraph described the impact of this hairdo with the following: 'You can forget the matinee idols, sporting stars and rebel rock stars of old, because the new haircut holy grail comes courtesy of a 27-year old former mechanic from Wolverhampton.

Source: Getty Images/David M. Benett / Getty Images for Converse.

that shapes their basic beliefs and values. They absorb a worldview that defines their relationships with others. The following cultural characteristics can affect marketing decision making.

Persistence of cultural values

People in a given society hold many beliefs and values. Their core beliefs and values have a high degree of persistence. For example, most Europeans believe in working, getting married, giving to charity and being honest. These beliefs shape more specific attitudes and behaviours found in everyday life. *Core* beliefs and values are passed on from parents to children and are reinforced by schools, churches, business and government.

Secondary beliefs and values are more open to change. Believing in marriage is a core belief; believing that people should get married early in life is a secondary belief. Marketers have some chance of changing secondary values but little chance of changing core values. For example, family-planning marketers could argue more effectively that people should get married later than that they should not get married at all.

Shifts in secondary cultural values

Although core values are fairly persistent, cultural swings do take place. Consider the impact of popular music groups, film stars and other celebrities on young people's hairstyling and clothing norms. As one example, in early 2014, a young mechanic was talent-spotted by a model agency – the concept of beauty being continually redefined in society – not for his height or facial features per se, but for his hairstyle. The impact his chosen style had on other models and street fashion was such that it led the *Telegraph* to run a story called 'Is this Britain's most influential haircut?'.[26] Marketers want to predict cultural shifts in order to spot new opportunities or threats. Some firms specialise in studying and predicting trends in popular culture. *the futures company* offers future forecasting services (formerly this was known as the Yankelovich Monitor), and has tracked consumer value trends for years. Clients can sign up to the Global MONITOR service from *the futures company* to see analysis and interpretation of the forces that shape consumers' lifestyles and their marketplace interactions.[27] The major cultural values of a society are expressed in people's views of themselves and others, as well as in their views of organisations, society, nature and the Universe.

People's views of themselves

People vary in their emphasis on serving themselves versus serving others. Some people seek personal pleasure, wanting fun, change and escape. Others seek self-realisation through religion, recreation or the avid pursuit of careers or other life goals. Some people see themselves as sharers and joiners; others see themselves as individualists. People use products, brands and services as a means of self-expression, and they buy products and services that match their views of themselves.

Marketers can target their products and services based on such self-views. For example, TOMS Shoes appeals to people who see themselves as part of the broader world community (see Marketing at Work 3.1).

People's views of others

In past decades, observers have noted several shifts in people's attitudes towards others. Recently, for example, many trend trackers have seen a new wave of 'cocooning' or 'nesting'. Due in part to the recessionary economy, people are going out less with others and are staying home more. One observer calls it 'Cocooning 2.0', in which people are 'newly intent on the simple pleasures of hearth and home'. Says another, 'The instability of the economy . . . creates uncertainty for consumers, and this uncertainty tends to make them focus more on being home and finding ways to save money. It's a return to more traditional values, like home-cooked meals.'[28]

People's views of organisations

People vary in their attitudes towards corporations, government agencies, trade unions, universities and other organisations. By and large, people are willing to work for major organisations and expect them, in turn, to carry out society's work.

The late 1980s saw a sharp decrease in confidence in and loyalty towards business and political organisations and institutions. In the workplace, there has been an overall decline in organisational loyalty. During the 1990s, waves of company downsizings bred cynicism and distrust. And more recently, corporate scandals at Enron, WorldCom, Tyco International and the financial crisis, for which many people reasonably blame the big banks, have resulted in a further loss of confidence in big business. Many people today see work not as a source of satisfaction but as a required chore to earn money to enjoy their non-work hours. This trend suggests that organisations need to find new ways to win consumer and employee confidence.

People's views of society

People vary in their attitudes towards their society; conservatives defend the status quo, liberals want to change it, malcontents want to leave it. People's orientation to their society influences their consumption patterns and attitudes towards the marketplace.

People's views of nature

People vary in their attitudes towards the natural world. Some feel ruled by it, others feel in harmony with it, and still others seek to master it. A long-term trend has been people's growing mastery over nature through technology and the belief that nature is bountiful. More recently, however, people have recognised that nature is finite and fragile, that it can be destroyed or spoiled by human activities.

This renewed love of things natural has created a sizeable 'lifestyles of health and sustainability' (LOHAS) market: consumers who seek out everything from natural, organic and nutritional products to fuel-efficient cars and alternative medicine. Business has responded by offering more products and services catering to such interests. The global market for organic food and drink is estimated to be worth around €45bn; Europe is the largest organic food market in the world, followed by North America in second place. Within Europe, Germany is the largest overall organic consumer followed by the UK, but although the Germans and British are avid consumers of organic produce, the share of the food market taken by organic products is highest in Switzerland and Austria, at 6 per cent, compared with 3 per cent in Germany and 1.6 per cent in the UK. Many European companies have emerged to exploit this large and growing market opportunity – for example, Biopark Markt GmbH in Germany (organic meat suppliers), St Merryn Meat Ltd in the UK (a slaughterhouse that supplies organic meat to supermarkets) and Bodin et Fils SA in France (the largest European supplier of organic poultry).

People's views of the Universe

Finally, people vary in their beliefs about the origin of the Universe and their place in it. It is very difficult to make generalisations about the religious faith of Europeans. Many European countries, such as France, Italy and Ireland, are predominantly Christian, while others, like Albania, are predominantly Muslim. The largest candidate for membership of the EU, Turkey, is overwhelmingly a Muslim country. However, the extent of religious observance and the significance of religion in people's lives varies considerably across the Continent.

Church attendance is much higher in Ireland than elsewhere in Europe, for example. The great majority of Irish people say that they attend a formal religious ceremony regularly, but only a minority of people in the UK say the same thing. In many parts of Europe there is evidence that attendance at religious ceremonies is declining. Nevertheless, religion itself, and cultural practices associated with religion, remain important factors influencing the behaviour of European consumers. For example, there is a tradition in the Roman Catholic Church of not eating meat on Fridays, but eating fish is deemed to be perfectly acceptable. Even though the religious basis for this tradition is not at all clear, the cultural tradition lives on and the Irish Sea Fisheries Board reports that 30 per cent of the wet fish sold in Ireland is sold on a Friday.[29]

MAKING CONNECTIONS Linking the concepts

Slow down and take a break. You've now read about a large number of environmental forces. How are all of these environments *linked* with each other? With company marketing strategy?

● How are major demographic forces linked with economic changes? With major cultural trends? How are the natural and technological environments linked? Think of an example of a company that has recognised one of these links and turned it into a marketing opportunity.

● Is the marketing environment uncontrollable – something that the company can only prepare for and react to? Or can companies be proactive in changing environmental factors? Think of a good example that makes your point, then read on.

RESPONDING TO THE MARKETING ENVIRONMENT

Many companies view the marketing environment as an uncontrollable element to which they must react and adapt. They passively accept the marketing environment and do not try to change it. They analyse the environmental forces and design strategies that will help the company avoid the threats and take advantage of the opportunities the environment provides.

Other companies take a *proactive* stance towards the marketing environment. Rather than simply watching and reacting, these firms take aggressive actions to affect the publics and forces in their marketing environment. Such companies hire lobbyists – people whose profession is to persuade politicians of a point of view – to influence legislation affecting their industries and stage media events to gain favourable press coverage. They run advertorials (advertisements expressing editorial points of view) to shape public opinion. They pursue legal actions and make complaints to regulators to keep competitors in line, and they form contractual agreements to control their distribution channels better.

Often, companies can find positive ways to overcome seemingly uncontrollable environmental constraint. However, marketing management cannot always control environmental forces. In many cases, it must settle for simply watching and reacting to the environment. For example, a company would have little success trying to influence geographic population shifts, the economic environment or major cultural values. But whenever possible, smart marketing managers will take a *proactive* rather than *reactive* approach to the marketing environment.

THE JOURNEY YOU'VE TAKEN Reviewing the concepts

In this chapter and the next two chapters, you'll examine the environments of marketing and how companies analyse these environments to understand the marketplace and consumers better. Companies must constantly watch and manage the marketing environment in order to seek opportunities and ward off threats. The marketing environment comprises all the actors and forces influencing the company's ability to transact business effectively with its target market.

1 Describe the environmental forces that affect the company's ability to serve its customers

The company's microenvironment consists of other actors close to the company that combine to form the company's value-delivery network or that affect its ability to serve its customers. It includes the company's internal environment – its several departments and management levels – as it influences marketing decision making. Marketing-channel firms – suppliers and marketing intermediaries, including resellers, physical distribution firms, marketing services agencies and financial intermediaries – cooperate to create customer value. Five types of customer markets include consumer, business, reseller, government and international markets. Competitors vie with the company in an effort to serve customers better. Finally, various publics have an actual or potential interest in or impact on the company's ability to meet its objectives.

The macroenvironment consists of larger societal forces that affect the entire microenvironment. The six forces making up the company's macroenvironment include demographic, economic, natural, technological, political and cultural forces. These forces shape opportunities and pose threats to the company.

2 Explain how changes in the demographic and economic environments affect marketing decisions

Demography is the study of the characteristics of human populations. Today's *demographic environment* shows a changing age structure, shifting family profiles, geographic population shifts, a better-educated and more white-collar population, and increasing diversity. The *economic environment* consists of factors that affect buying power and patterns. The economic environment is characterised by more consumer concern for value and shifting consumer spending patterns. Today's squeezed

consumers are seeking greater value – just the right combination of good quality and service at a fair price. The distribution of income also is shifting. The rich have grown richer, the middle class has shrunk and the poor have remained poor, leading to a two-tiered market. Many companies now tailor their marketing offers to two different markets – the affluent and the less affluent.

3 Identify the major trends in the firm's natural and technological environments

The *natural environment* shows three major trends: shortages of certain raw materials, higher pollution levels and more government intervention in natural resource management. Environmental concerns create marketing opportunities for alert companies. The marketer should watch for four major trends in the *technological environment*: the rapid pace of technological change, high R&D budgets, the concentration by companies on minor product improvements, and increased government regulation. Companies that fail to keep up with technological change will miss out on new product and marketing opportunities.

4 Explain the key changes in the political and cultural environments

The *political environment* consists of laws, agencies and groups that influence or limit marketing actions. The political environment has undergone three changes that affect marketing worldwide: increasing legislation regulating business, strong government agency enforcement, and greater emphasis on ethics and socially responsible actions. The *cultural environment* is made up of institutions and forces that affect a society's values, perceptions, preferences and behaviours. The environment shows long-term trends towards a 'we society', a lessening trust of institutions, greater appreciation for nature, and the search for more meaningful and enduring values.

5 Discuss how companies can react to the marketing environment

Companies can passively accept the marketing environment as an uncontrollable element to which they must adapt, avoiding threats and taking advantage of opportunities as they arise. Or they can take a *proactive* stance, working to change the environment rather than simply reacting to it. Whenever possible, companies should try to be proactive rather than reactive.

NAVIGATING THE KEY TERMS

NOTES AND REFERENCES

1 Information from Robert J. Benes, Abbie Jarman and Ashley Williams, '2007 NRA Sets Records', accessed at **www.chefmagazine.com/nra.htm**, September 2007; also **www.thecoca-colacompany.com/presscenter/presskit_fs.html** and **www.cokesolutions.com**, accessed November 2009.

2 World POPClock, US Census Bureau, accessed online at **www.census.gov**, August 2014. This website provides continuously updated projections of the US and world populations.

3 Adapted from information in Janet Adamy, 'Different Brew: Eyeing a Billion Tea Drinkers, Starbucks Pours It On in China', *Wall Street Journal,* 29 November 2006, p. A1. Also see 'Where the Money Is', *Financial Times,* 12 May 2007, p. 8; and Melissa Allison, 'Starbucks Thrives in China', *McClatchy-Tribune Business News,* 14 January 2009.

4 See 'China's Dependency-Ratio Turning Point' at the Huffington Post, 12 September 2014, and 'Asian Demography: The Flight from Marriage', *The Economist,* 20 August 2011, p. 19.

5 See **europa.eu/about-eu/facts-figures/living/index_en.htm**, accessed 15 August 2014.

6 Anushka Asthana and Vanessa Thorpe, 'Whatever happened to the original Generation X?', *Observer,* 23 January 2005, available from **http://www.guardian.co.uk/uk/2005/jan/23/britishidentity.anushkaasthana**

7 'Mixed Success: One Who Targeted Gen X and Succeeded – Sort Of', *Journal of Financial Planning,* February 2004, p. 15. Also see Neil Leslie, 'Farther Along on the X Axis', *American Demographics,* May 2004, pp. 21–4.

8 See 'Overlooked and Under X-Ploited', *American Demographics,* May 2004, p. 48; and Howard Schneider, 'Grunge Marketing', *Mortgage Banking,* November 2004, p. 106.

9 Jessica Tsai, 'Who, What, Where, When, Y', *Customer Relationship Management,* November 2008, pp. 24–8; and John Austin, 'Automakers Try to Reach Gen Y: Carmakers Look for New Marketing Approaches, Technological Advances to Attract Millennials', *McClatchy-Tribune Business News,* 1 February 2009.

10 See for example the *Telegraph* article 'Charting the rise of Generation Yawn: 20 is the new 40' at **www.telegraph.co.uk/women/womens-life/11061434/Charting-the-rise-of-Generation-Yawn-20-is-the-new-40.html**, accessed September 2014.

11 Statistics from the EU report 'European Social Statistics – 2013', available from **epp.eurostat.ec.europa.eu**

12 Statistics from the EU report 'Key Figures on Europe – 2013', available from **epp.eurostat.ec.europa.eu**

13 World Health Organization information obtained from **http://www.who.int/tobacco/global_data/country_profiles/euro/en/**, accessed 17 May 2008.

14 Information obtained from UNESCO at **stats.uis.unesco.org** and 'European Social Statistics – 2013', available from **epp.eurostat.ec.europa.eu**

15 'The Ethnic Population of England and Wales Broken Down by Local Authority', *Guardian*, **http://www.guardian.co.uk/news/datablog/2011/may/18/ethnic-population-england-wales#data**, accessed 29 August 2011.

16 Ellen Florian, 'Queer Eye Makes Over the Economy', *Fortune*, 9 February 2004, p. 38. See also Gillian K. Oakenfull and Timothy B. Greenlee, 'Queer Eye for a Gay Guy: Using Market-Specific Symbols in Advertising to Attract Gay Consumers Without Alienating the Mainstream', *Psychology and Marketing*, May 2005, pp. 421ff.

17 Howard L. Hughes, *Pink Tourism: Holidays of Gay Men and Lesbians* (Wallingford: CABI Publishing, 2006).

18 **http://www.youtube.com/manchestergayvillage**, accessed 29 August 2011.

19 **http://www.melbourne.com.au/gay.htm**, accessed 29 August 2011.

20 Information accessed at **http://www.germany-tourism.co.uk/EGB/attractions_events/gaygermany.htm**, 29 August 2011.

21 Information from 'Stagecoach Group Case Studies: Carbon Neutral Travel', accessed at **http://www.stagecoachgroup.com/scg/csr/casestudies/cntravel**, 29 August 2011; 'Pollution Prevention Pays', accessed at **http://solutions.3m.com/wps/portal/_l/en_US/_s.155/113842/_s.155/115848**, June 2005; 'Sustainability Key to UPS's Environmental Initiatives', accessed at **www.pressroom.ups.com/mediakits/factsheet/0,2305,1140,00.html**, June 2005.

22 See 'Wal-Mart Expands RFID Requirements', *McClatchy-Tribune Business News*, 30 January 2008; David Blanchard, 'Wal-Mart Lays Down the Law on RFID', *Industry Week*, May 2008, p. 72; David Blanchard, 'The Five Stages of RFID', *Industry Week*, January 2009, p. 50; and information accessed online at **www.autoidlabs.org**, April 2009.

23 R&D figures from 'R&D Expenditure', accessed at **http://epp.eurostat.ec.europa.eu/statistics_explained/index.php/R_%26_D_expenditure**

24 'Consolidated Versions of the Treaty on European Union and of the Treaty Establishing the European Community', *Official Journal of the European Communities*, 2002.

25 See Jack Neff, 'Unilever, P&G War Over Which Is Most Ethical', *Advertising Age*, 3 March 2008, p. 1; and information from **www.beautifullengths.com**, accessed August 2009.

26 Read the whole story at **http://www.telegraph.co.uk/men/fashion-and-style/10797932/Is-this-Britains-most-influential-haircut.html**, accessed October 2014.

27 **www.thefuturescompany.com**, accessed 1 September 2011.

28 Karen Von Hahn, '*Plus ça Change*: Get Set for Cocooning 2.0', *Globe and Mail* (Toronto), 3 January 2008, p. L1; and Liza N. Burby, 'Tips for Making Your Home a Cozy Nest, or "Hive"', *Newsday*, 23 January 2009, accessed at **www.newsday.com/services/newspaper/printedition/exploreli/ny-hocov6007466jan23,0,2603167.story**.

29 Information accessed at **http://www.independent.ie/national-news**, June 2008.

CHAPTER 4
MANAGING MARKETING INFORMATION

AFTER READING THIS CHAPTER, YOU SHOULD BE ABLE TO

- explain the importance of information to the company and its understanding of the marketplace
- define the marketing information system and discuss its parts
- outline the steps in the marketing research process
- explain how companies analyse and distribute marketing information
- discuss the special issues some marketing researchers face, including public policy and ethics issues

THE WAY AHEAD
Previewing the concepts

In the previous chapter, you learned about the complex and changing marketing environment. In this chapter, we'll continue our exploration of how marketers go about understanding the world in which they operate, their marketplaces and consumers. We'll look at how companies develop and manage information about important marketplace elements – about customers, competitors, products and marketing programmes. We'll examine marketing information systems designed to give managers the right information, in the right form, at the right time, to help them make better marketing decisions. We'll also take a close look at the marketing research process and at some special marketing research considerations. To succeed in today's marketplace, companies must know how to manage mountains of marketing information effectively.

We'll start the chapter with a story about how market research can help an organisation, an industry and even an entire country improve its marketing and maintain its competitive position.

VISIT SCOTLAND!

Recently, the Scottish Tourism Minister said at an event to mark the beginning of Scottish Tourism Week:

> **Tourism is one of the leading sectors of our economy. With record investment being pumped into the industry and overseas visitors at an all time high we are already outperforming the rest of the UK.**
>
> **We want to motivate everyone in Scotland, because tourism is everyone's business and this week should help us do that.**

The chair of VisitScotland – the public–private partnership with the task of supporting tourism in Scotland – added:

> **Scottish Tourism Week is an excellent opportunity to highlight how one of Scotland's largest and most sustainable industries helps support our economy.**
>
> **It's great to see our industry taking the lead in this way. Hundreds of countries are competing for the same visitors and we need to leave people feeling that there is always more to do in Scotland if we want to succeed in growing tourism revenues by 50 per cent in ten years.**[1]

Source: Alamy Images/Nagelestock.com

As commercial organisations face changing environments, so do nations. Until the 1960s, the Scottish economy was primarily based on manufacturing and engineering. These industries have steadily declined and now account only for a small proportion of national economic output. The Scottish economy has evolved along the lines followed by almost all developed nations – with an increasing proportion of the working population and GNP being involved with services. Figures released for the end of 2013 reveal that 72.3 per cent of Scottish GDP is generated by service industries. The Scottish tourism sector is worth £4.3bn in direct expenditure by overnight visitors.[2]

The Scottish Tourism Forum (the industry body) reports that tourism and heritage provide jobs for 215,000 people (8 per cent of the workforce) working for 20,000 businesses and that visitors to Scotland spent £4.8bn annually.[3] With numbers like these, it is no wonder that the state considers tourism to be a key plank in the future economic development of the nation – many parts of the country depend almost entirely on tourism for jobs and improvements to infrastructure.

Tourism is significant in economic and social terms in many parts of Europe. France, Spain, Italy, the UK, Germany and Austria are all in the world's top 10 in terms of tourist visits,[4] and of course many other European nations like Greece, Portugal, Malta and Cyprus rely very heavily on tourism. Competition is fierce – and the country which best understands these tourist customers and can provide them with the best experiences will maintain or increase their market share. Market research is a key means to this end.

It is because of this that the Scottish government co-sponsors VisitScotland.[5] Among other activities, such as campaigns to promote Scotland as a tourist destination around the world and providing training and services to Scottish tourism-related businesses, VisitScotland has the responsibility for collecting and processing information about tourism in Scotland and disseminating this information to interested parties – hotels, regional government, tourist attractions and so on. Scotland is not alone in this – similar organisations exist in almost every country in the world, including Germany and Greece.[6]

The national tourist board of Turkey reviewed its multi-million-dollar spend on advertising by collecting opinions from prospective tourists and then adjusted the mix of media used to improve effectiveness. This is the essence of market research and market intelligence systems – the need to understand the market requires information to be collected and analysed, and this processed information informs the decision making of managers in their day-to-day activities and also in their long-term strategy. The better the systems VisitScotland has in place to do this, the better these decisions will be, and the better the outlook for the tourism sector in Scotland.

As we will see, there are a great many ways to collect and process market information, but VisitScotland has two general ways in which it can get hold of information. It can buy or borrow information previously collected by another organisation (secondary data) and consider the implications of that information for its markets, or it can collect its own (primary data) according to its specific needs. Regardless, VisitScotland has the responsibility for using this information to create an overall picture of market-related trends and factors.

VisitScotland can obtain already existing market research information from a number of sources. In doing so, it tries to select information that is as accurate, relevant and up to date as possible. Let's have a look at some of the sources of previously collected information that VisitScotland uses.

The International Passenger Survey (IPS) is a survey of passengers entering and leaving the UK.[7] Each year, more than 250,000 people are interviewed – 1 in every 500 international travellers. The interview usually takes 3–5 minutes and contains questions about passengers' country of residence (for overseas residents) or country of visit (for UK residents), the reason for their visit, and details of their expenditure and fares. This survey is carried out by agencies of the UK government – not only to help with matters related to managing tourism specifically, but also for health and welfare services, as well as transport network development.

What can VisitScotland take from this data? The report shows that there has been a significant increase in the number of people coming to the UK for purposes of tourism – good news! Alas, the data also shows that there has been a much greater increase in the number of UK residents travelling abroad for a holiday – perhaps choosing France over a UK destination like Scotland. Some 31 per cent of visitors from Spain held UK passports, meaning they were likely to be UK expatriates living in Spain rather than Spanish tourists. Visits to the UK from the USA

were down, which is troubling given that other data suggests that these are the tourists who spend the most. The number of arrivals to the UK from Eastern Europe has increased remarkably in recent years. Should VisitScotland push for better language skills in this area, or perhaps invest more in promotion in Eastern Europe?

Newspapers and magazines often carry stories on tourism-related issues, and VisitScotland tries to keep up with these: How is Scotland being perceived by these journalists? What are the positives and negatives of their reports?[8] What about social media and search engines? Universities often publish reports or papers on commercial and social trends, and these can be a good source of advice for very specific objectives, such as branding a tourist destination like Scotland.[9]

Business intelligence organisations such as Euromonitor[10] and Mintel[11] collect information and publish reports on specific topics on countries, industries and even some large organisations. These are commercial products, and often carry price-tags in the thousands of euros – but the information will be up to date and relevant. Industry bodies like the world tourism organization also provide information.[12]

VisitScotland often collects its own data. Again, there are many choices and options – from whom and how the data is collected and so on. As examples, VisitScotland talks to hoteliers, restaurateurs and managers of tourist attractions to find out about their recent experiences. Doing so has told them that average occupancy rates at hostels has remained static over the last five years but that hotels and self-catering accommodation have seen increased usage. This has implications for managing the portfolio of accommodation in Scotland – perhaps hostels need to be made more appealing, perhaps there is an opportunity to raise the price of a hotel bedroom?

Most obviously, VisitScotland can talk to tourists past, present and potential. What did they like or dislike about their visit to Scotland? How was their experience and how could it be improved? Would they come back or recommend Scotland as a holiday destination to their friends and family?

As well as collecting and processing data, VisitScotland disseminates it. One recent report had several key findings with significant implications for the future of the tourism sector in Scotland – the information would allow better decisions to be made, which is what market research is all about! The report noted that in key markets like Japan and the USA, ageing populations meant that a tourist from these countries was increasingly likely to be retired and therefore unlikely to be bringing young children (and therefore able to visit outside of school holidays) but more likely to be concerned with steep hills or medical or dietary requirements. Younger tourists were visiting in increasing numbers from China and Russia. Tourists from all countries were increasingly likely to want to travel alone, but not want to be penalised by tour operators or hoteliers for doing so. Tourists still in employment had plenty of money to spend, but were likely to feel greater time pressure, preferring options other than a standard fortnight – how about long weekends or 10 days instead?[13]

A second report identified 10 different, distinct UK tourist segments, as well as profiling visitors from many countries.[14] Visitors from the Netherlands were very price sensitive, came to Scotland for the scenery and the space, and were unlikely to travel with children. Germans were particularly interested in short breaks but much preferred Edinburgh to Glasgow! Visitors from all nations were increasingly interested in active outdoor pursuits such as white-water rafting and mountain biking, rather than the passive enjoyment of scenery – and this has implications for the mix of resources to support these activities.

These efforts to keep abreast of trends in tourism are paying off – Scotland is maintaining market share in a global tourism industry impacted by economic uncertainty, and if the same dedication is shown to the collection, interpretation and dissemination of information in the future, then the objective of a 50 per cent increase in revenue is achievable!

Sources: See notes 1–14 at the end of this chapter. Contains public sector information licensed under the Open Government Licence v1.0.

In order to produce superior customer value and satisfaction, companies need information at almost every turn. As the story about tourism in Scotland shows, good products, services and marketing programmes begin with solid information on consumer needs and wants. Companies also need an abundance of information on competitors, resellers, and other actors and forces in the marketplace.

With the recent explosion of information technologies, even the smallest companies can now generate information in great quantities. In fact, this has become a significant problem – today's managers often receive too much information. One study found that with all the companies offering data, and with all the information now available through supermarket scanners, large retailers typically have the equivalent of 320 miles (512 km) of bookshelves of information on their products. Thus, running out of information is not a problem, but seeing through the 'data smog' is. 'In this oh-so-overwhelming Information age,' comments one observer, 'it's all too easy to be buried, burdened, and burned out by data overload.'[15]

Indeed, marketers frequently complain that they lack enough information of the right kind. They do not need *more* information, they need *better* information – information that is more appropriate and relevant to the issues and problems they face. Additionally, they need to make better *use* of the information they already have. A former CEO at Unilever once said that if Unilever only knew what it knows, it would double its profits. The meaning is clear: many companies compile vast mountains of information, but fail to manage and use it well.[16] Companies must design effective marketing information systems that give managers the right information, in the right form, at the right time, to help them make better marketing decisions.

A **marketing information system (MIS)** consists of people, equipment and procedures to gather, sort, analyse, evaluate and distribute needed, timely and accurate information to marketing decision makers. Figure 4.1 shows that the MIS begins and ends with information users – marketing managers, internal and external partners, and others who need marketing information to help them make decisions. First, it interacts with these information users to *assess information needs*. Next, it *develops needed information* from internal company databases, marketing intelligence activities and marketing research. Then it helps users to analyse information to put it in the right form for making marketing decisions and managing customer relationships. Finally, the MIS *distributes* the marketing information and helps managers *use* it in their decision making.

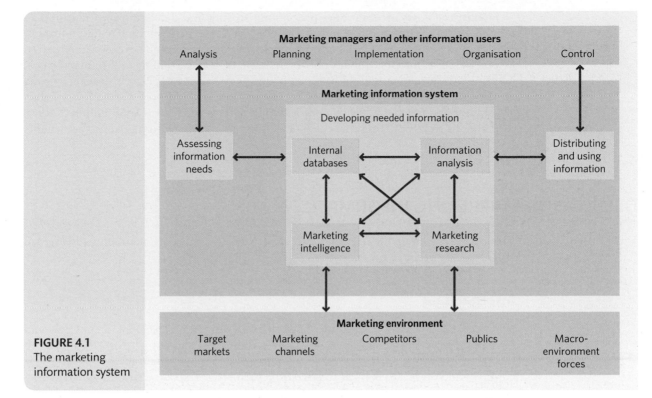

FIGURE 4.1
The marketing
information system

ASSESSING MARKETING INFORMATION NEEDS

The MIS primarily serves the company's marketing and other managers. However, it may also provide information to external partners, such as suppliers, resellers or marketing services agencies. For example, Asda gives key suppliers access to information on customer buying patterns and inventory levels – helping those suppliers to improve their own marketing decisions and in turn help Asda satisfy customer wants and needs better. Dell creates tailored Premium Pages for large customers, giving them access to product design, order status, and product support and service information. In designing an information system, the company must consider the needs of all of these users.

A good MIS balances the information users would *like* to have against what they really *need* and what is *feasible* to offer – the most common constraints being time and money. The company begins by interviewing managers to find out what information they would like. Some managers will ask for whatever information they can get without thinking carefully about what they really need. Too much information can be as harmful as too little. Other managers may omit things they ought to know, or they may not think to ask for some types of information they should have. For example, managers might need to know that a competitor plans to introduce a new product during the coming year. Because they do not know about the new product, they do not think to ask about it. The MIS must monitor the marketing environment in order to provide decision makers with information they should have to make key marketing decisions.

Sometimes the company cannot provide the needed information, either because it is not available or because of MIS limitations. For example, a brand manager might want to know how competitors will change their advertising budgets next year and how these changes will affect industry market shares. The information on planned budgets probably is not publicly available. Even if it is, the company's MIS may not be advanced enough to forecast resulting changes in market shares.

Finally, the costs of obtaining, processing, storing and delivering information can mount quickly. The company must decide whether the benefits of having additional information are worth the costs of providing it, but both value and cost are often hard to assess. By itself, information has no worth; its value comes from its *use*. In many cases, additional information will do little to change or improve a manager's decision, or the costs of the information may exceed the returns from the improved decision. Marketers should not assume that additional information will always be worth obtaining. Rather, they should weigh carefully the costs of getting more information against the benefits resulting from it.

DEVELOPING MARKETING INFORMATION

Marketers can obtain the needed information from *internal data*, *marketing intelligence* and of course *marketing research*.

Internal data

Many companies build extensive **internal databases** – electronic collections of consumer and market information obtained from data sources within the company network. We might call this the corporate memory the organisation has of the actions it has taken, the decisions it has made and the feedback it has received from partners, markets and customers. Marketing managers can readily access and work with information in the database to identify marketing opportunities and problems, plan programmes and evaluate performance.

Information in the database can come from many sources. The accounting department prepares financial statements and keeps detailed records of sales, costs and cash flows. Operations reports on production schedules, shipments and inventories. The marketing department furnishes information on customer transactions, demographics, psychographics and buying behaviour. The customer service department keeps records of customer satisfaction or service problems. The sales force reports on reseller reactions and competitor activities, and marketing channel partners provide data on point-of-sale transactions.

Here is an example of how one company uses its internal database to make better marketing decisions:

> Every four weeks, two-thirds of British households shop at Tesco. It takes nearly £1 in every £7 spent in the nation's shops – no one else comes close. And part of that success is down to Clubcard, which has tracked the shopping habits of up to 13 million British families for more than a decade. 'Contrary to popular belief, Tesco's most significant competitive advantage in the UK is not its scale,' Mike Tattersall, the retail analyst at Cazenove, wrote last year. 'We believe that Clubcard, which conveys an array of material benefits across virtually every discipline of its business, is Tesco's most potent weapon in the ongoing battle for market share.'
>
> Martin Hayward, director of consumer strategy and futures at Dunnhumby [Tesco's CRM agency], settles down in his chair in his small office around the corner from the lifts. 'We use your purchasing behaviour to create a picture of the kind of person you are,' he explains. Using Clubcard data, Dunnhumby can tell that you have a new baby, or that your children have left home. It can judge your social class and knows whether you are a good cook. It also gives Tesco clues about what it could sell more of – and to whom.
>
> Dunnhumby takes the information registered on Clubcards each time those 13 million families come into Tesco for their weekly shop, and turns it into 5 billion pieces of data. Each separate product bought has its own set of attributes. A ready meal can have up to 45 'values' ascribed to it: is it expensive, or cheap? Tesco-branded, or made by Birds Eye? An 'ethnic' recipe, or a traditional British dish? Clubcard is the Big Brother of the shopping world.

Air France–KLM: flying high with CRM

Michael Schellenberg, University of Strathclyde

Winning Gartner's 2004 CRM Excellence Award for outstanding CRM affirmed KLM Royal Dutch Airline's efforts to reorganise its CRM strategy. Gartner Inc., the leading commercial provider of research and analysis on the global IT industry, announced the airline as the winner for Europe, Middle East and Africa saying that 'the award highlighted the airline's ability to combine grand strategic vision with pragmatic execution'. Christina Zanchi, at that time Head of the newly created CRM Department, proudly witnessed prompt results for the recently implemented campaign 'CIOA' (Customer Insight, Analysis and Opportunities). This campaign was set into operation to 'obtain new customers and ensure the loyalty of established customers by providing continuous, permission-based and promotional communications, according to the customer's interests'. It aimed to:

- Identify various customer segments.
- Understand customer needs and preferences.
- Create targeted marketing and sales campaigns for specific segments.

Source: Getty Images/AFP.

- Monitor customer responses.
- Apply experiences to future campaigns.
- Steer customer buying and travelling behaviour.

A new single database was created from 12 that existed before to build a single view of the customer. The technology was used to manage the 'Circle of Contacts' (Figure 4.2) in order to implement better customer recognition at all customer interaction points.

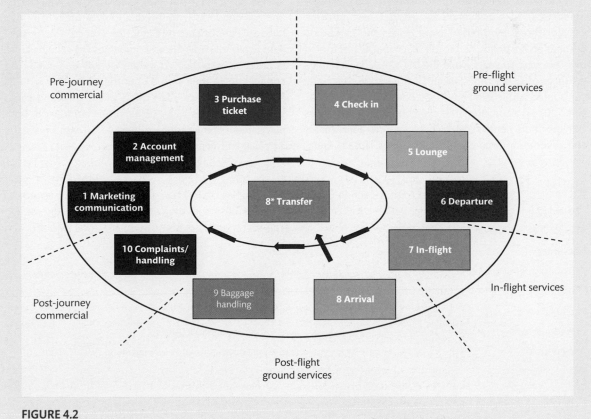

FIGURE 4.2
KLM 'Circle of Contacts'

Source: Stjin Viaene and Bjorn Cumps (2005) 'CRM excellence at KLM Royal Dutch Airlines', AMCIS 2005 Proceedings, Paper 37 (http://aisel.aisnet.org/amcis2005/37).

At each of the customer contact points, KLM aimed to communicate with the customer on a unique, one-to-one basis. Every touch point was understood as a critical 'moment of truth', making a real difference to the customer experience, which contributed to the mission of making 'every customer interaction into an opportunity to enhance the customer's buying and travel experience, and to increase and sustain company profitability'.

So far, so good. But CRM strategies wear out. In addition, KLM merged with Air France to form Air France–KLM. The merger of the two airlines involved the task of integrating both companies' CRM practices and both frequent-flyer programmes in order to offer the shared Flying Blue programme.

European Airline Industry

The European airline industry expects to see growth over the next few years. In 2013, the Association of European Airlines (AEA) saw growth of 1.6 per cent, adding 5.6 million more passenger journeys. Similar growth is expected to continue. The industry has historically been dominated by 'national flag carriers' (British Airways, Lufthansa, Air France and so on) that used to account for over 70 per cent of civilian passenger travel. However, low-cost carriers (LCCs), such as Ryanair and easyJet, have become a major threat by offering lower prices and extending destination portfolios; as a result seat capacity has tripled over the past 10 years while the LCCs have won a market share of 38 per cent. 'European airlines are constantly confronted with challenges that jeopardise their profitability. 2013 is a crucial year to overcome these challenges with the implemented cost-cuttings, capacity adjustments and revenue improvements,' said Athar Husain Khan,

Secretary General of AEA in 2013. The European airline industry is characterised by strong competition and over-supply, and many players are struggling to maintain their market share. Under these conditions airlines strive to establish, maintain and further develop emotional bonds with customers. More and more airlines have discovered the importance of keeping their most valuable customers and have focused on CRM or customer loyalty management in order to create additional value and to involve customers emotionally with the brand. The key question is: Who are our customers and what are their needs and aspirations? In many cases, however, instead of recognising CRM as a holistic strategy, they are still viewing it as synonymous with their frequent-flyer programmes. But effective CRM in the airline industry is a comprehensive strategy that manages all customer interactions in a consistent and value-orientated manner – with the frequent-flyer programmes being only one part of an integrated strategy.

Air France–KLM

KLM merged with Air France in 2004 forming the Air France–KLM Group, Europe's leading airline (Table 4.1). The core businesses are passenger transport, cargo shipment and aircraft maintenance. KLM and Air France each operate networks within a dual-hub strategy. The two hubs are Paris Charles de Gaulle (Air France) and Amsterdam Schiphol (KLM). Both companies kept their names in order to keep their corporate identity and emotional connection to their home countries. Together with its partners, Air France–KLM offers passengers and cargo shippers more than 250 destinations worldwide. Both KLM and Air France are members of SkyTeam, one of the global airline alliances.

TABLE 4.1 Facts and figures about Air France–KLM

Founded (merger)	2004
Employees worldwide	100,000
Revenue	€25bn
Total number of aircraft in the fleet	600
Total number of passengers transported in 2013	24 million
Load factor	82%
Headquarters	Paris – Charles de Gaulle Airport
Key people	Jean-Cyril Spinetta (CEO) Peter Hartmann (Vice-Chairman)

Source: airfranceklm.com.

New challenges along the way

In 2013 neither KLM nor Air France was ranked among the best 20 airlines in the annual Skytrax 'Best Airline' Awards (based on a survey of more than 18 million passengers and 200 airlines). Customer service and service quality are crucial factors in this assessment. Air France–KLM seems to have lost ground to Asian competitors such as Emirates, Qatar Airways and Singapore Airlines, which are highly customer-led and service-oriented players. Ten years after receiving an award for outstanding CRM, the airlines seem to be lagging behind their high-performing Asian counterparts. Even among European airlines Air France and KLM were lagging behind both major competitors like Turkish Airlines, Lufthansa and Swiss, and smaller players such as Austrian and Finnair (Table 4.2).

The KLM and Air France shared frequent-flyer programme, Flying Blue, has always been seen as a key component of the integrated CRM strategy. Flying Blue collects, stores and uses important information about the consumers and their preferences; identifies the customer at various points of contact; enables Air France–KLM to send out customised newsletters, and helps to establish a relationship with the customers.

Flying Blue members collect miles which they can convert into flights or other goods and services, partly provided by partnering firms (such as airlines, hotel chains, car rentals, financial services, consumer electronics and cinemas). Flying Blue has four different categories of customer: 'Ivory' (no minimum travel frequency required),

'Silver' (25,000 miles or 15 one-way flights per year), 'Gold' (40,000 miles or 30 flights) and 'Platinum' (70,000 miles or 60 flights). Each category provides different levels of services and benefits. Membership is free and anyone can sign up, whether a frequent flyer or not. Consequently, many Flying Blue (Ivory) members are not actually frequent flyers. Air France–KLM on the other hand benefits from the information provided by those individuals to provide sales opportunities.

Flying higher in 2013

Air France–KLM recognised that a generic frequent-flyer programme itself does not serve as a competitive advantage. Looking for improvements, the frequent-flyer programme Flying Blue went through major modifications aimed at improving its usability and functions in order to provide an improved customer experience. The enhanced 'Fly Blue' stores more information about the customer: it remembers the passenger's preferred seat, regular flight routes, preferred payment method and credit card details, specific dietary requirements, personal information of family members or other regular travel companions, passport details, and preferred language of communication online.

A new online chat system was also introduced. The chat box appears automatically on the individual's profile if one spends longer than normal on a section (perhaps the person is struggling to find their way around), with a service representative using this chat box to offer advice.

TABLE 4.2 The 2013 Skytrax 'Best Airline' Awards

Category	Best airline worldwide	Best cabin staff worldwide	Best airline in Europe
1	Emirates	Cathay Pacific	Turkish Airlines
2	Qatar Airways	Asiana Airlines	Lufthansa
3	Singapore Airlines	Malaysia Airlines	Swiss
4	ANA All Nippon	EVA Air	British Airways
5	Asiana Airlines	Singapore Airlines	Aegean Airlines
6	Cathay Pacific	ANA All Nippon	Austrian
7	Etihad Airways	Garuda Indonesia	Finnair
8	Garuda Indonesia	Qatar Airways	**KLM**
9	Turkish Airlines	Hainan Airlines	Virgin Atlantic
10	Qantas	Thai Airways	**Air France**

Source: airlinequality.com.

Online communication is in French, Dutch and English and aims to help with technical issues in particular (such as issues regarding browsers, operating systems, cookies and settings). Additionally, a call-back feature was installed. The new features were communicated thoroughly to the members online in order to keep them up to date with the modifications and to spread word of mouth.

Those improvements were noticed, and it was time for another award! This time, the 2013 'Freddie awards', an institution that honours outstanding frequent-flyer programmes, named Flying Blue in five categories: 'Best Earning Promotion', 'Best Elite Level', 'Best Redemption Ability', 'Best Program Of The Year', as well as 'Best Affinity Card' (Flying Blue American Express).

At the same time, having recognised CRM as a holistic, comprehensive strategy, Air France–KLM identified the need to further develop new CRM-related activities and to provide new offers to those who are in contact with the brand. To remain in the minds of infrequent customers Air France–KLM inaugurated the digital 'iFly Magazine'. Keeping in touch with those customers during the long time between bookings was thought to be important in establishing a new 'Circle of Contacts' (Figure 4.3).

'iFly' is sent to 1.5 million customers monthly to inspire and surprise them with unique content. The 'smart' digital magazine is built on three pillars: 'travel', 'Dutch heritage' and 'culture and innovation'. It is 'smart' because it helps to enrich customer profiles as clicks and online orientation behaviour are permanently tracked, since Air France–KLM aims to gain a wider perspective on its customers than just tracking sales. Those insights are stored in the customer profiles and used for other integrated communication tasks, enabling Air France–KLM to send relevant and targeted offers (emails) to those individuals.

Every issue of 'iFly' differentiates in content, design and message according to different target groups. The design and layout for male and female customers, and between frequent flyers and non-frequent flyers for example, vary substantially. As the reader becomes familiar with 'iFly', more time is spent reading and browsing through it, with the average reading time having increased from initially under five minutes up to eight minutes. Research also reveals that between 25 and 35 per cent of the readers feel that Air France–KLM's image has been positively changed by reading iFly; at least 27 per cent of the readers rate the digital magazine as very good or excellent and 70 per cent or more certainly would read the next issue, suggesting that a further step towards efficient and exciting CRM practices has been made.

Staying a high flyer

In an industry where the core service, getting people from A to B, is difficult to differentiate, creating and providing additional value through customer experience and CRM remains a crucial issue for airlines. Air France–KLM realises that it has to communicate with different target audiences on its own terms, and keep up with the ever-changing technology and the opportunities that it creates. The group's ability to do so will influence future success. The two partners that built Air France–KLM have a lot of work to do – bearing in mind that CRM strategies wear out.

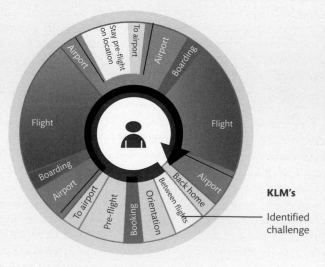

FIGURE 4.3
Air France–KLM 'new' Circle of Contacts

This information is also stored in a vast search engine that can be used by suppliers trying to launch products. Dunnhumby makes about £30 million a year selling Tesco data to more than 200 consumer goods companies, such as Procter & Gamble, Unilever and Nestlé. Within hours of launching a product or introducing a promotion into a local Tesco store, brand managers can track who is buying its products or responding to its promotions. Are they empty-nesters or young mums, lawyers or factory workers? 'If you understand who is buying and how they are buying, you can make better decisions,' Hayward says. 'The joy of our sample is that it is so large, and because Tesco is so representative of the country it is the best source of insight a supplier can get.'[17]

Internal databases usually can be accessed more quickly and cheaply than other information sources, but they also present some problems. Because internal information was often collected for other purposes, it may be incomplete or in the wrong form for making marketing decisions. For example, sales and cost data used by the accounting department for preparing financial statements must be adapted for use in evaluating the value of specific customer segment, sales force or channel performance. Data also ages quickly; keeping the database current requires a major effort. In addition, a large company produces mountains of information, which must be well integrated and readily accessible so that managers can find it easily and use it effectively. Managing so much data requires highly sophisticated equipment and techniques, but the human element must not be discounted either. Kwik-Fit, one of the largest companies in the European car repair industry, found that the information in its databases was badly corrupted and inaccurate.[18] The reason? Mechanics, who had the job of completing the paper forms which were inputted into the databases, did not take the job very seriously and would give customers joke names (Dr Acula, Mr M. Mouse) or leave contact information sections only partially complete.

Marketing intelligence

Marketing intelligence is the systematic collection and analysis of publicly available information about competitors and developments in the marketplace. The goal of marketing intelligence is to improve strategic decision making, assess and track competitors' actions, and provide early warning of opportunities and threats. VisitScotland will try to keep abreast of what is happening in other tourist destinations – especially near competitors like Ireland.

Competitive intelligence gathering has grown dramatically as more and more companies are now busily snooping on their competitors. Techniques range from quizzing the company's own employees and benchmarking competitors' products to researching the Internet, lurking around industry trade shows and even rooting through rivals' rubbish bins.

Much intelligence can be collected from people inside the company – executives, engineers and scientists, purchasing agents and the sales force. The company can also obtain important intelligence information from suppliers, resellers and key customers. Or it can get good information by observing competitors and monitoring their published information. It can buy and analyse competitors' products, monitor their sales, check for new patents and examine various types of physical evidence. In one case, Procter & Gamble admitted to 'dumpster diving' at rival Unilever's headquarters: 'P&G got its mitts on just about every iota of info there was to be had about Unilever's [hair-care] brands,' notes an analyst. However, when news of the questionable tactics reached top P&G managers, they were shocked. They immediately stopped the project and voluntarily set up negotiations with Unilever to right whatever competitive wrongs had been done. Although P&G claims it broke no laws, the company reported that the dumpster raids 'violated our strict guidelines regarding our business policies'.[19]

Competitors often reveal intelligence information through their annual reports, business publications, trade show exhibits, press releases, advertisements and web pages. The Internet is a vast source of competitor-supplied information. Using Internet search engines, marketers can search specific competitor names, events or trends and see what turns up. Moreover, most companies now place large amounts of information on their websites, providing details to attract customers, partners, suppliers, investors or franchisees. This can provide a wealth

Marketing intelligence: Procter & Gamble admitted to 'dumpster diving' at rival Unilever's Helene Curtis headquarters. When P&G's top management learned of the questionable practice, it stopped the project, voluntarily informed Unilever and set up talks to right whatever competitive wrongs had been done

Source: Getty Images/Andy Reynolds.

of useful information about competitors' strategies, markets, new products, facilities and other happenings. Of course, it is also important to keep track of what information competitors are releasing through their social media presence; for example, what are they saying on Twitter, on Facebook and at LinkedIn?

Something as simple as a competitor's job postings can be very revealing. For example, a few years back, while poking around on Google's company website, Microsoft's Bill Gates came across a 'help-wanted' page describing all of the jobs available at Google. To his surprise, he noted that Google was looking for engineers with backgrounds that had nothing to do with its web-search business but everything to do with Microsoft's core software businesses. Forewarned that Google might be preparing to become more than just a search engine company, Gates emailed a handful of Microsoft executives, saying, in effect, 'We have to watch these guys. It looks like they are building something to compete with us.' A marketing intelligence consultant noted that companies 'are often surprised that there's so much out there to know. They're busy with their day-to-day operations and they don't realise how much information can be obtained with a few strategic keystrokes.'[20]

Intelligence seekers can also pore through any of thousands of online databases. Some are free. For example, the European Patent Office (**www.epo.org**) manages patent applications across 37 European countries. For a fee, companies can subscribe to any of more than 3,000 online databases and information search services such as ProQuest Dialog, Hoover's, LexisNexis, Dow Jones News Retrieval and the Dun & Bradstreet Marketing Database.

The intelligence game goes both ways. Facing determined marketing intelligence efforts by competitors, most companies are now taking steps to protect their own information. For example, Unilever has begun widespread competitive intelligence training. Employees are taught not just how to collect intelligence information, but also how to protect company information from competitors. According to a former Unilever employee, 'We were even warned that spies from competitors could be posing as drivers at the mini-cab company we used.' Unilever even performs random checks on internal security. Says the former staff member, 'At one [internal marketing] conference, we were set up when an actor was employed to infiltrate the group. The idea was to see who spoke to him, how much they told him, and how long it took to realize that no one knew him. He ended up being there for a long time.'[21]

The growing use of marketing intelligence raises a number of ethical issues. Although most of the preceding techniques are legal, and some are considered to be shrewdly competitive, some may involve questionable ethics. Clearly, companies should take advantage of publicly available information. However, they should not stoop to snoop. With all the legitimate intelligence sources now available, a company does not have to break the law or accepted codes of ethics to get good intelligence.

MARKETING RESEARCH

In addition to information about competitor and marketplace events, marketers often need formal studies of specific situations. For example, Carrefour, the leading French retailer, wants to know what appeals will be most effective in its next corporate advertising campaign. Philips wants to know how many and what kinds of people will buy its next-generation plasma TVs. In such situations, marketing intelligence will not provide the detailed information needed. Managers will need marketing research.

Marketing research is the systematic design, collection, analysis and reporting of data relevant to a specific marketing situation facing an organisation. Companies use marketing research in a wide variety of situations. For example, marketing research can help marketers understand customer satisfaction and purchase behaviour. It can help them assess market potential and market share, or to measure the effectiveness of pricing, product, distribution and promotion activities.

Some large companies have their own research departments that work with marketing managers on marketing research projects. This is how P&G, Kraft, Citigroup and many other corporate giants handle marketing research. In addition, these companies – like their smaller counterparts – frequently hire outside research specialists to consult with management on specific marketing problems and conduct marketing research studies. Sometimes firms simply purchase data collected by outside firms to aid in their decision making – organisations like Mintel do very well by preparing and selling reports on specific topics, sectors and nations.

The marketing research process has four steps (see Figure 4.4): defining the problem and research objectives; developing the research plan; implementing the research plan; and interpreting and reporting the findings. What follows is an outline of this process. Market research can be a complex and occasionally technical business, but many books and online resources are available to assist.[22]

Defining the problem and research objectives

Marketing managers and researchers must work closely together to define the problem and agree on research objectives. The manager best understands the decision for which information is needed; the researcher best understands marketing research and how to obtain the information. Defining the problem and research objectives is often the hardest step in the research process. The manager may know that something is wrong, without knowing the specific causes.

After the problem has been defined carefully, the manager and researcher must set the research objectives. Typically, research objectives fall under three headings: exploratory, descriptive and causal. The objective of **exploratory research** is to gather preliminary information that will help define the problem and suggest hypotheses. The objective of **descriptive research** is to describe things, such as the market potential for a product or the demographics and attitudes of consumers who buy the product. The objective of **causal research** is to test hypotheses about cause-and-effect relationships. For example, would a 10 per cent decrease in the price of a tin of baked beans increase sales sufficiently to increase profits? Managers often start with exploratory research and later follow with descriptive or causal research.

The statement of the problem, and the research objectives, guide the entire research process. The manager and researcher should put the statement in writing to be certain that they agree on the purpose and expected results of the research.

Developing the research plan

Once the research problems and objectives have been defined, researchers must determine the exact information needed, develop a plan for gathering it efficiently and present the plan to management. The research plan outlines sources of existing data and spells out the specific research approaches, contact methods, sampling plans and instruments that researchers will use to gather new data.

Research objectives must be translated into specific information needs. For example, suppose that a Russian beer producer is thinking of entering Western European markets – like Baltika (see Chapter 6). With a great many markets to choose from, the company would need to research each of them to identify which would be the easiest to enter and establish

FIGURE 4.4
The marketing research process

Defining the problem and research objectives → Developing the research plan for collecting information → Implementing the research plan – collecting and analysing the data → Interpreting and reporting the findings

a profitable presence. What would it need to identify? What are the demographic, economic and lifestyle characteristics of its current customers – and is there a match for these profiled segments in a particular country? Much more detail would be required, such as:

- *Consumer-usage patterns for beer and other alcoholic drinks in the potential markets.* How much consumers drink, where and when. How do they perceive Russian beer when compared with domestic brands or other foreign (to the drinker) products?
- *Retailer reactions to the new Russian beers.* Failure to get retailer support could make it extremely difficult to reach customers, even if other research suggests that these customers would like the beer.
- *Forecasts of sales in both new and current markets.* Will the new markets require an expansion in production? Can current production and distribution networks be extended into the new markets?

Managers will need these and many other types and pieces of information to decide whether to enter the new markets.

The research plan should be presented in a *written proposal*. A written proposal is especially important when the research project is large and complex or when an outside firm carries it out. The proposal should cover the management problems addressed and the research objectives, the information to be obtained and the way the results will help management decision making. The proposal also should include research costs.

To meet the manager's information needs, the research plan can call for gathering secondary data, primary data, or both. **Secondary data** consist of information that already exists somewhere, having been collected for another purpose – VisitScotland draws on secondary data sources when it consults the reports of the International Passenger Survey. **Primary data** consists of information collected for the specific purpose at hand, such as when VisitScotland commissions interviews with tourists in Scotland.

Gathering secondary data

Researchers usually start by gathering secondary data. The company's internal database provides a good starting point. However, the company can also tap a wide assortment of external information sources, including commercial data services and government sources (see Exhibit 4.1).

EXHIBIT 4.1   Selected information sources

Media

The BBC website (news.bbc.co.uk) has excellent coverage of many business and marketing-related stories, as well as a wealth of financial data.

Le Monde is France's leading newspaper, in the original French (www.lemonde.fr/) and English-language (mondediplo.com/) versions.

Pravda (www.pravda.ru/) is available in Russian, English, Portuguese and Italian.

Der Spiegel (www.spiegel.de/international), the leading German newspaper, has an international edition in English.

The Economist (www.economist.com/) is a weekly business newspaper with a specific focus on economic and business issues. There is an excellent database and a very high quality of journalism.

The *Financial Times* (www.ft.com/) is a daily newspaper with a wealth of market data and business-related news.

Government data

The UK government has a large online library of statistics, many of which are relevant to marketing and market research (www.statistics.gov.uk) including demographic information and economic trends.

The Netherlands has an equivalent library (www.cbs.nl/nl-NL), available in English as well as Dutch.

Swedish government data is published in English and Swedish (www.scb.se/).

Austrian government statistics are available in German and English (www.statistik.at/).

An excellent directory of other national government statistics and data is provided by RBA (www.rba.co.uk/sources/stats.htm\#key).

National Embassies in other countries often produce reports and statistics to enable domestic firms to understand that foreign market. As an example, the British Embassy in Rome: https://www.gov.uk/government/world/organisations/british-embassy-rome.

Statistics, data, reports and other excellent sources of secondary data are produced by local government in cities and regions, such as for Glasgow in Scotland (www.glasgow.gov.uk), or Piraeus in Greece (www.pireas.com/en/companies).

The European Union has an enormous wealth of statistics, available in all European languages, including English (epp.eurostat.ec.europa.eu).

EFTA (European Free Trade Area) nations (www.efta.int/statistics) have a similar resource.

The Commonwealth of Independent States (CIS) – an alliance of former Soviet republics – has a collective resource as well (www.cisstat.com/eng/index.htm).

The United Nations commissions many research projects on a wide range of social, political and economic issues (www.un.org/en/).

Market research and market intelligence agencies and professional bodies

There are a great many professional market research agencies across Europe. Some cover the entire continent, others specialise in specific countries or sectors.

PMR covers Eastern Europe (www.research-pmr.com).

Large commercial, social and market research companies provide a lot of useful reports free of charge, covering a wide range of topics and geographical areas; examples are Ipsos MORI (www.ipsos-mori.com) and Millward Brown (www.millwardbrown.com).

Euromonitor (www.euromonitor.com) produces reports on specific commercial and social topics. These are commercial products with a substantial price-tag, but there are some free samples and most university and city libraries will have a selection of printed copies.

Similarly, Mintel (www.mintel.com) began by publishing reports on food and drink consumption, but has now expanded into most other industries.

ESOMAR (www.esomar.org) is a professional body which seeks to encourage higher ethical and professional standards across the industry. Many market research organisations are affiliated to ESOMAR and they have extensive training programmes.

The Market Research Society (www.mrs.org.uk) is a body which seeks to represent the interests of buyers and sellers of market research.

Industry bodies and pressure groups

Most industries have bodies which collect and publish data about that industry specifically in one country or across Europe.

The ABPI represents the UK pharmaceutical industry (www.abpi.org.uk).

VDA (www.vda.de) is the body representing the German car industry.

FoodDrink Europe (www.fooddrinkeurope.eu/) publishes data about activities in the European drinks industry.

The European Software Market Association (www.esoma.org/) represents software developers across Europe.

Eurochambres (www.eurochambres.be) is the umbrella organisation of European Chambers of Commerce.

For Internet data

ClickZ Stats/CyberAtlas (www.clickz.com/stats) brings together a wealth of information about the Internet and its users, from consumers to e-commerce.

Interactive Advertising Bureau (www.iab.net) covers statistics about advertising on the Internet.

Forrester Research (www.forrester.com/home/) provides information to support e-commerce marketing strategies.

Internet World Stats (www.internetworldstats.com) has demographic data on Internet use worldwide.

Companies can buy secondary data reports from outside suppliers. For example, ACNielsen sells data from a panel of 70,000 households across Europe with measures of trial and repeat purchasing, brand loyalty and buyer demographics.[23] Euromonitor sells reports compiling information on important social and lifestyle trends. These and other firms supply high-quality data to suit a wide variety of marketing information needs.[24]

Using commercial **online databases**, marketing researchers can conduct their own searches of secondary data sources. General database services such as ProQuest Dialog and LexisNexis put an incredible wealth of information at the keyboards of marketing decision makers. Beyond commercial websites offering information for a fee, almost every industry association, government agency, business publication and news medium offers free information to those tenacious enough to find their websites. There are so many websites offering data that finding the right ones can become an almost overwhelming task.

Secondary data can usually be obtained more quickly and at a lower cost than primary data. Also, secondary sources can sometimes provide data that an individual company cannot collect on its own – information that either is not directly available or would be too expensive to collect. For example, it would be too expensive for Nestlé to conduct a continuing retail store audit to find out about the market shares, prices and displays of competitors' brands. But it can buy the InfoScan service from Information Resources Inc., which provides this information from thousands of scanner-equipped supermarkets across Europe and the world.

Secondary data can also present problems. The needed information may not exist – researchers can rarely obtain all the data they need from secondary sources. For example, Baltika or any other Russian brewery will not find existing information about consumer reactions to Russian beers if it is the first such product in that market. Even when data can be found, it might not be very usable. The researcher must evaluate secondary information carefully to make certain it is *relevant* (fits research project needs), *accurate* (reliably collected and reported), *current* (up to date enough for current decisions) and *impartial* (objectively collected and reported).

Primary data collection

Secondary data provides a good starting point for research and often helps to define research problems and objectives. In most cases, however, the company must also collect primary data. Just as researchers must carefully evaluate the quality of secondary information, they also must take great care when collecting primary data. They need to make sure that it will be relevant, accurate, current and unbiased. Table 4.3 shows that designing a plan for primary data collection calls for a number of decisions on *research approaches, contact methods, sampling plan* and *research instruments*.

Research approaches

Research approaches for gathering primary data include observation, surveys and experiments. Each of these alternatives has inherent strengths and weaknesses, but it is generally correct to remember the adage: the right tool for the right job.[25] Here, we discuss each one in turn.

TABLE 4.3 Planning primary data collection

Research approaches	Contact methods	Sampling plan	Research instruments
Observation	Mail	Sampling unit	Questionnaire
Survey	Telephone	Sample size	Mechanical instruments
Experiment	Personal	Sampling procedure	
	Online		

Observational research

Observational research involves gathering primary data by observing relevant people, actions and situations. For example, a consumer packaged-goods marketer might visit supermarkets and observe shoppers as they browse the store, pick up and examine packages, and make buying decisions.[26] Or a bank might evaluate possible new branch locations by checking traffic patterns, neighbourhood conditions and the location of competing branches. Fisher-Price even set up an observation lab in which it could observe the reactions of little tots to new toys:

> The Fisher-Price Play Lab is a sunny, toy-strewn space where, for over 50 years, lucky kids have tested Fisher-Price prototypes. Today three boys and three girls, all four-year-olds, speed through the front door. Two boys tug quietly, but firmly, for the wheel of a new radio-controlled race set – a brand-new offering. The girls skid to a stop near a small sub development of dollhouses. And from behind the one way glass, toy designers study the action intently, occasionally stepping out to join the play. At the Play Lab, creation and (attempted) destruction happily coexist. Over an eight-week session with these kids, designers will test dozens of toy concepts, sending out crude models, then increasingly sophisticated revisions, to figure out what gets kids worked up into a new-toy frenzy.[27]

Observational research can obtain information that people are unwilling or unable to provide. An interesting recent development in observational research has been the use of eye-tracking devices that consumers wear like glasses as they do their shopping, enabling the researcher to see exactly what the consumer was looking at, and exactly how often.[28] In some cases, observation may be the only way to obtain the needed information. In contrast, some things simply cannot be observed, such as feelings, attitudes and motives, or private behaviour. Long-term or infrequent behaviour is also difficult to observe. Because of these limitations, researchers often use observation along with other data collection methods.

A wide range of companies now use *ethnographic research*. This involves sending trained observers to watch consumers in their 'natural habitat'.[29] The observers loiter in a pub or a bar, public transport hubs or a public space or park, and observe carefully how individuals and groups act and interact around products – food and drink products especially use this method. Ethnographic research often yields the kinds of intimate details that just do not emerge from traditional focus groups, where people know they are being watched and may moderate their actions accordingly.[30] To glean greater insights into buying behaviour, one company even went so far as to set up an actual retail store that serves as an ethnographic lab.

Survey research

Survey research, the most widely used method for primary data collection, is the approach best suited for gathering descriptive information. A company that wants to know about

Observational research: Fisher-Price set up an observation lab in which it could observe the reactions of little tots to new toys

Source: Photos of Fisher-Price Playlab used with permission of Fisher-Price, Inc., East Aurora, New York 14052.

people's knowledge, attitudes, preferences or buying behaviour can often find out by asking them directly.

Some firms provide marketers with a more comprehensive look at buying patterns through **single-source data systems**. These systems start with surveys of huge consumer panels – carefully selected groups of consumers who agree to participate in ongoing research. Then, they electronically monitor survey respondents' purchases and exposure to various marketing activities. Combining the survey and monitoring information gives a better understanding of the link between consumer characteristics, attitudes and purchase behaviour.

The major advantage of survey research is its flexibility – it can be used to obtain many different kinds of information in many different situations. However, survey research also presents some problems. Sometimes people are unable to answer survey questions because they cannot remember or have never thought about what they do and why. People may be unwilling to respond to unknown interviewers or about things they consider as sensitive topics – sexuality, relationships, politics, emotions and so on. Respondents may answer survey questions even when they do not know the answer in order to appear smarter or more informed. Or they may try to help the interviewer by giving pleasing answers. Finally, busy people may not take the time, or they might resent the intrusion into their privacy. As we will see in Marketing at Work 4.2, intrusions into privacy and control and ownership of personal data can be subtle and pervasive.

Experimental research

Whereas observation is best suited for exploratory research and surveys for descriptive research, **experimental research** is best suited for gathering causal information. Experiments involve selecting matched groups of subjects, giving them different treatments, controlling unrelated factors and checking for differences in group responses. Thus, experimental research tries to explain cause-and-effect relationships.

For example, before adding a new item to its menu, McDonald's might use experiments to test the effects on sales of two different prices it might charge. It could introduce the new item at one price in one city and at another price in another city. If the cities are similar, and if all other marketing efforts for the new item are the same, then differences in sales in the two cities could be related to the price charged.

Contact methods

Information can be collected by mail, telephone, personal interview or online. Each of these methods has inherent strengths and weaknesses that are contingent on the time, money and other resources available to the researchers (Table 4.4).

TABLE 4.4 Strengths and weaknesses of contact methods

	Mail	Telephone	Personal	Online
Flexibility	Poor	Good	Excellent	Good
Quantity of data that can be collected	Good	Fair	Excellent	Good
Control of interviewer effects	Excellent	Fair	Poor	Fair
Control of sample	Fair	Excellent	Good	Excellent
Speed of data collection	Poor	Excellent	Good	Excellent
Response rate	Fair	Good	Good	Good
Cost	Good	Fair	Poor	Excellent

Source: Donald S. Tull and Del I. Hawkins, *Marketing Research: Measurement and Method*, 7th edn (New York: Macmillan Publishing, 1993). Adapted with permission.

Mail, telephone and personal interviewing

Mail questionnaires can be used to collect large amounts of information at a low cost per respondent. Respondents may give more honest answers to more personal questions on a mail questionnaire than to an unknown interviewer in person or over the phone. Also, no interviewer is involved to bias the respondent's answers – perhaps by smiling or frowning at particular answers.

However, mail questionnaires are not very flexible – all respondents answer the same questions in a fixed order. Mail surveys usually take longer to complete and the response rate – the number of people returning completed questionnaires – is often very low. Finally, the researcher often has little control over the mail questionnaire sample. Even with a good mailing list, it is hard to control *who* at the mailing address fills out the questionnaire.

Telephone interviewing is one of the best methods for gathering information quickly, and it provides greater flexibility than mail questionnaires. Interviewers can explain difficult questions and, depending on the answers they receive, skip some questions or probe others. Response rates tend to be higher than with mail questionnaires, and interviewers can ask to speak to respondents with the desired characteristics or even by name.

However, with telephone interviewing, the cost per respondent is higher than with mail questionnaires. Also, people may not want to discuss personal questions with an interviewer. The method introduces interviewer bias – the way interviewers talk, how they ask questions and other differences may affect respondents' answers. Finally, different interviewers may interpret and record responses differently, and under time pressures some interviewers might even cheat by recording answers without asking questions.

Personal interviewing takes two forms – individual and group interviewing. *Individual interviewing* involves talking with people in their homes or offices, on the street, or in shopping malls. Such interviewing is flexible. Trained interviewers can guide interviews, explain difficult questions and explore issues as the situation requires. They can show subjects actual products, advertisements or packages, and observe reactions and behaviour. However, individual personal interviews may cost three to four times as much as telephone interviews, and because interviewers have more freedom in personal interviews, the problem of interviewer bias is greater.

Group interviewing consists of inviting 6–10 people to talk with a trained moderator about a product, service or organisation. Participants normally are paid a small sum for attending. The moderator encourages free and easy discussion, hoping that group interactions will bring out actual feelings and thoughts. At the same time, the moderator 'focuses' the discussion – hence the name, **focus group interviewing**. Researchers and marketers can watch the focus group discussions from behind one-way glass as they take place and the sessions are often audio or video recorded for subsequent in-depth analysis.

Focus group interviewing has become one of the major marketing research tools for gaining insight into consumer thoughts and feelings. However, focus group studies usually employ small sample sizes to keep time and costs down, and it may be hard to generalise from the results.

Today, many researchers are changing the way they conduct focus groups. Some are employing video-conferencing technology to connect marketers in distant locations with live focus group action. Using cameras and two-way sound systems, marketing managers in a far-off boardroom can look in and listen, even using remote controls to zoom in on faces and pan the focus group at will. Other researchers are changing the environments in which they conduct focus groups. To help consumers relax and to elicit more authentic responses, they are using settings that are more comfortable and more relevant to the products being researched. For example, they might conduct focus groups for cooking products in a kitchen setting, or focus groups for home furnishings in a living room setting. One research firm offers facilities that look just like anything from a living room or play room to a bar or even a courtroom.

Online marketing research

Advances in communication technologies have resulted in a number of high-tech contact methods. One is computer-assisted telephone interviewing (CATI), in which interviewers sit at computers, read questions from the screen and type in respondents' answers. Another is completely automated telephone surveys (CATS), in which respondents are dialled by computer and asked pre-recorded questions. They enter responses by voice or through the phone's touchpad.

Increasingly, marketing researchers are collecting primary data through **online (Internet) marketing research** – *Internet surveys, experiments, social media watching* and *online focus groups*. Internet research can take many forms.[31] A company can include a questionnaire on its website and offer incentives for completing it. Or it can use email, web links or web pop-ups to invite people to answer questions and possibly win a prize. The company can sponsor a chat room and introduce questions from time to time or conduct live discussions or virtual focus groups. A company can learn about the behaviour of online customers by following their *clickstreams* as they visit the website and move to other sites. A company can experiment with different prices, use different headlines, or offer different product features on different websites or at different times to learn the relative effectiveness of its offerings.

As you are probably aware, social media platforms like Facebook and Twitter are essentially machines for collecting and processing vast quantities of user data, much of it marketing related. You are the info-product of such companies, not the customer! For Facebook, the customers are who the data is packaged and sold to – and the advertisers who use some of the data to target ads better. As we will see later (see Chapter 12), many people have real concerns about the impact of this on individuals and society.

Web research offers some real advantages over traditional surveys and focus groups. The most obvious advantages are speed and low costs. Online focus groups require some advance scheduling, but results are practically instantaneous. For example, one soft-drinks company conducted an online survey to test teenager opinions of new packaging ideas. The 10- to 15-minute Internet survey included dozens of questions along with 765 different images of labels and bottle shapes. Some 600 teenagers participated over a three- to four-day period. Detailed analysis from the survey was available just five days after all the responses had come in – lightning quick compared with offline efforts.[32] Twitter call their data-stream 'the hosepipe'. As was seen in the previous chapter, companies can become aware very quickly how changes and initiatives have gone down with their customers and the wider public.

Internet research is also relatively low in cost. Participants can dial in for a focus group from anywhere in the world, eliminating travel, lodging and facility costs. For surveys, the Internet eliminates most of the postage, phone, labour and printing costs associated with other approaches. As a result, an Internet survey may be only 10–20 per cent as expensive as mail, telephone or personal surveys. Moreover, sample size has little influence on costs. Once the questionnaire is set up, there is little difference in cost between 10 and 10,000 respondents on the Web. Analysis of hundreds of thousands of Tweets can be done almost in real time at little to no cost.

Online surveys and focus groups are also excellent for reaching the hard to reach – the often elusive teenager, single, affluent and well-educated audiences. They are also good for reaching working mothers and other people who lead busy lives. These people can respond in their own space and at their own convenience. The Internet also works well for bringing together people from different parts of the country, especially those in higher income groups who cannot spare the time to travel to a central site.

Using the Internet to conduct marketing research does have some drawbacks. For one, restricted Internet access can make it difficult to get a broad cross-section of people. However, with Internet penetration now over 60 per cent across Europe as a whole, 84 per cent in the UK (80 per cent in France and 67 per cent in Spain, but only 44 per cent in Romania compared with 78 per cent in the USA),[33] this is less of a problem. However, another major problem is controlling who is in the sample. Without seeing respondents, it is difficult to know who they really are.

Even when you reach the right respondents, online surveys and focus groups can lack the dynamics of more personal approaches. The online world is devoid of the eye contact, body language and direct personal interactions found in traditional focus group research. And the Internet format – running, typed commentary and online 'emoticons' greatly restrict respondent expressiveness. 'You're missing all of the key things that make a focus group a viable method,' says the executive. 'You may get people online to talk to each other and play off each other, but it's very different to watch people get excited about a concept.'

To overcome such sample and response problems, many online research firms use opt-in communities and respondent panels. For example, online research firm Toluna provides access to 12 million opt-in panel members in more than 40 countries. Advances in technology – such as the integration of animation, streaming audio and video, and virtual environments – also help to overcome online sample and research dynamics limitations.

Perhaps the most explosive issue facing online researchers concerns consumer privacy. Some fear that unethical researchers will use the email addresses and confidential responses gathered through surveys to sell products after the research is completed. They are concerned about the use of electronic agents (such as Spambots or Trojans) that collect personal information without the respondents' consent. Failure to address such privacy issues could result in angry, less cooperative consumers and increased government intervention. Despite these concerns, online research now accounts for 8 per cent of all spending on quantitative marketing research, and most industry insiders predict healthy growth.[34]

Sampling plan

Marketing researchers usually draw conclusions about large groups of consumers by studying a small sample of the total consumer population. A **sample** is a segment of the population selected to represent the population as a whole. Ideally, the sample should be representative so that the researcher can make accurate estimates of the thoughts and behaviours of the larger population.

Designing the sample requires three decisions. First, *who* is to be surveyed (what *sampling unit*)? The answer to this question is not always obvious. For example, to study the decision-making process of a family purchasing a car, should the researcher interview the husband, the wife, other family members, salespeople, or all of these? The researcher must determine what information is needed and who is most likely to have it.

Second, *how many* people should be surveyed (what *sample size*)? Large samples give more reliable results than small samples. It is not necessary to sample the entire target market or even a large portion to get reliable results, however. If well chosen, samples of less than 1 per cent of a population can often give good reliability.

Third, *how* should the people in the sample be *chosen* (what *sampling procedure*)? Table 4.5 describes different kinds of samples. Using *probability samples,* each population member has a known chance of being included in the sample, and researchers can calculate confidence limits for sampling error. But when probability sampling costs too much or takes too much time, marketing researchers often take *non-probability samples,* even though their sampling error cannot be measured. These varied ways of drawing samples have different costs and time limitations as well as different accuracy and statistical properties. Which method is best depends on the needs of the research project.

Research instruments

In collecting primary data, marketing researchers have a choice of two main research instruments – the *questionnaire* and *mechanical devices*. The *questionnaire* is by far the most common instrument, whether administered in person, by phone or online.

Questionnaires are very flexible – there are many ways to ask questions. Closed-end questions include all the possible answers, and subjects make choices among them. Examples include multiple-choice questions and scale questions. Open-end questions allow respondents to answer in their own words. In a survey of airline users, Lufthansa might simply ask,

TABLE 4.5 Types of samples

Probability sample	
Simple random sample	Every member of the population has a known and equal chance of selection
Stratified random sample	The population is divided into mutually exclusive groups (such as age groups) and random samples are drawn from each group
Cluster (area) sample	The population is divided into mutually exclusive groups (such as streets) and the researcher draws a sample of the groups to interview
Non-probability sample	
Convenience sample	The researcher selects the easiest population members from which to obtain information
Judgement sample	The researcher uses his or her judgement to select population members who are good prospects for accurate information
Quota sample	The researcher finds and interviews a prescribed number of people in each of several categories

'What is your opinion of Lufthansa?' Or it might ask people to complete a sentence: 'When I choose an airline, the most important consideration is. . . .' These and other kinds of open-end questions often reveal more than closed-end questions because respondents are not limited in their answers. Open-end questions are especially useful in exploratory research, when the researcher is trying to find out what people think but not measuring how many people think in a certain way. Closed-end questions, on the other hand, provide answers that are easier to interpret and tabulate.

Researchers should also use care in the *wording* and *ordering* of questions. They should use simple, direct, unbiased wording. Questions should be arranged in a logical order. The first question should create interest, if possible, and difficult or personal questions should be asked last so that respondents do not become defensive. A carelessly prepared questionnaire usually contains many errors (see Exhibit 4.2).

Although questionnaires are the most common research instrument, researchers also use *mechanical devices* to monitor consumer behaviour. Nielsen Media Research attaches *people meters* to TV sets in selected homes to record who watches which programmes. Retailers use *checkout scanners* to record shoppers' purchases – a large amount of the data that Tesco, Aldi, Carrefour and other supermarkets has comes from this source.

EXHIBIT 4.2

Suppose that a marketing manager at a football club had prepared the following questionnaire to use in interviewing the parents of prospective youth season ticket holders. How would you assess each question?

1   What is your income to the nearest hundred euros? *People do not usually know their income to the nearest hundred euros, nor do they want to reveal their income that closely. Moreover, a researcher should never open a questionnaire with such a personal question.*

2   Are you a strong or weak supporter of children attending football matches? *What do 'strong' and 'weak' mean?*

3   Do your children behave themselves well while watching football? Yes ( ) No ( ) *'Behave' is a relative term. Furthermore, are yes and no the best response options for this question? Besides, will people answer this honestly and objectively? Why ask the question in the first place?*

4   What are the most salient and determinant attributes in your evaluation of food on sale at the stadium? *What are salient and determinant attributes? Don't use big words on me!*

5   Do you think it is right to deprive your child of the opportunity to become a fully committed fan of this club? *A loaded question. Given the bias, how can any parent answer yes?*

Other mechanical devices measure subjects' physical responses. For example, advertisers use eye cameras to study viewers' eye movements while watching ads – on what points their eyes focus first and how long they linger on any given ad component.

Implementing the research plan

The researcher next puts the marketing research plan into action. This involves collecting, processing and analysing the information. Data collection can be carried out by the company's marketing research staff or by outside firms. The data collection phase of the marketing research process is generally the most expensive and the most subject to error. Researchers should watch closely to make sure that the plan is implemented correctly. They must guard against problems with contacting respondents, with respondents who refuse to cooperate or who give biased answers, and with interviewers who make mistakes or take shortcuts.

Researchers must also process and analyse the collected data to isolate important information and findings. They need to check data for accuracy and completeness and code it for analysis. The researchers then tabulate the results and compute statistical measures.

Interpreting and reporting the findings

The market researcher must now interpret the findings, draw conclusions and report them to management. The researcher should not try to overwhelm managers with numbers and fancy statistical techniques. Rather, the researcher should present important findings that are useful in the major decisions faced by management.

However, interpretation should not be left only to the researchers. They are often experts in research design and statistics, but the marketing manager knows more about the problem and the decisions that must be made – the context. The best research is meaningless if the manager blindly accepts faulty interpretations from the researcher. Similarly, managers may be biased – they might tend to accept research results that show what they expected and to reject those that they did not expect or hope for. In many cases, findings can be interpreted in different ways, and discussions between researchers and managers will help point to the best interpretations. Thus, managers and researchers must work together closely when interpreting research results, and both must share responsibility for the research process and resulting decisions.[35]

MAKING CONNECTIONS Linking the concepts

We've covered a lot of territory. Let's take a breather and see if you can apply the marketing research process you've just studied.

- What specific kinds of research can VisitScotland use to learn more about its customers' preferences and buying behaviours? Sketch out a brief research plan for VisitScotland's next project.

- Could you use the marketing research process to analyse your career opportunities and job possibilities? (Think of yourself as a 'product' and employers as potential 'customers'.) What would your research plan look like?

ANALYSING MARKETING INFORMATION

Information gathered in internal databases and through marketing intelligence and marketing research usually requires more analysis. And managers may need help applying the information to their marketing decisions. This help may include advanced statistical analysis to learn more about the relationships within a set of data. Such analysis allows managers to go beyond means and standard deviations in the data and to answer questions about markets, marketing activities and outcomes.

Information analysis might also involve a collection of analytical models that will help marketers make better decisions. Each model represents some real system, process or outcome. These models can help answer the questions of *what if* and *which is best*. Marketing academics and consultants have developed numerous models to help marketing managers make better marketing mix decisions, design sales territories and sales call plans, select sites for retail outlets, develop optimal advertising mixes, and forecast new-product sales.

Customer relationship management

The question of how best to analyse and use individual customer data presents special problems. Most companies are awash with information about their customers. In fact, smart companies capture information at every possible customer *touch point*. These touch points include customer purchases, sales force contacts, service and support calls, website visits, satisfaction surveys, credit and payment interactions, market research studies and increasingly social media postings – every contact between the customer and the company.

The trouble is that this information is usually scattered widely across the organisation. It is buried deep in the separate databases and records of different company departments. To overcome such problems, many companies are now turning to **customer relationship management (CRM)** to manage detailed information about individual customers and carefully manage customer touch points in order to maximise customer loyalty.

CRM first burst onto the scene in the early 2000s. Many companies rushed in, implementing overly ambitious CRM programmes that produced disappointing results and many failures. More recently, however, companies have been moving ahead more cautiously and implementing CRM systems that really work. A Gartner Group study found that 60 per cent of the businesses surveyed were planning to adopt or expand their use of CRM. European companies spend around $2bn a year on CRM software alone. It is estimated that US companies currently spend about $74bn a year on CRM systems from companies such as Siebel Systems, Oracle, Microsoft and SAS.[36]

CRM consists of sophisticated software and analytical tools that integrate customer information from all sources, analyse it in depth and apply the results to build stronger customer relationships. CRM integrates everything that a company's sales, service and marketing teams know about individual customers to provide a 360-degree view of the customer relationship.

CRM analysts develop *data warehouses* and use sophisticated *data mining* techniques to unearth the riches hidden in customer data. A data warehouse is a company-wide electronic database of finely detailed customer information that needs to be sifted through for gems. The purpose of a data warehouse is not just to gather information, but to pull it together into a central, accessible location. Then, once the data warehouse brings the data together, the company uses high-powered data mining techniques to sift through the mounds of data and dig out interesting findings about customers.

By using CRM to understand customers better, companies can potentially provide higher levels of customer service and develop deeper customer relationships. They can use CRM

Experian is expert at helping its clients understand and develop relationships with their customers

Source: Logo and image courtesy of Experian.

to pinpoint high-value customers, target them more effectively, cross-sell the company's products and create offers tailored to specific customer requirements. Consider the contents of your wallet:

> In amongst cards for membership to a gym or to a club, and right by your bank and credit cards do you have other pieces of plastic from shops – cards that are commonly known as 'loyalty cards'? This is a very bad name for them, but the cards have become a key tool into generating customer insight. The next time you pass through a till, consider the enormous amount of information that you hand over. Your name, your method of payment, the time of day, the specific shop you are purchasing a specific set of products and services from. If you used the same retailer for a prolonged period of time then imagine the detailed profile of your shopping and consumption habits that the data from that loyalty card draws. Retailers have become quite excited by the possibilities here, and many have invested heavily in database related technology. The rationale for this is that the establishment of a customer database allows more highly targeted marketing and promotional initiatives.
>
> Some customers are concerned at what they consider to be invasions of their privacy. Others are worried that they encourage over-spending – take this quote from a participant in a recent study – *'Everybody knows how we're spending our money these days. Big Brother is watching us all the time, isn't he?'*. Others are disappointed that firms take all this information but still don't manage to make effective use of it in their communications and offers. The lessons here are that if a firm intends to implement a 'loyalty scheme' it must ensure that scheme will obtain valuable data that the organisation is capable of managing, analysing and interpreting and that the best means of maintaining the strength and vitality of the scheme is to ensure that joining it gives customers access to a higher level of service and satisfaction.[37]

CRM benefits do not come without cost or risk, not only in collecting the original customer data, but also in maintaining and mining it. The most common CRM mistake is to view CRM only as a technology and software solution. But technology alone cannot build profitable customer relationships. 'CRM is not a technology solution – you can't achieve . . . improved customer relationships by simply slapping in some software,' says a CRM expert. Instead, CRM is just one part of an effective overall *customer relationship management strategy*. 'Focus on the *R*,' advises the expert. 'Remember, a relationship is what CRM is all about.'[38]

When it works, the benefits of CRM can far outweigh the costs and risks. Based on regular polls of its customers, Siebel Systems claims that customers using its CRM software report an average 16 per cent increase in revenues and 21 per cent increase in customer loyalty and staff efficiency. 'No question that companies are getting tremendous value out of this,' says a CRM consultant. 'Companies [are] looking for ways to bring disparate sources of customer information together, then get it to all the customer touch points.' The powerful new CRM techniques can unearth 'a wealth of information to target that customer, to hit their hot button'.[39]

DISTRIBUTING AND USING MARKETING INFORMATION

Marketing information has no value until it is used to make better marketing decisions. Thus, the MIS must make the information readily available to the managers and others who make marketing decisions or deal with customers. In some cases, this means providing managers with regular performance reports, intelligence updates, and reports on the results of research studies.

But marketing managers may also need information for special situations and on-the-spot decisions. For example, a sales manager having trouble with a large customer may want a summary of the account's sales and profitability over the past year. Or a retail store manager who has run out of a bestselling product may want to know the current inventory levels in the chain's other stores. Increasingly, therefore, information distribution involves entering information into databases and making it available in a timely, user-friendly way.

Many firms use a company *intranet* to facilitate this process. The intranet provides ready access to research information, stored reports, shared work documents, contact information for employees and other stakeholders, and more. For example, iGo (**www.igo.com**), a catalogue and web retailer, integrates incoming customer service calls with up-to-date database information about customers' web purchases and email enquiries. By accessing this information on the intranet while speaking with the customer, iGo's service representatives can get a well-rounded picture of each customer's purchasing history and previous contacts with the company.

In addition, companies are increasingly allowing key customers and value network members to access account, product and other data on demand through *extranets*. Suppliers, customers, resellers and select other network members may access a company's extranet to update their accounts, arrange purchases and check orders against inventories to improve customer service. For example, one insurance firm allows its 200 independent agents access to a web-based database of claim information covering 1 million customers. This allows the agents to avoid high-risk customers and to compare claim data with their own customer databases.

Thanks to modern technology, today's marketing managers can gain direct access to the information system at any time and from virtually any location. They can tap into the system while working at a home office, from a hotel room, or from a local restaurant through a wireless network – any place where they can turn on a laptop and link up. Such systems allow managers to get the information they need directly and quickly and to tailor it to their own needs. From just about anywhere, they can obtain information from company or outside databases, analyse it using statistical software, prepare reports and presentations, and communicate directly with others in the network.

MAKING CONNECTIONS   Linking the concepts

Let's stop here for a bit – think back and be certain that you've got the 'big picture' concerning MISs.

- What's the overall goal of an MIS? How are the individual components linked and what does each contribute? Take another look at Figure 4.1 – it provides a good organising framework for the entire chapter.

- Apply the MIS framework to VisitScotland (as described in the chapter opening story). What does VisitScotland appear to be doing well? What else could it be doing?

OTHER MARKETING INFORMATION CONSIDERATIONS

This section discusses marketing information in two special contexts: marketing research in small businesses and non-profit organisations, and international marketing research. Finally, we look at public policy and ethical issues in marketing research.

Marketing research in small businesses and non-profit organisations

Just like larger firms, small organisations need market information. Start-up businesses need information about their industries, competitors, potential customers and reactions to new market offers. Existing small businesses must track changes in customer needs and wants, reactions to new products and changes in the competitive environment.

Managers of small businesses and non-profit organisations often think that marketing research can be done only by experts in large companies with big research budgets. True, large-scale research studies are beyond the budgets of most small businesses. However, many of the marketing research techniques discussed in this chapter can also be used by smaller organisations in a less formal manner and at little or no expense. Managers of small businesses and non-profit organisations can obtain good marketing information – often for free – simply by *observing* things around them. For example, aspirant retailers can evaluate new locations by observing vehicle and pedestrian traffic. They can monitor competitor advertising by collecting ads from local media. They can evaluate their customer mix by recording how many and what kinds of customers shop in the store at different times. In addition, many small business managers routinely visit their rivals and socialise with competitors to gain insights – it might even be argued that working for an organisation of the type you hope to set up yourself is an extended form of ethnographic research!

Managers can conduct informal *surveys* using small convenience samples. The director of an art museum can learn what visitors think about new exhibits by conducting informal focus groups – inviting small groups to lunch and having discussions on topics of interest. Retail salespeople can talk with customers visiting the store. Hospital managers can interview patients. Restaurant managers might make random phone calls during quiet periods to interview consumers about where they eat out and what they think of various restaurants in the area.

Managers can also conduct their own simple *experiments*. For example, by changing the themes in regular fundraising mailshots and watching the results, a non-profit manager can find out much about which marketing strategies work best. By varying newspaper advertisements, a store manager can learn the effects of things such as ad size and position, price coupons and media used.

Small organisations can obtain most of the secondary data available to large businesses. In addition, many associations, local media, chambers of commerce and government agencies provide special help to small organisations. The European Small Business Alliance (**www.esba-europe.org**) offers hints and tips on marketing and other aspects of business specifically tailored for small organisations. Topics range from starting, financing and expanding a small business to ordering business cards. Other excellent web resources for small businesses include the European Council for Small Businesses and Entrepreneurship (**www.ecsb.org**) and the UK government support services for small businesses (see **https://www.gov.uk/starting-up-a-business**). Most European governments also offer resources to assist small businesses, for example Poland (**www.pfp.com.pl**).

The business sections at local libraries can also be a good source of information. Local newspapers often provide information on local shoppers and their buying patterns. Finally, small businesses can collect a considerable amount of information at very little cost on the Internet. They can scour competitor and customer websites and use Internet search engines to research specific companies and issues.

In summary, secondary data collection, observation, surveys and experiments can all be used effectively by small organisations with small budgets. Although these informal research methods are less complex and less costly, they must still be conducted carefully. Managers must think carefully about the objectives of the research, formulate questions in advance, recognise the biases introduced by smaller samples and less skilled researchers, and conduct the research systematically.[40]

International marketing research

International marketing researchers follow the same steps as domestic researchers, from defining the research problem and developing a research plan to interpreting and reporting the results. However, these researchers often face more and different problems. Whereas domestic researchers deal with fairly homogeneous markets within a single country, international researchers deal with diverse markets in many different countries. This is a particular problem in Europe where many companies also operate in surrounding nations as an act of necessity, especially if the home markets are in countries with a relatively small population, Belgium being a good example. These varied markets often differ greatly in their levels of economic development, cultures and customs, and buying patterns.

In many foreign markets, the international researcher may have a difficult time finding good secondary data – in Europe, these resources are very well developed in the West, but are still in development in former Soviet republics. Some of the largest international research services do operate in many countries. For example, ACNielsen Corporation (owned by VNU NV, the world's largest marketing research company) has offices in more than 100 countries. And 65 per cent of the revenues of the world's 25 largest marketing research firms come from outside their home countries.[41]

However, most research firms operate in only a relative handful of countries. Thus, even when secondary information is available, it must usually be obtained from many different sources on a country-by-country basis, making the information difficult to combine or compare.

Because of the scarcity of good secondary data, international researchers must often collect their own primary data. Here again, researchers face problems not found domestically. For example, they may find it difficult simply to develop good samples. European researchers can use current telephone directories, census data and any of several sources of socio-economic data to construct samples. However, such information is less freely available and often of a much lower quality in many countries. Reaching respondents is often not so easy in some parts of the world. Researchers in Albania cannot rely on telephone, Internet and mail data collection – most data collection is door to door and concentrated in three or four of the largest cities. In some countries, few people have phones or good Internet connections. For example, the UK has 522 fixed telephone lines per thousand of the population and 338 broadband connections per thousand, Romania has 220 telephone lines per thousand and 160 broadband connections per thousand, while Slovakia has only 180 telephone lines and 148 broadband connections per thousand people. In some countries, the postal system is notoriously unreliable. In Brazil, for instance, an estimated 30 per cent of the mail is never delivered. In many developing countries, poor roads and transportation systems make certain areas hard to reach, making personal interviews difficult and expensive.[42]

Cultural differences from country to country cause additional problems for international researchers. Language is the most obvious obstacle. For example, questionnaires must be prepared in one language and then translated into the language of each country researched. Responses then must be translated back into the original language for analysis and interpretation. This adds to research costs and increases the risks of error. This is also a particular problem in Europe, with many countries having more than one officially recognised language – such as Belgium, Spain and Switzerland.

Translating a questionnaire from one language to another is anything but easy. Many idioms, phrases and statements mean different things in different cultures. For example, as

Some of the largest research services firms have large international organisations. ACNielsen has offices in more than 100 countries, including Germany and Japan.

Source: Alamy Images/Webstream.

a Danish executive noted: 'Check this out by having a different translator put back into English what you've translated from English. You'll get the shock of your life. I remember [an example in which] "out of sight, out of mind" had become "invisible things are insane".'[43]

Consumers in different countries also vary in their attitudes towards marketing research. People in one country may be very willing to respond; in other countries, non-response can be a major problem. Customs in some countries may prohibit people from talking with strangers. In certain cultures, research questions often are considered too personal. For example, in many Latin American countries, people may feel embarrassed to talk with researchers about their choices of shampoo, deodorant, or other personal-care products. Similarly, in most Muslim countries, mixed-gender focus groups are taboo, as is videotaping female-only focus groups.

Even when respondents are *willing* to respond, they may not be *able* to because of high functional illiteracy rates. And middle-class people in developing countries often make false claims in order to appear well-off. For example, in a study of tea consumption in India, over 70 per cent of middle-income respondents claimed that they used one of several national brands. However, the researchers had good reason to doubt these results – more than 60 per cent of the tea sold in India is unbranded generic tea.

Despite these problems, the recent growth of international marketing has resulted in a rapid increase in the use of international marketing research. Global companies have little choice but to conduct such research. Although the costs and problems associated with international research may be high, the costs of not doing it – in terms of missed opportunities and mistakes – might be even higher. Once recognised, many of the problems associated with international marketing research can be overcome or avoided.

Public policy and ethics in marketing research

Most marketing research benefits both the sponsoring company and its consumers. Through marketing research, companies learn more about consumers' needs, resulting in more satisfying products and services and stronger customer relationships. However, the misuse of marketing research can also harm or annoy consumers. Two major public policy and ethics issues in marketing research are intrusions of consumer privacy and the misuse of research findings.

Intrusions of consumer privacy

Many consumers feel positive about marketing research and believe that it serves a useful purpose. Some actually enjoy being interviewed and giving their opinions. However, others strongly resent or even mistrust marketing research. A few consumers fear that researchers might use sophisticated techniques to probe our deepest feelings or peek over our shoulders and then use this knowledge to manipulate our buying. Or they worry that marketers are building huge databases full of personal information about customers without their full knowledge and consent. (See Marketing at Work 4.2.)

Other consumers may have been taken in by previous 'research surveys' that actually turned out to be attempts to sell them something and some consumers confuse legitimate marketing research studies with telemarketing efforts and say 'no' before the interviewer can even begin. Most, however, simply resent the intrusion. They dislike mail, telephone or web surveys that are too long or too personal or that interrupt them at inconvenient times. Increasing consumer resentment has become a major problem for the research industry.

The research industry is considering several options for responding to this problem. ESOMAR, the European-wide body representing market research professionals, has working groups studying the problem and is hoping to establish best practice in a bid to halt

Doubleplusgood market research

The term *social media* is one that has become very popular in recent years. What it means depends upon who you ask, but many would describe it in terms of software and applications like Facebook, YouTube, Flickr and Google+. Functionality varies, but users are able to post messages publicly to specific groups, upload files like pictures or video, and note or indicate approval of the latest lolcat mash-up.

Stories about social media abound in the news – the number of users in a network, the online petition influencing government policy, the social and economic implications of these networks and communities. One very popular category of story is based on estimates of market value of the leading social media companies. In 2011, Twitter was valued at $8bn, a figure about which many people were sceptical. Then in 2013 Twitter became a publicly owned company through a public offering of shares, and by the middle of 2014 it had a market capitalisation (stock market value) of around £18bn. These speculative values can go down as well as up. Myspace, which was bought in 2005 for $600m, was sold on in mid-2011 for just $35m.[44]

Many of the reasons that these companies are valued so highly are marketing related. Brand building, customer relations and advertising are all activities for which social media have a very significant impact – Facebook alone achieved advertising revenue of $4bn in 2012.[45] The same is true – doubly true – of market research. Why is this? Almost regardless of what the users think the social media platform is for – keeping in contact with friends, sharing holiday snaps, etc. – these are, when considered objectively, giant machines for harvesting and processing data about the millions of people that use them.

So, if you are a user of (say) Facebook, exactly what sort of information are you voluntarily handing over? Obviously your name, a contact email address, a list of friends and acquaintances which you helpfully build up. You probably comment on things that you did or did not enjoy – and many of those will be product or service related. You can even 'like' brands, companies or organisations that you feel you have an affinity with. Then, images of you and your friends in your native environment. You might take part in opinion polling or an online game. For all of these and more, your actions and contributions are watched, recorded and analysed. Other social media platforms, like Foursquare, even have you sharing your location and route.

This is a level of detail and precision that is extraordinary in market research terms. The volume and quality of data being handed over – free of charge no less – to these companies are staggering.

No less significant are the social and cultural implications of these machines. Many of these focus around the topics of privacy and ownership of data. Here is something you might not have thought about. When you upload an image of yourself to share with friends, to whom does it belong? You might assume that it belonged to you. You'd be wrong. That box you ticked a couple of years ago to indicate your agreement with the terms and conditions? That was you agreeing that the ownership of all content you entered or uploaded is transferred away from you and towards the company supporting the platform.

Facebook has an information section on privacy which you can view at https://www.facebook.com/help/?faq.[46] It explains, among other things, how Facebook:

- Receives data from your mobile or computer when you access its site and that this may include information such as your location, your IP address or the pages you access.

- Receives data from you when you chat with Facebook or check out someone else's profile etc.

- Receives data from photos or videos you upload to its site (such as where and when you took the photo, for example).

- Receives data from other sites you visit if they use its platform.

- Receives data from advertisers if you contact them via an advert they placed on Facebook, although the data is combined with other people's after 180 days in such a way that it will no longer be associated with you.

- Uses the data it has gathered to serve you adverts that might be of interest, and to suggest friends you may want to tag etc.

These companies know a lot about you, and one of the ways they make money is by packaging vast quantities of personal data together and selling it. The advertising revenue is so great because the people paying for the advertising feel they have a much better *customer insight* into the people that will see the advert. Certainly much better than the equivalent advert on TV. This is the essence of the how and why of market research – collecting and processing information about your markets so that you can make better and more accurate decisions. The value of Myspace collapsed because the number of users – and hence the flow of data – was rapidly dwindling.

Worried yet? Even if you are blasé about the transfer of data from you to commercial organisations, there are perhaps issues you might not have thought about. Google – which I think we can agree knows a thing or two about collecting and interpreting information – has what is called a chief information officer, who I think we can agree knows a lot about collecting and processing information even by the standards of Google's workforce. His name is Ben Fried, and he believes that trust is one of the cornerstones of success at Google; so employees are free to get hold of whatever technology they like, even the company bikes if they think it will help them do their job better.[47]

The title of this box, 'Doubleplusgood', comes from George Orwell's book *1984*, and Orwellian is a term some have associated with this combined technological and social trend. The most famous phrase from that book is, of course, 'Big Brother is watching you'.

Social media platforms are machines to harvest personal information from their users

Source: Alamy Images/Anatolii Babii.

To conclude – one example of how this affects you and your future. Microsoft recently surveyed HR managers globally, asking them what use they made of social media in assessing candidates for jobs with their organisation. Its findings? The vast majority of HR recruiters are including information obtained about you from social media sources in your evaluation.[48] Still think that photo of you in your underwear and wearing a stolen traffic cone was a good idea? Oops!

and perhaps even reverse this trend. The industry also has considered adopting broad standards, perhaps based on the International Chamber of Commerce's International Code of Marketing and Social Research Practice. This code outlines researchers' responsibilities to respondents and to the general public. For example, it says that researchers should make their names and addresses available to participants. It also bans companies from representing activities such as database compilation or sales and promotional pitches as research.[49]

Many companies have now appointed a 'chief privacy officer' (CPO), whose job is to safeguard the privacy of consumers who do business with the company. The chief privacy officer for Microsoft says that his job is to come up with data policies for the company to follow, make certain that every program the company creates enhances customer privacy, and inform and educate company employees about privacy issues and concerns. Some 2,000 US companies already employ such privacy chiefs and this trend is spreading across Europe.[50]

American Express, which deals with a considerable volume of consumer information, has long taken privacy issues seriously. The company developed a set of formal privacy principles in 1991, and in 1998 it became one of the first companies to post privacy policies on its website. This penchant for customer privacy led American Express to introduce new services that protect consumers' privacy when they use an American Express card to buy items online. American Express views privacy as a way to gain competitive advantage – as something that leads consumers to choose one company over another.[51]

In the end, if researchers provide value in exchange for information, customers will gladly provide the information. For example, **Amazon.com**'s customers do not mind if the firm builds a database of products they buy in order to provide future product recommendations. This saves time and provides value. Similarly, Bizrate users gladly complete surveys rating e-tail sites because they can view the overall ratings of others when making purchase decisions. The best approach is for researchers to ask only for the information they need, to use it responsibly to provide customer value, and to avoid sharing information without the customer's permission.

Misuse of research findings

Research studies can be powerful persuasion tools; companies often use study results as claims in their advertising and promotion. Today, however, many research studies appear to be little more than vehicles for pitching the sponsor's products. In fact, in some cases the research surveys appear to have been designed just to produce the intended effect. Few advertisers openly rig their research designs or blatantly misrepresent the findings; most abuses tend to be subtle 'stretches'. Consider the following examples:

> A study by Chrysler contends that Americans overwhelmingly prefer Chrysler to Toyota after test-driving both. However, the study included just 100 people in each of two tests. More importantly, none of the people surveyed owned a foreign car brand, so they appear to be favourably predisposed to US brands.
>
> A Black Flag survey asked: 'A roach disk . . . poisons a roach slowly. The dying roach returns to the nest and after it dies is eaten by other roaches. In turn these roaches become poisoned and die. How effective do you think this type of product would be in killing roaches?' Not surprisingly, 79 per cent said effective.
>
> A poll sponsored by the disposable nappy industry asked: 'It is estimated that disposable nappies account for less than 2 per cent of the trash in today's landfills. In contrast, beverage containers, third-class mail, and yard waste are estimated to account for about 21 per cent of the trash in landfills. Given this, in your opinion, would it be fair to ban disposable nappies?' Again, not surprisingly, 84 per cent said no.[52]

Thus, subtle manipulations of the study's sample or the choice or wording of questions can greatly affect the conclusions reached.

In other cases, so-called independent research studies are actually paid for by companies with an interest in the outcome. Small changes in study assumptions or in how results are interpreted can subtly affect the direction of the results. For example, at least four widely quoted studies compare the environmental effects of using disposable nappies with those of using cloth nappies. The two studies sponsored by the cloth nappy industry conclude that cloth nappies are more environmentally friendly. Not surprisingly, the other two studies, sponsored by the disposable nappy industry, conclude just the opposite. Yet both appear to be correct *given* the underlying assumptions used.

Recognising that surveys can be abused, several associations have developed codes of research ethics and standards of conduct. For example, the Council of American Survey Research Organizations (CASRO) Code of Standards and Ethics for Survey Research outlines researcher responsibilities to respondents, including confidentiality, privacy and avoidance of harassment. It also outlines major responsibilities in reporting results to clients and the public.[53] In the end, however, unethical or inappropriate actions cannot simply be regulated away. Each company must accept responsibility for policing the conduct and reporting of its own marketing research to protect consumers' best interests and its own.

THE JOURNEY YOU'VE TAKEN Reviewing the concepts

In the previous chapter we discussed the marketing environment. In this chapter we've continued our exploration of how marketers go about understanding the marketplace and consumers. We've studied tools used to gather and manage information that marketing managers and others can use to assess opportunities in the marketplace and the impact of a firm's marketing efforts. After this brief pause for rest and reflection, we'll move on again in the next chapter to take a closer look at the object of all of this activity – consumers and their buying behaviour.

In today's complex and rapidly changing marketplace, marketing managers need more and better information to make effective and timely decisions. This greater need for information has been matched by the explosion of information technologies for supplying information. Using today's new technologies, companies can now obtain great quantities of information, sometimes even too much. Yet marketers often complain that they lack enough of the *right* kind of information or have an excess of the *wrong* kind. In response, many companies are now studying their managers' information needs and designing information systems to help managers develop and manage market and customer information.

1 Explain the importance of information to the company and its understanding of the marketplace

The marketing process starts with a complete understanding of the marketplace and consumer needs and wants. Thus, the company needs sound information in order to produce superior value and satisfaction for customers. The company also requires information on competitors, resellers, and other actors and forces in the marketplace. Increasingly, marketers are viewing information not only as an input for making better decisions, but also as an important strategic asset and marketing tool.

2 Define the marketing information system and discuss its parts

The *marketing information system (MIS)* consists of people, equipment and procedures to gather, sort, analyse, evaluate and distribute needed, timely and accurate information to marketing decision makers. A well-designed information system begins and ends with users. The MIS first *assesses information needs*. It primarily serves the company's marketing and other managers, but it may also provide information to external partners. Then, the MIS *develops information* from internal databases, marketing

intelligence activities and marketing research. *Internal databases* provide information on the company's own operations and departments. Such data can be obtained quickly and cheaply but often needs to be adapted for marketing decisions. *Marketing intelligence* activities supply everyday information about developments in the external marketing environment. *Market research* consists of collecting information relevant to a specific marketing problem faced by the company. Lastly, the MIS *distributes information* gathered from these sources to the right managers in the right form and at the right time.

3 Outline the steps in the marketing research process

The first step in the marketing research process involves *defining the problem and setting the research objectives*, which may be exploratory, descriptive or causal research. The second step consists of *developing a research plan* for collecting data from primary and secondary sources. The third step calls for *implementing the marketing research plan* by gathering, processing and analysing the information. The fourth step consists of *interpreting and reporting the findings*. Additional information analysis helps marketing managers apply the information and provides them with sophisticated statistical procedures and models from which to develop more rigorous findings.

Both *internal and external* secondary data sources often provide information more quickly and at a lower cost than primary data sources, and they can sometimes yield information that a company cannot collect by itself. However, the needed information might not exist in secondary sources. Researchers must also evaluate secondary information to ensure that it is *relevant, accurate, current and impartial*. Primary research must also be evaluated for these features. Each primary data collection method – *observational, survey* and *experimental* – has its own advantages and disadvantages. Each of the various primary research contact methods – mail, telephone, personal interview and online – also has its own advantages and drawbacks. Similarly, each contact method has its pluses and minuses.

4 Explain how companies analyse and distribute marketing information

Information gathered in internal databases and through marketing intelligence and marketing research usually requires more analysis. This may include advanced statistical analysis or the application of analytical models that will help marketers make better decisions. To analyse individual customer data, many companies have now acquired or developed special software and analysis techniques – called customer relationship management (CRM) – that integrate, analyse and apply the mountains of individual customer data contained in their databases.

Marketing information has no value until it is used to make better marketing decisions. Thus, the MIS must make the information available to the managers and others who make marketing decisions or deal with customers. In some cases, this means providing regular reports and updates; in other cases, it means making non-routine information available for special situations and on-the-spot decisions. Many firms use company intranets and extranets to facilitate this process. Thanks to modern technology, today's marketing managers can gain direct access to the information system at any time and from virtually any location.

5 Discuss the special issues some marketing researchers face, including public policy and ethical issues

Some marketers face special marketing research situations, such as those conducting research in small business, non-profit or international situations. Marketing research can be conducted effectively by small businesses and non-profit organisations with limited budgets. International marketing researchers follow the same steps as domestic researchers but often face more and different problems. All organisations need to respond responsibly to major public policy and ethical issues surrounding marketing research, including issues of intrusions of consumer privacy and misuse of research findings.

NAVIGATING THE KEY TERMS

NOTES AND REFERENCES

1 Press releases – which are a form of secondary data themselves – for the Scottish Parliament can be found at **www.scotland.gov.uk/News/Releases**

2 The silo of Scottish government data made available to the public can be found at: **www.scotland.gov.uk/topics**

3 The homepage of the Scottish Tourism forum is at **www.stforum.co.uk**; all figures 2011.

4 The homepage of the World Tourism Organization is at **www.world-tourism.org**

5 Online, VisitScotland is divided into two components, one at **www.visitscotland.com** and the other at **www.visitscotland.org** – the former is for customers and the latter for the industry.

6 The German national tourist board has pages in English at **www.germany-tourism.co.uk**; the Greek equivalent is at **www.gnto.gr**; for information on the adaptation of advertising strategy by the Turkish national tourist board see 'Turkey Tourism calls $45m global ad review' by Matt Williams, 1 September 2011, at **www.brandrepublic.com**

7 Further information on the UK International Passenger Survey is available from **http://www.ons.gov.uk/ons/about-ons/get-involved/taking-part-in-a-survey/information-for-households/a-to-z-of-household-and-individual-surveys/international-passenger-survey/index.html**

8 Example news stories: **travel.nytimes.com//2006/12/17/travel/17heads.html** and **travel. nytimes.com/2006/04/23/travel/23going.html**, both accessed August 2011.

9 S. Pike, 'Tourism Destination Branding Complexity', *Journal of Product and Brand Management,* 14(4), 2005, pp. 258–9.

10 Euromonitor can be found online at **www.euromonitor.com**

11 Mintel is at **www.mintel.com**

12 The homepage for the UNTWO can be found at **www.unwto.org**

13 Reports of this nature for the Scottish Tourism Industry can be found at **www.scotex-change.net/**

14 Regrettably this report is no longer available online, but **www.visitscotland.org** has several similar documents available for download.

15 See Blaine Mathieu, 'Turn Down the Noise: Tips for Managing Information Overload', *Information Management,* 30 August 2012; Leslie Langnau, 'Drowning in Data', *Material Handling Management,* December 2003, p. 22; Rick Mullin, 'Dealing with Information Overload', *Chemical and Engineering News,* 22 March 2004, p. 19; Evan Schuman, 'At Wal-Mart, World's Largest Retail Data Warehouse Gets Larger', *eWeek,* 13 October 2004, accessed at **www.eweek.com**; and Daniel Lyons, 'Too Much Information', *Forbes,* 13 December 2004, pp. 110–15.

16 See Philip Kotler, *Marketing Insights from A to Z* (Hoboken, NJ: Wiley, 2003), pp. 80–2.

17 Elizabeth Rigby, 'Eyes in the Till', *Financial Times,* 11 November 2006.

18 M.J. Harker, 'The Customer Perspective on Loyalty Cards', Academy of Marketing Conference, University of Gloucestershire, July 2004.

19 Andy Serwer, 'P&G's Covert Operation', *Fortune,* 17 September 2001, pp. 42–4. See also Andrew Crane, 'In the Company of Spies: When Competitive Intelligence Gathering Becomes Industrial Espionage', *Business Horizons,* May–June 2005, pp. 233ff.

20 Fred Vogelstein and Peter Lewis, 'Search and Destroy', *Fortune,* 2 May 2005.

21 James Curtis, 'Behind Enemy Lines', *Marketing,* 21 May 2001, pp. 28–9. See also George Chidi, 'Confessions of a Corporate Spy', *Inc.,* 2 February 2013, available at **http://www.inc .com/magazine/201302/george-chidi/confessions-of-a-corporate-spy.html**, accessed May 2014; Brian Caufield, 'Know Your Enemy', *Business 2.0,* June 2004, p. 89; and Michael Fielding, 'Damage Control: Firms Must Plan for Counterintelligence', *Marketing News,* 15 September 2004, pp. 19–20.

22 See, for example, A. Wilson, *Marketing Research: An Integrated Approach* (London: FT Prentice Hall, 2011); or R. Kent, *Marketing Research: Approaches, Methods and Applications in Europe* (London: Thomson, 2006).

23 ACNielsen press release: **www2.acnielsen.com/**, accessed August 2011.

24 For more on research firms that supply marketing information, see Jack Honomichl, 'Honomichl 50', special section, *Marketing News,* 15 June 2004, pp. H1–55. Other information from: **www.infores.com/public/global/content/consumernetwork/householdpanel. htm** and **http://www.yankelovich.com/monitor_new.asp**, July 2005.

25 D. Hanson and M. Grimmer, 'The Mix of Qualitative and Quantitative Research in Major Marketing Journals, 1993–2002', *European Journal of Marketing,* 41(1/2), 2007, pp. 58–70.

26 E. Gummesson, 'Access to Reality: Observations on Observational Methods', *Qualitative Market Research,* 10(2), 2007, pp. 130–4.

27 Sources for this example: 'Fisher Price Play Lab Celebrates 50 Years of Joy Filled Discovery', Fisher-Price press release available at **http://www.fisher-price.com/media/assets/ press_releases/Play%20Lab%2050th%20Press%20Release_FINAL.pdf**, accessed may 2014; Douglas McGray, 'Babes in R&D Toyland', *Fast Company,* December 2002, p. 46.

28 Tracy Harwood and Martin Jones, 'Mobile Eye-Tracking in Retail Research', in *Current Trends in Eye-Tracking Research*, ed. Mike Horsley, Matt Eliot, Bruce Allen Knight and Ronan Reilly, (Berlin: Springer), pp. 183–99.

29 Adapted from Linda Tischler, 'Every Move You Make', *Fast Company*, April 2004, pp. 73–5.

30 C. Nancarrow, A. Barker and L.T. Wright, 'Engaging the right mindset in qualitative marketing research', *Marketing Intelligence and Planning*, 19(4), 2001, pp. 236–44.

31 Ray Poynter, *The Handbook of Online and Social Media Research: Tools and Techniques for Market Researchers* (Chichester: Wiley, 2010); Alan Wilson and Nial Laskey, 'Internet Based Marketing Research: A Serious Alternative to Traditional Research Methods', *Marketing Intelligence and Planning*, 21(2), 2003, pp. 79–84.

32 This and other examples and quotes in this section, unless otherwise noted, are from 'Market Trends: Online Research Growing', accessed at **www.greenfieldcentral.com/ research_solutions/rsrch_solns_main.htm**, June 2003; Noah Shachtman, 'Web Enhanced Market Research', *Advertising Age*, 18 June 2001, p. T18; 'Cybersurveys Come of Age', *Marketing Research*, Spring 2003, pp. 32–7; Richard Lee, 'Stamford, Conn.-Based Market Research Firm Able to Reach Millions', *Knight Ridder Tribune Business News*, 6 May 2004, p. 1. See also Catherine Arnold, 'Not Done Net', *Marketing News*, April 2004, p. 17; and Richard Kottler, 'Eight Tips Offer Best Practices for Online MR', *Marketing News*, 1 April 2005, pp. 24–5.

33 From **www.internetworldstats.com/**; you can navigate to continent and then nation.

34 For more on Internet privacy, see James R. Hagerty and Dennis K. Berman, 'Caught in the Net: New Battleground over Web Privacy', *Wall Street Journal*, 27 August 2004, p. A1; 'The Spies in Your Computer', *Wall Street Journal*, 18 February 2004, p. A18; Susan Llewelyn Leach, 'Privacy Lost with the Touch of a Keystroke?', *Christian Science Monitor*, 10 November 2004, p. 15; and Alan R. Peslak, 'Internet Privacy Policies', *Information Resources Management Journal*, January–March 2005, pp. 29ff.

35 For a good discussion, see Deborah L. Vence, 'Better! Faster! Cheaper! Pick Any Three. That's Not a Joke', *Marketing News*, 1 February 2004, pp. 1, 31–2.

36 For European statistics see **www.computerwire.com/**; for US information, refer to David Harding, David Chiefetz, Scott DeAngelo and Elizabeth Ziegler, 'CRM's Silver Lining', *Marketing Management*, March–April 2004, pp. 27–32; and Ellen Neuborne, 'A Second Act of CRM', *Inc.*, March 2005, p. 40.

37 For a deeper exploration of this topic, see R. Christy, G. Oliver and J. Penn (1996) 'Relationship Marketing in Consumer Markets', *Journal of Marketing Management*, 12. pp. 175–87; L. O'Malley, and C. Tynan (2000) 'Relationship Marketing in Consumer Markets: Rhetoric or Reality', *European Journal of Marketing*, 34(7): 797–815; S. Sopanen (1996) 'Customer Loyalty Schemes in Retailing Across Europe', Templeton College, Oxford.

38 Michael Krauss, 'At Many Firms, Technology Obscures CRM', *Marketing News*, 18 March 2002, p. 5. See also Darrell K. Rigby and Dianne Ledingham, 'CRM Done Right', *Harvard Business Review*, November 2004, p. 129; and Barton Goldenberg, 'Let's Keep to the High Road', *CRM Magazine*, March 2005, p. 22.

39 See Adrian Payne and Penny Frow, *Strategic Customer Management: Integrating Relationship Management and CRM* (Cambridge: Cambridge University Press, 2013); Robert McLuhan, 'How to Reap the Benefits of CRM', *Marketing*, 24 May 2001, p. 35; Stewart Deck, 'Data Mining', *Computerworld*, 29 March 1999, p. 76; Jason Compton, 'CRM Gets Real', *Customer Relationship Management*, May 2004, pp. 11–12; and Neuborne, 'A Second Act of CRM', p. 40.

40 For some good advice on conducting market research in a small business, see 'Marketing Research . . . Basics 101', accessed at **https://www.sba.gov/content/marketing-101-basics**,

December 2014; and 'Researching Your Market', US Small Business Administration, accessed at **www.sba.gov/library/pubs/mt-8.doc**, June 2005.

41 Jack Honomichl, 'Despite Acquisitions, Firms' Revenue Dips', *Marketing News,* 13 August 2004, pp. H3–27; and the ACNielsen International Research website, accessed at **www.acnielsen.com/services/ir/**, July 2005.

42 Phone, PC and other country media statistics are from **www.nationmaster.com**, accessed May 2014.

43 Subhash C. Jain, *International Marketing Management,* 3rd edn (Boston, MA: PWS-Kent, 1990), p. 338. See also Debra L. Vence, 'Leave It to the Experts', *Marketing News,* 28 April 2003, p. 37.

44 A summary of the life history of Myspace, and analysis of the reasons behind the collapse in value, are available in the story by Andy Fixmer at **www.businessweek.com/news/2011-06-29/news-corp-calls-quits-on-myspace-with-specific-media-sale.html**, accessed August 2011.

45 A full report on revenue streams for social media platforms is available at great expense from the eMarketer website. A summary is free to view at **http://www.emarketer.com/Corporate/Coverage\#/results/1296/report**, December 2014.

46 Facebook provides extensive information on privacy related topics. This is continually updated as legislation and technology evolve. The information given here is based on data found at **https://www.facebook.com/help/?faq**, accessed May 2014.

47 **http://blogs.wsj.com/cio/2012/05/31/google-cio-runs-it-on-trust-and-transparency/**, accessed May 2014.

48 The report covers a great many issues on or about privacy and can be obtained free from **www.microsoft.com/privacy/**, accessed August 2011.

49 'ICC/ESOMAR International Code of Marketing and Social Research Practice', accessed at **http://www.esomar.org/uploads/public/knowledge-and-standards/codes-and-guidelines/ESOMAR_ICC-ESOMAR_Code_English.pdf**, December 2014. See also 'Respondent Bill of Rights,' accessed at **http://www.marketingresearch.org/respondent-bill-of-rights**, December 2014.

50 Catherine Siskos, 'In the Service of Guarding Secrets', *Kiplinger's Personal Finance,* February 2003, p. 26; John Schwartz, 'Chief Privacy Officers Forge Evolving Corporate Roles', *New York Times,* 12 February 2001, p. C1; Steve Ulfelder, 'CPOs: Hot or Not?', *Computerworld,* 15 March 2004, p. 40; and Bob Evans, 'Protecting Consumer Data Is Good Business', *InformationWeek,* 9 May 2005, p. 82.

51 Schwartz, 'Chief Privacy Officers Forge Evolving Corporate Roles', p. C1.

52 Cynthia Crossen, 'Studies Galore Support Products and Positions, But Are They Reliable?', *Wall Street Journal,* 14 November 1991, pp. A1, A9. Also see Allan J. Kimmel, 'Deception in Marketing Research and Practice: An Introduction', *Psychology and Marketing,* July 2001, pp. 657–61; and Alvin C. Burns and Ronald F. Bush, *Marketing Research* (Upper Saddle River, NJ: Prentice Hall, 2005), pp. 63–75.

53 Information accessed at **www.casro.org**, August 2011.

CHAPTER 5
CONSUMER AND BUSINESS BUYER BEHAVIOUR

AFTER STUDYING THIS CHAPTER, YOU SHOULD BE ABLE TO

- understand the consumer market and the major factors that influence consumer buyer behaviour
- identify and discuss the stages in the buyer decision process
- describe the adoption and diffusion process for new products
- define the business market and identify the major factors that influence business buyer behaviour
- list and define the steps in the business buying decision process

THE WAY AHEAD
Previewing the concepts

In the previous chapter, you studied how marketers obtain, analyse and use information to understand the marketplace and to assess marketing programmes. In this chapter, you'll continue your marketing journey with a closer look at the most important element of the marketplace – customers. The aim of marketing is to affect how customers think about and behave towards the organisation and its marketing offers. To affect the *whats*, *whens* and *hows* of buying behaviour marketers must first understand the *whys*. We look first at *final consumer* buying influences and processes and then at the buying behaviour of *business customers*. You'll see that understanding buying behaviour is an essential but very difficult task.

Our first point of interest is the huge Airbus A380, an aircraft that is designed to carry a lot of passengers, or a lot of freight, over vast distances. There is little doubt that the A380 is a brilliant conception, delivering not just massive carrying capacity and state-of-the-art technology, but also environmental benefits such as increased fuel efficiency and lower noise. But what is going to make or break the commercial success of this aircraft are the buying decisions made by airline executives; those buying decisions, in turn, are driven by the buying decisions of their customers. Let's take a look at what lies behind all of those important decisions.

AIRBUS A380

George S. Low, Associate Professor of Marketing, M.J. Neeley School of Business, Texas Christian University, USA

Marketing strategy situation

Airbus is one of the leading aircraft man-ufacturers in the global aircraft industry. The newest addition to its aircraft product line is the A380, an extremely large, two-floor aircraft that can be used as either a passenger or freight aircraft. Development of this project began in late 2000, with production beginning in early 2002. It was expected that the A380 would be ready for delivery by 2007; however, starting in 2005 delays began to occur because of manufacturing problems. Three delays occurred, and the delivery date was pushed back to 2010. These production delays have resulted in an expected $6bn loss in earnings along with

Source: Alamy Images/Antony Nettle.

a struggle to keep customers on board; FedEx has already pulled out of a deal for 10 A380s and bought Boeing's 777 instead. Airbus's top salesman, John Leahy, has responded to these delays by renegotiating contracts and attempt-ing to keep customers from bailing out like FedEx did. His strategy is to persuade customers to take discounts on future orders as opposed to the cash compensation they were originally expecting. Airbus knew there was risk involved when it came up with the plans for the A380, but it was not prepared for the delays, the loss in earnings, or the strain on the company's reputation.

Company background

Airbus is part of the Airbus Group (formerly the European Aeronautic Defence & Space Co., EADS). Airbus Group decided to invest in an organisation that could rival US aerospace giants, such as Boeing, and so created Airbus – the European equivalent. Airbus is based in France, but has offices throughout Europe and the USA, and deals with most of its costs in euros and sterling. The main mission of Airbus is to 'meet the needs of airlines and operators by producing the most modern and compre-hensive aircraft family on the market, complemented by the highest standard of product support'. Airbus remains environmentally conscious and continues to work towards building quieter and more fuel-efficient aircraft. The company has a good reputation in the minds of the

public but also has the reputation of being very politically oriented. Airbus is sometimes thought of as succeeding thanks to public subsidies, but not being a very robust commercial operation.

The global aviation industry is extremely cut-throat, so introducing any new product is risky, but there is a constant attempt to develop newer aircraft with bet-ter technology. At the same time, both passenger and freight air traffic are expected to grow over the next 10 years. The hope is that the A380, because of its very large capacity, will enable a growth in air journeys by both people and freight while restricting growth in the total number of flights. However, there is, of course, risk involved in the launching of the A380, since it is just as likely that no change in the industry will occur and the 'A380 is a very large aircraft for a very small market'.

Customers

The main customers that Airbus is focused on are the major airlines, paying passengers and freight customers. The large aircraft are able to provide something for eve-ryone since they can carry more cargo, but are also state of the art when it comes to luxury and style for high-pay-ing travellers. Some of the companies that have already ordered A380s are FedEx, UPS, Emirates, Thai Airways and Singapore Airlines. Singapore Airlines was first in line for deliveries of the aircraft, while FedEx was angered by the delays and pulled out of the deal.

There is a close relationship between the decisions made by operators of passenger airlines about which aircraft to buy and the decisions made by the airline operators' customers about which airline they will fly with. A lot of people are involved in making the decision about which aircraft an airline should buy. It is a long-term decision that will affect the future of the company. Airline engineers analyse the aircraft from a number of angles: operating efficiency, safety, maintenance costs and so on. Airline accountants focus on the lifetime costs associated with owning and operating the aircraft. The purchase price of an aircraft, despite being a very large sum of money, is only one part of the total costs involved in owning and operating the aircraft. Airline marketers are interested in how their customers will respond to the new aircraft. This, of course, involves understanding their own customers' behaviour, with a key focus on the different market segments that they serve. Passengers in first class pay top prices and expect the very best in terms of comfort and service. Business-class passengers want somewhere to get on with their work and maybe sleep in reasonable comfort to get ready for an important meeting. The rest of the passengers (i.e. most of us who ever fly) would like a pleasant journey, but mainly just want to arrive safely, on time and with their luggage intact. Before making the decision about which type of aircraft to buy, the airline operator analyses the extent to which each competing product can deliver the features and benefits that it wants to provide to its customers. Of course, different airlines themselves have different priorities: some are luxury airlines offering the best of everything, while others are budget airlines that aim to get you to your destination safely and on time but with a minimum of additional services. Consequently, different airlines, wishing to offer their customers different types of experience, will have different buying criteria when considering which aircraft to buy.

As well as passenger airlines, Airbus wants to sell the A380 to freight operators, like UPS and FedEx. These operators do not have to worry about the needs of passengers, but that does not make them any less demanding. The aircraft is one of the primary tools that these companies use to deliver on their promises to their customers. They sell their services to both businesses and consumers. Although you might only want to send a package across the Atlantic once a year (to your brother in the USA every Christmas), there are plenty of business customers that are sending lots of packages across the ocean every day. So the freight operators have to deliver a reliable, secure, high-speed service to both business customers and private consumers, and they know that the right choice of aircraft is vital if they are going to make this happen.

The A380

Airbus chose a double-deck configuration because the structure required is significantly lighter than a single deck one with twin tails. The design of the A380 was meant to be able to use existing airport infrastructure with minor modifications to the airports, and direct operating costs per seat of 15–20 per cent less than those for the 747-400. The A380 also has more floor space and more seating than the previous largest aircraft. The main cabin is about 20 inches (50 cm) wider than the Boeing 747's, and has economy passengers seated ten across, while the upper-deck economy class has eight seats across. Airbus wants to provide customers with wider seats and aisles for greater comfort. The name 380 was chosen because the 8 represents the cross-section of the twin decks. The wings are also quite long, almost 20 per cent longer than the 747's; even so, they are flexible and able to bend almost 4 metres during take-off and landing.

The innovative technology can be seen first by the pilots in the cockpit. The electronics include an environmental surveillance system which integrates weather radar, traffic alert and collision avoidance and a ground-proximity warning system. This allows pilots to see easily what type of weather they are flying into as well as what the weather will be in the next couple of hours. The technology also allows pilots to locate other aircraft easily and avoid any potential accidents, making the A380 safer for both customers and cargo. The ground-proximity system provides another safety feature as it makes landing easier for the pilots. Additionally, the A380 uses new technology in an attempt to have a larger range, lower fuel burn and emissions, and less noise. Airbus says it is more fuel efficient than a car – and it averages about 90.6 mpg (39 km per litre) per passenger.

Another luxury from the A380 is the low noise. The four huge Rolls-Royce engines emit little more than a low hum, even during take-off when engine noise is usually most noticeable. Landing is also quiet – the landing gear can barely be heard as it descends. It is easy to talk to passengers across the aisle and in adjoining rows without raising your voice. This provides the customers with a pleasant voyage as there is no annoying engine noise and conversation is not disrupted by turbulence or loud landings and take-offs. Sounds like a great product! But whether or not it succeeds depends on a whole range of buying decisions. Will airline operators believe that the A380 is the best aircraft to buy to serve their customers? Will freight operators be persuaded that it is the best product to meet the demands of their business and private customers? And, perhaps most important, will air passengers decide that they want to fly with operators who use the A380, because it makes their journeys that little bit more pleasant?

Sources: Doris Burke, 'Anatomy of an A380', *Fortune*, 5 March 2007, 155(4), pp. 101–8; Nelson D. Schwartz, 'Big Plane, Big Problems', *Fortune*, 5 March 2007, 155(4), pp. 95–8; Airbus Corporation website, http://www.airbus.com/en/corporate/ethics/ mission_values/; 'Airbus' New Flight Plan', *Wall Street Journal*, 9 March 2007; Rod Stone, 'Airbus Parent EADS Appoints Rudiger Grube as Co-Chairman', *Wall Street Journal*, 5 April 2007; Andrew Lee, 'The A380 is a Gamble Worth Taking', *The Engineer*, 10 February 2005; 'Airbus A380 Completes Test Flight', *BBC News*, 27 April 2005; Robert Wall, 'Schedule UPSet', *Aviation Week & Space Technology*, 5 March 2007, 166(10); 'The Airbus 380', Airliners.net, 9 April 2007, http://www.airliners.net/info/stats.main?id=29; Noelle Knox, 'A380 Makes Massive Debut', *USA Today*, 19 January 2005; 'Airbus A380: A Whale of a Plane!', *BBC News*, 10 May 2005; Carol Matlock, 'Aloft on Airbus' Giant New A380', BusinessWeek Online, 8 February 2007; Greg Lindsay, 'Airbust? A380 Hits Marketing Turbulence', *Advertising Age*, 2 April 2007, 78(14); Marc Graser, 'The Nonproduct Placement that Boosts Airbus', *Advertising Age*, 9 May 2005; Barbara Peterson, 'Airbus A380: Taking the Largest Passenger Jet for a Test Drive', *Popular Mechanics*, 22 March 2007, http://www.popularmechanics.com/bolgs/science_news/4213543.html.

The Airbus A380 example shows that many different factors affect business and consumer buying behaviour. Buying behaviour is never simple, yet understanding it is the essential task of marketing management. First we explore the dynamics of the consumer market and consumer buyer behaviour. We then examine business markets and the business buying process.

CONSUMER MARKETS AND CONSUMER BUYER BEHAVIOUR

Consumer buyer behaviour refers to the buying behaviour of final consumers – individuals and households who buy goods and services for personal consumption. All of these final consumers combine to make up the **consumer market**. The EU consumer market consists of more than 500 million people who consume many trillions of euros' worth of goods and services each year, making it one of the most attractive consumer markets in the world. The world consumer market consists of more than 7.1 *billion* people.[1]

Consumers around the world vary tremendously in age, income, education level and tastes. They also buy an incredible variety of goods and services. The ways in which these diverse consumers connect with each other and with other elements of the world around them influence their choices among various products, services and companies. Here we examine the fascinating array of factors that affect consumer behaviour.

Model of consumer behaviour

Consumers make many buying decisions every day. Most large companies research consumer buying decisions in great detail to answer questions about what consumers buy, where they buy, how and how much they buy, when they buy and why they buy. Marketers can study actual consumer purchases to find out what they buy, where and how much. But learning about the *whys* of consumer buying behaviour is not so easy – the answers are often locked deep within the consumer's head.

Penetrating the interior of the consumer's mind is no easy task. Often, consumers themselves do not know exactly what influences their purchases. 'Ninety-five per cent of the thought, emotion, and learning [that drive our purchases] occur in the unconscious mind – that is, without our awareness,' notes one consumer behaviour expert.[2]

The central question for marketers is: how do consumers respond to various marketing efforts the company might use? The starting point is the stimulus–response model of buyer behaviour shown in Figure 5.1. This figure shows that marketing and other stimuli enter the consumer's 'black box' and produce certain responses. Marketers must work out what is in the buyer's black box.

At the most basic level marketing stimuli consist of the 'marketing mix': product, price, place and promotion for goods, with the addition of people, physical evidence and process

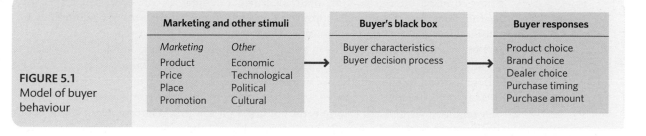

FIGURE 5.1
Model of buyer behaviour

for service products. Other stimuli include major forces and events in the buyer's environment: economic, technological, political and cultural. All these inputs enter the buyer's mind where they are turned into a set of observable buyer responses: product choice, brand choice, dealer choice, purchase timing and purchase amount.

The marketer wants to understand how the stimuli are changed into responses inside the consumer's mind. There are two components: first, the buyer's characteristics influence how he or she perceives and reacts to the stimuli; second, the buyer's decision process itself affects the buyer's behaviour. We look first at buyer characteristics as they affect buying behaviour and then discuss the buyer decision process.

Characteristics affecting consumer behaviour

Consumer purchases are influenced strongly by cultural, social, personal and psychological characteristics, as shown in Figure 5.2. For the most part, marketers cannot control such factors, but they must take them into account.

Cultural factors

Cultural factors exert a broad and deep influence on consumer behaviour. The marketer needs to understand the role played by the buyer's *culture*, *subculture* and *social class*.

Culture

Culture is the most basic cause of a person's wants and behaviour. Human behaviour is largely learned. Growing up in a society, a child learns basic values, perceptions, wants and behaviours from the family and other important institutions. For example, the former

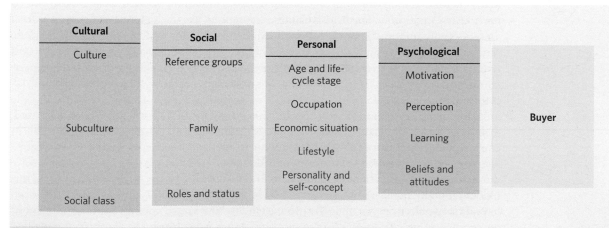

FIGURE 5.2
Factors influencing consumer behaviour

Prime Minister of the UK, Tony Blair, identified a number of core British values: creativity, tolerance, openness, adaptability, work and self-improvement, strong communities and families, fair play, rights and responsibilities, and an outward-looking approach to the world (no sniggering at the back!). Every group or society has a culture, and cultural influences on buying behaviour may vary greatly from country to country. Failure to adjust to these differences can result in ineffective marketing or embarrassing mistakes.

Marketers are always trying to spot *cultural shifts* in order to discover new products that might be wanted. For example, the cultural shift towards greater concern about health and fitness has created a huge industry for health and fitness services, exercise equipment and clothing, more natural foods and a variety of diets. The shift towards informality has resulted in more demand for casual clothing and simpler home furnishings.

Subculture

Each culture contains smaller **subcultures**, or groups of people with shared value systems based on common life experiences and situations. Subcultures include nationalities, religions, racial groups and geographic regions. Many subcultures make up important market segments, and marketers often design products and marketing programmes tailored to their needs. Ethnic minorities are an example of subculture groups. It is estimated that there are 5.5 million ethnic minority consumers in the UK, and the value of the ethnic minority market as a whole is estimated to be £12bn a year.[3] The UK has seen several waves of immigration during the last 60 years, including migrants from the Republic of Ireland, the Caribbean, the Indian subcontinent, Africa, Cyprus and Hong Kong. A new wave of immigration from Eastern Europe followed the expansion in 2004 and 2007. Several ethnic minority groups tend to have more children than the white indigenous population, making them an important target market for baby products companies and for any company that is targeting younger consumers. The ethnic minority market in the UK has a younger age structure than the indigenous population. For example, the 2011 Census showed that while 18 per cent of the White British population was aged over 65, this proportion was much smaller for members of ethnic minority groups, at 6 per cent of the Chinese ethnic group, and only 2 per cent of the Black African group.

In geographical terms, ethnic minority groups in the UK are heavily concentrated in the major cities of England, and nearly half live in Greater London. The high geographical concentration makes it easier to devise targeted marketing strategies for ethnic minority groups. However, while there are specialist ethnic minority media (such as radio stations, TV stations and newspapers) in the UK, they are nowhere near as well developed as in the USA.

The consumer buying behaviour of ethnic minority groups in the UK is influenced by many factors, among which income levels, religion and family structure can be considered particularly important. The British Chinese community has the highest average income level among ethnic minority groups, followed by African–Asians and by Indians. While these groups have relatively high average incomes, other ethnic groups such as the Pakistani and Bangladeshi communities have comparatively low average incomes. For many members of ethnic minority groups their religion is very important. The great majority of British Pakistanis and British Bangladeshis are Muslim, most white and Afro-Caribbean British people are Christian, while among the British Indian community several religions are represented, including Islam, Christianity, Hinduism and Sikhism. Religion can play an important role in consumer decisions. For example, Muslims are forbidden to eat certain foods or to consume alcohol, and may require specifically designed financial services products that do not involve the payment of interest (many Islamic scholars consider that interest is *haram*, meaning forbidden). Finally, family structures vary considerably between ethnic groups. Since they often have more children, ethnic minority groups tend to have larger families than the indigenous white community. Additionally, among some Asian subcultures the traditional extended family, where multiple generations live together under the same roof, still exists, although this structure seems to be in decline among British Asians.

Lloyds is offering services designed to meet the specific needs of people of the Islamic faith

Source: http://www.lloydsbank .com/current-accounts/ islamic-account.asp

Having identified a gap in the market for financial services aimed at the large Muslim minority in the UK, Lloyds Bank launched a range of sharia (Islamic law) approved financial services, including an Islamic current account and a sharia-approved home finance service (search Lloyds Islamic Account). Muslims signing up to any of these products could rest assured that their money would always be handled in accordance with sharia. The money that account holders placed with the bank would not be used for any interest-based business activities. In order to reassure Muslim customers of the integrity of the service, Lloyds recruited a committee of religious and legal advisers of the Islamic faith.

The worldwide population of people aged over 60 is growing faster than any other age group, and is expected to double to around 1.2 billion by 2025. Although other countries are also ageing, European countries are ageing faster than those of any other continent. By 2050 it is estimated that 35 per cent of Europe's population will be aged over 60. In the longer term the ageing population represents a considerable public policy challenge, since there will be fewer workers and more retired people. Major efforts by both governments and private firms are going into the promotion of pension plans to persuade younger people that they need to start saving early for retirement. For the moment, however, mature consumers are better off financially than are younger consumer groups. Because mature consumers have more time and money, they are an ideal market for exotic travel, restaurants, high-tech home entertainment products, leisure goods and services, designer furniture and fashions, financial services and healthcare services.[4]

Their desire to look as young as they feel also makes more mature consumers good candidates for cosmetics and personal-care products, health foods, fitness products and other items that combat the effects of ageing. The best strategy is to appeal to their active, multidimensional lives. For example, Kellogg's aired a TV spot for All-Bran cereal in which individuals ranging in age from 53 to 81 are featured playing ice hockey, water skiing, jumping hurdles and playing baseball, all to the tune of 'Wild Thing'. Meanwhile, Nintendo has been targeting older individuals who want to keep their minds sharp with its Dr. Kawashima's Brain Training software for the Nintendo DS.[5]

Social class

Almost every society has some form of social class structure. **Social classes** are society's relatively permanent and ordered divisions whose members share similar values, interests and behaviours. Social scientists have identified the 10 European social classes shown in Table 5.1.

Social class is not determined by a single factor, such as income, but is measured as a combination of occupation, income, education, wealth and other variables. In some social systems, members of different classes are reared for certain roles and cannot change their social positions. In Europe, however, the lines between social classes are not fixed and rigid; people can move to a higher social class or drop into a lower one. Marketers are interested in social class because people within a given social class tend to exhibit similar buying behaviour. Social classes show distinct product and brand preferences in areas such as clothing, home furnishings, leisure activity and cars.

Social factors

A consumer's behaviour is also influenced by social factors, such as the consumer's *small groups*, *family* and *social roles* and *status*.

Groups

A person's behaviour is influenced by many small **groups**. Groups that have a direct influence and to which a person belongs are called membership groups. In contrast, reference groups serve as direct (face-to-face) or indirect points of comparison or reference in forming a person's attitudes or behaviour. People are often influenced by reference groups to which they do not belong. For example, an aspirational group is one to which the individual wishes to belong, as when a young boy hopes someday to emulate Cristiano Ronaldo and play football for Portugal and for great club sides like Real Madrid and Manchester United.

Marketers try to identify the reference groups of their target markets. Reference groups expose a person to new behaviours and lifestyles, influence the person's attitudes and

TABLE 5.1 The European socio-economic classification

	ESeC class	Common term	Employment regulation
1	Large employers, higher grade professional, administrative and managerial occupations	Higher salariat	Service relationship
2	Lower grade professional, administrative and managerial occupations and higher grade technician and supervisory occupations	Lower salariat	Service relationship (modified)
3	Intermediate occupations	Higher grade white-collar workers	Mixed
4	Small employer and self-employed occupations (excl. agriculture etc.)	Petit bourgeoisie or independents	–
5	Self-employed occupations (agriculture etc.)	Petit bourgeoisie or independents	–
6	Lower supervisory and lower technician occupations	Higher grade blue-collar workers	Mixed
7	Lower services, sales and clerical occupations	Lower grade white-collar workers	Labour contract (modified)
8	Lower technical occupations	Skilled workers	Labour contract (modified)
9	Routine occupations	Semi- and non-skilled workers	Labour contract
10	Never worked and long-term unemployed	Unemployed	–

Source: https://www.iser.essex.ac.uk/archives/esec/user-guide/the-european-socio-economic-classification.

self-concept, and create pressures to conform that may affect the person's product and brand choices. The importance of group influence varies across products and brands. It tends to be strongest when the product is visible to others whom the buyer respects.

Manufacturers of products and brands subjected to strong group influence must figure out how to reach **opinion leaders** – people within a reference group who, because of special skills, knowledge, personality, or other characteristics, exert influence on others. Some experts call this 10 per cent of Europeans *the influentials* or *leading adopters*. These consumers 'drive trends, influence mass opinion and, most importantly, sell a great many products,' says one expert. They often use their big circle of acquaintances to 'spread their knowledge on what's good and what's bad'.[6]

Many marketers try to identify opinion leaders for their products and direct marketing efforts towards them. They use *buzz marketing* by enlisting or even creating opinion leaders to spread the word about their brands. Sneeze, a London marketing agency, uses *buzz marketing* to create successful word-of-mouth campaigns for its clients.

> Two or three years ago, a Premiership football club (I'm not allowed to tell you which one) was trying to sign up fans to its text bulletin service. For 25p a message (working out at around £100 a year), fans would get a text whenever something interesting happened at the club – team selections, injury updates, half-time scores, that sort of thing.
>
> Despite promoting the service in club literature, on its website, and with armies of attractive girls handing out leaflets on match days, the club could not get the rate of new subscriptions to rise above a disappointing 20 a week. So it hired a small marketing agency called Sneeze.
>
> 'We got a group of 14 or 16 actors, who were all football fans, but pretended to be fans [of the unnamed club],' explains Graham Goodkind, Sneeze's founder and chairman. 'And they went round bars and clubs around the ground, in groups of two, saying that one of their mates had been sacked from work because he kept on getting these text messages and talking to everyone about it, and his boss had had enough and given him the boot. So they were going round with this petition trying to get his job back – kind of a vaguely plausible story.
>
> 'And then the actors would pull out of their pocket some crumpled-up leaflet, which was for the text subscription service. They'd have a mobile phone in their pocket, and they'd show them how it worked. "What's the harm in that?" they'd say. And they could have these conversations with lots of people – that was the beauty of it. Two people could spend maybe 20 minutes or half an hour in each pub, working the whole pub. We did it at two home games and reckon we got about 4,000 people on the petition in total.'
>
> The petition went in the bin, of course, but subscriptions to the club's texting service soared. 'The week after we had done the activity it went up to 120 sign-ups,' says Goodkind, who is also boss of the Frank PR agency. 'Then you saw that after that it was 125, and the next week was 75, and the next week was 60. That was the talkability, because obviously if you get that service you tell your mates about it. We saw a massive effectiveness.'[7]

Family

Family members can strongly influence buyer behaviour. The family is the most important consumer buying organisation in society, and it has been researched extensively. Marketers are interested in the roles and influence of the husband, wife and children on the purchase of different products and services.

Husband–wife involvement varies widely by product category and by stage in the buying process. Buying roles change with evolving consumer lifestyles. For example, in many countries, the wife has traditionally been the main purchasing agent for the family in the areas of food, household products and clothing. But with a growing proportion of women holding jobs outside the home and the willingness of husbands to do more of the family's purchasing, all this is changing. The traditional division of labour between men and women in the family, with men earning the money and women running the home, is already a distant

Vauxhall got the message across to kids that the Zafira and the Meriva were designed with them in mind

Source: Vauxhall General Motors.

memory in many European countries and is breaking down elsewhere. The traditional buying roles of men and women are also breaking down.[8]

Such changes suggest that marketers in industries that have sold their products only to men or only to women are now courting the opposite sex. For example, women today account for 50 per cent of all technology purchases. So consumer electronics companies are increasingly designing products that are easier to use and more appealing to female buyers.

> As a growing number of women are embracing consumer electronics, engineers and designers are bringing a more feminine sensibility to products historically shaped by masculine tastes, habits and requirements. Designs are more 'feminine and softer', rather than masculine and angular. But many of the new touches are more subtle, like the wider spacing of the keys on a Sony ultraportable computer notebook. It accommodates the longer fingernails that women tend to have. Some of the latest mobile phones made by LG Electronics have the camera's automatic focus calibrated to arm's length. The company observed that young women are fond of taking pictures of themselves with a friend. Men, not so much. Nikon and Olympus recently introduced lines of lighter, more compact and easy-to-use digital single-lens-reflex cameras that were designed with women in mind because they tend to be a family's primary keeper of memories.[9]

Children may also have a strong influence on family buying decisions. For example, children as young as 6 may influence the family car purchase decision. Consequently, advertisers often take account of the interests of children when putting together campaigns. A very popular Vauxhall (Opel) campaign for the Zafira and Meriva multi-purpose vehicles used to feature three clever young boys, George, Harry and Amir, who had strong views on what a car should be able to do. However, marketers need to be conscious that both using children in advertising campaigns and running campaigns aimed at children are potentially controversial things to do. Advertisers who thoughtlessly target children with commercial messages are likely to be on the receiving end of a public relations backlash. Fortunately, the Advertising Standards Authority provides extensive advice on how to tackle the tricky issue of marketing to children in its 'Children and Advertising' guidelines (**http://www.asa .org.uk/News-resources/Hot-Topics**).

Roles and status

A person belongs to many groups – family, clubs, organisations. The person's position in each group can be defined in terms of both role and status. A role consists of the activities people are expected to perform according to the persons around them. Each role carries a status reflecting the general esteem given to it by society.

People usually choose products appropriate to their roles and status. Consider the various roles a working mother plays. In her company, she plays the role of a brand manager; in her family, she plays the role of wife and mother; at her favourite sporting events, she plays the role of avid fan. As a brand manager, she will buy the kind of clothing that reflects her role and status in her company.

Personal factors

A buyer's decisions are also influenced by personal characteristics such as the buyer's *age and life-cycle stage, occupation, economic situation, lifestyle* and *personality and self-concept*.

Age and life-cycle stage

People change the goods and services they buy over their lifetimes. Tastes in food, clothes, furniture and recreation are often age related. Buying is also shaped by the stage of the family life cycle – the stages through which families might pass as they mature over time. Marketers often define their target markets in terms of life-cycle stage and develop appropriate products and marketing plans for each stage.

Traditional family life-cycle stages include young singles and married couples with children. Today, however, marketers are increasingly catering to a growing number of alternative, non-traditional stages such as unmarried couples, singles marrying later in life, childless couples, same-sex couples, single parents, extended parents (those with young adult children returning home) and others.

Sony recently overhauled its marketing approach in order to target products and services to consumers based on their life stages. It created a new unit called the Consumer Segment Marketing Division, which has identified seven life-stage segments. They include, among others, Gen Y (under 25), Young Professionals/DINKs (Double Income No Kids, 25 to 34), Families (35 to 54) and Zoomers (55 and over).

Occupation

A person's occupation affects the goods and services bought. Blue-collar workers tend to buy more rugged work clothes, whereas executives buy more business suits. Marketers try to identify the occupational groups that have an above-average interest in their products and services. A company can even specialise in making products needed by a given occupational group. For example, Goliath Footwear from West Yorkshire in the UK specialises in rugged, durable, no-nonsense safety boots – including the Furnace Masters, a line of safety boots designed for people working with molten metals, which are heat resistant up to 300 degrees centigrade, and feature quick-release fasteners so that they can be removed speedily in the event of a molten-metal splash.

Economic situation

A person's economic situation will affect product choice. Marketers of income-sensitive goods watch trends in personal income, savings and interest rates. If economic indicators point to a recession, marketers can take steps to redesign, reposition and reprice their products closely. Some marketers target consumers who have lots of money and resources, charging prices to match. For example, Rolex positions its luxury watches as 'a tribute to elegance, an object of passion, a symbol for all time'. Other marketers target consumers with more modest means. Timex makes more affordable watches that are renowned for their reliability and durability, epitomised by the famous Timex Ironman Triathlon model, designed to withstand the toughest sporting conditions.

Lifestyle

People coming from the same subculture, social class and occupation may have quite different lifestyles. **Lifestyle** is a person's pattern of living as expressed in his or her psychographics. It involves measuring consumers' major AIO dimensions – Activities (work, hobbies, shopping, sports, social events), Interests (food, fashion, family, recreation) and Opinions (about themselves, social issues, business, products). Lifestyle captures something more than the person's social class or personality. It profiles a person's whole pattern of acting and interacting in the world.

Several research firms have developed lifestyle classifications. The most widely used is SRI Consulting's *Values and Lifestyles (VALS)* typology. VALS classifies people according to how they spend their time and money. It divides consumers into eight groups based on two major dimensions: primary motivation and resources. *Primary motivations* include ideals, achievement and self-expression. According to Strategic Business Insights Consulting, consumers who are primarily motivated by ideals are guided by knowledge and principles. Consumers who are primarily motivated by *achievement* look for products and services that demonstrate success to their peers. Consumers who are primarily motivated by *self-expression* desire social or physical activity, variety and risk. You can take the VALS survey yourself, if you like, to find out where you fit into the VALS categories: **http://www .strategicbusinessinsights.com/vals/presurvey.shtml**.

Consumers within each orientation are further classified into those with *high resources* and those with *low resources,* depending on whether they have high or low levels of income, education, health, self-confidence, energy and other factors. Consumers with either very high or very low levels of resources are classified without regard to their primary motivations (Innovators, Survivors). Innovators are people with so many resources that they exhibit all three primary motivations in varying degrees. In contrast, Survivors are people with so few resources that they do not show a strong primary motivation. They must focus on meeting needs rather than fulfilling desires.

One study identified five key food-related lifestyle segments in Croatia as follows:

- The relaxed segment, representing 13 per cent of the population. These people have no clear buying motives and the quality of food is not particularly important to them; they are influenced by friends and by the mass media. Buying and preparing food is not a major concern of this segment.

- The traditionalist segment accounts for 27 per cent of the population. Cooking and eating food are considered to be important social events for this segment, and members of the family like to help out at meal times. They enjoy shopping for food and like to experiment with new recipes.

- The modern segment, representing 32 per cent of the population. The members of this segment do not like to spend too much time on buying, preparing and cooking food; they make detailed shopping lists and plan their food shopping trips carefully. Their main motivation is to reduce the amount of time they spend on buying and cooking food.

- The concerned segment makes up only around 11 per cent of the population. These people are particularly interested in the safety and nutritional value of the food that they buy, and are convinced of the advantages of organic food. This segment tends to be relatively old and with above average incomes. Its members pay a lot of attention to the information on food product labels.

- The hedonist segment, representing 17 per cent of the population. This segment tends to comprise older consumers with lower than average education and income. Their main motivation is to enjoy the food that they eat. Women who belong to this segment spend a lot of time shopping for food and take pride in their cooking abilities.[10]

Lifestyle segmentation can also be used to understand how consumers use the Internet, computers and other technology. Forrester developed its 'Technographics' scheme, which segments consumers according to motivation, desire and ability to invest in technology. The framework splits people into ten categories, including:

- *Fast Forwards*: the biggest spenders on computer technology. Fast Forwards are career focused, time strapped, driven and top users of technology.

- *New Age Nurturers*: also big spenders. However, they are focused on technology for home uses, such as family education and entertainment.

- *Mouse Potatoes*: consumers who are dedicated to interactive entertainment and willing to spend for the latest in 'technotainment'.
- *Techno-Strivers*: consumers who are up-and-coming believers in technology for career advancement.
- *Media Junkies*: visual TV lovers who are especially interested in TV features like video-on-demand.
- *Sidelined Citizens*: technophobes and technology laggards, the least receptive to new technologies.[11]

Delta Airlines used Technographics to target online ticket sales better. It created marketing campaigns for time-strapped Fast Forwards and New Age Nurturers, and eliminated Technology Pessimists (those sceptical of technology) from its list of targets. When used carefully, the lifestyle concept can help marketers understand changing consumer values and how they affect buying behaviour.

Personality and self-concept

Each person's distinct personality influences his or her buying behaviour. **Personality** refers to the unique psychological characteristics that lead to relatively consistent and lasting responses to one's own environment. Personality is usually described in terms of traits such as self-confidence, dominance, sociability, autonomy, defensiveness, adaptability and aggressiveness. Personality can be useful in analysing consumer behaviour for certain product or brand choices. For example, coffee marketers have discovered that heavy coffee drinkers tend to be high on sociability. Thus, to attract customers, Starbucks and other coffee houses create environments in which people can relax and socialise over a cup of steaming coffee.

The idea is that brands also have personalities, and that consumers are likely to choose brands with personalities that match their own. A *brand personality* is the specific mix of human traits that may be attributed to a particular brand. One researcher identified five brand personality traits:

1 sincerity (down to earth, honest, wholesome and cheerful);
2 excitement (daring, spirited, imaginative and up to date);
3 competence (reliable, intelligent and successful);
4 sophistication (upper class and charming);
5 ruggedness (outdoorsy and tough).[12]

The researcher found that a number of well-known brands tended to be strongly associated with one particular trait: Levi's with 'ruggedness'; MTV with 'excitement'; CNN with 'competence'; and Campbell's with 'sincerity'. Hence, these brands will attract people who are high on the same personality traits.

Many marketers use a concept related to personality – a person's *self-concept* (also called *self-image*). The basic self-concept premiss is that people's possessions contribute to and reflect their identities; that is, 'we are what we have'. Thus, in order to understand consumer behaviour, the marketer must first understand the relationship between consumer self-concept and possessions.

Psychological factors

A person's buying choices are further influenced by four major psychological factors: *motivation, perception, learning* and *beliefs and attitudes*.

Motivation

A person has many needs at any given time. Some are biological, arising from states of tension such as hunger, thirst or discomfort. Others are psychological, arising from the need for recognition, esteem or belonging. A need becomes a motive when it is aroused to a sufficient

Brand personality: well-known brands tend to be strongly associated with one or more traits. Red Bull is associated with extreme 'excitement'

Source: Alamy Images/Tony Lockhart.

level of intensity. A **motive (drive)** is a need that is sufficiently pressing to direct the person to seek satisfaction. Psychologists have developed theories of human motivation. Two of the most popular – the theories of Sigmund Freud and Abraham Maslow – have quite different meanings for consumer analysis and marketing.

Sigmund Freud assumed that people are largely unconscious about the real psychological forces shaping their behaviour. He saw the person as growing up and repressing many urges. These urges are never eliminated or under perfect control; they emerge in dreams, in slips of the tongue, in neurotic and obsessive behaviour, or ultimately in psychoses.

Freud's theory suggests that a person's buying decisions are affected by subconscious motives that even the buyer may not fully understand. Thus, an ageing baby boomer who buys a sporty BMW 330Ci convertible might explain that he simply likes the feel of the wind in his thinning hair. At a deeper level, he may be trying to impress others with his success. At a still deeper level, he may be buying the car to feel young and independent again.

The term *motivation research* refers to qualitative research designed to probe consumers' hidden, subconscious motivations. Consumers often do not know or cannot describe just why they act as they do. Thus, motivation researchers use a variety of probing techniques to uncover underlying emotions and attitudes towards brands and buying situations. These sometimes bizarre techniques range from sentence completion, word association, and ink-blot or cartoon interpretation tests, to having consumers form daydreams and fantasies about brands or buying situations. Such projective techniques seem pretty strange, and some marketers dismiss such motivation research as mumbo-jumbo. But many marketers routinely use such touchy–feely approaches to dig deeply into consumer psyches and develop better marketing strategies.

Many companies employ teams of psychologists, anthropologists and other social scientists to carry out motivation research. One ad agency routinely conducts one-to-one, therapy-like interviews to delve into the inner workings of consumers. Another company asks consumers to describe their favourite brands as animals or cars (say, Volkswagens versus Peugeots) in order to assess the prestige associated with various brands. Still others rely on hypnosis, dream therapy, or soft lights and mood music to plumb the murky depths of consumer psyches.

Abraham Maslow sought to explain why people are driven by particular needs at particular times. Why does one person spend much time and energy on personal safety and another on gaining the esteem of others? Maslow's answer is that human needs are arranged in a hierarchy, as shown in Figure 5.3, from the most pressing at the bottom to the least pressing at the top.[13] They include *physiological* needs, *safety* needs, *social* needs, *esteem* needs and *self-actualisation* needs.

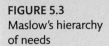

FIGURE 5.3
Maslow's hierarchy
of needs

Source: Haslow, Abraham H.,
Frager, Robert D., Fadiman,
James *Motivation and
Personality*, 3rd edn © 1987.
Printed and electronically
reproduced by permission of
Pearson Education, Inc., Upper
Saddle River, New Jersey.

A person tries to satisfy the most important need first. When that need is satisfied, it will stop being a motivator and the person will then try to satisfy the next most important need. For example, starving people (physiological need) will not take an interest in the latest happenings in the art world (self-actualisation needs), nor in how they are seen or esteemed by others (social or esteem needs), nor even in whether they are breathing clean air (safety needs). But as each important need is satisfied, the next most important need will come into play.

Perception

A motivated person is ready to act. How the person acts is influenced by his or her own perception of the situation. All of us learn by the flow of information through our five senses: sight, hearing, smell, touch and taste. However, each of us receives, organises and interprets this sensory information in an individual way. **Perception** is the process by which people select, organise and interpret information to form a meaningful picture of the world.

People can form different perceptions of the same stimulus because of three perceptual processes: selective attention, selective distortion and selective retention. People are exposed to a great many stimuli every day. For example, one analyst estimates that people are exposed to 3,000 to 5,000 ads every day.[14] It is impossible for a person to pay attention to all these stimuli. *Selective attention* – the tendency for people to screen out most of the information to which they are exposed – means that marketers have to work especially hard to attract the consumer's attention.

Even noticed stimuli do not always come across in the intended way. Each person fits incoming information into an existing mindset. *Selective distortion* describes the tendency of people to interpret information in a way that will support what they already believe. For example, if you distrust a company, you might perceive even honest ads from the company as questionable. Selective distortion means that marketers must try to understand the mindsets of consumers and how these will affect interpretations of advertising and sales information.

People will also forget much of what they learn. They tend to retain information that supports their attitudes and beliefs. Because of *selective retention*, consumers are likely to remember good points made about a brand they favour and to forget good points made about competing brands. Because of selective exposure, distortion and retention, marketers have to work hard to get their messages through. This fact explains why marketers use so much drama and repetition in sending messages to their market.

Interestingly, although most marketers worry about whether their offers will be perceived at all, some consumers worry that they will be affected by marketing messages without even knowing it – through *subliminal advertising*. In 1957, a researcher announced that he had flashed the phrases 'Eat popcorn' and 'Drink Coca-Cola' on a screen in a New Jersey movie theatre every five seconds for 1/300th of a second. He reported that although viewers did not consciously recognise these messages, they absorbed them subconsciously and bought 58 per cent more popcorn and 18 per cent more Coke. Suddenly advertisers and consumer protection groups became intensely interested in subliminal perception. Although the researcher later admitted to making up the data, the issue has not died. Some consumers still fear that they are being manipulated by subliminal messages. In fact, some recent research suggests that subliminal advertising can be effective, that it works better where consumers do not expect it and less well when they do expect it.[15]

On the other hand many marketers are very sceptical about subliminal advertising. Most advertisers scoff at the notion of an industry conspiracy to manipulate consumers through 'invisible' messages. Says one industry insider:

> [Some consumers believe we are] wizards who can manipulate them at will. Ha! Snort! Oh my sides! As we know, just between us, most of [us] have difficulty getting a 2 per cent increase in sales with the help of $50 million in media and extremely liminal images of sex, money, power, and other [motivators] of human emotion. The very idea of [us] as puppeteers, cruelly pulling the strings of consumer marionettes, is almost too much to bear.[16]

Learning

When people act, they learn. **Learning** describes changes in an individual's behaviour arising from experience. Learning theorists say that most human behaviour is learned. Learning occurs through the interplay of drives, stimuli, cues, responses and reinforcement.

A *drive* is a strong internal stimulus that calls for action. A drive becomes a motive when it is directed towards a particular *stimulus object*. For example, a person's drive for self-actualisation might motivate him or her to look into buying a digital camera. The consumer's response to the idea of buying a camera is conditioned by the surrounding cues. *Cues* are minor stimuli that determine when, where and how the person responds. For example, the person might spot several camera brands in a shop window, hear of a special sale price or discuss cameras with a friend. These are all cues that might influence a consumer's *response* to his or her interest in buying the product.

Suppose the consumer buys a Samsung digital camera. If the experience is rewarding, the consumer will probably use the camera more and more, and his or her response will be *reinforced*. Then, the next time the consumer shops for a camera, or for a similar product, the probability is greater that he or she will buy a Samsung product. The practical significance of learning theory for marketers is that they can build up demand for a product by associating it with strong drives, using motivating cues and providing positive reinforcement.

Beliefs and attitudes

Through doing and learning, people acquire beliefs and attitudes. These, in turn, influence their buying behaviour. A *belief* is a descriptive thought that a person has about something. Beliefs may be based on real knowledge, opinion or faith, and may or may not carry an emotional charge. Marketers are interested in the beliefs that people formulate about specific products and services, because these beliefs make up product and brand images that affect buying behaviour. If some of the beliefs are wrong and prevent purchase, the marketer will want to launch a campaign to correct them.

People have attitudes regarding religion, politics, clothes, music, food and almost everything else. *Attitude* describes a person's relatively consistent evaluations, feelings and tendencies towards an object or idea. Attitudes put people into a frame of mind of liking or disliking things, of moving towards or away from them. Our digital camera buyer may hold attitudes such as 'Buy the best', 'The Koreans make the most innovative electronics products in the world' and 'Creativity and self-expression are among the most important things in life.' If so, the Samsung camera would fit well into the consumer's existing attitudes.

Attitudes are difficult to change. A person's attitudes fit into a pattern, and to change one attitude may require difficult adjustments in many others. Thus, a company should usually try to fit its products into existing attitudes rather than attempt to change attitudes. Of course, there are exceptions in which the cost of trying to change attitudes may pay off handsomely. The traditional and dull Scottish breakfast of porridge oats has recently received a substantial boost from changes in lifestyles, greater awareness of healthy eating and some clever marketing:

> Oats have traditionally never enjoyed the sexiest image. But today even the most stylish and faddish foodie will happily admit to starting the day with a bowl of porridge.
>
> Wheat free, low on the Glycaemic Index – which means they are slow energy releasing – and low in calories and fat, oats tick all the boxes as a nutritious and versatile, food *du jour*.
>
> Unlike a slice of white bread or a sugary bowl of cereal for example, the complex carbs in oats help balance blood sugar levels and leave you feeling full up for longer – an excellent way to refuel and curb hunger pangs.
>
> Rich in fibre and protein, their nutritional benefits are also a huge plus. Studies have shown that oats can lower cholesterol, reduce high blood pressure and even improve libido. If further evidence was needed of their super-food status, Britain's longest-living man, David Henderson from Montrose, survived to the ripe old age of 109 and put his long life and good health down to his daily bowl of porridge.
>
> In an age when we are more aware than ever that we are what we eat, it was not long before the rather plain little oat underwent a glamorous makeover. Witness the Scott's Porage Oats advert featuring a young lady ogling up a ruggedly handsome porridge-eating Scotsman's kilt. Soon after this, oatcakes appeared in deliberately more modern flavours – Nairns brought out cracked black pepper oatcakes, closely followed by stem ginger, mixed berry and fruit and spice varieties. Word spread of their appeal as a versatile, healthy snack and before long, oats were flying off shelves in all their forms. Sainsbury's reported a 60 per cent increase in oat sales in the last six months, and according to reports by market researchers TNS last year, oats are now Britain's second favourite breakfast cereal, with the oat industry bringing in £79 million per year.
>
> Scots have long appreciated the benefits of oats. Native to Eurasia, they are the seeds of cereals belonging to the Avena genus and have been grown in Scotland for centuries. They have a lower summer heat requirement and greater tolerance of rain than cereals such as wheat, rye or barley, so are well suited to the Scottish climate. Our forefathers mixed them with a little fat to create oatcakes, one of the first convenience foods, a handy-sized and portable alternative to bread, but with the huge advantage that once baked they kept for long periods.
>
> Scottish chieftains carried around small sacks of oatmeal when travelling by horseback and baked oatcakes on the back of their iron shields for sustenance. Today a pack of emergency oatcakes in the pocket does the same job for the you-are-what-you-eat generation, proving that a good thing will stand the test of time.[17]

We can now appreciate the many forces acting on consumer behaviour. The consumer's choice results from the complex interplay of cultural, social, personal and psychological factors.

The buyer decision process

Now that we have looked at the influences that affect buyers, we are ready to look at how consumers make buying decisions. Figure 5.4 shows that the buyer decision process consists of five stages: *need recognition, information search, evaluation of alternatives, purchase decision* and *post-purchase behaviour*. Clearly, the buying process starts long before the actual purchase and continues long after. Marketers need to focus on the entire buying process rather than on just the purchase decision.

The figure suggests that consumers pass through all five stages with every purchase. But in more routine purchases, consumers often skip or reverse some of these stages. A woman buying her regular brand of toothpaste would recognise the need and go right to the

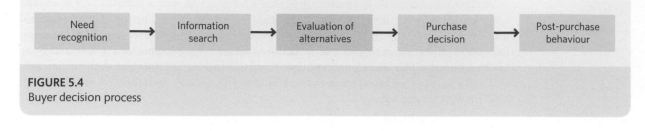

FIGURE 5.4
Buyer decision process

purchase decision, skipping information search and evaluation. However, we use the model in Figure 5.4 because it shows all the considerations that arise when a consumer faces a new and complex purchase situation.

Need recognition

The buying process starts with *need recognition*: the buyer recognises a problem or need. The need can be triggered by *internal stimuli* when one of the person's normal needs – hunger, thirst, sex – rises to a level high enough to become a drive. A need can also be triggered by *external stimuli*. For example, an advertisement or a discussion with a friend might get you thinking about buying a new car. At this stage, the marketer should research consumers to find out what kinds of needs or problems arise, what brought them about, and how they led the consumer to this particular product.

Information search

An interested consumer may or may not search for more information. If the consumer's drive is strong and a satisfying product is near at hand, the consumer is likely to buy it then. If not, the consumer may store the need in memory or undertake an *information search* related to the need. For example, once you have decided you need a new mobile phone, you will probably pay more attention to phone advertisements, phones owned by friends and conversations about phones. Or you may actively look for reading material, contact friends on Facebook and gather information in other ways. The amount of searching you do will depend on the strength of your drive, the amount of information you start with, the ease of obtaining more information, the value you place on additional information and the satisfaction you get from searching.

Consumers can obtain information from any of several sources. These include *personal sources* (family, friends, neighbours, acquaintances), *commercial sources* (advertising, sales-people, 'websites' dealers, packaging, displays), *public sources* (mass media, consumer-rating organisations, Internet searches) and *experiential sources* (handling, examining, using the product). The relative influence of these information sources varies with the product and the buyer. Generally, the consumer receives the most information about a product from commercial sources – those controlled by the marketer. The most effective sources, however, tend to be personal. Commercial sources normally *inform* the buyer, but personal sources *legitimise* or *evaluate* products for the buyer. As one marketer states, 'It's rare that an advertising campaign can be as effective as a neighbour leaning over the fence and saying, "This is a wonderful product". Increasingly, that "fence" is a digital one.' Consumers find sources of user-generated content – discussion forums, blogs, online review sites and social networking sites – three times more influential when making a purchase decision than conventional marketing methods such as TV advertising.[18]

As more information is obtained, the consumer's awareness and knowledge of the available brands and features increase. In your phone information search, you may learn about the several brands available. This might help you to drop certain brands from consideration. A company must design its marketing mix to make prospects aware of and knowledgeable about its brand. It should carefully identify consumers' sources of information and the importance of each source.

Evaluation of alternatives

We have seen how the consumer uses information to arrive at a set of final brand choices. How does the consumer choose among the alternative brands? The marketer needs to know about *alternative evaluation:* that is, how the consumer processes information to arrive at brand choices. Unfortunately, consumers do not use a simple and single evaluation process in all buying situations. Instead, several evaluation processes are at work.

The consumer arrives at attitudes towards different brands through some evaluation procedure. How consumers go about evaluating purchase alternatives depends on the individual consumer and the specific buying situation. In some cases, consumers use careful calculations and logical thinking. At other times, the same consumers do little or no evaluating; instead they buy on impulse and rely on intuition. Sometimes consumers make buying decisions on their own; sometimes they turn to friends, consumer guides or salespeople for buying advice.

Suppose you have narrowed your phone choices to three brands. And suppose that you are primarily interested in four attributes – style, features, guarantee and price. By this time, you have probably formed beliefs about how each brand rates on each attribute. Clearly, if one phone rated best on all the attributes, we could predict that you would choose it. However, the brands will no doubt vary in appeal. You might base your buying decision on only one attribute, and your choice would be easy to predict. If you wanted style above everything else, you would buy the phone that you think has the best styling. But most buyers consider several attributes, each with different importance. If we knew the importance that you assigned to each of the four attributes, we could predict your phone choice more reliably.

Marketers should study buyers to find out how they actually evaluate brand alternatives. If they know what evaluative processes go on, marketers can take steps to influence the buyer's decision.

Purchase decision

In the evaluation stage, the consumer ranks brands and forms purchase intentions. Generally, the consumer's *purchase decision* will be to buy the most preferred brand, but two factors can come between the purchase *intention* and the purchase *decision.* The first factor is the *attitudes of others.* If someone important to you thinks that you should buy the latest phone, then the chances of your buying an older model are reduced.

The second factor is *unexpected situational factors.* The consumer may form a purchase intention based on factors such as expected income, expected price and expected product benefits. However, unexpected events may change the purchase intention. For example, at the last minute you might see a persuasive negative online review, a close competitor might drop its price, or a friend might report being disappointed in your preferred phone. Thus, preferences and even purchase intentions do not always result in actual purchase choice.

Post-purchase behaviour

The marketer's job does not end when the product is bought. After purchasing the product, the consumer will be satisfied or dissatisfied and will engage in *post-purchase behaviour* of interest to the marketer. What determines whether the buyer is satisfied or dissatisfied with a purchase? The answer lies in the relationship between the *consumer's expectations* and the product's *perceived performance.* If the product falls short of expectations, the consumer is disappointed; if it meets expectations, the consumer is satisfied; if it exceeds expectations, the consumer is delighted.

If the consumer's perceptions of product performance fall a long way short of expectations, then the consumer will be very dissatisfied. This suggests that sellers should promise only what their brands can deliver so that buyers are satisfied. Some sellers might even understate product performance levels to boost later consumer satisfaction. This strikes many people as the opposite of what they think of as 'marketing', since they think that 'marketing' must mean telling people how fantastic your brand is, almost regardless of the truth. However, if you exaggerate the benefits your brand can deliver, then consumers' expectations will exceed their perceptions of what the product delivers and they will be dissatisfied. Then they will very likely tell their friends (both face to face and online) how dissatisfied they were, and the damage to your brand could be substantial.

Almost all major purchases result in **cognitive dissonance**, or discomfort caused by post-purchase conflict. After the purchase, consumers are satisfied with the benefits of the chosen brand and are glad to avoid the drawbacks of the brands not bought. However, every purchase involves compromise. Consumers feel uneasy about acquiring the drawbacks of the chosen brand and about losing the benefits of the brands not purchased. Thus, consumers feel at least some post-purchase dissonance for every purchase.[19]

Why is it so important to satisfy the customer? Customer satisfaction is a key to building profitable relationships with consumers – to keeping and growing consumers and reaping their customer lifetime value. Satisfied customers buy a product again, talk favourably to others about the product, pay less attention to competing brands and advertising, and buy other products from the company. Many marketers go beyond merely *meeting* the expectations of customers – they aim to *delight* the customer. The relatively little known Swedish mobile phone company Doro identified a way of delighting its key target market, older consumers, by providing them with mobiles that catered for the needs of the more mature consumer who may prefer a simpler phone with easy-to-use functions and nice, big, buttons on the keypad (see Marketing at Work 5.1).

Understanding what older consumers want

MARKETING AT WORK 5.1

By now there is no excuse for ignorance about the broad facts of the ageing population. Report after report has been produced on the subject, often commissioned by governments struggling to come to terms with the implications for public finances, pension provision, health services and care services for elderly people. This is certainly not just a European issue, since other countries such as Japan, China and even South Africa (which we will explore further a little later) are facing their own version of the same basic phenomenon. In essence, it is the simple arithmetic associated with tectonic shifts in national, continent-wide and global demographics. If the population gradually has fewer babies (a declining birth rate), and the age to which the average person can be expected to live (life expectancy) gradually increases, then inexorably the population will 'age'. This means that the average age of the population, which in this case is usually measured by the median, increases, and that the 'population pyramid' that shows the number of people in each age cohort changes shape. The way these things are usually drawn, with older people at the top and younger people at the bottom, means that it no longer looks much like a pyramid (fat at the bottom and thin at the top) but gradually begins to look like a simple tower (roughly the same width all the way up).

Mature consumers want mobile phones that are easy to use

Source: Getty Images/Bambu Productions.

While not *just* a European issue, the ageing population most certainly *is* a European issue. The median age of the population of the EU is forecast to increase from 40.1 in 2010 to 49.3 in 2060; by 2060 a third of the EU population will be aged over 65 (it is currently about a fifth); by

2060 there will be two people of working age for every person aged over 65 in the EU, while today there are four (this is known as the dependency ratio). It is important to remember that there are substantial variations between European countries. For example, Denmark and Finland are ageing more slowly than the European average (their median age will be in the low 40s in 2060), while Spain and Italy are ageing more quickly than the average (their median age will be in the mid-50s by 2060). Nevertheless, the overall European pattern is entirely clear – more, older people expecting pensions and healthcare, fewer younger people working and paying taxes.

If there is no excuse to be ignorant about the subject of ageing, then perhaps there is greater excuse to be ignorant about the marketing implications of the ageing population. Marketers have often been accused of largely ignoring the elderly and of being obsessed with everything to do with youth and youthfulness. Even today, much of the marketing directed at older people seems to be concerned with convincing them that there is no need to grow old (how to have younger looking skin, how to enjoy adventure sports in your retirement and so on) rather than focusing squarely on what older people want. The marketing industry still seems to believe that everyone over the age of 30 just wants to pretend that they are still young. However, the warnings have been around for quite a long time. As long ago as 1997 marketing professor Richard Leventhal tried to map out some of the marketing concepts and strategies that would be needed as marketers increasingly engaged with the older consumer. Above all, said Leventhal, marketers must not stereotype older consumers: 'Like sexism, ageism is stereotyping. Why are perceptions so far off? Why have we failed to set the record straight?' So the message is: do not stereotype older consumers; research them so as to understand their motivations, perceptions, desires, ambitions, aspirations and dreams just like you would any other important target market. Mind you, some of the generalisations that Leventhal provided us with back in 1997 still sound pretty much on the mark even today: 'They are sceptical above all else.' Older consumers have been subjected to marketing messages throughout their lives and if you try to fool them, or impress them with hype, they will very likely tune you out.

The ageing population is a global phenomenon. Even in India the median age of the population is forecast to rise substantially between 2010 and 2060, although only from the low base of 25 to a still fairly youthful 32. Indeed, even some African nations have begun to think about the implications of this kind of demographic time bomb. A research study by a team from the University of Cape Town, South Africa, looked at the consumer behaviour of affluent South Africans aged between 55 and 75. The great majority of the older consumers owned a mobile phone and had broadband Internet access. The study showed that older consumers in South Africa are most heavily influenced by TV advertising, but that web advertising and advertising on mobile phones are increasingly important. These consumers consider that they are under-represented in advertising because advertising largely focuses on young people; they think that advertising tends to portray older people as relatively unattractive, and as being 'stuck in their ways' rather than open to new experiences. In fact, in the South African case, it seemed as though marketers were still falling into the trap pointed out by Leventhal all those years ago and were treating older consumers stereotypically, and portraying them inaccurately in advertising material. To the clever marketer, this looks like a shining opportunity.

One brand that has zoomed in on the ageing population is the Swedish company Doro. It is a mobile phone brand – possibly one that you have not heard of, but one that has been very successful with its innovative niche marketing strategy. For example, there is the Doro Liberto 810 which is 'the perfect smartphone for beginners, full of convenient ways to communicate and enjoy access to email and the Internet', and the Doro PhonEasy 605 which is really easy to use: 'a robust, clamshell-style mobile phone for answering and ending calls with a simple flip. Dialling and texting is also very easy thanks to widely spaced, concave keys, predictive text and large, easy to read characters in phonebook and text messages.' You get the picture? These phones are very simple to use, most of them have physical keypads with large easy-to-read and easy-to-press keys, and the on-screen icons are large and easy to identify. Phones like this are ideal for people who maybe do not want to carry around a phone as a fashion statement, and perhaps are not too bothered about having the very latest social media app, but who want a phone that makes it easy for them to communicate with their nearest and dearest even though their sight, hearing and physical dexterity are not quite as good as they used to be. Many older people are in just that position. They do not need or want the latest, fastest or most fashionable phone; they want one that they can use. That is what Doro has delivered.

Sources: Justin Beneke, Nicole Frey, Ruth Chapman, Nontuthuzelo Mashaba and Tatum Howie, 'The Grey Awakening: A South African Perspective', *Journal of Consumer Marketing*, 28(2), 2011, pp. 114–24; Nicholas Thompson and Keith Thompson, 'Can Marketing Practice Keep up with Europe's Ageing Population?', *European Journal of Marketing*, 43(11–12), 2009, pp. 1281–8; Richard Leventhal, 'Aging Consumers and Their Effects on the Marketplace', *Journal of Consumer Marketing*, 14(4), 1997, pp. 276–81; 'The Global Later Lifers Market: How the Over 60s are Coming into Their Own – Executive Briefing', Euromonitor International, accessed at www.warc.com, June 2014; 'Ageing population: projections 2010–2060 for the EU27', The European Parliamentary Research Service, accessed at http://epthinktank.eu/2013-12-19/ageing-population-projections-2010-2060-for-the-eu27/, June 2014; http://www.doro.co.uk/

A dissatisfied consumer responds differently. Bad word of mouth often travels farther and faster than good word of mouth, whether face to face or online. It can quickly damage consumer attitudes about a company and its products. But companies cannot simply rely on dissatisfied customers to volunteer their complaints when they are dissatisfied. Most unhappy customers never tell the company about their problem. Therefore, a company should measure customer satisfaction regularly. It should set up systems that *encourage* customers to complain. In this way, the company can learn how well it is doing and how it can improve.

But what should companies do about dissatisfied customers? At a minimum, most companies offer free telephone numbers and websites to handle complaints and enquiries. For example, floorcare products company Vax offers extensive consumer advice to Australian consumers at **www.vax.com.au** and to British consumers at **www.vax.co.uk**, but is also very conscious that consumers may have individual problems that need the assistance of a customer care adviser. Vax explicitly asks for consumer feedback to use in improving its products:

> we are constantly updating and introducing new and innovative products with you, your home, your kids, your pets . . . and your budget in mind!
>
> We work with people like you to bring you the floorcare that you want. All your feedback is used by our Product Designers to create even better products for you. **http://www.vax .co.uk/about/**

By studying the overall buyer decision, marketers may be able to find ways to help consumers move through it. For example, if consumers are not buying a new product because they do not perceive a need for it, marketing might launch advertising messages that trigger the need and show how the product solves consumers' problems. If consumers know about the product but are not buying because they hold unfavourable attitudes towards it, the marketer must find ways either to change the product or to change consumer perceptions.

The buyer decision process for new products

We have looked at the stages buyers go through in trying to satisfy a need. Buyers may pass quickly or slowly through these stages, and some of the stages may even be reversed. Much depends on the nature of the buyer, the product and the buying situation.

We now look at how buyers approach the purchase of new products. A **new product** is a good, service or idea that is perceived by some potential customers as new. It may have been around for a while, but our interest is in how consumers learn about products for the first time and make decisions on whether to adopt them. We define the **adoption process** as 'the mental process through which an individual passes from first learning about an innovation to final adoption', and *adoption* as the decision by an individual to become a regular user of the product.[20]

Stages in the adoption process

Consumers go through five stages in the process of adopting a new product:

1　*Awareness*: The consumer becomes aware of the new product, but lacks information about it.
2　*Interest*: The consumer seeks information about the new product.
3　*Evaluation*: The consumer considers whether trying the new product makes sense.
4　*Trial*: The consumer tries the new product on a small scale to improve his or her estimate of its value.
5　*Adoption*: The consumer decides to make full and regular use of the new product.

This model suggests that the new product marketer should think about how to help consumers move through these stages. A manufacturer of three-dimensional televisions (3D TVs) may discover that many consumers in the interest stage do not move to the trial stage because of uncertainty and the large investment. If these same consumers were willing to use 3D TVs on a trial basis for a small fee, the manufacturer could consider offering a trial-use plan with an option to buy.

Individual differences in innovativeness

People differ greatly in their readiness to try new products. In each product area, there are 'consumption pioneers' and early adopters. Other individuals adopt new products much later. People can be classified into the adopter categories shown in Figure 5.5. After a slow start, an increasing number of people adopt the new product. The number of adopters reaches a peak and then drops off as fewer non-adopters remain. Innovators are defined as the first 2.5 per cent of the buyers to adopt a new idea (those beyond two standard deviations from mean adoption time); the early adopters are the next 13.5 per cent (between one and two standard deviations); and so on.

The five adopter groups have differing values. *Innovators* are adventurous – they try new ideas at some risk. *Early adopters* are guided by respect – they are opinion leaders in their communities and adopt new ideas early but carefully. The *early majority* are deliberate – although they are rarely leaders, they adopt new ideas before the average person. The *late majority* are sceptical – they adopt an innovation only after a majority of people have tried it.

Finally, *laggards* are tradition bound – they are suspicious of changes and adopt the innovation only when it has become something of a tradition itself.

This adopter classification suggests that an innovating firm should research the characteristics of innovators and early adopters and should direct marketing efforts towards them. In general, innovators tend to be relatively younger, better educated and higher in income than later adopters and non-adopters. They are more receptive to unfamiliar things, rely more on their own values and judgement, and are more willing to take risks. They are less brand loyal and more likely to take advantage of special promotions such as discounts, coupons and samples.

Influence of product characteristics on rate of adoption

The characteristics of the new product affect its rate of adoption. Some products catch on almost overnight (iPod), whereas others take a long time to gain acceptance (3D TV). Five characteristics are especially important in influencing an innovation's rate of adoption. For example, consider the characteristics of 3D TV in relation to the rate of adoption:

- *Relative advantage*: the degree to which the innovation appears superior to existing products. The greater the perceived relative advantage of using 3D TV – say, in picture quality and ease of viewing – the sooner 3D TVs will be adopted.

- *Compatibility*: the degree to which the innovation fits the values and experiences of potential consumers. For example, 3D TV is highly compatible with the lifestyles found in upper-middle-class homes. However, it is not very compatible with the programming and broadcasting systems currently available to consumers.

- *Complexity*: the degree to which the innovation is difficult to understand or use. Since 3D TVs are not very complex and, therefore, once more programming is available and prices come down, they will take less time to penetrate European homes than more complex innovations.

FIGURE 5.5
Adopter categorisation on the basis of relative time of adoption of innovations

Source: Reprinted with the permission of The Free Press, a division of Simon & Schuster, Inc. from *Diffusion of Innovations*, 5th edn, by Everett M. Rogers. Copyright © 1995, 2003 by Everett M. Rogers. Copyright © 1962, 1971, 1983 by The Free Press. All rights reserved.

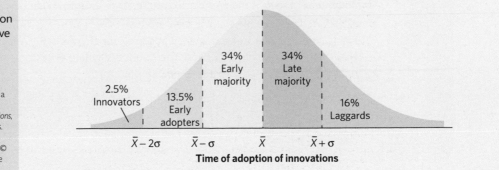

- *Divisibility*: the degree to which the innovation may be tried on a limited basis. Although 3D TVs are still rather expensive, to the extent that people can lease them with an option to buy, their rate of adoption will increase.
- *Communicability*: the degree to which the results of using the innovation can be observed or described to others. Because 3D TV lends itself to demonstration and description, its use will spread faster among consumers.

Other characteristics influence the rate of adoption, such as initial and ongoing costs, risk and uncertainty, and social approval. The new product marketer has to research all these factors when developing the new product and its marketing programme.

Consumer behaviour across international borders

Understanding consumer behaviour is difficult enough for companies marketing within the borders of a single country. For companies operating in many countries, however, understanding and serving the needs of consumers can be daunting. Although consumers in different countries may have some things in common, their values, attitudes and behaviours often vary greatly. International marketers must understand such differences and adjust their products and marketing programmes accordingly.

Sometimes the differences are obvious. For example, in the UK, where most people eat cereal regularly for breakfast, Kellogg's focuses its marketing on persuading consumers to select a Kellogg's brand rather than a competitor's brand. In France, however, where most people prefer croissants and coffee or no breakfast at all, Kellogg's advertising simply attempts to convince people that they should eat cereal for breakfast. Its packaging includes step-by-step instructions on how to prepare cereal. In India, where many consumers eat heavy, fried breakfasts and other consumers skip the meal altogether, Kellogg's advertising attempts to convince buyers to switch to a lighter, more nutritious breakfast diet.

Often, differences across international markets are more subtle. They may result from physical differences in consumers and their environments. For example, Japanese culture differs from European culture in several ways. In Japan, for example, humility and deference are considered great virtues, so pushy, hard-hitting sales approaches are considered offensive. Failing to understand such differences in customs and behaviours from one country to another can spell disaster for a marketer's international products and programmes.

Marketers must decide on the degree to which they will adapt their products and marketing programmes to meet the unique cultures and needs of consumers in various markets. On the one hand, they want to standardise their offerings in order to simplify operations and

MAKING CONNECTIONS Linking the concepts

Here's a good place to take some time out and apply the concepts you've examined in the first part of this chapter.

- Think about a specific major purchase you've made recently. What buying process did you follow? What major factors influenced your decision?
- Pick a company that we've discussed in a previous chapter – BT, Arla, Boots or another. How does the company you chose use its understanding of customers and their buying behaviour to build better customer relationships?
- Think about a company like Intel, which sells its products to computer makers and other businesses rather than to final consumers. How would Intel's marketing to business customers differ from Starbucks' marketing to final consumers? The second part of the chapter deals with this issue.

take advantage of cost economies. On the other hand, adapting marketing efforts within each country results in products and programmes that better satisfy the needs of local consumers. The question of whether to adapt or standardise the marketing mix across international markets has created a lively debate in recent years.

BUSINESS MARKETS AND BUSINESS BUYER BEHAVIOUR

In one way or another, most large companies sell to other organisations. Companies such as Airbus, Tata Steel, Caterpillar, Rolls-Royce and countless other firms sell *most* of their products to other businesses (in case you didn't know, Rolls-Royce doesn't make cars any more, it mainly makes aero-engines). Even large consumer products companies, which make products used by final consumers, must first sell their products to other businesses. For example, Procter & Gamble makes many familiar consumer brands – personal-care products like Dove, Lux, Sunsilk and Signal, home-care products such as Cif, Comfort, Domestos and Surf, food products like Bertolli, Knorr, Slim-Fast and Hellman's, and others. But to sell these products to consumers, Procter & Gamble must first sell them to the wholesalers and retailers that serve the consumer market.

Business buyer behaviour refers to the buying behaviour of the organisations that buy goods and services for use in the production of other products and services that are sold, rented or supplied to others. It also includes the behaviour of retailing and wholesaling firms that acquire goods to resell or rent them to others at a profit. In the *business buying process,* business buyers determine which products and services their organisations need to purchase, and then find, evaluate and choose among alternative suppliers and brands. *Business-to-business (B2B) marketers* must do their best to understand business markets and business buyer behaviour.

Business markets

The business market is *huge.* In fact, business markets involve far more money and goods than do consumer markets. For example, think about the large number of business transactions involved in the production and sale of a single set of Pirelli tyres. Various suppliers sell Pirelli the rubber, steel, equipment and other goods that it needs to produce the tyres. Pirelli then sells the finished tyres to retailers, who in turn sell them to consumers. Thus, many sets of *business* purchases were made for only one set of *consumer* purchases. In addition, Pirelli sells tyres as original equipment to manufacturers who install them on new vehicles, and as replacement tyres to companies that maintain their own fleets of company cars, trucks, buses or other vehicles.

Characteristics of business markets

In some ways, business markets are similar to consumer markets. Both involve people who assume buying roles and make purchase decisions to satisfy needs. However, business markets differ in many ways from consumer markets. The main differences are in *market structure and demand,* the *nature of the buying unit* and the *types of decisions and the decision process* involved.

Market structure and demand

The business marketer normally deals with *far fewer but far larger buyers* than the consumer marketer does. Even in large business markets, a few buyers often account for most of the purchasing. For example, when Pirelli sells replacement tyres to final consumers, its potential market includes the owners of the millions of cars currently in use in the EU and around the world. But Pirelli's fate in the business market depends on getting orders from one of only

The 'Intel Inside' slogan has been used for years to keep the Intel brand in the mind of the computer buyer

Source: Getty Images.

a handful of large car makers. Similarly, Black & Decker sells its power tools and outdoor equipment to tens of millions of consumers worldwide. However, it must sell these products through DIY retail outlets – such as B&Q and Wickes in the UK and Ireland, Brico in France and Spain, and Bauhaus in Germany – which provide its key routes to the market.

Business markets are also *more geographically concentrated*. Further, business demand is **derived demand** – it derives ultimately from the demand for consumer goods. Hewlett-Packard and Dell buy Intel microprocessor chips because consumers buy PCs. If consumer demand for PCs drops, so will the demand for computer chips.

Therefore, B2B marketers sometimes promote their products directly to final consumers to increase business demand. For example, Intel's long-running 'Intel Inside' advertising campaign sells PCs to buyers on the virtues of Intel microprocessors. The increased demand for Intel chips boosts demand for the PCs containing them, and both Intel and its business partners win.

Similarly, W.L. Gore promotes Gore-Tex directly to final consumers as a key branded ingredient in waterproof and breathable outdoor clothing – from mountaineering or sailing jackets through to winter ice-climbing boots. You see Gore-Tex hangtags on clothing lines such as Scarpa mountaineering boots, Henri-Lloyd sailing foul-weather gear, and The North Face walking and mountaineering jackets. By making Gore-Tex familiar and attractive to final buyers, W.L. Gore also makes the products containing it more attractive.

In B2B markets where businesses often sell to a few, large buyers, the process of developing relationships with customers is particularly important. This is illustrated in Marketing at Work 5.2.

GE: building B2B customer partnerships

Few brands are more global than GE. For more than 130 years, customers all over the world have used GE products – from light bulbs to refrigerators, cookers, clothes washers and dryers, microwave ovens, dishwashers, coffee makers, room air-conditioners, and hundreds of other products bearing the familiar script GE logo. The company's consumer finance unit – GE Money – helps finance these and other purchasers through credit cards, loans, mortgages and other financial services. GE even entertains us – its NBC Universal Division serves up a diverse fare of network and cable TV channels, movie entertainment and even theme parks. In all, GE offers a huge assortment of consumer products and services.

But here is a fact that would startle most consumers. Did you know that GE's consumer products contribute less than one-third of the company's total $183bn in annual sales? To the surprise of many, most of GE's business comes not from final consumers but from commercial and industrial customers across a wide range of industries. Beyond light bulbs and electronics, GE sells everything from medical imaging technologies, water processing systems and security solutions to power generation equipment, aircraft engines and diesel locomotives.

At a general level, marketing medical imaging technology or diesel locomotives to business customers is like selling refrigerators to final buyers. It requires a deep-down understanding of customer needs and customer-driven marketing strategies that create superior customer value. But that is about where the similarities end. In its business markets, GE, rather than selling to large numbers of small buyers, sells to a few very large buyers. Whereas it might be disappointing when a refrigerator buyer chooses a competing brand, losing a single sale to a large business customer can mean the loss of hundreds of millions of dollars in business.

Also, with GE's business customers, buying decisions are much more complex. An average consumer buying a refrigerator might do a little online research and then pop out to the local electrical store to compare models before buying one. In contrast, buying a batch of jet engines involves a tortuously long buying process, dozens or even hundreds of decision makers from all levels of the buying organisation, and layer upon layer of subtle and not-so-subtle buying influences.

To get an idea of the complexities involved in selling one of GE's industrial products, let's dig deeper into the company's GE Transportation Division and one of its bread-and-butter products, diesel locomotives. GE locomotives might not seem glamorous to you, but they are beautiful brutes to those who buy and use them. One GE Evolution series locomotive can pull the equivalent of 170 Boeing 747 'Jumbo Jet' airliners. It is not difficult to identify potential buyers for a 207 tonne, 4,400 horsepower GE locomotive with an average estimated cost of $2.2m per unit. The real challenge is to win buyers' business by building day-in, day-out and year-in, year-out partnerships with them based on superior products and close collaboration.

In the buying decision, locomotive performance plays an important role. In such big-ticket purchases, buyers carefully scrutinise factors such as cost, fuel efficiency and reliability. By most measures, GE's locomotives outperform competing engines on most of these dimensions. The company's innovative Evolution series locomotives, part of a broader GE 'ecomagination' initiative to build environmentally-friendly products, are now the most technically advanced, fuel-efficient and eco-friendly diesel-electric locomotives in history. Compared with their predecessors, they produce full power but cut fuel consumption by 5 per cent and reduce particulate pollution by 40 per cent. GE's next-generation Evolution Hybrid diesel-electric engines will reduce fuel consumption by another 15 per cent and emissions by as much as 50 per cent.

But locomotive performance is only part of the buying equation. GE wins contracts by partnering with business customers to help them translate that performance into moving their passengers and freight

more efficiently and reliably. CSX Transportation (CSXT), one of GE Transportation's largest customers, has purchased more than 300 GE Evolution locomotives since they were launched in 2005. According to a CSXT purchasing executive, the company 'evaluates many cost factors before awarding . . . a locomotive contract. Environmental impact, fuel consumption, reliability, serviceability [are] all key elements in this decision.' But also important is 'the value of our ongoing partnership with GE'.

A recent high-stakes international deal involving hundreds of GE locomotives demonstrates the potential importance, scope and complexity of some B2B decisions:

GE Transportation recently landed a huge $650 million contract to supply 310 Evolution locomotives to the Kazakhstan National Railway (KTZ) – the largest-ever order for locomotives delivered outside North America. Befitting its importance to not just the companies, but to their countries as well, the deal was inked at the Kazakhstan Embassy in Washington, DC. The signing was attended by high-level executives from both organisations, including the chief executive of GE Transportation and the president of KTZ.

The buying decision was based on a host of factors. KTZ wanted the very best performance technology available, and GE's Evolution locomotives fit the bill nicely. But the deal also hinged on many factors that had little to do with the engine performance. For example, important matters of international economics and politics came into play as well. Whereas the first 10 locomotives were built at GE's US plant, most of the remaining 300 locomotives will be assembled at a newly built, state-owned plant in Pavlodar, Kazakhstan.

Finally, the current contract was anything but an impulsive, one-and-done deal. Rather, it represented the culmination of years of smaller steps between the two organisations – the latest episode in a long-running relationship between GE and KTZ that dates back to the mid-1990s. The relationship accelerated in 2003 when GE won the first of several contracts for modernization kits that updated older KTZ locomotives. 'I am proud that KTZ and GE are extending our relationship,' said the CEO of GE Transportation. 'GE and Kazakhstan have a long and fruitful history of working together.'

Thanks to stories like this one, GE Transportation dominates the worldwide rail locomotive industry, now capturing a phenomenal 80 per cent market share.

More broadly, people throughout the entire GE organisation know that success in B2B markets involves more than just developing and selling superior products and technologies. Business customer buying decisions are made within the framework of a strategic, problem-solving partnership. 'We love the challenge of a customer's problem,' says the company on its GE Transportation website. 'Why? It's an opportunity for a true collaborative partnership. We enjoy the exchange of ideas, whether we're developing a brand new technology or applying existing technologies in innovative new ways. [We] go to great lengths to help our customers succeed.'

'Customer partnerships are at the center of GE and Ecomagination,' confirms GE's Chairman and CEO Jeffrey Immelt in a recent letter to shareholders. 'We are viewed as a technical partner by customers around the world.'

Sources: Quotes and other information from 'GE Transportation Endorses New Tier 3 and 4 Emission Regulations', *Business Wire*, 14 March 2008; 'General Electric Signs Contract to Supply 310 Evolution Series Locomotives to Kazakhstan', *Business Wire*, 28 September 2006; Jim Martin, 'GE to Seal $650 Million Deal', *Knight Ridder Tribune Business News*, 28 September 2006, p. 1; Rick Stouffer, 'GE Locomotives: 100 Years and Still Chuggin', *Knight Ridder Tribune Business News*, 23 September 2007; David Lustig, 'GE Unveils Hybrid Loco', *Railway Gazette International*, July 2007, p. 1; 'GE Transportation Delivers 3,000th GE Evolution® Series Locomotive to Kazakhstan Temir Zholy (KTZ)', *Business Wire*, 18 March 2009; 'Collaborating with Partners', accessed at www.getransportation.com, May 2009; and annual reports and various pages accessed at www.ge.com, October 2009.

Nature of the buying unit

Compared with consumer purchases, a business purchase usually involves *more decision participants* and a *more professional purchasing effort*. Often, business buying is done by trained purchasing agents who spend their working lives learning how to buy better. The more complex the purchase, the more likely it is that several people will participate in the decision-making process. Buying committees made up of technical experts and top management are common in the buying of major goods.

Beyond this, many companies are now upgrading their purchasing functions to 'supply management' or 'supplier development' functions. B2B marketers now face a new breed of higher-level, better-trained supply managers. These supply managers sometimes seem to know more about the supplier company than it knows about itself. Therefore, business marketers must have well-trained marketers and salespeople to deal with these well-trained buyers.

Types of decisions and the decision process

Business buyers usually face *more complex* buying decisions than do consumer buyers. Purchases often involve large sums of money, complex technical and economic considerations, and interactions among many people at many levels of the buyer's organisation. Because the purchases are more complex, business buyers may take longer to make their decisions. The business buying process also tends to be *more formalised* than the consumer buying process. Large business purchases usually call for detailed product specifications, written purchase orders, careful supplier searches and formal approval.

Finally, in the business buying process, buyer and seller are often much *more dependent* on each other. Consumer marketers are often at a distance from their customers. In contrast, B2B marketers may roll up their sleeves and work closely with their customers during all stages of the buying process – from helping customers define problems, to finding solutions, to supporting after-sale operation. They often customise their offerings to individual customer needs.

Business buyer behaviour

At the most basic level, marketers want to know how business buyers will respond to various marketing stimuli. Figure 5.6 shows a model of business buyer behaviour. In this model, marketing and other stimuli affect the buying organisation and produce certain buyer responses. As with consumer buying, the marketing stimuli for business buying consist of the four Ps: product, price, place and promotion (plus people, physical evidence and service delivery process for service products). Other stimuli include major forces in the environment: economic, technological, political, cultural and competitive. These stimuli enter the organisation and

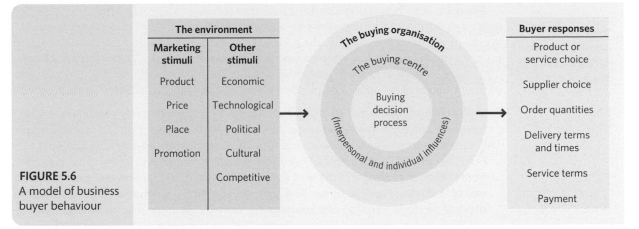

FIGURE 5.6
A model of business buyer behaviour

are turned into buyer responses: product or service choice; supplier choice; order quantities; and delivery, service and payment terms. In order to design good marketing mix strategies, the marketer must understand what happens within the organisation to turn stimuli into purchase responses.

Within the organisation, buying activity consists of two major parts: the buying centre, made up of all the people involved in the buying decision; and the buying decision process. The model shows that the buying centre and the buying decision process are influenced by internal organisational, interpersonal and individual factors as well as by external environmental factors.

The model in Figure 5.6 suggests four questions about business buyer behaviour. What buying decisions do business buyers make? Who participates in the buying process? What are the major influences on buyers? How do business buyers make their buying decisions?

Major types of buying situations

There are three major types of buying situations.[21] At one extreme is the *straight rebuy,* which is a fairly routine decision. At the other extreme is the *new task,* which may call for thorough research. In the middle is the *modified rebuy,* which requires some research.

In a **straight rebuy**, the buyer reorders something without any modifications. It is usually handled on a routine basis by the purchasing department. Based on past buying satisfaction, the buyer simply chooses from the various suppliers on its list. 'In' suppliers try to maintain product and service quality. They often propose automatic reordering systems so that the purchasing agent will save reordering time. 'Out' suppliers try to offer something new or exploit dissatisfaction so that the buyer will consider them.

In a **modified rebuy**, the buyer wants to modify product specifications, prices, terms or suppliers. The modified rebuy usually involves more decision participants than does the straight rebuy. The in suppliers may become nervous and feel pressured to put their best foot forward to protect an account. Out suppliers may see the modified rebuy situation as an opportunity to make a better offer and gain new business.

A company buying a product or service for the first time faces a **new-task situation**. In such cases, the greater the cost or risk, the larger the number of decision participants and the greater their efforts to collect information will be. The new-task situation is the marketer's greatest opportunity and challenge. The marketer not only tries to reach as many key buying influences as possible, but also provides help and information.

The buyer makes the fewest decisions in the straight rebuy and the most in the new-task decision. In the new-task situation, the buyer must decide on product specifications, suppliers, price limits, payment terms, order quantities, delivery times and service terms. The order of these decisions varies with each situation, and different decision participants influence each choice.

Many business buyers prefer to buy a packaged solution to a problem from a single seller. Instead of buying and putting all the components together, the buyer may ask sellers to supply the components *and* assemble the package or system. The sale often goes to the firm that provides the most complete system meeting the customer's needs. Thus, **systems selling** is often a key business marketing strategy for winning and holding accounts. For example, Veolia Environnement provides a complete solution for its customers' industrial waste problems:

Veolia Environnement is a 25 billion euro turnover company that few consumers will ever have heard of. Yet it operates all round the world, generating 48 per cent of its revenue from France, 33 per cent from elsewhere in Europe, 10 per cent from the Americas, and 9 per cent from the rest of the world. Veolia Environnement has subsidiaries in 27 European countries, from France and Portugal in the west to Russia in the east. Industrial waste management is one of Veolia's key business areas. The company can simply arrange to collect and dispose of waste products on behalf of manufacturing, commercial and public sector organisations, but promotes its 'integrated solutions and total waste management' to businesses that want their waste systems professionally managed from start to finish. For example, Veolia offers a complete range of integrated industrial site waste management services, including high pressure water jetting, tank and vessel cleaning, emergency response, chemical cleaning, on-site processing, chemical decontamination and land decontamination. Many municipal authorities across Europe also use Veolia's integrated waste management solutions to deliver their statutory obligation to provide waste and recycling services to local communities.[22]

Participants in the business buying process

Who does the buying of the trillions of euros' worth of goods and services needed by business organisations? The decision-making unit of a buying organisation is called its **buying centre**: all the individuals and units that participate in the business decision-making process. The buying centre includes all members of the organisation who play a role in the purchase decision process. This group includes the actual users of the product or service, those who make the buying decision, those who influence the buying decision, those who do the actual buying and those who control buying information.

The buying centre is not a fixed and formally identified unit within the buying organisation. It is a set of buying roles assumed by different people for different purchases. Within the organisation, the size and make-up of the buying centre will vary for different products and for different buying situations. For some routine purchases, one person – say, a buyer – may assume all the buying centre roles and serve as the only person involved in the buying decision. For more complex purchases, the buying centre may include 20 or 30 people from different levels and departments in the organisation.

The buying centre concept presents a major marketing challenge. The business marketer must learn who participates in the decision, each participant's relative influence and what evaluation criteria each decision participant uses. For example, the Malaysian company San Miguel Woven Products sells disposable surgical gowns to hospitals. It identifies the hospital personnel involved in this buying decision as the purchasing manager, the operating room administrator and the surgeons. Each participant plays a different role. The purchasing manager analyses whether the hospital should buy disposable gowns or reusable gowns. If analysis favours disposable gowns, then the operating room administrator compares competing products and prices and makes a choice. This administrator considers the gown's absorbency, antiseptic quality, design and cost, and normally buys the brand that meets requirements at the lowest cost. Finally, surgeons affect the decision later by reporting their satisfaction or dissatisfaction with the brand.

The buying centre usually includes some obvious participants who are involved formally in the buying decision. For example, the decision to buy a corporate jet will probably involve the company's CEO, chief pilot, a purchasing agent, some legal staff, a member of top management and others formally charged with the buying decision. It may also involve less obvious, informal participants, some of whom may actually make or strongly affect the buying decision. Sometimes, even the people in the buying centre are not aware of all the buying participants. For example, the decision about which corporate jet to buy may actually be made by a corporate board member who has an interest in flying and who knows a lot about aircraft. This board member may work behind the scenes to sway the decision. Many business buying decisions result from the complex interactions of ever-changing buying centre participants.

Major influences on business buyers

Business buyers are subject to many influences when they make their buying decisions. Some marketers assume that the major influences are economic. They think buyers will favour the supplier that offers the lowest price or the best product or the most service. They concentrate on offering strong economic benefits to buyers. However, business buyers respond to both economic and personal factors. Far from being cold, calculating and impersonal, business buyers are human and social as well. They react to both reason and emotion.

Today, most B2B marketers recognise that emotion plays an important role in business buying decisions. For example, you might expect that an advertisement promoting large trucks to corporate fleet buyers would stress objective technical, performance and economic factors. However, a recent ad for Volvo heavy-duty trucks shows two drivers arm-wrestling and claims, 'It solves all your fleet problems. Except who gets to drive.' It turns out that, in the face of an industry-wide driver shortage, the type of truck a fleet provides can help it to attract qualified drivers. The Volvo ad stresses the raw beauty of the truck and its comfort and roominess, features that make it more appealing to drivers. The ad concludes that Volvo trucks are 'built to make fleets more profitable and drivers a lot more possessive'.

Figure 5.7 lists various groups of influences on business buyers – environmental, organisational, interpersonal and individual. *Environmental factors* play a major role. For example, buyer behaviour can be heavily influenced by factors in the current and expected economic environment, such as the level of primary demand, the economic outlook and the cost of money. Another environmental factor is shortages in key materials. Many companies now are more willing to buy and hold larger inventories of scarce materials to ensure adequate supply. Business buyers are also affected by technological, political and competitive developments in the environment. Finally, culture and customs can strongly influence business buyer reactions to the marketer's behaviour and strategies, especially in the international marketing environment.

Business buyer behaviour is also influenced strongly by *organisational factors*. Each buying organisation has its own objectives, policies, procedures, structure and systems, and the business marketer must understand these factors well. Questions such as these arise: How many

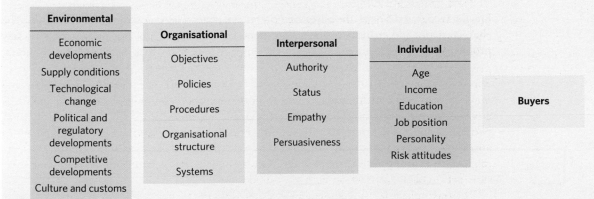

FIGURE 5.7
Major influences on business buyer behaviour

people are involved in the buying decision? Who are they? What are their evaluative criteria? What are the company's policies and limits on its buyers?

The buying centre usually includes many participants who influence each other, so *interpersonal factors* also influence the business buying process. However, it is often difficult to assess such interpersonal factors and group dynamics. Buying centre participants do not wear tags that label them as 'key decision maker' or 'not influential'. Nor do buying centre participants with the highest rank always have the most influence. Participants may influence the buying decision because they control rewards and punishments, are well liked, have special expertise, or have a special relationship with other important participants. Interpersonal factors are often very subtle. Whenever possible, business marketers must try to understand these factors and design strategies that take them into account.

Finally, business buyers are influenced by *individual factors*. Each participant in the business buying decision process brings in personal motives, perceptions and preferences. These individual factors are affected by personal characteristics such as age, income, education, professional identification, personality and attitudes towards risk. Also, buyers have different buying styles. Some may be technical types who make in-depth analyses of competitive proposals before choosing a supplier. Other buyers may be intuitive negotiators who are adept at pitting the sellers against one another for the best deal.

The business buying process

Figure 5.8 lists the eight stages of the business buying process.[23] Buyers who face a new-task buying situation usually go through all stages of the buying process. Buyers making modified or straight rebuys may skip some of the stages. We will examine these steps for the typical new-task buying situation.

Problem recognition

The buying process begins when someone in the company recognises a problem or need that can be met by acquiring a specific product or service. *Problem recognition* can result from internal or external stimuli. Internally, the company may decide to launch a new product that requires new production equipment and materials. Or a machine may break down and need new parts. Perhaps a purchasing manager is unhappy with a current supplier's product quality, service or prices. Externally, the buyer may get some new ideas at a trade show, see an ad, or receive a call from a salesperson who offers a better product or a lower price. In fact, in their advertising, business marketers often alert customers to potential problems and then show how their products provide solutions.

General need description

Having recognised a need, the buyer next prepares a general *need description* that describes the characteristics and quantity of the needed item. For standard items, this process presents few problems. For complex items, however, the buyer may have to work with others – engineers,

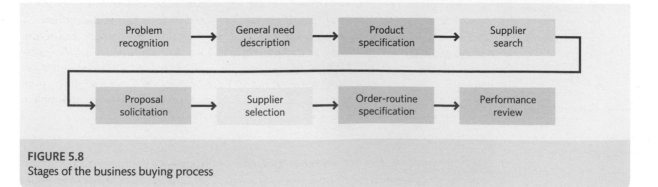

FIGURE 5.8
Stages of the business buying process

users, consultants – to define the item. The team may want to rank the importance of reliability, durability, price and other attributes desired in the item. In this phase, the alert business marketer can help the buyers define their needs and provide information about the value of different product characteristics.

Product specification

The buying organisation next develops the item's technical product specifications, often with the help of a value analysis engineering team. **Value analysis** is an approach to cost reduction in which components are studied carefully to determine if they can be redesigned, standardised, or made by less costly methods of production. The team decide on the best product characteristics and specify them accordingly. Sellers, too, can use value analysis as a tool to help secure a new account. By showing buyers a better way to make an object, outside sellers can turn straight rebuy situations into new-task situations that give them a chance to obtain new business.

Supplier search

The buyer now conducts a *supplier search* to find the best vendors. The buyer can compile a small list of qualified suppliers by reviewing trade directories, doing a computer search, or phoning other companies for recommendations. Today, more and more companies are turning to the Internet to find suppliers. For marketers, this has levelled the playing field – the Internet gives smaller suppliers many of the same advantages as larger competitors.

The newer the buying task, and the more complex and costly the item, the greater the amount of time the buyer will spend searching for suppliers. The supplier's task is to get listed in major directories and build a good reputation in the marketplace. Salespeople should watch for companies in the process of searching for suppliers and make certain that their firm is considered.

Proposal solicitation

In the *proposal solicitation* stage of the business buying process, the buyer invites qualified suppliers to submit proposals. In response, some suppliers will send only a catalogue or a salesperson. However, when the item is complex or expensive, the buyer will usually require detailed written proposals or formal presentations from each potential supplier.

Business marketers must be skilled in researching, writing and presenting proposals in response to buyer proposal solicitations. Proposals should be marketing documents, not just technical documents. Presentations should inspire confidence and should make the marketer's company stand out from the competition.

Supplier selection

The members of the buying centre now review the proposals and select a supplier or suppliers. During *supplier selection,* the buying centre often will draw up a list of the desired supplier attributes and their relative importance. Such attributes include product and service quality, on-time delivery, ethical corporate behaviour, honest communication and competitive prices. Other important factors include repair and servicing capabilities, technical aid and advice, geographic location, performance history and reputation. The members of the buying centre will rate suppliers against these attributes and identify the best suppliers.

Buyers may attempt to negotiate with preferred suppliers for better prices and terms before making the final selections. In the end, they may select a single supplier or a few suppliers. Many buyers prefer multiple sources of supplies to avoid being totally dependent on one supplier and to allow comparisons of prices and performance of several suppliers over time. Today's supplier development managers want to develop a full network of supplier partners that can help the company bring more value to its customers.

Order-routine specification

The buyer now prepares an *order-routine specification*. It includes the final order with the chosen supplier or suppliers and lists items such as technical specifications, quantity needed, expected time of delivery, return policies and warranties. In the case of maintenance, repair and operating items, buyers may use blanket contracts rather than periodic purchase orders. A blanket contract creates a long-term relationship in which the supplier promises to resupply the buyer as needed at agreed prices for a set time period.

Many large buyers now practise *vendor-managed inventory,* in which they turn over ordering and inventory responsibilities to their suppliers. Under such systems, buyers share sales and inventory information directly with key suppliers. The suppliers then monitor inventories and replenish stock automatically as needed.

Performance review

In this stage, the buyer reviews supplier performance. The buyer may contact users and ask them to rate their satisfaction. The *performance review* may lead the buyer to continue, modify or drop the arrangement. The seller's job is to monitor the same factors used by the buyer to make sure that the seller is giving the expected satisfaction.

The eight-stage buying process model provides a simple view of business buying as it might occur in a new-task buying situation. The actual process is usually much more complex. In the modified rebuy or straight rebuy situation, some of these stages would be compressed or bypassed. Each organisation buys in its own way, and each buying situation has unique requirements.

Different buying centre participants may be involved at different stages of the process. Although certain buying process steps usually do occur, buyers do not always follow them in the same order, and they may add other steps. Often, buyers will repeat certain stages of the process. Finally, a customer relationship might involve many different types of purchases ongoing at a given time, all in different stages of the buying process. The seller must manage the total customer relationship, not just individual purchases.

E-procurement: buying electronically and on the Internet

During the past few years, advances in IT have changed the face of the B2B marketing process. Electronic and online purchasing, often called *e-procurement,* has grown rapidly.

Companies can do e-procurement in any of several ways. They can conduct *reverse auctions,* in which they put their purchasing requests online and invite suppliers to bid for the business. Or they can engage in online *trading exchanges,* through which companies work collectively to facilitate the trading process. For example, Exostar ('A cloud-based integration platform for streamlined B2B collaboration', see **www.exostar.com**) is an online trading exchange that connects buyers and sellers in the aerospace and defence, life sciences and financial services industries. The huge exchange has connected more than 300 procurement systems and 40,000 trading partners in 20 countries around the world. Exostar itself is dwarfed in size by Alibaba, one of the biggest companies in the world and one which there is every chance you haven't heard of. At its IPO in September 2014, it was valued on the NYSE at $240bn, making it worth more than eBay and Amazon combined!

Companies can also set up their own *company buying sites.* For example, GE operates a company trading site on which it posts its buying needs and invites bids, negotiates terms and places orders. Or the company can create extranet links with key suppliers. For instance, companies can create direct procurement accounts with suppliers like Dell or Staples through which company buyers can purchase equipment, materials and supplies.

B2B marketers can help customers who wish to purchase online by creating well-designed, easy-to-use websites. For example, *BtoB* magazine rated management consulting and outsourcing firm Accenture's website as one of the 10 best B2B websites of 2010.

Research drove management consulting and outsourcing firm Accenture's latest website redesign. The company wanted visitors to the site to spend more time on it and interact with more content, so the new design had to be focused on user experience. 'The last thing we wanted to do was overwhelm people, but we wanted to find ways to bring them back again and again,' said Molly Spatara, senior director of Internet marketing. . . . Expert commentator, Kara Pernice (managing director of Nielsen Norman Group), says: 'It's easy to tell what Accenture does. It demonstrates achievements and is clear about its different offerings. Video is integrated in appropriate places. For example, you can read about analytics and there is a video right there so you can learn more. There are also related links, which offer people a path of places to go. And another great thing: contact information is always with you, which is invaluable for a b2b site because you eventually need to speak to someone.'[24]

E-procurement gives buyers access to new suppliers, lowers purchasing costs, and hastens order processing and delivery. In turn, business marketers can connect with customers online to share marketing information, sell products and services, provide customer support services and maintain ongoing customer relationships.

So far, most of the products bought online are MRO materials – Maintenance, Repair and Operations. For instance, the London Borough of Barnet purchases everything from chickens to light bulbs over the Internet. National Semiconductor has automated almost all of the company's 3,500 monthly requisitions to buy materials ranging from the sterile booties worn in its fabrication plants to state-of-the-art software. GE, one of the world's biggest purchasers, plans to be buying *all* of its general operating and industrial supplies online within the next few years.

The actual amount of money spent on these types of MRO materials pales in comparison with the amount spent on items such as aircraft parts, computer systems and steel tubing. Yet, MRO materials make up 80 per cent of all business orders and the transaction costs for order processing are high. Thus, companies have much to gain by streamlining the MRO buying process on the Web.

B2B e-procurement yields many benefits. First, it shaves transaction costs and results in more efficient purchasing for both buyers and suppliers. A web-powered purchasing programme eliminates the paperwork associated with traditional requisition and ordering procedures. E-procurement reduces the time between order and delivery. Time savings are particularly dramatic for companies with many overseas suppliers. Finally, beyond the cost and time savings, e-procurement frees purchasing people to focus on more strategic issues. For many purchasing professionals, going online means reducing drudgery and paperwork, and spending more time managing inventory and working creatively with suppliers.

The rapidly expanding use of e-procurement, however, also presents some problems. For example, at the same time that the Web makes it possible for suppliers and customers to share business data and even collaborate on product design, it can also erode decades-old customer–supplier relationships. Many buyers now use the power of the Web to pit suppliers against one another and to search out better deals, products and turnaround times on a purchase-by-purchase basis.

THE JOURNEY YOU'VE TAKEN Reviewing the concepts

This chapter is the last of three chapters that address understanding the marketplace and consumers. Here, we've looked closely at consumers and their buying behaviour. The EU consumer market consists of around 500 million people who consume many trillions of euros' worth of goods and services each year. The business market involves far more euros and items than the consumer market. Final consumers and business buyers vary greatly in their characteristics and circumstances. Understanding consumer and business buyer behaviour is one of the biggest challenges marketers face.

1 Describe the consumer market and the major factors that influence consumer buyer behaviour

The consumer market consists of all the individuals and households who buy or acquire goods and services for personal consumption. A simple stimulus–response model of consumer behaviour suggests that marketing stimuli and other major forces enter the consumer's 'black box'. This black box has two parts: buyer characteristics and the buyer's decision process. Once in the black box, the inputs result in observable buyer responses, such as product choice, brand choice, dealer choice, purchase timing and purchase amount.

Consumer buyer behaviour is influenced by four key sets of buyer characteristics: cultural, social, personal and psychological. Understanding these factors can help marketers to identify interested buyers and to shape products and appeals to serve consumer needs better. Culture is the most basic determinant of a person's wants and behaviour. People in different cultural, subcultural and social class groups have different product and brand preferences. Social factors – such as small-group and family influences – strongly affect product and brand choices, as do personal characteristics, such as age, life-cycle stage, occupation, economic circumstances, lifestyle and personality. Finally, consumer buying behaviour is influenced by four major sets of psychological factors: motivation, perception, learning, and beliefs and attitudes. Each of these factors provides a different perspective for understanding the workings of the buyer's black box.

2   Identify and discuss the stages in the buyer decision process

When making a purchase, the buyer goes through a decision process consisting of need recognition, information search, evaluation of alternatives, purchase decision and post-purchase behaviour. During need recognition, the consumer recognises a problem or need that could be satisfied by a product or service. Once the need is recognised, the consumer moves into the information search stage. With information in hand, the consumer proceeds to alternative evaluation and assesses brands in the choice set. From there, the consumer makes a purchase decision and actually buys the product. In the final stage of the buyer decision process, post-purchase behaviour, the consumer takes action based on satisfaction or dissatisfaction. The marketer's job is to understand the buyer's behaviour at each stage and the influences that are operating.

3   Describe the adoption and diffusion process for new products

The product adoption process comprises five stages: awareness, interest, evaluation, trial and adoption. New-product marketers must think about how to help consumers move through these stages. With regard to the diffusion process for new products, consumers respond at different rates, depending on consumer and product characteristics. Consumers may be innovators, early adopters, early majority, late majority or laggards. Each

group may require different marketing approaches. Marketers often try to bring their new products to the attention of potential early adopters, especially those who are opinion leaders.

4   Define the business market and identify the major factors that influence business buyer behaviour

The business market comprises all organisations that buy goods and services for use in the production of other products and services or for the purpose of reselling or renting them to others at a profit. As compared with consumer markets, business markets usually have fewer, larger buyers who are more geographically concentrated. Business demand is derived demand, and the business buying decision usually involves more, and more professional, buyers.

Business buyers make decisions that vary with the three types of buying situations: straight rebuys, modified rebuys and new tasks. The decision-making unit of a buying organisation – the buying centre – can consist of many different persons playing many different roles. The business marketer needs to know the following: Who are the major buying centre participants? In what decisions do they exercise influence and to what degree? What evaluation criteria does each decision participant use? The business marketer also needs to understand the major environmental, organisational, interpersonal and individual influences on the buying process.

5   List and define the steps in the business buying decision process

The business buying decision process itself can be quite involved, with eight basic stages: problem recognition, general need description, product specification, supplier search, proposal solicitation, supplier selection, order-routine specification and performance review. Buyers who face a new-task buying situation usually go through all stages of the buying process. Buyers making modified or straight rebuys may skip some of the stages. Companies must manage the overall customer relationship, which often includes many different buying decisions in various stages of the buying decision process.

Recent advances in IT have given birth to 'e-purchasing', by which business buyers are purchasing all kinds of products and services electronically, either through electronic data interchange (EDI) links or on the Internet. Such cyberbuying gives buyers access to new suppliers, lowers purchasing costs, and hastens order processing and delivery. However, it can also erode customer–supplier relationships and create potential security problems. Still, business marketers are increasingly connecting with customers online to share marketing information, sell products and services, provide customer support services and maintain ongoing customer relationships.

NAVIGATING THE KEY TERMS

NOTES AND REFERENCES

1 World POPClock, US Census Bureau, **www.census.gov**, July 2014. This website provides continuously updated projections of the US and world populations.

2 Brad Weiners, 'Getting Inside – Way Inside – Your Customer's Head', *Business 2.0*, April 2003, pp. 54–5.

3 Dawn Burton, 'Incorporating Ethnicity into Marketing Intelligence and Planning', *Marketing Intelligence and Planning*, 20(7), 2002, pp. 442–51; Ahmad Jamal, 'Marketing in a Multicultural World: The Interplay of Marketing, Ethnicity and Consumption', *European Journal of Marketing*, 37(11/12), 2003, pp. 1599–620; OFCOM, 'Ethnic Minority Groups and Communication Services, August 2013', accessed July 2014 at **http://stakeholders.ofcom.org.uk**.

4 See Nicholas Thompson and Keith Thompson, 'Can Marketing Practice Keep up with Europe's Ageing Population?', *European Journal of Marketing*, 43(11/12), 2009, pp. 1281–8.

5 Laura Petrecca, 'Savvy, Aging Boomers Buy into Pharma Mantra', *Advertising Age*, 8 July 2002, pp. S8–9; Peter Francese, 'Consumers Today', *American Demographics*, April 2003, pp. 28–9; Robin Goldwyn Blumenthal, 'Gray Is Good', *Barron's*, 22 March 2004, p. 37; Nintendo DS information from **www.nintendo.co.uk**, accessed 14 July 2011.

6 See Edward Keller and Jonathan Berry, *The Influentials* (New York: Free Press, 2003); John Battelle, 'The Net of Influence', *Business 2.0*, March 2004, p. 70; Alicia Clegg, 'Following the Leaders', *Marketing Week*, 30 September 2004, pp. 47–9; Ronald E. Goldsmith, 'The Influentials', *Journal of Product & Brand Management*, 2005, pp. 371–2; and Matthew Creamer, 'Study: Go Traditional to Influence Influencers', *Advertising Age*, 7 March 2005, p. 8.

7 L. Benedictus, 'Psst! Have you heard?' *Guardian*, 30 January 2007. Copyright Guardian News and Media Ltd 2007.

8 See Sharon Goldman Edry, 'No Longer Just Fun and Games', *American Demographics*, May 2001, pp. 36–8; Hillary Chura, 'Marketing Messages for Women Fall Short', *Advertising Age*, 23 September 2002, pp. 4, 14–15; and Pallavi Gogoi, 'I Am Woman, Hear Me Shop', *BusinessWeek Online*, 14 February 2005, accessed at **www.bwonline.com**.

9 Adapted from Michel Marriott, 'Gadget Designers Take Aim at Women', *New York Times*, 7 June 2007, p. C7. Also see Dean Takahashi, 'Philips Focuses on TVs Women Buyers', *McClatchy-Tribune Business News*, 6 January 2008.

10 T. Kesic and S. Piri-Rajh, 'Market Segmentation on the Basis of Food-Related Lifestyles of Croatian Families', *British Food Journal*, 105(3), 2003, pp. 162–74.

11 Information accessed at **www.forrester.com/**, 15 July 2011; and Colin Chung, 'Quantitative Research Approach to Understanding How Consumers Adopt Technology-Related Products and Services', accessed at **www.onetooneinteractive.com/advisor_chung.htl**, July 2005.

12 Jennifer Aaker, 'Dimensions of Measuring Brand Personality', *Journal of Marketing Research,* August 1997, pp. 347–56. See also Aaker, 'The Malleable Self: The Role of Self Expression in Persuasion', *Journal of Marketing Research,* May 1999, pp. 45–57; and Audrey Azoulay and Jean-Noel Kapferer, 'Do Brand Personality Scales Really Measure Brand Personality?', *Journal of Brand Management,* November 2003, p. 143.

13 See Abraham H. Maslow, 'A Theory of Human Motivation', *Psychological Review,* 50, 1943, pp. 370–96. See also Maslow, *Motivation and Personality,* 3rd edn (New York: HarperCollins, 1987); and Barbara Marx Hubbard, 'Seeking Our Future Potentials', *The Futurist,* May 1998, pp. 29–32.

14 See Louise Story, 'Anywhere the Eye Can See, It's Now Likely to See an Ad', *New York Times,* 15 January 2007, accessed at **www.nytimes.com**; Matthew Creamer, 'Caught in the Clutter Crossfire: Your Brand', *Advertising Age,* 1 April 2007, p. 35; and Ruth Mortimer, 'Consumer Awareness: Getting the Right Attention', *Brand Strategy,* 10 December 2008, p. 55.

15 T. Verwijmeren, J.C. Karremans, S.F. Bernritter, W. Stroebe and D.H.J. Wigboldus, 'Warning: You Are Being Primed! The Effect of a Warning on the Impact of Subliminal Ads', *Journal of Experimental Social Psychology,* 49(6), 2013, pp. 1124–9.

16 Bob Garfield, '"Subliminal" Seduction and Other Urban Myths', *Advertising Age,* 18 September 2000, pp. 4, 105; see also 'We Have Ways of Making You Think', *Marketing Week,* 25 September 2003, p. 14; and Si Cantwell, 'Common Sense: Scrutiny Helps Catch Catchy Ads', *Wilmington Star-News,* 1 April 2004, p. 1B.

17 C. Sawers, 'Porridge is the New Fast Food', *The Scotsman,* 17 August 2005.

18 Quotes and information from Yubo Chen and Jinhong Xie, 'Online Consumer Review: Word-of-Mouth as a New Element of Marketing Communication Mix', *Management Science,* March 2008, pp. 477–91; Douglas Pruden and Terry G. Vavra, 'Controlling the Grapevine', *Marketing Management,* July–August 2004, pp. 25–30; and Leo J. Shapiro & Associates, 'User-Generated Content Three Times More Influential Than TV Advertising on Consumer Purchase Decisions', *Marketing Business Weekly,* 28 December 2008, p. 34.

19 See Leon Festinger, *A Theory of Cognitive Dissonance* (Stanford, CA: Stanford University Press, 1957); Schiffman and Kanuk, *Consumer Behaviour* (Upper Saddle River, NJ: Pearson Education, 2009), pp. 219–20; Patti Williams and Jennifer L. Aaker, 'Can Mixed Emotions Peacefully Coexist?', March 2002, pp. 636–49; Adam Ferrier, 'Young Are Not Marketing Savvy; They're Suckers', *B&T Weekly,* 22 October 2004, p. 13; and 'Cognitive Dissonance and the Stability of Service Quality Perceptions', *Journal of Services Marketing,* 2004, pp. 433ff.

20 The following discussion draws from the work of Everett M. Rogers. See his *Diffusion of Innovations,* 5th edn (New York: Free Press, 2003). See also Eric Waarts, Yvonne M. van Everdingen and Jos van Hillegersberg, 'The Dynamics of Factors Affecting the Adoption of Innovations', *Journal of Product Innovation Management,* November 2002, pp. 412–23; Chaun-Fong Shih and Alladi Venkatesh, 'Beyond Adoption: Development and Application of a Use-Diffusion Model', *Journal of Marketing,* January 2004, pp. 59–72; and Richard R. Nelson, Alexander Peterhansl and Bhaven Sampat, 'Why and How Innovations Get Adopted: A Tale of Four Models', *Industrial and Corporate Change,* October 2004, pp. 679–99.

21 Patrick J. Robinson, Charles W. Faris and Yoram Wind, *Industrial Buying Behavior and Creative Marketing* (Boston, MA: Allyn & Bacon, 1967). See also James C. Anderson and James A. Narus, *Business Market Management,* 2nd edn (Upper Saddle River, NJ: Prentice Hall, 2004), ch. 3.

22 Based on information from **www.veoliaenvironnement.com**, accessed July 2011.

23 Robinson, Faris and Wind, *Industrial Buying Behavior,* op. cit., p. 14.

24 *Source:* **http://edit.btobonline.com/article/20100913/FREE/100919977/10-great-websites-accenture-com**, accessed 18 July 2011.

PART THREE

DESIGNING A CUSTOMER-DRIVEN MARKETING STRATEGY AND MARKETING MIX

PUTTING MARKETING INTO ACTION

Now that we've fully explored the context in which marketing is 'done' we move on to consider the details, decisions and processes of putting together a comprehensive marketing strategy.

CHAPTER 6

SEGMENTATION, TARGETING AND POSITIONING: BUILDING THE RIGHT RELATIONSHIPS WITH THE RIGHT CUSTOMERS

AFTER STUDYING THIS CHAPTER, YOU SHOULD BE ABLE TO

- define the three steps of target marketing: market segmentation, target marketing and market positioning
- list and discuss the major bases for segmenting consumer and business markets
- explain how companies identify attractive market segments and choose a target marketing strategy
- discuss how companies position their products for maximum competitive advantage in the marketplace

THE WAY AHEAD
Previewing the concepts

So far, you've learned what marketing is and also about the importance of understanding consumers and the marketplace environment. With that as background, you're now ready to delve deeper into marketing strategy and tactics. This chapter looks further into key marketing strategy decisions – how to divide up markets into meaningful customer groups (market segmentation), choose which customer groups to serve (target marketing), and create market offerings that best serve targeted customers (positioning). Then, the chapters that follow explore the tactical marketing tools – the four Ps – by which marketers bring these strategies to life.

As an opening example of segmentation, targeting and position at work, let's look first at Baltika, Russia's biggest brewer. The Baltika story provides a great example of how smart marketers use segmentation, targeting and positioning to succeed.

BALTIKA: SEGMENTING THE BEER MARKET IN RUSSIA AND THE WEST

Maria Smirnova, Graduate School of Management, St Petersburg State University, Russia

Ever heard of Baltika? If not, chances are you will become familiar with it shortly. Baltika is Russia's leading beer brand – to many Russians, Baltika is beer.

Baltika is considered by many to be the first, true, domestic Russian beer 'brand'. Previously, old Soviet products were state produced. Baltika Brewery was in fact originally opened as a state-owned and managed company before becoming a joint-stock company in the economic reforms of the 1990s and a Western-style limited company in 2014. It is now one of the world's biggest beer producers and Russia's largest FMCG company, running 10 breweries and directly employing 10,000 people in the production of more than 620 million hectolitres per year. Baltika owns more than 1,500 rail wagons to aid distribution – the second-biggest fleet after the Russian state railway.

Source: Getty Images.

From the very beginning, Baltika beer was conceived as a beer of the very highest European quality that would be brewed according to classical techniques. In order to achieve this, management invested in the reconstruction and development of the enterprise – bringing in advanced equipment and technologies to allow the production of the highest quality beers. The success of this programme has made Baltika the leader in the Russian beer market, a position that the company has held since 1996. This is no mean feat – contrary to Western perceptions, Russia is not the easiest country in which to market alcoholic drinks, particularly beer. Certainly, the country and its people have a reputation for enjoying drinking, but tough regulation and ingrained cultural preferences for other types of drinks in an increasingly competitive market mean that success has never been assured. Furthermore, unlike many other world beer markets, the Russian market is very fragmented and the shares of the main players are not large. Baltika is the one exception – the company is twice as big as its nearest competitor.

As a brand, Baltika is consistently rated amongst Russia's top three when evaluated on criteria of market position, stability and capacity for overcoming geographic borders and cultural barriers. Baltika today is Europe's first beer brand in terms of volume.

The right beer for the right drinker

Baltika has a portfolio of sub-brands, the most popular of which are the number '3' and '7' beers (see Table 6.1). The numbering system is unique to Baltika and Russia – marketing was not a concept widely understood in Soviet Russia, so rather than emotive or intriguing names, numbers were used instead. Over time, there has been no reason to change as everyone in Russia knows and understands the system. Baltika believes that the means to continued success lies in supplying 'the right beer to the right people' – that is, in segmenting the market and supplying each segment with an appropriate product. The company recognises that it is still in a developing market. Consumer brand loyalty is quite low and regional pride is high, so Baltika uses its network of breweries across Russia to provide consumers with 'local' products. Having this portfolio means that customers can still experiment and switch but stay with Baltika.

This is a very simple approach, but Baltika also uses more sophisticated marketing techniques to take the whole Russian market and break it down into segments. To do this Baltika uses a three-dimensional matrix model of the market created after extensive and continuing market research, with dimensions labelled 'price', 'need states' and 'occasions'. In this matrix, segments are given descriptive names like 'safe and smart', which represents conservative drinkers who prefer innovations and changes to their drinks to be minor; 'health and well-being', which contains those drinkers who are most concerned about

TABLE 6.1 Baltika brands

Brand name	Launched	Characteristics
Baltika No. 0	2001	Non-alcoholic
Baltika No. 1	1992	Light
Baltika No. 2 Pale	2004	Light and fresh
Baltika No. 3 Classic	1992	Golden and smooth
Baltika No. 4 Original	1992	Dark and bitter
Baltika No. 5 Gold	2002	Premium beer
Baltika No. 6 Porter	1995	Porter-type beer
Baltika No. 7 Export	1994	Premium export beer
Baltika No. 8 Wheat	2001	Fruity wheat beer
Baltika No. 9 Extra	1998	Strong and pale
Baltika Cooler	2006	Refreshing

the impact of beer on their health and waistline – Baltika introduced Russia's first non-alcoholic beer just for this segment, calling it Baltika No. 0. A third example of a segment is the 'sophisticates', who will pay a high price for a premium and exotic product. Baltika caters for this group by using its licensed production of Kronenbourg 1664 – a brand perceived as being complex and foreign.

Baltika markets its products to each segment by varying the way in which it uses pricing, packaging and promotional tools like advertising. For example, for the more price- and value-conscious drinkers, Baltika introduced 1 litre cans to be sold through supermarkets. For socialisers at bars who are paying more, the same beer is put into glass bottles with a distinctive shape.

Using its modelling, Baltika has noticed that some segments are growing more rapidly than others, and is hoping to track this evolving market environment by updating its portfolio through innovation and licensing – as it did with Baltika No. 0. As average income levels rise, drinkers are trading up from value brands (a segment in decline) to mid-price products in greater numbers, and the new brand – Baltika Cooler – has a 60 per cent share of this segment filled with young urbanites.

As the company grows, it is looking more and more to expand into international markets. Baltika recognises wisely that just because it has put a lot of effort into segmenting the Russian beer market, this does not mean that foreign markets can be broken up in the same way. The company believes that the strategic positioning of beer in international markets is essentially based around two main price segments – premium and mainstream – and that Baltika brands can best be positioned in Western markets as a premium/speciality beer. Close to home, in the CIS nations – which tend to be geographical neighbours of Russia – Baltika has fallen naturally into a premium position attractive to young, professional adults on good incomes who prefer a non-Western brand. Political unrest in and around Ukraine in 2014 might be turning the Russian heritage into a negative, though!

In the USA the leading brand Baltika exports is No. 9 (a strong beer that symbolises self-confidence), and the brand is promoted through sponsorship of sports events – especially ice hockey with its Eastern European following. The favourite alcoholic beverage for Russian Americans is beer. Among imported beers, Baltika is now their first preference.

This targeting of the Russian immigrant community in foreign markets is not limited to the USA. Baltika's President, Anton Artemiev, said recently, 'The UK is a country very much inhabited by Russian speakers' – in London alone there are 300,000 Russian-speaking people, many high-society people who spend a week in Moscow and a week in London, going back and forth.

Catering successfully for these ethnic/cultural segments has given Baltika a foothold in Western countries – but can it take the next step and move into the rest of the market? And what about countries in which there is no substantial ethnic Russian population? Further segmentation work will be required.

Sources: Institutional Investor Rating of Annual Russian Business Leader Studies, available from http://www.beer-union.com/search.php?search=Baltika; Baltika press releases, available from http://eng.baltika.ru/; stories from www.beer-union. com; Business Week Russia, 'The Best Russian Brands', http://www.ourfishbowl. com; 'Baltika Driving Russian Premium Beer Growth', from http://cee-foodindustry. com/; 'Stepping Out – A Story About Russian Companies Promoting their Brands Abroad', by Dmitri Frol, available from http://www.ethnicusa.com; 'Alcohol Preferences of Russian Americans', Global Advertising Strategies, Market Data, Research Products, 13 March 2006; "Baltika" Named Russia's Best Exporter; from www.fis.ru, 21 June 2007; interviews with Marcho Kuyumdzhiev, Vice President for Marketing, at Baltika Breweries, and Anna Balakina, Marketing Manager, International Marketing Group.

Companies today recognise that they cannot appeal to all buyers in the marketplace, or at least not to all buyers in the same way. Buyers are too numerous, too widely scattered and too varied in their needs and buying practices. Moreover, the companies themselves vary widely in their abilities to serve different segments of the market. Instead, a company must identify the parts of the market that it can serve best and most profitably. It needs to design strategies to build the *right* relationships with the *right* customers.

FIGURE 6.1
Steps in market segmentation, targeting and positioning

Thus, most companies are being choosier about the customers with whom they wish to build relationships. Most have moved away from mass marketing and towards *market segmentation and targeting* – identifying market segments, selecting one or more of them, and developing products and marketing programmes tailored to each. Instead of scattering their marketing efforts (the 'shotgun' approach), firms are focusing on the buyers who have greater interest in the values they create best (the 'rifle' approach).

Figure 6.1 shows the three major steps in target marketing. The first is **market segmentation** – dividing a market into smaller groups of buyers with distinct needs, characteristics or behaviours who might require separate products or marketing mixes. The company identifies different ways to segment the market and develops profiles of the resulting market segments. The second step is **target marketing** – evaluating each market segment's attractiveness and selecting one or more of the market segments to enter. The third step is **market positioning** – setting the competitive positioning for the product and creating a detailed marketing mix. We discuss each of these steps in turn.

MARKET SEGMENTATION

Markets consist of buyers, and buyers differ in one or more ways. They may differ in their wants, how they intend to use the product, resources, locations, buying attitudes and buying practices. Through market segmentation, companies divide large, heterogeneous markets into smaller segments that can be reached more efficiently and effectively with products and services that match their unique needs. In this section, we discuss four important segmentation topics: segmenting consumer markets, segmenting business markets, segmenting international markets and requirements for effective segmentation.

Segmenting consumer markets

There is no single way to segment a market. A marketer has to try different segmentation variables, alone and in combination, to find the best way to view the market structure. Table 6.2 outlines the major variables that might be used in segmenting consumer markets. Here we look at the major *geographic*, *demographic*, *psychographic* and *behavioural* variables.

Geographic segmentation

Geographic segmentation is about dividing the market into different geographical sectors. These sectors might be continents, nations, regions, cities or even a single street. A company may decide to operate in one or a few of these geographical areas – or to operate in all areas but pay attention to geographical differences in needs and wants, as Baltika does when using local breweries to brew local beers.[1]

TABLE 6.2 Major segmentation variables for consumer markets

Geographic	
World region or country	Europe (Western, Southern, Northern, Eastern), North America, Africa, Asia-Pacific, UK, Belgium, Kenya, Japan
Country region	French regions – Alsace, Limousin, Picardie; English counties – Yorkshire, Essex, Cornwall; Italian provinces – Campania, Lazio, Tuscany
Town/city size	Under 5,000; 5–20,000; 20–50,000; 50–100,000; 100–250,000; 250–500,000; 500–1,000,000; 1–4,000,000; over 4 million
Population density	Urban, suburban, rural
Climate	Mediterranean, arctic, temperate, tropical
Demographic	
Age	Under 6, 6–11, 12–19, 20–34, 35–49, 50–64, 65+
Gender	Male, female
Family size	1–2, 3–4, 5+
Life-cycle stage	Young, single; young married, no children; young, married with children; older, married with children; older, married, no children under 18; older, single; other
Income	Under £10,000; £10–20,000; £20–30,000; £30–50,000; £50–100,000; £100,000 and over
Occupation	Professional and technical; managers, officials and proprietors; clerical; sales; craftspeople; supervisors; operatives; farmers; retired; students; unemployed; homemakers
Education	Elementary or less; secondary; college; graduate; postgraduate
Religious beliefs	Buddhist, Christian, Muslim, Hindu, Jew, agnostic, atheist
Ethnicity	English, Irish, Scots, Welsh in the UK; Catalan, Castilian, Anadalusians in Spain; Flemings and Walloons in Belgium
Generation	Baby boomer, Generation X, Generation Y
Nationality	British, French, Spanish, Russian
Psychographic	
Social class	Lower lowers, upper lowers, working class, middle class, upper middles, lower uppers, upper uppers
Lifestyle	Achievers, strivers, survivors
Personality	Compulsive, gregarious, authoritarian, ambitious
Behavioural	
Occasions	Regular, special, one-off
Benefits	Quality, service, economy, convenience, speed
User status	Non-user, ex-user, potential user, first-time user, regular user
User rates	Light user, medium user, heavy user
Loyalty status	None, medium, strong, absolute
Readiness stage	Unaware, aware, informed, interested, desirous, intending to buy
Attitude towards product	Enthusiastic, positive, indifferent, negative, hostile

Many companies today are localising their products, advertising, promotion and sales efforts to fit the needs of individual regions, cities and even neighbourhoods. For example, Asda has supermarkets across the UK. The mix of products in the shop is influenced by the characteristics of the local area. Wealth levels, ethnic diversity, local industries and delicacies with a traditional geographic home will all have an impact on what is available and these products will often be sourced from the local area.

Asda stores in Scotland will stock a wider range of haggis, Lincolnshire stores have a wider variety of sausages and local favourites like 'chine' – a shoulder cut of pork, partly boned, filled with parsley, sold cooked and eaten cold. The rise in the number of people living in the UK of Polish origin is reflected by the addition of Polish foods and drinks to the shelves – brands like Zywiec beer and Pamapol ready meals. In time, some of these products will cross into the mainstream – the 1990s saw naan breads move from being a niche category product to the mass market.

If you think of the family board game Monopoly, you probably think of the London version. This was an adaptation of the original 1930s US version which had streets and landmarks from Atlantic City in New Jersey. The London version was marketed across the British Commonwealth set of nations – but there now exists a great variety of different sets. The German 'standard' version is based on Berlin, the French on Paris, the Norwegian on Oslo and the Austrian combines places from eight different cities across the country. The version for Swansea in Wales is printed in English and Welsh, and Belgian boards have French and Flemish text. Other than these national versions, many local cities across Europe have their own version – Rotterdam in the Netherlands, Milan in Italy and Barcelona and Seville in Spain. Cities are able to lobby the producer – Parker Brothers – to produce a version of their own city.

Other companies are seeking to cultivate as-yet-untapped geographic territory. For example, many multiple retailers in Germany have begun implementing plans for expansion into Eastern Europe, and Russian companies are hoping to exploit opportunities after consolidating their position in domestic markets – Baltika is not an exception in this regard.

In contrast, other retailers are developing new store concepts that will give them access to higher density urban areas. For example, IKEA is introducing stores in the centre of cities.[2] It is placing these stores in high-density markets, such as London and Amsterdam, where full-size stores are impractical. Similarly, Tesco has a large number of small 'cornerstore'-sized supermarkets called Tesco Express, locating them in central locations near concentrations of office workers and transportation hubs like stations, and it is no coincidence that Aldi often has supermarkets near concentrations of students.

Demographic segmentation

Demographic segmentation divides the market into groups based on variables such as age, gender, family size, family life cycle, income, occupation, education, religion, race, generation and nationality. Demographic factors are the most popular bases for segmenting customer groups. One reason is that consumer needs, wants and usage rates often vary closely in line with demographic variables. Another is that demographic variables are easier to measure than most other types of variables. Even when market segments are first defined using other bases, such as benefits sought or behaviour, their demographic characteristics must be known in order to assess the size of the target market and to reach it efficiently.

Age and life-cycle stage

Consumer needs and wants change with age. Some companies use **age and life-cycle segmentation**, offering different products or using different marketing approaches for different age and life-cycle groups. For example, Gap has branched out to target people at different ages and life stages. In addition to its standard line of clothing, the retailer now offers babyGap, GapKids, GapBody and GapMaternity.

Marketers must be careful to guard against stereotypes when using age and life-cycle segmentation, especially in this era of social change. For example, although some 70-year-olds require wheelchairs, others play tennis. Similarly, whereas some 40-year-old couples are sending their children off to university, others are just beginning new families. Thus, age is often a poor predictor of a person's life cycle, health, work or family status, needs and buying power. Companies marketing to mature consumers usually employ positive images and appeals. For example, ads for Dove 'Pro-Age' – designed to improve the elasticity and

Age and life-cycle segmentation: Dove recognises that middle-aged consumers use cosmetics for different purposes compared with the young

Source: Image courtesy of The Advertising Archives.

appearance of the 'maturing skin' of women over 50 – feature attractive older women and uplifting messages.[3]

Gender

Gender segmentation has long been used in clothing, cosmetics, toiletries and magazines. For example, Berghaus, manufacturers of gear for outdoor activities, has sought advice from female climbers and hikers at the design stage for the last 20 years. European car manufacturers like Renault, Seat and Fiat are producing cars with stylings, accessories and features specifically to appeal to women. Bramdean Asset Management now has a specific division – called Bramdiva – specialising in managing the wealth of women.[4]

Some consultancy companies, such as the aptly named *Pretty Little Head*, have sprung up to help (still) predominantly male senior managers avoid the dreadful mistake of trying to appeal to women via a strategy of 'shrink it and pink it' – taking products implicitly designed for men and making them smaller and more brightly coloured. Recent examples of how this can go badly wrong include Fujitsu with a 'female-oriented' laptop called 'Floral Kiss', and a chocolate bar from Cadbury's called 'Crispello' that highlighted its low-calorie value. The issue here is not that women do not want products that are different from those for men, but that they want them to be different in meaningful and beneficial ways. Under Armour – the US athletic clothing design firm – nearly fell into this trap, but realised in time that what was important was that its garments worked and supported the consumer, be they male or female.[5] Considering gender to be male versus female is rather binary and radical young things are suggesting that gender – and sexuality – is more of a continuum than a discrete category. Many marketers are focused on the potential of 'the pink pound' – the label given to the spending power of homosexuals – but there is something of a backlash from those in the LGBT communities against what they see as cynical manipulation.[6]

Income

Income segmentation has long been used by the marketers of products and services such as cars, boats, clothing, cosmetics, financial services and travel. Many companies target affluent consumers with luxury goods and convenience services. Stores such as Harrods in London or Quartier 206 in Berlin pitch everything from expensive jewellery and fine fashions to glazed Australian apricots priced at £20 a pound (450 g).[7] Credit card companies offer elite credit cards dripping with perks for those who spend thousands a month, rather than thousands a year.

To cater for its very best customers, Harrods has created its 'Harrods Rewards' programme. Every pound spent means one point credited to your account. Collect 500 points and you receive a gift voucher for £5 – but spend more and that is when the real benefits start. Make it to level 'Green' by spending between £500 and £5,000 in a year and you will be entitled to free delivery, complimentary tea and coffee in the lounges, and access to special in-store events such as couture fashion shows. Spending £5–10,000 takes you to 'Gold' level, meaning that alterations to clothes bought at Harrods are done without additional payment. Beyond 'Gold' there is 'Black', requiring an annual spend of more than £10,000. Achieving this brings you the services of a team of personal shoppers who will give you their full attention – as you recline comfortably in an armchair drinking camomile tea, they will bring products to you. Harrods is not the only company to recognise the potential of perks for cardholders – American Express has a card just for its very, very best customers and

MaW 6.1 shows how Savile Row tailors charge very high prices to the very limited number of men that can afford their handmade suits.

However, not all companies that use income segmentation target the affluent. For example, many retailers – such as Aldi and Lidl – successfully target low- and middle-income groups. More than half the sales in such stores come from shoppers with family incomes under £15,000. When Aldi scouts out locations for new stores, it looks for lower-middle-class districts where people wear cheaper shoes, drive old cars and often have students as neighbours.

Psychographic segmentation

Psychographic segmentation divides buyers into different groups based on social class, lifestyle or personality characteristics. People in the same demographic group can have very different psychographic make-ups.

Sebiro – segmentation in men's clothing

The Japanese have a word for a high-quality suit, *Sebiro*. Many languages incorporate words from other languages – through trade, political and social links and popular culture. Languages also change over time. They evolve, they are enriched by new words and others go out of fashion. English is a prime example. *Entrepreneur* comes from French, *chutney* from Hindi, *delicatessen* from German. So, where did the Japanese get the word Sebiro from? Etymologically, Sebiro is a corruption of the London street name Savile Row, a corruption being an informal or loose usage of a different term – we say bus, rather than omnibus, to describe the public transport vehicle. Say Sebiro out loud and you will hear a clear connection to the original. But why on Earth would the Japanese use a London street name as their word for a nice suit?

In the image here, we see a partial answer to this. Pictured are the Crown Prince Hirohito of Japan – the future Emperor Hirohito – and Edward, Prince of Wales, the future King Edward VIII. The historian Niall Ferguson explains:

From London to Tokyo, the well-dressed gentleman will be found within a Savile Row suit.

Source: Getty Images/General Photographic Agency.

> The Japanese prince was in London on a pre-wedding shopping spree. A Henry Poole representative had already sailed all the way to Gibraltar to take the Crown Prince's measurements, which were then cabled ahead to London. Henry Poole's ledger for the year in question shows the enormous order placed in Hirohito's name: military uniforms, embroidered waistcoats, dinner jackets, morning coats. A typical item in the list reads: 'A fancy cashmere suit, a blue cloth suit, and a striped flannel suit.' Hirohito was far from being the only

The list of past customers at Henry Poole is a list of the great and the good, and also the not-so-great and the downright bad.

Source: Rex Features/Times Newspapers (t); Alamy Images/Andrew Holt (b).

Poole has received warrants (public endorsements) from royalty across Europe and the world.

Savile Row

So how did Savile Row become synonymous with fine tailoring? In 1846 Henry Poole moved onto 'The Row' and was soon followed by other tailoring companies. Businesses often cluster together for reasons of convenience and natural or human resources – Silicon Valley in California being a prime example. Ede and Ravenscroft – who will likely supply you with your gown at graduation – moved to Savile Row in 1871. This Central London location put the tailors close to their well-to-do clients, making it more convenient for them to come and have clothes measured, adjusted and repaired. The bowler hat was invented on Savile Row, being designed for the gamekeepers of an aristocrat to wear in order to ensure protection from shot pheasants and angry poachers! Nearby to Savile Row is Jermyn Street, still home to makers of bespoke shirts, and makers of handmade shoes can be found locally, just as they could in the mid-nineteenth century. As society has changed, so have the clientele of Savile Row. Only a small percentage are still aristocrats; more come from Westminster, the financial power houses of the City of London and men who appreciate the finest suits money can buy and are willing to save up for them.

Compared with even a second- or third-tier high-street retailer, the total number of 'units' produced by Savile Row is tiny. The firms survive by producing a very limited number of suits for a highly select group of customers who represent a small fraction of 1 per cent of the total market and pay very high prices. All markets have these small but highly lucrative segments that are supplied by small but distinctive firms, whether it be cars from Lamborghini, watches from Philippe Patek, food hampers from Fortnum & Mason or Italian yachts from Riva. Never wanted a yacht? Go and look at pictures of a Riva Aquariva at www.riva-yacht.com – then you will!

Table 6.3 shows the different prices for suits from different retailers. Pricing is closely involved with

foreign dignitary in the market for an immaculately tailored English suit. Preserved in Henry Poole's basement are thousands of suit patterns for clients ranging from the last Emperor of Ethiopia, Haile Selassie, to the last Tsar of Russia, Nicholas II. Poole's most devoted customer was Jitendra Narayan, Maharaja of Cooch Behar, whose lifetime purchases of bespoke suits exceeded a thousand. In every case, the aim was the same: to be as well dressed as the perfect English gentleman.

As Niall Ferguson mentioned, Hirohito was by no means the only royal customer. Over the centuries, Henry

TABLE 6.3

Company	Suit price points	Target market
H&M	£115	16–25: first suit buyers, students
Banana Republic	£250–400	22–30: young professionals/first graduate job
Suitsupply	£259–699	25–40: dress-conscious professionals
Henry Poole & Co.	£2,600 and over	30–70: men for whom dress is of paramount importance

segmentation. Other than price, think how these companies target different market segments based on age, income, life stage and other factors. Which of them would you expect to shop at as a student, or a young professional, or as an old rich person?

Suitsupply

Suitsupply is a Dutch company, founded and wholly owned in the Netherlands by the entrepreneur Fokke de Jong. In just 15 years it has grown from one outlet in Amsterdam to more than fifty, spanning Europe with retail locations in – among others – Italy, Germany, the UK, Latvia and Lithuania. Outside Europe it has a well-established presence in the USA, and like many Western companies is beginning to find its way in China.

How and for whom Suitsupply makes suits is a lesson in market segmentation, targeting and positioning strategy. Suitsupply is known for selecting atypical retail locations – such as old townhouses in Canada and a penthouse and garden on top of a department store in Chicago. Despite this deliberate eclecticism, the locations are not just chosen for their uniqueness, but because they are in close proximity to the workplaces of men who wear suits to work. Financial districts in London, New York, Frankfurt and Paris get multiple stores. Suitsupply has recognised that the organic reasons that tailoring ended up on Savile Row still apply and has located itself accordingly – geographic and demographic segmentation. Indeed, one of its three London sites is at the end of Savile Row.

Does Suitsupply target all suit wearers equally in its marketing? No. It does not go for the bottom end of the market – suits sold by high-street firms like Marks & Spencer – which can retail for as little as €100. Nor does it go for the top end of the market, competing against the established full-bespoke service provided by tailors such as Henry Poole, Huntsman or Ozwald Boateng who can charge upwards of €3,000 a suit. Suitsupply has deliberately placed itself in the middle, targeting specifically men who want better quality and better fitting tailoring than is provided off the rack on the high street, but who do not have the means to afford the high-end product. Not a Nissan, not a Rolls-Royce, but a BMW.

So, geographical segmentation – through locations in urban centres with high densities of office-workers. Demographic segmentation – just clothing for men, and men on middle to high incomes. Psychographic segmentation – men involved in professional services where appearance is a factor. Behavioural segmentation – suits for men who know, or believe they know, the

Suitsupply seeks to position itself between the perfect luxury of Savile Row and the affordable prices of the high street. Better tailoring at an acceptable price for the urban professional

Source: Shutterstock.com/Viorel Sima (l); Shutterstock.com/Mark LaMoyne (r).

difference between poor- and good-quality suits, and who care about the clothes they wear.

It is a great position to be in, but how come there is room there for a new company to establish itself? Here is the view of Drake Bennett at *Bloomberg Businessweek*:

> **As men have bought fewer suits, stores such as Saks Fifth Avenue and Lord & Taylor, and France's Galeries Lafayette and Germany's Galeria Kaufhof, have shifted resources and floor space to more lucrative women's goods, including fragrances, accessories, and jewellery. As online shopping cuts their margins, the embattled department stores have accelerated the process, even though suits, with their higher prices and tailoring requirements, are the sort of thing people still prefer to buy in person. 'Suitsupply's future is extremely bright, because it's filling a vacuum that took two decades to create,' says Burt Flickinger III, managing director of Strategic Resource Group, a retail and consumer-goods consulting firm. 'The market's big enough for the company to continue to grow geometrically for the next few years.'**

The marketing environment has changed. Companies that used to cater for this segment have declined, disappeared or deliberately moved away, leaving a gap in the market that Suitsupply is acting to fill by positioning itself correctly.

So what is it like to be a Suitsupply customer? Assuming you are in the store and are serious about buying a suit, you will have options. The 'Blue Line' provides good-quality suits, retailing at £259. The suit is tailored with your choice of fabric and a range of basic alteration options that can be selected in the store, ensuring a unique and personally tailored suit. The 'Purple Line' suits start at £299. For the margin you get a wider range of fabrics to choose from and a greater number of basic fits from which your individual suit will be modified. Further up the price scale there is the 'Suit Up' range, offering more than 600 good-quality fabrics of all types and hand-finished detailing for buttons and cuffs. These retail from £469. At the very top of the scale is the 'Jort' range – named after Jort Kelder, a Dutch journalist and fashion guru. For £699 you get full canvassing, hand stitching and only the very highest quality materials.

Therein lies an important lesson in segmentation strategy. Not only must a company position itself against attractive, profitable segments, but also it must manage its range of products and services to cater for sub-groups within them.

Sources: http://www.retail-insider.com/retail-insider/tail-insider.com/2014-01/suitsupplys-1st-canadian-store-opens.html; http://www.businessweek.com/articles/2013-11-07/suitsupply-affordable-high-end-mens-suits-for-the-impatient-masses; N. Ferguson, *Civilization: The West and the Rest* (London: Penguin, 2011); 'Stitched up on Savile Row': http://news.bbc.co.uk/local/london/hi/people_and_places/newsid_8241000/8241730.stm; https://henrypoole.com/hp/wp-content/uploads/2013/03/hp-brochure1.pdf

In the previous chapter we discussed how the products people buy reflect their *lifestyles*. As a result, marketers often segment their markets by consumer lifestyles. Saga, which started by creating holiday packages for the over 50s, has expanded into a range of financial services for the elderly, and has found it necessary to offer a range of products that take account of the widely differing lifestyles – in regard to activity, desire to travel and plans for the future. Old people are not all the same, are planning to enjoy their retirement in different ways, and they certainly are not all planning on leaving their money to their children! Vegetarians, people with hobbies and dedicated supporters of a football team are examples of how lifestyle choices can impact on consumption decisions.[8]

Marketers have also used *personality* variables to segment markets. For example, marketing for Honda motor scooters *appears* to target young men about town. But it is *actually* aimed at a much broader personality group. One old ad, for example, showed a delighted child bouncing up and down on his bed while the announcer says, 'You've been trying to get there all your life.' The ad reminded viewers of the euphoric feelings they got when they broke away from authority and did things their parents told them not to do. Thus, Honda is appealing to the rebellious, independent child in all of us. In fact, 22 per cent of scooter riders are retired. 'The older buyers are buying them for kicks,' says one elderly customer. 'They never had the opportunity to do this as kids.'[9]

Behavioural segmentation

Behavioural segmentation divides buyers into groups based on their knowledge, attitudes, uses, or responses to a product. Many marketers believe that behaviour variables are the best starting point for building market segments.

Occasions

Buyers can be grouped according to occasions when they get the idea to buy, actually make their purchase, or use the purchased item. **Occasion segmentation** can help firms build up product usage. For example, eggs are most often consumed at breakfast. But the wonderfully named British Egg Information Service – an industry body – promotes the use of eggs in other meals, providing recipes and other resources in a bid to increase egg consumption.[10]

Some special days such as Mother's Day and Father's Day, were originally promoted partly to increase the sale of chocolates, flowers and especially cards – earning them the nickname of 'Hallmark Holidays'. Many marketers prepare special offers and ads for special days in the calendar. Cadbury begins heavy promotion of its Creme Eggs in the run-up to

Fortnum & Mason creates and markets luxury hampers for only the most special of occasions

Source: Courtesy of Fortnum and Mason.

Easter – after Easter, these campaigns come to an almost immediate halt. Some companies focus on specific, important events in people's lives. Anichini in Florence provides handmade clothes for christenings – important events in a traditionally Catholic country. Confetti provides a wide range of items for weddings – invitations, cake decorations and of course 174 different types of confetti![11]

Fortnum & Mason, Marks & Spencer and other firms providing ready-to-eat food use occasion segmentation in designing and marketing their comestibles. Fortnum & Mason offers specific sets of food and drink for weddings, birthdays, annual holidays, days at the races or a regatta, while Marks & Spencer picks slightly more mundane occasions to focus on – office meetings, children's parties and home entertaining. To receive a Fortnum & Mason's hamper of goodies is a wonderful thing.[12]

Benefits sought

A powerful form of segmentation is to group buyers according to the different benefits that they seek from the product. **Benefit segmentation** requires finding the major benefits people look for in the product class, the kinds of people who look for each benefit, and the major brands that deliver each benefit. For instance, our chapter-opening example pointed out that Baltika has identified many different segments of beer drinkers. Proctor & Gamble has a range of detergents matched to segments. Each segment seeks a unique combination of benefits, from cleaning and bleaching to economy, fabric softening, fresh smell, strength or mildness, and lots of suds or only a few.

Champion athletic wear segments its markets according to benefits that different consumers seek from their active wear. For example, 'Fit and Polish' consumers seek a balance between function and style – they exercise for results but want to look good doing it. 'Serious Sports Competitors' exercise heavily and live in and love their active wear – they seek performance and function. By contrast, 'Value-Seeking Mums' have low sports interest and low active wear involvement – they buy for the family and seek durability and value. Thus, each segment seeks a different mix of benefits. Champion must target the benefit segment or segments that it can serve best and most profitably using appeals that match each segment's benefit preferences.

User status

Markets can be segmented into non-users, ex-users, potential users, first-time users and regular users of a product. For example, blood banks cannot rely only on regular donors. They must also recruit new first-time donors and remind ex-donors – each will require different marketing appeals. Included in the potential user group are consumers facing life-stage changes – such as newly-weds and new parents – who can be turned into heavy users. For example, P&G acquires the names of parents-to-be and showers them with product samples and ads for its Pampers and other baby products in order to capture a share of their future purchases. It invites them to join **MyPampers.com**, giving them access to expert parenting advice, an email newspaper, and coupons and special offers.

Usage rate

Markets can also be segmented into light, medium and heavy product users. Heavy users are often a small percentage of the market but account for a high proportion of total consumption. For example, in the fast-food industry, heavy users make up only 20 per cent of patrons but eat up about 60 per cent of all the food served. A single heavy user, typically a single male in his 20s or 30s who does not know how to cook, might spend as much as £20 in a day at fast-food restaurants and visit them more than 20 times a month. Despite claims by some consumers that the fast-food chains are damaging their health, these heavy users are extremely loyal. 'They insist they don't need saving,' says one analyst, 'protesting that they are far from the clueless fatties anti-fast-food activists make them out to be.' Even the heaviest users 'would have to be stupid not to know that you can't eat only burgers and fries and not exercise,' he says.[13]

Interestingly, although fast-food companies such as Burger King, McDonald's and KFC depend a lot on heavy users and do all they can to keep them satisfied with every visit, these companies often target light users with their ads and promotions. The heavy users will visit the restaurants regardless. The company's marketing budget is instead focused on trying to convince light users that they want a burger in the first place.

Loyalty status

A market can also be segmented by consumer loyalty. Consumers can be loyal to brands (Berghaus), stores (John Lewis) and companies (Volvo). Buyers can be divided into groups according to their degree of loyalty. Some consumers are completely loyal – they buy one brand all the time. For example, Apple has customers, but it also has CUSTOMERS, a small but almost cult-like following of loyal users:

> It's the 'Cult of the Mac', and it's populated by 'macolytes'. Urbandictionary.com defines a *macolyte* as, 'One who is fanatically devoted to Apple products, especially the Macintosh computer. Also known as a Mac Zealot.' (Sample usage: 'He's a macolyte; don't even "think" of mentioning Microsoft within earshot.') How about Anna Zisa, a graphic designer from Milan who doesn't really like tattoos but stencilled an Apple tat on her behind. 'It just felt like the most me thing to have,' says Zisa. 'I like computers. The apple looks good and sexy.' Such fanatically loyal users helped keep Apple afloat during the lean years, and they are now at the forefront of Apple's burgeoning empire.[14]

Other consumers are somewhat loyal – they are loyal to two or three brands of a given product or favour one brand while sometimes buying others. Still other buyers show no loyalty to any brand. They either want something different each time they buy or buy whatever is on sale.

A company can learn a lot by analysing loyalty patterns in its market. It should start by studying its own loyal customers. For example, by studying 'macolytes', Apple can better pinpoint its target market and develop marketing appeals. By studying its less loyal buyers, the company can detect which brands are most competitive with its own. By looking at customers who are shifting away from its brand, the company can learn about its marketing weaknesses.

Using multiple segmentation bases

Marketers rarely limit their segmentation analysis to only one or a few variables. Rather, they are increasingly using multiple segmentation bases in an effort to identify smaller, better-defined target groups – as Baltika did with its modelling. Thus, a bank may not only identify a group of wealthy retired adults, but also, within that group, distinguish several segments based on their current income, assets, savings and risk preferences, housing and lifestyles.

One good example of multivariable segmentation is 'geodemographic' segmentation. Several business information services – such as Claritas, Experian, Acxiom and MapInfo – have arisen to help marketing planners link census and transaction data with consumer lifestyle patterns the better to segment their markets down to postcodes, streets and even households. One of the leading lifestyle segmentation systems is Experian's Mosaic consumer classification system. The Mosaic system classifies every UK household based on a host of demographic factors – such as age, educational level, income, occupation, family composition, ethnicity and housing – and behavioural and lifestyle factors – such as purchases, free-time activities and media preferences. Mosaic Global extends this across 590 million households in 26 countries. Utilising Mosaic, marketers can use where you live to paint a surprisingly precise picture of who you are and what you might buy.

Mosaic classifies UK households into 67 unique lifestyle types aggregated into 15 groups.[15] Its segments carry such exotic names as 'Global Power Brokers', 'Country Loving Elders' and 'Multicultural Towers'. 'Those image-triggered nicknames save a lot of time and technical research jargon explaining what you mean,' says one marketer. 'It's the names that bring the clusters to life,' says another.[16]

Regardless of what you call the categories, such systems can help marketers to segment people and locations into marketable groups of like-minded consumers. Each segment exhibits unique characteristics and buying behaviour. The category 'Asian Identities' recognises the rise of concentrated pockets of Asian ethnic minorities now residing in areas formerly occupied by the white working classes of the 1950s and requiring goods and services tailored to their cultural and social needs. The importance, increasing number and diversity of older customers are reflected by segmentation into different flavours – 'Bungalow Quietude' are the stay-at-home pensioners, favouring comfortable, familiar products and brands, while 'Beachcombers' are seeing more of the outdoors in the UK and beyond – thereby requiring a completely different mix of products and services to satisfy their different wants and needs.

Such segmentation provides a powerful tool for marketers of all kinds – from the simplest of products to the most complex of services and procedures. For example, the Bonati Institute, an advanced arthroscopic spinal surgery facility, used Prizm, a US equivalent of Mosaic, to help target prospective clients. The Institute wanted to know what its potential clients were like, where they lived and how to reach them. Claritas began by sorting 5,000 previous Bonati Institute patients into Prizm segments and ranking the segments according to their demographic, lifestyle and media behaviours. It found that the best target groups were middle-income consumers who were not aware of their orthopaedic-related choices. Armed with this information, the Institute devised a precisely targeted direct mail campaign to inform the best potential clients about a seminar series on spinal surgery technology. The results were immediate: seminar attendance increased by 20 per cent, producing a substantial increase in scheduled surgeries.[17]

Segmenting business markets

Consumer and business marketers use many of the same variables to segment their markets. Business buyers can be segmented geographically, demographically (industry, company size), or by benefits sought, user status, usage rate and loyalty status. Yet, business marketers also use some additional variables, such as customer *operating characteristics*, *purchasing approaches*, *situational factors* and *personal characteristics*. By going after segments instead of the whole market, companies can deliver just the right value proposition to each segment served and capture more value in return.

Almost every company serves at least some business markets. For example, you probably know American Express as a company that offers personal credit cards to consumers. But American Express also targets businesses in three other segments: merchants, corporations and small businesses. It has developed distinct marketing programmes for each segment. In the merchants' segment, American Express focuses on convincing new merchants to accept the card and on managing relationships with those that already do. For larger corporate customers, the company offers a corporate card programme, which includes extensive employee expenses and travel management services. It also offers this segment a wide range of asset management, retirement planning and financial education services. Finally, for small-business customers, American Express has created the OPEN: Small Business Network, 'the one place that's all about small business'. Small-business cardholders can access the network for everything from account and expense management software to expert small-business management advice and connecting with other small-business owners to share ideas and get recommendations.[18]

Many companies set up separate systems for dealing with larger or multiple-location customers. For example, Steelcase, a major producer of office furniture, first segments customers into 10 industries, including banking, insurance and electronics. Next, company salespeople work with independent Steelcase dealers to handle smaller, local or regional Steelcase customers in each segment. But many national, multiple-location customers, such as Exxon/Mobile or IBM, have special needs that may reach beyond the scope of individual dealers. So Steelcase uses national account managers to help its dealer networks handle its national accounts – we will talk more about this practice later (see Chapter 13).

Within a given target industry and customer size, the company can segment by purchase approaches and criteria. As in consumer segmentation, many marketers believe that *buying behaviour* and *benefits* provide the best basis for segmenting business markets.[19]

Segmenting international markets

Few companies have either the resources or the will to operate in all, or even most, of the countries that dot the globe. Although some large companies, such as Coca-Cola or Sony, sell products in more than 200 countries, most international firms focus on a smaller set. Operating in many countries presents new challenges. Different countries, even those that are close together, can vary greatly in their economic, cultural and political make-up. Thus, just as they do within their domestic markets, international firms need to group their world markets into segments with distinct buying needs and behaviours.

Companies can segment international markets using one or a combination of several variables. They can segment by *geographic location*, grouping countries by regions such as Western Europe, the Pacific Rim, the Middle East or Africa. Geographic segmentation assumes that nations close to one another will have many common traits and behaviours. Although this is often the case, there are many exceptions. For example, although Austria and Germany have much in common, both differ culturally and economically from the neighbouring Czech Republic. Even within a region, consumers can differ widely. For example, some marketers lump all Central and South American countries together. However, the Dominican Republic is no more like Brazil than Italy is like Sweden. Many Central and South Americans do not even speak Spanish, including 140 million Portuguese-speaking Brazilians and the millions in other countries who speak a variety of Indian dialects.

World markets can also be segmented on the basis of *economic factors*. For example, countries might be grouped by population income levels or by their overall level of economic development. A company's economic structure shapes its population's product and service needs and, therefore, the marketing opportunities it offers. Countries can be segmented by

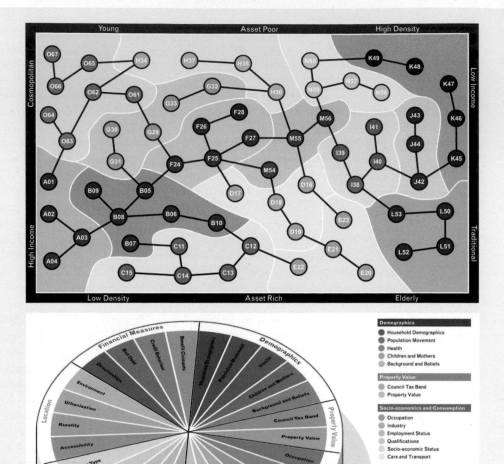

Demographics
- Household Demographics
- Population Movement
- Health
- Children and Mothers
- Background and Beliefs

Property Value
- Council Tax Band
- Property Value

Socio-economics and Consumption
- Occupation
- Industry
- Employment Status
- Qualifications
- Socio-economic Status
- Cars and Transport

Property Characteristics
- Housing Age
- Second Residences
- Amenities
- Tenure
- Building Type

Location
- Accessibility
- Rurality
- Urbanisation
- Environment

Financial Measures
- Directorships
- Bad Debt
- Credit Behaviour
- Benefit Claimants

Group	Description	%👤	%🏠	Type	Description	%👤	%🏠
A	Alpha Territory	4.28	3.54	A01	Global Power Brokers	0.32	0.30
				A02	Voices of Authority	1.45	1.18
				A03	Business Class	1.83	1.50
				A04	Serious Money	0.68	0.56
B	Professional Rewards	9.54	8.23	B05	Mid-Career Climbers	2.90	2.30
				B06	Yesterday's Captains	1.80	1.84
				B07	Distinctive Success	0.48	0.48
				B08	Dormitory Villagers	1.81	1.29
				B09	Escape to the Country	1.41	1.31
				B10	Parish Guardians	1.14	1.00
C	Rural Solitude	4.84	4.40	C11	Squires Among Locals	1.01	0.85
				C12	Country Loving Elders	1.32	1.31
				C13	Modern Agribusiness	1.61	1.36
				C14	Farming Today	0.53	0.53
				C15	Upland Struggle	0.36	0.34

D	Small Town Diversity	9.21	8.75	D16	Side Street Singles	1.21	1.17
				D17	Jacks of All Trades	2.60	1.99
				D18	Hardworking Families	2.87	2.63
				D19	Innate Conservatives	2.53	2.96
E	Active Retirement	3.41	4.34	E20	Golden Retirement	0.52	0.67
				E21	Bungalow Quietude	1.42	1.79
				E22	Beachcombers	0.57	0.60
				E23	Balcony Downsizers	0.90	1.29
F	Suburban Mindsets	13.16	11.18	F24	Garden Suburbia	2.82	2.14
				F25	Production Managers	2.31	2.63
				F26	Mid-Market Families	3.75	2.70
				F27	Shop Floor Affluence	2.82	2.73
				F28	Asian Attainment	1.45	0.98
G	Careers and Kids	5.34	5.78	G29	Footloose Managers	1.11	1.67
				G30	Soccer Dads and Mums	1.34	1.34
				G31	Domestic Comfort	1.24	1.09
				G32	Childcare Years	1.46	1.52
				G33	Military Dependants	0.19	0.17
H	New Homemakers	3.99	5.91	H34	Buy-to-Let Territory	1.08	1.79
				H35	Brownfield Pioneers	1.13	1.38
				H36	Foot on the Ladder	1.48	2.37
				H37	First to Move In	0.30	0.37
I	Ex-Council Community	10.60	8.67	I38	Settled Ex-Tenants	2.08	2.06
				I39	Choice Right to Buy	1.90	1.72
				I40	Legacy of Labour	3.46	2.68
				I41	Stressed Borrowers	3.15	2.20
J	Claimant Cultures	4.52	5.16	J42	Worn-Out Workers	1.82	2.30
				J43	Streetwise Kids	0.90	1.05
				J44	New Parents in Need	1.80	1.80
K	Upper Floor Living	4.30	5.18	K45	Small Block Singles	1.26	1.77
				K46	Tenement Living	0.62	0.80
				K47	Deprived View	0.36	0.50
				K48	Multicultural Towers	1.09	1.11
				K49	Re-Housed Migrants	0.97	0.99
L	Elderly Needs	4.04	5.96	L50	Pensioners in Blocks	0.89	1.31
				L51	Sheltered Seniors	0.67	1.12
				L52	Meals on Wheels	0.51	0.86
				L53	Low Spending Elders	1.98	2.68
M	Industrial Heritage	7.39	7.40	M54	Clocking Off	2.18	2.25
				M55	Backyard Regeneration	2.40	2.06
				M56	Small Wage Owners	2.81	3.09
N	Terraced Melting Pot	6.54	7.02	N57	Back-to-Back Basics	2.50	1.97
				N58	Asian Identities	1.06	0.88
				N59	Low-Key Starters	1.60	2.72
				N60	Global Fusion	1.38	1.44
O	Liberal Opinions	8.84	8.48	O61	Convivial Homeowners	1.74	1.68
				O62	Crash Pad Professionals	1.41	1.09
				O63	Urban Cool	1.25	1.10
				O64	Bright Young Things	1.36	1.52
				O65	Anti-Materialists	1.12	1.03
				O66	University Fringe	1.10	0.93
				O67	Study Buddies	0.87	1.14

One of the leading lifestyle segmentation systems is Experian's Mosaic consumer classification

Source: Used with kind permission of Experian.

political and legal factors such as the type and stability of government, receptivity to foreign firms, monetary regulations and the amount of bureaucracy. Such factors can play a crucial role in a company's choice of which countries to enter and how. *Cultural factors* can also be used, grouping markets according to common languages, religions, values and attitudes, customs and behavioural patterns.

Segmenting international markets based on geographic, economic, political, cultural and other factors assumes that segments should consist of clusters of countries. However, many companies use a different approach called **intermarket segmentation**. They form segments of consumers who have similar needs and buying behaviour even though they are located in different countries. For example, Mercedes-Benz targets the world's well-to-do, regardless of their country.

MTV targets the world's teenagers. The world's 1.2 billion teens have a lot in common: they study, shop and sleep. They are exposed to many of the same major issues: love, crime, homelessness, ecology and working parents. In many ways, they have more in common with each other than with their parents. 'Last year I was in seventeen different countries,' says one expert, 'and it's pretty difficult to find anything that is different, other than language, among a teenager in Japan, a teenager in the UK, and a teenager in China.' MTV bridges the gap between cultures, appealing to what teens around the world have in common. Sony, Reebok, Nike and many other firms also actively target global teens. For example, Sprite's 'Image is nothing – obey your thirst' theme appeals to teens the world over.[20]

Requirements for effective segmentation

Clearly, there are many ways to segment a market, but not all segmentations are effective. For example, buyers of table salt could be divided into blonde and brunette customers. But hair colour obviously does not affect the purchase of salt. Furthermore, if all salt buyers bought the same amount of salt each month, believed that all salt is the same, and wanted to pay the same price, the company would not benefit from segmenting this market.

To be useful, market segments must be:

● *Measurable*: The size, purchasing power and profiles of the segments can be measured. Certain segmentation variables are difficult to measure. For example, there are 8 million left-handed people in the UK[21] – almost equalling the combined populations of Norway and Ireland. Yet few products are targeted towards this left-handed segment. The major problem may be that the segment is hard to identify and measure. There is no data on the demographics of lefties, and national government census agencies do not keep track of left-handedness. Private data companies keep reams of statistics on other demographic segments but not on handedness.

● *Accessible*: The market segments can be effectively reached and served. Suppose a fragrance company finds that heavy users of its brand are single men and women who stay out late and socialise a lot. Unless this group lives or shops at certain places and is exposed to certain media, its members will be difficult to reach.

● *Substantial*: The market segments are large or profitable enough to serve. A segment should be the largest possible homogeneous group worth pursuing with a tailored marketing programme. It would not pay, for example, for a car manufacturer to develop cars especially for people whose height is greater than 7 feet (2.1 m).

● *Differentiable*: The segments are conceptually distinguishable and respond differently to different marketing mix elements and programmes. If married and unmarried women respond similarly to a sale on perfume, they do not constitute separate segments.

● *Actionable*: Effective programmes can be designed for attracting and serving the segments. For example, although one small airline identified seven market segments, its staff were too small to develop separate marketing programmes for each segment.

MAKING CONNECTIONS   Linking the concepts

Slow down a bit and smell the roses. How do the companies you do business with employ the segmentation concepts you're reading about here?

● Can you identify specific companies, other than the examples already presented, that practise the different types of segmentation just discussed?

● Using the segmentation bases you've just read about, segment the UK footwear market. Describe each of the major segments and sub-segments. Keep these segments in mind as you read the next section on target marketing.

TARGET MARKETING

Market segmentation reveals the firm's market segment opportunities. The firm now has to evaluate the various segments and decide how many and which segments it can serve best. We now look at how companies evaluate and select target segments.

Evaluating market segments

In evaluating different market segments, a firm must look at three factors: segment size and growth; segment structural attractiveness; and company objectives and resources. The company must first collect and analyse data on current segment sales, growth rates and expected profitability for various segments. It will be interested in segments that have the right size and growth characteristics. But 'right size and growth' is a relative matter. The largest, fastest-growing segments are not always the most attractive ones for every company. Smaller companies may lack the skills and resources needed to serve the larger segments. Or they may find these segments too competitive. Such companies may target segments that are smaller and less attractive in an absolute sense, but that are potentially more profitable for them.

The company also needs to examine major structural factors that affect long-term segment attractiveness.[22] For example, a segment is less attractive if it already contains many strong and aggressive *competitors*. The existence of many actual or potential *substitute products* may limit prices and the profits that can be earned in a segment. The relative *power of buyers* also affects segment attractiveness. Buyers with strong bargaining power relative to sellers will try to force prices down, demand more services, and set competitors against one another – all at the expense of seller profitability. Finally, a segment may be less attractive if it contains *powerful suppliers* who can control prices or reduce the quality or quantity of ordered goods and services.

Even if a segment has the right size and growth and is structurally attractive, the company must consider its own objectives and resources. Some attractive segments can be dismissed quickly because they do not mesh with the company's long-term objectives. Or the company may lack the skills and resources needed to succeed in an attractive segment. The company should enter only segments in which it can offer superior value and gain advantages over competitors.

Selecting target market segments

After evaluating different segments, the company must now decide which and how many segments it will target. A **target market** consists of a set of buyers who share common needs or characteristics that the company decides to serve.

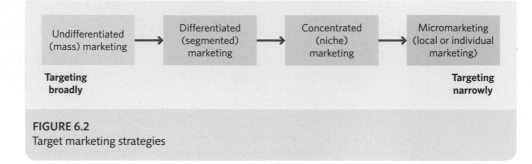

FIGURE 6.2
Target marketing strategies

Because buyers have unique needs and wants, a seller could potentially view each buyer as a separate target market. Ideally, then, a seller might design a separate marketing programme for each buyer. However, although some companies do attempt to serve buyers individually, most face larger numbers of smaller buyers and do not find individual targeting worthwhile. Instead, they look for broader segments of buyers. More generally, target marketing can be carried out at several different levels. Figure 6.2 shows that companies can target very broadly (undifferentiated marketing), very narrowly (micromarketing), or somewhere in between (differentiated or concentrated marketing).

Undifferentiated marketing

Using an **undifferentiated (mass) marketing** strategy, a firm might decide to ignore market segment differences and target the whole market with one offer. This mass-marketing strategy focuses on what is *common* in the needs of consumers rather than on what is *different*. The company designs a product and a marketing programme that will appeal to the largest number of buyers.

As noted earlier in the chapter, most modern marketers have strong doubts about this strategy. Difficulties arise in developing a product or brand that will satisfy all consumers. Moreover, mass marketers often have trouble competing with more focused firms that do a better job of satisfying the needs of specific segments and niches.

Differentiated marketing

Using a **differentiated (segmented) marketing** strategy, a firm decides to target several market segments and designs separate offers for each. General Motors tries to produce a car for every

Differentiated marketing: Estée Lauder offers hundreds of different products aimed at carefully defined segments, from its original Estée Lauder brand appealing to age 50+ baby boomers to Aveda, with earthy origins that appeal to younger New Age types

Source: Photos by Amanda Kamen.

'purse, purpose, and personality'. Gap Inc. has created three different retail store formats – Gap, Banana Republic and Old Navy – to serve the varied needs of different fashion segments. And Estée Lauder offers hundreds of different products aimed at carefully defined segments:

> Estée Lauder is an expert in creating differentiated brands that serve the tastes of different market segments. Five of the top-ten best-selling prestige perfumes in the United States belong to Estée Lauder. So do eight of the top-ten prestige make-up brands. There's the original Estée Lauder brand, with its gold and blue packaging, which appeals to older, 50+ baby boomers. Then there's Clinique, the company's most popular brand, perfect for the middle-aged mom with no time to waste and for younger women attracted to its classic free gift offers. For young, fashion-forward consumers, there's M.A.C., which provides make-up for clients like Girls' Aloud and Dita von Teese. For the young and trendy, there's the Stila line, containing lots of shimmer and uniquely packaged in clever containers. And, for the New Age type, there's upscale Aveda, with its salon, make-up and lifestyle products, based on the art and science of earthy origins and pure flower and plant essences, celebrating the connection between Mother Nature and human nature.[23]

By offering product and marketing variations to segments, companies hope for higher sales and a stronger position within each market segment. Developing a stronger position within several segments creates more total sales than undifferentiated marketing across all segments. Estée Lauder's combined brands give it a much greater market share than any single brand could. The Estée Lauder and Clinique brands alone reap a combined 40 per cent share of the prestige cosmetics market.

But differentiated marketing also increases the costs of doing business. A firm usually finds it more expensive to develop and produce, say, 10 units of ten different products than 100 units of one product. Developing separate marketing plans for the separate segments requires extra marketing research, forecasting, sales analysis, promotion planning and channel management. As well as this, trying to reach different market segments with different advertising increases promotion costs. Thus, the company must weigh increased sales against increased costs when deciding on a differentiated marketing strategy.

Concentrated marketing

A third market coverage strategy, **concentrated (niche) marketing**, is especially appealing when company resources are limited. Instead of going after a small share of a large market, the firm goes after a large share of one or a few smaller segments or niches. For example, Oshkosh Truck is the world's largest producer of airport rescue trucks and front-loading concrete mixers. Tetra sells 80 per cent of the world's tropical fish food, and Steiner Optical captures 80 per cent of the world's military binoculars market.

Through concentrated marketing, the firm achieves a strong market position because of its greater knowledge of consumer needs in the niches it serves and the special reputation it acquires. It can market more *effectively* by fine-tuning its products, prices and programmes to the needs of carefully defined segments. It can also market more *efficiently*, targeting its products or services, channels and communications programmes only towards consumers that it can serve best and most profitably.

Whereas segments are fairly large and normally attract several competitors, niches are smaller and may attract only one or a few competitors. Niching offers smaller companies an opportunity to compete by focusing their limited resources on serving niches that may be unimportant to or overlooked by larger competitors. Consider Apple. Rather than competing head-on with other PC makers as they slash prices and focus on volume, Apple invests in research and development, making it the industry trendsetter. For example, when the company introduced iTunes, it captured more than 70 per cent of the music download market. The iPad effectively owns the tablet market. Such innovation has created a loyal base of consumers who are willing to pay more for Apple's distinctive products.

Many companies start as nichers to get a foothold against larger, more resourceful competitors, then grow into broader competitors. For example, Ryanair began by providing a cheaper, no-frills service between southern Ireland and London using just one aeroplane – it is now a serious player in world aviation. In contrast, as markets change, some mega-marketers develop niche markets to create sales growth. For example, in recent years, Pepsi has introduced several niche products, such as Sierra Mist, Pepsi Edge, Mountain Dew Code Red and Mountain Dew LiveWire. Initially, these brands combined accounted for barely 5 per cent of Pepsi's overall soft-drinks sales. However, Sierra Mist has now blossomed into Pepsi's fastest-growing beverage brand, and Code Red and LiveWire have revitalised the Mountain Dew brand. Says Pepsi-Cola North America's chief marketing officer, 'The era of the mass brand has been over for a long time.'[24]

Today, the low cost of setting up shop on the Internet makes it even more profitable to serve seemingly minuscule niches. Small businesses, in particular, are realising riches from serving small niches on the Web. One 'webpreneur' who achieved astonishing results is the artist Jacquie Lawson. Jacquie sells e-cards to a dedicated and ever-growing number of subscribers who are willing to pay for the distinctiveness and personality of the designs.[25]

Concentrated marketing can be highly profitable. At the same time, it involves higher-than-normal risks. Companies that rely on one or a few segments for all of their business will suffer greatly if the segment turns sour. Or larger competitors may decide to enter the same segment with greater resources. For these reasons, many companies prefer to diversify in several market segments.

Micromarketing

Differentiated and concentrated marketers tailor their offers and marketing programmes to meet the needs of various market segments and niches. At the same time, however, they do not customise their offers to each individual customer. **Micromarketing** is the practice of tailoring products and marketing programmes to suit the tastes of specific individuals and locations. Rather than seeing a customer in every individual, micromarketers see the individual in every customer. Micromarketing includes *local marketing* and *individual marketing*.

Local marketing

Local marketing involves tailoring brands and promotions to the needs and wants of local customer groups – cities, neighbourhoods and even specific stores. Citibank provides different mixes of banking services in each of its branches, depending on neighbourhood demographics. Kraft helps supermarket chains identify the specific cheese assortments and shelf positioning that will optimise cheese sales in low-income, middle-income and high-income stores and in different ethnic communities.

Local marketing has some drawbacks. It can drive up manufacturing and marketing costs by reducing economies of scale. It can also create logistics problems as companies try to meet the varied requirements of different regional and local markets. Further, a brand's overall image might be diluted if the product and message vary too much in different localities.

Still, as companies face increasingly fragmented markets, and as new supporting technologies develop, the advantages of local marketing often outweigh the drawbacks. Local marketing helps a company to market more effectively in the face of pronounced regional and local differences in demographics and lifestyles. It also meets the needs of the company's first-line customers – retailers – who prefer more fine-tuned product assortments for their neighbourhoods.

Individual marketing

In the extreme, micromarketing becomes **individual marketing** – tailoring products and marketing programmes to the needs and preferences of individual customers. Individual marketing has also been labelled one-to-one marketing, mass customisation and markets-of-one marketing. We will discuss this issue in depth later in the section on direct marketing (see Chapter 13), but here is an outline.

The widespread use of mass marketing has obscured the fact that for centuries consumers were served as individuals: the tailor custom-made the suit, the cobbler designed shoes for

Individual marketing: the UK's Driver and Vehicle Licensing Authority (DVLA) recognises that some people will pay for personalised number plates for their cars

Source: DVLA, http://www. dvla-som-co.uk/home/. Crown Copyright.

the individual, the cabinetmaker made furniture to order. Today, however, new technologies are permitting many companies to return to customised marketing. More powerful computers, detailed databases, robotic production and flexible manufacturing – and interactive communication media such as email and the Internet – all have combined to foster 'mass customisation'. *Mass customisation* is the process through which firms interact one to one with masses of customers to design products and services tailor-made to individual needs.[26] As we will discuss later (see Chapter 14), technology even allows replication of replacement teeth and vertebrae that are identical to the organic originals.

Dell creates custom-configured computers and Ford lets buyers 'build a vehicle' from a palette of options. Marks & Spencer plc produces shirts custom-fitted for men who send in their specific measurements. Visitors to Nike's NikeID website can personalise their trainers by choosing from hundreds of colours and putting an embroidered word or phrase on the tongue. Even government agencies get in on the act. Visit the UK's vehicle licensing agency, DVLA, and you can choose your next licence plate letter/number combination.

Companies selling all kinds of products – from computers, foods, clothing and golf clubs to fire engines – are customising their offerings to the needs of individual buyers. 'Morelli's Gelato' in the Harrods Food Hall will produce a little tub of ice cream made up to your personal recipe in just 24 hours. Morelli's has been requested to produce ice creams for weddings (champagne and strawberry), flavours for the experimentally inclined (parmesan and pear), even the downright weird (fancy a tub of mushroom sorbet?). Someone did, and Morelli's had it ready the next day.

Consumer goods marketers are not the only ones going one to one. Business-to-business marketers are also finding new ways to customise their offerings. For example, John Deere manufactures seeding equipment that can be configured in more than 2 million versions to individual customer specifications. The seeders are produced one at a time, in any sequence, on a single production line.

Mass customisation provides a way to stand out against competitors. Consider Oshkosh Truck:

Oshkosh Truck specialises in making heavy-duty fire, airport-rescue, cement, garbage, snow-removal, ambulance and military vehicles. According to one account, 'Whether you need to plough your way through sand or snow, Oshkosh has your vehicle, by gosh.' Oshkosh has grown rapidly and profitably over the past decade. What's its secret? Mass customisation – the ability to personalise its products and services to the needs of individual customers. For example, when firefighters order a truck from Oshkosh, it's an event. They travel to the plant to watch the vehicle, which may cost as much as $800,000, take shape. The firefighters can choose from 19,000 options. A stripped-down fire truck costs $130,000, but 75 per cent of Oshkosh's customers order lots of extras, like hideaway stairs, ladders, special doors, compartments and firefighting foam systems for those difficult-to-extinguish fires. Some bring along paint chips so they can customise the colour of their fleet. Others are content just to admire the vehicles, down to the water tanks and hideaway ladders. 'Some chiefs even bring their wives; we encourage it,' says the president of Pierce Manufacturing, Oshkosh's firefighting unit. 'Buying a fire truck is a very personal thing.' Indeed, Pierce customers are in town so often that the Holiday Inn renamed its lounge the Hook and Ladder. Through such customisation and personalisation, Oshkosh has gained a big edge over its languishing larger rivals.[27]

Unlike mass production, which eliminates the need for human interaction, one-to-one marketing has made relationships with customers more important than ever. Just as mass production was the marketing principle of the last century, mass customisation is becoming a marketing principle for the twenty-first century. The world appears to be coming full circle – from the good old days when customers were treated as individuals, to mass marketing when nobody knew your name, and back again.

The move towards individual marketing mirrors the trend in consumer *self-marketing*. Increasingly, individual customers are taking more responsibility for determining which products and brands to buy. Consider two business buyers with two different purchasing styles. The first sees several salespeople, each trying to persuade him to buy his or her product. The second sees no salespeople but rather logs on to the Internet. She searches for information on available products; interacts electronically with various suppliers, users and product analysts; and then makes up her own mind about the best offer. The second purchasing agent has taken more responsibility for the buying process, and the marketer has had less influence over her buying decision.

As the trend towards more interactive dialogue and less advertising monologue continues, self-marketing will grow in importance. As more buyers look up consumer reports, join Internet product discussion forums, and place orders via the phone or online, marketers will have to influence the buying process in new ways. They will need to involve customers more in all phases of the product development and buying processes, increasing opportunities for buyers to practise self-marketing.

Choosing a target marketing strategy

Companies need to consider many factors when choosing a target marketing strategy. Which strategy is best depends on *company resources*. When the firm's resources are limited, concentrated marketing makes the most sense. The best strategy also depends on the degree of *product variability*. Undifferentiated marketing is more suited for uniform products such as grapefruit or steel. Products that can vary in design, such as cameras and cars, are more suited to differentiation or concentration. The *product's life-cycle stage* also must be considered. When a firm introduces a new product, it may be practical to launch only one version, and undifferentiated marketing or concentrated marketing may make the most sense. In the mature stage of the product life cycle, however, differentiated marketing begins to make more sense.

Another factor is *market variability*. If most buyers have the same tastes, buy the same amounts and react in the same way to marketing efforts, undifferentiated marketing is appropriate. Finally, *competitors' marketing strategies* are important. When competitors use differentiated or concentrated marketing, undifferentiated marketing can be suicidal. Conversely, when competitors use undifferentiated marketing, a firm can gain an advantage by using differentiated or concentrated marketing.

Socially responsible target marketing

Smart targeting helps companies to be more efficient and effective by focusing on the segments that they can satisfy best and most profitably. Targeting also benefits consumers – companies reach specific groups of consumers with offers carefully tailored to satisfy their needs. However, target marketing sometimes generates controversy and concern. The biggest issues usually involve the targeting of vulnerable or disadvantaged consumers with controversial or potentially harmful products.

For example, over the years, the breakfast cereal industry has been heavily criticised for its marketing efforts directed towards children. Critics worry that high-powered advertising appeals presented through the mouths of lovable animated characters will overwhelm children's defences. The marketers of toys and other children's products have been similarly battered, often with good justification.

Other problems arise when the marketing of adult products spills over into the kid segment – intentionally or unintentionally. For example, governments and citizen action groups have accused breweries of targeting under-age drinkers with 'alcopop'-type drinks. Some critics have even called for a complete ban on advertising to children in the UK, and in several European countries like Sweden severe restrictions are already in place.[28] To encourage responsible advertising, the Children's Advertising Review Unit, the US advertising industry's self-regulatory agency, has published extensive children's advertising guidelines that recognise the special needs of child audiences.

Cigarette, beer and fast-food marketers have also generated much controversy in recent years by their attempts to target vulnerable groups. For example, McDonald's and other chains have drawn criticism for pitching their high-fat, salt-laden fare to low-income people and the meteoric growth of the Internet and other carefully targeted direct media has raised fresh concerns about potential targeting abuses. The Internet allows increasing refinement of audiences and, in turn, more precise targeting. This might help makers of questionable products or deceptive advertisers to victimise more readily the most vulnerable audiences. Unscrupulous marketers can now send tailor-made deceptive messages directly to the computers of millions of unsuspecting consumers.

Not all attempts to target children, minorities or other special segments draw such criticism. In fact, most provide benefits to targeted consumers. For example, Colgate makes a large selection of toothbrushes and toothpaste flavours and packages for children – from Colgate Barbie, Blues Clues and SpongeBob SquarePants Sparkling Bubble Fruit toothpastes to Colgate Lego Bionicle and Bratz character toothbrushes.

Thus, in target marketing, the issue is not really *who* is targeted but rather *how* and for *what*. Controversies arise when marketers attempt to profit at the expense of targeted segments – when they unfairly target vulnerable segments or target them with questionable products or tactics. Socially responsible marketing calls for segmentation and targeting that serve not just the interests of the company, but also the interests of those targeted.

MAKING CONNECTIONS Linking the concepts

Time to coast for a bit and take stock.

- At the last Making Connections, you segmented the UK footwear market. Refer to Figure 6.2 and select two companies that serve this market. Describe their segmentation and targeting strategies. Can you come up with one that targets many different segments versus another that focuses on only one or a few segments?

- How does each company you chose differentiate its market offering and image? Has each done a good job of establishing this differentiation in the minds of targeted consumers? The final section in this chapter deals with such positioning issues.

POSITIONING FOR COMPETITIVE ADVANTAGE

Beyond deciding which segments of the market it will target, the company must decide what positions it wants to occupy in those segments. A **product's position** is the way the product is *defined by consumers* on important attributes – the place the product occupies in consumers' minds relative to competing products. 'Products are created in the factory, but brands are created in the mind,' says one positioning expert.[29]

In the car market, the Vauxhall (Opel) Astra and Ford Focus are positioned on economy, Mercedes and BMW on luxury, and Porsche and Ferrari on performance. Volvo positions powerfully on safety. And Toyota positions its fuel-efficient, hybrid Prius as a high-tech solution to the energy shortage. 'How far will you go to save the planet?', it asks.

Consumers are overloaded with information about products and services. They cannot re-evaluate products every time they make a buying decision. To simplify the buying process, consumers organise products, services and companies into categories and 'position' them in their minds. A product's position is the complex set of perceptions, impressions and feelings that consumers have for the product compared with competing products.

Consumers position products with or without the help of marketers. But marketers do not want to leave their products' positions to chance. They must *plan* positions that will give their products the greatest advantage in selected target markets, and they must design marketing mixes to create these planned positions.

Positioning maps

In planning their positioning strategies, marketers often prepare *perceptual positioning maps,* which show consumer perceptions of their brands versus competing products on important buying dimensions. Figure 6.3 shows a positioning map based on consumer perceptions of fashion retailers in the UK produced on behalf of Reiss.[30] In this example, the retailers are mapped on the basis of consumer perception of their prices and the level of 'fashion content', criteria that the researchers found to explain the situation best. Remember – these have not been objectively measured, it is all about consumer perception. From this map, Reiss can see that it is perceived as being relatively low priced and at about the midpoint with respect to fashion content. The map also shows which are its closest competitors – that is, the other fashion retailers that customers think of as being similar to Reiss. Management at Reiss must consider the implications of this map for its positioning strategy – is this where

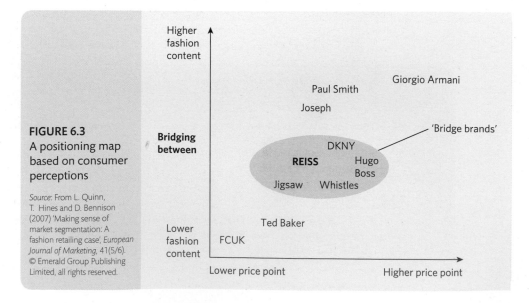

FIGURE 6.3
A positioning map based on consumer perceptions

Source: From L. Quinn, T. Hines and D. Bennison (2007) 'Making sense of market segmentation: A fashion retailing case', *European Journal of Marketing*, 41(5/6). © Emerald Group Publishing Limited, all rights reserved.

management wants the firm to be? If not, where is the preferred location, and what actions must be taken to manoeuvre the company there?

Choosing a positioning strategy

Some firms find it easy to choose their positioning strategy. For example, a firm well known for quality in certain segments will go for this position in a new segment if there are enough buyers seeking quality. But in many cases, two or more firms will go after the same position. Then, each will have to find other ways to set itself apart. Each firm must differentiate its offer by building a unique bundle of benefits that appeals to a substantial group within the segment.

The positioning task consists of three steps: identifying a set of possible competitive advantages upon which to build a position; choosing the right competitive advantages; and selecting an overall positioning strategy. The company must then effectively communicate and deliver the chosen position to the market.

Identifying possible competitive advantages

To build profitable relationships with target customers, marketers must understand customer needs better than competitors do and deliver more value. To the extent that a company can position itself as providing superior value, it gains **competitive advantage**. But solid positions cannot be built on empty promises. If a company positions its product as *offering* the best quality and service, it must then *deliver* the promised quality and service. Thus, positioning begins with actually *differentiating* the company's market offering so that it will give consumers superior value.

To find points of differentiation, marketers must think through the customer's entire experience with the company's product or service. An alert company can find ways to differentiate itself at every customer contact point. In what specific ways can a company differentiate itself or its market offer? It can differentiate along the lines of *product, services, channels, people* or *image*.

Product differentiation takes place along a continuum. At one extreme we find physical products that allow little variation: chicken, steel, aspirin. Yet even here some meaningful differentiation is possible. For example, many European farmers are successfully charging a premium price after adopting – or implying the adoption of – 'organic' production methods. At the other extreme are products that can be highly differentiated, such as cars, clothing and furniture. Such products can be differentiated on features, performance, or style and design. Thus, Volvo provides new and better safety features; Whirlpool designs its dishwasher to run more quietly; Bose positions its speakers on their striking design and sound characteristics. Similarly, companies can differentiate their products on such attributes as consistency, durability, reliability or reparability.

Beyond differentiating its physical product, a firm can also differentiate the services that accompany the product. Some companies gain *services differentiation* through speedy, convenient or careful delivery. For example, Ocado delivers groceries to your home, like many other companies, but will do so in a one-hour window of your choice and has an easy-to-use website. Installation services can also differentiate one company from another, as can repair services. Many a car buyer will gladly pay a little more and travel a little further to buy a car from a dealer that provides top-notch repair services.

Some companies gain service differentiation by providing customer training service or consulting services – data, information systems and advising services that buyers need.

Firms that practise *channel differentiation* gain competitive advantage through the way they design their channel's coverage, expertise and performance. Amazon.com, Dell and Avon set themselves apart with their high-quality direct channels. Caterpillar's success in the construction equipment industry is based on superior channels. Its dealers worldwide are renowned for their first-rate service.

Companies can gain a strong competitive advantage through *people differentiation* – hiring and training better people than their competitors do. Disney people are known to be friendly and upbeat. Singapore Airlines enjoys an excellent reputation, largely because of the grace of its flight attendants. People differentiation requires that a company selects its customer-contact people carefully and trains them well. For example, Disney trains its theme park people thoroughly to ensure that they are competent, courteous and friendly – from the hotel check-in agents, to the monorail drivers, to the ride attendants, to the people who sweep Main Street USA. Each employee is carefully trained to understand customers and to 'make people happy'.

Even when competing offers look the same, buyers may perceive a difference based on company or brand *image differentiation*. A company or brand image should convey the product's distinctive benefits and positioning. Developing a strong and distinctive image calls for creativity and hard work. A company cannot develop an image in the public's mind overnight using only a few advertisements. If Radisson means quality, this image must be supported by everything the company says and does in or around its hotels.

Symbols – such as the McDonald's golden arches, the Nike swoosh or Google's colourful logo – can provide strong company or brand recognition and image differentiation. The company might build a brand around a famous person, as Nike did in the 1980s with its Air Jordan basketball shoes. More recently it has tried to replicate this by sponsoring Tiger Woods. Alas, this has backfired somewhat, given his turbulent personal life. Some companies even become associated with colours, such as Sainsbury's (orange), IBM (blue) or UPS (brown). The chosen symbols, characters and other image elements must be communicated through advertising that conveys the company's or brand's personality.

Choosing the right competitive advantages

Suppose a company is fortunate enough to discover several potential competitive advantages. It must now choose the ones on which it will build its positioning strategy. It must decide *how many* differences to promote and *which ones*.

How many differences to promote?

Many marketers think that companies should aggressively promote only one benefit to the target market. Ad man Rosser Reeves, for example, said a company should develop a unique selling proposition (USP) for each brand and stick to it. Each brand should pick an attribute and tout itself as 'number one' on that attribute. Buyers tend to remember number one better, especially in an over-communicated society. Thus, Crest toothpaste consistently promotes its anti-cavity protection and Asda promotes low prices.

Other marketers think that companies should position themselves on more than one differentiator. This may be necessary if two or more firms are claiming to be best on the same attribute. Today, in a time when the mass market is fragmenting into many small segments, companies are trying to broaden their positioning strategies to appeal to more segments. For example, Lush produces cosmetics and toiletries that are not only handmade, but also from ingredients that have not been tested on animals, appealing to those who want either or both ethics and luxury in their toiletries. However, as companies increase the number of claims for their brands, they risk disbelief and a loss of clear positioning.

Which differences to promote?

Not all brand differences are meaningful or worthwhile; not every difference makes a good differentiator. Each difference has the potential to create company costs as well as customer benefits. A difference is worth establishing to the extent that it satisfies the following criteria:

- *Important*: The difference delivers a highly valued benefit to target buyers.
- *Distinctive*: Competitors do not offer the difference, or the company can offer it in a more distinctive way.
- *Superior*: The difference is superior to other ways that customers might obtain the same benefit.

Lush markets toiletries and cosmetics to customers who value 'freshness' and environmental friendliness

Source: Alamy Images/Alan King.

- *Communicable*: The difference is communicable and visible to buyers.
- *Pre-emptive*: Competitors cannot easily copy the difference.
- *Affordable*: Buyers can afford to pay for the difference.
- *Profitable*: The company can introduce the difference profitably.

Many companies have introduced differentiations that failed one or more of these tests. When the Westin Stamford Hotel in Singapore advertised that it was the world's tallest hotel, it was a distinction that was not important to most tourists – in fact, it turned many off. Polaroid's Polarvision, which produced instantly developed home movies, sank without trace too. Although Polarvision was distinctive and even pre-emptive, it was inferior to another way of capturing motion, namely camcorders. Thus, choosing competitive advantages upon which to position a product or service can be difficult, yet such choices may be crucial to success.

Selecting an overall positioning strategy

The full positioning of a brand is called the brand's **value proposition** – the full mix of benefits upon which the brand is positioned. It is the answer to the customer's question 'Why should I buy your brand?' Volvo's value proposition hinges on safety but also includes reliability, roominess and styling, all for a price that is higher than average but seems fair for this mix of benefits.

Figure 6.4 shows possible value propositions upon which a company might position its products. In the figure, the five green cells represent winning value propositions – positioning that gives the company competitive advantage. The red cells, however, represent losing value propositions. The centre yellow cell represents at best a marginal proposition. In the following sections, we discuss the five winning value propositions upon which companies can position their products: more for more, more for the same, the same for less, less for much less and more for less.

More for more

'More-for-more' positioning involves providing the most upscale product or service and charging a higher price to cover the higher costs. Radisson Hotels, Mont Blanc writing instruments, BMW cars – each claims superior quality, craftwork, durability, performance or style and charges a price to match. Not only is the market offering high in quality, but also it gives prestige to the buyer. It symbolises status and a loftier lifestyle. Often, the price difference exceeds the actual increment in quality.

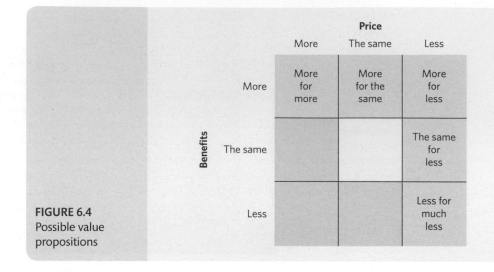

FIGURE 6.4
Possible value propositions

Sellers offering 'only the best' can be found in every product and service category, from hotels, restaurants, food and fashion to cars and household appliances. Consumers are sometimes surprised, even delighted, when a new competitor enters a category with an unusually high-priced brand. Starbucks coffee entered as a very expensive brand in a largely commodity category. Dyson came in as a premium vacuum cleaner with a price to match, touting 'No clogged bags, no clogged filters, and no loss of suction means only one thing. It's a Dyson.'

In general, companies should be on the lookout for opportunities to introduce a 'more-for-more' brand in any underdeveloped product or service category. Yet 'more-for-more' brands can be vulnerable. They often invite imitators who claim the same quality but at a lower price. Luxury goods that sell well during good times may be at risk during economic downturns when buyers become more cautious in their spending.

More for the same

Companies can attack a competitor's more-for-more positioning by introducing a brand offering comparable quality but at a lower price. For example, Toyota introduced its Lexus line with a 'more-for-the-same' value proposition versus Mercedes and BMW. Its headline read: 'Perhaps the first time in history that trading a £40,000 car for a £20,000 car could be considered trading up.' It communicated the high quality of its new Lexus through rave reviews in car magazines and through a widely distributed videotape showing side-by-side comparisons of Lexus and Mercedes cars. It published surveys showing that Lexus dealers were providing customers with better sales and service experiences than were Mercedes dealerships. Many Mercedes owners switched to Lexus, and the Lexus repurchase rate has been 60 per cent, twice the industry average.

The same for less

Offering 'the same for less' can be a powerful value proposition – everyone likes a good deal. For example, Dell offers equivalent quality computers at a lower 'price for performance'. Discount stores such as Wal-Mart and 'category killers' such as Toys 'R' Us and Tesco use this positioning. They do not claim to offer different or better products. Instead, they offer many of the same brands as department stores and speciality stores but at deep discounts based on superior purchasing power and lower-cost operations. Other companies develop imitative but lower-priced brands in an effort to lure customers away from the market leader. For example, AMD makes less expensive versions of Intel's market-leading microprocessor chips.

Less for much less

A market almost always exists for products that offer less and therefore cost less. Few people need, want or can afford 'the very best' in everything they buy. In many cases, consumers will gladly settle for less than optimal performance or give up some of the bells and whistles in exchange for a lower price. For example, many travellers seeking accommodation prefer not to pay for what they consider unnecessary extras, such as a pool, attached restaurant, or mints on the pillow. Hotel chains such Travelodge suspend some of these amenities and charge less accordingly.

'Less-for-much-less' positioning involves meeting consumers' lower performance or quality requirements at a much lower price. Retailers like Colruyt in Belgium, Dia-Mart in France and Lidl and Aldi across Europe (but originally from Germany) are examples of this type of positioning. Ryanair also practises less-for-much-less positioning. It charges incredibly low prices by not serving food, not assigning seats and not using travel agents (see Marketing at Work 6.2).

More for less

Of course, the winning value proposition would be to offer 'more for less'. Many companies claim to do this. And, in the short run, some companies can actually achieve such lofty positions. For example, when it first opened for business in the USA, Home Depot had arguably the best product selection, the best service and the lowest prices compared with local hardware stores and other home improvement chains.

Yet in the long run, companies will find it very difficult to sustain such best-of-both positioning. Offering more usually costs more, making it difficult to deliver on the 'for-less' promise. Companies that try to deliver both may lose out to more focused competitors. For example, facing determined competition from Asda, Sainsbury's must now decide whether it wants to compete primarily on superior service or on lower prices.

All said, each brand must adopt a positioning strategy designed to serve the needs and wants of its target markets. 'More for more' will draw one target market, 'less for much less' will draw another and so on. Thus, in any market, there is usually room for many different companies, each successfully occupying different positions.

The important thing is that each company must develop its own winning positioning strategy, one that makes it special to its target consumers. Offering only 'the same for the same' provides no competitive advantage, leaving the firm in the middle of the pack. Companies offering one of the three losing value propositions – 'the same for more', 'less for more' and 'less for the same' – will inevitably fail. Customers soon realise that they have been underserved, tell others and abandon the brand.

Ryanair's value proposition: less for much less

MARKETING AT WORK 6.2

All businesses start small, even airlines. Ryanair was founded in 1985, flying its single small aeroplane between Waterford in Ireland and London. As Table 6.4 shows, Ryanair has grown since 2000 to become the biggest international carrier in the world. Statistics from IATA show that it carried more than 80 million people across borders in 2014. It is now one of Europe's biggest carriers in terms of passengers per year – having experienced rapid growth since 2000. Measuring international travel only, Ryanair now flies 60 per cent more passengers than easyJet, twice as many as Emirates and getting on for three times the total international passengers of British Airways.[31]

Ryanair celebrated this in a (for it) appropriate way. Robin Kiely, Communications Chief, said in a press release commenting on achieving the top spot:

To celebrate being named the world's favourite airline once more, we have released 100,000 seats for sale across our European network, at prices from €19.99.

Up until 1992, Ryanair had no clear positioning strategy, and did well to break even. Then came the

TABLE 6.4 Top 100 airlines: ranked by traffic (passengers)*

International		
Rank	Airline	Thousands
1	Ryanair	81,395
2	easyJet	52,787
3	Lufthansa	50,739
4	Emirates	43,335
5	British Airways	33,803
6	Air France	33,118
7	Turkish Airlines	27,407
8	KLM	26,581
9	United Airlines	25,002
10	Delta Air Lines	23,086
11	Air Berlin	22,946
12	American Airlines	21,719
13	Cathay Pacific Airways	21,420
14	Lan Airlines	21,172
15	Qatar Airways	18,737
16	Singapore Airlines	18,666
17	Korean Air	16,223
18	Thai Airways International	16,029
19	SWISS	15,268
20	Qantas Airways	15,253
21	Scandinavian Airlines	15,052
22	Norwegian	14,704
23	Wizzair	13,500
24	Air Canada	12,763
25	China Airlines	12,606
26	Aeroflot Russian Airlines	11,991
27	Etihad Airways	11,519
28	Asiana Airways	11,384
29	Malaysia Airlines	10,786
30	Avianca	10,155

*IATA World Transport Statistics (2014 edition)

Source: IATA World Air Transport Statistics, http://www.iata.org/wats., International Air Transport Association (IATA)

appointment of a dynamic and focused new Chief Executive – Michael O'Leary. Given the task of turning round the organisation, O'Leary examined the business model of Southwest Airlines in the USA – the original low-cost carrier – and considered how that model could be imported into the newly deregulated EU airlines sector.[32] In essence, Ryanair adopted a positioning strategy of '*less for much less*' – to provide basic air travel with no frills or thrills at prices a fraction of those of its competitors.

In order to offer low prices on airfares while still making a profit, Ryanair is required to keep a very close eye on its costs – all organisations need to keep an eye on costs, but a fundamental requirement of Ryanair's positioning as a low-price carrier is a fixation with cost reduction and efficiency improvements. Indeed, Ryanair management has a reputation for being able to spot innovative new ways to save money.

How does Ryanair reduce costs? In a word, ruthlessly. Every aspect of the operation is continually under review to establish where costs can be trimmed – or passed on to others – and efficiency improved. In the words of Michael Cawley, Chief Operating Officer:

Can we do what we are doing at a reduced cost? Can we achieve what we want to achieve a different way? How can we hand on those cost savings to the customer? You cannot exist by just reducing prices. You can only exist profitably by reducing costs by at least as much.[33]

Ryanair only uses one type of aircraft, often purchased second-hand, namely Boeing 737-800s. This simplifies maintenance and repair, which in turn requires fewer support staff to manage and maintain the fleet. It also means that pilots only need to be qualified to fly the one type of aircraft, reducing retraining costs and giving both economies of scale and weight when negotiating with Boeing for spares or updates. The aeroplanes themselves are not equipped with the sophisticated passenger entertainment systems found on carriers like BA or Virgin – saving money on purchase and upkeep. In flight, passengers are not provided with complimentary meals, and must pay extra for any snacks or drinks they require. The implication of this is that, as well as an extra source of revenue on top of tickets, Ryanair can vastly simplify its logistical support systems.

Required by law to provide onboard safety information for passengers, Ryanair has chosen not to provide the usual plastic-coated sheets to be found next to the sickbags on most aeroplanes, but rather has them mounted on the back of the seat in front, meaning there are no stolen or damaged ones to be replaced. This parsimoniousness is continued in the rest of the interior fixtures and fittings – the seats do not recline, there are no detachable headrests and the windows have no blinds! Seats are upholstered in leather – not for luxury, but for reasons of longevity and ease of maintenance.

In choosing its routes, Ryanair avoids 'brand name' airports like Heathrow, Charles De Gaulle and Schiphol as an explicit part of its strategy, preferring to use less well-known regional hubs nearby, for example London Stansted, Paris-Beauvais and Eindhoven.[34] In doing so, Ryanair believes it improves turnaround time, is not required to pay premium fees for services and facilities like baggage-handling and refuelling, but the additional costs to passengers of significant transit distances at either end of the journey are often a sore point between Ryanair, customer groups and regulatory bodies.[35] Ryanair even grounds part of its fleet over the winter months when demand for flights is lower, a decision unique among airlines.[36]

Ryanair offers a classic 'less-for-much-less' proposition – the drive to cut costs is apparent across all of the firm's activities

Source: Ryanair.

The streamlining of ground operations, a one-model fleet and the use of regional airports have led to remarkable efficiency gains with respect to competitors. In 2003, Ryanair employed fewer than 2,000 staff to fly 24 million passengers. In the same year, Lufthansa required 39,000 employees to fly 37 million.[37] This is a per-employee productivity ratio of more than 12 to 1. Although other airlines have tried to replicate this and the ratio has decreased, Ryanair is still a clear leader.

The deviation from standard industry practice continues in areas of the business not directly connected with flying. Faced with a £3 million quotation for producing the first website for the firm, Ryanair instead turned to students at a local university, bargaining them down to less than £15,000.[38] Ryanair produces all its own advertisements in-house, rather than paying an external agency. This has sometimes led to confrontations with bodies such as the Advertising Standards Authority in the UK and its equivalents in other European countries like Belgium and Norway over the use of unpleasant, deceptive or inaccurate language in its communications.

Some 96 per cent of all tickets are sold via Ryanair. com, removing booking agency fees and most of the transaction costs. Some costs, such as fees payable to Visa or MasterCard for processing, are passed on to the passenger at the point of booking. Passengers also pay an additional fee for each item of luggage they wish to place in the hold.[39] At check-in, passengers are not assigned a specific seat.

Such ruthlessness does not always win friends or make good headlines. In recent times, Ryanair lost a case against a disabled passenger who acted to reclaim a fee imposed for the use of a wheelchair in the airports at either end of his journey. Ryanair's position that it was merely passing on the cost imposed on it by the airport operator failed to impress the County Court.[40] Indeed, while most passengers are satisfied, or at least feel they get what they pay for, an outcome of the strategy is that Ryanair has developed a poor reputation for customer service.[41] Several websites exist to report and collate stories about poor customer service from Ryanair.[42]

So what is the future for Ryanair? The company faces significant challenges in respect of legislation, taxation and concerns about the environmental impact of the aviation industry,[43] with Ryanair already fighting to have the sector less heavily regulated at the state and supra-state level within Europe, with specific targets of protectionism, state subsidy of national carriers and monopolies on airport management services.[44] Regardless, the obsession with cost control will stay, and the positioning of the business will remain '*less for much less*'.

Sources: See notes 31–44 at the end of this chapter.

Developing a positioning statement

Company and brand positioning should be summed up in a **positioning statement**. The statement should follow the form: *To (target segment and need) our (brand) is (concept) that (point of difference).*[45] For example:

> To young, active soft-drinks consumers who have little time for sleep, Red Bull is the soft drink that gives you more energy than any other brand because it has the highest level of caffeine. With Red Bull, you can stay alert and keep going even when you haven't been able to get a good night's sleep.

Note that the positioning first states the product's membership in a category (Red Bull is a soft drink, first marketed in Austria but based on a traditional Thai drink)[46] and then shows its point of difference from other members of the category (has more caffeine and distinctive ingredients like taurine). Placing a brand in a specific category suggests similarities that it might share with other products in the category. But the case for the brand's superiority is made on its points of difference.

Sometimes marketers put a brand in a surprisingly different category before indicating the points of difference. DiGiorno's is a frozen pizza whose crust rises when the pizza is heated. But instead of putting it in the frozen pizza category, the marketers positioned it in the delivered pizza category. Their ad shows party guests asking which pizza delivery service the host used. But, says the host, 'It's not delivery, its DiGiorno!' This helped highlight DiGiorno's fresh quality and superior taste over the normal frozen pizza.

Communicating and delivering the chosen position

Once it has chosen a position, the company must take strong steps to deliver and communicate the desired position to target consumers. All the company's marketing mix efforts must support the positioning strategy.

Positioning the company calls for concrete action, not just talk. If the company decides to build a position on better quality and service, it must first *deliver* that position. Designing the marketing mix – product, price, place and promotion – involves working out the tactical details of the positioning strategy. Thus, a firm that seizes on a more-for-more position knows that it must produce high-quality products, charge a high price, distribute through high-quality dealers and advertise in high-quality media. It must hire and train more service people, find retailers who have a good reputation for service, and develop sales and advertising messages that broadcast its superior service. This is the only way to build a consistent and believable more-for-more position.

Companies often find it easier to come up with a good positioning strategy than to implement it. Establishing a position or changing one usually takes a long time. In contrast, positions that have taken years to build can quickly be lost. Once a company has built the desired position, it must take care to maintain the position through consistent performance and communication. It must closely monitor and adapt the position over time to match changes in consumer needs and competitors' strategies. However, the company should avoid abrupt changes that might confuse consumers. Instead, a product's position should evolve gradually as it adapts to the ever-changing marketing environment.

THE JOURNEY YOU'VE TAKEN Reviewing the concepts

It's time to stop and stretch your legs. In this chapter, you've learned about the major elements of marketing strategy: segmentation, targeting and positioning. Marketers know that they cannot appeal to all buyers in their markets, or at least not to all buyers in the same way. Buyers are too numerous, too widely scattered and too varied in their needs and buying practices. Therefore, most companies today practise *target marketing* – identifying market segments, selecting one or more of them, and developing products and marketing mixes tailored to each.

1 Define the three steps of target marketing: market segmentation, target marketing and market positioning

Market segmentation is the act of dividing a market into distinct groups of buyers with different needs, characteristics or behaviours who might require separate products or marketing mixes. Once the groups have been identified, target marketing evaluates each market segment's attractiveness and selects one or more segments to serve. Target marketing involves designing strategies to build the right relationships with the right customers. Market positioning consists of deciding how best to serve target customers – setting the competitive positioning for the product and creating a detailed marketing plan.

2 List and discuss the major bases for segmenting consumer and business markets

There is no single way to segment a market. Therefore, the marketer tries different variables to see which give the best segmentation opportunities. For consumer marketing, the major segmentation variables are geographic, demographic, psychographic and behavioural. In *geographic segmentation*, the market is divided into different geographical units such as nations, regions, states, counties, cities or neighbourhoods. In *demographic segmentation*, the market is divided into groups based on demographic variables, including age, gender, family size, family life cycle, income, occupation, education, religion, race, generation and nationality. In *psychographic segmentation*, the market is divided into different groups based on social class, lifestyle or personality characteristics. In *behavioural segmentation*, the market is divided into groups based on consumers' knowledge, attitudes, uses or responses to a product.

Business marketers use many of the same variables to segment their markets. But business markets can also be segmented by business consumer *demographics* (industry, company size), *operating characteristics*, *purchasing approaches*, *situational factors* and *personal characteristics*.

The effectiveness of segmentation analysis depends on finding segments that are *measurable, accessible, substantial, differentiable* and *actionable*.

3 Explain how companies identify attractive market segments and choose a target marketing strategy

To target the best market segments, the company first evaluates each segment's size and growth characteristics, structural attractiveness, and compatibility with company objectives and resources. It then chooses one of four target marketing strategies – ranging from very broad to very narrow targeting. The seller can ignore segment differences and target broadly using *undifferentiated (or mass) marketing*. This involves mass producing, mass distributing and mass promoting the same product in about the same way to all consumers. Or the seller can adopt *differentiated marketing* – developing different market offers for several segments. *Concentrated marketing* (or *niche marketing*) involves focusing on only one or a few market segments. Finally, *micromarketing* is the practice of tailoring products and marketing programmes to suit the tastes of specific individuals and locations. Micromarketing includes *local marketing* and *individual marketing*. Which targeting strategy is best depends on company resources, product variability, product life-cycle stage, market variability and competitive marketing strategies.

4 Discuss how companies position their products for maximum competitive advantage in the marketplace

Once a company has decided which segments to enter, it must decide on its *market positioning* strategy – on which positions to occupy in its chosen segments. The positioning task consists of three steps: identifying a set of possible competitive advantages upon which to build a position; choosing the right competitive advantages; and selecting an overall positioning strategy. The brand's full positioning is called its *value proposition* – the full mix of benefits upon which the brand is positioned. In general, companies can choose from one of five winning value propositions upon which to position their products: more for more, more for the same, the same for less, less for much less or more for less. Company and brand positioning are summarised in positioning statements that state the target segment and need, positioning concept and specific points of difference. The company must then effectively communicate and deliver the chosen position to the market.

NAVIGATING THE KEY TERMS

Age and life-cycle
 segmentation 194
Behavioural segmentation 199
Benefit segmentation 200
Competitive advantage 215
Concentrated (niche) marketing 209
Demographic segmentation 194
Differentiated (segmented)
 marketing 208

Gender segmentation 195
Geographic segmentation 192
Income segmentation 195
Individual marketing 210
Intermarket segmentation 206
Local marketing 210
Market positioning 192
Market segmentation 192
Micromarketing 210

Occasion segmentation 199
Positioning statement 222
Product's position 214
Psychographic segmentation 196
Target market 207
Target marketing 192
Undifferentiated (mass)
 marketing 208
Value proposition 217

NOTES AND REFERENCES

1 See S. Paliwoda and S. Marinova, 'The Marketing Challenges Within the Enlarged Single European Market', *European Journal of Marketing,* 41(3/4), 2007, pp. 233–44.

2 BBC News, 'Ikea Store to Open in City Centre', **http://news.bbc.co.uk/1/hi/england/coventry_warwickshire/4649843.stm**, accessed 4 July 2005.

3 Dove has a set of pages promoting its products at **www.doveproage.com**

4 Bramdean's homepage is at **www.bramdean.com**

5 Read one woman's take on 'Shrinking and Pinking' in the *Telegraph* at 'Mad Men: Don't "Shrink It and Pink It" If You Want to Appeal to Women', **http://www.telegraph.co.uk/women/womens-business/10069878/Mad-men-Dont-shrink-it-and-pink-it-if-you-want-to-appeal-to-women.html**. Learn about Pretty Little Head from its homepage at **www.prettylittlehead.co.uk**

6 See for example the discussion on gay and lesbian views relating to commercialism is the *Guardian* column 'Are Gay People in the UK Divided by the Pink Pound?' at **http://www.theguardian.com/commentisfree/2013/oct/07/gay-people-uk-pink-pound**

7 Harrods can be found online at **www.harrods.com**; Quartier 206 at **www.quartier206.com**.

8 See for examples: J. Ansell, T. Harrison and T. Archibald, 'Identifying Cross-Selling Opportunities, Using Lifestyle Segmentation and Survival Analysis', *Marketing Intelligence & Planning,* 25(4), 2007, pp. 394–410; or S. Richbell and V. Kite, 'Night Shoppers in the "Open 24 Hours" Supermarket: A Profile', *International Journal of Retail & Distribution Management,* 35(1), 2007, pp. 54–68.

9 See Maureen Wallenfang, 'Appleton, Wis.-Area Dealers See Increase in Moped Sales', *Knight Ridder Tribune Business News,* 15 August 2004, p. 1; and Honda's website at **www.powersports.honda.com/scooters/**, July 2005.

10 This very British organisation can be found at **www.britegg.co.uk**

11 Confetti are at **www.confetti.co.uk**

12 Visit Fortnum & Mason at **www.fortnumandmason.com** – but not when you are hungry or poor!

13 See Jennifer Ordonez, 'Fast-Food Lovers, Unite!', *Newsweek,* 24 May 2004, p. 56.

14 See Alan T. Sarasevic, 'Author Plumbs Bottomless Depth of Mac Worship', *San Francisco Chronicle,* 12 December 2004.

15 The homepage for Experian is at **www.experian.co.uk**

16 John Fetto, 'American Neighborhoods' First Page', *American Demographics,* July–August 2003, p. 34.

17 Claritas can be found online at **www.claritas-solutions.com**

18 Information from **www.americanexpress.com**, accessed August 2011.

19 For more on segmenting business markets, see Turan Senguder, 'An Evaluation of Consumer and Business Segmentation Approaches', *Journal of the Academy of Business,* March 2003, pp. 618–24; and James C. Anderson and James A. Narus, *Business Market Management,* 2nd edn (Upper Saddle River, NJ: Prentice Hall, 2004), pp. 45–52.

20 See Arundhati Parmar, 'Global Youth United', *Marketing News,* 28 October 2002, pp. 1, 49; 'Teen Spirit', *Global Cosmetic Industry,* March 2004, p. 23; Johnnie L. Roberts, 'World Tour', *Newsweek,* 6 June 2005, pp. 34–6; and the MTV Worldwide website, **www.mtv.com**

21 BBC News, 'The Left Handed Liberation Front': **news.bbc.co.uk/1/hi/magazine/6943871. stm**, accessed September 2011.

22 See Michael Porter, *Competitive Advantage* (New York: Free Press, 1985), pp. 4–8, 234–6. For more recent discussions, see Stanley Slater and Eric Olson, 'A Fresh Look at Industry and Market Analysis', *Business Horizons,* January–February 2002, pp. 15–22; Kenneth Sawka and Bill Fiora, 'The Four Analytical Techniques Every Analyst Must Know: 2. Porter's Five Forces Analysis', *Competitive Intelligence Magazine,* May–June 2003, p. 57; and Philip Kotler and Kevin Lane Keller, *Marketing Management,* 12th edn (Upper Saddle River, NJ: Prentice Hall, 2006), pp. 342–3.

23 Nina Munk, 'Why Women Find Lauder Mesmerizing', *Fortune,* 25 May 1998, pp. 97–106; Christine Bittar, 'New Faces, Same Name', *Brandweek,* 11 March 2002, pp. 28–34; Robin Givhan, 'Estee Lauder, Sending a Message in a Bottle', *Washington Post,* 26 April 2004, p. C.01; and information accessed at **www.elcompanies.com**, **www.stila.com** and **www. macmakeup.com**, July 2011.

24 See Gerry Khermouch, 'Call it the Pepsi Blue Generation', *BusinessWeek,* 3 February 2003, p. 96; Kathleen Sampey, 'Sweet on Sierra Mist', *Adweek,* 2 February 2004, p. 20; and Nat Ives, 'Mountain Dew Double-Dose for Times Square Passers-By', *New York Times,* 8 April 2004, p. C9.

25 Gwendolyn Bounds, 'How an Artist Fell into a Profitable Online Card Business', *Wall Street Journal,* 21 December 2004, p. B1.

26 For a good discussion of mass customisation and relationship building, see Don Peppers and Martha Rogers, *Managing Customers Relationships: A Strategic Framework* (Hoboken, NJ: Wiley, 2004), ch. 10.

27 Adapted from information found in Mark Tatge, 'Red Bodies, Black Ink', *Forbes,* 18 September 2000, p. 114; 'Oshkosh Truck Corporation', *Hoover's Company Profiles,* 1 June 2005, p. 14345; and information accessed at **www.oshkoshcorporation.com**, August 2011.

28 Swedish government reports and press releases are available in Swedish and English and many other languages at **www.sweden.gov.se/**; the EU policy is outlined at **http:// europa.eu/legislation_summaries/audiovisual_and_media/l24030a_en.htm**, accessed September 2011.

29 Jack Trout, 'Branding Can't Exist without Positioning', *Advertising Age,* 14 March 2005, p. 28.

30 **http://www.reiss.co.uk/**; positioning map reproduced from L. Quinn, T. Hines and D. Bennison, 'Making Sense of Market Segmentation: A Fashion Retailing Case', *European Journal of Marketing,* 41(5/6), 2007, pp. 439–65.

31 The homepage of Ryanair is at **www.ryanair.com**. For corporate information see **corporate.ryanair.com/**

32 R. Lachenauer and George Stalk Jr, 'Hardball: Five Killer Strategies for Trouncing the Opposition', *Harvard Business Review,* 1 April 2004.

33 Interview available at **www.ericsson.com**, accessed September 2011.

34 Strategy Document: **www.ryanair.com/**, accessed September 2011.

35 BBC News, 'Ryanair's Eurostar Claim Banned', available at **http://news.bbc.co.uk/1/hi/business/6957882.stm**, accessed September 2011.

36 Kevin Done, 'Ryanair Jumps on Cost-Cutting Move', *Financial Times,* accessed at **http://www.ft.com/**, September 2011.

37 A. Ruddock, 'Keeping up with O'Leary', *Management Today,* September 2003, p. 48.

38 Book review by Heather Stewart on 'A Life in Full Flight', *Guardian,* accessed at **http://books.guardian.co.uk/reviews/biography/0,,2146959,00.html**, September 2011.

39 Neasa MacErlean, 'Ryanair Risks Throwing the Passengers Out with the Baggage', *Guardian,* accessed at **http://money.guardian.co.uk/consumernews/story/0,2152518,00.html**, September 2011.

40 BBC News, 'Ryanair Wheelchair Case Continues', accessed at **http://news.bbc.co.uk/1/hi/england/essex/3994913.stm**, September 2011.

41 RTE News, 'Ryanair Launches New Customer Charter', accessed at **www.rte.ie/news/2002/0917/ryanair-business.html,** September 2011.

42 There are several of these: **www.ryanaircampaign.org** is a typical example.

43 Press release: 'Air Travel and the Environment' from **http://www.direct.gov.uk/en/environmentandgreenerliving/greenertravel/dg_064429**, September 2011.

44 Gill Plinner, 'Ryanair Files Complaint with Regulators Against BAA', *Financial Times,* accessed at **www.ft.com**, September 2011.

45 See Bobby J. Calder and Steven J. Reagan, 'Brand Design', in Dawn Iacobucci (ed.), *Kellogg on Marketing* (New York: Wiley, 2001), p. 61.

46 Redbull online at **www.redbull.com**

CHAPTER 7
PRODUCT, SERVICES AND BRANDING STRATEGY

AFTER STUDYING THIS CHAPTER, YOU SHOULD BE ABLE TO

- define *product* and the major classifications of products and services
- describe the decisions companies make regarding their individual products and services, product lines and product mixes
- discuss branding strategy – the decisions companies make in building and managing their brands
- identify the four characteristics that affect the marketing of a service and the additional marketing considerations that services require
- discuss two additional product issues: socially responsible product decisions and international product and services marketing

THE WAY AHEAD
Previewing the concepts

Now that you've had a good look at marketing strategy, we'll take a deeper look at the marketing mix – the tactical tools that marketers use to implement their strategies. In this and the next chapter we'll study how companies develop and manage products and brands. Then, in the chapters that follow, we'll look at pricing, distribution and marketing communication tools. The product is usually the first and most basic marketing consideration. We'll start with a seemingly simple question: what *is* a product? As it turns out, however, the answer is not so simple.

First stop on this leg of the journey: a supremely elegant English brand that has become known around the world as a statement of sophistication, taste and quality – Dunhill. What is the magic ingredient that makes a brand invented for pioneering, and usually very eccentric, English motoring gentlemen in the nineteenth century relevant to well-off consumers of good taste around the world today? How is it that a brand that was invented to sell motoring accessories in England nearly 120 years ago can be used to sell gorgeous pens, fragrances and chess sets today?

ALFRED DUNHILL LTD: RECONCILING TRADITION AND INNOVATION IN PRODUCT AND BRAND MANAGEMENT

Dr Kim Lehman and Dr John Byrom, School of Management, University of Tasmania, Australia

Alfred Dunhill would probably not be surprised if he were to walk into a twenty-first-century Dunhill store. Certainly he might if he were to visit a store in Shanghai, Dubai, Hong Kong or New Delhi, since he would only know the original retail outlet in St James's, London – which remains the spiritual home of Alfred Dunhill Ltd – and the New York and Paris stores. While he might be surprised by the global reach of the brand, he would still see some of his famous motoring accessories dotted about. But he would surely recognise that aura of discreet, but nonetheless luxurious, style and the continuation of his own fascination with innovative high-quality products. Still, Dunhill has come a long way since Alfred took over his father's saddlery business in 1893. It ranks as one of the most well-known British brands in the world. It is still seen as one of those masculine, but gentlemanly, brands that hark back to times gone by. Swiss-based luxury goods conglomerate Compagnie Financière Richemont SA owns Dunhill, alongside a harem of other height-of-luxury brands like IWC, Purdey and Cartier.

What would no doubt please Alfred Dunhill, and remind him of his own day, is the way Dunhill still specialises in the market it helped to create all those years ago, supplying gentlemen's luxury accessories, designed in the English style. When Dunhill's tagline was 'Everything for the car but the motor', the firm aimed to provide the still embryonic motoring market with all the extras drivers might need, since cars were little more than a chassis and an engine at the time. Alfred coined the term 'Motorites' for the products he invented to sell in his elegant shop in central London. That market, though, was made up largely of wealthy, eccentric men prepared to brave technology most people thought would not last very long. Nowadays there may well not be enough gentleman adventurers to form a viable market segment for any firm, but an astute firm will retain the 'spirit' of the past, repackage it for the modern consumer, and carefully manage its products and brand to suit.

Keeping the traditions of the brand alive needs to be a priority for firms, like Dunhill, that seek to incorporate their history into their marketing communications. This is no different from a firm that, for example, is known for its value for money. Such a firm would incorporate into its branding communications clues to the consumer as to where its products sit in relation to others – their position in other words – then use branding to build an image

Dunhill's marketing emphasises classic British style

Source: The Advertising Archives (t); Alamy Images/Hugh Threlfall (b).

upon which the consumer can draw when it comes time to purchase.

Branding, then, encompasses the associations that come to mind when consumers think about a brand, as well as all instances of contact that customers may have with a brand. For Dunhill, its retail stores and licensed outlets must reinforce the brand. Linked to this is how Dunhill uses brand identity, which involves those facets of the brand that represent the brand visually and verbally – logos, taglines, colours and so on. These facets are constructions of the firm concerned. Dunhill crafts a brand identity to support its position as a retailer of superior, luxury goods for men, continually and consistently communicating the message of tradition and heritage through its advertising. The firm understands that simply claiming a tradition since 1893 is not sufficient to impress today's highly informed consumers. It must be demonstrated in a tangible way.

A significant part of the Dunhill brand is its reputation for innovation and invention. This is true even in relation to its retail outlets. The current London store has a fitting room with a unique lighting system that can reproduce the natural lighting of any city in the world at any time of the day. A gentleman, no matter where he may be from, can assess his suit in just the right lighting! Clearly, Dunhill has never been merely about the 'gentlemanly' product range; it was also about that quirky, eccentric side to the English identity. One example often told is Alfred Dunhill's invention of 'Bobby-finders', a combined binocular/goggle that claimed to be useful in detecting police hiding by the roadside, waiting to catch unsuspecting motorists who might be speeding.

Source: Alamy Images/Photos 12.

Stemming from a speeding ticket handed out to Alfred, the 'Bobby-finder' is one slightly eccentric example. There are, though, numerous, more mainstream instances of product innovation. The 'Unique' petrol cigarette lighter became almost a cult item – in one of the most famous moments in cinema history, we were introduced to James Bond as he lights a cigarette using a Dunhill lighter first sold in 1927.

Today, on a more commercial level, the firm exploits this tradition of innovation by drawing on the products of the past. Dunhill maintains an archive of products that feels like a first-class museum, which is used as a source of inspiration for its designers. Items in the archive have provided the inspiration for new products that can be as innovative today as those in the archive were in years gone by. The archive plays a core role in the business. It serves as a reminder of the brand's history, of the variety and quality of products over the years, and is a source of inspiration to energise the creative team to continue that tradition. In a manner of speaking, Dunhill view its archive as an embodiment of the DNA of the brand. There is, then, a storehouse of corporate memory that competing firms can only dream of.

The products that come from this reference to the past are not just reproductions of previous items. The archive 'informs' the design, it does not control it. There is little value in designing, manufacturing and retailing a product that does not communicate with the current market. One example of how this works for Dunhill is its 'Sidecar' collection, launched in 2004. This collection, which included a range of writing instruments and leather goods, was inspired by the motorcycle sidecars produced by Dunhill in its early years – part of the firm's 'Motorites for Motorcyclists' that first appeared in a 1905 product catalogue. One product in the Sidecar collection particularly illustrates the Dunhill philosophy. A limited-edition fountain pen, the Sidecar Limousette, was included, with only 1,893 produced, to celebrate the year in which Alfred Dunhill took over the business. These subtleties are part of the English style that is carefully cultivated by Dunhill.

It is this very 'Englishness' that is perhaps at the heart of the brand's appeal in the global marketplace. Dunhill has now successfully packaged its brand for a number of international markets. Alfred Dunhill opened his first New York store in 1921 and the Paris store in 1924. The latter, in Rue de la Paix, has become something of a landmark in the French capital, much as the St James's store has in London. In the 1920s, to be able to state 'London, Paris, New York' on your marque was symbolic of an internationally successful brand. It was not until 1966 that Dunhill ventured to Asia, opening a store in Hong Kong in that year. Now Dunhill is represented throughout the Far East, the Indian subcontinent and the Middle East. These 'outposts' of the Dunhill brand, the wholly owned stores in particular, all communicate the same message as the original three stores – style, restrained luxury and quality gentlemen's accoutrements. Indeed, items from the Dunhill archive collection sometimes travel throughout the firm's global network, tangibly to reinforce the brand's heritage. It would not be unusual to see a collection of 1930s' Dunhill Art Deco silver and lacquer cigarette lighters and timepieces on display in the Tokyo store, for example. Both the London and Paris stores have continual exhibition displays from the Dunhill archive, including many items from the very early motoring days. Visitors are literally immersed in the Dunhill brand!

For Dunhill, then, there are two things that are fundamental to its appeal to sophisticated, wealthy customers. The first is authenticity – of the brand and of the products. That authenticity is underpinned by the history and traditions of the firm. A customer might say: 'I go to Dunhill because I know Dunhill has been around for a hundred years, and it stands for something.' Buying into that tradition, that heritage – very important in the Asian market – is an important facet of the Dunhill brand that needs to be carefully managed. However, the brand image can only survive so long as the products are perceived as stylish, well designed and beautifully made, and deliver on the brand promise. Of course, the product must also make the buyers feel good about themselves, and make other people feel impressed – perhaps make the buyer feel 20 years younger, or look taller and a lot more sexy! Remember, luxury products are about much more than their physical attributes. They are also about feeling good.

The second fundamental aspect of the Dunhill brand is its relevance to the current market and its consumer. So, while there is no doubt that authenticity and heritage are very important, the product line has to be in tune with the spirit of the times. If it is not, it will fail – consumers are not going to buy simply because of the heritage of the brand. In other words, a heritage brand, if it is not counterbalanced by good-quality products with a contemporary feel, can actually become a millstone, because the image of the brand will be diluted, relegating it to being thought of as simply old-fashioned.

The challenge for brands like Dunhill, that rely on their heritage as part of their branding, is to reconcile this with the constant need to remain relevant to the modern consumer. Global retailing, where the same stores appear in every major city, means that consumers throughout the world can now choose from a myriad of luxury brands, many with similar brand promises. In some ways Dunhill has a distinct advantage. It has always had a reputation for producing quirky, innovative, but, above all, high-quality men's accessories. It can take risks with its products, and revisit classic ideas and designs. But it would be an unwise strategy to lose sight of those facets of the brand that made it famous. Perhaps the trick might be to remain true to Alfred Dunhill's original vision. He aimed to fill his store with products customers could not find anywhere else. People would visit London, come to Dunhill, and expect to find something new, different and exciting. That is a product and branding strategy still valid in today's world – and one which still works for Dunhill.

Clearly, there is a lot more to the products Dunhill sells than simply a nice pen or a bottle of perfume – Dunhill sells something far more complex than just consumer commodities. This chapter begins with a deceptively simple question: what is a product? After answering this question, we look at ways to classify products in consumer and business markets. Then we discuss the important decisions that marketers make regarding individual products, product lines and product mixes. Next, we look into the critically important issue of how marketers build and manage brands. Finally, we examine the characteristics and marketing requirements of a special form of product – services.

WHAT IS A PRODUCT?

We define a **product** as anything that can be offered to a market for attention, acquisition, use or consumption that might satisfy a want or need. Products include more than just tangible goods. Broadly defined, products include physical objects, services, events, persons, places, organisations, ideas or mixes of these entities. Throughout this text, we use the term *product* broadly to include any or all of these entities. Thus, an Apple iPad, a Toyota Avensis and a tin of Dulux paint are products. But so are a skiing holiday, HSBC banking services and advice from your doctor.

Because of their importance in the world economy, services are given our special attention. **Services** are a form of product that consists of activities, benefits or satisfactions offered for sale that are essentially intangible and do not result in the ownership of anything. Examples are banking, hotel, airline, retail, accounting and home repair services. We will look at services more closely later in this chapter.

Products, services and experiences

Product is a key element in the overall *market offering*. Marketing mix planning begins with formulating an offering that brings value to target customers. This offering becomes the basis upon which the company builds profitable relationships with customers.

The Guinness
Brewery Storehouse,
Dublin, Ireland

Source: Alamy Images/AR
Photo.

A company's market offering often includes both tangible goods and services. Each component can be a minor or a major part of the total offer. We used to think of some products as being *pure tangible goods*, such as soap, toothpaste or salt, with few or no services accompanying the product, but these days even bottles of water have a customer service helpline. You should call them, they are probably bored and lonely. At the other extreme are *pure services*, for which the offer consists only of a service. Examples include having your teeth checked by a dentist, or financial services. Between these two extremes, however, many goods-and-services combinations are possible.

Because of a proliferation of products and competitors, many companies are moving to a new level in creating value for their customers. To differentiate their offers, beyond simply making products and delivering services, they are creating and managing customer *experiences* with their products or company.

Experiences have always been important in the entertainment industry – Disney has long manufactured memories through its movies and theme parks. Today, however, all kinds of firms are recasting their traditional goods and services to create experiences. For example, Ireland's top visitor attraction is the Guinness Storehouse in Dublin. Hundreds of thousands of people visit every year to enjoy the complete Guinness *experience*. This is a great deal more than simply enjoying a drink of Ireland's world famous stout:

> Traditionally the unique attraction of Ireland as a tourist destination has been the level and depth of contact tourists have with Irish people. This is especially the case with tourists who wish to connect with their Irish heritage and who consider Ireland to be a second home. As an internationally recognised and acclaimed visitor experience the Guinness Storehouse has consistently been the top visitor attraction in Ireland since it opened its doors in late 2000. Diageo, which Guinness is part of, have successfully leveraged the association of Ireland as a destination and the rich history attached to the Guinness brand into a viable and leading focal point for tourists when they visit Ireland.[1]

Companies that market experiences realise that customers are really buying much more than just products and services. They are buying what those offers will *do* for them.

Levels of product and services

Product planners need to think about products and services on three levels (see Figure 7.1). Each level adds more customer value. The most basic level is the *core benefit*, which addresses the question *what is the buyer really buying?* When designing products, marketers must first define the core, problem-solving benefits or services that consumers seek. A woman buying lipstick buys more than lip colour. Charles Revson of Revlon saw this early: 'In the factory, we make cosmetics; in the store, we sell hope.' And young parents buying a Sony Cybershot

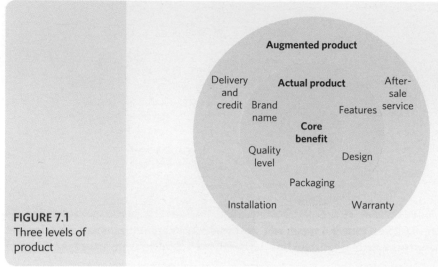

FIGURE 7.1
Three levels of
product

are buying more than a digital camera. They are buying a convenient, high-quality way to capture important moments and memories.

At the second level, product planners must turn the core benefit into an *actual product*. They need to develop product and service features, design, a level of quality, a brand name and packaging. For example, the Sony digital camera is an actual product. Its name, parts, styling, features, packaging and other attributes have all been combined carefully to deliver the core benefit of capturing memories.

Finally, product planners must build an *augmented product* around the core benefit and actual product by offering additional consumer services and benefits. Sony must offer more than just a digital camera. It must provide consumers with a complete solution to their picture-taking problems. Thus, when consumers buy a Sony digital camera, Sony and its dealers might also give buyers a warranty on parts and workmanship, instructions on how to use the camera, software to process the images, and copious online services providing help, support and a community of fellow customers.

Consumers see products as complex bundles of benefits that satisfy their needs. When developing products, marketers must first identify the *core* consumer needs the product will satisfy. They must then design the *actual* product and find ways to *augment* it in order to create the bundle of benefits that will provide the most satisfying customer experience.

Product and service classifications

Products and services fall into two broad classes based on the types of consumers that use them – *consumer products* and *industrial products*. Broadly defined, products also include other marketable entities such as experiences, organisations, persons, places and ideas.

Consumer products

Consumer products are products and services bought by final consumers for personal consumption. Marketers usually classify these products and services further based on how consumers go about buying them. Consumer products include *convenience products, shopping products, speciality products* and *unsought products*. These products differ in the ways consumers buy them and therefore in how they are marketed (see Table 7.1).

Convenience products are consumer products and services that the customer usually buys frequently, immediately and with a minimum of comparison and buying effort. Examples include soap, chocolate, newspapers and fast food. Convenience products are usually inexpensive, and marketers place them in many locations to make them readily available when customers need them.

TABLE 7.1 Marketing considerations for consumer products

	Type of consumer product			
Marketing considerations	**Convenience**	**Shopping**	**Speciality**	**Unsought**
Customer buying behaviour	Frequent purchase, little planning, little comparison or shopping effort, low customer involvement	Less frequent purchase, much planning and shopping effort, comparison of brands on price, quality, style	Strong brand preference and loyalty, special purchase effort, little comparison of brands, low price sensitivity	Little product awareness, knowledge (or, if aware, little or even negative interest)
Price	Low price	High price	Higher price	Varies
Distribution	Widespread distribution, convenient locations	Selective distribution in fewer outlets	Exclusive distribution in only one or a few outlets per market area	Varies
Promotion	Mass promotion by the producer	Advertising and personal selling by both producer and resellers	More carefully targeted promotion by both producer and resellers	Aggressive advertising and personal selling by producer and resellers
Examples	Toothpaste, magazines, laundry detergent	Major appliances, TVs, furniture, clothing	Luxury goods, such as Rolex watches or fine crystal	Life insurance, Red Cross blood donations

Shopping products are less frequently purchased consumer products and services that customers compare carefully on suitability, quality, price and style. When buying shopping products and services, consumers spend a lot of time and effort gathering information and making comparisons. Examples include furniture, clothing, used cars, major appliances, and hotel and airline services. Marketers usually distribute their shopping products through fewer outlets but provide deeper sales support to help customers in their comparison efforts.

Speciality products are consumer products and services with unique characteristics or brand identification for which a significant group of buyers is willing to make a special purchase effort. Examples include specific brands and types of cars, high-priced photographic equipment, designer clothes and the services of medical or legal specialists. A Porsche sports car, for example, is a speciality product because buyers are usually willing to travel great distances to buy one. Buyers normally do not compare speciality products. They invest only the time needed to reach dealers carrying the wanted products.

Unsought products are consumer products that the consumer either does not know about or knows about but does not normally think of buying. Most major new innovations are unsought until the consumer becomes aware of them through advertising. Classic examples of known but unsought products and services are life insurance, pre-planned funeral services and personal pensions. By their very nature, unsought products require a lot of advertising, personal selling and other marketing efforts.

Industrial products

Industrial products are those purchased for further processing or for use in conducting a business. Thus, the distinction between a consumer product and an industrial product is based on the *purpose* for which the product is bought. If a consumer buys a lawnmower for use around the home, the lawnmower is a consumer product. If the same consumer buys the same lawnmower for use in a landscaping business, the lawnmower is an industrial product.

The three groups of industrial products and services include materials and parts, capital items, and supplies and services. *Materials and parts* include raw materials and manufactured materials and parts. Raw materials consist of farm products (wheat, cotton, livestock, fruits, vegetables) and natural products (fish, wood, crude oil, iron ore). Manufactured materials and parts consist of component materials (iron, yarn, cement, wires) and component parts (small motors, tyres, castings). Most manufactured materials and parts are sold directly to industrial users. Price and service are the major marketing factors; branding and advertising tend to be less important. Components brought together make the whole, much as a child builds a model from Lego bricks.

Capital items are industrial products that aid the buyer's production or operations, including installations and accessory equipment. Installations consist of major purchases such as buildings (factories, offices) and fixed equipment (generators, drill presses, large computer systems). Accessory equipment includes portable factory equipment and tools (hand tools, fork-lift trucks) and office equipment (computers, fax machines, desks). They have a shorter life than installations and simply aid the production process.

The final group of business products is *supplies and services*. Supplies include operating supplies (lubricants, coal, paper, pencils) and repair and maintenance items (paint, nails, brooms). Supplies are the convenience products of the industrial field because they are usually purchased with a minimum of effort or comparison. Business services include maintenance and repair services (window cleaning, computer repair) and business advisory services (legal, management consulting, advertising). Such services are usually supplied under contract.

Organisations, persons, places and ideas

In addition to tangible products and services, in recent years marketers have broadened the concept of a product to include other market offerings – organisations, persons, places and ideas.

Organisations often carry out activities to 'sell' the organisation itself. *Organisation marketing* consists of activities undertaken to create, maintain or change the attitudes and behaviour of target consumers towards an organisation. Both profit and not-for-profit organisations practise organisation marketing. Business firms sponsor public relations or corporate advertising campaigns to polish their images. *Corporate image advertising* is a major tool that companies use to market themselves to various publics. For example, Dutch bank ABN AMRO ads say, 'While some are focused on us, we are focused on you', and the French oil company Total tells us that: 'Our energy is your energy.' Similarly, not-for-profit organisations, such as churches, universities, charities, museums and performing arts groups, market their organisations in order to raise funds and attract members or patrons.

People can also be thought of as products. *Person marketing* consists of activities undertaken to create, maintain or change attitudes or behaviour towards particular people. People ranging from presidents, entertainers and sports figures to professionals such as doctors, lawyers and architects use person marketing to build their reputations and increase business. Businesses, charities, sports teams and other organisations also use person marketing. Creating or associating with well-known personalities often helps these organisations achieve their goals better. That is why companies such as Nike, Kia Motors and Emporio Armani line up to sponsor star tennis champion Rafa Nadal, and Andy Murray was able to exploit his win at Wimbledon by endorsing brands like Rado, Adidas and RBS.[2]

The skilful use of person marketing can turn a person's name into a powerhouse brand. You can buy a wide range of clothing marketed under the Björn Borg brand name, a

Nigella Lawson is an example of someone who has spent years crafting a public persona

Source: Photoshot Holdings Limited/Zuma.

vast array of golfing gear endorsed by Ryder Cup golf star Sergio Garcia, and you can make yourself smell nice with a Roger Federer cologne set. It is not just athletes – celebrity chef Nigella Lawson has successfully established her own personal brand through a number of TV series and books which have attracted viewers and readers in their millions across the globe. Of course, when there are problems in the real lives of these individuals, those become headline news.

Place marketing involves activities undertaken to create, maintain or change attitudes or behaviour towards particular places. Cities, states, regions and even entire nations compete to attract tourists, new residents, conventions, and company offices and factories. Stratford-upon-Avon in England promotes itself as the birthplace of Shakespeare, Dublin – 'the fair city' – advertises itself as a cultural capital with a youthful population where everyone will have fun, while Durban, South Africa, calls itself 'the playground of the Zulu kingdom', promoting both its African heritage and its beautiful coastline. The Iceland Tourist Board invites visitors to Iceland by advertising that it has 'Discoveries the Entire Year'. Icelandair, the only airline that serves the island, partners with the tourist board to sell world travellers on the wonders of Iceland – everything from geothermal spas and glacier tours to midnight golf and clubbing.[3]

Ideas can also be marketed. In one sense, all marketing is the marketing of an idea, whether it is the general idea of brushing your teeth or the specific idea that Arm & Hammer Enamel Care toothpaste will help to protect the enamel on your teeth. Here, however, we narrow our focus to the marketing of *social ideas*. This area has been called **social marketing,** defined by the Social Marketing Institute as the use of commercial marketing concepts and tools in programmes designed to influence individuals' behaviour to improve their well-being and that of society.[4]

Social marketing programmes include public health campaigns to reduce smoking, alcoholism, drug abuse and overeating. Other social marketing efforts include environmental campaigns to promote wilderness protection, clean air and conservation. Still others address issues such as family planning, human rights and racial equality. The European Commission has recently developed a pan-European multimedia advertising campaign to try to convince Europeans to stop smoking, or never to start smoking in the first place – take a look at the start of Chapter 16 if you would like to know more about this now.

But social marketing involves much more than just advertising – the Social Marketing Institute (SMI) encourages the use of a broad range of marketing tools. 'Social marketing goes well beyond the promotional "*P*" of the marketing mix to include every other element to achieve its social change objectives,' says the SMI's executive director.[5]

PRODUCT AND SERVICE DECISIONS

Marketers make product and service decisions at three levels: individual product decisions, product line decisions and product mix decisions. We discuss each in turn.

Individual product and service decisions

Figure 7.2 shows the important decisions in the development and marketing of individual products and services. We will focus on decisions about *product attributes, branding, packaging, labelling* and *product support services.*

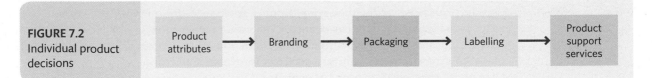

FIGURE 7.2
Individual product decisions

Product attributes → Branding → Packaging → Labelling → Product support services

Product and service attributes

Developing a product or service involves defining the benefits that it will offer. These benefits are communicated and delivered by product attributes such as *quality, features* and *style and design*.

Product quality

Product quality is one of the marketer's major positioning tools. Quality has a direct impact on product or service performance; thus, it is closely linked to customer value and satisfaction. In the narrowest sense, quality can be defined as 'freedom from defects'. But most customer-centred companies go beyond this narrow definition. Instead, they define quality in terms of creating customer value and satisfaction. For example, Siemens defines quality this way: 'Quality is when our customers come back and our products don't.'[6] We emphasised above that a product may be either a tangible good or an intangible service, and in a service business quality has been defined as 'the extent to which the service delivered meets the customer's expectations'.[7]

Total quality management (TQM) is an approach in which all the company's people are involved in constantly improving the quality of products, services and business processes. Companies large and small have credited TQM with greatly improving their market shares and profits. Over the years, however, many companies have encountered problems in implementing TQM. Some companies viewed TQM as a magic cure-all and created token total quality programmes that applied quality principles only superficially. Still others became obsessed with narrowly defined TQM principles and lost sight of broader concerns for customer value and satisfaction. As a result, many such programmes failed, causing a backlash against TQM.

When applied in the context of creating customer satisfaction, however, *total quality* principles remain a requirement for success. Although many firms no longer use the TQM label, for most top companies customer-driven quality has become a way of doing business. Today, companies are taking a 'return on quality' approach, viewing quality as an investment and holding quality efforts accountable for bottom-line results.[8]

Product quality has two dimensions – level and consistency. In developing a product, the marketer must first choose a *quality level* that will support the product's positioning. Here, product quality means *performance quality* – the ability of a product to perform its functions. For example, a BMW provides higher performance quality than a Fiat: it is better engineered and lasts longer. Companies rarely try to offer the highest possible performance quality level – few customers want or can afford the high levels of quality offered in products such as a Rolls-Royce car, a €1,500 Louis Vuitton handbag or a Rolex watch. Instead, companies choose a quality level that matches target market needs and the quality levels of competing products.

Beyond quality level, high quality can mean high levels of consistency. Here, product quality means *conformance quality* – freedom from defects and *consistency* in delivering a targeted level of performance. All companies should strive for high levels of conformance quality. In this sense, a Ford can have just as much quality as a Rolls-Royce. Although a Ford does not have all the same features as a Rolls-Royce, it can as consistently deliver the quality that customers pay for and expect.

Many companies today have turned customer-driven quality into a potent strategic weapon. They have created customer satisfaction and value by consistently and profitably meeting customers' needs and preferences for quality.

Product features

A product can be offered with varying features. A stripped-down model, one without any extras, is the starting point. The company can create higher level models by adding more features. Features are a competitive tool for differentiating the company's product from competitors' products. Being the first producer to introduce a needed and valued new feature is one of the most effective ways to compete.

How can a company identify new features and decide which ones to add to its product? The company should periodically survey buyers who have used the product and ask these questions: How do you like the product? Which specific features of the product do you like most? Which features could we add to improve the product? The answers provide the company with a rich list of feature ideas. The company can then assess each feature's *value* to customers versus its *cost* to the company. Features that customers value little in relation to costs should be dropped; those that customers value highly in relation to costs should be added.

Product style and design

Another way to add customer value is through distinctive product style and design. Design is a larger concept than style. Style simply describes the appearance of a product. Styles can be eye catching or yawn producing. A sensational style may grab attention and produce pleasing aesthetics, but it does not necessarily make the product perform better. Unlike style, design is more than skin deep – it goes to the very heart of a product. Good design contributes to a product's usefulness as well as to its looks.

Good design begins with a deep understanding of customer needs. More than simply creating product or service attributes, it involves shaping the customer's product-use experience. Consider the design process behind Invotek's Strawboard.

Invotek Solutions began life as Poole Partitionings in 1973, a specialist manufacturer of simple aluminium frames:

> Like most companies in the partitioning business, Invotek's traditional material of choice has always been plasterboard. It's cheap, fireproof and relatively soundproof.
>
> But there's a problem. Not only is the material not biodegradable, but gypsum-based products such as plasterboard can also be hazardous if combined with other unstable products in landfill. New regulations tackling this issue led Invotek to seek a better, more sustainable alternative.
>
> For Simon Coleman, Commercial Director at Invotek, the change in regulations represented more of an opportunity than a threat to his business: 'It gave us the chance to explore a potentially radical solution,' he explains. 'We could have chosen a mainstream alternative, such as chipboard, ply or MDF, but since they all have environmentally unsound production processes, we didn't feel we'd be making a significant impact to our own environmental footprint.'
>
> Instead, after some intensive desk research, Coleman came across the possibility of using a by-product of wheat straw.
>
> Coleman approached Compak UK, an agrifibre engineering business which manufactures solid compressed sheets from straw waste. The two companies began collaborating on the development of an entirely new partitioning solution.
>
> Invotek's five-strong team of designers was central to the development of the new solution, from the production process and manufacturing specifications to the appearance of the finished product. As with any groundbreaking innovation, there were a number of challenges to be overcome, but nothing the team couldn't handle. 'Over the years we have developed a culture of innovation and design,' says Coleman. 'It means we can respond better to customers' needs, and we are agile enough to adapt our solutions and solve any problems as they arise.'
>
> The resulting product – Strawboard – is biodegradable, easily recycled, produced from a sustainable source, structurally sound, easy to fit and secure, resistant to fire and high impacts and performs well in acoustic testing.
>
> 'It wasn't enough just to be environmentally friendly, Strawboard has to perform both practically and financially,' says Coleman. 'We have to be able to demonstrate to environmentally considerate architects and interior designers that Strawboard not only complies with long-term waste acceptance criteria, but provides a very adaptable alternative for plaster surfaces and partitioning.'
>
> The first project using the new material went ahead in July 2006 with the refurbishment of school classrooms at Winton Primary School in Bournemouth. Shortly after, Invotek

Invotek developed Strawboard as a cost-effective, biodegradable, environmentally-friendly new product for use in its partitioning products

Source: http://www.invotekltd. co.uk/new_developments/ strawboard_paneling.html. Courtesy of Invotek Systems.

was short-listed for Most Innovative Product at the 100% Detail/RIBA Journal Innovations Awards.

Since then, it's not just the company name that has changed. Constant design innovation, driven by customer demand, new materials and cutting-edge techniques, has transformed the business. Invotek now boasts an extensive product range, employs 40 people and turned over an impressive £5.5 million in 2004.

Simon Coleman says the company has experienced a 'natural evolution' from its engineering roots and has become an increasingly design-led business. 'The only way to gain competitive advantage in this sector is to offer something unique,' he says. 'And to do that you have to design something.'

Design is central to Invotek's product development, and it's the customers and users who drive the innovation process. 'We listen to what customers say and value their input,' says Coleman. 'In a competitive industry like partitioning you have to be one step ahead.' Listening to the feedback of its customer base – largely architects and designers – Invotek is able to anticipate new trends and capitalise on opportunities. 'Customers are our eyes and ears,' says Coleman. 'They drive our appetite for design and innovation. If enough people are asking for a particular type of product or service then we try to find out how we can give it to them.'

As a result, Invotek has continued to refine its product range. Even though the original Invotek 75 range, developed in 1975, still accounts for approximately 50 per cent of total sales, the past 30 years have seen the range expanded to include a number of other products including glass partitions and movable wall systems. 'Flexibility is an important factor for our customers and we have sought to respond to their needs by adapting what we do best,' says Coleman.

And the Strawboard launch was similarly a response to customer demand for a sustainable alternative to plasterboard. 'It's not just the regulators that are driving the need for more sustainable solutions; our customers want them too,' Coleman explains. 'Our first project with Strawboard was in a school, and it was important for them to be able to source building materials manufactured with the environment in mind.'

He, and the rest of the company, are determined to keep innovating. 'Innovative products such as Strawboard are the result of our continual investment in design, research and development,' says Coleman, 'and those disciplines have been the cornerstones of our consistent growth over the years.'[9]

Thus, product designers should think less about product attributes and technical specifications and more about how customers will use and benefit from the product.

Branding

Perhaps the most distinctive skill of professional marketers is their ability to build and manage brands. A **brand** is a name, term, sign, symbol or design, or a combination of these, that identifies the maker or seller of a product or service. Consumers view a brand as an important part of a product, and branding can add value to a product. For example, most consumers would perceive a bottle of Chanel perfume as a high-quality, expensive product. But the same perfume in an unmarked bottle would probably be viewed as lower in quality, even if the fragrance was identical.

Branding has become so strong that today hardly anything goes unbranded. Salt is packaged in branded containers, common screws and staples are packaged with a distributor's label, and car parts – spark plugs, tyres, filters – bear brand names that differ from those of the car makers.

Branding helps buyers in many ways. Brand names help consumers identify products that might benefit them. Brands also say something about product quality and consistency – buyers who always buy the same brand know that they will get the same features, benefits and quality each time they buy. Branding also gives the seller several advantages. The brand name becomes the basis on which a whole story can be built about a product's special qualities. The seller's brand name and trademark provide legal protection for unique product features that otherwise might be copied by competitors. And branding helps the seller to segment markets. For example, Nestlé can offer Cheerios, Shredded Wheat, Shreddies, Fitnesse and many other cereal brands, not just one general product for all consumers.

Building and managing brands is perhaps the marketer's most important task. We will discuss branding strategy in more detail later in the chapter.

Packaging

Packaging involves designing and producing the container or wrapper for a product. The package includes a product's primary container (the tube holding Colgate Total toothpaste). It may also include a secondary package that is thrown away when the product is about to be used (the cardboard box containing the tube of Colgate). Finally, it can include a shipping package necessary to store, identify and ship the product (a corrugated box carrying six-dozen tubes of Colgate). Labelling – printed information appearing on or with the package – is also part of packaging.

Traditionally, the primary function of the package was to contain and protect the product. In recent times, however, numerous factors have made packaging an important marketing tool. Increased competition and clutter on retail store shelves mean that packages must now perform many sales tasks – from attracting attention, to describing the product, to making the sale.

Companies are realising the power of good packaging to create instant consumer recognition of the company or brand. For example, in an average supermarket, which stocks 45,000 items, the typical shopper passes by some 300 items per minute, and more than 70 per cent of all purchases are decided on in the store. In this highly competitive environment, the package may be the seller's last chance to influence buyers. So, for many companies, the packaging has become a key communications medium.[10] Think of the Toblerone pyramid box and the curves of the classic Coke bottle.

Innovative packaging can give a company an advantage over competitors. Sometimes even seemingly small packaging improvements can make a big difference. For example, Heinz revolutionised the 170-year-old condiments industry by inverting the good old ketchup bottle, letting customers quickly squeeze out even the last bit of ketchup. At the same time, it adopted a 'fridge-door-fit' shape that not only slots into shelves more easily, but also has a cap that is simpler for children to open. In the four months following the introduction of the new package, sales jumped 12 per cent. What is more, the new package does double duty as a promotional tool. Says a packaging analyst, 'When consumers see the Heinz logo on the fridge door every time they open it, it's taking marketing inside homes.'[11]

In contrast, poorly designed packages can cause headaches for consumers and lost sales for the company. This has been an issue of significance for Amazon, which has a programme called Frustration Free Packaging that is meant to prevent what it has labelled 'wrap-rage' – the anxiety and stress and anger caused by packaging seemingly impenetrable to those with limited strength or dexterity, such as more elderly customers. In making packaging decisions, the company is one of a growing number also heeding environmental concerns and trying to increase the proportion of items using environmentally responsible packaging materials.

Labelling

Labels may range from simple tags attached to products to complex graphics that are part of the package. They perform several functions. At the very least, the label *identifies* the product or brand, such as the name Outspan stamped on oranges. The label might also *describe* several things about the product – who made it, where it was made, when it was made, its contents, how it is to be used and how to use it safely. Finally, the label might help to *promote* the product and support its positioning.

For example, in the never-ending search for ways to stand out, the clothing industry seems to be rediscovering the promotional value of the product label:

> Some clothing labels send strong messages. A 'booklet tag' hanging from a workout garment might reinforce the brand's positioning, describing in detail how the garment is used by certain high-profile athletes or what types of special materials are used in its construction. Other brasher statements include pocket flashers and 'lenticular tags', which generate 3-D or animation effects. At the other extreme, tagless heat-transfer labels are replacing sewn-in woven labels, promising ultimate comfort. Even low-key labels are using more brilliant colours or elaborate graphics, beautifying the product and reinforcing the brand message. Rich treatments on labels add pizzazz to luxury items; futuristic tags support emerging technical, man-made fabrications; tags adorned with playful characters evoke a sense of fun for kids' garments. 'The product label is a key cog in branding strategy,' says a labelling expert. 'The look, feel, or even smell of the label – if done creatively – can complement a brand.'[12]

Along with the positives, labelling also raises concerns. There has been a long history of legal concerns about packaging and labels. Labels can mislead customers, fail to describe important ingredients, or fail to include needed safety warnings. As a result, several European laws regulate labelling, while individual countries have their own laws which often supplement EU legislation. Agreed EU-wide controls on food labelling were introduced with Directive 79/112 in 1979. Additional controls have been added and amendments introduced to produce a complex array of labelling requirements. In 2000, the original 1979 Directive and its amendments were consolidated into a single new Directive – 2000/13/EC.

Directive 2000/13/EC is concerned with the labelling of foodstuffs to be delivered to the final consumer, and those to be delivered to catering outlets such as restaurants and canteens. The basic principle is that the labelling must not mislead the purchaser about the product, for example with respect to the characteristics, quantity, properties or origins of the foodstuff. Article 3 of the Directive specifies a range of information that must be provided on all foodstuffs, including a list of ingredients, the shelf life, details of origin, the name and address of the manufacturer, and any special storage conditions or conditions of use. You are probably aware of the confusion that can be caused when some products are labelled as 'sell by' or 'best before' and others are labelled as 'use by'. This has led to enormous waste of food as consumers play it safe by unnecessarily disposing of food that is still edible.

Product support services

Customer service is another element of product strategy. A company's offer usually includes some support services, which can be a minor or a major part of the total offering. Later in the chapter we will discuss services as products in themselves. Here, we discuss services that augment actual products.

The first step is to survey customers periodically to assess the value of current services and to obtain ideas for new ones. For example, the Department for Work and Pensions – a large UK governmental department of state – canvassed opinion on the affordability and availability of childcare services with particular attention paid to how well services integrated with schools, which regulations limited or made worse current service provision, and how childcare services could be used as part of a strategy to move people from benefits back into paid employment. Interested parties could take part in local discussions or complete feedback forms in print or online.[13]

Many companies are now using a sophisticated mix of phone, email, Internet and interactive voice and data technologies to provide support services that were not possible before. For example, HP offers a complete set of sales and after-sale services. It promises, 'HP Total Care – expert help for every stage of your computer's life. From choosing it, to configuring it, to protecting it, to tuning it up – all the way to recycling it.' Customers can click onto the HP Total Care service portal that offers online resources for HP products and 24/7 tech support, which can be accessed via email, instant online chat, and telephone.[14]

Product line decisions

Beyond decisions about individual products and services, product strategy also calls for building a product line. A **product line** is a group of products that are closely related because they function in a similar manner, are sold to the same customer groups, are marketed through the same types of outlets, or fall within given price ranges. For example, Nike produces several lines of athletic shoes and clothing, Nokia produces several lines of telecommunications products, and HSBC produces several lines of financial services.

The major product line decision involves *product line length* – the number of items in the product line. The line is too short if the manager can increase profits by adding items; the line is too long if the manager can increase profits by dropping items. The company should manage its product lines carefully. Product lines tend to lengthen over time, and most companies eventually need to prune unnecessary or unprofitable items from their lines to increase overall profitability. Managers need to conduct a periodic *product line analysis* to assess each product item's sales and profits and to understand how each item contributes to the line's performance.

Product line length is influenced by company objectives and resources. For example, one objective might be to allow for upselling. Thus BMW wants to move customers up from its 1-series and 3-series models to 5- and 7-series models. Another objective might be to allow cross-selling: HP sells printers as well as cartridges. Still another objective might be to protect against economic swings: Arcadia Group runs several different chains of clothing stores catering for different target markets and different income categories to try to reduce the impact of economic fluctuations (these include Burton, Dorothy Perkins, Miss Selfridge, Evans and Top Shop).

A company can lengthen its product line in two ways: by *line stretching* or by *line filling*. *Product line stretching* occurs when a company lengthens its product line beyond its current range. The company can stretch its line downwards, upwards or both ways.

Companies located at the upper end of the market can stretch their lines *downwards*. A company may stretch downwards to plug a market hole that otherwise would attract a new competitor or to respond to a competitor's attack on the upper end. Or it may add low-end products because it finds faster growth taking place in the low-end segments. DaimlerChrysler stretched its Mercedes line downwards for all these reasons. Facing a slow-growth luxury car market and attacks by Japanese car makers on its high-end positioning, it successfully introduced its Mercedes C-Class cars. These models sell in the €30,000 range without harming the firm's ability to sell other Mercedes at much higher prices.

Companies at the lower end of a market can stretch their product lines *upwards*. Sometimes, companies stretch upwards in order to add prestige to their current products. Or they may be attracted by a faster growth rate or higher margins at the higher end. For example, each of the leading Japanese car companies introduced an upmarket automobile: Toyota launched Lexus, Nissan launched Infinity and Honda launched Acura. They used entirely new names rather than their own names.

Companies in the middle range of the market may decide to stretch their lines in *both directions*. Marriott did this with its hotel product line. Along with regular Marriott hotels, it has added new branded hotel lines to serve both the upper and lower ends of the market. Renaissance aims to attract and please top executives; Marriott, upper and middle managers; Courtyard, salespeople and other 'road warriors'; and Fairfield Inn, vacationers and business travellers on a tight travel budget. ExecuStay by Marriott provides temporary housing for those relocating or away on long-term assignments of 30 days or longer. Marriott's Residence Inn provides a relaxed, residential atmosphere – a home away from home for people who travel for a living. Marriott TownePlace Suites provide a comfortable atmosphere at a moderate price for extended-stay travellers. And Marriott SpringHill Suites have 25 per cent more space than an average hotel room – offering a separate living and work space for business travellers.[15] The major risk with this strategy is that some travellers will trade down after finding that the lower price hotels in the Marriott chain give them pretty much everything they want. However, Marriott would rather capture its customers who move downwards than lose them to competitors.

An alternative to product line stretching is *product line filling* – adding more items within the present range of the line. There are several reasons for product line filling: reaching for extra profits, satisfying dealers, using excess capacity, being the leading full-line company and plugging holes to keep out competitors. Dyson added further models of vacuum cleaners to its range for specific uses and purposes such as for use on hardwood floors, to fit into small storage spaces in city-centre apartments and to pick up pet-hairs. However, line filling is overdone if it results in cannibalisation and customer confusion. The company should ensure that new items are noticeably different from existing ones.

Product mix decisions

An organisation with several product lines has a product mix. A **product mix (or product portfolio)** consists of all the product lines and items that a particular seller offers for sale. Avon's product mix consists of five major product lines: beauty products, wellness products, jewellery and accessories, gifts and 'inspirational' products (inspiring gifts, books, music and home accents). Each product line consists of several sublines. For example, the beauty line breaks down into make-up, skin care, bath and beauty, fragrance, salon and spa, and outdoor protection products. Each line and subline has many individual items. Altogether, Avon's product mix includes 1,300 items. In contrast, 3M markets more than 60,000 products, a typical hypermarket stocks 100,000 to 120,000 items, and GE manufactures as many as 250,000 items.

A company's product mix has four important dimensions: width, length, depth and consistency. Product mix *width* refers to the number of different product lines the company carries. For example, Colgate markets a fairly wide product mix, consisting of dozens of brands that you can 'trust to care for yourself, your home, and the ones you love'. This product mix is organised into five major product lines: oral care, personal care, household care, fabric care and pet nutrition.

Product mix *length* and *depth* refer to the total number of items the company carries within its product lines (length) and the number of items carried within a specific line (depth). Consider two major consumer products companies, Unilever and Colgate. Unilever typically carries many brands within each line. For example, its personal-care line includes Lifebuoy, Lux, Pond's, Sunsilk and Dove (product line length). The Dove brand alone is used on soaps, body washes, shampoos, conditioners and deodorants (product line depth). To illustrate product line *depth* further, consider Colgate's line of toothpastes, which come in 11 varieties, ranging from Colgate Total, Colgate Tartar Control, Colgate

2in1 and Colgate Cavity Protection to Colgate Sensitive, Colgate Fresh Confidence, Colgate Max Fresh, Colgate Simply White, Colgate Sparkling White, Colgate Kids Toothpastes and Colgate Baking Soda & Peroxide. Then, each variety comes in its own special forms and formulations. For example, you can buy Colgate Total in regular, mint fresh stripe, whitening paste and gel, advanced fresh gel or 2in1 liquid gel versions.[16]

Finally, the *consistency* of the product mix refers to how closely related the various product lines are in end use, production requirements, distribution channels, or in some other way. Colgate's product lines are consistent in so far as they are consumer products that go through the same distribution channels. The lines are less consistent in so far as they perform different functions for buyers.

These product mix dimensions provide the methods of defining the company's product strategy. The company can increase its business in four ways. It can add new product lines, widening its product mix. In this way, its new lines build on the company's reputation in its other lines. The company can lengthen its existing product lines to become a more full-line company. Or it can add more versions of each product and thus deepen its product mix. Finally, the company can pursue more product line consistency – or less – depending on whether it wants to have a strong reputation in a single field or in several fields.

BRANDING STRATEGY: BUILDING STRONG BRANDS

Some analysts see brands as *the* major enduring asset of a company, outlasting the company's specific products and facilities. John Stewart, co-founder of Quaker Oats, once said, 'If this business were split up, I would give you the land and bricks and mortar, and I would keep the brands and trademarks, and I would fare better than you.' A former CEO of McDonald's agrees: 'If every asset we own, every building, and every piece of equipment were destroyed in a terrible natural disaster, we would be able to borrow all the money to replace it very quickly because of the value of our brand. . . . The brand is more valuable than the totality of all these assets.'[17]

Thus, brands are powerful assets that must be carefully developed and managed. In this section, we examine the key strategies for building and managing brands.

Brand equity

Brands are more than just names and symbols. Brands represent consumers' perceptions and feelings about a product and its performance – everything that the product or service *means* to consumers. In the final analysis, brands exist in the minds of consumers.

The real value of a strong brand is its power to capture consumer preference and loyalty. Brands vary in the amount of power and value they have in the marketplace. Some brands, such as Coca-Cola, Mercedes, Nike, Disney and others, become larger-than-life icons that maintain their power in the market for years, even generations. These brands win in the marketplace not simply because they deliver unique benefits or reliable service. Rather, they succeed because they forge deep connections with customers.

A powerful brand has high *brand equity*. **Brand equity** is the positive differential effect that knowing the brand name has on customer response to the product or service. Branding consultancy Interbrand specialises in analysing, interpreting and valuing brands. Its analysis considers the competitive strength of the brand, the role the brand plays in the purchase decision, and the financial performance of the branded products or services. In evaluating brand strength Interbrand believes it has identified 10 key factors,[18] and these are listed in Table 7.2.

A brand must be distinct, or consumers will have no reason to choose it over other brands. But the fact that a brand is highly differentiated does not necessarily mean that consumers

TABLE 7.2 Interbrand's key brand strength factors

Internal	External
Clarity Clarify internally about what the brand stands for and its values, positioning and proposition. Clarity, too, about target audiences, customer insights, and drivers. Because so much hinges on this, it is vital that these are articulated and shared across the organisation	**Authenticity** The brand is soundly based on an internal truth and capability. It has a defined heritage and a well-grounded value set. It can deliver against the (high) expectations that customers have of it
Commitment Internal commitment to brand, and a belief internally in the importance of brand. The extent to which the brand receives support in terms of time, influence and investment	**Relevance** The fit with customer/consumer needs, desires and decision criteria across all relevant demographics and geographies
Protection How secure the brand is across a number of dimensions: legal protection, proprietary ingredients or design, scale or geographical spread	**Differentiation** The degree to which customers/consumers perceive the brand to have a differentiated positioning distinctive from the competition
Responsiveness The ability to respond to market changes, challenges and opportunities. The brand should have a sense of leadership internally, and a desire and ability to constantly evolve and renew itself	**Consistency** The degree to which a brand is experienced without fail across all touch points or formats
	Presence The degree to which a brand feels omnipresent and is talked about positively by consumers, customers and opinion formers in both traditional and social media
	Understanding Not only is the brand recognised by customers, but also there is an in-depth knowledge and understanding of its distinctive qualities and characteristics. (Where relevant, this will extend to consumer understanding of the company that owns the brand)

will buy it. The brand must stand out in ways that are relevant to consumers' needs. But even a differentiated, relevant brand is far from a shoe-in. Before consumers will respond to the brand, they must first know about and understand it. And that familiarity must lead to a strong, positive consumer–brand connection.

A brand with strong brand equity is a very valuable asset. *Brand valuation* is the process of estimating the total financial value of a brand. According to Interbrand, the world's most valuable brands in 2014 were Apple at $118bn followed by Google at $107bn and Coca-Cola at $82bn. The most valuable European brands in the top 100 were Mercedes-Benz and BMW, both at around $32bn, with Louis Vuitton some way behind on $25bn.[19]

High brand equity provides a company with many competitive advantages. A powerful brand enjoys a high level of consumer brand awareness and loyalty. Because consumers expect stores to carry the brand, the company has more leverage in bargaining with resellers. Because the brand name carries high credibility, the company can more easily launch line and brand extensions, as when Coca-Cola used its well-known brand to introduce Diet Coke and recently Coke Life, and when Unilever extended the Dove brand to include shampoos and conditioners. A powerful brand offers the company some defence against fierce price competition.

Above all, a powerful brand forms the basis for building strong and profitable customer relationships. Therefore, the fundamental asset underlying brand equity is *customer equity* – the value of the customer relationships that the brand creates. A powerful brand is important, but what it really represents is a profitable set of loyal customers. The proper focus of marketing is building customer equity, with brand management serving as a major marketing tool.

Building strong brands

Branding poses challenging decisions to the marketer. Figure 7.3 shows that the major brand strategy decisions involve brand positioning, brand name selection, brand sponsorship and brand development.

Brand positioning

Marketers need to position their brands clearly in target customers' minds. They can position brands at any of three levels.[20] At the lowest level, they can position the brand on *product attributes*. Thus, marketers of Aquafresh toothpaste can talk about the product's innovative ingredients and good taste. However, attributes are the least desirable level for brand positioning. Competitors can easily copy attributes. More important, customers are not interested in attributes as such; they are interested in what the attributes will do for them.

A brand can be better positioned by associating its name with a desirable *benefit*. Thus, Aquafresh marketers can go beyond the brand's ingredients and talk about the resulting decay prevention or teeth whitening benefits. Some successful brands positioned on benefits are Volvo (safety), Duracell (extended use), The North Face (adventure), FedEx (guaranteed on-time delivery), Nike (performance) and Lexus (quality).

The strongest brands go beyond attribute or benefit positioning. They are positioned on strong *beliefs and values*. These brands deliver emotional benefits. Thus, Aquafresh's marketers can talk not just about ingredients and decay-prevention benefits, but about how these give customers 'a whole new experience of clean'.[21] Successful brands engage customers on a deep, emotional level. Brands such as Starbucks, Christian Louboutin and Apple rely less on a product's tangible attributes and more on creating surprise, passion and excitement surrounding a brand.

When positioning a brand, the marketer should establish a mission for the brand and a vision of what the brand must be and do. A brand is the company's promise to deliver a specific set of features, benefits, services and experiences consistently to the buyers. The brand promise must be simple and honest. The Travel Inn hotel chain, for example, offers clean rooms, low prices and good service but does not promise expensive furniture or large bathrooms. In contrast, Ritz-Carlton offers luxurious rooms and a truly memorable experience but does not promise low prices.

Brand name selection

A good name can add greatly to a product's success. However, finding the best brand name is a difficult task. It begins with a careful review of the product and its benefits, the target market and proposed marketing strategies. After that, naming a brand becomes part science, part art and a measure of instinct (see Marketing at Work 7.1).

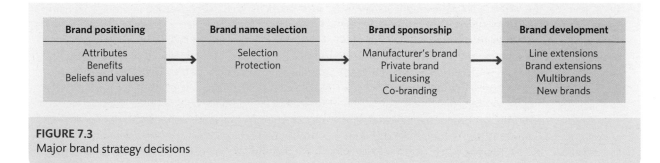

FIGURE 7.3
Major brand strategy decisions

Naming brands: just how much does a name matter?

MARKETING AT WORK 7.1

Late 2013 saw the almost simultaneous launch of two new gaming consoles from Sony and Microsoft. Sony played it safe – the PlayStation 3 would be followed by . . . the PlayStation 4. Microsoft took a different strategy. The previous generation console was called the Xbox 360, so the new one (the third in the series) would be called . . . Xbox One.

Why pick this name? When challenged on it, Jeff Henshaw – who heads up Xbox projects at Microsoft – said:

It only takes a little while before you realize what's going on underneath that name. There's something very powerful about it. Xbox One really embodies the concept that this is the first device, the combination of this very powerful console that brings all its eight cores, 8GB of RAM, super fast memory, super powerful dedicated audio and video processing subsystems. There's incredible power in this device, married with the next generation of Kinect for really enabling those subtle interactions between you and your entertainment. So to us, One is really the embodiment that this becomes one device that addresses all the entertainment that you want to enjoy on your TV, and brings it to you in a way that's so simple, that it can be the only input you have connected through your television. It is truly the one place to go for all this. So One ends up being a deeply meaningful thing to us here. It's almost a bar that we are striving to achieve, and I think we nailed it really well with the Xbox One.

Regrettably for Jeff, the combination of letters and graphic design of the chosen name and logo has led to many calling it the Xbone. Whether that will come to be a name of affection or disdain remains to be seen.

It is not just new products that go through the naming process. Fairly recently, UK consumers found one of their favourite insurance companies – Norwich Union – persuading them that in the future it should be called 'Aviva', and that this was a really good idea. It is reasonable to suppose that rather a lot of those consumers were a bit confused by the whole idea. After all, Norwich Union had great brand recognition in the UK, and the name is derived from the name of a town in eastern England (Norwich) where the company was founded in 1797; not a particularly famous town outside the UK, but a well-loved town by the British, famous for a football team of modest success (known as 'the Canaries' because they play in yellow kit – their fans are known as the 'Yellow Army'), and close to some family-friendly holiday resorts on the North Sea coast. So, Norwich, a well-liked town, and Norwich Union, a well-known name.

Why, then, 'Aviva'? The name has no literal meaning in English, although it does raise associations with French (*à vivre*) and Spanish (*viva*) expressions with which many English people are familiar, and which have generally 'lively' meanings. The Aviva company was formed in 2002 by a merger between Norwich Union and CGU plc, with the aim of creating an insurance company to compete on the global stage. CGU plc itself had a 'modern' sounding name; names formed solely of letters became something of a fashion in the 1990s (e.g. British Telecommunications became simply BT). CGU was formed in 1998 when insurance companies Commercial Union and General Accident merged. In May 2002, this company merged with Norwich Union to form CGNU, and then in April 2002 the shareholders approved the change of name to Aviva. So, by the time that Aviva was trying to persuade British consumers to drop 'Norwich Union' and to think 'Aviva' as the top-of-mind brand name, Aviva had been the legal company name for nearly seven years.

The strategic reasoning behind the name change was explained on the Aviva website:

As a global company, we need a name and a brand that will be recognised anywhere. The name Aviva brings together more than 40 different trading names around the world. It's perfect for us because it's short, memorable and feels positive and lively.

Of course, another key advantage of 'Aviva' over 'Norwich Union' is that it takes a lot less effort to type! If you take a quick look at the standard English-language computer keyboard you will see that the least accomplished keyboard user can probably manage a–v–i–v–a without too much difficulty (you might also reflect that a–v–a–v–a would have been even easier). Why is this important? Well, the truth is that more and more consumer insurance services, like car insurance, travel insurance and home insurance, are being sold direct over the Internet. So a name that is easy to remember, easy to type and easy to spell is a definite advantage. In fact, 'Norwich' is a particular problem even for people born and brought up in England because of that silent 'w' in the middle; it is an easily misspelt word. Online marketing of insurance is a cut-throat business. If the consumer does not get the desired website first time around, then it is very easy to opt for another provider, particularly if the name is simpler to type.

By the way, there really is an insurance company – one of Aviva's rivals – called 'AXA', and its website is 'axa.com'. This company was created in 1982 by the amalgamation of a French and a Canadian insurance company; the name AXA was adopted in 1985 long before anyone had the slightest idea that it would be so convenient for the Internet age. For people using an English-language 'QWERTY' keyboard it is difficult to think of a simpler name to type.

Now, there are probably quite a few sceptics out there who think that names cannot matter all that much. Surely, you might argue, it is a question of how good a service the company is selling, what kind of price it offers and the perceived value delivered to the customer that make the difference, not the name. There is nothing wrong with that argument. However, there are a lot of companies out there offering excellent products and services at highly competitive prices that deliver high levels of customer value. A supposedly 'little thing' like the name just might make enough difference to matter. In their bestselling book *Freakonomics*, Steven Levitt and Stephen Dubner presented some fascinating, perhaps disturbing, information about the link between an individual person's name and their life-chances. Extensive evidence from the USA in the 1990s shows big differences between the better-off and the poorer members of society in terms of the names given to children. The chances are very strong that Alexandra and her brother Benjamin come from a well-off, highly educated white family, while Cody and his sister Amber come from a badly-off, poorly educated white family. This does *not* mean that the choice of a child's name directly affects the child's life-chances. However, it clearly *does* mean that people's names carry a lot of extra information over and above simply how to address them. In simple terms, names *matter*. The same goes for companies and brands.

In recent years the trend in marketing and business has been away from the rather meaningless names that were preferred in the 1990s, and towards names that

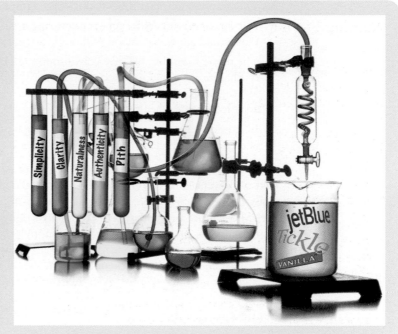

Naming brands: there is some science to it, and some basic rules to be heeded, but there is also a big dose of art and more than a little instinct

Source: John Kuczala.

have some intrinsic significance. Management consultant 'Accenture' and the business-to-business online service provider 'Covisint' represented the previous wave of names; they both sound interesting, but appear to mean nothing in particular. Such names probably work best when there are few of them, so that the curiosity of the name intrigues the customer. 'Phones4U' carries real meaning for the customer (a 'sub' is short for 'submarine', which bears a passing resemblance to the kind of bread sold in Subway fast-food franchises; Phones4U did very much what it says on the tin – but this was not able to protect it from its suppliers!). Of course, 'Aviva', with which we started this case study, is not a particularly meaningful name. Which makes it all the more intriguing to see whether the new name will succeed with customers.

Sources: Interview with Jeff Henshaw at http://news.cnet.com/8301-10805_3-57585620-75/microsoft-talks-xbox-one-naming-privacy-and-more-q-a/; www.aviva.com; www.open2.net/management_organisation/online_branding.html; www.axa.com; Steven D. Levitt and Stephen J. Dubner, *Freakonomics: A Rogue Economist Explores the Hidden Side of Everything* (London: Penguin, 2006).

Desirable qualities for a brand name include the following:

1 It should suggest something about the product's benefits and qualities. Examples: Aquafresh (toothpaste), Jungle Formula (insect repellent), Mr Sheen (furniture polish).

2 It should be easy to pronounce, recognise and remember. Short names help. Examples: Daz, Dove, Cif. But longer ones are sometimes effective. Examples: 'Vanish Carpet Powershot' carpet cleaner, 'I Can't Believe It's Not Butter' margarine.

3   The brand name should be distinctive. Examples: Lexus, Kodak, Oracle.

4   It should be extendable: **Amazon.com** began as an online bookseller but chose a name that would allow expansion into other categories.

5   The name should translate easily into foreign languages. Before spending $100 million to change its name to Exxon, Standard Oil of New Jersey tested several names in 54 languages in more than 150 foreign markets. It found that the name Enco referred to a stalled engine when pronounced in Japanese.

6   It should be capable of registration and legal protection. A brand name cannot be registered if it infringes on existing brand names.

Once chosen, the brand name must be protected. Many firms try to build a brand name that will eventually become identified with the product category. Brand names such as Kleenex, Levi's, Sellotape, Elastoplast and Formica have succeeded in this way. However, their very success may threaten the company's rights to the name. Many originally protected brand names – such as cellophane, aspirin, nylon, kerosene, linoleum, yo-yo, trampoline, escalator, thermos and shredded wheat – are now generic names that any seller can use. To protect their brands, marketers present them carefully using the word 'brand' and the registered trademark symbol, as in 'Elastoplast®'.

Brand sponsorship

A manufacturer has four sponsorship options. The product may be launched as a *manufacturer's brand* (or national brand), as when Kellogg's and IBM sell their output under their own manufacturer's brand names. Or the manufacturer may sell to resellers who give it a *private brand* (also called a *store brand* or *distributor brand*). Although most manufacturers create their own brand names, others market *licensed brands*. Finally, two companies can join forces and *co-brand* a product.

Manufacturers' brands versus private brands

Manufacturers' brands have long dominated the retail scene. In recent times, however, an increasing number of retailers and wholesalers have created their own **private brands (or store brands)**. And in many industries, these private brands are giving manufacturers' brands a real run for their money:

> It seems that almost every retailer now carries its own store brands. In the UK Tesco offers several different options across its own 'Tesco' range of brands. You can have the standard Tesco brand (for example, Tesco Daily Care freshmint toothpaste), the low-priced 'value' brand (for example, Tesco Value Kitchen Towel), or the premium 'finest' brand (for example, Tesco Finest Aftersun Lotion). The Spar chain of supermarkets, which you can find in virtually every European country, stocks a wide variety of Spar branded products in many different product categories: 'Each of the SPAR brand goods has been developed and benchmarked against our competitors to ensure that we're offering the best possible product for the price, and of course, the kind of quality you expect. SPAR brand gives you an outstanding alternative to the major brands that will help you save money.'[22]

In the so-called *battle of the brands* between manufacturers' and private brands, retailers have many advantages. They control what products they stock, where they go on the shelf, what prices they charge and which ones they will feature in local circulars. Most retailers also charge manufacturers *slotting fees* – payments from the manufacturers before the retailers will accept new products and find 'slots' for them on their shelves.

Private brands can be hard to establish and costly to stock and promote. However, they also yield higher profit margins for the reseller. And they give resellers exclusive products that cannot be bought from competitors, resulting in greater store traffic and loyalty. Retailers price their store brands lower than comparable manufacturers' brands, thereby appealing

Apple are just one of a growing number of retailers that have created their own store brands

Source: Alamy Images/ David Pearson

to budget-conscious shoppers, especially in difficult economic times. And most shoppers believe that store brands are often made by one of the larger manufacturers anyway.

To fend off private brands, leading brand marketers will have to invest in R&D to bring out new brands, new features and continuous quality improvements. BMW's placing in the top echelon of brands is due in no small part to heavy investment in R&D. Its 2013 annual report gave it as nearly 6 per cent of total revenues. Roche spent more than $10bn in 2013, 20 per cent of total revenue, a not atypical proportion for the leading pharmaceutical brands like their fellow Swiss Novartis and the French Sanofi. Companies must also design strong advertising programmes to maintain high awareness and preference. They must find ways to 'partner' with major distributors in a search for distribution economies and improved joint performance.

Licensing

Most manufacturers take years and spend millions to create their own brand names. However, some companies license names or symbols previously created by other manufacturers, names of well-known celebrities, or characters from popular films and books. For a fee, any of these can provide an instant and proven brand name.

Clothing and accessories sellers pay large royalties to adorn their products – from blouses to ties, and linens to luggage – with the names or initials of well-known fashion innovators such as Calvin Klein, Tommy Hilfiger, Gucci or Armani. Sellers of children's products attach an almost endless list of character names to clothing, toys, school supplies, linens, dolls, lunch boxes, cereals and other items. Licensed character names range from classics such as Sesame Street, Disney, Peanuts, Winnie the Pooh, the Muppets and Scooby Doo characters to the more recent Ice Age, Bob the Builder, Peppa Pig and Harry Potter characters.

Name and character licensing has grown rapidly in recent years. Annual retail sales of licensed products worldwide have grown from only $4bn in 1977 to $55bn in 1987 and more than $185bn today. Licensing can be a highly profitable business for many companies. Three of the top licences in 2013 belonged to Disney – Disney Princesses, Winnie the Pooh and the Pixar cartoon Cars – with Star Wars and Hello Kitty rounding out the top five. Further down was a new entrant – Angry Birds (see Chapter 14 for more on that phenomenon). It is not always an easy ride for the licensor, though, with Nickelodeon forced to bow to consumer pressure and withdraw from deals involving junk food tie-ups and Dora-the-Explorer.[23]

Co-branding

Although companies have been **co-branding** products for many years, there has been a recent resurgence in co-branded products. Co-branding occurs when two established brand names of different companies are used on the same product, and has been defined as 'pairing two or more branded products (constituent brands) to form a separate and unique product (composite brand)'.[24] For example, car maker Ford and fashion brand Eddie Bauer co-branded a sport utility vehicle – the Ford Explorer, Eddie Bauer edition. According to Swedish expert Henrik Uggla:

> Corporate brands can exploit pre-established benefits and credibility by licensing ingredient brands. . . . Gore-Tex collaborates with strong corporate brands such as Ecco and BOSS, it has stronger purchase intent scores in the apparel category than corporate brands such as Nike, Levi's and Ecco. . . . The Adidas corporate [sic] have reinforced its brand values and reached new target groups through corporate co-branding with the New Zealand Rugby Union and the All Blacks.[25]

In most co-branding situations, one company licenses another company's well-known brand to use in combination with its own.[26]

Co-branding offers many advantages. Because each brand dominates in a different category, the combined brands create broader consumer appeal and greater brand equity. Co-branding also allows a company to expand its existing brand into a category it might otherwise have difficulty entering alone.

Co-branding also has limitations. Such relationships usually involve complex legal contracts and licences. Co-branding partners must carefully coordinate their advertising, sales promotion and other marketing efforts. Finally, when co-branding, each partner must trust that the other will take good care of its brand.

Brand development

A company has four choices when it comes to developing brands (see Figure 7.4). It can introduce *line extensions* (existing brand names extended to new forms, sizes and flavours of an existing product category), *brand extensions* (existing brand names extended to new product categories), *multibrands* (new brand names introduced in the same product category) or *new brands* (new brand names in new product categories).

Line extensions

Line extensions occur when a company introduces additional items in a given product category under the same brand name, such as new flavours, forms, colours, ingredients or package sizes. Thus, Nestlé introduced several line extensions to its Ski yoghurt range, including new yogurt flavours, Ski Up & Go yogurt with cereal and fruit, Ski Smooth (with no fruit pieces) and Ski Fat Free. The vast majority of all new-product activity consists of line extensions.

A company might introduce line extensions as a low-cost, low-risk way to introduce new products. Or it might want to meet consumer desires for variety, to use excess capacity, or simply to command more shelf space from resellers. However, line extensions involve some risks. An overextended brand name might lose its specific meaning, or heavily extended brands can cause consumer confusion or frustration.

		Product category	
		Existing	**New**
Brand name	**Existing**	Line extension	Brand extension
	New	Multibrands	New brands

FIGURE 7.4
Brand development strategies

Want a Coke? Not so easy. Pick from more than 16 varieties. In zero-calorie versions alone, Coke comes in three subbrands – Diet Coke, Diet Coke with Splenda, and Coca-Cola Zero. Throw in the flavoured and free versions – Diet Vanilla Coke, Diet Cherry Coke, Diet Coke with Lemon, Diet Coke with Lime, and Caffeine-Free Diet Coke – and you reach a dizzying eight diets from Coke. And that doesn't count 'mid-calorie' Coca-Cola C2. Each subbrand has its own hype – Diet Coke lets you 'live your life', while Coke Zero gives you 'real Coca-Cola taste and zero calories'. And Coca-Cola C2 has 'half the carbs, half the calories, all the great taste'. But it's unlikely that many consumers fully appreciate the differences. Instead, the glut of extensions will likely cause what one expert calls 'profusion confusion'. Laments one cola consumer, 'How many versions of Diet Coke do they need?'[27]

Another risk is that sales of an extension may come at the expense of other items in the line. A line extension works best when it takes sales away from competing brands, not when it 'cannibalises' the company's other items.

Brand extensions

A **brand extension** involves the use of a successful brand name to launch new or modified products in a new category. For example, Kimberly-Clark extended its market-leading Huggies brand from disposable nappies to a full line of toiletries for tots, from shampoos, lotions and nappy-rash ointments to baby wash, disposable washcloths and disposable changing pads. Victorinox extended its venerable Swiss Army brand from multi-tool knives to products ranging from cutlery and ballpoint pens to watches, luggage and apparel.

A brand extension gives a new product instant recognition and faster acceptance. It also saves the high advertising costs usually required to build a new brand name. At the same time, a brand extension strategy involves some risk. While Richard Branson's business empire Virgin has succeeded with ventures ranging from the original record stores to railway travel and an airline, it has also failed with several attempted brand extensions – into vodka, clothing and cosmetics, for example.[28] The extension may confuse the image of the main brand. And if a brand extension fails, it may harm consumer attitudes towards the other products carrying the same brand name. Further, a brand name may not be appropriate to a particular new product, even if it is well made and satisfying – would you consider buying Texaco milk or HSBC sausages? Companies that are tempted to transfer a brand name must research how well the brand's associations fit the new product.[29]

Multibrands

Companies often introduce additional brands in the same category. Thus, Procter & Gamble markets many different brands in each of its product categories. Multibranding offers a way to establish different features and appeal to different buying motives. It also allows a company to lock up more reseller shelf space.

A major drawback of multibranding is that each brand might obtain only a small market share, and none may be very profitable. The company may end up spreading its resources over many brands instead of building a few brands to a highly profitable level. These companies should reduce the number of brands they sell in a given category and set up tighter screening procedures for new brands.

New brands

A company might believe that the power of its existing brand name is waning and a new brand name is needed. Or a company may create a new brand name when it enters a new product category for which none of the company's current brand names is appropriate. For example, Virgin Atlantic created the 'Little Red' brand to compete in the budget air travel sector. Japan's Matsushita uses separate names for its different families of consumer electronics products: Panasonic, Technics, National and Quasar.

As with multibranding, offering too many new brands can result in a company spreading its resources too thin. And in some industries, such as consumer packaged goods, consumers

Brand extensions:
Victorinox, originally
known for 'Swiss
Army' pocket knives,
now offers a range
of high-quality
consumer products

Source: Victorinox.

and retailers have become concerned that there are already too many brands, with too few differences between them. Thus, Procter & Gamble, Nestlé and other large consumer product marketers are now pursuing *megabrand* strategies – weeding out weaker brands and focusing their marketing budgets only on brands that can achieve the number 1 or number 2 market-share positions in their categories.

Managing brands

Companies must manage their brands carefully. First, the brand's positioning must be continuously communicated to consumers. Major brand marketers often spend huge amounts on advertising to create brand awareness and to build preference and loyalty. For example, McDonald's spends more than $1bn a year to promote its brand in the USA alone.[30]

Such advertising campaigns can help to create name recognition, brand knowledge and maybe even some brand preference. However, the fact is that brands are not maintained by advertising but by the *brand experience*. Today, customers come to know a brand through a wide range of contacts and touch points. These include advertising, but also personal experience with the brand, word of mouth, personal interactions with company people, company web pages and many other contacts. The company must put as much care into managing these touch points as it does into producing its ads. A former Disney executive agrees: 'A brand is a living entity, and it is enriched or undermined cumulatively over time, the product of a thousand small gestures.'[31]

The brand's positioning will not take hold fully unless everyone in the company lives the brand. Therefore the company needs to train its people to be customer centred. Even better, the company should carry on internal brand building to help employees to understand and be enthusiastic about the brand promise. Many companies go even further by training and encouraging their distributors and dealers to serve their customers well. But it is important to remember that brands and branding are key issues for small businesses, not just for multinational organisations with large product portfolios. Small companies need to develop and nurture their brand and its position in the market just as carefully as the well-known international consumer products companies. In Marketing at Work 7.2 we can see how a small Irish company, Cloon Keen, worked very hard to establish its brand at a premium position in the market for scented candles.

All of this suggests that managing a company's brand assets can no longer be left only to brand managers. Brand managers do not have enough power or scope to do all the things necessary to build and enhance their brands. Moreover, brand managers often pursue short-term results, whereas managing brands as assets calls for longer term strategy. Thus, some companies are now setting up brand asset management teams to manage their major brands. Canada Dry and Colgate-Palmolive have appointed *brand-equity managers* to maintain and protect their brands' images, associations and quality, and to prevent short-term actions by over-eager brand managers from hurting the brand.

Finally, companies need periodically to audit their brands' strengths and weaknesses.[32] They should ask: Does our brand excel at delivering benefits that consumers truly value? Is the brand properly positioned? Do all of our consumer touch points support the brand's positioning? Do the brand's managers understand what the brand means to consumers? Does the brand receive proper, sustained support? The brand audit may turn up brands that need more support, brands that need to be dropped, or brands that must be rebranded or repositioned because of changing customer preferences or new competitors.

Cloon Keen Atelier: developing a premium brand

Ann M. Torres, Marketing Department, Cairns Graduate School of Business and Economics, National University of Ireland

Margaret Mangan, co-founder of Cloon Keen Atelier, always had a passion for scent; she believes scent forms the heart of her products. Cloon Keen develops high-quality products where fragrance, design and functionality are blended carefully to create a mood of authenticity and pleasure. The challenge for Cloon Keen, a small operator, is to pursue a strategy that reinforces its chosen market position as it develops new products and markets.

In June 2002, Margaret Mangan and Julian Checkley established Cloon Keen Candles in Galway, Ireland, and began making their hand-poured candles. In the early days of their start-up, Margaret spent a number of weeks travelling around Ireland to find shops that are a good fit for Cloon Keen candles, primarily high-end gift and craft shops as well as upmarket home interior and furniture shops with a modern flair. Margaret's sales drive was successful, as she secured orders from over 60 retailers across the country. To its credit, Cloon Keen has retained about 90 per cent of its original retailers. Despite its achievement with retailers, the firm is shifting its focus towards developing its own retail initiatives, which are ultimately more profitable.

In August 2005, Cloon Keen Atelier opened its retail premises in the heart of Galway city. In designing the shop interior, the firm took particular care to develop an atmosphere that reflected the brand. The shop has a warm, modern look that is clean and uncluttered, but not quite minimalist. An opening in Ceardlann Spiddal Craft Village in July 2006 was an opportunity for Cloon Keen to open another retail outlet in Spiddal, Co. Galway. Conveniently located 15 km from Galway city, Ceardlann is also a scenic tourist destination, where visitors can see Cloon Keen's master chandlers pour candles, and can then purchase the finished product from the adjoining shop. Although the studio shop reflects aspects found in the Kirwan's Lane venue, the Ceardlann retail venue was tailored to showcase the craft studio and its environs. The effect is sufficiently similar to recognise Cloon Keen's *look*, but suitably different to intrigue customers with variety.

How do you create a premium, branded candle product? Cloon Keen employs the expertise of three perfumers to create fragrances exclusively for their range of scented candles; they never use generic scents. The quality of fragrance is especially important. Cloon Keen uses authentic aromas, which do not smell harsh, bitter or 'chemical'. Superior quality wax and cotton wicks are used to ensure optimum absorption and diffusion of fragrance. The craft for producing premium candles requires a highly scientific approach. For example, each scent requires a different wick to ensure the candle burns effectively; spicy scents require a thicker cotton wick than sweet scents. Additionally, softer wax is more effective in scented candles, as harder wax disperses fragrance poorly. Cloon Keen assembles 300 to 400 units per week, which increases to 1,500 to 2,000 units per week during the busiest period between September and December. The next product venture is a line of Cloon Keen branded soaps, creams and lotions in two scents: Lavender and Linden Blossom. In time, the plan is to create a signature perfume to serve as the brand's hallmark.

Price is a key issue in positioning the products in the premium sector of the market. Cloon Keen produces two lines of premium-scented candles. The gourmet collection, priced at €33 per unit, is packaged in tins and is a playful, funky product. It comes in scents such as Basil and Lime Pesto, Crazy as Coconut, Just Baked Apple Pie, Fresh Linen and Swedish Sauna. Irish consumers generally prefer the softer floral scents in the gourmet range, such as Wild Irish Lavender and Galway Honeysuckle; these floral scents are among Cloon Keen's best sellers. The spa collection of luxury candles offers more sophisticated, subtle scents such as Exotic Woods and Fig Tree; its sumptuous packaging reflects its more sensuous, indulgent qualities. Cloon Keen's pricing strategy reflects its positioning as a quality producer. Margaret and Julian follow a policy of offering exceptionally high quality for the price they charge and regularly monitor rivals' price levels to ensure their products remain competitive.

Cloon Keen actively manages its brand. Margaret and Julian believe that Cloon Keen's brand values have greatly facilitated in generating word of mouth to build a loyal customer base. The brand is based on offering accessible pricing for superior products and a unique store experience through its upscale store design, attentive customer service and product presentation. Cloon Keen strives for authenticity in its branding approach. The combination of smell, touch and sight in its retail ambiance is meant to inspire and heighten the customer's experience. As a speciality retailer, Cloon Keen is being positioned as a worthy alternative to the high-priced designer brands offered in department stores.

Margaret and Julian use traditional media, primarily press features in quality news and fashion magazines, such as *Image, Irish Tatler* and *The Gloss.* Select sponsorship, such as the launch of the new *Irish Times* building and the *Irish Tatler* magazine, has been fruitful in generating awareness and opportunities for feature articles in the press. Merchandising within the shops, branding and product packaging have been Cloon Keen's strongest forms of promotion. Margaret and Julian are interested in using electronic media, to generate the opportunity for audience involvement. Interactivity can facilitate brand objectives and be a powerful tool for eliciting an immediate response from customers. Cloon Keen aims to build a website, not only to serve as an online retail environment, but also as a platform to initiate a lifestyle blog, which would work as a source for stimulating viral marketing. In a coup, a Cloon Keen candle was part of Ireland's official gift to the family of President Obama on St Patrick's Day, 2013 – worth a blog post!

Source: Shutterstock/Andreka.

So far, Cloon Keen's branding strategy seems to have paid off. Even with fairly limited promotional efforts, Cloon Keen has garnered a loyal customer base, as 80 per cent are repeat customers. Its marketing efforts primarily target working women, aged 25 to 50 years, who have traditionally purchased premium scented candles and skin-care products in department stores. They use these high-quality products on a daily basis as affordable luxuries. Cloon Keen's loyal customers are well travelled, have reasonably high levels of disposable income, are open to trying new products and are increasingly seeking better pricing without sacrificing high quality and service. Cloon Keen's strategy has also been successful in attracting other consumers beyond its primary target, such as metrosexual males, who are attracted to the good-quality toiletries, as well as young teenage girls, who are attracted to Cloon Keen's gourmet range of candles.

One of the main purposes of the branding and product development strategy has been to differentiate Cloon Keen from its competitors. The company operates in two overlapping markets: candles and home fragrances, as well as the personal-care market. There are numerous rivals that manufacture functionally similar products, sold through a variety of channels. Many of these rivals have substantially greater resources, better name recognition and sell through broader distribution channels. Some of these competitors are speciality retailers of personal-care products, including international chains such as The Body Shop and L'Occitane, as well as local speciality retailers, such as The Burren Perfumery. The lack of significant barriers to entry in this market may result in new competition, including possible imitators to Cloon Keen.

The challenge for Cloon Keen Atelier is to find the optimum market position that provides a strategic advantage among robust competition. How will it maintain the high quality, good value and premium position in the market against new competitors? And how can Cloon Keen effectively promote itself and communicate with customers to the extent that it may be considered a lifestyle brand, rather than just a product brand?

Sources: The Cloon Keen Atelier example has been informed by the following reports: Datamonitor Reports, 'Market Watch: Personal Care', March 2006; 'Personal Care: Industry Update', August 2006; 'Hand and Body Care in Ireland Industry Profile', December 2006; Euromonitor International Reports, 'Country Market Insight: Retailing Ireland', September 2006; 'Skin Care: Ireland', May 2006; 'Cosmetics and Toiletries: World', February 2007; 'Air Care: Ireland', March 2007; Margaret Mangan, co-owner of Cloon Keen Atelier, provided information in relation to the firm. The author thanks Margaret Mangan and Julian Checkley, of Cloon Keen Atelier, for their time and assistance in the writing of this case. Blog post on the gift to Michelle Obama at http://blog.cloonkeenatelier.com/antique-library-for-mrs-obama/

SERVICES MARKETING

Services have grown dramatically in recent years. Services account for the largest proportion of economic activity in the EU, although the percentage of economic activity (measured by the percentage of the workforce employed in the service industries) varies considerably from country to country. For example, in the UK about three-quarters of the workforce is employed in services, and the figure is very similar for Sweden. However, in Germany and Ireland a smaller proportion works in services. Germany has retained more of its manufacturing industries than other rich European countries, while Ireland has retained a fairly large agricultural sector. Nevertheless, even in these countries the service sector is the largest part of the economy. And the service sector is growing in size all across Europe. Services are growing fast in the world economy, making up an increasing share of all international trade. For example, in 2012, exports of services from the UK amounted to €222bn, while tiny Luxembourg exported €55bn – towering over the much more populous Greece at €27bn. In total, the EU sold €507bn of services to the rest of the world.[33]

Service industries vary greatly. *Governments* offer services through courts, employment services, hospitals, the armed forces, police and fire services, postal service and schools. *Private not-for-profit organisations* offer services through museums, charities, churches, universities and hospitals. A large number of *business organisations* offer services – airlines, banks, hotels, insurance companies, consulting firms, medical and legal practices, entertainment companies, property (estate) agents, retailers and others.

Nature and characteristics of a service

A company must consider four special service characteristics when designing marketing programmes: *intangibility*, *inseparability*, *variability* and *perishability* (see Figure 7.5).

Service intangibility means that services cannot be seen, tasted, felt, heard or smelled before they are bought. For example, people undergoing cosmetic surgery cannot see the result before the purchase. Airline passengers have nothing but a ticket (these days, often an e-ticket) and the promise that they and their luggage will arrive safely at the intended destination, hopefully at the same time. To reduce uncertainty, buyers look for 'signals' of service quality. They draw conclusions about quality from the place, people, price, equipment and communications that they can see.

Therefore, the service provider's task is to make the service tangible in one or more ways and to send the right signals about quality. One analyst calls this *evidence management*, in which the service organisation presents its customers with organised, honest evidence of its capabilities. The famous US not-for-profit medical service provider the Mayo Clinic practises good evidence management:

> When it comes to hospitals, it's very hard for the average patient to judge the quality of the 'product'. You can't try it on, you can't return it if you don't like it, and you need an advanced degree to understand it. And so, when we're considering a medical facility, most of us unconsciously turn detective, looking for evidence of competence, caring, and integrity. The Mayo Clinic doesn't leave that evidence to chance. By carefully managing a set of

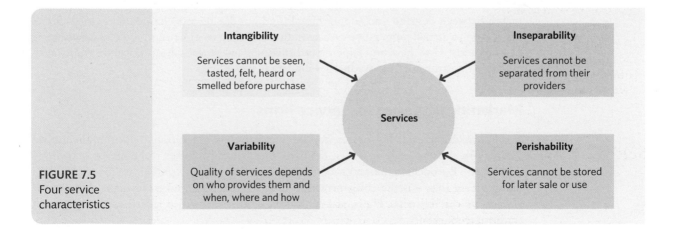

FIGURE 7.5
Four service characteristics

visual and experiential clues, Mayo offers patients and their families concrete evidence of its strengths and values. For example, staff people at the clinic are trained to act in a way that clearly signals its patient-first focus. 'My doctor calls me at home to check on how I am doing,' marvels one patient. 'She wants to work with what is best for my schedule.' Mayo's physical facilities also send the right signals. They've been carefully designed to relieve stress, offer a place of refuge, create positive distractions, convey caring and respect, signal competence, accommodate families, and make it easy to find your way around. Looking for external confirmation? Go online and hear directly from those who've been to the clinic or who work there. Mayo now uses social networking – everything from blogs to Facebook and YouTube – to enhance the patient experience. For example, on the Sharing Mayo Clinic blog (http://sharing.mayoclinic.org), patients and their families retell their Mayo experiences and Mayo employees offer behind-the-scenes views. The result? Exceptionally positive word of mouth and abiding customer loyalty have allowed Mayo Clinic to build what is arguably the most powerful brand in healthcare with very little advertising. 'The quality of the [patient] experience is key,' says Dr Thoraf Sundt, a heart surgeon and chair of Mayo's marketing committee.[34]

Very similar strategies are pursued by similar private healthcare organisations in Europe, such as the UK-based BUPA, which is now expanding internationally and operates in Spain through its Sanitas subsidiary and in Ireland as Quinn Healthcare.

Physical goods are produced, then stored, later sold and still later consumed. In contrast, services are first sold, then produced and consumed at the same time. **Service inseparability** means that services cannot be separated from their providers, whether the providers are people or machines. If a service employee provides the service, then the employee becomes a part of the service. Because the customer is also present as the service is produced, *provider–customer interaction* is a special feature of services marketing. Both the provider and the customer affect the service outcome.

Service variability means that the quality of services depends on who provides them as well as when, where and how they are provided. For example, some hotels – say, Ibis – have reputations for providing better service than others. Still, within a given Ibis hotel, one registration-desk employee may be cheerful and efficient, whereas another standing just a few feet away may be unpleasant and slow. Even the quality of a single Ibis employee's service varies according to his or her energy and frame of mind at the time of each customer encounter.

Service perishability means that services cannot be stored for later sale or use. Some dentists charge patients for missed appointments because the service value existed only at that point and disappeared when the patient did not show up. The perishability of services is not a problem when demand is steady. However, when demand fluctuates, service firms often have difficult problems. For example, because of rush-hour demand, public transport companies have to own much more equipment than they would if demand were even throughout the day. Thus, service firms often design strategies for producing a better match between demand and supply. Hotels and holiday resorts charge lower prices in the off-season to attract more guests. And restaurants hire part-time employees to serve during peak periods. How have you experienced this as a customer? Cheap travel on trains mid-morning onwards, Orange Wednesday cinema tickets.

Marketing strategies for service firms

Just like manufacturing businesses, good service firms use marketing to position themselves strongly in chosen target markets. Retailer John Lewis promises to be 'never knowingly undersold'. European banking group Santander tells us that 'Together, we are Santander', emphasising that it is the customers who make deposits and take out loans that are the essence of the business. These and other service firms establish their positions through traditional marketing mix activities.

However, because services differ from tangible products, they often require additional marketing approaches. In a product business, products are fairly standardised and can sit on shelves waiting for customers. But in a service business, the customer and frontline service employee *interact* to create the service. Thus, service providers must interact effectively with customers to create superior value during service encounters. Effective interaction, in turn, depends on the skills of frontline service employees and on the support processes backing these employees.

The service profit chain

Successful service companies focus their attention on *both* their customers and their employees. They understand the **service–profit chain**, which links service firm profits with employee and customer satisfaction. This chain consists of five links:

- Internal service quality: superior employee selection and training, a quality work environment and strong support for those dealing with customers, which results in . . .
- Satisfied and productive service employees: more satisfied, loyal and hardworking employees, which results in . . .
- Greater service value: more effective and efficient customer value creation and service delivery, which results in . . .
- Satisfied and loyal customers: satisfied customers who remain loyal, repeat purchase and refer other customers, which results in . . .
- Healthy service profits and growth: superior service firm performance.[35]

Therefore, reaching service profits and growth goals begins with taking care of those who take care of customers. In fact, Starbucks CEO Howard Schultz goes so far as to say that 'customers always come in second – employees matter more'. The idea is that happy employees will unleash their enthusiasm on customers, creating even greater customer satisfaction. 'If the battle cry of the company [is] to exceed the expectations of our customers,' says Schultz, 'then as managers, we [must] first exceed the expectations of our people.'[36]

Thus, service marketing requires more than just traditional external marketing using the four Ps. Figure 7.6 shows that service marketing also requires *internal marketing* and *interactive marketing*. **Internal marketing** means that the service firm must effectively train and motivate its customer-contact employees and supporting service people to work as a *team* to provide customer satisfaction. Marketers must get everyone in the organisation to be customer centred. In fact, internal marketing must *precede* external marketing.

Interactive marketing means that service quality depends heavily on the quality of the buyer–seller interaction during the service encounter. In product marketing, product quality often depends little on how the product is obtained. But in services marketing, service quality depends on both the service deliverer and the quality of the delivery. Service marketers, therefore, have to master interactive marketing skills.

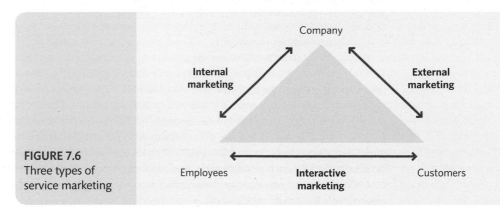

FIGURE 7.6
Three types of
service marketing

In today's marketplace, companies must know how to deliver interactions that are not only 'high touch' but also 'high tech'. For example, customers can log on to the Deutsche Bank Private Wealth Management site and access account information, investment research, real-time stock prices and personal financial advice. Customers seeking more personal interactions can contact service reps by phone or visit a local Deutsche Bank branch office. Thus, Deutsche Bank has mastered interactive marketing at all three levels – calls, clicks *and* visits.

Today, as competition and costs increase, and as productivity and quality decrease, more services marketing sophistication is needed. Service companies face three major marketing tasks: they want to increase their *service differentiation, service quality* and *service productivity*.

Managing service differentiation

In these days of intense price competition, service marketers often complain about the difficulty of differentiating their services from those of competitors. To the extent that customers view the services of different providers as similar, they care less about the provider than the price.

The solution to price competition is to develop a differentiated offer, delivery and image. The *offer* can include innovative features that set one company's offer apart from competitors' offers. Some hotels offer car hire, banking and business centre services in their lobbies and high-speed Internet connections in their rooms. Airlines differentiate their offers through frequent-flyer award programmes and special services. For example, Qantas offers personal entertainment screens at every seat and 'Skybeds' for international business-class flyers. Lufthansa provides wireless Internet access and real-time surfing to every seat – it makes 'an airplane feel like a cyber café'. And British Airways offers spa services at its arrivals lounge at Heathrow Airport. Says one ad: 'You can step off the plane and straight into a shower, a robe, even a Molton Brown facial – all while your suit is being pressed.'

Service companies can differentiate their service *delivery* by having more able and reliable customer-contact people, by developing a superior physical environment in which the service product is delivered, or by designing a superior delivery process. For example, many grocery chains now offer online shopping and home delivery as a better way to shop than having to drive, park, queue up and carry groceries home.

Finally, service companies also can work on differentiating their *images* through symbols and branding. Telecommunications group BT adopted the 'world' symbol to demonstrate its commitment to offering global services. Other well-known service symbols include the red and white HSBC 'triangles' symbol, McDonald's Golden Arches, and the London Underground signage has been world famous for 100 years.

Managing service quality

One of the major ways a service firm can differentiate itself is by delivering consistently higher quality than its competitors do. Like manufacturers before them, most service industries have now joined the customer-driven quality movement. And like product marketers, service providers need to identify what target customers expect concerning service quality.

Unfortunately, service quality is harder to define and judge than is product quality. For instance, it is harder to agree on the quality of a haircut than on the quality of a hair dryer. Customer retention is perhaps the best measure of quality – a service firm's ability to hang on to its customers depends on how consistently it delivers value to them.[37]

Top service companies set high service quality standards. They watch service performance closely, both their own and that of competitors. They do not settle for merely good service; they aim for 100 per cent defect-free service. A 98 per cent performance standard may sound good, but using this standard, 310,000 UPS packages would be lost each day, 10 words would be misspelled on each printed page, and drinking water would be unsafe seven days a year.

Unlike product manufacturers who can adjust their machinery and inputs until everything is perfect, service quality will always vary, depending on the interactions between employees and customers. As hard as they try, even the best companies will have an occasional late delivery, burnt steak or grumpy employee. However, good *service recovery* can turn angry customers into loyal ones. In fact, good recovery can win more customer purchasing and loyalty than if things had gone well in the first place. Therefore, companies should take steps not only to provide good service every time, but also to recover from service mistakes when they do occur.

The first step is to *empower* frontline service employees – to give them the authority, responsibility and incentives they need to recognise, care about and tend to customer needs. At Radisson, for example, well-trained employees go through the 'Yes I Can!' training programme to give them the confidence to do whatever it takes, on the spot, to keep guests happy. They are also expected to help management ferret out the cause of guests' problems and to inform managers of ways to improve overall hotel service and guests' comfort.

Managing service productivity

With their costs rising rapidly, service firms are under great pressure to increase service productivity. They can do so in several ways. They can train current employees better or hire new ones who will work harder or more skilfully. Or they can increase the quantity of their service by giving up some quality. The provider can 'industrialise the service' by adding equipment and standardising production, as in McDonald's assembly-line approach to fast-food retailing. Finally, the service provider can harness the power of technology. Although we often think of technology's power to save time and costs in manufacturing companies, it also has great – and often untapped – potential to make service workers more productive.

However, companies must avoid pushing productivity so hard that doing so reduces quality. Attempts to industrialise a service or to cut costs can make a service company more efficient in the short term. But they can also reduce its longer term ability to innovate, maintain service quality or respond to consumer needs and desires. In short, they can take the 'service' out of service.

ADDITIONAL PRODUCT CONSIDERATIONS

Here, we discuss two additional product policy considerations: social responsibility in product decisions and issues of international product and service marketing.

Product decisions and social responsibility

Product decisions have attracted much public attention. Marketers should consider carefully public policy issues and regulations involving acquiring or dropping products, patent protection, product quality and safety, and product warranties.

Regarding new products, governments may prevent companies from adding products through acquisitions if the effect threatens to reduce competition. Companies dropping products must be aware that they have legal obligations, written or implied, to their suppliers, dealers and customers who have a stake in the dropped product. Companies must also obey patent laws when developing new products. A company cannot make its product illegally similar to another company's established product.

Manufacturers must comply with specific laws regarding product quality and safety. The European Food Safety Authority is responsible for maintaining food standards within the EU, and individual countries have their own authorities, such as the Food Safety Authority of Ireland, and the Food Standards Agency in the UK. Several EU laws protect consumers from unsafe and adulterated food, drugs and cosmetics. Safety legislation has been passed to regulate fabrics, chemical substances, vehicles, toys, and drugs and poisons. If consumers have been injured by a product that has been designed defectively, they can sue manufacturers or dealers.

This phenomenon has resulted in huge increases in product liability insurance premiums, causing big problems in some industries. Some companies pass these higher rates along to

Sodastream has turned consumer concern about environmental impacts of consumption to its advantage by demonstrating its green credentials in respect of recycling and shipping

Source: Getty Images/Ariel Jerozolimski/Bloomberg via Getty Images.

consumers by raising prices. Others are forced to discontinue high-risk product lines. Some companies are now appointing 'product stewards', whose job is to protect consumers from harm and the company from liability by proactively identifying potential product problems.

These issues represent difficulties for some companies, but opportunities for others. Sodastream has revitalised its fortunes by being able to show that its sodas are far more environmentally sound – bottles are reused and only the syrup and not the water is transported around the globe.

International product and services marketing

International product and service marketers face special challenges. First, they must figure out what products and services to introduce and in which countries. Then, they must decide how much to standardise or adapt their products and services for world markets.

On the one hand, companies would like to standardise their offerings. Standardisation helps a company to develop a consistent worldwide image. It also lowers the product design, manufacturing and marketing costs of offering a large variety of products. On the other hand, markets and consumers around the world differ widely. Companies must usually respond to these differences by adapting their product offerings. Something as simple as an electrical outlet can create big product problems:

> Those who have travelled across Europe know the frustration of electrical plugs, different voltages, and other annoyances of international travel. . . . Philips, the electrical appliance manufacturer, has to produce 12 kinds of irons to serve just its European market. The problem is that Europe does not have a universal [electrical] standard. The ends of irons bristle with different plugs for different countries. Some have three prongs, others two; prongs protrude straight or angled, round or rectangular, fat, thin, and sometimes sheathed. There are circular plug faces, squares, pentagons, and hexagons. Some are perforated and some are notched. One French plug has a niche like a keyhole. Looking for a fix? One online travel service sells an elaborate 10-piece adapter plug set for international travellers for $65.00.[38]

Packaging also presents new challenges for international marketers. Packaging issues can be subtle. For example, names, labels and colours may not translate easily from one country to another. A firm using yellow flowers in its logo might fare well in the USA but meet with disaster in Mexico, where a yellow flower symbolises death or disrespect. Similarly, although Nature's Gift might be an appealing name for gourmet mushrooms in the USA, it would be deadly in Germany, where *gift* means poison. Packaging may also have to be tailored to meet the physical characteristics of consumers in various parts of the world. For instance, soft drinks are sold in smaller cans in Japan to fit the smaller Japanese hand better.

Thus, although product and package standardisation can produce benefits, companies must usually adapt their offerings to the unique needs of specific international markets.

Service marketers also face special challenges when going global. Some service industries have a long history of international operations. For example, the commercial banking industry was one of the first to grow internationally. Banks had to provide global services in order to meet the foreign exchange and credit needs of their home-country clients wanting to sell overseas. In recent years, many banks have become truly global. For example, Germany's Deutsche Bank has nearly 3,000 branches in 70 countries, with regional hubs in New York, Singapore, Dubai, Tokyo and London.[39]

Professional and business services industries such as accounting, management consulting and advertising have only recently globalised. The international growth of these firms followed the globalisation of the client companies they serve. For example, as their clients began to employ worldwide marketing and advertising strategies, advertising agencies responded by globalising their own operations. McCann-Erickson Worldwide, a global advertising agency, operates in more than 110 countries. It serves international clients such as Coca-Cola, GM, ExxonMobile, Microsoft, MasterCard, Johnson & Johnson and Unilever in markets ranging from the USA and Canada to Korea and Kazakhstan. Moreover, McCann-Erikson is one company in the Interpublic Group of companies, an immense, worldwide network of advertising and marketing services companies.[40]

Retailers are among the latest service businesses to go global. As their home markets become saturated, US retailers such as Wal-Mart, Toys 'R' Us, Office Depot and Saks Fifth Avenue are expanding into faster-growing markets abroad. For example, Wal-Mart operates in 15 countries. Other retailers are making similar moves. Asian shoppers can now buy European products in French-owned Carrefour stores. Carrefour, the world's second-largest retailer behind Wal-Mart, now operates around 10,000 stores in 34 countries, with over 1,500 in France, over 3,000 elsewhere in Europe, over 1,100 in Latin America and 600 in Asia.[41]

The trend towards growth of global service companies will continue, especially in banking, airlines, telecommunications and professional services. Today service firms are no longer simply following their manufacturing customers. Instead, they are taking the lead in international expansion.

THE JOURNEY YOU'VE TAKEN Reviewing the concepts

A product is more than a simple set of tangible features. In fact, many marketing offers consist of combinations of both tangible goods and services, ranging from *pure tangible goods* at one extreme to *pure services* at the other. Each product or service offered to customers can be viewed on three levels. The *core product* consists of the core problem-solving benefits that consumers seek when they buy a product. The *actual product* exists around the core and includes the quality level, features, design, brand name and packaging. The *augmented product* is the actual product plus the various services and benefits offered with it, such as warranty, free delivery, installation and maintenance.

1 Define product and the major classifications of products and services

Broadly defined, a *product* is anything that can be offered to a market for attention, acquisition, use or consumption that might satisfy a want or need. Products include physical objects but also services, events, persons, places, organisations, ideas or mixes of these entities. *Services* are products that consist of activities, benefits or satisfactions offered for sale that are essentially intangible, such as banking, hotel, telephone and home repair services.

Products and services fall into two broad classes based on the types of consumers that use them. *Consumer products* – those bought by final consumers – are usually classified according to consumer shopping habits (convenience products, shopping products, speciality products and unsought products). *Industrial products* – purchased for further processing or for use in conducting a business – include materials and parts, capital items, and supplies and services. Other marketable entities – such as organisations, persons, places and ideas – can also be thought of as products.

2 **Describe the decisions companies make regarding their individual products and services, product lines and product mixes**

Individual product decisions involve product attributes, branding, packaging, labelling and product support services. *Product attribute* decisions involve product quality, features, and style and design. *Branding* decisions include selecting a brand name and developing a brand strategy. *Packaging* provides many key benefits, such as protection, economy, convenience and promotion. Package decisions often include designing *labels*, which identify, describe and possibly promote the product. Companies also develop *product support services* that enhance customer service and satisfaction and safeguard against competitors.

Most companies produce a product line rather than a single product. A *product line* is a group of products that are related in function, customer-purchase needs or distribution channels. *Line stretching* involves extending a line downwards, upwards or in both directions to occupy a gap that might otherwise by filled by a competitor. In contrast, *line filling* involves adding items within the present range of the line. All product lines and items offered to customers by a particular seller make up the *product mix*. The mix can be described by four dimensions: width, length, depth and consistency. These dimensions are the tools for developing the company's product strategy.

3 **Discuss branding strategy – the decisions companies make in building and managing their brands**

Some analysts see brands as *the* major enduring asset of a company. Brands are more than just names and symbols – they embody everything that the product or service *means* to consumers. *Brand equity* is the positive differential effect that knowing the brand name has on customer response to the product or service. A brand with strong brand equity is a very valuable asset.

In building brands, companies need to make decisions about brand positioning, brand name selection, brand sponsorship and brand development. The most powerful *brand positioning* builds around strong consumer beliefs and values. *Brand name selection* involves finding the best brand name based on a careful review of product benefits, the target market and proposed marketing strategies. A manufacturer has four *brand sponsorship* options: it can launch a *manufacturer's brand* (or national brand), sell to resellers who use a *private brand*, market *licensed brands*, or join forces with another company to *co-brand* a product. A company also has four choices when it comes to developing brands. It can introduce *line extensions*, *brand extensions*, *multibrands* or *new brands*.

Companies must build and manage their brands carefully. The brand's positioning must be continuously communicated to consumers. Advertising can help. However, brands are not maintained by advertising but by the *brand experience.* Customers come to know a brand through a wide range of contacts and interactions. The company must put as much care into managing these touch points as it does into producing its ads. Thus, managing a company's brand assets can no longer be left only to brand managers. Some companies are now setting up brand asset management teams to manage their major brands. Finally, companies must periodically audit their brands' strengths and weaknesses. In some cases, brands may need to be repositioned because of changing customer preferences or new competitors. Other cases may call for completely *rebranding* a product, service or company.

4 **Identify the four characteristics that affect the marketing of a service and the additional marketing considerations that services require**

Services are characterised by four key characteristics: they are *intangible*, *inseparable*, *variable* and *perishable.* Each characteristic poses problems and marketing requirements. Marketers work to find ways to make the service more tangible, to increase the productivity of providers who are inseparable from their products, to standardise the quality in the face of variability, and to improve demand movements and supply capacities in the face of service perishability.

Good service companies focus attention on *both* customers and employees. They understand the *service profit chain*, which links service firm profits with employee and customer satisfaction. Services marketing strategy calls not only for external marketing, but also for *internal marketing* to motivate employees and *interactive marketing* to create service delivery skills among service providers. To succeed, service marketers must create *competitive differentiation*, offer high *service quality* and find ways to increase *service productivity.*

5 **Discuss two additional product issues: socially responsible product decisions and international product and services marketing**

Marketers must consider two additional product issues. The first is *social responsibility*. This includes public policy issues and regulations involving acquiring or dropping products, patent protection, product quality and safety, and product warranties. The second involves the special challenges facing international product and service marketers. International marketers must decide how much to standardise or adapt their offerings for world markets.

NAVIGATING THE KEY TERMS

Brand **241**
Brand equity **245**
Brand extension **253**
Co-branding **251**
Consumer product **234**
Convenience product **234**
Industrial product **235**
Interactive marketing **259**
Internal marketing **259**

Line extension **252**
Packaging **241**
Private brand (or store brand) **250**
Product **232**
Product line **243**
Product mix (or product portfolio) **244**
Product quality **238**
Services **232**

Service inseparability **258**
Service intangibility **257**
Service perishability **258**
Service–profit chain **259**
Service variability **258**
Shopping product **235**
Social marketing **237**
Speciality product **235**
Unsought product **235**

NOTES AND REFERENCES

1 Based on material from **http://www.business2000.ie/cases/cases_8th/case18.htm**, July 2009.

2 Both these top sportsmen list their main sponsors front and centre on their homepages. See **http://www.rafaelnadal.com** and **http://www.andymurray.com/partners/rado/**, both accessed January 2014.

3 For more on marketing places, see Philip Kotler, Donald Haider and Irving J. Rein, *Marketing Places* (New York: Free Press, 2008).

4 Available online at **www.social-marketing.org/aboutus.html**, accessed 18 July 2011.

5 See Rob Gould and Karen Gutierrez, 'Social Marketing Has a New Champion', *Marketing News*, 7 February 2000, p. 38. Also see Alan R. Andreasen, *Social Marketing in the 21st Century* (Thousand Oaks, CA: Sage, 2006); Philip Kotler and Nancy Lee, *Social Marketing: Improving the Quality of Life*, 3rd edn (Thousand Oaks, CA: Sage, 2008); and **www.social-marketing.org**, October 2009.

6 Quotes and definitions from Philip Kotler, *Kotler on Marketing* (New York: Free Press, 1999), p. 17; and **www.asq.org/glossary/q.html**, July 2009.

7 Abby Ghobadian, Simon Speller and Matthew Jones, 'Service Quality: Concepts and Models', *International Journal of Quality & Reliability Management*, **11**(9), 1994, pp. 43–66.

8 See Roland T. Rust, Anthony J. Zahorik and Timothy L. Keiningham, 'Return on Quality (ROQ): Making Service Quality Financially Accountable', *Journal of Marketing*, April 1995, pp. 58–70; Roland T. Rust, Christine Moorman and Peter R. Dickson, 'Getting Return on Quality: Revenue Expansion, Cost Reduction, or Both?', *Journal of Marketing*, October 2002, pp. 7–24; and Roland T. Rust, Katherine N. Lemon and Valerie A. Zeithaml, 'Return on Marketing: Using Customer Equity to Focus Marketing Strategy', *Journal of Marketing*, January 2004, p. 109.

9 Reproduced with permission: **www.designcouncil.org.uk**

10 See 'Supermarket Facts', accessed at **www.fmi.org/facts_figs/?fuseaction=superfact**, January 2014.

11 Sonja Reyes, 'Ad Blitz, Bottle Design Fuel Debate over Heinz's Sales', *Brandweek*, 12 February 2007, accessed at **www.brandweek.com/bw/news/recent_display.jsp?vnu_content_id=1003544497**

12 Based on Thomas J. Ryan, 'Labels Grow Up', *Apparel*, February 2005, pp. 26–9.

13 This informal consultative process is outlined at **https://www.gov.uk/government/consultations/childcare-commission-informal-consultation** (February 2014). By the time you read this book, the civil servants may well have reported back.

14 See the HP Total Care site at **http://www8.hp.com/uk/en/support-drivers/total-care/total-care.html**, accessed December 2013.

15 Information accessed online at **www.marriott.com**, August 2011.

16 Information about Colgate's product lines accessed at **www.colgate.com/app/Colgate/US/Corp/Products.cvsp**, August 2011.

17 See 'McAtlas Shrugged', *Foreign Policy*, May–June 2001, pp. 26–37; and Philip Kotler and Kevin Lane Keller, *Marketing Management*, 13th edn (Upper Saddle River, NJ: Prentice Hall, 2009), p. 254.

18 For details on this and much more on Interbrand's work, see **http://www.interbrand.com/en/best-global-brands/2013/best-global-brands-methodology.aspx**, accessed January 2014.

19 'Best Global Brands 2014', Interbrand, accessed at **bestglobalbrands.com**, October 2014. This annual report appears in autumn each year and is always worth a read.

20 See Scott Davis, *Brand Asset Management*, 2nd edn (San Francisco: Jossey-Bass, 2002). For more on brand positioning, see Kotler and Keller, *Marketing Management*, op. cit., ch. 10.

21 Read about Aquafresh at **www.aquafresh.co.uk**, accessed November 2013.

22 Spar naturally has a corporate and retail website to peruse; find it at **http://www.spar.co.uk**, January 2014.

23 An overview of the licensing industry can be found at **http://www.licensingpages.com/insight/industry-overview/**, accessed December 2013. For more on the most valuable licenses, see the Forbes story 'Disney Princess Tops List of the 20 Best-Selling Entertainment Products' at **http://www.forbes.com/sites/jennagoudreau/2012/09/17/disney-princess-tops-list-of-the-20-best-selling-entertainment-products/**, accessed December 2013. See also 'Dora the Explorer Takes the Lead as Sales Growth Elevates Property to Megabrand Status as Number-One Toy License in 2006', *PR Newswire*, 8 February 2007; Clint Cantwell, '$187 Billion Global Licensing Industry Comes to Life at Licensing International Expo 2008', *Business Wire*, 6 June 2008; 'Nickelodeon Expands Product Offerings and Debuts New Properties for Kids and Teens at Licensing 2008 International Show', 10 June 2008, accessed at **http://biz.yahoo.com/prnews/080610/nytu056.html?.v=101**; and 'SpongeBob SquarePants Swims to the Cricut', *Business Wire*, 28 January 2009.

24 Judith H. Washburn, Brian D. Till and Randi Priluck, 'Co-branding: Brand Equity and Trial Effects', *Journal of Consumer Marketing*, 17(7), 2000, pp. 591–604.

25 Henrik Uggla, 'The Corporate Brand Association Base: A Conceptual Model for the Creation of Inclusive Brand Architecture', *European Journal of Marketing*, 40(7/8), 2006, pp. 785–802.

26 Laura Liebeck, 'Two Tastes Can Be Better Than One', *Retail Merchandiser*, February 2005, p. 20.

27 Based on information from Kate McArthur, 'Cannibalization a Risk as Coke Diet Brand Tally Grows to Seven', *Advertising Age*, 28 March 2005, pp. 3, 123; and 'Coca-Cola Zero Pops Into Stores Today', *Atlanta Business Chronicle*, 13 June 2005, accessed at **http://atlanta.bizjournals.com/atlanta/stories/2005/06/13/daily7.html**

28 For more on Virgin's successful and unsuccessful attempts at brand extensions, see the paper at **http://www.brandchannel.com/papers_review.asp?sp_id=634**, July 2011.

29 For more on the use of line and brand extensions and consumer attitudes towards them, see Subramanian Balachander and Sanjoy Ghose, 'Reciprocal Spillover Effects: A Strategic Benefit of Brand Extensions', *Journal of Marketing*, January 2003, pp. 4–13;

Eva Martinez and Leslie de Chernatony, 'The Effect of Brand Extension Strategies Upon Brand Image', *Journal of Consumer Marketing,* 2004, p. 39; and Devon DeiVecchio and Danile Smith, 'Brand-Extension Price Premiums: The Effect of Perceived Fit and Extension Product Category Risk', *Journal of Academy of Marketing Science,* Spring 2005, pp. 184–92.

30 Businessweek has a recent story about the top 10 US advertisers – 'The 10 Biggest Advertisers In America, Ranked By Dollars Spent Annually' at **http://www.businessinsider.com/ the-10-biggest-advertisers-in-america-ranked-by-dollars-spent-annually-2013-7?op=1**, accessed January 2014.

31 Stephen Cole, 'Value of the Brand', *CA Magazine,* May 2005, pp. 39–40.

32 See Kevin Lane Keller, 'The Brand Report Card', *Harvard Business Review,* January 2000, pp. 147–57; Kevin Lane Keller, *Strategic Brand Management,* 2nd edn (Upper Saddle River, NJ: Prentice Hall, 2003), pp. 766–7; and David A. Aaker, 'Even Brands Need Spring Cleaning', *Brandweek,* 8 March 2004, pp. 36–40.

33 *Eurostat: International Trade in Services.* Available at **http://epp.eurostat.ec.europa.eu/ statistics_explained/index.php/International_trade_in_services**, accessed January 2014.

34 Portions adapted from information in Leonard Berry and Neeli Bendapudi, 'Clueing in Customers', *Harvard Business Review,* February 2003, pp. 100–6; with additional information and quotes from Jeff Hansel, 'Mayo Hits the Blogosphere', *McClatchy-Tribune Business News,* 22 January 2009; and **www.mayoclinic.org**, August 2009.

35 See James L. Heskett, W. Earl Sasser Jr and Leonard A. Schlesinger, *The Service Profit Chain: How Leading Companies Link Profit and Growth to Loyalty, Satisfaction, and Value* (New York: Free Press, 1997); Heskett, Sasser and Schlesinger, *The Value Profit Chain: Treat Employees Like Customers and Customers Like Employees* (New York: Free Press, 2003); and Garry A. Gelade and Stephen Young, 'Test of the Service Profit Chain Model in the Retail Banking Sector,' *Journal of Occupational and Organisational Psychology,* March 2005, pp. 1–22.

36 Jeremy B. Dann, 'How to Find a Hit as Big as Starbucks', *Business 2.0,* May 2004, pp. 66–8.

37 For discussions of service quality, see Valerie A. Zeithaml, A. Parasuraman and Leonard L. Berry, *Delivering Quality Service: Balancing Customer Perceptions and Expectations* (New York: Free Press, 1990); Zeithaml, Berry and Parasuraman, 'The Behavioral Consequences of Service Quality', *Journal of Marketing,* April 1996, pp. 31–46; Y.H. Hung, M.L. Huang and K.S. Chen, 'Service Quality Evaluation by Service Quality Performance Matrix', *Total Quality Management & Business Excellence,* January 2003, pp. 79–89; and Bo Edvardsson, 'Service Quality: Beyond Cognitive Assessment', *Managing Service Quality,* **2**(2), pp. 127–31.

38 See Philip Cateora, *International Marketing,* 8th edn (Homewood, IL: Irwin, 1993), p. 270; David Fairlamb, 'One Currency – But 15 Economies', *BusinessWeek,* 31 December 2001, p. 59; and **www.walkabouttravelgear.com/elect.htm**, July 2005.

39 Information accessed online at **www.db.com**, February 2014.

40 Information accessed online at **www.interpublic.com** and **www.mccann.com**, 19 July 2011.

41 Information accessed online at **www.walmartstores.com** and **www.carrefour.com**, November 2013.

CHAPTER 8
DEVELOPING NEW PRODUCTS AND MANAGING THE PRODUCT LIFE CYCLE

AFTER STUDYING THIS CHAPTER, YOU SHOULD BE ABLE TO

- explain how companies find and develop new-product ideas
- list and define the steps in the new-product development process
- describe the stages of the product life cycle
- describe how marketing strategies change during the product's life cycle

THE WAY AHEAD
Previewing the concepts

In the previous chapter, you learned how marketers manage individual brands and entire product mixes. In this chapter, we'll look into two additional product topics: developing new products and managing products through their life cycles. New products are the lifeblood of an organisation. However, new-product development is risky and many new products fail. So, the first part of this chapter lays out a process for finding and growing successful new products. Once introduced, marketers want their products to enjoy a long and happy life. In the second part of the chapter, you'll see that every product passes through several life-cycle stages and that each stage poses new challenges requiring different marketing strategies and tactics.

For openers, consider Google, one of the world's most innovative companies. Google seems to come up with an almost unending flow of amazing new technologies and services. If it has to do with finding, refining or using information, there's probably an innovative Google solution for it. At Google, innovation isn't just a process, it's in the very spirit of the place.

CHAPTER CONTENTS

GOOGLE: INNOVATION AT THE SPEED OF LIGHT[1]

Google is wildly innovative. *Fast Company* magazine lists the world's most innovative companies, and Google regularly ranks in the top five; in 2014 it was number 1. Google is also spectacularly successful. Despite formidable competition from giants such as Microsoft and Yahoo, Google's share in its core business – online search – has climbed to a decisive 90 per cent, dwarfing the combined market share of its two closest competitors.

Source: Getty Images/Bloomberg.

But Google has grown to become much more than just an Internet search and advertising company. Google's mission is 'to organise the world's information and make it universally accessible and useful'. In Google's view, information is a kind of natural resource, one to be mined and refined and universally distributed. That idea unifies what would otherwise appear to be a widely diverse set of Google projects, such as mapping the world, searching the Web on a mobile phone screen, or even providing for early detection of flu epidemics. If it has to do with harnessing and using information, Google's got it covered in some new innovative way.

Google knows how to innovate. At many companies, new-product development is a cautious, step-by-step affair that might take a year or two to unfold. In contrast, Google's freewheeling new-product development process moves at the speed of light. The nimble innovator implements major new services in less time than it takes competitors to refine and approve an initial idea. For example, a Google senior project manager describes the lightning-quick development of iGoogle, Google's customisable homepage:

> It was clear to Google that there were two groups [of Google users]: people who loved the site's clean, classic look and people who wanted tons of information there – email, news, local weather [for those who wanted a fuller home page]. iGoogle started out with me and three engineers. I was 22, and I thought, 'This is awesome.' Six weeks later, we launched the first version in May. The happiness metrics were good, there was healthy growth, and by September, we had [iGoogle fully operational with] a link on Google.com.

Such fast-paced innovation would boggle the minds of product developers at most other companies, but at Google it is standard operating procedure. 'That's what we do,' says Google's VP for Search Products and User Experience:

> The hardest part about indoctrinating people into our culture is when engineers show me a prototype and I'm like, 'Great, let's go!' They'll say, 'Oh, no, it's not ready.' I tell them, 'The Googly thing is to launch it early on Google Labs [a site where users can try out experimental Google applications] and then to iterate, learning what the market wants – and making it great.'

Adds a Google engineering manager, 'We set an operational tempo: when in doubt, do something. If you have two paths and you're not sure which is right, take the fastest path.'

Google's famously chaotic innovation process has unleashed a seemingly unending flurry of diverse products, ranging from an email service (Gmail), an online payment service (Google Checkout) and a photo sharing service (Google Picasa) to a universal platform for mobile phone applications (Google Android), a cloud-friendly web browser (Chrome), an online office suite, projects for mapping and exploring the world (Google Maps and Google Earth), and even an early-warning system for flu outbreaks in your area (FluTrends).

According to Google CEO Eric Schmidt, when it comes to new-product development at Google, there are no two-year plans. The company's new-product planning looks ahead only four to five months. Schmidt says that he would rather see projects fail quickly than see a carefully planned, long drawn-out project fail. Google continuously reviews its portfolio and is not scared to kill off products if they no longer fit or are not working or performing as hoped. That remains true even when it has user bases in the millions – groups who have often voiced their displeasure at their toys being taken away but have found their pleas falling on deaf ears. Google Reader, Meebo and the social network Orkut – all dead and gone.

The list above consists of products that are software based. As you are almost certainly aware, the last few years have seen Google get into physical, tangible electronics products. Chromebook netbook computers running the Chrome browser with add-ons to make it an operating system and the notorious Google Glasses lead the charge in wearable technologies.

Google is open to new-product ideas from about any source. What ties it all together is the company's passion for helping people find and use information. Innovation is the responsibility of every Google employee. Google engineers are encouraged to spend 20 per cent of their time developing their own new-product ideas. And all new Google ideas are quickly tested in beta form by the ultimate judges – those who will use them. According to one observer:

Any time you cram some 20,000 of the world's smartest people into one company, you can expect to grow a garden of unrelated ideas. Especially when you give some of those geniuses one workday a week – Google's famous '20 per cent time' – to work on whatever projects fan their passions. And especially when you create Google Labs, a website where the public can kick the tires on half-baked Google creations. Some Labs projects go on to become real Google services, and others are quietly snuffed out.

Even though Google Labs have now closed down, the ethos behind them moves on. In the final analysis, at Google, innovation is more than a process – it is part of the company's DNA. 'Where does innovation happen at Google? It happens everywhere,' says a Google research scientist.

Talk to Googlers at various levels and departments, and one powerful theme emerges: whether they are designing search engines for the blind or preparing meals for their colleagues, these people feel that their work can change the world. The marvel of Google is its ability to continue to instil a sense of creative fearlessness and ambition in its employees. Prospective employees are often asked, 'If you could change the world using Google's resources, what would you build?' But here, this is not a goofy or even theoretical question: Google wants to know, because thinking – and building – on that scale is what Google does. This, after all, is the company that wants to make available online every page of every book ever published. Smaller gauge ideas die of disinterest. When it comes to innovation, Google *is* different. But the difference is not tangible. It is in the air, in the spirit of the place.

Sound like a company you might want to work for? Every year Google runs the *Google Online Marketing Challenge* – look it up and get a team entered.

Sources: See note 1 at the end of this chapter.

As the Google story suggests, companies that excel at developing and managing new products reap big rewards. Every product seems to go through a life cycle — it is born, goes through several phases and eventually dies as newer products come along that better serve consumer needs. This product life cycle presents two major challenges. First, because all products eventually decline, a firm must be good at developing new products to replace ageing ones (the challenge of *new-product development*). Second, the firm must be good at adapting its marketing strategies in the face of changing tastes, technologies and competition as products pass through life-cycle stages (the challenge of *product life-cycle strategies*). We first look at the problem of finding and developing new products and then at the problem of managing them successfully over their life cycles.

NEW-PRODUCT DEVELOPMENT STRATEGY

Given the rapid changes in consumer tastes, technology and competition, companies must develop a steady stream of new products and services. A firm can obtain new products in two ways. One is through *acquisition* — by buying a whole company, a patent or a licence to produce someone else's product. Facebook recently did this with the virtual reality tech company Oculus Rift. The other is through **new-product development** in the company's own R&D department.

GlaxoSmithKline does this when developing new drugs. By *new products* we mean original products, product improvements, product modifications and new brands that the firm develops through its own R&D efforts. In this chapter, we concentrate on new-product development.

Innovation can be very risky. These days the Sony name is associated with a wide range of successful consumer electronics products and many successful innovations, but in the 1970s and 1980s Sony was famous as the company that introduced the Betamax video recorder format – a format that lost decisively in the marketplace to the alternative VHS format. Later the whole electronics industry fought in the Blu-ray vs HD-DVD wars, only to be conquered by newer downloadable formats supplied by Netflix and Apple. In fact the Internet has spawned a whole new generation of product failures, including **CyberRebate.com** (who offered to give customers all of their money back after they bought something), CueCat (a cute bar-code reader offering quick access to advertising websites), iLoo (Internet-enabled toilet) and the infamous **Pets.com**.

New products continue to face tough odds. Studies indicate that more than 90 per cent of all new consumer products fail within two years. Tens of thousands of new consumer food, beverage and beauty products are launched each year. But on average only 2 per cent of them are considered successful. New industrial products appear to fare better but still face failure rates as high as 30 per cent.[2] App stores for smartphones see launches of upwards of a thousand apps per day. Less than one per day goes on to have any commercial success and a terrifying (for app developers anyway) proportion of them are never downloaded at all – snowed under by hundreds of rivals.

Why do so many new products fail? There are several reasons. Although an idea may be good, the company may overestimate market size. The actual product may be poorly designed. Or it might be incorrectly positioned, priced too high or poorly advertised. A high-level executive might push a favourite idea despite poor marketing research findings. Sometimes the costs of product development are higher than expected, and sometimes competitors fight back harder than expected. However, the reasons behind some new-product failures seem pretty obvious. Try the following on for size:[3]

Strolling the aisles of the NewProductWorks collection at GfK Strategic Innovation's Resource Center is like finding yourself in a new-product history museum. Many of the more than 110,000 products on display were quite successful. Others, however, were abject flops. Behind each of these flops are squandered dollars and hopes and the classic question, 'What were they thinking?' Some products failed because they simply failed to bring value to customers – for example, Look of Buttermilk Shampoo, Cucumber antiperspirant spray or Premier smokeless cigarettes. Smokeless cigarettes? What were they thinking? Other companies failed because they attached trusted brand names to something totally out of character. Can you imagine swallowing Ben-Gay aspirin? Or how about Gerber Singles food for adults (perhaps the tasty pureed sweet-and-sour pork or chicken Madeira)? Other misbegotten attempts to stretch a good name include Cracker Jack cereal, Exxon fruit punch, Smucker's premium ketchup, Fruit of the Loom laundry detergent, and Harley-Davidson cake-decorating kits. Really, what were they thinking?

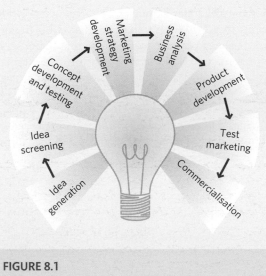

FIGURE 8.1
Major stages in new-product development

So companies face a problem – they must develop new products, but the odds weigh heavily against success. In all, to create successful new products, a company must understand its consumers, markets and competitors, and develop products that deliver superior value to customers. It must carry out strong new-product planning and set up a systematic *new-product development process* for finding and growing new products. Figure 8.1 shows the eight major steps in this process.

Idea generation

New-product development starts with **idea generation** – the systematic search for new-product ideas. A company typically has to generate many ideas in order to find a few good ones. Major sources of new-product ideas include internal sources and external sources such as customers, competitors, distributors and suppliers, and others.

Internal idea sources

Using *internal sources*, the company can find new ideas through formal R&D. However, in one recent survey, 750 global CEOs reported that only 14 per cent of their innovation ideas came from traditional R&D. Instead, 41 per cent came from employees and 36 per cent from customers.[4]

Thus, companies can pick the brains of employees – from executives to scientists, engineers, and manufacturing staff to salespeople. Many companies are making it everybody's business to come up with great ideas and are searching internally and externally for the next one. For example, Internet networking company Cisco has set up an internal wiki called Idea Zone or I-Zone, through which any Cisco employee can propose an idea for a new product or comment on or modify someone else's proposed idea. Since its inception, I-Zone has generated hundreds of ideas and Cisco selects ideas that draw the most activity for further development.[5]

Some companies have developed successful 'intrapreneurial' programmes that encourage employees to think up and develop new-product ideas. For example, Samsung built a special Value Innovation Programme (VIP) Centre in Suwon, South Korea, to encourage and support internal new-product innovation:

> The VIP Centre is the total opposite of Samsung's typical office facilities – which feature grey computers on grey desks inside grey walls – where workers adhere to strict Confucian traditions and would never dream of questioning a superior or making a wacky suggestion. Instead, the VIP Centre features workrooms, dorm rooms, training rooms, a kitchen, and a basement filled with games, a gym and sauna. Grass sprouts from the ceilings, doors are covered with funhouse mirrors, and walls are covered with chalk drawings of ideas. Inside the centre, Samsung researchers, engineers, and designers sport Viking and bumblebee hats, play with Elmo toys and inflatable dolphins, and throw around ideas without regard to rank. Recent ideas sprouting from the VIP Centre include a 102-inch plasma HDTV and a process to reduce material costs on a multifunction printer by 30 per cent. The centre has helped Samsung, once known as the maker of cheap knock-off products, become one of the world's most innovative and profitable consumer electronics companies.[6]

External idea sources

Companies can also obtain good new-product ideas from any of a number of external sources. For example, *distributors and suppliers* can contribute ideas. Distributors are close to the market and can pass along information about consumer problems and new-product possibilities. Suppliers can tell the company about new concepts, techniques and materials that can be used to develop new products. *Competitors* are another important source. Companies watch competitors' ads to get clues about their new products. They buy competing new products, take them apart to see how they work, analyse their sales, and decide whether they should bring out a new product of their own. Other idea sources include trade magazines, shows and seminars; government agencies; advertising agencies; marketing research firms; university and commercial laboratories; and inventors.

Some companies seek the help of outside new-product consultancies and design firms, such as IDEO or ZIBA for new-product ideas and designs. For example, when Cranium needed innovative new ideas for extending its popular family board game, it turned to award-winning design firm IDEO. A team of IDEO and Cranium designers began with the core premise that the games should focus on laughter, togetherness and creativity rather than competition. For inspiration, the team observed people who exemplified the Cranium characters – Word Worm, Creative Cat, Data Head and Star Performer – and then tested prototypes in actual game-playing sessions with families. Based on customer insights gained from these observations and interactions, the IDEO–Cranium team developed four new popular character-based games.[7]

Many companies are also turning to online collaborative communities to help solve new-product problems. For example, collaborative network InnoCentive puts its corporate clients ('seekers') in touch with its global network of more than 100,000 scientists ('solvers'). The seeker companies post 'challenges', and solvers can earn up to $100,000 for providing solutions. For example, P&G wanted to create a dishwashing detergent smart enough to reveal when just the right amount of soap has been added to a sink full of dirty dishes. After seeing the problem posted on InnoCentive, an Italian chemist working from her home laboratory, Giorgia Sgargetta, solved the problem by creating a new kind of dye that turns dishwater blue when a certain amount of soap is added. Her reward: $30,000. P&G estimates that more than 50 per cent of its new-product innovations today have elements that originated outside the company, up from 15 per cent in 2000.[8]

Perhaps the most important source of new-product ideas is *customers* themselves. The company can analyse customer questions and complaints to find new products that better solve consumer problems. Or a company can actively solicit ideas from customers. For example, Apple releases multiple versions of new software to limited numbers of customers and key developers. By letting these expert users play with it to destruction, weak spots, defects, and ways and means to improve the user experience for the typical user can be found, removed and implemented respectively. Sugru, the makers of the cult self-setting rubber, asks users to send in photos of how they have used the product to effect repairs. Sugru can incorporate these ideas into its own advertising and informational materials and consider how related problems could also be solved using their products – a virtuous circle of improvement.[9]

Customers often create new products and uses on their own, and companies can benefit by putting them on the market. For example, for years customers were spreading the word that Avon Skin-So-Soft bath oil and moisturiser was also a terrific bug repellent. Whereas some consumers were content simply to bathe in water scented with the fragrant oil, others carried it in their backpacks to mosquito-infested campsites or kept a bottle on the decks of their beach houses. Avon turned the idea into a complete line of Skin-So-Soft Bug Guard products, including Bug Guard Mosquito Repellent Towelettes and Bug Guard Plus, a combination moisturiser, insect repellent and sunscreen.[10]

Finally, beyond simply gathering new products from customers, companies can work with customers to create new products. Through customer co-creation, companies involve customers directly in the innovation process in multiple ways at various points. For example, the LEGO Group used customer co-creation to develop its most popular product ever, LEGO MINDSTORMS:[11]

> The LEGO MINDSTORMS build-it-yourself robot was initially an internal effort in partnership with MIT. Within three weeks of its introduction, however, more than 1,000 intrigued customers formed their own web community to outdo each other in making it better. Rather than fight the idea of co-creation (as Sony did with its Robot Dog), the LEGO Group embraced it. The next generation of LEGO MINDSTORMS featured user-defined parts. Then, the LEGO Group made customer co-creation official by creating the MINDSTORMS Development Programme (MDPs), through which it selected the most avid MINDSTORMS fans – 100 pioneers, inventors and innovators from across the globe – to play with LEGO MINDSTORMS and create innovative new features and applications. The MDP's share their ideas with other customers and invite feedback. The MINDSTORMS co-creation experience

also spawned the LEGO Factory, where users can design products, create 3-D models on the web, design packaging (which the LEGO Group will manage), and sell the products on the LEGO site.

Although customer input on new products yields many benefits, companies must be careful not to rely *too* heavily on what customers say. For some products, especially highly technical ones, customers may not know what they need. 'You can't ask people what they want if it's around the next corner,' said the late Apple founder and former CEO, Steve Jobs. 'And even when they think they know what they want,' adds an innovation management consultant, 'merely giving people what they want isn't always enough. People want to be surprised; they want something that's better than they imagined, something that stretches them in what they like.'[12]

Idea screening

The purpose of idea generation is to create a large number of ideas. The purpose of the succeeding stages is to *reduce* that number. The first idea reducing stage is **idea screening**, which helps spot good ideas and drop poor ones as soon as possible. Product development costs rise greatly in later stages, so the company wants to go ahead only with the product ideas that will turn into profitable products.

Many companies require their executives to write up new-product ideas on a standard form that can be reviewed by a new-product committee. The write-up describes the product, the target market and the competition. It makes some rough estimates of market size, product price, development time and costs, manufacturing costs and rate of return. The committee then evaluates the idea against a set of general criteria.

For example, at the large Japanese consumer products business Kao Company, the new-product committee asks questions such as these: Is the product truly useful to consumers and society? Is it good for our particular company? Does it mesh well with the company's objectives and strategies? Do we have the people, skills and resources to make it succeed? Does it deliver more value to customers than do competing products? Is it easy to advertise and distribute? Many companies have well-designed systems for rating and screening new-product ideas. The Swedish pharmaceutical company Orexo has a Product Development Committee that meets regularly to develop criteria for establishing the priority to be given to new-product ideas.[13] Companies that can direct efforts more often towards the best and most commercially exploitable ideas, and waste less time and effort on dead-end or marketplace duds, will outcompete those companies that cannot or do not.

Concept development and testing

An attractive idea must be developed into a **product concept**. It is important to distinguish between a product idea, a product concept and a product image. A *product idea* is an idea for a possible product that the company can see itself offering to the market. A *product concept* is a detailed version of the idea stated in meaningful consumer terms. To put it another way, a product idea is the company explaining the product to itself, and a product concept is the company explaining the product to customers. A *product image* is the way consumers perceive an actual or potential product, it is their view of the concept as presented to them.

Concept development

One idea for the future of motoring is the fuel-cell-powered car. This car's non-polluting fuel-cell system runs directly on hydrogen, which powers the fuel cell with only water as a by-product. It is highly fuel efficient and gives the new car an environmental advantage over even today's economical petrol–electric hybrid cars.

The Volkswagen HyMotion fuel-cell-powered Touran

Source: Volkswagen Group.

For example, VW has developed prototypes based on the Touran and the Passat family vehicles. These cars accelerate quickly, reach speeds of 140 kilometres per hour, and have a driving range far in excess of battery-powered electric cars.[14]

The next task is to develop this new product into alternative product concepts, find out how attractive each concept is to customers, and choose the best one. The following are product concepts for the fuel-cell electric car:

- *Concept 1* A moderately priced super-mini designed as a second family car to be used around town. The car is ideal for running errands and visiting friends.
- *Concept 2* A medium-cost sports coupé appealing to young people.
- *Concept 3* An inexpensive medium-sized 'green' car appealing to environmentally con- scious people who want practical, low-polluting transportation.
- *Concept 4* A high-end 4×4 appealing to those who love the space 4×4s provide but dislike the poor fuel economy.

Concept testing

Concept testing calls for testing new-product concepts with groups of target consumers. The concepts may be presented to consumers symbolically or physically. Here, in words, is concept 3:

> An efficient, fun-to-drive, fuel-cell-powered, electric, medium-sized car that seats four. This hydrogen-powered high-tech wonder provides practical and reliable transporta- tion with virtually no pollution. It goes at up to 140 kilometres per hour and, unlike battery-powered electric cars, it never needs recharging. It's priced, fully equipped, at €25,000.

For some concept tests, a word or pictorial description might be sufficient. However, a more concrete and physical presentation of the concept will increase the reliability of the concept test. After being exposed to the concept, consumers then may be asked to react to it by answering questions such as those in Exhibit 8.1.

The answers to such questions will help the company decide which concept has the strongest appeal. For example, the last question asks about the consumer's intention to buy. Suppose 10 per cent of consumers say they 'definitely' would buy, and another 5 per cent say 'probably'. The company could project these figures to the full population in this target group to estimate sales volume. Even then, the estimate is uncertain because people do not always carry out their stated intentions.

EXHIBIT 8.1

1   Do you understand the concept of a fuel-cell-powered electric car?

2   Do you believe the claims about the car's performance?

3   What are the major benefits of the fuel-cell-powered electric car compared with a conventional car?

4   What are its advantages compared with a battery-powered electric car?

5   What improvements in the car's features would you suggest?

6   For what uses would you prefer a fuel-cell-powered electric car to a conventional car?

7   What would be a reasonable price to charge for the car?

8   Who would be involved in your decision to buy such a car? Who would drive it?

9   Would you buy such a car (definitely, probably, probably not, definitely not)?

Marketing strategy development

Suppose you decided to develop concept 3 for the fuel-cell-powered electric car. The next step is **marketing strategy development** – designing an initial marketing strategy for introducing this car to the market.

The *marketing strategy statement* consists of three parts. The first part describes the target market, the planned product positioning, and the sales, market share and profit goals for the first few years. Thus:

> The target market is younger, well-educated, moderate to high-income individuals, couples or small families seeking practical, environmentally responsible transportation. The car will be positioned as more fun to drive and less polluting than today's internal combustion engine or hybrid cars. It is also less restricting than battery-powered electric cars, which must be recharged regularly. The company will aim to sell 100,000 cars in the first year, at a loss of not more than €15 million. In the second year, the company will aim for sales of 120,000 cars and a profit of €25 million.

The second part of the marketing strategy statement outlines the product's planned price, distribution and marketing budget for the first year:

> The fuel-cell-powered electric car will be offered in three colours – red, white and blue – and will have optional air-conditioning and automatic transmission features. It will sell at a retail price of €25,000 – with 15 per cent off the list price to dealers. Dealers who sell more than ten cars per month will get an additional discount of 5 per cent on each car sold that month. An advertising budget of €50 million will be split 50–50 between a European media campaign and local advertising. Advertising will emphasise the car's fun spirit and low emissions. During the first year, €100,000 will be spent on marketing research to find out who is buying the car and their satisfaction levels.

The third part of the marketing strategy statement describes the planned long-term sales, profit goals and marketing mix strategy:

> The company intends to capture a 3 per cent long-run share of the total car market and achieve an after-tax return on investment of 15 per cent. To achieve this, product quality will start high and be improved over time. Price will be raised in the second and third years if competition permits. The total advertising budget will be raised each year by about 10 per cent. Marketing research will be reduced to €60,000 per year after the first year.

Business analysis

Once management has decided on its product concept and marketing strategy, it can evaluate the business attractiveness of the proposal. **Business analysis** involves a review of the sales, costs and profit projections for a new product to find out whether they satisfy the company's objectives. If they do, the product can move to the product development stage.

To estimate sales, the company might look at the sales history of similar products and conduct surveys of market opinion. It can then estimate minimum and maximum sales to assess the range of risk. After preparing the sales forecast, management can estimate the expected costs and profits for the product, including marketing, R&D, operations, accounting and finance costs. The company then uses the sales and costs figures to analyse the new product's financial attractiveness.

Product development

So far, for many new-product concepts, the product may have existed only as a word description, a drawing or perhaps a crude mock-up. If the product concept passes the business test, it moves into **product development.** Here, R&D or the engineering department develops the product concept into a physical product. The product development step, however, now calls for a large jump in investment. It will show whether the product idea can be turned into a workable product.

The R&D department will develop and test one or more physical versions of the product concept. R&D hopes to design a prototype that will satisfy and excite consumers and that can be produced quickly and at budgeted costs. Developing a successful prototype can take days, weeks, months or even years.

Often, products undergo rigorous tests to make sure that they perform safely and effectively, or that consumers will find value in them. Here are some examples of such product tests:

> Thunk. Thunk. Thunk. Behind a locked door in the basement of Louis Vuitton's elegant Paris headquarters, a mechanical arm hoists a brown-and-tan handbag a half-meter off the floor – then drops it. The bag, loaded with an 8-pound weight, will be lifted and dropped, over and over again, for four days. This is Vuitton's test laboratory, a high-tech torture chamber for its fabled luxury goods. Another piece of lab equipment bombards handbags with ultraviolet rays to test resistance to fading. Still another tests zippers by tugging them open and shutting them 5,000 times. There's even a mechanised mannequin hand, with a Vuitton charm bracelet around its wrist, being shaken vigorously to make sure none of the charms falls off.
>
> At Gillette, almost everyone gets involved in new-product testing. Every working day at Gillette, 200 volunteers from various departments come to work unshaven, troop to the second floor of the company's gritty South Boston plant, and enter small booths with a sink and mirror. There they take instructions from technicians on the other side of a small window as to which razor, shaving cream, or aftershave to use. The volunteers evaluate razors for sharpness of blade, smoothness of glide, and ease of handling. In a nearby shower room, women perform the same ritual on their legs, underarms, and what the company delicately refers to as the 'bikini area.' 'We bleed so you'll get a good shave at home,' says one Gillette employee.[15]

A new product must have the required functional features and also convey the intended psychological characteristics. The fuel-cell electric car, for example, should strike consumers as being well built, comfortable and safe. Management must learn what makes consumers decide that a car is well built. To some consumers, this means that the car has 'solid-sounding' doors. To others, it means that the car is able to withstand heavy impact in crash tests. Consumer tests are conducted in which consumers test-drive the car and rate its attributes.

Because of an unorthodox but successful test-marketing approach, Innocent smoothies are now available in many countries

Source: Innocent Ltd.

Test marketing

If the product passes functional and consumer tests, the next step is **test marketing,** the stage at which the product and marketing programmes are introduced into more realistic market settings. Test marketing gives the marketer experience with marketing the product before going to the great expense of full introduction. It lets the company test the product and its entire marketing programme – positioning strategy, advertising, distribution, pricing, branding and packaging, and budget levels.

The amount of test marketing needed varies with each new product. Test marketing costs can be high, and it takes time that may allow competitors to gain advantages. When the costs of developing and introducing the product are low, or when management is already confident about the new product, the company may do little or no test marketing. In fact, test marketing by consumer goods firms has been declining in recent years. Companies often do not test-market simple line extensions or copies of successful competitor products.

However, when the stakes are high test marketing is important. This could be when a large company is introducing a new product that requires a big investment, or when management is not sure of the product or marketing programme. On the other hand, there are other reasons why test marketing can be very important, such as when you are planning to give up your job to set up your own business, like the founders of drinks company Innocent:

In the summer of 1998, when we had developed our first smoothie recipes but were still nervous about giving up our proper jobs, we bought £500 worth of fruit, turned it into smoothies and sold them from a stall at a little music festival in London. We put up a big sign saying 'Do you think we should give up our jobs to make these smoothies?' and put out a bin saying 'YES' and a bin saying 'NO' and asked people to put the empty bottle in the right bin. At the end of the weekend the 'YES' bin was full so we went in the next day and resigned.[16]

In another example, Australian Wool Innovation, the International Wool Textile Organisation and Australian Wool Services carried out a collaborative test marketing project with two prominent US retailers, Saks Fifth Avenue and Dillards. The aim was to establish whether direct consumer marketing of high-quality wool fabrics would have a positive influence on sales of fine wool garments.[17]

Commercialisation

Test marketing gives management the information needed to make a final decision about whether to launch the new product. If the company goes ahead with **commercialisation** – introducing the new product into the market – it will face high costs. The company may have to build or rent a manufacturing facility. And it may have to spend, in the case of a new consumer-packaged good, between €10m and €200m for advertising, sales promotion and other marketing efforts in the first year.

The company launching a new product must first decide on introduction *timing*. If VW's new fuel-cell electric car will eat into the sales of the company's other cars, its introduction may be delayed. If the car can be improved further, or if the economy is weak, the company may wait until the following year to launch it. However, if competitors are ready to introduce their own fuel-cell models, VW may push to introduce the car sooner.

Next, the company must decide *where* to launch the new product – in a single location, a region, a national market, the EU market or the international market. Few companies have the confidence, capital and capacity to launch new products into full national, EU or international distribution. They will develop a planned *market rollout* over time. In particular, small companies may enter attractive cities or regions one at a time. Larger companies, however, may quickly introduce new models into several regions, into a full national market, or even go for a pan-European launch.

Organising for new-product development

Many companies organise their new-product development process into the orderly sequence of steps shown in Figure 8.1, starting with idea generation and ending with commercialisation. Under this **sequential product development** approach, one company department works individually to complete its stage of the process before passing the new product along to the next department and stage. This orderly, step-by-step process can help bring control to complex and risky projects. But it can also be dangerously slow. In fast-changing, highly competitive markets, such slow but sure product development can result in product failures, lost sales and profits, and crumbling market positions. Pharmaceutical companies usually use this method, as developing new drugs is immensely expensive and subject to severe regulation and oversight by governments – a firm could not move on to testing the new drug on humans before many prior stages and their associated paperwork had been completed.

In order to get their new products to market quicker, many companies are adopting a faster, team-oriented approach called **simultaneous (or team-based) product development** (or collaborative product development). Under this approach, company departments work closely together through cross-functional teams, overlapping the steps in the product development process to save time and increase effectiveness. Instead of passing the new product from department to department, the company assembles a team of people from various departments that stay with the new product from start to finish. Such teams usually include people from the marketing, finance, design, manufacturing and legal departments, and even supplier and customer companies.[18]

Top management gives the product development team general strategic direction but no clear-cut product idea or work plan. It challenges the team with stiff and seemingly contradictory goals – 'turn out carefully planned and superior new products, but do it quickly' – and then gives the team whatever freedom and resources they need to meet the challenge. In the sequential process, a bottleneck at one phase can seriously slow the entire project. In the simultaneous approach, if one functional area hits snags, it works to resolve them while the team move on. Although inherently more complicated and difficult to manage, this system can lead to huge competitive advantages, especially when time-to-market is key.

The European automotive industry has achieved tremendous benefits by adopting simultaneous development. Under the old sequential approach, the company's marketing departments passed a new-product idea to designers, who worked in isolation to prepare concepts that they then sent along to product engineers. The engineers, also working by themselves, developed expensive prototypes and passed these to manufacturing, which tried to find a way to build the new product. Finally, after many years and dozens of costly design compromises and delays, marketing was asked to sell the new product, which it often found to be priced too high or sadly out of date. Now, all of the departments work together in a single project team to develop new products. This has resulted in reduced time-to-market for European car makers, enabling them to compete more effectively with their competitors from the Far East and the USA.

The simultaneous team-based approach does have some limitations. Very fast product development can be riskier and more costly than the slower, more orderly sequential approach. Moreover, it often creates increased organisational tension and confusion. And the company must take care that rushing a product to market does not adversely affect its quality – the objective is not to create products faster, but to create them *better* and faster.

Despite these drawbacks, in rapidly changing industries facing increasingly shorter product life cycles, the rewards of fast and flexible product development far exceed the risks. Companies that get new and improved products to the market faster than competitors often gain a big competitive edge. They can respond more quickly to emerging consumer tastes and charge higher prices for more advanced designs. As one car industry executive states, 'What we want to do is get the new car approved, built, and in the consumer's hands in the shortest time possible. . . . Whoever gets there first gets all the marbles.'[19]

Thus, new-product success requires more than simply thinking up a few good ideas, turning them into products and finding customers for them. It requires a systematic approach for finding new ways to create valued customer experiences, from generating and screening new-product ideas to creating and rolling out want-satisfying products to customers.

More than this, successful new-product development requires a whole-company commitment. At companies known for their new-product prowess – such as Google, Apple, IDEO, 3M, Procter & Gamble and Electrolux – the entire culture encourages, supports and rewards innovation (see Marketing at Work 8.1). The company can appoint a respected senior person to be the company's innovation manager. It can set up web-based idea management software and encourage all company stakeholders – employees, suppliers, distributors, dealers – to become involved in finding and developing new products. It can assign a cross-functional innovation management committee to evaluate proposed new-product ideas and help bring good ideas to market. It can create recognition programmes to reward those who contribute the best ideas.

The innovation management system approach yields two favourable outcomes. First, it helps create an innovation-oriented company culture. It shows that top management supports, encourages and rewards innovation. Second, it will yield a larger number of new-product ideas, among which will be found some especially good ones. The good new ideas will be more systematically developed, producing more new-product successes. No longer will good ideas wither for the lack of a sounding board or a senior product advocate.

Thus, new-product success requires more than simply thinking up a few good ideas, turning them into products and finding customers for them. It requires a holistic approach for finding new ways to create valued customer experiences, from generating and screening new-product ideas to creating and rolling out want-satisfying products to customers.

Electrolux: cleaning up with customer-centred, team-based new-product development

MARKETING AT WORK 8.1

You will never meet Catherine, Anna, Maria or Monica. But the future success of Swedish home appliances maker Electrolux depends on what these four women think. Catherine, for instance, a type A career woman who is a perfectionist at home, loves the idea of simply sliding her laundry basket into a washing machine, instead of having to lift the clothes from the basket and into the washer. That product idea has been moved onto the fast track for consideration.

So, just who are Catherine and the other women? Well, they don't actually exist. They are composites based on in-depth interviews with some 160,000 consumers from around the globe. To divine the needs of these mythical customers, 53 Electrolux employees – in teams that included designers, engineers and marketers hailing from various divisions – gathered in Stockholm recently for a week-long brainstorming session. The Catherine team began by ripping photographs out of a pile of magazines and sticking them onto poster boards. Next to a picture of a woman wearing a sharply tailored suit, they scribbled some of Catherine's attributes: driven, busy and a bit overwhelmed.

With the help of these characters, Electrolux product developers are searching for the insights they'll need to dream up the next batch of hot products. It's a new way of doing things for Electrolux, but then again, a lot is new at the company. When Chief Executive Keith McLoughlin took the helm in 2011, Electrolux – which sells products under the Electrolux, AEG and Zanussi brands – faced a number of key challenges, notably rapid global growth in raw material prices, slow economic growth in the European economies worst hit by the financial crisis, and intensifying competition from the Far East.

McLoughlin had to do something radical, especially in the area of new-product innovation. So he began breaking down barriers between departments and forcing his designers, engineers and marketers to work together to come up with new products. He also introduced an intense focus on the customer. He set out to become 'the leader in our industry in terms of systematic development of new products based on consumer insight'.

At the Stockholm brainstorming session, for example, group leader Kim Scott urges everyone 'to think of yourselves as Catherine'. The room buzzes with discussion. Ideas are refined, sketches drawn up. The group settles on three concepts: Breeze, a clothes steamer that also removes stains; an Ironing Centre, similar to a trouser press but for shirts; and Ease, the washing machine that holds a laundry basket inside its drum.

Half the group races off to the machine shop to turn out a prototype for Breeze, while the rest stay upstairs to bang out a marketing plan. Over the next hour, designer Lennart Johansson carves and sandpapers a block of peach-coloured polyurethane until a contraption that resembles a cross between an electric screwdriver and a handheld vacuum begins to emerge. The designers in the group want the Breeze to be smaller, but engineer Giuseppe Frucco points out that would leave too little space for a charging station for the 1,500-watt unit.

For company veterans such as Frucco, who works at Electrolux's fabric care research and development centre in Porcia, Italy, this dynamic group approach is a refreshing change: 'We never used to create new products together,' he says. 'The designers would come up with something and then tell us to build it.' The new way saves time and money by avoiding the technical glitches that crop up as a new design moves from the drafting table to the factory floor. The ultimate goal is to come up with new products that consumers will gladly pay a premium for: gadgets with drop-dead good looks and clever features that ordinary people can understand without having to pore through a thick users' manual. 'Consumers are prepared to pay for good design and good performance,' says the CEO.

Few companies have pulled off the range of hot new offerings that Electrolux has. One clear hit is a cordless stick and hand vacuum, called the Rapido in Europe, and the Pronto in the USA. Available in an array of metallic hues with a rounded, ergonomic design, this is the Cinderella of vacuums. Too attractive to be locked up in the broom closet, it calls out to be displayed in your kitchen. In Europe, it now commands 50 per cent of the market for stick vacs, a coup for a product with fewer than two years on the market. The Pronto is cleaning up in the United States, too. Stacy Silk, a buyer at retail chain Best Buy, says it is one of her hottest sellers, even though it retails for around $100, double the price of comparable models. A recent check at Best Buy's online site shows that the Pronto is currently out of stock. 'The biggest thing is the aesthetics,' Silk says. 'That gets people to walk over and look.'

Electrolux is crafting such new products even while moving away from many traditional customer research tools. The company relies less heavily on focus groups and now prefers to interview people in their homes where they can be videotaped pushing a vacuum or shoving laundry into the washer. 'Consumers think they know what they want, but they often have trouble articulating it,' says Electrolux's senior vice-president for global design. 'But when we watch them, we can ask, "Why do you do that?" We can change the product and solve their problems.'

This customer-centred, team-based new-product development approach is producing results. Under the new approach, new-product launches have almost doubled in quantity, and the proportion of new-product launches that result in outsized unit sales is now running at 50 per cent of all introductions, up from around 25 per cent

Developing and launching innovative new products is at the heart of the Electrolux marketing strategy

Source: Getty Images/Martin Poole.

previously. As a result, Electrolux's sales, profits and share price are all up sharply.

It all boils down to understanding consumers and giving them what they need and want. According to a recent Electrolux annual report:

All new products are born out of the Group's process for consumer-driven product development. Extensive consumer interviews and visits to consumers' homes have enabled Electrolux to identify global social trends and needs, to which new products are tailored.

Thanks to such thinking, Electrolux has now grown to become the world's biggest household appliances company. Catherine and the other women would be pleased.

Sources: Portions adapted from Ariene Sains and Stanley Reed, 'Electrolux Cleans Up', *BusinessWeek*, 27 February 2006, pp. 42–3; *Electrolux Annual Report*, 2010, accessed at www.electrolux.com, May 2011; Additional information from Caroline Perry, 'Electrolux Doubles Spend with New Strategy', *Marketing Week*, 16 February 2006, pp. 7–9.

MAKING CONNECTIONS Linking the concepts

Think about new products and how companies find and develop them.

● Suppose that you're on a panel to nominate the 'best new products of the year'. What products would you nominate and why? See what you can learn about the new-product development process for one of these products.

● Applying the new-product development process you've just studied, develop an idea for an innovative new snack-food product and sketch out a brief plan for bringing it to market. Relax and have some fun with this.

PRODUCT LIFE-CYCLE STRATEGIES

After launching the new product, management wants the product to enjoy a long and happy life. Although it does not expect the product to sell for ever, the company wants to earn a decent profit to cover all the effort and risk that went into launching it. Management is aware that each product will have a life cycle, although its exact shape and length are not known in advance.

Figure 8.2 shows a typical **product life cycle** (PLC) – the course that a product's sales and profits take over its lifetime. The product life cycle has five distinct stages:

1 *Product development* begins when the company finds and develops a new-product idea. During product development, sales are zero and the company's investment costs mount.

2 *Introduction* is a period of slow sales growth as the product is introduced in the market. Profits are non-existent in this stage because of the heavy expenses of product introduction.

3 *Growth* is a period of rapid market acceptance and increasing profits.

4 *Maturity* is a period of slowdown in sales growth because the product has achieved acceptance by most potential buyers. Profits level off or decline because of increased marketing outlays to defend the product against competition.

5 *Decline* is the period when sales fall off and profits drop.

Not all products follow this product life cycle. Some products are introduced and die quickly; others stay in the mature stage for a long, long time. Some enter the decline stage and are then cycled back into the growth stage through strong promotion or repositioning. Brands such as American Express, Budweiser, Coca-Cola, Gillette, Western Union, Wells Fargo and Tabasco, for instance, are still going strong in their respective categories after

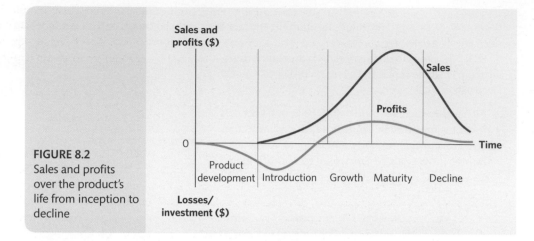

FIGURE 8.2
Sales and profits over the product's life from inception to decline

100+ years. Newspaper brands that were born over a century ago are now turning themselves into online services fit for the twenty-first century: *The Times* newspaper (**www.timesonline.co.uk**) has been published since 1788 and *The Economist* (**www.economist.com**) since 1843.

The PLC concept can describe a *product class* (petrol-powered cars), a *product form* (family hatchback car) or a *brand* (the Ford Focus). The PLC concept applies differently in each case. Product classes have the longest life cycles – the sales of many product classes stay

The Economist newspaper is over 150 years old and has fully embraced the online revolution

Source: The Economist Newspaper Limited, London.

in the mature stage for a long time. Product forms, in contrast, tend to have the standard PLC shape. Product forms such as 'dial telephones' and 'compact discs' passed through a regular history of introduction, rapid growth, maturity and decline. Product forms you are using today will do this as well – your tablet computers, your smartphones, the branded food products you eat – all will change and evolve.

A specific brand's life cycle can change quickly because of changing competitive attacks and responses. For example, although laundry soaps (product class) and powdered detergents (product form) have enjoyed fairly long life cycles, the life cycles of specific brands have tended to be much shorter.

The PLC concept can also be applied to what are known as styles, fashions and fads. Their special life cycles are shown in Figure 8.3. A **style** is a basic and distinctive mode of expression. For example, styles appear in homes (the Swiss chalet style, the English cottage style and so on), clothing (formal, casual) and art (realist, surrealist, abstract). Once a style is invented, it may last for generations, passing in and out of vogue. A style has a cycle showing several periods of renewed interest. A **fashion** is a currently accepted or popular style in a given field. Fashions tend to grow slowly, remain popular for a while and then decline slowly.

A **fad** is a temporary period of unusually high sales driven by consumer enthusiasm and immediate product or brand popularity.[20] It may be part of an otherwise normal life cycle, as in the case of recent surges in the sales of ripped jeans. Or the fad may comprise a brand's or product's entire life cycle. Morph suits, loom bands – these come and go and often have lifespans comparable with mayflies. Other examples of such fads include Rubik's Cube, lava lamps, Troll Dolls and Furbies.[21]

The PLC concept can be applied by marketers as a useful framework for describing how products and markets work. And when used carefully, the PLC concept can help in developing good marketing strategies for different stages of the PLC. But using the PLC concept for forecasting product performance or for developing marketing strategies presents some practical problems. For example, managers may have trouble identifying which stage of the PLC the product is in, or pinpointing when the product moves into the next stage. They may also find it hard to determine the factors that affect the product's movement through the stages. In practice, it is difficult to forecast the sales level at each PLC stage, the length of each stage and the shape of the PLC curve. Using the PLC concept to develop marketing strategy also can be difficult because strategy is both a cause and a result of the PLC. The product's current PLC position suggests the best marketing strategies, and the resulting marketing strategies affect product performance in later life-cycle stages.

Moreover, marketers should not blindly push products through the traditional stages of the PLC. Instead, marketers often defy the 'rules' of the life cycle and position their products in unexpected ways. By doing this companies can rescue products foundering in the maturity phase of their life cycles and return them to the growth phase. Or they can leapfrog obstacles that could slow the product down, and catapult new products forward into the growth phase.

We looked at the product development stage of the PLC in the first part of the chapter. We now look at strategies for each of the other life-cycle stages.

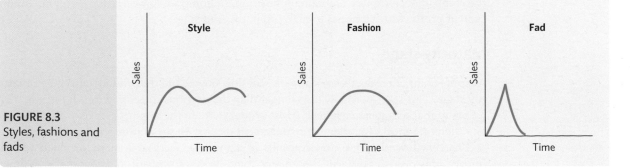

FIGURE 8.3
Styles, fashions and fads

Introduction stage

The **introduction stage** starts when the new product is first launched. Introduction takes time and sales growth is apt to be slow. Well-known products such as instant coffee, frozen foods and HDTVs lingered for many years before they entered a stage of rapid growth.

In this stage, as compared with other stages, profits are negative or low because of the low sales and high distribution and promotion expenses. A lot of money is needed to attract distributors and build their inventories. Promotional spending is relatively high to inform consumers of the new product and get them to try it. Because the market is not generally ready for product refinements at this stage, the company and its few competitors produce basic versions of the product. These firms focus their selling on those buyers who are the most ready to buy.

A company, especially the *market pioneer,* must choose a launch strategy that is consistent with the intended product positioning. It should understand that the initial strategy is just the first step in a grander marketing plan for the product's entire life cycle. If the pioneer chooses its launch strategy to make big short-term profits it may be sacrificing long-run revenue for the sake of short-run gain. As the pioneer moves through later stages of the life cycle, it will have continuously to formulate new pricing, promotion and other marketing strategies. It has the best chance of building and retaining market leadership if it plays its cards correctly from the start. These issues were given great consideration by Tesla, when devising the marketing plan for its electrically powered vehicles.

Growth stage

If the new product satisfies the market, it will enter a **growth stage,** in which sales will start climbing quickly. The early adopters will continue to buy, and later buyers will start following their lead, especially if they hear favourable word of mouth. Attracted by the opportunities for profit, new competitors will enter the market. Apple has proved that the tablet market is extremely lucrative. Competitors have moved to provide products to compete with iPads and more will surely follow. They will introduce new product features and the market will expand and evolve. The increase in competitors leads to an increase in the number of distribution outlets and sales jump just to build reseller inventories. Prices remain where they are or fall only slightly. Companies keep their promotion spending at the same or a slightly higher level. Educating the market remains a goal, but now the company must also meet the competition.

Profits increase during the growth stage, because promotional costs are spread over a large volume and unit manufacturing costs fall as a result of economies of scale. The firm uses several strategies to sustain rapid market growth as long as possible. It improves product quality and adds new product features and models. It enters new market segments and new distribution channels. It shifts some advertising from building product awareness to building product conviction and purchase, and it aims to lower prices at the right time to attract more buyers.

In the growth stage, the firm faces a trade-off between high market share and high current profit. By spending a lot of money on product improvement, promotion and distribution, the company can capture a dominant position. In doing so, however, it gives up maximum current profit, which it hopes to make up in the next stage.

Maturity stage

At some point, a product's sales growth will slow down, and the product will enter a **maturity stage.** This stage normally lasts longer than the previous stages and it poses strong challenges to marketing management. Most products are in the maturity stage of the life cycle and therefore most of marketing management deals with the mature product.

The slowdown in sales growth results in many producers with many products to sell. In turn, this overcapacity leads to greater competition. Competitors begin marking down prices, increasing their advertising and sales promotions, and upping their R&D budgets to find better versions of the product. These steps lead to a drop in profit. Some of the weaker competitors start dropping out and the industry eventually contains only well-established competitors.

Although many products in the mature stage appear to remain unchanged for long periods, most successful ones are actually evolving to meet changing consumer needs. Product managers should do more than simply maintain or defend their mature products – they need to keep thinking of ways to improve. They should consider modifying the market, product and marketing mix.

In *modifying the market*, the company tries to increase the consumption of the current product. It may look for new users and new market segments. For example, manufacturers of professional power tools, such as Robert Bosch GmbH, are constantly aware that their highly specified products also appeal to the high-end domestic do-it-yourself market.

The manager may also look for ways to increase usage among present customers. Online retailer Amazon (**amazon.com**, **amazon.de**, **amazon.fr**, **amazon.co.uk**) does this by sending permission-based emails to regular customers letting them know when their favourite authors publish new books or their favourite TV series is available to buy as a boxset. The WD-40 Company has shown a real knack for expanding the market by finding new uses for its popular substance. The original product, WD-40, was invented as an industrial degreasing agent in 1953, and was only launched as a consumer product five years later after the employees of the company had found it very useful around the home and garage. Today, the WD-40 Company still sells the original degreaser, and a range of other cleaning and lubricating products, in many markets around the world – with European offices in the UK, Spain, Germany, the Netherlands, Italy, Austria and France.

In 2000, the company launched a search to uncover 2,000 unique uses for WD-40. After receiving 300,000 individual submissions, it narrowed the list to the best 2,000 and posted it on the company's website. Some consumers suggest simple and practical uses. One teacher uses WD-40 to clean old chalkboards in her classroom. 'Amazingly, the boards started coming to life again,' she reports. 'Not only were they restored, but years of masking and Scotch tape residue came off as well.' Others, however, report some pretty unusual applications. One man uses WD-40 to polish his glass eye; another uses it to remove a prosthetic leg. And did you hear about the nude burglary suspect who had wedged himself in a vent at a café in Denver? The fire department extracted him with a large dose of WD-40. Or how about the Mississippi naval officer who used WD-40 to repel an angry bear? Then there's the college student who wrote to say that a friend's nightly amorous activities in the next room were causing everyone in his dorm to lose sleep – he solved the problem by treating the squeaky bedsprings with WD-40.[22]

The company might also try *modifying the product* – changing characteristics such as quality, features or style to attract new users and to inspire more usage. It might improve the product's quality and performance – its durability, reliability, speed, taste. It can improve the product's styling and attractiveness. Thus, car manufacturers restyle their cars to attract buyers who want a new look; modified and improved (or 'face-lifted') versions of popular models like the VW Golf and the Renault Clio come along regularly. The makers of consumer food and household products introduce new flavours, colours, ingredients or packages to revitalise consumer buying. Or the company might add new features that expand the product's usefulness, safety or convenience. For example, Sony keeps adding new styles and features to its portable music player lines, and Volvo adds new safety features to its cars.

Finally, the company can try *modifying the marketing mix* – improving sales by changing one or more marketing mix elements. It can cut prices to attract new users and competitors' customers. It can launch a better advertising campaign or use aggressive sales promotions – trade deals, money-off, premiums and contests. In addition to pricing and promotion, the company can also move into larger market channels, using mass merchandisers, if these channels are growing. The company can also offer new or improved services to buyers.

Decline stage

The sales of most product forms and brands eventually dip. Slow or quick, death always comes sooner or later. Vinyl LPs were killed by cassettes which were killed by CDs which were killed by MP3 files. Sales may plunge to zero, or they may drop to a low level where they continue for many years – it is still possible to buy video cassette tapes and machines. This is the **decline stage**.

Sales decline for many reasons, including technological advances, shifts in consumer tastes and increased competition. As sales and profits decline, some firms withdraw from the market. Those remaining may prune their product offerings. They may drop smaller market segments and marginal trade channels, or they may cut the promotion budget and reduce their prices further.

Carrying a weak product can be very costly to a firm, and not just in profit terms. There are many hidden costs. A weak product may take up too much of management's time. It often requires frequent price and inventory adjustments. It requires advertising and sales force attention that might be better used to make 'healthy' products more profitable. A product's failing reputation can cause customer concerns about the company and its other products. The biggest cost may well lie in the future. Keeping weak products delays the search for replacements, creates a lopsided product mix, hurts current profits and weakens the company's foothold on the future.

For these reasons, companies need to pay more attention to their ageing products. The firm's first task is to identify those products in the decline stage by regularly reviewing sales, market shares, costs and profit trends. Then, management must decide whether to maintain, harvest or drop each of these declining products.

Management may decide to *maintain* its brand without change in the hope that competitors will leave the industry. Or management may decide to reposition or reinvigorate the brand in the hope of moving it back into the growth stage of the PLC. Procter & Gamble has done this with several brands, including Mr Clean and Old Spice.

Management may decide to *harvest* the product, which means reducing various costs (plant and equipment, maintenance, R&D, advertising, sales force) and hoping that sales hold up. If successful, harvesting will increase the company's profits in the short term. Or management may decide to *drop* the product from the line. It can sell it to another firm or simply liquidate it at salvage value. In recent years, Procter & Gamble has sold off a number of lesser or declining brands. If the company plans to find a buyer, it will not want to run down the product through harvesting. A declining brand may prove useful to another company, particularly where it has a gap to fill in its product portfolio – see Marketing at Work 8.2.

VW and Alfa Romeo: German engineering with Italian chic?

MARKETING AT WORK 8.2

'VW in hot pursuit of Alfa' is not the kind of headline you might expect to read. Is this a special issue of *Police, Camera, Action!* devoted to unusual car chases where paunchy, middle-aged, balding men in boring family cars chase sunglass-wearing, youthful, muscle-bound male models driving sexy motors? Well, no, it's a *Financial Times* story explaining that, despite being rebuffed several times in their efforts to acquire the Alfa Romeo brand from Fiat/General Motors, Volkswagen AG are still hot on the trail of the iconic Italian car marque, aiming to add it to the growing portfolio of automotive brands it already owns.

You could be forgiven for thinking that the brand image of Alfa Romeo was about as far from VW as you can get. The motoring correspondent of the *Financial Times* thinks a rather unflattering comparison between Alfa Romeo vehicles and Hollywood hunks used to be the order of the day: 'Like the Alpha Male of movie mythology these cars were good looking and unreliable in equal measure. Always fast, the appeal of their smooth charm diminished with every breakdown and those looks quickly faded courtesy of notoriously poor bodywork.' But times have changed, and today Alfa makes fairly reliable cars that do not rust. Unfortunately, it also make cars that not many people want to buy. So why would VW, a company with a virtually unparalleled reputation for German engineering excellence and quality, want to acquire an Italian brand that is famous for manufacturing fast fashion statements that break down and rust?

Well, in the first place, Fiat/GM seem to have been doing a pretty good job of turning Alfa around. In 1995 Alfa Romeo pulled out of the US market after selling only 400 cars, but today they have plans to re-enter the market and sell 85,000 cars a year in the USA based on the launch of an attractive, and reliable, new product range. In Europe, Alfa's cute, new MiTo is tackling the BMW Mini in the retro chic segment of the market, and winning great reviews from the critics: 'Alfa Romeo's MiTo is compact, looks fun to drive and exudes a sort of cool-yet-hot Italianness. . . . In many ways this is the future of cars as objects to enjoy,' according to one motoring journalist. The marketing dream at Alfa Romeo is to retain the reputation for Italian chic, while losing the reputation for making cars that break down.

However, one industry expert thinks that the main reason for VW's interest in Alfa is that the fashionable and upmarket image of the Italian brand will enable the German company to plug an important gap in its product portfolio:

Source: Volkswagen Group.

Source: Getty Images/Valentin Flauraud/Bloomberg.

It could provide a solution to VW's current strategic dilemma facing its highly successful Audi brand. . . . Audi is being forced to cover too much ground in its efforts to compete against both Mercedes, with its more staid luxury sedan cars, and BMW, with its sporty image. This risks diluting Audi's strategic focus and hence it would be perhaps best to allow Audi to concentrate wholly on competing against Mercedes. So acquiring Alfa Romeo would give VW a new vehicle to take on BMW.

The VW product portfolio spans seven automobile brands (VW, Audi, Skoda, Bentley, Seat, Bugatti and Lamborghini) and two commercial vehicle brands (VW commercial vehicles and Scania). This makes VW the epitome of a European company: it owns brands that originate from seven European countries, selling nearly 10 million vehicles in 2013 in 157 countries, leading to revenue of €197bn and giving a 25 per cent share of sales in Western Europe and 11 per cent of total global car sales.

Each of VW's brands has its own image with consumers, and within each brand the company manufactures a wide range of models that are designed to appeal to different customer segments. For example, the Skoda Octavia is a large family car that provides excellent value for money and will appeal to the economy-minded family driver, while the Audi A1 is a premium ultra-compact vehicle that offers style and sophistication (for a price) and could be sold either as a second car to an affluent family, or as a style statement to a young business executive. The core VW brand itself was rated 34th in the Interbrand list of the best global brands, while the VW Group's luxury Audi brand stood at 51st place in the global best brand list and Porsche at 64th.

Maintaining a clear position in the market for some of VW's brands is easier than for others. Lamborghini, Bugatti and Bentley are legendary, classic European automobile brands, each with its own unique history and mythology. For example, a Bentley won the most famous automobile endurance race in the world – the Le Mans

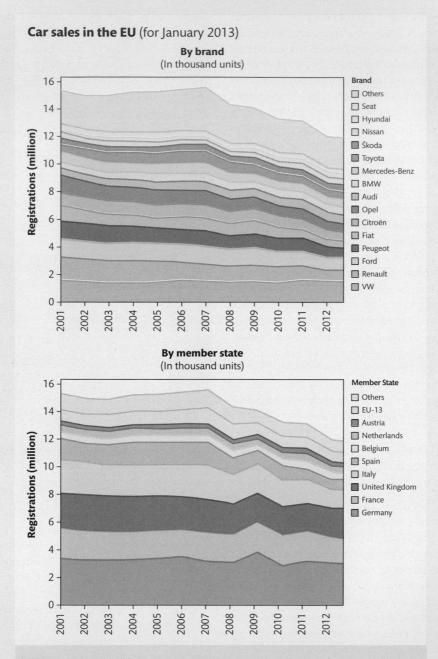

FIGURE 8.4

VW and Germany top the chart for European car sales, so why could it want to buy a much smaller Italian rival?

Source: Thomson Reuters?

24-Hour Race – five out of the first ten times it was run (amazingly, between 2000 and 2010 the same race was won eight times by an Audi). For the less mythological brands it is a little more difficult. During the economic crisis of 2008–12 advertising for the VW brand switched to the slogan 'unbelievable value' to emphasise just how much car you were getting for your money, but risking some confusion with other value-for-money brands in the portfolio, notably Skoda and Seat.

In some ways the positioning of the Audi brand presents the greatest challenge. It has become the most successful luxury car brand in the world, but perhaps the VW Group is asking too much of a single brand. Can it continue to position itself as a rival to the comfortable, relaxed luxury of Mercedes-Benz, and to the edgier, sporting luxury of BMW? If VW gets its hands on the Alfa Romeo brand, and endows it with the unmistakable aura of German quality, perhaps that will give VW a new and potent weapon in its competitive struggle for European luxury car supremacy.

Sources: 'Volkswagen Achieving Ambitious Sales Goals at Expense of Profitability', *Forbes*, 16 March 2014; 'The Revival of Alfa Romeo', *The Economist*, 28 August 2010; Paul Betts, 'A Reputation Is Hanging on Alfa Romeo's Renaissance', *Financial Times*, 11 December 2009; John Reed and Daniel Schäfer, 'VW in Hot Pursuit of Alfa Romeo', *Financial Times*, 3 December 2010; Matthew Pettipher, 'Alfa Romeo Mito 1.4TB', *Financial Times*, 14 January 2010; *Audi 2013 Annual Report*, available at www.volkswagenag.com, accessed 14 August 2014; *Best Global Brands 2013*, available at www.interbrand.com, accessed 5 August 2014; John Simister, 'Alfa Mito', *Independent*, 6 July 2008.

Table 8.1 summarises the key characteristics of each stage of the PLC. The table also lists the marketing objectives and strategies for each stage.

TABLE 8.1 Summary of life-cycle characteristics, objectives and strategies

Characteristics	Introduction	Growth	Maturity	Decline
Sales	Low sales	Rapidly rising sales	Peak sales	Declining sales
Costs	High cost per customer	Average cost per customer	Low cost per customer	Low cost per customer
Profits	Negative	Rising profits	High profits	Declining profits
Customers	Innovators	Early adopters	Middle majority	Laggards
Competitors	Few	Growing number	Stable number beginning to decline	Declining number
Marketing objectives				
	Create product awareness and trial	Maximise market share	Maximise profit while defending market share	Reduce expenditure and milk the brand
Strategies				
Product	Offer a basic product	Offer product extensions, service, warranty	Diversify brand and models	Phase out weak items
Price	Use cost-plus	Price to penetrate market	Price to match or beat competitors	Cut price
Distribution	Build selective distribution	Build intensive distribution	Build more intensive distribution	Go selective: phase out unprofitable outlets
Advertising	Build product awareness among early adopters and dealers	Build awareness and interest in the mass market	Stress brand differences and benefits	Reduce to level needed to retain hard-core loyals
Sales promotion	Use heavy sales promotion to entice trial	Reduce to take advantage of heavy consumer demand	Increase to encourage brand switching	Reduce to minimal level

THE JOURNEY YOU'VE TAKEN   Reviewing the concepts

A company's current products face limited lifespans and must be replaced by newer products. But new products can fail – the risks of innovation are as great as the rewards. The key to successful innovation lies in a total-company effort, strong planning and a systematic *new-product development* process.

1   Explain how companies find and develop new-product ideas

Companies find and develop new-product ideas from a variety of sources. Many new-product ideas stem from *internal sources.* Companies conduct formal research and development, pick the brains of their employees and brainstorm at executive meetings. Other ideas come from *external sources.* By conducting surveys and focus groups and analysing *customer* questions and complaints, companies can generate new-product ideas that will meet specific consumer needs. Companies track *competitors'* offerings and inspect new products, dismantling them, analysing their performance and deciding whether to introduce a similar or improved product. *Distributors and suppliers* are close to the market and can pass along information about consumer problems and new-product possibilities.

2   List and define the steps in the new-product development process

The new-product development process consists of eight sequential stages. The process starts with *idea generation.* Next comes *idea screening*, which reduces the number of ideas based on the company's own criteria. Ideas that pass the screening stage continue through *product concept development*, in which a detailed version of the new-product idea is stated in meaningful consumer terms. In the next stage, *concept testing*, new-product concepts are tested with a group of target consumers to determine whether the concepts have strong consumer appeal. Strong concepts proceed to *marketing strategy development*, in which an initial marketing strategy for the new product is developed from the product concept. In the *business analysis* stage, a review of the sales, costs and profit projections for a new product is conducted to determine whether the new product is likely to satisfy the company's objectives. With positive results here, the ideas become more concrete through *product development* and *test marketing* and finally are launched during *commercialisation.*

3   Describe the stages of the product life cycle

Each product has a *life cycle* marked by a changing set of problems and opportunities. The sales of the typical product follow an S-shaped curve made up of five stages. The cycle begins with the *product development stage* when the company finds and develops a new-product idea. The *introduction stage* is marked by slow growth and low profits as the product is distributed to the market. If successful, the product enters a *growth stage*, which offers rapid sales growth and increasing profits. Next comes a *maturity stage* when sales growth slows down and profits stabilise. Finally, the product enters a *decline stage* in which sales and profits dwindle. The company's task during this stage is to recognise the decline and to decide whether it should maintain, harvest or drop the product.

4   Describe how marketing strategies change during the product's life cycle

In the *introduction stage*, the company must choose a launch strategy consistent with its intended product positioning. Much money is needed to attract distributors and build their inventories and to inform consumers of the new product and achieve trial. In the *growth stage*, companies continue to educate potential consumers and distributors. In addition, the company works to stay ahead of the competition and sustain rapid market growth by improving product quality, adding new product features and models, entering new market segments and distribution channels, shifting advertising from building product awareness to building product conviction and purchase, and lowering prices at the right time to attract new buyers. In the *maturity stage*, companies continue to invest in maturing products and consider modifying the market, the product and the marketing mix. When *modifying the market*, the company attempts to increase the consumption of the current product. When *modifying the product*, the company changes some of the product's characteristics – such as quality, features or style – to attract new users or inspire more usage. When *modifying the marketing mix*, the company works to improve sales by changing one or more of the marketing mix elements. Once the company recognises that a product has entered the *decline stage*, management must decide whether to *maintain* the brand without change, hoping that competitors will drop out of the market; *harvest* the product, reducing costs and trying to maintain sales; or *drop* the product, selling it to another firm or liquidating it at salvage value.

NAVIGATING THE KEY TERMS

NOTES AND REFERENCES

1 Extracts and quotes from or adapted from information found in Chuck Salter, 'Google: The Faces and Voices of the World's Most Innovative Company', *Fast Company,* June 2014, pp. 74–88; 'The World's Most Innovative Companies', *Fast Company,* July 2014; 'Google Shines a Light on Innovation', *Computer Weekly,* 9–15 September 2008, p. 3; Jessica Guynn, 'Internet: Google's Results Defy Downturn', *Los Angeles Times,* 17 October 2008, p. C1; David Pogue, 'Geniuses at Play, On the Job', *New York Times,* 26 February 2009, p. B1; also **www.google.com**, accessed August 2014.

2 See Alison Stein Wellner, 'The New Science of Focus Groups', *American Demographics,* March 2003, p. 30; Kevin J. Clancy and Peter C. Krieg, 'Surviving Innovation', *Marketing Management,* March–April 2003, pp. 14–20; 'Market Research: So What's the Big Idea?', *Marketing Week,* 11 March 2004, p. P37; and Deborah Ball *et al.,* 'Just What You Need!', *The Wall Street Journal,* 28 October 2004, p. B1.

3 Information and examples from Robert M. McMath and Thom Forbes, *What Were They Thinking? Money-Saving, Time-Saving, Face-Saving Marketing Lessons You Can Learn from Products That Flopped* (New York: Times Business, 1999), various pages; Beatriz Cholo, 'Living with Your "Ex": A Brand New World', *Brandweek,* 5 December 2005, p. 4; and **www.gfkamerica.com/newproductworks**, October 2009.

4 For an academic paper on this topic, see James E. Burroughs *et al.,* 'Facilitating and Rewarding Creativity During New Product Development', *Journal of Marketing,* 75(4), 2011, pp. 53–67. For lighter reading, look at John Peppers and Martha Rogers, 'The Buzz on Customer-Driven Innovation', *Sales & Marketing Management,* June 2007, p. 13.

5 See Rik Kirkland, 'Cisco's Display of Strength', *Fortune,* 12 November 2007, pp. 90–100; Richard Martin, 'Collaboration Cisco Style', *InformationWeek,* 28 January 2008, p. 30; and 'Cisco on Cisco: Web 2.0 in the Enterprise', March 2008, accessed at **www.cisco.com**

6 Based on material from Anna Fifield, 'Samsung Sows for the Future with Its Garden of Delights', *Financial Times,* 4 January 2008, p. 13; and Peter Lewis, 'A Perpetual Crisis Machine', *Fortune,* 19 September 2005, pp. 58–67. Also see 'Camp Samsung', BusinessWeek Online, 3 July 2006, accessed at **www.businessweek.com**

7 Example from **www.ideo.com/work/item/game-suite**, accessed June 2014.

8 Jeff Howe, 'Join the Crowd', *Independent* (London), 2 September 2008, p. 2.

9 Learn about Sugru at **Sugru.com**. For an academic appreciation of consumer co-creation, check out Wayne D. Hoyer *et al.,* 'Consumer Co-creation in New Product Development', *Journal of Service Research,* 13(3), 2010, pp. 283–96.

10 Information accessed online at **www.avon.com**, June 2014. Also see **http://ezinearti-cles.com/?Avons-SSS-Flea-Control---Plus-Many-Other-Uses-to-Go-Green!&id=1819677**, accessed June 2009.

11 Example adapted from information in Kevin O'Donnell, 'Where Do the Best Ideas Come From? The Unlikeliest Sources', *Advertising Age*, 14 July 2008, p. 15; also at **http://mindstorms.lego.com/MeetMDP/default.aspx** and **http://mindstorms.lego.com/community/default.aspx**, accessed May 2014. MINDSTORMS® and LEGO® are registered trademarks of the LEGO Group.

12 Quotes from Robert Gray, 'Not Invented Here', *Marketing*, 6 May 2004, pp. 34–7; and Betsy Morris, 'What Makes Apple Golden?' *Fortune*, 17 March 2008, pp. 68–74.

13 See **www.orexo.com**

14 See 'Power of the Future: Volkswagen Van with Fuel Cell', *Volkswagen Media Room*, accessed at **http://media.vw.com/article_display.cfm?article_id=9441**, May 2011; and Steven Ashley, 'On the Road to Fuel-Cell Cars', *Scientific American*, 1 March 2005, p. 62; 'Test Drive: Volkswagen's Hydrogen Fuel-Cell Concept', **www.popsci.com**, accessed May 2011.

15 Examples adapted from those found in Emily Nelson, 'Focus Groupies: P&G Keeps Cincinnati Busy with All Its Studies – While Her Sons Test Old Spice, Linda Geil Gets Swabbed', *The Wall Street Journal*, 24 January 2002, p. A1; and Carol Matlack, 'The Vuitton Machine', *BusinessWeek*, 22 March 2004, pp. 98–102.

16 Visit Innocent Drinks at **www.innocentdrinks.co.uk**, accessed July 2014.

17 **http://www.just-style.com/news/wool-industry-signs-saks-dillards-in-us-marketing-bid_id94025.aspx**, accessed May 2011.

18 How best to speed up new product development is an area of interest for researchers in marketing. Have a look at Jiyao Chen, Richard R. Reilly and Gary S. Lynn, 'New Product Development Speed: Too Much of a Good Thing?', *Journal of Product Innovation Management*, 29(2), 2012, pp. 288–303; or alternatively, Gerda Gemser and Mark A.A.M. Leenders, 'Managing cross-functional cooperation for new product development success', *Long Range Planning*, 44(1), 2011, pp. 26–41.

19 For a review of research on new-product development, see Ernst Holger, Wayne D. Hoyer and Carsten Rübsaamen, 'Sales, Marketing and R&D Cooperation across New Product Development Stages: Implications for Success', *Journal of Marketing*, September 2010, pp. 80–92; John Nicholas, Ann Ledwith and Helen Perks, 'New Product Development Best Practice in SME and Large Organisations: Theory vs Practice', *European Journal of Innovation Management*, 14(2), pp. 227–51; Z. Ayag, 'An Integrated Approach to Evaluating Conceptual Design Alternatives in a New Product Development Environment', *International Journal of Production Research*, 15 February 2005, pp. 27–37; and Ken Kono, 'Planning Makes Perfect', *Marketing Management*, April 2005, pp. 31–5. For an interesting view of an alternative new-product development process, see Bruce Nussbaum, 'The Power of Design', *BusinessWeek*, 17 May 2004, pp. 86–94.

20 This definition is based on one found in Bryan Lilly and Tammy R. Nelson, 'Fads: Segmenting the Fad-Buyer Market', *Journal of Consumer Marketing*, 20(3), 2003, pp. 252–65.

21 See 'Scooter Fad Fades, as Warehouses Fill and Profits Fall', *The Wall Street Journal*, 14 June 2001, p. B4; Katya Kazakina, 'Toy Story: Yo-Yos Make a Big Splash', *The Wall Street Journal*, 11 April 2003, p. W10; and Robert Johnson, 'A Fad's Father Seeks a Sequel', *New York Times*, 30 May 2004, p. 3.2.

22 See 'The Official List of 2000+ Uses': **http://www.wd40.com/uses-tips/**, accessed February 2014.

CHAPTER 9

PRICING: UNDERSTANDING AND CAPTURING CUSTOMER VALUE

AFTER STUDYING THIS CHAPTER, YOU SHOULD BE ABLE TO

- understand the importance of customer value perceptions and company costs when setting prices
- identify and define the other important internal and external factors affecting a firm's pricing decisions
- describe the major strategies for pricing imitative and new products
- explain how companies find a set of prices that maximises the profits from the total product mix
- discuss how companies adjust their prices to take into account different types of customers and situations
- discuss key issues related to initiating and responding to price changes

THE WAY AHEAD
Previewing the concepts

We continue your marketing journey with a look at a second major marketing mix tool – pricing. Firms successful at creating customer value with the other marketing mix activities must capture this value in the prices they earn. According to one pricing expert, pricing involves 'harvesting your profit potential'.[1] If effective product development, promotion and distribution sow the seeds of business success, effective pricing is the harvest. Yet, despite its importance, many firms do not handle pricing well. In this chapter, we begin with the question, 'What is a price?' Next, we look at customer value perceptions, costs and other factors that marketers must consider when setting prices. Finally, we examine pricing strategies for new-product pricing, product mix pricing, price adjustments and dealing with price changes.

Pricing decisions can make or break a company. For openers, consider Primark, whose low-cost, everyday-low-price strategy years have helped it to become a top high-street fashion retailer. Everything that Primark does is focused on the goal of delivering clothes that people want at prices that other retailers cannot match.

PRIMARK – THE HIGH COST OF LOW PRICES?

Clothing retailer Primark is one of Europe's most spectacular retailing successes. When it opened a flagship store on London's Oxford Street, eager customers queued through the night and blocked the whole street just to be among the first visitors. How did Primark achieve this kind of success? Well, in simple terms, by offering the kind of clothes that young women want to buy at prices that are so low they might be thought to be 'loss leaders' or 'sale prices'. But Primark does not do loss leaders or sale prices, it just does low prices in all of its stores all of the time: 'everyday low pricing' or EDLP in today's jargon. This raised suspicions that Primark's prices are too good to be true. How can Primark offer good products at such low prices? Why can their rivals not match them?

The position of Primark's management is that its clothing is manufactured under exactly the same conditions as the clothing sold by other major high-street chains. The low prices that Primark offers its customers are not achieved through a special 'trick' and the labour conditions at Primark's suppliers are just the same as the conditions at factories supplying other major high-street clothing stores – note that those are both relative, not absolute, statements and we will return to consider them shortly. Meanwhile, the question is, then, if there is no 'special trick', just how does it manage to deliver the products that customers want at prices that are so strikingly low?

Primark Stores Ltd is a subsidiary of Associated British Foods, a diversified international food, ingredients and retail group with global sales of £10.2bn and 97,000 employees in 44 countries. The company employs in excess of 27,000 people. In the UK, in terms of market share, Primark is ranked as the fourth-largest clothing retailer and was named both Fashion Retail Business of the Year (over £125m turnover) and International Fashion Retailer of the Year by Drapers in 2013, as well as picking up 'Best Affordable Fashion' Award at the ITV Lorraine High Street Fashion Awards in the same year.

Recently Primark has been expanding rapidly with new stores opening in France, Spain, the Netherlands, Portugal, Germany, Belgium and the Canary Islands so that, as of early 2014, Primark had a total of 260 stores trading.

Primark explains its success in terms of:

- super-competitive prices (the result of technology, efficient distribution, supply and volume buying); and
- mainstream market product quality (high-street locations, superior store interiors, clear focus on the target market).

Source: Getty Images/Peter Macdiarmid.

Primark targets young, fashion-conscious under 35s, offering them high-quality fashion basics at value-for-money prices. Almost half of sales are in womenswear. A quarter of sales are in menswear and childrenswear, with other items constituting the remaining sales. Buying and merchandising teams in Reading (UK) and Dublin (Ireland) travel internationally to source and buy up-to-the-minute fashion basics that best reflect each season's key fashion trends. Primark's offer to the customer is one of high-quality merchandise, at value for money, backed by Primark's service promise. Primark prides itself on its loyal customer base. According to the company:

A strong consumer proposition has been developed for the Primark brand and embodied in the line 'Look Good, Pay Less' which communicates Primark's value-based offering in a precise manner, to its core target audience. The purpose of the advertising in the first instance is to support this strong

value proposition and secondly to tailor the media solution to the store. Communication models are created and the imagery of the advertising is young, modern and dynamic to reflect the core target audience. A combination of media is used to create, impact upon and tightly target new customers.

This all leaves the main question unanswered. It is not hard to see that offering customers desirable products in convenient high-street locations and at rock-bottom prices is a recipe for success. Everything about Primark is designed to deliver low costs and low prices. The entire business proposition is built around delivering value to customers. There is a constant emphasis on keeping overhead and operating costs low. Profit margins are lower than the industry average. Primark only invests in advertising that it knows will make a difference, and avoids high-profile, expensive image-building advertising; the management team believe that their customers know what the company stands for and that positive word-of-mouth advertising from satisfied customers is the best kind of promotion. Above all, Primark keeps its product designs simple, concentrates on the most popular sizes, and then buys products in large quantities so benefiting from economies of scale.

Now let us return to those two statements about the working conditions of those employed on behalf of Primark and other high-street fashion retailers. Primark published a code of conduct in respect of terms and conditions of these workers which until 2013 read as follows:

- Employment is freely chosen.
- Freedom of association and the right to collective bargaining are respected.
- Working conditions are safe and hygienic.
- Child labour shall not be used.
- Living wages are paid.
- Working hours are not excessive.
- No discrimination is practised.
- Regular employment is provided.
- No harsh or inhumane treatment is allowed.
- No bribery or corruption will be tolerated.

In April 2013, though, the world was shocked to hear of the Rana Plaza disaster, in which a large building in Dhaka, Bangladesh, collapsed. The building contained a number of factories producing garments under contract for Western retailers. Other than Primark, clothes were being made for familiar European high-street names such as Benetton, Mango and El Corte Ingles. In total 1,132

people died, almost exclusively young women and children. A further 2,500 were injured. The reality of employment in these factories was brought into the light. Unsafe buildings, 19-hour shifts, no right to unionise, locked fire escapes, pitiful salaries – 10 pence per hour – being just a few of the issues that emerged in the aftermath.

Paul Lister, Head of Corporate Governance at Primark's parent company, Associated British Foods, said in an interview with the BBC: 'We looked on in horror. We knew our clothes were in the building, and we accepted responsibility.'

The events in April caused a lot of soul searching within Primark, or at least public image management. Shortly after the disaster, Primark contributed $2m to help fund support efforts for the injured and bereaved and a press release outlined additional efforts.

Our key activities have included:

–Setting up helpdesks near the factory site which allowed us to identify victims and assess their immediate needs.

–Emergency food aid distribution to over 1265 households for five weeks, in partnership with a NGO.

–Paying short-term financial assistance to 3639 workers and their families, equivalent to six months' salary.

–On October 24th 2013, we committed to provide a third round of financial support, equivalent to a further three months salary, for the workers of the factory that made our garments. At the same time, we called on other brands involved in the Rana Plaza disaster to make a contribution by paying short-term aid to the workers (or their dependents) who made clothes for their own labels. We pledged that if these brands did not come forward to offer support, we would regardless offer this third round of support again to all the workers of Rana Plaza.

–Providing support for workers who remain in hospital or are receiving medical treatment, working with the United Federation of Garment Workers, a trade union body. The support provided medicines and medical check-ups for patients, and food and accommodation for patients and their relatives.

–Developing a programme to provide appropriate long-term compensation and support services for the workers and families who were working in the factory that produced garments for Primark. This long-term compensation scheme has been devised by the company with assistance from external experts, and involves medical and vulnerability assessments. These assessments will be carried out

with the support of Dhaka University – Department of Vulnerability Studies and Disaster Management, Dhaka University medical faculty, independent doctors, along with the unions and our NGO implementation partners. The company's scheme has been tabled with the ILO. Other retail brands are considering whether to adopt this scheme as an industry-wide framework for delivering compensation.

–Carrying out building surveys in Bangladesh to assess the structural integrity of factories from which we source garments. We are on track to complete all surveys by the end of 2014.

–Becoming a signatory to the Accord on Fire and Building Safety in Bangladesh. The Accord is a pioneering contract between almost 100 apparel brands and retailers, international and local trade unions and NGOs to ensure sustainable improvements to working conditions in the Bangladesh Garment Industry.

Is that a progressive organisation taking responsibility for its impact on people and society or cynical damage control? Was it sufficient or too little, too late? That is debatable. Certainly it was more than some companies equally implicated were prepared to do, such as Wal-Mart. One final point for you to consider – next time you are shopping for a new outfit, perhaps take a moment to consider the high cost of cheap clothing.

Sources: www.primark.co.uk; www.primark-bangladesh.com; www.bbc.co.uk; Guardian, 'Fashion Chains Sign Accord to Help Finance Safety in Bangladesh Factories', 13 May 2013.

As the Primark case study shows, companies today face a fierce and fast-changing pricing environment. Increasing customer price consciousness has put many companies in a 'pricing vice'. In the USA they call this the 'Wal-Mart phenomenon', reflecting the aggressive pricing policies adopted by the world's largest retailer. So far Wal-Mart has established only a fairly small presence in Europe, with the acquisition of Asda in the UK. However, Wal-Mart is increasing its global presence and now operates more than 11,000 stores in 26 markets outside the continental USA that bring in $466bn per year, roughly in line with the GDP of each of Argentina, Poland and Belgium.[2] The sort of retail power that Wal-Mart exerts in the USA is making its presence felt across the globe. In response, it seems that almost every company is looking for ways to slash prices, and that is hurting their profits.

Yet, cutting prices is often not the best answer. Reducing prices unnecessarily can lead to lost profits and damaging price wars. It can signal to customers that the price is more important than the customer value a brand delivers. Instead, companies should sell value, not price. They should persuade customers that paying a higher price for the company's brand is justified by the greater value they gain. The challenge is to find the price that will let the company make a fair profit by harvesting the customer value it creates. For example, the IKEA business vision is to create a better everyday life for as many people as possible, and it aims to do this 'by offering a wide range of well-designed, functional home furnishing products at prices so low that as many people as possible will be able to afford them'.[3] IKEA aims to make a profit itself by offering customers real value.

WHAT IS A PRICE?

In the narrowest sense, **price** is the amount of money charged for a product or service. More broadly, price is the sum of all the values that customers give up in order to gain the benefits of having or using a product or service. Historically, price has been the major factor affecting buyer choice. In recent decades, non-price factors have gained increasing importance. However, price still remains one of the most important elements affecting a firm's market share and profitability.

Price is the only element in the marketing mix that produces revenue; all other elements represent costs. Price is also one of the most flexible elements of the marketing mix. Unlike product features and channel commitments, prices can be changed quickly. At the same time, pricing is the number 1 problem facing many marketing executives, and many companies do not handle pricing well. One frequent problem is that companies are too quick to reduce prices in order to get a sale rather than convincing buyers that their product's greater value is worth a higher price. Other common mistakes include pricing that is too cost oriented rather than customer value oriented, and pricing that does not take the rest of the marketing mix into account.

Some managers view pricing as a big headache, preferring instead to focus on the other marketing mix elements. However, smart managers treat pricing as a key strategic tool for creating and capturing customer value. Prices have a direct impact on a firm's bottom line. According to one expert, on average a 5 per cent increase in price increases profits by 22 per cent.[4] More importantly, as a part of a company's overall value proposition, price plays a key role in creating customer value and building customer relationships.

FACTORS TO CONSIDER WHEN SETTING PRICES

The price the company charges will fall somewhere between one that is too high to produce any demand and one that is too low to produce a profit. Figure 9.1 summarises the major considerations in setting price. Customer perceptions of the product's value set the ceiling for prices. If customers perceive that the price is greater than the product's value, they will not buy the product. Product costs set the floor for prices. If the company prices the product below its costs, company profits will suffer. In setting its price between these two extremes, the company must consider a number of factors, including its overall marketing strategy and mix, the nature of the market and demand, competitors' strategies and prices, and a number of other internal and external factors.

Customer perceptions of value

In the end, the customer will decide whether a product's price is right. Pricing decisions, like other marketing mix decisions, must start with customer value. When customers buy a product, they exchange something of value (the price) in order to get something of value (the benefits of having or using the product). Effective, customer-oriented pricing involves understanding how much value consumers place on the benefits they receive from the product and setting a price that captures this value.

Value-based pricing

Good pricing begins with a complete understanding of the value that a product or service creates for customers. **Value-based pricing** uses buyers' perceptions of value, not the seller's cost, as the key to pricing. Value-based pricing means that the marketer cannot design a product and marketing programme and then set the price. Price is considered along with the other marketing mix variables *before* the marketing programme is set.

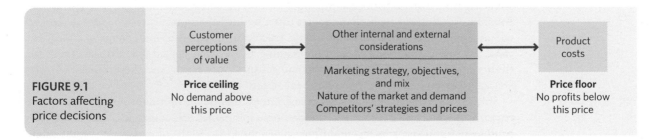

FIGURE 9.1
Factors affecting price decisions

Customer perceptions of value ←→ Other internal and external considerations ←→ Product costs

Marketing strategy, objectives, and mix
Nature of the market and demand
Competitors' strategies and prices

Price ceiling
No demand above this price

Price floor
No profits below this price

FIGURE 9.2
Value-based pricing
versus cost-based
pricing

Source: Nagle, Thomas;
Holden, Reed, *The Strategy
and Tactics of Pricing: A Guide
to Profitable Decision Making*,
3rd, © 2002. Printed and
Electronically reproduced
by permission of Pearson
Education, Inc., Upper Saddle
River, New Jersey.

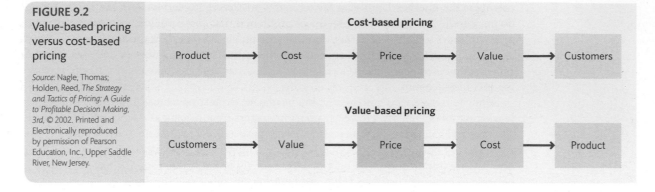

Figure 9.2 compares value-based pricing with cost-based pricing. Cost-based pricing is product driven. The company designs what it considers to be a good product, adds up the costs of making the product, and sets a price that covers costs plus a target profit. Marketing must then convince buyers that the product's value at that price justifies its purchase. If the price turns out to be too high, the company must settle for lower mark-ups or lower sales, both resulting in disappointing profits.

Value-based pricing reverses this process. The company sets its target price based on customer perceptions of the product value. The targeted value and price then drive decisions about product design and what costs can be incurred. As a result, pricing begins with analysing consumer needs and value perceptions, and price is set to match consumers' perceived value.

It is important to remember that 'good value' is not always the same as 'low price'. For example, the German luxury goods manufacturer Montblanc, part of the Swiss firm Compagnie Financière Richemont SA, sells exclusive pens for hundreds of euros – a less expensive pen might write just as well, but some consumers place great value on the intangibles they receive from a 'fine writing instrument'. Similarly, a Steinway piano – any Steinway piano – costs a lot. But to those who own one, a Steinway is a great value:

> A Steinway grand piano typically runs anywhere from €40,000 to €165,000. The most popular model sells for around €72,000. But ask anyone who owns one and they'll tell you that, when it comes to Steinway, price is nothing, the Steinway experience is everything. Steinway makes very high quality pianos – handcrafting each Steinway requires up to one full year. But more important, owners get the Steinway mystique. The Steinway name evokes images of classical concert stages and the celebrities and performers who've owned and played Steinway pianos across more than 155 years.
>
> But Steinways aren't just for world-class pianists and the wealthy. Ninety-nine per cent of all Steinway buyers are amateurs who perform only in their homes. To such customers, whatever a Steinway costs, it's a small price to pay for the value of owning one. As one Steinway owner puts it, 'My friendship with the Steinway piano is one of the most important and beautiful things in my life'. Who can put a price on such feelings?[5]

A company using value-based pricing must find out what value buyers assign to different competitive offers. However, companies often find it hard to measure the value customers will attach to their products. For example, calculating the cost of ingredients in a meal at a good restaurant is relatively easy. But assigning a value to other satisfactions such as taste, environment, relaxation, conversation and status is very hard. And these values will vary for both different consumers and different situations.

Still, consumers will use these perceived values to evaluate a product's price, so the company must work to measure them. Sometimes, companies ask consumers how much they would pay for a basic product and for each benefit added to the offer. Or a company might conduct experiments to test the perceived value of different product offers. According to an old Russian proverb, there are two fools in every market – one who asks too much and one who asks too little. If the seller charges more than the buyers' perceived value, the company's sales will suffer. If the seller charges much less than buyers' perceived value, its products sell very well, but they produce less revenue than they would if they were priced at the level of perceived value.

We now examine two types of value-based pricing: *good value pricing* and *value-added pricing*.

Good value pricing

During the past decade, marketers have noted a fundamental shift in consumer attitudes towards price and quality. Many companies have changed their pricing approaches to bring them into line with changing economic conditions and consumer price perceptions. More and more, marketers have adopted **good value pricing** strategies – offering just the right combination of quality and good service at a fair price.

In many cases, this has involved introducing less expensive versions of established, brand name products. For example, Armani offers the less expensive, more casual Armani Exchange fashion line. In other cases, good value pricing has involved redesigning existing brands to offer more quality for a given price or the same quality for less.

An important type of good value pricing at the retail level is *everyday low pricing (EDLP)*. EDLP involves charging a constant, everyday low price with few or no temporary price discounts. In contrast, *high–low pricing* involves charging higher prices on an everyday basis but running frequent promotions to lower prices temporarily on selected items. Think of any recent TV adverts you've seen for sofas – most likely heavy discounts were flagged to get attention. In recent years, high–low pricing has given way to EDLP in retail settings, ranging from Peugeot car dealerships to Carrefour or Tesco supermarkets, to upmarket department stores such as John Lewis.

Value-added pricing

In many business-to-business marketing situations, the challenge is to build the company's *pricing power* – its power to escape price competition and to justify higher prices and margins without losing market share. To do this, many companies adopt **value-added pricing** strategies. Rather than cutting prices to match competitors, they attach value-added features and services to differentiate their offers and thus support higher prices.

When a company finds its major competitors offering a similar product at a lower price, the natural tendency is to try to match or beat that price. Although the idea of undercutting a competitor's prices and watching customers flock in is tempting, there are dangers. Price cutting can lead to price wars that erode the profit margins of all competitors in an industry. Or worse, discounting a product can cheapen it in the minds of customers. This greatly reduces the seller's power to maintain profitable prices in the long term.

So, how can a company keep its pricing power when a competitor undercuts its price? Often, the best strategy is not to price below the competitor, but rather to price above and convince customers that the product is worth it. The company should ask, 'What is the value of the product to the customer?', then stand up for what the product is worth. In this way, the company shifts the focus from price to value. 'Even in today's economic environment, it's not about price,' says a pricing expert. 'It's about keeping customers loyal by providing service they can't find anywhere else.'[6] A past master at value-added marketing is the German kitchen fixtures and fittings specialist Miele:

> The motto at Miele is *'Immer Besser'* which translated means 'Forever Better'. This motto was conceived over 100 years ago by the founders and remains our company motto today, permeating through every aspect of our business. We pride ourselves on having the best products with unsurpassed quality and below are the elements that really set out the Miele difference.

Quality and reliability:

- All products are designed for 20 years' use.
- Products are subjected to rigorous endurance testing during development.
- Every product we produce goes through an end line test before passing quality control.
- Many products are then randomly checked against further quality criteria.
- Strict quality control for us means peace of mind for you.

Performance:

- Miele is consistently independently tested in many product categories and consistently comes out on top.
- Whether its washing dishes, clothes or cooking a meal, Miele products deliver optimal results no matter how big or small the task.
- What's more, optimal results are married with gentle performance, which is vital for good fabric care and glassware for example.[7]

So, that is what Miele itself has to say, but what independent evidence is there that it delivers enhanced value to customers, and that customers are prepared to pay for it? Well, the UK independent consumer testing organisation Which? made Miele its 'best domestic appliance brand' for the fifth time in 2013. In fact, virtually every Miele product tested by Which? wins the coveted title of a Which? 'Best Buy'. It is the quality of the build and the reliability and performance of its products that enable Miele to charge premium prices. For example, you can buy many brands of washing machine, such as Beko, Hoover or Servis, for around €200. But if you want a Miele, you will have to pay considerably more; even if you shop around, you are unlikely to find one priced below €500. Miele delivers better value to the customer, and customers are prepared to pay for it.[8]

Company and product costs

Whereas customer value perceptions set the price ceiling, costs set the floor for the price that the company can charge. The company wants to charge a price that both covers all its costs for producing, distributing and selling the product, and delivers a fair rate of return for its effort and risk. A company's costs may be an important element in its pricing strategy. Many companies, such as Ryanair and Aldi, work to become the 'low-cost producers' in their industries. Companies with lower costs can set lower prices that result in greater sales and profits.

The emphasis at Miele is on delivering products with excellent quality and reliability that justify a price premium over other brands. Independent customer test organisations consistently give Miele products the highest ratings

Source: Miele.

Types of costs

A company's costs take two forms, fixed and variable. **Fixed costs** (also known as overheads) are costs that do not vary with production or sales level. For example, a company must pay each month's bills for rent, heating, interest and managerial salaries, whatever the company's output. **Variable costs** vary directly with the level of production. Each PC produced by Dell involves a cost of microprocessors, wires, plastic, packaging and other inputs. These costs tend to be the same for each unit of the same model produced. They are called variable because their total varies with the number of units produced – the more computers produced, the higher the variable costs. **Total costs** are the sum of the fixed and variable costs for any given level of production. Management wants to charge a price that will at least cover the total production costs at a given level of production.

The company must watch its costs carefully. If it costs the company more than competitors to produce and sell its product, the company will have to charge a higher price or make less profit, putting it at a competitive disadvantage.

Cost-based pricing

The simplest pricing method is **cost-plus pricing** – adding a standard mark-up to the cost of the product. For example, an electrical retailer might pay a manufacturer €20 for a toaster and mark it up to sell at €30, a 50 per cent mark-up on cost. The retailer's gross margin is €10. If the store's operating costs amount to €8 per toaster sold, the retailer's profit margin will be €2.

The manufacturer that made the toaster probably used cost-plus pricing. If the manufacturer's standard cost of producing the toaster was €16, it might have added a 25 per cent mark-up, setting the price to the retailers at €20. Similarly, construction companies submit job bids by estimating the total project cost and adding a standard mark-up for profit. Lawyers, accountants, architects and other professionals typically price by adding a standard mark-up to their costs. Some sellers tell their customers they will charge cost plus a specified mark-up; for example, aerospace companies price this way to the government.

Using standard mark-ups to set prices is generally not a good idea. Any pricing method that ignores customer value and competitor prices is not likely to lead to the best price. Still, mark-up pricing remains popular for many reasons. First, sellers are more certain about costs than about customer value perceptions and demand. By tying the price to cost, sellers simplify pricing – they do not have to make frequent adjustments as demand changes. Second, when all firms in the industry use this pricing method, prices tend to be similar and price competition is thus minimised. Third, many people feel that cost-plus pricing is fairer to both buyers and sellers. Sellers earn a fair return on their investment but do not take advantage of buyers by raising prices when buyers' demand is very high.

Another cost-oriented pricing approach is **break-even pricing**, or a variation called **target profit pricing**. The firm tries to determine the price at which it will break even or make the target profit it is seeking. Target pricing uses the concept of a *break-even chart*, which shows the total cost and total revenue expected at different sales volume levels. Figure 9.3 shows a break-even chart for the toaster manufacturer discussed here. Fixed costs are €6m regardless of sales volume, and variable costs are €5 per unit. Variable costs are added to fixed costs to form total costs, which rise with volume. The slope of the total revenue curve reflects the price. Here, the price is €15 (e.g. the company's revenue is €12m on 800,000 units, or €15 per unit).

At the €15 price, the company must sell at least 600,000 units to *break even* (break-even volume = fixed costs ÷ (price − variable costs) = €6,000,000 ÷ (€15 − €5) = 600,000). That is, at this level, total revenues will equal total costs of €9m. If the company wants a target profit of €2m, it must sell at least 800,000 units to obtain the €12m of total revenue needed to cover the costs of €10m plus the €2m of target profits. In contrast, if the company charges a higher price, say €20, it will not need to sell as many units to break even or to achieve its target profit. In fact, the higher the price, the lower the company's break-even point.

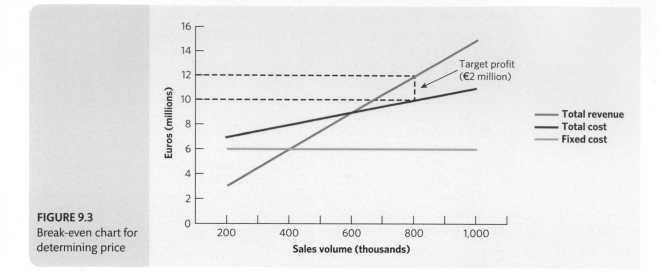

FIGURE 9.3
Break-even chart for
determining price

The major problem with this analysis, however, is that it fails to consider customer value and the relationship between price and demand. As the *price* increases, *demand* decreases, and the market may not buy even the lower volume needed to break even at the higher price. For example, suppose the company calculates that, given its current fixed and variable costs, it must charge a price of €30 for the product in order to earn its desired target profit. But marketing research shows that few consumers will pay more than €25. In this case, the company will have to reduce its costs in order to lower the break-even point so that it can charge the lower price consumers expect.

Thus, although break-even analysis and target profit pricing can help the company to determine minimum prices needed to cover expected costs and profits, they do not take the price–demand relationship into account. When using this method, the company must also consider the impact of price on sales volume needed to realise target profits and the likelihood that the needed volume will be achieved at each possible price.

Other internal and external considerations affecting price decisions

Customer perceptions of value set the upper limit for prices, and costs set the lower limit. However, in setting prices within these limits, the company must consider a number of other internal and external factors. Internal factors affecting pricing include the company's overall marketing strategy, objectives and marketing mix, as well as other organisational considerations. External factors include the nature of the market and demand, competitors' strategies and prices, and other environmental factors.

Overall marketing strategy, objectives and mix

Price is only one element of the company's broader marketing strategy. Thus, before setting price, the company must decide on its overall marketing strategy for the product or service. If the company has selected its target market and positioning carefully, then its marketing mix strategy, including price, will be fairly straightforward. For example, when Toyota developed its Lexus brands to compete with German luxury performance cars in the higher income segment, this required charging a high price. In contrast, when it introduced its Aygo model, a small car with excellent fuel economy and low running costs aimed at budget-conscious car buyers, this positioning required charging a low price. Thus, pricing strategy is heavily influenced by decisions on market positioning.

General pricing objectives might include survival, current profit maximisation, market-share leadership, or customer retention and relationship building. At a more specific level, a company can set prices to attract new customers or to retain profitably existing ones. It can set prices low to prevent competition from entering the market or set prices at competitors' levels to stabilise the market. It can price to keep the loyalty and support of resellers or to avoid government intervention. Prices can be reduced temporarily to create excitement for a brand. Or one product may be priced to help the sales of other products in the company's line. Thus, pricing may play an important role in helping to accomplish the company's objectives at many levels.

Price is only one of the marketing mix tools that a company uses to achieve its marketing objectives. Price decisions must be coordinated with product design, distribution and promotion decisions to form a consistent and effective marketing programme. Decisions made for other marketing mix variables may affect pricing decisions. For example, a decision to position the product on high-performance quality will mean that the seller must charge a higher price to cover higher costs. And producers whose resellers are expected to support and promote their products may have to build larger reseller margins into their prices.

Companies often position their products on price and then tailor other marketing mix decisions to the prices they want to charge. Here, price is a crucial product-positioning factor that defines the product's market, competition and design. Many firms support such price-positioning strategies with a technique called **target costing**, a potent strategic weapon. Target costing reverses the usual process of first designing a new product, determining its cost and then asking, 'Can we sell it for that?' Instead, it starts with an ideal selling price based on customer value considerations, and then targets costs that will ensure that the price is met.

Other companies de-emphasise price and use other marketing mix tools to create *non-price* positions. Often, the best strategy is not to charge the lowest price, but rather to differentiate the marketing offer to make it worth a higher price. For example, Sony builds more value into its consumer electronics products and charges a higher price than many competitors. Customers recognise Sony's higher quality and are willing to pay more to get it. Some marketers even *feature* high prices as part of their positioning (see Marketing at Work 9.1). For example, Belgian beer brand Stella Artois has long been advertised as 'reassuringly expensive', with the 'expensive' image of the brand designed to convey both quality and European sophistication to the customer.

Rolex: much more than just a watch

MARKETING AT WORK 9.1

Recently *Media* magazine reported on the market for luxury watches in China. The prospects are good: 'Having a Swiss-made watch clasped around one's wrist is a talisman of attainment for Chinese men. A watch is a must,' says Sandy Chen, Research Director, TNS China. 'When buying up, they start with a luxury watch, next comes the luxury car, and last is the luxury apartment. Men compare and discuss watches, and they need a watch of a certain quality to be part of the social circle.' The most aspirational brand in this very aspirational market? Rolex. Apparently, if you want to demonstrate your success in the world's second-largest (and soon to be largest) economy, then nothing beats a Rolex watch. This is good news for luxury goods manufacturers in general, and for Rolex SA in particular, at a time when the European market for luxury goods looks like stagnating in the face of poor prospects for long-term growth. The fast-growing Asian economies are showing a craving for the very best brands that Europe can offer.

One branding expert claims that, 'If there were a fight to be the perfect brand, Rolex could be the heavyweight titleholder.' After all, the simple function of telling the time can be served extremely well by more or less any watch costing more than a few euros these days. More complex functions can be delivered by, say, a watch from one of those solid and dependable brands, Timex or Casio. For around €50 you can more or less carry a multi-function computer on your wrist that will tell you the time in several time zones, light up at night, and capture multiple lap times on your jog round the park. Agreed, there are some people who will not find these utilitarian products all that attractive, but for the style conscious there are

Owning a Rolex signals membership of an exclusive group

Source: Alamy Images/carlo draisci.

the ubiquitous and stylish Swatch products, which, again for a very reasonable price, you can own in psychedelic colours, fluorescent shades, or adorned with your favourite cartoon character. For no more than €200 you can, if you desire, own several watches to meet more or less every purpose – sport, leisure, evening wear, work, travel, swimming . . . you name it. Clearly, a Rolex is delivering something very special to its owner, something that has nothing to do with accurate time-keeping or even aesthetic appeal (which is not to deny that a Rolex is generally very easy on the eye).

An economist would tell you that the unique charm of a Rolex is that it is a 'position good'. That is to say, its most important purpose is not utilitarian but to assert the social position of the wearer. Human beings are social animals with a strong sense of hierarchy, and one of the psychological forces driving them to work harder and to achieve more is the desire to attain social status. What better way to assert social status, and to demonstrate material success, than by carrying round on one's wrist a product costing €10,000 whose essential functions are undifferentiable from those of a product costing €50?

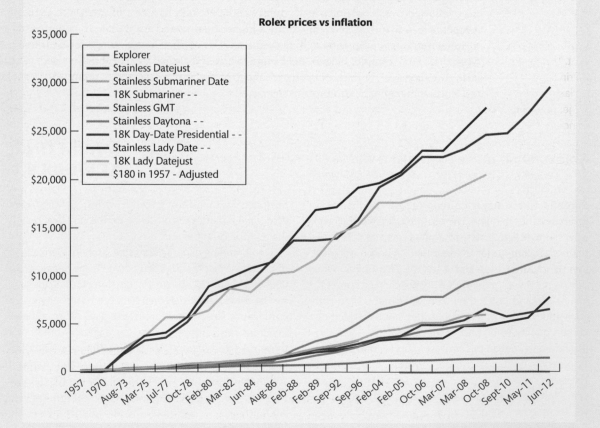

That is €50 to be able to tell what time it is, and €9,950 to show that the owner belongs to a highly exclusive social category. A marketer might explain this using Maslow's hierarchy of needs (see Chapter 5). We can reasonably suppose that the basic, physiological needs of a Rolex owner have been met. Owning a Rolex, however, clearly contributes to the satisfaction of esteem needs, and simultaneously to the social need to be seen to belong to a valued peer group.

How have Rolex processes changed over time? If you refer to the chart, you'll observe that it shows prices for some of the company's key watch models against time. The classic Rolex Submariner – which adorned the wrist of James Bond – retailed for just $180 in 1957. For the last year for which we have hard numbers (2012) we see it was listed at about $8,000. That is an increase of 45 times the original price! How and why has this occurred? There are several reasons, the most important of which are inflation, exchange rates and branding. Let's take the last first. About 60 years ago, a Rolex watch was quite a utilitarian tool for professionals in specific contexts. Divers used the Submariners (and don't forget – it is Commander James Bond of the Royal Navy), pilots used the GMT model to help with multiple time zones. The brand has evolved over time into the epitome of luxury it is today. Inflation erodes the value of currency. The average inflation rate for the US dollar between 1957 and 2014 was 3.8 per cent. This means that the same $180 it cost to buy a Submariner in 1957 would be equivalent to $1,471 in 2014 dollars. Currencies depreciate at different rates as each is subject to political and national bank policy, but the Swiss franc has long been regarded as a safe haven for cash investors, meaning that the exchange rate between Swiss francs and US dollars has shifted quite considerably and so Rolex has had to adjust prices to account for both inflation and exchange rates. This is the reason for the uneven spread of the price lists – in periods of low volatility, prices can remain the same. In periods of high volatility – such as the financial crisis of 2008 – prices need to be changed more often to keep up. These issues affect every company that trades internationally.

Irrespective of the impact of inflation and investors, let's make no mistake about it – a Rolex is a fabulous example of the Swiss watchmaker's art. The original company was founded by Hans Wilsdorf in 1905, with the trademark Rolex registered in 1908. Rolex has to its credit several important advances in watch technology: the first waterproof watch (publicised in a swim across the English Channel in 1927); the first date-adjusting watch; and the original diver's watch – the Rolex Sea-Dweller, released in 1967, was certified down to depths of 1,220 metres. Rolex watches were used by members of the expedition on the first successful ascent of Mount Everest in 1953.

Naturally, Rolex is very careful about the kind of people and events with which it associates its brand. Not just any sporting or cultural event, nor just any sportsman or woman, meet the demanding Rolex standards. In tennis, think Wimbledon Championships and all-time great Roger Federer, while in the arts think the Teatro alla Scalla in Milan and superstar ballerina Sylvie Guillem. Rolex associates its brand with the most successful people and the most successful events in the cultural and sporting worlds, and carefully selects the type of sporting and cultural event to reflect the preferences, and above all the aspirations, of the highly motivated, driven and successful people who are in the target market. Above all, the message is exclusivity. The Rolex brand is associated with exceptional people and events; it epitomises European, and particularly Swiss, tradition, precision and excellence. For the expenditure of a mere few thousand euros you can buy yourself a small piece of this exclusivity, and you can establish yourself as a member of this most sought-after club. Now, when you think of it that way, it's not really an expensive watch at all, is it?

Sources: Glen Smith, 'Luxury Watches Find Booming Market in China', *Media*, 10 September 2009; David Taylor, 'Rolex Watches: A Timeless Example of Building a Brand Champion', *Central Penn Business Journal*, 3 December 2010, available from www.centralpennbusiness.com, accessed 15 April 2011; John E. Brozek, 'Everest: A Pinnacle of Achievement for Rolex', *International Watch*, April 2004; Company Profile: Compagnie Financière Richemont AG, Datamonitor, 2010. Further information obtained from: www.rolex.com; www.sylvieguillem.com; and www.rogerfederer.com; accessed 15 April 2011. Rolex price lists obtained from the spreadsheet published at www.minus4plus6.com/PriceEvolution.htm, accessed January 2014.

Thus, marketers must consider the total marketing strategy and mix when setting prices. If the product is positioned on non-price factors, then decisions about quality, promotion and distribution will strongly affect price. If price is a crucial positioning factor, then price will strongly affect decisions made about the other marketing mix elements. But even when featuring price, marketers need to remember that customers rarely buy on price alone. Instead, they seek products that give them the best value in terms of benefits received for the price paid.

Organisational considerations

Management must decide who within the organisation should set prices. Companies handle pricing in a variety of ways. In small companies, prices are often set by top management rather than by the marketing or sales departments. In large companies, pricing is typically handled by divisional or product line managers. In industrial markets, salespeople may be allowed to negotiate with customers within certain price ranges. Even so, senior management sets the pricing objectives and policies, and it often approves the prices proposed by lower-level management or salespeople.

In industries in which pricing is a key factor (airlines, aerospace, steel, railways, oil companies), companies often have pricing departments to set the best prices or to help others in setting them. These departments report to the marketing department or top management. Others who have an influence on pricing include sales managers, production managers, finance managers and accountants.

The market and demand

As noted earlier, good pricing starts with an understanding of how customers' perceptions of value affect the prices they are willing to pay. Both consumer and industrial buyers balance the price of a product or service against the benefits of owning it. Thus, before setting prices, the marketer must understand the relationship between price and demand for its product. In this section, we take a deeper look at the price–demand relationship and how it varies for different types of markets. We then discuss methods for analysing the price–demand relationship.

Pricing in different types of markets

The seller's pricing freedom varies with different types of markets. Economists recognise four types of markets, each presenting a different pricing challenge.

Under *pure competition* (also known as *perfect competition*), the market consists of many buyers and sellers trading in a uniform commodity such as wheat, copper or financial securities. No single buyer or seller has much effect on the going market price. A seller cannot charge more than the going price, because buyers can obtain as much as they need at that price. Nor would sellers charge less than the market price, because they can sell all they want at this price. If price and profits rise, new sellers can easily enter the market. In a purely competitive market, marketing research, product development, pricing, advertising and sales promotion play little or no role. Sellers in these markets do not spend much time on marketing strategy.

Under *monopolistic competition,* the market consists of many buyers and sellers who trade over a range of prices rather than a single market price. A range of prices occurs because sellers can differentiate their offers to buyers. Either the physical product can be varied in quality, features or style, or the accompanying services can be varied. Buyers see differences in sellers' products and will pay different prices for them. Sellers try to develop differentiated offers for different customer segments and, in addition to price, freely use branding, advertising and personal selling to set their offers apart. Thus, Dulux paint is differentiated through strong branding and advertising, reducing the impact of price. Because there are many competitors in such markets, each firm is less affected by competitors' pricing strategies than in oligopolistic markets. You probably know about the concept of monopoly, but how about *monopsony?* That is the mirror image of a monopoly – many sellers, but just one buyer. Examples of monopsony would include most armaments, where companies can get into deep trouble by selling to parties other than the state!

Under *oligopolistic competition,* the market consists of a few sellers who are highly sensitive to each other's pricing and marketing strategies. The product can be uniform (steel, aluminium) or non-uniform (cars, computers). There are few sellers because it is difficult for new sellers to enter the market. Each seller is alert to competitors' strategies. If a steel company slashes its price by 10 per cent, buyers will quickly switch to this supplier. The other steelmakers must respond by lowering their prices or increasing their services.

In a *pure monopoly*, the market consists of one seller. The seller may be a government monopoly, a private regulated monopoly or simply a private company that has a monopoly because it has introduced a unique, new product. In many European countries telecommunications services were, until recently, run by government monopolies, but in recent years it has become normal to allow competition (take a look back at the case study with which we opened Chapter 2). Utility services, such as water and gas, are often run by private companies (such as the French firm SUEZ Environnement – formerly Suez Lyonnaise des Eaux) but regulated by the government. W.L. Gore is a good example of a company that obtained a monopoly through the introduction of a unique product, namely the Gore-Tex waterproof and breathable membrane used extensively in both consumer and industrial products. In a regulated monopoly, the government appoints a regulator whose job it is to see that the monopolist charges reasonable prices, offering good value to the customer and fair returns to shareholders. Non-regulated monopolies are free to price at what the market will bear. However, they do not always charge the full price for a number of reasons: a desire not to attract competition, a desire to penetrate the market faster with a low price, or a fear of government regulation.

Analysing the price–demand relationship

Each price the company might charge will lead to a different level of demand. The relationship between the price charged and the resulting demand level is shown in the **demand curve** in Figure 9.4. The demand curve shows the number of units the market will buy in a given time period at different prices that might be charged. In the normal case, demand and price are inversely related; that is, the higher the price, the lower the demand. Thus, the company would sell less if it raised its price from P_1 to P_2. In short, consumers with limited budgets probably will buy less of something if its price is too high.

In the case of prestige goods, the demand curve sometimes slopes upwards. This is because consumers believe that higher prices mean higher quality, and because higher prices can deliver product exclusivity – for example, think about the beautiful Rolex watches we explored in Marketing at Work 9.1. The market position only works because the watches are so expensive. Or think about buying an exclusive product that you don't buy very often, let's say champagne. Would you really want to buy champagne (i.e. real champagne, from the region of France around Reims and Epernay) for €7 a bottle? Most of us think that the more you pay for champagne, the better it is.

Many companies try to measure their demand curves by estimating demand at different prices. The type of market makes a difference. In a monopoly, the demand curve shows the total market demand resulting from different prices. If the company faces competition, its demand at different prices will depend on whether competitors' prices stay constant or change with the company's own prices. For example, in a town with several competing petrol stations, if one petrol retailer raises its price when the others do not, then one would expect demand for its petrol to decline sharply because customers will buy from the lower-priced competitors.

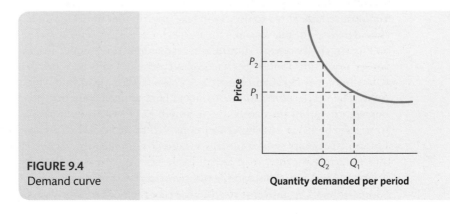

FIGURE 9.4
Demand curve

Price elasticity of demand

Marketers also need to be aware of **price elasticity** – how responsive demand will be to a change in price. If demand hardly changes with a small change in price, we say demand is *inelastic*. If demand changes greatly, we say the demand is *elastic*.

If demand is elastic rather than inelastic, sellers will consider lowering their prices because a lower price will produce more total revenue. This practice makes sense as long as the extra costs of producing and selling more do not exceed the extra revenue. At the same time, most firms want to avoid pricing that turns their products into commodities. In recent years, forces such as deregulation and the instant price comparisons afforded by the Internet and other technologies have increased consumer price sensitivity, even turning products like mobile phones, laptop computers and music into commodities in some consumers' eyes. Marketers need to work harder than ever to differentiate their offerings when many different competitors are selling virtually the same product at a comparable or lower price. More than ever, companies need to understand the price sensitivity of their customers and prospects and the trade-offs people are willing to make between price and product characteristics.

Competitors' strategies and prices

In setting its prices, the company must also consider competitors' costs, prices and market offerings. Consumers will base their judgements of a product's value on the prices that competitors charge for similar products. A consumer who is considering the purchase of a Sony digital camera will evaluate Sony's customer value and price against the value and prices of comparable products made by Nikon, Kodak, Canon and others.

In addition, the company's pricing strategy may affect the nature of the competition it faces. If Sony follows a high-price, high-margin strategy, it may attract competition. A low-price, low-margin strategy, however, may stop competitors or drive them out of the market. Sony needs to benchmark its costs and value again competitors' costs and value. It can then use these benchmarks as a starting point for its own pricing.

In assessing competitors' pricing strategies, the company should ask several questions. First, how does the company's market offering compare with competitors' offerings in terms of customer value? If consumers perceive that the company's product or service provides greater value, the company can charge a higher price. If consumers perceive less value relative to competing products, the company must either charge a lower price or change customer perceptions to justify a higher price.

Next, how strong are current competitors and what are their current pricing strategies? If the company faces a host of smaller competitors charging high prices relative to the value they deliver, it might charge lower prices to drive weaker competitors out of the market. If the market is dominated by larger, low-price competitors, the company may decide to target unserved market niches with value-added products at higher prices. For example, your local independent bookshop isn't likely to win a price war against Amazon.com, Carrefour, Tesco or Waterstones. It would be wiser to add special customer services and personal touches that justify higher prices and margins. Alternatively, you could do what French independent booksellers united to do – lobby the government to bring in a legislative change making 'free delivery' illegal.[9]

Finally, the company should ask, 'How does the competitive landscape influence customer price sensitivity?' For example, customers will be more price sensitive if they see few differences between competing products. They will buy whichever product costs the least. The more information customers have about competing products and prices before buying, the more price sensitive they will be. Easy product comparisons help customers to assess the value of different options and to decide what prices they are willing to pay. Finally, customers will be more price sensitive if they can switch easily from one product alternative to another.

What principle should guide decisions about what price to charge relative to those of competitors? The answer is simple in concept but often difficult in practice: no matter what price you charge – high, low, or in between – be certain to give customers superior value for that price.

Other external factors

When setting prices, the company also must consider a number of other factors in its external environment. *Economic conditions* can have a strong impact on the firm's pricing strategies. Economic factors such as boom or recession, inflation and interest rates affect pricing decisions because they affect both consumer perceptions of the product's price and value and the costs of producing a product.

The recent economic recession has caused consumers to think very hard about the price they pay, and often to seek out cheaper alternatives. The most obvious response to the new economic realities is to cut prices and offer deep discounts. And thousands of companies have done just that. Lower prices make products more affordable and help spur short-term sales. However, such price cuts can have undesirable long-term consequences. 'Tempted to cut prices?' asks one pricing consultant. 'You're not alone. With slumping sales, many businesses have been quick to offer discounts. But price cuts raise some tough questions: Will deep discounts cheapen your brand? Once you cut prices, can you raise them again? How do you deal with narrower margins?'[10]

Remember, even in tough economic times, consumers do not buy based on prices alone. They balance the price they pay against the value they receive. For example, according to a recent survey, despite selling its shoes for as much as €150 a pair, Nike commands the highest consumer loyalty of any brand in the footwear segment.[11] Customers perceive the value of Nike's products and the Nike ownership experience to be well worth the price. Thus, no matter what price they charge – low or high – companies need to offer great *value for money*.

The company must also consider what impact its prices will have on other parties in its environment. How will *resellers* react to various prices? The company should set prices that give resellers a fair profit, encourage their support and help them to sell the product effectively. The *government* is another important external influence on pricing decisions. Finally, *social concerns* may have to be taken into account. In setting prices, a company's short-term sales, market share and profit goals may have to be tempered by broader societal considerations. An example of this would be concerns about the impact of very low-cost alcohol on the well-being of young people. We will examine public policy issues in pricing later in the chapter.

MAKING CONNECTIONS Linking the concepts

The concept of customer value is critical to good pricing and to successful marketing in general. Slow down for a minute and be certain that you appreciate what value really means.

- In an earlier example, we explained that there are customers who regard a Steinway piano as a real bargain even at €75,000. Does this fit with your idea of value?

- Pick two competing brands from a familiar product category (watches, perfume, consumer electronics, restaurants) – one priced low and the other priced high. Which, if either, offers the greatest value?

- Does 'value' mean the same thing as 'low price'? How do these concepts differ?

We have now seen that pricing decisions are subject to an incredibly complex array of customer, company, competitive and environmental forces. To make things even more complex, a company sets not a single price but rather a *pricing structure* that covers different items in its line. This pricing structure changes over time as products move through their life cycles. The company adjusts product prices to reflect changes in costs and demand and to account for variations in buyers and situations. As the competitive environment changes, the company considers when to initiate price changes and when to respond to them.

We now examine the major dynamic pricing strategies available to marketers. In turn, we look at *new-product pricing strategies* for products in the introductory stage of the product life cycle, *product mix pricing strategies* for related products in the product mix, *price adjustment strategies* that account for customer differences and changing situations, and strategies for initiating and responding to *price changes*.

NEW-PRODUCT PRICING STRATEGIES

Pricing strategies usually change as the product passes through its life cycle – we talked about those earlier (see Chapter 8). The introductory stage is especially challenging. Companies bringing out a new product face the challenge of setting prices for the first time. They can choose between two broad strategies: *market-skimming pricing* and *market-penetration pricing*.

Market-skimming pricing

Many companies that invent new products set high initial prices to 'skim' revenues layer by layer from the market. Sony frequently uses this strategy, called **market-skimming pricing**. When Apple first introduced the iPhone, it charged an initial price of as much as $599 per phone. The phones were purchased only by customers who really wanted the sleek new gadget and could afford to pay a high price for it. Six months later, Apple dropped the price to $399 for an 8GB model and $499 for the 16GB model to attract new buyers. Within a year, it dropped prices again to $199 and $299. In this way, Apple skimmed the maximum amount of revenue from the various segments of the market.[12]

Market skimming makes sense only under certain conditions. First, the product's quality and image must support its higher price, and enough buyers must want the product at that price. Second, the costs of producing a smaller volume cannot be so high that they cancel the advantage of charging more. Finally, competitors should not be able to enter the market easily and undercut the high price. Both Microsoft and Sony will be using this strategy with the new generation of games consoles, as they did for the last.

Market-penetration pricing

Rather than setting a high initial price to skim off small but profitable market segments, some companies use **market-penetration pricing**. They set a low initial price in order to *penetrate* the market quickly and deeply – to attract a large number of buyers quickly and win a large market share. The high sales volume results in falling costs, allowing the company to cut its price even further. For example, Aldi, Lidl and other discount retailers use penetration pricing. IKEA used penetration pricing when it entered the Chinese market. Usually Western brands go for a high-value, high-price position in China, but IKEA found that Chinese consumers were browsing its store and then going to cheap local competitors who provided good copies of IKEA merchandise. So IKEA decided to source many of its products locally and to slash its prices. As a result, Chinese consumers flocked to the IKEA stores in China.

Several conditions must be met for this low-price strategy to work. First, the market must be highly price sensitive so that a low price produces more market growth. Second, production and distribution costs must fall as sales volume increases. Finally, the low price must help keep out the competition, and the penetration pricer must maintain its low-price position – otherwise, the price advantage may be only temporary.

PRODUCT MIX PRICING STRATEGIES

The strategy for setting a product's price often has to be changed when the product is part of a product mix. In this case, the firm looks for a set of prices that maximises the profits on the total product mix. Pricing is difficult because the various products have related demand and costs and face different degrees of competition. We now take a closer look at the five product mix pricing situations summarised in Table 9.1: *product line pricing, optional-product pricing, captive-product pricing, by-product pricing* and *product bundle pricing*.

Product line pricing

Companies usually develop product lines rather than single products. For example, you can buy a small Samsung TV for the bedroom or kitchen and it will cost around €300, but if you want the top-of-the-range 65-inch Samsung model it is going to cost you more like €7,500, and there is a whole range of models in between. If you want to buy a Canon digital camera, then even for the simpler models (rather than the more expensive and more complicated models with exchangeable lenses) you can pay anything from €100 for a basic model to €450 for a model with top-of-the-range features.

In **product line pricing**, management must decide on the price steps to set between the various products in a line.

The price steps should take into account cost differences between the products in the line, customer evaluations of their different features and competitors' prices. In many industries, sellers use well-established *price points* for the products in their line. Thus, the Dutch Suitsupply might carry men's suits at three price levels: €275, €365 and €495. The customer will probably associate low-, average- and high-quality suits with the three price points. Even if the three prices are raised a little, men normally will buy suits at their own preferred price points. The seller's task is to establish perceived quality differences that support the price differences.

Optional-product pricing

Many companies use **optional-product pricing** – offering to sell optional or accessory products along with their main product. For example, a car buyer may choose to order air-conditioning, satellite navigation and leather seats. An airline might offer extra legroom or a more generous baggage allowance.

Pricing these options is tricky. Car companies have to decide which items to include in the base price and which to offer as options. Until recent years, the major US car companies' normal pricing strategy was to advertise a stripped-down model at a base price to bring people into showrooms and then to devote most of the showroom space to showing option-loaded cars at higher prices. The economy model was stripped of so many comforts and conveniences that most buyers rejected it. European and Japanese car manufacturers had always tended to offer more in the base price model, and eventually GM and other US car makers followed their example and included more desirable features in the base models. Most advertised prices today represent a well-equipped car.

TABLE 9.1 Product mix pricing strategies

Strategy	Description
Product line pricing	Setting price steps between product line items
Optional-product pricing	Pricing optional or accessory products sold with the main product
Captive-product pricing	Pricing products that must be used with the main product
By-product pricing	Pricing low-value by-products to get rid of them
Product bundle pricing	Pricing bundles of products sold together

Captive-product pricing

Companies that make products that must be used along with a main product are using **captive-product pricing**. Examples of captive products are razor blades, video games and printer cartridges. Producers of the main products (razors, video games consoles and printers) often price them low and set high mark-ups on the supplies. Thus, Gillette sells low-priced razors but makes money on the replacement cartridges. HP makes very low margins on its printers but very high margins on printer cartridges and other supplies. Sony and other video games makers sell games consoles at low prices and obtain the majority of their profits from the video games. Sales of video games software are worth about four times as much in market value as sales of the games consoles themselves.

In the case of services, this strategy is called *two-part pricing*. The price of the service is broken into a *fixed fee* plus a *variable usage rate*. Theme parks such as Disneyland Paris charge an admission fee that gives customers access to most of the attractions, but then hope that customers will pay more for the food, drinks, merchandise and other services – like photographs taken of you on the roller-coasters – when they visit the park. Sports events, such as professional football and tennis, charge an admission fee and then offer customers a range of additional products and services to buy – again, merchandise, like football shirts and player photographs, is a big part of this. Mobile phone companies charge a flat rate for a fixed number of call minutes and SMS text messages, then charge for extra minutes and texts over what the plan allows. The service firm must decide how much to charge for the basic service and how much for the variable usage. The fixed amount should be low enough to induce usage of the service; profit can be made on the variable fees.

By-product pricing

In producing processed meats, petroleum products, chemicals and other products, there are often by-products. If the by-products have no value and if getting rid of them is costly, this will affect the pricing of the main product. Using **by-product pricing**, the manufacturer will seek a market for these by-products and should accept any price that covers more than the cost of storing and delivering them.

By-products can even turn out to be profitable. For example, papermaker MeadWestvaco has turned what was once considered chemical waste into profit-making products:

> MeadWestvaco created a separate company, Asphalt Innovations, which creates useful chemicals entirely from the by-products of MeadWestvaco's wood-processing activities. In fact, Asphalt Innovations has grown to become the world's biggest supplier of specialty chemicals for the paving industry. Using the salvaged chemicals, paving companies can pave roads at a lower temperature, create longer-lasting roads, and more easily recycle road materials when roads need to be replaced. What's more, salvaging the by-product chemicals eliminates the costs and environmental hazards once associated with disposing of them.[13]

By-products can be a valuable source of revenue. Animal manure can be converted into excellent fertiliser

Source: Westland Horticultural.

Sometimes, companies do not realise how valuable their by-products are. For example, most zoos do not realise that one of their by-products – their occupants' manure – can be an excellent source of additional revenue. Chessington Zoo in London sells the manure from its tigers to people who want to deter domestic cats from entering their property – apparently the scent of tiger manure is enough to scare off even the most determined pet cat. More widely than this, of course, animal manure is a natural by-product of many agricultural activities (raising animals) and is a very desirable input to other agricultural activities (growing crops). So chicken farmers can sell the manure that their chickens produce to companies that will process it into chicken manure pellets for use by farmers or by gardeners. General farmyard manure is a highly desirable, natural fertiliser and soil improver which you can buy from any garden centre or agricultural supplier.

Product bundle pricing

Using **product bundle pricing**, sellers often combine several of their products and offer the bundle at a reduced price. For example, fast-food restaurants bundle a burger, fries and a soft drink at a combo price. Theatres and sports teams sell season tickets at less than the cost of single tickets. Resorts sell specially priced holiday packages that include airfare, accommodations, meals and entertainment. And computer makers include attractive software packages with their PCs. Price bundling can promote the sales of products that consumers might not otherwise buy, but the combined price must be low enough to get them to buy the bundle.[14]

PRICE ADJUSTMENT STRATEGIES

Companies usually adjust their basic prices to account for various customer differences and changing situations. Here we examine the seven price adjustment strategies summarised in Table 9.2: *discount and allowance pricing, segmented pricing, psychological pricing, promotional pricing, geographical pricing, dynamic pricing* and *international pricing*.

Discount and allowance pricing

Most companies adjust their basic price to reward customers for certain responses, such as early payment of bills, volume purchases and off-season buying. These price adjustments – called *discounts* and *allowances* – can take many forms.

The many forms of **discounts** include a *cash discount,* a price reduction to buyers who pay their bills promptly. A typical example is '2/10, net 30,' which means that although payment is due within 30 days, the buyer can deduct 2 per cent if the bill is paid within 10 days. Utility companies often do this with the gas and electricity companies. A *quantity discount* is a price reduction to buyers who buy large volumes. Such discounts provide an incentive to the customer to buy more from one given seller, rather than from many different sources.

A *functional discount* (also called a *trade discount*) is offered by the seller to trade-channel members who perform certain functions, such as selling, storing and record keeping. A *seasonal discount* is a price reduction to buyers who buy merchandise or services out of season. For example, lawn and garden equipment manufacturers offer seasonal discounts to

TABLE 9.2 Price adjustment strategies

Strategy	Description
Discount and allowance pricing	Reducing prices to reward customer responses such as paying early or promoting the product
Segmented pricing	Adjusting prices to allow for differences in customers, products or locations
Psychological pricing	Adjusting prices for psychological effect
Promotional pricing	Temporarily reducing prices to increase short-term sales
Geographical pricing	Adjusting prices to account for the geographical location of customers
Dynamic pricing	Adjusting prices continually to meet the characteristics and needs of individual customers and situations
International pricing	Adjusting prices for international markets

retailers during the autumn and winter months to encourage early ordering in anticipation of the heavy spring and summer selling seasons. Seasonal discounts allow the seller to keep production steady during an entire year.

Allowances are another type of reduction from the list price. For example, *trade-in allowances* are price reductions given for turning in an old item when buying a new one. Trade-in allowances are common in the car industry but are also becoming more common with smartphones, which contain valuable elements and components which can be recycled profitably. *Promotional allowances* are payments or price reductions to reward dealers for participating in advertising and sales support programmes.

Segmented pricing

Companies will often adjust their basic prices to allow for differences in customers, products and locations. In **segmented pricing**, the company sells a product or service at two or more prices, even though the difference in prices is not based on differences in costs.

Segmented pricing takes several forms. Under *customer-segment* pricing, different customers pay different prices for the same product or service. Museums, for example, may charge a lower admission for students and for retired people. Under *product-form pricing*, different versions of the product are priced differently but not necessarily according to differences in their costs.

Using *location pricing,* a company charges different prices for different locations, even though the cost of offering each location is the same. For instance, concert halls vary their seat prices because of audience preferences for certain locations, and UK universities charge higher tuition fees for students from outside the EU. Finally, using *time pricing,* a firm varies its price by the season, the month, the day and even the hour. Some public utilities vary their prices to commercial users by time of day and weekend versus weekday. Holiday resorts may give weekend and seasonal discounts. Rail fares vary – expensive for those travelling to work in the early morning, but cheaper for leisure travellers during the day.

In the airline industry, segmented pricing is called *revenue management*. The airlines, for example, routinely set prices hour by hour – even minute by minute – depending on seat availability, demand and competitor price changes. European air travellers are now used to logging on to a budget airline's website to get a price for a flight – say, from Frankfurt to Barcelona for a fun weekend – and then, when they check back an hour or two later (or even a minute or two), finding that the price has changed. That is the consumer experience of dynamic time pricing in the budget airline industry.

Segmented pricing: at any given moment, easyJet may have many thousands of prices in the market. All of those prices need to be managed, all of the time

Source: Alamy Images/G.I. Dobner.

For segmented pricing to be an effective strategy, certain conditions must exist. The market must be segmentable and the segments must show different degrees of demand. The costs of segmenting and watching the market cannot exceed the extra revenue obtained from the price difference. Of course, the segmented pricing must also be legal. Most importantly, segmented prices should reflect real differences in customers' perceived value. Otherwise, in the long run, the practice will lead to customer resentment and ill will.

Psychological pricing

Price says something about the product. For example, many consumers use price to judge quality. A €100 bottle of perfume may contain only €3 worth of scent, but some people are willing to pay the €100 because this price indicates something special.

In using **psychological pricing**, sellers consider the psychology of prices and not simply the economics. For example, consumers usually associate price with quality; they generally assume that a higher-priced product also offers higher quality. When they can judge the quality of a product by examining it or by calling on past experience with it, they use price less to judge quality. But when they cannot judge quality because they lack the information or skill, price becomes an important quality signal:

> Some years ago, Heublein produced Smirnoff, then America's leading vodka brand. Smirnoff was attacked by another brand, Wolfschmidt, which claimed to have the same quality as Smirnoff but was priced at one dollar less per bottle. To hold on to market share, Heublein considered either lowering Smirnoff's price by one dollar or holding Smirnoff's price but increasing advertising and promotion expenditures. Either strategy would lead to lower profits and it seemed that Heublein faced a no-win situation. At this point, however, Heublein's marketers thought of a third strategy. They *raised* the price of Smirnoff by one dollar! Heublein then introduced a new brand, Relska, to compete with Wolfschmidt. More-over, it introduced yet another brand, Popov, priced even *lower* than Wolfschmidt. This clever strategy positioned Smirnoff as the elite brand and Wolfschmidt as an ordinary brand, producing a large increase in Heublein's overall profits. The irony is that Heublein's three brands were pretty much the same in taste and manufacturing costs. Heublein knew that a product's price signals its quality. Using price as a signal, Heublein sold roughly the same product at three different quality positions.

Another aspect of psychological pricing is **reference prices** – prices that buyers carry in their minds and refer to when looking at a given product. The reference price might be formed by noting current prices, remembering past prices or assessing the buying situation. Sellers can influence or use these consumers' reference prices when setting price. For example, a company could display its product next to more expensive ones in order to imply that it belongs in the same class. Department stores often sell women's clothing in separate departments differentiated by price: clothing found in the more expensive department is assumed to be of better quality.

For most purchases, consumers do not have all the skill or information they need to figure out whether they are paying a good price. They do not have the time, ability or inclination to research different brands or stores, compare prices and get the best deals. Instead, they may rely on certain cues that signal whether a price is high or low. For example, the fact that a product is sold in a prestigious department store might signal that it is worth a higher price.

Interestingly, such pricing cues are often provided by sellers. A retailer might show a high manufacturer's suggested price next to the marked price, indicating that the product was originally priced much higher. Or the retailer might sell a selection of familiar products for which consumers have accurate price knowledge at very low prices, suggesting that the store's prices on other, less familiar products are low as well. The use of such pricing cues has become a common marketing practice (see Marketing at Work 9.2).

Quick, what's a good price for . . . ? We'll give you a cue

It's Saturday morning and you stop by your local supermarket to pick up a few items for tonight's garden barbecue. Cruising the aisles, you're bombarded with price signs, all suggesting that you just can't beat this store's deals. A 4 kg bag of Heat Beads barbecue briquettes goes for only £3.97. Cans of Heinz Baked Beans are four for £1.86. An aisle display advertises big bags of Walker's potato crisps at an 'everyday low price' of just £1.99. And a sign on top of a huge mass of Coke 10-packs advertises two for £5.50.

These certainly look like good prices, but *are* they? If you're like most shoppers, you don't really know. In a *Harvard Business Review* article, two pricing researchers conclude: 'for most of the items they buy, consumers don't have an accurate sense of what the price should be'. In fact, customers often do not even know what prices they are actually paying. In one recent study, researchers asked supermarket shoppers the price of an item just as they were putting it into their shopping carts. Less than half the shoppers gave the right answer.

To know for sure if you're paying the best price, you'd have to compare the marked price with past prices, prices of competing brands and prices in other stores. For most purchases, consumers just do not bother. Instead, they rely on a most unlikely source. 'Remarkably . . . they rely on the retailer to tell them if they're getting a good price,' say the researchers. 'In subtle and not-so-subtle ways, retailers send signals [or pricing cues] to customers, telling them whether a given price is relatively high or low.' In their article, the researchers outline the following common retailer pricing cues:

- *Sale signs.* The most straightforward retail pricing cue is a sale sign. It might take any of several familiar forms: 'Sale!', 'Reduced!', 'New low price!', 'Price after discount!' or 'Now two for only . . . !' Such signs can be very effective in signalling low prices to consumers and increasing sales for the retailer. The researchers' studies in retail stores and mail-order catalogues reveal that using the word 'sale' beside a price (even without actually varying the price) can increase demand by more than 50 per cent.
- While sales sign can be effective, overuse or misuse can damage both the seller's credibility and its sales.

Pricing cues such as sales signs and prices ending in 9 can be effective in signalling low prices to consumers and increasing sales for the retailer

Source: Getty Images/Tim Boyle.

Unfortunately, some retailers do not always use such signs truthfully. Still, consumers trust sale signs. Why? 'Because they are accurate most of the time,' say the researchers. 'And besides, customers are not that easily fooled.' They quickly become suspicious when sale signs are used improperly.

- *Prices ending in 9.* Just like a sale sign, a 9 at the end of a price often signals a bargain. You see such prices everywhere. For example, browse the websites of discounters such as Aldi or Carrefour and you will see that a lot of prices end in 9. 'In fact, this pricing tactic is so common', say the researchers, 'you'd think customers would ignore it. Think again. Response to this pricing cue is remarkable.' Normally, you'd expect that demand for an item will fall as the price goes up. Yet in one study involving women's clothing, raising the price of a dress from €34 to €39 *increased* demand by a third. By comparison, raising the price from €34 to €44 yielded no difference in demand.

But are prices ending in 9 accurate as pricing cues? 'The answer varies,' the researchers report:

Some retailers do reserve prices that end in 9 for their discounted items. For instance, J. Crew and Ralph Lauren generally use 00-cent endings on regularly priced merchandise and 99-cent endings on discounted items. Comparisons of prices at major department stores reveal that this is common, particularly for apparel. But at some stores, prices that end in 9 are a miscue – they are used on all products regardless of whether the items are discounted.

- *Signpost pricing (or loss-leader pricing).* Unlike sale signs or prices that end in 9, signpost pricing is used on frequently purchased products about which consumers tend to have accurate price knowledge. For example, you probably know a good price on a 10-pack of Coke when you see one. New parents usually know how much they should expect to pay for disposable nappies. Research suggests that customers use the prices of such 'signpost' items to gauge a store's overall prices. If a store has a good price on Coke or Pampers or Persil, they reason, it probably also has good prices on other items.

  Retailers have long known the importance of signpost pricing, often called 'loss-leader pricing'. They offer selected signpost items at or below cost to pull customers into the store, hoping to make money on the shopper's other purchases.

- *Price-matching guarantees.* Another widely used retail pricing cue is price matching, whereby stores promise to meet or beat any competitor's price. Department store John Lewis, for example, uses 'Never Knowingly Undersold' as its catchphrase. If you find a better price within 28 days on something you bought at John Lewis, the retailer will refund the difference. While this is certainly a promise that John Lewis will fulfil if necessary, it is not a promise that it expects to have to meet very often, because the company monitors prices carefully and always aims to give the lowest local price for every product.

  Evidence suggests that customers perceive that stores offering price-matching guarantees have overall lower prices than competing stores, especially in markets where they perceive price comparisons to be relatively easy. But are such perceptions accurate? 'The evidence is mixed,' say the researchers. Consumers can usually be confident that they will pay the lowest price on eligible items. However, some manufacturers make it hard to take advantage of price-matching policies by introducing 'branded variants' – slightly different versions of products with different model numbers for different retailers. At a broader level, some pricing experts argue that price-matching policies are not really targeted at customers. Rather, they may serve as a warning to competitors: 'If you cut your prices, we will, too.' If this is true, price-matching policies might actually reduce price competition, leading to higher overall prices.

Used properly, pricing cues can help consumers. Careful buyers really can take advantage of signals such as sale signs, 9-endings, loss leaders and price guarantees to locate good deals. Used improperly, however, these pricing cues can mislead consumers, tarnishing a brand and damaging customer relationships.

The researchers conclude:

Customers need price information, just as they need products. They look to retailers to provide both. Retailers must manage pricing cues in the same way that they manage quality. . . . No retailer . . . interested in [building profitable long-term relationships with customers] would purposely offer a defective product. Similarly, no retailer who [values customers] would deceive them with inaccurate pricing cues. By reliably signalling which prices are low, companies can retain customers' trust – and [build more solid relationships].

Sources: Quotes and other information reprinted by permission of *Harvard Business Review*; excerpt from 'Mind Your Pricing Cues' by Eric Anderson and Duncan Simester, September 2003, Copyright © 2003 by the Harvard Business School Corporation; all rights reserved. See also Joydeep Srivastava and Nicholas Lurie, 'Price-Matching Guarantees as Signals of Low Store Prices: Survey and Experimental Evidence', *Journal of Retailing*, 80(2), 2004, pp. 117–28; and Michael J. Barone, Kenneth C. Manning and Paul W. Minard, 'Consumer Response to Retailers' Use of Partially Comparative Pricing', *Journal of Marketing*, July 2004, pp. 37–47.

Even small differences in price can signal product differences. Consider a stereo priced at €300 compared with one priced at €299.95. The actual price difference is only 5 cents, but the psychological difference can be much greater. For example, some consumers will see the €299.95 as a price in the €200 range rather than the €300 range. The €299.95 will more likely be seen as a bargain price, whereas the €300 price suggests more quality. Some psychologists argue that each digit has symbolic and visual qualities that should be considered in pricing. Thus, 8 is round and even and creates a soothing effect (not to mention being considered lucky by the Chinese), whereas 7 is angular and creates a jarring effect.

Promotional pricing

With **promotional pricing**, companies will temporarily price their products below list price and sometimes even below cost to create buying excitement and urgency. Promotional pricing takes several forms. Supermarkets and department stores will price a few products as *loss leaders* to attract customers to the store in the hope that they will buy other items at normal mark-ups. For example, supermarkets often sell disposable nappies at less than cost in order to attract family buyers who make larger average purchases per trip. Sellers will also use *special-event pricing* in certain seasons to draw more customers. That is why a lot of retailers have post-Christmas sales to attract shoppers back into their stores.

Manufacturers sometimes offer *cash rebates* ('cash back') to consumers who buy the product from dealers within a specified time; the manufacturer sends the rebate directly to the customer. Rebates have been popular with car companies and producers of durable goods and small appliances, but they are also used with consumer packaged goods. Some manufacturers offer *low-interest financing, longer warranties* or *free maintenance* to reduce the consumer's 'price'. This practice has become a favourite of the car industry. Or the seller may simply offer *discounts* from normal prices to increase sales and reduce inventories.

Promotional pricing, however, can have adverse effects. Used too frequently and copied by competitors, price promotions can create 'deal-prone' customers who wait until brands go on sale before buying them. Or constantly reduced prices can erode a brand's value in the eyes of customers. Marketers sometimes use price promotions as a quick fix instead of working through the difficult process of developing effective longer term strategies for building their brands. In fact, one observer notes that price promotions can be addictive for both the company and the customer: 'Price promotions are the brand equivalent of heroin: easy to get into but hard to get out of. Once the brand and its customers are addicted to the short-term high of a price cut it is hard to wean them away to real brand building . . . . But continue and the brand dies by 1,000 cuts.'[15]

The frequent use of promotional pricing can also lead to industry price wars. Such price wars usually play into the hands of only one or a few competitors – those with the most efficient operations. The point is that promotional pricing can be an effective means of generating sales for some companies in certain circumstances. But it can be damaging for other companies or if taken as a steady diet.

MAKING CONNECTIONS Linking the concepts

Here's a good place to take a brief break. Think about some of the companies and industries you deal with that are 'addicted' to promotional pricing.

● Many industries have created 'deal-prone' consumers through the heavy use of promotional pricing – fast food, cars, airlines, tyres, furniture and others. Pick a company in one of these industries and suggest ways that it might deal with this problem.

● How does the concept of value relate to promotional pricing? Does promotional pricing add to or detract from customer value?

Geographical pricing

A company must also decide how to price its products for customers located in different parts of the country or world. Should the company risk losing the business of more distant customers by charging them higher prices to cover the higher shipping costs? Or should the company charge all customers the same prices regardless of location? We will look at five **geographical pricing** strategies for the following hypothetical situation.

The Peerless Paper Company is located in Rotterdam, Holland, and sells paper products to customers all over Europe. The cost of transport is high and affects the companies from whom customers buy their paper. Peerless wants to establish a geographical pricing policy. It is trying to determine how to price a €10,000 order to three specific customers: Customer A (Oslo, Norway), Customer B (Milan, Italy) and Customer C (Lisbon, Portugal).

One option is for Peerless to ask each customer to pay the shipping cost from the Rotterdam factory to the customer's location. All three customers would pay the same factory price of €10,000, with Customer A paying, say, €100 for shipping; Customer B, €150; and Customer C, €250. Called *FOB-origin pricing,* this practice means that the goods are placed *free on board* (hence *FOB*) a carrier. At that point the title and responsibility pass to the customer, who pays the freight from the factory to the destination. Because each customer picks up its own cost, supporters of FOB pricing feel that this is the fairest way to assess freight charges. The disadvantage, however, is that Peerless will be a high-cost firm to distant customers.

Uniform-delivered pricing is the opposite of FOB pricing. Here, the company charges the same price plus freight to all customers, regardless of their location. The freight charge is set at the average freight cost. Suppose this is €150. Uniform-delivered pricing therefore results in a higher charge to the Oslo customer (who pays €150 freight instead of €100) and a lower charge to the Lisbon customer (who pays €150 instead of €250). Although the Oslo customer would prefer to buy paper from another local paper company that uses FOB-origin pricing, Peerless has a better chance of winning over the Portuguese customer. Other advantages of uniform-delivered pricing are that it is fairly easy to administer and it lets the firm advertise its price internationally.

Zone pricing falls between FOB-origin pricing and uniform-delivered pricing. The company sets up two or more zones. All customers within a given zone pay a single total price; the more distant the zone, the higher the price. For example, Peerless might set up a Northern Europe zone and charge €100 freight to all customers in this zone, and a Southern Europe zone in which it charges €250. In this way, the customers within a given price zone receive no price advantage from the company. For example, customers in Milan and Lisbon pay the same total price to Peerless. The complaint, however, is that the Milan customer is paying part of the Lisbon customer's freight cost.

Using *basing-point pricing,* the seller selects a given city as a 'basing point' and charges all customers the freight cost from that city to the customer location, regardless of the city from which the goods are actually shipped. For example, Peerless might set Paris as the basing point and charge all customers €10,000 plus the freight from Paris to their locations. This means that a Rotterdam customer pays the freight cost from Paris to Rotterdam, even though the goods may be shipped from Rotterdam. If all sellers used the same basing-point city, delivered prices would be the same for all customers and price competition would be eliminated. Industries such as sugar, cement, steel and vehicles used basing-point pricing for years, but this method has become less popular today. Some companies set up multiple basing points to create more flexibility: they quote freight charges from the basing-point city nearest to the customer.

Finally, the seller who is anxious to do business with a certain customer or geographical area might use *freight-absorption pricing.* Using this strategy, the seller absorbs all or part of the actual freight charges in order to get the desired business. The seller might reason that if it can get more business, its average costs will fall and more than compensate for its extra freight cost. Freight-absorption pricing is used for market penetration and to hold onto increasingly competitive markets.

Dynamic pricing

Throughout most of history, prices were set by negotiation between buyers and sellers. *Fixed price* policies – setting one price for all buyers – is a relatively modern idea that arose with the development of large-scale retailing at the end of the nineteenth century. Today, most prices are set this way. However, some companies are now reversing the fixed pricing trend. They are using **dynamic pricing** – adjusting prices continually to meet the characteristics and needs of individual customers and situations.

For example, think about how the Internet has affected pricing. From the mostly fixed pricing practices of the past century, the Web seems now to be taking us back into a new age of fluid pricing. The flexibility of the Internet allows web sellers instantly and constantly to adjust prices on a wide range of goods based on demand dynamics (sometimes called *real-time pricing*). In other cases, customers control pricing by bidding on auction sites such as eBay or negotiating on sites such as Priceline. Still other companies customise their offers based on the characteristics and behaviours of specific customers.[16]

Dynamic pricing offers many advantages for marketers. For example, Internet sellers such as Amazon (through its **.com** and national web addresses in Europe) can mine their databases to gauge a specific shopper's desires, measure his or her means, instantaneously tailor products to fit that shopper's behaviour, and price products accordingly.

Many direct marketers monitor inventories, costs and demand at any given moment and adjust prices instantly. For example, Dell uses dynamic pricing to achieve real-time balancing of supply and demand for computer components.

Buyers also benefit from the Web and dynamic pricing. A wealth of websites – such as PriceRunner, Ciao, ShopGenie and shopzilla – give instant product and price comparisons from thousands of vendors. For example, Ciao (**www.ciao.de** in Germany, **www.ciao.fr** in France, **www.ciao.co.uk** in the UK, **www.ciao.es** in Spain, and so on) lets shoppers browse by category or search for specific products and brands. It then searches the Web and reports back links to sellers offering the best prices. In addition to simply finding the vendor with the best price, customers armed with price information can often negotiate lower prices.

Buyers can also negotiate prices at online auction sites and exchanges. Suddenly the centuries-old art of haggling is back in vogue. Want to sell that antique pickle jar that's been collecting dust for generations? Post it on eBay, the world's biggest online flea market. Want to name your own price for a hotel room or hire car? Visit Priceline (**www.priceline.de** in Germany, **www.priceline.fr** in France, **www.priceline.co.uk** in the UK, **www.priceline.es** in Spain, and so on) or another reverse auction site.

International pricing

Companies that market their products internationally must decide what prices to charge in the different countries in which they operate. In some cases, a company can set a uniform worldwide price. For example, Boeing sells its aircraft at about the same price everywhere, whether in the USA, Europe or a Third World country. However, most companies adjust their prices to reflect local market conditions and cost considerations.

The price that a company should charge in a specific country depends on many factors, including economic conditions, competitive situations, laws and regulations, and development of the wholesaling and retailing system. Consumer perceptions and preferences also may vary from country to country, calling for different prices. Or the company may have different marketing objectives in various world markets, which require changes in pricing strategy. For example, Samsung might introduce a new product into mature markets in highly developed countries with the goal of quickly gaining mass-market share – this would call for a penetration pricing strategy. In contrast, it might enter a less developed market by targeting smaller, less price-sensitive segments; in this case, market-skimming pricing makes sense.

Costs play an important role in setting international prices. Travellers abroad are often surprised to find that goods that are relatively inexpensive at home may carry outrageously higher price-tags in other countries. A pair of Levi's jeans might sell for €90 in Paris and only €30 in New York. A McDonald's Big Mac selling for a modest €2.90 in the USA might cost €6.00 in Reykjavik, Iceland, and an Oral-B toothbrush selling for €2.49 in the UK may cost €10 in China. Conversely, a Gucci handbag going for only €140 in Milan, Italy, might fetch €240 in the USA. In some cases, such *price escalation* may result from differences in selling strategies or market conditions. In most instances, however, it is simply a result of the higher costs of selling in another country – the additional costs of product modifications, shipping and insurance, import tariffs and taxes, exchange-rate fluctuations and physical distribution.

Price has become a key element in the international marketing strategies of companies attempting to enter emerging markets, such as China, India and Brazil. Consider Unilever's pricing strategy for developing countries:

> There used to be one way to sell a product in developing markets, if you bothered to sell there at all: slap on a local label and market at premium prices to the elite. Unilever – maker of such brands as Dove, Lipton and Vaseline – changed that. Instead, it built a following among the world's poorest consumers by shrinking packages to set a price even consumers living on $2 a day could afford. The strategy was forged about 25 years ago when Unilever's Indian subsidiary found its products out of reach for millions of Indians. To lower the price while making a profit, Unilever developed single-use packets for everything from shampoo to laundry detergent, costing just pennies a pack. The small, affordable packages put the company's premier brands within reach of the world's poor. Today, Unilever continues to woo cash-strapped customers with great success. For example, its approachable pricing helps explain why Unilever now captures 70 per cent of the Brazil detergent market.[17]

Thus, international pricing presents some special problems and complexities. We discuss international pricing issues in more detail later (see Chapter 15).

PRICE CHANGES

After developing their pricing structures and strategies, companies often face situations in which they must initiate price changes or respond to price changes by competitors.

Initiating price changes

In some cases, the company may find it desirable to initiate either a price cut or a price increase. In both cases, it must anticipate possible buyer and competitor reactions.

Initiating price cuts

Several situations may lead a firm to consider cutting its price. One such circumstance is excess capacity. Another is falling market share in the face of strong price competition. In such cases, the firm may aggressively cut prices to boost sales and share. But as the airline, fast-food and other industries have learned in recent years, cutting prices in an industry loaded with excess capacity may lead to price wars as competitors try to hold onto market share.

A company may also cut prices in a drive to dominate the market through lower costs. Either the company starts with lower costs than its competitors, or it cuts prices in the hope of gaining market share that will further cut costs through larger volume. Dell has used this strategy effectively in the PC market.

Initiating price increases

A successful price increase can greatly increase profits. For example, if the company's profit margin is 3 per cent of sales, a 1 per cent price increase will increase profits by 33 per cent if sales volume is unaffected. A major factor in price increases is cost inflation. Rising costs squeeze profit margins and lead companies to pass cost increases along to customers. Another factor leading to price increases is over-demand: when a company cannot supply all that its customers need, it may raise its prices, ration products to customers, or both.

When raising prices, the company must avoid being perceived as a price gouger. Customers have long memories, and they will eventually turn away from companies or even whole industries that they perceive as charging excessive prices. There are some techniques for avoiding this problem. One is to maintain a sense of fairness surrounding any price increase. Price increases should be supported by company communications telling customers why prices are being raised. Making low-visibility price moves first is also a good technique: some examples include dropping discounts, increasing minimum order sizes, and curtailing production of low-margin products. The company sales force should help business customers find ways to economise.

Wherever possible, the company should consider ways to meet higher costs or demand without raising prices. For example, it can consider more cost-effective ways to produce or distribute its products. It can shrink the product or substitute less expensive ingredients instead of raising the price, as candy bar manufacturers often do. Or it can 'unbundle' its market offering, removing features, packaging or services and separately pricing elements that were formerly part of the offer. IBM, for example, now offers training and consulting as separately priced services.

Buyer reactions to price changes

Customers do not always interpret price changes in a straightforward way. They may view a price *cut* in several ways. For example, what would customers think if Chanel No. 5 perfume, for which '*la feminité est intemporelle*' ('femininity is timeless'), were to cut its price in half? Or what if Sony suddenly cut its PC prices drastically? You might think that the computers are about to be replaced by newer models or that they have some fault and are not selling well. You might think that Sony is abandoning the computer business and may not stay in this business long enough to supply future parts. You might believe that quality has been reduced. Or you might think that the price will come down even further and that it will pay to wait and see.

Similarly, a price *increase*, which would normally lower sales, may have some positive meanings for buyers. What would you think if Sony *raised* the price of its latest PC model? On the one hand, you might think that the item is very 'hot' and may be unobtainable unless you buy it soon. Or you might think that the computer is an unusually good performer. On the other hand, you might think that Sony is greedy and charging what the market will bear.

Competitor reactions to price changes

A firm considering a price change has to worry about the reactions of its competitors as well as those of its customers. Competitors are most likely to react when the number of firms involved is small, when the product is uniform and when the buyers are well informed about products and prices.

How can the firm anticipate the likely reactions of its competitors? The problem is complex because, like the customer, the competitor can interpret a company price cut in many ways. It might think the company is trying to grab a larger market share, or that it is doing

A high price adds to the aura of exclusivity associated with prestigious brands such as Chanel

Source: Getty Images/ WireImage.

poorly and trying to boost its sales. Or it might think that the company wants the whole industry to cut prices to increase total demand.

The company must guess each competitor's likely reaction. If all competitors behave alike, this amounts to analysing only a typical competitor. In contrast, if the competitors do not behave alike – perhaps because of differences in size, market shares or policies – then separate analyses are necessary. However, if some competitors will match the price change, there is good reason to expect that the rest will also match it.

Responding to price changes

Here we reverse the question and ask how a firm should respond to a price change by a competitor. The firm needs to consider several issues: Why did the competitor change the price? Is the price change temporary or permanent? What will happen to the company's market share and profits if it does not respond? Are other competitors going to respond? Besides these issues, the company must also consider its own situation and strategy and possible customer reactions to price changes.

Figure 9.5 shows the ways a company might assess and respond to a competitor's price cut. Suppose the company learns that a competitor has cut its price and decides that this price cut is likely to harm company sales and profits. It might simply decide to hold its current price and profit margin. The company might believe that it will not lose too much market share, or that it would lose too much profit if it reduced its own price. Or it might decide that it should wait and respond when it has more information on the effects of the competitor's price change. However, waiting too long to act might let the competitor get stronger and more confident as its sales increase.

If the company decides that effective action can and should be taken, it might make any of four responses. First, it could *reduce its price* to match the competitor's price. It may decide that the market is price sensitive and that it would lose too much market share to the lower-priced competitor. Cutting the price will reduce the company's profits in the short term. Some companies might also reduce their product quality, services and marketing communications to retain profit margins, but this will ultimately hurt long-term market share. The company should try to maintain its quality as it cuts prices.

Alternatively, the company might maintain its price but *raise the perceived value* of its offer. It could improve its communications, stressing the relative value of its product over that of the lower-priced competitor. The firm may find it cheaper to maintain price and spend money to improve its perceived value than to cut price and operate at a lower margin.

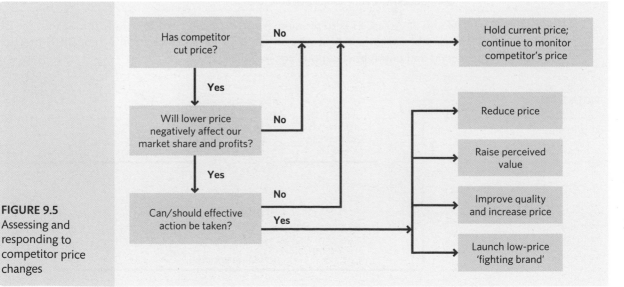

FIGURE 9.5
Assessing and responding to competitor price changes

Or the company might *improve quality and increase price,* moving its brand into a higher price–value position. The higher quality creates greater customer value which justifies the higher price. In turn, the higher price preserves the company's higher margins.

Finally, the company might *launch a low-price 'fighting brand'* – adding a lower-priced item to the line or creating a separate lower-priced brand. This is necessary if the particular market segment being lost is price sensitive and will not respond to arguments of higher quality.

PUBLIC POLICY AND PRICING

Price competition is a core element of a free market economy. In setting prices, companies are not usually free to charge whatever prices they wish. Many European and national laws govern the rules of fair play in pricing. In addition, companies must consider broader societal pricing concerns. Legislation is in place in all of the world's major economies to prohibit anti-competitive pricing practices. For example, in Europe the most important legislation affecting pricing is Article 81 of the EU Treaty.

Figure 9.6 shows the major public policy issues in pricing. These include potentially damaging pricing practices within a given level of the channel (price fixing and predatory pricing) and across levels of the channel (retail price maintenance, discriminatory pricing and deceptive pricing).[18]

In the EU, anti-competitive business practices are prohibited by Article 81 of the EU Treaty:

> The following shall be prohibited as incompatible with the common market: all agreements between undertakings, decisions by associations of undertakings and concerted practices which may affect trade between Member States and which have as their object or effect the prevention, restriction or distortion of competition within the common market, and in particular those which:
>
> a. directly or indirectly fix purchase or selling prices or any other trading conditions;
> b. limit or control production, markets, technical development, or investment;
> c. share markets or sources of supply;
> d. apply dissimilar conditions to equivalent transactions with other trading parties, thereby placing them at a competitive disadvantage;
> e. make the conclusion of contracts subject to acceptance by the other parties of supplementary obligations which, by their nature or according to commercial usage, have no connection with the subject of contracts.[19]

The aim of Article 81 is to promote free competition and free trade throughout the EU. Many member states have their own further legislation to prevent anti-competitive practices in general and unfair pricing practices specifically.

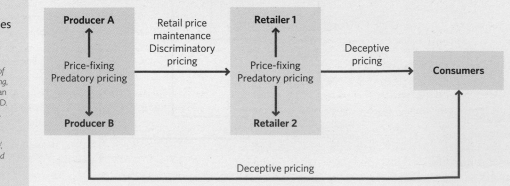

FIGURE 9.6
Public policy issues in pricing

Source: Reprinted with permission from *Journal of Public Policy and Marketing,* published by the American Marketing Association, L.D. Compeau and D. Grewel, 'Pricing and Public Policy: A Research Agenda and Overview of Special Issue', *Journal of Public Policy and Marketing*, Spring 1999, pp. 3–10, Figure 1.

THE JOURNEY YOU'VE TAKEN Reviewing the concepts

Before you leave pricing behind, let's review the important concepts. *Price* can be defined as the sum of all the values that customers give up in order to gain the benefits of having or using a product or service. Pricing decisions are subject to an incredibly complex array of company, environmental and competitive forces.

1 Discuss the importance of understanding customer value perceptions and company costs when setting prices

Good pricing begins with a complete understanding of the value that a product or service creates for customers and setting a price the captures that value. The price the company charges will fall somewhere between one that is too high to produce any demand and one that is too low to produce a profit.

Customer perceptions of the product's value set the ceiling for prices. If customers perceive that the price is greater than the product's value, they will not buy the product. At the other extreme, company and product costs set the floor for prices. If the company prices the product below its costs, its profits will suffer.

Costs are an important consideration in setting prices. However, cost-based pricing is product driven. The company designs what it considers to be a good product and sets a price that covers costs plus a target profit. If the price turns out to be too high, the company must settle for lower mark-ups or lower sales, both resulting in disappointing profits. Value-based pricing reverses this process. The company sets its target price based on customer perceptions of the product value. The targeted value and price then drive decisions about product design and what costs can be incurred. As a result, pricing begins with analysing customer needs and value perceptions, and price is set to match customers' perceived value.

2 Identify and define the other important external and internal factors affecting a firm's pricing decisions

Other *internal* factors that influence pricing decisions include the company's overall marketing strategy, objectives, mix and organisation for pricing. Price is only one element of the company's broader marketing strategy. If the company has selected its target market and positioning carefully, then its marketing mix strategy, including price, will be fairly straightforward. Some companies position their products on price and then tailor other marketing mix decisions to the prices they want to charge.

Other companies de-emphasise price and use other marketing mix tools to create *non-price* positions.

Common pricing objectives might include survival, current profit maximisation, market-share leadership, or customer retention and relationship building. Price decisions must be coordinated with product design, distribution and promotion decisions to form a consistent and effective marketing programme. Finally, in order to coordinate pricing goals and decisions, management must decide who within the organisation is responsible for setting price.

Other external pricing considerations include the nature of the market and demand, competitors' strategies and prices, and environmental factors such as the economy, reseller needs and government actions. The seller's pricing freedom varies with different types of markets. Ultimately, the customer decides whether the company has set the right price. The customer weighs the price against the perceived values of using the product – if the price exceeds the sum of the values, consumers will not buy. So the company must understand concepts like demand curves (the price–demand relationship) and price elasticity (consumer sensitivity to prices). Consumers also compare a product's price with the prices of competitors' products. A company therefore must learn the customer value and prices of competitors' offers.

3 Describe the major strategies for pricing imitative and new products

Pricing is a dynamic process. Companies design a *pricing structure* that covers all their products. They change this structure over time and adjust it to account for different customers and situations. Pricing strategies usually change as a product passes through its life cycle. In pricing innovative new products, it can follow a *skimming policy* by initially setting high prices to 'skim' the maximum amount of revenue from various segments of the market. Or it can use *penetration pricing* by setting a low initial price to penetrate the market deeply and win a large market share.

4 Explain how companies find a set of prices that maximises the profits from the total product mix

When the product is part of a product mix, the firm searches for a set of prices that will maximise the profits from the total mix. In *product line pricing*, the company decides on price steps for the entire set of products it offers. In addition, the company must set prices for *optional products* (optional or accessory products included with the main product), *captive products* (products that are required for use of the main product), *by-products* (waste or residual products produced when making the main product) and *product bundles* (combinations of products at a reduced price).

5   **Discuss how companies adjust their prices to take into account different types of customers and situations**

Companies apply a variety of *price adjustment strategies* to account for differences in consumer segments and situations. One is *discount and allowance pricing*, whereby the company establishes cash, quantity, functional or seasonal discounts or varying types of allowances. A second strategy is *segmented pricing*, whereby the company sells a product at two or more prices to accommodate different customers, product forms, locations or times. Sometimes companies consider more than economics in their pricing decisions, using *psychological pricing* to better communicate a product's intended position. In *promotional pricing*, a company offers discounts or temporarily sells a product below list price as a special event, sometimes even selling below cost as a loss leader. Another approach is *geographical pricing*, whereby the company decides how to price to near and distant customers.

Dynamic pricing involves adjusting prices continually to meet the characteristics and needs of individual customers and situations. Finally, *international pricing* means that the company adjusts its price to meet conditions and expectations in different world markets.

6   **Discuss the key issues related to initiating and responding to price changes**

When a firm considers initiating a price change, it must consider customers' and competitors' reactions. There are different implications to initiating price cuts and initiating price increases. Buyer reactions to price changes are influenced by the meaning customers see in the price change. Competitors' reactions flow from a set reaction policy or a fresh analysis of each situation.

There are also many factors to consider in responding to a competitor's price changes. The company that faces a price change initiated by a competitor must try to understand the competitor's intent as well as the likely duration and impact of the change. If a swift reaction is desirable, the firm should pre-plan its reactions to different possible price actions by competitors. When facing a competitor's price change, the company might sit tight, reduce its own price, raise perceived value, improve quality and raise price, or launch a fighting brand.

NAVIGATING THE KEY TERMS

NOTES AND REFERENCES

1 Thomas T. Nagle and Reed K. Holden, *The Strategy and Tactics of Pricing*, 4th edn (Upper Saddle River, NJ: Prentice Hall, 2005), ch. 1.

2 Information obtained online at **http://corporate.walmart.com/our-story**, accessed January 2014.

3 Information obtained online at **http://franchisor.ikea.com**, accessed 7 May 2007.

4 A. Hinterhuber, 'Towards Value-Based Pricing – An Integrative Framework for Decision Making', *Industrial Marketing Management*, 33, 2004, pp. 765–78.

5 Based on information from Anne Marie Chaker, 'For a Steinway, I Did It My Way', *The Wall Street Journal*, 22 May 2008; also **www.steinway.com/steinway** and **www.steinway .com/steinway/quotes.shtml**, accessed November 2009.

6 Erin Stout, 'Keep Them Coming Back for More', *Sales & Marketing Management*, February 2002, pp. 51–2. See also Hinterhuber, 'Towards Value-Based Pricing – An Integrative Framework for Decision Making', *op. cit.*, pp. 765ff; and Helen Atkinson, 'Adding New Value', *Traffic World*, 28 March 2005, pp. 18–22.

7 Extract from **www.miele.co.uk**, accessed January 2014.

8 Information from **www.which.co.uk**, accessed 19 July 2011.

9 See the *Financial Times* story: 'France Targets Amazon to Protect Bookshops' at **FT.com**

10 Ryan McCarthy, 'Pricing: How Low Can You Go?' *Inc.*, March 2009, pp. 91–2.

11 Kenneth Hein, 'Study: Trumps Price among Shoppers,' *Brandweek*, 2 March 2009, p. 6.

12 See Brian Chen, 'WWDC: Apple Slashes Prices with iPhone 3G, Shipping in July', 9 June 2008, accessed at **www.macworld.com/article/133838/2008/06/iphone3g.html**; and Olga Kharif, 'Can Apple Keep a Shine on the iPhone?' BusinessWeek Online, 18 March 2009, accessed at **www.businessweek.com**

13 Michael Buettner, 'Charleston, S.C.-Based Asphalt Innovations Turns Waste into Helpful Product', *Knight Ridder Tribune Business News*, 18 October 2004, p. 1.

14 See Nagle and Hogan, *The Strategy and Tactics of Pricing*, 4th edn (Upper Saddle River, NJ: Prentice Hall, 2007), pp. 244–7; Bram Foubert and Els Gijsbrechts, 'Shopper Response to Bundle Promotions for Packaged Goods', *Journal of Marketing Research*, November 2007, pp. 647–62; Roger M. Heeler *et al.*, 'Bundles = Discount? Revisiting Complex Theories of Bundle Effects', *Journal of Product & Brand Management*, 16(7), 2007, pp. 492–500; and Timothy J. Gilbride *et al.*, 'Framing Effects in Mixed Price Bundling', *Marketing Letters*, June 2008, pp. 125–40.

15 Tim Ambler, 'Kicking Price Promotion Habit Is Like Getting Off Heroin – Hard', *Marketing*, 27 May 1999, p. 24. See also Robert Gray, 'Driving Sales at Any Price?', *Marketing*, 11 April 2002, p. 24; Lauren Kellere Johnson, 'Dueling Pricing Strategies', *MIT Sloan Management Review*, Spring 2003, pp. 10–11; and Peter R. Darke and Cindy M.Y. Chung, 'Effects of Pricing and Promotion on Consumer Perceptions: It Depends on How You Frame It', *Journal of Retailing*, 2005, pp. 35–47.

16 Louise Story, 'Online Pitches Made Just for You', *New York Times*, 6 March 2008.

17 Based on information found in 'The World's Most Influential Companies: Unilever', *BusinessWeek*, 22 December 2008, p. 47; and **www.unilever.com/sustainability/people/consumers/affordability/**, accessed June 2009.

18 For discussions of these issues, see Dhruv Grewel and Larry D. Compeau, 'Pricing and Public Policy: A Research Agenda and Overview of Special Issue', *Journal of Public Policy and Marketing*, Spring 1999, pp. 3–10; and Michael V. Marn, Eric V. Roegner and Craig C. Zawada, *The Price Advantage* (Hoboken, NJ: Wiley, 2004), Appendix 2.

19 Information online at **http://europa.eu**, accessed 20 July 2011.

CHAPTER 10
MARKETING CHANNELS AND SUPPLY CHAIN MANAGEMENT

AFTER STUDYING THIS CHAPTER, YOU SHOULD BE ABLE TO

- explain why companies use distribution channels and discuss the functions these channels perform
- discuss how channel members interact and how they organise to perform the work of the channel
- identify the major channel alternatives open to a company
- explain how companies select, motivate and evaluate channel members
- discuss the nature and importance of marketing logistics and integrated supply chain management

THE WAY AHEAD
Previewing the concepts

We now arrive at the third marketing mix tool – distribution. Firms rarely work alone in creating value for customers and building profitable customer relationships. Instead, most are only a single link in a larger supply chain and distribution channel. As such, an individual firm's success depends not only on how well *it* performs, but also on how well its *entire distribution channel* competes with competitors' channels. To be good at customer relationship management, a company must also be good at partner relationship management. The first part of this chapter explores the nature of distribution channels and the marketer's channel design and management decisions. We then examine physical distribution – or logistics – an area that is growing dramatically in importance and sophistication. In the next chapter, we'll look more closely at two major channel intermediaries – retailers and wholesalers.

To get us started, we'll take a close look at a medium-sized Spanish paint company, Pinturas Fierro, which has had to solve quite a few distribution and logistical issues as it has grown and entered international markets. Good management of the distribution system has been a key component in enabling this family firm to survive and thrive for over 70 years. Read on and see why.

PINTURAS FIERRO: SLOW BUT SAFE GROWTH

Jesús Cambra Fierro

Pinturas Fierro is a Spanish family company devoted to the production and distribution of paint for industrial use, such as the car and the decoration industries; the company also produces solvents and other auxiliary products. It demonstrates some characteristic features for a medium-sized business: a fairly small number of employees, management of the business handled by the owners, and relatively few specialists in management positions. The company was created in 1930 by the family that owns and runs it today. Currently the third generation runs the company while the fourth generation is receiving training in the fields of chemistry and business administration in order to take over control and management of the company in the future.

The retail team at Pinturas Fierro
Source: Photo by Jesús Cambra Fierro.

Since its creation the company has been characterised by great dynamism and an eagerness to grow. Initially, the company was a small local shop that sold paint, varnish and accessories. When the founder's son took charge of the business, in 1943, the location changed to the commercial area of Barbastro, their home town in northern Spain, and they established a provincial and regional network for the exclusive distribution of the most highly respected paint brands in Spain (such as Titan and Valentine). During this period the company became well established in its home region and began to expand into neighbouring France. In the early 1980s the important decision was made to invest in manufacturing facilities for paint, varnish and solvents. The first production activities coincided with the arrival of the third generation into the company's management in 1986. However, although members of the family had excellent knowledge of chemistry they had little training in business management, and this began to hamper the company's development. After a period of consolidation, during which managerial skills were developed, the business began to look for expansion opportunities nationally and internationally.

Today the company is divided into two fundamental areas: first, production and distribution (wholesaling) to industrial customers; and, second, distribution (wholesaling) to commercial customers and retailers. The company has 16 employees, and in 2005 sales turnover amounted to €4.5m. The centre of operations is still in the Spanish market, especially in Aragon, Catalonia, industrial areas of Madrid, Valencia and Andalusia; there is an international presence through non-exclusive distributors in France, northern Italy and, on a smaller scale, in Portugal and Morocco.

Throughout most of the history of Pinturas Fierro the company has relied less on formal management principles and more on the intuitive business sense of the owners. Because the people that have run the company always knew that they were dealing with the present and future of their family, they were never tempted to take on excessive risks. Besides, they were chemists rather than businessmen. This has led to a fairly cautious approach to business expansion, with a clear focus on producing high-quality products even if this meant that prices sometimes had to be higher than those of rivals.

Let's now take a look at how the company has managed its expansion, and how it has consistently and carefully augmented the distribution channels that it employs. The first stage of the expansion was characterised by the creation of a simple distribution network, covering 75–100 kilometres from the physical location of the firm. The problem here was that the area is mountainous (near the Pyrenees) and the transport infrastructure was poorly developed. However, the company exploited the absence of competitors interested in the area. This territory was neither attractive nor profitable for distant companies, whereas, for Pinturas Fierro, it was its home territory and all it needed was a driver with a van who could make deliveries and handle logistical matters. Using this simple commercial network the company obtained exclusive dealership within the local area for several of the most prestigious national and international brands, like Valentine and Titan.

However, the growing business led to the need to increase the stock of products stored and to have actual space for it. The company acquired two fairly small warehouses in the same town, one for paints and varnishes, the other for accessory products.

The 1980s saw further expansion of the business and the addition of a new product line: accessory machinery. This line included air compressors and power generators. However, this increased the complexity of the management task considerably. New brands like Peugeot and Pintuc were added to the portfolio, and it became clear that the company needed more space in which to exhibit and store the products, and to offer technical support. In particular, in this industry, customers often give equipment maintenance a low priority, and expect the dealer to sort out any problems quickly when equipment breaks down. Customer service is a priority.

During this period more employees were hired: one as warehouse manager, one to handle the accounts and administration, and two as commercial salespeople. Two delivery vehicles were acquired and agreements on physical distribution were signed with specialised companies so that commercial staff no longer had to handle the physical distribution of the product. As a result the sales team could spend more time on existing customers and prospecting for new customers.

As transport infrastructure improved in the 1980s, so several competing companies became interested in the home territory of Pinturas Fierro. At the same time several new brands emerged with very aggressive pricing strategies. All these factors reduced profit margins and meant that the company had to handle a wider range of brands. In any case, Pinturas Fierro had been able to build a commercial network perfectly adapted to the physical and social features of the territory. The company had a good reputation for the technical training of its salespeople, its commitment to meet customer deadlines, the size of its product portfolio and its willingness to meet the specific needs of every customer.

As the company developed its production facilities and began to sell its own products, rather than simply to distribute those of other companies, new challenges emerged. Establishing distribution channels, and handling logistics, for its own products became matters of serious concern. Key target markets were in the industrial centres of Catalonia and, inevitably, in Madrid, where the concentration of business was highest. Although Pinturas Fierro wanted to establish exclusive distributorships, it was not well known as a manufacturer and so found this very difficult. Consequently, it decided to sell its products through distributors that also handled other brands. The company looked for

distributors who specialised in industrial customers with a wide portfolio. Potential distributors were invited to the factory so that they could learn about the production process and how the product could be customised to meet the needs of particular industrial customers. Pinturas Fierro managers regularly visited Madrid and Barcelona to meet potential customers. This way they both demonstrated their support to the distributor and surveyed the actual needs of the market. This information, together with the feedback generated by the distributor, considerably enriched the company's knowledge of the market.

What about international markets? They were considered to be of secondary importance compared with getting established in Spain. But by the 1990s the management felt that the company was mature enough to expand internationally. The route selected to enter foreign markets was by exporting, building relationships with distributors in international markets in the same way that it had built relationships with Spanish distributors. Expanding into inter-national markets was expected to enhance the reputation of the company back home in Spain. Pinturas Fierro followed a typical internationalisation strategy for a medium-sized firm, making the nearby countries of France and Italy their first targets. The company has taken part in trade missions and international trade fairs. Gradually the proportion of exports in total sales has been increasing.

What are the challenges that Pinturas Fierro faces in the future? The company, true to its origins, still sells to the retail trade and still distributes the Valentine and Titan brands. Although the retail trade is fairly small, it has always been there and has always provided funds for the company's new ventures. Further, the management of the business is emotionally attached to the retail trade and would not want to see it go. The company has been working on enlarging the central main warehouse and the manufacturing facilities, and investing in new, improved logistics technology designed to improve physical stock management. Working relationships with suppliers are very satisfactory, and the managers are working hard to maintain and improve them. Similarly, the company understands that its distributors are the principal point of contact with the customers, and so will continue to invest time and effort in developing excellent distributor relationships. The challenge of further internationalisation is always present. The company is hampered because few employees can speak a foreign language, and, in any case, it currently has limited production capacity with which to expand further in international markets. However, as the next generation of the family comes into the business, fully trained in modern management and marketing techniques, perhaps they will take the plunge and launch Pinturas Fierro decisively into the international arena.

Sources: Based on interviews with the owners and managers.

Just like Pinturas Fierro, most firms cannot bring value to customers by themselves. Instead, they must work closely with other firms in a larger value-delivery network.

SUPPLY CHAINS AND THE VALUE-DELIVERY NETWORK

Producing a product or service and making it available to buyers requires building relationships not just with customers, but also with key suppliers and resellers in the company's *supply chain*. This supply chain consists of 'upstream' and 'downstream' partners. Upstream from the company is the set of firms that supply the raw materials, components, parts, information, finances and expertise needed to create a product or service. Marketers, however, have traditionally focused on the 'downstream' side of the supply chain – on the *marketing channels* or *distribution channels* that look forward towards the customer. Downstream marketing-channel partners, such as wholesalers and retailers, form a vital connection between the firm and its customers.

Both upstream and downstream partners may also be part of other firms' supply chains. But it is the unique design of each company's supply chain that enables it to deliver superior value to customers. An individual firm's success depends not only on how well *it* performs, but also on how well its entire supply chain and marketing channel competes with competitors' channels.

The term *supply chain* may be too limited – it takes a *make-and-sell* view of the business. It suggests that raw materials, productive inputs and factory capacity should serve as the starting point for market planning. A better term would be *demand chain* because it suggests a *sense-and-respond* view of the market. Under this view, planning starts with the needs of target customers, to which the company responds by organising a chain of resources and activities with the goal of creating customer value.

Even a demand-chain view of a business may be too limited, because it takes a step-by-step, linear view of purchase–production–consumption activities. With the advent of the Internet and other technologies, however, companies are forming more numerous and complex relationships with other firms. For example, Ford manages numerous supply chains. It also sponsors or transacts on many B2B websites and online purchasing exchanges as needs arise. Like Ford, most large companies today are engaged in building and managing a continuously evolving *value-delivery network*.

As defined earlier (see Chapter 2), a value-delivery network is made up of the company, suppliers, distributors and ultimately customers who 'partner' with each other to improve the performance of the entire system. For example, Samsung, a leading manufacturer of mobile phones, manages a whole community of suppliers and assemblers of semiconductor components, plastic cases, colour displays and accessories. Its network also includes offline and online resellers. All of these diverse partners must work effectively together to bring superior value to Samsung's customers.

This chapter focuses on marketing channels – on the downstream side of the value-delivery network. However, it is important to remember that this is only part of the full value network. To bring value to customers, companies need upstream supplier partners just as they need downstream channel partners. Increasingly, marketers are participating in and influencing their company's upstream activities as well as its downstream activities. More than marketing-channel managers, they are becoming full value network managers.

The chapter examines four major questions concerning marketing channels. What is the nature of marketing channels and why are they important? How do channel firms interact and organise to do the work of the channel? What problems do companies face in designing and managing their channels? What role do physical distribution and supply chain management play in attracting and satisfying customers? We will look later at marketing-channel issues from the viewpoint of retailers and wholesalers (see Chapter 11).

THE NATURE AND IMPORTANCE OF MARKETING CHANNELS

Few producers sell their goods directly to the final users. Instead, most use intermediaries to bring their products to market. They try to forge a **marketing channel** (or **distribution channel**) – a set of interdependent organisations that help make a product or service available for use or consumption by the consumer or business user.

A company's channel decisions directly affect every other marketing decision. Pricing depends on whether the company works with national discount chains, uses high-quality speciality stores, or sells directly to consumers via the Web. The firm's sales force and communications decisions depend on how much persuasion, training, motivation and support its channel partners need. Whether a company develops or acquires certain new products may depend on how well those products fit the capabilities of its channel members.

Companies often pay too little attention to their distribution channels, sometimes with damaging results. In contrast, many companies have used imaginative distribution systems to *gain* a competitive advantage. FedEx's creative and imposing distribution system made it a leader in express delivery. Dell revolutionised its industry by selling PCs directly to consumers rather than through retail stores. Amazon pioneered the sales of books and a wide range of other goods via the Internet.

Distribution channel decisions often involve long-term commitments to other firms. For example, companies such as PSA Peugeot Citroën, Samsung or Toshiba can easily change their advertising, pricing or promotion programmes. They can scrap old products and introduce new ones as market tastes demand. But when they set up distribution channels through contracts with franchisees, independent dealers or large retailers, they cannot readily replace these channels with company-owned stores or websites if conditions change. Therefore, management must design its channels carefully, with an eye on tomorrow's likely selling environment as well as today's.

How channel members add value

Why do producers give some of the selling job to channel partners? After all, doing so means giving up some control over how and to whom they sell their products. Producers use intermediaries because they create greater efficiency in making goods available to target markets. Through their contacts, experience, specialisation and scale of operation, intermediaries usually offer the firm more than it can achieve on its own.

Figure 10.1 shows how using intermediaries can provide economies. Figure 10.1A shows three manufacturers, each using direct marketing to reach three customers. This system requires nine different contacts. Figure 10.1B shows the three manufacturers working through one distributor, which contacts the three customers. This system requires only six contacts. In this way, intermediaries reduce the amount of work that must be done by both producers and consumers.

From an economic point of view the role of marketing intermediaries is to transform the assortments of products made by producers into the assortments wanted by consumers. Producers make narrow assortments of products in large quantities, but consumers want broad assortments of products in small quantities. Marketing-channel members buy large quantities from many producers and break them down into the smaller quantities and broader assortments wanted by consumers.

For example, Nestlé makes millions of KitKat bars each day, but you want to buy only a few bars at a time. So big food, drug and discount retailers, such as Carrefour, Lidl, Aldi and Tesco, buy KitKat by the truckload and stock it on their stores' shelves. In turn, you can buy a single KitKat, along with a shopping trolley full of small quantities of toothpaste, shampoo and other related products as you need them. Thus, intermediaries play an important role in matching supply and demand.

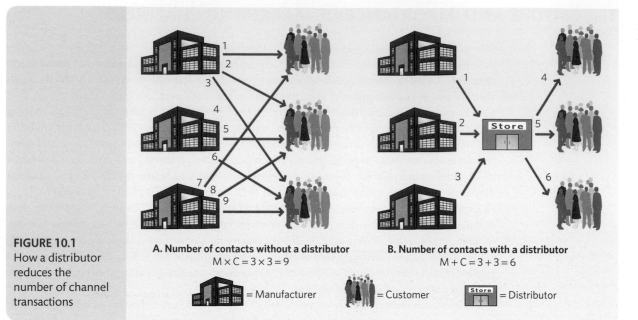

FIGURE 10.1
How a distributor reduces the number of channel transactions

A. Number of contacts without a distributor
$M \times C = 3 \times 3 = 9$

B. Number of contacts with a distributor
$M + C = 3 + 3 = 6$

= Manufacturer   = Customer   = Distributor

In making products and services available to consumers, channel members add value by bridging the major time, place and possession gaps that separate goods and services from those who would use them. Members of the marketing channel perform many key functions. Some help to complete transactions:

- *Information*: Gathering and distributing marketing research and intelligence information about actors and forces in the marketing environment needed for planning and aiding exchange.
- *Promotion*: Developing and spreading persuasive communications about an offer.
- *Contact*: Finding and communicating with prospective buyers.
- *Matching*: Shaping and fitting the offer to the buyer's needs, including activities such as manufacturing, grading, assembling and packaging.
- *Negotiation*: Reaching an agreement on price and other terms of the offer so that ownership or possession can be transferred.

Others help to fulfil the completed transactions:

- *Physical distribution*: Transporting and storing goods.
- *Financing*: Acquiring and using funds to cover the costs of the channel work.
- *Risk taking*: Assuming the risks of carrying out the channel work.

The question is not *whether* these functions need to be performed – they must be – but rather *who* will perform them. To the extent that the manufacturer performs these functions, its costs go up and its prices have to be higher. When some of these functions are shifted to intermediaries, the producer's costs and prices may be lower, but the intermediaries must charge more to cover the costs of their work. In dividing the work of the channel, the various functions should be assigned to the channel members who can add the most value for the cost.

Number of channel levels

Companies can design their distribution channels to make products and services available to customers in different ways. Each layer of marketing intermediaries that performs some

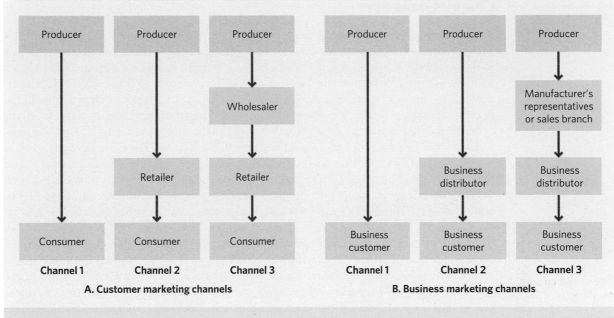

FIGURE 10.2
Consumer and business marketing channels

work in bringing the product and its ownership closer to the final buyer is a **channel level**. Because the producer and the final consumer both perform some work, they are part of every channel.

The *number of intermediary levels* indicates the *length* of a channel. Figure 10.2A shows several consumer distribution channels of different lengths. Channel 1, called a **direct marketing channel**, has no intermediary levels; the company sells directly to consumers. For example, both Avon and Essentially Yours sell cosmetic products through home and office sales parties and on the Web; Interflora sells flowers, gifts and greeting cards direct by telephone and online. The remaining channels in Figure 10.2A are **indirect marketing channels**, containing one or more intermediaries.

Figure 10.2B shows some common business distribution channels. The business marketer can use its own sales force to sell directly to business customers, or it can sell to various types of intermediaries, who in turn sell to these customers. Consumer and business marketing channels with even more levels can sometimes be found, but less often. From the producer's point of view, a greater number of levels mean less control and greater channel complexity. Moreover, all of the institutions in the channel are connected by several types of *flows*. These include the *physical flow* of products, the *flow of ownership*, the *payment flow*, the *information flow* and the *promotion flow*. These flows can make even channels with only one or a few levels very complex.

CHANNEL BEHAVIOUR AND ORGANISATION

Distribution channels are more than simple collections of firms tied together by various flows. They are complex behavioural systems in which people and companies interact to accomplish individual, company and channel goals. Some channel systems consist only of informal interactions among loosely organised firms. Others consist of formal interactions guided by strong organisational structures. Moreover, channel systems do not stand still – new types of intermediaries emerge and whole new channel systems evolve. Here we look at channel behaviour and at how members organise to do the work of the channel.

Channel behaviour

A marketing channel consists of firms that have partnered for their common good. Each channel member depends on the others. For example, a Peugeot dealer depends on Peugeot to design cars that meet consumer needs. In turn, Peugeot depends on the dealer to attract consumers, persuade them to buy Peugeot cars, and service cars after the sale. Each Peugeot dealer also depends on other dealers to provide good sales and service that will uphold the brand's reputation. In fact, the success of individual Peugeot dealers depends on how well the entire Peugeot marketing channel competes with the channels of other auto manufacturers.

Each channel member plays a specialised role in the channel. For example, Sony's role is to produce consumer electronics products that consumers will like and to create demand through national advertising. The role of electrical retailers like Fnac and Currys is to display these Sony products in convenient locations, to answer buyers' questions and to complete sales. The channel will be most effective when each member takes on the tasks it can do best.

Ideally, because the success of individual channel members depends on overall channel success, all channel firms should work together smoothly. They should understand and accept their roles, coordinate their activities and cooperate to attain overall channel goals. However, individual channel members rarely take such a broad view. Cooperating to achieve overall channel goals sometimes means giving up individual company goals. Although channel members depend on one another, they often act alone in their own short-term best interests. They often disagree on who should do what and for what rewards. Such disagreements over goals, roles and rewards generate **channel conflict**.

Horizontal conflict occurs among firms at the same level of the channel. For instance, some Peugeot dealers in Madrid might complain that other dealers in the city steal sales from them by pricing too low or by advertising outside their assigned territories. Or Holiday Inn franchisees might complain about other Holiday Inn operators overcharging guests or giving poor service, hurting the overall Holiday Inn image.

Channel conflict: Goodyear's conflicts with its independent dealers have caused hard feelings and flattened the company's replacement tyre sales

Source: Getty Images/Mike Ehrmann.

Vertical conflict, conflicts between different levels of the same channel, is even more common. For example, Goodyear created hard feelings and conflict with its premier independent-dealer channel when it began selling through mass-merchant retailers. For more than 60 years, Goodyear sold replacement tyres exclusively through its premier network of 5,300 independent Goodyear dealers. In mid-1992, however, Goodyear jolted its dealers by agreeing to sell its tyres through Sears auto centres. Similar pacts soon followed with Wal-Mart and Sam's Club, pitting dealers against the nation's most potent retailers. Goodyear claimed that the change was essential. Value-minded tyre buyers were increasingly buying from cheaper, multibrand discount outlets and department stores. By selling exclusively through its dealer network, Goodyear simply was not putting its tyres where many consumers were going to buy them. Unfortunately, as Goodyear expanded into the new channels, it took few steps to protect its prized exclusive-dealer network.

Not surprisingly, Goodyear's aggressive moves into new channels set off a surge of channel conflict, and dealer relations deteriorated rapidly. Some of Goodyear's best dealers defected to competitors. Other angry dealers struck back by taking on competing brands of cheaper private-label tyres. Such dealer actions weakened the Goodyear name, and the company's replacement tyre sales – which made up 73 per cent of its revenues – went flat, dropping the company into a profit funk more than a decade long. Although Goodyear has since repaired fractured dealer relations, it still has not fully recovered. 'We lost sight of the fact that it's in our interest that our dealers succeed,' admits a Goodyear executive.[1]

Some conflict in the channel takes the form of healthy competition. Such competition can be good for the channel – without it, the channel could become passive and non-innovative. But severe or prolonged conflict, as in the case of Good-year, can disrupt channel effectiveness and cause lasting harm to channel relationships. Companies should manage channel conflict to keep it from getting out of hand.

Vertical marketing systems

For the channel as a whole to perform well, each channel member's role must be specified and channel conflict must be managed. The channel will perform better if it includes a firm, agency or mechanism that provides leadership and has the power to assign roles and manage conflict.

Historically, *conventional distribution channels* have lacked such leadership and power, often resulting in damaging conflict and poor performance. One of the biggest channel developments over the years has been the emergence of *vertical marketing systems* that provide channel leadership. Figure 10.3 contrasts the two types of channel arrangements.

A **conventional distribution channel** consists of one or more independent producers, wholesalers and retailers. Each is a separate business seeking to maximise its own profits, perhaps even at the expense of the system as a whole. No channel member has much control over the other members, and no formal means exists for assigning roles and resolving channel conflict.

In contrast, a **vertical marketing system (VMS)** consists of producers, wholesalers and retailers acting as a unified system. One channel member owns the others, has contracts with them or wields so much power that they must all cooperate. The VMS can be dominated by the producer, wholesaler or retailer.

We look now at three major types of VMSs: *corporate, contractual* and *administered*. Each uses a different means for setting up leadership and power in the channel.

Corporate VMS

A **corporate VMS** integrates successive stages of production and distribution under single ownership. Coordination and conflict management are attained through regular organisational channels. For example, French car manufacturer Citroën has local subsidiary companies responsible for selling in national markets, such as Citroën Espana, Citroën Deutschland and Citroën UK.[2] The fantasy games company Games Workshop designs, manufactures, distributes and retails its own range of products, so retaining complete control over the

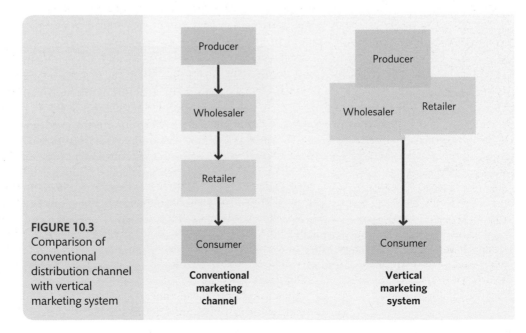

FIGURE 10.3
Comparison of conventional distribution channel with vertical marketing system

entire VMS.[3] And little-known Italian eyewear maker Luxottica produces many famous eyewear brands – including Ray-Ban, Vogue, Anne Klein, Ferragamo and Bvlgari. It then sells these brands through two of the world's largest optical chains, LensCrafters and Sunglass Hut, which it also owns.[4]

Contractual VMS

A **contractual VMS** consists of independent firms at different levels of production and distribution who join together through contracts to obtain more economies or sales impact than each could achieve alone. Coordination and conflict management are attained through contractual agreements among channel members.

The **franchise organisation** is the most common type of contractual relationship – a channel member called a *franchisor* links several stages in the production–distribution process. Although McDonald's is undoubtedly the best known franchise in Europe, as it is around the world, Europe boasts many home-grown franchises. Almost every kind of business has been franchised – from hotels and fast-food restaurants to dental centres and dating agencies, from wedding consultants and maid services to fitness centres and undertaker services. The largest European franchise operations include '5 *à sec*' dry-cleaners from France, Paellador restaurants from Spain, Groszek convenience stores from Poland and Chemex International commercial cleaning services from the UK.[5]

There are three types of franchises. The first type is the *manufacturer-sponsored retailer franchise system* – for example, Peugeot and its network of independent franchised dealers. The second type is the *manufacturer-sponsored wholesaler franchise system* – Coca-Cola licenses bottlers (wholesalers) in various markets who buy Coca-Cola syrup concentrate and then bottle and sell the finished product to retailers in local markets. The third type is the *service-firm-sponsored retailer franchise system* – examples are found in the commercial cleaning business (Chemex International, Swisher), the fast-food service business (McDonald's, Paellador) and the hotel business (Mercure, Ibis, Travelodge).

The fact that most consumers cannot tell the difference between contractual and corporate VMSs shows how successfully the contractual organisations compete with corporate chains.

Administered VMS

In an **administered VMS**, leadership is assumed not through common ownership or contractual ties, but through the size and power of one or a few dominant channel members.

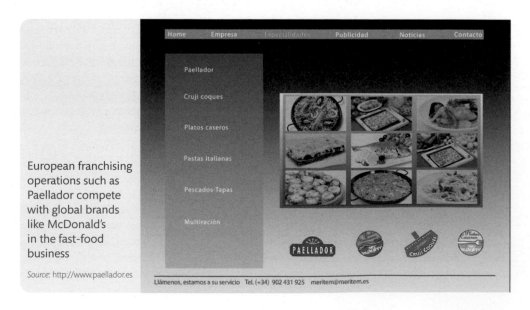

European franchising operations such as Paellador compete with global brands like McDonald's in the fast-food business

Source: http://www.paellador.es

Manufacturers of a top brand can obtain strong trade cooperation and support from resellers. For example, Danone, Louis Vuitton and L'Oréal can command unusual cooperation from resellers regarding displays, shelf space, promotions and price policies. Large retailers such as Carrefour and Tesco can exert strong influence on the manufacturers that supply the products they sell.

Horizontal marketing systems

Another channel development is the **horizontal marketing system**, in which two or more companies at one level join together to follow a new marketing opportunity. By working together, companies can combine their financial, production or marketing resources to accomplish more than any one company could alone.

Companies might join forces with competitors or non-competitors. They might work with each other on a temporary or permanent basis, or they may create a separate company. For example, banks often install automated teller machines (ATMs) on the premises of major retailers, delivering mutual benefits to the customer, the retailer and the bank itself. Similarly, both the coffee bar company Costa and the bookshop chain Waterstones clearly believe that their businesses benefit from having Costa coffee bars located in Waterstones stores. Customers can stay in the store longer, rather than leaving to find a separate coffee shop when their book browsing makes them thirsty.

Such channel arrangements also work well globally. For example, because of its excellent coverage of international markets, Nestlé jointly sells General Mills' cereal brands in 80 countries outside North America. Similarly, Coca-Cola and Nestlé formed a joint venture, Beverage Partners Worldwide, to market ready-to-drink coffees, teas and flavoured milks in more than 40 countries worldwide. Coke provides worldwide experience in marketing and distributing beverages, and Nestlé contributes two established brand names – Nescafé and Nestea.[6]

Multichannel distribution systems

In the past many companies used a single channel to sell to a single market or market segment. Today, with the proliferation of customer segments and channel possibilities, more and more companies have adopted **multichannel distribution systems** – often called *hybrid marketing channels*. Such multichannel marketing occurs when a single firm sets up two or more marketing channels to reach one or more customer segments. The use of multichannel systems has increased greatly in recent years.

Figure 10.4 shows a hybrid channel. In the figure, the producer sells directly to consumer segment 1 using direct mail catalogues, telemarketing and the Internet, and reaches

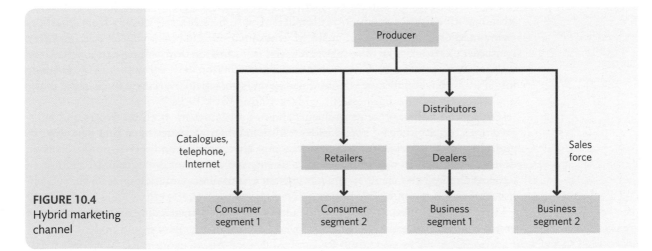

FIGURE 10.4
Hybrid marketing channel

consumer segment 2 through retailers. It sells indirectly to business segment 1 through distributors and dealers and to business segment 2 through its own sales force.

These days, almost every large company and many small ones distribute through multiple channels. The Spanish banking organisation Grupo Santander is well established in both Europe and Latin America, and reaches customers by telephone, over the Internet and through its branch offices. The office supplies company Staples originated in the USA but now operates in 22 countries, with stores in the UK, Germany, the Netherlands, Portugal, and catalogue businesses in several other European countries including Italy, Spain, Poland and Hungary. Staples markets through its traditional retail outlets, a direct-response Internet site, virtual malls and 30,000 links on affiliated sites.

Siemens uses multiple channels to serve dozens of segments and niches, ranging from large corporate and institutional buyers to small businesses to home office buyers. The Siemens sales force sells the company's IT equipment and services to large and mid-size business customers. Siemens also sells through a network of distributors and value-added resellers, which sell Siemens computers, systems and services to a variety of special business segments. Both business and home office buyers can buy directly from Siemens by phone or online from the company's websites (the corporate website is **www.siemens.com**, and from there you can navigate to individual country websites such as **www.siemens.ua**, the Ukrainian site).

Multichannel distribution systems offer many advantages to companies facing large and complex markets. With each new channel, the company expands its sales and market coverage and gains opportunities to tailor its products and services to the specific needs of diverse customer segments. But such multichannel systems are harder to control, and they generate conflict as more channels compete for customers and sales. For example, when Siemens began selling directly to customers through its own website, many of its retail dealers were concerned that they might lose sales.

Changing channel organisation

Changes in technology and the explosive growth of direct and online marketing are having a profound impact on the nature and design of marketing channels. One major trend is towards **disintermediation** – a big term with a clear message and important consequences. Disintermediation occurs when product or service producers cut out intermediaries and go directly to final buyers, or when radically new types of channel intermediaries displace traditional ones.

Thus, in many industries traditional intermediaries are dropping by the wayside. For example, companies such as Dell and easyJet sell directly to final buyers, cutting retailers out of their marketing channels altogether. In other cases, new forms of resellers are displacing traditional intermediaries. For example, e-commerce has grown rapidly, taking business from traditional bricks-and-mortar retailers. Consumers can buy flowers from Interflora (**www.interflora.com**), clothes from H&M (**www.hm.com**), and books, videos, toys, jewellery, consumer electronics and almost anything else from **amazon.com** or their national Amazon website (**www.amazon.co.uk**, **www.amazon.fr**, **www.amazon.de**) – all without ever stepping into a traditional retail store. Disintermediation is a particularly strong force in the music and computer gaming businesses (see Marketing at Work 10.1).

Disintermediation presents problems and opportunities for both producers and intermediaries. To avoid being swept aside, traditional intermediaries must find new ways to add value in the supply chain. To remain competitive, product and service producers must develop new channel opportunities, such as Internet and other direct channels. However, developing these new channels often brings them into direct competition with their established channels, resulting in conflict.

To ease this problem, companies often look for ways to make going direct a plus for the entire channel. For example, Bosch knows that many customers would prefer to buy its

Steam-powered marketing: disintermediation in the computer game industry

Disintermediation is a fancy word, but the idea is quite simple: the removal of intermediaries from the supply chain or marketing channel.

A traditional channel for something like baked beans would include the farmer growing the beans, merchants buying beans from many farmers and shipping them to processors like Heinz, who also brand and package them before passing them on to retailers, perhaps via a wholesaler. Each of those businesses does specific jobs that create added value, and has specific goals, and each is rewarded with a proportion of the price that the end user pays in order to have the key ingredient for that gourmet meal – beans on toast. Rewards are not equal between the members of the supply chain. Maybe the retailer takes 40 per cent of the final selling price while the originator of the raw materials – in this case a farmer – probably receives between a tenth and a twentieth of that: 2–4 per cent. If you were a farmer, you might think this unfair, and wonder whether you could cut out some intermediaries and increase your share of the revenue. It is possible for cooperative groups of farmers to consider integrating activities closer to the customer into their own business model – activities like processing, packaging and even branding. In practice this kind of 'forward integration' is very difficult. It is considerably easier for a major retailer to integrate activities further away from the customer into its business model, in a process of 'backward integration'.

However, what is difficult for farmers is not so difficult for producers in some other markets. In particular, disintermediation is much easier where the product comprises data, so that it can be delivered digitally. Apple has disintermediated the supply chain for music – bands supply music to labels like Sony BMG and Virgin, who pass MP3 files to Apple for sale through the iTunes online store and customers buy their music (and films and TV programmes) directly. This eliminates the physical shipping of CDs and other media, and bypasses high-street retailers like HMV. Some artists like Radiohead, David Byrne and David Bowie have gone a step further – offering their music direct to fans with essentially no intermediaries.

That these products are data based is the key attribute – the consumers receive the product electronically via an Internet connection and there is no need for a physical component to the offering – as long as the ones and zeros can be rearranged back into the appropriate structure, the product can be delivered. The same principle also applies to software, and has become extremely important in the computer gaming software market.

Steam is the dominant player in the downloadable games market for PC games, with an estimated 75 per cent market share and 75 million active user accounts at the beginning of 2013. Year-on-year sales have increased by more than 100 per cent for five years. What does Steam do from the perspective of customers? It enables them to buy and download games software without requiring physical media such as a DVD. Even better, their purchased games can be updated, repaired or improved by 'patches' distributed automatically. They can download additional content to extend the value and life of the games and participate in online communities – perhaps discussing best strategy, asking for help with puzzles or gossiping about upcoming titles.

Steam is as much a brand as a piece of software – it gives a screen presence to an otherwise invisible organisation. The community aspect allows Valve Corporation, the creators of Steam, to create, build and maintain relationships with its customers. Steam creates marketing opportunities for Valve in three key areas – marketing communications, customer insight and partnering.

At a basic level, Steam enables the transmission of near-traditional advertisements as image or video files. After exiting a game, users can be presented with a series of advertisements tailored to their interests. The online forums and communities allow peer-to-peer word of mouth to snowball. Steam users can receive special offers such as discounts on current or future titles or early access to the hottest new releases. Demo versions of a game can be downloaded and trialled. Purchasers of a game might be given a 'guest pass' to allow a pal to join them on an adventure for a week before having to decide whether to pay for the full game. These promotions can be tailored and targeted very specifically to identified segments.

What about customer insight? The transmission of data between Steam and users is by no means one way. Data flows back from the user to Valve. As well as the obvious information about games bought and means and method of payment, the system collects information about how long was spent playing each game, how the individual interacts with the wider community – either in a forum or in a multi-player game – and how well or badly the player is doing, not to mention all the personal information incorporated within the user's online profile. Additionally, Steam returns information about adverts seen and demos and media files downloaded. Steam generates a picture – detailed down to the atomic level of who their customers are and the how, why and what of the technology they are using to enjoy their games.

Steam also allows Valve Corporation to partner with other game publishers. In negotiations with these other companies, Valve can make the enticing offer of being able to supply to end users more quickly, and far more cheaply than traditional distribution networks – with Valve taking a per-unit fee for incorporating the title into the sales and management functions of Steam. Currently, more than 3,000 titles from more than 100 publishers are available for download.

So, customers are getting access, convenience and value. Valve is able to gain significant insight and construct a highly effective marketing communications programme while simultaneously increasing the proportion of the end-user price the company realises and taking fees from other developers. Everyone (excepting the retailers) must be happy, yes?

Alas, no. Switching to Steam as a method of distribution has caused problems for consumers, Valve and other publishers. Let's consider consumer issues first. Even with today's technology the downloading process can represent a serious bottleneck. Even if you have signed up to superfast broadband, when a hot new title is released the demand for download bandwidth can be such that speeds slow to a trickle. If the Internet connection goes down during download then the game may not be able to validate itself against Steam's anti-piracy systems, meaning it won't work. If a new patch to repair or improve a game is released, the auto-install function within Steam may mean that that game is not playable until downloading and installation of the patch is complete, and that wait could be several hours. Economic issues also exist. If a consumer buys a game on the high street on physical media, that copy can be sold on or used in part exchange against another title. With only an electronic copy, no such potential exists. Furthermore, the flexibility of the online store allies itself with information held on that customer to present a price in his or her local currency, and many consumers are aware of and resent the fact that different prices are charged in different markets. Finally, the very fact that such a quantity of information is passed back through Steam is a concern to users worried about privacy – and such concerns may result in

Brands such as Steam enable the customer to buy and download games software without requiring physical media such as a DVD

Source: Alamy Images/Patriotic Alien.

further regulation, limitation and control of such activities generally.

For Valve, the situation is not black and white either. Steam requires considerable investment and support in respect of time and money – that global network of servers is expensive. Word of mouth about new releases can be enormously beneficial to sales if positive, but if a title garners negative comments in the Steam forums then that can depress sales significantly.

For other publishers – like Sega and Activision – Steam offers an attractive alternative to traditional distribution and retailing strategies. But they have to face the concern that Valve is a competitor as well as a distribution channel. Valve operates Steam as a game delivery channel, but it also develops and markets its own games.

Unquestionably, disintermediation has worked brilliantly as a strategy for Valve Corporation. Is there any chance that this strategy might eventually run out of steam?

Sources: 'What is iTunes?', available from http://www.apple.com/itunes/what-is/, accessed February 2010; 'Stardock Reveals Impulse, Steam Market Share Estimates', available from http://www.gamasutra.com/php-bin/news_index.php?story=26158, accessed February 2010; 'Direct2Drive: Recent Digital Distribution Market Estimates "Misinformation At Best"', available from http://www.gamasutra.com/view/news/26292/Direct2Drive_Recent_Digital_Distribution_Market_Estimates_Misinformation_At_Best.php, accessed February 2010; 'Our Products – Heinz Baked Beans', available from http://www.heinz.co.uk/Products/Beans/Ranges/Beanz/Heinz-Baked-Beanz, accessed February 2010; J.F. Mills and V. Camek, 'The Risks, Threats and Opportunities of Disintermediation: A Distributor's View', *International Journal of Physical Distribution and Logistics Management*, 34(9), 2004, pp. 714–27; 'Valve Corporation History', available from http://www.mobygames.com/company/valve-corporation/history, accessed February 2010; 'Steam Realises Extraordinary Growth in 2009', available from http://store.steampowered.com/news/3390/, accessed February 2010; 'Leading Platform for PC Games Now Serving Over 25 Million Accounts', available from http://www.valvesoftware.com/news.php?id=3390, accessed February 2010.

Rather than selling directly from its own website, Bosch refer buyers to resellers' websites or stores

Source: Alamy Images/ PhotoAlto.

power tools and outdoor power equipment online. But selling directly through its website would create conflicts with important and powerful retail partners. So, while Bosch's website provides detailed information about the company's products, you cannot buy a Bosch cordless screwdriver, rotary hammer, power saw or anything else there. Instead, the Bosch site provides a 'dealer locator' tool that refers you to resellers' websites and stores. Thus, Bosch's direct marketing helps both the company and its channel partners.

CHANNEL DESIGN DECISIONS

We now look at several channel decisions that manufacturers face. In designing marketing channels, manufacturers struggle between what is ideal and what is practical. A new firm with limited capital usually starts by selling in a limited market area. Deciding on the best channels might not be a problem. The problem might simply be how to convince one or a few good intermediaries to handle the line.

If successful, the new firm can branch out to new markets through the existing intermediaries. In smaller markets, the firm might sell directly to retailers; in larger markets, it might sell through distributors. In one region, it might grant exclusive franchises; in another, it might sell through all available outlets. Then, it might add a web store that sells directly to hard-to-reach customers. In this way, channel systems often evolve to meet market opportunities and conditions.

For maximum effectiveness, however, channel analysis and decision making should be more purposeful. Designing a channel system calls for analysing consumer needs, setting channel objectives, identifying major channel alternatives and evaluating them.

Analysing consumer needs

As noted previously, marketing channels are part of the overall *customer value-delivery network*. Each channel member adds value for the customer. Thus, designing the marketing channel starts with finding out what target consumers want from the channel. Do consumers want to buy from nearby locations or are they willing to travel to more distant centralised locations? Would they rather buy in person, over the phone, through the mail or via the Internet? Do they value breadth of assortment or do they prefer specialisation? Do consumers want many add-on services (delivery, credit, repairs, installation) or will they obtain these elsewhere? The faster the delivery, the greater the assortment provided, and the more add-on services supplied, the greater the channel's service level.

Providing the fastest delivery, greatest assortment and most services may not be possible or practical. The company and its channel members may not have the resources or skills needed to provide all the desired services. Also, providing higher levels of service results in higher costs for the channel and higher prices for consumers. The company must balance consumer needs not only against the feasibility and costs of meeting these needs, but also against customer price preferences. The success of discount retailing shows that consumers will often accept lower service levels in exchange for lower prices.

Setting channel objectives

Companies should state their marketing-channel objectives in terms of targeted levels of customer service. Usually, a company can identify several segments wanting different levels of service. The company should decide which segments to serve and the best channels to use in each case. In each segment, the company wants to minimise the total channel cost of meeting customer service requirements.

The company's channel objectives are also influenced by the nature of the company, its products, its marketing intermediaries, its competitors and the environment. For example, the company's size and financial situation determine which marketing functions it can handle itself and which it must give to intermediaries. Companies selling perishable products may require more direct marketing to avoid delays and too much handling.

In some cases, a company may want to compete in or near the same outlets that carry competitors' products. In other cases, producers may avoid the channels used by competitors. Mary Kay Cosmetics, for example, sells direct to consumers through its corps of more than 1.8 million independent beauty consultants in 35 markets worldwide, among them Finland, Moldova, Norway, Poland, Slovakia and Ukraine, rather than going head-to-head with other cosmetics makers for scarce positions in retail stores. Directline markets insurance directly to consumers via the telephone and the Web rather than through agents.

Finally, environmental factors such as economic conditions and legal constraints may affect channel objectives and design. For example, in a depressed economy, producers want to distribute their goods in the most economical way, using shorter channels and dropping unneeded services that add to the final price of the goods.

Identifying major alternatives

When the company has defined its channel objectives, it should next identify its major channel alternatives in terms of *types* of intermediaries, the *number* of intermediaries and the *responsibilities* of each channel member.

Types of intermediaries

A firm should identify the types of channel members available to carry out its channel work. Most companies face many channel member choices. For example, computer manufacturer Dell has used two distinct channel distribution strategies over the years. One of those is to sell directly to final consumers and business buyers only through its sophisticated phone and Internet marketing channel, and directly to large corporate, institutional and government buyers using its direct sales force. However, to reach more consumers and to match competitors such as HP, Dell has also employed an indirect distribution strategy of selling through retailers and 'value-added resellers', who are independent distributors and dealers who develop computer systems and applications tailored to the special needs of small and medium-sized business customers. Dell has used both the direct and the indirect channel strategies in response to conditions in the marketplace and competitor action.

Using many types of resellers in a channel provides both benefits and drawbacks. For example, by selling through retailers and value-added resellers in addition to its own direct channels, Dell is able to reach more and different kinds of buyers. However, those are more difficult to manage and control. And the direct and indirect channels will compete with each other for many of the same customers, causing potential conflict.

Number of marketing intermediaries

Companies must also determine the number of channel members to use at each level. Three strategies are available: intensive distribution, exclusive distribution and selective distribution. Producers of convenience products and common raw materials typically seek **intensive distribution** – a strategy in which they stock their products in as many outlets as possible. These products must be available where and when consumers want them. For example, toothpaste, confectionery and other similar items are sold in millions of outlets to provide maximum brand exposure and consumer convenience. Nestlé, Danone, Cadbury and other consumer goods companies distribute their products in this way.

By contrast, some producers purposely limit the number of intermediaries handling their products. The extreme form of this practice is **exclusive distribution**, in which the producer gives only a limited number of dealers the exclusive right to distribute its products in their territories. Exclusive distribution is often found in the distribution of luxury cars and exclusive women's clothing. For example, Bentley dealers are few and far between – even large cities may have only one dealer. By granting exclusive distribution, Bentley gains stronger distributor selling support and more control over dealer prices, promotion, credit and services. Exclusive distribution also enhances the car's image and allows for higher mark-ups.

Between intensive and exclusive distribution lies **selective distribution** – the use of more than one, but fewer than all, of the intermediaries who are willing to carry a company's products. Most TV, furniture and home appliance brands are distributed in this manner. For example, Zanussi-Electrolux, Beko and Miele sell their major appliances through dealer networks and selected large retailers. By using selective distribution, they can develop good working relationships with selected channel members and expect a better-than-average selling effort. Selective distribution gives producers good market coverage with more control and less cost than does intensive distribution.

Responsibilities of channel members

The producer and intermediaries need to agree on the terms and responsibilities of each channel member. They should agree on price policies, conditions of sale, territorial rights and specific services to be performed by each party. The producer should establish a list price and a fair set of discounts for intermediaries. It must define each channel member's territory, and it should be careful about where it places new resellers.

Mutual services and duties need to be spelled out carefully, especially in franchise and exclusive distribution channels. For example, McDonald's provides franchisees with promotional support, a record-keeping system, training at Hamburger University and general management assistance. In turn, franchisees must meet company standards for physical facilities, cooperate with new promotion programmes, provide requested information and buy specified food products.

Evaluating the major alternatives

Suppose a company has identified several channel alternatives and wants to select the one that will best satisfy its long-term objectives. Each alternative should be evaluated against economic, control and adaptive criteria.

Using *economic criteria,* a company compares the likely sales, costs and profitability of different channel alternatives. What will be the investment required by each channel alternative, and what returns will result? The company must also consider *control issues.* Using intermediaries usually means giving them some control over the marketing of the product, and some intermediaries take more control than others. Other things being equal, the company prefers to keep as much control as possible. Finally, the company must apply *adaptive criteria*. Channels often involve long-term commitments, yet the company wants to keep the channel flexible so that it can adapt to environmental changes. A channel that involves long-term commitments must deliver superior economic returns or better control.

Designing international distribution channels

International marketers face many additional complexities in designing their channels. Each country has its own unique distribution system that has evolved over time and changes very slowly. These channel systems can vary widely from country to country. Thus, global marketers usually adapt their channel strategies to the existing structures within each country.

In some markets, the distribution system is complex and hard to penetrate, consisting of many layers and large numbers of intermediaries.

For example, many Western companies find Japan's distribution system difficult to navigate. It is steeped in tradition and very complex, with many distributors touching one product before it makes it to the store shelf. Many Western firms have had great difficulty breaking into the closely knit, tradition-bound Japanese distribution network.

At the other extreme, distribution systems in developing countries may be scattered, inefficient or altogether lacking. For example, China and India are huge markets, each with populations well over a billion people. However, because of inadequate distribution systems, most companies can profitably access only a small portion of the population located in each country's most affluent cities. 'China is a very decentralised market,' notes a China trade expert. '[It's] made up of two dozen distinct markets sprawling across 2,000 cities. Each has its own culture. . . . It's like operating in an asteroid belt.' China's distribution system is so fragmented that logistics costs to wrap, bundle, load, unload, sort, reload and transport goods amount to more than 22 per cent of the nation's GDP, far higher than in most other countries. (In Europe logistics costs generally account for just over 10 per cent of a nation's GDP.) After years of effort, even the best overseas companies admit that they have been unable to assemble an efficient supply chain in China.[7]

Thus, international marketers face a wide range of channel alternatives. Designing efficient and effective channel systems between and within various country markets poses a difficult challenge. We discuss international distribution decisions later (see Chapter 15).

CHANNEL MANAGEMENT DECISIONS

Once the company has reviewed its channel alternatives and decided on the best channel design, it must implement and manage the chosen channel. Channel management calls for selecting, managing and motivating individual channel members and evaluating their performance over time.

Selecting channel members

Producers vary in their ability to attract qualified marketing intermediaries. Some producers have no trouble signing up channel members. For example, with a globally prestigious motor car brand such as Lexus, there will never be any difficulty in attracting dealers in practically any part of Europe or the rest of the world. But things are different for a less prestigious brand such as Skoda, particularly in the rich economies of Western Europe.

When selecting intermediaries, the company should determine what characteristics distinguish the better ones. It will want to evaluate each channel member's years in business, other lines carried, growth and profit record, cooperativeness and reputation. If the intermediaries are sales agents, the company will want to evaluate the number and character of other lines carried and the size and quality of the sales force. If the intermediary is a retail store that wants exclusive or selective distribution, the company will want to evaluate the store's customers, location and future growth potential.

Managing and motivating channel members

Once selected, channel members must be continuously managed and motivated to do their best. The company must sell not only *through* the intermediaries, but also *to* and *with* them. Most companies see their intermediaries as first-line customers and partners. They practise strong *partner relationship management (PRM)* to forge long-term partnerships with channel members. This creates a marketing system that meets the needs of both the company *and* its marketing partners.

In managing its channels, a company must convince distributors that they can succeed better by working together as a part of a cohesive value-delivery system.[8] Thus, Procter & Gamble and Tesco work together to create superior value for final consumers. They jointly plan merchandising goals and strategies, inventory levels, and advertising and promotion plans. Similarly, heavy-equipment manufacturer Caterpillar and its worldwide network of independent dealers work in close harmony to find better ways to bring value to customers.

> Caterpillar produces innovative, high-quality products. Yet the most important reason for Caterpillar's dominance is its distribution network of 181 outstanding independent dealers worldwide. Caterpillar and its dealers work as partners. According to a former Caterpillar CEO: 'After the product leaves our door, the dealers take over. They are the ones on the front line. They're the ones who live with the product for its lifetime. They're the ones customers see.' When a big piece of Caterpillar equipment breaks down, customers know that they can count on Caterpillar and its outstanding dealer network for support. Dealers play a vital role in almost every aspect of Caterpillar's operations, from product design and delivery to product service and support.
>
> Caterpillar really knows its dealers and cares about their success. It closely monitors each dealership's sales, market position, service capability and financial situation. When it sees a problem, it jumps in to help. In addition to more formal business ties, Caterpillar forms close personal ties with dealers in a kind of family relationship. Caterpillar and its dealers feel a deep pride in what they are accomplishing together. As the former CEO puts it, 'There's a camaraderie among our dealers around the world that really makes it more than just a financial arrangement. They feel that what they're doing is good for the world because they are part of an organisation that makes, sells, and tends to the machines that make the world work.'[9]

As a result of its partnership with dealers, Caterpillar dominates the world's markets for heavy construction, mining and logging equipment. Its familiar yellow tractors, crawlers, loaders, bulldozers and trucks capture some 40 per cent of the worldwide heavy-equipment business, twice that of number 2, Komatsu.

Many companies are now installing integrated high-tech PRM systems to coordinate their whole-channel marketing efforts. Just as they use customer relationship management (CRM) software systems to help manage relationships with important customers, companies can now use PRM and supply chain management (SCM) software to help recruit, train, organise, manage, motivate and evaluate relationships with channel partners.

Evaluating channel members

The producer must regularly check channel member performance against standards such as sales quotas, average inventory levels, customer delivery time, treatment of damaged and lost goods, cooperation in company promotion and training programmes, and services to the customer. The company should recognise and reward intermediaries who are performing well and adding good value for consumers. Those who are performing poorly should be assisted or, as a last resort, replaced. A company may periodically 'requalify' its intermediaries and prune the weaker ones.

PUBLIC POLICY AND DISTRIBUTION DECISIONS

For the most part, companies are legally free to develop whatever channel arrangements suit them. In fact, the laws affecting channels seek to prevent the exclusionary tactics of some companies that might keep another company from using a desired channel. Most channel law deals with the mutual rights and duties of the channel members once they have formed a relationship.

Many producers and wholesalers like to develop exclusive channels for their products. When the seller allows only certain outlets to carry its products, this strategy is called *exclusive distribution*. When the seller requires that these dealers do not handle competitors' products, its strategy is called *exclusive dealing*. Both parties can benefit from exclusive arrangements. The seller obtains more loyal and dependable outlets, and the dealers obtain a steady source of supply and stronger seller support. But exclusive arrangements also exclude other producers from selling to these dealers. This situation brings exclusive dealing contracts under the scope of Article 85(1) of the EU Treaty. One of the principal objectives of establishing the EU was to bring about conditions of free trade, so it is not surprising to find that matters to do with free competition, which can include 'vertical agreements' between channel members, were addressed in the treaty upon which the EU was founded. Article 85(1) prohibits actions which 'have as their object or effect the prevention, restriction or distortion of competition'. In practice, many forms of vertical agreement are allowed under EU competition law, but this is a complex area in which advice from a lawyer with expertise in EU law is likely to be necessary.

Exclusive dealing often includes *exclusive territorial agreements*. The producer may agree not to sell to other dealers in a given area, or the buyer may agree to sell only in its own territory. The first practice is normal under franchise systems as a way to increase dealer enthusiasm and commitment. It is also perfectly legal – a seller has no legal obligation to sell through more outlets than it wishes. The second practice, whereby the producer tries to keep a dealer from selling outside its territory, is a much more contentious issue.

Producers of a strong brand sometimes sell it to dealers only if the dealers will take some or all of the rest of the line. This is called full-line forcing. Such *tying agreements* are not necessarily illegal, but the legal situation will vary depending on the specific anti-competition laws in individual European countries. The practice may prevent consumers from freely choosing among competing suppliers of these other brands.

Finally, producers are free to select their dealers, but their right to terminate dealers is somewhat restricted. In general, sellers can drop dealers 'for cause'. However, they cannot drop dealers if, for example, the dealers refuse to cooperate in a doubtful legal arrangement, such as exclusive dealing or tying agreements.

MARKETING LOGISTICS AND SUPPLY CHAIN MANAGEMENT

In today's global marketplace, selling a product is sometimes easier than getting it to customers. Companies must decide on the best way to store, handle and move their products and services so that they are available to customers in the right assortments, at the right time and in the right place. Physical distribution and logistics effectiveness have a major impact on both customer satisfaction and company costs. Here we consider the nature and importance of logistics management in the supply chain, goals of the logistics system, major logistics functions and the need for integrated supply chain management.

Nature and importance of marketing logistics

To some managers, marketing logistics means only trucks and warehouses. But modern logistics is much more than this. **Marketing logistics** (or **physical distribution**) involves planning, implementing and controlling the physical flow of goods, services and related information from points of origin to points of consumption to meet customer requirements at a profit. In short, it involves getting the right product to the right customer in the right place at the right time.

In the past, physical distribution typically started with products at the plant and then tried to find low-cost solutions to get them to customers. However, today's marketers prefer customer-centred logistics thinking, which starts with the marketplace and works backwards to the factory, or even to sources of supply. Marketing logistics involves not only *outbound distribution* (moving products from the factory to resellers and ultimately to customers) but also *inbound distribution* (moving products and materials from suppliers to the factory) and *reverse distribution* (moving broken, unwanted or excess products returned by consumers or resellers). That is, it involves the entire **supply chain management** – managing upstream and downstream value-added flows of materials, final goods and related information among suppliers, the company, resellers and final consumers, as shown in Figure 10.5.

The logistics manager's task is to coordinate activities of suppliers, purchasing agents, marketers, channel members and customers. These activities include forecasting, information systems, purchasing, production planning, order processing, inventory, warehousing and transportation planning.

Companies today are placing greater emphasis on logistics for several reasons. First, companies can gain a powerful competitive advantage by using improved logistics to give customers better service or lower prices. Second, improved logistics can yield tremendous cost savings to both the company and its customers. As much as 20 per cent of an average product's price is accounted for by shipping and transport alone. This far exceeds the cost of advertising and many other marketing costs. Third, the explosion in product variety has created a need for improved logistics management. For example, 100 years ago a typical grocery store carried only 270 items. The store manager could keep track of this inventory on about 10 pages of notebook paper stuffed in a shirt pocket. Today, the average supermarket carries a bewildering stock of more than 25,000 items. A Carrefour Hypermarché carries more than 100,000 products, 30,000 of which are grocery products. Ordering, shipping, stocking and controlling such a variety of products presents a sizeable logistics challenge.

Finally, improvements in IT have created opportunities for major gains in distribution efficiency. Today's companies are using sophisticated supply chain management software, web-based logistics systems, point-of-sale scanners, uniform product codes, satellite tracking, and electronic transfer of order and payment data. Such technology lets them manage the flow of goods, information and finances quickly and efficiently through the supply chain.

Goals of the logistics system

Some companies state their logistics objective as providing maximum customer service at the least cost. Unfortunately, no logistics system can *both* maximise customer service *and* minimise distribution costs. Maximum customer service implies rapid delivery, large inventories, flexible assortments, liberal returns policies and other services – all of which raise

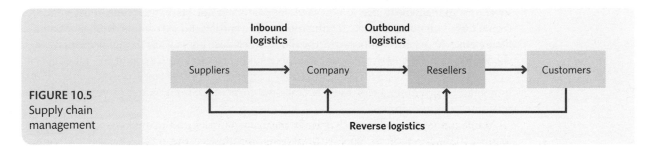

FIGURE 10.5
Supply chain management

distribution costs. In contrast, minimum distribution costs imply slower delivery, smaller inventories and larger shipping lots – which represent a lower level of overall customer service.

The goal of marketing logistics should be to provide a *targeted* level of customer service at the least cost. A company must first research the importance of various distribution services to customers and then set desired service levels for each segment. The objective is to maximise *profits*, not sales. Therefore, the company must weigh the benefits of providing higher levels of service against the costs. Some companies offer less service than their competitors and charge a lower price. Other companies offer more service and charge higher prices to cover higher costs.

Major logistics functions

Given a set of logistics objectives, the company is ready to design a logistics system that will minimise the cost of attaining these objectives. The major logistics functions include *warehousing, inventory management, transportation* and *logistics information management*.

Warehousing

Production and consumption cycles rarely match. Most companies have to store their tangible goods while waiting to sell them. For example, Flymo, Bosch, Honda and other lawnmower manufacturers run their factories all year long and store up products for the heavy spring and summer buying seasons. The storage function overcomes differences in needed quantities and timing, ensuring that products are available when customers are ready to buy them.

A company must decide on *how many* and *what types* of warehouses it needs and *where* they will be located. The company might use either *storage warehouses* or *distribution centres*. Storage warehouses store goods for moderate to long periods. **Distribution centres** are designed to move goods rather than just store them. They are large and highly automated warehouses designed to receive goods from various plants and suppliers, take orders, fill them efficiently and deliver goods to customers as quickly as possible.

For example, Tesco operates a network of 20 distribution centres in the UK, serving the needs of over 1,250 UK stores. As Tesco expands internationally it opens similar distribution centres in other countries. For example, in addition to distribution centres in many parts of the UK, Tesco has distribution centres in Ireland, Slovakia, Poland, Hungary and the Czech Republic. A typical Tesco distribution centre employs around 500 people and handles 100 million cases of products every year.

Like almost everything else these days, warehousing has seen dramatic changes in technology in recent years. Older, multi-storeyed warehouses with outdated materials-handling methods are steadily being replaced by newer, single-storeyed *automated warehouses* with advanced, computer-controlled materials-handling systems requiring few employees. Computers and scanners read orders and direct lift trucks, electric hoists or robots to gather goods, move them to loading docks and issue invoices.

Inventory management

Inventory management also affects customer satisfaction. Here, managers must maintain the delicate balance between carrying too little inventory and carrying too much. With too little stock, the firm risks not having products when customers want to buy. To remedy this, the firm may need costly emergency shipments or production. Carrying too much inventory results in unnecessarily high inventory carrying costs and stock obsolescence. Thus, in managing inventory, firms must balance the costs of carrying larger inventories against resulting sales and profits.

Many companies have greatly reduced their inventories and related costs through *just-in-time* logistics systems. With such systems, producers and retailers carry only small inventories of parts or merchandise, often only enough for a few days of operations. For example, computer manufacturer Dell is now Ireland's largest exporter. Dell is a master just-in-time producer and carries just 3–4 days of inventory, whereas competitors might carry 40 days or even 60.[10] New stock arrives exactly when needed, rather than being stored in inventory until being used. Just-in-time systems require accurate forecasting along with fast, frequent and flexible delivery so that new supplies will be available when needed. However, these systems result in substantial savings in inventory carrying and handling costs.

Marketers are always looking for new ways to make inventory management more efficient. In the not too distant future, handling inventory might even become fully automated. For example, we have already discussed RFID or 'smart tag' technology (see Chapter 3), by which small transmitter chips are embedded in or placed on products and packaging on everything from flowers and razors to tyres. 'Smart' products could make the entire supply chain – which accounts for nearly 75 per cent of a product's cost – intelligent and automated. Companies using RFID would know, at any time, exactly where a product is located physically within the supply chain. 'Smart shelves' would not only tell them when it is time to reorder, but also place the order automatically with their suppliers. Such exciting new IT applications will revolutionise distribution as we know it. Many large and resourceful marketing companies, such as Procter & Gamble, IBM and Wal-Mart, are investing heavily to make full use of RFID technology a reality.[11]

Transportation

The choice of transportation carriers affects the pricing of products, delivery performance and condition of the goods when they arrive – all of which will affect customer satisfaction. In shipping goods to its warehouses, dealers and customers, the company can choose among five main transportation modes, namely truck, rail, water, pipeline and air, along with an alternative mode for digital products: the Internet.

Trucks have in recent years increased their share of transportation steadily and offer some advantages that are hard to match. Trucks are highly flexible in their routing and time schedules, and they can usually offer faster service than railways. They are efficient for short hauls of high-value merchandise. Trucking firms have added many services in recent years. For example, French trucking company Société Norbert Dentressangle SA and most other major carriers now offer everything from satellite tracking and 24-hour shipment information to logistics planning software and 'border ambassadors' who expedite cross-border shipping operations. Norbert Dentressangle is a typical example of a large-scale European trucking operation. Although the company is based in France, 65 per cent of its business serves destinations outside France, and on average the company clocks up 650 crossings of the English Channel every day.

Increasingly, transport operators like Norbert Dentressangle of France have to take account of environmental factors in their strategic planning

Source: Courtesy of Renault Trucks Ltd.

However, Norbert Dentressangle and other European transport operators (such as Kühne und Nagel AG of Germany) are all having to face up to the issue of CO_2 emissions; transport in general is a major contributor to Europe's CO_2 emissions, and road transport contributes much the largest share of overall transport emissions. Trucking companies are striving to increase the efficiency of their operations, but with the current European focus on reducing CO_2 emissions in the struggle to avert climate change, they will no doubt come under ever-increasing pressure to reduce the environmental impact of their business.

Railways are one of the most cost-effective modes for shipping large amounts of bulk products – coal, sand, minerals, and farm and forest products – over long distances. In recent years, railways have increased their customer services by designing new equipment to handle special categories of goods, providing flatcars for carrying truck trailers by rail (piggyback), and providing in-transit services such as the diversion of shipped goods to other destinations en route and the processing of goods en route.

Water carriers transport large amounts of goods by ships and barges on European coastal and inland waterways. Although the cost of water transportation is very low for shipping bulky, low-value, non-perishable products such as sand, coal, grain, oil and metallic ores, water transportation is the slowest mode and may be affected by the weather. Both rail transport and water transport produce less CO_2 per kilometre than road transport, so that European policy makers prefer these transport modes to road transport wherever possible.

Pipelines, which account for about 16 per cent of cargo tonne-kilometres, are a specialised means of shipping oil, natural gas and chemicals from sources to markets. Most pipelines are used by their owners to ship their own products.

Although *airfreight* contributes only a small percentage of freight kilometres, this is still an important freight transportation mode. Airfreight rates are much higher than rail or truck rates, but airfreight is ideal when speed is needed or distant markets have to be reached. Among the most frequently airfreighted products are perishables (fresh fish, cut flowers) and high-value, low-bulk items (technical instruments, jewellery). Companies find that airfreight also reduces inventory levels, packaging costs and the number of warehouses needed. Of course, air transport performs relatively poorly on environmental grounds (e.g. in terms of CO_2 emissions). Some consumer activists are encouraging consumers to avoid products that have been transported by air, in order to discourage the use of airfreight other than for essential purposes.

The *Internet* carries digital products from producer to customer via satellite, cable modem or telephone wire. Software firms, the media, music companies and education all make use of the Internet to transport digital products. While these firms primarily use traditional transportation to distribute CDs, newspapers and more, the Internet holds the potential for lower product distribution costs. Whereas aircraft, trucks and trains move freight and packages, digital technology moves information bits.

Shippers also use **intermodal transportation** – combining two or more modes of transportation. *Piggyback* describes the use of rail and trucks; *fishyback,* water and trucks; *train-ship,* water and rail; and *airtruck,* air and trucks. Combining modes provides advantages that no single mode can deliver. Each combination offers advantages to the shipper. For example, not only is piggyback cheaper than trucking alone, but it also provides flexibility, convenience and potential environmental benefits.

In choosing a transportation mode for a product, shippers must balance many considerations: speed, dependability, availability, cost and others. Thus, if a shipper needs speed, air and truck are the prime choices. If the goal is low cost, then water or pipeline might be best. Increasingly, shippers will also have to take account of the environmental impact of their operations, because of pressure from European policy makers and consumers.

Logistics information management

Companies manage their supply chains through information. Channel partners often link up to share information and to make better joint logistics decisions. From a logistics perspective, information flows such as customer orders, billing, inventory levels and even customer data are closely linked to channel performance. The company wants to design a simple, accessible, fast and accurate process for capturing, processing and sharing channel information.

Information can be shared and managed in many ways – by mail or telephone, through salespeople, or through traditional or Internet-based *electronic data interchange (EDI)*, the computerised exchange of data between organisations. EDI has existed since well before the emergence of the Internet, and has been advocated as a mechanism by which the less developed countries of Europe can improve their economic conditions. For example, EDI was developed in Slovenia in the 1990s, with a focus on the automotive, trade, transportation and financial sectors, in order to promote economic growth.[12] Some car manufacturers make the use of EDI compulsory for any supplier that wants to do business with them.[13]

In some cases, suppliers might actually be asked to generate orders and arrange deliveries for their customers. Many large retailers – such as Tesco and Homebase – work closely with major suppliers such as Procter & Gamble or Black & Decker to set up *vendor-managed inventory (VMI)* systems or *continuous inventory replenishment* systems. Using VMI, the customer shares real-time data on sales and current inventory levels with the supplier. The supplier then takes full responsibility for managing inventories and deliveries. Some retailers even go so far as to shift inventory and delivery costs to the supplier. Such systems require close cooperation between the buyer and seller.

Integrated logistics management

Today, more and more companies are adopting the concept of **integrated logistics management**. This concept recognises that providing better customer service and trimming distribution costs require *teamwork*, both inside the company and among all the marketing-channel organisations. Inside, the company's various departments must work closely together to maximise the company's own logistics performance. Outside, the company must integrate its logistics system with those of its suppliers and customers to maximise the performance of the entire distribution system.

Cross-functional teamwork inside the company

In most companies, responsibility for various logistics activities is assigned to many different functional units – marketing, sales, finance, operations, purchasing. Too often, each function tries to optimise its own logistics performance without regard for the activities of the other functions. However, transportation, inventory, warehousing and order processing activities interact, often in unexpected ways. Lower inventory levels reduce inventory carrying costs. But they may also reduce customer service and increase costs from stockouts, back orders, special production runs and costly fast-freight shipments. Because distribution activities involve strong trade-offs, decisions by different functions must be coordinated to achieve better overall logistics performance.

The goal of **integrated supply chain management** is to harmonise all of the company's logistics decisions. Close working relationships among functions can be achieved in several ways. Some companies have created permanent logistics committees, made up of managers responsible for different physical distribution activities. Companies can also create supply chain manager positions that link the logistics activities of functional areas. For example, Procter & Gamble has created supply managers who manage all of the supply chain activities for each of its product categories. Many companies have a vice president of logistics with cross-functional authority. Finally, companies can employ sophisticated, system-wide supply chain management software, now available from a wide range of software enterprises large and small, from SAP and Oracle to Infor and Logility. The worldwide market for supply chain management software grew by 7.1 per cent to over $8.3bn in 2012 and continues to grow fast.[14] The important thing is that the company must coordinate its logistics and marketing activities to create high market satisfaction at a reasonable cost.

Building logistics partnerships

Companies must do more than improve their own logistics. They must also work with other channel partners to improve whole-channel distribution. The members of a distribution channel are linked closely in creating customer value and building customer relationships. One company's distribution system is another company's supply system. The success of each channel member depends on the performance of the entire supply chain. For example, Carrefour can charge the lowest retail prices only if its entire supply chain – consisting of thousands of merchandise suppliers, transport companies, warehouses and service providers – operates at maximum efficiency.

Smart companies coordinate their logistics strategies and forge strong partnerships with suppliers and customers to improve customer service and reduce channel costs. Many companies have created *cross-functional, cross-company teams*. Other companies partner through *shared projects*. For example, many large retailers are working closely with suppliers on in-store programmes. Clearly, both the supplier and the customer benefit from such partnerships. The point is that all supply chain members must work together in the cause of serving final consumers.

Third-party logistics

Most big companies love to make and sell their products. But many loathe the associated logistics 'grunt work'. They detest the bundling, loading, unloading, sorting, storing, reloading, transporting, customs clearing and tracking required to supply their factories and to get products out to customers. They hate it so much that a growing number of firms now outsource some or all of their logistics to **third-party logistics (3PL) providers**.

These '3PLs' – companies such as CEVA Logistics, UPS Supply Chain Services or FedEx Logistics – help clients to tighten up sluggish, overstuffed supply chains, slash inventories and get products to customers more quickly and reliably. CEVA Logistics employs over 50,000 people and operates from over 1,000 locations in over 100 countries. In 2008 CEVA Romania, a subsidiary of CEVA Logistics, announced that it had taken over the planning and supply of Pirelli tyres from Pirelli's warehouse in Slatina to all Romanian customers.[15] According to a recent survey of chief logistics executives at Fortune 500 companies, 81 per cent of these companies use third-party logistics (also called *outsourced logistics* or *contract logistics*) services.[16]

Zara: fast fashions – *really* fast

MARKETING AT WORK 10.2

Fashion retailer Zara is growing fast. It sells 'cheap chic' – stylish designs that resemble those of big-name fashion houses but at moderate prices. Zara is the prototype for a new breed of 'fast-fashion' retailers, companies that recognise and respond to the latest fashion trends quickly and nimbly. While competing retailers are still working out their designs, Zara has already put the latest fashion into its stores and is moving on to the next big thing.

Zara has attracted a near cult-like clientele in recent years. Following the recent economic crisis, even affluent shoppers are swarming to buy Zara's stylish but affordable offerings. Thanks to Zara's rapid growth, the sales, profits and store presence of its parent company, Spain-based Inditex, have more than quadrupled since 2000. That makes Inditex the world's largest clothing retailer with nearly 6,000 stores.

Zara clearly sells the right goods for the present times. This success comes not just from *what* it sells. Perhaps more important, success comes from how and how fast Zara's cutting-edge distribution system *delivers* what it sells to eagerly awaiting customers. Zara delivers fast fashion – *really* fast fashion. Through vertical integration, Zara controls all phases of the fashion process, from design and manufacturing to distribution through its own managed stores. The company's integrated supply system makes Zara faster, more flexible and more efficient than international competitors such as Gap, Benetton and H&M. Zara can take a new fashion concept through design, manufacturing and store-shelf placement in as little as two weeks, whereas competitors often take six months or more. And the resulting low costs let Zara offer the very latest mid-market chic at downmarket prices.

The whole process starts with input about what consumers want. Zara store managers act as trend spotters. They patrol store aisles using handheld computers, reporting in real time what is selling and what is not. They talk with customers to learn what they are looking for but not yet finding. At the same time, Zara trend seekers roam fashion shows in Paris and concerts in Tokyo, looking for young people who might be wearing something new or different. Then, they are on the phone to company headquarters in tiny La Coruña, Spain, reporting on what they have seen and heard. Back home, based on this and other feedback, the company's team of 300 designers conjures up a prolific flow of hot new fashions.

Once the designers have done their work, production begins. But rather than relying on a hodgepodge of slow-moving suppliers in Asia, as most competitors do, Zara makes 40 per cent of its own fabrics and produces more than half of its own clothes. Even outsourced manufacturing goes primarily to local contractors. Almost all clothes sold in Zara's stores worldwide are made quickly and efficiently at or near company headquarters in the remote northwest corner of Spain.

Finished goods then feed into Zara's modern distribution centres, which ship finished products immediately and directly to stores around the world, saving time, eliminating the need for warehouses and keeping inventories low. The highly automated centres can sort, pack, label and allocate up to 80,000 items an hour.

Again, the key word describing Zara's distribution system is *fast*. The time between receiving an order at the distribution centre and the delivery of goods to a store averages 24 hours for European stores and a maximum of 48 hours for American or Asian stores. Zara stores receive small shipments of new merchandise two to three times each week, compared with competing chains' outlets, which get large shipments seasonally, usually just four to six times per year.

Speedy design and distribution allow Zara to introduce a lot of new fashions – far more than its competitors. The combination of a large number of new fashions delivered in frequent small batches gives Zara stores a continually updated merchandise mix that brings customers back more often. Zara customers visit the store an average of 17 times per year, compared with less than five customer visits at competing stores. Fast turnover also results in less outdated and discounted merchandise. Because Zara makes what consumers already want or are now wearing, it does not have to guess what will be hot six months out.

In all, Zara's carefully integrated design and distribution process gives the fast-moving retailer a tremendous competitive advantage. Its turbocharged system gets out the goods customers want, when they want them – maybe even before:

A couple of summers ago, Zara managed to latch onto one of the season's hottest trends in just four weeks. The process started when trend-spotters spread the word back to headquarters: white eyelet – cotton with tiny holes in it – was set to become white-hot. A quick telephone survey of Zara store managers confirmed that the fabric could be a winner, so in-house designers got down to work. They zapped patterns electronically to Zara's factory across the street, and the fabric was cut. Local subcontractors stitched white-eyelet V-neck belted dresses and finished them in less than a week. The €129 dresses were inspected, tagged, and transported through a tunnel under the street to a distribution centre. From there, they were quickly dispatched to Zara stores from Berlin to Tokyo – where they were flying off the racks just two days later.

Sources: Cecilie Rohwedder, 'Zara Grows as Retail Rivals Struggle', *The Wall Street Journal*, 26 March 2009, p. B1; 'Inditex Outperforms with Growth in All Its Markets', *Retail Week*, 27 March 2009, accessed at www.retail-week.com; Kerry Capell, 'Fashion Conquistador', *BusinessWeek*, 4 September 2006, pp. 38–9; Cecilie Rohwedder, 'Turbocharged Supply Chain May Speed Zara Past Gap as Top Clothing Retailer', *The Globe and Mail*, 26 March 2009, p. B12; information from the Inditex Press Dossier, accessed at http://www.inditex.com/en/media/press_dossier, December 2014, and from Inditex FY2013 Results Presentation, December 2014, accessed at http://www.inditex.com/en/investors/investors_relations/results_presentations

Companies use third-party logistics providers for several reasons. First, because getting the product to market is their main focus, these providers can often do it more efficiently and at lower cost. Outsourcing typically results in 15 per cent to 30 per cent cost savings. Second, outsourcing logistics frees a company to focus more intensely on its core business. Finally, integrated logistics companies understand increasingly complex logistics environments. This can be especially helpful to companies attempting to expand their global market coverage. For example, companies distributing their products across Europe face a bewildering array of environmental restrictions that affect logistics, including packaging standards, truck size and weight limits, and noise and emissions pollution controls. By outsourcing its logistics, a company can gain a complete pan-European distribution system without incurring the costs, delays and risks associated with setting up its own system.

THE JOURNEY YOU'VE TAKEN Reviewing the concepts

So, what have you learned about distribution channels and integrated supply chain management? Marketing-channel decisions are among the most important decisions that management faces. A company's channel decisions directly affect every other marketing decision. Management must make channel decisions carefully, incorporating today's needs with tomorrow's likely selling environment. Some companies pay too little attention to their distribution channels, but others have used imaginative distribution systems to gain competitive advantage.

1 Explain why companies use marketing channels and discuss the functions these channels perform

Most producers use intermediaries to bring their products to market. They try to forge a *marketing channel* (or *distribution channel*) – a set of interdependent organisations involved in the process of making a product or service available for use or consumption by the consumer or business user. Through their contacts, experience, specialisation and scale of operation, intermediaries usually offer the firm more than it can achieve on its own.

Marketing channels perform many key functions. Some help *complete* transactions by gathering and distributing *information* needed for planning and aiding exchange; by developing and spreading persuasive *communications* about an offer; by performing *contact* work – finding and communicating with prospective buyers; by *matching* – shaping and fitting the offer to the buyer's needs; and by entering into *negotiation* to reach an agreement on price and other terms of the offer so that ownership can be transferred. Other functions help to *fulfil* the completed transactions by offering *physical distribution* – transporting and storing goods; *financing* – acquiring and using funds to cover the costs of the channel work; and *risk taking* – assuming the risks of carrying out the channel work.

2 Discuss how channel members interact and how they organise to perform the work of the channel

The channel will be most effective when each member is assigned the tasks it can do best. Ideally, because the success of individual channel members depends on overall channel success, all channel firms should work together smoothly. They should understand and accept their roles, coordinate their goals and activities, and cooperate to attain overall channel goals. By cooperating, they can more effectively sense, serve and satisfy the target market. In a large company, the formal organisation structure assigns roles and provides needed leadership. But in a distribution channel made up of independent firms, leadership and power are not formally set. Traditionally, distribution channels have lacked the leadership needed to assign roles and manage conflict. In recent years, however, new types of channel organisations have appeared that provide stronger leadership and improved performance.

3 Identify the major channel alternatives open to a company

Each firm identifies alternative ways to reach its market. Available means vary from direct selling to using one, two, three or more intermediary *channel levels*. Marketing channels face continuous and sometimes dramatic change. Three of the most important trends are the growth of *vertical, horizontal* and *multichannel marketing systems*. These trends affect channel cooperation, conflict and competition. *Channel design* begins with assessing customer channel service needs and company channel objectives and constraints. The company then identifies the major channel alternatives in terms of the *types* of intermediaries, the *number* of intermediaries and the *channel responsibilities* of each. Each channel alternative must be evaluated according to economic, control and adaptive criteria. Channel management calls for selecting qualified intermediaries and motivating them. Individual channel members must be evaluated regularly.

4 Explain how companies select, motivate and evaluate channel members

Producers vary in their ability to attract qualified marketing intermediaries. Some producers have no trouble signing up channel members. Others have to work hard to line up enough qualified intermediaries. When selecting intermediaries, the company should evaluate each channel member's qualifications and select those who best fit its channel objectives. Once selected, channel members must be continuously motivated to do their best. The company must sell not only *through* the intermediaries, but *to* them. It should work to forge long-term partnerships with its channel partners to create a marketing system that meets the needs of both the manufacturer *and* the partners. The company must also regularly check channel member performance against established performance standards, rewarding intermediaries who are performing well and assisting or replacing weaker ones.

5 Discuss the nature and importance of marketing logistics and integrated supply chain management

Just as firms are giving the marketing concept increased recognition, more business firms are paying attention to *marketing logistics* (or *physical distribution*). Logistics is an area of potentially high cost savings and improved customer satisfaction. Marketing logistics addresses not only *outbound distribution,* but also *inbound distribution* and *reverse distribution.* That is, it involves entire *supply chain management* – managing value-added flows between suppliers, the company, resellers and final users. No logistics system can both maximise customer service and minimise distribution costs. Instead, the goal of logistics management is to provide a *targeted* level of

service at the least cost. The major logistics functions include *order processing, warehousing, inventory management* and *transportation.*

The *integrated supply chain management concept* recognises that improved logistics requires teamwork in the form of close working relationships across functional areas inside the company and across various organisations in the supply chain. Companies can achieve logistics harmony among functions by creating cross-functional logistics teams, integrative supply manager positions, and senior-level logistics executives with cross-functional authority. Channel partnerships can take the form of cross-company teams, shared projects and information-sharing systems. Today, some companies are outsourcing their logistics functions to third-party logistics (3PL) providers to save costs, increase efficiency, and gain faster and more effective access to global markets.

NAVIGATING THE KEY TERMS

NOTES AND REFERENCES

1 See Kevin Kelleher, 'Giving Dealers a Raw Deal', *Business 2.0,* December 2004, pp. 82–4; Jim MacKinnon, 'Goodyear Boasts of Bright Future', *McClatchy-Tribune Business News,* 9 April 2008; Andrea Doyle, 'Forging Ahead', *Successful Meetings,* May 2009, pp. 36–42; and information accessed at **www.goodyear.com**, September 2009.

2 **www.citroen.com**, accessed June 2014.

3 **http://investor.games-workshop.com/our-business-model/**, accessed June 2014.

4 Information accessed at **www.kroger.com** and **http://www.luxottica.com/en/company/about-us/company-profile**, June 2014.

5 Information accessed at **www.franchiseeurope.com**, June 2014.

6 Information accessed at **http://www.nestle.com/Brands/Cereals/Pages/CerealsCatalogue.aspx**, June 2014.

7 Quotes and information from Normandy Madden, 'Two Chinas', *Advertising Age,* 16 August 2004, pp. 1, 22; Russell Flannery, 'China: The Slow Boat', *Forbes,* 12 April 2004, p. 76; Jeff Berman, 'US Providers Say Logistics in China on the Right Track', *Logistics Management,* March 2007, p. 22; Jamie Bolton, 'China: The Infrastructure Imperative', *Logistics Management,* July 2007, p. 63; and China trade facts from **http://cscmp.org/press/fastfacts.asp**, March 2009.

8 For more on channel relationships, see 'Supply Chain Challenges', *Harvard Business Review,* July 2003, pp. 65–73; James C. Anderson and James A. Narus, *Business Market Management,* 2nd edn (Upper Saddle River, NJ: Prentice Hall, 2004), ch. 9; Jeffery K. Liker and Thomas Y. Choi, 'Building Deep Supplier Relationships', *Harvard Business Review,* December 2004, pp. 104–13; and David Hannon, 'Supplier Relationships Key to Future Success', *Purchasing,* 2 June 2005, pp. 25–9.

9 Quotes and other information from Alex Taylor III, 'Caterpillar', *Fortune,* 20 August 2007, pp. 48–54; Donald V. Fites, 'Make Your Dealers Your Partner', *Harvard Business Review,* March–April 1996, pp. 84–95; and information accessed at **www.caterpillar.com**, June 2014.

10 'Dell Computers: A Case Study in Low Inventory', *Inventory Management Review,* accessed at **http://www.inventorymanagementreview.org**, June 2014, 'Adding a Day to Dell', *Traffic World,* 21 February 2005, p. 1; and William Hoffman, 'Dell Ramps Up RFID', *Traffic World,* 18 April 2005, p. 1.

11 See 'Walmart Relaunches EPC RFID Effort Starting with Men's Jeans and Basics', *RFID Journal,* 23 July 2010, accessed at **http://www.rfidjournal.com**, June 2014; 'A Worldwide Look at RFID', *Supply Chain Management Review,* April 2007, pp. 48–55; 'Wal-Mart Says Use RFID Tags or Pay Up', *Logistics Today,* March 2008, p. 4; and David Blanchard, 'The Five Stages of RFID', *Industry Week,* 1 January 2009, p. 50.

12 Donald J. McCubbrey and Joze Gricar, 'The EDI Project in Slovenia: A Case Study and Model for Developing Countries', *Information Technology and People,* 8(2), 1995, pp. 6–16.

13 Thomas W. Lauer, 'Side-Effects of Mandatory EDI Order Processing in the Automotive Supply Chain', *Business Process Management Journal,* 6(5), 2000, pp. 366–75.

14 See **http://www.gartner.com/newsroom/id/2488715**, accessed June 2014; Bob Trebilcock, 'Top 20 Supply Chain Management Software Suppliers', *Modern Material Handling,* 1 July 2008, accessed at **www.mmh.com/article/CA6574264.html**; and 'The 2009 Supply & Demand Chain Executive 100', *Supply & Demand Chain Executive,* June–July 2009, accessed at **www.sdcexec.com**

15 **http://www.cevalogistics.com**, accessed 22 July 2011.

16 See 'Add Value to Your Supply Chain – Hire a 3PL', *Materials Management and Distribution,* January–February 2004, p. A3; and Paul Stastny, 'Outsourcing Global Supply Chain Management', *Canadian Transportation Logistics,* March 2005, pp. 32–4.

CHAPTER 11
RETAILING AND WHOLESALING

AFTER STUDYING THIS CHAPTER, YOU SHOULD BE ABLE TO

- explain the roles of retailers and wholesalers in the distribution channel
- describe the major types of retailers and give examples of each
- identify the major types of wholesalers and give examples of each
- explain the marketing decisions facing retailers and wholesalers

THE WAY AHEAD
Previewing the concepts

In the previous chapter, you learned the basics of distribution channel design and management. Now, we'll look more deeply into the two major intermediary channel functions, retailing and wholesaling. You already know something about retailing – you're served every day by retailers of all shapes and sizes and there is a good chance you've had some experience of working in a retail environment. However, you probably know much less about the horde of wholesalers that work behind the scenes. In this chapter, we'll navigate through the characteristics of different kinds of retailers and wholesalers, the marketing decisions they make and trends for the future.

To start the tour, we'll look at Aldi. This German supermarket chain is known as a hard discounter – a retailer that sells goods without requiring customers to pay for extras like strong brands or extra packaging.

ALDI: DON'T DISCOUNT THEM

Sean Ennis, Department of Marketing, University of Strathclyde, Scotland

Albrecht Discount (Aldi) was established by two brothers in Germany in the 1950s. It emerged in response to the economic difficulties experienced by German society after the Second World War. The two brothers had a major disagreement in 1962 and the company was split into two separate operations: Aldi Nord (concentrating mainly in Denmark, France, the Benelux countries and Poland) and Aldi Sud (focusing its efforts in the UK, Ireland, Austria and Slovenia). Both entities now cooperate in a friendly manner. As a retailer, its underlying philosophy has evolved from the basic principle of offering low prices, focusing on own-branded products, carrying a limited number of items (1,000 as compared with 25,000 in the traditional supermarkets) and operating in a basic no-frills store, with minimal staffing. This approach contrasts strongly with other retailers in an environment where most European consumers have come to expect a wide choice of brands at varying price points.

Source: Alamy Images/Vario Images GmbH & Co. KG.

In an interview the former Managing Director of Aldi in the UK, Paul Foley, outlined the Aldi strategy by offering the following observations: 'If you sell more versions of a product, you need a bigger store – the customer will still only buy one product. Aldi stores are a cross between a supermarket, a street market and a warehouse.'[1]

Some retailers try to cater for all segments – Aldi very deliberately does not. Foley went on to say:

> **the bottom end of the market is not that attractive to us. They don't have much money, they don't travel very far and they are very brand conscious. The very top of the market – where the amount of money spent on food is a very small amount of disposable income – is not attractive either. But everything in the middle is fair game.**

Certainly in the UK, Aldi would appear to be making inroads into the ABC1 social category, where 50 per cent of its customers fall. As economic times get harder, Aldi is becoming a more attractive proposition to the middle-class shopper hoping to make savings. Indeed, Aldi has promised its customers a saving of £30 on a £100 weekly shop when compared with the 'Big Four' supermarkets (Tesco, Asda, Sainsbury's and Morrisons). How can it deliver on this bold promise?

Because it carries so few items, it can purchase very large quantities from its suppliers and is therefore able to offer lower prices. It applies rigorous cost control procedures over all aspects of its operations. The stores are spartan and facilitate ease of handling and display – another source for cost reduction. Long queues at the checkouts and minimal staffing reinforce this image of low-cost, low-service operations. Aldi does little or no advertising, apart from periodic newsletters that it circulates locally, and specialises in selling staple products such as food, beverages, sanitary articles and other inexpensive household items. Store managers use handheld devices to place their orders in the evening and the store is replenished the next day. This puts Aldi into the category known as the 'hard discounter': an operation that pushes prices even lower than the traditional discounters – for cultural and historical reasons, this retailing category is strongly associated with Germany, Lidl being another prime example.

In terms of international expansion, Aldi finances its new store openings from its cash resources, avoiding potential exposure to high loans. The company shuns publicity and moves quietly into new markets. This quiet expansion has taken Aldi to 3.5 per cent of the total European market. In comparison, the market leader – Carrefour – has captured 6.8 per cent.

Shopping culture significantly influences how well or badly Aldi performs in a given market. Until recently, Aldi and Lidl struggled to capture a significant slice of the UK market, which is dominated by companies such as Tesco, Sainsbury's, Asda and Morrisons. Almost 70 per cent of food sales fall into the hands of these companies. Traditionally, UK shoppers have been more interested in purchasing well-known branded products. Many dislike the idea of buying 'own brands' or little known European brands. By contrast, in its home market of Germany – the third-biggest retail market in the world, after the USA and Japan – Aldi is in pole position and discounters hold sway. No social stigma is associated with shopping in such stores there and, as a consequence, the focus on low price works very effectively.

Despite the low, low prices, Aldi has done its best to build up a reputation for selling good-quality products. Cabinet displays at Aldi head office attest to this observation – where over 50 awards and citations recognising the quality of various products sit proudly on display. Surveys consistently show that, in the German market, Aldi is perceived as the third most respected brand (after Siemens and BMW).

Aldi continues to refine various aspects of its retail strategy. Until recently, of the 1,000 items carried, only 15 fell into the branded category: such brands as Marmite, Tetley Teabags and Budweiser. Then, Aldi started to stock a limited number of premium brands such as the Italian confectioner Ferrero, and consumer goods brands from Procter & Gamble and Kimberley Clark.

The recession and credit crunch in many European markets meant that Aldi presented an even more attractive option to shoppers on increasingly tight budgets. The tough economic times from 2008 to 2013 mean that these shoppers have had to look for smarter and more innovative ways of maximising their value from declining disposable incomes. Aldi provides an attractive alternative.

Certainly in the UK, Aldi has been expanding even faster than the 'Big Four' competitors. Its target is to open one store a week until 1,200 stores are established. Although only holding 3 per cent of the UK market share, the effective management of its costs means that it is very profitable. It will be interesting to see whether Aldi continues to make inroads into the dominance of the traditional supermarkets such as Tesco and Sainsbury's. Even if there is a sustained economic recovery, some analysts believe that Aldi will continue to thrive. Not long ago retail industry experts believed that, once there were signs of an economic recovery, shoppers would return to the big-name supermarket chains such as Tesco. However, a different analysis is now regarded as very plausible: shoppers have discovered that they can enjoy high-quality products at relatively modest prices and have overcome their suspicion of the hard discounting stores, so perhaps they will stick with Aldi even if they feel better off. In any event, Aldi has clearly developed a successful value proposition, making it one of the most profitable and successful retailers in Europe.

Source: See note 1 at the end of this chapter.

The Aldi story sets the stage for examining the fast-changing world of today's resellers. This chapter looks at *retailing* and *wholesaling*. In the first section, we look at the nature and importance of retailing, major types of store and non-store retailers, the decisions retailers make and the future of retailing. In the second section, we discuss these same topics as they relate to wholesalers.

RETAILING

What is retailing? We all know that Tesco, Carrefour and H&M are retailers, but so are Avon representatives, **Amazon.com**, the local Travelodge and a hair stylist in the beauty salon. **Retailing** includes all the activities involved in selling products or services directly to final consumers for their personal, non-business use. Many institutions – manufacturers, wholesalers and retailers – do retailing. But most retailing is done by **retailers**: businesses whose sales come *primarily* from retailing.

Although most retailing is done in retail stores, in recent years *non-store retailing* has been growing much faster than has store retailing. Non-store retailing includes selling to final consumers through direct mail, catalogues, telephone, the Internet, home-shopping TV, home and office parties, door-to-door contact, vending machines and other direct selling approaches. We discuss such direct marketing approaches in detail later (see Chapter 13). In this chapter, we focus on store retailing.

Types of retailers

Retail stores come in all shapes and sizes and new retail types keep emerging. The most important types of retail stores are described in Exhibit 11.1 and discussed in the following sections. They can be classified in terms of several characteristics, including the *amount of service* they offer, the breadth and depth of their *product lines*, the *relative prices* they charge and how they are *organised*.

EXHIBIT 11.1 | **Major store retailer types**

Speciality stores

Carry a narrow product line with a deep assortment, such as clothing stores, sporting-goods stores like JD Sports, furniture stores, florists and bookshops. A clothing store would be a *single-line* store, a men's clothing store would be a *limited-line store* and a men's custom-shirt store would be a *super-speciality* store. Examples: Zara, Gap, JD Sports.

Department stores

Carry several product lines – typically clothing, home furnishings and household goods – with each line operated as a separate department managed by a specialist buyer or merchandiser. Examples: John Lewis, Macy's, Le Printemps and Gostiny Dvor.

Supermarkets

A relatively large, low-cost, low-margin, high-volume, self-service operation designed to serve the consumer's total needs for grocery and household products. Examples: Carrefour, Aldi, Tesco.

Convenience stores

Relatively small stores located near residential areas, open long hours seven days a week, and carrying a limited line of high-turnover convenience products at slightly higher prices. Examples: 7-Eleven, Londis, Opencor.

Discount stores

Carry standard merchandise sold at lower prices with lower margins and higher volumes. Examples: Wal-Mart, Target.

Off-price retailers

Sell merchandise bought at less than regular wholesale prices and sold at less than retail, often leftover goods, overruns and irregulars obtained at reduced prices from manufacturers or other retailers. These include *factory outlets* owned and operated by manufacturers (example: the collection at Serravalle); *independent off-price retailers* owned and run by entrepreneurs or by divisions of larger retail corporations (example: TK Maxx – known as TJ Maxx outside the UK, Ireland and Germany); and *warehouse (or wholesale) clubs* selling a limited selection of brand name groceries, appliances, clothing and other goods at deep discounts to consumers who pay membership fees (example: Costco).

Superstores

Very large stores traditionally aimed at meeting consumers' total needs for routinely purchased food and non-food items. Includes *category killers*, which carry a deep assortment in a particular category and have a knowledgeable staff (examples: Tesco, Petsmart, Staples); *supercentres*, combined supermarket and discount stores (example: Wal-Mart Supercenters); and *hypermarkets* with up to 220,000 square feet (20,400 square metres) of space combining supermarket, discount and warehouse retailing (examples: Carrefour, Pyrca).

Amount of service

Different products require different amounts of service and customer service preferences vary. Retailers may offer one of three levels of service: self-service, limited service and full service.

Self-service retailers serve customers who are willing to perform their own 'locate–compare–select' process to save money. Self-service is the basis of all discount operations and is typically used by sellers of convenience goods (such as supermarkets) and nationally branded, fast-moving shopping goods (such as Marks & Spencer and Debenhams).

Limited-service retailers, such as Carphone Warehouse, provide more sales assistance because they carry more shopping goods about which customers need information – expensive electronic items, for example. Their increased operating costs result in higher prices. In *full-service retailers,* such as speciality stores and first-class department stores, salespeople assist customers in every phase of the shopping process – think Harrods. Full-service stores usually carry more speciality goods for which customers like to be 'waited on'. They provide more services resulting in much higher operating costs, which are passed along to customers as higher prices.

Product line

Retailers also can be classified by the length and breadth of their product assortments. Some retailers, such as **speciality stores**, carry narrow product lines with deep assortments within those lines. Today, speciality stores are flourishing. The increasing use of market segmentation, market targeting and product specialisation has resulted in a greater need for stores that focus on specific products and segments.

In contrast, **department stores** carry a wide variety of product lines. In recent years, department stores have been squeezed between more focused and flexible speciality stores on the one hand, and more efficient, lower-priced discounters on the other. In response, many have added promotional pricing to meet the discount threat. Others have stepped up the use of store brands and single-brand 'designer shops' to compete with speciality stores – as Marks & Spencer does with Per Una clothing for women. Still others are trying mail order, telephone and web selling. Service remains the key differentiating factor. Retailers such as John Lewis in the UK, El Corte Inglés in Spain and Portugal, and other high-end department stores are doing well by emphasising high-quality service.

Supermarkets are the most frequently shopped type of retail store. In Europe they are facing slower sales growth because of slower population growth, saturation of the market and increasing restrictions on new shop development.

Thus, most supermarkets are making improvements to attract more customers. In the battle for 'share of stomachs', many large supermarket chains are moving upscale, providing improved store environments and higher quality food offerings, such as in-store bakeries, gourmet deli counters and fresh seafood departments – 'It's not just food, it's M&S Food.' Others are cutting costs, establishing more efficient operations and lowering prices in order to compete more effectively against the discounters like Lidl and Aldi – Asda has taken this route. Many of the major European supermarket chains offer home delivery for groceries bought online – the British Retail Consortium estimates that 9 per cent of all retail transactions are now conducted online.[2] Many speculate on the current and future size of the online portion of retail markets, but Mintel, the market intelligence agency, has suggested it was about €114bn across the EU in 2010, representing about 5 per cent of all retail transactions, and Forrester Research predicts that EU online retailing will be worth €191bn by 2017.[3]

Convenience stores are small stores that carry a limited line of high-turnover convenience goods like newspapers, snacks and drinks. There are chains of these all over Europe – Narvesan in Norway and Pressbyrån in Sweden were both founded in the nineteenth century (the latter specialising in small outlets in railway stations), Londis (London and District Independent Shopkeepers) in the UK, the Spanish Opencor and, of course, Spar over much of the continent (originally Dutch in origin).[4] These specialists are increasingly being joined by small-format versions of the leading grocers, such as the Tesco Express and Sainsbury Local chains.

Convenience stores are becoming ever more sophisticated retailing environments

Source: Alamy Images/TNT Magazine.

Superstores are much larger than regular supermarkets and offer a large assortment of routinely purchased food products, non-food items and services. Wal-Mart acquired Asda in 1999, and has developed the chain to replicate the US format of very large combination food and discount stores in the EU – Wal-Mart has 2,500 of these in the USA alone.[5]

Recent years have also seen the explosive growth of superstores that are actually giant speciality stores, the so-called **category killers**. They feature stores the size of aircraft hangars that carry a very deep assortment of a particular line with a knowledgeable staff. Category killers are prevalent in a wide range of categories, including books, baby gear, toys, electronics, home improvement products, linens and towels, party goods, sporting goods, even pet supplies. Another superstore variation, a *hypermarket,* is a huge superstore, perhaps as large as *six* football pitches. This is a format that emerged in Europe before the USA – Carrefour pioneered hypermarkets in France, and now generates three-quarters of its sales from its four key EU markets in France, Italy, Spain and Belgium. It is also rapidly expanding in China and Eastern Europe.[6]

Finally, for some retailers, the product line is actually a service. Service retailers include hotels, banks, airlines, cinemas, restaurants, garages, hair salons and dry cleaners.

Relative prices

Retailers can also be classified according to the prices they charge (see Exhibit 11.1). Most retailers charge regular prices and offer normal quality goods and customer service. Others offer higher quality goods and service at higher prices. The retailers that feature low prices are discount stores and 'off-price' retailers.

Discount stores

A **discount store** sells standard merchandise at lower prices by accepting lower margins and selling higher volume. The early discount stores cut expenses by offering few services and operating in warehouse-like facilities in low-rent, heavily populated areas. Today's discounters have improved their store environments and increased their services, while at the same time keeping prices low through lean, efficient operations. If France brought Europe and the world the hypermarket, then Germany can claim to be the home of the two most significant discounters in Europe – Aldi and Lidl. Other significant players include the Danish Netto and the Spanish DIA. These discounters are increasingly influencing the retail scene as a whole, as we saw in the opening case about Aldi.

Off-price retailers

As the major discount stores traded up, a new wave of **off-price retailers** moved in to fill the ultra-low price, high-volume gap. Ordinary discounters buy at regular wholesale prices and accept lower margins to keep prices down. In contrast, off-price retailers buy at less than regular wholesale prices and charge consumers less than regular retail prices. Off-price retailers can be found in all areas, from food, clothing and electronics to no-frills banking and discount brokerages.

The three main types of off-price retailers are *independents, factory outlets* and *warehouse clubs.* **Independent off-price retailers** are either owned and run by entrepreneurs or divisions of larger retail corporations. Although many off-price operations are run by smaller independents, most large off-price retailer operations are owned by bigger retail chains. Well known off-price retailers in Europe include TK Maxx, Matalan and Makro.

Factory outlets are producer-operated stores sometimes grouped together in *factory outlet malls* and *value retail centres*, where dozens of outlet stores offer prices as low as 50 per cent below retail on a wide range of items. Factory outlet malls have become one of the hottest growth areas in retailing. While common in the USA, these are still relatively scarce in Europe. Serravalle Designer Outlet, near Piedmont in Italy, offers good deals on brands like Cerruti and Dolce and Gabbana. In the UK, Bicester Village is one of a very few examples – owned and operated by a company called Value Retail which specialises in this type of retail environment.[7]

Brands such as Polo Ralph Lauren, Giorgio Armani, Gucci and Versace are increasingly appearing in these outlets, causing department stores to protest to the manufacturers of these brands. Given their higher costs, the department stores have to charge more than the off-price outlets. Manufacturers counter that they send last year's merchandise and seconds to the factory outlet malls, not the new merchandise that they supply to the department stores. Still, the department stores are concerned about the growing number of shoppers willing to make weekend trips to stock up on branded merchandise at substantial savings.

Organisational approach

Although many retail stores are independently owned, others band together under some form of corporate or contractual organisation. The major types of retail organisations – *corporate chains, voluntary chains, retailer cooperatives, franchise organisation*s and *merchandising conglomerate*s – are described in Table 11.1.

Chain stores are two or more outlets that are commonly owned and controlled. They have many advantages over independents. Their size allows them to buy in large quantities at lower prices and gain promotional economies. They can hire specialists to deal with areas such as pricing, promotion, merchandising, inventory control and sales forecasting.

The great success of corporate chains caused many independents to band together in one of two forms of contractual associations. One is the *voluntary chain* – a wholesaler-sponsored group of independent retailers that engages in group buying and common merchandising (see Chapter 10). In Germany, Edeka supermarkets operate like this. The other form of contractual association is the *retailer cooperative* – a group of independent retailers that bands together to set up a jointly owned, central wholesale operation and conducts

TABLE 11.1 Major types of retail organisation

Type	Description	Examples
Corporate chain stores	Two or more outlets that are commonly owned and controlled, employ central buying and merchandising, and sell similar lines of merchandise. Corporate chains appear in all types of retailing, but they are strongest in department stores, food stores, chemists, shoe stores and women's clothing stores	Zara, WHSmith
Voluntary chains	Wholesaler-sponsored groups of independent retailers engaged in bulk buying and common merchandising	Londis, Edeka
Retailer co-operatives	Groups of independent retailers who set up a central buying organisation and conduct joint promotion efforts	Euronics
Franchise organisations	Contractual association between a franchiser (a manufacturer, wholesaler or service organisation) and franchisees (independent businesspeople who buy the right to own and operate one or more units in the franchise system). Franchise organisations are normally based on some unique product, service or method of doing business, or on a trade name or patent, or on goodwill that the franchiser had developed	McDonald's, Subway, Pizza Hut, The Body Shop
Merchandising conglomerate	A free-form corporation that combines several diversified conglomerates retailing lines and forms under central ownership, along with some integration of their distribution and management functions	Dixons Retail plc

joint merchandising and promotion efforts. A good example of this would be the Euronics network of independent electrical retailers.[8] These organisations give independents the buying and promotion economies they need to match the prices of larger chains.

Another form of contractual retail organisation is a **franchise**. The main difference between franchise organisations and other contractual systems (voluntary chains and retail cooperatives) is that franchise systems are normally based on some unique product or service, on a method of doing business, or on the trade name, goodwill or patent that the franchiser has developed. Franchising has been prominent in fast foods, health and fitness centres, hairdressing, car hire and dozens of other product and service areas.

But franchising covers a lot more than just burgers and fitness centres. Franchises have sprung up to meet just about any need. The Swedish company Husse has more than 300 franchisees across Europe, each delivering pet food directly to owners' homes. Benetton is a famous Italian clothing company with franchises all over the globe – but Italy also has smaller businesses like Calzedonia offering franchises in its specialities of swimwear and hosiery, and in Austria and Germany Musikschule Fröhlich offers private music lessons through its franchise partners.[9]

Franchises now command a significant presence on most European high streets. Benetton, McDonald's, Subway and Toni&Guy are present in most UK towns and cities, and across the continent companies like Etam, Bang & Olufsen, Depato and Lacoste follow suit.[10]

One of the best known and most successful franchisers, McDonald's, now has more than 26,000 restaurants in 119 countries serving nearly 40 million customers a day.[11]

Finally, *merchandising conglomerates* are corporations that combine several different retailing forms under central ownership. For example, Dixons Retail plc (formerly known as DSG International) operates retail outlets like PC World and Currys. Outside the UK it also own Elkjøp and Gigantti in Scandinavia, UniEuro in Italy and Kotsovolus in Greece. Such diversified retailing, similar to a multibranding strategy, provides superior management systems and economies that benefit all the separate retail operations.

MAKING CONNECTIONS Linking the concepts

Slow down and think about all the different kinds of retailers you deal with regularly, many of which overlap in the products they carry.

- Pick a familiar product – camera, microwave, item of clothing. Shop for this product at two very different store types, say a discount store or category killer on the one hand, and a department store or smaller speciality store on the other. Compare the stores on product assortment, services and prices. If you were going to buy the product, where would you buy it and why?

- What does your shopping trip suggest about the futures of the competing store formats that you sampled?

Retailer marketing decisions

Retailers are always searching for new marketing strategies to attract and retain customers. In the past, retailers attracted customers with unique product assortments and more or better services. Today, retail assortments and services are looking more and more alike. National brand manufacturers, in their drive for volume, have placed their branded goods everywhere. Such brands are found not only in department stores, but also in mass-merchandise discount stores, off-price discount stores and on the Web. Thus, it is now more difficult for any one retailer to offer exclusive merchandise.

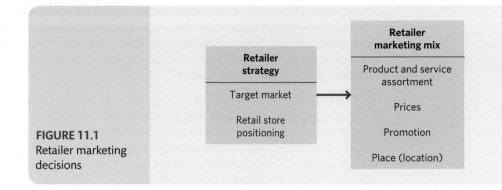

FIGURE 11.1
Retailer marketing
decisions

Service differentiation among retailers has also diminished. Many department stores have trimmed their services, whereas discounters have increased theirs. Customers have become smarter and more price sensitive. They see no reason to pay more for identical brands, especially when service-level differences are shrinking. For all these reasons, many retailers today are rethinking their marketing strategies.

As shown in Figure 11.1, retailers face major marketing decisions about their *target market and positioning, product assortment and services, price, promotion* and *place*.

Target market and positioning decision

Retailers first must define their target markets and then decide how they will position themselves in these markets. Should the store focus on upscale, mid-scale or downscale shoppers? Do target shoppers want variety, depth of assortment, convenience or low prices? Until they define and profile their markets, retailers cannot make consistent decisions about product assortment, services, pricing, advertising, store decor, or any of the other decisions that must support their positions.

Too many retailers fail to define their target markets and positions clearly. They try to have 'something for everyone' and end up satisfying no market well. In contrast, successful retailers define their target markets well and position themselves strongly. Asda positions itself on being good value for money, Aldi on low-price goods without branding or packaging, Tesco on range and Marks & Spencer on quality.

Product assortment and services decision

Retailers must decide on three major product variables: *product assortment, services mix* and *store atmosphere*.

The retailer's *product assortment* should differentiate the retailer while matching target shoppers' expectations. One strategy is to offer merchandise that no other competitor carries, such as private brands or national brands on which it holds exclusives. For example, department store chain House of Fraser gets exclusive rights to carry well-known designers' labels. It also offers an exclusive men's fashion line under its own Linea private brand. Another strategy is to feature blockbuster merchandising events – Debenhams is known for running spectacular 24-hour sales at very short notice. Finally, the retailer can differentiate itself by offering a highly targeted product assortment – Long Tall Sally carries clothing for tall and large women, Games Workshop carries a range of table-top games and hobby materials.

The *services mix* can also help set one retailer apart from another. For example, some retailers invite customers to ask questions or consult service representatives in person or via phone or keyboard. B&Q offers a diverse mix of services to do-it-yourselfers, from 'how-to' classes to a proprietary credit card.

The *store's atmosphere* is another element in the reseller's product arsenal. Every store has a physical layout that makes moving around in it either hard or easy. Each store has a 'feel'; one store is cluttered, another cheerful, a third plush, a fourth sombre. The retailer must design an atmosphere that suits the target market and moves customers to buy. In the USA, Urban Outfitters sets itself apart by creating a unique store environment, and this atmosphere is deliberately recreated in the European outlets in, among other places, Glasgow, Dublin, Copenhagen and Antwerp:

> The inside of an Urban Outfitters store is a far cry from the stark, cookie-cutter interiors you'll find at Gap or Express. 'Shopping here should be like a treasure hunt,' says Laura O'Connor, Urban's 34-year-old general merchandising manager. O'Connor and her team give every store the feel of a boutique. Urban delivers small batches of new merchandise daily to keep things fresh. New and recycled fashions are sold alongside housewares (think beaded curtains and cocktail shakers), encouraging serious browsing and creating a thrill-of-the-hunt vibe suited to a thrift store. Visual arts teams at each store – typically four artists per location – overhaul each store's look every two weeks. The men's department at one store – this week, at least – is wallpapered with newspaper sports pages dyed pink. That art deco jewellery? O'Connor got the idea while visiting a museum in Prague. The quick-changing assortments and decor get customers stopping in often to see what's new, while the 'organised clutter' design keeps them around by selling unexpected items side by side. Urban even places Xboxes and vintage arcade games in its menswear sections so bored boyfriends won't pressure female shoppers to leave. As a result, Urban's customers stay an average of 45 minutes per visit – more than twice as long as shoppers linger in most clothing stores. That helps the company's stores generate $596 in sales per square foot each year – 80 per cent more than at Limited and Express. That, in turn, makes Urban Outfitters one of the best-performing clothing chains around.[12]

A modern shopping mall can be immense. With 10 floors, Cevahir in Istanbul is Europe's largest

Other retailers practise 'experiential retailing'. At Inglesport, consumers can try out climbing equipment on a huge wall in the store, or they can test Gore-Tex jackets by going under a simulated rain shower. At London's Master Spa, shoppers are invited to wear their bathing suits during a 'tub test'. Similarly, Smeg – Italy's largest producer of kitchen appliances – helps its dealers to install its products in realistic kitchen mock-ups.[13]

Increasingly, retailers are turning their stores into theatres that transport customers into unusual, exciting shopping environments. Many believe the largest shopping mall in Europe is Istanbul's Cevahir Mall with an enormous 350 shops on 10 floors. Of this huge space, a mere 58,000 square metres is given over to the Atlantis Entertainment Centre, which incorporates an indoor roller-coaster and several IMAX cinema screens, as well as a theatre. Others champion Dolce Vita Tejo in Portugal. Deciding which is the biggest depends on the criteria you choose, such as floor area, number of stores, sales turnover or number of visitors.[14]

All of this confirms that retail stores are much more than simply assortments of goods. They are environments to be experienced by the people who shop in them. Store atmospheres offer a powerful tool by which retailers can differentiate their stores from those of competitors.

Price decision

A retailer's price policy must fit its target market and positioning, product and service assortment, and competition. All retailers would like to charge high mark-ups and achieve high volume,

Henry Poole will make an outfit measured to fit you – and only you

Source: Alamy Images/Kirsty Mclaren.

but the two seldom go together. Most retailers seek *either* high mark-ups on lower volume (most speciality stores) *or* low mark-ups on higher volume (mass merchandisers and discount stores).

Thus, Henry Poole & Co. – a bespoke tailors on Savile Row in London – will custommake a suit or even an outfit appropriate to visit a royal palace that will fit you, and only you, exactly. How much does this cost? As the saying goes: 'If you have to ask, you can't afford it.'

At the other extreme, TK Maxx sells brand name clothing at discount prices, settling for a lower margin on each sale but selling at a much higher volume.

Retailers must also decide on the extent to which they will use sales and other price promotions. Some retailers use no price promotions at all, competing instead on product and service quality rather than on price. For example, it is difficult to imagine Henry Poole holding a two-for-the-price-of-one sale. Other retailers practise '*high–low*' *pricing* – charging higher prices on an everyday basis, coupled with frequent sales and other price promotions to increase store traffic, clear out unsold merchandise, create a low-price image or attract customers who will buy other goods at full prices. Still others – such as Asda, Tesco and other mass retailers – practise *everyday low pricing* (EDLP), charging constant, everyday low prices with few sales or discounts. Which strategy is best depends on the retailer's marketing strategy and the pricing approaches of competitors.[15]

Promotion decision

Retailers use any or all of the promotion tools – advertising, personal selling, sales promotion, public relations and direct marketing – to reach consumers. They advertise in newspapers and magazines and on radio, TV and the Internet. Advertising may be supported by newspaper inserts and direct mail. Personal selling requires careful training of salespeople in how to greet customers, meet their needs and handle their complaints. Sales promotions may include instore demonstrations, displays, contests and visiting celebrities. Public relations activities, such as press conferences and speeches, store openings, special events, newsletters, magazines and public service activities, are always available to retailers. Most retailers have also set up websites, offering customers information and other features, and often selling merchandise directly.

Place decision

Retailers often point to three critical factors in retailing success: *location, location* and *location*! It is very important that retailers select locations that are accessible to the target market in areas that are consistent with the retailer's positioning. Small retailers may have to settle for whatever locations they can find or afford. Large retailers, however, usually employ specialists who select locations using advanced methods.

Most stores today cluster together to increase their customer pulling power and to give consumers the convenience of one-stop shopping. Historically, European shopping districts have tended to evolve rather than be designed. An excellent example of this is the street in York called The Shambles. Shambles derives from an ancient word – *shamel* – related to open-air meat markets. The combination of smells, noises, chaos and claustrophobia of these medieval streets has led to the modern meaning of the word to describe things being in a mess.[16] Urban planning is a relatively modern concept, meaning these districts do not have an organised layout, have poor infrastructure and facilities, and usually are not big enough for modern purposes. Without very significant reconstruction, there are a limited number of ways to improve these areas – pedestrianisation becoming an increasingly popular option.

A **shopping centre** is a group of retail businesses planned, developed, owned and managed as a unit. A *regional shopping centre,* or *regional shopping mall,* the largest and most dramatic shopping centre, can have several hundred stores and attract customers from a wide area. The Metro Centre in Gateshead, Bluewater in Kent, the Galeria Kazimierz in Cracow and the Olympia in Munich are all good examples; the Cevahir Mall, mentioned above, sits on the historical trade hub between Europe and Asia.

A *community shopping centre* contains between 15 and 40 retail stores. It normally contains a branch of a department store or variety store, a supermarket, speciality stores, professional offices and sometimes a bank. Most shopping centres are there to support the needs of a city district or a complete town. In Europe some of these are quite old. Glasgow has the Argyll Arcade from 1827 and Paris has many that survive from the first half of the nineteenth century, with evocative names like *Passage Choiseul, Passage des Panoramas* and *Grand-Cerf.*[17] Many more, generally rather ugly modern examples, exist – like Kringlan in the centre of Reykjavik.

A recent addition to the shopping centre scene is the so-called *retail park*. These huge unenclosed shopping centres consist of a group of retail stores, including large, free-standing anchors such as IKEA, Staples and Next. Each store has its own entrance, with parking directly in front for shoppers who wish to visit only one store. Retail parks have increased rapidly in number during the past few years to challenge traditional indoor malls.

The current trend is towards value-oriented outlet malls and retail parks on the one hand, and smaller 'lifestyle centres' on the other. These lifestyle centres – smaller malls with upscale stores, convenient locations and expensive atmospheres – are usually located near affluent residential districts and cater to the retail needs of consumers in their areas. The future of malls 'will be all about creating places to be rather than just places to buy'.[18]

The future of retailing

Retailers operate in a harsh and fast-changing environment, which offers threats as well as opportunities. For example, the industry suffers from chronic overcapacity, resulting in fierce competition for customers. Consumer demographics, lifestyles and shopping patterns are changing rapidly, as are retailing technologies. To be successful, then, retailers will have to choose target segments carefully and position themselves strongly. They will have to take the following retailing developments into account as they plan and execute their competitive strategies.

New retail forms and shortening retail life cycles

New retail forms continue to emerge to meet new situations and consumer needs, but the life cycle of new retail forms is getting shorter. Department stores took about 100 years to reach the mature stage of the life cycle; more recent forms, such as warehouse stores, reached maturity in about 10 years. In such an environment, seemingly solid retail positions can crumble quickly – C&A, the Dutch clothing retailer, had been a presence on the UK high street for 75 years. In 2000, it took the decision to close down all 113 of its UK shops, making nearly 5,000 staff redundant. The reason? A previously strong position selling

Movers and shakers: leaders in European retailing

MARKETING AT WORK 11.1

Every year, Interbrand – the market intelligence agency – produces a series of reports in which it discusses and debates the strongest brands in different sectors. One of these reports looks at retail brands and ranks brand strength in different countries. The size, market share and financial performance of the companies behind these brands is of course important in Interbrand's methodology, but other criteria like market responsiveness and influence, appeal to customers, and the credibility and quality of the products and services provided also have significance. So, these are not necessarily the biggest companies in European retail, but they could be said to be setting the pace – 'moving and shaking'. Let's take a look at the top-ranked companies in four key European retail markets: France, Germany, Spain and the UK.

France

The French supermarket sector – and *supermarket* being a concept invented in France – is dominated by Carrefour. Indeed, Carrefour is of a size to be a titan in world retailing, second only to Wal-Mart on a global scale and making strong headway in Asian markets, an area where Tesco has not done as well as it would have liked. Auchan – another supermarket chain – is itself dominated by Carrefour in terms of global presence, brand strength and number of retail outlets. Auchan is privately owned by one of France's richest families and is steered by the patriarch of that family – Gérard Mulliez. Leroy Merlin is also part of the Mulliez empire and is France's leading DIY/home improvement chain. One estimate is that retailers controlled by the Mulliez family enjoy annual sales of about $100bn. L'Occitane and Sephora are familiar names outside France, the former trading on its heritage in Provence

and the latter bought out by LVMH (Louis Vuitton and Moet Hennessy) 15 years ago. The name comes from a combination of *sephos* (the Greek word for 'beauty') and *Zipporah* (Mrs Moses). Look at the homepage for Conforama and you will immediately think of analogues like Amazon, IKEA and Argos. Darty is the market leader in France for domestic appliances whereas Decathlon has the leadership position for sporting goods across Europe. FNAC focuses on entertainment and leisure hardware and software and is praised for its successful segmentation strategy in a challenging and rapidly evolving marketing environment. Finally for France we have Casino. Despite the name, this is another supermarket chain. While not a market leader by any means, Casino scores highly for its social and environmental ideals and practices and is seen as a company to watch on a global scale.

Germany

As we saw in France, leading retailers are quite often supermarkets. The reason for this is a simple question with a complicated answer, but it is safe to assume key factors include the range and number of goods, the regular and repeated visits by shoppers and a large number of stores. In Germany, Interbrand has only ranked seven retailers. Aldi is selected as its number 1 retail brand. Aldi is a trusted company in Germany, well regarded for the quality of products and the treatment of its workforce – we learned a lot about it in the opening pages of this chapter. Edeka, Lidl, Kaufland and REWE are four more supermarket chains, Edeka leading the pack in terms of annual revenue in the German market while Lidl has high hopes for its new private brand 'Ein gutes Stück Heimat', which translates as 'a good piece of home'. Kaufland

Across Europe, retailers are finding different ways to succeed and grow

Sources: Alamy Images/Iain Masterton (left); Getty Images/ AFP (middle top); Getty Images/Bloomberg (middle bottom); Alamy Images/ M. Itani (top right); Alamy Images/Paul Mayall/Germany (bottom right).

meanwhile sees its best hopes for expansion as being in Eastern Europe and REWE is rapidly expanding through an aggressive programme of takeovers. In fourth place is MediaMarkt – Europe's leading consumer electronics retailer. An innovative company, it had Germany's first video-on-demand service and is currently trialling branded vending machines containing gadgets at airports and rail stations. dm is a drugstore chain competing strongly on the basis of sustainability and recently winning an award for being the best 'sustainable' retailer in Germany.

Spain

Interbrand has ranked nine retailers in Spain, and there is a very heavy representation from fashion brands. Indeed, unlike in France, Germany and the UK, the top-ranked retail brand in Spain is not a supermarket but rather Zara, a fashion retailer that is using the speed and efficiency of its buying and logistics to beat competitors. El Corte Inglés (which translates as 'The English Cut', conveying the same sense of chic that the phrase *Italian styled* might) is a name that reflects the role of British traders and manufacturers of cloth in the eighteenth and nineteenth centuries. Founded in Madrid, the company is the largest chain of department stores in Europe and promises customers that a product will be waiting for collection within 24 hours if it is not in stock at that moment. Mango is a second fashion retailer, and is opening stores rapidly in developing fashion markets like China and Russia. Staff at Mercadona – Spain's cheapest supermarket – are trained to refer to customers as 'the bosses'. DIA is focusing on meeting the

needs of families in respect of grocery shopping, and has also revamped uniforms and store formats as part of a company-wide branding shake-up. Of the remaining four brands listed in Interbrand's top retail brands in Spain, three – Bershka, Massimo Dutti and Desigual – are fashion brands, and the fourth, Tous, is a jewellery brand. Nobody can doubt that the Spaniards love their fashion brands!

United Kingdom

Many of the names on the UK list will be familiar to you. Tesco is the third company along with Carrefour and Wal-Mart that dominate global retailing, and Marks & Spencer and Boots will be companies you've known all your life. Next and Argos are successfully meeting the challenge of becoming 'click-and-brick' retailers by incorporating online retail alongside their high-street presence. Fully half of the UK top 10 is made up of supermarkets – with Sainsbury's, Morrisons, Waitrose and Asda all on the list. Asda of course has the backing of the mighty Wal-Mart, and it will be very interesting to see how it takes on Tesco in its home market. A fascinating recent newcomer to the UK list is the online fashion retailer asos. It was founded only in 2000, is based in the fashionable Camden area of north London, and is rapidly expanding across Europe and the rest of the world from its UK base.

Asia

How about outside Europe? Markets like China and India have rapidly developing retail sectors. If you refer to Table 11.2, though, you might be forgiven for thinking

TABLE 11.2 Leading brands in European and Asian retail

	France	Germany	Spain	UK	Asia-Pacific
1	Carrefour	Aldi	Zara	Tesco	Woolworths
2	Auchan	Lidl	Mango	M&S	Uniqlo
3	Sephora	Edeka	Bershka	Boots	Coles
4	Leroy Merlin	MediaMarkt	El Corte Inglés	Asda	Lotte
5	L'Occitane	Kaufland	Mercadona	Next	Chow Tan Fook
6	Conforama	dm	Massimo Dutti	Sainsbury's	FairPrice
7	Decathlon	REWE	DIA	Argos	Lawson
8	Darty		Desigual	asos	Bunnings
9	FNAC		Tous	Waitrose	SM
10	Casino			Morrisons	Matahari

Source: 'Best Retail Brands 2014' from Interbrand, www.interbrand.com

that many of those retailers do not sound very Asian. Partly this is to do with history – firms being founded by colonial powers in places like Hong Kong or Shanghai, or manufacturers moving down the supply chain so they also have a retail presence in key markets. Woolworths is a sister company of the UK chain that ceased trading in 2009. Expansion from the Australian domestic market has seen the company become a significant player in other Pacific Rim nations. Uniqlo is a Japanese clothing retailer, specialising in simple elegant designs of staple wardrobe pieces. The company is establishing a stronger presence in the West. The remainder of the Asia-Pacific top 10 represent an exotic mixture of countries of origin and retail sectors. There are three department store businesses, namely Lotte from Korea, Coles from Australia and Matahari from Indonesia, and two grocery store businesses, SM from the Philippines and FairPrice from Singapore. That just leaves Chow Tai Fook, the chain or jewellery stores from China, Bunnings Warehouse, the top DIY chain in Australia, and Lawson, a Japanese chain of convenience stores.

A lesson to take from this? Even though the lists are heavy with supermarkets, the variety of strategies and focus is obvious. There is room for different customer value propositions in the retail sector. Some retailers focus largely or exclusively on price, others on quality of products and services, others on speed of logistics or convenience. All provide value to the customer, just in different ways.

Sources: This material was compiled using the 'Best Retail Brands 2014' report by Interbrand, available freely from **www.interbrand.com**. Estimate of the size of the Mulliez retail empire from 'Gérard Mulliez' Auchan: France's Wal-Mart Goes Global' by Carol Matlack at **www.businessweek.com**. View the Lidl *Ein gutes Stück Heimat'* range at **www.ein-gutes-stueck-heimat.de**. Other information from respective corporate websites and annual reports.

value-for-money clothing had been eroded by new retailers like Matalan undercutting prices and established companies like Gap and Next taking away profitable segments.[19] The UK retail sector has seen some famous companies disappear – most notably Woolworths.

Many retailing innovations are partially explained by the **wheel-of-retailing concept**.[20] According to this concept, many new types of retailing forms begin as low-margin, low-price, low-status operations. They challenge established retailers that have become 'fat' by letting their costs and margins increase. The new retailers' success leads them to upgrade their facilities and offer more services. In turn, their costs increase, forcing them to increase their prices. Eventually, the new retailers become like the conventional retailers they replaced. The cycle begins again when still newer types of retailers evolve with lower costs and prices. The wheel-of-retailing concept seems to explain the initial success and later troubles of department stores, supermarkets and discount stores, and the recent success of off-price retailers.

Growth of non-store retailing

Most of us still make most of our purchases the old-fashioned way: we go to the shop, find what we want, queue patiently to hand over our cash or credit card, and bring home our purchases. However, consumers now have an array of alternatives, including mail order, TV, phone and online shopping. Shoppers are increasingly avoiding the hassles and crowds by doing more of their shopping by phone or computer – music, films, software have been especially affected by this. Although such retailing advances may threaten some traditional retailers, they offer exciting opportunities for others. Most store retailers have now developed direct retailing channels. In fact, more online retailing is conducted by 'click-and-brick' retailers than by 'click-only' retailers – the presence on the high street reassuring consumers looking at the website in respect of factors like reliability, service standards, and warranty and repair issues.[21]

Online retailing is the newest form of non-store retailing. All types of retailers now use the Web as an important marketing tool. The online sales of giant bricks-and-mortar retailers, such as Tesco, John Lewis and Marks & Spencer, are increasing rapidly. Several large click-only retailers – **Amazon.com**, online auction site eBay, online travel companies such as Travelocity and Expedia, and others – are now making it big on the Web. At the other extreme, hordes of niche marketers are using the Web to reach new markets and expand their sales. Today's more sophisticated search engines and comparison shopping sites (**Shopping.com**, kelkoo, Shopzilla and others) put almost any e-tailer within a mouse click or two's reach of millions of customers.

Still, much of the anticipated growth in online sales will go to multichannel retailers – the click-and-brick marketers who can successfully merge the virtual and physical worlds. Do you get groceries delivered to your door after ordering them online? If so, which company do you pick and why? Home delivery is becoming increasingly important for many major retailers – and minor ones who want to become major.[22]

Retail convergence

Today's retailers are increasingly selling the same products at the same prices to the same consumers in competition with a wider variety of other retailers. For example, you can buy books at outlets ranging from independent local bookshops to superstores such as Waterstones or websites such as **Amazon.com**. When it comes to brand name appliances, department stores, discount stores, home improvement stores, off-price retailers, electronics superstores and a slew of websites all compete for the same customers. This merging of consumers, products, prices and retailers is called *retail convergence*:

> Retail convergence is the coming together of shoppers, goods and prices. Customers of all income levels are shopping at the same stores, often for the same goods. Old distinctions such as discount store, speciality store and department store are losing significance: the successful store must match a host of rivals on selection, service and price. Where you go for what you want – that has created the biggest challenge facing retailers. Consider fashion. Once the exclusive of the wealthy, fashion now moves just as quickly from the runways of New York and Paris to retailers at all levels. Ralph Lauren sells in department stores and in the Marshall's at the strip mall. Designer Stephen Sprouse, fresh off a limited edition of Louis Vuitton handbags and luggage, has designed a summer line of clothing and other products for Target.[23]

Such convergence means greater competition for retailers and greater difficulty in differentiating offerings. The competition between chain superstores and smaller, independently owned stores has become particularly heated. In the USA, Wal-Mart has been accused of destroying independents in countless small towns around the country. In the UK, this is becoming a significant issue for retailers like Tesco.[24]

Yet the news is not all bad for smaller companies. Many small, independent retailers are thriving. They are finding that sheer size and marketing muscle are often no match for the personal touch that small stores can provide or the speciality niches that small stores fill for a devoted customer base.

The rise of mega-retailers

The rise of huge mass merchandisers and speciality superstores, the formation of vertical marketing systems and a rash of retail mergers and acquisitions have created a core of superpower mega-retailers. Through their superior information systems and buying power, these giant retailers can offer better merchandise selections, good service and strong price savings to consumers. As a result, they grow even larger by squeezing out their smaller, weaker competitors. Amazon killed Borders, iTunes has just about killed HMV.

The mega-retailers are also shifting the balance of power between retailers and producers. A relative handful of retailers now control access to enormous numbers of consumers, giving them the upper hand in their dealings with manufacturers. In Europe, this concentration and the problems it can cause are most marked in the supermarket sector.[25]

Growing importance of retail technology

Retail technologies are becoming critically important as competitive tools. Progressive retailers are using advanced IT and software systems to produce better forecasts, control inventory costs, order electronically from suppliers, send information between stores, and even sell to customers within stores. They are adopting checkout scanning systems, online transaction processing, electronic data interchange, in-store TV and improved merchandise handling systems.

Perhaps the most startling advances in retailing technology concern the ways in which today's retailers are connecting with customers. Many retailers now routinely use technologies such as touch-screen kiosks, customer loyalty cards, electronic shelf labels and signs, handheld shopping assistants, smart cards, self-scanning systems and virtual reality displays.

Global expansion of major retailers

Retailers with unique formats and strong brand positioning are increasingly moving into other countries. Many are expanding internationally to escape mature and saturated home markets. Over the years, several giant US retailers – McDonald's, Gap, Toys 'R' Us – have become globally prominent as a result of their great marketing prowess. Others, such as the world's largest retailer, Wal-Mart, are rapidly establishing a global presence. Wal-Mart, which now operates more than 7,000 stores in 14 countries abroad, sees exciting global potential, potential which is already being exploited by the three European retailers in the global top five – Carrefour, Tesco and Germany's Metro.[26]

French discount retailer Carrefour, the world's second-largest retailer after Wal-Mart, has embarked on an aggressive mission to extend its role as a leading international retailer – with nearly 15,000 stores worldwide selling goods to the value of €82bn it is rapidly catching up with Wal-Mart, and is pursued in turn by Tesco.

Retail stores as 'communities'

With the rise in the number of people living alone, working at home, or living in isolated and sprawling suburbs, there has been a resurgence of establishments that, regardless of the product or service they offer, also provide a place for people to get together. These places include cafés, tea shops, juice bars, bookshops, superstores, children's play spaces and farmers' markets. Today's bookshops have become part bookshop, part library, part living room and part coffee house.

Bricks-and-mortar retailers are not the only ones creating community. Others have also built virtual communities on the Internet – there is a thriving subculture around eBay and Amazon and many smaller, more locally focused online retailers.

MAKING CONNECTIONS Linking the concepts

Time out! So-called experts have long predicted that non-store retailing eventually will replace store retailing as our primary way to shop. What do you think?

- Shop for a good book on the Amazon website (**www.amazon.co.uk**), taking time to browse the site and see what it has to offer. Next, shop at a nearby Waterstones or other bookshop. Compare the two shopping experiences. Where would you rather shop? On what occasions? Why?

- A Starbucks café creates something of a sense of community. How does a McDonald's compare in this respect?

WHOLESALING

Wholesaling includes all activities involved in selling goods and services to those buying for resale or business use. We call **wholesalers** those firms engaged *primarily* in wholesaling activities.

Wholesalers buy mostly from producers and sell mostly to retailers, industrial consumers and other wholesalers. As a result, many of the largest and most important wholesalers are largely unknown to final consumers. For example, you may never have heard of a Dutch firm called The Greenery, even though as one of Europe's largest wholesalers of fruit and vegetables you probably eat food supplied by it – see Marketing at Work 11.2 for more detail.

The Greenery: a fresh approach

Everyone knows that eating fresh fruit and vegetables is good for you, and most people do not eat enough of them. But what are the key buying decision criteria that consumers take into account when choosing their fruit and vegetables? That is something about which food marketers have a pretty good idea. Number 1, consumers want great taste and freshness. After that, several important criteria vie for position, but something that unites them is a sense that fresh fruit and vegetables are more than just 'fuel to keep human beings running properly'; they are more important than that. Many people like to think that their food was produced locally, and that they are supporting local farmers when they buy; a related issue is sustainability, since consumers would generally prefer, where possible, to buy food that has not been transported over vast distances. Consumers believe that locally produced food is trustworthy, healthy and authentic. So if you are a European food distribution company working directly with hundreds of fruit and vegetable growers in Europe, that puts you in a strong position to sell fruit and vegetables to the lucrative European market. Dutch cooperative The Greenery is just such a company.

The Greenery supplies fresh produce to almost all of the major European supermarkets and to similar outlets in North America and the Far East. Around 2,500 people are employed by the company across the globe but mainly in the three Dutch centres at Bleiswijk, Maasland and Barendrecht. These ultra-modern high-tech facilities have every possible aid to make bringing in fragile produce (pre-packed by their suppliers) and directing it to the right customer as efficient and quick as possible, using 150 specially equipped and fitted lorries.

In a cooperative the members are the owners of the company, so all of the shares in The Greenery are owned by the producers who are members of the horticultural cooperative 'The Greenery UA'. The 1,500 producer-owned member companies market all their products via The Greenery. The main activity of the company is to provide a complete range of vegetables, fruit and mushrooms to supermarket chains in Europe, North America and the Far East throughout the year – generating revenue of about €2bn annually. Other major target groups

are catering companies and industrial processing companies that use the produce in their own operations rather than retailing it.

As an intermediary, The Greenery requires good relationships with buyers and sellers, and the relationships The Greenery has with producers in the Netherlands and abroad give the company direct access to the source of the best produce. Organising the shortest possible chain and optimally matching supply to demand are top priorities – the quicker, the better, the fresher – and old vegetables are donated to charity, not sold. Food safety, sustainability, innovation and logistical efficiency also have a high priority in all The Greenery's activities.

Because of this, programmes to supply the same product all year round are developed in collaboration with customers and suppliers. During one season the products come from Spain, whereas during another season they are grown in the Netherlands. An example of this is a special all-year tomato supply programme for a large chain of supermarkets in the Benelux countries. The Greenery is able to offer this kind of customised concept thanks to its own product quality expertise and its extensive market information network and long-term relationships with professional producers – both in the Netherlands and in the rest of the world.

Food safety and product quality are also continuously subjected to a strict monitoring programme, in which The Greenery supervises and works closely together with all partners in the chain so that what appears on the supermarket shelf is as fresh and as healthy as possible – and that organic and non-organic produce are never mixed or mislabelled. As part of its commitment to sustainability and ethical trade, The Greenery trains and works with small-scale farmers in Third World countries. Operating in many markets, The Greenery is very aware of national differences. In the German market price is key, but in Benelux and the UK there is rapid growth in organic and convenience products.

At the end of each year, you will find The Greenery working very closely with its UK customers and all its suppliers to prepare for a very short healthy-eating boom immediately after Christmas. This is never a long-term logistical exercise because previous experience suggests the boom lasts no more than three weeks. Kevin Doran, Managing Director of The Greenery UK, said:

> **The first week after Christmas always sees a huge increase in salad sales. It is not clear if this is because of a wave of New Year resolutions to adopt a healthier diet or just a reaction to the excesses of Christmas week. If it is a result of New Year resolutions, the resolutions appear not to be kept for long – because within three weeks the peak of sales has declined back to the average winter level.**

Typically, in the first week of the new year, The Greenery ships 20 per cent more than its average weekly winter volume of tomatoes and cucumbers – that is several hundred additional tonnes of tomatoes. To ensure that supermarkets can meet the demands of shoppers with a short-term appetite for fresh produce at the start of the year, The Greenery schedules harvesting of salad vegetables over the Christmas period so that they can be delivered to stores immediately after the holidays. This means planning well in advance to ensure that growers have sown crops under glass in time to meet the post-Christmas rush.

What does the future hold for The Greenery? Chief Executive Office Philip Smits is optimistic, expecting to see better returns, an improved position in the retail market, and expects 'that we'll have a strong position in the local-for-local market'. The important concept of the 'local-for-local market' brings us right back to where we started with the question of what consumers are looking for when they buy fruit and vegetables. Buying locally

The Greenery is a leading European wholesaler of fresh produce – it probably supplies your local supermarket

Source: Shutterstock.com/Kondor83.

grown produce is becoming ever more important to consumers in Europe and in The Greenery's overseas markets, such as the USA. Remember, The Greenery has a strong Dutch heritage, and the Netherlands is famous for its high-quality fruit, vegetable and flower production. The world-renowned expertise of the Dutch horticultural industry is being exploited to improve fruit and vegetable production with The Greenery's partners worldwide. Consumers want their fruit and vegetables to be really fresh, taste great and be locally produced. The Greenery is on a mission to deliver what the consumer wants.

Sources: 'The Greenery Annual Report 2010' and Corporate Brochure, available from www.thegreenery.com; and press releases from Smye Holland Associates, available from www.smye-holland.com; 'Implementation of SAP Signals Next Phase in The Greenery', online resource available at http://www.freshplaza.com/article/105357/Implementation-of-SAP-signals-next-phase-in-The-Greenery, accessed August 2014; Jurriaan Visser, Jacques Trienekens and Paul van Beek, "Opportunities for Local for Local Food Production: A Case in Dutch Fruit and Vegetables", *International Journal on Food System Dynamics*, 4(1), 2013, pp. 417–37.

But why are wholesalers used at all? For example, why would a producer use wholesalers rather than selling directly to retailers or consumers? Simply put, wholesalers add value by performing one or more of the following channel functions:

- *Selling and promoting*: Wholesalers' sales forces help manufacturers reach many small customers at a lower cost. The wholesaler has more contacts and is often more trusted by the buyer than the distant manufacturer.

- *Buying and assortment building*: Wholesalers can select items and build assortments needed by their customers, thereby saving the consumers a lot of work.

- *Bulk breaking*: Wholesalers save their customers money by breaking large lots into small quantities.

- *Warehousing*: Wholesalers hold inventories, thereby reducing the inventory costs and risks of suppliers and customers.

- *Transportation*: Wholesalers can provide quicker delivery to buyers because they are closer than the producers.
- *Financing*: Wholesalers finance their customers by giving credit, and they finance their suppliers by ordering early and paying bills on time.
- *Risk bearing*: Wholesalers absorb risk by taking title and bearing the cost of theft, damage, spoilage and obsolescence.
- *Market information*: Wholesalers give information to suppliers and customers about competitors, new products and price developments.
- *Management services and advice*: Wholesalers often help retailers train their salespeople, improve store layouts and displays, and set up accounting and inventory control systems.

Types of wholesalers

Wholesalers fall into three major groups (see Table 11.3): *merchant wholesalers, brokers and agents* and *manufacturers' sales branches and offices*. **Merchant wholesalers** are the largest single group of wholesalers, accounting for roughly 50 per cent of all wholesaling. Merchant wholesalers include two broad types: full-service wholesalers and limited-service wholesalers. *Full-service wholesalers* provide a full set of services, whereas the various *limited-service wholesalers* offer fewer services to their suppliers and customers. The several different types of limited-service wholesalers perform varied specialised functions in the distribution channel.

Brokers and *agents* differ from merchant wholesalers in two ways: they do not take title to goods and they perform only a few functions. Like merchant wholesalers, they generally specialise by product line or customer type. A **broker** brings buyers and sellers together and assists in negotiation. **Agents** represent buyers or sellers on a more permanent basis. *Manufacturers' agents* (also called manufacturers' representatives) are the most common type of agent wholesaler. The third major type of wholesaling is that done in **manufacturers' sales branches and offices** by sellers or buyers themselves rather than through independent wholesalers.

Wholesaler marketing decisions

Wholesalers now face growing competitive pressures, more demanding customers, new technologies and more direct-buying programmes on the part of large industrial, institutional and retail buyers. As a result, they have had to take a fresh look at the marketing strategies. As with retailers, their marketing decisions include choices of target markets, positioning and the marketing mix – product assortments and services, price, promotion and place (see Figure 11.2).

Target market and positioning decision

Like retailers, wholesalers must define their target markets and position themselves effectively – they cannot serve everyone. They can choose a target group by size of customer (only large retailers), type of customer (convenience stores only), need for service (customers who need credit) or other factors. Within the target group, they can identify the more profitable customers, design stronger offers and build better relationships with them. They can propose automatic reordering systems, set up management training and advising systems, or even sponsor a voluntary chain. They can discourage less profitable customers by requiring larger orders or adding service charges to smaller ones.

Marketing mix decisions

Like retailers, wholesalers must decide on product assortment and services, prices, promotion and place. The wholesaler's 'product' is the assortment of *products and services* that it offers. Wholesalers are under great pressure to carry a full line and to stock enough for

TABLE 11.3 Major types of wholesalers

Type	Description
Merchant wholesalers	Independently owned businesses that take title to the merchandise they handle. In different trades they are called *jobbers*, *distributors* or *mill supply houses*. Include full-service wholesalers and limited-service wholesalers:
Full-service wholesalers	Provide a full line of services, carrying stock, maintaining a sales force, offering credit, making deliveries and providing management assistance. There are two types:
Wholesale merchants	Sell primarily to retailers and provide a full range of services. General merchandise wholesalers carry several merchandise lines, whereas general line wholesalers carry one or two lines in great depth. Speciality wholesalers specialise in carrying only part of a line. Examples: health food wholesalers, seafood wholesalers
Industrial distributors	Sell to manufacturers rather than to retailers. Provide several services, such as carrying stock, offering credit and providing delivery. May carry a broad range of merchandise, a general line or a speciality line
Limited-service wholesalers	Offer fewer services than full-service wholesalers. Limited-service wholesalers are of several types:
Cash-and-carry wholesalers	Carry a limited line of fast-moving goods and sell to small retailers for cash. Normally do not deliver. Example: a small fish store retailer may drive to a cash-and-carry fish wholesaler, buy fish for cash and bring the merchandise back to the store
Truck wholesalers (or truck jobbers)	Perform primarily a selling and delivery function. Carry limited lines of semi-perishable merchandise (such as milk, bread, snack foods), which they sell for cash as they make their rounds to supermarkets, small groceries, hospitals, restaurants, factory cafeterias and hotels
Drop shippers	Do not carry inventory or handle the product. On receiving an order, they select a manufacturer, who ships the merchandise directly to the customer. The drop shipper assumes title and risk from the time the order is accepted to its delivery to the customer. They operate in bulk industries, such as coal, steel and heavy equipment
Rack jobbers	Serve grocery and health/beauty retailers, mostly in non-food items. They send delivery trucks to stores, where the delivery people set up toys, paperbacks, hardware items, health and beauty aids, or other items. They price the goods, keep them fresh, set up point-of-purchase displays and keep inventory records. Rack jobbers retain title to the goods and invoice the retailers only for the goods sold to consumers
Producers' cooperatives	Are owned by farmer members and assemble farm produce to sell in local markets. The coop's profits are distributed to members at the end of the year. They often attempt to improve product quality and promote a coop brand name, such as Sun Maid raisins or Sunkist oranges
Mail-order wholesalers	Send catalogues to retail, industrial and institutional customers featuring jewellery, cosmetics, speciality foods and other small items. Maintain no outside sales force. Main customers are businesses in small outlying areas. Orders are filled and sent by mail, truck or other transportation
Brokers and agents	Do not take title to goods. Main function is to facilitate buying and selling, for which they earn a commission on the selling price. Generally specialise by product line or customer type
Brokers	Chief function is bringing buyers and sellers together and assisting in negotiation. They are paid by the party who hired them and do not carry inventory, get involved in financing or assume risk. Examples: food brokers, property brokers, insurance brokers and security brokers
Agents	Represent either buyers or sellers on a more permanent basis than brokers do. There are several types:
Manufacturers' agents	Represent two or more manufacturers of complementary lines. A formal written agreement with each manufacturer covers pricing, territories, order handling, delivery service and warranties, and commission rates. Often used in such lines as clothing, furniture and electrical goods. Most manufacturers' agents are small businesses, with only a few skilled salespeople as employees. They are hired by small manufacturers who cannot afford their own field sales forces and by large manufacturers who use agents to open new territories or to cover territories that cannot support full-time salespeople

(Continued)

TABLE 11.3 *Continued*

Type	Description
Selling agents	Have contractual authority to sell a manufacturer's entire output. The manufacturer either is not interested in the selling function or feels unqualified. The selling agent serves as a sales department and has significant influence over prices, terms and conditions of sale. Found in product areas such as textiles, industrial machinery and equipment, coal and coke, chemicals and metals
Purchasing agents	Generally have a long-term relationship with buyers and make purchases for them, often receiving, inspecting, warehousing and shipping the merchandise to the buyers. They provide helpful market information to clients and help them obtain the best goods and prices available
Commission merchants	Take physical possession of products and negotiate sales. Normally, they are not employed on a long-term basis. Used most often in agricultural marketing by farmers who do not want to sell their own output and do not belong to producers' cooperatives. The commission merchant takes a truckload of commodities to a central market, sells it for the best price, deducts a commission and expenses, and remits the balance to the producers
Manufacturers' and retailers' branches and offices	Wholesaling operations conducted by sellers or buyers themselves rather than through independent wholesalers. Separate branches and offices can be dedicated to either sales or purchasing
Sales branches and offices	Set up by manufacturers to improve inventory control, selling and promotion. *Sales branches* carry inventory and are found in industries such as lumber and automotive equipment and parts. *Sales offices* do not carry inventory and are most prominent in dry-goods industries
Purchasing officers	Perform a role similar to that of brokers or agents but are part of the buyer's organisation. Many retailers set up purchasing offices in major market centres such as Paris and Moscow

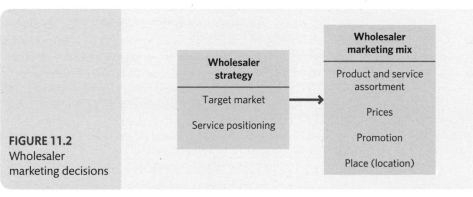

FIGURE 11.2
Wholesaler marketing decisions

immediate delivery. But this practice can damage profits. Wholesalers today are cutting down on the number of lines they carry, choosing to carry only the more profitable ones. Wholesalers are also rethinking which services count most in building strong customer relationships and which should be dropped or charged for. The key is to find the mix of services most valued by their target customers.

Price is also an important wholesaler decision. Wholesalers usually mark up the cost of goods by a standard percentage – say, 20 per cent. Expenses may run at 17 per cent of the gross margin, leaving a profit margin of 3 per cent. In grocery wholesaling, the average profit margin is often less than 2 per cent. Wholesalers are trying new pricing approaches. They may cut their margin on some lines in order to win important new customers. They may ask suppliers for special price breaks when they can turn them into an increase in the supplier's sales.

Although *promotion* can be critical to wholesaler success, most wholesalers are not promotion minded. Their use of trade advertising, sales promotion, personal selling and public relations is largely scattered and unplanned. Many are behind the times in personal selling – they still see selling as a single salesperson talking to a single customer instead of as a team effort to sell, build and service major accounts. Wholesalers also need to adopt some of the non-personal promotion techniques used by retailers. They need to develop an overall promotion strategy and to make greater use of supplier promotion materials and programmes.

Finally, *place* is important – wholesalers must choose their locations, facilities and web locations carefully. Wholesalers typically locate in low-rent, low-tax areas and tend to invest little money in their buildings, equipment and systems. As a result, their materials handling and order processing systems are often outdated. In recent years, however, large and progressive wholesalers are reacting to rising costs by investing in automated warehouses and online ordering systems. The Greenery has invested heavily in these because of the fragile and perishable nature of the produce it works with. Typically, orders are fed from the retailer's system directly into the wholesaler's computer, and the items are picked up by mechanical devices and automatically taken to a shipping platform where they are assembled. Most large wholesalers are using technology to carry out accounting, billing, inventory control and forecasting. Modern wholesalers are adapting their services to the needs of target customers and finding cost-reducing methods of doing business.

Trends in wholesaling

The wholesaling industry faces considerable challenges. The industry remains vulnerable to one of the most enduring trends of the last decade – fierce resistance to price increases and the winnowing out of suppliers who are not adding value based on cost and quality. Progressive wholesalers constantly watch for better ways to meet the changing needs of their suppliers and target customers. They recognise that, in the long run, their only reason for existence comes from adding value by increasing the efficiency and effectiveness of the entire marketing channel. For example, most people in the UK will be familiar with WHSmith, the leading high-street newsagent. Less well known is the fact that until 2006 the company also operated an extremely successful wholesale operation for papers and magazines. This is now an independent company, originally called Smiths News but in 2014 renamed Connect Group, with an annual turnover of £1.8bn that delivers 60 million items per week to 22,000 retail customers – and then collects the items that were not sold the next day. In order to assist this process, the company has invested heavily in technology. Its Connect2U website allows each customer to manage its account online, assisting greatly with stock control and order management – critical areas with such a rapid turnaround.[27]

The distinction between large retailers and large wholesalers continues to blur. Many retailers now operate formats such as wholesale clubs and hypermarkets that perform many wholesale functions. In return, many large wholesalers are setting up their own retailing operations. For example, SuperValu is the largest food wholesaler in the USA, and it is also one of the country's largest food retailers. Almost half of the company's $40bn in sales comes from its Bigg's, Cub Foods, Save-A-Lot, Farm Fresh, Hornbacher's, Laneco, Metro, Scott's Foods, Shop 'n' Save, and Shoppers Food Warehouse stores.[28]

Wholesalers will continue to increase the services they provide to retailers – retail pricing, cooperative advertising, marketing and management information reports, accounting services, online transactions and others. Rising costs on the one hand, and the demand for increased services on the other, will put the squeeze on wholesaler profits. Wholesalers who do not find efficient ways to deliver value to their customers will soon drop by the wayside. However, the increased use of computerised, automated and web-based systems will help wholesalers to contain the costs of ordering, shipping and inventory holding, boosting their productivity.

THE JOURNEY YOU'VE TAKEN Reviewing the concepts

Pull in here and reflect on this retailing and wholesaling chapter, the last of two chapters on distribution channels. In this chapter, we first looked at the nature and importance of retailing, major types of retailers, the decisions retailers make and the future of retailing. We then examined these same topics for wholesalers. Although most retailing is conducted in retail stores, in recent years non-store retailing has increased rapidly. In addition, although many retail stores are independently owned, an increasing number are now banding together under some form of corporate or contractual organisation. Wholesalers, too, have experienced recent environmental changes, most notably mounting competitive pressures. They have faced new sources of competition, more demanding customers, new technologies and more direct-buying programmes on the part of large industrial, institutional and retail buyers.

1 **Explain the roles of retailers and wholesalers in the distribution channel**

Retailing and wholesaling consist of many organisations bringing goods and services from the point of production to the point of use. *Retailing* includes all activities involved in selling goods or services directly to final consumers for their personal, non-business use. *Wholesaling* includes all the activities involved in selling goods or services to those who are buying for the purpose of resale or for business use. Wholesalers perform many functions, including selling and promoting, buying and assortment building, bulk breaking, warehousing, transporting, financing, risk bearing, supplying market information, and providing management services and advice.

2 **Describe the major types of retailers and give examples of each**

Retailers can be classified as *store retailers* and *non-store retailers*. Although most goods and services are sold through stores, non-store retailing has been growing much faster than has store retailing. Store retailers can be further classified by the *amount of service* they provide (self-service, limited service or full service), *product line sold* (speciality stores, department stores, supermarkets, convenience stores, superstores and service businesses) and *relative prices* (discount stores and off-price retailers). Today, many retailers are banding together in corporate and contractual *retail organisations* (corporate chains, voluntary chains and retailer cooperatives, franchise organisations and merchandising conglomerates).

3 **Identify the major types of wholesalers and give examples of each**

Wholesalers fall into three groups. First, *merchant wholesalers* take possession of the goods. They include *full-service wholesalers* (wholesale merchants, industrial distributors) and *limited-service wholesalers* (cash-and-carry wholesalers, truck wholesalers, drop shippers, rack jobbers, producers' cooperatives and mail-order wholesalers). Second, *brokers and agents* do not take possession of the goods but are paid a commission for aiding buying and selling. Finally, *manufacturers' sales branches and offices* are wholesaling operations conducted by non-wholesalers to bypass the wholesalers.

4 **Explain the marketing decisions facing retailers and wholesalers**

Each retailer must make decisions about its target markets and positioning, product assortment and services, price, promotion and place. Retailers need to choose target markets carefully and position themselves strongly. Today, wholesaling is holding its own in the economy. Progressive wholesalers are adapting their services to the needs of target customers and are seeking cost-reducing methods of doing business. Faced with slow growth in their domestic markets and developments such as the North American Free Trade Agreement and EU enlargement, many large wholesalers are also now going global.

NAVIGATING THE KEY TERMS

NOTES AND REFERENCES

1 'The Retail Boss Who Says He Can Save you £30 a Week', interview by Julia Finch, City Editor, *Guardian,* 11 July 2008, p. 27.

2 The British Retail Consortium has plenty of information on the UK retail sector and can be found at **www.brc.org.uk**

3 Forrester Research is a market intelligence agency like Euromonitor and Mintel. Many of its reports are at EU level and some on the EU retail sector, for example 'Western European Online Retail Forecast, 2012 to 2017' from **www.forrester.com**

4 SPAR can be found online at **www.spar-international.com**. Pressbyran are at **www.pressbyran.se** and Openco at **www.elcorteingles.es/opencor/**

5 Wal-Mart has a major impact on the global retail market and can be found online at **www.walmartstores.com**

6 'Carrefour Annual Report 2010', available from **http://www.carrefour.com**

7 Serravalle Designer Outlet is located online at **www.mcarthurglen.it/serravalle/** and Bicester Village at **www.bicestervillage.com**. Value Retail can be found at **www.valueretail.com/**

8 The homepage for the Euronics group is at **www.euronics.co.uk** and Edeka at **www.edeka.com**

9 Learn all about Husse petfoods at **www.husse.com**; Calzedonia are at **http://www.calzedonia.it/en/** (English text version) and the German-language homepage of the music schools at **www.musikschule-froehlich.de**

10 Extensive information about European franchises can be found at **www.franchiseeurope.com**

11 McDonald's corporate web pages are at **www.mcdonalds.co.uk**

12 Adapted from Susanna Hamner, 'Lessons from a Retail Rebel', *Business 2.0,* June 2005, pp. 62–4.

13 See **www.inglesport.com** and **www.masterspas.co.uk**. Also **www.smeguk.com**

14 The homepage of the Cevahir mall with plenty of facts and figures is at **http://www.istanbulcevahir.com/en-EN/home/29.aspx**

15 For a good discussion of retail pricing and promotion strategies, see Kathleen Seiders and Glenn B. Voss, 'From Price to Purchase', *Marketing Management,* November–December 2005, pp. 38–43.

16 For a potted history see **www.insideyork.co.uk/shambles**

17 Mike Bygrave, 'Welcome to the World's First Shopping Malls', *Independent on Sunday,* http://www.independent.co.uk/travel/europe/welcome-to-the-worlds-first-shopping-malls-298190.html, accessed December 2014. An example of the early Parisian passages can be read about at www.passagesetgaleries.org/texts/passages/2fiches_passages/fiches/choiseul.html, accessed August 2011.

18 Dean Starkman, 'The Mall, Without the Haul – "Lifestyle Centers" Slip Quietly into Upscale Areas, Mixing Cachet and "Curb Appeal"', *The Wall Street Journal,* 25 July 2001, p. B1; 'To Mall or Not to Mall?', *Buildings,* June 2004, p. 99; Arlyn Tobian Gajilan, 'Wolves in Shops' Clothing', *Fortune Small Business,* February 2005, pp. 17–18; and information accessed on the International Council of Shopping Centers website, www.icsc.org, August 2005.

19 Read about the withdrawal of C&A from the UK market, *BBC News,* 'C&A Quit UK', news.bbc.co.uk/1/hi/business/792028.stm, accessed August 2011; C&A homepage at www.c-and-a.com

20 See Malcolm P. McNair and Eleanor G. May, 'The Next Revolution of the Retailing Wheel', *Harvard Business Review,* September–October 1978, pp. 81–91; Stephen Brown, 'The Wheel of Retailing: Past and Future', *Journal of Retailing,* Summer 1990, pp. 143–7; Stephen Brown, 'Variations on a Marketing Enigma: The Wheel of Retailing Theory', *Journal of Marketing Management,* 7(2), 1991, pp. 131–55; Jennifer Negley, 'Retrenching, Reinventing and Remaining Relevant', *Discount Store News,* 5 April 1999, p. 11; Don E. Schultz, 'Another Turn of the Wheel', *Marketing Management,* March–April 2002, pp. 8–9; and Carol Krol, 'Staples Preps Easier E-Commerce Site', *B to B,* 14 March 2005, pp. 3–4.

21 See Sungwook Min and Mary Wolfinbarger, 'Market Share, Profit Margin, and Marketing Efficiency of Early Movers, Bricks and Clicks, and Specialists in E-Commerce', *Journal of Business Research,* August 2005, pp. 1030ff.

22 See for example the French retailer Auchan at www.auchan.fr and read about its expansion into Poland via Internet home delivery operations: 'Auchan Launches Online Grocery Delivery', www.just-food.com/news/auchan-launches-online-grocery-delivery_id115217.aspx, accessed August 2011.

23 Excerpt adapted from Alice Z. Cuneo, 'What's in Store?', *Advertising Age,* 25 February 2002, pp. 1, 30–1. See also Robert Berner, 'Dark Days in White Goods for Sears', *BusinessWeek,* 10 March 2003, pp. 78–9.

24 An example of a lengthy dispute between a local community and Tesco can be read about at 'Town's Tesco Plans Remain on Hold', *BBC News,* news.bbc.co.uk/1/hi/wales/mid/7371372.stm, accessed August 2011. See other examples of similar issues at www.thisismoney.co.uk/news/article.html?in_article_id=417691&in_page_id=2 and 'Manningtree to fight Tesco superstore plan' by Charles Clover at http://www.telegraph.co.uk/news/earth/hands-off-our-land/8862574/Ledbury-fights-to-resist-the-superstores.html, accessed December 2014.

25 For examples of Government and other agency pressures on the retail sector, see 'UK Supermarket Sector Set for Shake-up', *BBC News,* news.bbc.co.uk/1/hi/business/7245944.stm, accessed August 2011.

26 Read the full report: 'Global Powers of Retailing 2011' at www.deloitte.com, accessed August 2011.

27 Information about Connect2U is available from the pages at www.connect2u.co.uk; Connect Group is at www.connectgroupplc.com

28 Facts accessed at www.supervalu.com, Corporate Profile, July 2014.

CHAPTER 12

COMMUNICATING CUSTOMER VALUE: ADVERTISING, SALES PROMOTION AND PUBLIC RELATIONS

AFTER STUDYING THIS CHAPTER, YOU SHOULD BE ABLE TO

- discuss the process and advantages of integrated marketing communications in communicating customer value
- define the five promotion tools and discuss the factors that must be considered in shaping the overall promotion mix
- describe and discuss the major decisions involved in developing an advertising programme
- explain how sales promotion campaigns are developed and implemented
- explain how companies use public relations to communicate with their publics

THE WAY AHEAD
Previewing the concepts

We'll forge ahead now into the last of the marketing mix tools – promotion. Companies must do more than just create customer value. They must also use promotion to communicate that value clearly and persuasively. You'll find that promotion is not a single tool but rather a mix of several tools. Ideally, under the concept of *integrated marketing communications*, the company will carefully coordinate these promotion elements to deliver a clear, consistent and compelling message about the organisation and its products. We'll begin by introducing you to the various promotion mix tools. Next, we'll examine the rapidly changing communications environment and the need for integrated marketing communications. Finally, we'll look more closely at three of the promotion tools – advertising, sales promotion and public relations. In the next chapter, we'll visit the other two promotion mix tools, personal selling and direct marketing.

To start this chapter, let's look behind the scenes at a campaign to improve the perception of Renault cars in Germany.

CHAPTER CONTENTS

RENAULT: HOW A SAUSAGE, A SUSHI ROLL, A CRISPBREAD AND A BAGUETTE HAVE AFFECTED CAR SALES IN EUROPE

Barbara Caemmerer, Professeur Associée de Marketing, ESSCA, Paris

In Europe, the country-of-origin is a strong factor impacting on consumers' decision making when buying a car – particularly in the five key markets of Germany, France, Italy, Spain and the UK.[1] Industry data shows that most of the top 10 bestselling cars in Germany – the biggest car market in the EU – are produced by Volkswagen, BMW or DaimlerChrysler, while the French and Italians prefer cars that originate in their home markets.[2] This ethnocentric loyalty is the result of clever marketing communications campaigns which have created country-specific, favourable brand images. For example, for German consumers *safety* is one very important criterion when choosing a new car – and they perceive the Mercedes and Volkswagen brands as being the market leaders in this attribute.[3]

Source: Nordpol+ Hamburg Agentur für Kommunikation GmbH.

Therefore, Joerg-Alexander Ellhof, Director of Marketing Communications at Renault Germany, faced a particular challenge when the French headquarters decided that Renault had to expand its share in the German market. After a phase of thorough market research, he decided that the only way forward was directly to attack the main German competitors as well as other major car import brands on the attribute of *safety*. He believed that a creative, well-integrated marketing communications campaign could have a strong positive impact on the organisation's fortunes in the German market. However, the task seemed to be immense as – in order to gain market share – he had to convince German car buyers that Renault, a French car manufacturer, was actually building safer cars than the German heavyweights themselves!

Fortunately, Renault had factual evidence for this proposition, as eight of its car models won the Euro NCAP (European New Car Assessment Programme) Crashtest competition with five stars.[4] This result made Renault officially the manufacturer of the safest cars in Europe – a very good basis on which to build the marketing communications campaign! But various questions remained: How could the campaign be implemented? Which agencies should be involved? What elements of the marketing communications mix should be used? What should the creative execution look like? How should it be evaluated?

After a pitching process during which various agencies were invited to present their campaign suggestions, the Renault marketing department decided to work with two agencies, Publicis[5] and Nordpol+, on the project. While Publicis is a large and well-established international advertising agency network, Nordpol+ was a relatively new agency with only 25 employees, but had been attracting great industry attention over the prior 10 years thanks to its extraordinarily creative approaches to campaign planning and design.[6]

The overarching strategic marketing communications objective for the campaign was to increase consumers' awareness of Renault's positive safety attributes and thus enhance desire for the brand among German consumers. Therefore, it was decided to use the following message content for the communications campaign: '*Die sichersten Autos kommen aus Frankreich*' ('The safest cars come from France'). It was the task of the agencies to identify how this message could be conveyed to the target audience in the most effective and efficient manner. Nordpol+ recommended that the key marketing communications mix elements used in this campaign should consist of cinema advertising, supported by viral marketing initiatives and TV screenings, as well as a new company website that would link into the theme of the campaign.[7] Publicis was responsible for the print advertisements that would also stress the safety message throughout (title: *'Niemand hat mehr üer Sicherheit zu erzählen als Renault'*; 'No one has more to say about safety than Renault').[8]

In order to stress the superlative that the *safest* cars come from France, Nordpol+ and Renault decided that the commercial had to demonstrate that Renault cars were safer in comparison with those of other car manufacturers from competing countries-of-origin, mainly Germany, Japan and Sweden. To reinforce the factual basis for this claim, the agency decided to recreate in detail the Euro NCAP Crashtest scenario for the commercial. However, instead of showing how cars with crashtest dummies slam into the barriers, the agency decided to film the collision of stereotypical national food items with the walls! First, a giant German sausage is driven into the barrier – bursting into thousands of pieces. The same thing happens to a Japanese sushi roll and a Swedish crispbread: both pretty much disintegrate on impact. The last contestant is a soft French baguette which is thrust into the barrier and – surprise – it survives the test with hardly any damage as it can fully absorb the shock (through crumpling and uncrumpling its front). The scenes are shown in slow motion and the forceful images stand in stark contrast to the accompanying music, the passionate song *'J'attendrai'* ('I will wait') by singer Rina Ketty, which was recorded in 1939.

During the campaign, the market research agency tns sofres[9] was commissioned to track changes in consumers' attitudes to evaluate the effectiveness and efficiency of the marketing communications initiatives used. The data suggests that this commercial – 'Crashtest' – created by Nordpol+ was very successful in changing consumer attitudes towards the brand. There was a strong increase in awareness levels of the safety of Renault cars as well as in intentions to purchase a car from Renault. The two key factors that contributed to this success were the creative execution of the commercial as well as the media strategy that was used to reach the intended audience (in particular, potential new car buyers, male, 30–49 years old, with an income of more than €2,000 a month).

Besides the creative execution of the commercial, Nordpol+ and Renault also had to think about what media channels they could use to reach their key target audience. They identified multiplex cinemas, the Internet and TV as appropriate channels and a good media mix – with each channel supporting the other. 'Crashtest' was shown in multiplex cinemas across 141 German cities. In support of the cinema launch, a viral campaign was started that initiated the diffusion of the commercial on the Internet – by viewers sending the link on to each other by email. Within a few weeks thousands of viewers had seen 'Crashtest' on YouTube. The campaign was extended through the broadcasting of the commercial in two-week periods on TV. In support of the TV campaign the commercial was screened again in cinemas. Finally, 'Crashtest' could be seen continuously on TV in commercial breaks during selected programmes. Overall, the advert was available for nearly a year. In parallel to the TV campaign, an additional website was developed that was directly linked to the campaign message: **www.sicher.de** (*sicher* = safe). On this website users could identify how safe their car was, according to the latest Euro NCAP Crashtest results. In addition, the interactive website contained a wide range of additional information on car and road safety.

The unique creative execution as well as the well-integrated integration of messages and media channels used played a crucial role in making this campaign effective and efficient. But it is not only the consumers who have been impressed. The campaign won various prestigious advertising prizes, for example at the ADC (Art Director's Club) Awards and the international advertising festival in Cannes – a result that both client Renault and agency Nordpol+ can be very proud of. For Ellhof the success of the campaign clearly reflects that creativity can be effective and efficient. While the French headquarters of Renault was first sceptical about the rather unconventional approach to the campaign, it has recently suggested that the 'Crashtest' commercial should be launched in a further 13 European countries. Renault HQ believes that Renault Germany has found a very good way of convincing consumers that Renault is building the safest cars in Europe – and as the campaign has been successful in the German market, why should it not have similar effects in other countries, too?

The audience has been screaming for more. . . . After the successful implementation of the campaign, client and agency went back to the drawing board to create follow-up commercials for 'Crashtest'. The result? The website **www.sicher.de** *now* also hosts two new viral commercials called 'Ballett' and 'Kollision', both created by Nordpol+. They have spread quickly through viewers' recommendations across the Web and have had an impressive number of hits on the YouTube website. Cinema and TV screenings have also been used in support of the viral campaign. Linking into the 'Crashtest' theme, 'Ballett' shows the eight Renault NCAP five-star models in a desert in South Africa performing a ballet dance. Built into the performance are quite a few coordinated (but serious!) crashes – however, all cars survive with minor damage and all are able to dance until the end of the piece. The commercial ends with the tagline, *'Das sicherste Ensemble der Welt'* ('The world's safest ensemble') and a shot of the eight Renault models. The other follow-up commercial, 'Kollision', is also closely linked to the crashtest theme but, instead of bursting food items, the commercial features scenes of people colliding with each other. Judging from their facial expressions, it is pretty clear that the Sumo wrestlers hurt themselves quite badly during their fight – so do the Swedish and German folk dancers when they bump into each other during a performance. Only the French are exceptionally well coordinated: an elegantly dressed man and woman are about to collide – but instead of hurting themselves they start kissing . . . the tagline of the commercial is '*Der beste Schutz bei einem Zusammenstoss kommt aus Frankreich*' ('In case of a collision the best protection comes from France').

Isn't this exactly the sort of story we expect from the French? The Germans seem to love it – let's see what the rest of the European nations will think.

Sources: With special thanks to Jörg Ellhof and Anne Fritzemeier. For full source details, see notes 1–9 at the end of this chapter.

Building good customer relationships calls for more than just developing a good product, pricing it attractively and making it available to target customers. Companies must also communicate that value to customers, and what they communicate should not be left to chance. All of their communications must be planned and blended into a carefully integrated marketing communications programme. Just as good communication is important in building and maintaining any kind of relationship, it is a crucial element in a company's efforts to build profitable customer relationships.

THE PROMOTION MIX

A company's total **promotion mix** (or **marketing communications mix**) consists of the specific blend of advertising, sales promotion, public relations, personal selling and direct marketing tools that the company uses persuasively to communicate customer value and build customer relationships. Definitions of the five major promotion tools follow:[10]

- **Advertising:** Any paid form of non-personal presentation and promotion of ideas, goods or services by an identified sponsor.
- **Sales promotion:** Short-term incentives to encourage the purchase or sale of a product or service.
- **Public relations:** Building good relations with the company's various publics by obtaining favourable publicity, building up a good corporate image, and handling or heading off unfavourable rumours, stories and events.
- **Personal selling:** Personal presentation by the firm's sales force for the purpose of making sales and building customer relationships.
- **Direct marketing:** Direct connections with carefully targeted individual consumers both to obtain an immediate response and to cultivate lasting customer relationships – the use of telephone, mail, fax, email, the Internet and other tools to communicate directly with specific consumers.

Each category involves specific promotion tools used to communicate with consumers. For example, advertising includes broadcast, print, online, outdoor and other forms. Sales promotion includes discounts, coupons, displays and demonstrations. Personal selling includes sales presentations, trade shows and incentive programmes. Public relations includes press releases, sponsorships, special events and Twitter. And direct marketing includes catalogues, telephone marketing, kiosks, the Internet and more.

At the same time, marketing communication goes beyond these specific promotion tools. The product's design, its price, the shape and colour of its package, and the stores that sell it – all communicate something to buyers. Thus, although the promotion mix is the company's primary communication activity, the entire marketing mix – promotion and product, price and place – must be coordinated for greatest communication impact.

INTEGRATED MARKETING COMMUNICATIONS

In past decades, marketers have perfected the art of mass marketing – selling highly stand-ardised products to masses of customers. In the process, they have developed effective mass-media communications techniques to support these mass-marketing strategies. Large companies routinely invested millions or even billions in TV, social media or other mass-media advertising, reaching tens of millions of customers with a single advert. Today, how-ever, marketing managers face some new marketing communications realities.

The new marketing communications landscape

Three major factors are changing the face of today's marketing communications. First, as mass markets have fragmented, marketers are shifting away from mass marketing. More and more, they are developing focused marketing programmes designed to build closer relation-ships with customers in more narrowly defined micromarkets. Second, as the volume of data we hand over as customers via social media and loyalty cards grows ever larger, companies can use this to build up a more detailed picture of what appeals to us as individuals – markets-of-one. Less *broad*casting, more *narrow*casting.

Improved IT has also caused striking changes in the ways in which companies and cus-tomers communicate with each other. Many of these issues are covered in more depth later (see Chapter 14), but even young children and those lacking in technical savvy are research-ing, engaging, interacting and critiquing companies, brands and products via blogs, social media and company-sponsored web pages. The technology also gives consumers more con-trol over the nature and timing of messages they choose to send and receive.

The shifting marketing communications model

The shift towards segmented marketing and the explosive developments in information and communications technology have had a dramatic impact on marketing communications. Just as mass marketing once gave rise to a new generation of mass-media communications, the shift towards targeted marketing and the changing communications environment are giving birth to a new marketing communications model. Although TV, magazines and other mass media remain very important, their dominance is now declining. Advertisers are now adding a broad selection of more specialised and highly targeted media to reach smaller customer segments with more personalised messages. The new media range from speciality magazines and TV channels to product placements in TV programmes and video games, to Internet catalogues and email and even displays that can evaluate a passer-by and show an appropriate advert – see Marketing at Work 12.1.

Some advertising industry experts even predict a doom-and-gloom 'chaos scenario', in which the old mass-media communications model will collapse entirely. They believe that marketers will increasingly abandon traditional mass media in favour of new digital technologies – from websites and email to mobile phone content and video-on-demand – technologies that allow conversations with small clusters of consumers who are proactively choosing what advertising to consume.[11]

As mass-media costs rise, audiences shrink, and more and more viewers use SkyPlus+ and other digital video recorder (DVR) systems to skip past disruptive TV commercials, the sceptics predict the demise of the old mass-media mainstay – the 30-second TV commer-cial. They point out that many large advertisers are now shifting their advertising budgets away from broadcast TV in favour of more targeted, cost-effective, interactive and engag-ing media that appear on non-TV screens like tablets, phones and home computers. Now advertisers have to reach consumers in less conventional ways – on the street, on a mobile phone, online and, as we will see shortly, in-game.

Other industry insiders, however, see a more gradual shift to the new marketing communi-cations model. They note that broadcast TV and other mass media still capture the lion's share of the promotion budgets of most major marketing firms, a fact that is not likely to change quickly. One advertising expert explains: 'TV audiences remain coveted, because – shrinking though they are – they represent the last vestige of mass media and marketing, or as [one executive asserts] "the last surviving conglomeration of human beings in the living room"'.[12] That being said, many European nations lead the world in terms of the proportion of the advertising budget that is spent on online advertising – the UK now spends more on online advertising than TV advertising, the first country in the world in which this has happened.[13]

Thus, it seems likely that the new marketing communications model will consist of a gradually shifting mix of both traditional mass media and a wide array of exciting new, more targeted, more personalised media. 'We need to reinvent the way we market to consumers,' says A.G. Lafley, recently retired Chief Executive of Procter & Gamble. 'Mass marketing still has an important role, [but] we need new models to initially coexist with mass marketing, and eventually to succeed it.'[14]

The need for integrated marketing communications

The shift towards a richer mix of media and communication approaches poses a problem for marketers. Consumers today are bombarded by commercial messages from a broad range of sources. But consumers do not distinguish between message sources the way marketers do. In the consumer's mind, messages from different media and promotional approaches all become part of a single message about the company. Conflicting messages from these different sources can result in confused company images, brand positions and customer relationships.[15]

All too often, companies fail to integrate their various communications channels. The result is a hodgepodge of communications to consumers. Mass-media advertisements say one thing, while a price promotion sends a different signal, and a product label creates still another message. Company sales literature says something altogether different and the company's website seems out of sync with everything else – including unhelpful Twitter messages from employees!

The problem is that these communications often come from different parts of the company. Advertising messages are planned and implemented by the advertising department or an advertising agency. Personal selling communications are developed by sales management. Other company specialists are responsible for public relations, sales promotion events, Internet marketing and other forms of marketing communications.

However, whereas these companies have separated their communications tools, customers will not, and it is because of this that more and more companies are adopting the concept of **integrated marketing communications (IMC)**. Under this concept, as illustrated in Figure 12.1, the company carefully integrates its many communications channels to deliver a clear, consistent and compelling message about the organisation and its brands.[16]

IMC calls for recognising all contact points where the customer may encounter the company and its brands. Each *brand contact* will deliver a message, whether good, bad or indifferent. The company wants to deliver a consistent and positive message with each contact. IMC leads to a total marketing communications strategy aimed at building strong customer relationships by showing how the company and its products can help customers solve their problems.

IMC ties together all of the company's messages and images. The company's advertising and personal selling communications have the same message, look and feel as its email promotions. And its public relations materials project the same image as its website.[17] For example, print adverts for Peugeot build consumer preference for the brand. But the ads also point viewers to the company's website, which offers lots of help and very little hype. The site helps serious car buyers build and price a model, find a local showroom online, and learn more about the cars and the company. Later, at the showroom, Peugeot-trained salespeople communicate on a one-to-one basis while customers test-drive the cars.

In the past, no one person or department was responsible for thinking through the communication roles of the various promotion tools and coordinating the promotion mix. To help implement IMC, some companies appoint a marketing communications director who has overall responsibility for the company's communications efforts. This helps to produce

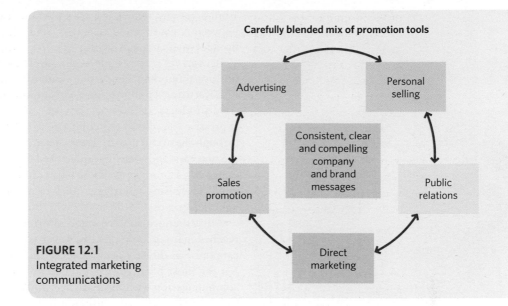

FIGURE 12.1
Integrated marketing
communications

better communications consistency and greater sales impact. It places the responsibility in someone's hands – where none existed before – to unify the company's image as it is shaped by thousands of company activities.

IMC involves identifying the target audience and shaping a well-coordinated promotional programme to elicit the desired audience response. Too often, marketing communicators focus on creating immediate brand awareness, image or preference in the target market. But this approach to communications is too short-sighted. Today, marketers are viewing communications as helping to *manage the customer relationship over time*. Because customers differ, communications programmes need to be developed for specific segments, niches and even individuals. And, in these days of new interactive digital communications technologies, companies must ask not only 'How can we reach our customers?' but also 'How can we find ways to let our customers reach us?'

SHAPING THE OVERALL PROMOTION MIX

The concept of IMC suggests that the company must blend the promotion tools carefully into a coordinated *promotion mix*. But how does the company determine what mix of promotion tools it will use? Companies within the same industry differ greatly in the design of their promotion mixes. For example, Avon spends most of its promotion funds on personal selling and direct marketing, whereas Rimmel spends heavily on consumer advertising. Acer relies on advertising and promotion to retailers, whereas Dell uses more direct marketing. We now look at factors that influence the marketer's choice of promotion tools.

The nature of each promotion tool

Each promotion tool has unique characteristics and costs. Marketers must understand these characteristics in shaping the promotion mix.

Advertising

Advertising can reach masses of geographically dispersed buyers at a low cost per exposure, and it enables the seller to repeat a message many times. For example, TV advertising can reach huge audiences who are watching significant sports or entertainment events. About 380 million people across 200 countries watched Real Madrid beat Atlético Madrid in the final of the UEFA European Champions League in 2014 – a mere fraction of the more than

www.rimmellondon.com

COLOUR
FOR KEEPS

FOOD-PROOF, KISS-PROOF
IO HOUR COLOUR AND GLOSS

NEW INFINITE COLOUR LIPSTICK

2 STEPS TO HEAVEN   1. Unveil long-lasting colour 2. Gloss and glow.
RESISTS EVERYTHING   Nibble, kiss – the Colourhold™ formula stays true.
BREAK THE RULES   For colour, for shine, for keeps.

RIMMEL
LONDON

Rimmel spends heavily on consumer advertising

Source: Image Courtesy of The Advertising Archives.

1 billion who watched at least a part of the World Cup Final between Argentina and Germany on any one of hundreds of broadcasting channels worldwide.[18]

Beyond its reach, large-scale advertising says something positive about the seller's size, popularity and success. Because of advertising's public nature, consumers tend to view advertised products as more legitimate. Advertising is also very expressive – it allows the company to dramatise its products through the artful use of visuals, print, sound and colour. On the one hand, advertising can be used to build up a long-term image for a product (such as Coca-Cola ads). On the other hand, advertising can trigger quick responses (as when Debenhams advertises a 24-hour sale with little advance warning).

Advertising also has some shortcomings. Although it reaches many people quickly, advertising is impersonal and cannot be as directly persuasive as can company salespeople. For the most part, advertising can only carry on a one-way communication with the audience, and the audience does not feel that it has to pay attention or respond. In addition, advertising can be very costly. Although some advertising forms, such as newspaper and radio advertising, can be done on smaller budgets, other forms, such as network TV advertising, require very large budgets.

Personal selling

Personal selling is the most effective tool at certain stages of the buying process, particularly in building up buyers' preferences, convictions and actions. It involves personal interaction between two or more people, so each person can observe the other's needs and characteristics and make quick adjustments. Personal selling also allows all kinds of customer relationships to spring up, ranging from matter-of-fact selling relationships to personal friendships. An effective salesperson keeps the customer's interests at heart in order to build a long-term relationship. Finally, with personal selling, the buyer usually feels a greater need to listen and respond, even if the response is a polite 'No thank you.'

These unique qualities come at a cost, however. A sales force requires a longer-term commitment than does advertising – advertising can be turned on and off, but sales force size is harder to change. Personal selling is also the company's most expensive promotion tool, often costing hundreds of pounds per call. Many firms spend up to three times as much on personal selling as they do on advertising.

Sales promotion

Sales promotion includes a wide assortment of tools – coupons, contests, money-off deals, premiums and others – all of which have many unique qualities. They attract consumer attention, offer strong incentives to purchase, and can be used to dramatise product offers and to boost sagging sales. Sales promotions invite and reward quick response – whereas advertising says 'Buy our product', sales promotion says 'Buy it now'. Sales promotion effects are often short-lived, however, and often are not as effective as advertising or personal selling in building long-term brand preference and customer relationships.

Public relations

Public relations is very believable – news stories, features, sponsorships and events seem more real and believable to readers than ads do. Public relations can also reach many prospects who avoid salespeople and ads – the message gets to the buyers as 'news' rather than as a sales-directed communication. And, as with advertising, public relations can dramatise a company or product. Marketers tend to underuse public relations or to use it as an after-thought, yet a well-thought-out public relations campaign used with other promotion mix elements can be very effective and economical.

Direct marketing

Although there are many forms of **direct marketing** – telephone marketing, direct mail, online marketing and others – they all share four distinctive characteristics. Direct market-ing is *non-public:* the message is normally directed to a specific person. Direct marketing is *immediate* and *customised:* messages can be prepared very quickly and can be tailored to appeal to specific consumers. Finally, direct marketing is *interactive:* it allows a dialogue between the marketing team and the consumer, and messages can be altered depending on the consumer's response. Thus, direct marketing is well suited to highly targeted marketing efforts and to building one-to-one customer relationships.

Promotion mix strategies

Marketers can choose from two basic promotion mix strategies – *push* promotion or *pull* promotion. Figure 12.2 contrasts the two strategies. The relative emphasis on the specific promotion tools differs for push and pull strategies. A **push strategy** involves 'pushing' the product through marketing channels to final consumers. The producer directs its market-ing activities (primarily personal selling and trade promotion) towards channel members to induce them to carry the product and to promote it to final consumers.

Using a **pull strategy**, the producer directs its marketing activities (primarily advertising and consumer promotion) towards final consumers to induce them to buy the product. If the pull strategy is effective, consumers will then demand the product from channel members, who will in turn demand it from producers. Thus, under a pull strategy, consumer demand 'pulls' the product through the channels.

Some industrial goods companies use only push strategies; some direct-marketing com-panies use only pull. However, most large companies use some combination of both. For example, Heinz uses mass-media advertising and consumer promotions to pull its products and a large sales force and trade promotions to push its products through the channels. In recent years, consumer goods companies have been decreasing the pull portions of their

FIGURE 12.2
Push versus pull promotion strategies

mixes in favour of more push. This has caused concern that they may be driving short-term sales at the expense of long-term brand equity.

Companies consider many factors when designing their promotion mix strategies, including *type of product/market* and the *product life-cycle stage*. For example, the importance of different promotion tools varies between consumer and business markets. Business-to-consumer (B2C) companies usually 'pull' more, putting more of their funds into advertising, followed by sales promotion, personal selling and then public relations. In contrast, business-to-business (B2B) marketers tend to 'push' more, putting more of their funds into personal selling, followed by sales promotion, advertising and public relations. In general, personal selling is used more heavily with expensive and risky goods and in markets with fewer and larger sellers.

Now that we have examined the concept of IMC and the factors that firms consider when shaping their promotion mixes, let's look more closely at the specific marketing communications tools.

MAKING CONNECTIONS Linking the concepts

Pull over here for a few minutes. Flip back through and link the parts of the chapter you've read so far.

● How do the integrated marketing communications (IMC) and promotion mix concepts relate to one another?

● How has the changing communications environment affected the ways in which companies communicate with you about their products and services? If you were in the market for a new car, where might you hear about various available models? Where would you search for information?

ADVERTISING

Advertising can be traced back to the very beginnings of recorded history. The Romans painted walls to announce gladiator fights, and the Phoenicians painted pictures promoting their wares on large rocks along parade routes. Modern advertising, however, is a far cry from these early efforts. Billions upon billions are spent every year on advertising. Exact figures are hard to come by – and lag a couple of years behind – but estimates for global expenditure in 2014 put it at around $550bn. Let's take just one country – Belgium. One of the more affluent European nations certainly, but far from being the largest in terms of population (less than 11 million). mandmglobal – an advertising research company – gives an estimate of advertising expenditure of $4.8bn in 2015 and a list of the top 10 advertisers in Belgium. In first place is Procter & Gamble, in second place Belgacom – a telecoms company – and in third place Vlaamse Media Maatschappij, which is a domestic media conglomerate; visit them at **medialaan.net**. How about some detail for media and sectors? EACA (the European Association of Communications Agencies) has some figures. Food products were top with $182m, followed by cars ($120m) and pharmaceuticals. In respect of media, TV is still king on a global level with about 40 per cent of the total. Online/mobile combined are catching up and it is expected they will overtake TV in the next five years. In some markets this has already occurred.[19]

Which companies are spending the most on advertising? AdAge has an annual list of the top 100. There are plenty of names you'd recognise – like Procter & Gamble, BMW and Diageo. Also some names that might not be as familiar to you – either because you know the brand but not the formal company name, or because the company doesn't operate near you. Kao Corp, Henkel, Yum Brands all fall under that category. Coca-Cola spent more than $3bn on advertising globally in 2013: $400m in the USA, twice that in Europe and three times that in the Asia-Pacific region. In the UK the leader is BSkyB with £264m, with Procter & Gamble in second place on £178m and BT third with £150m (Table 12.1). Across Europe, the top spenders vary by country: in France it is the entertainment/telecoms conglomerate Vivendi; in Italy it is Fiat; and in the Republic of Ireland it is the national government ($72m).[20] Why would the state be the number 1 advertiser? The answer is of course that advertising is a good way to inform and persuade, whether the purpose is to sell Coca-Cola or new environmentally-friendly regulations or to promote new social marketing objectives.

Marketing management must make four important decisions when developing an advertising programme (see Figure 12.3): setting advertising objectives; setting the advertising budget; developing advertising strategy (message decisions and media decisions); and evaluating advertising campaigns.

TABLE 12.1 Top advertisers in the UK (£), 2014

Rank	Advertiser	Expenditure (2013)	Expenditure (2012)	% Year on year
1	British Sky Broadcasting Ltd	264,338,785	241,106,331	9.63
2	Procter & Gamble Ltd	177,257,396	195,182,834	−9.18
3	BT Ltd	149,788,119	179,677,909	−16.63
4	Unilever Uk Ltd	119,100,702	138,979,674	−14.30
5	Tesco Plc	116,269,526	117,403,761	−0.96
6	Asda Stores Ltd	97,035,247	109,139,356	−11.09
7	Talktalk Grp	92,545,979	48,486,735	90.86
8	Virgin Media	88,357,222	106,062,440	−16.69
9	Wm Morrison Supermarkets Plc	81,522,591	76,681,050	6.31
10	DFS Furniture Co. Ltd	75,682,183	79,895,687	−5.27
11	Vodafone Ltd	74,594,746	58,193,426	28.18
12	McDonald's Restrs Ltd	72,148,548	55,670,024	29.60
13	Reckitt Benckiser (UK) Ltd	68,980,070	76,107,639	−9.36
14	L'Oréal Paris	63,593,242	69,284,114	−8.21
15	Nestle	63,150,743	57,586,017	9.66
16	Lloyds Bank Plc	62,299,430	52,128,303	19.51
17	Sainsburys Supermarkets Ltd	60,440,611	60,698,553	−0.42
18	Microsoft Ltd	60,156,751	40,027,216	50.28
19	British Gas Plc	60,135,852	64,785,302	−7.17
20	Aldi Stores Ltd	56,594,569	43,321,903	30.63
21	Boots The Chemists Ltd	56,129,214	53,525,341	4.86
22	DSG Intl Holdings Plc	54,242,348	46,957,991	15.51
23	Samsung (UK) Ltd	53,564,819	64,510,309	−16.96
24	EE Everything Everywhere Ltd	53,115,591	87,196,029	−39.08
25	Marks & Spencer	50,710,168	67,739,402	−25.13

Source: http://www.marketingmagazine.co.uk/article/1289560/top-100-uk-advertisers-bskyb-increases-lead-p-g-bt-unilever-reduce-adspend

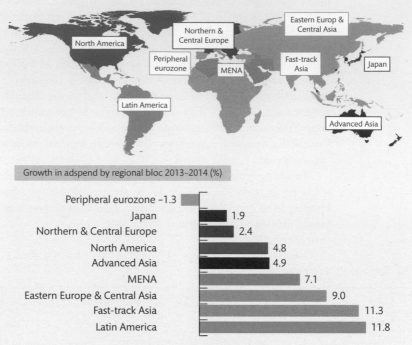

Growth in adspend by regional bloc 2013–2014 (%)

Peripheral eurozone	-1.3
Japan	1.9
Northern & Central Europe	2.4
North America	4.8
Advanced Asia	4.9
MENA	7.1
Eastern Europe & Central Asia	9.0
Fast-track Asia	11.3
Latin America	11.8

(a) Forecast by regional bloc

	2013	Adspend		2016	Adspend
1	USA	167,299	1	USA	191,433
2	Japan	53,015	2	China	57,374
3	China	40,951	3	Japan	56,252
4	Germany	23,184	4	Germany	24,145
5	UK	20,448	5	UK	23,870
6	Brazil	16,380	6	Brazil	20,199
7	Australia	13,118	7	Australia	14,330
8	France	12,809	8	Indonesia	14,213
9	Canada	11,570	9	South Korea	13,795
10	South Korea	10,612	10	France	13,092

(b) Top ten ad markets (US$ million, current prices, currency conversion at 2012 average rates).

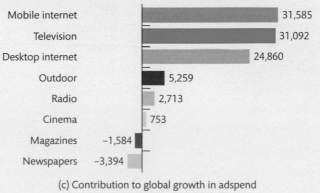

Medium	Value
Mobile internet	31,585
Television	31,092
Desktop internet	24,860
Outdoor	5,259
Radio	2,713
Cinema	753
Magazines	-1,584
Newspapers	-3,394

(c) Contribution to global growth in adspend by medium 2013-2016 (US$m)

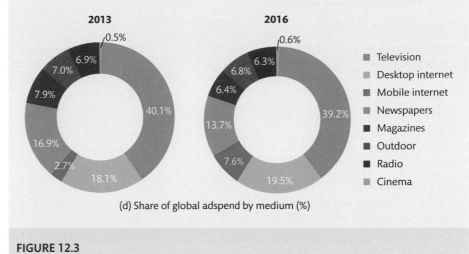

2013

0.5%
6.9%
7.0%
7.9%
16.9%
2.7%
18.1%
40.1%

2016

0.6%
6.3%
6.8%
6.4%
13.7%
7.6%
19.5%
39.2%

- Television
- Desktop internet
- Mobile internet
- Newspapers
- Magazines
- Outdoor
- Radio
- Cinema

(d) Share of global adspend by medium (%)

FIGURE 12.3
Zenith Optimedia data gives us a better understanding of the where and how of advertising expenditures in a globalised economy

Source: Zenith Optimedia adspend forecasts via brandrepublic.com. Reproduced from Brand Republic magazine with the permission of the copyright owner, Haymarket Business Publications Limited.

Setting advertising objectives

The first step is to set *advertising objectives* (Figure 12.4). These objectives should be based on past decisions about the target market, positioning and marketing mix, which define the job that advertising must do in the total marketing programme.

An **advertising objective** is a specific communication *task* to be accomplished with a specific *target* audience during a specific period of *time*. Advertising objectives can be classified by primary purpose – whether the aim is to *inform, persuade* or *remind*. Table 12.2 lists examples of each of these objectives.

Informative advertising is used heavily when introducing a new product category – think of the iPad. In this case, the objective is to build primary demand. Thus, early producers of

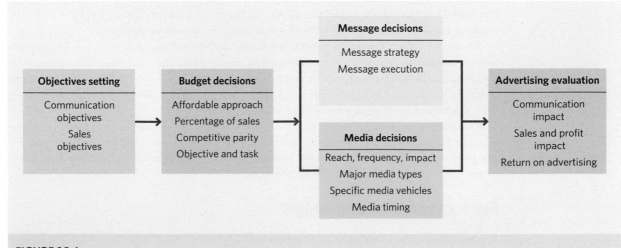

Objectives setting	Budget decisions	Message decisions	Media decisions	Advertising evaluation

Message decisions

Message strategy
Message execution

Objectives setting

Communication objectives

Sales objectives

Budget decisions

Affordable approach
Percentage of sales
Competitive parity
Objective and task

Media decisions

Reach, frequency, impact
Major media types
Specific media vehicles
Media timing

Advertising evaluation

Communication impact

Sales and profit impact

Return on advertising

FIGURE 12.4
Major decisions in advertising

TABLE 12.2 Possible advertising objectives

Informative advertising	
Telling the market about a new product	Describing available services
Suggesting new uses for a product	Correcting false impressions
Informing the market of a price change	Reducing consumers' fears
Explaining how the product works	Building a company image
Persuasive advertising	
Building brand preference	Persuading customer to purchase now
Encouraging switching to your brand	Persuading customer to receive a sales call
Changing customer's perception of product attributes	
Reminder advertising	
Building and maintaining the customer	Reminding consumer where to buy the product
Reminding consumer that the product may be needed in the near future	relationship
	Keeping it in the customer's mind during off-seasons

DVD players first had to inform consumers of the image quality and convenience benefits of the new product when compared with video recorders, then repeat the trick with Blu-ray and again with digital-media-based technologies. *Persuasive advertising* becomes more important as competition increases. Here, the company's objective is to build selective demand. For example, once tablet computers became established, Apple began trying to persuade consumers that *its* brand offered the best quality for their money. As technology moves on, Apple must repeat this with the later product evolutions.

Some persuasive advertising has become *comparative advertising,* in which a company directly or indirectly compares its brand with one or more other brands. Comparative advertising has been used for products ranging from soft drinks, beer and pain relievers to computers, batteries, car hire and credit cards. For example, in its classic comparative campaign, the car-hire company Avis positioned itself against market-leading Hertz by claiming, 'We're number two, so we try harder.'

More recently, Three – the mobile telecoms company – wanted to compare its price plans with those of its rivals. Three produced a TV advert in which its lower pricing was highlighted next to air bubbles containing the numbers for rival price plans, these bubbles (a theme prominent in the adverts of its arch-competitor O2) popping each time to emphasise Three's superior value. Apollo, a company manufacturing fire alarms, produced a poster showing its wider range of products when compared with that of a rival, Rafiki. The German advertising agency BBDO created a clever comparison to benefit its client FedEx by creating imagery to imply that UPS relied on FedEx to deliver its packages.[21]

Advertisers use comparative advertising with caution. All too often such ads invite competitor responses, resulting in an advertising war that neither competitor can win – or breaking the EU's strict rules and regulations in this area. Three was taken to the European Court of Justice by O2. The court ruled that while the use of the bubbles did infringe on O2's trademarks, the comparison itself was not unfair.[22]

Reminder advertising is important for mature products – it helps to maintain customer relationships and keep consumers thinking about the product. Expensive Coca-Cola TV ads primarily build and maintain the Coca-Cola brand relationship rather than informing or persuading customers to buy in the short term.

Setting the advertising budget

After determining its advertising objectives, the company next sets its *advertising budget* for each product. No matter what method is used, setting the advertising budget is no easy task. Here, we look at four common methods used to set the total budget for advertising:

the *affordable method*, the *percentage-of-sales method*, the *competitive-parity method* and the *objective-and-task method*.[23]

Affordable method

Some companies use the **affordable method**: they set the promotion budget at the level they think the company can afford. Small businesses often use this method, reasoning that the company cannot spend more on advertising than it has. They start with total revenues, deduct operating expenses and capital outlays, and then devote some portion of the remaining funds to advertising. Unfortunately, this method of setting budgets completely ignores the effects of promotion on sales. It tends to place advertising last among spending priorities, even in situations in which advertising is critical to the firm's success. It leads to an uncertain annual promotion budget, which makes long-range market planning difficult.

Percentage-of-sales method

Other companies use the **percentage-of-sales method**, setting their promotion budget at a certain percentage of current or forecasted sales. Or they budget a percentage of the unit sales price. The percentage-of-sales method has advantages. It is simple to use and helps management think about the relationships between promotion spending, selling price and profit per unit.

Despite these claimed advantages, however, the percentage-of-sales method has little to justify it. It wrongly views sales as the *cause* of promotion rather than as the *result*. It bases the ad budget on the availability of funds rather than on marketing needs and opportunities. Larger brands tend to receive more advertising, whether they need it or not. Meanwhile, smaller or failing brands receive less spending even though they may need more. Also, under the percentage-of-sales method, because the budget varies with year-to-year sales, long-range planning is difficult. Finally, the method does not provide any basis for choosing a *specific* percentage, except what has been done in the past or what competitors are doing.

Competitive-parity method

Still other companies use the **competitive-parity method**, setting their promotion budgets to match competitors' outlays. They monitor competitors' advertising or get industry promotion spending estimates from publications or trade associations, and then set their budgets based on the industry average.

Two arguments support this method. First, competitors' budgets represent the collective wisdom of the industry. Second, spending what competitors spend helps prevent promotion wars. Unfortunately, neither argument is valid. There are no grounds for believing that the competition has a better idea of what a company should be spending on promotion than does the company itself. Companies differ greatly, and each has its own special promotion needs. Finally, there is no evidence that budgets based on competitive parity prevent promotion wars.

Objective-and-task method

The most logical budget-setting method is the **objective-and-task method**, whereby the company sets its promotion budget based on what it wants to accomplish with promotion. This budgeting method entails the following:

1 defining specific promotion objectives;
2 determining the tasks needed to achieve these objectives;
3 estimating the costs of performing these tasks;
4 summing these costs to obtain the proposed promotion budget.

The objective-and-task method is the best method for setting advertising budgets. It forces management to spell out its assumptions about the relationship between money spent and promotion results. But it is also the most difficult method to use. Often, it is hard to figure out which specific tasks will achieve specific objectives. For example, suppose HTC wants 60 per cent awareness for its latest handset during the six-month introductory period. What specific advertising messages and media schedules should HTC use to attain this objective? How much would these messages and media schedules cost? HTC management would have to consider such questions, even though they are hard to answer.

Developing advertising strategy

Advertising strategy consists of two major elements: creating advertising *messages* and selecting advertising *media*. In the past, companies often viewed media planning as secondary to the message creation process. The creative department first created good advertisements, and then the media department selected the best media for carrying these advertisements to desired target audiences. This often caused friction between creatives and media planners.

Today, however, media fragmentation, soaring media costs and more focused target marketing strategies have promoted the importance of the media planning function. More and more, advertisers are orchestrating a closer harmony between their messages and the media that deliver them. Among the more noteworthy ad campaigns based on tight media creative partnerships is the pioneering campaign for Absolut vodka, made by V&S Absolut Spirits.

> Since the iconic 'bottle' campaign began in 1979, the Absolut team and its ad agency meet once a year with a slew of magazines to set Absolut's media schedule. The agency's creative department then creates media-specific ads. The result is a wonderful assortment of very creative ads for Absolut, tightly targeted to audiences of the media in which they appear. For example, an 'Absolut Bravo' ad in playbills has roses adorning a clear bottle, while business magazines contain an 'Absolut Merger' foldout. In New York-area magazines, 'Absolut Manhattan' ads feature a satellite photo of Manhattan, with Central Park assuming the distinctive outline of an Absolut bottle. In London, ads show the famous entry to the Prime Minister's residence at No. 10 Downing Street with the door in the shape of an Absolut bottle. An 'Absolute Primary' ad run during the political season featured the well-known bottle spattered with mud. In 'Absolut Love', run in February to celebrate Valentine's Day, two Absolut bottles embrace, silhouetted by a shining heart in the background. In some cases, the creatives even develop ads for magazines not yet on the schedule, such as a clever 'Absolut Centrefold' ad for *Playboy* magazine. The ad portrayed a clear, unadorned playmate bottle ('11-inch bust, 11-inch waist, 11-inch hips'). In all, Absolut has developed more than 1,500 ads for the more than two-decades-old campaign. At a time of soaring media costs and cluttered communication channels, a closer cooperation between creative and media people has paid off handsomely for Absolut. Largely as a result of its breakthrough advertising, in the United States, Absolut remains the nation's number one imported vodka and the number three liquor brand overall. The Absolut ads have developed a kind of cult following, and Absolut is one of only three original brands to be inducted into the American Advertising Hall of Fame.[24]

Creating the advertising message

No matter how big the budget, advertising can succeed only if advertisements gain attention and communicate well. Good advertising messages are especially important in today's costly and cluttered advertising environment. The average number of receivable TV channels per household has skyrocketed from low single figures in the 1950s to more than 100 today, alongside the thousands of magazines from which to choose. Add the countless radio stations and a continuous barrage of catalogues, direct mail, and out-of-home media and online, and consumers are being bombarded with ads at home, at work and at all points in between. How many ads do you see each day? Estimates vary wildly. One expert estimates that the average person is exposed to some 1,600 ad messages a day. Another puts the number at an eye-popping 5,000 ads a day – and some people are not happy about that level of saturation.[25]

As Figure 12.3 indicated, the most rapidly growing types of advertising are placed on social media and web pages. Adverts go where the attention is, and increasing amounts of attention are being paid to the screens of computers, tablets and phones. As you probably know from your own use, browsers like Chrome, Safari and Internet Explorer allow extensions – small pieces of code attached to those pieces of software to allow extra functionality. Many of these ease or enhance the use of social media sites like Pinterest or shopping sites like Amazon. Others, though, are installed by users to manage their experience in other ways. One key extension is called AdBlock. As you might guess from the name, it checks information received from web pages and makes an informed judgement as to whether that content is an ad or not. If it thinks it is, that content is blocked and replaced with blank space – unless that user has 'white-listed' ads from that particular company. How popular is this communally produced piece of code? It had 300 million installations by mid-2014, making it the most popular extension across all of the main browser options.[26]

Breaking through the clutter

If all this advertising clutter bothers some consumers, it also causes big problems for advertisers. Take the situation facing TV advertisers. As well as the significant costs of creating and filming their commercial – which is usually in the region of £200,000 to £300,000 – they must also pay for it to be broadcast. Rates vary considerably, being a function of the length, time of day, time of year, broadcaster and expected share of the total audience the particular channel captures. Here is an example. ITV broadcasts a set of channels across the UK, but the main one is ITV1. A 30-second advert, showing mid-morning, would cost about £8,000 a time. The same advert shown during peak time in the evening would cost £83,000. Having your advert shown only in part of the country costs less. Channel 5 quotes prices for the same two time slots of about £2,000 and £17,000 – reflecting generally smaller audiences.[27]

Until recently, TV viewers were pretty much a captive audience for advertisers. But today's digital wizardry has given consumers a rich new set of information and entertainment choices. With the growth in cable and satellite TV, the Internet and video-on-demand (VOD), today's viewers have many more options. Digital technology has also armed consumers with an arsenal of weapons for choosing what they watch or do not watch. Increasingly, consumers are choosing *not* to watch ads. They 'zap' commercials by fast-forwarding through recorded programmes. With the remote control, they mute the sound during a commercial or 'zip' around the channels to see what else is on. Studies have found that nearly half of all TV viewers now switch channels when the commercial break starts.

Adding to the problem is the rapid growth of digital-video-recorder-based and VOD systems like SkyPlus+. Many of these systems allow commercial breaks to be omitted from recordings, missing the adverts altogether. The number of viewers using such systems is expected to increase rapidly over the next few years, meaning that an ever-increasing proportion of the viewing public will be able to watch programming on their own time terms, with or without commercials.

Thus, advertisers can no longer force-feed the same old clichéd ad messages to captive consumers through traditional media. Just to gain and hold attention, today's advertising messages must be better planned, more imaginative, more entertaining and more rewarding to consumers. Fail and your intended audience will be making tea, emptying their bladders, watching a different channel or looking at blank space on the page.

Message strategy

The first step in creating effective advertising messages is to plan a message strategy – to decide what general message will be communicated to consumers. The purpose of advertising is to get consumers to think about or react to the product or company in a certain way. People will react only if they believe that they will benefit from doing so. Thus, developing an effective message strategy begins with identifying customer benefits that can be used as advertising appeals. Ideally, advertising message strategy will follow directly from the company's broader positioning and customer value strategies.

Message strategy statements tend to be plain, straightforward outlines of benefits and positioning points that the advertiser wants to stress. The advertiser must next develop a compelling *creative concept* – or '*big idea*' – that will bring the message strategy to life in a distinctive and memorable way. At this stage, simple message ideas become great ad campaigns. Usually, a copywriter and art director will team up to generate many creative concepts, hoping that one of these concepts will turn out to be the big idea. The creative concept may emerge as a visualisation, a phrase or a combination of the two.

Narrowcasting – Savile Row and science fiction

MARKETING AT WORK 12.1

Throughout this chapter, much mention has been made of advertisements and other forms of marketing communications being *broadcast* to audiences measuring in the millions. The splintering of the mass TV audiences of the 1960s and 1970s across hundreds of channels recently has combined with rapid and significant changes in technology to allow *narrowcasting* of messages tailored and adjusted sometimes to the level of the individual. What does this mean? The advert targeted at you isn't a one-size-fits-all production, seen by everyone who reads that web page or shops at that store or watches that Champions League match, but rather is a bespoke item – made to measure based on who and what you are. The former is a shapeless T-shirt from H&M, the latter a tailored suit from Savile Row.

The film *Minority Report* used person-specific advertising as part of its dystopia. Now it is a reality

Source: The Kobal Collection.

It is becoming more commonplace for marketing letters and leaflets – even postcards – to be adapted to the individual, by swapping out generic text and images and swapping in person-specific snippets – their name, where they have recently travelled, products they may have bought previously. As you experience on a daily basis, the same is true of materials delivered to you online. Now, though, narrowcasting is getting truly hi-tech.

Let's take a look at some of the technology behind – and some of the social and legal implications in front of – narrowcasting, as given in a recent news story from the *LA Times*.

Once the stuff of science fiction and high-tech crime fighting, facial recognition technology has become one of the newest tools in marketing, even though privacy concerns abound.

Picture this: You stop in front of a digital advertising display at a mall and suddenly an ad pops up touting makeup, followed by one for shoes and then one for butter pecan ice cream. It seems to know you're a woman in your late twenties and, in fact, it does. When you looked at the display, it scanned your facial features and tailored its messages to you.

The Venetian resort, hotel and casino in Las Vegas has started using it on digital displays to tailor suggestions for restaurants, clubs and entertainment to passersby. Kraft Foods Inc. and Adidas say they are planning to experiment with it.

The commercial applications of facial recognition are in contrast to those being used by law enforcement to identify specific individuals. Companies, at least at this point, mostly just want to pinpoint a demographic based on age and gender to tailor their ads. But even this facial recognition-lite alarms privacy advocates, given that it could greatly popularise and expand use of the technology.

Intel Corp., which makes such software, said it's widely adaptable. 'You can put this technology into kiosks, vending machines, digital signs,' said Christopher O'Malley, director of retail marketing for Intel's embedded and communications group. 'It's going to become a much more common thing in the next few years.'

So far, the technology is in most use commercially in Japan, where a variety of businesses use it to customise ads. 'It's not just clothing stores or restaurant chains,' said Joseph Jasper, spokesman for NEC Corp., which makes display screens used for facial recognition-driven ads. Banks, for example, use it to target customers based on their ages, separating out older customers from young people who are more likely to be opening their first account.

The technology works by digitally measuring the distance between the eyes, the width of the nose, the length of a jawline and other data points. Law enforcement agencies that use facial recognition – as was done during the recent London riots – compare the measurements against photos in database.

But for most marketing uses, the measurements are compared to standardised codes that represent features typical of males and females in various age brackets.

Adidas is working with Intel to install and test digital walls with facial recognition in a handful of stores either in the U.S. or Britain. If a woman in her 50s walks by and stops, 60% of the shoes displayed will be for females in her age bracket, while the other 40% will be a random sprinkling of other goods.

'If a retailer can offer the right products quickly, people are more likely to buy something,' said Chris Aubrey, vice president of global retail marketing for Adidas.

Kraft said it's in talks with a supermarket chain, which it would not identify, to test face-scanning kiosks. 'If it recognises that there is a female between 25 to 29 standing there, it may surmise that you are more likely to have young children at home and give suggestions on how to spice up Kraft Macaroni & Cheese for the kids,' said Donald King, the company's vice president of retail experience.

In the science fiction film *Minority Report*, Tom Cruise plays a character on the run from the authorities. To make his escape, he takes the extreme step of retina replacement surgery to avoid detection by security cameras that are constantly searching for him. In one scene in the film, he stumbles through a shopping mall, and artificially intelligent advertising display screens greet him using the name of the original owner of the retinas and make offers based on that man's past consumption history! That takes us onto an important social and legal issue – what effect might this have on privacy?

Privacy advocates worry the technology is one more way for companies to quietly gather data about people without their permission or even knowledge. In June, Facebook Inc. rolled out a facial recognition feature worldwide that could pinpoint individuals. It was used to automatically identify friends when you uploaded photos of them onto the social network. When members realised this was happening, many loudly objected, calling it creepy and invasive. The feature still exists, but the company apologised and made it more clear how users can opt out.

The non-profit Electronic Privacy Information Center said such uses of facial recognition have the potential to violate civil liberties and give governments too much power. 'What if the government starts compiling a database of everyone who shows up to protests?' asked Marc Rotenberg, executive director of the group. 'There are so many 1st Amendment and human rights concerns. It's a slippery slope. When you think about facial recognition, you have to ask the questions, "Why is it being done?" "Who is it being done to?" "How is that information used?" and "What is it linked to?" '

David C. Thompson, an attorney at Munger, Tolles & Olson who specialises in privacy law, said the use of facial recognition can catch and expose people during very sensitive moments of their lives, such as going to an abortion clinic or a cancer treatment center. 'The problem is that there are things we do that we don't need a permanent record of,' Thompson said. 'I don't need other people to know where I've been and what I'm doing.'

Ed Warm, co-owner of Joe's Bar in Chicago, said many customers were excited about the SceneTap app that gave them the demographics of the crowd in the bar on any given night, but were clueless that facial recognition technology made it possible. 'Frankly, almost no one seemed to care how it worked,' Warm said.

Sami Ari, a 27-year-old social media marketer, is one of about 8,000 people who have downloaded the app. He knew it was facial recognition at work and didn't mind it. 'I use it at least once a week to find a cool place for me and my friends to hang out,' said Ari, who describes himself as 'hyper social'. 'It's not that scary,' he added. 'I always get upset at new Facebook privacy settings, and then I get over it.'

Your reality now includes this science fiction. Apple incorporated what it called iBeacon response into its smartphone and tablet software. Go near one of those iBeacons with your devices and it may well send you a tailored advert based on location and other factors about you. More generally, that technique is referred to as Location Based Marketing. They send you messages, because they know who and where you are.

Do you agree with Sami? *Minority Report* was a decade ago. Good science fiction predicts the future. *1984* and *Brave New World* were written much longer ago – 1948 and 1931 respectively. If you think *Big Brother* is just a TV show you need to do some reading!

Sources: Case edited and compiled from: Shan Li and David Sarno, 'Advertisers Start Using Facial Recognition to Tailor Pitches', *LA Times*, 21 August 2011; and Richard Gray, 'Minority Report-style Advertising Billboards to Target Consumers', *Daily Telegraph*, 1 August 2010.

The creative concept will guide the choice of specific appeals to be used in an advertising campaign. *Advertising appeals* should have three characteristics. First, they should be *meaningful*, pointing out benefits that make the product more desirable or interesting to consumers. Second, appeals must be *believable* – consumers must believe that the product or service will deliver the promised benefits.

However, the most meaningful and believable benefits may not be the best ones to feature. Appeals should also be *distinctive* – they should tell how the product is better than the competing brands. For example, the most meaningful benefit of owning a wristwatch is that it keeps accurate time, yet few watch ads feature this benefit. Instead, based on the distinctive benefits they offer, watch advertisers might select any of a number of advertising themes. Dolce & Gabbana consistently features style and fashion, whereas Rolex stresses luxury and status.

Message execution

The advertiser now has to turn the big idea into an actual ad execution that will capture the target market's attention and interest. The creative team must find the best style, tone, words and format for executing the message. Any message can be presented in different execution styles, such as the following:

- *Slice of life*: This style shows one or more 'typical' people using the product in a normal setting. For example, two mothers at a picnic discuss the nutritional benefits of Dairylea cheese spread.
- *Lifestyle*: This style shows how a product fits in with a particular lifestyle. For example, an ad for Mongoose mountain bikes shows a serious biker traversing remote and rugged but beautiful terrain, and states, 'There are places that are so awesome and so killer that you'd like to tell the whole world about them. But please, *don't*.'
- *Fantasy*: This style creates a fantasy around the product or its use. For instance, many ads are built around dream themes. Gap even introduced a perfume named Dream. Ads show a woman sleeping blissfully and suggests that the scent is 'the stuff that clouds are made of'.
- *Mood or image*: This style builds a mood or image around the product or service, such as beauty, love or serenity. Few claims are made about the product except through suggestion. For example, ads for Singapore Airlines feature soft lighting and refined flight attendants pampering relaxed but happy customers.
- *Musical*: This style shows people or cartoon characters singing about the product. For example, one of the most famous ads in history was a Coca-Cola ad built around the song 'I'd Like to Teach the World to Sing'.

- *Personality symbol*: This style creates a character that represents the product. The character might be *animated* (Tony the Tiger for Kellogg's cereals) or *real* (the Marlboro man).

- *Technical expertise*: This style shows the company's expertise in making the product. Thus, Maxwell House shows one of its buyers carefully selecting coffee beans, and Gallo tells about its many years of wine-making experience.

- *Scientific evidence:* This style presents survey or scientific evidence that the brand is better or better liked than one or more other brands. For years, Crest toothpaste has used scientific evidence to convince buyers that Crest is better than other brands at fighting cavities.

- *Testimonial evidence or endorsement*: This style features a highly believable or likeable source endorsing the product. It could be ordinary people saying how much they like a given product or a celebrity presenting the product. For example, Lucozade supported its Isotonic brand with a series of adverts featuring professional sports coaches saying how important hydration was for top sportsmen.

When selecting an execution strategy, advertisers must be very careful to consider if their advert might be perceived to be patronising, arrogant or socially unacceptable – especially if the offended groups are key to the commercial success of the product![28]

The advertiser also must choose a *tone* for the ad. Procter & Gamble always uses a positive tone: its ads say something very positive about its products. P&G usually avoids humour

Heathcliff lept over the balcony, strode into the bedroom and pressed his lips firmly against Megan's. "Not now," she yawned.

Advertisers often try to use humour to create awareness and interest in their products and brands

Source: Image courtesy of The Advertising Archives.

Drift off with Britain's leading bed specialist.

Dreams

that might take attention away from the message. In contrast, many advertisers now use edgy humour to break through the commercial clutter.

The advertiser must use memorable and attention-getting *words* in the ad. For example, rather than claiming simply that 'a BMW is a well-engineered automobile', BMW uses more creative and higher impact phrasing: 'The ultimate driving machine.' It is not Häagen-Dazs is 'a tasty luxury ice cream', but rather 'Our passport to indulgence: passion in a touch, perfection in a cup, summer in a spoon, one perfect moment.'

Finally, *format* elements make a difference in an ad's impact as well as in its cost. A small change in ad design can make a big difference in its effect. In a print ad, the *illustration* is the first thing the reader notices – it must be strong enough to draw attention. Next, the *headline* must effectively entice the right people to read the copy. Finally, the *copy* – the main block of text in the ad – must be simple but strong and convincing. Moreover, these three elements must effectively work *together* persuasively to present customer value.

Selecting advertising media

The major steps in media selection are:

1   deciding on *reach*, *frequency* and *impact*;
2   choosing among major *media types*;
3   selecting specific *media vehicles*; and
4   deciding on *media timing*.

Deciding on reach, frequency and impact

To select media, the advertiser must decide on the reach and frequency needed to achieve advertising objectives. Reach is a measure of the percentage of people in the target market who are exposed to the ad campaign during a given period of time. For example, the advertiser might try to reach 70 per cent of the target market during the first three months of the campaign. Frequency is a measure of how many times the average person in the target market is exposed to the message. For example, the advertiser might want an average exposure frequency of three.

The advertiser also must decide on the desired *media impact* – the *qualitative value* of a message exposure through a given medium. For example, for products that need to be demonstrated, messages on TV may have more impact than messages on radio because TV uses sight *and* sound. The same message in one newspaper (say, the *Financial Times*) may be more believable than in another (say, the *Daily Mail*). In general, the more reach, frequency and impact the advertiser seeks, the higher the advertising budget will have to be.

Choosing among major media types

The media planner has to know the reach, frequency and impact of each of the major media types. As summarised in Table 12.3, the major media types are newspapers, TV, direct mail, radio, magazines, outdoor and the Internet. Each medium has advantages and limitations. Media planners consider many factors when making their media choices. They want to choose media that will effectively and efficiently present the advertising message to target customers. Thus, they must consider each medium's impact, message effectiveness and cost.

The mix of media must be re-examined regularly. For a long time, TV and magazines have dominated the media mixes of national advertisers, with other media often neglected. However, as discussed at the start of the chapter, the media mix appears to be shifting.

TABLE 12.3 Profiles of major media types

Medium	Advantages	Limitations
Newspapers	Flexibility; timeliness; good local market coverage; broad acceptability; high believability	Short life; poor reproduction quality; small pass-along audience
Television	Good mass-marketing coverage; low cost per exposure; combines sight, sound and motion; appealing to the senses	High absolute costs; high clutter; fleeting exposure; less audience selectivity
Direct mail	High audience selectivity; flexibility; no ad competition within the same medium; allows personalisation	Relatively high cost per exposure; 'junk mail' image
Radio	Good local acceptance; high geographic and demographic selectivity; low cost	Audio only, fleeting exposure; low attention ('the half-heard' medium); fragmented audiences
Magazines	High geographic and demographic selectivity; credibility and prestige; high-quality reproduction; long life and good pass-along readership	Long ad purchase lead time; high cost; no guarantee of position
Outdoor	Flexibility; high repeat exposure; low cost; low message competition; good positional selectivity	Little audience selectivity; creative limitations
Internet/social media	High selectivity; low cost; immediacy; interactive capabilities; growing amount of consumer attention	Demographically skewed audience; relatively low impact; can be blocked automatically

As mass-media costs rise, audiences shrink and exciting new digital media emerge, many advertisers are finding new ways to reach consumers. They are supplementing the traditional mass media with more specialised and highly targeted media that cost less and target more effectively – switching from a broad to a narrow focus.

For example, cable and satellite TV systems are booming. Such systems allow narrow programming formats such as all sports, all news, nutrition, arts, home improvement and gardening, cooking, travel, history, finance and others that target select groups. BSkyB and other cable operators are even testing systems that will let them target specific types of ads to specific types of customers. For example, only pet owners would see ads from pet food companies. Advertisers can take advantage of such 'narrowcasting' to target specific market segments. Satellite TV and set-top box-based broadcast media seem to make good sense with their multitude of channels, each with a specific set of audience characteristics. But, increasingly, ads are popping up in far less likely places. In their efforts to find less costly and more highly targeted ways to reach consumers, advertisers have discovered a dazzling collection of 'alternative media', including computer games (see Marketing at Work 12.2).

Another important trend affecting media selection is the rapid growth in the number of 'media multitaskers', people who absorb more than one medium at a time. One term you might have heard recently describes what you yourself are likely to do: 'dual screening' – dividing your attention between two screens, quite likely a TV and a laptop or tablet. A marketing trend company reveals that:

A third of the population now owns a tablet, up 152 per cent since this February, while the number of people using tablets while they are watching TV rose 225 per cent during the same period.[29]

Media planners need to take such media interactions into account when selecting the types of media they will use.

Advertising in computer games

Video games are big business. We've all grown used to seeing them advertised on TV and online alongside cars, beers and their rivals for entertainment spending – movies. This case isn't about the advertising *of* video games, it's about the advertising *in* video games.

Why is this a significant issue for marketers? In recent years, advertising professionals have become increasingly concerned that traditional media are being ignored by key consumer segments – especially young men and/or highly educated urban residents. Research suggests that these and others key groups are spending less and less time watching TV and instead using the Internet and playing games, whether it be on a PC, a console or on a handheld device like a mobile phone or iPad. Worse, even if they are watching TV, the commercial break is a period when their attention switches from the big-screen TV to the small one in their hands, meaning all those expensively produced and transmitted adverts razzle-dazzle to an audience that is not even looking.

Advertising in video games is part of the response – go where the attention actually is. You'll have experienced this during your games of Candy Crush and other free-to-play smartphone games where your experience will include adverts at the top or bottom of the screen. If you play marquee titles like FIFA on a console you'll be well used to seeing branding and advertising as part of the recreated world these games show.

> 'What's unique about videogames is that people are immersed in the gameplay, with their eyes glued to the TV screen. So it's pretty hard – if not impossible – for people to tune out in-game advertising, and not to recall the ads they see while playing,' explains Jordan L. Howard, founder and CEO of Reloaded.[30]

Electronic Arts, one of the world's largest video games companies, has released a free online version of its popular Battlefield games, called *Battlefield Heroes*. Why would it do this? EA intends that the money lost from not selling the game will be more than made up for by means of reduced costs (no mass production and distribution) and by advertising revenue from brand managers keen to place their products where they might be seen by these elusive groups. Adverts will not appear in the game itself, but rather during pauses as a new game is waiting to start, or a new level is loading. EA is periodically releasing new content – levels, equipment – which will come with updated ads from new sponsors.[31]

Electronic Arts is also heavily involved with some of the bestselling video gaming franchises of all time. Adam Dawson of the Digital Journal takes up the story in a column arguing that in-game advertising is the future of the entire industry:

> **Sports series such as Fifa, Madden and NBA 2K feature more product placement than any other game genre, creating a lifelike experience with brand sponsored replays, brand sponsored statistical graphics, pop up ads and advertisements posted throughout the digitally recreated stadiums. Examples being the Sprite Slam Cam in NBA 2K, Old Spice Swagger ratings in Madden, and numerous ads surrounding the field in Fifa.**
>
> **Though placing traditional ads in games is effective, there are interactive methods which incorporate the use of actual products in the game. Some games require players to use items that exist in the real world in order to progress. For example, in Splinter Cell: Pandora Tomorrow protagonist Sam Fisher uses his Sony Ericsson phone to talk to his superiors, cycle through his inventory and photograph terrorists. Another example is the Japanese version of Metal Gear Solid: Peace Walker where Snake can eat Doritos, spray himself with Axe, and drink Pepsi or Mountain Dew to regain health.[32]**

Gatorade reported a 24 per cent increase in sales following the placement of branding and advertising within the latest iteration of the Madden American Football game.[33]

The growth and potential of these media have not gone unnoticed by established companies. Historically advertising agencies have often specialised in one type of medium – print, cinema or TV. To those we now have a growing number of agencies who are creating and placing adverts into games or producing marketing materials for the $40bn games industry. One such company is Intergi (**www.intergi.com**) who have worked on recent blockbuster games such as Skyrim, Call of Duty and Saints Row. Activision now works with the market research agency Nielsen to collect and interpret audience measurement figures for computer game adverts. Google and Yahoo have already invested heavily, and Microsoft recently bought out a specialist outfit called Massive.

Microsoft sees its early lead in the in-game advertising market as a strategic opportunity that fits well into the

Adverts are everywhere these days – this neon sign was added to the game world of Splinter Cell

Source: http://www.trendwatching.com/img/briefing/2006-07//SplinterCell_axe.jpg

TABLE 12.4 Game ads – recall numbers

Key metric	Gamers not exposed to ads	Gamers exposed to ads	Increase
Brand familiarity	20%	40%	+100%
Brand rating	14%	25%	+79%
Purchase consideration	28%	47%	+68%
Ad recall	38%	55%	+45%
Positive ad rating	30%	41%	+37%

Source: www.massiveincorporated.com, Massive, Inc.

company's overall advertising strategy. Why? Table 12.4 shows that Massive believes in-game advertising has an impact way above that of TV or audio advertising for key demographic groups.

> 'The idea is to have advertisements appear and fit in naturally to the games just as they would in real life,' said Jay Sampson, vice president of North American and Asia Pacific sales for Massive, Microsoft's in-game advertising marketplace. 'But these advertisements are also dynamic. So the ads can be updated or changed by the advertiser at any time.'
>
> 'Emerging media, like in-game advertising, is a huge component of our overall strategy,' said Matthew Carr, senior director of Microsoft Digital Advertising Solutions. 'We're already in a leadership position here. And we see this as being where the future growth will be.'[34]

Does advertising your products in a game bring any advantages? IGA World-wide, a company specialising in matching brands with games, believes that in fact there are five clear advantages, and that work done for them by Nielsen supports this:[35]

1 *Realism* – as the real world is filled with advertising, the plausibility and credibility of game worlds can be enhanced by incorporating brand imagery and simulated posters/displays in the game setting. Nielsen found that most gamers actually liked the extra realism ads brought to the games – whether the AXE (Lynx) deodorant neon sign in Splinter Cell or a Coke vending machine in Second Life.

2 *Non-interruptive* – we all hate pop-up ads on websites, and we grow impatient in waiting for an interstitial to close, but would we think our gaming experience had been lessened by a Toyota ad appearing on a hoarding as we screamed round the Nürburgring, or the advertising for Adidas or Nike around the pitch in many football games?

3 *Engaging* – as one 'media futures' advertising executive said: 'The killer benefit of gaming is attention. We live in a multimedia world and you can't guarantee people will take any notice of your TV ad, but gamers have to concentrate on what they're doing, or their character dies. Your message is much more likely to get through.'[36] If the product and brand can be incorporated into the game in a credible way this enhances the engagement immensely – the neon AXE sign in Splinter Cell was designed into the game so that it became an obstacle the gamer has to negotiate. Once this is accomplished, the in-game hero then uses the sign to tether a rope line to as he abseils his way towards the bad guys.

4 *Recall, awareness and purchase intention* – if brands are making the game more realistic and enjoyable, then gamers will be much more likely to recall those products at a later date and also be more likely to consider purchasing them.

5 *Measurable* – the number of people that see a TV ad or drive past a roadside hoarding can only be estimated. Some online multi-player games produce extraordinarily accurate and detailed data about the in-game behaviour of players – where they were, what they looked at and for how long. This data is fascinating for social scientists as well as brand managers.

So are all brands suitable for in-game advertising? The answer appears to be no – with two reasons. First, if the brand is not one which could credibly appear in the context of the game, it will look inauthentic. Second, some groups are becoming increasingly concerned that in-game ads may be just too effective with certain vulnerable groups – such as young children, as one newspaper columnist reports:

> What is also striking is that advergaming is almost entirely unregulated. The Advertising Standards Agency in the UK oversees adverts that play before a game starts, but not adverts within the game, which are classed as sponsorship.
>
> 'I think the ASA ought to have its brief expanded to cover computer games properly,' says John Beyer, a director of Mediawatch UK, the lobby group formerly known as the National Viewers' and Listeners' Association.

So far, tobacco advertising has been kept out of computer games by the software companies themselves. For example, Sony, which publishes the current Formula One game, and Electronic Arts, which used to publish it, both refuse tobacco adverts. Also, a game with alcohol advertising would be unlikely to get an age rating below 18 from Pan European Game Information, the trade body that certifies games as suitable for particular age groups. Even so, Electronic Arts and Activision, among other publishers, have worked with fast-food companies despite growing concerns about levels of obesity in the population. More adverts in games are also likely to lead to more calls for regulation.[37]

Sources: See notes 30–37 at the end of this chapter.

Selecting specific media vehicles

The media planner now must choose the best media vehicles – specific media within each general media type. For example, TV vehicles include *Coronation Street* and ITV's *X-Factor.* Magazine vehicles include *Vogue,* the Italian *Corriere della Sera* and *FHM*.

Media planners must compute the cost per thousand persons reached by a vehicle. A full-page colour advert in the *Daily Telegraph* costs about £60,000 per day – and daily readership averages around 2.1 million, meaning that the cost per thousand is about £29. In the *Guardian,* a similar advert will cost £18,000 but, with a readership of 1.1 million, a cost per thousand of £16.[38] The media planner ranks each magazine by cost per thousand and favours those magazines with the lower cost per thousand for reaching target consumers. The media planner must also consider the costs of producing ads for different media. Whereas newspaper ads may cost very little to produce, flashy TV ads may cost millions.

In selecting specific media vehicles, the media planner must balance media costs against several media effectiveness factors. First, the planner should evaluate the media vehicle's *audience quality*. For a Huggies disposable nappy advertisement, for example, *You and Your Baby* magazine would have a high exposure value; *GQ* would have a low exposure value. For the numbers given above for the *Telegraph* and *Guardian,* the planner must consider the make-up of the readership – the *Guardian* may be cheaper per thousand, but is a higher proportion of the *Telegraph*'s readership more likely to conform to the targeted segments, those interested in luxury cars, for example? Second, the media planner should consider *audience attention*. Readers of *Vogue,* for example, typically pay more attention to ads than do *The Economist* readers. Third, the planner should assess the vehicle's *editorial quality* – the *Financial Times* is more believable and prestigious than the *Daily Mail, Der Spiegel* is more credible than *Bild*.

Deciding on media timing

The advertiser must also decide how to schedule the advertising over the course of a year. Suppose sales of a product peak in December and drop in March. The firm can vary its advertising to follow the seasonal pattern, to oppose the seasonal pattern, or to be the same all year. Most firms do some seasonal advertising – for example, before major annual events or holidays like Christmas, Easter and Valentine's Day. Some marketers do only seasonal advertising. For instance, Bell's advertises its whisky only in the period leading up to Christmas.

Finally, the advertiser has to choose the pattern of the ads. *Continuity* means scheduling ads evenly within a given period. *Pulsing* means scheduling ads unevenly over a given time period. Thus, 52 ads could either be scheduled at one per week during the year or be pulsed in several bursts. The idea behind pulsing is to advertise heavily for a short period to build awareness that carries over to the next advertising period. Those who favour pulsing feel that it can be used to achieve the same impact as a steady schedule but at a much lower cost. However, some media planners believe that although pulsing achieves minimal awareness, it sacrifices depth of advertising communications.

Evaluating advertising effectiveness and return on advertising investment

Advertising accountability has become a hot issue for most companies. Increasingly, top management is asking 'What return are we getting on our advertising investment?' and 'How do we know that we're spending the right amount?' According to a recent survey by the US Association of National Advertisers (ANA), measuring advertising's efficiency and effectiveness is the number 1 issue in the minds of today's advertisers. In the survey, 61.5 per cent of respondents said that it is important that they define, measure and take action in the area of advertising accountability.[39]

Advertisers should regularly evaluate two types of advertising results: communication effects and the sales and profit effects. Measuring the *communication effects* of an ad or ad campaign tells whether the ads and media are communicating the ad message well. Individual ads can be tested before or after they are run. Before an ad is placed, the advertiser can show it to consumers, ask how they like it, and measure message recall or attitude changes resulting from it. After an ad is run, the advertiser can measure how the ad affected consumer recall or product awareness, knowledge and preference. Pre- and post-evaluations of communication effects can be made for entire advertising campaigns as well.

Advertisers have become pretty good at measuring the communication effects of their ads and ad campaigns. However, the *sales and profits* effects of advertising are often much harder to measure. For example, what sales and profits are produced by an ad campaign that increases brand awareness by 20 per cent and brand preference by 10 per cent? Sales and profits are affected by many factors besides advertising – such as product features, price and availability.

One way to measure the sales and profit effects of advertising is to compare past sales and profits with past advertising expenditures. Another way is through experiments. For example, to test the effects of different advertising spending levels, Coca-Cola could vary the amount it spends on advertising in different market areas and measure the differences in the resulting sales and profit levels. More complex experiments could be designed to include other variables, such as differences in the ads or media used.

However, because so many factors affect advertising effectiveness, some controllable and others not, measuring the results of advertising spending remains an inexact science. Despite the growing importance of advertising accountability, only 19 per cent of the ANA study respondents were satisfied with their ability to measure return on advertising investments. When asked if they would be able to 'forecast the impact on sales' of a 10 per cent cut in advertising spending, 63 per cent said no.

Other advertising considerations

In developing advertising strategies and programmes, the company must address two additional questions. First, how will the company organise its advertising function – who will perform which advertising tasks? Second, how will the company adapt its advertising strategies and programmes to the complexities of international markets?

Organising for advertising

Different companies organise in different ways to handle advertising. In small companies, advertising might be handled by someone in the sales department. Large companies set up advertising departments whose job it is to set the advertising budget, work with the ad agency and handle other advertising not done by the agency. Most large companies use outside advertising agencies because they offer several advantages.

How does an **advertising agency** work? Advertising agencies were started in the mid- to late 1800s by salespeople and brokers who worked for the media and received a commission for selling advertising space to companies. As time passed, the salespeople began to help customers prepare their ads. Eventually, they formed agencies and grew closer to the advertisers than to the media.

Today's agencies employ specialists who can often perform advertising tasks better than can the company's own staff. Agencies also bring an outside point of view to solving the company's problems, along with lots of experience from working with different clients and situations. So, today, even companies with strong advertising departments of their own use advertising agencies.

Some advertising agencies are huge – WPP in London is the biggest in the world (£11.3bn in 2013), the US-based Omnicon Group exceeded $14.5bn in the same year and the French Publicis Group is in third place (€6bn).[40] Most large advertising agencies have the staff and resources to handle all phases of an advertising campaign for their clients, from creating a marketing plan to developing ad campaigns and preparing, placing and evaluating ads.

International advertising decisions

International advertisers face many complexities not encountered by domestic advertisers. The most basic issue concerns the degree to which global advertising should be adapted to the unique characteristics of various country markets. Some large advertisers have attempted to support their global brands with highly standardised worldwide advertising, with campaigns that work as well in Bangkok as they do in Birmingham or Berlin. For example, Range Rover has created a worldwide brand image of ruggedness and reliability; Coca-Cola's Sprite brand uses standardised appeals to target the world's youth. Ads for Gillette's Venus razors are almost identical worldwide, with only minor adjustments to suit the local culture.

Standardisation produces many benefits – lower advertising costs, greater global advertising coordination and a more consistent worldwide image. But it also has drawbacks. Most importantly, it ignores the fact that country markets differ greatly in their cultures, demographics and economic conditions. Thus, most international advertisers 'think globally but act locally'. They develop global advertising *strategies* that make their worldwide advertising efforts more efficient and consistent. Then they adapt their advertising *programmes* to make them more responsive to consumer needs and expectations within local markets.[41] For example, Coca-Cola has a pool of different commercials that can be used in or adapted to several different international markets. Some can be used with only minor changes – such as language – in several different countries. Local and regional managers decide which commercials work best for which markets.

Global advertisers face several special problems. Advertising media costs and availability differ vastly from country to country, for instance. Countries also differ in the extent to which they regulate advertising practices. Many countries have extensive systems of laws restricting how much a company can spend on advertising, the media used, the nature of advertising claims and other aspects of the advertising programme. Such restrictions often require advertisers to adapt their campaigns from country to country. For example, alcoholic products cannot be advertised or sold in Muslim countries. In many countries, Sweden and Norway for example, food ads are banned from kid's TV. To play it safe, McDonald's advertises itself as a family restaurant in Sweden. Comparative ads, while acceptable and even common in the USA and Canada, are less commonly used in the UK, unacceptable in Japan, and illegal in India and Brazil. When it goes wrong for a company, it can go badly wrong. Google makes a lot of money through attaching ads to web pages. In 2011 it paid a fine of $500m to avoid criminal prosecution by US authorities for attaching ads for Canadian pharmacies who were illegally posting drugs to US addresses.[42]

China has restrictive censorship rules for TV and radio advertising; for example, the words 'the best' are banned, as are ads that 'violate social customs' or present women in 'improper ways'. McDonald's recently avoided government sanctions there by publicly apologising for an ad that crossed cultural norms by showing a customer begging for a discount. Similarly, Coca-Cola's Indian subsidiary was forced to end a promotion that offered prizes, such as a trip to Hollywood, because it violated India's established trade practices by encouraging customers to buy in order to 'gamble'.[43]

Thus, although advertisers may develop global strategies to guide their overall advertising efforts, specific advertising programmes must usually be adapted to meet local cultures and customs, media characteristics and advertising regulations.

MAKING CONNECTIONS Linking the concepts

Think about what goes on behind the scenes for the ads we all tend to take for granted.

- Pick a favourite print or TV ad. Why do you like it? Do you think that it's effective? Can you think of an ad that people like that may not be effective?

- Dig a little deeper and learn about the campaign *behind* your ad. What are the campaign's objectives? What is its budget? Assess the campaign's message and media strategies. Looking beyond your own feelings about the ad, is the campaign likely to be effective?

SALES PROMOTION

Advertising often works closely with another promotion tool, sales promotion. *Sales promotion* consists of short-term incentives to encourage purchase or sales of a product or service. Whereas advertising offers reasons to buy a product or service, sales promotion offers reasons to buy *now*.

Examples of sales promotions are found everywhere. A free-standing insert in the Sunday newspaper contains a coupon offering £1 off an album download. An email from **Ocado.com** offers a £5 discount on your next home delivery. The display at the end of the aisle in the local supermarket tempts impulse buyers with a wall of beer multi-packs. A businessman buys a new Sony laptop and gets a free carrying case, or a family buys a new car and receives a rebate of £500. A DIY chain might receive a 10 per cent discount on selected Black & Decker portable power tools if it agrees to advertise them in local newspapers. Sales promotion includes a wide variety of promotion tools designed to stimulate earlier or stronger market response.[44]

Rapid growth of sales promotion

Sales promotion tools are used by most organisations, including manufacturers, distributors, retailers and not-for-profit institutions. They are targeted towards final buyers (*consumer promotions*), retailers and wholesalers (*trade promotions*), business customers (*business promotions*) and members of the sales force (*sales force promotions*).

Sales promotion is viewed as an effective short-term sales tool in many companies, but there are significant problems. Externally, a company faces more competition and competing brands are less differentiated. Second, increasingly competitors are using sales promotion to help differentiate their offers. Third, advertising efficiency has declined because of rising costs, media clutter and legal restraints. Finally, consumers have become more deal oriented, and ever-larger retailers are demanding more deals from manufacturers.

The growing use of sales promotion has resulted in *promotion clutter,* similar to advertising clutter. Consumers are increasingly tuning out promotions, weakening their ability to trigger immediate purchase. Manufacturers are now searching for ways to rise above the clutter, such as offering larger coupon values or creating more dramatic point-of-purchase displays.

The next chapter has a case on Groupon, a company combining direct marketing, Internet media and sales promotion to take couponing into the twenty-first century.

In developing a sales promotion programme, a company must first set sales promotion objectives and then select the best tools for accomplishing these objectives.

Sales promotion objectives

Sales promotion objectives vary widely. Sellers may use *consumer promotions* to increase short-term sales or to help build long-term market share. Objectives for *trade promotions* include getting retailers to carry new items and more inventory, getting them to advertise the product and give it more shelf space, and getting them to buy ahead. For the *sales force,* objectives include getting more sales force support for current or new products or getting salespeople to sign up new accounts. Sales promotions are usually used together with advertising, personal selling or other promotion mix tools. Consumer promotions must usually be advertised and can add excitement and pulling power to ads. Trade and sales force promotions support the firm's personal selling process.

In general, rather than creating only short-term sales or temporary brand switching, sales promotions should help to reinforce the product's position and build long-term *customer relationships.* If properly designed, every sales promotion tool has the potential to build both short-term excitement and long-term consumer relationships. Increasingly, marketers are avoiding 'quick-fix', price-only promotions in favour of promotions designed to build brand equity. Examples include all of the 'frequency marketing programmes' and loyalty clubs that have mushroomed in recent years. Most hotels, supermarkets and airlines now offer frequent-guest/buyer/flyer programmes offering rewards to regular customers. For example, Air France offers a loyalty programme called Flying Blue, a programme that targets its core market of not-so-frequent leisure travellers.

Major sales promotion tools

Many tools can be used to accomplish sales promotion objectives. Descriptions of the main consumer, trade and business promotion tools follow.

Consumer promotion tools

The main *consumer promotion tools* include samples, coupons, cash refunds, price packs, premiums, advertising specialities, patronage rewards, point-of-purchase displays and demonstrations, and contests, sweepstakes and games.

Samples are offers of a trial amount of a product. Sampling is the most effective – but most expensive – way to introduce a new product or to create new excitement for an existing one. Some samples are free; for others, the company charges a small amount to offset its cost. The sample might be delivered door to door, sent by mail, handed out in a store, attached to another product or featured in an ad. Sometimes, samples are combined into sample packs, which can then be used to promote other products and services. Sampling can be a powerful promotion tool. Consider this example of cough sweets originating in Fleetwood, UK:

> Fisherman's Friend throat lozenges used sampling as the centrepiece of a very successful brand-building programme. It began by passing out 250,000 samples of its lozenges at more than 25 fairs, sporting events, and other happenings where it was a sponsor. Each sample contained an invitation to visit the Fisherman's Friend website, where customers could enter

a contest to win a Mini Cooper by submitting a slogan to be used in the future 'Tell a Friend' (about Fisherman's Friend) ad campaign. The sampling promotion was a complete success. US sales of Fisherman's Friend lozenges grew 115 per cent for the year, 25 per cent better than expectations. Some 5,000 people submitted a slogan for the company's new ad campaign. The winner suggested the slogan 'Lose a Cough. Gain a Friend', which is now featured in ads and on the website. The successful sampling campaign continues via the company's website, which invites consumers to sign up themselves and a friend to receive free samples of Fisherman's Friend in the mail.[45]

Coupons are certificates that give buyers a saving when they purchase specified products. Coupons can promote early trial of a new brand or stimulate sales of a mature brand. However, as a result of coupon clutter, redemption rates have been declining in recent years and the industry body is concerned about how these trends and challenges can be met.[46] Thus, most major consumer goods companies are issuing fewer coupons and targeting them more carefully by using more and better data about the customer and/or using social media to have them delivered to appropriate people more often. Marketers are also cultivating new outlets for distributing coupons, such as supermarket shelf dispensers, electronic point-of-sale coupon printers, or even text messaging systems. Text message couponing is popular in Europe, India and Japan, and it is slowly gaining popularity in the USA. For instance, if a local nightclub is having a slow night, it can log in and blast out a special offer coupon.

Cash refunds (or rebates) are like coupons except that the price reduction occurs after the purchase rather than at the retail outlet. The consumer sends a 'proof of purchase' to the manufacturer, who then refunds part of the purchase price by mail. For example, Citroën often offers customers a mix of cash refunds and part exchange on new cars and Barratt offers relatively substantial rebates to people who buy newly built houses from it.

Price packs (also called money-off deals) offer consumers savings off the regular price of a product. The reduced prices are marked by the producer directly on the label or package. Price packs can be single packages sold at a reduced price (such as two for the price of one), or two related products banded together (such as a toothbrush and toothpaste). Price packs are very effective – even more so than coupons – in stimulating short-term sales.

Premiums are goods offered either free or at low cost as an incentive to buy a product, ranging from toys included with kids' products to phone cards and DVDs. A premium may come inside the package (in-pack), outside the package (on-pack) or through the mail. Kellogg's is a past master at this – its *Galactic Gadgets* promotion offered *Star Wars* prizes via an assortment of channels. Packages of Frosted Flakes contained a free light-up Saberspoon. Other cereals offered an R2-D2 snack bowl that beeps and whistles. And if your specially marked package of Pop-Tarts played Darth Vader music, you won a Darth Vader Voice Changer.

Advertising specialities, also called *promotional products,* are useful articles imprinted with an advertiser's name, logo or message that are given as gifts to consumers. Typical items include T-shirts and other apparel, pens, coffee mugs, calendars, key rings, mouse pads, matches, tote bags, coolers, golf balls and caps. Such items can be very effective. In a recent study, 71 per cent of all consumers surveyed had received at least one promotional product in the last 12 months; 76 per cent of those were able to recall the advertiser's name on the promotional product they received, compared with only 53 per cent who could recall the name of an advertiser in a print publication they had read in the past week.[47]

Patronage rewards are cash or other awards offered for the regular use of a certain company's products or services. For example, airlines offer frequent-flyer plans, awarding points for miles travelled that can be turned in for free airline trips. And supermarkets issue frequent-shopper cards that dole out a wealth of discounts at the checkout. Baskin-Robbins offers frequent-purchase awards – for every 10 purchases, customers receive a free ice cream.

Point-of-purchase (POP) promotions include displays and demonstrations that take place at the point of purchase or sale. Think of your last visit to the local Tesco, WHSmith or Boots. Chances are good that you were tripping over aisle displays, promotional signs, 'shelf talkers' or demonstrators offering free tastes of featured food products. Unfortunately, many retailers do not like to handle the hundreds of displays, signs and posters they receive from manufacturers each year. Manufacturers have responded by offering better POP materials, tying them in with TV or print messages, and offering to set them up.

Contests, sweepstakes and *games* give consumers the chance to win something, such as cash, trips or goods, by luck or through extra effort. A *contest* calls for consumers to submit an entry – a jingle, guess, suggestion – to be judged by a panel that will select the best entries. A *sweepstake* calls for consumers to submit their names for a draw. A *game* presents consumers with something – bingo numbers, missing letters – every time they buy, which may or may not help them win a prize. A sales contest urges dealers or the sales force to increase their efforts, with prizes going to the top performers.

Trade promotion tools

Manufacturers direct more sales promotion cash towards retailers and wholesalers (78 per cent) than to consumers (22 per cent).[48] Trade promotion can persuade resellers to carry a brand, give it shelf space, promote it in advertising and push it to consumers. Shelf space is so scarce these days that manufacturers often have to offer price-offs, allowances, buy-back guarantees, or free goods to retailers and wholesalers to get products on the shelf and, once there, to keep them on it.

Manufacturers use several trade promotion tools. Many of the tools used for consumer promotions – contests, premiums, displays – can also be used as trade promotions. Or the manufacturer may offer a straight discount off the list price on each case purchased during a stated period of time (also called a *price-off, off-invoice* or *off-list*). Manufacturers also may offer an allowance (usually so much off per case) in return for the retailer's agreement to feature the manufacturer's products in some way. An *advertising allowance* compensates retailers for advertising the product. A *display allowance* compensates them for using special displays.

Manufacturers may offer *free goods,* which are extra cases of merchandise, to resellers who buy a certain quantity or who feature a certain flavour or size. They may offer *push money* – cash or gifts to dealers or their sales forces to 'push' the manufacturer's goods. Manufacturers may give retailers free *speciality advertising items* that carry the company's name, such as pens, pencils, calendars, paperweights, memo pads and mouse mats.

Business promotion tools

Companies spend billions each year on promotion to industrial customers. *Business promotion tools* are used to generate business leads, stimulate purchases, reward customers and motivate salespeople. Business promotion includes many of the same tools used for consumer or trade promotions. Here, we focus on two additional major business promotion tools – conventions and trade shows, and sales contests.

Many companies and trade associations organise *conventions and trade shows* to promote their products. Firms selling to the industry show their products at the trade show. Vendors receive many benefits, such as opportunities to find new sales leads, contact customers, introduce new products, meet new customers, sell more to present customers, and educate customers with publications and audio-visual materials. Trade shows also help companies reach many prospects not reached through their sales forces. Some trade shows are huge. For example, at the BAUMA mining and construction equipment trade show in Munich, Germany, some 3,256 exhibitors from 52 countries presented their latest product innovations in half a million square metres of space to more than 420,000 attendees from 200 countries.[49]

A *sales contest* is a contest for salespeople or dealers to motivate them to increase their sales performance over a given period. Sales contests motivate and recognise good company performers, who may receive trips, cash prizes or other gifts. Some companies award points for performance, which the receiver can turn in for any of a variety of prizes. Sales contests work best when they are tied to measurable and achievable sales objectives (such as finding new accounts, reviving old accounts or increasing account profitability).

Developing the sales promotion programme

Beyond selecting the types of promotions to use, marketers must make several other decisions in designing the full sales promotion programme. First, they must decide on the *size of the incentive*. A certain minimum incentive is necessary if the promotion is to succeed; a larger incentive will produce more sales response. The marketer also must set *conditions for participation*. Incentives might be offered to everyone or only to select groups.

Marketers must also decide how to *promote and distribute the promotion* programme itself. A money-off coupon could be given out in a package, at the store, via the Internet or in an advertisement. Each distribution method involves a different level of reach and cost. Increasingly, marketers are blending several media into a total campaign concept. The *length of the promotion* is also important. If the sales promotion period is too short, many prospects (who may not be buying during that time) will miss it. If the promotion runs too long, the deal will lose some of its 'act now' force.

Evaluation is also very important. Many companies fail to evaluate their sales promotion programmes, and others evaluate them only superficially. Yet marketers should work to measure the returns on their sales promotion investments, just as they should seek to assess the returns on other marketing activities. The most common evaluation method is to compare sales before, during and after a promotion. Marketers should ask: Did the promotion attract new customers or more purchasing from current customers? Can we hold on to these new customers and purchases? Will the long-term customer relationship and sales gains from the promotion justify its costs?

Clearly, sales promotion plays an important role in the total promotion mix. To use it well, the markcter must define the sales promotion objectives, select the best tools, design the sales promotion programme, implement the programme and evaluate the results. Moreover, sales promotion must be coordinated carefully with other promotion mix elements within the IMC programme.

PUBLIC RELATIONS

Another major mass-promotion tool is *public relations* – building good relations with the company's various publics by obtaining favourable publicity, building up a good corporate image, and handling or heading off unfavourable rumours, stories and events. Public relations departments may perform any or all of the following functions:[50]

- *Press relations or press agency:* Creating and placing newsworthy information in the news media to attract attention to a person, product or service.
- *Product publicity:* Publicising specific products.
- *Public affairs:* Building and maintaining national or local community relations.
- *Lobbying:* Building and maintaining relations with legislators and government officials to influence legislation and regulation.
- *Investor relations:* Maintaining relationships with shareholders and others in the financial community.
- *Development:* Public relations with donors or members of non-profit organisations to gain financial or volunteer support.

Public relations is used to promote products, people, places, ideas, activities, organisations and even nations. Companies use public relations to build good relations with consumers, investors, the media and their communities. Trade associations have used public relations to rebuild interest in declining commodities such as eggs, apples, milk and potatoes. The state of New York turned its image around when its 'I ♥™ New York!' publicity and advertising campaign took root, bringing in millions more tourists. Whole nations have used public relations to attract more tourists, foreign investment and international support.

The role and impact of public relations

Public relations can have a strong impact on public awareness at a much lower cost than advertising can. The company does not pay for the space or time in the media. Rather, it pays for staff to develop and circulate information and to manage events. If the company develops an interesting story, it could be picked up by several different media, having the same effect as advertising that would cost millions. And it would have more credibility than advertising.[51]

Public relations results can sometimes be spectacular. Think how each new Harry Potter book launch was used to turn a commercial release into a social and cultural event. The launches of the seven Harry Potter novels became increasingly linked in with promotional efforts as the series neared its conclusion. For the release of the final book, J.K. Rowling read out excerpts to 500 competition winners at the Natural History Museum in London, while tens of thousands of children took part in activities around the world involving costumes, parties and freebies – a frenzy whipped up by the publishers. The result? One UK supermarket chain sold 250,000 copies in nine hours of trading.

Despite its potential strengths, public relations is sometimes described as a marketing stepchild because of its often limited and scattered use. The public relations department is usually located at corporate headquarters. Its staff are so busy dealing with various publics – stockholders, employees, legislators, the press – that public relations programmes to support product marketing objectives may be ignored. Marketing managers and public relations practitioners do not always talk the same language. Many public relations practitioners see their job as simply communicating. In contrast, marketing managers tend to be much more interested in how advertising and public relations affect brand building, sales and profits, and customer relationships.

This situation is changing, however. Although public relations still captures only a small portion of the overall marketing budgets of most firms, it is playing an increasingly important brand-building role. Public relations can be a powerful brand-building tool. Two well-known marketing consultants even go so far as to conclude that advertising does not build brands, public relations does. The consultants proclaim that the dominance of advertising is over, and that public relations is quietly becoming the most powerful marketing communications tools. One recent book was called *The Rise of PR and the Fall of Advertising*:

The birth of a brand is usually accomplished with [public relations], not advertising. Our general rule is [PR] first, advertising second. [Public relations] is the nail, advertising the hammer. [PR] creates the credentials that provide the credibility for advertising. . . . Anita Roddick built the Body Shop into a major brand with no advertising at all. Instead, she travelled the world on a relentless quest for publicity. . . . Until recently Starbucks Coffee Co. didn't spend a hill of beans on advertising, either. In ten years, the company spent less than $10 million on advertising, a trivial amount for a brand that delivers annual sales of [in the billions].

Public relations results can sometimes be spectacular. The release of the last book in the Harry Potter series saw events globally reported

Source: Getty Images.

> Wal-Mart Stores became the world's largest retailer . . . with very little advertising. . . .
> On the Internet, **Amazon.com** became a powerhouse brand with virtually no advertising.[52]

While most advertisers would not agree about the 'fall of advertising' part of the title, the point is a good one. Advertising and public relations should work hand in hand to build and maintain brands.

Major public relations tools

Public relations (PR) uses several tools. One of the major tools is *news*. PR professionals find or create favourable news about the company and its products or people. Sometimes news stories occur naturally, and sometimes the PR person can suggest events or activities that would create news. *Speeches* can also create product and company publicity. Increasingly, company executives must field questions from the media or give talks at trade associations or sales meetings, and these events can either build or hurt the company's image. Another common PR tool is *special events,* ranging from news conferences, press tours, grand openings and fireworks displays to laser shows, hot-air balloon releases, multimedia presentations, star-studded spectaculars, or educational programmes designed to reach and interest target publics. Increasingly, PR professionals are taking social media more seriously.

PR people also prepare *written materials* to reach and influence their target markets. These materials include annual reports, brochures, articles, and company newsletters and magazines. *Audio-visual materials,* such as films, podcasts and apps, are being used increasingly as communication tools. *Corporate identity materials* can also help create a corporate identity that the public immediately recognises. Logos, stationery, brochures, signs, business forms, business cards, buildings, uniforms, and company cars and trucks – all become marketing tools when they are attractive, distinctive and memorable. Finally, companies can improve public goodwill by contributing money and time to *public service activities.*

As we discussed earlier (see Chapter 5), many marketers are now also designing *buzz marketing* campaigns to generate excitement and favourable word of mouth for their brands. Buzz marketing creates publicity by getting consumers themselves to spread information about a product or service to others in their communities. Procter & Gamble understands the importance of buzz. It created a separate marketing arm called Tremor, which has enlisted an army of buzzers to create word of mouth not just about P&G products, but for those of other client companies as well.

Another recent PR development is *mobile marketing* – travelling promotional tours that bring the brand to consumers. Mobile marketing has emerged as an effective way to build one-to-one relationships with targeted consumers. These days, it seems that almost every company is putting its show on the road – the German firm mm Promotions provides vehicles and mobile-exhibit design for a large number of firms. Recent 'tours' have included Electrolux, Samsung, Nivea and the trade union IG Metall. These tours take new products, free samples, literature and salespeople out and about – bringing the company to where potential customers are. Charmin's 'Potty Palooza' serves as a rolling showcase for – you guessed it – toilet paper and makes an appearance at music festivals where its facilities are appreciated.

A company's website can be a good PR vehicle. Consumers and members of other publics can visit the site for information and entertainment. Such sites can be extremely popular and can also be ideal for handling crisis situations. In all, in this age where 'it's easier to disseminate information through email marketing, blogs, and online chat', notes an analyst, 'public relations is becoming a valuable part of doing business in a digital world'.[53]

As with the other promotion tools, in considering when and how to use product PR, management should set PR objectives, choose the PR messages and vehicles, implement the PR plan and evaluate the results. The firm's PR should be blended smoothly with other promotional activities within the company's overall IMC effort.

THE JOURNEY YOU'VE TAKEN Reviewing the concepts

In this chapter, you've learned how companies use integrated marketing communications to communicate customer value. Modern marketing calls for more than just creating customer value by developing a good product, pricing it attractively and making it available to target customers. Companies also must clearly and persuasively *communicate* that value to current and prospective customers. To do this, they must blend five communication mix tools, guided by a well-designed and implemented integrated marketing communications strategy.

1 **Discuss the process and advantages of integrated marketing communications in communicating customer value**

Recent shifts towards targeted or one-to-one marketing, coupled with advances in information and communications technology, have had a dramatic impact on marketing communications. As marketing communicators adopt richer but more fragmented media and promotion mixes to reach their diverse markets, they risk creating a communications hotchpotch for consumers. To prevent this, more companies are adopting the concept of *integrated marketing communications (IMC)*. Guided by an overall IMC strategy, the company works out the roles that the various promotion tools will play and the extent to which each will be used. It carefully coordinates the promotional activities and the timing of when major campaigns take place. Finally, to help implement its integrated marketing strategy, the company appoints a marketing communications director who has overall responsibility for the company's communications efforts.

2 **Define the five promotion tools and discuss factors that must be considered in shaping the overall promotion mix**

A company's total *promotion mix* – also called its *marketing communications mix* – consists of the specific blend of *advertising, personal selling, sales promotion, public relations* and *direct marketing* tools that the company uses persuasively to communicate customer value and build customer relationships. Advertising includes any paid form of non-personal presentation and promotion of ideas, goods or services by an identified sponsor. In contrast, public relations focuses on building good relations with the company's various publics by obtaining favourable unpaid publicity. Personal selling is any form of personal presentation by the firm's sales force for the

purpose of making sales and building customer relationships. Firms use sales promotion to provide short-term incentives to encourage the purchase or sale of a product or service. Finally, firms seeking immediate response from targeted individual customers use non-personal direct marketing tools to communicate with customers.

The company wants to create an integrated *promotion mix*. It can pursue a *push* or a *pull* promotional strategy, or a combination of the two. The best specific blend of promotion tools depends on the type of product/market and the product life-cycle stage. People at all levels of the organisation must be aware of the many legal and ethical issues surrounding marketing communications.

3 **Describe and discuss the major decisions involved in developing an advertising programme**

Advertising – the use of paid media by a seller to inform, persuade and remind about its products or organisation – is a strong promotion tool that takes many forms and has many uses. *Advertising decision making* involves decisions about the objectives, the budget, the message, the media and, finally, the evaluation of results. Advertisers should set clear *objectives* as to whether the advertising is supposed to inform, persuade or remind buyers. The advertising *budget* can be based on what is affordable, on sales, on competitors' spending, or on the objectives and tasks. The *message decision* calls for planning a message strategy and executing it effectively. The *media decision* involves defining reach, frequency and impact goals; choosing major media types; selecting media vehicles; and deciding on media timing. Message and media decisions must be closely coordinated for maximum campaign effectiveness. Finally, *evaluation* calls for evaluating the communication and sales effects of advertising before, during and after the advertising is placed and measuring advertising return on investment.

4 **Explain how sales promotion campaigns are developed and implemented**

Sales promotion covers a wide variety of short-term incentive tools – coupons, premiums, contests, buying allowances – designed to stimulate final and business consumers, the trade and the company's own sales force. Sales promotion spending has been growing faster than advertising spending in recent years. A sales promotion campaign first calls for setting sales promotion objectives (in general, sales promotions should be *consumer relationship building*). It then calls for developing and implementing the sales promotion programme by using consumer promotion tools (*samples, coupons, cash refunds* or *rebates, price packs, premiums, advertising specialities, patronage rewards* and others); trade promotion tools (*discounts, allowances, free goods, push money*); and business promotion tools (*conventions, trade shows, sales contests*). The sales promotion effort should be coordinated carefully with the firm's other promotion efforts.

5 **Explain how companies use public relations to communicate with their publics**

Public relations involves building good relations with the company's various publics. Its functions include *press agency, product publicity, public affairs, lobbying, investor relations* and *development*. Public relations can have a strong impact on public awareness at a much lower cost than advertising can, and public relations results can sometimes be spectacular. Despite its potential strengths, however, public relations sometimes sees only limited and scattered use. Public relations tools include *news, speeches, special events, buzz marketing, mobile marketing, written materials, audio-visual materials, corporate identity materials* and *public service activities*. A company's website can be a good public relations vehicle. In considering when and how to use product public relations, management should set public relations objectives, choose the public relations messages and vehicles, implement the public relations plan and evaluate the results. public relations should be blended smoothly with other promotional activities within the company's overall integrated marketing communications effort.

NAVIGATING THE KEY TERMS

Advertising **399**
Advertising agency **420**
Advertising objective **405**
Affordable method **407**
Competitive-parity method **407**
Direct marketing **401**

Integrated marketing
 communications (IMC) **398**
Objective-and-task method **407**
Percentage-of-sales method **407**
Personal selling **400**

Promotion mix (or marketing
 communications mix) **396**
Public relations **400**
Pull strategy **401**
Push strategy **401**
Sales promotion **400**

NOTES AND REFERENCES

1 See 'Europas Automarktstartet 2006' at **www.netzeitung.de**

2 Michael Loeffler, 'A Multinational Examination of the "(Non-)domestic Product" Effect', *International Marketing Review*, 19(4/5), 2002, p. 482.

3 German Effie Awards – Automotive. Full report available in German from **www.gwa.de**, accessed July 2014. Select 'Awards and Events' from the sidebar.

4 The homepage for the Euro NCAP organisation is at **www.euroncap.com**

5 The online presence for Publicis can be found at **www.publicis.com**. Nordpol+ can be found at **www.nordpol.com**

6 See the story '*Mit Nordpol auf Kreativer Expedition*' in the German-language newspaper **www.welt.de**, accessed August 2014.

7 Search for Renault on the GWA site at **www.gwa.de**

8 Search for Renault on the Publicis site at **www.publicis.com**

9 The homepage for this agency is at **www.tns-sofres.com**

10 The first four of these definitions are adapted from Peter D. Bennett, *The AMA Dictionary of Marketing Terms*, 2nd edn (New York: McGraw-Hill, 2004). Other definitions can be found at **https://www.ama.org/resources/Pages/Dictionary.aspx**, January 2015.

11 Bob Garfield, 'The Chaos Scenario', *Advertising Age,* 4 April 2005, pp. 1, 57ff; and 'Readers Respond to "Chaos Scenario"', *Advertising Age,* 18 April 2005, pp. 1ff.

12 Garfield, ibid., p. 57.

13 Mark Sweney, 'Internet Overtakes Television to Become Biggest Advertising Sector in the UK', available from **www.guardian.co.uk**, accessed July 2014. The Internet Advertising Bureau also has many facts, figures and stories about Internet advertising and can be found at **www.iabuk.net**

14 Jack Neff, 'P&G Chief: We Need New Model Now', *Advertising Age,* 15 November 2004, pp. 1, 53.

15 See O. Holm, 'Integrated Marketing Communication: From Tactics to Strategy', *Corporate Communications: An International Journal,* 11(1), 2006, pp. 23–33.

16 Don E. Schultz and Heidi Schultz, *IMC: The Next Generation* (New York: McGraw-Hill, 2004).

17 For more on integrated marketing communications, see Chris Fill, *Marketing Communications* (Harlow: Pearson Education, 2013).

18 Champions League viewing figures from: **www.uefa.com/uefachampionsleague/news/newsid=2111684.html**, accessed August 2014.

19 Estimates for 2014 global advertising spend from 'Carat Forecasts 5% Growth in Global Advertising Spend During 2015' at **www.thedrum.com**; facts on figures on media-type proportions from 'Executive summary: Advertising Expenditure Forecasts December' by ZenithOptima, available from **http://www.zenithoptimedia.com/wp-content/uploads/2013/12/Adspend-forecasts-December-2013-executive-summary.pdf**. Belgian numbers from **mandmglobal.com/media-passport/belgium/market-data.aspx**, accessed September 2014.

20 Figures for UK advertising in 2013 from Ben Bold, 'Top 100 UK Advertisers: BSkyB Increases Lead as P&G, BT and Unilever Reduce Adspend', *Marketing Magazine,* **www.marketingmagazine.co.uk**. The AdAge annual report on advertising expenditure is comprehensive and detailed. Regrettably it is also very expensive and only a small amount of data is available as a free sample – see the Datacenter at **www.adage.com**

21 FedEx example from **adsoftheworld.com**, by BBDO at **www.bbdo.de**, accessed July 2014.

22 See the story at 'O2 and 3 Bubble Trade Mark Dispute Sent to Europe' from **www.out-law.com**, accessed July 2014.

23 For more on advertising budgets, see George E. Belch and Michael A. Belch, *Advertising and Promotion: An Integrated Marketing Communications Perspective,* 9th edn (New York: McGraw-Hill, 2011).

24 Information from Gary Levin, '"Meddling" in Creative More Welcome', *Advertising Age,* 9 April 1990, pp. S4, S8; 'Absolut Vodka Turns 25 Tomorrow', press release, 19 April 2004, accessed at **www.absolut.com**

25 **Adbusters.org** is a group which campaigns against the prevalence of advertising and often has interesting and insightful anti-advertising articles.

26 Read about the what and how of AdBlock at **adblockplus.org**

27 Channel 5 figures from **www.five.tv**; ITV estimates from 'In The Picture' at **www.itpmag.demon.co.uk**; both accessed July 2014.

28 One common means of causing offence is through gender stereotyping. See for example M. Eisend, J. Plagemann and J. Sollwedel, 'Gender Roles and Humor in Advertising: The Occurrence of Stereotyping in Humorous and Nonhumorous Advertising and Its Consequences for Advertising Effectiveness', *Journal of Advertising,* 43(3), 2014, pp. 256–73; and Y.K. Lee, 'Gender Stereotypes as a Double-Edged Sword in Political Advertising: Persuasion Effects of Campaign Theme and Advertising Style', *International Journal of Advertising,* 33(2), 2014, pp. 203–34.

29 This quote from 'ITV Marks 225% Hike in Dual-screening TV Habits' from The Drum at **http://www.thedrum.com/news/2013/07/16/itv-marks-225-hike-dual-screening-tv-habits**

30 This quote from 'In-game Advertising Is Worth $1+ Billion a Year – Is PS4's Future Commercial?' in a column from PlayStation – Official Magazine UK at **www.officialplaystationmagazine.co.uk/2013/11/01/when-ads-invade-games-in-game-advertising-is-worth-over-1-billion-a-year/**

31 Richard Wray, 'EA Looks to Ads in Free Games', from **www.guardian.co.uk**, accessed July 2014. See also an academic study on in-game advertising by M. Yeu, H.S. Yoon, C.R. Taylor and D.H. Lee, 'Are Banner Advertisements in Online Games Effective?'. *Journal of Advertising,* 42(2–3), 2013, pp. 241–50.

32 Quote from the article 'Op-Ed: The Future of Advertising Lies Within Video Games' available from **www.digitaljournal.com/a-and-e/gaming/op-ed-the-potential-of-advertising-in-video-games/article/375665**

33 Entertainment Software Association, 'In-game Advertising' at **www.theesa.com/**

34 Edited from 'Microsoft Demos In-game Advertising' at **www.news.cnet.com**, accessed July 2011.

35 This section compiled from The Internet Advertising Bureau's report on in-games advertising – available from **www.iabuk.net**, and IGA Worldwide at **www.igaworldwide.com**; both accessed July 2014.

36 From IAB 'Report on In-game Advertising', p. 10, available from **www.iabuk.net**, accessed July 2014.

37 From: 'Game On for Advertisers', *Daily Telegraph* at **www.telegraph.co.uk/**, accessed July 2014.

38 *Telegraph* rates from **www.telegraph.co.uk/advertising/**; *Guardian* rates and readership from **www.adinfo-guardian.co.uk**, accessed July 2014.

39 Stuart Elliot, 'How Effective Is This Ad, in Real Numbers? Beats Me', *The New York Times,* 20 July 2005, p. C8.

40 Company revenues taken from 2013 annual reports at **omnicomgroup.com**, **www.wpp .com** and **publicisgroupe.com** respectively. Profiles of top global advertisers from Adage, 'Agency Profiles Yearbook 2014', available from **www.adage.com** – subscription required.

41 See M.R. Nelson and Hye-Jin Paek, 'A Content Analysis of Advertising in a Global Magazine Across Seven Countries: Implications for Global Advertising Strategies', *International Marketing Review,* 24(1), 2007, pp. 64–86; and Kara Chan, Lyann Li, Sandra Diehl and Ralf Terlutter, 'Consumers' Response to Offensive Advertising: A Cross Cultural Study', *International Marketing Review,* 24(5), 2007, pp. 606–28.

42 For a report on this see *The Wall Street Journal* article by Thomas Catan and Amir Efrati, 'Google Near Deal in Drug Ad Crackdown', at **www.wsj.com**, accessed July 2014.

43 See recent studies such as J. Garrett and R. 'International Advertising Research: A Literature Review 1990-2010', *International Journal of Management,* 30(1), 2013; or J.G. Kliatchko and D.E. Schultz, 'Twenty Years of IMC: A Study of CEO and CMO Perspectives in the Asia-Pacific Region', *International Journal of Advertising,* 33(2), 2014, pp. 373–90.

44 See Alexandra Jardine and Laurel Wentz, 'It's a Fat World After All', *Advertising Age,* 7 March 2005, p. 3; George E. Belch and Michael A. Belch, *Advertising and Promotion* (New York: McGraw-Hill/Irwin, 2004), pp. 666–8; and Jonathan Cheng, 'China Demands Concrete Proof of Ads', *The Wall Street Journal,* 8 July 2005, p. B1.

45 'Casting the Net Wider', *Candy Industry,* February 2005, p. 24; Damian J. Troise, 'Fisherman's Friend Coughs Up Mini Cooper for Slogan Contest Winner', *Knight Ridder Tribune Business News,* 25 February 2005, p. 1; and **www.fishermansfriendusa.com**

46 The Institute of Promotional Marketing can be found at **www.theipm.org.uk**

47 See 'Promotional Products – Impact, Exposure, and Influence' at Promotional Products Association International website, **www.ppai.org**, May 2005.

48 'Rusty Relations', *Convenience Store News,* 3 August 2005, accessed at **www.csnews.com**

49 Numbers from **www.bauma.de**, accessed July 2014.

50 Adapted from Scott Cutlip, Allen Center and Glen Broom, *Effective Public Relations,* 11th edn (Upper Saddle River, NJ: Prentice Hall, 2012), ch. 1.

51 See for example K. Takano, 'McDonald's Japan: A Case Study of Effective Public Relations', *Public Relations Review,* 39(1), 2013, pp. 60–2.

52 Al Ries and Laura Ries, 'First Do Some Publicity', *Advertising Age,* 8 February 1999, p. 42. Also see Al Ries and Laura Ries, *The Fall of Advertising and the Rise of PR* (New York: HarperBusiness, 2002). For points and counterpoints, see O. Burtch Drake, '"Fall" of Advertising? I Differ', *Advertising Age,* 13 January 2003, p. 23; Robert E. Brown, 'Book Review: The Fall of Advertising & the Rise of PR', *Public Relations Review,* March 2003, pp. 91–3; and Mark Cheshire, 'Roundtable Discussion – Making & Moving the Message', *The Daily Record,* 30 January 2004, p. 1.

53 See for example I. Himelboim, G.J. Golan, B.B. Moon and R.J. Suto, 'A Social Networks Approach to Public Relations on Twitter: Social Mediators and Mediated Public Relations', *Journal of Public Relations Research,* 26(4), 2014, pp. 359–79.

CHAPTER 13

COMMUNICATING CUSTOMER VALUE: PERSONAL SELLING AND DIRECT MARKETING

AFTER STUDYING THIS CHAPTER, YOU SHOULD BE ABLE TO

- discuss the role of a company's salespeople in creating value for customers and building customer relationships
- identify and explain the six major sales force management steps
- discuss the personal selling process, distinguishing between transaction-oriented marketing and relationship marketing
- define direct marketing and discuss its benefits to customers and companies
- identify and discuss the major forms of direct marketing

THE WAY AHEAD
Previewing the concepts

In this chapter, we examine two more promotion mix tools – personal selling and direct marketing. Both involve direct connections with customers aimed at communicating customer-unique value and building profitable customer relationships.

In the previous chapter, you learned about communicating customer value through integrated marketing communications (IMC), and about three specific elements of the marketing communications mix: advertising, sales promotion and publicity. In this chapter, we'll consider the final two IMC elements – personal selling and direct marketing. Personal selling is the interpersonal arm of marketing communications, in which the sales force interacts with customers and prospects to build relationships and make sales. Direct marketing consists of direct connections with carefully targeted consumers both to obtain an immediate response and to cultivate lasting customer relationships. Actually, direct marketing can be viewed as more than just a communications tool. In many ways it constitutes an overall marketing approach – a blend of communication and distribution channels all rolled into one. As you read on, remember that although this chapter examines personal selling and direct marketing as separate tools, they must be carefully integrated with other elements of the marketing promotion mix.

When someone says 'salesperson', what image comes to mind? Or how about 'direct marketing'? Perhaps you think about a stereotypical glad-hander who's out to lighten your wallet by selling you something you don't really need. Think again. Today, for most companies, personal selling and direct marketing play an important role in building profitable customer relationships. Let's take a look at how Philips, one of the biggest electronic goods companies in the world, manages its relationships with key customers.

INNOVATING IN BUSINESS RELATIONSHIPS: HOW PHILIPS WORKS WITH INTERNATIONAL RETAILERS

Beth Rogers, Principal Lecturer, University of Portsmouth Business School, UK

International retailers like Wal-Mart, Carrefour and the Metro Group are sophisticated organisations, selling thousands of products in thousands of stores. For fast-moving consumer goods suppliers, these powerful customers have been getting bigger and fewer. Managing a business relationship with them requires particular focus from suppliers – there is little margin for error in such a competitive environment. So how do consumer goods companies respond?

The Philips brand

Headquartered in the Netherlands, Philips is one of the most highly respected and innovative companies in the world, and one of the top 10 global electronics companies. In 2014, Philips had sales of €24bn, 120,000 employees in more than 100 countries and over 50,000 patents. Its brand promise 'sense and simplicity' encapsulates its mission to enhance consumers' lives with simple-to-use, high-performing products. The company began producing carbon filament lamps in 1891. Now Philips is a market leader in medical diagnostic imaging and patient monitoring systems, energy-efficient lighting solutions, personal-care and home appliances, and of course consumer electronics.

For consumer goods, the retailer is a vital link in the delivery process to consumers. Obviously, Philips has a number of product divisions and regional offices. A customer like international retailer Carrefour, which operates in 30 different countries, has visits from over 250 Philips representatives and many more 'touch points' with Philips's operational staff.

The drivers for key account management

From the mid-1990s, the balance of power in supply chains has favoured customers, especially large retailers who are able to leverage their volume requirements to drive down suppliers' prices. Fast-moving consumer goods companies were seeing their largest customers become the least profitable. A small powerful group of international retailers has emerged, with large market shares, and it wants to deal with suppliers on a global

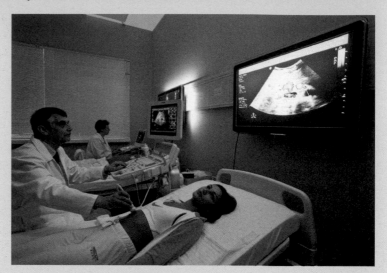

As well as individuals, Philips needs to manage relationships with other types of customers – like hospitals

Source: Courtesy of Philips Electronics.

basis. These retailers expect their organisational needs to be the focus of supplier processes. So, companies with a product-based organisational structure were faced with a considerable challenge as customers demanded consistency across their product portfolio, which in Philips's case means from light bulbs and kettles to TVs and MP3 players, all across international boundaries.

Carrefour asked Philips for a global contract in 1998, at a time when Philips was regionally organised. Philips piloted this, appointing a dedicated global account manager, developing an account plan and a contact network, and managing coordination across product and geographical units using an intranet site. The pilot was successful. The process was soon applied to other key accounts, starting in retail, but spreading to other sectors. Business with these global customers grew fast. By 2004, the top 25 customers were responsible for 30 per cent of sales, and were also responsible for a significant proportion of growth. Some customers represented more revenue than some countries.

To develop further, Philips needed to move away from working with customers on a transactional basis. Integrating with each customer's processes to increase the efficiency and effectiveness of the business relationship was critical to achieving competitive advantage. And it was still important to be price competitive.

'One Philips' approach to international retailers

In 2004, Philips set up an International Retail Board, headed up by a member of the Board of Management. The board are responsible for a 'One Philips' approach to international retailers. Cross-divisional key account teams were set up to ensure the best level of communication and process coordination to establish and maintain long-term partnerships, combining Philips's knowledge of the behaviour of the end users of their products with the retailer's insight into the way people shop. The board approached their task with a consistent and objective process.

First of all, customers were segmented on the basis of weighted scores for anticipated future performance with the customer, the fit of Philips's capabilities to the customer's requirements, and the customer's willingness to work cooperatively. On the basis of the weighted scores, Philips matched resources and service levels to the strategic importance of each account. Top-scoring accounts have multinational key account teams and senior management contact.

Philips is very aware of the importance of 'being easy to do business with'. The International Retail Management team designed processes that would eliminate hassle for its customers. These included joint business review processes at multiple levels in the organisation, and connectivity of the Philips operational processes to the retail value chain. Account planning was and is critical to this process development. The account plans include analysis of the market from the customers' point of view to identify their strategic priorities, and mapping Philips's strengths and weaknesses to the account's opportunities. The account managers concentrate on just three strategic programmes within the account. The plans are discussed with the customer in exploratory workshops. The customer, who will sign them off, agrees measurement criteria and process.

The International Retail Management team also designed a competency framework to ensure selection of account managers with appropriate skills. The account manager must be a business manager, which requires many more skills than a sales role. Philips develops some account managers from within the company but also recruits from outside. There is a single competency framework for marketing and sales, encompassing account management. This gives people within Philips varied career development paths. Talented sales and marketing employees are groomed to become global key account managers through extensive training and development activities. They attend basic courses, for example teaming up with buyers on negotiation skills. They progress to more advanced courses that are mapped to competency profiles. More than 3,000 employees have trained in sales, account management or category management. Philips also conducts joint training with retailers on consumer insight. Talent is shared between different parts of Philips, and cross-divisional moves are encouraged to ensure cultural flexibility.

Team member selection is also carefully organised across product divisions, regional offices and relevant functions such as logistics, planning, marketing and information systems. Everyone in account teams (including product managers and engineers) is trained in sales awareness.

Knowledge transfer is vital in key account teams operating across functional, product and geographical lines. Philips is implementing a 'One CRM' (Customer Relationship Management) system that provides a common platform for communications and knowledge sharing, a single view of the key account's data, and various elements of key account team process support. These include a contact matrix – a map of customer 'touch points' that underpins the forward plan for meetings with customers – and an archive of contact reports. The global account manager cannot negotiate everything for every category with global customers – team members need to be involved. The more contacts there are between Philips and the customer, the closer the business relationship becomes.

Internal activity recording processes are also robust, for example Philips's information systems can measure sales, gross margin and earnings before interest and taxes (EBIT) per customer.

It took a while for senior decision makers in Philips to get used to discussing individual customers in depth. Slots for discussion of key accounts were introduced onto the agenda of management meetings. Account managers were trained to use these slots to generate discussion and get feedback and direction. Account managers are empowered to provide business solutions for customers, but the senior managers have to understand the risks and allocate the resources to support implementation. Reviews are also conducted with customers using customer scorecards to measure the success of the collaboration. Key performance indicators encompass financial performance (including growth and cost reduction), customer satisfaction, process improvements and learning achieved.

Recognition and success

Philips has benchmarked its key account management performance against other leading FMCG companies and identified clear areas of strength such as people competency management and account profitability measurement.

More importantly, the programme is contributing to financial and non-financial company objectives. Philips aims for 'mind space' as well as shelf space. Philips wants to be seen as the best supplier partner for the retail trade – one that understands consumers and can help retailers improve their category performances.

Undoubtedly the Philips brand carries weight with the world's most influential retailers. In the USA, when The Home Depot chose Philips as its key supplier of branded light bulbs, Jerry Edwards, Executive Vice President of Merchandising, said: 'Philips was selected for its product innovation and brand awareness as well as its delivery reliability and its dedication to environmental conservation.' But to build a strategic relationship with a supplier demonstrates the trust that is developed and underpinned by the Philips account management programme.

Philips has received supplier awards from Comet, Wal-Mart, Carrefour and Sam's USA, demonstrating that 'sense and simplicity' is inherent in the way Philips does business with its key accounts.

In good economic times. This strategy led to profitable growth, achieved through board-level focus, a robust segmentation, investment in key account competencies, knowledge management, strategic account planning and rigorous measurement, including net customer profitability. In times of cutbacks, these strong relationships have become assets vital to the continued prosperity of the company!

Continuous improvement

Future plans for the 'One Philips' global key account management approach include implementation of more focused cross-functional teams, sharing more information, strengthening key account management capabilities, leverage success with category management initiatives, integrating account management with recently acquired companies and applying account management practices to other channels.

Sources: This case study was compiled with guidance from Bart Logghe, Senior Director, IKAM Competence Centre at Philips, and from financial reports available at www.philips.com

PERSONAL SELLING

Robert Louis Stevenson once noted that 'everyone lives by selling something'. We are all familiar with the sales forces used by business organisations to sell products and services to customers around the world. But sales forces are also found in many other kinds of organisations. For example, political parties have recruiters, and museums, galleries and charities use fundraisers to contact donors and raise money. In the first part of this chapter, we examine the role of personal selling in the organisation, sales force management decisions and the personal selling process.

The nature of personal selling

Selling is one of the oldest professions in the world. The people who do the selling go by many names: salespeople, sales representatives, account executives, sales consultants, sales engineers, agents, district managers and account development reps to name just a few of the politer ones.

People hold many stereotypes of salespeople – including some unfavourable ones. 'Salesman' may bring to mind the image of Arthur Miller's pitiable Willy Loman in *Death of a Salesman* or Ralph Ineson as Chris Finch in *The Office*. These examples depict salespeople as having unpleasant personalities or being loners, travelling their territories, trying to foist their wares on unsuspecting or unwilling buyers.

However, modern salespeople are a far cry from these unfortunate stereotypes. Today, most salespeople are well-educated, well-trained professionals who work to build and maintain long-term customer relationships. They listen to their customers, assess customer needs and organise the company's efforts to solve customer problems. Consider Boeing, the aerospace giant competing in the rough-and-tumble worldwide commercial aircraft market. It takes more than fast talk and a warm smile to sell expensive aircraft:

Professional selling: it takes more than fast talk and a warm smile to sell high-tech aircraft at $100m or more a copy. Success depends on building solid, long-term relationships with customers

Source: Alamy Images/Jack Sullivan.

Selling high-tech aircraft at $100 million or more a copy is complex and challenging. A single big sale can easily run into billions of dollars. Boeing salespeople head up an extensive team of company specialists – sales and service technicians, financial analysts, planners, engineers – all dedicated to finding ways to satisfy airline customer needs. The selling process is nerve-rackingly slow – it can take two or three years from the first sales presentation to the day the sale is announced. After getting the order, salespeople then must stay in almost constant touch to keep track of the account's equipment needs and to make certain the customer stays satisfied. Success depends on building solid, long-term relationships with customers, based on performance and trust. 'When you buy an airplane, it is like getting married,' says the head of Boeing's commercial airplane division. 'It is a long-term relationship.'[1]

The term **salesperson** covers a wide range of positions. At one extreme, a salesperson might be largely an *order taker,* such as the department store salesperson standing behind the till. At the other extreme are *order getters,* whose positions demand *creative selling* and *relationship building* for products and services ranging from appliances, industrial equipment and aircraft to insurance and IT services. Here, we focus on the more creative types of selling and on the process of building and managing an effective sales force.

The role of the sales force

Personal selling is the interpersonal arm of the promotion mix. Advertising consists largely of one-way, non-personal communication with target consumer groups. In contrast, personal selling involves two-way, personal communication between salespeople and individual customers – whether face to face, by telephone, through video or Skype conferences, or by other means. Personal selling can be more effective than advertising in more complex selling situations. Salespeople can probe customers to learn more about their problems, then adjust the marketing offer and presentation to fit the special needs of each customer.

The role of personal selling varies from company to company. Some firms have no salespeople at all – for example, companies that sell only online like Amazon or through catalogues like Argos; or companies that sell through manufacturer's reps, sales agents or brokers. In most firms, however, the sales force plays a major role. In companies that sell business products and services, such as IBM or DuPont, the company's salespeople work directly with customers. In consumer product companies such as Procter & Gamble and Nike, the sales force plays an important behind-the-scenes role. It works with wholesalers and retailers to gain their support and to help them be more effective in selling the company's products.

The sales force serves as a critical link between a company and its customers. In many cases, salespeople serve both masters – the seller and the buyer. First, they *represent the company to customers*. They find and develop new customers and communicate information about the company's products and services. They sell products by approaching customers, presenting their products, answering objections, negotiating prices and terms, and closing sales. In addition, salespeople provide customer service and carry out market research and intelligence work.[2]

At the same time, salespeople *represent customers to the company*, acting inside the firm as 'champions' of customers' interests and managing the buyer–seller relationship. Salespeople relay customer concerns about company products and actions back inside to those who can handle them. They learn about customer needs and work with other marketing and non-marketing people in the company to develop greater customer value. The old view was that salespeople should worry about sales and the company should worry about profit. However, the current view holds that salespeople should be concerned with more than just producing *sales* – they should work with others in the company to produce *customer value* and *company profit*.

MANAGING THE SALES FORCE

We define **sales force management** as the analysis, planning, implementation and control of sales force activities. It includes designing sales force strategy and structure and recruiting, selecting, training, compensating, supervising and evaluating the firm's salespeople. These major sales force management decisions are shown in Figure 13.1 and are discussed in the following sections.

Designing sales force strategy and structure

Marketing managers face several sales force strategy and design questions: How should salespeople and their tasks be structured? How big should the sales force be? Should salespeople sell alone or work in teams with other people in the company? Should they sell in the field or by telephone? We address these issues below.[3]

Sales force structure

A company can divide up sales responsibilities along any of several lines. The decision is simple if the company sells only one product line to one industry with customers in many locations. In that case the company would use a *territorial sales force structure*. However, if the company sells many products to many types of customers, it might need a *product sales force structure*, a *customer sales force structure* or a combination of the two.

Territorial sales force structure

In the **territorial sales force structure,** each salesperson is assigned to an exclusive geographical area and sells the company's full line of products or services to all customers in that territory. This territory might be a city, a region or, in certain business markets with relatively few

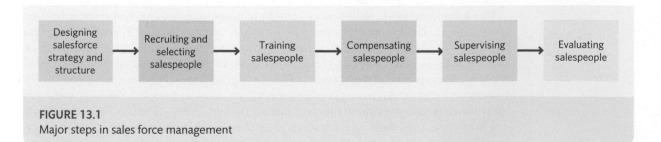

FIGURE 13.1
Major steps in sales force management

customers, even a country. This organisation clearly defines each salesperson's job and fixes accountability. It also increases the salesperson's desire to build local customer relationships that, in turn, improve selling effectiveness. Finally, because each salesperson travels within a limited geographical area, travel expenses are relatively small.

A territorial sales organisation is often supported by many levels of sales management positions – here are a couple of example sales structures. H+H Celcon supplies building materials to the construction industry. The nature of the product and the markets mean that salespeople must visit sites and advise customers on choice of specific product and agree on delivery schedules. The UK is divided into three territories: Scotland, Eastern and Western (which includes Wales). Each territory has a divisional sales manager. These DSMs each manage a team of salespeople, who subdivide the territory into smaller sectors. In turn, the DSMs all report to the national sales director, who has overall control and also has oversight of the internal sales team who take orders from the firm's head office in Middlesex. That is quite a simple structure, appropriate for a mid-sized firm. Loquendo, which sells speech recognition software, had an even simpler structure when it was just starting out – it had one sales team for inside Italy where the firm was founded, and a second team for the 'rest of the world'.[4] As Loquendo grew, the 'rest of the world' was split and teams assigned to key markets in the USA and more specific territories in Europe – London, Madrid, Munich and Paris.

Product sales force structure

Salespeople must know their products – especially when the products are numerous and complex. This need, together with the growth of product management, has led many companies to adopt a **product sales force structure**, in which the sales force sells along product lines. For example, Hewlett-Packard uses different sales forces for its consumer products and for its industrial products. The consumer products sales force deals with simple products that are distributed intensively, whereas the industrial products sales force deals with complex products that require technical understanding.

The product structure can lead to problems, however, if a single large customer buys many different company products. For example, Nestlé is divided into several business divisions across Europe – pet foods, confectionery and cereals among others. Each of these divisions is further broken down into units handling several related products or brands and having their own sales teams. Many of these sales teams will interact with the same customer – perhaps on the same day. These extra costs must be compared with the benefits of better product knowledge and attention to individual products.

Customer sales force structure

More and more companies are now using a **customer sales force structure**, in which they organise the sales force along customer or industry lines. Separate sales forces may be set up for different industries, for serving current customers versus finding new ones, and for major accounts versus regular accounts. Many companies even have special sales forces set up to handle the needs of individual large customers. For example, Black & Decker has one sales organisation supporting sales through DIY retailers like B&Q in the UK, and Leroy Merlin, which has a significant market share in France and Spain, and a second supporting sales to commercial/professional users through companies like Screwfix.

Organising the sales force around customers can help a company build closer relationships with important customers. For example, 20 years ago, IBM shifted from a product-based structure to a customer-based one. Before the shift, droves of salespeople representing different IBM software, hardware and services divisions might call on a single large client, creating confusion and frustration. However, such large customers wanted a 'single face', one point of contact for all of IBM's vast array of products and services.

Following the restructuring, a single IBM 'client executive' works with each large customer and manages a team of IBMers who work with the customer. One client executive describes his role this way: 'I am the owner of the business relationship with the client. If the client has a problem, I'm the one who pulls together software or hardware specialists or consultants.' According to a sales organisation expert, 'This structure puts salespeople in the position of being advisers to clients, and it also allows them to offer holistic solutions to clients' business problems.'[5] Such an intense focus on customers is widely credited for IBM's dramatic turnaround in the 1990s.

Complex sales force structures

When a company sells a wide variety of products to many types of customers over a broad geographical area, it often combines several types of sales force structures. Salespeople can be specialised by customer and territory, by product and territory, by product and customer, or by territory, product and customer. No single structure is best for all companies and situations. Each company should select a sales force structure that best serves the needs of its customers and fits its overall marketing strategy.

Sales force size

Once the company has set its structure, it is ready to consider *sales force size*. Sales forces may range in size from only a few salespeople to many tens of thousands. Some sales forces are huge – for example, Glaxo employs 34,000, PepsiCo 36,000, and The Hartford Financial Services Group, which sells investment and insurance services globally, employs a staggering 100,000. Across the 500 largest companies in the world, there are estimated to be 24 million salespeople.[6] Salespeople constitute one of the company's most productive – and most expensive – assets. Therefore, increasing their number will increase both sales and costs.

Many companies use some form of *workload approach* to set sales force size. Using this approach, a company first groups accounts into different classes according to size, account status or other factors related to the amount of effort required to maintain them. It then determines the number of salespeople needed to call on each class of accounts the desired number of times. The company might think as follows: Suppose we have 1,000 Type-A accounts and 2,000 Type-B accounts. Type-A accounts require 36 calls a year and Type-B accounts require 12 calls a year. In this case, the sales force's *workload* – the number of calls it must make per year – is 60,000 calls [(1,000 × 36) + (2,000 × 12) = 36,000 + 24,000 = 60,000]. Suppose our average salesperson can make 1,000 calls a year. Thus, the company needs 60 salespeople (60,000 ÷ 1,000).[7]

Other sales force strategy and structure issues

Sales management must also decide who will be involved in the selling effort and how various sales and sales support people will work together.

Outside and inside sales forces

The company may have an **outside sales force** (or field sales force), an **inside sales force**, or both. Outside salespeople travel to call on customers in the field. Inside salespeople conduct business from their offices via telephone, the Internet or visits from buyers.

Some inside salespeople provide support for the outside sales force, freeing it to spend more time selling to major accounts and finding new prospects. For example, *technical sales support people* provide technical information and answers to customers' questions. *Sales assistants* provide clerical back-up for outside salespeople. They call ahead and confirm appointments, follow up on deliveries and answer customers' questions when outside salespeople cannot be reached.

Other inside salespeople do more than just provide support. *Telemarketers* and *web sellers* use the phone and Internet to find new leads and qualify prospects or to sell and service accounts directly. Telemarketing and web selling can be very effective, less costly ways to sell to smaller, harder-to-reach customers. Depending on the complexity of the product and customer, for example, a telemarketer can make from 20 to 33 decision-maker contacts a day, compared with the average of 4 that an outside salesperson can make. And whereas an average business-to-business field sales call costs £170, a routine industrial telemarketing call costs only about £3 and a complex call about £10.[8]

For some smaller companies, telephone and web selling may be the primary sales approaches. However, larger companies also use these tactics. For example, IBM uses phone and Internet reps to pitch IBM solutions to and nurture relationships with its small and mid-size (SMB) customers. IBM's roughly 1,200 inside reps now generate 30 per cent of IBM's revenues from SMB clients.

For many types of products and selling situations, phone or web selling can be as effective as a personal sales call. Notes a DuPont telemarketer: 'I'm more effective on the phone. [When you're in the field], if some guy's not in his office, you lose an hour. On the phone, you lose 15 seconds. . . . Through my phone calls, I'm in the field as much as the rep is.' There are other advantages: 'Customers can't throw things at you,' quips the rep, 'and you don't have to outrun dogs.'[9] What is more, although they may seem impersonal, the phone and Internet can be surprisingly personal when it comes to building customer relationships.

Both inside and outside salespeople now have a growing array of tools at their disposal for interacting with and serving customers. For example, the Internet offers explosive potential for restructuring sales forces and conducting sales operations. More and more companies are now using the Internet to support their personal selling efforts – not just for selling, but for everything from training salespeople to conducting sales meetings and servicing accounts.

Team selling

As products become more complex, and as customers grow larger and more demanding, a single salesperson simply cannot handle all of a large customer's needs. Instead, most companies now use **team selling** to service large, complex accounts. Sales teams can unearth problems, solutions and sales opportunities that no individual salesperson could. Such teams might include experts from any area or level of the selling firm – sales, marketing, technical and support services, R&D, engineering, operations, finance and others. In team selling situations, the salesperson shifts from 'soloist' to 'orchestrator'.

In many cases, the move to team selling mirrors similar changes in customers' buying organisations. 'Today, we're calling on teams of buying people, and that requires more fire-power on our side,' says one sales vice president. 'One salesperson just can't do it all – can't be an expert in everything we're bringing to the customer. We have strategic account teams, led by customer business managers, who basically are our quarterbacks.'[10]

Some companies, such as IBM, Xerox and Procter & Gamble, have used teams for a long time. P&G sales reps are organised into 'customer business development (CBD) teams'. Each CBD team is assigned to a major P&G customer, such as Tesco, Sainsbury's or Boots. Teams consist of a customer business development manager, several account executives (each responsible for a specific category of P&G products) and specialists in marketing strategy, operations, information systems, logistics and finance. This organisation places the focus on serving the complete needs of each important customer. It lets P&G 'grow business by working as a "strategic partner" with our accounts, not just as a supplier. Our goal: to grow their business, which also results in growing ours.'[11]

Team selling does have some pitfalls. For example, selling teams can confuse or over-whelm customers who are used to working with only one salesperson. Salespeople who are used to having customers all to themselves may have trouble learning to work with and trust others on a team. Finally, difficulties in evaluating individual contributions to the team selling effort can create some sticky compensation issues.

Recruiting and selecting salespeople

At the heart of any successful sales force operation is the recruitment and selection of good salespeople. The performance difference between an average salesperson and a top salesperson can be substantial. In a typical sales force, the top 30 per cent of the salespeople might bring in 60 per cent of the sales. Thus, careful salesperson selection can greatly increase overall sales force performance. Beyond the differences in sales performance, poor selection results in costly turnover. When a salesperson quits, the costs of finding and training a new

Great salespeople: the best salespeople possess intrinsic motivation, disciplined work style and the ability to close a sale – not to mention the ability to build relationships with customers

Source: Schibsted/Gustav Martensson.

salesperson – plus the costs of lost sales – can be very high. Also, a sales force with many new people is less productive and turnover disrupts important customer relationships.[12]

What sets great salespeople apart from all the rest? In an effort to profile top sales performers, Gallup Management Consulting Group, a division of the well-known Gallup polling organisation, interviewed hundreds of thousands of salespeople. Its research suggests that the best salespeople possess four key talents: intrinsic motivation, disciplined work style, the ability to close a sale and, perhaps most important, the ability to build relationships with customers.

Super salespeople are motivated from within. 'Different things drive different people – pride, happiness, money, you name it,' says one expert. 'But all great salespeople have one thing in common: an unrelenting drive to excel.' Some salespeople are driven by money, a hunger for recognition or the satisfaction of competing and winning. Others are driven by the desire to provide service and to build relationships. The best salespeople possess some of each of these motivations.

Whatever their motivations, salespeople must also have a disciplined work style. If salespeople are not organised and focused, and if they do not work hard, they cannot meet the ever-increasing demands customers make these days. Great salespeople are tenacious about laying out detailed, organised plans, then following through in a timely, disciplined way. Says one sales trainer, 'Some people say it's all technique or luck. But luck happens to the best salespeople when they get up early, work late, stay up till two in the morning working on a proposal, or keep making calls when everyone is leaving at the end of the day.'

Other skills mean little if a salesperson cannot close the sale. So what makes for a great closer? For one thing, it takes unyielding persistence. 'Great closers are like great athletes,' says one sales trainer. 'They're not afraid to fail, and they don't give up until they close.' Great closers also have a high level of self-confidence and believe that they are doing the right thing.

Perhaps most important in today's relationship marketing environment, top salespeople are customer problem solvers and relationship builders. They have an instinctive understanding of their customers' needs. Talk to sales executives and they will describe top performers in these terms: Empathetic. Patient. Caring. Responsive. Good listeners. Honest. Top performers can put themselves on the buyer's side of the desk and see the world through their customers' eyes. They do not want just to be liked, they want to add value for their customers.

When recruiting, a company should analyse the sales job itself and the characteristics of its most successful salespeople to identify the traits needed by a successful salesperson in its industry. Then, it must recruit the right salespeople. The human resources department looks for applicants by getting names from current salespeople, using employment agencies, placing classified ads, searching the Web and working through college placement services. Another source is to attract top salespeople from other companies. Proven salespeople need less training and can be immediately productive.

Recruiting will attract many applicants from whom the company must select the best. The selection procedure can vary from a single informal interview to lengthy testing and interviewing. Many companies give formal tests to sales applicants. Tests typically measure sales aptitude, analytical and organisational skills, personality traits and other characteristics. But test scores provide only one piece of information in a set that includes personal characteristics, references, past employment history and interviewer reactions.

Training salespeople

New salespeople may spend anywhere from a few weeks or months to a year or more in training. Then, most companies provide continuing sales training via seminars, sales meetings and the Web throughout the salesperson's career.[13] Although training can be expensive, it can also yield dramatic returns. For example, one recent study showed that sales training conducted by a major telecommunications firm paid for itself in 16 days and resulted in a six-month return on investment of 812 per cent. Similarly, Nabisco analysed the return on its two-day professional selling programme, which teaches sales reps how to plan for and make professional presentations. Although it cost about £500 to put each sales rep through the programme, the training resulted in additional sales of more than £60,000 per rep and yielded almost £10,000 of additional profit per rep.[14]

Training programmes have several goals. First, salespeople need to know about customers and how to build relationships with them. So the training programme must teach them about different types of customers and their needs, buying motives and buying habits. And it must teach them how to sell effectively and train them in the basics of the selling process. Salespeople also need to know and identify with the company, its products and its competitors. So an effective training programme teaches them about the company's objectives, organisation, chief products and markets, and about the strategies of major competitors.

Today, many companies are adding web-based training to their sales training programmes. Such training may range from simple text-based product information to Internet-based sales exercises that build sales skills to sophisticated simulations that recreate the dynamics of real-life sales calls. Networking equipment and software maker Cisco Systems[15] has learned that using the Internet to train salespeople offers many advantages.

Keeping a large sales force up to speed on hundreds of complex, fast-changing products can be a daunting task. Under the old training process, newly hired Cisco salespeople travelled to a central location for several five-day training sessions each year. 'We used to fly people in and put them through a week of death-by-PowerPoint,' says a Cisco training executive. This approach involved huge programme-development and travel costs. Perhaps worse, it cost salespeople precious lost opportunity time spent away from their customers. To address these issues, Cisco launched an internal e-learning portal through which Cisco's salespeople around the world can plan, track, develop, and measure their skills and knowledge.

The e-learning site links salespeople to tens of thousands of web-based learning aids. Learning involves the blending of audio and video, live broadcasts of classes and straight content. Content can be turned into an MP3 file, viewed on-screen, downloaded to the computer, even printed out in magazine form. Under the e-learning system, Cisco can conduct a single training session that reaches up to 3,000 people at once, worldwide, by broadcasting it over the company's global intranet. Live events can then be archived as video-on-demand modules for viewers who missed the live broadcast. The system also provides electronic access to Cisco experts or 'e-mentors', who can respond via email or phone, or meet learners in a virtual lab, connect to their screens, and walk them through exercises. The e-learning portal has improved training by giving Cisco salespeople anywhere, anytime access to a vast system of training resources. At the same time, it has cut field-training costs by 40 per cent to 60 per cent while boosting salesperson 'face time' with customers by 40 per cent.[16]

Compensating salespeople

To attract good salespeople, a company must have an appealing compensation plan. Compensation is made up of several elements – a fixed amount, a variable amount, expenses and fringe benefits. The fixed amount, usually a salary, gives the salesperson some stable income. The variable amount, which might be commissions or bonuses based on sales performance, rewards the salesperson for greater effort and success.

Management must decide what *mix* of these compensation elements makes the most sense for each sales job. Different combinations of fixed and variable compensation give rise to four basic types of compensation plans: straight salary, straight commission, salary plus bonus, and salary plus commission. A study of sales force compensation plans showed that 70 per cent of all companies surveyed use a combination of base salary and incentives. The average plan consisted of about 60 per cent salary and 40 per cent incentive pay.[17]

The sales force compensation plan can both motivate salespeople and direct their activities. Compensation should direct the sales force towards activities that are consistent with overall marketing objectives. Table 13.1 illustrates how a company's compensation plan should reflect its overall marketing strategy. For example, if the strategy is to grow rapidly and gain market share, the compensation plan might include a larger commission component, coupled with a new account bonus to encourage high sales performance and new account development. In contrast, if the goal is to maximise current account profitability, the compensation plan might contain a larger base salary component with additional incentives for current account sales or customer satisfaction.

In fact, more and more companies are moving away from high-commission plans that may drive salespeople to make short-term grabs for business. They worry that a salesperson who is pushing too hard to close a deal may ruin the customer relationship. Instead, companies are designing compensation plans that reward salespeople for building customer relationships and growing the long-term value of each customer.

Supervising and motivating salespeople

New salespeople need more than a territory, compensation and training – they need supervision and motivation. The goal of *supervision* is to help salespeople 'work well' by doing the right things in the right ways. The goal of *motivation* is to encourage salespeople to 'work hard' and energetically towards sales force goals. If salespeople work well and work hard, they will realise their full potential, to their own and the company's benefit.

Companies vary in how closely they supervise their salespeople. Many help their salespeople to identify target customers and set call norms. Some may also specify how much

TABLE 13.1 The relationship between overall marketing strategy and sales force compensation

	Strategic goal		
	To gain market share rapidly	**To solidify market leadership**	**To maximise profitability**
Ideal salesperson	An independent self-starter	A competitive problem solver	A team player A relationship manager
Sales focus	Deal making Sustained high effort	Consultative selling	Account penetration
Compensation role	To capture accounts To reward high performance	To reward new and existing account sales	To manage the product mix To encourage team selling To reward account management

Source: Compensation and Benefits Review by Sam T. Johnson, Copyright © 1993 by Sage Publications. Reprinted by permission of Sage Publications.

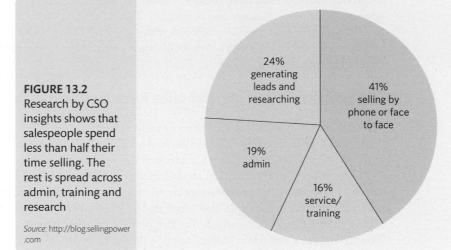

FIGURE 13.2
Research by CSO insights shows that salespeople spend less than half their time selling. The rest is spread across admin, training and research

Source: http://blog.sellingpower.com

time the sales force should spend prospecting for new accounts and set other time management priorities. One tool is the weekly, monthly or annual *call plan* that shows which customers and prospects to call on and which activities to carry out. Another tool is *time-and-duty analysis*. In addition to time spent selling, the salesperson spends time travelling, waiting, taking breaks and doing administrative chores.

Figure 13.2 shows how salespeople spend their time. On average, actual face-to-face selling time accounts for less than 30 per cent of total working time! Companies are always looking for ways to save time – simplifying record keeping, finding better sales call and routing plans, supplying more and better customer information, and using phones, email or video conferencing instead of travelling.

Many firms have adopted *sales force automation systems* – computerised, digitised sales force operations that let salespeople work more effectively at any time, anywhere. It is a rare salesman or woman who is not lugging around a laptop, smartphone containing customer contact and relationship management software. Armed with these technologies, salespeople can more effectively and efficiently profile customers and prospects, analyse and forecast sales, schedule sales calls, make presentations, prepare sales and expense reports, and manage account relationships. The result is better time management, improved customer service, lower sales costs and higher sales performance.[18]

Beyond directing salespeople, sales managers must also motivate them. Some salespeople will do their best without any special urging from management. To them, selling may be the most fascinating job in the world. But selling can also be frustrating. Salespeople often work alone and they must sometimes travel away from home. They may face aggressive competing salespeople and difficult customers. Therefore, salespeople often need special encouragement to do their best.

Management can boost sales force morale and performance through its organisational climate, sales quotas and positive incentives. *Organisational climate* describes the feeling that salespeople have about their opportunities, value and rewards for a good performance. Some companies treat salespeople as if they are not very important and performance suffers accordingly. Other companies treat their salespeople as valued contributors and allow virtually unlimited opportunity for income and promotion. Not surprisingly, these companies enjoy higher sales force performance and less staff turnover.[19]

Many companies motivate their salespeople by setting **sales quotas** – standards stating the amount they should sell and how sales should be divided among the company's products. Compensation is often related to how well salespeople meet their quotas. Companies also use various positive incentives to increase sales force effort. Sales meetings provide social occasions, breaks from routine, chances to meet and talk with 'company brass', and opportunities to air feelings and to identify with a larger group. Companies also sponsor *sales contests* to spur the sales force to make a selling effort above what would normally be expected. Other incentives include honours, merchandise and cash awards, trips and profit-sharing plans.

Evaluating salespeople and sales force performance

We have thus far described how management communicates what salespeople should be doing and how it motivates them to do it. This process requires good feedback. And good feedback means getting regular information about salespeople to evaluate their performance.

Management gets information about its salespeople in several ways. The most important source is *sales reports*, including weekly or monthly work plans and longer term territory marketing plans. Salespeople also write up their completed activities on *call reports* and submit *expense reports* for which they are partly or wholly repaid. The company can also monitor the sales and profit performance of the salesperson's territory. Additional information comes from personal observation, customer surveys and talks with other salespeople.

Using various sales force reports and other information, sales management evaluates members of the sales force. It evaluates salespeople on their ability to 'plan their work and work their plan'. Formal evaluation forces management to develop and communicate clear standards for judging performance. It also provides salespeople with constructive feedback and motivates them to perform well.

On a broader level, management should evaluate the performance of the sales force as a whole. Is the sales force accomplishing its customer relationship, sales and profit objectives? Is it working well with other areas of the marketing and company organisation? Are sales force costs in line with outcomes? As with other marketing activities, the company wants to measure its *return on sales investment*.

MAKING CONNECTIONS Linking the concepts

Take a break and re-examine your thoughts about salespeople and sales management.

- When someone says 'salesperson', what image comes to mind? Have your perceptions of salespeople changed after what you've just read? How? Be specific.

- Apply each of the steps in sales force management shown in Figure 13.1 to the chapter-opening Philips example.

- Find and talk with someone employed in professional sales. Ask about and report on how this salesperson's company designs its sales force and recruits, selects, trains, compensates, supervises and evaluates its salespeople. Would you like to work as a salesperson for this company?

THE PERSONAL SELLING PROCESS

We now turn from designing and managing a sales force to the actual personal selling process. The **selling process** consists of several steps that the salesperson must master. These steps focus on the goal of getting new customers and obtaining orders from them. However, most salespeople spend much of their time maintaining existing accounts and building long-term customer *relationships*. We discuss the relationship aspect of the personal selling process in a later section.

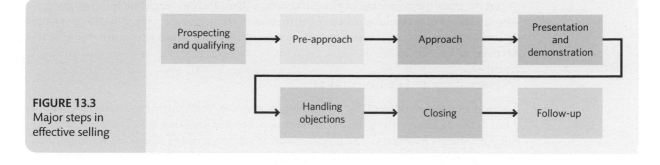

FIGURE 13.3
Major steps in effective selling

Steps in the selling process

As shown in Figure 13.3, the selling process consists of seven steps: prospecting and qualifying, pre-approach, approach, presentation and demonstration, handling objections, closing, and follow-up.

Prospecting and qualifying

The first step in the selling process is **prospecting** – identifying qualified potential customers. Approaching the right potential customers is crucial to selling success. As one expert puts it: 'If the sales force starts chasing anyone who is breathing and seems to have a budget, you risk accumulating a roster of expensive-to-serve, hard-to-satisfy customers who never respond to whatever value proposition you have.' He continues, 'The solution to this isn't rocket science. [You must] train salespeople to actively scout the right prospects.' Another expert concludes: 'Increasing your prospecting effectiveness is the fastest single way to boost your sales.'[20]

The salesperson must often approach many prospects to get just a few sales. Although the company supplies some leads, salespeople need skill in finding their own. The best source is referrals. Salespeople can ask current customers for referrals and cultivate other referral sources, such as suppliers, dealers, non-competing salespeople and bankers. They can also search for prospects in directories or on the Web and track down leads using the telephone and direct mail. Or they can drop in unannounced on various offices (a practice known as 'cold calling').

Salespeople also need to know how to *qualify* leads – that is, how to identify the good ones and screen out the poor ones. Prospects can be qualified by looking at their financial ability, volume of business, special needs, location and possibilities for growth.

Pre-approach

Before calling on a prospect, the salesperson should learn as much as possible about the organisation (what it needs, who is involved in the buying) and its buyers (their characteristics and buying styles). This step is known as the **pre-approach**. The salesperson can consult standard industry and online sources, acquaintances and others to learn about the company. The salesperson should set *call objectives,* which may be to qualify the prospect, to gather information or to make an immediate sale. Another task is to decide on the best approach, which might be a personal visit, a phone call or a letter. The best timing should be considered carefully because many prospects are busiest at certain times. Finally, the salesperson should give thought to an overall sales strategy for the account.

Approach

During the **approach** step, the salesperson should know how to meet and greet the buyer and get the relationship off to a good start. This step involves the salesperson's appearance, opening lines and the follow-up remarks. The opening lines should be positive to build goodwill from the beginning of the relationship. This opening might be followed by some key questions to learn more about the customer's needs or by showing a display or sample to attract the buyer's attention and curiosity. As in all stages of the selling process, listening to the customer is crucial.

Presentation and demonstration

During the **presentation** step of the selling process, the salesperson tells the product 'story' to the buyer, presenting customer benefits and showing how the product solves the customer's problems. The problem-solver salesperson fits better with today's marketing concept than does a hard-sell salesperson or the glad-handing extrovert. Buyers today want solutions, not smiles; results, not razzle-dazzle. They want salespeople who listen to their concerns, understand their needs, and respond with the right products and services.

This *need-satisfaction approach* calls for good listening and problem-solving skills. 'To me, sales is listening to customers, finding out what they want, finding out what their concerns are, and then trying to fill them,' notes one experienced salesperson. 'Listening is basically the foundation for success.' Another salesperson suggests, 'It's no longer enough to have a good relationship with a client. You have to understand their problems. You have to feel their pain.' One sales manager suggests that salespeople need to put themselves in their customers' shoes: 'Make yourself a customer and see first-hand how it feels,' he says.[21]

The qualities that buyers *dislike most* in salespeople include being pushy, late, deceitful, and unprepared or disorganised. The qualities they *value most* include good listening, empathy, honesty, dependability, thoroughness and follow-through. Great salespeople know how to sell, but more importantly they know how to listen and to build strong customer relationships.

Handling objections

Customers almost always have objections during the presentation or when asked to place an order. The problem can be either logical or psychological, and objections are often unspoken. In **handling objections,** the salesperson should use a positive approach, seek out hidden objections, ask the buyer to clarify any objections, take objections as opportunities to provide more information, and turn the objections into reasons for buying. Every salesperson needs training in the skills of handling objections.

Closing

After handling the prospect's objections, the salesperson now tries to close the sale. Some salespeople do not get around to **closing** or do not handle it well. They may lack confidence, feel guilty about asking for the order or fail to recognise the right moment to close the sale. Salespeople should know how to recognise closing signals from the buyer, including physical actions, comments and questions. For example, the customer might sit forward and nod approvingly or ask about prices and credit terms. Salespeople can use one of several closing techniques. They can ask for the order, review points of agreement, offer to help write up the order, ask whether the buyer wants this model or that one, or note that the buyer will lose out if the order is not placed now. The salesperson may offer the buyer special reasons to close, such as a lower price or an extra quantity at no charge.

Follow-up

The last step in the selling process – **follow-up** – is necessary if the salesperson wants to ensure customer satisfaction and repeat business. Right after closing, the salesperson should complete any details on delivery time, purchase terms and other matters. The salesperson then should schedule a follow-up call when the initial order is received, to make sure there is proper installation, instruction and servicing. This visit would reveal any problems, assure the buyer of the salesperson's interest and reduce any buyer concerns that might have arisen since the sale.

Personal selling and customer relationship management

The steps in the selling process as just described are *transaction oriented* – their aim is to help salespeople close a specific sale with a customer. But in most cases, the company is not simply seeking a sale: it has targeted a major customer that it would like to win and keep. The company would like to show that it has the capabilities to serve the customer over the long haul in a mutually profitable *relationship*. The sales force usually plays an important role in building and managing profitable customer relationships.

Today's large customers favour suppliers who can sell and deliver a coordinated set of products and services to many locations, and who can work closely with customer teams to improve products and processes. For these customers, the first sale is only the beginning of the relationship. Unfortunately, some companies ignore these relationship realities. They sell their products through separate sales forces, each working independently to close sales. Their technical people may not be willing to lend time to educate a customer. Their engineering, design and manufacturing people may have the attitude that 'it's our job to make good products and the salesperson's to sell them to customers'. Their salespeople focus on pushing products towards customers rather than listening to customers and providing solutions.

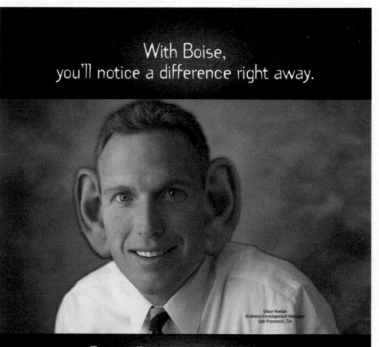

Building customer relationships: smart companies listen to customers, understand their needs and carefully coordinate the whole company's efforts towards creating customer value

Source: © Copyright 1994–2004 Boise Cascade Corporation. All rights reserved.

Other companies, however, recognise that winning and keeping accounts requires more than making good products and directing the sales force to close lots of sales. It requires listening to customers, understanding their needs, and carefully coordinating the whole company's efforts to create customer value and to build lasting relationships.

DIRECT MARKETING

Many of the marketing and promotion tools that we examined in previous chapters were developed in the context of *mass marketing:* targeting broad markets with standardised messages and offers distributed through intermediaries. Today, however, with the trend towards more narrowly targeted marketing, many companies are adopting *direct marketing,* either as a primary marketing approach or as a supplement to other approaches. We talked about this in the last chapter – *broadcasting vs narrowcasting.* In this section, we explore the world of direct marketing before the next chapter takes us on to the latest evolution in marketing communications – efforts based around the use of social media. The use of social media by marketers has generated so much attention that the fact that most marketing is still done by non-social media is sometimes forgotten.

Direct marketing consists of direct connections with carefully targeted individual consumers both to obtain an immediate response and to cultivate lasting customer relationships. Direct marketers communicate directly with customers, often on a one-to-one, interactive basis. Using detailed databases, they tailor their marketing offers and communications to the needs of narrowly defined segments or even individual buyers.

Beyond brand and image building, direct marketers usually seek a direct, immediate and measurable consumer response. For example, Dell interacts directly with customers, by telephone or through its website, to design built-to-order systems that meet customers' individual needs. Buyers order directly from Dell, and Dell quickly and efficiently delivers the new computers to their homes or offices.

The new direct marketing model

Early direct marketers – catalogue companies, direct mailers and telemarketers – gathered customer names and sold goods mainly by mail and telephone. Today, however, fired by rapid advances in database technologies and new marketing media – especially the Internet – direct marketing has undergone a dramatic transformation.

In previous chapters, we discussed direct marketing as direct distribution, as marketing channels that contain no intermediaries. We also included direct marketing as one element of the promotion mix, as an approach for communicating directly with consumers. In fact, direct marketing is both these things.

Most companies still use direct marketing as a supplementary channel or medium for marketing their goods. Thus, BMW markets mostly through mass-media advertising and its high-quality dealer network but also supplements these channels with direct marketing. Its direct marketing includes promotional materials mailed directly to prospective buyers and a web page (**www.bmw.com**) that provides consumers with information about various models, competitive comparisons, financing and dealer locations. Similarly, most department stores sell the majority of their merchandise off their store shelves but also sell through direct mail and online catalogues.

However, for many companies today, direct marketing is more than just a supplementary channel or medium. For these companies, direct marketing – especially in its most recent transformation, namely Internet marketing and e-commerce – constitutes a complete model for doing business. More than just another marketing channel or advertising medium, this new *direct model* is rapidly changing the way companies think about building relationships with customers. Indeed, if you did a survey of current marketing professionals and you asked them about the future of IMC, a large majority of the responses would include the phrases 'social media' and 'relationship building' – but we will leave that topic to be discussed fully later (see Chapter 14).

Rather than using direct marketing and the Internet only as supplemental approaches, firms employing the direct model use it as the only approach. Some of these companies, such as Dell, **Amazon.com** and eBay, began as only direct marketers. Other companies – such as Cisco Systems, Charles Schwab and many others – have transformed themselves into direct marketing superstars. One company that perhaps best exemplifies this new direct marketing model is Groupon (see Marketing at Work 13.1). Groupon has built its entire approach to the marketplace around direct marketing.

Groupon: making life less boring through direct marketing on the Web

MARKETING AT WORK 13.1

When 28-year-old Pittsburgh native and part-time Internet entrepreneur, Andrew Mason, decided to convert the old-fashioned coupon into an exciting online direct marketing system, the Internet had its next great thing. Groupon was born: an e-coupon website, aiming to connect neighbourhood businesses with prospective customers through deep discounts, distributed online by direct marketing.

With seed money from his former employer, Mason co-founded Groupon in 2008 and became its first CEO. Starting the business with a seven-man team in a small Chicagoan office, the basic premise of Groupon in its early days was to give lifestyle-conscious locals a daily recommendation on the trendiest things to do, eat, see or buy in their city. Local businesses ('merchants' in Groupon jargon) ranging from ice-cream shops to yoga studios to skydiving operators would be broadcast in a funny and striking way on Groupon's website for just a day. To get listed, merchants had to give a one-time price discount of at least 50 per cent on their products and services. In direct response to such a 'deal of the day', a minimum number of buyers – typically between 25 and 50 – had to sign up within 24 hours. If not enough people were interested, the deal would simply expire and no money changed hands. Provided the deal was on, buyers were charged automatically after the deal had ended and a printable voucher was emailed

The world's first Groupon: A daily deal for the Motel Bar, located just downstairs from the first Groupon office in Chicago, Illinois. After that first deal, businesses across the city were hooked and joined. Shortly thereafter, the company expanded into other cities across the USA, Canada and abroad. Within less than two years Groupon was on the spot in the major cities of 36 countries worldwide with more than 10,000 employees

Source: Courtesy of Groupon Inc.

to them. Shoppers could then individually redeem their 'Groupon' voucher, commonly within 6–12 months' time, at the featured merchant.

By putting this web-crafty twist on the boring old coupon and attaching cooperative purchasing to it, Groupon had created a powerful direct marketing medium attractive to brick-and-mortar businesses with limited marketing budgets and/or a lack of skill to advertise online on their own.

While buyers had the chance to explore hidden shopping and leisure gems of their city for a song, merchants mainly benefited from getting exposure to an untapped and, for them, widely inaccessible online target audience.

At the same time it was very convenient both to measure and to control overall effectiveness of a Groupon campaign for merchants. A successful deal automatically brought in a minimum amount of new customers. On the other hand, the desired maximum number could be capped in order to avoid running the risk of being swamped by massive surges of voucher holders. As opposed to classical advertising (such as printed newspaper ads) where one could only *hope* that initial expenditures turned into leads, Groupon's direct model delivered effective and traceable marketing results in terms of new customers. Similarly a Groupon campaign did not require any upfront costs. Yet for their middleman service, Groupon kept 50 per cent of the voucher's face value as a finder's fee. The other half was paid out to the merchants once they had returned all redeemed vouchers. Hence, in the end, merchants, customers and Groupon were all getting their slice of the pie.

Other businesses across Chicago caught on instantly after they had gotten wind of the business model's inherent win–win situation and Groupon began to open branches in various US and Canadian metropolises. Through major acquisitions of international clones (those firms having copied the website, but marketed it under a different name in other countries), Groupon also entered the international stage soon thereafter. By acquiring the German-based and already European-wide established Holtzbrinck venture, CityDeal, in early 2010, the company gained momentum in important European markets such as Germany, Austria, Switzerland, Italy, France, Belgium and the UK. By the end of 2010, Groupon had subsidiaries in the major cities of 36 countries worldwide with over 10,000 employees.

However, Groupon's stunningly rapid success was not entirely owed to the simple, yet equally clever website that featured discounted local goods and services utilising humorous copy. A further touch point with end buyers was maintained by email marketing, which was responsible for distributing the deals to customers' inboxes day in, day out. As Mason highlighted in 2011: 'the first thing we try to do when we're driving people to the site is to get them to sign up for our mailing list. The way we explain the value proposition to customers is: "Have an Email delivered to you every day with an awesome deal."'

What started as a simple mailing list in each city would soon turn into an extensive direct mail system built around Groupon's 'deal of the day' website supported by a comprehensive customer database. In fact, the company's database contained not only email addresses of Groupon subscribers, but also whole customer profiles which began to evolve based on demographic (age, gender, profession, yearly income), geographic (location), psychographic (interests) and behavioural (browsing and purchasing history) characteristics.

With Groupon having become more diversified over time in terms of featuring simultaneously a rich variety of deals from different categories and industries each day, the database became increasingly significant with regard to deal customisation. Hence, among other things, it was used to sketch personalised emails, previewing primarily those deals that were thought to be most appealing to the targeted customer. For example, a 26-year-old, single, female, Berlin-based university graduate with a yearly income of over €40,000 would have found in her inbox every morning a Groupon mail with links to deals such as: 'a wellness weekend at a regional day spa with a friend for 70% off' or a voucher for 'clothing at a fashion store in the hip Kreuzberg-district for 25€ worth 50€'.

Having embraced the online direct model to its heart, Groupon also invested heavily in online display advertising and Google adwords to encourage more people to subscribe. Groupon mainly placed banner ads on targeted websites, often in the form of pop-ups showing the Groupon logo and a 'call-to-action link'. By clicking on the link, prospective subscribers were redirected to the Groupon landing page in their region.

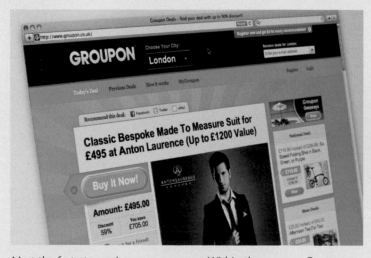

Meet the fastest-growing company ever: Within three years, Groupon cracked the $1bn revenue mark with its direct model, making Internet giants such as Amazon and Google look old

Source: Alamy Images/M4OS Photos.

With this highly effective direct marketing ecosystem entailing an e-coupon website in combination with direct email machinery and a customer database to push deals into the right market segments, Groupon became the new darling of the Internet press. Mason and his entourage were heralded as the 'fastest growing company ever' by *Forbes* Magazine and in November 2011 the company went public, valued at almost $13bn.

Nonetheless, sales slumped in the following months in virtually all markets and stock prices constantly fell after the IPO. As a consequence many critics of the business model appeared. Did the company grow too fast? Was the direct model not sustainable at all? Horror stories of dissatisfied merchants whose businesses capsized under mammoth waves of voucher holders due to poor consulting by a pressurised Groupon salesforce made the rounds. Further, analysts blamed the company for creating 'voucher fatigue' thanks to floods of emails in customers' inboxes.

Groupon's management reacted by starting to relaunch its US website with a different design and transforming it into a searchable and browsable 'deal marketplace'. Shortly thereafter overseas operations did the same. With the new design and functionality, customers could instantly search for specific local shopping activities of their interest, instead of waiting for them to arrive in their mailboxes at some point. The collective buying element was dropped out of Groupon's business apparatus and deals would run longer without disappearing immediately after they had expired. This gave buyers more flexibility and merchants benefited from being incorporated into Google's search indexes after a period of time.

'Groupon has mastered serendipity, but it has not always been good at giving people a place to shop for things they are already looking to buy,' summarised Jeff Holden, Senior Vice President of Product Management, these moves being necessary both to counteract decreasing sales and to respond to rapidly changing consumer needs in the digital landscape.

In line with a new 'marketplace' strategy, customers were also encouraged to browse through a vast array of both discounted product goods and travel offerings stocked in Groupon's own inventories. These were available on a national basis and delivered to buyers' homes via Groupon's free delivery service. The newly launched direct-to-consumer retail sales arm, Groupon Goods, and travel channel Groupon Getaways made it possible.

As a consequence, Groupon has undergone a major transformation from a sole local 'deal-of-a-day' intermediary to an online retail outlet and discount travel agent using a comprehensive web-based catalogue to market directly to consumers. As of late, this online catalogue still relies on a vast array of traditional local deals, yet is increasingly displaying a variety of Groupon-owned inventory, spanning categories such as food, health, fitness, home, technology, auto, leisure and travel offerings via both the Goods and Getaways channels.

In summary, Groupon has shifted its entire strategy from the previously email-based push model to a more pull-oriented marketplace approach where customers decide when and what to buy. To complement this approach of letting customers actively seek out their preferred offerings, more emphasis is being put on the Groupon app on mobile devices. The company intends to become the benchmark for mobile commerce in the near future with its web-based

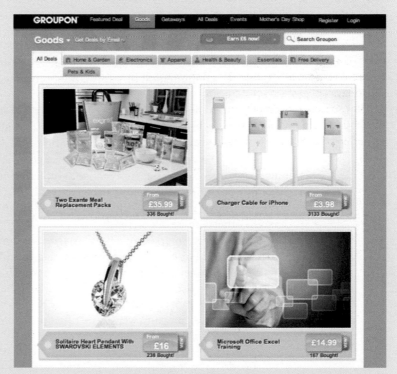

Transformation from local e-coupon website to online catalogue: In addition to daily local deals, Groupon features through Groupon Goods and Getaways a wide variety of quality inventory at a discount ranging from diamond jewellery and designer sunglasses to mattresses, computer tablets, 3D HDTVs, toys and travel packages

Source: Groupon UK, 2014.

catalogue of discounted local and nationwide offerings. 'We have the chance to be one of the truly great Internet businesses of the world and maybe the great mobile-commerce company of the next decade,' says Eric Lefkovsky, successor CEO to the rich and retired Andrew Mason.

By early 2014 nearly 50 per cent of global transactions were completed on mobile devices and more than 70 million people had downloaded the Groupon app worldwide. By contrast, direct email accounted for less than 40 per cent of North American transactions in 2013. Despite these promising numbers, the goal of becoming the starting point for all mobile commerce may be seen as overambitious. According to an industry analyst: 'the goods and travel markets that Groupon wants to succeed in are extremely competitive with very well-entrenched competitors, such as Amazon, eBay, Priceline or Expedia.'

It will be interesting to see if Groupon can bear up against these giant competitors with their new direct pull model in the near future. One thing is certain: the past has shown that Groupon is always good for a fresh and exciting surprise, which is in line with Andrew Mason's claim: 'Life is too short to be a boring company. . .'

Sources: This case was compiled using information from the Groupon corporate website, its international homepages (Germany and the UK) and annual reports available at www.groupon.com

Benefits and growth of direct marketing

Whether employed as a complete business model or as a supplement to a broader integrated marketing mix, direct marketing brings many benefits to both buyers and sellers. As a result, direct marketing is growing very rapidly.

For buyers, direct marketing is convenient, easy to use and private. From the comfort of their homes or offices, they can browse mail catalogues or company websites at any time of the day or night. Direct marketing gives buyers ready access to a wealth of products and information, at home and around the globe. Finally, direct marketing is immediate and interactive – buyers can interact with sellers by phone or on the seller's website to create exactly the configuration of information, products or services they desire, then order them on the spot.

For sellers, direct marketing is a powerful tool for building customer relationships. Using database marketing, today's marketers can target small groups or individual consumers, tailor offers to individual needs, and promote these offers through personalised communications. Direct marketing can also be timed to reach prospects at just the right moment. Because of its one-to-one, interactive nature, the Internet is an especially potent direct marketing tool. Direct marketing also gives sellers access to buyers that they could not reach through other channels. For example, the Internet provides access to *global* markets that might otherwise be out of reach.

Finally, direct marketing can offer sellers a low-cost, efficient alternative for reaching their markets. For example, direct marketing has grown rapidly in B2B marketing, partly in response to the ever-increasing costs of marketing through the sales force. When personal sales calls can cost £170 per contact, they should be made only when necessary and to high-potential customers and prospects. Lower cost-per-contact media – such as telemarketing, direct mail and company websites – often prove more cost effective in reaching and selling to more prospects and customers.

As a result of these advantages to both buyers and sellers, direct marketing has become the fastest-growing form of marketing. According to the Direct Marketing Association, more than one pound in eight spent on promotion is spent on direct marketing in the UK, with billions of items mailed out annually.

Customer databases and direct marketing

Effective direct marketing begins with a good customer database. A **customer database** is an organised collection of comprehensive data about individual customers or prospects, including geographic, demographic, psychographic and behavioural data. The database gives companies 'a snapshot of how customers look and behave'. A good customer database can be a potent relationship-building tool. 'If there's been any change in the past decade it's the knowledge we now can have about our customers,' says one expert. 'Strategically, the most essential tool is our customer database. A company is no better than what it knows.'[22]

Many companies confuse a customer database with a customer mailing list. A customer mailing list is simply a set of names, addresses and telephone numbers. A customer database contains much more information. In consumer marketing, the customer database might contain a customer's demographics (age, income, family members, birthdays), psychographics (activities, interests and opinions) and buying behaviour (buying preferences and the recency, frequency and monetary value – RFM – of past purchases).[23] In B2B marketing, the customer profile might contain the products and services the customer has bought; past volumes and prices; key contacts (and their ages, birthdays, hobbies and favourite foods); competitive suppliers; status of current contracts; estimated customer spending for the next few years; and assessments of competitive strengths and weaknesses in selling and servicing the account.

Some of these databases are huge. Dunnhumby, who manage database services on behalf of Tesco, have a database codenamed 'Crucible':

> The company refuses to reveal the information it holds, yet Tesco is selling access to this database to other big consumer groups, such as Sky, Orange and Gillette. 'It contains details of every consumer in the UK at their home address across a range of demographic, socio-economic and lifestyle characteristics,' says the marketing blurb of Dunnhumby, the Tesco subsidiary in question. It has 'added intelligent profiling and targeting' to its data through a software system called Zodiac. This profiling can rank your enthusiasm for promotions, your brand loyalty, whether you are a 'creature of habit' and when you prefer to shop.[24]

Companies use their databases in many ways. They use databases to locate good potential customers and to generate sales leads. They can mine their databases to learn about customers in detail, and then fine-tune their market offerings and communications to the special preferences and behaviours of target segments or individuals. In all, a company's database can be an important tool for building stronger long-term customer relationships.

> When it revealed that families were not buying nappies or other baby supplies in their weekly shop, further research showed they were instead paying some 20 per cent more to buy these items at nearby Boots pharmacies because they trusted the Boots brand when it came to looking after their babies. So Tesco began a baby club, offering advice on pregnancy and mothering. Within two years almost four of every ten expectant parents in Britain were members and the firm had seized almost a quarter of the mother and baby market.
>
> Some quirky correlations also pop out of the data. Take the fact that families buying baby wipes also buy more beer, mainly because fathers of young children have less time to go to the pub. Tesco's response: mailing families with infants discount coupons for toys and beer.[25]

Like many other marketing tools, database marketing requires a special investment. Companies must invest in computer hardware, database software, analytical programs, communication links and skilled personnel. The database system must be user friendly and available to various marketing groups, including those in product and brand management, new-product development, advertising and promotion, direct mail, telemarketing, web marketing, field sales, order fulfilment and customer service. A well-managed database should lead to sales and customer relationship gains that will more than cover its costs.

Intrusions by governmental institutions into personal data have been a hot topic recently. Facebook, Google and a number of other firms have been found to allow access to personal and private messages to both US and European security services. Such actions have unsurprisingly raised concerns among users of those online services. What is less well known is that such agencies also have access to data held by Dunnhumby from Tesco Clubcards. From this statistical experts have been able to produce models predicting who is, and who is not, a likely terrorist based on shopping data that is believed to be extremely accurate – especially when compared with other types of data where unpleasant behaviours and intentions might be deliberately masked.

Forms of direct marketing

The major forms of direct marketing – as shown in Figure 13.4 – include personal selling, telephone marketing, direct mail marketing, catalogue marketing, direct response TV marketing, kiosk marketing and online marketing. We examined personal selling in depth earlier in this chapter and will look closely at online marketing later (see Chapter 14). Here, we examine the other direct marketing forms.

Telephone marketing

Telephone marketing involves using the telephone to sell directly to consumers and business customers. B2B marketers use telephone marketing extensively, accounting for more than 60 per cent of all telephone marketing sales.

Marketers use *outbound* telephone marketing to sell directly to consumers and businesses. *Inbound* Freefone 0800 numbers are used to receive orders from TV and print ads, direct mail or catalogues. The use of 0800 numbers has taken off in recent years as more and more companies have begun using them.

Properly designed and targeted telemarketing provides many benefits, including purchasing convenience and increased product and service information. However, the explosion in unsolicited outbound telephone marketing over the years annoys many consumers, who object to the almost daily 'junk phone calls' that stop them getting on with their lives. In the UK, a further problem was created by what are termed 'silent calls'. Silent calls occur

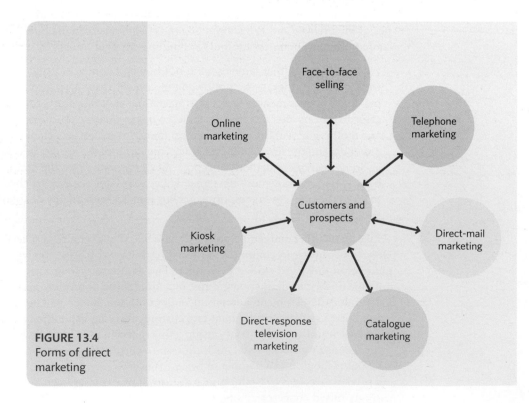

FIGURE 13.4
Forms of direct marketing

when automated calling systems, used by call centres for telemarketing, market research, debt collection and other purposes, generate more calls than the available call centre agents can deal with. When the person dialled answers the telephone, there is no agent available, resulting in silence on the line. These abandoned calls can cause significant anxiety and annoyance. This was a special concern with vulnerable groups like the elderly and young children. In response to this, Ofcom, the government body responsible for regulating the communications sector, changed its policy and now has much stricter control over the telemarketing industry – with heavy fines for those that break the rules.[26] Additionally, residents can now opt out of receiving telemarketing calls by subscribing to the database managed by the Telephone Preference Service[27] – a related group to the Mail Preference Service to be discussed shortly.

A number of large UK businesses have suffered severe government-imposed sanctions as punishments for mis-selling financial services products such as payment protection insurance and mortgages to millions of customers. As of late 2014, the current total of compensation paid out runs to £18bn.[28] This mis-selling occurred when vulnerable or ignorant customers were unfairly treated by sales agents, and usually this happened by phone rather than face to face. This crisis has created severe challenges for the industry body, the Institute of Direct Marketing.[29]

Two major forms of telemarketing – inbound consumer telemarketing and outbound B2B telemarketing – remain strong and growing. Interestingly, preference lists appear to be helping most direct marketers more than they are hurting them. Many of these marketers are shifting their call centre activity from making cold calls on often resentful customers to managing existing customer relationships. They are developing 'opt-in' calling systems, in which customers invite phone, email and other contacts that provide useful information and offers. These 'sales tactics have [produced] results as good as – or even better than – telemarketing,' declares one analyst. 'The opt-in model is proving [more] valuable for marketers [than] the old invasive one.'[30]

Direct mail marketing

Direct mail marketing involves sending an offer, announcement, reminder or other item to a person at a particular address. Using highly selective mailing lists, direct marketers send out millions of mail pieces each year – letters, ads, brochures, samples or audio-visual carrying media such as pendrives.

Direct mail is well suited to direct, one-to-one communication. It permits high target market selectivity, can be personalised, is flexible and allows easy measurement of results. Although the cost per thousand people reached is higher than with mass media such as TV or magazines, the people who are reached are much better prospects. Direct mail has proved successful in promoting all kinds of products, from books, magazine subscriptions and insurance to gift items, clothing, gourmet foods and industrial products. Direct mail is also used heavily by charities to raise millions of pounds each year.

The Direct Mail Information Service (DMIS) recently produced a list of factors which make direct mail recipients more likely to respond. These factors, phrased as a list of statements with which customers could agree or disagree, included:[31]

- I'm already a customer/have dealt with the company – 73.4 per cent
- I feel it is relevant to me – 72.3 per cent
- I have heard of the brand name – 69.4 per cent
- I am interested in/considering this type of product/service – 68.4 per cent
- It is correctly addressed – 67.5 per cent
- It looks like it contains a free sample – 62.9 per cent
- It has the name of the company on the envelope – 62.6 per cent

In the past, all direct mail was paper based and sent through the post. Recently, however, new forms of delivery have become popular, such as *voice mail* and *email*. Voice mail is subject to the same preference list restrictions as telemarketing, so its use has been limited in recent years. However, email is booming as a direct marketing tool. Today's email messages have moved far beyond the drab text-only messages of old. The new breed of email ad uses animation, interactive links, streaming video and personalised audio messages to reach out and grab attention. You may think of email as being old hat compared with social media and instant messaging, but you must remember that Twitter and WhatsApp are minority pursuits, and the vast bulk of the population are not sophisticated users of these platforms but are still using email daily.

Email and other new forms deliver direct mail at incredible speeds compared with a post office's 'snail mail' pace. Yet, much like mail delivered through traditional channels, they may be resented as 'junk mail' or spam if sent to people who have no interest in them. For this reason, smart marketers are targeting their direct mail carefully so as not waste their money and recipients' time. They are designing permission-based programs, sending email ads only to those who want to receive them.

Companies like Groupon are exploiting these trends – matching their large databases of customers with local businesses that want to promote themselves but do not have the resources or skill to do so alone.[32]

Catalogue marketing

Advances in technology, along with the move towards personalised, one-to-one marketing, have resulted in exciting changes in **catalogue marketing**.

With the stampede to the Internet, more and more catalogues are going digital. Most print cataloguers have added web-based catalogues to their marketing mixes, and a variety of new web-only cataloguers have emerged. One recent study found that consumers now make 36 per cent of their catalogue purchases online. However, although the Internet has provided a new avenue for catalogue sales, all you have to do is check your post to know that printed catalogues remain the primary medium. Research shows that print catalogues generate many of those online orders. Customers who receive print catalogues are more likely to buy online, and they spend more than customers who did not receive catalogues.

Catalogue marketing has grown explosively during the past 25 years. Some newer companies like Boden and The White Company have used it to establish themselves – their target markets appreciate a printed catalogue and are not enthusiastic users of the Internet.[33] Some large retailers – such as Argos and Next – sell a full line of merchandise through catalogues. IKEA annually prints 38 different editions of its catalogue, in 17 languages and distributed in 28 countries – the number printed per year is estimated at 175 million – three times the number of bibles.[34] In recent years, these giants have been challenged by thousands of speciality catalogues that serve highly specialised market niches. Consumers can buy just about anything from a catalogue. The N. Brown group of companies includes firms that produce catalogues focusing on fashion for the over 50s and footwear for those with larger than typical feet. Birkenstock has been selling its sandals across Germany and the rest of the world through a catalogue for the last 30 years.

Web-based catalogues present a number of benefits compared with printed catalogues. They save on production, printing and mailing costs. Whereas print catalogue space is limited, online catalogues can offer an almost unlimited amount of merchandise. Web catalogues also allow real-time merchandising: products and features can be added or removed as needed, and prices can be adjusted instantly to match demand. Finally, online catalogues can be spiced up with interactive entertainment and promotional features, such as games, contests and daily specials.

Along with the benefits, however, web-based catalogues also present challenges. Whereas a print catalogue is intrusive and creates its own attention, web catalogues are passive and must be marketed. Attracting new customers is much more difficult for a web catalogue than for a print catalogue. Thus, even cataloguers who are sold on the Web are not likely to abandon their print catalogues.

Direct response TV marketing

Direct response TV marketing takes one of two major forms. The first is *direct response advertising*. Direct marketers air TV ads, often 60 or 120 seconds long, which persuasively describe a product and give customers a free-phone number or website for ordering. TV viewers also often encounter (usually when they should be in bed) full 30-minute or longer advertising programmes, or *infomercials*, for a single product.

For years, infomercials have been associated with somewhat questionable pitches for juicers and other kitchen gadgets, get-rich-quick schemes and nifty ways to stay in shape without working very hard at it. Traditionally, they have 'almost been the Wild West of advertising, where people make rules for themselves as they go along,' says Jack Kirby, Chairman of the Electronic Retailing Association.[35] In recent years, however, a number of large companies – Johnson & Johnson, Procter & Gamble, Disney, Revlon, IBM, Land Rover, Anheuser-Busch – have begun using infomercials to sell their wares over the phone, refer customers to retailers, send out coupons and product information, recruit members or attract buyers to their websites. An estimated 20 per cent of all new infomercials now come to you courtesy of Fortune 1000 companies.[36] According to Kirby, it is 'time to really set some standards and move forward'.

Direct response TV commercials are usually cheaper to make and the media purchase is less costly. Moreover, results are easily measured. Unlike most media campaigns, direct response ads always include an 0800 number or web address, making it easier for marketers to track the impact of their pitches.

Home shopping channels, another form of direct response TV marketing, are TV programmes or entire channels dedicated to selling goods and services. Some home shopping channels, such as the Quality Value Channel (QVC), Price-drop TV and Ideal World, broadcast 24 hours a day – the advent of digital TV and set-top boxes giving them time and space. On QVC, the programme's hosts offer bargain prices on products ranging from jewellery, lamps, collectable dolls and clothing to power tools and consumer electronics – usually obtained by the home shopping channel at close-out prices. QVC estimates it has a reach of 200 million households worldwide.[37]

Kiosk marketing

As consumers become more comfortable with computer and digital technologies, many companies are placing information and ordering machines – called *kiosks* (in contrast to vending machines, which dispense actual products) – in stores, airports and other locations. Kiosks are popping up everywhere these days, from self-service hotel and airline check-in devices to in-store ordering kiosks that let you order merchandise not carried in the store.

In-store Fujifilm kiosks let customers transfer pictures from memory sticks, mobile phones and other digital storage devices, edit them and make high-quality colour prints. Jessops has kiosks in its own and other stores that allow customers to edit, manage and print digital photographs. Kiosks in Boots stores allow customers to print out personalised coupons for special offers. BMI uses kiosks for check-in procedures for those passengers with hand luggage only who do not want to queue. Similar systems for tickets are available at many cinemas. Argos uses kiosks to let customers check if an item is in stock – the catalogue and the kiosk work together to reduce significantly the cost-to-serve of a typical customer. Should you enter an unemployment office, it is likely you will be able to use a kiosk that will help you sift through the job and training vacancy options. Some high-street music retailers are experimenting with kiosks that allow customers to choose between the physical media of a CD or an equivalent set of MP3 tracks that can be immediately added to a player – all before the customer leaves the store.[38]

MAKING CONNECTIONS Linking the concepts

Hold up a moment and think about the impact of direct marketing on your life.

● When was the last time you *bought* something via direct marketing? What did you buy and why did you buy it direct? When was the last time you *rejected* a direct marketing offer? Why did you reject it? Based on these experiences, what advice would you give to direct marketers?

● For the next week, keep track of all the direct marketing offers that come your way via direct mail and catalogues, telephone, direct response TV and the Internet. Then analyse the offers by type, source, and what you liked or disliked about each offer and the way it was delivered. Which offer best hit its target (you)? Which missed by the widest margin?

Integrated direct marketing

Too often, a company's different direct marketing efforts are not well integrated with one another or with other elements of its marketing and promotion mixes. For example, a firm's media advertising may be handled by the advertising department working with a traditional advertising agency. Meanwhile, its direct mail and catalogue business may be handled by direct marketing specialists, while its website is developed and operated by an outside Internet firm. Even within a given direct marketing campaign, too many companies use only a 'one-shot' effort to reach and sell to a prospect or a single vehicle in multiple stages to trigger purchases.

A more powerful approach is **integrated direct marketing**, which involves using carefully coordinated multiple-media, multiple-stage campaigns. Such campaigns can greatly improve response. Whereas a direct mail piece alone might generate a 2 per cent response, adding a website and free-phone phone number might raise the response rate by 50 per cent. Then, a well-designed outbound email campaign might lift response by an additional 500 per cent. Suddenly, a 2 per cent response has grown to 15 per cent or more by adding interactive marketing channels to a regular mailshot.

More elaborate integrated direct marketing campaigns can be used. Consider the multi-media, multi-stage campaign shown in Figure 13.5. Here, the paid ad creates product awareness and stimulates phone, mail or web enquiries. The company immediately sends direct mail or email responses to those who enquire. Within a few days, the company follows up with an outbound telemarketing call or email seeking an order. Some prospects will order by phone or on the company's website; others might request a face-to-face sales call. In such a campaign, the marketer seeks to improve response rates and profits by adding media and stages that contribute more to additional sales than to additional costs.

We saw earlier how Dell has mastered direct marketing, but that is a huge organisation with a lot of resources. Can direct marketing be implemented by smaller companies, and can

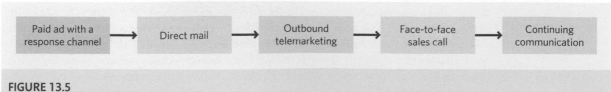

FIGURE 13.5
An integrated direct marketing campaign

they successfully integrate it with other elements of their promotion mix? In Marketing at Work 13.2 one small businessman reflects on his recent experiences. Groupon – a company we have already mentioned – acts as an intermediary, allowing small or local businesses to use powerful direct marketing techniques.

Armorica Cookware: integrated direct marketing in a small firm

MARKETING AT WORK 13.2

Armorica is a specialist cookware retailer based in Petersfield, Hampshire. Owners Bill and Valerie Brown have recently started direct marketing to publicise both their high-street outlet and complementary online shop. Bill describes the methods used and how the campaigns have increased sales:

> We had been advertising in some of the bigger home magazines for a while, but it was expensive and we weren't getting the response rates we'd hoped for. We investigated several direct-marketing methods and decided to start with a leaflet drop.
>
> Our trade organisation, the British Hardware Federation (BHF), produces a twice-yearly product catalogue for members. The catalogue is printed by the BHF with several pages of generic content but is tailored for individual retailers with logos and outlet-specific information.

Armorica retails a wide range of kitchen gadgets and utensils

Source: Alamy Images/Foodfolio.

> You end up with a professional-looking sales tool at a fraction of the price of doing it all yourself. We did an initial drop of 15,000 leaflets to local addresses. In the month following the drop, we experienced a 35 per cent uplift in sales compared to the previous year.
>
> We have a database of over 600 customers, managed by our web design company, and we're especially careful to abide by the opt-out rules that prohibit contacting customers who have asked not to be sent information.
>
> We send out a six-weekly Armorica newsletter to all eligible contacts, updating them on new products and special offers in-store and on the website. To add value and encourage retention, we also include a practical article in each issue, for example, tips on how to choose good kitchen knives.
>
> We regularly review our direct-marketing activities to assess the return on investment. While you have to put your money where your mouth is and try new things, you also need to know you're not wasting resources. We ask for customer feedback and track sales volumes following each activity.
>
> Direct marketing is only as good as the quality of the material you send out. If a particular leaflet drop or newsletter isn't as successful as we'd hoped, we'll look at ways to develop it, for example by including a voucher redeemable by quoting a reference number or bringing the leaflet into the shop.
>
> We're fortunate that our products are of universal appeal to most households, so 'blanket mailing' our database has been quite successful. However, certain product categories appeal more to certain types of customer, so we're looking at ways to segment our database and target specific groups.
>
> When we started the website last year, we initially thought that it would have to be marketed separately to the shop. With experience, we found that the two sales channels complement rather than compete with each other, so we now use direct marketing to promote both.

Source: Adapted from 'Here's How Direct Marketing Improved my Business', available at www.businesslink.gov.uk; visit Armorica online at www.armorica.co.uk

Public policy and ethical issues in direct marketing

Direct marketers and their customers usually enjoy mutually rewarding relationships. Occasionally, however, a darker side emerges. The aggressive and sometimes shady tactics of a few direct marketers can bother or harm consumers, giving the entire industry a black eye. Abuses range from simple excesses that irritate consumers to instances of unfair practices or even outright deception and fraud. The direct marketing industry has also faced growing concerns about invasion of privacy issues.

Irritation, unfairness, deception and fraud

Direct marketing excesses sometimes annoy or offend consumers. Most of us dislike direct response TV commercials that are too loud, too long and too insistent. Especially bothersome are dinnertime or late-night phone calls. Beyond irritating consumers, some direct marketers have been accused of taking unfair advantage of impulsive or less sophisticated buyers. TV shopping channels and programme-long 'infomercials' targeting TV-addicted shoppers seem to be the worst culprits. They feature smooth-talking hosts, elaborately staged demonstrations, claims of drastic price reductions, 'while they last' time limitations, and unequalled ease of purchase to tempt buyers who have low sales resistance. Even well-known direct mailers have been accused of deceiving consumers.

Other direct marketers pretend to be conducting research surveys when they are actually asking leading questions to screen or persuade consumers. Fraudulent schemes, such as investment scams or phoney collections for charity, have also multiplied in recent years. Crooked direct marketers can be hard to catch: direct marketing customers often respond quickly, do not interact personally with the seller and usually expect to wait for delivery. By the time buyers realise that they have been duped, the thieves are usually somewhere else plotting new schemes. The modern-day evolution of mail fraud is known as 'click-fraud' – rather than a bogus letter, an email or website is used to extract personal financial details or is part of any number of online scams.[39]

Invasion of privacy

Invasion of privacy is perhaps the toughest public policy issue now confronting the direct marketing industry. These days, it seems that almost every time consumers enter a prize draw, apply for a credit card, take out a magazine subscription, or order products by mail, telephone or the Internet, their names are entered into some company's already bulging database. Using sophisticated computer technologies, direct marketers can use these databases to 'micro-target' their selling efforts.

Consumers often benefit from such database marketing – they receive more offers that are closely matched to their interests. However, many critics worry that marketers may know *too* much about consumers' lives and that they may use this knowledge to take unfair advantage of consumers. At some point, they claim, the extensive use of databases intrudes on consumer privacy.

For example, they ask, should BT be allowed to sell marketers the names of customers who frequently call the 0800 numbers of catalogue companies? Should a company such as American Express be allowed to make data on its millions of cardholders worldwide available to merchants who accept AmEx cards? Is it right for credit bureaux to compile and sell lists of people who have recently applied for credit cards – people who are considered prime direct marketing targets because of their spending behaviour?

In their drives to build databases, companies sometimes get carried away. For example, when first introduced, Intel's Pentium III chip contained an embedded serial number that allowed the company to trace users' equipment. When privacy advocates complained, Intel disabled the feature. Similarly, Microsoft caused substantial privacy concerns when one version of its Windows software used a 'Registration Wizard' that snooped into users' computers. When users went online to register, without their knowledge Microsoft 'read' the configurations of their PCs to learn about the major software products they were running. When this became known, users protested loudly and Microsoft abandoned the practice. These days, it is not only the large companies that can access such private information. The explosion of IT has put these capabilities into the hands of almost any business. Such access to and use of information has caused much concern and debate among companies, consumers and public policy makers. Consumer privacy has become a major regulatory issue.

If you use iTunes, then you will probably be familiar with the 'Genius' component. iTunes uses software and your history of past purchases to suggest other tracks you might like to buy. This selection will be constructed by an assessment of your previous purchases and tracks played using the iTunes player – even if not bought from Apple – and those tracks bought by other similar customers. Amazon does something similar – calling it *'the page that you made'*. In 2007, Apple started selling what it called 'DRM-free' tracks. Each track sold is labelled electronically, and should the music end up on a file-sharing service, Apple will be able to detect to whom it was originally sold.[40]

The direct marketing industry is addressing issues of ethics and public policy. The Federation of Direct and Interactive Marketing Associations (FEDMA) is the industry body of the European direct marketing industry. Its national members are direct marketing associations (DMAs) representing users, service providers and media/carriers of direct marketing. FEDMA also has more than 200 direct company members. FEDMA has a mosaic of self-regulatory schemes, many of which are to do with industry standards in respect of personal privacy and personal data management and control.[41] Most European countries operate what are known as 'preference services' which allow individuals (and companies) to signify that they do not want to receive 'junk mail'. In some cases these services are run by the state, in others by national direct marketing industry bodies. In the UK, for example, the Direct Marketing Association runs the Mailing Preference Service, while in the Czech Republic it is run by ADMAZ and in France by FEVAD.[42] Take-up of these services varies wildly by country. In the UK, more than 1.8 million people have signed on, but in Ireland it is less than 1,000.

Direct marketers know that, left unaddressed, such problems will lead to increasingly negative consumer attitudes, lower response rates, and calls for more restrictive local and national legislation. 'Privacy and customer permission have become the cornerstones of customer trust, [and] trust has become the cornerstone to a continuing relationship,' says one expert. Companies must 'become the custodians of customer trust and protect the privacy of their customers'.[43]

Most direct marketers want the same things that consumers want: honest and well-designed marketing offers targeted only towards consumers who will appreciate and respond to them. Direct marketing is just too expensive to waste on consumers who do not want it.

THE JOURNEY YOU'VE TAKEN Reviewing the concepts

Let's revisit this chapter's key concepts. The chapter is the second of two chapters covering the final marketing mix element – promotion. The previous chapter dealt with advertising, sales promotion and public relations. This one investigates personal selling and direct marketing.

Personal selling and direct marketing are both direct tools for persuasively communicating customer value and building customer relationships. Selling is the interpersonal arm of the communications mix. To be successful in personal selling, a company must first build and then manage an effective sales force. Firms must also be good at direct marketing, the process of forming one-to-one connections with customers. Today, many companies are turning to direct marketing in an effort to reach carefully targeted customers more efficiently and to build stronger, more personal, one-to-one relationships with them.

1   Discuss the role of a company's salespeople in creating value for customers and building customer relationships

Most companies use salespeople, and many companies assign them an important role in the marketing mix. For companies selling business products, the firm's salespeople work directly with customers. Often, the sales force is the customer's only direct contact with the company and therefore may be viewed by customers as representing the company itself. In contrast, for consumer product companies that sell through intermediaries, consumers usually do not meet salespeople or even know about them. The sales force works behind the scenes, dealing with wholesalers and retailers to obtain their support and help them become effective in selling the firm's products.

As an element of the promotion mix, the sales force is very effective in achieving certain marketing objectives and carrying out such activities as prospecting, communicating, selling and servicing, and information gathering. But with companies becoming more market oriented, a customer-focused sales force also works to produce both *customer satisfaction* and *company profit*. The sales force plays a key role in developing and managing profitable *customer relationships*.

2   Identify and explain the six major sales force management steps

High sales force costs necessitate an effective sales management process consisting of six steps: designing sales force strategy and structure, recruiting and selecting, training, compensating, supervising and evaluating salespeople, and sales force performance.

In designing a sales force, sales management must address strategy issues such as what type of sales force structure will work best (territorial, product, customer or complex structure); how large the sales force should be; who will be involved in the selling effort; and how its various sales and sales support people will work together (inside or outside sales forces and team selling).

To hold down the high costs of hiring the wrong people, salespeople must be recruited and selected carefully. In recruiting salespeople, a company may look to job duties and the characteristics of its most successful salespeople to suggest the traits it wants in its salespeople and then look for applicants through recommendations of current salespeople, employment agencies, classified ads, the Internet and by contacting college students. In the selection process, the procedure can vary from a single informal interview to lengthy testing and interviewing. After the selection process is complete, training programmes familiarise new salespeople not only with the art of selling, but also with the company's history, its products and policies, and the characteristics of its market and competitors.

The sales force compensation system helps to reward, motivate and direct salespeople. In compensating salespeople, companies try to have an appealing plan, usually close to the going rate for the type of sales job and needed skills. In addition to compensation, all salespeople need supervision, and many need continuous encouragement because they must make many decisions and face many frustrations. Periodically, the company must evaluate their performance to help them do a better job. In evaluating salespeople, the company relies on getting regular information gathered through sales reports, personal observations, customers' letters and complaints, customer surveys and conversations with other salespeople.

3   Discuss the personal selling process, distinguishing between transaction-oriented marketing and relationship marketing

The art of selling involves a seven-step selling process: prospecting and qualifying, pre-approach, approach, presentation and demonstration, handling objections, closing and follow-up. These steps help marketers close a specific sale and as such are *transaction oriented*. However, a seller's dealings with customers should be guided by the larger concept of *relationship marketing*. The company's sales force should help to orchestrate a whole-company effort to develop profitable long-term relationships with key customers based on superior customer value and satisfaction.

4   Define direct marketing and discuss its benefits to customers and companies

Direct marketing consists of direct connections with carefully targeted individual consumers both to obtain an immediate response and to cultivate lasting customer relationships. Using detailed databases, direct marketers tailor their offers and communications to the needs of narrowly defined segments or even individual buyers.

For buyers, direct marketing is convenient, easy to use and private. It gives them ready access to a wealth of products and information, at home and around the globe. Direct marketing is also immediate and interactive, allowing buyers to create exactly the configuration of information, products or services they desire, then order them on the spot. For sellers, direct marketing is a powerful tool for building customer relationships. Using database marketing, today's marketers can target small groups or individual consumers, tailor offers to individual needs and promote these offers through personalised communications. It also offers them a low-cost, efficient alternative for reaching their markets. As a result of these advantages to both buyers and sellers, direct marketing has become the fastest-growing form of marketing.

5 Identify and discuss the major forms of direct marketing

The main forms of direct marketing include personal selling, telephone marketing, direct mail marketing, catalogue marketing, direct response television marketing, kiosk marketing and online marketing. We discuss personal selling in the first part of this chapter and will examine online marketing in detail in the next chapter.

Telephone marketing consists of using the telephone to sell directly to consumers. Direct mail marketing consists of the company sending an offer, announcement, reminder or other item to a person at a specific address.

Recently, new forms of 'mail delivery' have become popular, such as email marketing. Some marketers rely on catalogue marketing, or selling through catalogues mailed to select customers, or made available in stores or on the Web. Direct response television marketing has two forms: direct response advertising or infomercials and home shopping channels. Kiosks are information and ordering machines that direct marketers place in stores, airports and other locations. Online marketing involves online channels and e-commerce, which electronically link consumers with sellers.

NAVIGATING THE KEY TERMS

NOTES AND REFERENCES

1 Quote from Laurence Zuckerman, 'Selling Airplanes with a Smile', *New York Times*, 17 February 2002, p. 3.2; see also '7 Digital 7', *Forbes*, 21 June 2004, p. 117; and 'China's Appetite for 737 Shows No Sign of Slowing', *Knight Ridder Tribune Business News*, 11 May 2005, p. 1.

2 For an overview of some of the key issues in sales and sales teams development, see the first chapter in the academic text *Oxford Handbook of Sales and Sales Management* by D.W. Cravens, L. Meunier-FitzHugh and N.F. Piercy (Oxford: Oxford University Press, 2011).

3 For further reading see: W.G. Biemans and M.M. Brencic, 'Designing the Marketing–Sales Interface in B2B Firms', *European Journal of Marketing*, 41(3/4), 2007, pp. 257–73.

4 Visit Loquendo online at **www.loquendo.com** – available in five languages.

5 Quotes and other information from Geoffrey Brewer, 'Love the Ones You're With', *Sales & Marketing Management*, February 1997, pp. 38–45; and Erin Stout, 'Blue Skies Ahead?', *Sales & Marketing Management*, March 2003, pp. 25–9.

6 'Selling Power 500' report, available from **www.sellingpower.com**, accessed September 2014.

7 For more on this and other methods for determining sales force size, see Douglas J. Dalrymple, William L. Cron and Thomas E. DeCarlo, *Sales Management*, 8th edn (New York: Wiley, 2004), pp. 112–16.

8 J. Kuruzovich, 'Sales Technologies, Sales Force Management, and Online Infomediaries', *Journal of Personal Selling & Sales Management*, 33(2), 2013, pp. 211–24 is an academic paper which looks at the key aspects of using technology in sales – such as cost savings.

9 See Martin Everett, 'Selling by Telephone', *Sales & Marketing Management*, December 1993, pp. 75–9. See also Terry Arnold, 'Telemarketing Strategy', *Target Marketing*, January 2002, pp. 47–8.

10 William F. Kendy, 'No More Lone Rangers', *Selling Power*, April 2004, pp. 70–4. See also Jon Bacot, 'Team Selling: A Winning Approach', *Paperboard Packaging*, April 2005, pp. 44–50.

11 'Customer Business Development', http://www.pgcareers.com, accessed September 2014.

12 For an overview of some of the key issues in respect of recruitment, development and retention of top salespeople try D. Giannakis and M.J. Harker, 'Strategic Alignment Between Relationship Marketing and Human Resource Management in Financial Services Organizations', *Journal of Strategic Marketing*, 22(5), 2014, pp. 1–24.

13 See Sergio Román and Salvador Ruiz, 'A Comparative Analysis of Sales Training in Europe: Implications for International Sales Negotiations', *International Marketing Review*, 20(3), 2003, pp. 304–27.

14 Robert Klein, 'Nabisco Sales Soar after Sales Training', *Marketing News*, 6 January 1997, p. 23; and Geoffrey James, 'The Return of Sales Training', *Selling Power*, May 2004, pp. 86–91.

15 Learn about Cisco Systems at www.cisco.com – go to 'Training and Events' for an outline of some of the online training that Cisco provides itself.

16 See 'SMM's Best of Sales and Marketing: Best Trained Sales Force – Cisco Systems', *Sales & Marketing Magazine*, September 2001, pp. 28–9; 'Cisco Systems Canada Wins 2002 National Award for Learning Technologies in the Workplace', 8 May 2002, accessed at newsroom.cisco.com; and 'E-Learning: Field Training – How Cisco Spends Less Time in the Classroom and More Time with Customers' from www.cisco.com

17 See *Dartnell's 30th Sales Force Compensation Survey*, Dartnell Corporation, August 1999; and Galea, '2005 Compensation Survey', *Sales & Marketing Management*, May 2005, pp. 24–9.

18 For extensive discussions of sales force automation, see the May 2005 issue of *Industrial Marketing Management*, which is devoted to the subject.

19 For an outline of some of the issues that sales force turnover can cause, read Gavin Dunaway, 'Sales Force, Turnover Blamed for Yahoo!'s Slip in Display Revenue Growth', at www.themediabriefing.com, accessed September 2014.

20 Quotes from Bob Donath, 'Delivering Value Starts with Proper Prospecting', *Marketing News*, 10 November 1997, p. 5; and Bill Brooks, 'Power-Packed Prospecting Pointers', *Agency Sales*, March 2004, p. 37.

21 Quotes from Dana Ray, 'Are You Listening?', *Selling Power*, October 2004, pp. 24–7; Erin Stout, 'Throwing the Right Pitch', *Sales & Marketing Management*, April 2001, pp. 61–3; Andy Cohen, 'Customers Know Best', *Sales & Marketing Management*, January 2003, p. 10; and William F. Kendy, 'How to Be a Good Listener', *Selling Power*, April 2004, pp. 41–4.

22 Alicia Orr Suman, 'Ideas You Can Take to the Bank! 10 Big Things All Direct Marketers Should Be Doing Now', *Target Marketing*, February 2003, pp. 31–3; and Mary Ann Kleinfelter, 'Know Your Customer', *Target Marketing*, January 2005, pp. 28–31.

23 See A. Osarenkhoe and A. Bennani, 'An Exploratory Study of Implementation of Customer Relationship Management Strategy', *Business Process Management Journal*, 13(1), 2007, pp. 139–64.

24 Heather Tomlinson and Robert Evans, 'Tesco Stocks up on Inside Knowledge of Shoppers' Lives', at **www.guardian.co.uk**, accessed September 2014; visit Dunnhumby at **www.dunnhumby.com**

25 'Fresh, But Far From Easy' from *The Economist* at **www.economist.com**, accessed September 2014.

26 'TalkTalk and Tiscali UK Fined £3 Million for Breaching Consumer Rules' at **media.ofcom.org.uk**, accessed September 2014.

27 Read and learn about the TPS at **www.tpsonline.org.uk**

28 Reuters have a good story summarising one industry and its mis-selling compensation crisis, 'UK Banks Forced to Re-open 2.5 Million Insurance Mis-Selling Cases', at **http://uk.reuters.com/article/2014/08/29/uk-britain-banks-misselling-idUKKBN0GT0ZD20140829**

29 Visit the IDM at **www.theidm.com** and read about how it is evolving in M. Cornwell, 'A Snapshot of the IDM's Future', *Journal of Direct, Data and Digital Marketing Practice*, 14(4), 2013, pp. 287–8.

30 Ira Teinowitz, '"Do Not Call" Does Not Hurt Direct Marketing', *Advertising Age*, 11 April 2005, p. 3.

31 Statistics from the Direct Marketing Information Service – now incorporated into the Direct Marketing Association which can be found at **www.dma.org.uk**

32 Visit Groupon at **www.groupon.com**. Read more about the company and its markets at 'Ignore the Groupon Hate: Group Buying Isn't Dying – It's Just Getting Started' by Dan Frommer at **www.businessinsider.com**, accessed September 2014.

33 See 'Catalogue Marketing – There's a New Class of Consumer' at **www.themarketer.co.uk**, accessed September 2011.

34 Read about the IKEA catalogue at **www.ikea.com** – visit the press room/student centre for up-to-date info and press releases; accessed September 2014.

35 Nat Ives, 'Infomercials Clean Up Their Pitch', *New York Times*, 12 April 2004, p. C1.

36 Thomas Mucha, 'Stronger Sales in Just 28 Minutes', *Business 2.0*, June 2005, pp. 56–60.

37 QVC corporate facts and figures from **www.qvcuk.com**, accessed September 2014. See also C.R. Mafé and S.S. Blas, 'Teleshopping Adoption by Spanish Consumers', *Journal of Consumer Marketing*, 24(4), 2007, pp. 242–50, for the situation in one European country.

38 See Andrea Clements, 'Belfast Company that Could Revolutionise the Way we Buy Music', at **www.belfasttelegraph.co.uk**, accessed September 2014.

39 See '"Middle-man" Services Add New Layer to Online Scams' in the Irish Times at **www.irishtimes.com/business/technology/middle-man-services-add-new-layer-to-online-scams-1.1887268**, accessed January 2015.

40 Read about how musicians and intermediaries try to prevent piracy now: Ian Youngs, 'Stars Step up War on Music Leaks', **www.news.bbc.co.uk**, accessed September 2014. See how user information was not used appropriately at 'Apple Addresses iTunes Concerns', **www.news.bbc.co.uk**, accessed September 2014.

41 Visit FEDMA online at **www.fedma.org**

42 These lists can be found online at **www.mpsonline.org.uk**, **www.admaz.cz** and **www.fevad.com** respectively; FEDMA can be found at **www.fedma.org** – all accessed September 2014.

43 Debbie A. Connon, 'The Ethics of Database Marketing', *Information Management Journal*, May–June 2002, pp. 42–4.

PART FOUR

EXTENDING MARKETING

CAN MARKETING SAVE THE WORLD?

Already in this book we have covered a very large number of issues and topics on and related to marketing. This final part draws back a little and considers the impact of marketing on our societies and cultures, and discusses whether marketing ideas and processes can be used to make the world a slightly better place.

CHAPTER 14
MARKETING IN THE DIGITAL AGE

AFTER STUDYING THIS CHAPTER, YOU SHOULD BE ABLE TO

- discuss how the digital age is affecting both consumers and the marketers who serve them
- explain how companies have responded to the Internet and other powerful new technologies with e-business strategies, and how these strategies have resulted in benefits to both buyers and sellers
- describe the four major e-marketing domains
- discuss how companies go about conducting e-marketing to deliver more value profitably to customers
- overview the promise and challenges that e-commerce presents for the future

THE WAY AHEAD
Previewing the concepts

We've learned that the aim of marketing is to create value *for* customers in order to capture value *from* consumers in return. Good marketing companies win, keep and grow customers by understanding customer needs, designing customer-driven marketing strategies, constructing value-delivering marketing programmes, and building customer and marketing partner relationships. In the final three chapters, we'll extend this concept to three special areas – marketing in the digital age, global marketing, and marketing ethics and social responsibility. Although we've visited these topics regularly in each previous chapter, because of their special importance we will focus exclusively on them in this part.

In this chapter, we look into marketing in the rapidly changing digital environment. Marketing strategy and practice have undergone dramatic changes during the past decade. Major technological advances in respect of hardware and software have had a major impact on buyers and the marketers who serve them. To thrive in this digital age – even to survive – marketers must rethink their strategies and adapt them to today's changing environment.

We'll begin by looking at how recent innovations may mean that in the very near future we'll be printing out products at home, and what that might mean for retailers, logistics companies and traditional manufacturers – not to mention consumers.

PRINTING THE FUTURE

Disruptive technologies

New technologies change products, consumers and thereby markets. The impact of many if not most technologies is minor or incremental. Things last a little longer, cost a little less, perform a little better or have a reduced impact on the environment. Some technologies, though, have incredible effects on how we all live our lives, to the extent that after just a few years we cannot imagine living life without them and younger generations take the radically transformed world as normal.

Take audio technology. You might think of LPs as being ancient technology, but in the period shortly after their introduction in the 1930s by Columbia it became easier to enjoy recorded music in the home. As that technology was refined, the quality of recording became excellent and spurred on social, cultural and sexual revolutions in the 1960s. The audio compact cassette from Philips took over in the late 1960s, being a more robust, less easily damageable format which – miracle of miracles – allowed home recording and rerecording on equipment that became cheap and easy to use. Sony and Philips cooperated in researching and developing the compact disc, which allowed recorded media not just in audio format but also with video. The hegemony of the CD lasted until the 1990s, when DVD and Blu-ray discs briefly reigned until music and video moved to being stored in file formats on hard drives and solid state memory.

Now you probably carry round a small handheld player or phone, containing thousands of pieces of music and perhaps hundreds of hours of video within an object that weighs just a couple of hundred grams and that can be connected wirelessly to online catalogues containing millions of tracks and movies, some of which are even legal!

At each evolution and generation of technology – after each period of *disruption* – the ability to enjoy and consume audio entertainment has become easier, cheaper, less restricted and more common.

One of the greatest tech advances in history, and thereby one which caused considerable disruption, was the bringing together by Johannes Gutenberg of movable type and a wooden press – the *printing press* – in the fifteenth century. This allowed for the first time the production of books on a mass scale, pushing and developing a more literate, educated and informed society into the renaissance. Gutenberg spent a lot of his later life in trouble with the church and the state, thanks to the mess he was deemed to have caused.

Such radical transformations are rare, but it is possible that we are now on the cusp of another one – *additive manufacturing*. You've probably heard of this, but under another name – 3D printing. So what is it, and how and why might it prove to be such a radical change?

What is 3D printing?

Even though audio cassette technology existed in the Second World War, it was not until two decades later that it became a commonly owned consumer technology. At the time of writing in 2014, home 3D printers are available but are not cheap, sophisticated or easy to use. That will come with time. As an interconnected set of technologies, 3D printing dates back to the 1980s, when stereolithography – using ultraviolet (UV) lasers to manipulate special heat-sensitive plastics – was introduced as an industrial method of quickly producing product mock-ups and models, sometimes called *rapid prototyping*. Producing prototypes was more rapid because the computer-generated designs could be relayed direct to the printer and created straight away, without need for much human input – especially long and complex bureaucratic exchanges between different elements of the same company!

So how does the actual 3D printing process work?

If you look closely (with a microscope) at a page of text from your home printer, you'll see the letters don't just stain the paper, they're actually sitting slightly on top of the surface of the page.

In theory, if you printed over that same page a few thousand times, eventually the ink would build up enough layers on top of each other to create a solid 3D model of each letter. That idea of building a physical form out of tiny layers is how the first 3D printers worked.

The 3D printing process turns a whole object into thousands of tiny little slices, then makes it from the bottom-up, slice by slice. Those tiny layers stick together to form a solid object. Each layer can be very complex, meaning 3D printers can create moving parts like hinges and wheels as part of the same object. You could print a whole bike – handlebars, saddle, frame, wheels, brakes, pedals and chain – ready assembled, without using any tools. It's just a question of leaving gaps in the right places.

The Independent

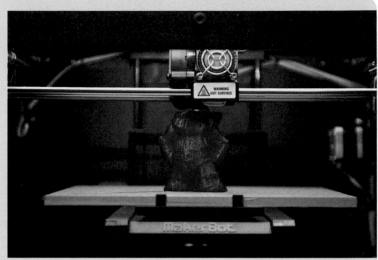

Early adopters are learning how to use the technology to produce quite remarkable items

Sources: Alamy Images/Rik Hamilton (tl); Piero Cruciatti (tr).

While initially only simple and fragile manufactures from weak and brittle plastic were achievable, it soon became possible to produce more complex and larger items, and to manufacture them from many different materials – not just stronger plastics, but also metals and ceramics. The industrial version of the technology is now so sophisticated and developed that replacement components for jet fighters can be produced and fitted and crucial parts of the human body can be repaired or replaced. One Chinese man had part of his spine replaced by a 3D printed vertebra, a British team recently performed a hip replacement operation using a custom sized and shaped hipbone, and replacement teeth that are exact replicas of the originals are being manufactured in the USA.

So why is this relevant to students of marketing? The answer lies in the disruption the new technology will cause in established market and marketing frameworks and structures. As Internet platforms like Google and Facebook have melted and reformed marketing in respect of advertising, branding and customer relations, 3D printing may well radically restructure other aspects of the marketing function and the means and mechanisms by which value is delivered to the customer.

The marketing impact

As audio recordings become a retail product, and then a product that shifted through multiple formats before disappearing from the high street onto the Internet – leaving HMV and a number of other companies in retail and adjacent sectors as empty shells – what impacts might 3D printing have as a mass-market consumer phenomenon?

Let's take *retailing* as our first example. Why do retailers exist? What is their fundamental rationale? By collecting any number of products together under one roof, and providing a safe and handy place in which to shop, retailers provide convenience. In return for this they receive and keep a good proportion of the end-user price. But what if the desired product could be printed out at home? Why not select what you want from an extensive catalogue and with just a few more clicks have it created in your own home? Sound fanciful? Early uses for home 3D printing machines include replacement components for glasses and home appliances – specialist items that might not be easily or instantly obtainable outside major population centres. You might think food retailers would be safe, but the technology already exists to print carbohydrate heavy foods like pasta and there have already been experiments with chocolate! What takes the biscuit? *Space pizza.*

Because the health and happiness of astronauts is paramount, NASA granted contractor Systems & Materials Research $125,000 to develop a pizza printer. The prototype uses shelf-stable powdered food and oils, offering nutrition whilst minimizing garbage on board a space vehicle. It first prints a layer of dough onto a heated plate that bakes the dough and then lays down a tomato base that has been stored in powdered form and mixed with water and oil. Last comes a printed 'protein layer'.
BusinessWeek

Retailers work hand in hand with *distributors* to make sure the right products are in the right place at the right time. If consumers are printing out products at home, and there is a reduced need to visit a retail store to get what is wanted, then the companies that help to keep those stores full will not be as necessary as they once were. Trucks once carried millions of CDs across Europe each week. As the mass market moved onto file formats, fewer and fewer trucks were needed. If that process is replicated with physical goods, then it could have an immense impact on even Europe's largest logistics firms, companies such as Schenker, Delamode and Norbert Dentressangle.

So much for shops and trucks. What about the *manufacturers?* If they are also designers and innovators they will be safer, but many manufacturers produce products on behalf of other companies. Would you print out the next Apple product at home if you could? Why pay those manufacturers to do a job that no longer needs doing? That would be a question for both you and Apple.

Those examples look pretty negative for the respective parties. Would certain types of company benefit? It is quite likely that the answer is yes. As bands like Radiohead have been able to cut out intermediaries to distribute their music direct to fans, perhaps we might see product designers selling designs direct to the consumers who will print them out? Forget Apple, how about receiving something direct from Jony Ive? Companies like Maker-Bot, which is one of the early pioneers in consumer 3D printing tech, are clearly hoping to move into the mass market and shift millions of units of one of the few things probably still necessary – the printers themselves.

As well as the hardware, 3D printing requires software. There are already dozens of software development houses that are producing and refining code, and their number and size will only get bigger as the market grows. It would not be at all surprising to find new intermediaries emerging. They might collect and sell on designs for home printing, or collect and redistribute fees for design

leasing or owning – a model that would actually be pretty similar to Apple's immensely profitable iTunes – essentially a digital warehouse and database.

Legal and regulatory frameworks have struggled to keep up with the digital revolution. Illegally downloaded torrents of films and music and the harvesting and selling of personal data by social networks are just two examples; 3D home printing would add to this pressure on governments and regulatory bodies to catch up. What, for example, would stop you from printing out multiple copies of the same item, even if you've only paid for one? If you scanned and then replicated a product, would there be sanctions? What is MakerBot going to do if you buy one of its 3D printers and then use it to replicate dozens more?

It is unlikely you would mind if your neighbours were printing out pizzas, but what if they were printing out guns? One organisation has already released working designs for handguns into the public domain. If you can print out chocolate, would you also be able to print out explosives? How about credit cards, or banknotes?

Always remember, you live in interesting times.

Sources: An overview of the academic perspective on these issues can be found in the paper by Matthew S. O'Hern and Lynn R. Kahle, 'The Empowered Customer: User-Generated Content and the Future of Marketing', *Global Economics and Management Review*, 18(1), 2013, pp. 22–30.

The *Independent* newspaper has a good overview of 3D printing at www.independent.co.uk/life-style/gadgets-and-tech/features/3d-printing-for-dummies-how-do-3d-printers-work-8668937.html; see also Mashable article at mashable.com/2013/03/28/3d-printing-explained/

The *Guardian* has examples of how 3D printed products are already changing medical practice and *BusinessWeek* talks about foods:

http://www.theguardian.com/business/2014/aug/24/medical-implants-drive-3d-printer-growth

www.businessweek.com/articles/2014-01-28/all-the-food-thats-fit-to-3d-print-from-chocolates-to-pizza

One of the leaders in the nascent field of home 3D printing machines is MakerBot. Find it at www.makerbot.com and a column giving examples of legal issues confronting the growing industry at www.wired.co.uk/news/archive/2014-05/16/3d-printed-guns

As this case makes clear, recent technological advances have created a digital age. Widespread use of powerful and affordable hardware and software such as smartphones, apps and other powerful new technologies is having a dramatic impact on marketers and buyers. In this chapter, we examine how marketing strategy and practice are having to change constantly to take advantage of today's new technologies.[1]

THE DIGITAL AGE

It is likely that you'll know quite a bit about these technologies already, but some of the terminology is bandied about very loosely so we'll define a few terms first for the sake of clarity. **Intranets** are networks that connect people within a company to each other and to the company network – sets of pages and online resources available only to those in that organisation, even if the geographical spread of these people is global. If you're currently studying, it's likely that your college or university will have an intranet for staff and students – you can access the library, download class materials and perhaps even find out how well you did in your assessments. **Extranets** connect a company with its suppliers, distributors and other outside partners – big retailers and wholesalers use these to manage the movement of goods more effectively. The **Internet**, a vast public web of computer networks, connects users of all types all around the world to each other and to an amazingly large information repository.

The wonderful world of Internet statistics

This chapter – just like all the others – contains many facts and figures. It is in the nature of Internet-related statistics and estimates that any accuracy they may possibly have had will be momentary – the rapidity and fluidity of the medium, and the inherent difficulty in obtaining accurate information, mean many such figures are guesstimates at best, wild speculation at worst. During the lifespan of this and any book, technologies, capacities and activities can increase or reduce by several orders of magnitude. That warning being given, let's have a peek into the wonderful world of Internet statistics.

With the creation of the World Wide Web and web browsers in the 1990s, the Internet was transformed from a mere communication tool into a certifiably revolutionary technology. The Internet continues to grow explosively. It is estimated that about 3 billion people have regular access to the Internet – less than half the world. In detail, we can see that Internet use is not evenly distributed across the globe – nearly 85 per cent of North Americans have access but only one in five Africans. Generally there is a significant correlation between wealth and development levels and Internet usage. Europe has about 70 per cent of its population as regular users, but this varies very significantly by country. Ukraine comes near the bottom of the league with about a third online, while the Netherlands and Iceland are at the top with more than 90 per cent. The UK and Germany are towards the top end while France, Italy and the Czech Republic are catching up but still behind.[2]

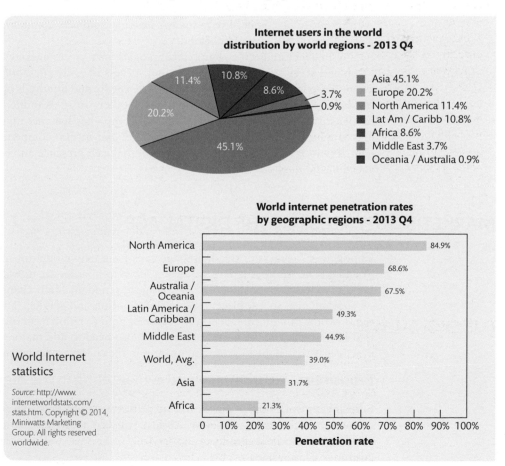

World Internet statistics

You may think of the Internet as being an English-speaking phenomenon, and indeed English is the most common language used on web pages. Unsurprisingly Chinese is in second place and Spanish, French, German, Italian and Portuguese make up most of the rest of the top 10.[3] Quality of access varies just as much as quantity. One recent report found that broadband users in France and Sweden had an average connection speed of 17mbps, nearly three times that of Germany, six times that of the UK and fifteen times that of Spain.[4] Even within countries access can vary widely – rural parts of Portugal, Russia and Scotland (the highlands and islands) are not well served, even when a major city in the same country might be. Residents of London get twice the speed of those living in Belfast.[5] This does matter – the changing culture and demographics of web usage and availability mean that marketers cannot treat all Internet customers the same.[6]

This explosive worldwide growth in Internet usage forms the heart of the digital age. The Internet has been *the* revolutionary technology of the new millennium, empowering consumers and businesses alike. Proof? The rise of social media is just one small aspect of the way in which the way we experience the world has been transformed by Internet-enabled technologies. If this is something you have grown up with, it may seem commonplace, but if you ask someone who was around before the Web, they may be able to convince you just what a radical change it has been to all aspects of how a life is lived. In respect of marketing, the Internet enables consumers and companies to access and share huge amounts of information with just a few mouse clicks. Recent studies have shown that more and more consumers are accessing information on the Internet before making major life decisions. One in three consumers relies heavily on the Internet to gather information about buying a car, finding a job, dealing with a major illness or making investment decisions. Nielsen recently estimated that the average UK Internet user spent some 45 hours a month online – with about 27 hours of that at home and one in four minutes spent using social media. In Italy the equivalent total for work and home combined was 43 hours and in France 60 hours.[7] As a result, to be competitive in today's new marketplace, companies must adopt Internet technology or risk being left behind.

The Internet and other digital technologies have given marketers a whole new way to reach and serve customers. The amazing success of early *click-only* companies – the so-called dot-coms such as **Amazon.com**, eBay, Expedia and hundreds of others – caused existing *brick-and-mortar* manufacturers and retailers to re-examine how they served their markets. Now, almost all these traditional companies have set up their own online sales and communications channels, becoming *click-and-mortar* competitors. It is hard to find a company today that does not have a substantial web presence and cannot be contacted by social media methods.

MARKETING STRATEGY IN THE DIGITAL AGE

Conducting business in the digital age calls for a new model for marketing strategy and practice. The Internet is revolutionising how companies create value for customers and build customer relationships. The digital age has fundamentally changed customers' notions of convenience, speed, price, product information and service. Thus, today's marketing requires new thinking and action. Companies need to retain most of the skills and practices that have worked in the past. But they will also need to add major new competencies and practices if they hope to grow and prosper in the changing digital environment.

E-business, e-commerce and e-marketing in the digital age

E-business involves the use of electronic platforms – intranets, extranets and the Internet – to conduct a company's business. Almost every company has set up a website to inform about and promote its products and services. Others use websites simply to build stronger customer relationships.

Most companies have also created intranets to help employees communicate with each other and to access information found in the company's systems. For example, some 14,000 employees regularly log on to the P&G intranet, mNet, to receive training and to research marketing news from around the world. Companies also set up extranets with their major suppliers and distributors to enable information exchange, orders, transactions and payments.

E-commerce is more specific than e-business. E-business includes all electronics-based information exchanges within or between companies and customers. In contrast, e-commerce involves buying and selling processes supported by electronic means, primarily the Internet. *E-markets* are 'market*spaces*', rather than physical market*places*. Sellers use e-markets to offer their products and services online. Buyers use them to search for information, identify what they want, and place orders using credit or other means of electronic payment.

E-commerce includes *e-marketing* and *e-purchasing (e-procurement)*. **E-marketing** is the marketing side of e-commerce. It consists of company efforts to communicate about, promote, and sell products and services over the Internet. Thus, **Amazon.com**, **LLBean.com** and **Dell.com** conduct e-marketing at their websites. The flip side of e-marketing is e-purchasing, the buying side of e-commerce. It consists of companies purchasing goods, services and information from online suppliers. In business-to-business buying, e-marketers and e-purchasers come together in huge e-commerce networks.

E-commerce and the Internet bring many benefits to both buyers and sellers. Let's review some of these major benefits.

Benefits to buyers

Internet buying benefits both final buyers and business buyers in many ways. It can be *convenient*. Customers do not have to battle traffic, find parking spaces, and trek through shops and aisles to find and examine products. They can do comparative shopping by surfing websites. Web marketers never close their doors. Buying is *easy* and *private* – at least, your friends and family won't necessarily know what you are shopping for, even if Google and Facebook do. Customers encounter fewer buying hassles and do not have to face salespeople or open themselves up to persuasion and emotional pitches. Business buyers can learn about and buy products and services without waiting for and tying up time with salespeople.

In addition, the Internet often provides buyers with greater product access and selection. Unrestrained by physical boundaries, web sellers can offer an almost unlimited selection to consumers almost anywhere in the world. Just compare the incredible selections offered by many web merchants with the more meagre assortments of their bricks-and-mortar counterparts. For example, log on to **Bulbs.com**, 'the web's no. 1 light bulb superstore', and you'll have instant access to every imaginable kind of light bulb or lamp – incandescent bulbs, fluorescent bulbs, projection bulbs, surgical bulbs, automotive bulbs, you name it. No physical store could offer handy access to such a vast selection.

E-commerce channels also give buyers access to a wealth of comparative *information* about companies, products and competitors. Good sites often provide more information in more useful forms than even the most solicitous salesperson can. For example, **Amazon.com** offers top 10 product lists, extensive product descriptions, expert and user product reviews, and recommendations based on customers' previous purchases.

Companies can now provide applications for use with portable devices like Apple's iPhone so that customers can view and buy wherever they are

Source: Getty Images/Evrim Aydin/Anadolu Agency.

Finally, online buying is *interactive* and *immediate*. Buyers can often interact with the seller's site to create exactly the configuration of information, products or services they desire, then order or download them on the spot. Moreover, the Internet gives consumers a greater measure of control. Like nothing else before it, the Internet has empowered consumers. These days, people looking to buy a new laptop or mobile phone will research prices, performance and possibilities online. They may not actually purchase online, but when they come to buy, they will be armed with much more knowledge. This is the new reality of consumer control.

Benefits to sellers

E-commerce also yields many benefits to sellers. First, the Internet is a powerful tool for *customer relationship building*. Because of its one-to-one, interactive nature, companies can interact online with customers to learn more about specific needs and wants. In turn, online customers can ask questions and volunteer feedback. Based on this ongoing interaction, companies can increase customer value and satisfaction through product and service refinements.

The Internet and other electronic channels can also *reduce costs* and *increase speed and efficiency*. By using the Internet to link directly to suppliers, factories, distributors and customers, businesses can cut costs and pass on savings to customers. Internet-only marketer **Amazon.com** avoids the expense of maintaining a store and the related costs of rent, insurance and utilities. Because customers deal directly with sellers, online selling often results in lower costs and improved efficiencies for channel and logistics functions such as order processing, inventory handling, delivery and trade promotion. Finally, communicating electronically often costs less than communicating on paper through the mail. For instance, a company can produce digital catalogues for much less than the cost of printing and mailing paper ones.

E-marketing can also offer greater *flexibility*. It allows marketers to make ongoing adjustments to offers and programmes, or to make immediate and timely announcements and offers. For example, easyJet and other budget airlines can micromanage their pricing structures to take into account demand for seats, and they can notify customers about changes, delays or other problems very promptly. Argos can use its website to update its online catalogue on a continual basis, something simply not possible with the printed version.

Finally, the Internet is a truly *global* medium that allows buyers and sellers to click from one country to another in seconds. A web surfer from Paris or Istanbul can access an online L.L. Bean catalogue as easily as someone living in Freeport, Maine, the direct retailer's home town. Even small e-marketers find that they have ready access to global markets.[8]

E-MARKETING DOMAINS

The four major e-marketing domains are shown in Figure 14.1 and discussed below. They include B2C (business to consumer), B2B (business to business), C2C (consumer to consumer) and C2B (consumer to business).

		Targeted to consumers	Targeted to businesses
	Initiated by business	B2C (business to consumer)	B2B (business to business)
FIGURE 14.1 E-marketing domains	**Initiated by consumer**	C2C (consumer to consumer)	C2B (consumer to business)

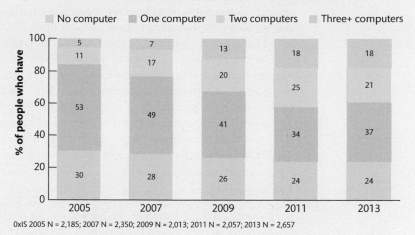

Number of computers in the household by years (QH9)

OxIS 2005 N = 2,185; 2007 N = 2,350; 2009 N = 2,013; 2011 N = 2,057; 2013 N = 2,657

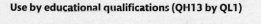

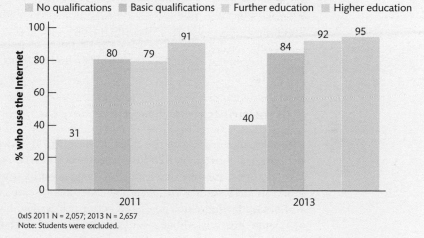

Use by educational qualifications (QH13 by QL1)

OxIS 2011 N = 2,057; 2013 N = 2,657
Note: Students were excluded.

The Oxford Internet
Survey

Source: From Dutton, William
H. & Blank, Grant with Groselj,
Darja. (2013) Cultures of
the Internet: The Internet in
Britain, Oxford Internet Survey
2013. Oxford Internet Institute.
University of Oxford., http://
oxis.oii.ox.ac.uk/wp-content/
uploads/2014/11/OxIS-2013.
pdf, Source: Oxford Internet
Survey (Dutton & Blank. 2013).

B2C (business to consumer)

The popular press has paid the most attention to **B2C (business-to-consumer) e-commerce** –
the online selling of goods and services to final consumers. Online consumer buying continues to grow at a healthy rate. Industry body Ecommerce Europe believes it was worth €311bn
in 2013 and is confident of its prediction of €625bn in 2016. This is not evenly spread across
Europe, though, with the UK (€96 billion), Germany (€50 billion) and France (€45 billion)
together representing 61 per cent of the total European B2C e-commerce sector and of
the 3.5 billion packages sent across Europe that contain products bought online. Globally,
eMarketer reckons a current total of $1.5 trillion with two-thirds in the Asia-Pacific, North
American and Western European regions – a total to grow to $2.4 trillion by 2017.[9]

Online consumers

Not all types of people use the Internet to the same degree, or in the same proportion.
Although the gender gap has narrowed significantly in the last 10 years, there is still an
imbalance towards men. Age is a significant factor – while ever-increasing numbers of the
over 55s are browsing online, a much higher proportion of the young do so. In fact, the

Oxford Internet Survey reported that one in three retired people were online, as were more than half of those of working age but almost all of those of student age were regular Internet users. It also reported that Internet usage was correlated very strongly with both education and income – 90 per cent of those earning more than £50,000 per year were online, compared with less than a third of those on £12,500 or less.[10]

Internet consumers differ from traditional offline consumers in their approaches to buying and in their responses to marketing. The exchange process via the Internet has become more customer initiated and customer controlled. Traditional marketing targets a somewhat passive audience. In contrast, e-marketing targets people who actively select which websites they will visit, Twitter accounts they follow and Facebook pages they like and thereby what marketing information they will receive about which products and under what conditions. Thus, the new world of e-commerce requires new marketing approaches.

B2C websites

Consumers can find a website for buying almost anything. The Internet is most useful for products and services when the shopper seeks greater ordering convenience or lower costs.[11] The Internet also provides great value to buyers looking for information about differences in product features and value. However, consumers find the Internet less useful when buying products that must be touched or examined in advance. Still, even here there are exceptions. For example, who would have thought that tens of thousands of people would order cars online each year without seeing and trying them first?

People now go online to order a wide range of goods – clothing from Gap, furniture from IKEA, major appliances from Currys, flowers from Interflora or even financial services from Egg.

B2B (business to business)

Although the media give the most attention to B2C websites, consumer goods sales via the Web are dwarfed by **B2B (business-to-business) e-commerce.** B2B marketers use trading networks, auction sites, spot exchanges, online product catalogues, barter sites and other online resources to reach new customers, serve current customers more effectively, and obtain buying efficiencies and better prices. The biggest company you've never heard of is quite possibly Alibaba – a Chinese B2B portal that is larger than Amazon and eBay combined in respect of turnover and market value.

Within Europe, there is evidence to suggest that there are significant national, industry/sector and functional differences affecting not only the *number* of businesses that trade online, but also, for those that do, the *proportion* of business done online. Industries and sectors with a strong ICT dimension like telecommunications are much more heavily involved with B2B e-commerce than more traditional industries like footwear manufacture or construction. Nationally, some countries stand out: 78 per cent of Danish companies are involved with e-commerce, but only 6 per cent in Bulgaria; the significance of e-commerce in respect of overall turnover also varies greatly, representing 31 per cent in Ireland, but only 2 per cent in Greece.[12]

Most major B2B marketers now offer product information, customer purchasing and customer support services online. For example, corporate buyers can visit Sun Microsystems' website (**www.sun.com**), select detailed descriptions of Sun's products and solutions, request sales and service information, and interact with staff members. Some major companies conduct almost all of their business on the Web. Networking equipment and software maker Cisco Systems takes more than 80 per cent of its orders over the Internet.

Some B2B e-commerce takes place in **open trading exchanges** – huge e-market spaces in which buyers and sellers find each other online, share information and complete transactions efficiently. For example, **PlasticsNet.com**, an Internet marketplace for the plastics product industry, connects over 90,000 monthly visitor/buyers with more than 200 suppliers.

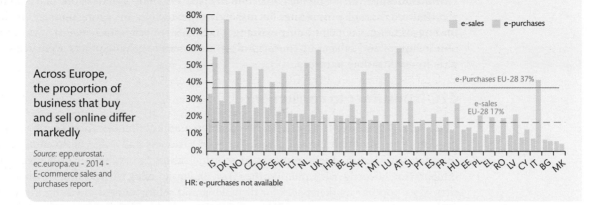

Across Europe, the proportion of business that buy and sell online differ markedly

Source: epp.eurostat. ec.europa.eu - 2014 - E-commerce sales and purchases report.

HR: e-purchases not available

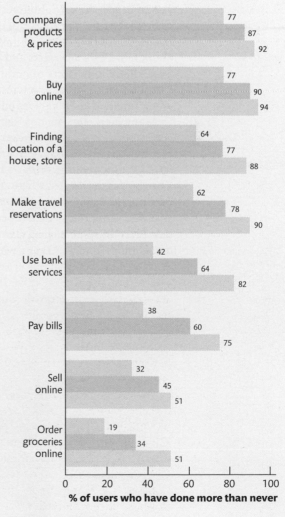

Buying and using services online by income (QC30 by SC2)

■ Less than £12,500 ■ £12,500–£30,000
■ £30,000 or more

The Oxford Internet Survey

Source: From Dutton, William H. & Blank, Grant with Groselj, Darja. (2013) Cultures of the Internet: The Internet in Britain, Oxford Internet Survey 2013. Oxford Internet Institute. http://oxis.oii.ox.ac.uk/wp-content/uploads/2014/11/OxIS-2013. pdf, Source: Oxford Internet Survey (Dutton & Blank. 2013).

OxIS current users: 2013 N = 2,083

However, despite the use of such open e-marketspaces, a lion's share of all B2B e-commerce is conducted through private sites. Increasingly, online sellers are setting up their own **private trading exchanges**. Open trading exchanges facilitate transactions between a wide range of online buyers and sellers. In contrast, a private trading exchange links a particular seller with its own trading partners.

C2C (consumer to consumer)

Much **C2C (consumer-to-consumer) e-commerce** and communication occur on the Web between interested parties over a wide range of products and subjects. In some cases, the Internet provides an excellent means by which consumers can buy or exchange goods or information directly with one another. For example, eBay, Amazon and other auction sites offer popular marketspaces for displaying and selling almost anything, from art and antiques, coins, stamps and jewellery to computers and consumer electronics. EBay's C2C online trading community consists of more than 150 million users worldwide – 19 million of them in the UK. In 2013, \$212bn of goods were sold – more than \$6,700 *every second*.[13] On a much smaller scale we have similar setups like Etsy, where the emphasis is on handmade and crafted items rather than on second-hand goods, and many of the sellers are also the creators.

In other cases, C2C involves interchanges of information through Internet forums that appeal to specific special-interest groups. Such activities may be organised for commercial or non-commercial purposes. An example is web logs, or *blogs,* which can be about anything, from politics or football to haiku or cooking. EBay uses these to keep investors informed about news – hirings, facts and figures, legislative impact and so on. One social media platform that allows peers to curate and share themed collections of images which are often consumption related is Pinterest. It is similar to sites such as Flickr in respect of relying on *user-generated content* in its business models.[14]

Many marketers are now tapping into blogs as a medium for reaching carefully targeted consumers. One way is to advertise on an existing blog or to post content there. For example, web-savvy Nike created an 'Art of Speed' microsite on blog site Gawker.[15] The 'Art of Speed' showcased the work of 15 innovative filmmakers who interpreted the idea of speed. The showcase gave Nike high-quality exposure within a small audience. 'Gawker is a very influential site among a community that appreciates creativity, film, and interesting projects and who are going to dig deeper and find out the back story,' said Nike's communications manager. 'In some circles, Gawker has more authenticity than Nike,' says an online communications analyst. 'That's why blogs really work for advertisers, because of the credibility

Etsy is much smaller than eBay, and focuses on crafted items sold direct by their creators

Source: Shutterstock.com/ Mark Shoon.

of the blog.'[16] Other companies set up their own blogs. For example, Procter & Gamble launched a blog site (**www.sparklebodyspray.com**) to promote its Secret Sparkle Body Spray to tween girls (7- to 12-year-olds). The site features character blogs based on each of four Sparkle Body Spray girls – Rose, Vanilla, Tropical and Peach. Each character's writing takes on a personality similar to a real pre-teen girl. They blog about things girls are purported to be interested in, from fashion to celebrity gossip to sports. Says Secret's brand manager, 'the character blog concept [allows] each visitor to create her own experience'.[17]

As a marketing tool, blogs offer some advantages. They can offer a fresh, original, personal and cheap way to reach today's fragmented audiences. However, the blogosphere is cluttered and difficult to control. 'Blogs may help companies bond with consumers in exciting new ways, but they won't help them control the relationship,' says a blog expert. Such web journals remain largely a C2C medium. 'If anything, blogs will continue tipping the balance of power toward the consumer,' says the expert. 'That isn't to suggest companies can't influence the relationship or leverage blogs to engage in a meaningful relationship, but the consumer will remain in control.'

In all, C2C means that online buyers do not just consume product information – increasingly, they create it. They join Internet interest groups and type in hashtags to share information, with the result that 'word of web' is joining 'word of mouth' as an important buying influence. Word about good companies and products travels fast. Word about bad companies and products travels even faster. Many sites, including **eComplaints.com**, **ConsumerReview.com** and **Consumerist.com**, have cropped up to provide consumers with a forum where they can air complaints and share information about product and service experiences. Further adding to the chaos we have social media platforms like Twitter and Facebook, where C2C interactions take place without intervention or editorial control. This is becoming a key issue for many companies, as when a customer contacts them about an issue, plenty of other people know that it happened, and can witness the action or inaction of the company in response.

HMV is a company that probably wishes the Internet had never been invented. Not only has it meant that its main product categories – entertainment media on discs – have been trampled by files distributed online via legal and illegal methods, but also it experienced the swift and brutal backlash of its social media presence going out of control when senior management decided to implement wide-scale restructuring. The Huffington Post ran with the story almost in real time:

> Staff from HMV's head office have gone rogue on the company's official Twitter account, tweeting that loyal staff are being 'executed' and the brand they love destroyed. The tweets, which began on Thursday afternoon, describe an HR meeting where 60 staff have been made redundant. It is not confirmed which staff are being referred to, but they are believed to be in the company's head office.
>
> Tweeting with the hashtag \#hmvXFactorFiring, the anonymous tweeter took over the @HMVtweets account.
>
> The tweeter apologised from having been away from the verified account for so long, and revealed the account had originally been set up by an unpaid intern. 'Sorry we've been quiet for so long. Under contract, we've been unable to say a word, or – more importantly – tell the truth,' the Twitter account wrote.
>
> Senior managers appeared to be struggling to shut the feed down, with tweets being deleted within minutes, but the perpetrator continuing to post.
>
> 'We're tweeting live from HR where we're all being fired! Exciting!!' the first one read.
>
> 'There are over 60 of us being fired at once! Mass execution of loyal employees who love the brand.'
>
> Panic in head office appeared to ensue. 'Just overheard our Marketing Director (he's staying, folks) ask "How do I shut down Twitter?"' the account reported.[18]

Marketers are realising that the issues and trends discussed in social media often move into the mainstream consciousness of the culture of the society over time – the thoughts and opinions of key opinion formers can be used to develop an understanding of the current Zeitgeist, critical in markets where fashions and trends can change quickly. One online magazine goes so far as to measure the importance of blogs on online culture and produces a continually updating 'Top 100' of the most influential blogs.[19]

C2B (consumer to business)

The final e-commerce domain is **C2B (consumer-to-business) e-commerce**. Thanks to the Internet, today's consumers are finding it easier to communicate with companies. Most companies now invite prospects and customers to send in suggestions and questions via company websites. Beyond this, rather than waiting for an invitation, consumers can search out sellers on the Web, learn about their offers, initiate purchases and give feedback. Using the Web, consumers can even drive transactions with businesses, rather than the other way around. For example, using **Priceline.com**, would-be buyers bid for airline tickets, hotel rooms, hire cars and even home mortgages, leaving the sellers to decide whether to accept their offers.

Consumers can also use websites such as **PlanetFeedback.com** to ask questions, offer suggestions, lodge complaints or deliver compliments to companies. The site provides letter templates for consumers to use based on their moods and reasons for contacting the company. The site then forwards the letters to the customer service manager at each company and helps to obtain a response. 'About 80 per cent of the companies respond to complaints, some within an hour,' said a PlanetFeedback spokesperson.[20]

MARKETING ON THE WEB

Companies of all types are now marketing online. In this section, we first discuss the different types of e-marketers shown in Figure 14.2. Then we examine how companies go about conducting online marketing.

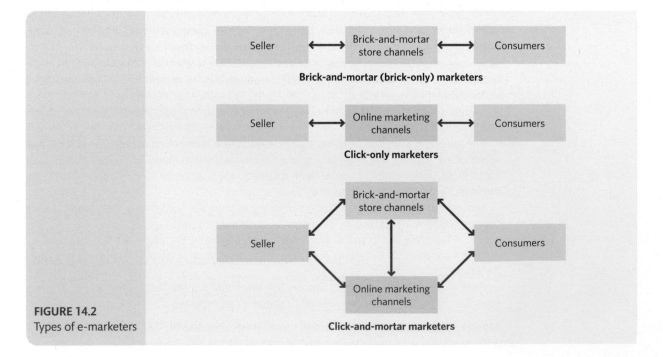

FIGURE 14.2
Types of e-marketers

Click-only versus click-and-mortar e-marketers

The Internet gave birth to a new species of e-marketers – the *click-only* dot-coms – which operate only online without any brick-and-mortar market presence. In addition, most traditional *brick-and-mortar* companies have now added e-marketing operations, transforming themselves into *click-and-mortar* competitors.[21]

Click-only companies

Click-only companies come in many shapes and sizes. They include *e-tailers* – dot-coms that sell products and services directly to final buyers via the Internet. Examples include **Amazon.com**, Expedia and **iwantoneofthose.com**. Netflix streams movies, standing on the grave of companies like Blockbuster.

The click-only group also includes *search engines* and *portals,* such as Google, MSN and Yahoo, which began as search engines and later added services such as news, weather, stock reports, entertainment and storefronts, hoping to become the first port of entry to the Internet. *Shopping* or *price comparison sites,* such as **Froogle.com**, **Dooyoo.co.uk**, **Pricerunner.co.uk** and **Bizrate.com**, give instant product and price comparisons from thousands of sellers – often with feedback ratings from customers attached.

Internet service providers (ISPs) such as Deutsche Telekom's T-Online, the Italian Tiscali and of course BT are click-only companies that provide Internet and email connections for a fee. *Transaction sites,* such as auction site eBay, take commissions for transactions conducted on their sites. The hype surrounding such click-only web businesses reached astronomical levels during the 'dot-com gold rush' of the late 1990s, when avid investors drove dot-com stock prices to dizzying heights. However, the investing frenzy collapsed in the year 2000, and many high-flying, overvalued dot-coms came crashing back to Earth. Dot-coms failed for many reasons. Some rushed into the market without proper research or planning. Often their primary goal was simply to launch an initial public offering (IPO) while the market was hot. Many relied too heavily on spin and hype instead of developing sound marketing strategies. They spent lavishly offline on mass marketing to attract new customers to their sites instead of building loyalty and purchasing among current customers. As one industry watcher concluded, many dot-coms failed because they gave a lot of thought to the razzmatazz and very little to the business model. Such companies should start by rethinking how they create value for customers. How can they leverage their web-only models to compete effectively against traditional brick-and-mortar competitors on the one hand, and against the newer click-and-mortar competitors on the other?

A decade and a half later, are we seeing a similar bubble in respect of social media companies like Twitter and Facebook? Opinion is divided. Some see the streams of customer shopping and behaviour data as being immensely valuable, Twitter calls its 'The Hosepipe'. Others, though, point to the speed with which social media platforms can collapse or fall out of favour and the push-back against invasions of privacy by citizen action groups and legislators. If Facebook were to lose the right to collect and sell user data, what would it be worth then?

Click-and-mortar companies

As the Internet grew, some established companies rushed to open websites providing information about their companies and products. However, most resisted adding e-commerce to their sites. They worried that this would produce *channel conflict* – that by selling their products or services online they would be competing with their offline retailers and agents. For example, Hewlett-Packard feared that its retailers would drop HP's computers if the company sold the same computers directly online. Merrill Lynch hesitated to introduce online stock trading, fearing that its own brokers would rebel.

These companies struggled with the question of how to conduct online sales without cannibalising the sales of their own stores, resellers or agents. However, they soon realised that the risks of losing business to online competitors were even greater than the risks of angering channel partners. If they did not cannibalise these sales, online competitors soon would. Thus, most established brick-and-mortar companies are now prospering as **click-and-mortar companies.**

For example, Office Depot's more than 1,600 office-supply superstores rack up annual sales of $12bn in more than 55 countries. But you might be surprised to learn that Office Depot's fastest recent growth has come not from its traditional brick-and-mortar channels, but from the Internet – this is despite buying up other stationery supplies companies like the French firm Guilbert and Papirius of the Czech Republic.[22] The company sells $5bn worth of these goods online – to businesses and individuals. Other retailers are finding the same thing – firms like Tesco and Carrefour recognise online retailing as being increasingly important to the whole of their operations.

Most click-and-mortar marketers have found ways to resolve channel conflicts. For example, Gibson Guitars found that although its dealers were outraged when it tried to sell guitars directly to consumers, the dealers did not object to direct sales of accessories such as guitar strings and parts. Avon worried that direct online sales might cannibalise the business of its Avon ladies, who had developed close relationships with their customers. Fortunately, Avon's research showed little overlap between existing customers and potential web customers. Avon shared this finding with the reps and then moved into online marketing. As an added bonus for the reps, Avon also offered to help them set up their own websites.

Despite potential channel conflict issues, many click-and-mortar companies are now having more online success than their click-only competitors. The list of the top 10 online retailers is divided evenly between click-only and click-and-mortar.[23]

What gives the click-and-mortar companies an advantage? Established companies such as John Lewis, Dixons, House of Fraser and Debenhams have known and trusted brand names and greater financial resources. They have large customer bases, deeper industry knowledge and experience, and good relationships with key suppliers. By combining online marketing and established brick-and-mortar operations, they can offer customers more options.

For example, consumers can choose the convenience and assortment of online shopping 24 hours a day, the more personal and hands-on experience of in-store shopping, or both. Customers can buy merchandise online and then easily return unwanted goods to a nearby store.

MAKING CONNECTIONS Linking the concepts

Think about the relative advantages and disadvantages of *click-only*, *brick-and-mortar* and *click-and-mortar* retailers.

- Visit the Amazon website. Search for a specific book or film – perhaps one that's not too well known – and go through the buying process.
- Now visit www.waterstones.com and shop for the same book or film. Then visit a Waterstones store and shop for the item there.
- What advantages does Amazon have over Waterstones? What disadvantages? How does your local independent bookshop fare against these two competitors?

Setting up an online marketing presence

Clearly, all companies need to consider moving online. Companies can conduct e-marketing in any of the four ways shown in Figure 14.3: creating a website, placing ads and promotions online, setting up or participating in web communities, or using email.

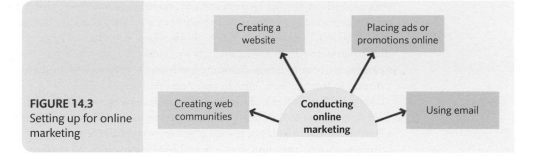

FIGURE 14.3
Setting up for online marketing

Creating a website

For most companies, the first step in conducting e-marketing is to create a website. However, beyond simply creating a website, marketers must design an attractive site and find ways to get consumers to visit the site, stay around and come back often.

Types of websites

Websites vary greatly in purpose and content. The most basic type is a **corporate website**. These sites are designed to build customer goodwill and to supplement other sales channels, rather than to sell the company's products directly. For example, although you can buy ice cream and other items at the gift shop on **benjerry.com**, the site's primary purpose is to enhance customer relationships. At the site, you can learn all about Ben & Jerry's company philosophy, products and locations. Or you can visit the Fun Stuff area and send a free e-card to a friend, subscribe to the Chunk Mail newsletter, or while away time playing Scooper Challenge or Virtual Checkers.

Corporate websites typically offer a rich variety of information and other features in an effort to answer customer questions, build closer customer relationships and generate excitement about the company. They generally provide information about the company's history, its mission and philosophy, and the products and services that it offers. They might also tell about current events, company personnel, financial performance and employment opportunities. Most corporate websites also provide entertainment features to attract and hold visitors. Finally, the site might also provide opportunities for customers to ask questions or make comments through email before leaving the site.

Other companies create a **marketing website.** These sites engage consumers in an interaction that will move them closer to a direct purchase or other marketing outcome. Such sites might include a catalogue, shopping tips and promotional features such as sales events or

Corporate website: although you can buy some ice cream at the Ben & Jerry's website, the site's primary purpose is to enhance customer relationships. At the site, you can learn all about the Ben & Jerry's company and do lots of 'fun-related stuff'

Source: http://www.benjerry.co.uk/

contests. For example, visitors to **SonyStyle.com** can search through dozens of categories of Sony products, review detailed features and specifications lists for specific items, read expert product reviews and check out the latest hot deals. They can place an order for the desired Sony products online and pay by credit card, all with a few mouse clicks. Companies aggressively promote their marketing websites in offline print and broadcast advertising and through 'banner-to-site' ads that pop up on other websites.

Mini USA operates a marketing website at **www.miniusa.com**. Once a potential customer clicks in, the car maker wastes no time trying to turn the enquiry into a sale, and then into a long-term relationship. The site offers a garage full of useful information and interactive selling features, including detailed and fun descriptions of current Mini models, tools for designing your very own Mini, information on dealer locations and services, and even tools for tracking your new Mini from factory to delivery.

> Before Angela DiFabio bought her Mini Cooper last September, she spent untold hours on the company's website, playing with dozens of possibilities before coming up with the perfect combination: A chili-peppered exterior, white racing stripes on the hood, and a 'custom rally badge bar' on the grill. When DiFabio placed her order with her dealer, the same build-your-own tool – and all the price and product details it provided – left her feeling like she was getting a fair deal. 'He even used the site to order my car,' she says. While she waited for her Mini to arrive, DiFabio logged on to Mini's website every day, this time using its 'Where's My Baby?' tracking tool to follow her car, like an expensive FedEx package, from the factory in Britain to its delivery. 'To be able to check the process made the wait exciting. It definitely gave me a feeling of control in the process,' says DiFabio. It's not that Mini's technology is groundbreaking. Rather, it makes an impact on the customer experience because of how it's integrated with the brand: it's fun, it's individual, it makes users feel like part of the clan. The website does more than just provide information or sell products or services. It keeps customers engaged, and when they're more engaged, they're usually happier, too.[24]

Designing effective websites

Creating a website is one thing; getting people to visit the site is another. The key is to create enough value and excitement to get consumers to come to the site, stick around and come back again. Today's web users are quick to abandon any website that does not measure up. One research team found that many users will give a web page two seconds to give them the information they want – if it fails this test they disappear elsewhere. This means that companies must constantly update their sites to keep them current, fresh and useful – not to mention quick! Doing so involves time and expense, but the expense is necessary if the e-marketer wishes to cut through the increasing online clutter.

In addition, many online marketers spend heavily on good old-fashioned advertising and other offline marketing avenues to attract visitors to their sites. For example, Mitsubishi recently ran a series of ads to draw visitors to its Galant website. The ad featured a cliff-hanger of a crash-avoidance test comparing the manoeuvrability of a Gallant GTS versus a Toyota Camry – to find out what happened, viewers had to go to the website.[25]

For some types of products, attracting visitors is easy. Consumers buying new cars, computers or financial services will be open to information and marketing initiatives from sellers. Marketers of lower involvement products, however, may face a difficult challenge in attracting website visitors. If you're in the market for a computer and you see a banner ad that says, 'The top 10 computers under £500', you'll be likely to click on the banner. But what kind of ad would get you to visit a site like **dentalfloss.com**?[26]

For low-interest products, the company can create a corporate website to answer customer questions, build goodwill and excitement, supplement selling efforts through other channels and collect customer feedback. Kimberly-Clark does this with a website for its leading toilet-paper brand. Making use of the long-standing association with puppies, the website offers simple games for children as well as competitions for their parents.[27]

A key challenge is designing a website that is attractive on first view and interesting enough to encourage repeat visits. To attract new visitors and to encourage revisits, suggest experts, e-marketers should pay close attention to the seven Cs of effective website design:[28]

- *Context*: the site's layout and design.
- *Content*: the text, pictures, sound and video that the website contains.
- *Community*: the ways that the site enables user-to-user communication.
- *Customisation*: the site's ability to tailor itself to different users or to allow users to personalise the site.
- *Communication*: the ways the site enables site-to-user, user-to-site, or two-way communication.
- *Connection*: the degree to which the site is linked to other sites.
- *Commerce*: the site's capabilities to enable commercial transactions.

And to keep customers coming back to the site, companies need to embrace yet another 'C' – constant change.

At the very least, a website should be easy to use and physically attractive. Ultimately, however, websites must also be *useful*. 'The bottom line: people seek substance over style, usefulness over flash,' says one analyst. 'They want to get what they want quickly. Surfers should know almost immediately upon accessing your site why they should stick around, what's in it for them.'[29] Thus, effective websites contain deep and useful information, interactive tools that help buyers find and evaluate products of interest, links to other related sites, changing promotional offers and entertaining features that lend relevant excitement.

From time to time, a company needs to reassess its website's attractiveness and usefulness. One way is to invite the opinion of site-design experts. But a better way is to have users themselves evaluate what they like and dislike about the site. This can be done via a questionnaire or by allowing users to leave comments. Such feedback is useful for all organisations in managing their web presence, whether they are the EU or a local council – these organisations can learn who is using their website and how they are using it, or would like to use it.[30]

Placing ads and promotions online

As consumers spend more and more time on the Internet, many companies are shifting more of their marketing budget to *digital advertising* to build their brands or to attract visitors to their websites. The amount spent on digital advertising has increased exponentially, and this rate of increase is not expected to slow down in the foreseeable future. As can be seen in

Applying the 7Cs of effective website design, is this a good site?

Source: Pearson Education Ltd.

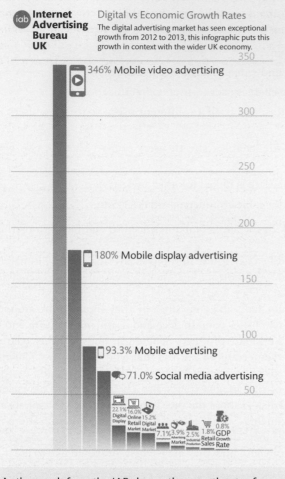

As the graph from the IAB shows, the growth rates for online advertising of all types have been rapid, but spending on mobile advertising is seeing incredible growth

the nearby chart provided by IABUK – the UK industry body – the rate of growth for advertising spend on social media networks is extraordinary, but is in turn dwarfed by the rate of change of spending on mobile marketing. As proportions of the whole across Europe, TV still has the biggest single share with 28 per cent, online/mobile now takes the silver medal with 24 per cent, displacing newspaper advertising, which drops to third place with 19 per cent. There are marked difference between countries – the UK leads the way in respect of the share of online/mobile spend, followed by France and Germany.[31]

Forms of online advertising

Online ads might appear anywhere on an Internet user's screen. The most common form of online advertising is the banner ad – banner-shaped ads found at the top, bottom, left, right, or centre of a web page. Banners go by many names, including tickers (banners that move across the screen), skyscrapers (tall, skinny banner ads at the side of a web page) and rectangles (block ads appearing in the middle of the screen). Most banner ads contain links to the advertiser's website. For instance, a web surfer looking up airline schedules or fares might encounter a flashing banner that screams, 'Rent a car from Hertz and get up to 2 days free!' Clicking on the ad takes consumers to the Hertz website, where they can redeem the promotion.

Interstitials are online ads that appear between screen changes on a website, especially while a new screen is loading. For example, visit **www.marketwatch.com** and you'll probably see a 10-second ad for Visa, Verizon or another sponsor before the homepage loads. *Pop-up*s are online ads that appear suddenly in a new window in front of the window being viewed. Such ads can multiply out of control, creating a major annoyance. As a result, Internet services and web browser providers have developed applications that let users block most pop-ups. But not to worry. Many advertisers have now developed *pop-unders*, new windows that evade pop-up blockers by appearing behind the page you're viewing.

Another hot growth area for online advertising is *search-related ads* (or *contextual advertising*), in which text-based ads and links appear alongside search engine results on sites such as Google and Yahoo. What advertisers love about these is that they pay per click – that is, if the advert is ignored, then it does not cost the advertiser anything. This compares very favourably with a print ad, for which the rates are fixed dependent on the number of copies of the paper or magazine printed.

Finally, with the increase in broadband Internet access, many companies are developing exciting, new *rich media* advertisements, which incorporate animation, video, sound and interactivity. Rich media ads attract and hold consumer attention better than traditional banner ads. They employ techniques such as float, fly and snapback – animations that jump out and sail over the web page before retreating to their original space.

All of the above forms of advertising and promotion can be encountered on your phone. Creating successful campaigns using such a small screen is not easy, and many companies are in danger of becoming annoyances, rather than added value or possible choice. Mobile-marketer is a news website for the industry. In its run-through of what it saw as successful campaigns for 2013 it included one from Fiat, who used a phone interstitial to bring people to a highly interactive and engaging site incorporating Vine and Instagram videos. Another was by JetBlue, who, rather than relying on video, used the inbuilt microphone to tempt viewers into engagement by promising rewards for successfully 'talking pigeon', whereby cooing activated the voice recognition software which passed you on to the full site.[32] One method particular to the phone is the incorporation of ads into otherwise free-to-play games. Candy Crush is one such game you may well be familiar with.

Other forms of online promotion

Other forms of online promotion include content sponsorships, microsites, alliances and affiliate programmes, and viral advertising.

Content sponsorships are another form of Internet promotion. Many companies gain name exposure on the Internet by sponsoring special content on various websites, such as news or financial information or special-interest topics. For example, Betfair sponsors the Fantasy Football portion of the *Daily Telegraph*'s website, and the Edinburgh Fringe Festival website is sponsored by a panel of firms including the Royal Bank of Scotland and Magners Cider. Smaller, more focused websites for niche interests also gain sponsorship of their websites – the UK Games Expo in Birmingham is sponsored by firms like Wizards of the Coast – who market 'Magic: The Gathering' collectable card games. These companies pay for the sponsorship and in return receive exclusive ad and sponsorship recognition alongside the content. Sponsorships are best placed in carefully targeted sites where they can offer relevant information or service to the audience. Similarly, e-marketers can also go online with *microsites* – limited areas on the Web managed and paid for by an external company. For example, an insurance company might create a microsite on a car-buying site, offering insurance advice for car buyers and at the same time offering good insurance deals. Increasingly, firms are adopting this strategy on social media platforms and building a presence there as they would on a high street.

Internet companies can also develop *alliances and affiliate programmes,* in which they work with other companies, online and offline, to 'promote each other'. **Amazon.com** has more than 900,000 affiliates who post Amazon banners on their websites. And Yahoo, whose ad revenue makes up 84 per cent of its total worldwide revenue, has become a fertile ground for alliances with film studios and TV production companies. In one episode of the US version of *The Apprentice,* teams created and marketed a new flavour of Ciao Bella ice cream. Although Ciao Bella had previous sold its ice cream in only 18 stores in New York and San Francisco, Yahoo convinced the manufacturer to place the new product in 760 stores around the country. An end-of-episode promotion urged viewers to visit Yahoo's local online search engine to look for the store nearest them. The product sold out by 5 p.m. the next day. And thanks to Yahoo's registration database, it was able to provide Ciao Bella with the demographic characteristics of respondents.[33]

Finally, online marketers use viral marketing, the Internet version of word-of-mouth marketing. Viral marketing involves creating a website, Twitter hashtag, or other marketing event that is so infectious that customers will want to pass it along to their friends. Because customers pass the message or promotion along to others, viral marketing can be very inexpensive. And when the information comes from a friend, the recipient is much more likely to open and read it. 'The idea is to get your customers to do your marketing for you,' notes a viral marketing expert.[34] When these tactics work, they can create a real buzz around your brand. If done badly, they can fall foul of legislation or create a backlash.

Some firms have gone to extreme lengths – bordering on or even passing legal and moral boundaries. L'Oréal set up a fake blog called *Journal de ma Peau* ('Diary of my Skin'), in order to promote Peel Microabrasion, an anti-wrinkle product. 'Claire' – the purported author of the blog – did not in fact exist, and her endorsement of the product was merely a creation of the company. This tactic spectacularly backfired when the truth became known – many potential consumers were outraged and the negative word of mouth and publicity was significant. Recent changes in legislation at the EU level mean that such actions are now illegal – and of course unethical.

The future of online advertising

It is likely that in the near future, online and mobile advertising spend will form the bulk of expenditure for most if not all companies. For the moment, TV is still king, and in some specific segments older forms like radio and cinema are still very important. Any good IMC programme will be blending promotional messages across media types and platforms. When campaigns successfully integrate online and offline advertising, the synergy created can be immense – as GroupM found:

> The research found that TV is stronger at telling people about a new brand they haven't heard of before (74 per cent), sparking interest in a brand (74 per cent), providing new information about a brand people are already aware of (72 per cent) and persuading people to try a brand or product (59 per cent). Online advertising can also have these effects but performs relatively better at helping people decide which brands are relevant (50 per cent), causing a re-evaluation of a brand (41 per cent) and giving enough information to make a purchase decision (41 per cent). The findings demonstrated that people have different motivations for watching TV and using the Internet. Although there are overlaps in reasons for use, the Internet is accessed primarily for finding information (75 per cent) and communication (66 per cent), while TV is mainly used for entertainment (80 per cent) and relaxation (73 per cent). Importantly, it also found that consumers are now much more aware of the existence and role of TV and online advertising and what they can do with it for themselves. It was clear from the findings that they appreciate the complete package that TV and online, when used together, offers them. Good news for advertisers concerned with any supposed anti-advertising sentiment.[35]

According to a P&G marketer, online marketing is 'a permission-based way to offer consumers more information about a product than can be shared in a typical 30-second spot. It opens a two-way exchange where we can better educate consumers about our products.'[36]

The popularity of blogs and other web forums has resulted in a rash of commercially sponsored websites called web communities, which take advantage of the C2C properties of the Internet. Such sites, whether from independent companies, consumer community creations or hosted on intermediaries, allow members to congregate online and exchange views on issues of common interest. They are the cyberspace equivalent to a Starbucks coffee house, a place where everybody knows your email address and Twitter name.

For example, **iVillage.com** is a web community in which women can exchange views and obtain information, support and solutions on families, food, fitness, relationships, relaxation, home and garden, news and issues, or just about any other topic. The site draws more than 16 million unique visitors a month, putting it in a league with magazines such as *Cosmopolitan*, *Glamour* and *Vogue*. Another is **Chess.com**, a home for those who like to play chess online.[37]

Such communities are often attractive to advertisers because they draw frequent, lengthy visits from consumers with common interests and well-defined demographics.

Marketing applications: from Angry Birds to Happy Marketers   MARKETING AT WORK 14.1

Apps

What is an app? The name is an abbreviation for *application* – a piece of software with a set of capabilities and functions. Microsoft Word is an application, and so is the web browser Chrome. What the abbreviated name refers to, though, is a relatively small and self-contained piece of software that has a very specific and focused purpose. Most so-called smartphones come with several of these pre-installed. The calendar is an app, the contacts directory is an app, the web browser is an app and so on. What makes apps worthy of particular interest is the after-markets – apps offered for sale by third parties to smartphone users. Let's quickly review some quite dazzling facts and figures.

How many apps – products – are there? Given the number of platforms and operating systems and means to obtain them, no one knows for sure, and the number

Source: Alamy Images/Pumpkinpie.

Marketing of a game-app

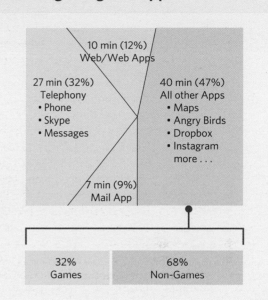

App usage by category

Source: Appsfire.com

is growing too rapidly to get a good fix, but Apple has indicated that for its smartphones and portable devices (iPhones, iPads) there were at least 1.5 million choices by mid-2014. The online store (which itself is a piece of software) only opened in July 2008. Arithmetic tells us then that in about 2,200 days, the apps added to the list of choices to buy from the store increased by 700 a day, per day, every day!

Just because there are so many products to choose from, it does not mean that people are buying them, though, does it? Let's check that out as well. How many of these applications have been downloaded from the store onto Apple devices? Note the word 'downloaded' rather than 'sold' – an issue we will come to later. Apple does know that – it knows it perfectly. Apple recently held a sales promotion with a large prize for the person who downloaded the 50-billionth app. That digital music, marketed through software portals like iTunes, has revolutionised the marketing and consumption of music is surely beyond question. The rapidity with which the marketplace changed beyond recognition from what it was even a decade ago has been breathtaking. One research group has recently compared the growth in sales of digital music with the growth in sales of apps. Music had a four-year head start over apps, but apps have now caught up and are accelerating into the distance.

If those are the headline figures, do we know anything a bit more specific about how people are using and consuming apps? Indeed we do. One online collective has examined this issue and has some tentative findings to report:

1 A typical iPhone user has downloaded about 80 apps to add to the 20 pre-installed by Apple.

2 Users spend upwards of 80 minutes a day using these apps.

3 Just over two-thirds of the apps downloaded were 'free'.

Having developed some focus and context, we can now turn to some specific marketing related issues for game-apps and examine some specific examples of practice.

Where to start? How about channel strategy? If your app is for an Apple device, there is only one choice – the App Store as part of iTunes. Apple takes 30 per cent of the price that the end user pays – and decides whether or not it wants to retail the app at all – sometimes a problem if your app contains adult-orientated material like sex, violence and profanity. In return for that substantial slice of the pie, Apple hosts the app on its servers for download and integrate it into the online catalogue, as well as managing feedback and payment.

If your business is involved with traditional physical goods, the feedback you get from your channels can be delayed, incomplete or inaccurate. This makes good decision making difficult. This is not true for apps. The graphic shows the sales chart of a game called Flight Control – an early success in the App Store. Most developers keep such data close to their chests, but after time made it less commercially sensitive, Firemint was willing to share publicly. As you can see, even with millions of copies sold, Firemint knows exactly how many were sold overall, how many in specific national markets and the impact of significant events like a change in price, some publicity or even just a release of an updated version. Within each market it also knows its ranking in the sales charts. Similar data is available for country of sale. When you have this level of detail and precision, making good decisions is easier.

TABLE 14.1 Pricing of apps in the Apple App Store

	Count by price – active apps			
Month	Apps	Games	Total	% of total
Free	754,335	192,560	946,895	68.86
0.99	140,953	54,392	195,345	14.21
1.99	67,870	17,337	85,207	6.20
2.99	39,552	11,727	51,279	3.73
3.99	18,637	2,087	20,724	1.51
4.99	24,264	3,400	27,664	2.01
5.99	6,233	386	6,619	0.48
6.99	3,919	726	4,645	0.34
7.99	2,828	135	2,963	0.22
8.99	2,120	82	2,202	0.16
9.99	10,693	1,044	11,737	0.85
Total apps	1,090,471	284,679	1,375,150	
Total cost to buy all apps	$1,572,202.64	$193,644.81	$1,765,847.45	
Average app price	$1.44	$0.68	$1.28	

Source: http://www.pocketgamer.biz/metrics/app-store/app-prices/

After distribution and sales management, perhaps it is time to look at pricing. Further interesting things are happening here as the nature of apps means that great flexibility is possible. The price of an app can be changed almost instantly, meaning that price can easily be used as a promotional tool or to establish a user base for future exploitation. Apps can even be offered free via the Apple App Store. Why would any company give away its product? There are some good reasons. As just mentioned, the short- to medium-term objective might be to establish a reputation or gain publicity and attention. Once achieved the app can have a price change upwards. Electronic Arts uses this tactic regularly. Slashing prices across its range of games, it quickly occupies most of the top 10 positions on the charts. After Christmas or other seasonal events, when millions of owners have just unwrapped their new Apple devices, EA reaps the benefit from its games being front and centre. Some apps are deliberately released with only a portion of the functionality operable. If the user wants to get the full benefits, then a payment must be made. If this were a car, we might refer to that as a test drive. If the app sample is not to the liking of the user, then there is no cognitive dissonance – no money was wasted. This switching on of the functionality

of the app is not even as simple as an on–off switch. The app creators might have adopted a pricing model called freemium – a word you will hear increasingly often in the future. Freemium means the app itself is free or very low cost to download, but once installed the user must make what is called an in-app purchase to unlock portions of functionality. In game terms, this might mean extra levels to play through for a few pennies, or new items for in-game characters to be equipped with. This model is one which is increasingly attractive with app developers as it means they

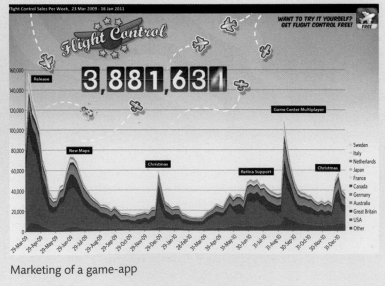

Marketing of a game-app

Source: Firemint.com

can create a stream of revenue from each user, rather than a one-off payment, and achieve this without the substantial costs of developing an app from scratch.

Angry Birds – product and promotion

We have taken a very brief look at elements of pricing and place in the context of app marketing. The basic framework of the marketing mix has of course two further elements: product and promotion. Before we finish, let's consider those – and do so in the context of possibly the most famous game-app of all time – Angry Birds! An app by Rovio of Finland, it is an inaugural member of Apple's App Hall of Fame. Angry Birds has sold an astonishing 2 billion copies. No app has sold more. In the global, all-time app hall of fame, Angry Birds and follow-on products are at numbers 18, 10, 5 and 1. For context, WhatsApp is at number 6.

Let's hear from an interview with the lead designer – Niklas Hed – where the discussion turns to the ethos and process of the games genesis and evolution:

Rovio was perfectly positioned to take advantage. It had learnt a lot from the triumphs and failures of its past games. It also had copious notes from focus groups it had organised over the years, during which Niklas and his colleagues had watched people playing games from behind a glass screen and recorded what the players found difficult, what excited them, what they found boring. The information from these sessions had then been used to produce a blueprint of the 'perfect' mobile game. The checklist ran to several thousand words, but, one of the main things they learnt was that each level had to feel achievable.

'It's important that players don't feel that the game is punishing them,' Niklas says. 'If you fail a level you blame yourself. If the pigs laugh at you, you think: "I need to try one more time."'

They also knew it was important that any game they designed could be played in short bursts – occupying those periods of 'downtime', such as queuing for a coffee or waiting for a bus, that had formerly been devoted to staring into space or, perhaps, reflecting on life.

'You have to be able to play the game right away,' Niklas says. 'We didn't want any loading times.'

It was this principle that led to the introduction of the catapult, the game's central feature. Players know immediately what to do with it and it makes the game more intuitive.

The game also had to appeal to both video game 'virgins' and hard-core enthusiasts. 'We knew it had to be simple but it couldn't be too simple,' Niklas says.

The promotion of the game was based on a very simple strategy. Rovio noted that Apple tended to highlight apps in the store with strong colourful characters present in the game itself and imagery used in logo design. This meant the characters in the game became front and centre in design – and the name became Angry Birds rather than, say, Catapult. Examining potential partners to publish the game (games studios design and build, publishers market) Rovio plumped for a company called Chillingo which had a good relationship with Apple and a track record of successful publicity campaigns. The strategy worked; Apple selected the game as a highlight of the apps in the store – that generated publicity which led to downloads, which led to almost totally positive reviews (word of mouth) between consumers, which led to more sales and so on in a virtuous circle that has required next to nothing in terms of traditional advertising expenditure.

Even more interesting than the way the game was promoted is the way in which the game itself became so strong as a brand that it has been used to help promote other products and has even led to game-related merchandise – Rovio is selling a million plush toys *and* a million Angry Birds T-shirts every month! There is even a tie-in with an animated film called *Rio*. The clincher in respect of Angry Birds now being a 'transmedia franchise'? Angry Birds being included as part of a promotion in a Super Bowl advertisement. Look forward to the animated series!

So, has Rovio discovered the magic formula which it can exploit to guarantee success time after time? Alas no. Although follow-ups to the original Angry Birds apps like Angry Birds – Star Wars sold very well to the huge base of addicts, further releases have not done so well. A partial return to the winning themes of Angry Birds with a game called Bad Piggies flattered to deceive with very high initial sales that collapsed to a few thousand a day. Most developers would kill for that level of success, but Angry Birds has been installed more than a million times a day since its release six years ago.

To have one mega-product, dwarfing all others in the company portfolio, is a two-edged sword that many companies face – just ask McDonald's about Big Macs and Coca-Cola about its red cans. So, perhaps marketing apps is not completely different from normal physical products after all?

Sources: Case compiled from: Apple 'The App Store Has Reached 50 Billion Downloads' from www.apple.com/itunes/50-billion-app-countdown, accessed July 2014; Stats on Apple App Store sales and pricing from PocketGamer at www.pocketgamer.biz/metrics/app-store/app-prices/, 'Infographic: iOS Apps vs Web Apps', from blog.appsfire.com/infographic-ios-apps-vs-web-apps, accessed September 2011; Chillingo, 'About Us', from http://www.chillingo.com/about.htm, accessed September 2011; Horace Dedieu, 'More Than 60 Apps Have Been Downloaded for Every IOS Device Sold', from www.asymco.com/2011/01/16/more-than-60-apps-have-been-downloaded-for-every-ios-device-sold/, accessed September 2011; Develop; Firemint, 'Flight Control Sales Per Week', from firemint.com, accessed September 2011 and no longer available post-merger with IronMonkeys to form a new studio – Firemonkeys at www.firemonkeys.com.au/

Interview segment from P. Kendell, 'Angry Birds: The Story Behind iPhone's Gaming Phenomenon', *Daily Telegraph*, from www.telegraph.co.uk/technology/video-games/8303173/Angry-Birds-the-story-behind-iPhones-gaming-phenomenon.html, accessed February 2011.

S. Pulman, 'Angry Birds: Casual Gaming to Transmedia Franchise?', from http://transmythology.com/2011/01/17/angry-birds-casual-gaming-to-transmedia-franchise/, accessed 2011.

Using email and social media

A recent study of email marketing in Europe suggested that we get twice as many commercial messages as work-related and personal emails combined – a result of the estimated €2bn spent annually by marketers.[38] To compete effectively in this ever more cluttered email environment – not to mention the increasing sophistication of virus blockers and other software – marketers are designing 'enriched' email messages – animated, interactive and personalised messages full of streaming audio and video. And they are targeting these attention grabbers more carefully to those who want them and will act upon them. Consider how Apple uses its weekly email – *New Music Tuesday*. Around the world, millions of iTunes users receive an email that has been customised to them individually. Apple does this by matching up the new releases that week with records of who bought what from the iTunes Store, meaning that you are much more likely to see news and links to music you would be interested in than if you had received the same standardised email as everyone else. As with other types of online marketing, companies must be careful that they do not cause resentment among Internet users who are already overloaded with 'junk email'. The explosion of **spam** – unsolicited, unwanted commercial email messages that clog up our emailboxes – has produced consumer frustration and anger. According to one research company, spam accounts for as much as 90 per cent of all email.[39]

Email marketers walk a fine line between adding value for consumers and being intrusive. Companies must beware of irritating consumers by sending unwanted emails to promote their products. Legislation recently enacted across Europe and increasingly around the world is requiring that marketers should ask customers for permission to email marketing pitches. They should also tell recipients how to 'opt in' or 'opt out' of email promotions at any time. This approach, known as *permission-based marketing*, has become a standard model for email marketing.

More recently, the use of social media as a marketing tool has received a great deal of attention. It is quite likely that you have your own Pinterest or Twitter profile – and you may have devoted significant time to personalising it. One estimate about the use of Twitter suggests that 10 per cent of messages involve a brand name. As we saw in Marketing at Work 14.1, social media are used by marketers for more than promotion – and online promotions selected using the data volunteered by users can be a powerful promotional tool – just ask Google and Facebook.

THE PROMISES AND CHALLENGES OF THE DIGITAL AGE

As we discussed earlier (see Chapter 3), understanding the marketing environment – the context of business – is crucial for any organisation to survive, let alone thrive. Let's then take a look at some of the issues and problems and opportunities that the rise of the digital age has caused.

New intermediaries

First – intermediaries. Earlier in the book the role of wholesalers, retailers and the like was discussed in the context of having an impact on the operation of a company and the perception of it by consumers. New or evolved categories or intermediaries now exist. We saw for example that Steam has revolutionised the way games are distributed (see Chapter 10), and you'd have to be living in a cave not to have heard about iTunes and the impact that has had on the music, film and TV industries. Companies like Priceline and Expedia – who collate and aggregate deals from a spectrum of suppliers – have caused what is called *price transparency* – and this has had a tremendous impact on firms in the various insurance industries, among many others. Google is a new intermediary for almost any organisation. If Google is not hosting or matching your advertising then it will be the instrument consumers use to research about a particular product or organisation. Google is what you probably think of when you think of search engines, but in other markets firms like Yandex (Russia) and Baidu (China) hold sway.[40]

What new categories of intermediary are coming? The opening case on 3D printing suggested some possibilities in respect of home production of manufactured products.[41]

Society and culture

The digital age has had an undeniable impact on society and culture. Most of us would agree that movie, sports and music stars have what might be called a *personal brand* – their public image and perception. David Beckham is a past master at personal brand management. Tiger Woods used to be. In your use of social media, have you been developing your own personal brand? Choice of colours, choice of what information is made publicly available, choice of images, choice of endorsements? Be careful – Microsoft sponsored a recent study that found that many HR operatives are including a profile based on your social media use in their evaluations of you as a job candidate.[42] Some firms are exploiting the information and user-generated content to make money – Flickr do it with images, YouTube with video clips and Blogger with public diaries. Next time you're on a forum, look at the adverts that will be there in return for the space being provided – see **Fark.com** or the comments sections at the *Guardian* or other newspapers. Other firms incorporate observed online trends into their advertising, lolcats being one tragic example, and sometimes in sophisticated ways – see **Burberry.com** and its 'Art of the Trench' galleries.[43]

At Nike ID you can design an athletic shoe to your personal specification – mass customisation

Source: Getty Image.

Mass customisation and new markets

The Industrial Revolution was all about mass production. Standardisation. Many companies are now experimenting with the possibilities that the Internet allows in respect of what is termed mass customisation – products tailored to specific requirements. The concept is not that new. Car manufacturers like Toyota have long had a system where the goal is to build a car only if it has already been sold – and the colour, engine size, fittings and model have been chosen by the customer. Companies like Marks & Spencer are trying this with clothing. The customer selects the design of the shirt and the material it is to be made from. Further selections are made for collar shape, buttons and even whether the garment should have initials. Once the information is collected and the payment made, that specific shirt is made for that specific customer. A leader in the concept of mass customisation is Nike, which has a sophisticated online tool for customers to design and build their own shoes and sports clothing.

As the Internet presents new opportunities and challenges to businesses, the same applies to not-for-profit organisations like charities. The recent experiences of the International Committee of the Red Cross are a good example of how the Internet can impact across many marketing-related issues – see Marketing at Work 14.2 for more on this.

The International Committee of the Red Cross

Ann M. Torres, Marketing Department, Cairns Graduate School of Business and Economics, National University of Ireland

The International Committee of the Red Cross (ICRC), established in 1863, is a neutral organisation that works towards ensuring humanitarian protection. The ICRC, headquartered in Geneva, Switzerland, operates in more than 80 countries and employs more than 12,000 staff. It is the world's oldest non-religious organisation dedicated to humanitarian relief and it has a unique place in international law; it is identified by the four 1949 Geneva Conventions as an *impartial humanitarian body* and is mandated by public international law to assist victims of war and violence.

The ICRC's delegations and missions primarily employ nationals of the countries in which it works to carry out a range of activities, such as assisting civilians, individuals deprived of their freedom, dispersed families, the wounded and sick of existing or emerging conflict; preventive action through the cooperation with the national societies; as well as humanitarian coordination and diplomacy. The ICRC and its societies work to uphold seven fundamental principles: humanity, impartiality, neutrality, independence, voluntary service, unity and universality. The principle of humanity forms the central purpose of the ICRC's activities, which is 'to prevent and alleviate human suffering, without discrimination, and to protect human dignity'.

As a consequence of its increased international presence, the ICRC has received more media attention, but as an organisation it is still poorly understood. In July 2001, a review of the Red Cross brand in 15 countries by advertising agency Young & Rubicam found that while the ICRC 'had a high status in all of the 15 countries, people weren't sure what the Red Cross actually did'. Surprisingly, this lack of understanding persists despite the fact the ICRC has won four Nobel Peace Prizes. More importantly, the ICRC began to reassess what it wanted to be known for. As a result, a greater portion of ICRC's marketing communication efforts have been devoted to informing relevant audiences, including the general public, by availing itself

Thousands of Internally Displaced People (IDPs) gather in a field to receive food aid from the Red Cross near a camp for IDPs in the town of Kibati, just north of the provincial capital of Goma, on 5 November 2008. The humanitarian situation remained catastrophic in the North Kivu region, where over 1 million people had been displaced by fighting the week before

Source: Getty Images/Roberto Schmidt/AFP.

of new media to increase its reach – and a major part of this effort has been in revamping the online presence of the organisation.

The ICRC website (www.icrc.org) is among its most valuable communication tools – not only as a means to communicate with the general public, but also as a central channel through which it can distribute information and reports to relevant audiences – without having to rely on national governments. It is available in seven languages and consultation of the website continues to rise worldwide. Peak usage of the ICRC website typically occurs around incidents of extraordinary disaster or armed conflict – when the website hosts help and advice for victims and appeals to donors for help. Traffic peaks in correlation with tragedies – Japan in 2011, for example. In response to operational needs and public communication requirements, the ICRC continues to add new functions to its website, such as the launch of an RSS feed – a system that makes it possible to deliver newly published press releases and other documents directly to people's desktops. Considerable efforts have also been made to improve the website's editorial content so as to 'strengthen the ICRC's positioning as a global and independent humanitarian organisation'.

Recently the ICRC's Marketing Unit has pursued a number of large-scale research studies so as to develop its communication strategies and to raise 'awareness and influence attitudes on issues of importance' more effectively. The ICRC has focused on two areas of research: examining the communication needs of key audiences, regionally and globally; and measuring perceptions of and attitudes towards humanitarian action, the humanitarian environment, as well as the ICRC logo and emblems. Much of this research has been carried out more quickly at less cost because of the Internet, and the medium is now a key marketing tool in meeting these objectives.

Source: Alamy Images/M4OS Photos.

Indeed, the findings from the ICRC's research studies informed its print, TV and Internet campaign strategy, *Abuse Grows Hatred*. The multimedia campaign focused on detention and emphasised the need to abide by the rules of the Geneva Conventions, which prohibit the abuse of detainees. The campaign goes further, stating that abuse and torture perpetuate a cycle of violence. The animated film, created by the agency VCCP City, 'dramatises the point that the ill treatment of prisoners breeds hatred within the families, communities and countries of the imprisoned' (VCCP 2006: 1). The Internet proved to be by far the most effective and value-for-money medium through which to distribute this message worldwide.

Learning from this success, the ICRC, as the official charity partner of UEFA for EURO 2008 and 2012, launched an online fundraising campaign www.scorefortheredcross.org. The campaign in 2008 prompted Internet users to make donations in support of the Red Cross, where each donation was transformed into virtual goals for the donor's favourite side among the 16 qualifiers. The football team with the most goals would win the title of the Most Humanitarian Team of EURO 2008; the campaign's winning team turned out to be Germany, followed by Spain and the Netherlands. The proceeds from the campaign were designated for landmine victims in Afghanistan and to local projects of the 16 European Red Cross societies associated with the campaign: 'This collaboration with the sporting world in a festive competition like EURO 2008 represents an opportunity for the ICRC. It lays the basis for raising the awareness of a large public in a playful way about sensitive topics of humanitarian concern, such as the situation of mine victims in Afghanistan.' The UEFA website also has a link to the ICRC site and frequently provides information about ICRC activities online.

As it has learned to use the Internet more effectively, the ICRC has become a more sophisticated user of social media platforms. Twitter especially has helped with getting campaigns off to a rapid and globalised start, and is also an excellent means of distributing key info to those in sudden need of guidance – or as instant reinforcement or rebuttals of points others have made. Facebook allows disseminating of images and longer form media which is easily sharable and is a cheap and quick way of raising awareness. By integrating itself into these social media networks, the ICRC is easily and cheaply able to place itself at the heart of our personal networks, obtaining the attention and funds without which it cannot achieve its objectives. *This is what we are, and this is what we do* – in real time.

Sources: The ICRC can be found on Twitter@ICRC and on Facebook at https://www.facebook.com/ICRC. Quotes and information relating to the ICRC example have been drawn from L.A. Casey and D.B. Rivkin, 'Double-red-crossed', *The National Interest*, 22 March 2005, No. 79, pp. 63–9; Department for International Development, 'Working in Partnership with the International Committee of the Red Cross 2002–2006', 2003; D.P. Forsythe, *The Humanitarians: The International Committee of the Red Cross* (Cambridge: Cambridge University Press, 2005); M. Griffin, 'Emblem Crossed Out by a Crystal', *The Age*, 19 September 2005; International Committee of the Red Cross, 'Discover the ICRC', September 2005; ICRC, 'ICRC 2005 Annual Report', May 2006; ICRC, 'Emblems of Humanity: The International Red Cross and Red Crescent Movement', July 2007; ICRC, 'ICRC 2006 Annual Report', May 2007; ICRC, 'Study on Operational and Commercial and Other Non-Operational Issues Involving the Use of the Emblems', October 2007; ICRC, 'Score for the Red Cross – Flash Video Spot', May 2008; R. Murphy, 'International Red Cross and Red Crescent Movement: Lecture Notes', 2007, The Centre for Human Rights, National University of Ireland, Galway; Standing Commission of the Red Cross and Red Crescent, 'Strategy for the International Red Cross and Red Crescent', November 2001; VCCP, 'VCCP Creates Detention Ad for ICRC', August 2006. The VCCP campaign's animated film may be viewed at http://www.icrc.org/web/eng/siteeng0.nsf/html/video-spot-detention-010706. The video spot for the ICRC/UEFA online campaign for EURO 2008 can be seen at http://www.icrc.org/web/eng/siteeng0.nsf/html/score-for-the-red-cross-ytfilm-050508. The ICRC logo and emblems can be seen at http://www.icrc.org/web/eng/siteeng0.nsf/htmlall/emblem?OpenDocument

The Web's darker side – legal and ethical issues

From a broader societal viewpoint, Internet marketing practices have raised a number of ethical and legal questions. In previous sections, we have touched on some of the negatives associated with the Internet, such as unwanted email and the annoyance of pop-up ads. Here we examine concerns about consumer online privacy and security, and other legal and ethical issues.

Online privacy and security

The nature, sustainability and protection of privacy in the digital world is an issue confronting all of us as citizens and consumers. Companies like Google and Facebook are in essence nothing more than giant machines designed and built to harvest data continually from millions upon millions of users. The quid pro quo is *'we provide the services you enjoy free of charge, you provide us with your personal info'*. We agree to this pact every time we log in or do a search.

How sensitive is this issue for companies like Facebook? When we asked to include snippets of its privacy policy in this book – its nominally publicly stated privacy policy – we were refused permission to do so. Why such sensitivity? If Facebook was restricted in what user data it could collect, and was also restricted in what it could do with such data, for example selling it on to other parties, what would the business be worth then? Would it still be tens of billions?

Consumers are becoming increasingly aware about their data being harvested, sold and used. Many are not happy, and want to see companies like Google and Facebook better regulated and controlled by legal frameworks that need to evolve significantly to take account of the rapidly changing technological and social landscape. These concerns have led to pressure groups being formed, and legal cases being brought before European courts. The *Guardian* regularly reports on this issue:

> Schrems is claiming damages of 500 euros (£397) per supporter in the courts in Vienna for alleged data protection violations by Facebook, including over the US Prism spy programme.
>
> The action is being taken against the Irish subsidiary of the New York-listed web giant.
>
> Schrems has been challenging the social network's use of data through his Europe-v-facebook.org campaign and the Data Protection Commission in Ireland and has more than 20 active complaints of alleged data breaches filed with the watchdog.
>
> The class action claims Facebook Ireland is in breach of European law on users' data and it violates rights by tracking internet use on external sites, including the use of 'like' buttons.
>
> It also attacks Facebook's analysis of users through what it calls 'big data' systems.
>
> Schrems claims the company supports the Prism surveillance programme, the US secret service's worldwide monitoring and data mining exposed by the whistleblower Edward Snowden.
>
> Facebook has several weeks to respond to Schrems's claims.
>
> An earlier landmark battle launched in Ireland to find out what Facebook tells US spy chiefs was referred to the European court of justice by a judge in Dublin last month.[44]

Many consumers also worry about *online security*. They fear that unscrupulous snoopers will eavesdrop on their online transactions or intercept their credit card numbers and make unauthorised purchases. In a recent survey, eight out of ten online shoppers in the UK were concerned about typing in their credit card details.[45] In turn, companies doing business online fear that others will use the Internet to invade their computer systems for the purposes of commercial espionage or even sabotage. There appears to be an ongoing competition between the technology of Internet security systems and the sophistication of those seeking to break them.

In response to such online privacy and security concerns, most national and suprana-tional governments have attempted to legislate – but the technological and geographical complexity of many issues is a legal minefield. If a shopper in Sweden is browsing the web-site of a company that is registered in Belgium but is hosted on a server in the Netherlands and pays for her goods using a credit card registered in the UK from a Swiss bank, then which laws do and do not apply if the goods are faulty, if the goods are illegal, if there is a fraud? What taxes are payable? Which governments and agencies have access to personal data generated by that transaction? That is a possible and relatively simplistic illustration of some of the potential issues. Here is a recent example from the world of media:

> Two British newspaper publishers have been fined in French courts because they violated French privacy laws. The publishers were liable because the articles were viewed in France on the Internet. Olivier Martinez, famous in the UK as an ex-boyfriend of Kylie Minogue, sued Mirror Group Newspapers (MGN) and Associated Newspapers for breach of France's strict privacy laws after the newspapers published stories suggesting Martinez and Minogue had recommenced their relationship, which had ended a year previously. The stories also detailed their movements together in Paris earlier this year. MGN was sued because of an article at sundaymirror.co.uk, while Associated was sued over articles at dailymail.co.uk and thisislondon.co.uk. For each title the publishers were ordered to pay €4,500.

> The Tribunal de Grande Instance de Paris rejected claims that it did not have the right to hear the case. It had jurisdiction because the online versions of the articles were viewable in France, it found. Though he was only awarded €4,500 per publication, Martinez had claimed €30,000 in total in a series of privacy cases about articles making the same allegations.

> His lawyer, Emmanuel Asmar, told out-law.com that French courts usually ordered small payouts. The significance of the case was not financial, he said, but in the setting of a prec-edent that UK publications could be liable under French privacy legislation. 'The big thing is that for the first time the [court] considered that UK publishers are liable for their contents in France since it is viewable here and the UK is a member of the EU,' he said.

> A related case from earlier this year was notable because it held one publisher responsi-ble for material published on its site by another publisher via an RSS syndication feed. That case was also taken by Asmar but on behalf of *La Vie en Rose* director Olivier Dahan. He successfully sued three websites for publishing stories about him and actress Sharon Stone via an RSS feed.

> Martinez also won in a case against three websites earlier this year when a court ruled that by publishing a link to offending material the blogs were liable for the privacy invasions of that material.[46]

Of special concern are the privacy and safety of children. Social networking sites like Bebo, Facebook and Myspace are increasingly being used not just by teenagers, but also by younger children. On these sites they are exposed to advertising intended for older children or adults, uncontrolled imagery in other users' profiles and are potentially exposed to abuse from peers and adults. Across Europe, efforts to mitigate these problems and promote safe use of the Internet by children is led by INSAFE.[47] This body, sponsored and endorsed by the EU, is active on four main fronts in respect of online child safety – fighting against illegal content, tackling unwanted and harmful content (whether images or software), promoting a safer online environment and raising awareness among parents of online issues. Are such efforts necessary? One group found that three out of four attempts by under-18 boys to buy pornography and '18' rated video games were successful, and that an increasing number of teenagers were buying alcohol online.[48]

Many companies have responded to consumer privacy and security concerns with actions of their own. To help foster customer trust, companies such as Expedia have conducted voluntary audits of their privacy and security policies. Since 2000, Expedia has employed PricewaterhouseCoopers to run privacy audits of its online services. Expedia's privacy pol-icy gives customers complete control over the use of the personal information they share with the online travel booker. Expedia also has an independent auditor regularly assess its web security technology and procedures.[49]

Still others are taking a broadly industry-wide approach. Founded in 1996, TRUSTe is a non-profit, self-regulatory organisation that works with a number of large corporate sponsors, including Microsoft and AT&T, to audit companies' privacy and security measures and help consumers navigate the Web safely. According to the company's website, 'TRUSTe believes that an environment of mutual trust and openness will help make and keep the Internet a free, comfortable, and richly diverse community for everyone.' To reassure consumers, the company lends it 'trustmark' stamp of approval to websites that meet its privacy and security standards.[50]

Other legal and ethical issues

Beyond issues of online privacy and security, consumers are also concerned about Internet fraud, including identity theft, investment fraud and financial scams.

One common form of Internet fraud is *phishing,* a type of identity theft that uses deceptive emails and fraudulent websites to fool users into divulging their personal data. Some of these messages are obvious attempts at frauds, other are more subtle or more credible – seemingly using plausible email addresses or web links in order to catch the unwary. Even though web users are becoming more sophisticated, a significant proportion of people can be caught out.

Phishing also damages the brand identities of legitimate online marketers who have worked to build user confidence in web and email transactions. Fortunately, companies and governments are taking action. ENISA – the European Network Information Security Agency – is an EU-wide body which coordinates efforts to prevent, address and respond to network and information security problems.[51]

There are also concerns about *segmentation and discrimination* on the Internet. Some social critics and policy makers worry about the so-called *digital divide* – the gap between those who have access to the latest Internet and information technologies and those who do not. They are concerned that in this information age, not having equal access to information can be a social and economic handicap. Socially, lack of Internet access can be an issue for those looking for jobs, somewhere to study, and those considering to whom to give their vote. Economically, at an individual or household level, those who can afford a computer and an Internet connection can browse at Amazon – perhaps saving £5 on a book priced at £20 on the high street. Those without the access pay the high-street price – the rich pay less, the poor pay more. Does that strike you as fair? You may recall from the beginning of this chapter how degree and quality of Internet access was so strongly correlated with income and education. This issue scales up across regions and nations – almost all of Europe is an Internet literate and savvy society, used to viewing, evaluating and analysing vast quantities of data, but the same cannot be said for much of Africa and Asia. The eighteenth and nineteenth centuries saw the Industrial Revolution in the West – should we now speak of the digital revolution as the next step?

Despite these challenges and issues, companies large and small are quickly integrating online marketing into their marketing strategies and mixes. As it continues to grow, online marketing will prove to be a powerful tool for building customer relationships, improving sales, communicating company and product information, and delivering products and services more efficiently and effectively.[52]

THE JOURNEY YOU'VE TAKEN Reviewing the concepts

Recent technological advances have created a digital age. To thrive in this digital environment, marketers are adding some Internet thinking to their strategies and tactics. This chapter discusses how marketers are adapting.

1 Discuss how the digital age is affecting both consumers and the marketers who serve them

Much of today's business operates on digital information, which flows through connected networks. Intranets, extranets and the Internet now connect people and companies with each other and with important information. The Internet has grown explosively to become *the* technology of the new millennium, empowering consumers and businesses alike with the blessings of connectivity. Of course, some groups are more blessed than others.

The Internet and other new technologies have changed the ways that companies reach and serve their markets. The Internet enables consumers and companies to access and share huge amounts of information with just a few mouse clicks. In turn, the Internet and other digital technologies have given marketers a whole new way to reach and serve customers. New Internet marketers and channel relationships have arisen to replace some types of traditional marketers. The new technologies are helping marketers to tailor their offers effectively to targeted customers or even to help buyers customise their own marketing offers. It Is hard to find a company today that does not have a substantial web presence.

2 Explain how companies have responded to the Internet and other powerful new technologies with e-business strategies, and how these strategies have resulted in benefits to both buyers and sellers

Conducting business in the digital age calls for a new model of marketing strategy and practice. Companies need to retain most of the skills and practices that have worked in the past. However, they must also add major new competencies and practices if they hope to grow and prosper in the digital environment. E-business is the use of electronic platforms to conduct a company's business. E-commerce involves buying and selling processes supported by electronic means, primarily the Internet. It includes e-marketing (the selling side of e-commerce) and e-purchasing (the buying side of e-commerce).

E-commerce benefits both buyers and sellers. For buyers, e-commerce makes buying convenient and private, provides greater product access and selection, and makes available a wealth of product and buying information. It is interactive and immediate and gives the consumer a greater measure of control over the buying process. For sellers, e-commerce is a powerful tool for building customer relationships. It also increases the sellers' speed and efficiency, helping to reduce selling costs. E-commerce also offers great flexibility and better access to global markets.

3 Describe the four major e-marketing domains

Companies can practise e-commerce in any or all of four domains. B2C (business-to-consumer) e-marketing is initiated by businesses and targets final consumers. Despite setbacks following the 'dot-com gold rush' of the late 1990s, B2C e-commerce continues to grow at a healthy rate. Although online consumers are still somewhat higher in income and more technology oriented than traditional buyers, the cyberspace population is becoming much more mainstream and diverse. This growing diversity opens up new e-commerce targeting opportunities for marketers. Today, consumers can buy almost anything on the Web.

B2B (business-to-business) e-commerce dwarfs B2C e-commerce. Most businesses today operate websites or use B2B trading networks, auction sites, spot exchanges, online product catalogues, barter sites or other online resources to reach new customers, serve current customers more effectively, and obtain buying efficiencies and better prices. Business buyers and sellers meet in huge marketspaces – or open trading networks – to share information and complete transactions efficiently. Or they set up private trading networks that link them with their own trading partners.

Through C2C (consumer-to-consumer) e-marketing, consumers can buy or exchange goods and information directly from or with one another. Examples include online auction sites, forums and web logs (blogs). Finally, through C2B (consumer-to-business) e-commerce, consumers are now finding it easier to search out sellers on the Web, learn about their products and services, and initiate purchases. Using the Web, customers can even drive transactions with business, rather than the other way around.

4 Discuss how companies can go about conducting e-marketing profitably to deliver more value to customers

Companies of all types are now engaged in e-commerce. The Internet gave birth to the *click-only* dot-coms, which operate only online. In addition, many traditional brick-and-mortar companies have now added e-marketing operations, transforming themselves into *click-and-mortar* competitors. Many click-and-mortar companies are now having more online success than their click-only competitors.

Companies can conduct e-marketing in any of four ways: creating a website, placing ads and promotions online, setting up or participating in web communities, or using online email. The first step typically is to set up a website. Beyond simply setting up a site, however, companies must make their sites engaging, easy to use and useful in order to attract visitors, hold them and bring them back again.

E-marketers can use various forms of **online advertising** to build their Internet brands or to attract visitors to their websites. Beyond online advertising, other forms of online promotion include content sponsorships, microsites, alliances and affiliate programmes, and **viral marketing**, the Internet version of word-of-mouth marketing. Online marketers can also participate in **web communities**, which take advantage of the C2C properties of the Web. Finally, email marketing has become a hot new e-marketing tool for both B2C and B2B marketers.

5 Overview the promise and challenges that e-commerce presents for the future

E-commerce continues to offer great promise for the future. For most companies, online marketing will become an important part of a fully integrated marketing mix. For others, it will be the major means by which they serve the market. Eventually, the 'e' will fall away from e-business or e-marketing as companies become more adept at integrating e-commerce with their everyday strategy and tactics. However, e-commerce also faces many challenges. One challenge is web profitability – surprisingly few companies, especially the web-only dot-coms, are using the web profitably. The other challenge concerns legal and ethical issues – issues of online privacy and security, Internet fraud and the digital divide. Despite these challenges, companies large and small are quickly integrating online marketing into their marketing strategies and mixes.

NAVIGATING THE KEY TERMS

B2B (business-to-business) e-commerce **482**
B2C (business-to-consumer) e-commerce **481**
C2B (consumer-to-business) e-commerce **486**
C2C (consumer-to-consumer) e-commerce **484**

Click-and-mortar companies **488**
Click-only companies **487**
Corporate website **489**
E-business **478**
E-commerce **479**
E-marketing **479**
Extranet **477**
Internet **477**

Intranet **476**
Marketing website **489**
Online advertising **506**
Open trading exchanges **482**
Private trading exchanges **484**
Spam **498**
Viral marketing **506**
Web communities **506**

NOTES AND REFERENCES

1 In just one chapter it simply is not possible to consider many of the key issues in depth. For more detail try books like D. Chaffey and P.R. Smith, *eMarketing eXcellence: Planning and optimizing your digital marketing* (Abingdon: Routledge, 2014).

2 Data from **www.internetworldstats.com**, September 2014 – note that the bottom of each section lists the sources of the data that has been used to compile the graphs and charts.

3 'Top Ten Languages in the Internet' from **www.internetworldstats.com/**, accessed September 2014.

4 ITIF Broadband Rankings available from **www.itif.org** – alongside many other sets of data on technology issues in society.

5 See for example the story 'NI "Last" for UK Broadband Speeds', from *BBC News,* at news.bbc.co.uk, accessed July 2014.

6 See I. Burgmann, J. Philip, P.J. Kitchen and R. Williams, 'Does Culture Matter on the Web?', *Marketing Intelligence & Planning,* 24(1), 2006, pp. 62–76.

7 Data from Nielsen NetRatings, **www.nielsen-online.com**, accessed September 2011.

8 See P. Harrigan, E. Ramsey and P. Ibbotson, 'e-CRM in SMEs: An Exploratory Study in Northern Ireland', *Marketing Intelligence & Planning,* 26(4), 2008, pp. 385–404.

9 See Ecommerce Europe press release at **http://www.ecommerce-europe.eu/press/2013/05/press-release-european-e-commerce-to-reach-312-billion-in-2012-19-growth**, accessed May 2014. An article on worldwide B2C facts and figures can be found at **http://www.emarketer.com/Article/Global-B2C-Ecommerce-Sales-Hit-15-Trillion-This-Year-Driven-by-Growth-Emerging-Markets/1010575**, accessed May 2014.

10 Oxford Internet Survey 2013, available from **www.oii.ox.ac.uk**

11 See for example the price aggregator Priceline at **www.priceline.com**

12 Facts and figures from **http://epp.eurostat.ec.europa.eu/statistics_explained/index.php/E-commerce_statistics**, accessed August 2014.

13 Data from **http://www.ebay-mediacentre.co.uk/About-eBay/About-eBay-29.aspx**, accessed September 2014.

14 See **Pinterest.com**. User-generated content is becoming a big issue; one paper to help you get a grasp of the key topics would be M.S. O'Hern and L.R. Kahle, 'The Empowered Customer: User-Generated Content and the Future of Marketing', *Global Economics and Management Review,* 18(1), 2013, pp. 22–30.

15 Gawker can be found online at **www.gawker.com**

16 Chris Oser, 'Nike Assays Blog as Marketing Tool', *Advertising Age,* 14 June 2004, p. 26.

17 'The Secret Is Out: Secret Sparkle Body Spray Launches New Website', 16 May 2005, accessed at **www.imc2.com**; and Jack Neff, 'Strong Enough for a Man But Made for a Tween', *Advertising Age,* 25 April 2005, p. 26.

18 The full report is available from the Huffington Post at **http://www.huffingtonpost.co.uk/2013/01/31/hmv-twitter-goes-rogue-60-staff_n_2589922.html**

19 See **www.technorati.com**

20 Michelle Slatalla, 'Toll-Free Apology Soothes Savage Beast', *New York Times,* 12 February 2004, p. G4; and information from **www.planetfeedback.com/consumer**, August 2004.

21 An academic overview of these issues can be found in the paper by J.J. Kacen, J.D. Hess and W.Y. Kevin Chiang, 'Bricks or Clicks? Consumer Attitudes Toward Traditional Stores and Online Stores', *Global Economics and Management Review,* 18(1), 2013, pp. 12–21.

22 Information from **www.officedepot.co.uk**, accessed May 2014.

23 For a guide to the companies at the top of the online e-tailing charts, see **www.internetre-tailer.com** – search for the annual 'Top 500' report.

24 Adapted from Jena McGregor, 'High-Tech Achiever: MINI USA', *Fast Company,* October 2004, p. 86, with information from **www.miniusa.com**, August 2005.

25 Marty Bernstein, 'Mitsubishi Super Bowl Ad Lures Viewer to Internet', *Automotive News,* 29 March 2004, p. 56B.

26 That site does exist – but it looks like no one has been there in quite a while!

27 Visit Andrex online at **www.andrex.co.uk**

28 Jeffrey F. Rayport and Bernard J. Jaworski, *e-Commerce* (New York: McGraw-Hill, 2001), p. 116. Also see Goutam Chakraborty, 'What Do Customers Consider Important in B2B Websites?', *Journal of Advertising,* March 2003, p. 50; and David Sparrow, 'Get 'Em to Bite', *Catalogue Age,* 1 April 2003, pp. 35–6.

29 Reid Goldsborough, 'Creating Web Sites for Web Surfers', *Black Issues in Higher Education*, 17 June 2004, p. 120.

30 Organisations large and small do this – at the EU level there is europa.eu/survey_en.htm and at the local council level there is **www.rutland.gov.uk**

31 Visit the Internet Advertising Bureau at **www.iabeurope.eu** – many of the reports require membership or a fee, but there are samples of data available free of charge in the 'Knowledge Base'. Top-line figures are freely available from **www.iabuk.net**, accessed September 2014.

32 Visit **mobilemarketer.com** to read about current trends and news stories on the rapidly growing mobile marketing industry. Their Top Ten campaigns of 2013 can be found at **http://www.mobilemarketer.com/cms/news/advertising/16847.html**

33 Kris Oser, 'Video in Demand', *Advertising Age*, 4 April 2005, pp. S1–S5.

34 Pete Snyder, 'Wanted: Standards for Viral Marketing', *Brandweek*, 28 June 2004, p. 21.

35 Edited from 'Double the Power of Advertising', *Marketing Week*, **www.marketingweek.com/2008/05/22/double-the-power-of-advertising/** (Centaur Media).

36 Jack Neff, 'Taking Package Goods to the Net', *Advertising Age*, 11 July 2005, pp. 51–53.

37 Visit and play chess online at **www.chess.com** – surely more interesting than Modern Warfare 3?

38 See a summary of the report at Forrester Research, **www.forrester.com/Research/Document/Excerpt/0,7211,43165,00.html**, accessed September 2011.

39 Read the story: Darren Waters, 'Spam Blights E-Mail 15 Years On', at news.bbc.co.uk, accessed September 2011.

40 Only ever tried Google? Experiment with a few others – Yandex at **www.yandex.com** or Baidu at **www.baidu.com**

41 A good paper on the companies taking advantage of these opportunities is by N. Savage, 'Technology: Building Opportunities', *Nature*, 509(7501), 2014, pp. 521–3.

42 Microsoft has an entire site devoted to privacy issues at **www.microsoft.com/privacy**

43 See the Burberry 'Art of the Trenches' galleries at **www.artofthetrench.com**, accessed September 2011.

44 For the full story read 'Lawyer Suing Facebook Overwhelmed with Support' at **http://www.theguardian.com/technology/2014/aug/06/facebook-privacy-action-austria-max-schrems**, accessed August 2014.

45 Read the story: Kieron Guilfoyle, 'Security Matters: Why Online Shoppers Need an Education', at **www.ft.com**, accessed September 2011.

46 Edited from **www.out-law.com/page-9155**, September 2011.

47 For examples see **www.saferinternet.org** and ec.europa.eu/information_society/

48 The story in full: Joe Lynam, 'Tackling Under-Age Online Sales', at **news.bbc.co.uk**, September 2011.

49 Information on Expedia at **www.expedia.com**

50 Information on TRUSTe accessed at **www.truste.com**

51 For more on this organisation, visit **www.enisa.europa.eu**

52 See J.A. Schibrowsky, J.W. Peltier and A. Nill, 'The State of Internet Marketing Research: A Review of the Literature and Future Research Directions', *European Journal of Marketing*, 41(7/8), 2007, pp. 722–33.

CHAPTER 15
THE GLOBAL MARKETPLACE

AFTER STUDYING THIS CHAPTER, YOU SHOULD BE ABLE TO

- discuss how the international trade system and economic, political–legal and cultural environments affect a company's international marketing decisions
- describe three key approaches to entering international markets
- explain how companies adapt their marketing mixes for international markets
- identify the three major forms of international marketing organisation

THE WAY AHEAD
Previewing the concepts

It's difficult to find an area of marketing that doesn't contain at least some international issues. In this chapter, we'll focus on the special considerations that companies face when they market their products and brands globally. Advances in communications, transportation and other technologies have made the world a much smaller place. Today, almost every firm, large or small, faces international marketing issues. In this chapter, we'll examine six major decisions that marketers make in going global.

Our first story of issues and problems that arise from marketing in other countries is the example of Volkswagen and its trials and tribulations in China.

CHAPTER CONTENTS

VOLKSWAGEN IN CHINA: THE PEOPLE'S CAR IN THE PEOPLE'S REPUBLIC

Wing Lam, Durham University

'China used to be an easy game. Not anymore.'[1]

No Western company entering China has experienced such a roller-coaster experience as Volkswagen (VW), the German automobile giant. When China started its economic reforms and gradually opened its door to foreign investors in the early 1980s, many foreign companies were reluctant to invest, either because of state restrictions on technology transfer or because of concerns about protecting patents from Chinese partners. VW was the very first and the only foreign car maker to form a joint venture with a Chinese partner in the 1980s, signing a joint-venture agreement with Shanghai Automotive Industry Corp., to form the Shanghai Volkswagen Automotive Co. (SVW), and soon after another with First Automobile Works (FAW) in the northern Chinese city of Changchun in 1990 to produce Jetta, Golf, Bora and Audi branded sedans in China.[2]

When the joint venture started in 1985, there were only a handful of domestic car makers in China, all of them state owned. VW as the only real alternative fascinated Chinese buyers and initially proved to be very successful. Despite operating at full production capacity, waiting lists still grew, creating a thriving black market in VW cars. By the mid-1990s, almost all Shanghai taxis were VW Santana cars. In 2007, VW set a new sales record of 910,491 vehicles, up 28 per cent from 2006.[3] Sales were definitely on the up and up. Sounds like a complete success story? A closer examination suggests otherwise.

Despite its record sales figures, VW's market leader position in China has been steadily eroding since China joined the WTO in 2001 – this opened the market to other joint ventures and motivated domestic manufacturers to improve themselves radically. While the number of cars sold is impressive, it represents a shrinking proportion of the overall market – sales are growing rapidly, but the market is growing much more rapidly. VW's once-dominant market share has gone from 59 per cent in 1998 to 26 per cent in 2004 to 18 per cent in 2007. In 2005, General Motors overtook VW to become the sales leader in China.[4]

So what went wrong?

Model as brand

Despite VW's early success in China, it failed to establish the VW brand. As a consequence, VW Santana, its very first model when the joint venture was formed in 1985, gained more recognition than the VW corporate brand. For the majority of Chinese, Santana is a brand in its own

Remember to end the party before the last subway train because after all, you don't have a POLO GP.

Source: Volkswagen Group.

right, many consumers failing to realise its connection with VW. A worry for VW is that the Santana is an obsolete model and its popularity is declining as the domestic car makers catch up with the technology, while increased purchasing power and preferences make other Western brands attractive and available. When VW began assembling cars in China in the 1980s, the government was the main customer – individuals now account for more than half of China's car market.[5]

Distribution channels

Another issue facing VW China is the collaboration with its two Chinese joint ventures, which have separate marketing, sales and distribution channels. In other words, they are not working together to develop the VW brand, but are competing against each other in the same market segments. According to VW China, the rationale behind VW's two separate distribution channels is that vehicles of FAW-Volkswagen target more success-oriented customers, while Shanghai VW targets urban trendsetters.[6] It can be argued that the separate sales and distribution networks limit VW's ability to gather customer data, which may contribute to poor product decisions.[7] To make matters more complicated, VW's Chinese partner, Shanghai Automotive Industry Corp (SAIC), signed a joint venture with VW China's biggest competitor, General Motors, in 1997. Even more perturbing is that SAIC launched its own cars in China in late 2006, directly competing with both VW and GM.

Many of VW's competitors, especially the new foreign and local smaller car manufacturers, have much smaller distribution networks than the well-established VW network, but they do not seem to have any problems in competing with VW. The problem is not the size or degree of cooperation/competition of the two VW joint ventures, but their ability to gather market information and, most importantly, their abilities to respond to consumers' needs.

Responding to customer needs

Shaken by the rapid decline in market share, VW reorganised its China operation to place more decision-making power there. The key objective is actively to understand consumers and respond to their needs. According to the vice president of sales and marketing of Volkswagen Group China, 'VW previously segmented the market along more traditional demographic lines, such as age and income. It placed vehicles in low-, middle- and high-end price groups. In order to better respond to consumer needs, VW now divides Chinese consumers into 48 customer groups based on factors such as income and lifestyles.'[8]

Knowing consumers is one thing, responding to their needs is another. VW's previous attempt to meet customer needs included its launch of the Golf in July 2003 as a business car at RMB147,000 (€14,640). After poor sales, VW repositioned the Golf as a family car and cut its price to €13,470. Another example was its small car Gol; it was launched in May 2003 at the very low price of €7,400. The fact that it did not have air-conditioning – a necessity in China's summer – has made it very unattractive to Chinese consumers. VW was forced to relaunch the Gol with an air-conditioner and radio to meet the basic requirements of its consumers.

VW's German-centred decision making still hinders quick responses to the increasingly sophisticated Chinese consumer needs in a rapidly evolving Chinese market environment. According to one Chinese VW employee, a senior product design engineer in Shanghai, 'Our ideas are rarely respected. Every single suggestion has to go through the headquarters in Germany. It is quite obvious that a junior engineer in Germany has more power than a local engineer with over 20 years' engineering experience in VW China.' VW's rigid structure and product development procedures offer little help – for every single new design, even parts or small accessories, the local design team has to draw up a manual as thick as a phone book. The 'phone book' then needs to be sent to Germany for approval. Even a minor change suggested by a junior engineer in Germany would mean that the whole design

team in China have to draw up another 'phone book' from scratch. It is very common for experienced engineers to draw up over a dozen 'phone books' in order to get one new part approved. For an industry like car making, this practice is understandable as quality and reliability are the top priorities. In fact, the Chinese staff appreciate it as good practice quality control. However, from the designers' point of view, to devote most of their time working on the 'phone books' largely kills off their creativity in respect of improving the product, never mind their motivation to respond to consumers' needs. In fact, the organisational culture of VW has little to do with customer orientation, as perceived by its employees in their product design departments. The result is obvious: the decision makers do not necessarily know the consumers' needs while those who know the consumers have little influence or are distracted by other duties and requirements.

The 'white ceiling'

VW is proud of its staff development programme for its local Chinese staff. According to the company, training for Chinese employees is one of VW's paramount goals in China. Apprenticeships and advanced training schemes for local personnel are conducted in Germany and abroad as well as in China itself.[9] Many current and former employees of VW China agree that they benefited enormously from the training offered by VW. However, things started to turn sour when the local managers hit the 'white ceiling' – a look at any of VW China's department organisation charts shows that most managerial positions above a certain level are taken by German managers.

Frustrated by the feeling that they have little say in decision making, and little chance of promotion to a senior managerial position, a significant number of experienced local staff leave VW each year for better job prospects. Many of them stay in the same industry, working for VW's parts suppliers or, most worryingly for VW, its competitors. Inadvertently, VW has become the de facto training school for China's car industry.[10]

The way forward

Traditionally VW China focused its marketing on promoting individual cars. For the first time in nearly 20 years, VW launched a marketing campaign to build corporate brand identity.[11] Additionally, and just as importantly, the People's Car company in the People's Republic is working hard to retain its own staff by introducing sincere localisation of senior managerial posts in order to encourage creativity and innovation in China, in order to serve better another group of people, their customers.

Sources: See notes 1–11 at the end of this chapter.

International trade goes back thousands of years in Europe – from the Greeks and Romans in ancient times, through the Vikings and then the Venetians, to the modern day

Source: Alamy Images/Rob Bartree.

Almost all companies begin by serving their local markets. These customers are closer, more convenient to serve and are most easily understood by the firm. Managers do not immediately need to learn other languages, deal with strange and changing currencies, face another set of political and legal uncertainties, or adapt their products to different customer needs and expectations in other nations and cultures. In essence, the domestic market is relatively easy and relatively safe. Some cultures have historically been better at this than others, by virtue of possibility or necessity – Germany has long been a world leader in terms of exports, exploiting its strengths in engineering. Italy and Greece are two European nations with Mediterranean-centred trading patterns dating back more than 25 centuries, and a company in Switzerland or Luxembourg will have international markets only a few kilometres away. Archaeologists recently discovered coins from Damascus, Persia and Africa in Sweden – brought back by Viking traders in the ninth century.[12] Napoleon called England 'a nation of shopkeepers', and the financial instruments used by London-based bankers such as the Rothschilds played as much a part in his eventual downfall as did Waterloo.

Some nations have historically been less active international traders. Japan closed its borders to most foreign influences in the middle of the seventeenth century, only reopening them 200 years later after some gunboat diplomacy by the USA. US companies themselves have until recently existed in a mostly homogeneous market with many tens of millions of customers domestically – and this has reduced the imperative to make a priority of overseas markets.

GLOBAL MARKETING IN THE TWENTY-FIRST CENTURY

Today, however, the situation is very different. The world is shrinking rapidly with the advent of faster communications, transportation and financial flows. Products developed in one country – Gucci handbags, Sony electronics, McDonald's hamburgers, BMWs – are finding enthusiastic acceptance in other countries. We would not be surprised to hear about a German businessman wearing an Italian suit meeting a French friend at a Japanese restaurant in Moscow who later returns home to drink Scotch whisky and watch Spanish football on a Korean TV.

International trade is booming. Since 1969 the number of multinational corporations in the world has grown from 7,000 to more than 63,000. Some of these multinationals are true giants. In fact, of the largest 100 'economies' in the world, only 47 are countries. The remaining 53 are multinational corporations. ExxonMobil, one of the world's largest companies, has annual revenues greater than the GDP of all but the world's 20 largest countries.[13]

In 2010, the WTO reported that world trade had – after a decade of growth – shrunk in the face of a global recession. Despite this, the volume and value of goods traded internationally were immense. China's growth had seen it overtake Germany to become the leading exporter in the world – with the USA declining to third place. Taken as a whole, Europe was responsible for 42 per cent of all global exports – three times that of the USA and four times that of China – powered by the 'big 4' of Germany, France, Italy and the UK. China also became the second-largest importer of goods, after the USA.[14] The destination of exports also revealed that three-quarters of European trade went to another European nation. If you've been wondering why the EU causes such a fuss, that should tell you.

Many companies have long been successful at international marketing – Unilever, Coca-Cola, BMW, KPMG, Sony, Toyota, BP, Nokia, Nestlé, Royal Bank of Scotland, Boeing, McDonald's – and dozens of others have made the world their market. Michelin, the oh-so-French tyre manufacturer, now does a third of its business in the USA and Mexico; Johnson & Johnson, the maker of quintessentially all-American products like Band-Aids and Johnson's Baby Shampoo, does 42 per cent of its business abroad.[15]

But while global trade is growing, global competition is intensifying. Foreign firms are expanding aggressively into new international markets, and home markets are no longer as rich in opportunity. Few industries are now safe from foreign competition. If companies delay taking steps towards internationalising, they risk being shut out of growing markets in Western and Eastern Europe, China and the Pacific Rim, Russia and elsewhere. Firms that stay at home to play it safe might not only lose their chances to enter other markets, but also risk losing their home markets.[16] Domestic companies that never thought about foreign competitors suddenly find these competitors on their own doorstep.

Ironically, although the need for companies to go abroad is greater today than in the past, so are the risks. Companies that go global may face highly unstable governments and currencies, restrictive government policies and regulations, and high trade barriers. Corruption is also an increasing problem – officials in some countries often award business not to the best bidder, but to the highest briber. This is not an issue that is likely to go away, but in this age of easy exchange and dissemination of information, it is a lot harder to keep it quiet – organisations like Transparency International challenge governments, societies and businesses on corruption-related issues. For example, Sweden's Volvo was fined £3.5m for illegally bypassing UN trade restrictions in Iraq.[17]

A **global firm** is one that, by operating in more than one country, gains marketing, production, R&D and financial advantages that are not available to purely domestic competitors. The global company sees the world as one market. It minimises the importance of national boundaries and develops 'transnational' brands. It raises capital, obtains materials and components, and manufactures and markets its goods wherever it can do the best job. For example, Otis Elevator gets its elevator door systems from France, small geared parts from Spain, electronics from Germany and special motor drives from Japan. It uses the USA only for systems integration. 'Borders are so twentieth century,' says one global marketing expert. 'Transnationals take "stateless" to the next level.'[18]

This does not mean that small and medium-sized firms must operate in a dozen countries to succeed. These firms can practise *global niching*. But the world is becoming smaller, and every company operating in a global industry – whether large or small – must assess and establish its place in world markets.

The rapid move towards globalisation means that all companies will have to answer some basic questions: What market position should we try to establish in our country, in our economic region and globally? Who will our global competitors be, and what are their strategies and resources? Where should we produce or source our products? What strategic alliances should we form with other firms around the world?

As shown in Figure 15.1, a company faces six major decisions in international marketing. We will discuss each decision in detail in this chapter.

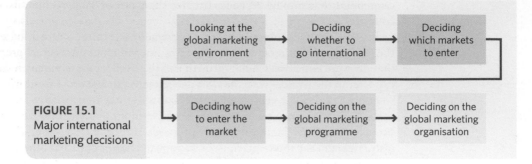

FIGURE 15.1
Major international
marketing decisions

LOOKING AT THE GLOBAL MARKETING ENVIRONMENT

Before deciding whether to operate internationally, a company must understand the international marketing environment. That environment has changed a great deal in the last two decades, creating both new opportunities and new problems.

The international trade system

Companies looking abroad must start by understanding the international *trade system*. When selling to another country, a firm may face restrictions on trade between nations. Foreign governments may charge *tariffs,* taxes on certain imported products designed to raise revenue or to protect domestic firms. Or they may set *quotas,* limits on the amount of foreign imports that they will accept in certain product categories. The EU currently has quotas for the import of products as varied as light bulbs, shoes and many agricultural commodities. The purpose of a quota is sometimes to conserve foreign exchange/rates but more usually to protect local industry and employment. Firms may also face *exchange controls*, which limit the amount of foreign exchange and the exchange rate against other currencies.

The company may also face *non-tariff trade barriers,* such as biases against non-domestic company bids or restrictive product standards that go against current product features:

> One of the cleverest ways the Japanese have found to keep foreign manufacturers out of their domestic market is to plead 'uniqueness'. Japanese skin is different, the government argues, so foreign cosmetics companies must test their products in Japan before selling there. The Japanese say their stomachs are small and have room for only the mikan, the local tangerine, so imports of oranges are limited. Now the Japanese have come up with what may be the flakiest argument yet: their snow is different, so ski equipment should be too.[19]

At the same time, certain forces *help* trade between nations. Examples include the General Agreement on Tariffs and Trade (GATT) and various regional free trade agreements. In Europe, the biggest is, of course, the EU, although there are others, like EFTA (European Free Trade Association – members include Iceland and Norway) and CEFTA (Central European Free Trade Association – members include Croatia, Serbia and Albania).

The World Trade Organization and GATT

The GATT is a 65-year-old treaty designed to promote world trade by reducing tariffs and other international trade barriers. Since the treaty's inception in 1948, member nations have met in eight rounds of GATT negotiations to reassess trade barriers and set new rules for international trade. The first seven rounds of negotiations reduced the average worldwide tariffs on manufactured goods from 45 per cent to just 5 per cent.[20]

The most recently completed GATT negotiations, dubbed the Uruguay Round, dragged on for seven long years before concluding in 1993. It reduced the world's remaining merchandise tariffs by 30 per cent – one concern of many economists is that the recent economic turbulence might reverse that trend. The agreement also extended GATT to cover trade in agriculture and a wide range of services, and it toughened international protection of copyrights, patents, trademarks and other intellectual property. Although the financial impact of such an agreement is difficult to measure, research suggests that cutting agriculture, manufacturing and services trade barriers by one-third would boost the world economy by $613bn, the equivalent of adding another Australia to the world economy.[21]

Beyond reducing trade barriers and setting global standards for trade, the Uruguay Round set up the World Trade Organization (WTO) to enforce GATT rules.[22] In general, the WTO acts as an umbrella organisation, overseeing GATT, mediating global disputes and imposing trade sanctions. The previous GATT organisation never possessed such authority. A new round of GATT negotiations, the Doha Round, began in Doha, Qatar, in late 2001 and was set to conclude in January 2005. Although progress has been made – notably the 'Bali Package' of arrangements to streamline trade achieved in 2013 – by mid-2014 the Doha Round had still not reached a final conclusion.[23] The WTO had 160 member nations in June 2014.

Regional free trade zones

Certain countries have formed *free trade zones* or **economic communities**. These are groups of nations organised to work towards common goals in the regulation of international trade. One such community is the EU. Originally formed in 1957 as the European Economic Community (EEC), it set out to create a single European market by reducing barriers to the free flow of products, services, finances and labour among member countries and developing policies on trade with non-member nations. Today, the EU represents one of the world's single largest markets. Its current 28 member states (Croatia is the newest member, having joined in 2013, while Turkey and Macedonia are among the states hoping to join) contain over 500 million consumers.[24]

As a result of increased unification, European companies have grown bigger and more competitive. Perhaps an even greater concern, however, is that lower barriers *inside* Europe will create only thicker *outside* walls. Some observers envisage a 'Fortress Europe' that gives favours to firms from EU countries but hinders outsiders by imposing obstacles – this is especially a concern for African nations, but also for the USA and China.

Progress towards European unification has been slow – many doubt that complete unification can or should be achieved. In recent years, 18 member states have taken a significant

Economic communities: the EU represents one of the world's largest single markets. Its current 28 member states contain more than 493 million consumers and account for 20 per cent of the world's exports

Source: Alamy Images/BL Images Ltd.

step towards unification by adopting the euro as a common currency – but this project is now under pressure and it remains to be seen whether or not it can be sustained in the long term. At the macroeconomic level the euro may be causing discomfort to national governments, but the adoption of the euro has decreased much of the currency risk associated with doing business in Europe from the perspective of firms, making member states with previously weak currencies more attractive markets.[25]

However, even with the adoption of the euro, it is unlikely that the EU will ever go against 2,000 years of tradition and become the 'United States of Europe'. A community with dozens of different languages and cultures will always have difficulty coming together and acting as a single entity. Still, although only partly successful so far, unification has made Europe a global force with which to reckon, with a combined EU annual GDP of more than $16 trillion.[26]

Following the apparent success of the EU and NAFTA, the North American Free Trade Agreement,[27] the Central American Free Trade Agreement (CAFTA) established a free trade zone between the USA and Costa Rica, the Dominican Republic, El Salvador, Guatemala, Honduras and Nicaragua in 2005. There have also been a number of international meetings to investigate the establishment of a Free Trade Area of the Americas, but so far these discussions have not borne fruit.

Other free trade areas have formed in Latin America and South America. For example, MERCOSUR links nine Latin American and South American countries, and the Andean Community (CAN, for its Spanish initials) links five more. In late 2004, MERCOSUR and CAN agreed to unite, creating the South American Community of Nations (CSN), which will be modelled after the EU. Complete integration between the two trade blocs was agreed in 2008 and all tariffs between the nations are to be eliminated by 2019. With a population of more than 367 million, a combined economy of more than $2.8 trillion a year, and exports worth $181bn, the CSN will make up the largest trading bloc after NAFTA and the EU.[28]

Although the recent trend towards free trade zones has caused great excitement and new market opportunities, some see it as a mixed blessing. For example, in Germany and France, trade unions like IG Metall and Force Ouvrière fear that EU expansion will lead to the exodus of manufacturing jobs to Central and Eastern Europe, where wage rates are much lower. Environmentalists worry that companies that are unwilling to play by the strict rules of the EU or North America will relocate in Mexico or China, where pollution regulation is more lax.[29]

Each nation has unique features that must be understood. A nation's readiness for different products and services and its attractiveness as a market to foreign firms depend on its economic, political, legal and cultural environments.

Economic environment

The international marketer must study each country's economy. Two economic factors reflect the country's attractiveness as a market: the country's industrial structure and its income distribution.

The country's *industrial structure* shapes its product and service needs, income levels and employment levels. The four types of industrial structures are as follows:

- *Subsistence economies*: In a subsistence economy, the vast majority of people engage in simple agriculture. They consume most of their output and barter the rest for simple goods and services. They offer few market opportunities.

- *Raw-material-exporting economies*: These economies are rich in one or more natural resources but poor in other ways. Much of their revenue comes from exporting these resources. Examples are Chile (tin and copper), Democratic Republic of Congo (copper, cobalt and coffee) and Saudi Arabia (oil). These countries are good markets for large equipment, tools and supplies, and trucks. If there are many foreign residents or a wealthy upper class, they are also a market for luxury goods.

● *Industrialising economies*: In an industrialising economy, manufacturing accounts for 10–20 per cent of the country's economy. Examples include Egypt, India and Brazil. As manufacturing increases, the country needs more imports of raw textile materials, steel and heavy machinery, and fewer imports of finished textiles, paper products and vehicles. Industrialisation typically creates a new rich class and a small but growing middle class, both demanding new types of imported goods.

● *Industrial economies*: Industrial economies are major exporters of manufactured goods, services and investment funds. They trade goods among themselves and also export them to other types of economies for raw materials and semi-finished goods. The varied manu-facturing activities of these industrial nations and their large middle class make them rich markets for all sorts of goods. Many European nations have this form of industrial struc-ture – but some argue that a more realistic description of the most developed European nations would be 'post-industrial economies', where production of goods and products forms a minority of an economy that is dominated by services – such as the UK and Germany with their large financial services sectors.

The second economic factor is the country's *income distribution*. Industrialised nations may have low-, medium- and high-income households. In contrast, countries with subsist-ence economies may consist mostly of households with very low family incomes. Still other countries may have households with only either very low or very high incomes. However, even poor or developing economies may be attractive markets for all kinds of goods, includ-ing luxuries. For example, many luxury brand marketers are rushing to take advantage of China's rapidly developing consumer markets:

> More than half of China's 1.3 billion consumers can barely afford rice, let alone luxuries. According to the World Bank, more than 400 million Chinese live on less than $2 a day. For now, only some 1 per cent of China's population (about 13 million people) earns enough to even consider purchasing luxury-brand products. Yet posh brands – from Gucci and Cartier to BMW and Bentley – are descending on China in force. How can purveyors of $2,000 hand-bags, $20,000 watches, and $1 million limousines thrive in a developing economy? Easy, says a Cartier executive. 'Remember, even medium-sized cities in China . . . have populations larger than Switzerland's. So it doesn't matter if the percentage of people in those cities who can afford our products is very small.'
>
> Dazzled by the pace at which China's booming economy is minting millionaires and swelling the ranks of the middle class, luxury brands are rushing to stake out shop space, tout their wares, and lay the foundations of a market they hope will eventually include as many as 100 million conspicuous consumers. 'The Chinese are a natural audience for luxury goods,' notes one analyst. After decades of socialism and poverty, China's elite are suddenly 'keen to show off their newfound wealth'.
>
> Europe's fashion houses are happy to assist. Giorgio Armani . . . hosted a star-studded fashion show to celebrate the opening of his 12,000-square-foot flagship store on Shanghai's waterfront . . . and promised 30 stores in China before the 2008 Beijing Olympics. Gucci recently opened stores in Hangzhou and Chengdu, bringing its China total to six. And it's not just clothes. Cartier, with nine stores in China and seven on the drawing board, has seen its China sales double for the past several years. Car makers, too, are racing in. BMW recently cut the ribbon on a new Chinese factory that has the capacity to produce 50,000 BMWs a year. Audi's sleek A6 has emerged as the car of choice for the Communist Party's senior ranks, despite its $230,000 price tag. Bentley, which sold 70 cars in China in 2003 – including 19 limousines priced at more than $1 million each – boasts three dealerships in China, as does Rolls-Royce.[30]

Thus, country and regional economic environments will affect an international mar-keter's decisions about which global markets to enter and how.

Political–legal environment

Nations differ greatly in their political–legal environments. In considering whether to do business in a given country, a company should consider factors such as the country's attitudes towards international buying, government bureaucracy, political stability and monetary regulations.

Some nations are very receptive to foreign firms; others are less accommodating. For example, India has tended to bother foreign businesses with import quotas, currency restrictions and other limitations that make operating there a challenge. In contrast, neighbouring Asian countries such as Singapore and Thailand court foreign investors and shower them with incentives and favourable operating conditions. Political stability is another issue. India's government is notoriously unstable – the country has elected 10 new governments in the past 20 years, and there is a history of high-level political assassinations – increasing the risk of doing business there. Although most international marketers still find India's huge market attractive, the unstable political situation will affect how they handle business and financial matters. However, things may change after the Bharatiya Janata Party (BJP) won the 2014 Indian general election, and with their leader Narendra Modi becoming the country's Prime Minister, since Modi is considered to be a business-friendly politician.[31]

Companies must also consider a country's monetary regulations. Sellers want to take their profits in a currency of value to them. Ideally, the buyer can pay in the seller's currency or in other world currencies. Short of this, sellers might accept a blocked currency – its removal from the country is restricted by the buyer's government – if they can buy other goods in that country that they need themselves or can sell elsewhere for a needed currency. Besides currency limits, a changing exchange rate also creates high risks for the seller.

Most international trade involves cash transactions. Yet many nations have too little hard currency to pay for their purchases from other countries. They may want to pay with other items instead of cash, which has led to a growing practice called **countertrade**. Countertrade takes several forms. *Barter* involves the direct exchange of goods or services, as when Azerbaijan imports wheat from Romania in exchange for crude oil, and Vietnam exchanges rice for fertiliser and coconuts from the Philippines. Another form is *compensation* (or *buyback*), whereby the seller sells a plant, equipment or technology to another country and agrees to take payment in the resulting products. Thus, Japan's Fukusuke Corporation sold knitting machines and raw textile materials to Shanghai clothing manufacturer Chinatex in exchange for finished textiles produced on the machines. The most common form of countertrade is *counterpurchase,* in which the seller receives full payment in cash but agrees to spend some of the money in the other country. For example, Boeing sells aircraft to India and agrees to buy Indian coffee, rice, castor oil and other goods and sell them elsewhere.[32]

Countertrade deals can be very complex. For example, a few years ago DaimlerChrysler agreed to sell 30 trucks to Romania in exchange for 150 Romanian jeeps, which it then sold to Ecuador for bananas, which were in turn sold to a German supermarket chain for the then German currency (the Deutschmark). Through this roundabout process, DaimlerChrysler finally obtained payment in German money.

Cultural environment

Each country has its own traditions, norms and taboos. When designing global marketing strategies, companies must understand how culture affects consumer reactions in each of its world markets. In turn, they must also understand how their strategies affect local cultures.

The impact of culture on marketing strategy

The seller must examine the ways consumers in different countries think about and use certain products before planning a marketing programme. There are often surprises. For example, the average French man uses almost twice as many cosmetics and grooming aids as his wife. The Germans and the French eat more packaged, branded spaghetti than do Italians. Italian children like to eat chocolate bars between slices of bread as a snack. Women in Tanzania will not give their children eggs for fear of making them bald or impotent.

Companies that ignore such differences can make some very expensive and embarrassing mistakes. Here is an example:

> McDonald's and Coca-Cola managed to offend the entire Muslim world by putting the Saudi Arabian flag on their packaging. The flag's design includes a passage from the Koran, and Muslims feel very strongly that their Holy Writ should never be tossed in the garbage. Nike faced a similar situation in Arab countries when Muslims objected to a stylised 'Air' logo on its shoes, which resembled 'Allah' in Arabic script. Nike apologised for the mistake and pulled the shoes from distribution.[33]

Business norms and behaviour also vary from country to country. For example, Western executives often like to get right down to business and engage in fast and tough face-to-face bargaining. However, Japanese and other Asian businesspeople often find this behaviour offensive. They prefer to start with polite conversation, and they rarely say no in face-to-face conversations. As another example, South Americans like to sit or stand very close to each other when they talk business – in fact, almost nose to nose. Business executives need to be briefed on these kinds of factors before conducting business in another country.[34]

By the same token, companies that understand cultural nuances can use them to advantage when positioning products internationally. Consider the following examples of how European products have adapted to local conditions in the increasingly important market of China:

> A product marketed with a well-designed and localised name creates an instant connection with local consumers, yet maintains the prestige and perceptions of high quality that are frequently associated with foreign products. Carrefour, a French hypermarket chain, localised its name into '家乐福,' or 'jia le fu' when entering the Chinese market. This name literally translates as 'Happy Family'. However, the individual characters bring with them the associations of harmony, luck and prosperity – a highly desirable combination in Chinese thought.
>
> Sometimes, localising a product's appearance can also mean changing the product's physical presentation to fit in with cultural events. Häagen-Dazs, the epitome of fine ice cream, localised its product appearance to capitalise on Chinese holidays, which are peak buying seasons throughout China. To fit in with the local culture, Häagen-Dazs produced ice cream in the form of a Chinese moon cake. By doing so, it could both charge a premium price for the 'foreign experience', while taking advantage of a surge in sales usually enjoyed only by bakeries. To localise the content means adjusting the product to the local language, measurement system, currency and local ideals. The sophisticated international magazine on fashion, beauty, and style – *Elle* – not only localises the content into Chinese language, but it also sensitises to local cultural ideals and has adapted its content to profile Chinese models, publish more conservative editorials, and advertise beauty products that appeal to the Chinese ideals of beauty such as whitening cream for a paler complexion.[35]

Thus, understanding cultural traditions, preferences and behaviours can help companies not only to avoid embarrassing mistakes, but also to take advantage of cross-cultural opportunities.

The impact of marketing strategy on cultures

Whereas marketers worry about the impact of culture on their global marketing strategies, others may worry about the impact of marketing strategies on global cultures. For example, some critics argue that 'globalisation' really means 'Americanisation'. Globalisation as a concept or topic is not one that is seen positively in all corners of the world. In France, for example, there is real concern and debate about the connection between the culture of business and the culture of society as whole – a recent survey found that only one in three French think a free-market economy is the best way to develop the nation. Of course, France is home to many of the leading global brands, and French companies have operations all round the world – one-third of Europe's top 100 companies are French in origin.[36]

Critics worry that the more people around the world are exposed to Western lifestyles in the food they eat, the stores they shop in and the TV shows and films they watch, the more they will lose their individual cultural identities. They contend that exposure to Western values and products erodes other cultures and Westernises the world – see Marketing at Work 15.1 for the story of how the Big Mac went East.

McDonald's: serving customers around the world

MARKETING AT WORK 15.1

The first McDonald's stand popped up in California in 1954, and what could be more American than burger-and-fries fast food? But as it turns out, the quintessentially all-American company now sells more burgers and fries outside the country than within. Nearly 65 per cent of McDonald's $23.5bn of sales come from outside the USA, and its international sales are growing at close to twice the rate of domestic sales.

McDonald's today is a truly global enterprise. Its 32,000 restaurants serve more than 58 million people in more than 100 countries each day. Few firms have more international marketing experience than McDonald's. But going global has not always been easy, and McDonald's has learned many important lessons in its journeys overseas. To see how far McDonald's has come, consider its experiences in Russia, a market that is very different culturally, economically and politically from our own.

McDonald's first set its sights on Russia (then a part of the Soviet Union) in 1976, when George Cohon, Head of McDonald's in Canada, took a group of Soviet Olympics officials to a McDonald's while they visited for the Montreal Olympic Games. Cohon was struck by how much the Soviets liked McDonald's hamburgers, fries and other fare. Over the next 14 years, Cohon flew to Russia more than 100 times, first to get Soviet permission for McDonald's to provide food for the 1980 Moscow Olympics, and later to be allowed to open McDonald's restaurants in the country. He quickly learned that no one in Russia had any idea what a McDonald's was. The Soviets turned Cohon down flat on both requests.

Source: Getty Images/AFP.

Finally, in 1988, as Premier Mikhail Gorbachev began to open the Russian economy, Cohon forged a deal with the city of Moscow to launch the first Russian McDonald's in Moscow's Pushkin Square. But obtaining permission was only the first step. Actually opening the restaurant brought a fresh set of challenges. Thanks to Russia's large and bureaucratic government structure, McDonald's had to obtain some 200 separate signatures just to open the single location. It had difficulty finding reliable suppliers for even such basics as hamburgers and buns. So McDonald's forked out over $45m to build a facility to produce these things itself. It even brought in technical experts from Canada with special strains of disease-resistant seed to teach Russian farmers how to grow Russet Burbank potatoes for French fries, and it built its own pasteurising plant to ensure a plentiful supply of fresh milk.

When the Moscow McDonald's at Pushkin Square finally opened its doors in January 1990, it quickly won the hearts of Russian consumers. However, the company faced still more hurdles. The Pushkin Square restaurant is huge – 26 cash registers and 900 seats (compared with 40 to 50 seats in a typical McDonald's). The logistics of serving customers on such a scale was daunting, made even more difficult by the fact that few employees or customers understood the fast-food concept.

Although Western consumers were well acquainted with McDonald's, the Russians were clueless. So, in order to meet its high standards for customer satisfaction in this new market, the US fast feeder had to educate employees about the time-tested McDonald's way of doing things. It trained Russian managers at Hamburger University and subjected each of 630 new employees (most of whom did not know a chicken McNugget from an Egg McMuffin) to 16 to 20 hours of training on such essentials as cooking meat patties, assembling Filet-O-Fish sandwiches and giving service with a smile. Back in those days, McDonald's even had to train consumers – most Muscovites had never seen a fast-food restaurant. Customers waiting in line were shown videos telling them everything from how to order and pay at the counter, to how to put their coats over the backs of their seats, to how to handle a Big Mac.

However, the new Moscow McDonald's got off to a spectacular start. An incredible 50,000 customers swarmed to the restaurant during its first day of business. And in its usual way, McDonald's began immediately to build community involvement. On opening day, it held a kick-off party for 700 Muscovite orphans and then donated all opening-day proceeds to the Moscow Children's Fund.

Today, McDonald's is thriving in Russia. The Pushkin Square location is now the busiest McDonald's in the world, and Russia is the crown jewel in McDonald's global empire. The company's 240 restaurants in 40 Russian cities each serve an average of 850,000 diners a year – twice the per-store traffic of any of the other 122 countries in which McDonald's operates.

Despite the long lines of customers, McDonald's has been careful about how rapidly it expands in Russia. In recent years, it has reined in its rapid growth strategy and focused instead on improving product and service quality and profitability. The goal is to squeeze more business out of existing restaurants and to grow slowly but profitably. One way to do that is to add new menu items to draw in consumers at different times of the day. So, as it did many years ago in the USA, McDonald's in Russia is now adding breakfast items.

Although only about 5 per cent of Russians eat breakfast outside the home, more commuters in the big cities are leaving home earlier to avoid heavy traffic. The

company hopes that the new breakfast menu will encourage commuters to stop off at McDonald's on their way to work. However, when the fast-food chain added breakfast items, it stopped offering its traditional hamburger fare during the morning hours. When many customers complained of 'hamburger withdrawal', McDonald's introduced the Fresh McMuffin, an English muffin with a sausage patty topped with cheese, lettuce, tomato, and special sauce. The new sandwich became an instant hit.

To reduce the lines inside restaurants and to attract motorists, McDonald's is also introducing Russian consumers to drive-thru windows. At first, many Russians just did not get the concept. Instead, they treated the drive-thru window as just another line, purchasing their food there, parking, and going inside to eat. Also, Russian cars often do not have cupholders, so drive-thru customers bought fewer drinks. However, as more customers get used to the concept, McDonald's is putting drive-thru and walk-up windows in about half of its new stores.

So, that is a look at McDonald's in Russia. But just as McDonald's has tweaked its formula in Russia, it also adjusts its marketing and operations to meet the special needs of local consumers in other major global markets. To be sure, McDonald's is a global brand. Its restaurants around the world employ a common global strategy – convenient food at affordable prices. And no matter where you go in the world – from Moscow to Montreal or Shanghai to Cheboygan, Michigan – you'll find those good old golden arches and a menu full of Quarter Pounders, Big Macs, fries, milkshakes and other familiar items. But within that general strategic framework, McDonald's adapts to the subtleties of each local market. Says a McDonald's Europe executive, 'Across Europe with 40 different markets, there are 40 sets of tastes. There are also differences within each market. We are a local market but a global brand.'

In the past, US companies paid little attention to international trade. If they could pick up some extra sales through exporting, that was fine. But the big market was at home, and it teemed with opportunities. The home market was also much safer. Managers did not need to learn other languages, deal with strange and changing currencies, face political and legal uncertainties, or adapt their products to different customer needs and expectations. Today, however, the situation is much different. Organisations of all kinds, from Coca-Cola, IBM and Google to MTV and even the NBA, have gone global.

Sources: Quotes and other information from Janet Adamy, 'Steady Diet: As Burgers Boom in Russia, McDonald's Touts Discipline', *The Wall Street Journal,* 16 October 2007, p. A1; Fern Glazer, 'NPD: QSR Chains Expanding Globally Must Also Act Locally', *Nation's Restaurant News,* 22 October 2007, p. 18; 'McDonald's Eyes Russia with 40 New Stores', www.reuters.com; and information from www.mcdonalds.com

DECIDING WHETHER TO GO INTERNATIONAL

Not all companies need to venture into international markets to survive. Operating domestically is easier and safer. Managers do not need to learn another country's language and laws. They do not have to deal with unstable currencies, face additional political and legal uncertainties, or redesign their products to suit different customer expectations. However, companies that operate in global industries, where their strategic positions in specific markets are affected strongly by their overall global positions, must compete on a worldwide basis to succeed.

Any of several factors might draw a company into the international arena. Global competitors might attack the company's home market by offering better products or lower prices. The company might want to counter-attack these competitors in their home markets to tie up their resources. Or the company's home market might be stagnant or shrinking, and foreign markets may present higher sales and profit opportunities. Or the company's customers might be expanding abroad and require international servicing.

Before going abroad, the company must weigh several risks and answer many questions about its ability to operate globally. Can the company learn to understand the preferences and buyer behaviour of consumers in other countries? Can it offer competitively attractive products? Will it be able to adapt to other countries' business cultures and deal effectively with foreign nationals? Do the company's managers have the necessary international experience? Has management considered the impact of regulations and the political environments of other countries?

Because of the difficulties of entering international markets, most companies do not act until some situation or event thrusts them into the global arena. Someone – a domestic exporter, a foreign importer, a foreign government – may ask the company to sell abroad. Or the company may be saddled with overcapacity and need to find additional markets for its goods.

DECIDING WHICH MARKETS TO ENTER

Before going abroad, the company should try to define its international *marketing objectives and policies*. It should decide what *volume* of foreign sales it wants. Most companies start small when they go abroad. Some plan to stay small, seeing international sales as a small part of their business. Other companies have bigger plans, seeing international business as equal to or even more important than their domestic business.

The company also needs to choose *how many* countries it wants to market in. Companies must be careful not to spread themselves too thin or to expand beyond their capabilities by operating in too many countries too soon. Next, the company needs to decide on the *types* of countries to enter. A country's attractiveness depends on the product, geographical factors, income and population, political climate and other factors. The seller may prefer certain country groups or parts of the world. In recent years, many major new markets have emerged, offering both substantial opportunities and daunting challenges.

After listing possible international markets, the company must carefully evaluate each one. It must consider many factors. For example, Colgate's decision to enter the Chinese market seems fairly straightforward: China's huge population makes it the world's largest toothpaste market. And given that only 20 per cent of China's rural dwellers now brush daily, this already huge market can grow even larger. Yet Colgate must still question whether market size *alone* is reason enough to invest heavily in China.

Colgate must ask some important questions: Will it be able to overcome cultural barriers and convince Chinese consumers to brush their teeth regularly? Does China provide for the needed production and distribution technologies? Can Colgate compete effectively with dozens of local competitors, a state-owned brand managed by Unilever and Procter & Gamble's Crest?

TABLE 15.1 Indicators of market potential

Demographic characteristics	Socio-cultural factors
Education Population size and growth Population age composition	Consumer lifestyles, beliefs and values Business norms and approaches Social norms Languages
Geographic characteristics	**Political and legal factors**
Climate Country size Population density – urban, rural Transportation structure and market accessibility	National priorities Political stability Government attitudes towards global trade Government bureaucracy Monetary and trade regulations
Economic factors	
GDP size and growth Income distribution Industrial infrastructure Natural resources Financial and human resources	

Will the Chinese government remain stable and supportive? Colgate's current success in China suggests that it could answer yes to all of these questions. By aggressively pursuing promotional and educational programmes – from massive ad campaigns to visits to local schools to sponsoring oral-care research – Colgate has expanded its market share from 7 per cent in 1995 to 35 per cent in 2005. Still, the company's future in China is filled with uncertainties.[37]

Possible global markets should be ranked on several factors, including market size, market growth, cost of doing business, competitive advantage and risk level. The goal is to determine the potential of each market, using indicators such as those shown in Table 15.1. Then the marketer must decide which markets offer the greatest long-term return on investment.

DECIDING HOW TO ENTER THE MARKET

Once a company has decided to sell in a foreign country, it must determine the best mode of entry. Its choices are *exporting, joint venturing* and *direct investment*. Figure 15.2 shows three market entry strategies, along with the options each one offers. As the figure shows, each succeeding strategy involves more commitment and risk, but also more control and potential profits.

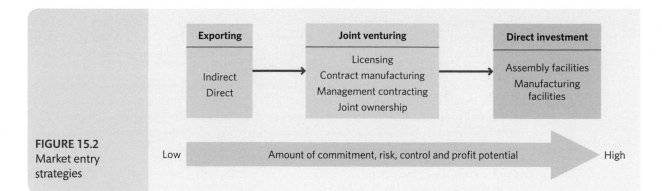

FIGURE 15.2 Market entry strategies

Exporting

The simplest way to enter a foreign market is through **exporting**. The company may passively export its surplus production from time to time, or it may make an active commitment to expand exports to a particular market. In either case, the company produces all its goods in its home country. It may or may not modify them for the export market. Exporting involves the least change in the company's product lines, organisation, investments or mission – making it by far the simplest method to enter a foreign market.

Companies typically start with *indirect exporting*, working through independent international marketing intermediaries. Indirect exporting involves less investment because the firm does not require an overseas marketing organisation or set of contacts. It also involves less risk. International marketing intermediaries bring know-how and services to the relationship, so the seller normally makes fewer mistakes.

Sellers may eventually move into *direct exporting*, whereby they handle their own exports. The investment and risk are somewhat greater in this strategy, but so is the potential return. A company can conduct direct exporting in several ways. It can set up a domestic export department that carries out export activities. It can set up an overseas sales branch that handles sales, distribution and perhaps promotion. The sales branch gives the seller more presence and programme control in the foreign market and often serves as a display centre and customer service centre. The company can also send home-based salespeople abroad at certain times in order to find business. Finally, the company can do its exporting either through foreign-based distributors who buy and own the goods or through foreign-based agents who sell the goods on behalf of the company.

Joint venturing

A second method of entering a foreign market is **joint venturing** – joining with foreign companies to produce or market products or services. Joint venturing differs from exporting in that the company joins with a host-country partner to sell or market abroad. VW did this with its Chinese partners. It differs from direct investment in that an association is formed with someone in the foreign country. There are four types of joint ventures: licensing, contract manufacturing, management contracting and joint ownership.[38]

Licensing

Licensing is a simple way for a manufacturer to enter international marketing. The company enters into an agreement with a licensee in the foreign market. For a fee or royalty, the licensee buys the right to use the company's manufacturing process, trademark, patent, trade secret or other item of value. The company thus gains entry into the market at little risk; the licensee gains production expertise or a well-known product or name without having to start from scratch.

Coca-Cola markets internationally by licensing bottlers around the world and supplying them with the syrup needed to produce the product. In Japan, Budweiser beer flows from Kirin breweries, and Tokyo Disneyland is owned and operated by Oriental Land Company under licence from the Walt Disney Company. GW Pharmaceuticals strikes deals with Japanese partners to produce their new drugs in the UK.

Licensing has potential disadvantages, however. The firm has less control over the licensee than it would over its own production facilities – the Danish toy company, Lego, recently took over production at its licensed partner's production facility in the Czech Republic for strategic reasons, but this company – Flextronics – will continue production in Mexico.[39] Furthermore, if the licensee is very successful, the firm has given up these profits, and if and when the contract ends it may find it has created a competitor.

Contract manufacturing

Another option is **contract manufacturing** – the company contracts with manufacturers in the foreign market to produce its product or provide its service. Boots, the large UK pharmaceutical retailer, has a division which manufactures health and beauty products for many other companies like French Connection, Toni&Guy and Soltan sunblock in the UK, France and Germany.[40] For these brands there are potential drawbacks – decreased control over the manufacturing process and loss of potential profits on manufacturing. The benefits are the chance to start faster, with less risk, and the later opportunity either to form a partnership with or to buy out the local manufacturer.

Management contracting

Under **management contracting**, the domestic firm supplies management know-how to a foreign company that supplies the capital. The domestic firm exports management services rather than products. Hilton uses this arrangement in managing hotels around the world.

Management contracting is a low-risk method of getting into a foreign market, and it yields income from the beginning. The arrangement is even more attractive if the contracting firm has an option to buy some share in the managed company later on. The arrangement is not sensible, however, if the company can put its scarce management talent to better uses or if it can make greater profits by undertaking the whole venture. Management contracting also prevents the company from setting up its own operations for a period of time.

Joint ownership

Joint ownership ventures consist of one company joining forces with foreign investors to create a local business in which they share joint ownership and control. A company may buy an interest in a local firm, or the two parties may form a new business venture. Joint ownership may be needed for economic or political reasons. The firm may lack the financial, physical or managerial resources to undertake the venture alone. Or a foreign government may require joint ownership as a condition for entry.

Inchcape is a leading car retailer, with operations in Austria, Belgium, Greece, the UK and many other countries outside Europe. Wishing to enter the growing Russian market, it went into partnership with a local organisation, the Olimp Group, several years ago. Having gained experience of this new market, it bought out Olimp and now has sole ownership of the operation.[41] Tesco now operates in many countries – in Thailand it partners with a local company called Lotus to provide stores of a similar format to the Tesco Express shops in the UK – 24-hour convenience stores.[42] Lotus provides local knowledge, contacts and familiarity, and Tesco brings its expertise in logistics and distribution, as well as the customer-centred ethos that has helped it dominate in its home market.

Direct investment

The biggest involvement in a foreign market comes through **direct investment** – the development of foreign-based assembly or manufacturing facilities. If a company has gained experience in exporting and if the foreign market is large enough, foreign production facilities offer many advantages. The firm may have lower costs in the form of cheaper labour or raw materials, foreign government investment incentives and freight savings. The firm may improve its image in the host country because it creates jobs – perhaps developing a deeper relationship with government, customers, local suppliers and distributors, allowing it to adapt its products to the local market better. Finally, the firm keeps full control over the investment and therefore can develop manufacturing and marketing policies that serve its long-term international objectives.

The main disadvantage of direct investment is that the firm faces many risks, such as restricted or devalued currencies, falling markets or government changes. In some cases, a firm has no choice but to accept these risks if it wants to operate in the host country.

> ### MAKING CONNECTIONS Linking the concepts
>
> Slow down here and think again about Volkswagen's global marketing issues.
>
> ● To what extent can Volkswagen standardise for the Chinese market? What marketing strategy and programme elements can be similar to those used in Europe and other parts of the Western world? Which ones must be adapted? Be specific.
>
> ● To what extent can Volkswagen standardise its products and programmes for the UK market? Which elements can be standardised and which must be adapted?
>
> ● To what extent are Volkswagen's 'globalisation' efforts contributing to 'Westernisation' of countries and cultures around the world? What are the positives and negatives of such cultural developments?

DECIDING ON THE GLOBAL MARKETING PROGRAMME

Companies that operate in one or more foreign markets must decide how much, if at all, to adapt their marketing strategies and programmes to local conditions. At one extreme are global companies that use a **standardised marketing mix**, selling largely the same products and using the same marketing approaches worldwide. At the other extreme is an **adapted marketing mix**. In this case, the producer adjusts the marketing mix elements to each target market, bearing more costs but hoping for a larger market share and return.

The question of whether to adapt or standardise the marketing strategy and programme has been much debated in recent years. On the one hand, some global marketers believe that technology is making the world a smaller place, and that consumer needs around the world are becoming more similar. This paves the way for 'global brands' and standardised global marketing. Global branding and standardisation, in turn, result in greater brand power and reduced costs from economies of scale. See Table 15.2 for the brands that have achieved world domination.

On the other hand, the marketing concept holds that marketing programmes will be more effective if tailored to the unique needs of each targeted customer group. If this concept applies within a country, it should apply even more in international markets. Despite global convergence, consumers in different countries still have widely varied cultural backgrounds. They still differ significantly in their needs and wants, spending power, product preferences and shopping patterns. Because these differences are hard to change, most marketers adapt their products, prices, channels and promotions to fit consumer desires in each country.[43]

However, global standardisation is not an all-or-nothing proposition but rather a matter of degree. Most international marketers suggest that companies should 'think globally but act locally' – that they should seek a balance between standardisation and adaptation. These marketers advocate a 'glocal' strategy in which the firm standardises certain core marketing elements and localises others. The corporate level gives global strategic direction; local units focus on individual consumer differences across global markets. Simon Clift, Head of Marketing for global consumer goods giant Unilever, puts it this way: 'We're trying to strike a balance between being mindlessly global and hopelessly local.'[44]

McDonald's operates this way. It uses the same basic fast-food operating model in its restaurants around the world but adapts its menu to local tastes. In Korea, it sells roast pork on a bun with a garlicky soy sauce. In India, where cows are considered sacred,

TABLE 15.2 Top global brands

Rank	Brand	Country/Region	Sector	Brand value ($m)	Change in brand value
1	Apple	USA	Electronics	118,863	21%
2	Google	USA	Internet services	107,439	15%
3	Coca-Cola	USA	Beverages	81,563	3%
4	IBM	USA	Business services	72,244	−8%
5	Microsoft	USA	Computer software	61,154	3%
6	GE	USA	Diversified	45,480	−3%
7	Samsung	Korea	Electronics	45,462	15%
8	Toyota	Japan	Automotive	42,392	20%
9	McDonald's	USA	Restaurants	42,254	1%
10	Mercedes-Benz	Germany	Automotive	34,338	8%
11	BMW	Germany	Automotive	34,214	7%
12	Intel	USA	Electronics	34,153	−8%
13	Disney	USA	Media	32,223	14%
14	Cisco	USA	Business services	30,936	6%
15	Amazon	USA	Online retail	29,478	25%
16	Oracle	USA	Technology	25,980	8%

Source: Adapted from Interbrand Rankings, available from http://bestglobalbrands.com/2014/ranking/

McDonald's serves McChicken, Filet-O-Fish, McVeggie (a vegetable burger), Pizza McPuffs, McAlooTikki (a spiced-potato burger) and the Maharaja Mac – two all-chicken patties, special sauce, lettuce, cheese, pickles and onions on a sesame-seed bun. McDonald's in France sells beer. Similarly, L'Oréal markets truly global brands – including, among others, Maybelline, Garnier, Lancôme, Kiehl's and Biotherm, as well as Ralph Lauren and Giorgio Armani Parfums, always adapting its brands to meet the cultural nuances of each local market:

> How does a French company with a British CEO successfully market a Japanese version of an American lipstick in Russia? Ask L'Oréal, which sells more than $18 billion worth of cosmetics, hair-care products and fragrances each year in 150 countries, making it the world's biggest cosmetics company. L'Oréal markets its brands globally by understanding how they appeal to cultural nuances in specific local markets. For L'Oréal, that means finding local brands, sprucing them up, positioning them for a specific target market, and exporting them to new customers all over the globe. Then, to support this effort, the company spends $4 billion annually to tailor global marketing messages to local cultures.
>
> For example, in 1996, the company bought the stodgy American make-up producer, Maybelline. To reinvigorate and globalise the brand, it moved the unit's headquarters from Tennessee to New York City and added 'New York' to the label. The resulting urban, street-smart, Big Apple image played well with the mid-price positioning of the workaday make-up brand. The makeover earned Maybelline a 20 per cent market share in its category in Western Europe. The young urban positioning also hit the mark in Asia, where few women realise that the trendy 'New York' Maybelline brand belongs to French cosmetics giant L'Oréal. When CEO Lindsey Owens-Jones recently addressed a UNESCO conference, nobody batted an eyelid when he described L'Oréal as 'the United Nations of Beauty'.[45]

The question of finding the right balance between a global approach and a local approach to international marketing remains relevant. Marketing at Work 15.2 looks at this issue as it affects European marketers striving to build a strong position in the Chinese market.

Doing business with China: culture matters

MARKETING AT WORK 15.2

China is an obsession with European marketers. If you search for 'marketing to China' on Google you will get hundreds of millions of hits. A great many of these hits will direct you to business consulting organisations, to market research companies, to international trading businesses, to academic institutions and to business magazines all offering advice and support on how the European marketer can build a business in the Chinese market. China is big business; marketing to China is big business; and even providing advice to marketers on how to make it big in China has become big business.

You don't have to look far to find out why China is considered to be so important by international marketers operating out of European businesses. According to one of those Google hits, in this case a report from the highly esteemed business journal *Forbes*:

Why is China taking off now? Essentially, the government has given people the right to go shopping . . . ten million new Chinese consumers enter the market each year. In 2010, China's consumer market was estimated to be worth $1.7 trillion. Credit Suisse projects that the burgeoning domestic consumer market could grow to nearly $16 trillion within a decade.

In simple terms, there are a great many people in China (around 1.3 billion right now); the Chinese government has set an agenda to increase the size of the economy rapidly; and more and more Chinese people are becoming well-educated, getting good jobs and aspiring to a high standard of living.

In order to succeed in China, European marketers need strong brands, good insight into Chinese culture and access to the right marketing channels. This is the fastest-growing consumer market in the world, and it is becoming increasingly cluttered with both international brands and local Chinese brands seeking to get their share of the action. So building brand awareness and creating a positive brand perception are crucial marketing goals. Most Western marketers believe that they need to adapt their brand to the different conditions found in China. However, it is a difficult balancing act. On the one hand, many Chinese people aspire to own well-known Western brands like Adidas and BMW, but, on the other hand, Chinese marketing experts insist that success in China requires understanding of and sensitivity towards Chinese cultural values. In order to understand Chinese culture many businesspeople and academic researchers have used anthropological methods. Anthropology is the study

of human culture and is often associated with research conducted among aboriginal people living in remote areas such as the Amazon rainforest in South America. However, these days anthropological methods are used to study industrialised cultures too and are taken seriously by marketers who want really to understand the deeper factors that underlie decisions made by consumers in the marketplace.

Research into Chinese culture has identified a number of important ideas that European marketers need to understand. Probably the most important of these is *guanxi* ('gwang shee'), which refers to two Chinese characters, *guan* meaning gate and *xi* meaning connection. So *guanxi* refers to a network of relationships and social connections based on mutual interests and benefits. Important terms related to *guanxi* are *xinyong* ('zin yong') and *renqing* ('ren ching'), which respectively mean 'trust' and 'favour'. Both *xinyong* and *renqing* will be found within a *guanxi* relationship. People who have a *guanxi* relationship will have mutual trust, and will do favours for each other. While the Western idea of relationship marketing is usually built on relatively impersonal tools such as customer relationship management (CRM) systems and database marketing, the Chinese conception of business relationships built on *guanxi* is much more personal. Two professors from Hong Kong universities, Adolphus Wan and Ken Ng, studied the use of *guanxi* in the relationship marketing strategies of domestic Chinese banks and foreign banks trying to establish themselves in China. The domestic Chinese banks made considerable use of *guanxi*, while the foreign banks relied more on conventional relationship marketing techniques (such as CRM), but were at a disadvantage compared with the domestic banks because they found it more difficult to build *guanxi* relationships.

One of the most successful European services to attract Chinese business in recent years has been higher education. While many European universities have attracted large numbers of Chinese students to study in Europe, a few universities have taken the more difficult step of setting up a campus in China. The first foreign university to take this step was the University of Nottingham, which set up the University of Nottingham, Ningbo, China (UNNC) in 2004 (shortly after, in 2005, the University of Nottingham opened its second overseas campus near Kuala Lumpur in Malaysia). UNNC provides an English-style higher education experience to around 5,000 students drawn primarily from China but also from other countries in the Far East. The University of Nottingham identified a market opportunity based around the rapid growth of the middle classes in China, their admiration for the British higher education system, and the natural concern some more conservative middle-class Chinese parents felt about sending their children half-way round the world to study. The solution – to offer them a British education at a more affordable cost and without the need to cross the globe.

While all cultures naturally value their children and want to maximise their life chances, the present generation of Chinese young people have been valued particularly highly because of the so-called 'one-child policy'. In order to restrict population growth, since the 1970s much of the Chinese population has been restricted to having only one child per family. The long-term effects of this policy have yet to be felt and could be serious (who will be around to look after all the old folks?), but so far the main outcome has been a tremendous concentration of resources on a generation of 'only children'. This has been good news for the European universities that have helped educate many of them, and for the European luxury brands for which many of these so-called Little Emperors (and Empresses) have acquired a taste. However, the inevitable long-term outcome seems likely to be a rapidly ageing Chinese population over the next few

European marketers need to understand Chinese culture

Source: Eyevine Ltd/Mark Leong/Redux.

decades. China will continue to create intriguing possibilities for European marketers for the foreseeable future.

Sources: 'Marketing to the New Chinese Consumer', Forbes INSIGHTS, 2011, accessed at http://images.forbes.com/forbesinsights/StudyPDFs/Marketing_to_the_Chinese_Consumer.pdf, June 2014; Katy Tian and Luis Borges, 'Cross-Cultural Issues in Marketing Communications: An Anthropological Perspective of International Business', *International Journal of China Marketing*, 2(1), 2011, pp. 110–26; Adolphus Wan and Ken Ng, 'The Significance of *Guanxi* in Relationship Marketing: Perspectives of Foreign Banks in China', *International Journal of China Marketing*, 3(2), 2013, pp. 72–99; Fang Yang, 'Marketing Strategy for Foreign Universities in China: A Case Study of the University of Nottingham, Ningbo', *International Journal of China Marketing*, 3(1), 2012, pp. 140–52; Jonathan Wilson and Ross Brennan, 'Doing Business in China: Is the Importance of *Guanxi* Diminishing?', *European Business Review*, 22(6), 2010, pp. 652–65.

Product

Five strategies allow for adapting product and marketing communication to a global market (see Figure 15.3).[46] We first discuss the three product strategies and then turn to the two communication strategies.

Straight product extension means marketing a product in a foreign market without any change. Top management tells its marketing people, 'Take the product as is and find

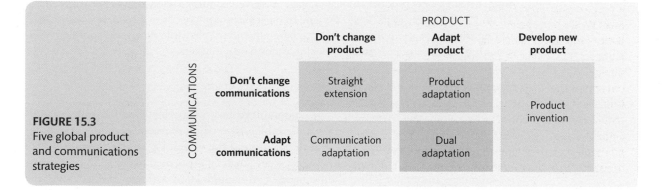

FIGURE 15.3
Five global product and communications strategies

		PRODUCT		
		Don't change product	Adapt product	Develop new product
COMMUNICATIONS	Don't change communications	Straight extension	Product adaptation	Product invention
	Adapt communications	Communication adaptation	Dual adaptation	

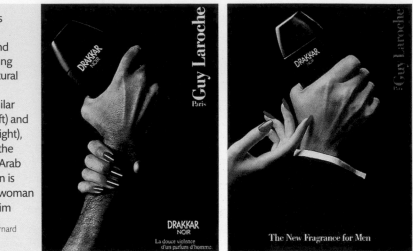

Some companies standardise their advertising around the world, adapting only to meet cultural differences. Guy Laroche uses similar ads in Europe (left) and Arab countries (right), but tones down the sensuality in the Arab version – the man is clothed and the woman barely touches him

Source: Courtesy of Bernard Matussiere.

customers for it.' The first step, however, should be to find out whether foreign consumers use that product and what form they prefer.

Straight product extension has been successful in some cases and disastrous in others. Kellogg's cereals, Gillette razors, Heineken beer and Black & Decker tools are all sold successfully in about the same form around the world. But General Foods introduced its standard powdered Jell-O in the British market only to find that British consumers prefer a solid wafer or cake form. Likewise, Philips began to make a profit in Japan only after it reduced the size of its coffeemakers to fit into smaller Japanese kitchens and its shavers to fit smaller Japanese hands. Straight extension is tempting because it involves no additional product development costs, manufacturing changes or new promotion. But it can be costly in the long run if products fail to satisfy foreign consumers.

Product adaptation involves changing the product to meet local conditions or wants. For example, Procter & Gamble's Vidal Sassoon shampoos contain a single fragrance world-wide, but the amount of scent varies by country: more in Europe but less in Japan, where subtle scents are preferred. Gerber serves Japanese baby food that might turn the stomachs of many Western consumers – local favourites include flounder and spinach stew, cod roe spaghetti, mugwort casserole, and sardines ground up in white radish sauce. And Finnish mobile phone maker Nokia customises its mobile phones for every major market. Developers build in rudimentary voice recognition for Asia where keyboards are a problem and raise the ring volume so phones can be heard on crowded Asian streets.

Product invention consists of creating something new for a specific country market. This strategy can take two forms. It might mean maintaining or reintroducing earlier product forms that happen to be well adapted to the needs of a given country. Volkswagen continued to produce and sell its old VW Beetle model in Mexico until just recently. Or a company might create a new product to meet a need in a given country. For example, Sony added the 'U' and 'UX' ranges to its VAIO PC line to meet the unique needs of Japanese consumers – among which was a requirement for it to be small and usable while the user is standing, even though it would not have much appeal in other world markets.

Promotion

Companies can either adopt the same communication strategy they used in the home market or change it for each local market. Consider advertising messages. Some global companies use a standardised advertising theme around the world. Of course, even in highly standardised communications campaigns, some small changes might be required to adjust for language and minor cultural differences. For example, Guy Laroche uses virtually the

TABLE 15.3 How Coca-Cola spends its advertising money globally

Measured media spending in millions of US dollars			
By region	**2012**	**2011**	**% chg**
Africa	71.0	54.6	30.1
Asia and Pacific	1,113.2	987.6	12.7
Europe	830.5	989.8	−16.1
Latin America	289.9	289.5	0.1
Middle East	322.9	178.9	80.5
Canada	16.8	21.5	−21.9
Subtotal media outside the USA	2,644.3	2,522.0	4.9
US media spending	384.6	391.4	−1.7
Worldwide	3,028.9	2,913.4	4.0

Source: http://adage.com/datacenter/globalmarketers2013#706

same ads for its Drakkar Noir fragrances in Europe as in Arab countries. However, it subtly tones down the Arab versions to meet cultural differences in attitudes towards sensuality. Table 15.3 shows how one global advertiser, Coca-Cola, spends large amounts of money advertising throughout all regions of the world.

Colours are also changed sometimes to avoid taboos in other countries. Purple is associated with death in most of Latin America, white is a mourning colour in Japan and green is associated with sickness in Malaysia. Even names must be changed. Kellogg's had to rename Bran Buds cereal in Sweden, where the name roughly translates as 'burned farmer'. And in the Americas, Mitsubishi changed the Japanese name of its Pajero SUV to Montero – it seems that *pajero* in Spanish is a slang term for sexual self-gratification.

Other companies follow a strategy of **communication adaptation**, fully adapting their advertising messages to local markets. Kellogg's ads in the USA promote the taste and nutrition of Kellogg's cereals versus competitors' brands. In France, where consumers drink little milk and do not eat much for breakfast, Kellogg's ads must convince consumers that cereals are a tasty and healthful breakfast. In India, where many consumers eat heavy, fried breakfasts, Kellogg's advertising convinces buyers to switch to a lighter, more nutritious breakfast diet.

Similarly, Coca-Cola sells its low-calorie beverage as Diet Coke in North America, the UK and the Middle and Far East, but as Light elsewhere. According to Diet Coke's global brand manager, in Spanish-speaking countries Coke Light ads 'position the soft drink as an object of desire, rather than as a way to feel good about yourself, as Diet Coke is positioned in the US and UK'. This 'desire positioning' plays off research showing that 'Coca-Cola Light is seen in other parts of world as a vibrant brand that exudes a sexy confidence'.[47]

Media also need to be adapted internationally because media availability varies from country to country. TV advertising time is very limited in Europe, for instance ranging from four hours a day in France to none in Scandinavian countries. Advertisers must buy time months in advance, and they have little control over airtimes. Magazines also vary in effectiveness. For example, magazines are a major medium in Italy and a minor one in Austria. Newspapers are mostly national in the UK but are only local in Spain.[48]

Price

Companies also face many problems in setting their international prices. For example, how might Black & Decker price its power tools globally? It could set a uniform price all around the world, but this amount would be too high a price in poor countries and not high enough in rich ones. It could charge what consumers in each country would bear, but this strategy ignores differences in the actual costs from country to country. Finally, the company could use a standard mark-up of its costs everywhere, but this approach might price Black & Decker out of the market in some countries where costs are high.

To deal with such issues, P&G adapts its pricing to local markets. For example, in Asia it has moved to a tiered pricing model.

> When P&G first entered Asia, it used the approach that had made it so successful in the United States. It developed better products and charged slightly higher prices than competitors. It also charged nearly as much for a box of Tide or bottle of Pantene in Asia as it did in North America. But such high prices limited P&G's appeal in Asian markets, where most consumers earn just a few dollars a day. So last year P&G adopted a tiered pricing strategy to help compete against cheaper local brands while also protecting the value of its global brands. It slashed Asian production costs, streamlined distribution channels, and reshaped its product line to create more affordable prices. For example, it introduced a 320-gram bag of Tide Clean White for 23 cents, compared with 33 cents for 350 grams of Tide Triple Action. Clean White doesn't offer such benefits as stain removal and fragrance, and it contains less advanced cleaning enzymes. But it costs less to make and outperforms every other brand at the lower price level. The results of P&G's new tiered pricing have been dramatic. Using the same approach for toothpaste, P&G now sells more Crest in China than in the United States. Its Olay brand is the best-selling facial cream in China and Rejoice is the bestselling shampoo.[49]

Regardless of how companies go about pricing their products, their foreign prices probably will be higher than their domestic prices for comparable products. A Gucci handbag may sell for the equivalent of $60 in Italy and $240 in the USA. Why? Gucci faces a *price escalation* problem. It must add the cost of transportation, tariffs, importer margin, wholesaler margin and retailer margin to its factory price. Depending on these added costs, the product may have to sell for two to five times as much in another country to make the same profit. For example, a pair of Levi's jeans that sells for $30 in the USA typically fetches $63 in Tokyo and $88 in Paris. Typically, a computer that sells for $1,000 in New York may cost £1,000 in the UK – nearly twice as much, depending on exchange rates. A Ford car priced at $20,000 in the USA might sell for more than $80,000 in South Korea.

Another problem involves setting a price for goods that a company ships to its foreign subsidiaries. If the company charges a foreign subsidiary too much, it may end up paying higher tariff duties even while paying lower income taxes in that country. If the company charges its subsidiary too little, it can be charged with *dumping*. Dumping occurs when a company either charges less than its costs or less than it charges in its home market. Various governments and multi-state bodies like the EU and NAFTA watch for dumping abuses, and they often force companies to set the price charged by other competitors for the same or similar products. For example, in 2013 the European Commission took anti-dumping action against Chinese solar panels, arguing that Chinese producers were selling solar panels below cost in the EU and so were threatening 25,000 jobs in the European solar industry. Globally, Chinese exports were the target of 37 per cent of these actions and this issue – and the complex legal and diplomatic questions it raises – is becoming of increasing importance between China and its trading partners.[50]

Recent economic and technological forces have had an impact on global pricing. For example, in much of the EU the transition to the euro has reduced the amount of price differentiation. Since, within the single currency area, consumers can often quickly see price differentiation between countries, companies are being forced to harmonise prices across the countries that have adopted the single currency. Consumers are willing and able to drive a few kilometres over a border to make a substantial saving – a real and growing issue in countries like Austria and Germany where Polish prices are often markedly lower. Companies and marketers that offer something genuinely unique or essential products or services will be least affected by such 'price transparency'.

For Marie-Claude Lang, a 72-year-old retired Belgian postal worker, the euro is the best thing since bottled water – or French country sausage. Always on the prowl for bargains, Ms Lang is now stalking the wide aisles of an Auchan hypermarket in Roncq, France, a 15-minute drive from her Wervick home . . . . Ms Lang has been coming to France every other week for years to stock up on bottled water, milk, and yogurt. But the launch of the euro . . . has opened her eyes to many more products that she now sees cost less across the border. Today she sees that 'saucisse de campagne' is cheaper 'by about five euro cents', a savings she didn't notice when she had to calculate the difference between Belgian and French francs.[51]

The Internet has also made global price differences more obvious. When firms sell their wares over the Internet, customers can see how much products sell for in different countries. They might even be able to order a given product directly from the company location or dealer offering the lowest price. This will force companies towards more standardised international pricing.

International distribution: distribution channels vary greatly from nation to nation, as this photo from the streets of Beijing suggests.

Source: Alamy Images/mikecranephotography.com.

Distribution channels

The international company must take a **whole-channel view** of the problem of distributing products to final consumers. Figure 15.4 shows the three major links between the seller and the final buyer. The first link, the *seller's headquarters organisation*, supervises the channels and is part of the channel itself. The second link, *channels between nations*, moves the products to the borders of the foreign nations. The third link, *channels within nations*, moves the products from their foreign entry point to the final consumers. Some manufacturers may think their job is done once the product leaves their hands, but they would do well to pay more attention to its handling within foreign countries.

Channels of distribution within countries vary greatly from nation to nation. First, there are the large differences in the *numbers and types of intermediaries* serving each foreign market. For example, a European company marketing in China must operate through a frustrating maze of state-controlled wholesalers and retailers. Chinese distributors often carry competitors' products and frequently refuse to share even basic sales and marketing

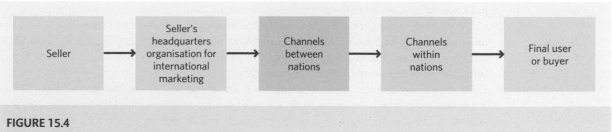

FIGURE 15.4
Whole-channel concept for international marketing

information with their suppliers. Hustling for sales is an alien concept to Chinese distributors, who are used to selling all they can obtain. Working with or getting around this system sometimes requires much time and investment.

When Coke first entered China, for example, customers bicycled up to bottling plants to get their soft drinks. Many shopkeepers still do not have enough electricity to run soft drink coolers. Now, Coca-Cola has set up direct distribution channels, investing heavily in refrigerators and trucks, and upgrading wiring so that more retailers can install coolers. The company has also built an army of more than 10,000 sales representatives that makes regular visits on resellers, often on foot or bicycle, to check on stocks and record sales. 'Coke and its bottlers have been trying to map every supermarket, restaurant, barbershop, or market stall where a can of soda might be consumed,' notes an industry observer. 'Those data help Coke get closer to its customers, whether they are in large hypermarkets, Spartan noodle shops, or schools.' Still, to reach the most isolated spots in the country, Coca-Cola relies on some pretty unlikely business partners – teams of delivery donkeys. 'Massive advertising budgets can drum up demand,' says another observer, 'but if the distribution network doesn't exist properly or doesn't work, the potential of China's vast market cannot be realised.'[52]

Another difference lies in the *size and character of retail units* abroad. Whereas large-scale retail chains dominate in much of Europe, much retailing in other countries is done by many small, independent retailers. In India, millions of retailers operate tiny shops or sell in open markets. Their mark-ups are high, but the actual price is lowered through haggling. Supermarkets could offer lower prices, but supermarkets are difficult to build and open because of many economic and cultural barriers. Incomes are low, and people prefer to shop daily for small amounts rather than weekly for large amounts. They also lack storage and refrigeration to keep food for several days. Packaging is not well developed because it would add too much to the cost. These factors have kept large-scale retailing from spreading rapidly in developing countries.

A further issue is that of grey markets. These are created when manufactured products are exported from their domestic market and then resold back to a retailer in that home market by a foreign intermediary. Companies like Adidas and Levi Strauss have suffered from this as they set prices in the Far East at a much lower level than in Western Europe and North America – retailers in these nations can pay for the goods to be imported back to them and still undercut the domestic retail price charged by companies which bought from the manufacturers directly.

DECIDING ON THE GLOBAL MARKETING ORGANISATION

Companies manage their international marketing activities in at least three different ways: most companies first organise an export department, then create an international division and finally become a global organisation.

A firm normally gets into international marketing by simply shipping out its goods. If its international sales expand, the company organises an *export department* with a sales manager and a few assistants. As sales increase, the export department can expand to include various marketing services so that it can actively go after business. If the firm moves into joint ventures or direct investment, the export department will no longer be adequate.

Many companies get involved in several international markets and ventures. A company may export to one country, license to another, have a joint ownership venture in a third and own a subsidiary in a fourth. Sooner or later it will create *international divisions* or subsidiaries to handle all its international activity.

International divisions are organised in a variety of ways. An international division's corporate staff consist of marketing, manufacturing, research, finance, planning and personnel specialists. They plan for and provide services to various operating units, which can be organised in one of three ways. The operating units can be *geographical organisations,* with country managers who are responsible for salespeople, sales branches, distributors and licensees in their respective countries. Or the units can be *world product groups,* each responsible for worldwide sales of different product groups. Finally, operating units can be *international subsidiaries*, each responsible for its own sales and profits.

Many firms have passed beyond the international division stage and become truly *global organisations*. They stop thinking of themselves as national marketers who sell abroad and start thinking of themselves as global marketers. The top corporate management and staff plan worldwide manufacturing facilities, marketing policies, financial flows and logistical systems. The global operating units report directly to the chief executive or executive committee of the organisation, not to the head of an international division. Executives are trained in worldwide operations, not just domestic *or* international. The company recruits management from many countries, buys components and supplies where they cost the least, and invests where the expected returns are greatest.

Moving further into the twenty-first century, major companies must become more global if they hope to compete. As foreign companies successfully invade their domestic markets, companies must move more aggressively into foreign markets. They will have to change from companies that treat their international operations as secondary, to companies that view the entire world as a single borderless market.

THE JOURNEY YOU'VE TAKEN Reviewing the concepts

It's time to stop and think back about the global marketing concepts you covered in this chapter. Companies today can no longer afford to pay attention only to their domestic market, regardless of its size. Many industries are global industries, and firms that operate globally achieve lower costs and higher brand awareness. At the same time, global marketing is risky because of variable exchange rates, unstable governments, protectionist tariffs and trade barriers, and several other factors. Given the potential gains and risks of international marketing, companies need a systematic way to make their global marketing decisions.

1 **Discuss how the international trade system and economic, political–legal and cultural environments affect a company's international marketing decisions**

A company must understand the global marketing environment, especially the international trade system. It must assess each foreign market's economic, political-legal and cultural characteristics. The company must then decide whether it wants to go abroad and consider the potential risks and benefits. It must decide on the volume of international sales it wants, how many countries it wants to market in and which specific markets it wants to enter. This decision calls for weighing the probable rate of return on investment against the level of risk.

2 **Describe three key approaches to entering international markets**

The company must decide how to enter each chosen market – whether through exporting, joint venturing or direct investment. Many companies start as exporters, move to joint ventures and finally make a direct

investment in foreign markets. In exporting, the company enters a foreign market by sending and selling products through international marketing intermediaries (indirect exporting) or the company's own department, branch or sales representative or agents (direct exporting). When establishing a joint venture, a company enters foreign markets by joining with foreign companies to produce or market a product or service. In licensing, the company enters a foreign market by contracting with a licensee in the foreign market, offering the right to use a manufacturing process, trademark, patent, trade secret or other item of value for a fee or royalty.

3 **Explain how companies adapt their marketing mixes for international markets**

Companies must also decide how much their products, promotion, price and channels should be adapted for each foreign market. At one extreme, global companies use a standardised marketing mix worldwide. Others use an adapted marketing mix, in which they adjust the marketing mix to each target market, bearing more costs but hoping for a larger market share and return.

4 **Identify the three major forms of international marketing organisation**

The company must develop an effective organisation for international marketing. Most firms start with an export department and graduate to an international division. A few become global organisations, with worldwide marketing planned and managed by the top officers of the company. Global organisations view the entire world as a single, borderless market.

NAVIGATING THE KEY TERMS

Adapted marketing mix **528**
Communication adaptation **533**
Contract manufacturing **527**
Countertrade **520**
Direct investment **527**
Economic communities **517**

Exporting **526**
Global firm **515**
Joint ownership **527**
Joint venturing **526**
Licensing **526**
Management contracting **527**

Product adaptation **532**
Standardised marketing mix **528**
Straight product extension **531**
Whole-channel view **535**

NOTES AND REFERENCES

1 D. Roberts, 'GM and VW: How Not to Succeed in China', *BusinessWeek*, 5 September 2005, p. 94.

2 Volkswagen China official website **http://www.vw.com.cn/cds/?menu_uid=551**, accessed 8 January 2008.

3 'VW's China Sales Reach Record', *International Business Times*, 8 January 2008, **http://www.ibtimes.com**, accessed 18 January 2008.

4 A. Webb, 'GM Tops VW for China Sales Lead', *Automotive News*, 79(6161), 2005, p. 6; and Xinhua, China News Agency, **http://news.xinhuanet.com/english/2008-01/11/content_7401796.htm**, accessed 24 January 2008.

5 A. Webb, 'As its Sales Plunge in China, VW Tries a New Approach', *Automotive News*, 80(6176), 2005, p. 24B.

6 Volkswagen China official website **http://www.vw.com.cn/cds/?menu_uid=567**, accessed 12 January 2008.

7 A. Webb, 'China Skid: Where VW Went Wrong', *Automotive News Europe*, 9(13), 2004, pp. 1–28.

8 A. Webb, 'As Its Sales Plunge in China, VW Tries a New Approach', *Automotive News*, 80(6176), 2005, p. 24B.

9 Volkswagen China official website **http://www.vw.com.cn/cds/?menu_uid=565**, accessed 15 January 2008.

10 Volkswagen China official website **http://www.vw.com.cn/cds/?menu_uid=565**, accessed 15 January 2008.

11 N. Madden, 'VW Hopes to Pull Chinese Heartstrings', *Automotive News*, 78(6103), 2004, p. 28.

12 Read the background in English: 'Swedes Find Viking-era Arab Coins' at *BBC News*, **www.bbc-co.uk/news**; and in the original Swedish at Silverskattfran Vikingatidenfunnen, **www.raa.se**, accessed September 2011.

13 George Melloan, 'Feeling the Muscles of the Multinationals', *The Wall Street Journal*, 6 January 2004, p. A19.

14 Numbers from WTO, 'International Trade Statistics', available from **www.wto.org**, accessed September 2011.

15 See 'Compagnie Générale des Établissements Michelin', *Hoover's Company Records*, 15 July 2005, p. 41240; and 'Johnson & Johnson', *Hoover's Company Records*, 15 July 2005, p. 10824.

16 See U. Golob and K. Podnar, 'Competitive Advantage in the Marketing of Products within the Enlarged European Union', *European Journal of Marketing*, 41(3/4), 2007,

pp. 245–56; and S. Paliwoda and S. Marinova, 'The Marketing Challenges Within the Enlarged Single European Market', *European Journal of Marketing,* 41(3/4), 2007, pp. 233–44.

17 For context on this see the Transparency International pages at **www.transparency.org** and the Volvo press releases from **www.volvo.com** – search for Iraq; see also **http://news.bbc .co.uk/1/hi/business/7307432.stm**, accessed July 2014.

18 Steve Hamm, 'Borders Are So 20th Century', *BusinessWeek,* 22 September 2003, pp. 68–73.

19 'The Unique Japanese', *Fortune,* 24 November 1986, p. 8. See also James D. Southwick, 'Addressing Market Access Barriers in Japan Through the WTO', *Law and Policy in International Business,* Spring 2000, pp. 923–76; and US Commercial Service, *Country Commercial Guide Japan, FY 2005,* ch. 5, accessed at **www.buyusa.gov**, 18 June 2005.

20 Read '*What is the WTO?*', at **www.wto.org/**, accessed September 2011.

21 This prediction made in 'WTO Annual Report 2004', and '10 Benefits of the WTO Trading System', accessed at **www.wto.org**. We'll never know if it was true.

22 Read more about the history and future of the GATT in 'Timeline: World Trade Organization' from *BBC News,* **www.bbc.co.uk/news**, accessed September 2011.

23 The complete story: 'Fearful or Cheerful? The Prospects for the World Trade Talks', *The Economist,* **www.economist.com**, accessed September 2011; and, information from the WTO website, **http://www.wto.org/english/tratop_e/dda_e/dda_e.htm**, accessed July 2014.

24 'See The European Union at a Glance', at europa.eu/about-cu/facts-figures/economy for a top-line overview of the EU economy; and **http://europa.eu/about-eu/countries/index _en.htm**, accessed July 2014.

25 'Overviews of European Union Activities: Economic and Monetary Affairs', accessed at **europa.eu/pol/emu/**, September 2011.

26 IMF data from 'World Economic Outlook Database', **www.imf.org**, accessed September 2011.

27 Read more about NAFTA via **www.nafta.org**.

28 Richard Lapper, 'South American Unity Still a Distant Dream', *Financial Times,* 9 December 2004, accessed at **www.news.ft.com**; and Mary Turck, 'South American Community of Nations', Resource Center of the Americas, accessed at **www.americas.org**, August 2005.

29 Read 'A Large Black Cloud' from *The Economist* at **www.economist.com**, accessed September 2011.

30 Adapted from information found in Clay Chandler, 'China Deluxe', *Fortune,* 26 July 2004, pp. 148–56. See also 'Selling to China's Rich and Not So Rich', *Strategic Directions,* June 2005, pp. 5–8; and Lisa Movius, 'Luxury's China Puzzle', *WWD,* 15 June 2005, p. 1. See also David Woodruff, 'Ready to Shop until They Drop', *BusinessWeek,* 22 June 1998, pp. 104–8; and James MacAonghus, 'Online Impact of a Growing Europe', *New Media Age,* 12 February 2004, p. 15.

31 See Om Malik, 'The New Land of Opportunity', *Business 2.0,* July 2004, pp. 72–9; also coverage of the 2014 Indian general election at **http://www.bbc.co.uk/news/world- asia-26869578**, accessed July 2014.

32 Ricky Griffin and Michael Pustay, *International Business,* 4th edn (Upper Saddle River, NJ: Prentice Hall, 2005), pp. 522–3.

33 Rebecca Piirto Heath, 'Think Globally', *Marketing Tools,* October 1996, pp. 49–54; and 'The Power of Writing', *National Geographic,* August 1999, pp. 128–9.

34 For other examples and discussion, see **www.executiveplanet.com**, December 2005; *Dun & Bradstreet's Guide to Doing Business Around the World* (Upper Saddle River, NJ: Prentice Hall, 2000); Ellen Neuborne, 'Bridging the Culture Gap', *Sales & Marketing*

Management, July 2003, p. 22; Richard Pooley, 'When Cultures Collide', *Management Services,* Spring 2005, pp. 28–31; and Helen Deresky, *International Management,* 5th edn (Upper Saddle River, NJ: Prentice Hall, 2006).

35 Adapted from 'Importance of Adapting to the Chinese Market' from **www.renmenbi.com**, accessed September 2011.

36 Information from Lucy Ash, 'France Versus the World', from *BBC News,* **www.bbc.co.uk /news**

37 See Jack Neff, 'Submerged', *Advertising Age,* 4 March 2002, p. 14; and Ann Chen and Vijay Vishwanath, 'Expanding in China', *Harvard Business Review,* March 2005, pp. 19–21.

38 For a good discussion of joint venturing, see James Bamford, David Ernst and David G. Fubini, 'Launching a World-Class Joint Venture', *Harvard Business Review,* February 2004, pp. 91–100.

39 See Lego at **www.lego.com** and Flextronics at **www.flextronics.com**

40 Read more about BCM at its online home: **http://www.bcm-manufacturing.com/**

41 Visit Inchcape online at **www.inchcape.com**; some context to the story in the *Financial Times* – Stanley Pignal, 'Inchcape Takes Full Ownership in Russia', **www.ft.com**, accessed July 2014.

42 Read more about Tesco and its operations in Asia at **www.tescolotus.com**. Some context: the story 'Global Tendrils' in *The Economist* at **www.economist.com**, accessed July 2014.

43 See A. Schuh, 'Brand Strategies of Western MNCs as Drivers of Globalization in Central and Eastern Europe', *European Journal of Marketing,* 41(3/4), 2007, pp. 274–91; and T.L. Powers and J.J. Loyka, 'Market, Industry, and Company Influences on Global Product Standardization', *International Marketing Review,* 24(6), 2007, pp. 678–94.

44 For good discussions, see Laura Mazur, 'Globalization Is Still Tethered to Local Variations', *Marketing,* 22 January 2004, p. 18; Johny K. Johansson and Ilkka A. Ronkainen, 'The Brand Challenge: Are Global Brands the Right Choice for Your Company?', *Marketing Management,* March/April 2004; Douglas B. Holt, John A. Quelch and Earl L. Taylor, 'How Global Brands Compete', *Harvard Business Review,* September 2004, pp. 68–75; and Boris Sustar and Rozana Sustar, 'Managing Marketing Standardization in a Global Context', *Journal of American Academy of Business,* September 2005, pp. 302–10.

45 Quotes and other information from Richard Tomlinson, 'L'Oréal's Global Makeover', *Fortune,* 30 September 2002, p. 141; Gail Edmondson, 'The Beauty of Global Branding', *BusinessWeek,* 28 June 1999, pp. 70–5; Jeremy Josephs, 'O-J's Powers of Seduction Hard to Resist', 25 March 2003, accessed at **www.jeremyjosephs.com**; 'Consumer Products Brief: L'Oréal', *The Wall Street Journal,* 23 February 2004, p. 1; Vito J. Racanelli, 'Touching Up', 16 February 2004, pp. 18–19; Ross Tucker, 'L'Oréal Global Sales Rise', *WWD,* 18 February 2005; and information accessed at **www.loreal.com**, September 2005.

46 Warren J. Keegan, *Global Marketing Management,* 7th edn (Upper Saddle River, NJ: Prentice Hall, 2002), pp. 346–51. See also Phillip Kotler and Kevin Lane Keller, *Marketing Management,* 12th edn (Upper Saddle River, NJ: Prentice Hall, 2006), pp. 677–84.

47 Kate MacArthur, 'Coca-Cola Light Employs Local Edge', *Advertising Age,* 21 August 2000, pp. 18–19; and 'Case Studies: Coke Light Hottest Guy', Advantage Marketing, msn India, accessed at **http://advantage.msn.co.in**, 15 March 2004.

48 See Alicia Clegg, 'One Ad One World?', *Marketing Week,* 20 June 2002, pp. 51–2; and George E. Belch and Michael A. Belch, *Advertising and Promotion: An Integrated Marketing Communications Perspective,* 6th edn (New York: McGraw-Hill, 2004), pp. 666–8.

49 Adapted from Normandy Madden and Jack Neff, 'P&G Adapts Attitude Toward Local Markets', *Advertising Age,* 23 February 2004, p. 28; and information found in 'P&G Hits No. 1 in China', *SPC Asia,* November 2004, p. 3.

50 See the Chinese side of the story by reading 'China Dissatisfied with EU Anti-Dumping Duties', **www.chinadaily.com.cn**, accessed September 2011; for the story about alleged Chinese dumping of solar panels see **http://www.theguardian.com/business/2013/jun/04 /eu-tarriffs-dumping-china-solar-panels**, accessed July 2014.

51 Sarah Ellison, 'Revealing Price Disparities, the Euro Aids Bargain-Hunters', *The Wall Street Journal*, 30 January 2002, p. A15.

52 See Patrick Powers, 'Distribution in China: The End of the Beginning', *China Business Review,* July–August 2001, pp. 8–12; Drake Weisert, 'Coca-Cola in China: Quenching the Thirst of a Billion', *The China Business Review,* July–August 2001, pp. 52–5; Gabriel Kahn, 'Coke Works Harder at Being the Real Thing in Hinterland', *The Wall Street Journal,* 26 November 2002, p. B1; Leslie Chang, Chad Terhune and Betsy McKay, 'A Global Journal Report; Rural Thing – Coke's Big Gamble in Asia', *The Wall Street Journal,* 11 August 2004, p. A1; and Jo Bowman, 'Target: Managing Channels', 22 October 2004, p. S8.

CHAPTER 16
ETHICS, SOCIAL RESPONSIBILITY AND SUSTAINABILITY

AFTER STUDYING THIS CHAPTER, YOU SHOULD BE ABLE TO

- identify the major social criticisms of marketing
- define *consumerism*, *environmentalism* and *sustainability* and explain how they affect marketing strategies
- describe the principles of socially responsible marketing
- explain the role of ethics in marketing

THE WAY AHEAD
Previewing the concepts

You've almost completed your introductory marketing travels. In this final chapter, we'll focus on marketing as a social institution. First, we'll look at some common criticisms of marketing as it affects individual consumers, other businesses and society as a whole. Then we'll examine consumerism, environmentalism, sustainability and other citizen and public actions to keep marketing in check. Finally, we'll see how companies themselves can benefit from actively pursuing socially responsible, sustainable and ethical practices that bring value not just to individual customers, but to society as a whole. You'll see that social responsibility, sustainable and ethical actions are more than just the right thing to do; many people claim they are also good for business.

Before travelling on, let's take a look at one of the longest-running issues in ethics, social responsibility and business, namely the marketing of tobacco products. Today everybody knows that smoking is really bad for your health, but that was not always the case. Did the tobacco companies ever deceive customers about the risks to their health from smoking? Is it morally right to make a profit from selling a product that has well-known health risks? What has the EU been doing to try to persuade people to give up smoking? Read on.

HELP – FOR A LIFE WITHOUT TOBACCO

Dr Louise Hassan, Senior Lecturer in Marketing, Lancaster University

Consumers engage in a lot of risky behaviour with potentially damaging consequences for themselves, which also can have a serious impact on the health of others, and on the social and financial well-being of society at large. Most of this risky behaviour (such as binge drinking, speeding and gambling) carries an immediate risk; smoking, on the other hand, is aptly called the secret killer. Smoking is now known to be one of the most hazardous forms of behaviour that a consumer can engage in. Despite this, many young people still take up the habit. Research has shown that taking up smoking is one of the most negative lifestyle choices that an individual can make, with 50 per cent of lifelong smokers dying prematurely because of their habit. Medical data shows that smokers on average live 10 years fewer than non-smokers. In fact smoking

Source: http://en.help-eu.com/pages/index-abzo_pl-ABSURD-ZONE.html. The HELP 'For a life without tobacco' campaign is an initiative of the European Commission's Health and Consumer Directorate (DG SANCO).

is thought to be the cause of 30 per cent of all cancer deaths in developed countries. Many illnesses can also be caused by smoking; for instance, smoking is known to cause impotence and blindness. Given these stark facts, national governments, the European Commission and health organisations such as the World Health Organization (WHO) continue to work separately and in partnership to reduce the harm caused by tobacco. Indeed the first ever public health treaty, called the Framework Convention on Tobacco Control, is a global effort to tackle the burden of tobacco across the world by providing guidelines on implementable tobacco control policies. So far over 160 countries have signed up to this treaty, with over 130 countries ratifying and implementing its guidelines.

Most countries have targets to reduce smoking, while some countries aim to be entirely smoke-free within the next 50 years. However, there is a lack of consensus on the use of tobacco by consumers and the role of marketing by tobacco companies. Separately, many societies are exploring how marketing, in the form of social marketing, can help to turn the tide and reduce tobacco consumption.

There are various perspectives on the role of tobacco companies in our society. Some people argue that

growing tobacco provides jobs and helps a country's economy, others argue that smoking is a personal choice and that in a free society tobacco companies should be allowed to advertise their products and to use other marketing tools, such as price promotions, to increase sales, market share and the size of the overall market. Many countries, such as the USA, Germany and Switzerland, still allow limited tobacco advertising (in newspapers and on hoardings). However, a substantial amount of research into the marketing practices of tobacco companies has demonstrated that legitimate criticisms can be made against them.

First, the tobacco industry did use deceitful practices to encourage young people to take up smoking and worried smokers to switch to so-called 'light' cigarettes through brand imagery and advertising. Other promotional activities took place in bars where marketing representatives of the tobacco companies distributed branded goods, such as branded lighters, matches and bar mats. In a court judgment in the USA, Judge Kessler concluded that the tobacco industry had deceived the general public concerning the health risks of smoking over the last 50 years. For these reasons the tobacco companies have been widely criticised, with some consumers now viewing tobacco companies as illegitimate and deceitful. This has been reinforced by public campaigns such as the Truth Campaign in the USA, resulting in increased anti-smoking attitudes among young people.

Second, it is known that advertising tobacco products increases tobacco consumption and that only a complete ban on all forms of tobacco promotion is effective. Other elements of the marketing mix have also been found to be effective in reducing tobacco consumption. Increasing the price of tobacco products decreases the likelihood of young people taking up the habit; tobacco branding can lead to greater intention to smoke. Governments therefore have a key legislative role in the control of tobacco products and tobacco marketing practices in order to protect public health. One aspect of the government's role is to demarket tobacco. Demarketing can be defined as the aspect of marketing that deals with discouraging customers in general or a certain class of customers in particular on either a temporary or permanent basis. In terms of demarketing tobacco many measures can be used, such as smoking bans in public places, a reduction in the number of outlets allowed to sell tobacco, higher taxation on tobacco, free comprehensive smoking cessation support as well as informative and targeted anti-smoking social advertising campaigns.

Within the EU, the European Commission (EC) has been taking steps to reduce tobacco consumption. An important EC tobacco control initiative is the 'HELP – for a life without tobacco' campaign which ran from 2005 to 2010. This large-scale anti-smoking advertising campaign ran across the 25 EU member states (at January 2007; when Bulgaria and Romania joined, the most recent wave of advertisements was also screened in these two new member states). The HELP campaign's main component was a series of TV advertisements using identical visual content with equivalent voice-over messages in the native language of each member state. The overall aims of the HELP campaign were to highlight the harmful effects of both active and passive smoking, encourage smokers to think more responsibly about their habit (such as the harm it can do to non-smokers) and to consider quitting. Although smokers are a key target group for anti-smoking campaigns (indeed, around 27 per cent of the EU's population are smokers), non-smokers are an increasingly important group given the emphasis across the EU and the world on the harms caused by passive or second-hand smoking. Young people are also a key target group because most experimentation with smoking occurs during adolescence so that anti-smoking advertisements need to promote not only cessation but also prevention. Accordingly the HELP campaign was aimed at adolescents and young adults, typically those aged 15 to 34.

Targeting such a large, varied and multicultural audience with a uniform advertising campaign is a challenge for any marketer, even with a large budget. The budget for the HELP campaign of around €72m, although one of the largest budgets for a social marketing campaign, was still modest compared with the expenditure on advertising of large multinational corporations. In order to ensure that such a campaign works effectively across countries, extensive pre-testing of advertising concepts is required. The style or persuasive approach of the adverts must also be considered. In the past, different approaches have been used to tackle social problems through advertising. Some authors have found that exposure to an anti-smoking fear appeal can reduce smoking behaviour, others criticise the use of fear as inappropriate. Humour is also used, but humour varies from culture to culture.

Given these observations, the EC and the advertising agency in charge of the development of the HELP campaign used the concept of the 'absurdity of smoking' as a general theme for the campaign. In order to highlight the absurdity of smoking a 'party whistle' was adopted as the substitute for cigarettes in each of the four adverts developed for the campaign. This also reinforces the common creative element of the campaign across each of the adverts. The adverts used throughout the campaign covered the three themes of prevention, cessation and passive smoking (in social situations and in the home). Over the course of the campaign different lengths of adverts were used. Initially, longer 30-second adverts were produced and aired, with reinforcement spots of 10-second and 20-second adverts. January and February were chosen as the main advertising periods, partly because advertising space is less expensive during these months, but additionally because the New Year period is often a time for reflection with many smokers making resolutions to quit. Advertising national quit-line telephone numbers and the HELP campaign website (which contains tips on avoiding smoking, on stopping, and advice about passive smoking) is very important in assisting those wishing to find out more. It is also important to place adverts on multiple (national and pan-European) channels and at times when the target audience is likely to be watching TV, such as during popular soap operas or dramas.

But in today's multichannel era, is TV advertising enough to engage a young target audience? Obviously not, since young people spend more time surfing the Internet than watching TV. Therefore the HELP campaign has pioneered a multichannel approach to engage its target group, using Internet advertising, an 'absurd zone' on the campaign website with games and an email coaching cessation programme, as well as a linked viral marketing campaign. Additionally, interactive and entertaining national events and roadshows took place in many EU capitals. Another key aspect of the HELP campaign was the annual post-exposure evaluation. This allows an independent assessment across each member state of the level of awareness of the televised campaign, as well as consumers' attitude and liking for the campaign, comprehension of the campaign message and thinking about smoking as a result of the campaign. The results of the evaluation show that awareness of the campaign increased year on year, with 60 per cent of the target group aware of the campaign. More importantly, message comprehension and liking of the campaign across the member states is consistently very high. Furthermore, over 55,000 people across the EU took part in the email coaching programme in 2007 alone, while 200,000 have taken part in carbon dioxide testing and over 3 million people viewed the first viral marketing campaign. Together with the significant press coverage and over 46,000 advertising TV spots as well as 4.2 million hits on the campaign website, these results show that the diverse nature of the campaign generated a huge overall response from the target audience.

Drawing together these findings, the HELP campaign provides a model example of a successful social advertising campaign in terms of engaging with consumers. However, time will tell whether or not smoking uptake or prevalence has been reduced across the EU. Governments require a multifaceted approach to social advertising which allows people to examine their behaviour in a constructive and non-judgemental way. In order to reach a diverse target group, multiple approaches such as Internet advertising and viral marketing are required. Today's social marketer cannot simply rely on TV advertising as the only way to tackle social problems.[1]

Sources: The author would like to thank the European Commission and all those involved in the development and management of the HELP campaign. This case study was written in 2008. The HELP – for a life without tobacco campaign ended in 2010, with this case discussing Stage 1 of the campaign which took place between 2005 and 2008. For full source details see note 1 at the end of this chapter.

Responsible marketers discover what consumers want and respond with market offerings that create value for buyers in order to capture value in return. The *marketing concept* is a philosophy of customer value and mutual gain. Its practice leads the economy by an invisible hand to satisfy the many and changing needs of millions of consumers.

Not all marketers follow the marketing concept, however. In fact, some companies use questionable marketing practices, and some marketing actions that seem innocent in themselves strongly affect the larger society. Not so long ago the consensus was that tobacco companies should be free to sell cigarettes and smokers should be free to buy them. But, as we saw above, this private transaction involves larger questions of public policy. For example, the smokers are harming their health and may be shortening their own lives. Smoking places a financial burden on the smoker's family and on society at large. Other people around smokers may suffer discomfort and harm from second-hand smoke. Marketing cigarettes to adults might also influence young people to begin smoking. That is why the marketing of tobacco products has sparked substantial debate and negotiation in recent years.[2] In Europe, as the 'HELP – for a life without tobacco' example showed, governments are taking increasingly strong measures to reduce tobacco consumption.

This chapter examines the social effects of private marketing practices. We examine several questions: What are the most frequent social criticisms of marketing? What steps have private citizens taken to curb marketing ills? What steps have legislators and government agencies taken to curb marketing ills? What steps have enlightened companies taken to carry out socially responsible and ethical marketing that creates value for both individual customers and society as a whole?

SOCIAL CRITICISMS OF MARKETING

Marketing receives much criticism. Some of this criticism is justified; much is not. Social critics claim that certain marketing practices hurt individual consumers, society as a whole and other business firms.

Marketing's impact on individual consumers

Consumers have many concerns about how well the Western marketing system serves their interests. Surveys usually show that consumers hold mixed or even slightly unfavourable attitudes towards marketing practices. Consumer advocates, government agencies and other critics have accused marketing of harming consumers through high prices, deceptive practices, high-pressure selling, shoddy or unsafe products, planned obsolescence and poor service to disadvantaged consumers.

High prices

Many critics charge that the Western marketing system causes prices to be higher than they would be under more 'sensible' systems. They point to three factors: *high costs of distribution, high advertising and promotion costs* and *excessive mark-ups.*

High costs of distribution

A long-standing charge is that greedy intermediaries mark up prices beyond the value of their services. Critics charge that there are too many intermediaries, that intermediaries are inefficient, or that they provide unnecessary or duplicate services. As a result, distribution costs too much and consumers pay for these excessive costs in the form of higher prices.

How do resellers answer these charges? They argue that intermediaries do work that would otherwise have to be done by manufacturers or consumers. Mark-ups reflect services that consumers themselves want – more convenience, larger stores and assortments, more service, longer store hours, opportunities to return unwanted goods, and others. In fact, they argue, retail competition is so intense that margins are actually quite low. For example, after taxes, supermarket chains are typically left with barely 1 per cent profit on their sales. If some resellers try to charge too much relative to the value they add, other resellers will step in with lower prices. Low-price stores such as Aldi, Lidl and other discounters pressure their competitors to operate efficiently and keep their prices down.[3]

High advertising and promotion costs

Modern marketing is also accused of pushing up prices to finance heavy advertising and sales promotion. For example, a dozen tablets of a heavily promoted brand of pain reliever sell for the same price as 100 tablets of less promoted brands, even though they all contain the same active ingredients. Differentiated products – cosmetics, detergents, toiletries – include promotion and packaging costs that can amount to 40 per cent or more of the manufacturer's price to the retailer. Critics charge that much of the packaging and promotion adds only psychological value to the product rather than functional value.

Marketers respond that advertising does add to product costs, but it also adds value by informing potential buyers of the availability and merits of a brand. Brand name products may cost more, but branding gives buyers assurances of consistent quality. Moreover, consumers can usually buy functional versions of products at lower prices. However, they *want* and are willing to pay more for products that also provide psychological benefits – that make them feel wealthy, attractive or special. Also, heavy advertising and promotion may be necessary for a firm to match competitors' efforts – the business would lose 'share of mind' if it did not match competitive spending. At the same time, companies are cost-conscious about promotion and try to spend their money wisely.

Excessive mark-ups

Critics also charge that some companies mark up goods excessively. They point to the drug industry, where a pill costing 5 cents to make may cost the consumer €2 to buy. They point to the high rates of interest charged by lending companies on loans made to some of the poorest members of society, and to the high charges for car repair and other services.

Marketers respond that most businesses try to deal fairly with consumers because they want to build customer relationships and repeat business. Most consumer abuses are unintentional. When shady marketers do take advantage of consumers, they should be reported to consumer associations and to government agencies. Marketers also respond that consumers often do not understand the reasons for high mark-ups. For example, the prices of successful new medicines must cover their own development and operating costs *plus* the high research and development costs of formulating and testing many experimental drugs that never make it to market because they turn out to be ineffective or dangerous. And while the interest rates charged on short-term loans by so-called 'pay-day loan companies' seem extraordinary (in July 2014, for example, **www.wonga.com** was quoting a 'representative rate' of 5,853 per cent), the companies counter that these are intended to be very short-term loans for people who would otherwise be unable to borrow money, and that the high risk of default and high administrative charges justify the price. Recent years have seen these companies work very hard to ensure that customers understand exactly what they are getting and how much it will cost, but criticism has continued and it seems to be inevitable that further regulation will be imposed and the industry will be significantly curtailed.[4]

Deceptive practices

Marketers are sometimes accused of deceptive practices that lead consumers to believe they will get more value than they actually do. Deceptive practices fall into three groups: pricing, promotion and packaging. *Deceptive pricing* includes practices such as falsely advertising 'factory' or 'wholesale' prices or a large price reduction from an unrealistically high retail list price. *Deceptive promotion* includes practices such as misrepresenting the product's features or performance or luring the customers to the shop for a bargain that is out of stock. *Deceptive packaging* includes exaggerating the package contents through subtle design, using misleading labelling or describing size in misleading terms.

The toughest problem is defining what is 'deceptive'. For instance, an advertiser's claim that its stimulant drink 'gives you wings', showing cartoon people sprouting wings and flying away, is not intended to be taken literally. Instead, the advertiser might claim, it is 'puffery' – innocent exaggeration for effect. One noted marketing thinker, Theodore Levitt, once claimed that advertising puffery and alluring imagery are bound to occur – and that they may even be desirable: 'There is hardly a company that would not go down in ruin if it refused to provide fluff, because nobody will buy pure functionality . . . . Worse, it denies . . . people's honest needs and values. Without distortion, embellishment, and elaboration, life would be drab, dull, anguished, and at its existential worst.'[5]

However, others claim that puffery and alluring imagery can harm consumers in subtle ways, and that consumers must be protected through education:

> The real danger to the public . . . comes not from outright lies – in most cases facts can ultimately be proven and mistakes corrected. But . . . advertising uses [the power of images and] emotional appeals to shift the viewer's focus away from facts. Viewers who do not take the trouble to distinguish between provable claims and pleasant but meaningless wordplay end up buying 'the sizzle, not the steak' and often paying high. The best defence against misleading ads . . . is not tighter controls on [advertisers], but more education and more critical judgment among . . . consumers. Just as we train children to be wary of strangers offering candy, to count change at a store, and to kick the tires before buying a used car, we must make the effort to step back and judge the value of . . . advertisements, and then master the skills required to separate spin from substance.[6]

Marketers argue that most companies avoid deceptive practices because such practices harm their business in the long run. Profitable customer relationships are built upon a foundation of value and trust. If consumers do not get what they expect, they will switch to more reliable products. In addition, consumers usually protect themselves from deception. Most consumers recognise a marketer's selling intent and are careful when they buy, sometimes to the point of not believing completely true product claims.

High-pressure selling

Salespeople are sometimes accused of high-pressure selling that persuades people to buy goods they had no thought of buying. It is often said that insurance, property and cars are *sold*, not *bought*. Salespeople are trained to deliver smooth, fully prepared talks to entice purchase. They sell hard because sales contests promise big prizes to those who sell the most.

But in most cases, marketers have little to gain from high-pressure selling. Such tactics may work in one-off selling situations for short-term gain. However, increasingly marketers have become convinced that the route to long-term business profitability is through building long-term relationships with customers in order to keep customers coming back (customer retention) because they believe that they receive excellent value. High-pressure or deceptive selling can do serious damage to such relationships. For example, imagine a Procter & Gamble account manager trying to pressure a Carrefour buyer, or an IBM salesperson trying to browbeat a Siemens IT manager. It simply would not work.

Shoddy, harmful or unsafe products

Another criticism concerns poor product quality or function. One complaint is that, too often, products are not made well and services are not performed well. A second complaint is that many products deliver little benefit, or that they might even be harmful. For example, many critics have pointed out the dangers of today's fat-laden fast food.

There is widespread concern that the long-term health of young people is being put at risk because of poor dietary habits, and in many Western countries there has been talk of an 'obesity epidemic' which could lead to chronic health problems and premature death for many people.[7] Who is to blame for the obesity problem? And what should responsible food companies do about it? As with most social responsibility issues, there are no easy answers. Several fast-food companies, including McDonald's, have worked to improve their products and make their menus and their customers healthier. However, to be honest, the staples of the fast-food menu are still items such as French fries, burgers and deep-fried chicken, often seasoned with quite a lot of salt. For one perspective on this issue, a perspective that does not flatter the fast-food industry, you could watch documentary maker Morgan Spurlock's famous film *Super Size Me* (find the film details at **http://www.imdb.com/title/tt0390521**). This kind of perspective tends to suggest that fast-food firms are being socially irresponsible. But the companies themselves would say that they offer healthy options on the menu, and that they are simply delivering the products that consumers want.[8] We explore the issues further in Marketing at Work 16.1.

The international obesity debate: who's to blame?

MARKETING AT WORK 16.1

As you've no doubt heard, many countries in the Western world are facing an obesity epidemic. Everyone seems to agree on the problem. But still unresolved is another weighty issue: who's to blame? Is it the fault of self-indulgent consumers who just can't say no to sticky buns, fat burgers and other tempting treats? Or is it the fault of greedy food marketers who are cashing in on vulnerable consumers, turning us into a nation of overeaters?

Around 10 per cent of British children are classified as 'obese', and 31,000 premature deaths in the UK each year are attributed to poor diet combined with insufficient exercise. The British government has concluded that this is a major social problem and is committed to a public health strategy to minimise the long-term harm. In the USA the 'obesity epidemic' is even more severe, with 31.1 per cent of adults and 15.8 per cent of children aged 6–11 being classified as obese, based on data for the period 1999–2002. Meanwhile, the European Consumers' Organisation, BEUC, claims that in some European countries more than half the adult population is overweight and that one child in five is obese (**www.beuc.eu**).

So, here's that weighty question again. If we know that we're overweight and that it's bad for us, why do we keep putting on the pounds? Who's to blame? The answer, of course, depends on who you ask. However, these days, lots of people are blaming food marketers. In the obesity debate, food marketers have become a favourite target of almost everyone, from politicians, public policy makers and the press to overweight consumers themselves. And some food marketers are looking pretty much guilty as charged.

Take the American burger chain Hardee's, for example. At a time when other fast-food chains such as McDonald's, Wendy's and Subway were getting 'leaner', Hardee's introduced the decadent Thickburger, featuring one-third of a pound of Angus beef. It followed up with the *Monster* Thickburger: two one-third of a pound Angus beef patties, four strips of bacon and three slices of American cheese, all nestled in a buttered sesame-seed bun slathered with mayonnaise! The Monster Thickburger weighs in at a whopping 1,420 calories and 108 grams of fat, far greater than the government's recommended fat intake for an entire day (the company conveniently provides a nutritional calculator at **http://www.hardees.com/menu/nutritional_calculator_landing** so you can work this out for yourself).

Surely, you say, Hardee's made a colossal blunder here. Not so! At least, not from a profit viewpoint. Sales at Hardee's 2,050 outlets have climbed 20 per cent since it introduced the Thickburger line, resulting in fatter profits and a tripling of Hardee's stock price. It seems that some consumers, especially in Hardee's target market of young men aged 18–34, just love fat burgers. A reporter asked a 27-year-old construction worker who was downing a Monster Thickburger if he'd thought about its effect on his health. 'I've never even thought about it,' he replied, 'and to be honest, I don't really care. It just tastes good.'

Hardee's certainly isn't hiding the nutritional facts. Here's how it describes Thickburgers on its website:

> **There's only one thing that can slay the hunger of a young guy on the move: the Thickburger line at Hardee's. With nine cravable varieties, including the classic Original Thickburger and the monument to decadence, the Monster Thickburger, quick-service goes premium with 100% Angus beef and all the**

Celebrity chef Jamie Oliver has made a determined effort to improve the nutritional quality of the lunches provided in British schools

Source: © Peter Dench/Corbis.

> **fixings. . . . If you want to indulge in a big, delicious, juicy burger, look no further than Hardee's.**

So, should Hardee's hang its head in shame? Is it being socially irresponsible by aggressively promoting over-indulgence to ill-informed or unwary consumers? Or is it simply practising good marketing, creating more value for its customers by offering a big juicy burger that clearly satisfies their taste buds, and letting them make their own choices? Critics claim the former; industry defenders claim the latter.

The question of blame gets even murkier when it comes to child obesity. The debate rages over the marketing of everything from fast food and soft drinks in school cafeterias to cereal, biscuits, cakes and other 'not-so-good-for-you' products targeted towards kids and teens, who are seen as especially vulnerable to seductive or misleading marketing pitches. Once again, many public and private advocacy groups point the finger at food marketers. They worry that a 5-year-old watching cute characters and fun ads for a sugary breakfast cereal or chocolate confectionery during a Saturday morning cartoon show probably understands little about good nutrition. These critics have called on food marketers to adopt voluntarily more responsible children's marketing practices. In the UK this issue really hit the headlines when one of the country's leading celebrity chefs, Jamie Oliver, weighed into the argument about the nutritional quality of school meals. After hosting a popular TV show, *Jamie's School Dinners*, the chef was invited to meet influential politicians to promote his argument that the nutritional quality of school meals was dreadful, and that it undermined the ability of children to concentrate in school while putting their long-term health at risk. At first everyone seemed to agree with Jamie that something had to be done to provide schoolchildren with nutritious, freshly cooked lunches made from wholesome ingredients. Government ministers rapidly aligned themselves with Jamie's good-food agenda. Then the debate became more acrimonious, with some people even calling the likeable Jamie a 'food fascist'; newspapers and TV stations gave coverage to 'angry mums' who gathered at school gates during the lunch break to provide their offspring with the sugary and fatty products that were now prohibited from the school premises. Things did not get any easier in 2010 when Jamie took his healthy eating message to the USA, where the TV audience seemed largely unimpressed.

So, back to that big question: who's to blame for the obesity epidemic? Is it the marketers who promote unhealthy but irresistible fare to vulnerable consumers? Or is it the fault of consumers themselves for failing to take personal responsibility for their own health and well-being? It's a weighty decision for many food marketers. And, as is the case with most social responsibility issues, finding the answer to that question is even harder than trying to take off some of those extra pounds.

Sources: Sarah Ellison, 'Kraft Limits on Kid's Ads May Cheese Off Rivals', *The Wall Street Journal*, 13 January 2005, p. B3; Steven Gray, 'At Fast-Food Chains, Era of the Giant Burger (Plus Bacon) Is Here', *The Wall Street Journal*, 27 January 2005, p. B1; 'Obesity Research Ignites Calls for Food Ad Curbs', *Marketing Week*, 5 May 2005, p. 8; http://www.jamieoliver.com/schooldinners/; Peter Walker, 'Jamie Oliver Retreats from America to Fly the Flag for Pub Food', *Guardian*, 26 May 2011, accessed online at http://www.guardian.co.uk/lifeandstyle/2011/may/26/jamie-oliver-television-jamies-great-britain

A third complaint concerns product safety. Product safety has been a problem for several reasons, including company indifference, increased product complexity and poor quality control. For years, consumers' associations across Europe, such as BEUC (the European Consumers' Organisation), CAI (the Consumers' Association of Ireland) and Which? in the UK, have reported various hazards in tested products: electrical dangers in appliances, carbon monoxide poisoning from room heaters, injury risks from lawnmowers and faults in car design among many others. The organisations' testing and other activities have helped consumers make better buying decisions and encouraged businesses to eliminate product flaws.

However, most manufacturers *want* to produce high-quality goods. The way a company deals with product quality and safety problems can damage or help its reputation. Companies selling poor-quality or unsafe products risk damaging conflicts with consumer groups and regulators. Moreover, unsafe products can result in product liability suits and large awards for damages. More fundamentally, consumers who are unhappy with a firm's products may avoid future purchases and talk other consumers into doing the same. Thus, quality errors can have severe consequences. Today's marketers know that customer-driven quality results in customer value and satisfaction, which in turn creates profitable customer relationships.

Planned obsolescence

Critics have also argued that some producers follow a programme of planned obsolescence, causing their products to become obsolete before they actually should need replacement. For example, consider this writer's tale about an ageing mobile phone:

Today, most people, myself included, are all agog at the wondrous outpouring of new technology, from mobile phones to iPods, iPhones, laptops, BlackBerries, and on and on. I have a drawer filled with the detritus of yesterday's hottest products, now reduced to the status of fossils. I have video cameras that use tapes no longer available, laptops with programs incompatible with anything on today's market, portable CD players I no longer use, and more. But what really upsets me is how quickly some still-useful gadgets become obsolete, at least in the eyes of their makers.

I recently embarked on an epic search for a cord to plug into my wife's mobile phone to recharge it. We were travelling and the poor phone kept bleating that it was running low and

Planned obsolescence: printer companies continually introduce new cartridge models and tweak designs. 'You've got planned obsolescence,' says the owner of Laser Logic, a small cartridge refilling company. 'It's kind of like *Mission Impossible:* at the end of this tape, the toner cartridge will self-destruct.'

Source: Reprinted with permission from Lawrence Journal-World.

the battery needed recharging. So, we began a search – from big-box technology superstores to smaller suppliers and the mobile phone companies themselves – all to no avail. Finally, a salesperson told my wife, 'That's an old model, so we don't stock the charger any longer.' 'But I only bought it last year,' she sputtered. 'Yeah, like I said, that's an old model,' he replied without a hint of irony or sympathy. The proliferation and sheer waste of this type of practice is mind-boggling.[9]

Critics charge that some producers continually change consumer concepts of acceptable styles to encourage more and earlier buying. An obvious example is constantly changing clothing fashions. A particular example is the case of replica football shirts for national teams and famous football clubs; it is alleged that teams issue new shirts too frequently, and that the prices charged for them are too high for many fans to afford. In 2003, the UK Office of Fair Trading fined several businesses, including Manchester United Football Club, for illegally fixing the price of replica shirts.[10] Other producers are accused of holding back attractive functional features, then introducing them later to make older models obsolete. Critics claim that this occurs in the consumer electronics and computer industries.

Marketers respond that consumers *like* style changes; they get tired of the old goods and want a new look in fashion or a new design in cars. No one has to buy the new look, and if too few people like it, it will simply fail. For most technical products, customers *want* the latest innovations, even if older models still work. Companies that withhold new features run the risk that competitors will introduce the new feature first and steal the market. For example, consider PCs. Some consumers grumble that the consumer electronics industry's constant push to produce 'faster, smaller, cheaper' models means that they must continually buy new machines just to keep up. Others, however, can hardly wait for the latest model to arrive. Much of so-called planned obsolescence is the working of the competitive and technological forces in a free society – forces that lead to ever-improving goods and services.

Poor service to disadvantaged consumers

Finally, the Western marketing system has been accused of serving disadvantaged consumers poorly. For example, critics claim that the urban poor often have to shop in smaller stores that carry inferior goods and charge higher prices. The presence of large national chain stores in low-income neighbourhoods would help to keep prices down. However, the critics accuse major chain retailers of 'red-lining', drawing a red line around disadvantaged neighbourhoods and avoiding placing stores there.

Similar red-lining charges have been levelled at the insurance, consumer lending, banking and healthcare industries. Home and car insurers have been accused of assigning higher premiums to people with poor credit ratings. The insurers claim that individuals with bad credit tend to make more insurance claims, and that this justifies charging them higher premiums. However, critics and consumer advocates have accused the insurers of a new form of red-lining. Says one writer, 'This is a new excuse for denying coverage to the poor, elderly, and minorities.'[11]

MAKING CONNECTIONS Linking the concepts

Time to take a few moments for reflection. Few marketers *want* to abuse or anger consumers – it's simply not good business. Instead, as you know well by now, most marketers work to build long-term, profitable relationships with customers based on real value and caring. Still, some marketing abuses do occur.

- Think back over the past three months or so and list the instances in which you've suffered a marketing abuse such as those just discussed. Analyse your list. What kinds of companies were involved? Were the abuses intentional? What did the situations have in common?

- Pick one of the instances you listed and describe it in detail. How might you go about righting this wrong? Write out an action plan and then do something to remedy the abuse. If we all took such actions when wronged, there would be far fewer wrongs to right!

Marketing's impact on society as a whole

The Western marketing system has been accused of adding to several 'evils' in society at large. Advertising has been a special target.

False wants and too much materialism

Critics have argued that the marketing system encourages too much interest in material possessions. People are judged by what they *own* rather than by who they *are*. This drive for wealth and possessions hit new highs in the 1980s and 1990s, when phrases such as 'greed is good' and 'shop till you drop' seemed to characterise the times.

In the last decade, many social scientists have noted a reaction against the opulence and waste of the previous decades and a return to more basic values and social commitment. However, our infatuation with material things continues. This is causing widespread concern, in particular about the materialistic attitudes of children. Research undertaken in the UK for the Children's Society in 2007 revealed that 89 per cent of adults believed that today's children were more materialistic than previous generations. The Chief Executive of the society, Bob Reitemeier, said: 'A crucial question raised by the inquiry is whether childhood should be a space where developing minds are free from concentrated sales techniques', and the former Archbishop of Canterbury (head of the Church of England), Dr Rowan Williams, said: 'The selling of lifestyles to children creates a culture of material competitiveness and promotes acquisitive individualism at the expense of the principles of community and cooperation.' Clearly there are influential figures in society who believe that marketing activities are responsible for creating an unhealthy obsession with material things.[12] Some authors have argued that the 'Credit Crunch' was partly fuelled by the unrealistic ambitions of consumers, driven by marketing campaigns that persuaded them to spend regularly more than they could afford. The consequence was a massive increase in consumer debt, which was one contributory factor to the economic and financial woes of many Western countries in 2009–12.[13]

The critics do not view this interest in material things as a natural state of mind but rather as a matter of false wants created by marketing. Businesses hire top advertising agencies to stimulate people's desires for goods and advertisers use the mass media to create materialistic models of the good life. People work harder to earn the necessary money. Their purchases increase the output of industry and industry in turn uses advertising to stimulate more desire for the industrial output. Thus, marketing is seen as creating false wants that benefit industry more than they benefit consumers.

Many marketers would say that these criticisms overstate the power of business to create needs. People are quite sceptical of advertising material. Marketers are most effective when they appeal to existing wants rather than when they attempt to create new ones. Furthermore, people seek information when making important purchases and often do not rely on single sources. Even minor purchases that may be affected by advertising messages lead to repeat purchases only if the product delivers the promised customer value. Finally, the high failure rate of new products shows that companies are not able to control demand.

On a deeper level, our wants and values are influenced by many factors including family, peer groups, religion, ethnic background and education. If Europeans are highly materialistic, these values arise out of basic socialisation processes that go much deeper than business and mass media could produce alone.

Too few social goods

Business has been accused of overselling private goods at the expense of public goods. As private goods increase, they often require more public services that may not be available. For example, an increase in car ownership (private good) requires more roads, traffic control, parking spaces and police services (public goods). The overselling of private goods results in 'social costs'. For cars, the social costs include traffic congestion, air pollution, fuel shortages, and deaths and injuries from car accidents.

A way must be found to restore a balance between private and public goods. One option is to make producers bear the full social costs of their operations. The government could require car manufacturers to build cars with even more safety features, more efficient engines and better pollution control systems. The car companies would then raise their prices to cover extra costs. If buyers found the price of some cars too high, however, the producers of these cars would disappear. Demand would then move to those producers that could support the sum of the private and social costs.

A second option is to make consumers pay the social costs. For example, many cities around the world are starting to impose 'congestion charges' in an effort to reduce traffic congestion. To try to unclog its streets, the City of London introduced a congestion charge in 2003. By 2014 the charge was £11.50 per day per car to drive into the congestion charging area, approximately 8 square miles (20 km²) in the very heart of the city. The London congestion charge was introduced under one mayor, the left-leaning Ken Livingstone, and has subsequently been endorsed by another mayor, the right-leaning Boris Johnson. Regardless of political differences, it seems that the principle of charging a substantial amount of money to virtually all cars driven into the centre of London is now well established. The charge has not only reduced the number of cars entering the zone by 21 per cent, but also raised money to invest in London's public transport system.[14] Other cities in Europe and elsewhere have developed schemes with the same aims as the London congestion charge, although the methods of implementation vary. For example, Stockholm has a very similar congestion charge, while Singapore has a more comprehensive 'electronic road pricing' scheme with charges that vary depending on time and location. Several other major cities are actively considering the introduction of such schemes.

Cultural pollution

Critics charge the marketing system with creating *cultural pollution*. Our senses are being constantly assaulted by marketing and advertising. Advertisements interrupt serious programmes; pages of advertisements obscure magazines; posters obscure beautiful scenery; spam fills our inboxes. These interruptions continually pollute people's minds with messages of materialism, sex, power or status.

Many people would see these as powerful criticisms, but marketers can try to answer the charges of 'commercial noise' with these arguments. First, they hope that their advertisements reach primarily the target audience. Because of mass-communication channels, some of them are bound to reach people who have no interest in the product and are therefore bored or annoyed. People who buy magazines addressed to their interests rarely complain about the advertisements because the magazines advertise products of interest; if you buy the motorcycle magazine *Road Racing Ireland* or the magazine for lovers of audio equipment *Hi-Fi World* then you probably look forward to reading the advertisements as well as the articles.

Second, advertisements make much of TV and radio free to users and keep down the costs of magazines and newspapers. Many people think this is a small price to pay for these benefits. For example, in many large cities you can pick up one or more free newspapers during the rush hour, paid for completely out of advertising revenue; and judging by the number of people reading such newspapers on the train home, they seem to be popular! Finally, today's consumers have alternatives. For example, they can dodge TV advertisements by using their remote control, or avoid them altogether on many cable or satellite channels. Thus, to hold consumer attention, advertisers are making their work more entertaining and informative.

Too much political power

Another criticism is that business wields too much political power. Large companies in a wide range of industry sectors, including oil, tobacco, pharmaceuticals and alcohol, spend money on public relations material and on specialist PR consultants who lobby (i.e. try to influence) people in positions of political power. Advertisers are accused of holding too much power over the mass media, limiting media freedom to report independently and objectively. The critics ask: How can magazines afford to tell the truth about the low nutritional value of packaged foods when these magazines are being subsidised by advertisers who produce high-sugar, high-fat food products low in nutritional content? How can the major TV companies criticise the practices of the large car companies when such companies invest billions of euros a year in broadcast advertising?

This debate has run for years, and will continue to run for a long time to come. European industries, in fact industries worldwide, do promote and protect their own interests. They have a right to put their views to politicians and to use the mass media. However, their influence can become too great because they wield so much economic power and have so much money to spend on promoting their own point of view. Nevertheless, there are organisations – notably some of the consumer associations that we mentioned earlier in the chapter – that consistently call big business to account and, in their turn, lobby politicians to ensure that there is a counterbalance to the power of big businesses.

Marketing's impact on other businesses

Critics also argue that a company's marketing practices can harm other companies and reduce competition. Three problems are involved: acquisitions of competitors, marketing practices that create barriers to entry and unfair competitive marketing practices.

Critics claim that firms are harmed and competition reduced when companies expand by acquiring competitors rather than by developing their own new products. The large number of acquisitions and rapid pace of industry consolidation over the past several decades have caused concern that vigorous young competitors will be absorbed and that competition will be reduced. In virtually every major industry – retailing, entertainment, financial services, utilities, transportation, vehicles, telecommunications, healthcare – the number of major competitors is shrinking.

Business acquisition is a complex subject. Acquisitions can sometimes be good for society. The acquiring company may gain economies of scale that lead to lower costs and lower prices. A well-managed company may take over a poorly managed company and improve its efficiency. An industry that was not very competitive might become more competitive after the acquisition. But acquisitions can also reduce competition and, therefore, are closely regulated by governments.

Critics have also charged that marketing practices prevent new companies from entering an industry. Large marketing companies can use patents and heavy promotional spending, and can tie up suppliers or dealers to keep out or drive out competitors. Those concerned with the regulation of anti-competitive behaviour recognise that some barriers are the natural result of the economic advantages of doing business on a large scale. There are some industries, like aircraft manufacturing, that can only be done efficiently if they are done on a massive scale.

Finally, some firms have actually used unfair competitive marketing practices with the intention of hurting or destroying other firms. They may set their prices below costs, threaten to cut off business with suppliers, or discourage the buying of a competitor's products. Various laws work to prevent such predatory competition. It is difficult, however, to prove that the intent or action was really predatory.

Nevertheless, there is clear evidence that companies' marketing approaches, particularly their approaches to pricing, sometimes break the law. For example, in 2009, after a five-year investigation, the UK's competition watchdog, the Office of Fair Trading, announced that it had imposed fines totalling £129.5m on construction firms in England that were found guilty of illegal price collusion. The offence of which the firms were found guilty was 'cover pricing', but the news media had a range of more colourful terms for this practice: 'price rigging', 'price fixing', 'illegal bid rigging' and even, simply, 'scam'. Because of this illegal collusion, some organisations buying construction services (including businesses, public authorities and charities) were believed to have paid too much for various building works.[15] Clearly, marketers must strive at all times to operate within the relevant domestic and European laws on competition.

CITIZEN AND PUBLIC ACTIONS TO REGULATE MARKETING

Because some people view business as the cause of many economic and social ills, grassroots movements have arisen from time to time to keep business in line. The two major movements have been *consumerism* and *environmentalism*.

Consumerism

Businesses have been the target of organised consumer movements on three occasions. The first consumer movement took place in the early 1900s. It was fuelled by rising prices, revelations about conditions in the meat industry and scandals in the drug industry. The second consumer movement, in the mid-1930s, was sparked by an upturn in consumer prices during the Great Depression and another drugs scandal.

The third movement began in the 1960s. Consumers had become better educated, products had become more complex and potentially hazardous, and people were unhappy with US institutions. A prominent champion of consumer rights called Ralph Nader appeared on the scene to force many issues, and other well-known writers, such as the Canadian economist John Kenneth Galbraith, accused big business of wasteful and unethical practices. Since then, many consumer groups have been organised and several consumer protection laws have been passed. The consumer movement has spread internationally and is particularly strong in Europe.

But what is the consumer movement? **Consumerism** is an organised movement of citizens and government agencies to improve the rights and power of buyers in relation to sellers. Traditional sellers' rights include:

- The right to introduce any product in any size and style, provided it is not hazardous to personal health or safety; or, if it is, to include proper warnings and controls.

- The right to charge any price for the product provided no discrimination exists among similar kinds of buyers.

- The right to spend any amount to promote the product provided it is not defined as unfair competition.

- The right to use any product message provided it is not misleading or dishonest in content or execution.

- The right to use any buying incentive programmes provided they are not unfair or misleading.

Traditional *buyers' rights* include:

- The right not to buy a product that is offered for sale.

- The right to expect the product to be safe.

- The right to expect the product to perform as claimed.

Comparing these rights, many believe that the balance of power lies on the seller's side. True, the buyer can refuse to buy. But critics feel that the buyer has too little information, education and protection to make wise decisions when facing sophisticated sellers. Consumer advocates call for the following additional consumer rights:

- The right to be well informed about important aspects of the product.

- The right to be protected against questionable products and marketing practices.

- The right to influence products and marketing practices in ways that will improve the 'quality of life'.

Each proposed right has led to more specific proposals by consumerists. The right to be informed includes the right to know the true interest on a loan (truth in lending), the true cost per unit of a brand (unit pricing), the ingredients in a product (ingredient labelling), the nutritional value of foods (nutritional labelling), product freshness (open dating) and the true benefits of a product (truth in advertising). Proposals related to consumer protection include strengthening consumer rights in cases of business fraud, requiring greater product safety and giving more power to government agencies. Proposals relating to quality of life include controlling the ingredients that go into certain products and packaging, reducing the level of advertising 'noise' and putting consumer representatives on company boards to protect consumer interests.

Consumers not only have the *right* but also the *responsibility* to protect themselves instead of leaving this function to someone else. Consumers who believe they got a bad deal have several remedies available, including contacting the company or the media, contacting European, national or local agencies, and going to small-claims courts.

Sustainability

Whereas consumerists consider whether the marketing system is efficiently serving consumer wants, environmentalists are concerned with marketing's effects on the environment and with the costs of serving consumer needs and wants. **Environmentalism** is an organised movement of concerned citizens, businesses and government agencies to protect and improve people's living environment.

Environmentalists are not against marketing and consumption; they simply want people and organisations to operate with more care for the environment. The marketing system's goal, they assert, should not be to maximise consumption, consumer choice or consumer satisfaction, but rather to maximise life quality. And 'life quality' means not only the quantity and quality of consumer goods and services, but also the quality of the environment. Environmentalists want environmental costs included in both producer and consumer decision making.

The first wave of modern environmentalism was driven by environmental groups and concerned consumers in the 1960s and 1970s. They were concerned with damage to the ecosystem caused by strip-mining, forest depletion, acid rain, loss of the atmosphere's ozone layer, toxic wastes and litter. They also were concerned with the loss of recreational areas and with the increase in health problems caused by bad air, polluted water and chemically treated food.

The second environmentalism wave was driven by government, which passed laws and regulations during the 1970s and 1980s governing industrial practices affecting the environment. This wave hit some industries hard. Steel companies and utilities had to invest billions in pollution control equipment and costlier fuels. The car industry had to introduce expensive emission controls in cars. The packaging industry had to find ways to reduce litter. These industries and others have often resented and resisted environmental regulations, especially when they have been imposed too rapidly to allow companies to make proper adjustments. Many of these companies claim they have had to absorb large costs that have made them less competitive.

The first two environmentalism waves have now merged into a third and stronger wave in which companies are accepting responsibility for doing no harm to the environment. They are shifting from protest to prevention, and from regulation to responsibility. More and more companies are adopting policies of **environmental sustainability** – developing strategies that both sustain the environment *and* produce profits for the company. According to one strategist, 'The challenge is to develop a *sustainable global economy:* an economy that the planet is capable of supporting indefinitely . . . . [It's] an enormous challenge – and an enormous opportunity.'[16] One company that has been striving to be at the forefront of sustainability is the retailer Marks & Spencer. To find out more about how it has been pursuing the sustainability agenda, take a look at Marketing at Work 16.2.

The Marks & Spencer and Oxfam Clothes Exchange

MARKETING AT WORK 16.2

Professor Ken Peattie, BRASS Research Centre, Cardiff Business School, Wales

During the twenty-first century the most significant challenges faced by marketers, and the products, brands and companies they represent, will be linked to aspects of the sustainable development agenda. The relatively unconstrained economic growth of the twentieth century had social and environmental consequences that now threaten the future stability of our society and our economy, and the environmental systems on which we depend. Governments, businesses and many non-governmental organisations (NGOs) are increasingly seeking to address growing concerns about the sustainability of future economic development by taking more account of issues such as climate change, global poverty, resource depletion, waste, biodiversity and population growth.

Marks & Spencer's 'Plan A'

In January 2007 Marks & Spencer launched its £200m eco-plan 'Plan A', one of the most ambitious strategies to address sustainability concerns to be developed by a leading company. The 100-point plan sought to address the key sustainability challenges that the business faced, grouped under five headings:

- *Climate change:* with the aim of making the business carbon neutral by 2012.
- *Waste:* with the aim of eliminating waste to landfill from its operations by 2012.
- *Sustainable sourcing:* particularly to extend M&S's use of organic and free-range produce.
- *Ethical trading standards:* to use the power of M&S as an own-brand retailer to improve the livelihoods of its suppliers and supplier communities worldwide.
- Helping customers and employees to live a healthier lifestyle.

In unveiling the plan, M&S Chief Executive, Stuart Rose, commented:

Every business and individual needs to do their bit to tackle the enormous challenges of climate change and waste. While M&S will continue to sell great quality, stylish and innovative products, our customers, employees and shareholders now expect us to take bold steps and do business differently and responsibly. We believe a responsible business can be a profitable business. We are calling this 'Plan A'

because there is no 'Plan B' . . . . This is a deliberately ambitious and, in some areas, difficult plan. We don't have all the answers but we are determined to work with our suppliers, partners and government to make this happen. Doing anything less is not an option.

Honouring Pledge 44

One reason why Plan A was so ambitious was that many of its pledges represented a bold public commitment to change made before the company had fully worked out how that commitment might be met. This was the case for Pledge 44 about helping customers to reduce their waste clothing by 'making sure that, within five years, you need throw none of our clothing away as waste after you've finished with it. We will start by researching alternatives into clothing disposal, including donation, composting and recycling.' In doing so, M&S would help to address the problem of the estimated 1 million tonnes of clothing annually going into landfill in the UK, much of it suitable for reuse or recycling. The obvious solution for Pledge 44 might have been an in-house clothes reclamation and recycling scheme, but this posed a significant reverse logistics challenge for a retail operation geared towards providing rather than reacquiring products. Instead, it was the emphasis on partnership that was central to the Plan A project that inspired a solution.

Oxfam is one of the UK's best known charities with a campaigning and disaster relief remit that seeks to tackle poverty and promote development globally. Many of the issues that Oxfam campaigns on, including climate change, fairer trade and the emerging global food crisis, are also central to the strategic agenda for a major food and clothing retailer such as M&S. Since the company sought to maintain good relationships with campaigning charities and other NGOs, it was natural for it to enter into a dialogue with Oxfam on a range of Plan A issues linked to its ethical trading and sustainable sourcing responsibilities and commitments. During this dialogue the realisation grew that there was an opportunity for the two organisations to go beyond talking together, and instead to work together on a mutually beneficial project. With a network of over 750 high-street shops throughout the UK, Oxfam represented the most extensive retail network involved in recycling second-hand goods, particularly clothes. It was also the only UK charity with its own textile sorting operation, Wastesaver, based in Huddersfield. This meant that even the clothes it handled that were unsuitable for resale in the UK could be reused in other countries or recycled in other ways. For M&S, Oxfam represented the perfect partner for a scheme to recycle customers'

used and excess clothing. For Oxfam, the quality of M&S items made them strong sellers within its shops, and an increased flow of M&S items represented a potentially valuable income boost with which to fund its development and disaster relief campaigns. From this opportunity the 'M&S and Oxfam Clothes Exchange' cause-related marketing campaign was born.

The strategic fit between the priorities, needs and capabilities of the two organisations was obvious. There was also a good strategic fit between the strengths of the two brands within their respective worlds, the geographical locations of their stores, and in the nature of their loyal core groups of customers/supporters. Culturally, tactically and operationally, however, there were a number of issues to resolve. For Oxfam a cause-related marketing partnership with a commercial retailer, even one with the strong ethical credentials of M&S, was a new departure. It carried with it an element of reputational risk should M&S find itself involved in any ethical controversies linked to another aspect of its operations, particularly those close to the heart of Oxfam's agenda such as the treatment of workers in poorer countries. For M&S, it meant an operational link with an organisation that was a social enterprise and not a conventional commercial business, and which depended to a large extent on volunteer workers. So the partnership dialogue to establish the scheme included an operational audit of the Huddersfield Wastesaver facilities to ensure that any operational risks for M&S were addressed, and a review of all elements of the ethical agenda for M&S to ensure that any reputational risks for Oxfam were addressed.

There were some other unusual aspects to the scheme. Although it was a strategically important campaign, it was developed without specific performance targets. Since it was considered central to honouring Pledge 44, and was also a relatively unique campaign for which no obvious precedents or benchmarks existed, it was established on a 'try it and see' basis. The scheme was also developed in considerable secrecy to prevent competitors becoming aware of what was planned. Therefore, instead of the normal regional trial to assess the success of such a scheme, a national launch was planned. The nationwide scope and emphasis on secrecy together posed a challenge given that the scheme's success depended on informing and training (and gaining the support of) 23,000 Oxfam staff and volunteers in 790 shops and 65,000 M&S employees across its 375 stores. This was tackled by holding back informing and training people until two weeks before the launch, at which point the Oxfam store managers who had been brought together in London ostensibly for a national 'training day' instead found themselves being briefed and trained on the new joint venture with M&S.

Launching the Clothes Exchange

The scheme was announced, on a six-month trial basis, in January 2008 to mark the first anniversary of Plan A. To add impetus to the campaign launch, the two organisations commissioned market research into the nation's wardrobes from YouGov. This showed that an estimated 2.4 billion items (representing 46 per cent of people's clothes) had sat in a wardrobe without being worn once in the past year. Consumers in the 25–34 age group had the most expensive unworn clothes collection, worth an average of £228. As unworn clothes they were providing no value to the consumer, yet represented a store of value that could be converted into clothes that Oxfam could use to fund its work tackling poverty and which other consumers could purchase and benefit from.

As Oxfam Director Barbara Stocking said:

> **This partnership is an enormous opportunity and Oxfam is very excited to be working with M&S to help make a real difference to global poverty. Recycling and reusing clothes – and anything else we can sell – has always been central to Oxfam's fundraising, as well as being good for the environment. Through our unique textile sorting facility and the resourcefulness and skills of our specialist staff, Oxfam is able to make the most from all the clothes we receive. People's unwanted clothes really will raise much needed money to help people living in poverty.**

The offer to M&S customers was that if they made a donation to Oxfam containing at least one piece of M&S labelled clothing or accessory (excluding underwear and swimwear), they would be given a special M&S and Oxfam Clothes Exchange voucher. The voucher was valid for one month, and provided a £5 discount at M&S if customers spent more than £35 on clothing, beauty or products for the home. The deal was structured to reward people through the discount voucher, rather than simply to appeal to their ethical instincts by asking for surplus M&S clothes to be donated to Oxfam. The one-month expiry date on the coupon also acted as a motivator to encourage people to follow through on obtaining the personal benefits from making their clothes donation.

The details of the scheme were communicated to customers through several channels. The launch, backed by a national press advertising campaign, attracted widespread media coverage. Point-of-sale material was developed for use within both M&S stores and Oxfam shops in the UK and Republic of Ireland; it was featured in the M&S customer magazine and through both organisations' websites. The communications campaign generated considerable public interest and follow-up research showed it reached an audience of approximately 45 million people and generated public relations benefits valued at £4.5m.

The results

The success of the scheme was obvious after only seven weeks when progress was first reviewed. In those seven weeks, Oxfam had issued 140,884 vouchers in exchange for an average of 4.85 items per donation. A total of 683,287 items were donated, representing a 40 per cent increase on normal donations and equating to an estimated 341 tonnes of clothing which might otherwise have ended up in landfill. By the end of the first six months of the scheme, the forecast additional income for Oxfam would represent around £1.5m (on an annual basis) to invest in its campaigns. Frontline feedback also suggested that the scheme had attracted thousands of people into an Oxfam shop for the first time, and as the scheme progressed it became clear that its stakeholders approved.

From the M&S perspective, of the vouchers issued during those first seven weeks, over 48 per cent were redeemed (which compares with a typical redemption rate for such vouchers of only 2 per cent). The average value of the basket of goods purchased by customers redeeming vouchers was also just over double the average customer basket, and by the end of the first six months the scheme was generating an average of around £1m per month in additional sales. The scheme was exemplary in delivering the 'triple bottom-line' benefits sought by commercial sustainability strategies. It

The Clothes Exchange, jointly organised with the global charity Oxfam, is one mechanism by which Marks & Spencer is implementing its 'Plan A' commitment to tackle climate change and waste

Source: © Oxfam and © Marks and Spencer plc.

generated valuable funds for Oxfam to spend on social causes in poorer countries. On an annual basis it would benefit the environment by diverting 2 million items of clothing away from landfill. Commercially it benefited M&S through additional sales volume and it benefited consumers by delivering wardrobe space to some and

new (to them) clothing to others, and an ethical 'glow' from supporting Oxfam to all of them.

Sources: The author would like to thank Mike Barry, Head of Corporate Responsibility, Marks & Spencer, and David McCullough, Trading Director Oxfam, and Fee Gilfeather, Trading Communications & Marketing Manager Oxfam, for their help in developing this case study.

Figure 16.1 shows a grid that companies can use to gauge their progress towards environmental sustainability. At the most basic level, a company can practise *pollution prevention*. This involves more than pollution control – cleaning up waste after it has been created.

Pollution prevention means eliminating or minimising waste before it is created. Companies emphasising prevention have responded with 'green marketing' programmes – developing ecologically safer products, recyclable and biodegradable packaging, better pollution controls and more energy-efficient operations.

For example, French transport company Norbert Dentressangle has taken steps to improve fuel efficiency and reduce the emissions from its large fleet of trucks. This includes specific, tough targets for the annual reduction of greenhouse gas emissions, which will be achieved by operating more efficient trucks, reducing the distances that trucks have to cover when empty and optimising vehicle loading to reduce unnecessary miles travelled.

At the next level, companies can practise *product stewardship* – minimising not just pollution from production but all environmental impacts throughout the full product life cycle and all the while reducing costs. Many companies are adopting *design for environment (DFE)* practices, which involve thinking ahead to design products that are easier to recover reuse or recycle. DFE not only helps to sustain the environment, but also can be highly profitable for the company. The Commission for Architecture and the Built Environment (CABE) has produced a briefing paper for builders, architects and government organisations offering them advice on how to 'design in' environmental sustainability to construction projects. The aim is to address environmental matters at the very earliest stage in a construction project, for example at the point where the urban planners start to think about where a new housing development should be built.[17]

FIGURE 16.1
The environmental sustainability grid

Source: Reprinted by permission of *Harvard Business Review*. Exhibit from 'Beyond Greening: Strategies for a Sustainable World', by Stuart L. Hart, January–February 1997, p. 74. Copyright © 1997 by the Harvard Business School Publishing Corporation: all rights reserved.

	Internal	External
Tomorrow	**New environmental technology** — Is the environmental performance of our products limited by our existing technology base? / Is there potential to realise major improvements through new technology?	**Sustainability vision** — Does our corporate vision direct us towards the solution of social and environmental problems? / Does our vision guide the development of new technologies, markets, products and processes?
Today	**Pollution prevention** — Where are the most significant waste and emission streams from our current operations? / Can we lower costs and risks by eliminating waste at the source or by using it as useful input?	**Product stewardship** — What are the implications for product design and development if we assume responsibility for a product's entire life cycle? / Can we add value or lower costs while simultaneously reducing the impact of our products?

At the third level, companies look to the future and plan for *new environmental technologies*. Many organisations that have made good sustainability headway are still limited by existing technologies. To develop fully sustainable strategies, they will need to develop new technologies. For example, in 2005 the Korean car company Hyundai opened its New Environmental Technology R&D Centre in Seoul. The building itself was developed according to environmental standards (including a vacuum toilet system that uses one-tenth as much water as conventional toilets), while the purpose of the R&D facility is to develop the next generation of vehicles and environmental technologies that will cause far less environmental damage than today's cars. This includes projects looking at fuel-cell cars, increasing the recyclability of the materials used in cars, and reducing the use of ferrous (iron-based) materials in car manufacturing.

Finally, companies can develop a *sustainability vision,* which serves as a guide to the future. It shows how the company's products and services, processes and policies must develop and what new technologies must be established to get there. This vision of sustainability provides a framework for pollution control, product stewardship and environmental technology.

Most companies today focus on the lower left quadrant of the grid in Figure 16.1, investing most heavily in pollution prevention. Some forward-looking companies practise product stewardship and are developing new environmental technologies. Few companies have well-defined sustainability visions. Emphasising only one or a few quadrants in the environmental sustainability grid can be short-sighted. Investing only in the bottom half of the grid puts a company in a good position today but leaves it vulnerable in the future. In contrast, a heavy emphasis on the top half suggests that a company has good environmental vision but lacks the skills needed to implement it. Thus, companies should work at developing all four dimensions of environmental sustainability. The EC has created a scheme called the European Business Awards for the Environment to promote just this kind of corporate behaviour. Every two years, a number of European companies are selected as the award winners because of their efforts to promote environmentally-conscious business. In 2012, the winners of these awards came from all over Europe including Belgium (Unicore – a materials technology company), Slovakia (Slovenské elektrárne – a power generating company) and the UK (Marks & Spencer for its Plan A – see Marketing at Work 16.2).

Environmentalism creates some special challenges for global marketers. As international trade barriers come down and global markets expand, environmental issues are having an ever-greater impact on international trade. Countries in Western Europe, North America and other developed regions are evolving strict environmental standards. The EU recently passed 'end-of-life' regulations affecting vehicles and consumer electronics products. The EU's Eco-Management and Audit Scheme provides guidelines for environmental self-regulation.[18]

However, environmental policies still vary widely from country to country. Countries such as Denmark, Germany, Japan, the UK and the USA have fully developed environmental policies and high public expectations. But major countries such as China, India, Brazil and Russia are in only the early stages of developing such policies. Moreover, environmental factors that motivate consumers in one country may have no impact on consumers in another. For example, PVC soft-drinks bottles cannot be used in Switzerland or Germany. However, they are preferred in France, which has an extensive recycling process for them. Thus, international companies have found it difficult to develop standard environmental practices that work around the world. Instead, they are creating general policies and then translating these policies into tailored programmes that meet local regulations and expectations.

Public actions to regulate marketing

Concerns among the general public about marketing practices will usually lead to government attention and possibly to legislative proposals. Ideas for new laws will be debated – many will be defeated, others will be modified and a few will become workable laws.

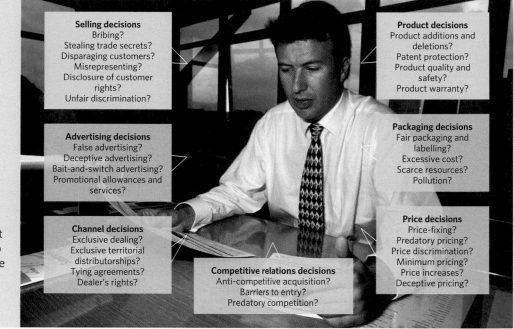

Selling decisions
Bribing?
Stealing trade secrets?
Disparaging customers?
Misrepresenting?
Disclosure of customer rights?
Unfair discrimination?

Product decisions
Product additions and deletions?
Patent protection?
Product quality and safety?
Product warranty?

Advertising decisions
False advertising?
Deceptive advertising?
Bait-and-switch advertising?
Promotional allowances and services?

Packaging decisions
Fair packaging and labelling?
Excessive cost?
Scarce resources?
Pollution?

Channel decisions
Exclusive dealing?
Exclusive territorial distributorships?
Tying agreements?
Dealer's rights?

Competitive relations decisions
Anti-competitive acquisition?
Barriers to entry?
Predatory competition?

Price decisions
Price-fixing?
Predatory pricing?
Price discrimination?
Minimum pricing?
Price increases?
Deceptive pricing?

FIGURE 16.2
Major marketing decision areas that may be called into question under the law

Source: Photo is © Helen Rogers/Alamy Images.

Many of the laws that affect marketing were discussed earlier (see Chapter 3). The task is to translate these laws into the language that marketing executives understand as they make decisions about competitive relations, products, price, promotion and channels of distribution. Figure 16.2 illustrates the major legal issues facing marketing management.

BUSINESS ACTIONS TOWARDS SOCIALLY RESPONSIBLE MARKETING

At first, many companies opposed consumerism and environmentalism. They thought the criticisms were either unfair or unimportant. But by now most companies have accepted the new consumer rights, at least in principle. They might oppose certain pieces of legislation as inappropriate ways to solve specific consumer problems, but they recognise the consumer's right to information and protection. Many of these companies have responded positively to consumerism and environmentalism as a way to create greater customer value and to strengthen customer relationships.

Sustainable marketing

The philosophy of **sustainable marketing** holds that a company's marketing should support the best long-term performance of the marketing system. Sustainable marketing consists of five principles: *consumer-oriented marketing, innovative marketing, customer value marketing, sense-of-mission marketing* and *societal marketing.*

Consumer-oriented marketing

Consumer-oriented marketing means that the company should view and organise its marketing activities from the consumer's point of view. It should work hard to sense, serve and satisfy the needs of a defined group of customers. Every good marketing company that we have discussed in this text has had this in common: an all-consuming passion for delivering superior value to carefully chosen customers. Only by seeing the world through its customers' eyes can the company build lasting and profitable customer relationships. By creating value *for* consumers, the company can capture value *from* consumers in return.

Innovative marketing

The principle of **innovative marketing** requires the company always to be seeking real product and marketing improvements. The company that overlooks new and better ways to do things will eventually lose customers to another company that has found a better way. An excellent example of an innovative marketer is Samsung Electronics:

> A decade ago, Samsung was a copycat consumer electronics brand you bought off a shipping pallet at Costco if you couldn't afford a Sony. But today, the brand holds a high-end, cutting-edge aura. In 1996, Samsung Electronics made an inspired decision. It turned its back on cheap knock-offs and set out to overtake rival Sony. The company hired a crop of fresh, young designers, who unleashed a torrent of new products – not humdrum, me-too products, but innovative and stylish products, targeted to high-end users. Samsung called them 'lifestyle works of art' – from brightly coloured mobile phones and elegantly thin DVD players to flat-panel TV monitors that hung on walls like paintings. Every new product had to pass the 'Wow!' test. If it didn't get a 'Wow!' reaction during market testing, it went straight back to the design studio.[19]

Samsung supported this worldwide goal with substantial advertising expenditure, and reconsidered its distribution strategy so that Samsung products were to be found in upmarket retail outlets where consumers are prepared to pay above-average prices for premium-quality products with innovative features. Over the last decade Samsung has successfully repositioned itself as a producer of innovative, high-quality electronics products.

Customer value marketing

According to the principle of **customer value marketing,** the company should put most of its resources into customer-value-building marketing investments. Many things marketers do – one-shot sales promotions, minor packaging changes, direct response advertising – may raise sales in the short term but add less *value* than would fundamental improvements in the product's quality, features or convenience. Sustainable marketing calls for building long-term consumer loyalty and relationships by continually improving the value consumers receive from the firm's market offering.

Sense-of-mission marketing

Sense-of-mission marketing means that the company should define its mission in broad *social* terms rather than narrow *product* terms. When a company defines a social mission, employees feel better about their work and have a clearer sense of direction. For example, Ben & Jerry's ice cream brand is known all over the world (since 2000 Ben & Jerry's has been a business unit of the Anglo-Dutch consumer goods giant Unilever), and defined in narrow terms the mission of Ben & Jerry's might be 'to sell ice cream'. However, Ben & Jerry's states its mission more broadly, as one of 'linked prosperity', including product, economic and social missions (see **http://www.benjerry.com/values/**). Founders Ben Cohen and Jerry Greenfield pioneered the concept of 'values-led business' or 'caring capitalism'. Their mission was to use business to make the world a better place:

> From its beginnings in 1978, Ben & Jerry's bought only hormone-free milk and cream and used only organic fruits and nuts to make its ice cream, which it sold in environmentally-friendly containers. It went to great lengths to buy from minority and disadvantaged suppliers. From its early Rainforest Crunch to its more recent One Sweet Whirled flavours and awareness campaigns, Ben & Jerry's championed a host of social and environmental causes over the years. And from the start, Ben & Jerry's donated a whopping 7.5 per cent of pre-tax profits to support projects that exhibited 'creative problem-solving and hopefulness . . . relating to children and families, disadvantaged groups, and the environment'. By the mid-1990s, Ben & Jerry's had become [America's] number-two super-premium ice cream brand.

However, having a 'double bottom line' of values and profits is no easy proposition. Through the 1990s, as competitors not shackled by their 'principles before profits' missions invaded its markets, Ben & Jerry's growth and profits flattened. Perhaps this was why in 2000, after several years of disappointing financial returns, Ben & Jerry's was acquired by Unilever. Looking back, the company appears to have focused too much on social issues at the expense of sound business management. Cohen once commented, 'There came a time when I had to admit "I'm a businessman." And I had a hard time mouthing those words.'[20]

Such experiences taught the socially responsible business movement some hard lessons. The result is a new generation of activist entrepreneurs – not social activists with big hearts who hate capitalism, but well-trained business managers and company builders with a passion for a cause. Innocent Smoothies is a good example of this new kind of caring company with a highly professional approach to business and marketing. It says, 'We want to leave things a little bit better than we find them. We strive to do business in a more enlightened way, where we take responsibility for the impact of our business on society and the environment, and move these impacts from negative to neutral, or better still, positive.' This is from a company that started up in 1999 and has now achieved an annual turnover of over £100m, and is the most prominent UK smoothie brand. In 2009 Innocent received some criticism from its loyal fans for accepting an investment from Coca-Cola. However, in 2010 Innocent was voted among the ten 10 UK 'thought leadership brands' in a poll of 1,000 business leaders, indicating that the strong values of the founders were alive and well in the company.[21]

Societal marketing

Following the principle of **societal marketing**, a sustainable marketing company makes marketing decisions by considering consumers' wants and interests, the company's requirements and society's long-term interests. The company is aware that neglecting consumer and societal long-term interests is a disservice to consumers and society. Alert companies view societal problems as opportunities.

A societally oriented marketer wants to design products that are not only pleasing but also beneficial. The difference is shown in Figure 16.3. Products can be classified according to their degree of immediate consumer satisfaction and long-term consumer benefit. **Deficient products**, such as bad-tasting and ineffective medicine, have neither immediate appeal nor long-term benefits. **Pleasing products** give high immediate satisfaction but may hurt consumers in the long run. Examples include cigarettes and junk food. **Salutary products** have low appeal but may benefit consumers in the long run; for instance, seat belts

Many entrepreneurial businesses today, like Innocent Drinks, strive to make both profits and a wider contribution to society

Source: Innocent Ltd.

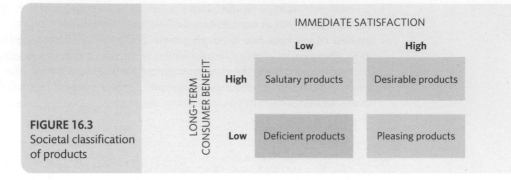

FIGURE 16.3
Societal classification
of products

and air bags. **Desirable products** give both high immediate satisfaction and high long-term benefits, such as a tasty *and* nutritious breakfast food.

MAKING CONNECTIONS Linking the concepts

Pause here, hold your place with your finger, and go back and take another look at the societal marketing concept section in Chapter 1.

● How does Figure 1.4 apply to the sustainable marketing section in this chapter?

● Use the five principles to assess the actions of a company that you believe exemplifies socially responsible marketing. (If you can't think of one, use Unilever or one of the other companies discussed in this chapter.)

● Use the principles of sustainable marketing to assess the actions of a company that you believe falls short of socially responsible marketing.

Examples of desirable products abound. Low-energy-consumption, long-life light bulbs are a well-known example, and they are widely available through the biggest retailers (such as Tesco and Carrefour) who stock major brands such as Philips and GE. Toyota's hybrid Prius family car gives both a quiet ride and fuel efficiency. Miele's range of washing machines and dishwashers is recommended by consumer organisations for their excellent performance, and also deliver better energy efficiency and lower water consumption than standard brands.

Companies should try to turn all of their products into desirable products. The challenge posed by pleasing products is that they sell very well but may end up hurting the consumer. The product opportunity, therefore, is to add long-term benefits without reducing the product's pleasing qualities. The challenge posed by salutary products is to add some pleasing qualities so that they will become more desirable in consumers' minds.

Marketing ethics

Good ethics are a cornerstone of sustainable marketing. In the long run, unethical marketing harms customers and society as a whole. Further, it eventually damages a company's reputation and effectiveness, jeopardising the company's very survival. Thus, the sustainable marketing goals of long-term consumer and business welfare can be achieved only through ethical marketing conduct.

Conscientious marketers face many moral dilemmas. The best thing to do is often unclear. Because not all managers have fine moral sensitivity, companies need to develop *corporate marketing ethics policies* – broad guidelines that everyone in the organisation must follow.

These policies should cover distributor relations, advertising standards, customer service, pricing, product development and general ethical standards.

The finest guidelines cannot resolve all the difficult ethical situations the marketer faces. Exhibit 16.1 lists some difficult ethical situations marketers could face during their careers. If marketers choose immediate sales-producing actions in all these cases, their marketing behaviour might well be described as immoral or even amoral. If they refuse to go along with *any* of the actions, they might be ineffective as marketing managers and unhappy because of the constant moral tension. Managers need a set of principles that will help them work out the moral importance of each situation and decide how far they can go in good conscience.

But *what* principle should guide companies and marketing managers on issues of ethics and social responsibility? One philosophy is that such issues are decided by the free market and legal system. Under this principle, companies and their managers are not responsible for making moral judgements. Companies can, according to this principle, in good conscience do whatever the market and legal systems allow.

A second philosophy puts responsibility not on the system but in the hands of individual companies and managers. This more enlightened philosophy suggests that a company should have a 'social conscience'. Companies and managers should apply high standards of ethics and morality when making corporate decisions, regardless of 'what the system allows'. History provides an endless list of examples of company actions that were legal but highly irresponsible.

EXHIBIT 16.1   Some Morally Difficult Situations in Marketing

1   You work for a cigarette company. Public policy debates over the past few years now leave no doubt in your mind that cigarette smoking and cancer are closely linked. Although your company currently runs an 'if you don't smoke, don't start' promotion campaign, you believe that other company promotions might encourage young (although legal age) non-smokers to pick up the habit. What would you do?

2   Your R&D department has changed one of your products slightly. It is not really 'new and improved', but you know that putting this statement on the package and in advertising will increase sales. What would you do?

3   You have been asked to add a stripped-down model to your line that could be advertised to pull customers into the store. The product will not be very good, but salespeople will be able to switch buyers up to higher-priced units. You are asked to give the green light for the stripped-down version. What would you do?

4   You are thinking of hiring a product manager who has just left a competitor's company. She would be more than happy to tell you all the competitor's plans for the coming year. What would you do?

5   One of your top dealers in an important territory has recently had family troubles and his sales have slipped. It looks like it will take him a while to straighten out his family trouble. Meanwhile you are losing many sales. Legally, you can terminate the dealer's franchise and replace him. What would you do?

6   You have a chance to win a big account that will mean a lot to you and your company. The purchasing agent hints that a 'gift' would influence the decision. Your assistant recommends sending a fine high-definition colour TV set to the buyer's home. What would you do?

7   You have heard that a competitor has a new product feature that will make a big difference in sales. The competitor will demonstrate the feature in a private dealer meeting at the annual trade show. You can easily send a spy to this meeting to learn about the new feature. What would you do?

8   You have to choose between three advertising campaigns outlined by your agency. The first (a) is a soft-sell, honest, straight-information campaign. The second (b) uses sex-loaded emotional appeals and exaggerates the product's benefits. The third (c) involves a noisy, somewhat irritating commercial that is sure to gain audience attention. Pre-tests show that the campaigns are effective in the following order: (c), (b) and (a). What would you do?

9   You are interviewing a capable female applicant for a job as salesperson. She is better qualified than the men just interviewed. Nevertheless, you know that some of your important customers prefer dealing with men and you will lose some sales if you hire her. What would you do?

Each company and marketing manager must work out a philosophy of socially responsible and ethical behaviour. Under the societal marketing concept, each manager must look beyond what is legal and allowed and develop standards based on personal integrity, corporate conscience and long-term consumer welfare. Dealing with issues of ethics and social responsibility in an open and forthright way helps to build strong customer relationships based on honestly and trust. In fact, many companies now routinely include consumers in the social responsibility process. Consider toy maker Mattel:

> In autumn 2007, the discovery of lead paint on several of its best-selling products forced Mattel to make worldwide recalls on millions of toys. Threatening as this was, rather than hesitating or hiding the incident, the company's brand advisors were up to the challenge. Their quick, decisive response helped to maintain consumer confidence in the Mattel brand, even contributing to a 6 per cent sales increase over the same period the year before. Just who were these masterful 'brand advisors'? They were the 400 mums with kids aged 3 to 10 comprising The Playground Community, a private online network launched by Mattel's worldwide consumer insights department in June 2007 to 'listen to and gain insight from mums' lives and needs'. Throughout the crisis, The Playground Community members kept in touch with Mattel regarding the product recalls and the company's forthright response plan, even helping to shape the post-recall promotional strategy for one of the affected product lines. Even in times of crisis, 'brands that engage in a two-way conversation with their customers create stronger, more trusting relationships', says a Mattel executive.[22]

As with environmentalism, the issue of ethics provides special challenges for international marketers. Business standards and practices vary a great deal from one country to the next. For example, whereas bribes and kickbacks are illegal for EU firms, they are common business practice in some other countries. The World Bank estimates that bribes worth more than $1 trillion per year are paid out worldwide. One study showed that the most flagrant bribe-paying firms were from India, Russia and China. Other countries where corruption is common include Iraq, Myanmar and Haiti. The least corrupt were companies from Iceland, Finland, New Zealand and Denmark.[23]

The question arises as to whether a company must lower its ethical standards to compete effectively in countries with lower standards. The answer? No. Companies should make a commitment to a common set of shared standards worldwide.

Many industrial and professional associations have suggested codes of ethics and many companies are now adopting their own codes. For example, the American Marketing Association's code of ethics is shown in Exhibit 16.2. Companies are also developing programmes to teach managers about important ethical issues and help them find the proper responses. They hold ethics workshops and seminars and set up ethics committees. Furthermore, most major EU companies have appointed high-level ethics officers to champion ethical issues and to help resolve ethical problems and concerns facing employees.

Consider Allied Irish Bank (AIB), which has a CSR Committee that is a subcommittee of the main AIB board – 'CSR', by the way, stands for Corporate Social Responsibility, which is the headline term used for corporate ethical, social and environmental responsibility in many businesses today. At AIB there is a very detailed 20-page Code of Conduct for all Employees of the AIB Group, which provides detailed guidance to employees about how they are expected to conduct their business ethically. This includes advice on dealing with customer information and protecting customer privacy, dealing with colleagues and ensuring that there is fairness in all employment practices, and advice on general business practice such as forbidding bribery and advising great caution in the acceptance of small gifts or hospitality.[24]

Still, written codes and ethics programmes do not ensure ethical behaviour. Ethical and social responsibility requires a total corporate commitment. In order to have the best chance of making the corporate ethical code work in practice, companies are advised to keep the code as short as possible, provide employees with concrete examples of correct behaviour,

Most large European businesses, like Allied Irish Bank, have codes of ethics that make it clear to employees what is considered ethical, and unethical, behaviour in pursuing profits for the firm

Source: http://aibgroup.com

| EXHIBIT 16.2 | **American Marketing Association: Ethical norms and values for marketers** |

Ethical Norms

As Marketers, we must:

1 *Do no harm.* This means consciously avoiding harmful actions or omissions by embodying high ethical standards and adhering to all applicable laws and regulations in the choices we make.

2 *Foster trust in the marketing system.* This means striving for good faith and fair dealing so as to contribute toward the efficacy of the exchange process as well as avoiding deception in product design, pricing, communication, and delivery of distribution.

3 *Embrace ethical values.* This means building relationships and enhancing consumer confidence in the integrity of marketing by affirming these core values: honesty, responsibility, fairness, respect, transparency and citizenship.

Ethical Values

Honesty – to be forthright in dealings with customers and stakeholders. To this end, we will:

- Strive to be truthful in all situations and at all times.
- Offer products of value that do what we claim in our communications.
- Stand behind our products if they fail to deliver their claimed benefits.
- Honor our explicit and implicit commitments and promises.

   Responsibility – to accept the consequences of our marketing decisions and strategies. To this end, we will:

- Strive to serve the needs of customers.
- Avoid using coercion with all stakeholders.

- Acknowledge the social obligations to stakeholders that come with increased marketing and economic power.
- Recognize our special commitments to vulnerable market segments such as children, seniors, the economically impoverished, market illiterates and others who may be substantially disadvantaged.
- Consider environmental stewardship in our decision-making.

Fairness – to balance justly the needs of the buyer with the interests of the seller. To this end, we will:

- Represent products in a clear way in selling, advertising and other forms of communication; this includes the avoidance of false, misleading and deceptive promotion.
- Reject manipulations and sales tactics that harm customer trust.
- Refuse to engage in price fixing, predatory pricing, price gouging or 'bait-and-switch' tactics.
- Avoid knowing participation in conflicts of interest.
- Seek to protect the private information of customers, employees and partners.

Respect – to acknowledge the basic human dignity of all stakeholders. To this end, we will:

- Value individual differences and avoid stereotyping customers or depicting demographic groups (e.g., gender, race, sexual orientation) in a negative or dehumanizing way.
- Listen to the needs of customers and make all reasonable efforts to monitor and improve their satisfaction on an ongoing basis.
- Make every effort to understand and respectfully treat buyers, suppliers, intermediaries and distributors from all cultures.
- Acknowledge the contributions of others, such as consultants, employees and coworkers, to marketing endeavors.
- Treat everyone, including our competitors, as we would wish to be treated.

Transparency – to create a spirit of openness in marketing operations. To this end, we will:

- Strive to communicate clearly with all constituencies.
- Accept constructive criticism from customers and other stakeholders.
- Explain and take appropriate action regarding significant product or service risks, component substitutions or other foreseeable eventualities that could affect customers or their perception of the purchase decision.
- Disclose list prices and terms of financing as well as available price deals and adjustments.

Citizenship – to fulfill the economic, legal, philanthropic and societal responsibilities that serve stakeholders. To this end, we will:

- Strive to protect the ecological environment in the execution of marketing campaigns.
- Give back to the community through volunteerism and charitable donations.
- Contribute to the overall betterment of marketing and its reputation.
- Urge supply chain members to ensure that trade is fair for all participants, including producers in developing countries.

Source: https://archive.ama.org/Archive/AboutAMA/Pages/Statement%20of%20Ethics.aspx

demonstrate that the code receives serious support from top managers, provide training to employees and frequently reinforce the message that ethics is important, and demonstrate that breaches of the code are taken very seriously.[25]

THE JOURNEY YOU'VE TAKEN Reviewing the concepts

Well – here you are at the end of your introductory marketing travels. In this chapter, we've closed with many important concepts involving marketing's sweeping impact on individual consumers, other businesses and society as a whole. You learned that responsible marketers discover what consumers want and respond with the right market offerings, priced to give good value to buyers and profit to the producer. A marketing system should deliver customer value and improve the quality of consumers' lives. In working to meet consumer needs, marketers may take some actions that are not to everyone's liking or benefit. Marketing managers should be aware of the main *criticisms of marketing*.

1 **Identify the major social criticisms of marketing**

Marketing's *impact on individual consumer welfare* has been criticised for its high prices, deceptive practices, high-pressure selling, shoddy or unsafe products, planned obsolescence and poor service to disadvantaged consumers. Marketing's *impact on society* has been criticised for creating false wants and too much materialism, too few social goods, cultural pollution and too much political power. Critics have also criticised marketing's *impact on other businesses* for harming competitors and reducing competition through acquisitions, practices that create barriers to entry and unfair competitive marketing practices. Some of these concerns are justified; some are not.

2 **Define consumerism and environmentalism and explain how they affect marketing strategies**

Concerns about the marketing system have led to citizen action movements. Consumerism is an organised social movement intended to strengthen the rights and power of consumers relative to sellers. Alert marketers view it as an opportunity to serve consumers better by providing more consumer information, education and protection. Environmentalism is an organised social movement seeking to minimise the harm done to the environment and quality of life by marketing practices. The first wave of modern environmentalism was driven by environmental groups and concerned consumers, whereas the second wave was driven by government, which passed laws and regulations governing industrial practices impacting on the environment. Moving into the twenty-first century,

the first two environmentalism waves are merging into a third and stronger wave in which companies are accepting responsibility for doing no environmental harm. Companies now are adopting policies of environmental sustainability – developing strategies that both sustain the environment and produce profits for the company.

3 **Describe the principles of socially responsible marketing**

Many companies originally opposed these social movements and laws, but most of them now recognise a need for positive consumer information, education and protection. Some companies have followed a policy of sustainable marketing, which holds that a company's marketing should support the best long-term performance of the marketing system. Sustainable marketing consists of five principles: consumer-oriented marketing, innovative marketing, customer value marketing, sense-of-mission marketing and societal marketing.

4 **Explain the role of ethics in marketing**

Increasingly, companies are responding to the need to provide company policies and guidelines to help their managers deal with questions of marketing ethics. Of course, even the best guidelines cannot resolve all the difficult ethical decisions that individuals and firms must make. But there are some principles that marketers can choose among. One principle states that such issues should be decided by the free market and legal system. A second, and more enlightened principle, puts responsibility not on the system but in the hands of individual companies and managers. Each firm and marketing manager must work out a philosophy of socially responsible and ethical behaviour. Under the societal marketing concept, managers must look beyond what is legal and allowable and develop standards based on personal integrity, corporate conscience and long-term consumer welfare.

Because business standards and practices vary from country to country, the issue of ethics poses special challenges for international marketers. The growing consensus among today's marketers is that it is important to make a commitment to a common set of shared standards worldwide.

NAVIGATING THE KEY TERMS

Consumerism **556**
Consumer-oriented marketing **563**
Customer value marketing **564**
Deficient products **565**
Desirable products **566**

Environmental sustainability **558**
Environmentalism **557**
Innovative marketing **564**
Pleasing products **565**
Salutary products **565**

Sense-of-mission marketing **564**
Societal marketing **565**
Sustainable marketing **563**

NOTES AND REFERENCES

1 *Sources:* M.J. Thun, C.A. Day-Lally, E.E. Calle *et al.*, 'Excess Mortality Among Cigarette Smokers: Changes in a 20-year Interval', *American Journal of Public Health*, 85, 1995, pp. 1223–30; R. Doll, R. Peto, J. Boreham and I. Sutherland, 'Mortality in Relation to Smoking: 50 Years' Observations on Male British Doctors', *British Medical Journal*, 328, 2004, pp. 1519–27; D.M. Mannino, M. Klevens and W.D. Flanders, 'Cigarette Smoking: An Independent Risk Factor for Impotence?', *American Journal of Epidemiology*, 140, 1994, pp. 1003–8; on blindness, see **http://www.rnib.org.uk/xpedio/groups/public/documents/publicwebsite/public_smokingbrusselspr.hcsp; http://www.who.int/gb/fctc/**; *Choosing Health: Making Healthy Choices Easier*, Department of Health (2004); **http://www.tobaccoleaf.org/about_tobacco/index.asp?op=7&l=en;** R.W. Pollay, 'Targeting Youth and Concerned Smokers: Evidence from Canadian Tobacco Industry Documents', *Tobacco Control*, 9, 2000, pp. 136–47; S.K. Katz and A.M. Lavack, 'Tobacco Related Bar Promotions: Insights from Tobacco Industry Documents', *Tobacco Control*, 11 (Suppl. I), 2002, pp. i92–101; **http://www.usatoday.com/news/washington/2006-08-17-tobacco-lawsuit_x.htm;** M.C. Farrelly, C.G. Healton, K.C. Davis, P. Messeri, J.C. Hersey and M.L. Haviland, 'Getting to the Truth: Evaluating National Tobacco Countermarketing Campaigns', *American Journal of Public Health*, 92(6), 2002, pp. 901–7; R.L. Andrews and G.R. Franke, 'The Determinants of Cigarette Consumption: A Meta-Analysis', *Journal of Public Policy and Marketing*, 10 (Spring), 1991, pp. 81–100; H. Saffer and F. Chaloupka, 'The Effect of Tobacco Advertising Bans on Tobacco Consumption', *Journal of Health Economics*, 19, 2000, pp. 1117–37; F.J. Chaloupka and H. Wechsler, 'Price, Tobacco Control Policies and Smoking Among Young Adults', *Journal of Health Economics*, 16, 1997, pp. 359–73; I.C. Grant, L.M. Hassan, G. Hastings, A.-M. MacKintosh and D. Eadie, 'The Influence of Branding on Adolescent Smoking Behaviour: Exploring the Mediating Role of Image and Attitudes', *Journal of Nonprofit and Voluntary Sector Marketing*, DOI: 10.1002/nvsm.329, 2007; P. Kotler and S.J. Levy, 'Demarketing, Yes, Demarketing', *Harvard Business Review*, 49(6), 1971, pp. 74–80 [p. 75]; US Department of Health and Human Services, *Preventing Tobacco Use Among Young People: A Report of the Surgeon General* (Atlanta, GA: Centers for Disease Control and Prevention, Office on Smoking and Health, 1994); K.H. Smith and M.-A. Stutts, 'Effects of Short-Term Cosmetic Versus Long-Term Health Fear Appeals in Anti-Smoking Advertisements on the Smoking Behaviour of Adolescents', *Journal of Consumer Behaviour*, 3, 2003, pp. 157–77; G. Hastings, M. Stead and J. Webb, 'Fear Appeals in Social Marketing: Strategic and Ethical Reasons for Concern', *Psychology and Marketing*, 21, 2004, pp. 961–86; D.L. Alden, W.D. Hoyer and C. Lee, 'Identifying Global and Culture-Specific Dimensions of Humor in Advertising: A Multinational Analysis', *Journal of Marketing*, 57, 1993, pp. 64–75; **http://www.eiaa.net/news/eiaa-articles-details.asp?lang=1&id=154;** 'The HELP Programme 2005–2007: Moving Towards a Smoke-Free Europe', accessed at **http://ec.europa.eu/health/ph_determinants/life_style/Tobacco/help/docs/2_years**

2 See Winnie Hu, 'The Smoking Ban: Clean Air, Murky Economics', *The New York Times,* 28 December 2003, p. 1.1; 'Smoking Bans Have Their Place, but Outside Isn't One of Them', *The Washington Post,* 5 February 2004, p. T.04; and 'EU Regulations: EU-Wide Ban on Tobacco Ads Imminent', *EIU ViewsWire,* 8 July 2005.

3 See Alex Lawson and Ben Chu, "Aldi and Lidl Seize Market Share from Big Players", *Independent,* 9 April 2014, available at **http://www.independent.co.uk/news/business/news/aldi-and-lidl-seize-market-share-from-big-players-9247375.html**, accessed July 2014.

4 See 'FCA Proposes Price Cap for Payday Lenders', 15 July 2014, available at **http://www.fca.org.uk/news/fca-proposes-price-cap-for-payday-lenders**, accessed July 2014.

5 Theodore Levitt, 'The Morality (?) of Advertising', *Harvard Business Review,* July–August 1970, pp. 84–92. For counterpoints, see James Heckman, 'Don't Shoot the Messenger: More and More Often, Marketing is the Regulators' Target', *Marketing News,* 24 May 1999, pp. 1, 9.

6 Lane Jennings, 'Hype, Spin, Puffery, and Lies: Should We Be Scared?', *The Futurist,* January–February 2004, p. 16. For recent examples of deceptive advertising, see 'Tropicana Settles Complaint by FTC over Misleading Ads', *The Wall Street Journal,* 3 June 2005, p. B4; and Monty Phan, 'City Sues Wireless Firms', 22 July 2005, accessed at **www.newsday.com**

7 Ross Brennan, Stephan Dahl and Lynne Eagle, 'Persuading Young People to Make Healthy Nutritional Decisions', *Journal of Marketing Management,* 2010, 26(7/8), pp. 635–55.

8 'McDonald's to Cut "Super Size" Option', *Advertising Age,* 8 March 2004, p. 13; Dave Carpenter, 'Hold the Fries, Take a Walk', *The News & Observer,* 16 April 2004, p. D1; Michael V. Copeland, 'Ronald Gets Back in Shape,' *Business 2.0,* January/February 2005, pp. 46–7; David P. Callet and Cheryl A. Falvey, 'Is Restaurant Food the New Tobacco?', *Restaurant Hospitality,* May 2005, pp. 94–6; and Kate McArthur, 'BK Offers Fat to the Land', *Advertising Age,* 4 April 2005, pp. 1, 60.

9 Adapted from David Suzuki, 'We All Pay for Technology', *Niagara Falls Review,* 15 March 2007, p. A4. For more discussion, see Joseph Guiltinan, 'Creative Destruction and Destructive Creations: Environmental Ethics and Planned Obsolescence', *Journal of Business Ethics,* May 2009, pp. 19–28.

10 **www.which.co.uk/reports_and_campaigns/consumer_rights/campaigns/**, accessed July 2014.

11 See Brian Grow and Pallavi Gogoi, 'A New Way to Squeeze the Weak?', *BusinessWeek,* 28 January 2002, p. 92; Todd Cooper, 'Redlining Rears Its Ugly Head', *US Banker,* August 2003, p. 64; Marc Lifsher, 'Allstate Settles Over Use of Credit Scores', *Los Angeles Times,* 2 March 2004, p. C.1; and Judith Burns, 'Study Finds Links in Credit Scores, Insurance Claims', *The Wall Street Journal,* 28 February 2005, p. D3.

12 'Children "Damaged" by Materialism', **http://news.bbc.co.uk**, accessed 14 May 2008; and 'Reflections on Childhood – Lifestyle', report produced by GfK Social Research for The Children's Society, 20 September 2007, available from **http://news.bbc.co.uk/1/shared/bsp/hi/pdfs/25_02_08_childhood.pdf**

13 John A. Quelch, 'Selling Out the American Dream', *Harvard Business School Working Knowledge,* 6 November 2008, accessed at **http://hbswk.hbs.edu/item/6071.html**; Leonard Stern, 'Aspiration Gap Behind Downward Cycle in US', *Calgary Herald* (Canada), 9 November 2008, p. A11; and Keilo Morris, 'Brief: OSHA Cites Wal-Mart in Trampling Death', *McClatchy-Tribune Business News,* 26 May 2009.

14 Information obtained from **http://www.tfl.gov.uk/roadusers/congestioncharging/**, accessed July 2014.

15 Ross Brennan, Louise Canning and Ray McDowell, *Business to Business Marketing,* pp. 349–51 (London: Sage, 2014).

16   Stuart L. Hart, 'Beyond Greening: Strategies for a Sustainable World', *Harvard Business Review,* January–February 1997, pp. 66–76. Also see Subhabrata Bobby Banerjee, Easwar S. Iyer and Rajiv K. Kashyap, 'Corporate Environmentalism: Antecedents and Influence of Industry Type', *Harvard Business Review,* April 2003, pp. 106–22; Christopher Laszlo, *The Sustainable Company: How to Create Lasting Value through Social and Environmental Performance* (Washington, DC: Island Press, 2003); Volkert Beekman, 'Sustainable Development and Future Generations', *Journal of Agriculture and Environmental Ethics,* 17(1), 2004, p. 3; and Bill Hopwood, Mary Mellor and Geoff O'Brien, 'Sustainable Development: Mapping Different Approaches', *Sustainable Development,* February 2005, pp. 38ff.

17   'Sustainable Design, Climate Change and the Built Environment', briefing paper from the Commission for Architecture and the Built Environment, available at **http://webarchive.nationalarchives.gov.uk/20110118095356/** and **http:/www.cabe.org.uk/publications/sustainable-design-and-climate-change**, accessed July 2014.

18   'Introducing EMAS', accessed at **http://www.iema.net/emas**, July 2014.

19   Information and quotes from Andy Milligan, 'Samsung Points the Way for Asian Firms in Global Brand Race', *Media,* 8 August 2003, p. 8; Katherine Chen, Michael Jakielski, Nadia Luhr and Joseph Mayer-Salman, 'DigitAll', student paper at the University of North Carolina at Chapel Hill, Spring 2003; Gerry Khermouch, 'The Best Global Brands', *BusinessWeek,* 5 August 2002, p. 92; Leslie P. Norton, 'Value Brand', *Barron's,* 22 September 2003, p. 19; and Samsung Electronics Co. Ltd, *Hoover's Company Capsules,* 15 March 2004; 'Cult Brands', *BusinessWeek Online,* 2 August 2004, accessed at **www.businessweek.com**; and Samsung Annual Reports and other information accessed at **www.samsung.com**, September 2005.

20   Information from Mike Hoffman, 'Ben Cohen: Ben & Jerry's Homemade, Established in 1978', *Inc,* 30 April 2001, p. 68; and the Ben & Jerry's website at **www.benjerry.com**, July 2014.

21   Andrew Clark, 'Innocent and John Lewis Break into Poll of Leading Brands as Ethics Becomes Good Business', *Observer,* 14 November 2010, accessed at **http://www.guardian.co.uk/business/2010/nov/14/innocent-john-lewis-most-influential-brands**, accessed July 2014; also information from **http://www.innocentdrinks.co.uk**, accessed July 2014.

22   Jyoti Thottam, "Why Mattel Apologised to China", *Time,* 21 September 2007, available at **http://content.time.com/time/business/article/0,8599,1664428,00.html**, accessed July 2014; Louise Story, "Lead Paint Prompts Mattel to Recall 967,000 Toys", *New York Times,* 2 August 2007, available at **http://www.nytimes.com/2007/08/02/business/02toy.html/**, accessed July 2014.

23   See The World Bank, 'The Costs of Corruption', 8 April 2004, accessed at **www.worldbank.org**; Joseph A. McKinney and Carlos W. Moore, 'International Bribery: Does a Written Code of Ethics Make a Difference in Perceptions of Business Professionals?', *Journal of Business Ethics,* April 2008, pp. 103–11; and *Corruption Perceptions Index 2013,* Transparency International, available at **http://www.transparency.org/research/gcr/overview**, accessed July 2014.

24   'Code of Business Conduct for all Employees of AIB Group', edition of May 2012, available at **http://www.aib.ie/**, accessed July 2014.

25   Mark S. Schwartz, 'Effective Corporate Codes of Ethics: Perceptions of Code Users', *Journal of Business Ethics,* 55, 2004, pp. 323–43.

APPENDIX 1
MARKETING PLAN

THE MARKETING PLAN: AN INTRODUCTION

As a marketer, you'll need a good marketing plan to provide direction and focus for your brand, product or company. With a detailed plan, any business will be better prepared to launch a new product or build sales for existing products. Non-profit organisations also use marketing plans to guide their fundraising and outreach efforts. Even government agencies put together marketing plans for initiatives such as building public awareness of proper nutrition and stimulating area tourism.

The purpose and content of a marketing plan

Unlike a business plan, which offers a broad overview of the entire organisation's mission, objectives, strategy and resource allocation, a marketing plan has a more limited scope. It serves to document how the organisation's strategic objectives will be achieved through specific marketing strategies and tactics, with the customer as the starting point. It is also linked to the plans of other departments within the organisation. Suppose a marketing plan calls for selling 200,000 units annually. The production department must gear up to make that many units, the finance department must arrange funding to cover the expenses, the human resources department must be ready to hire and train staff, and so on. Without the appropriate level of organisational support and resources, no marketing plan can succeed.

Although the exact length and layout will vary from company to company, a marketing plan usually contains the sections described in Chapter 2. Smaller businesses may create shorter or less formal marketing plans, whereas corporations frequently require highly structured marketing plans. To guide implementation effectively, every part of the plan must be described in considerable detail. Sometimes a company will post its marketing plan on an internal website, which allows managers and employees in different locations to consult specific sections and collaborate on additions or changes.

The role of research

Marketing plans are not created in a vacuum. To develop successful strategies and action programmes, marketers need up-to-date information about the environment, the competition and the market segments to be served. Often, analysis of internal data is the starting point for assessing the current marketing situation, supplemented by marketing intelligence and research investigating the overall market, the competition, key issues, and threats and opportunities. As the plan is put into effect, marketers use a variety of research techniques to measure progress towards objectives and identify areas for improvement if results fall short of projections.

Finally, marketing research helps marketers learn more about their customers' requirements, expectations, perceptions and satisfaction levels. This deeper understanding provides a foundation for building competitive advantage through well-informed segmenting, targeting, differentiating and positioning decisions. Thus, the marketing plan should outline what marketing research will be conducted and how the findings will be applied.

The role of relationships

The marketing plan shows how the company will establish and maintain profitable customer relationships. In the process, however, it also shapes a number of internal and external relationships. First, it affects how marketing personnel work with each other and with other departments to deliver value and satisfy customers. Second, it affects how the company works with suppliers, distributors and strategic alliance partners to achieve the objectives listed in the plan. Third, it influences the company's dealings with other stakeholders, including government regulators, the media and the community at large. All of these relationships are important to the organisation's success, so they should be considered when a marketing plan is being developed.

From marketing plan to marketing action

Companies generally create yearly marketing plans, although some plans cover a longer period. Marketers start planning well in advance of the implementation date to allow time for marketing research, thorough analysis, management review and coordination between departments. Then, after each action programme begins, marketers monitor ongoing results, compare them with projections, analyse any differences and take corrective steps as needed. Some marketers also prepare contingency plans for implementation if certain conditions emerge. Because of inevitable and sometimes unpredictable environmental changes, marketers must be ready to update and adapt marketing plans at any time.

For effective implementation and control, the marketing plan should define how progress towards objectives will be measured. Managers typically use budgets, schedules and performance standards for monitoring and evaluating results. With budgets, they can compare planned expenditures with actual expenditures for a given week, month or other period. Schedules allow management to see when tasks were supposed to be completed – and when they were actually completed. Performance standards track the outcomes of marketing programmes to see whether the company is moving towards its objectives. Some examples of performance standards are: market share, sales volume, product profitability and customer satisfaction.

SAMPLE MARKETING PLAN FOR SONIC

This section takes you inside the sample marketing plan for Sonic, a hypothetical start-up company. The company's first product is the Sonic 1000, a high-quality smartphone. Sonic will be competing with Apple, Samsung, Huawei, Sony and other well-established rivals in a crowded, fast-changing marketplace for smartphones that combine communication, entertainment and storage functionality. The annotations explain more about what each section of the plan should contain and why.

Executive summary

Executive summary
This section summarises the main goals, recommendations and points as an overview for senior managers who will read and approve the marketing plan. Generally a table of contents follows this section, for management convenience.

Sonic is preparing to launch a new high-quality smartphone, the Sonic 1000, in a mature market. Our product offers a competitively unique combination of advanced features and functionality at a value-added price. We are targeting specific segments in the consumer and business markets, taking advantage of opportunities indicated by higher demand for easy-to-use smartphones with expanded communications, entertainment and storage functionality.

The primary marketing objective is to achieve first-year European sales of 500,000 units. The primary financial objectives are to achieve first-year sales revenues of €75m, keep first-year losses to less than €8m and break even early in the second year.

Current marketing situation

Current marketing situation
In this section, marketing managers discuss the overall market, identify the market segments they will target, and provide information about the company's current situation.

Sonic, founded 18 months ago by two entrepreneurs with experience in the tablet computer market, is about to enter the maturing smartphone market. Multi-function mobile phones, email devices and wireless communication devices have become commonplace for both personal and professional use. Research shows that in Western Europe mobile phone sales were 43.6 million units in the first quarter of 2014, showing growth of 1.5 per cent on the previous year, while smartphone sales were 31.6 million (73 per cent of all mobile phone sales) in the same period, showing growth of 10 per cent over the previous year.

Competition is therefore more intense even as demand flattens, industry consolidation continues, and pricing pressures squeeze profitability. Worldwide, Samsung is the market leader for mobile phone sales, with Apple in second place. In the Western European market, Samsung is again the market leader (with a 40 per cent share) followed by Apple (19 per cent). To gain market share in this dynamic environment, Sonic must carefully target specific segments with features that deliver benefits valued by each customer group.

Market description
Describing the targeted segments in detail provides context for the marketing strategies and detailed action programmes discussed later in the plan.

Market description

Sonic's market consists of consumers and business users who prefer to use a single device for communication, information storage and exchange, and entertainment on the go. Specific segments being targeted during the first year include professionals, corporations, students, entrepreneurs and medical users. Table A1.1 shows how the Sonic 1000 addresses the needs of targeted consumer and business segments.

TABLE A1.1 Segment needs and corresponding features/benefits of Sonic

Targeted segment	Customer need	Corresponding feature/benefit
Professionals (consumer market)	• Stay in touch conveniently and securely while on the go • Perform many functions hands-free without carrying multiple gadgets	• Built-in mobile phone and push-to-talk to communicate anywhere at any time; wireless email/web access from anywhere; Linux operating system less vulnerable to hackers • Voice-activated applications are convenient; GPS function, advanced camera add value
Students (consumer market)	• Perform many functions hands-free without carrying multiple gadgets • Express style and individuality	• Compatible with numerous applications (apps) and peripherals for convenient, cost-effective communication and entertainment • Wardrobe of smartphone cases for individual style
Corporate users (business market)	• Security and adaptability for proprietary tasks • Obtain driving directions to business meetings	• Customisable to fit corporate tasks and networks; Linux-based operating system less vulnerable to hackers • Built-in GPS allows voice-activated access to directions and maps
Entrepreneurs (business market)	• Organise and access contacts, schedule details, business and financial files • Get in touch fast	• Hands-free, wireless access to calendar, address book, information files for checking appointments and data, connecting with contacts • Push-to-talk instant calling speeds up communications
Medical users (business market)	• Update, access and exchange medical records • Photograph medical situations to maintain a visual record	• Removable memory card and hands-free, wireless information recording reduces paperwork and increases productivity • Built-in advanced camera allows fast and easy photography, stores images for later retrieval

Benefits and product features
Table A1.1 clarifies the benefits that product features will deliver to satisfy the needs of customers in each targeted segment.

Buyers can choose between models based on several different operating systems, including systems from Microsoft, BlackBerry and Android, plus Linux variations. Sonic licenses a Linux-based system because it is somewhat less vulnerable to attack by hackers and viruses. Removable memory cards are popular smartphone options. Sonic is equipping its first entry with an ultra-fast 32-gigabyte removable memory card for information and entertainment storage. Technology costs are decreasing even as capabilities are increasing, which makes value-priced models more appealing to consumers and to business users with older devices who want to trade up to new, high-end multi-function units.

Product review

Product review
The product review summarises the main features of all of the company's products, organised by product line, type of customer, market or order of product introduction.

Our first product, the Sonic 1000, offers the following standard features with a Linux OS:

- built-in dual mobile phone/Internet phone functionality and push-to-talk instant calling;
- digital music/video/television recording, wireless downloading and playback;
- wireless web and email, text messaging and instant messaging;
- 5-inch hi-definition colour screen for easy viewing;
- organisation functions, including calendar, address book and synchronisation;
- global positioning system for directions and maps;
- integrated 10-megapixel digital camera;
- ultra-fast 32-gigabyte removable memory card with upgrade potential;
- interchangeable case wardrobe of different colours and patterns;
- voice recognition functionality for hands-free operation.

First-year sales revenues are projected to be €75m, based on sales of 500,000 Sonic 1000 units at a wholesale price of €150 each. During the second year, we plan to introduce the Sonic 2000, also with a Linux OS, as a higher end smartphone product offering the following standard features:

- global phone and messaging compatibility;
- translation capabilities to send English text as German text (other languages to be offered as add-on options);
- integrated 20-megapixel camera.

Competitive review

Competitive review
The purpose of a competitive review is to identify key competitors, describe their market positions and briefly discuss their strategies.

The emergence of lower-priced smartphones, including the Apple iPhone, has increased competitive pressure. Key competitors include the following:

- *Samsung*: The market leader, offering value, style and functionality. Samsung is a strong competitor, offering a variety of smartphones for consumer and business segments. Some of its smartphones are available for specific telecommunications carriers and some are 'unlocked', ready for any compatible telecommunications network. Its recent products, such as the Galaxy 4 and Galaxy 5, have proved enormously popular and are comparable with Apple products in terms of style and desirability.
- *Apple*: The stylish, popular iPhone 6 (and related versions such as the 6 Plus) follow in the footsteps of iconic products that have inspired very high levels of consumer loyalty. Apple uses its own proprietary operating system. The connectivity between Apple smartphones and other Apple devices such as iPads and MacBooks is attractive to many users, while others find it unappealing to be so tied in to a single brand.
- *Nokia*: No longer the market leader in smartphones, but still a competitor to take seriously, Nokia offers a wide range of products for consumers and professionals. Many of Nokia's smartphones offer full keyboards, similar to Research in Motion models, but

stripped-down models are available for users who do not require the full keyboard and full multimedia capabilities.

- *Huawei*: This Chinese brand is seeking to build on its huge success in the Chinese market to grow in worldwide markets including Europe. Up to this point consumers regard Huawei as a relatively inexpensive option that offers good value for money but cannot compete with Apple and Samsung in terms of innovation and style. However, there is no doubt that Huawei has every intention of competing on the same level as the market leaders.

- *Sony*: Recent years have seen Sony suffering a setback in the consumer electronics market. For a long time Sony products were the undisputed leaders in terms of innovation and style, but this is no longer the case. Nevertheless, Sony has a range of very respectable smartphone products and it would be unwise to underestimate this well-resourced and innovative competitor.

Despite this strong competition, Sonic can carve out a definite image and gain recognition among the targeted segments. Our voice recognition system for completely hands-off operation is a critical point of differentiation for competitive advantage. Also, offering enhanced GPS as a standard feature gives us a competitive edge compared with similarly priced smartphones. Moreover, our product is faster than most and runs the Linux OS, which is an appealing alternative for customers concerned about security. Table A1.2 shows a sample of competitive products and prices.

Channels and logistics review

In this section, marketers list the most important channels, provide an overview of each channel arrangement, and identify developing issues in channels and logistics.

Channels and logistics review

Sonic-branded products will be distributed through a network of retailers in the top 50 Western European markets. Among the most important channel partners being contacted are:

- *Independent high street retailers*: Independent retailers, notably Carphone Warehouse, will carry Sonic products.

TABLE A1.2 Sample of competitive products and pricing

Competitor	Model	Features	Price
Samsung	Galaxy S5	2800 mAh battery providing extended battery life Quad core high-performance processor Water and dust resistant	€35 per month on a contract
Apple	iPhone 6	16GB memory Stylish aluminium and glass construction Retina display 8-megapixel iSight camera Touch ID	€45 per month on a contract
Nokia	Lumia 930	High-quality video recording with hi-definition sound 5-inch screen Available in a range of bright colours	€30 per month on a contract
Sony	Xperia Z3	High-quality scratch-resistant construction Digital noise cancelling feature Waterproof	€45 per month on a contract
Huawei	Ascend P7	13-megapixel camera Hi-definition screen Corning Gorilla Glass	€25 per month on a contract

- *Network operator stores*: Sonic products will feature in O2 stores and EE stores.
- *Online retailers*: Amazon will carry Sonic products and, for a promotional fee, will give Sonic prominent placement on its homepage during the introduction.

Initially, our channel strategy will focus on France, Germany and the UK; according to demand, we plan to expand into Spain, Italy and beyond, with appropriate logistical support.

Strengths, weaknesses, opportunities and threat analysis

Sonic has several powerful strengths on which to build, but our major weakness is lack of brand awareness and image. The major opportunity is demand for multimedia smartphones that deliver a number of valued benefits, eliminating the need for customers to carry more than one device. We also face the threat of ever-higher competition from consumer electronics manufacturers, as well as downward pricing pressure. Table A1.3 summarises Sonic's main strengths, weaknesses, opportunities and threats.

Strengths

Strengths
Strengths are internal capabilities that can help the company reach its objectives.

Sonic can build on three important strengths:

1 *Innovative product*: The Sonic 1000 offers state-of-the-art functions including a high-quality camera, GPS, access to a wide range of downloadable apps, hi-definition screen and high-quality audio.

2 *Security*: Our smartphone uses a Linux-based operating system that is less vulnerable to hackers and other security threats that can result in stolen or corrupted data.

3 *Pricing*: Our product is priced lower than competing multi-function models – none of which offer the same bundle of features – which gives us an edge with price-conscious customers.

Weaknesses

Weaknesses
Weaknesses are internal elements that may interfere with the company's ability to achieve its objectives.

By waiting to enter the smartphone market until some consolidation of competitors has occurred, Sonic has learned from the successes and mistakes of others. Nonetheless, we have two main weaknesses:

1 *Lack of brand awareness*: Sonic has no established brand or image, whereas Apple and others have strong brand recognition. We will address this issue with aggressive promotion.

TABLE A1.3 Sonic's strengths, weaknesses, opportunities and threats

Strengths	Weaknesses
• Highly competitive range of functions and apps • Security due to Linux-based operating system • Value pricing	• Lack of brand awareness and image • Heavier and thicker than most competing models
Opportunities	**Threats**
• Increased demand for multimedia, multi-function smartphones • Cost-efficient technology	• Intense competition • Downward pricing pressure • Compressed product life cycle

2   *Physical specifications*: The Sonic 1000 is slightly heavier and thicker than most competing models because it incorporates multiple features, offers sizeable storage capacity and is compatible with numerous peripheral devices. To counteract this weakness, we will emphasise our product's benefits and value-added pricing, two compelling competitive strengths.

Opportunities

Sonic can take advantage of two major market opportunities:

1   *Increasing demand for multimedia smartphones with multiple functions*: The market for multimedia, multi-function devices is growing much faster than the market for single-use devices. Growth will accelerate as dual-mode capabilities become mainstream, giving customers the flexibility to make phone calls over cell or Internet connections. Smartphones are already commonplace in public, work and educational settings, which is boosting primary demand. Also, customers who bought entry-level models are replacing older models with more advanced models.

2   *Cost-efficient technology*: Better technology is now available at a lower cost than ever before. Thus, Sonic can incorporate advanced features at a value-added price that allows for reasonable profits.

Threats

We face three main threats at the introduction of the Sonic 1000:

1   *Increased competition*: More companies are entering the Western European market with smartphone models that offer some but not all of the features and benefits provided by Sonic's product. Therefore, Sonic's marketing communications must stress our clear differentiation and value-added pricing.

2   *Downward pressure on pricing*: Increased competition and market-share strategies are pushing smartphone prices down. Still, our objective of seeking a 10 per cent profit on second-year sales of the original model is realistic, given the lower margins in this market.

3   *Compressed product life cycle*: Smartphones have reached the maturity stage of their life cycle more quickly than earlier technology products. We have contingency plans to keep sales growing by adding new features, targeting additional segments and adjusting prices as needed.

Objectives and issues

We have set aggressive but achievable objectives for the first and second years of market entry.

First-year objectives

During the Sonic 1000's initial year on the market, we are aiming for unit sales volume of 500,000.

Second-year objectives

Our second-year objectives are to sell a combined total of 1 million units of our two models and to break even early in this period.

Issues

In relation to the product launch, our major issue is the ability to establish a well-regarded brand name linked to a meaningful positioning. We will invest heavily in marketing to create a memorable and distinctive brand image projecting innovation, quality and value. We also must measure awareness and response so we can adjust our marketing efforts as necessary.

Marketing strategy

Sonic's marketing strategy is based on a positioning of product differentiation. Our primary consumer target is middle- to upper-income professionals who need one portable device to coordinate their busy schedules, communicate with family and colleagues, get driving directions and be entertained on the go. Our secondary consumer target is high school, college and graduate students who want a multimedia, dual-mode device. This segment can be described demographically by age (16–30) and education status.

Our primary business target is mid- to large-sized corporations that want to help their managers and employees stay in touch and input or access critical data when out of the office. This segment consists of companies with more than €25m in annual sales and more than 100 employees. We are also targeting entrepreneurs and small-business owners as well as medical users who want to update or access patients' medical records while reducing paperwork.

Positioning

Using product differentiation, we are positioning the Sonic as the most versatile, convenient, value-added model for personal and professional use. Our marketing will focus on the hands-free operation of multiple communication, entertainment and information capabilities differentiating the Sonic 1000.

Product strategy

The Sonic 1000, including all the features described in the earlier product review section, will be sold with a one-year warranty. We will introduce a more compact, powerful high-end model (the Sonic 2000) during the following year. Building the Sonic brand is an integral part of our product strategy. The brand and logo (Sonic's distinctive yellow thunderbolt) will be displayed on the product and its packaging and reinforced by its prominence in the introductory marketing campaign.

Pricing strategy

The Sonic 1000 will be introduced at €150 wholesale/€199 estimated retail price per unit. We expect to lower the price of this first model when we expand the product line by launching the Sonic 2000, to be priced at €175 wholesale per unit. These prices reflect a strategy of (1) attracting desirable channel partners and (2) taking share from Apple, Samsung and other established competitors.

Distribution strategy

Our channel strategy is to use selective distribution, marketing Sonic smartphones through well-known stores and online retailers. During the first year, we will add channel partners until we have coverage in all major Western European markets and the product is included in the major electronics catalogues and on websites. We will also investigate distribution through mobile phone outlets maintained by major carriers such as EE. In support of our channel partners, Sonic will provide demonstration products, detailed specification handouts and full-colour photos and displays featuring the product. Finally, we plan to arrange special payment terms for retailers that place volume orders.

Marketing communications strategy

By integrating all messages in all media, we will reinforce the brand name and the main points of product differentiation. Research about media consumption patterns will help our advertising agency choose appropriate media and timing to reach prospects before and during product introduction. Thereafter, advertising will appear on a pulsing basis to maintain brand awareness and communicate various differentiation messages. The agency will also coordinate public relations efforts to build the Sonic brand and support the differentiation message. To create buzz, we will host a user-generated video contest on our website. To attract, retain and motivate channel partners for a push strategy, we will use trade sales promotions and personal selling. Until the Sonic brand has been established, our communications will encourage purchases through channel partners rather than from our website.

Marketing research

Using research, we are identifying the specific features and benefits that our target market segments value. Feedback from market tests, surveys and focus groups will help us develop the Sonic 2000. We are also measuring and analysing customers' attitudes towards competing brands and products. Brand awareness research will help us determine the effectiveness and efficiency of our messages and media. Finally, we will use customer satisfaction studies to gauge market reaction.

Marketing organisation

Sonic's Chief Marketing Officer, Jane Melody, holds overall responsibility for all of the company's marketing activities. Figure A1.1 shows the structure of the eight-person marketing organisation. Sonic has hired Worldwide Marketing to handle national sales campaigns, trade and consumer sales promotions, and public relations efforts.

Action programmes

The Sonic 1000 will be introduced in February. We will use the following summaries of the action programmes during the first six months of next year to achieve our stated objectives.

January

We will launch a €200,000 trade sales promotion campaign and exhibit at the major industry trade shows to educate dealers and generate channel support for the product launch

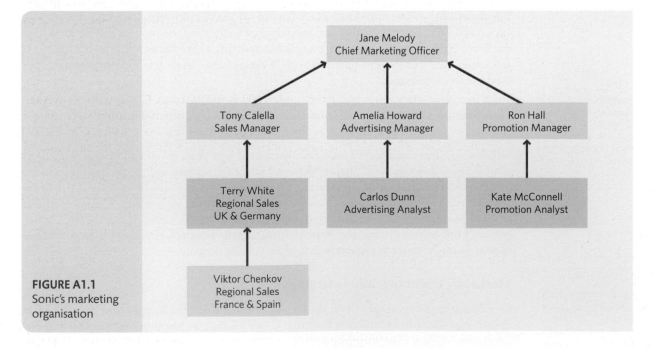

FIGURE A1.1
Sonic's marketing organisation

in February. Also, we will create buzz by providing samples to selected product reviewers, opinion leaders, influential bloggers and celebrities. Our training staff will work with retail sales personnel at major chains to explain the Sonic 1000's features, benefits and advantages.

February

We will start an integrated print/radio/Internet campaign targeting professionals and consumers. The campaign will show how many functions the Sonic smartphone can perform and emphasise the convenience of a single, powerful handheld device. This multimedia campaign will be supported by point-of-sale signage as well as online-only ads and video tours.

March

As the multimedia advertising campaign continues, we will add consumer sales promotions such as a contest in which consumers post videos to our website, showing how they use the Sonic in creative and unusual ways. We will also distribute new point-of-purchase displays to support our retailers.

April

We will hold a trade sales contest offering prizes for the salesperson and retail organisation that sells the most Sonic smartphones during the four-week period.

May

We plan to roll out a new national advertising campaign this month. The radio ads will feature celebrity voices telling their Sonic smartphones to perform functions such as initiating a phone call, sending an email, playing a song or video, and so on. The stylised print and online ads will feature avatars of these celebrities holding their Sonic smartphones.

June

Our radio campaign will add a new voice-over tagline promoting the Sonic 1000 as a graduation gift. We will also exhibit at the semi-annual electronics trade show and provide channel partners with new competitive comparison handouts as a sales aid. In addition, we will tally and analyse the results of customer satisfaction surveys for use in future promotions and to provide feedback for product and marketing activities.

Budgets

Budgets
Managers use budgets to project profitability and plan for each marketing programme's expenditures, scheduling and operations.

Total first-year sales revenue for the Sonic 1000 is projected at €75m, with an average wholesale price of €150 per unit and variable cost per unit of €100 for unit sales volume of 500,000. We anticipate a first-year loss of up to €8m on the Sonic 1000 model. Break-even calculations indicate that the Sonic 1000 will become profitable after the sales volume exceeds 650,000, early in the product's second year. Our break-even analysis of Sonic's first smartphone product assumes per-unit wholesale revenue of €150 per unit, variable cost of €100 per unit and estimated first-year fixed costs of €32,500,000. Based on these assumptions, the break-even calculation is

$$\frac{€32,500,000}{€150/unit - €100/unit} = 650,000 \text{ units}$$

Controls

Controls
Controls help management assess results after the plan is implemented, identify any problems or performance variations and initiate corrective action.

We are planning tight control measures to monitor closely quality and customer service satisfaction. This will enable us to react very quickly in correcting any problems that may occur. Other early warning signals that will be monitored for signs of deviation from the plan include monthly sales (by segment and channel) and monthly expenses. Given the market's volatility, we are developing contingency plans to address fast-moving environmental changes such as new technology and new competition.

Sources: Background information and market data adapted from 'Hospital Uses PDA App for Patient Transport', *Health Data Management*, June 2007, p. 14; 'Smartphones Get Smarter, Thanks in Part to the iPhone', *InformationWeek*, 21 July 2007; Chris Nutall and others, 'Apple Set to Slash iPhone Prices to Lift Sales', *Financial Times*, 10 June 2008, p. 20; Olga Kharif and Roger O. Crockett, 'Motorola's Market Share Mess', *BusinessWeek*, 10 July 2008, www.businessweek.com; 'Follow the Leader', *The Economist*, 14 June 2008, pp. 78–80; Laura M. Holson, 'Phone Giants Fight to Keep Subscribers', *New York Times*, 23 July 2008, p. C1; Adam Lashinsky, 'Palm Fights Back (Against Apple)', *Fortune*, 8 June 2009, pp 88–92; Moon Ihlwan, 'Samsung Smartphones Take on iPhones, Blackberrys', *BusinessWeek Online*, 23 June 2009.

APPENDIX 2
MARKETING METRICS

One aspect of marketing not discussed in detail within the text is marketing metrics. This refers to a wide range of figures that can be calculated to measure the effectiveness and efficiency of marketing activities. Ultimately, in a privately owned profit-seeking business, the goal of marketing is to contribute to the creation – some people would say to the *maximisation* – of the business owners' equity (the value of the business to the owners). In a publicly quoted company (one that is listed on the stock exchange) this means striving to increase, and arguably to maximise, the value of the business to its shareholders, simply called *shareholder value*. However, these ultimate goals – useful though they are for guiding marketing strategy – are a little too abstract to be used for daily guidance in marketing management, so that more straightforward metrics concerned with sales, costs and certain ratios are commonly applied. This appendix describes three major areas underlying the calculation of marketing metrics: the *profit-and-loss account, analytic ratios* and *mark-ups and mark-downs*.

PROFIT-AND-LOSS ACCOUNT

The profit-and-loss account and the balance sheet are the two main financial statements used by companies. The **balance sheet** shows the assets, liabilities and net worth of a company at a given time. The **profit-and-loss account** (or **income statement**) is the more important of the two for marketing information. It shows company sales, cost of goods sold and expenses during a specified time period. By comparing the profit and loss account from one time period with the next, the firm can spot favourable or unfavourable trends and take appropriate action.

Table A2.1 shows the financial year 2013–14 profit-and-loss account for Charles Smith Menswear, a men's clothing retailer in Manchester, UK. This statement is for a retailer; the profit-and-loss account for a manufacturer would be somewhat different – specifically, the section on purchases within the 'cost of goods sold' area would be replaced by 'cost of goods manufactured'.

The outline of the profit-and-loss account follows a logical series of steps to arrive at the firm's £25,000 net profit figure:

Net sales	£300,000
Cost of goods sold	−175,000
Gross margin	£125,000
Expenses	−100,000
Net profit	£25,000

The first part of the profit-and-loss account details the amount that Smith received for the goods sold during the year. The sales figures consist of three items: *gross sales, returns and allowances* and *net sales*. **Gross sales** comprise the

TABLE A2.1 Profit-and-loss account: Charles Smith Menswear: Year ending 31 March 2014

Gross sales			£325,000
Less: Sales returns and allowances			£25,000
Net sales			£300,000
Cost of goods sold			
Opening inventory, 1 April, at cost		£60,000	
Gross purchases	£165,000		
Less: Purchase discounts	£15,000		
Net purchases	£150,000		
Plus: Freight-in	£10,000		
Net cost of delivered purchases		£160,000	
Costs of goods available for sale		£220,000	
Less: Closing inventory, 31 March, at cost		£45,000	
Cost of goods sold			£175,000
Gross margin			£125,000
Expenses			
Selling expenses			
Sales, salaries and commissions	£40,000		
Advertising	£5,000		
Delivery	£5,000		
Total selling expenses		£50,000	
Administrative expenses			
Office salaries	£20,000		
Office supplies	£5,000		
Miscellaneous (outside consultant)	£5,000		
Total administrative expenses		£30,000	
General expenses			
Rent	£10,000		
Heat, light, telephone	£5,000		
Miscellaneous (insurance, depreciation)	£5,000		
Total general expenses		£20,000	
Total expenses			£100,000
Net profit			£25,000

total amount charged to customers during the year for merchandise purchased in Smith's store. As expected, some customers returned merchandise because of damage or a change of mind. If the customer gets a full refund or full credit on another purchase, we call this a *return*. Or the customer may decide to keep the item if Smith will reduce the price. This is called an *allowance*. By subtracting returns and allowances (£25,000) from gross sales (£325,000), we arrive at net sales (£300,000) – what Smith earned in revenue from a year of selling merchandise.

The second major part of the profit-and-loss account calculates the amount of sales revenue Smith retains after paying the costs of the merchandise. We start with the inventory (or stock) in the store at the beginning of the year. During the year, Smith bought £165,000 worth of suits, trousers, shirts, ties, jeans and other goods. Suppliers gave the store discounts totalling £15,000, so that net purchases were £150,000. Because the store is located outside the main city centre, Smith had to pay an additional £10,000 to get the products delivered, giving the firm a net cost of £160,000. Adding the beginning inventory, the cost of goods available for sale amounted to £220,000. The £45,000 ending inventory of clothes in the store on 31 March is then subtracted to come up with the £175,000 **cost of goods sold**. Here again we have followed a logical series of steps to calculate the cost of goods sold:

Amount Smith started with (opening inventory)	£60,000
Net amount purchased	+150,000
Any added cost to obtain these purchases	+10,000
Total cost of goods Smith had available for sale during year	£220,000
Amount Smith had left over (closing inventory)	−45,000
Cost of goods actually sold	£175,000

The difference between what Smith paid for the merchandise (£175,000) and what it sold it for (£300,000) is called the **gross margin** (£125,000).

In order to show the profit Smith 'cleared' at the end of the year, we must subtract from the gross margin the *expenses* incurred while doing business. *Selling expenses* for this shop included two sales employees, local newspaper and radio advertising, and the cost of delivering merchandise to customers after alterations. Selling expenses totalled £50,000 for the year. *Administrative expenses* included the salary for an office manager, office supplies such as stationery and business cards, and miscellaneous expenses including an administrative audit conducted by an outside consultant. Administrative expenses totalled £30,000 in 2013–14. Finally, the general expenses of rent, utilities, insurance and depreciation came to £20,000. Total expenses were therefore £100,000 for the year. By subtracting expenses (£100,000) from the gross margin (£125,000), we arrive at the net profit of £25,000 for Smith during 2013–14.

ANALYTIC RATIOS

The profit-and-loss account provides the figures needed to compute some crucial ratios. Typically these ratios are called **operating ratios** – the ratio of selected profit-and-loss account items to net sales. They let marketers compare the firm's performance in one year with that in previous years (or with industry standards and competitors in the same year). The most commonly used operating ratios are the *gross margin percentage*, the *net profit percentage*, the *operating expense percentage* and the *returns and allowances percentage*.

Ratio	Formula	Computation from Table A2.1
Gross profit percentage	$= \dfrac{\text{gross profit}}{\text{net sales}}$	$\dfrac{£125,000}{£300,000} = 42\%$
Net profit percentage	$= \dfrac{\text{net profit}}{\text{net sales}}$	$\dfrac{£25,000}{£300,000} = 8\%$
Operating expense percentage	$= \dfrac{\text{total expenses}}{\text{net sales}}$	$\dfrac{£100,000}{£300,000} = 33\%$
Return and allowances percentage	$= \dfrac{\text{returns and allowances}}{\text{net sales}}$	$\dfrac{£25,000}{£300,000} = 8\%$

Another useful ratio is the *stock turnover rate* (also called *inventory turnover rate*). The stock turnover rate is the number of times the stock (or inventory) turns over or is sold during a specified time period (often one year). It may be computed on a cost, selling price or units basis. Thus the formula can be

$$\text{Stock turnover rate} = \frac{\text{cost of goods sold}}{\text{average inventory at cost}}$$

or

$$\text{Stock turnover rate} = \frac{\text{selling price of goods sold}}{\text{average selling price inventory}}$$

or

$$\text{Stock turnover rate} = \frac{\text{sales in units}}{\text{average inventory in units}}$$

We will use the first formula to calculate the stock turnover rate for Smith:

$$\frac{£175,000}{(£60,000 + £45,000)/2} = \frac{£175,000}{£52,500} = 3.3$$

That is, Smith's inventory turned over 3.3 times in 2013–14. Normally, the higher the stock turnover rate, the higher the management efficiency and company profitability.

Return on investment (ROI) is frequently used to measure managerial effectiveness. It uses figures from the firm's profit-and-loss account and balance sheet. A commonly used formula for computing ROI is

$$\text{ROI} = \frac{\text{net profit}}{\text{sales}} \times \frac{\text{sales}}{\text{investment}}$$

You may have two questions about this formula: Why use a two-step process when ROI could be computed simply as net profit divided by investment? And what exactly is 'investment'?

To answer these questions, let's look at how each component of the formula can affect the ROI. Suppose Smith has a total investment of £150,000. Then ROI can be computed as follows:

$$\text{ROI} = \frac{£25,000 \text{ (net profit)}}{£300,000 \text{ (sales)}} \times \frac{£300,000 \text{ (sales)}}{£150,000 \text{ (investment)}} = 8.3\% \times 2 = 16.6\%$$

Now suppose that Smith had worked to increase its share of market. It could have had the same ROI if its sales had doubled while pound profit and investment stayed the same (accepting a lower profit ratio to get higher turnover and market share):

$$\text{ROI} = \frac{£25,000 \text{ (net profit)}}{£600,000 \text{ (sales)}} \times \frac{£600,000 \text{ (sales)}}{£150,000 \text{ (investment)}} = 4.16\% \times 4 = 16.6\%$$

Smith might have increased the ROI by increasing net profit through more cost cutting and more efficient marketing:

$$\text{ROI} = \frac{£50,000 \text{ (net profit)}}{£300,000 \text{ (sales)}} \times \frac{£300,000 \text{ (sales)}}{£150,000 \text{ (investment)}} = 16.6\% \times 2 = 33.2\%$$

Another way to increase ROI is to find some way to get the same levels of sales and profits while decreasing investment (perhaps by cutting the size of Smith's average inventory):

$$\text{ROI} = \frac{£25,000 \text{ (net profit)}}{£300,000 \text{ (sales)}} \times \frac{£300,000 \text{ (sales)}}{£75,000 \text{ (investment)}} = 8.3\% \times 4 = 33.2\%$$

What is 'investment' in the ROI formula? *Investment* is often defined as the total assets of the firm. But many analysts now use other measures of return to assess performance.

These measures include *return on net assets (RONA), return on shareholders' equity (ROE)* or *return on assets managed (ROAM)*. Because investment is measured at a point in time, we usually compute ROI as the average investment between two time periods (say, 1 April of one year and 31 March of the next). The objective in using any of these measures is to determine how well the company has been using its resources. As inflation, competitive pressures and cost of capital increase, such measures become increasingly important indicators of marketing and company performance.

MARK-UPS AND MARK-DOWNS

Retailers and wholesalers must understand the concepts of **mark-ups** and **mark-downs**. They must make a profit to stay in business and the mark-up percentage affects profits. Mark-ups and mark-downs are expressed as percentages.

There are two different ways to compute mark-ups – on *cost* or on *selling price*:

$$\text{Mark-up percentage on cost} = \frac{\text{pounds mark-up}}{\text{cost}}$$

$$\text{Mark-up percentage on selling price} = \frac{\text{pounds mark-up}}{\text{selling price}}$$

Smith must decide which formula to use. If Smith bought shirts for £15 and wanted to mark them up £10 to a price of £25, its mark-up percentage on cost would be £10/£15 = 67.7 per cent. If Smith based mark-up on selling price, the percentage would be £10/£25 = 40 per cent. In calculating mark-up percentage, most retailers use the selling price rather than the cost.

Suppose Smith knew its cost (£12) and desired mark-up on price (25 per cent) for a man's tie, and wanted to compute the selling price. The formula is

$$\text{Selling price} = \frac{\text{cost}}{1 - \text{mark-up}}$$

$$\text{Selling price} = \frac{£12}{0.75} = £16$$

As a product moves through the channel of distribution, each channel member adds a mark-up before selling the product to the next member. This 'mark-up chain' is shown for a suit purchased by a Smith customer for £200:

		Amount (£)	% of selling price
Manufacturer	Cost	108	90
	Mark-up	12	10
	Selling price	120	100
Wholesaler	Cost	120	80
	Mark-up	30	20
	Selling price	150	100
Retailer	Cost	150	75
	Mark-up	50	25
	Selling price	200	100

The retailer whose mark-up is 25 per cent does not necessarily enjoy more profit than a manufacturer whose mark-up is 10 per cent. Profit also depends on how many items with that profit margin can be sold (stock turnover rate) and on operating efficiency (expenses).

Sometimes a retailer wants to convert mark-ups based on selling price to mark-ups based on cost, and vice versa. The formulae are

$$\text{Mark-up percentage on selling price} = \frac{\text{mark-up percentage on cost}}{100\% + \text{mark-up percentage on selling cost}}$$

$$\text{Mark-up percentage on cost} = \frac{\text{mark-up percentage on cost}}{100\% - \text{mark-up percentage on selling cost}}$$

Suppose Smith found that its competitor was using a mark-up of 30 per cent based on cost and wanted to know what this would be as a percentage of selling price. The calculation would be

$$\frac{30\%}{100\% + 30\%} = \frac{30\%}{130\%} = 23\%$$

Because Smith was using a 25 per cent mark-up on the selling price for suits, it felt that its mark-up was suitable compared with that of the competitor.

Near the end of the summer Smith still had an inventory of casual summer trousers in stock. Therefore, it decided to use a *mark-down,* a reduction from the original selling price. Before the summer it had purchased 20 pairs at £10 each, and it had since sold 10 pairs at £20 each. It marked down the other pairs to £15 and sold 5 pairs. We compute its *mark-down ratio* as follows:

$$\text{Mark-down percentage} = \frac{\text{pounds markdown}}{\text{total net sales in pounds}}$$

The pound mark-down is £25 (5 pairs at £5 each) and total net sales are £275 (10 pairs at £20 + 5 pairs at £15). The ratio, then, is £25/£275 = 9%.

Larger retailers usually compute mark-down ratios for each department rather than for individual items. The ratios provide a measure of relative marketing performance for each department and can be calculated and compared over time. Mark-down ratios can also be used to compare the performance of different buyers and salespeople in a store's various departments.

NAVIGATING THE KEY TERMS

APPENDIX 3
CAREERS IN MARKETING

Now that you've read this book about marketing, you have a good idea of what the field entails. You may be wondering whether or not marketing is something you should study in more depth in the rest of your degree or what sorts of careers are available to graduate marketers.

Marketing is a very broad field offering a wide variety of career options and many of these offer constant challenges, stimulating problems, the opportunity to work with people and excellent advancement opportunities. This appendix helps you discover what types of marketing jobs best match your special skills and interests, describes marketing career paths open to you and suggests some information resources.

MARKETING CAREERS TODAY

The field of marketing is booming in the twenty-first century, with entry-level marketing salaries usually only slightly below those for engineering and chemistry but equal to or exceeding starting salaries in economics, finance, accountancy, general business and the liberal arts. Moreover, if you succeed in an entry-level marketing position, it's likely that you will be promoted quickly to higher levels of responsibility and salary. In addition, because of the consumer and product knowledge you'll gain in these jobs, marketing positions provide excellent training for the highest levels in an organisation.

Overall marketing facts and trends

In conducting your job search, consider the following facts and trends that are changing the world of marketing:

- *Technology*: Technology is changing the way marketers work. For example, price coding allows instantaneous retail inventorying. Software for marketing training, forecasting and other functions is changing the ways we market. If you make yourself into a graduate with good skills in respect of using and managing social media towards a marketing end, then you'll be attractive to prestigious employers. That means more than checking your Facebook status every 10 minutes! It means having a detailed grasp of the machines under the surface and how and why they impact on marketers and marketing. Whereas advertising firms have traditionally recruited 'generalists' in account management, 'generalist' has now taken on a whole new meaning – advertising account executives must now have both broad and specialised knowledge.

- *Diversity*: The number of women and minorities in marketing continues to rise. For example, women now outnumber men by nearly two to one as advertising account executives. As marketing becomes more global, the need for diversity in marketing positions will continue to increase, opening new opportunities for people who can empathise and operate in China and India and Brazil as well as Europe.

- *Global*: Companies such as Coca-Cola, McDonald's, Apple, Tesco and Procter & Gamble have become multinational, with offices and manufacturing operations in hundreds of countries. Indeed, such companies often make more profit from sales outside their home country than from within. And it is not just the big companies that are involved in international marketing. Organisations of all sizes have moved into the global arena. Many new marketing opportunities and careers will be directly linked to the expanding global marketplace. The globalisation of business also means that you will need more culture, language and people skills in the marketing world of the twenty-first century.

- *Not-for-profit organisations*: Increasingly, universities, arts organisations, libraries, hospitals and other not-for-profit organisations are recognising the need for effectively marketing their 'products' and services to various publics. This awareness has led to new marketing positions – with these organisations hiring their own marketing directors or using outside marketing specialists.

MARKETING JOBS

This section describes some of the key marketing positions.

Advertising

Advertising is one of today's hottest fields in marketing.

Job descriptions

Key advertising positions include copywriter, art director, production manager, account executive and media planner/buyer:

- *Copywriters* write advertising copy and help find the concepts behind the written words and visual images of advertisements.
- *Art directors,* the other part of the creative team, help translate the copywriters' ideas into dramatic visuals called 'layouts'. Agency artists develop print layouts, package designs, television layouts (called 'storyboards'), corporate logotypes, trademarks and symbols.
- *Production managers* are responsible for physically creating advertisements, in-house or by contracting through outside production houses.
- *Account development executives* research and understand clients' markets and customers and help develop marketing and advertising strategies to impact them.
- *Account executives* serve as liaisons between clients and agencies. They coordinate the planning, creation, production and implementation of an advertising campaign for the account.
- *Media planners (or buyers)* determine the best mix of online, television, radio, newspaper, magazine and other media for the advertising campaign.

Skills needed, career paths and typical salaries

Work in advertising requires strong people skills in order to interact closely with an often difficult and demanding client base. In addition, advertising attracts people with high skills in planning, problem solving, creativity, communication, initiative, leadership and presentation. Advertising involves working under high levels of stress and pressure created by unrelenting deadlines. Advertisers frequently have to work long hours to meet deadlines for a presentation. But work achievements are very apparent, with the results of creative strategies observed by thousands or even millions of people as Google, Facebook and television distribute the final advertisements around the globe.

Because they are so sought after, positions in advertising sometimes require a postgraduate qualification. But there are many jobs open for business, graphics arts and liberal arts undergraduates. Advertising positions often serve as gateways to higher level management. Moreover, with large advertising agencies opening offices all over the world, there is the possibility of eventually working on global campaigns.

Starting advertising salaries are relatively low compared with some other marketing jobs because of strong competition for entry-level advertising jobs. You may even want to consider working for free to break in – perhaps help a small local company or charity with its social media marketing? Pay will increase quickly as you move into account executive or other management positions. For more facts and figures, see the web pages of *Advertising Age,* a key advertising industry publication (www.adage.com).

Brand and product management

Brand and product managers plan, direct and control business and marketing efforts for their products. They are involved with research and development, packaging, manufacturing, sales and distribution, advertising, promotion, market research, and business analysis and forecasting.

Job descriptions

A company's brand management team consist of people in several positions.

- *Brand managers* guide the development of marketing strategies for a specific brand.
- *Assistant brand managers* are responsible for certain strategic components of the brand.
- *Product managers* oversee several brands within a product line or product group.
- *Product category managers* direct multiple product lines in the product category.
- *Market analysts* research the market and provide important strategic information to the project managers.
- *Project directors* are responsible for collecting market information on a marketing or product project.
- *Research directors* oversee the planning, gathering and analysing of all organisational research.

Skills needed, career paths and typical salaries

Brand and product management requires high problem-solving, analytical, presentation, communication and leadership skills, as well as the ability to work well in a team. Product management requires long hours and involves the high pressure of running large projects. In consumer goods companies, the newcomer joins a brand team as an assistant and learns the ropes by doing numerical analyses and watching senior brand people. This person eventually heads the team and later moves on to manage a larger brand, then several brands. Many industrial goods companies also have product managers. Product management is one of the best training grounds for future corporate officers. Product management also offers good opportunities to move into international marketing. Product managers command relatively high salaries. Starting pay tends to be higher than in other marketing categories such as advertising or retailing. Statistically speaking, this is a very common path for marketing graduates, a reflection of the number of brands that need to be managed.

Sales, sales management

Sales and sales management opportunities exist in a wide range of profit and non-profit organisations and in product and service organisations, including financial, insurance, consulting and government organisations.

Job descriptions

Key jobs include consumer sales, industrial sales, national account manager, service support, sales trainers, sales management and telesales:

- *Consumer sales* involves selling consumer products and services through retailers.
- *Industrial sales* includes selling products and services to other businesses.
- *National account managers (NAM)* oversee a few very large accounts.
- *Service support* personnel support salespeople during and after the sale of a product.
- *Sales trainers* train new recruits and provide refresher training for all sales personnel.
- *Sales management* includes a sequence of positions ranging from district manager to vice president of sales.
- The *teleseller* (not to be confused with the home consumer telemarketer) offers service and support to field salespeople.

Salespeople enjoy active professional lives, working outside the office and interacting with others. They manage their own time and activities. Competition for top jobs can be intense. Every sales job is different, but some positions involve extensive travel, long work days and working under pressure, which can negatively impact on personal life. You can also expect to be transferred more than once between company headquarters and regional offices. Some people are natural sellers, and others are not. Persisting in pursuing a career in sales when you don't have the knack is a brutal way to live your life.

Skills needed, career paths and typical salaries

Selling is a people profession in which you'll work with people every day, all day long. Besides people skills, sales professionals need sales and communication skills. Most sales positions also require high problem-solving, analytical, presentation and leadership ability as well as creativity and initiative. Teamwork skills are increasingly important.

Career paths lead from salesperson to district, regional and higher levels of sales management and, in many cases, to the top management of the firm. Today, most entry-level sales management positions require a degree. Increasingly, people seeking selling jobs are acquiring sales experience from placements and internships or from a part-time job before graduating. Although there is a high turnover rate (one in four people leave their jobs in a year), sales positions are great springboards to leadership positions, with more CEOs starting in sales than in any other entry-level position. Possibly this explains why competition for top sales jobs is intense.

Starting base salaries in sales may be moderate, but compensation is often supplemented by significant commission, bonus or other incentive plans. In addition, many sales jobs include a company car or car allowance. Successful salespeople are among most companies' highest paid employees – and they've earned it.

Other marketing jobs

Retailing

Retailing provides an early opportunity to assume marketing responsibilities. Key jobs include store manager, regional manager, buyer, department manager and salesperson. *Store managers* direct the management and operation of an individual store. *Regional managers* manage groups of stores and report performance to headquarters. *Buyers* select and buy the merchandise that the store carries. The *department manager* acts as store manager of a department, such as clothing, but on the department level. The *salesperson* sells merchandise to retail customers. Retailing can involve relocation, but generally there is little travel unless you're a buyer. Retailing requires high levels of people and sales skills because retailers are constantly in contact with customers. Enthusiasm, willingness and communication skills are very helpful for retailers, too.

Retailers work long hours, but their daily activities are often more structured than some types of marketing positions. Starting salaries in retailing tend to be low, but pay increases as you move into management or some retailing speciality job. As online retailing surges and grows, people with parallel skills to the above are needed – hybrids between retailing and logistics that can work in high-intensity environments like Amazon and eBay. Long hours? Yes – 24 hours a day, 365 days a year baby!

Marketing research

Marketing researchers interact with managers to define problems and identify the information needed to resolve them. They design research projects, prepare questionnaires and samples, analyse data, prepare reports, and present their findings and recommendations to management. They must understand statistics, consumer behaviour, psychology and sociology. Career opportunities exist with manufacturers, retailers, some wholesalers, trade and industry associations, marketing research firms, advertising agencies, and government and private non-profit agencies. In the era of 'big data' marketing researchers must be able to obtain, process and present on datasets involving detailed information on millions of customers and relationships.

New-product planning

People interested in new-product planning can find opportunities in many types of organisations. They usually need a good background in marketing, marketing research and sales forecasting; they need organisational skills to motivate and coordinate others; and they may need a technical background. Usually, these people work first in other marketing positions before joining the new-product department. As we've noted throughout the book, physical products hold the key ground but the future is software-based products like apps and designs for 3D printers. You'll need to be able to engage with hi-tech and be able to communicate effectively using the technical languages of your colleagues in engineering and software design.

Marketing logistics (physical distribution)

Marketing logistics, or physical distribution, is a large and dynamic field, with many career opportunities. Major transportation carriers, manufacturers, wholesalers and retailers all employ logistics specialists. Increasingly, marketing teams include logistics specialists, and marketing managers' career paths include marketing logistics assignments. Training in quantitative methods, finance, accountancy and marketing will provide you with the necessary skills for entering the field. For online businesses this means managing capacity to ensure products and services reach the customer through the Internet – such as server farms – or working efficiently to shift physical products as quickly as possible to end users. Google drone delivery anyone?

Public relations

Most organisations have public relations staff to anticipate problems with various publics, handle complaints, deal with media and build the corporate image. People interested in public relations should be able to speak and write clearly and persuasively, and they should have a background in journalism, communications or marketing. The challenges in this job are highly varied and very people oriented. Imagine being in charge of the Twitter account for a large corporation. Scary or exciting?

Non-profit services

The key jobs in non-profit organisations include marketing directors, directors of development, event coordinators, publication specialists and fundraising volunteers. The *marketing director* is in charge of all marketing activities for the organisation. The *director of development* organises, manages and directs the fundraising campaigns that keep a non-profit organisation in existence. An *event coordinator* directs all aspects of fundraising events, from initial planning through to implementation. The *publication specialist* oversees publications designed to promote awareness of the organisation. Although typically an unpaid position, the *intern/volunteer* performs various marketing functions, and this work can be an important step to gaining a full-time position. The non-profit sector is typically not for someone who is money driven. Rather, most non-profit organisations look for people with a strong sense of community spirit and the desire to help others. So starting pay is usually lower than in other marketing fields. However, the bigger the organisation, the better your chance of increasing your income rapidly when moving into upper management.

How to make yourself employable as a marketer

You are marketing yourself. Recognise this fact and reflect on the implications it has for whether or not you will achieve your goals. Do you have a plan? What are your personal objectives? Is there an industry/company you would like to work for? How about a specific job role – those outlined above or some other position? What skills and knowledge and experiences would make you appropriate for that position or that company? When you're making choices about classes or training courses – even the specific subject of an assignment – can you extract extra value from the situation so that when you're in front of an interview panel you can tell them how you analysed their industry, studied their competitors, researched their product range, gained skills in market research?

The phrase '*it's not what you know, it's who you know*' has some validity. If you don't have the good fortune to have a close friend or relative who can push opportunities your way, then make some connections. Create a profile for yourself on a professional networking site like LinkedIn. Do it properly. Get a few pals to do the same – develop your relationships with friends, family and tutors and you'll soon be amazed at what and who appear in your network. Offline, are there clubs for budding entrepreneurs you could join? How about societies involving technology or languages or cultures?

A difficulty many young people have is their lack of experience. Every little helps. Organise a small event, help to manage a club or society. Look for opportunities to demonstrate initiative and enterprise – enter a competition like the Google Online Marketing Challenge. Work experience is also very helpful. Large and prominent companies get inundated with requests for placements. Think laterally – find and investigate small firms and organisations close to you. Is there a local business that needs a small piece of research doing but can't afford an MR company? Perhaps its newspaper advertisements are old and dull? Perhaps you could use your knowledge to provide some informal training in using social media to promote the company? All these possibilities exist for small charities as well. Small firms are more flexible – you'll have opportunities to do something more real and more significant than you might if you'd ended up making tea at Tesco.

When the moment of truth comes and you're sitting in front of three middle-aged people in suits, be what you want to appear to them as – proactive, someone with a plan, someone with skills, someone who has looked for opportunities, someone who has allied intelligence with dedication, someone who can point to achievements above and beyond graduating.

In short, get organised, get scheming – you'll make your own luck.

OTHER RESOURCES

Professional marketing associations and organisations are another source of information about careers. Marketers belong to many such societies. You may want to contact some of the following in your job search:

- The Chartered Institute of Marketing is the UK professional body – but is growing rapidly in Europe and Asia as well: www.cim.co.uk
- The European Marketing Confederation is a continent-wide professional organisation: www.emc.be
- *Marketing Week* might best be described as the profession's newspaper. Like most other newspapers it has sections on jobs and job hunting: www.marketingweek.co.uk
- *Sales and Marketing Jobs* does what it says on the tin, being a specialist in listing marketing and sales positions: www.sales-and-marketing-jobs.co.uk/
- Many national newspapers have sections specifically for marketing and sales. The *Guardian* is good for non-profit-related jobs and also media and creative careers. The *Telegraph* and *The Times* tend to have more brand management and/or market research positions.

GLOSSARY

Adapted marketing mix An international marketing strategy for adjusting the marketing mix elements to each international target market, bearing more costs but hoping for a larger market share and return.

Administered VMS A Vertical Marketing System that coordinates successive stages of production and distribution, not through common ownership or contractual ties, but through the size and power of one of the parties.

Adoption process The mental process through which an individual passes from first hearing about an innovation to final adoption.

Advertising Any paid form of non-personal presentation and promotion of ideas, goods or services by an identified sponsor.

Advertising agency A marketing services firm that assists companies in planning, preparing, implementing and evaluating all or portions of their advertising programmes.

Advertising objective A specific communication task to be accomplished with a specific target audience during a specific period of time.

Affordable method Setting the promotion budget at the level management thinks the company can afford.

Age and life-cycle segmentation Dividing a market into different age and life-cycle groups.

Agent A wholesaler who represents buyers or sellers on a relatively permanent basis, performs only a few functions and does not take title to goods.

Allowance Promotional money paid by manufacturers to retailers in return for an agreement to feature the manufacturer's products in some way.

Approach The step in the selling process in which the salesperson meets the customer for the first time.

B2B (business-to-business) e-commerce Using B2B trading networks, auction sites, spot exchanges, online product catalogues, barter sites and other online resources to reach new business customers, serve current customers more effectively, and obtain buying efficiencies and better prices.

B2C (business-to-consumer) e-commerce The online selling of goods and services to final consumers.

Baby boomers The generation of people born in Europe and North America during the baby boom following the Second World War and lasting until the early 1960s.

Behavioural segmentation Dividing a market into groups based on consumer knowledge, attitude, use or response to a product.

Benefit segmentation Dividing the market into groups according to the different benefits that consumers seek from the product.

Brand A combination of name, term, sign, symbol or design, intended to identify the goods or services of one seller or group of sellers and to differentiate them from those of competitors.

Brand equity The positive differential effect that knowing the brand name has on customer response to the product or service.

Brand extension Using a successful brand name to launch a new or modified product in a new category.

Break-even pricing Setting price to break even on the costs of making and marketing a product; or setting price to make a target profit.

Broker A wholesaler that does not take title to goods and whose function is to bring buyers and sellers together and assist in negotiation.

Business analysis A review of the sales, costs and profit projections for a new product to find out whether these factors satisfy the company's objectives.

Business buyer behaviour The buying behaviour of the organisations that buy goods and services for use in the production of other products and services or for the purpose of reselling or renting them to others at a profit.

Business portfolio The collection of businesses and products that make up the company.

Buying centre All the individuals and units that participate in the business buying decision process.

By-product pricing Setting a price for by-products in order to make the main product's price more competitive.

C2B (consumer-to-business) e-commerce Online exchanges in which consumers search out sellers, learn about their offers and initiate purchases, sometimes even driving transaction terms.

C2C (consumer-to-consumer) e-commerce Online exchanges of goods and information between final consumers.

Captive-product pricing Setting a price for products that must be used along with a main product, such as blades for a razor and film for a camera.

Catalogue marketing Direct marketing through print, video or electronic catalogues that are mailed to selected customers, made available in stores or presented online.

Category killer Giant speciality store that carries a very deep assortment of a particular line and is staffed by knowledgeable employees.

Causal research Marketing research to test hypotheses about cause-and-effect relationships.

Chain stores Two or more outlets that are owned and controlled in common, have central buying and merchandising, and sell similar lines of merchandise.

Channel conflict Disagreement among marketing channel members on goals and roles – who should do what and for what rewards.

Channel level A layer of intermediaries that performs some work in bringing the product and its ownership closer to the final buyer.

Click-and-mortar companies Traditional brick-and-mortar companies that have added e-marketing to their operations.

Click-only companies The so-called dot-coms, which operate only online without any brick-and-mortar market presence.

Closing The step in the selling process in which the salesperson asks the customer for an order.

Co-branding The practice of using the established brand names of two different companies on the same product.

Cognitive dissonance Buyer psychological discomfort following a purchase arising from anxiety that the buying decision was sub-optimal.

Commercialisation Introducing a new product into the market.

Communication adaptation A global communication strategy of fully adapting advertising messages to local markets.

Competitive advantage An advantage over competitors gained by offering consumers or business buyers greater value, either through lower prices or by providing more benefits that justify higher prices.

Competitive-parity method Setting the promotion budget to match competitors' outlays.

Concentrated (niche) marketing A market coverage strategy in which a firm goes after a large share of one or a few segments or niches.

Concept testing Testing new-product concepts with a group of target consumers to find out if the concepts have strong consumer appeal.

Consumer buyer behaviour The buying behaviour of final consumers – individuals and households who buy goods and services for personal consumption.

Consumer market All the individuals and households who buy or acquire goods and services for personal consumption.

Consumer product Product bought by final consumer for personal consumption, or perhaps as a gift.

Consumerism An organised movement of citizens and government agencies to improve the rights and power of buyers in relation to sellers.

Consumer-oriented marketing The philosophy of enlightened marketing that holds that the company should view and organise its marketing activities from the consumer's point of view.

Contract manufacturing A joint venture in which a company contracts with manufacturers in a foreign market to produce its product or provide its service.

Contractual VMS A Vertical Marketing System in which independent firms at different levels of production and distribution join together through contracts to obtain more economies or sales impact than they could achieve alone.

Convenience product Consumer product that the customer usually buys frequently, immediately and with a minimum of comparison and buying effort.

Convenience store A small store located near a residential area that is open long hours seven days a week and carries a limited line of high-turnover convenience goods.

Conventional distribution channel A channel consisting of one or more independent producers, wholesalers and retailers, each a separate business seeking to maximise its own profits even at the expense of profits for the system as a whole.

Corporate VMS A Vertical Marketing System that combines successive stages of production and distribution under single ownership – channel leadership is established through common ownership.

Corporate website A website designed to build customer goodwill and to supplement other sales channels, rather than to sell the company's products directly.

Cost-plus pricing Adding a standard mark-up to the cost of the product, for example 10 per cent.

Countertrade International trade involving the direct or indirect exchange of goods for other goods instead of cash.

Cultural environment Institutions and other forces that affect society's basic values, perceptions, preferences and behaviours.

Culture The set of basic values, perceptions, wants and behaviours learned by a member of society from family and other important institutions.

Customer database An organised collection of comprehensive data about individual customers or prospects, including geographic, demographic, psychographic and behavioural data.

Customer equity The total combined customer lifetime values of all of the company's customers.

Customer lifetime value The value of the entire stream of purchases that the customer would make over a lifetime of patronage. Often quoted as an amount lost to the company if the customer disappears.

Customer perceived value The customer's evaluation of the difference between all the benefits and all the costs of a marketing offer relative to those of competing offers.

Customer relationship management Nominally to do with the process of creating, developing and maintaining relationships with customers, more typically and accurately referring to the management and use of customer information in databases.

Customer sales force structure A sales force organisation under which salespeople specialise in selling only to certain customers or industries.

Customer satisfaction The extent to which a product's perceived performance matches a buyer's expectations.

Customer value marketing An approach to marketing that emphasises the creation and enhancement of customer value as a route to competitive success.

Decline stage The product life-cycle stage in which a product's sales decline.

Deficient products Products that have neither immediate appeal nor long-term benefits.

Demand curve A curve that shows the number of units the market will buy in a given time period, at different prices that might be charged.

Demands Wants that are backed by buying power.

Demographic segmentation Dividing the market into groups based on demographic variables such as age, sex, family size, family life cycle, income, occupation, education, religion, race and nationality.

Demography The study of human populations in terms of size, density, location, age, gender, ethnicity, occupation and other statistics.

Department store A retail organisation that carries a wide variety of product lines – typically clothing, home furnishings and household goods; each line is operated as a separate department managed by specialist buyers or merchandisers.

Derived demand Business demand that ultimately comes from (derives from) the demand for consumer goods.

Descriptive research Marketing research to better describe marketing problems, situations or markets, such as the market potential for a product or the demographics and attitudes of consumers.

Desirable products Products that give both high immediate satisfaction and high long-term benefits.

Differentiated (segmented) marketing A market coverage strategy in which a firm decides to target several market segments and designs separate offers for each.

Direct investment Entering a foreign market by developing foreign-based assembly or manufacturing facilities.

Direct mail marketing Direct marketing by sending an offer, announcement, reminder or other item to a person at a particular address.

Direct marketing Direct connections with carefully targeted individual consumers both to obtain an immediate response and to cultivate lasting customer relationships – the use of telephone, mail, fax, email, the Internet and other tools to communicate directly with specific consumers.

Direct marketing channel A marketing channel that has no intermediary levels.

Direct response TV marketing Direct marketing via television, including direct response television advertising or infomercials and home shopping channels.

Discount A straight reduction in price on purchases during a stated period of time.

Discount store A retail institution that sells standard merchandise at lower prices by accepting lower margins and selling at higher volume.

Disintermediation The cutting out of marketing channel intermediaries by product or service producers, or the displacement of traditional resellers by radical new types of intermediaries.

Distribution centre A large, highly automated warehouse designed to receive goods from various plants and suppliers, take orders, fill them efficiently and deliver goods to customers as quickly as possible.

Distribution channel See Marketing channel.

Diversification A strategy for company growth through starting up or acquiring businesses outside the company's current products and markets.

Downsizing Reducing the business portfolio by eliminating products or business units that are not profitable or that no longer fit the company's overall strategy.

Dynamic pricing Adjusting prices continually to meet the characteristics and needs of individual customers and situations.

E-business The use of electronic platforms – intranets, extranets and the Internet – to conduct a company's business.

E-commerce Buying and selling processes supported by electronic means, primarily the Internet.

Economic community A group of nations organised to work towards common goals in the regulation of international trade.

Economic environment Factors that affect consumer buying power and spending patterns.

E-marketing The marketing side of e-commerce – company efforts to communicate about, promote, and sell products and services over the Internet.

Engel's laws Differences noted over a century ago by Ernst Engel in how people shift their spending across food, housing, transport, healthcare, and other goods and services categories as family income rises.

Environmental sustainability A management approach that involves developing strategies that both sustain the environment and produce profits for the company.

Environmentalism An organised movement of concerned citizens and government agencies to protect and improve people's living environment.

Exchange The act of obtaining a desired object from someone by offering something in return.

Exclusive distribution Giving a limited number of dealers the exclusive right to distribute the company's products in their territories.

Experimental research The gathering of primary data by selecting matched groups of subjects, giving them different treatments, controlling related factors and checking for differences in group responses.

Exploratory research Marketing research to gather preliminary information that will help define problems and suggest hypotheses.

Exporting Entering a foreign market by selling goods produced in the company's home country, often with little modification.

Extranet A network that connects a company with its suppliers and distributors, often paired with an intranet (see below).

Factory outlet Off-price retailing operation that is owned and operated by a manufacturer and that normally carries the manufacturer's surplus, discontinued or irregular goods.

Fad A fashion that enters quickly, is adopted with great zeal, peaks early and declines very quickly.

Fashion A currently accepted or popular style in a given field.

Fixed costs Costs that do not vary with production or sales level.

Focus group interviewing Personal interviewing that involves inviting typically 6 to 10 people to gather for a few hours with a trained interviewer to talk about a product, service or organisation. The interviewer 'focuses' the group discussion on important issues.

Follow-up The last step in the selling process in which the salesperson follows up after the sale to ensure customer satisfaction and repeat business.

Franchise A contractual association between a manufacturer, wholesaler or service organisation (a franchisor) and independent businesspeople (franchisees) who buy the right to own and operate one or more units in the franchise system.

Franchise organisation A contractual vertical marketing system in which a channel member, called a franchisor, links several stages in the production–distribution process.

Gender segmentation Dividing a market into different groups based on gender.

Generation X The generation of people born between 1965 and 1976 in the 'birth dearth' following the baby boom.

Generation Y The children of the baby boomers, born between 1977 and 1994.

Geographic segmentation Dividing a market into different geographical units such as nations, states, regions, counties, cities or neighbourhoods.

Geographical pricing Setting price based on the buyer's geographical location.

Global firm A firm that operates and/or markets products and services in many nations – potentially in radically different ways. Typically a very large firm with well-known brands.

Good value pricing Good value pricing means offering just the right combination of quality and good service at a fair price.

Group Two or more people who interact to accomplish individual or mutual goals.

Growth–share matrix A portfolio planning method that evaluates a company's strategic business units in terms of their market growth rate and relative market share. SBUs are classified as stars, cash cows, question marks or dogs.

Growth stage The product life-cycle stage in which a product's sales start climbing quickly.

Handling objections The step in the selling process in which the salesperson seeks out, clarifies and overcomes customer objections to buying.

Horizontal marketing system A channel arrangement in which two or more companies at one level join together to follow a new marketing opportunity. (See Vertical marketing system.)

Idea generation The systematic search for new-product ideas.

Idea screening Screening new-product ideas in order to spot good ideas and drop poor ones as soon as possible.

Income segmentation Dividing a market into different income groups.

Independent off-price retailer Off-price retailer that is either owned and run by entrepreneurs or is a division of a larger retail corporation.

Indirect marketing channel Channel containing one or more intermediary levels.

Individual marketing Tailoring products and marketing programmes to the needs and preferences of individual customers – also labelled 'markets-of-one marketing', 'customised marketing' and 'one-to-one marketing'.

Industrial product Product bought by individuals and organisations for further processing or for use in conducting a business.

Innovative marketing A principle of sustainable marketing that requires that a company seeks real product and marketing improvements.

Inside sales force Inside salespeople who conduct business from their offices via telephone, the Internet or visits from prospective buyers.

Integrated direct marketing Direct marketing campaigns that use multiple vehicles and multiple stages to improve response rates and profits.

Integrated logistics management The logistics concept that emphasises teamwork, both inside the company and among all the marketing channel organisations, to maximise the performance of the entire distribution system.

Integrated marketing communications (IMC) The concept under which a company carefully integrates its many communications channels to deliver a clear, consistent and compelling message about the organisation and its products.

Integrated supply chain management The integrated supply chain management concept recognises that improved logistics requires teamwork in the form of improved working relationships across functional areas inside the company and across various organisations in the supply chain.

Intensive distribution Stocking the product in as many outlets as possible.

Interactive marketing Marketing by a service firm that recognises that perceived service quality depends heavily on the quality of buyer–seller interaction, either face to face or using Internet-related tools.

Intermarket segmentation Forming segments of consumers who have similar needs and buying behaviour even though they are located in different countries.

Intermodal transportation Combining two or more modes of transportation.

Internal databases Electronic collections of consumer and market information obtained from data sources within the company network.

Internal marketing Marketing by a service firm to train and effectively motivate its customer-contact employees and all the supporting service people to work as a team to provide customer satisfaction.

Internet A vast public web of computer networks, which connects users of all types all around the world to each other and to an amazingly large 'information repository'.

Intranet A network that connects people within a company to each other and to the company network and excludes those outside this network (see Extranet).

Introduction stage The product life-cycle stage in which the new product is first distributed and made available for purchase.

Joint ownership A joint venture in which a company joins investors in a foreign market to create a local business in which the company shares joint ownership and control.

Joint venturing Entering foreign markets by joining with other companies to produce or market a product or service.

Learning Changes in an individual's behaviour arising from experience.

Licensing A method of entering a foreign market in which the company enters into an agreement with a licensee in the foreign market, offering the right to use a manufacturing process, trademark, patent, trade secret or other item of value for a fee or royalty.

Lifestyle A person's pattern of living as expressed in his or her activities, interests and opinions.

Line extension Using a successful brand name to introduce additional items in a given product category under the same brand name, such as new flavours, forms, colours, added ingredients or package sizes.

Local marketing Tailoring brands and promotions to the needs and wants of local customer groups – cities, neighbourhoods and even specific stores.

Macroenvironment The larger societal forces that affect the microenvironment – demographic, economic, legal, technological, political and cultural forces.

Management contracting A joint venture in which the domestic firm supplies the management know-how to a foreign company that supplies the capital; the domestic firm exports management services rather than products.

Manufacturers' sales branches and offices Wholesaling by sellers or buyers themselves rather than through independent wholesalers.

Market The set of all actual and potential buyers of a product or service.

Market development A strategy for company growth by identifying and developing new market segments for current company products.

Market offering Some combination of products, services, information or experiences offered to a market to satisfy a need or want.

Market penetration A strategy for company growth by increasing sales of current products to current market segments without changing the product.

Market-penetration pricing Setting a low price for a new product in order to attract a large number of buyers and a large market share.

Market positioning Arranging for a product to occupy a clear, distinctive and desirable place relative to competing products in the minds of target consumers.

Market segment A group of consumers who respond in a similar way to a given set of marketing efforts.

Market segmentation Dividing a market into distinct groups with distinct needs, characteristics or behaviours who might require separate products or marketing mixes.

Market-skimming pricing Setting a high price for a new product to skim maximum revenues layer by layer from the segments willing to pay the high price; the company makes fewer but more profitable sales.

Marketing The process by which companies create value for customers and build strong customer relationships in order to capture value from customers in return. The AMA defines marketing as 'an organizational function and a set of processes for creating, communicating, and delivering value to customers and for managing customer relationships in ways that benefit the organization and its stakeholders'.

Marketing audit A comprehensive, systematic, independent and periodic examination of a company's environment, objectives, strategies and activities to determine problem areas and opportunities and to recommend a plan of action to improve the company's marketing performance.

Marketing channel A set of interdependent organisations that help make a product or service available for use or consumption by the consumer or business user.

Marketing concept The marketing management philosophy that holds that achieving organisational goals depends on knowing the needs and wants of target markets and delivering the desired satisfactions better than competitors do.

Marketing control The process of measuring and evaluating the results of marketing strategies and plans, and taking corrective action to ensure that objectives are achieved.

Marketing environment The actors and forces outside marketing that affect marketing management's ability to build and maintain successful relationships with target customers.

Marketing implementation The process that turns marketing strategies and plans into marketing actions in order to accomplish strategic marketing objectives.

Marketing information system (MIS) People, equipment and procedures to gather, sort, analyse, evaluate and distribute needed, timely and accurate information to marketing decision makers.

Marketing intelligence The systematic collection and analysis of publicly available information about competitors and developments in the marketing environment.

Marketing intermediaries Firms that help the company to promote, sell and distribute its goods to final buyers; they include resellers, physical distribution firms, marketing service agencies and financial intermediaries.

Marketing logistics (or physical distribution) The tasks involved in planning, implementing and controlling the physical flow of materials, final goods and related information from points of origin to points of consumption to meet customer requirements at a profit.

Marketing management The art and science of choosing target markets and building profitable relationships with them.

Marketing mix The set of controllable tactical marketing tools – product, price, place and promotion – that the firm blends to produce the response it wants in the target market.

Marketing myopia The mistake of paying more attention to the specific products a company offers than to the benefits and experiences produced by those products.

Marketing research The systematic design, collection, analysis and reporting of data relevant to a specific marketing situation facing an organisation.

Marketing strategy The marketing logic by which the business unit hopes to achieve its marketing objectives.

Marketing strategy development Designing an initial marketing strategy for a new product based on the product concept.

Marketing supply chain management See Supply chain management.

Marketing website A website that engages consumers in interactions that will move them closer to a direct purchase or other marketing outcome.

Maturity stage The stage in the product life cycle in which sales growth slows or levels off.

Merchant wholesaler Independently owned business that takes title to the merchandise it handles.

Microenvironment The actors close to the company that affect its ability to serve its customers – the company, suppliers, marketing intermediaries, customer markets, competitors and publics.

Micromarketing The practice of tailoring products and marketing programmes to the needs and wants of specific individuals and local customer groups – includes local marketing and individual marketing.

Mission statement A statement of the organisation's purpose – what it wants to accomplish in the larger environment.

Modified rebuy A business buying situation in which the buyer wants to modify product specifications, prices, terms or suppliers.

Motive (drive) A need that is sufficiently pressing to direct the person to seek satisfaction of the need.

Multichannel distribution system A distribution system in which a single firm sets up two or more marketing channels to reach one or more customer segments.

Natural environment Natural resources that are needed as inputs by marketers or that are affected by marketing activities.

Needs States of felt deprivation.

New product A good, service or idea that is perceived by some potential customers as new.

New-product development The development of original products, product improvements, product modifications and new brands through the firm's own R&D efforts.

New-task situation A business buying situation in which the buyer purchases a product or service for the first time.

Objective-and-task method Developing the promotion budget by (1) defining specific objectives, (2) determining the tasks that must be performed to achieve these objectives, and (3) estimating the costs of performing these tasks. The sum of these costs is the proposed promotion budget.

Observational research The gathering of primary data by observing relevant people, actions and situations.

Occasion segmentation Dividing the market into groups according to occasions when buyers get the idea to buy, actually make their purchase or use the purchased item.

Off-price retailer Retailer that buys at less than regular wholesale prices and sells at less than retail. Examples are factory outlets, independents and warehouse clubs.

Online advertising Advertising that appears while consumers are surfing the Web, including banners, interstitials, pop-ups and other forms.

Online databases Computerised collections of information available from online commercial sources or via the Internet.

Online (Internet) marketing research Collecting primary data through Internet surveys and online focus groups.

Open trading exchanges Huge e-marketspaces in which B2B buyers and sellers find each other online, share information and complete transactions efficiently. An 'eBay' for the commercial world.

Opinion leader Person within a reference group who, because of special skills, knowledge, personality or other characteristics, exerts influence on others.

Optional-product pricing The pricing of optional or accessory products along with a main product.

Outside sales force (or field sales force) Outside salespeople who travel to call on customers in the field.

Packaging The activities of designing and producing the container or wrapper for a product.

Partner relationship management Working closely with partners in other company departments and outside the company jointly to bring greater value to customers.

Percentage-of-sales method Setting the promotion budget at a certain percentage of current or forecasted sales or as a percentage of the unit sales price.

Perception The process by which people select, organise and interpret information to form a meaningful picture of the world.

Personal selling Personal presentation by the firm's sales force for the purpose of making sales and building customer relationships.

Personality The unique psychological characteristics that lead to relatively consistent and lasting responses to one's own environment.

Pleasing products Products that give high immediate satisfaction but may hurt consumers in the long run.

Political environment Laws, government agencies and pressure groups that influence and limit various organisations and individuals in a given society.

Portfolio analysis The process by which management evaluates the products and businesses making up the company.

Positioning statement A statement that summarises company or brand positioning – it takes this form: To (target segment and need) our (brand) is (concept) that (point of difference).

Pre-approach The step in the selling process in which the salesperson learns as much as possible about a prospective customer before making a sales call.

Presentation The step in the selling process in which the salesperson tells the product 'story' to the buyer, highlighting customer benefits.

Price The amount of money charged for a product or service, or the sum of all the values that customers give up in order to gain the benefits of having or using a product or service.

Price elasticity A measure of the sensitivity of demand to changes in price.

Primary data Information collected for the specific purpose at hand.

Private brand (or store brand) A brand created and owned by a reseller of a product or service.

Private trading exchanges B2B trading networks that link a particular seller with its own trading partners.

Product Anything that can be offered to a market for attention, acquisition, use or consumption that might satisfy a want or need.

Product adaptation Adapting a product to meet local conditions or wants in foreign markets.

Product bundle pricing Combining several products and offering the bundle at a reduced price.

Product concept A detailed version of the new-product idea stated in meaningful consumer terms. Part of the new-product development process.

Product development (1) A strategy for company growth by offering modified or new products to current market segments.

Product development (2) Developing the product concept into a physical product in order to ensure that the product idea can be turned into a workable product.

Product life cycle The course of a product's sales and profits over its lifetime. It involves five distinct stages: product development, introduction, growth, maturity and decline.

Product line A group of products that are closely related because they function in a similar manner, are sold to the same customer groups, are marketed through the same types of outlets or fall within given price ranges.

Product line pricing Setting the price steps between various products in a product line based on cost differences between the products, customer evaluations of different features and competitors' prices.

Product–market expansion grid A portfolio planning tool for identifying company growth opportunities through market penetration, market development, product development or diversification.

Product mix (or product portfolio) The set of all product lines and items that a particular seller offers for sale.

Product quality The ability of a product to perform its functions; it includes the product's overall durability, reliability, precision, ease of operation and repair, and other valued attributes.

Product sales force structure A sales force organisation under which salespeople specialise in selling only a portion of the company's products or lines.

Product's position The way the product is defined by consumers on important attributes – the place the product occupies in consumers' minds relative to competing products.

Production concept The idea that consumers will favour products that are available and highly affordable and that the organisation should therefore focus on improving production and distribution efficiency – 'we will sell what we can make'.

Promotion mix (or marketing communications mix) The specific mix of advertising, personal selling, sales promotion, public relations and direct marketing that a company uses to communicate customer value persuasively and build customer relationships.

Promotional pricing Temporarily pricing products below the list price, and sometimes even below cost, to increase short-term sales.

Prospecting The step in the selling process in which the salesperson identifies qualified potential customers.

Psychographic segmentation Dividing a market into different groups based on social class, lifestyle or personality characteristics.

Psychological pricing A pricing approach that considers the psychology of prices and not simply the economics; the price is used to say something about the product.

Public Any group that has an actual or potential interest in, or impact on, an organisation's ability to achieve its objectives.

Public relations Building good relations with the company's various publics by obtaining favourable publicity, building up a good 'corporate image', and handling or heading off unfavourable rumours, stories and events.

Pull strategy A promotion strategy that calls for spending a lot on advertising and consumer promotion to build up consumer demand that will pull the product through channels.

Push strategy A promotion strategy that calls for using the sales force and trade promotion to push the product through channels.

Reference prices Prices that buyers carry in their minds and refer to when they look at a given product.

Relationship marketing Often defined in opposition to transactional marketing (see below), in that relationship marketing espouses long-term 'management of customers' rather than on a transaction-by-transaction basis. A term often misused to describe loyalty cards.

Retailer Business whose sales come primarily from retailing.

Retailing All activities involved in selling goods or services directly to final consumers for their personal, non-business use.

Return on marketing (or marketing ROI) The net return from a marketing investment divided by the costs of the marketing investment. Often difficult to measure with any degree of accuracy.

Sales force management The analysis, planning, implementation and control of sales force activities. It includes designing sales force strategy and structure, and recruiting, selecting, training, supervising, compensating and evaluating the firm's salespeople.

Sales promotion Short-term incentives to encourage the purchase or sale of a product or service.

Sales quota A standard that states the amount a salesperson should sell and how sales should be divided among the company's products.

Salesperson An individual acting for a company by performing one or more of the following activities: prospecting, communicating, servicing and information gathering.

Salutary products Products that have low appeal but may benefit consumers in the long term.

Sample A segment of the population selected for marketing research to represent the population as a whole.

Secondary data Information that already exists somewhere, having been collected for another purpose.

Segmented pricing Selling a product or service at two or more prices, where the difference in prices is not based on differences in costs.

Selective distribution The use of more than one, but fewer than all, of the intermediaries who are willing to carry the company's products.

Selling concept The idea that consumers will not buy enough of the firm's products unless it undertakes a large-scale selling and promotion effort.

Selling process The steps that the salesperson follows when selling, which include prospecting and qualifying, pre-approach, approach, presentation and demonstration, handling objections, closing and follow-up.

Sense-of-mission marketing A principle of enlightened marketing that holds that a company should define its mission in broad social terms rather than narrow product terms.

Sequential product development A new-product development approach in which one company department works to complete its stage of the process before passing the new product along to the next department and stage.

Service Any activity or benefit that one party can offer to another that is essentially intangible and does not result in the ownership of anything.

Service inseparability A major characteristic of services – they are produced and consumed at the same time and cannot be separated from their providers, whether the providers are people or machines.

Service intangibility A major characteristic of services – they cannot be seen, tasted, felt, heard or smelled before they are bought.

Service perishability A major characteristic of services – they cannot be stored for later sale or use.

Service–profit chain The chain that links service firm profits with employee and customer satisfaction.

Service variability *A major characteristic of* services – their quality may vary greatly, depending on who provides them and when, where and how.

Share of customer The portion of the customer's purchasing that a company gets in its product categories.

Shopping centre A group of retail businesses planned, developed, owned and managed as a unit. Also commonly known as a shopping mall.

Shopping product Consumer good that the customer, in the process of selection and purchase, characteristically compares on such bases as suitability, quality, price and style.

Simultaneous (or team-based) product development An approach to developing new products in which various company departments work closely together, overlapping the steps in the product development process to save time and increase effectiveness.

Single-source data systems Electronic monitoring systems that link consumers' exposure to television advertising and promotion (measured using television meters) with what they buy in stores (measured using store checkout scanners).

Social class Relatively permanent and ordered divisions in a society, the members of which share similar values, interests and behaviours.

Social marketing The design, implementation and control of programmes seeking to increase the acceptability of a social idea, cause or practice among a target group.

Societal marketing A principle of enlightened marketing that holds that a company should make good marketing decisions by considering consumers' wants, the company's requirements, consumers' long-term interests and society's long-term interests.

Spam Unsolicited, unwanted commercial email messages.

Speciality product Consumer product with unique characteristics or brand identification for which a significant group of buyers is willing to make a special purchase effort.

Speciality store A retail store that carries a narrow product line with a deep assortment within that line.

Standardised marketing mix An international marketing strategy for using basically the same product, advertising, distribution channels and other elements of the marketing mix in all the company's international markets.

Straight product extension Marketing a product in a foreign market without any change.

Straight rebuy A business buying situation in which the buyer routinely reorders something without any modifications.

Strategic planning The process of developing and maintaining a strategic fit between the organisation's goals and capabilities and its changing marketing opportunities. It involves defining a clear company mission, setting supporting objectives, designing a sound business portfolio and coordinating functional strategies.

Style A basic and distinctive mode of expression.

Subculture A group of people with shared value systems based on common life experiences and situations.

Supermarket Large, low-cost, low-margin, high-volume, self-service store that carries a wide variety of food, laundry and household products.

Superstore A store much larger than a regular supermarket that carries a large assortment of routinely purchased food and non-food items and offers services such as dry cleaning, post office, photo finishing, cheque cashing, bill paying, café, car care and pet care.

Supply chain management Managing upstream and downstream value-added flows of materials, final goods and related information among suppliers, the company, resellers and final consumers.

Survey research The gathering of primary data by asking people questions about their knowledge, attitudes, preferences and buying behaviour.

Sustainable marketing This is an approach to marketing that focuses on the long-term viability of marketing strategies and their effects on wider social and ecological systems within which business enterprises are embedded.

SWOT analysis An overall evaluation of the company's strengths (S), weaknesses (W), opportunities (O) and threats (T). A part of the preparation required in drawing up a marketing plan.

Systems selling Buying a packaged solution to a problem from a single seller, thus avoiding all the separate decisions involved in a complex buying situation.

Target costing Pricing that starts with an ideal selling price, then targets costs that will ensure that the price is met.

Target market A set of buyers sharing common needs or characteristics that the company decides to serve.

Target marketing The process of evaluating each market segment's attractiveness and selecting one or more segments to enter.

Target profit pricing See Break-even pricing.

Team selling Using teams of people from sales, marketing, engineering, finance, technical support, and even upper management, to service large, complex accounts.

Technological environment Forces that create new technologies, creating new product and market opportunities.

Telephone marketing Using the telephone to sell directly to customers.

Territorial sales force structure A sales force organisation that assigns each salesperson to an exclusive geographical territory in which that salesperson sells the company's full line.

Test marketing The stage of new-product development in which the product and marketing programme are tested in more realistic market settings.

Third-party logistics (3PL) provider An independent logistics provider that performs any or all of the functions required to get its client's product to market.

Total costs The sum of the fixed and variable costs for any given level of production.

Undifferentiated (mass) marketing A market coverage strategy in which a firm decides to ignore market segment differences and go after the whole market with one offer.

Unsought product Consumer product that the consumer either does not know about or knows about but does not normally think of buying.

Value-added pricing Attaching value-added features and services to differentiate a marketing offer and support higher prices, rather than cutting prices to match competitors.

Value analysis An approach to cost reduction in which components are studied carefully to determine if they can be redesigned, standardised or made by less costly methods of production.

Value-based pricing Setting price based on buyers' perceptions of value rather than on the seller's cost.

Value chain The series of departments that carry out value-creating activities to design, produce, market, deliver and support a firm's products.

Value-delivery network The network made up of the company, suppliers, distributors and ultimately customers who 'partner' with each other to improve the performance of the entire system.

Value proposition The full positioning of a brand – the full mix of benefits upon which it is positioned.

Variable costs Costs that vary directly with the level of production.

Vertical marketing system (VMS) A distribution channel structure in which producers, wholesalers and retailers act as a unified system. One channel member owns the others, has contracts with them or has so much power that they all cooperate. (See Horizontal marketing system.)

Viral marketing The Internet version of word-of-mouth marketing – websites, email messages or other marketing events that are so infectious that customers will want to pass them along to friends.

Wants The form needs take as shaped by culture and individual personality. (See Needs.)

Web communities Websites upon which members can congregate online and exchange views on issues of common interest.

Wheel-of-retailing concept A concept of retailing that states that new types of retailers usually begin as low-margin, low-price, low-status operations but later evolve into higher-priced, higher-service operations, eventually becoming like the conventional retailers they replaced.

Whole-channel view Designing international channels that take into account all the necessary links in distributing the seller's products to final buyers, including the seller's headquarters organisation, channels among nations and channels within nations.

Wholesaler A firm engaged primarily in wholesaling activity.

Wholesaling All activities involved in selling goods and services to those buying for resale or business use.

INDEX